PHYSICS

CHEMISTRY

MEDICINE

PSYCHOLOGY

MATHEMATICS

EARTH SCIENCES

SOCIAL SCIENCES

Geoscience
Anthropology
Political Science
Sociology
History
Zoology
Economics
Geography
Gerontology
General Medicine
Psychiatry
Communications
Management
Education
Library Science
Information
Applied Math
Nursing
Paleontology
Psychology
Statistics
Ophthalmo
Public
Astro

Food
Pharmacology
Microbiology
Virology
Plant Sciences
Respiratory Medicine
Pediatrics
Endocrinology
Polymers
Gastroenterology
Agriculture
Veterinary Medicine
Ecology
Condensed Matter
Gynecology
Material Sciences
Geoscience
Marine Biology
Computer Science
Genetics
Toxicology
Pathology
Biochemistry
Hematology
Nuclear Physics
Sports Sciences
Organic Chemistry
Analytical Chemistry
Rheumatology
Emergency Medicine
Meteorology
Plant Chemistry
Chemical Engineering
Biotechnology
Physical Sciences
Electrical Engineering

John T.
Cacioppo
University of Chicago

Laura A.
Freberg
California Polytechnic
State University,
San Luis Obispo

Discovering
Psychology
The Science *of* Mind

WADSWORTH
CENGAGE Learning

Australia • Brazil • Japan • Korea • Mexico • Singapore • Spain • United Kingdom • United States

WADSWORTH
CENGAGE Learning

Discovering Psychology: The Science of Mind
John T. Cacioppo and Laura A. Freberg

Publisher: Jon-David Hague

Sr. Development Group Manager: Jeremy Judson

Assistant Editors: Kelly Miller and Lauren Moody

Editorial Assistants: Sheli DeNola and Travis Holland

Media Editor: Mary Noel

Marketing Manager: Jessica Egbert

Marketing Assistant: Janay Pryor

Sr. Marketing Communications Manager: Laura
   Localio

Content Project Manager: Charlene M. Carpentier

Design Director: Rob Hugel

Art Director: Vernon Boes

Print Buyer: Karen Hunt

Rights Acquisitions Specialist: Tom McDonough

Production Service: Lachina Publishing Services

Text Designer: Diane Beasley

Developmental Art Editor: Lisa Torri

Photo Editor: Trina McManus

Photo Researcher: Stephen Forsling

Text Researcher: Karyn Morrison

Copy Editor: Carolyn Crabtree, Lachina Publishing
   Services

Illustrators: Argosy Publishing, Inc., and Lachina
   Publishing Services

Cover Designer: Irene Morris

Cover image: Stefano Tiraboschi/Fotolia

Compositor: Lachina Publishing Services

For product information and technology assistance, contact us at
Cengage Learning Customer & Sales Support, 1-800-354-9706

For permission to use material from this text or product, submit all requests online at **www.cengage.com/permissions**
Further permissions questions can be e-mailed to
permissionrequest@cengage.com

Library of Congress Control Number: 2011940901

Student Edition:
ISBN-13: 978-0-618-18550-4
ISBN-10: 0-618-18550-X

Loose-leaf Edition:
ISBN-13: 978-1-111-83627-6
ISBN-10: 1-111-83627-2

Wadsworth
20 Davis Drive
Belmont, CA 94002-3098
USA

Cengage Learning is a leading provider of customized learning solutions with office locations around the globe, including Singapore, the United Kingdom, Australia, Mexico, Brazil, and Japan. Locate your local office at **www.cengage.com/global**.

Cengage Learning products are represented in Canada by Nelson Education, Ltd.

To learn more about Wadsworth, visit **www.cengage.com/Wadsworth**

Purchase any of our products at your local college store or at our preferred online store **www.CengageBrain.com**.

Printed in Canada
1 2 3 4 5 6 7 15 14 13 12

About the Authors

John T. Cacioppo is the Tiffany and Margaret Blake Distinguished Service Professor and Director of the Center for Cognitive and Social Neuroscience at the University of Chicago. He is the Chair of the Psychology Section of the American Association for the Advancement of Science and the President of the Society for Social Neuroscience, and he is a past President of four other scientific societies including the Association for Psychological Science. He is the recipient of numerous awards, including the National Academy of Sciences Troland Research Award, the American Psychological Association Distinguished Scientific Contribution Award, the Society for Experimental  Social Psychology Scientific Impact Award, the Presidential Citation from the American Psychological Association, and the Society for Personality and Social Psychology Theoretical Innovation Prize. He has served as Editor and Associate Editor of various journal boards, and currently serves on the Council of the Center for Scientific Review at the National Institutes of Health.

Laura A. Freberg is Professor of Psychology at California Polytechnic State University, San Luis Obispo, where she teaches courses in Introductory Psychology, Biological Psychology, and Sensation and Perception. Recently, to better understand the needs of the online education community, Laura also began teaching Social Psychology for Argosy University Online. Laura's teaching career began over 35 years ago when she taught her first college course at Pasadena City College at the age of 23. She has received Faculty Member of the Year recognition from Cal Poly Disabilities Resource Center three times (1991, 1994, and 2009) for her work with students with dis-  abilities. She enjoys using technology and social media in the classroom, and is a syndicated expert blogger for Live Right Live Well! She serves as the Bylaws and Archives Committee Chair for the Society for Social Neuroscience.

Brief Contents

Contents

1 The Science of Mind
The Discipline of Psychology

© Argosy Publishing, Inc.

2 The Measure of Mind

Methods of Psychology

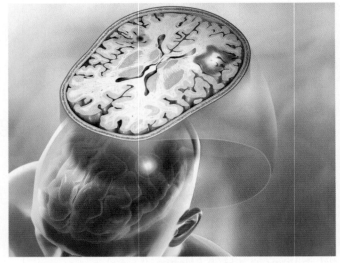

© Argosy Publishing, Inc.

3 The Evolving Mind
Nature and Nurture Intertwined

© Argosy Publishing, Inc.

4 The Biological Mind
The Physical Basis of Behavior

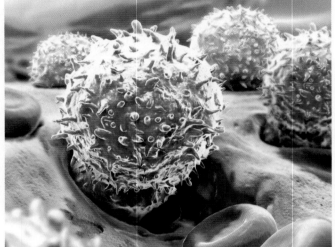

© Argosy Publishing, Inc.

5 The Perceiving Mind

Sensation and Perception

© Argosy Publishing, Inc.

6 The Aware Mind

Elements of Consciousness

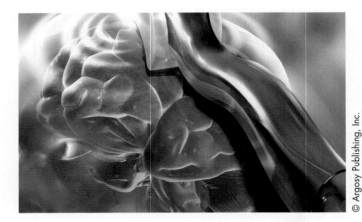

© Argosy Publishing, Inc.

7 The Feeling Mind
Motivation and Emotion

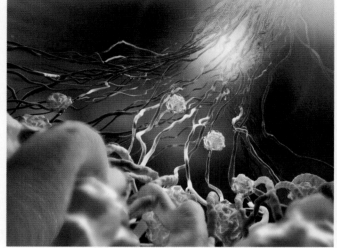

© Argosy Publishing, Inc.

8 The Adaptive Mind

Learning

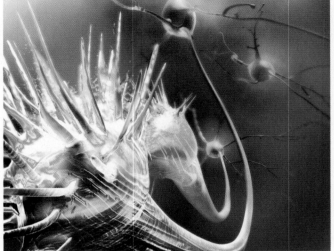

© Argosy Publishing, Inc.

9 The Knowing Mind
Memory

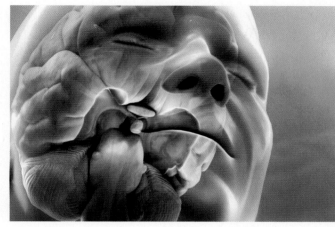

© Argosy Publishing, Inc.

10 The Thinking Mind

Thinking, Language, and Intelligence

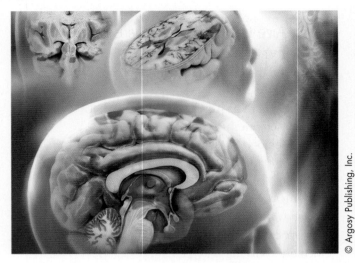

© Argosy Publishing, Inc.

11 The Developing Mind

Life-Span Development

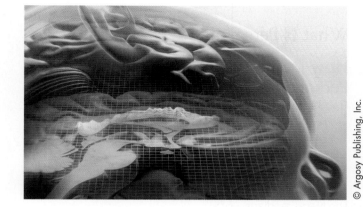

© Argosy Publishing, Inc.

12 The Individual Mind

Personality and the Self

© Argosy Publishing, Inc.

13 The Connected Mind

Social Psychology

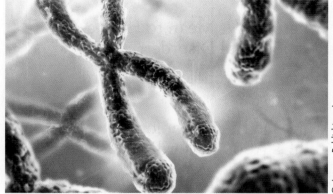

© Argosy Publishing, Inc.

14 The Troubled Mind

Psychological Disorders

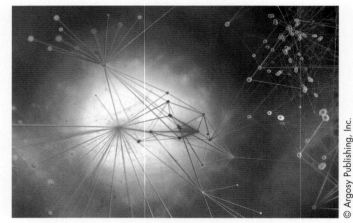

© Argosy Publishing, Inc.

15 Healing the Troubled Mind

Therapy

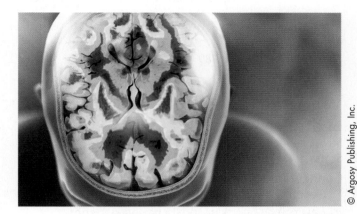

© Argosy Publishing, Inc.

16 The Healthy Mind

Stress and Coping, Health Psychology, and Positive Psychology

© Argosy Publishing, Inc.

Preface

Adapted from "Mapping the Backbone of Science," by Kevin W. Boyack et al., 2005, Scientometrics, 64(3). With kind permission from Springer Science+Business Media.

With *Discovering Psychology*, we sought to produce a textbook that reflects psychology's rightful place as a hub science, a discipline that draws from and is cited by research in many other fields. In a scientific community increasingly dominated by interdisciplinary teams, we would like students to see psychology not as an isolated area of study but as one that integrates a broad range of knowledge into a true science of mind.

The science of psychology developed in the 20th century as a collection of loosely organized, independent subspecialties. Ten years into the 21st century, the discipline is moving rapidly toward maturity as an integrative, multidisciplinary science. Not only are psychologists forming rich collaborations with scholars in other fields, from business to education to medicine, but we are returning to original conceptions of psychology put forward by thinkers such as William James, who sought a complete understanding of the human mind and was not content to view psychology from narrow, isolated perspectives. We share a mutual excitement about this evolution of psychological science and also a mutual impatience with the slow pace at which existing introductory psychology textbooks—most of which were first written in the 20th century—have adjusted to this sea change.

For many years, the introductory psychology course has served primarily as a jumping-off point for advanced courses in the field, and the textbooks prepared to support the course have reflected this goal. Each chapter provided a capsule of stand-alone information designed to acquaint the student with the terminology and hypotheses of a single psychological perspective. We see the introductory course as providing a unique opportunity to discuss *all* of psychology in one place and at one time. This approach allows us to reflect on the intersections between various perspectives as they inform the whole of our understanding of the human mind. Given that most students in our introductory classes will take only this one course in the field, we have a responsibility to provide a comprehensive structure that will support their lifelong learning and understanding of human behavior.

> We see the introductory course as providing a unique opportunity to discuss *all* of psychology in one place and at one time.

Our goal is to bring the teaching of introductory psychology fully into the 21st century, and we view the first edition of *Discovering Psychology* as a solidly grounded bridge toward this goal. The structure of the bridge is a traditional chapter organization. The piers on which the bridge rests are the foundational theories of the discipline developed in the late 19th and early 20th centuries. The steel beams of which the bridge is composed consist of the theories and research painstakingly developed throughout the 20th century, and the rivets, trusses, and tie rods that hold the bridge together are integrative themes. Finally, the smooth roadbed that transports students across the bridge is a clear, inviting, warm, and lively writing style.

As active instructors ourselves in the introductory psychology classroom, we recognize the balance busy faculty members must find between their preparation for class and their many other duties. Our intent is to make the transition from a 20th-century textbook to a 21st-century textbook as seamless and effortless as possible for faculty and students alike. Our discussions of complex issues, such as heritability and its application to intelligence, include sufficient information for students and instructors to explain each issue. Clear writing, frequent examples, and engaging pedagogy energize students and provide the support needed for success. After completing the course, students will be able to appreciate the distinction between how laypeople and psychologists think about human behavior.

As citizens of the 21st century, community leaders, and influencers, college graduates will need a firm foundation in the understanding of human behavior to confront successfully the myriad issues of privacy, genetic manipulation, free will, human dignity, health, and well-being that will face them in the future. *Discovering Psychology* is designed to provide that foundation.

In his 1899 book, *Talks to Teachers*, William James wrote, "[I]n teaching, you must simply work your pupil into such a state of interest in what you are going to teach him that every other object of attention is banished from his mind; then reveal it to him so impressively that he will remember the occasion to his dying day; and finally fill him with devouring curiosity to know what the steps in connection with the subject are." We think psychology can produce just such enthusiasm in our students, if presented the right way.

> [I]n teaching, you must simply work your pupil into such a state of interest in what you are going to teach him that every other object of attention is banished from his mind; then reveal it to him so impressively that he will remember the occasion to his dying day; and finally fill him with devouring curiosity to know what the steps in connection with the subject are.
>
> —William James

Our Approach

Integrative and Functionalist Foundation

Early writings about psychology were integrated and inclusive rather than insular and reductionistic. Diverse elements of behavior were combined into the whole. William James (1890) cautions us about the risks of missing the big picture by breaking the phenomenon of mind into little pieces. Mental life for James was not an entity that can be "chopped into bits." Despite the long-lived popularity of his dominant psychology textbook, James did not prevail. Psychology soon split into camps of scholars who viewed behavior and mental life through their own single, narrow perspectives, rarely speaking with those who held different views and producing curricula and textbooks that emphasized the parts rather than the whole.

As psychological science became more and more siloed in the 20th century, its origins in the late 19th century as a unified whole were forgotten. In 20th-century introductory psychology textbooks, the writings and experiments of Wundt, Titchener, and James are described as the discipline's prehensile tail, long ago lost and interesting only from a historical perspective. The organization of the study of mind into separate, disconnected chapters not only transformed the topics of psychology into islands without bridges but actually built barriers to students' understanding of the connectedness between them. A "memory" cannot be fully understood from one isolated point of view; only when the evolutionary, social, cognitive, biological, developmental, clinical, and individual difference perspectives are combined can it be thoroughly grasped. James (1890) warns us that when mental phenomena are "superficially considered, their variety and complexity is such as to leave a chaotic impression on the observer." This confusion, unfortunately, is the legacy for many of our students exposed only to outdated textbooks in psychology.

Breaking from the approach of 20th-century textbooks, we reflect throughout our text on the integrative influences of the founders in our functionalist approach to the material. We seek not only to describe behavior but to answer questions about why a particular behavior occurs. Behavior through this lens is neither random nor unexplainable and shifts into focus when we consider its goals and functions. For example, people do not just experience feelings of loneliness, but loneliness acts as a warning signal to remind us of the importance of social connectedness.

Our book is subtitled "The Science of Mind," and, unlike other contemporary texts with their occasional references to "mind," the word appears in each of the chapter titles, highlighting the scientific study of the nature and behavior of the mind. Throughout the book, we emphasize the relationship between rigorous scientific methods and observations, and the implications of these observations for competing theories about the structure and operations of the mind.

Integrative Approach

Integration in this textbook extends in two directions, both within psychology and between psychology and other disciplines. We hope to highlight for students the many connections within the discipline of psychology as well as the connections between psychology and other disciplines. Many introductory psychology textbooks share our goal of providing integration, but we would like to make our methods of achieving this goal explicit.

1. Within the body of each chapter, we make frequent connections to material in other chapters, forming bridges between subtopics. For example, in a discussion of our predisposition towards social behavior in our chapter on social psychology chapter, we say:

   Evidence that this need for social contact has been incorporated into our genetic heritage can be found in our development and biology. As we discussed in our chapters on development and on motivation and emotion, the age at which children experience distress due to separation from caregivers peaks at around 18 months across a diverse set of cultures (Kagan, Kearsley, & Zelazo, 1978). In our chapter on biological psychology, we discussed how the same parts of the brain are activated when a participant experiences physical pain and the pain of social exclusion (Eisenberger, Lieberman, & Williams, 2003; Kross, Berman, Mischel, Smith, & Wager, 2011).

2. We use frequent examples from other parts of the discipline to illustrate principles within a chapter. For example, when we discuss latent inhibition in the learning chapter, we illustrate that principle by linking to clinical research about latent inhibition, creativity, and schizophrenia and to social psychology work on prejudice.

3. We specifically identify and explore seven integrative perspectives that weave the standard topics more closely together: **social psychology/ social neuroscience, cognition, evolution, biology, development, personality/individual differences,** and **clinical psychology**. In keeping with the standard organization of introductory psychology textbooks, the fundamentals of these perspectives are covered in distinct chapters, and the threads of each perspective are woven into all the chapters. These perspectives are explained in greater detail in the following section.

4. Each chapter includes one or more examples of six features, which are described in more detail in a later section: **Chapter Opener and Prologue, Thinking Scientifically, Experiencing Psychology, Psychology as a Hub Science, Connecting to Research, Interpersonal Relationships From a [Chapter Topic] Perspective,** and **Chapter Reflections**. These features are designed to promote active learning and to increase student interest, and two of these in particular (Interpersonal Relationships From a [Chapter Topic] Perspective and Psychology as a Hub Science) also contribute to our integrative approach.

Integrative Perspectives

In each chapter, we pay especially close attention to the contributions of each of the following perspectives to the topic at hand.

Evolutionary The contemporary mind is the product of behaviors that allowed our ancestors to survive in their hunter-gatherer societies 100,000 years ago. When we discuss topics such as individual emotion and motivation, human development, and group behavior, we pause to remind students that humans cooperate, punish defectors, love, hate, feel lonely, manipulate others, and reproduce following many of the same rules that have worked for people for millennia, even when such behaviors might have unanticipated consequences in our modern societies.

Social English writer and poet John Donne was absolutely correct in stating that "no man is an island." We are a social species, and much of our behavior can be understood in terms of how it maintains our social relatedness with one another. The consequences of failing to maintain connectedness are severe. For example, in the discussion of pain perception, we note that when people perceive that they have been socially excluded, activity can be observed in parts of the brain that also respond to physical pain. Being left out hurts.

Cognitive The human being is above all else a thinking organism, and the way we process information impacts our behavior. Whether we are considering the development of behavior, learned behavior, or the aberrations of behavior that accompany psychological disorders, an understanding of how we think provides considerable insight. For instance, we understand that an effective way to improve depressed people's moods is to help them restructure the way they process information. Instead of students thinking that flunking an exam means they are not good enough to attend college, we can encourage them to think that although flunking an exam isn't fun, it's not the end of the world, and that they can make some changes that will lead to better performance next time.

Biological We believe that all introductory students, even those who will never take another psychology course, will gain a better understanding of contemporary psychology in the context of the relationships between biological processes and behavior. For example, when we discuss attraction and close relationships, we mention data showing that viewing a photograph of somebody we love, as opposed to somebody we just like, activates the brain's reward circuits and decreases activity in areas associated with social judgment. Love not only is somewhat socially blind but also really does feel good.

Developmental The structures and processes of behavior, as well as behavior itself, change over time. Knowing that most children achieve a theory of mind by the age of 4 years not only is relevant to our understanding of children and their behavior but also informs discussions of the development of language and social skills and the deficits found in individuals with autism.

Clinical We can understand behavior by observing what works, but it is also highly useful to see what happens when things go wrong. Just as the neuroscientist learns about normal brain function by observing changes following the damage caused by a stroke, we can also learn much about behavior by observing how it changes due to a psychological disorder. For example, in the chapter on sensation and perception, we consider the impact of schizophrenia on the perception of smell and facial expression, and in the chapter on the self, we explore the impact of autism on social behavior.

Individual Differences/Personality Behavioral systems are particularly prone to variation, and we illustrate how such variation can be regarded as important data in its own right. In addition to exploring individual differences within the context of personality, we integrate this facet with other perspectives. For example, we discuss individual differences within the framework of a general perspective of the population as a whole and illustrate how this perspective can be used to address the nature of the mechanisms that give rise to a specific behavior.

Features

Extensive literature supports the idea that an engaged and cognitively active student is more likely to master content. Although students are accustomed to textbooks, their approaches to learning have been impacted by technologies that transfer information at an ever-increasing pace with a strong emphasis on rapidly presented visual images. Consequently, it becomes all too easy to go through the motions of reading a text without really thinking about what you have read. We have incorporated six features designed to model good textbook reading practices in students, while maintaining a high level of interest and understanding.

Chapter Opener and Prologue To introduce and engage interest in upcoming chapter material, many textbooks use a vignette or case study, accompanied by either a fine art piece or a photo that is not discussed further. We begin each chapter with a combination of two images that spread across the left page onto the right page for impact—one gives the "big picture" while the other gives the "micro view" of the same topic. The prologue guides the student through the significance of the images. We use the terms *zoom in* and *zoom out* to emphasize the need to understand the underpinnings of a psychological phenomenon without losing the impact of its larger context. For example, in the biological psychology chapter, the opening images show a woman watching two friends converse (zoom out) and a beautiful image of a white blood cell exiting bone marrow (zoom in). Does the woman feel like part of the conversation or does she feel left out? Depending on how she perceives her situation, biological cascades are set in motion that prepare her immune system for fighting either the viruses found in close social contact or the bacteria that might be more of a risk when a person is solitary. The reader is drawn into the reciprocal relationships that exist between biology and behavior.

Psychology as a Hub Science This integrative feature broadens the discussion of a psychological topic to include ways in which it is engaged in cooperative science with other disciplines, from medicine to the social sciences. It is accompanied by a graphic adapted from a citation analysis by Boyack, Klavens, and Borner (2005) that shows psychology citations as nodes with connections to other related disciplines. This graphic highlights the connections between psychology and the relevant disciplines of psychiatry, nursing, public health, emergency medicine, pharmacology, and obstetrics and gynecology. Given these connections, psychology has a central role to play in our efforts to deal with economic collapses, the spread of pandemics, energy conservation, the spread of terrorism, rising health care costs, and our crumbling educational system. For example, cardiovascular disease is surely a medical condition, but contemporary scientists recognize that a full understanding of this killer requires consideration of psychological domains, including stress appraisal and reactivity and a person's social context.

Experiencing Psychology This interactive feature provides ways for students to connect the course material to their own lives and interests. Some hands-on examples are the Epworth Sleepiness Scale in the consciousness chapter, Coren's handedness scale in the biological psychology chapter, and Anderson and Dill's video game violence and aggression instruments in the research methods chapter. In other cases, this feature provides longer-term opportunities for students to apply their learning, such as working to reduce the frequency of a bad habit.

Thinking Scientifically This interactive feature models critical thinking skills for students by providing them with opportunities to critique the progress of science. For example, students are guided through five steps of critical thinking while evaluating data about the economy and marriage rates published in the news.

Connecting to Research To emphasize psychology as a science, this feature explores either a classic or a very contemporary study relevant to the chapter's material and comments on its significance to the field. Sections on the question, methods, results, and conclusions provide a guided introduction for the student to the essentials of the peer-reviewed literature. From Wertheimer's classic study of apparent motion to the discovery of mirror neurons to Quiroga and colleagues' patient with the "Halle Berry" cell, students are given insight into what psychological scientists do.

Interpersonal Relationships From a [Chapter Topic] Perspective In keeping with the integrative mission of this textbook, the goal of this feature is to demonstrate how the information in a particular chapter can be applied to a single topic—building and maintaining important relationships. This issue is personally meaningful to college students, especially first-year students, and it applies across the board—regardless of gender, race, ethnicity, sociocultural background, sexual orientation, or level of academic preparation. The feature has two main purposes: (1) to engage and maintain student interest throughout the text and (2) to stitch together into an integrative, thematic quilt the patchwork of traditional introductory psychology topic areas.

Chapter Reflections We envision our prologue and Chapter Reflections features as bookends for each chapter. In the prologue, we introduce a way of thinking about psychology that will be elaborated in the body of the chapter. In the chapter-ending narrative section of Chapter Reflections, we tie all the loose ends together. This feature is not a summary of the material for studying purposes; rather, it is a discussion of how the student can now see the material differently for having studied the chapter.

Organization

The chapter organization of this text matches the sequencing of topics as they are commonly presented in introductory psychology courses, but with two slight variations.

1. *The inclusion of a separate chapter on nature and nurture intertwined.* In addition to expanding the usual coverage of the "nature" side of the nature-nurture interaction underlying human behavior found in chapters on biological psychology and sensation and perception, this chapter addresses the fascinating interactions between genetics and experience through a discussion of epigenetics. These typically technical topics are made accessible through the frequent use of examples and application to the everyday experiences of the typical college student.

2. *The placement of the social psychology chapter after personality and before disorders and treatment, and ending the book on a positive note.* The traditional approach is to view the topic of personality strictly as a prologue to the topic of disorders and to view the topic of social psychology as having nothing to do with either of those topics. The sequencing in our text enables us to integrate personality into the fabric of students' understanding of mind—the whole person, the self—and finally our collective selves, because as social animals, that is the whole of what we are. The personality chapter concludes with a discussion of the self. This discussion of the self serves as a bridge from individual minds to connected minds, which covers social psychology. Following chapters on disorders and their treatments, we end the textbook on an upbeat note with a chapter on stress, coping, health, and positive psychology. The purpose of this organization is to give students a complete foundation of understanding of the human mind, of the whole of what we are, so that they are fully prepared to grasp the nuances involved in both psychological disorder and health.

Acknowledgments

We would like to thank William James for bringing so many disparate threads of scholarship together to form the backbone of what continues to be the study of psychology.

Cengage Learning Team We are very grateful to our Cengage Learning team. Jon-David Hague shared our vision for this textbook from the outset and went many extra miles to make it a reality. Jeremy Judson, Jessica Egbert, Vernon Boes, Charlene Carpentier, Mandy Walden, Thomas Finn, Trina McManus, Lisa Torri, Stephen Forsling, Jessica Alderman, Sheli DeNola, Dan Moneypenny, and Mary Falcon gave us their full support through each step of the process. We also thank Michelle Shiota of Arizona State University and instructional designer Jan Johnson.

Manuscript Reviewers

We thank our colleagues for their diligent and thoughtful readings of early drafts of this first edition. Their suggestions pointed the way to make this a better book.

Full Manuscript Reviewers

John Allen, *University of Arizona*

Ted Barker, *Northwest Florida State College*

Mark Basham, *Regis University*

Kyle Baumbauer, *Texas A&M University*

Kathy Becker-Blease, *Oregon State University*

Rachel Blaser, *University of San Diego*

Christina M. Brown, *Saint Louis University*

Eric Bruns, *Campbellsville University*

Kathryn Caldwell, *Ithaca College*

Aimee A. Callender, *Auburn University*

David Campbell, *Humboldt State University*

Brian D. Carpenter, *Washington University, St. Louis*

Lawrence Cohen, *University of Delaware*

Brian Cowley, *Park University*

Verne Cox, *University of Texas, Arlington*

Natalie Dautovich, *University of Alabama*

Robert DuBois, *Waukesha County Technical College*

Kimberly Duff, *Cerritos College*

Darlene Earley, *Southern Union State Community College*

Kathy Erickson, *Pima Community College*

Carlos Escoto, *Eastern Connecticut State University*

Kendall Eskine, *Loyola University New Orleans*

Melanie Evans, *Eastern Connecticut State University*

Debra Lynn Frame, *University of Cincinnati*

Andrea Friedrich, *University of Kentucky*

Stephen L. Forssell, *George Washington University*

Perry Fuchs, *University of Texas, Arlington*

Philip Gable, *University of Alabama*

Bridgett Galvin, *Framingham State College*

Deborah Garfin, *Georgia State University*

Bryan Gibson, *Central Michigan University*

Allen Gorman, *Angelo State University*

Ruth Grahn, *Connecticut College*

Ruth M. Grant, *Sacred Heart University*

Anthony Greene, *University of Wisconsin, Milwaukee*

Christina Grimes, *Duke University*

Scott Gustafson, *University of Mississippi*

Erin E. Hardin, *Texas Tech University*

Robert J. Hines, *University of Arkansas, Little Rock*

Linda Jackson, *Michigan State University*

Irene P. Kan, *Villanova University*

Craig Kinsley, *University of Richmond*

Megan L. Knowles, *Franklin and Marshall College*
Jordan Labouff, *Baylor University*
Carrie Lane, *Florida State University*
Jennifer Lee, *Cabrillo College*
Fabio Leite, *Ohio State University, Lima*
Robin Lightner, *University of Cincinnati*
Christine Lofgren, *University of California, Irvine*
Nicolette Lopez, *University of Texas, Arlington*
David Malcolm, *Fordham University*
Michael Mangan, *University of New Hampshire*
Abigail Marsh, *Georgetown University*
Anna Medina, *Gonzaga University*
Sean P. Meegan, *University of Utah*
Antoinette Miller, *Clayton State University*
Robin K. Morgan, *Indiana University Southeast*
Hajime Otani, *Central Michigan University*
Marion Perlmutter, *University of Michigan, Ann Arbor*
Gabriel Radvansky, *University of Notre Dame*
Cynthia Reidi, *Morrisville State College*
Ann E. Renken, *University of Southern California*
Heather J. Rice, *Washington University, St. Louis*
Michael Roberts, *DePauw University*
Catherine Sanderson, *Amherst College*
Patrick Saxe, *State University of New York, New Paltz*
Luis Schettino, *Lafayette College*
David Schroeder, *University of Arkansas*
Dennis Shaffer, *Ohio State University, Mansfield*
Donald Sharpe, *University of Regina*
Mikle Don South, *Brigham Young University*
Brian Thomas, *Baldwin-Wallace College*
Lisa Thomassen, *Indiana University, Bloomington*
Anre Venter, *University of Notre Dame*
Craig Vickio, *Bowling Green State University*
Mark Walter, *Salisbury University*
Shannon Welch, *University of Idaho*
John Wright, *Washington State University*
Erin Young, *Texas A&M University*

Focus Group Reviewers

Judith Addelston, *Valencia College, East*
Anthony Ahrens, *American University*
Roxanna Andersen, *Palm Beach State College, Boca Raton*
Stacy Anderson, *Florida Gulf Coast University*
Richard Bernstein, *Broward College, South*
Kathleen Bey, *Palm Beach State College, Lake Worth*
Sara Broaders, *Northwestern University*
John Timothy Cannon, *University of Scranton*
John Connor, *Daytona State College*

David Seth Crystal, *Georgetown University*
Jennifer Engler, *York College of Pennsylvania*
Gregory Harris, *Polk State College*
Jeffrey Henriques, *University of Wisconsin, Madison*
Jennifer Johnson, *Bloomsberg University*
Todd Joseph, *Hillsborough Community College, Dale Mabry*
Irene Kan, *Villanova University*
Kevin Keating, *Broward College, North*
Cheri Kittrell, *State College of Florida, Manatee-Sarasota*
Debra Laino, *Philadelphia University*
Natalie Lawrence, *James Madison University*
Daniel McConnell, *University of Central Florida*
Ronald Morrison, *Daytona State College*
Kevin O'Neil, *Florida Gulf Coast University*
Gwendolyn Parsons-Spurrier, *Hillsborough Community College, Ybor City*
Lois Pasapane, *Palm Beach State College, Lake Worth*
Ronnie Rothschild, *Broward College, Central*
Sharleen Sakai, *Michigan State University*
Alex Sharpe, *Santa Fe College*
Caroline Shelton-Toney, *Polk State College*
William Suits, *Seminole State College of Florida*
Cyril Svoboda, *University of Maryland University College*
Clarissa Thompson, *University of Oklahoma*
Terry Trepper, *Purdue University, Calumet*
Katherine Urquhart, *Lake Sumter Community College*
Lona Whitmarsh, *Fairleigh Dickinson University*

We also thank Suzanne Corkin for reading and commenting on sections describing the amnesic patient H.M.

Finally, we could not have done this without the patience and support of our families: Stephanie, Christina, and Anthony (JTC) and Roger, Kristin, Karen, and Karla (LF).

Taste buds contained in the papillae of the tongue are far more
responsive to bitter tastes than to sweet tastes.

The Science of Mind

The Discipline of Psychology

1

Learning Objectives

1 Explain the subject matter that psychologists study, addressing the meaning of *mind* and psychology's role as a hub science.

2 Analyze the respective contributions of philosophy and the physical sciences as the "roots" of modern psychology.

3 Compare and contrast the early movements in psychology—structuralism, Gestalt psychology, functionalism, behaviorism, psychodynamic theory, and humanism—in terms of leading figures, core principles, and contributions to modern psychology.

4 Differentiate the seven major perspectives of modern psychology in terms of typical research questions, research methods, and focal causes of behavior.

5 Analyze the ways in which the seven major perspectives can be integrated to address a single psychological problem or topic.

6 Explain why psychology's role as a "hub science" allows psychologists to pursue a wide range of career paths with respect to professional specialties and research areas.

© Argosy Publishing, Inc.

Studying the science of psychology can lead you to see yourself and other people in completely new ways. A lifetime of observation teaches us many things about our own behavior and about the behavior of others, but psychological science can uncover new and exciting explanations for behavior that we otherwise might miss. Let's begin with a seemingly simple and familiar example: our ability to taste. We all know a lot about taste—what we like or dislike, the different qualities of taste, and so on. You might even be aware that some types of taste seem stronger than others. Most of us can taste sweetness in a solution of one part sugar in 200 parts water; this ability shows an impressive taste

© Masterfile/Radius Images

3

sensitivity, to be sure. As remarkable as this sensitivity appears to be, however, people can detect one part bitter substance (like quinine) in 2 *million* parts water. This contrast in taste sensitivity between sweet and bitter does not reflect the actual difference between sweet and bitter substances—that is, bitter tastes are not 10,000 times stronger than sweet tastes, but that is how we experience them. Why would we have such a vast difference in sensitivity between these tastes?

Our observations of taste do not help us out much in answering this question, but psychology can. As it turns out, our greater sensitivity to bitter tastes is highly adaptive: Most poisons or toxins taste bitter, and if you want to stay alive, it is more important to avoid swallowing poison than to enjoy something sweet. Being far more sensitive to tastes that are bitter is a trait that has served our species well, because it helps us avoid eating things that could potentially kill us. Psychology helps us understand why we do the things we do by providing a context for understanding behavior.

To gain that understanding, psychology has to act like the zoom feature in Google Earth. In some parts of this textbook, we will be zooming in on human behaviors, like looking at the highly magnified image at the beginning of the chapter of the tongue, which allows us to taste, and tracing the messages about taste sent from the tongue to the brain. At other times, we'll zoom back out again to take in the larger picture, to better understand why the boy on the previous page is giving his bitter-tasting broccoli a skeptical look.

Psychologists zoom in to the study of the mind using in-depth perspectives, which we will be describing in this chapter. For example, we can look at the little boy's reaction to his broccoli from a developmental perspective, which tells us that taste sensitivity decreases over the lifespan. Or, using the social perspective, we can think about social influences like culture on food preferences. Cottage cheese, enjoyed by many Americans, is viewed with disgust in some other parts of the world. Fruit bat pie, a delicacy in Palau, might not be a popular item for a campus dining facility in the United States.

Although single perspectives can tell us a lot about a phenomenon like our sensitivity to bitter tastes, no one perspective can give us a complete answer. The best view of all comes from zooming back out again by putting multiple perspectives together into a whole. You can learn a lot about your house from Google Earth by zooming in, but when you see how your home fits into the larger scene of city, state, country, and planet, that viewpoint adds something special to your understanding.

We'll start by learning more about psychology's main perspectives, along with a little background about their origins. At that point, we'll be in a better position to understand how these perspectives come together to give us the big picture. ⚙

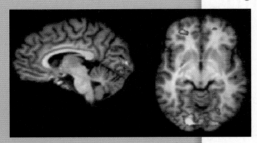

Introspection is the personal observation of our own thoughts, feelings, and behaviors. Because we are not perfect observers of the operations of our own minds, psychologists developed other methods that provide truly scientific insight into the mind. In this functional magnetic resonance imaging (fMRI) scan, areas of the brain that were activated when the participant was hungry are highlighted. Through technology, researchers can better understand how the brain regulates hunger. From D. Fuhrer, S. Zysset, & M. Stumvoll, "Brain Activity in Hunger and Satiety: An Exploratory Visually Stimulated fMRI Study," in *Obesity* (2008) 16: 945–950. © Nature Publishing Group.

What Is Psychology?

The study of the **mind** is as fascinating as it is complex. Psychological scientists view the mind as a way of talking about the brain and its activities, including thought, emotion, and behavior. A quick look at this textbook's table of contents will show you the variety of approaches to *mind* that you will encounter along this voyage, such as the thinking mind (cognitive psychology) and the troubled mind (abnormal psychology).

The word **psychology** is a combination of two Greek words: *psyche* (or *psuche*), or "soul," and *logos*, "the study of." For the ancient Greeks, the use of the word "soul" was closer to our modern view of a spirit or mind. *Logos* is the source of all our "ologies," such as biology, anthropology, and so on. Literally translated, therefore, *psychology* means "the study of the mind."

Contemporary definitions of psychology refine this basic meaning. Most psychologists today define their field as *the scientific study of behavior and mental processes*—that is, the scientific study of the mind.

The phrase *behavior and mental processes* has undergone several changes over the history of psychology. *Behavior* refers to any action that we can observe. As we will see in our chapter on research methods, observation has been an important tool for psychologists from the very early days of the discipline. Notice, too, that our definition does not specify whose behavior is to be examined. Although the bulk of psychology focuses on human behavior, animal behavior has been an essential part of the discipline, both for its own sake and for the sake of comparison with human behavior.

The study of *mental processes* has been highly dependent on the methods available to psychologists. Early efforts to study mental processes were generally unsatisfactory, as they relied on the use of **introspection**, or the personal observation of your own thoughts, feelings, and behaviors. Because it is difficult for others to confirm an individual's introspections, this subjective approach does not lend itself well to the scientific method. If you say that you are feeling hungry, how can anyone else really know if your observation is accurate or not? In the last 30 years, however, revolutions in the methods used to observe brain activity have allowed psychologists to revisit the question of mental processes with much greater objectivity and success.

As you learn more about psychology, some conclusions will seem obvious to you. After all, we already know a great deal about the mind from our own experiences. In other cases, the conclusions of psychological research might challenge your firmly held beliefs. You may be surprised to learn that having a "good cry" can make you feel worse instead of better, or that people are less likely to come to another person's aid when they are part of a crowd of observers than when they are the only ones available to help. Sometimes, we even believe ideas that contradict each other. Everyone knows that opposites attract and that birds of a feather flock together. It takes the science of psychology to determine when and under what conditions these beliefs are actually correct.

mind The brain and its activities, including thought, emotion, and behavior.

psychology The scientific study of behavior and mental processes.

introspection Personal observation of your own thoughts, feelings, and behavior.

What Are Psychology's Roots?

Psychology is a relatively young discipline, dating back only to the 1870s. However, topics that interest modern psychologists go back much farther in the history of human thought. People living as long ago as 6000–5000 BCE in Assyria described their dreams (Restak, 1988). Among these accounts are descriptions of being chased, which are still among the most common dreams experienced by people (Nielsen et al., 2003). See ● Figure 1.1 for common dream themes that many people experience.

The psychology family tree includes two major roots: **philosophy** and the **physical sciences.** Psychologists answer questions traditionally posed by philosophers by borrowing the methods of the physical sciences. We examine scientific methods in detail in our next chapter.

Philosophers and psychologists share an interest in questions regarding the nature of the self, the effects of early experience, the existence of free will, and the origin of knowledge. Both disciplines consider the relative balance of biological factors (nature) and environmental factors (nurture) in the resulting human behavior. Both attempt to determine the relationships between self-interest and the welfare of the community, between body and mind, and between humans and the other species with whom we share the planet. Although we typically consider questions of the unconscious mind

philosophy The discipline that systematically examines basic concepts, including the source of knowledge.

physical science Any science that studies nonliving matter, including physics, chemistry, astronomy, and geology.

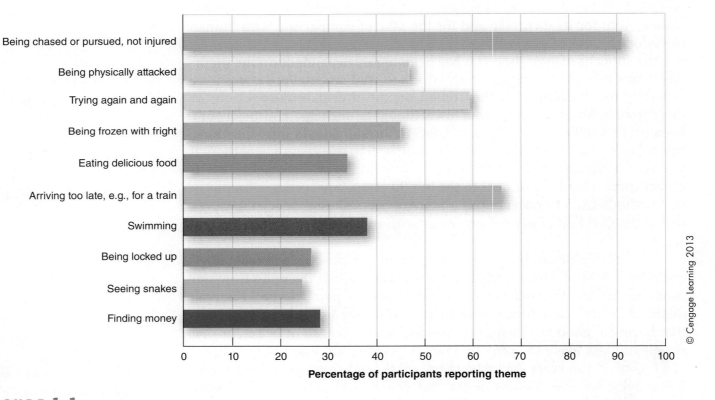

© Cengage Learning 2013

FIGURE 1.1

Many People Report Dreams With the Same Themes. Although we don't understand why we dream about certain things, many people report similar themes in their dreams. *Source: Adapted from Nielsen et al. (2003).*

and abnormal behavior to be the realm of the psychologist, philosophers investigated these issues thousands of years before the first psychologist was born.

The Philosophers' Questions   A comprehensive survey of the philosophical roots of psychology is beyond the scope of an introductory textbook like this one, but we can provide you with a small sample of this heritage. The point we would like you to take away from this discussion is that many of the questions you will read about in this textbook are not unique to psychology, but have fascinated thinkers for thousands of years. What is the mind? What is the relationship between the body and mind? Is the mind inborn or is it formed through experience?

The ancient Greek philosopher Plato (427–347 BCE) was one of the earliest thinkers to tackle the question "What is the mind?" Plato's version of the mind featured three parts that must be in balance: reason, spirit, and appetite. He compared these parts to a team of horses (spirit and appetite) guided by a driver (reason). Plato's division of the mind is echoed in the more modern work of Sigmund Freud (1856–1939). Freud also divided the mind into three parts: the id (inborn aggressive and sexual impulses), the ego (the self), and the superego (conscience). Later in this textbook, we will see that Freud's concept of the ego serves the role of Plato's driver, overseeing and balancing the two horses: the impulses of the id and the restrictions imposed by the superego. You might relate to the dilemma of the driver (reason/ego) when you are faced with an opportunity to indulge an impulse (id) while hearing that little voice in the back of your head (superego) telling you that this really isn't a very good idea.

Plato viewed the mind as a charioteer (reason) driving two horses (spirit and appetite).

Another question with ancient roots asks about the relationship between body and mind, a topic that we will explore further in our chapter on biological psychology. On one side of the question were thinkers who believed in *dualism,* or the idea that body and mind are quite different and separate. To the dualist, our bodies are physical, but our minds are something nonphysical and somewhat more mysterious. Arguing against this point of view were the proponents of *monism,* the idea that mind and body are not separate. Another way of thinking about monism is to assume that the mind is the result of activity in the brain. Does one of these positions seem closer to your own way of thinking than the other?

The ancient Greek philosophers were nearly evenly split between monism and dualism. Democritus (460–370 BCE) and Aristotle (384–322 BCE) argued in favor of monism, while Pythagoras (580–500 BCE), Socrates (469–399 BCE), and Plato believed in dualism. As the classical world of Greece and Rome gave way, monism moved to the background while medieval Christian thinkers wrote about a dualism between body and soul. Dualism continued to dominate discussion during the Renaissance. The French philosopher René Descartes (1596–1650) was a vocal proponent of dualism. He saw the body as mechanical but the mind as a nonphysical entity not suitable for scientific inquiry.

© Beaux Arts/Alamy

René Descartes (1596–1650) believed in mind-body dualism, or the separation of the physical body from the nonphysical mind.

Contemporary scientists studying the brain support monism, but they agree with Descartes' belief that the mind and body influence one another. In our biological psychology chapter, we emphasize the reciprocal relationships between biology and behavior. Our biology clearly impacts our behavior, as when hormones released during times of stress increase our heart rate and make our palms sweaty, but our behavior also affects our biology, as the situations we choose to enter (e.g., skydiving) influence the release of stress hormones. This reciprocal influence between biology and behavior can be seen in social situations, too. We know that among primates, males' testosterone levels predict their amount of sexual activity. At the same time, however, the males' testosterone levels increase in the presence of larger numbers of available and receptive females (Cacioppo & Berntson, 1992). That is, the social context affects the physiology of the male primates.

Just as philosophers disagreed about the relationship of mind and body, they argued about whether the mind's knowledge was inborn or the product

Psychology
as a Hub Science

Psychology Connects to Other Disciplines

Psychology is all about people, and there are very few occupations that do not require an understanding of people and their behavior. An architect cannot design a functional space without

Psychology

considering how people respond to crowding. An attorney cannot cross-examine a witness without an understanding of memory, motivation, emotion, and stress. A teacher cannot encourage students to reach their potential without an understanding of child development. The study of psychology, then, provides you with better insight into and understanding of many different occupations and fields of study.

You have probably seen applications that allow you to map your friendship networks on social media, with shorter links indicating greater connectivity than longer links and

with larger bubbles indicating more overlapping friendships with another person. Kevin Boyack and his colleagues generated a similar map of the sciences (see ● Figure 1.2), but used reference lists in journal articles instead of friendship networks (Boyack, Klavans, & Börner, 2005). The resulting analysis shows that psychology is one of the major "hub" sciences, with strong connections to the medical sciences, the social sciences, and education. In our upcoming chapters, we will highlight these connections with examples that are relevant to each particular chapter. ⊗

of experience. Some philosophers, including Descartes, argued that ideas and emotions were innate or inborn. More commonly, philosophers beginning with Aristotle believed that all knowledge is gained through sensory experience. Beginning in the 17th century, this idea flourished in the British philosophical school of *empiricism*. The empiricists viewed the mind as a "blank slate" at birth that was filled with ideas gained by observing the world. As one of the major empiricists, John Locke (1632–1704), wrote in *An Essay Concerning Human Understanding*:

> Let us then suppose the mind to be, as we say, white paper void of all characters, without any ideas. How comes it to be furnished? . . . To this I answer, in one word, from EXPERIENCE. (Locke, 1690, II.1.2)

Empiricism contributed two important ideas that continue to influence contemporary psychologists. First, empiricism is the foundation for science itself, which allows us to gain knowledge through careful and systematic observation, resulting in "empirical" results.

Aristotle (384–322 BCE) argued in favor of monism and believed that we gain knowledge through our senses.

John Locke (1632–1704) and other empiricist philosophers believed that the mind was a "blank slate" at birth and that knowledge was gained through experience.

© National Trust Photo Library/ Art ResoUrce, NY

© www.BibleLandPictures.com/Alamy

FIGURE 1.2

Psychology as a Hub Science. This map of science was generated by comparing citations from over 1 million papers published in more than 7,000 journals since 2000. Psychology appears among the seven major areas of science, indicated in the map by large fonts. The other six major areas are social sciences, mathematics, physics, chemistry, earth sciences, and medicine. *Source:* Adapted from "Mapping the Backbone of Science," by Kevin W. Boyack et al., 2005, *Scientometrics, 64*(3). With kind permission from Springer Science+Business Media.

The empiricists had a profound influence on the foundations of American political thought—All of us are created equal. For generations, Europe had been ruled by people who were born into positions of power instead of earning the privilege of leading through hard work and education. If knowledge is not innate or inborn, any of us can learn enough to grow up to be President.

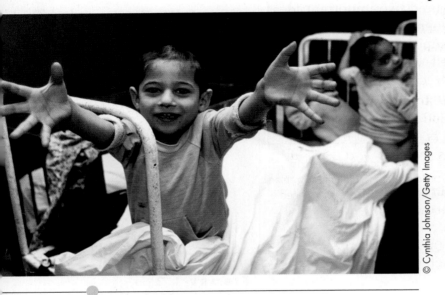

© Cynthia Johnson/Getty Images

Desperate conditions in Romanian orphanages in the 1970s left many children without the experiences they needed for optimum cognitive or social development.

Second, empiricism guided the 20th-century behaviorists, psychologists who examined behaviors that were the result of experience and that could be directly observed. The behaviorists' contributions to psychology will be discussed in detail in our chapter on learning.

The philosophical debate about the source of knowledge is echoed in psychology as researchers consider the relative contributions of inborn or innate factors (nature) and experience (nurture) to particular behaviors. You might have heard people debate the importance of genes (nature) or good schools (nurture) on shaping the intelligence of children, a topic we discuss in a later chapter on cognition and intelligence. Contemporary psychology no longer views the question of nature and nurture as either/or. Instead, we see the mind as a result of complex interactions between inborn characteristics and experiences. We might have a genetic predisposition for intelligent behavior, but intelligence depends on experience, too. During the 1970s, children in Romanian orphanages experienced extremely deprived social conditions due to a lack of funding for their care. The children had few opportunities to interact with other people or with the environment. They spent most of their days in cots surrounded by sheets, preventing them from even seeing other children. Children who were adopted from these orphanages at young ages were able to recover, but the children who had endured years of deprivation experienced permanent cognitive deficits (Ames, 1997). In our chapters on genetics and development, we will revisit these debates in depth.

If philosophers and psychologists ask the same questions, what makes these two fields different from each other? As we noted earlier, the structure and operations of the mind are not always obvious, even to the most brilliant philosopher, and the scientific methods of the psychologist helped develop additional theories of the mind and behavior. The branching of psychology from philosophy was gradual. Nineteenth-century philosophers began to argue for the experimental study of human behavior, and some, like Alexander Bain (1818–1903), wrote psychology textbooks and founded psychology journals. As philosophical ideas were tested scientifically, new explanations for the mind and behavior began to emerge, and the march toward psychological science as an independent discipline became irreversible.

The Physical Scientists' Methods

Running along a parallel track to the early philosophers, ancient physicians were laying the foundation of our biological knowledge of the brain and nervous system, discussed in greater detail in our chapter on biological psychology. During this pursuit, physicians helped develop the scientific methods that would become central to contemporary psychology and previewed the application of the knowledge they gained to the improvement of individual well-being.

Although some confusion occurred along the way, as in Aristotle's belief that the mind was located in the heart, ancient people had a rudimentary understanding that the head and later the brain were important for mental life. As long as 7,000 years ago, healers using a technique known as trepanation drilled holes in a person's skull to cure some unspecified conditions, possibly headache or hallucination. Subsequent growth of the skull bones indicates that some patients actually survived this procedure. The early Egyptians correctly understood that paralysis of a part of the body was due to brain damage and that such damage was permanent (Breasted, 1930).

As early as 500 BCE, Greek physicians began to systematically dissect human bodies. Not only did they correctly conclude that the brain was the organ of memory, thinking, and understanding, but they noticed the connection of the brain to the sense organs, such as the eyes, and recognized that the brain is the source of many emotional problems. Later Greek physicians offered a rudimentary theory of personality that remained popular until the 19th century. According to this approach, personality would be affected by the relative amounts of four different body fluids: yellow bile (a type of gastric fluid), black bile, blood, and phlegm. For example, a person with a sad disposition suffered from excess black bile, whereas a person with a lot of blood would be cheerful. Medical practices such as "bleeding" a patient were applications of this theory.

For many centuries, the whole of medicine remained a primitive business. Beginning in the 17th and 18th centuries, scientists armed with new technologies, including the light microscope (see ● Figure 1.3), began to make a series of important new discoveries about the human body and mind. For example, they demonstrated that a single sensory nerve carried one type of information, instead of multiple types. You might have already duplicated this research yourself while rubbing your sleepy eyes—you see a flash of light. The nerves serving the retina of the eye do not know how to process information about touch or pressure. When stimulated, they are capable of one and only one type of message—light. These types of discoveries about the physical aspects of the mind convinced scientists that, contrary to Descartes' conclusions, the mind really could be studied scientifically.

The work of Hermann von Helmholtz (1821–1894) on the speed of nerve signaling provided further evidence that the mind had a physical basis. Von Helmholtz asked his participants to push a button when they felt a touch. If a thigh were touched, participants reacted faster than when the toe was touched. Because the toe is farther from the brain than the thigh, signals from the toe required more time to reach the brain. Von Helmholtz used these differences in reaction time to show that voluntary behavior did

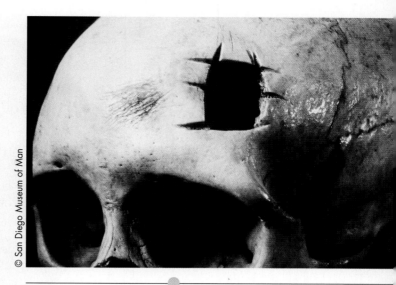

© San Diego Museum of Man

Ancient people might have attempted to cure headaches, seizures, or psychological disorders by drilling holes in the skull. Bone growth around the hole indicates that some of these patients survived the procedure.

© Photos.com

The traditional red-and-white barber's pole has its roots in the practice of bloodletting to treat diseases, which was often carried out in barber shops. The red-and-white stripes represent bloody bandages wrapped around a pole.

FIGURE 1.3

Microscopes Changed the World of Science. This light microscope was used by Anton von Leeuwenhoek to discover red blood cells in 1676. Microscopes opened a whole new world to scientists interested in living things.

A = A screw for adjusting the height of the object being examined
B = A metal plate serving as the body
C = A skewer to impale the object and rotate it
D = The lens itself, which was spherical

The work of Hermann von Helmholtz (1821–1894) on reaction time helped establish the mind as something that could be studied scientifically.

not occur instantaneously as previously thought. The fact that behavior is *not* instantaneous, but requires time for the system to process physical signals, contributed to a more scientific, less mystical view of the nervous system.

At the same time that the philosophers began to incorporate physiological and psychological concepts into their work, the physical scientists began to explore the questions asked by the philosophers. The gradual merger of these approaches resulted in a series of experiments that looked more and more like contemporary psychology. Scientists began to ask questions about the relationships between physical stimulation and its resulting sensations. For example, Gustav Fechner (1801–1889) was able to identify the softest sound a person could hear by randomly presenting sounds of different intensities, to which a participant would respond "yes" or "no." When the "yes" responses reached 50%, Fechner concluded that the sound was within the range that the human ear could detect. The stage was set for a modern science of psychology.

Summary 1.1

Highlights in the Philosophical and Scientific Roots of Psychology

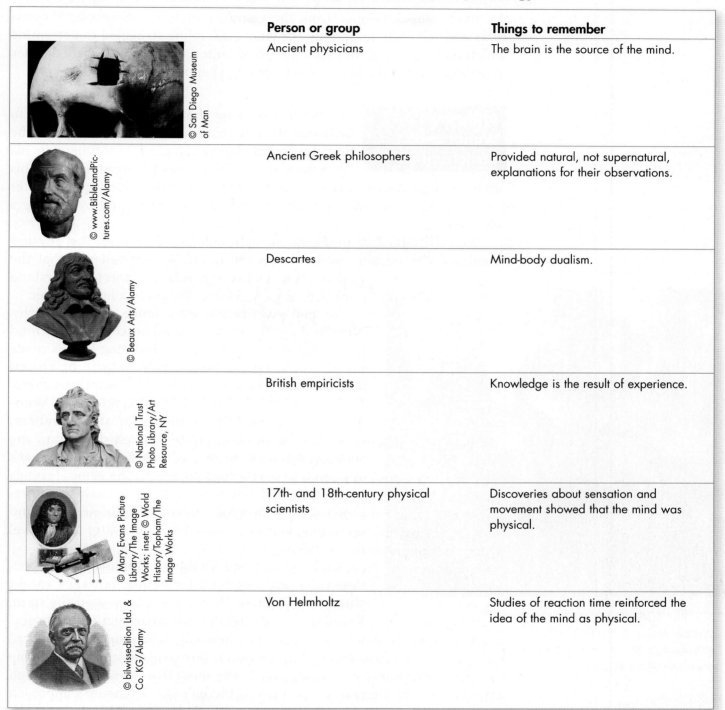

	Person or group	Things to remember
© San Diego Museum of Man	Ancient physicians	The brain is the source of the mind.
© www.BibleLandPictures.com/Alamy	Ancient Greek philosophers	Provided natural, not supernatural, explanations for their observations.
© Beaux Arts/Alamy	Descartes	Mind-body dualism.
© National Trust Photo Library/Art Resource, NY	British empiricists	Knowledge is the result of experience.
© Mary Evans Picture Library/The Image Works; inset: © World History/Topham/The Image Works	17th- and 18th-century physical scientists	Discoveries about sensation and movement showed that the mind was physical.
© bilwissedition Ltd. & Co. KG/Alamy	Von Helmholtz	Studies of reaction time reinforced the idea of the mind as physical.

How Did the Science of Psychology Begin?

As psychology developed from the gradual merger of philosophical questions and scientific reasoning, the young discipline struggled to determine which questions and methods were best suited to its goals. Lively debates arose among psychologists who helped to shape the field.

The credit for being the first psychologist goes to **Wilhelm Wundt** (1832–1920), who conducted the first documented psychological experiment in his laboratory at the University of Leipzig in 1879. This landmark experiment was a simple test of reaction time. How quickly after hearing a ball drop onto a platform could a person respond by striking a telegraph key?

Wundt, trained in medicine and physiology, was one of the physical scientists who became interested in the mind. Wundt believed that the goal of a new science of psychology was to understand consciousness, which we discuss in a later chapter.

Wundt saw mental experience as a hierarchy. The mind constructs an overall perception (the food I'm eating tastes good) out of building blocks made up of separate sensations (such as taste or vision) and emotional responses. One of Wundt's students, Edward Titchener (1867–1923), expanded on Wundt's views to establish a theory of **structuralism,** in which the mind could be broken down into the smallest elements of mental experience. Titchener's approach to psychology paralleled the general trends in the physical sciences of his day, such as efforts in chemistry to break molecules into elements and attempts by physicists to describe matter at the level of the atom.

Both Wundt and Titchener employed introspection as an experimental technique, but they meant somewhat different things when they used the term. Recall that we earlier defined introspection as observing your own thoughts, feelings, and behaviors. Wundt's approach to introspection is illustrated by his reaction time experiment with the falling ball. This experiment is introspective in the sense that pressing a telegraph key indicates an internal state—I heard the ball fall. Titchener's approach to introspection was more consistent with the building block approach to experience. He would instruct his research participants to describe an object, perhaps a cup, in great detail (size, color, shape, and so on), hoping that these details would serve as the building blocks for the mind's overall perception of the cup.

© INTERFOTO/Alamy

Wilhelm Wundt (1832–1920), seated in this photo, is considered to be the first experimental psychologist.

structuralism An approach in which the mind is broken into the smallest elements of mental experience.

Gestalt Psychology

The structuralists' effort to break behavior down into its essential elements was rejected by a group of early 20th-century German psychologists, including Kurt Koffka, Max Wertheimer, and Wolfgang Köhler, who founded **Gestalt psychology.** *Gestalt,* although lacking a clear translation into English, means "form" or "whole." The Gestalt psychologists believed that breaking a "whole" perception into its building blocks, as advocated by the structuralists, would result in the loss of some important psychological information. For example, take a look at the middle image in ● Figure 1.4. It is the same in both the top and bottom rows, yet in the context of the first row, most people would interpret the image as the letter B. In the context of the bottom row, however, the image looks like the number 13. The structuralists would have a difficult time explaining why the same visual building blocks could lead to such different conclusions.

While largely known for their work in perception, the Gestalt psychologists also had wide-ranging interests in learning, memory, motivation, and group dynamics. The influence of Gestalt psychologists will resurface in our later discussions of perception and cognitive psychology, the study of thinking and information processing.

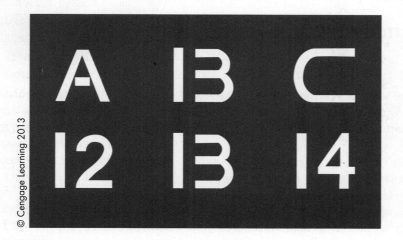
© Bettmann/CORBIS

Max Wertheimer (1880–1943) was one of the founders of Gestalt psychology.

William James and Functionalism

While the structuralists and Gestalt psychologists continued their debate, a new type of psychology emerged, partly in response to the publication of Charles Darwin's *The Origin of Species* in 1859 and *The Descent of Man* in 1871. **Functionalism** viewed behavior as purposeful, since it led to survival. Nineteenth-century United States politics and culture, which valued individuality, practicality, and frontier survival, embraced functionalism. Instead of restricting themselves to exploring the

© Cengage Learning 2013

FIGURE 1.4

Gestalt Psychologists Challenged Structuralism. Participants usually see the middle figure as a B when instructed to look at the first row, but see a 13 when instructed to read the second row. The structuralists, who believed that experiences could be reduced to small building blocks, would have difficulty explaining these results. In contrast, Gestalt psychologists, who emphasized the role of context or the "whole" in perception, would have no difficulties at all.

Gestalt psychology An approach to psychology that saw experience as different than the sum of its elements.

functionalism An approach to psychology that saw behavior as purposeful and contributing to survival.

William James (1842–1910) proposed functionalism, an approach to the mind that viewed behavior as purposeful.

structure of the mind, functionalists were more interested in *why* behavior and mental processes worked in a particular way. To answer these questions, functionalists broadened their research techniques beyond the introspection used by Wundt and Titchener.

Functionalism's chief proponent was **William James** (1842–1910), whose textbook, *Principles of Psychology* (1890), dominated the field of psychology for 50 years. At Harvard University, James offered a course in psychology and established a laboratory in 1875, four years before Wundt's first lab. However, James's lab served primarily as a demonstration lab for his course rather than a research lab like Wundt's. Because of psychology's emphasis on research contributions, Wundt is still given credit for being the first psychologist.

There are few topics in psychology that James did not address in his *Principles,* and many of his ideas sound thoroughly modern. For example, James coined the term *stream of consciousness* to describe the flow of ideas people experience while awake. Throughout his discussions of mental processes and behavior, James emphasized the role of evolution. For the functionalist, the value of an activity depended on its consequences. Behaviors that enhance survival are repeated, and those that are either irrelevant

Connecting *to* Research

The Experiment That Launched Gestalt Psychology

The Gestalt movement traces its origin to a single experiment conducted by Max Wertheimer in 1912 that demonstrated the apparent movement of objects (Wertheimer, 1912).

According to historians, Wertheimer was inspired to conduct his study after playing with a toy stroboscope, which he bought from a vendor at a train station (Boring, 1942). If you look through the slits in the rotating disk of a stroboscope, like the one in ● Figure 1.5, It looks like the images behind the disk are moving, somewhat like an old cartoon. Most of us would probably just enjoy

the toy, but Wertheimer immediately saw a deeper meaning, which he tested in his experiment.

The Question: *Can the perceived movement between two stimuli be explained in structuralist terms? If Wundt and the structuralists were correct and all perceptions could be broken down into their elements, then we would not "see" movement when viewing stationary stimuli.*

METHODS

Wertheimer used a stroboscope to control the timing of the appearance of two black lines (one vertical and

the other horizontal) against a white background. The first line would appear and then disappear, followed some time later by the appearance and disappearance of the second line. The amount of time between the disappearance of the first line and the appearance of the second, which depended on the speed with which the wheel on the stroboscope was turned, varied from trial to trial, and the observers noted whether they perceived movement or not.

RESULTS

When the interval between the appearance of the two lines was

or damaging to survival are abandoned. If we dream, it must be because dreaming improves our chances of survival. If we enjoy ice cream, it must be because eating sweet, high-fat foods enhances survival—at least it did for our ancestors, for whom famine was a much more likely problem than obesity.

It is difficult to overestimate the impact of William James on psychology. Although he really didn't establish a particular "school" or train large numbers of students as did Wundt or other early psychologists, James's ideas have become so dominant in psychology that we no longer refer to any separate "functionalist" approach. Structuralism came and went, but all contemporary psychologists are generally functionalists at heart. As described by psychology historians, "As a systematic point of view, functionalism was an overwhelming success, but largely because of this success it is no longer a distinct school of psychology. It was absorbed into the mainstream psychology. No happier fate could await any psychological point of view" (Chaplin & Krawiec, 1979, p. 53).

James, like the Gestalt psychologists, rejected the notion that you can study the mind by breaking it into elements or building blocks, as this division would result in a loss of understanding. As psychology entered the 20th century, this "big picture" approach of William James eventually broke up into a variety of separate perspectives, as psychologists attempted to gain understanding by limiting their research to particular aspects of the mind and behavior.

© Corbis Bridge/Alamy

Courtesy of the Wellesley College Archives

Mary Whiton Calkins (1863–1930) was a student of William James at Harvard, although she could not officially register due to her gender. She studied memory and the self and served as president of the American Psychological Association in 1905.

© SSPL/Science Museum/ The Image Works

FIGURE 1.5

A Toy Stroboscope Helped Launch Gestalt Psychology. Studying a toy stroboscope, which produces a perception of movement, inspired Wertheimer to question Wundt and the structuralists. How could the perception of movement in the image be explained by basic sensations if there were no real sensations to see in the first place?

about 30 milliseconds (a millisecond is one one-thousandth of a second), the observers reported that the lines appeared and disappeared together. With intervals longer than 60 milliseconds, observers reported seeing one line that moved from a vertical to horizontal orientation.

CONCLUSIONS

Wertheimer realized that his participants were "seeing" something— movement—that could not be explained by the sensations of lines appearing and disappearing. Wundt and the structuralists must be wrong— there is more to perception than just sensing elements, like lines. An application of Wertheimer's work can be seen in the "moving" words in scrolling electric signs, which are really just groups of lights flashing on and off. ✪

© A. Vossberg/Visum/The Image Works

Scrolling signs take advantage of the apparent movement observed by Wertheimer. Nothing in the sign is moving at all, but perception of movement results when the lights flash on and off in sequence.

Beginning at the dawn of the 20th century, the "mental processes" in our definition of psychology took a backseat to observable behavior for the better part of the next 50 years, as psychologists following the perspective of **behaviorism** concentrated on observable, measurable behaviors. As part of their effort to measure behavior carefully, many behaviorists restricted their research to studies using animals. Armed with Darwin's evidence linking humans to animals, the behaviorists comfortably drew parallels between their observations of animals and their assumptions about human behavior. In particular, behaviorists were fascinated by learning, which we define as any persistent change in behavior due to experience. We will examine the behaviorists' contributions to this area in depth in a later chapter on learning.

While studying digestion, Ivan Pavlov (1849–1936), seated second from left, realized that his dogs could learn that certain signals meant food was on the way.

Ivan Petrovitch Pavlov (1849–1936) had a particularly significant impact on the course of behaviorism and psychology. While studying digestion in dogs, he realized that the dogs' salivation in response to the arrival of the handler or to being harnessed for an experiment indicated that the dogs had associated, or linked, these signals with the arrival of food. The dogs' ability to use this learned association to anticipate important future events was a remarkable advantage in terms of survival. This type of learning is now referred to as classical or Pavlovian conditioning, which we will discuss in detail in our chapter on learning.

Psychology textbooks would not spend too much time on Pavlov if his research applied only to salivating dogs. Although classical conditioning occurs in rather primitive organisms, including fruit flies, snails, and slugs, it also occurs quite frequently in humans. Many of our emotional responses associated with environmental cues are the result of this type of learning. If you feel especially anxious prior to taking an exam, you can thank classical conditioning. If you are repulsed by the idea of eating a food that you once consumed just before becoming ill, this is again a likely result of classical conditioning. A war veteran who experiences distress while filling a pickup truck with diesel fuel (a common battlefield smell) is also likely to be experiencing the results of classical conditioning.

John B. Watson (1878–1958) began experimenting with learning in rats, and independently came to many of the same conclusions as Pavlov. Watson also echoed the "blank slate" approach of the British empiricist philosophers in his emphasis on the role of experience in forming human behavior. In a famous speech given in 1926, Watson made the following claim:

> Give me a dozen healthy infants, well-formed, and my own specified world to bring them up in and I'll guarantee to take any one at

behaviorism An approach to psychology that features the study and careful measurement of observable behaviors.

random and train him to become any type of specialist I might select—a doctor, lawyer, artist, merchant-chief, and yes, even into beggarman and thief, regardless of his talents, penchants, tendencies, abilities, vocations and race of his ancestors. (Watson, 1925, p. 10)

Later in Watson's career, he applied his understanding of behavior to the budding American advertising industry. By 1930, Watson was earning $70,000 per year as an advertising executive, an astronomical salary for the time and quite different from the $3,000 per year he earned as a professor. After discovering that blindfolded participants couldn't tell the difference between brands of cigarettes, Watson concluded that to be successful, a product must be associated with an appealing image. The advertising industry was never the same, and today's advertisers continue to apply Watson's principles. Old Spice aftershave achieved great success with its ads featuring NFL wide receiver Isaiah Mustafa, implying that using Old Spice would make a man more "manly."

Watson's legacy in psychology was enormous. He changed the goal of the discipline from Wundt's desire to understand consciousness to the prediction and control of behavior. He also restricted psychology to the study of observable behavior. As we will see in our section on research methods and throughout this text, even those psychologists who are interested in internal events, like the visual recognition of an object, seek related observable behaviors, such as brain images, reaction time, or other similar measures.

Like Pavlov's, Watson's approach to psychology focused on the relationships between environmental cues and behavior. Other behaviorists were much more interested in the effects of consequences on behavior, an idea that was derived from basic functionalism. **Edward Thorndike** (1874–1949) proposed a law of effect, which suggested that behaviors followed by pleasant or helpful outcomes would be more likely to occur in the future, whereas behaviors followed by unpleasant or harmful outcomes would be less likely to occur. Thorndike based his law on observations of cats' behavior in a puzzle box he had constructed (see ● Figure 1.6). To escape the box, a cat was required to complete a sequence of behaviors. Through trial-and-error learning, the cat would escape faster and faster on

© AP Photo/Noor Khan

Classical conditioning helps us understand the links we make between environmental cues and our emotions. If a soldier associated the smell of diesel fuel with traumatic experiences, smelling diesel fuel at a gas station back home can trigger distress.

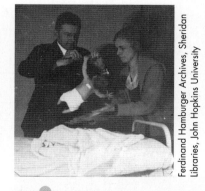

Ferdinand Hamburger Archives, Sheridan Libraries, John Hopkins University

John B. Watson (1878–1958) was a strong believer in the "blank slate" approach of the earlier empiricist philosophers. After working as a psychology professor, he applied his knowledge of human behavior to advertising.

© Daniel Tanner/WENN.com/Newscom

Watson applied his understanding of behaviorism to advertising with great success. He believed that a product would sell better if it were paired with an appealing image.

FIGURE 1.6

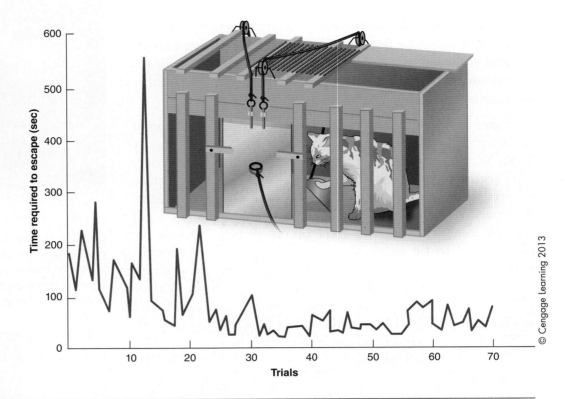

Thorndike's Law of Effect Emerged From Observations of Cats. If you own a cat, you probably know that cats don't like to be enclosed in boxes. Edward Thorndike (1874–1949) studied the escape strategies of a cat to build his Law of Effect.

© Cengage Learning 2013

B. F. Skinner (1904–1990) was interested in the effects of reward and punishment on future behavior.

© Nina Leen/Time & Life Pictures/Getty Images

successive trials. In other words, the cat repeated effective behaviors and abandoned ineffective ones.

Like Thorndike, **B. F. Skinner** (1904–1990) was very interested in the effects of consequences on how frequently behaviors were performed. Skinner shared Watson's belief that psychology did not benefit from any consideration of consciousness or internal mental states. Skinner believed that inner, private states such as thinking and feeling existed, but he viewed them as behaviors that followed the same rules as public behaviors, like driving a car (Jensen & Burgess, 1997). He not only reduced his study of behavior to the actions of rats and pigeons in adapted cages that came to be known as *Skinner boxes,* but he was very comfortable generalizing from the behavior of rats and pigeons to complex human behaviors. In spite of its strong focus on a limited set of animals and situations, Skinner's behaviorism has provided a wealth of beneficial applications. Smokers attempting to quit, doctors and nurses engaged in self-paced continuing education courses, and children receiving treatment for autism are all likely to be benefiting from Skinner's efforts.

By the 1950s, the behaviorists' disinterest in mental states and activity was challenged by scientists from diverse fields, including linguistics and computer science, leading to a cognitive revolution. Cognition covers the very private and internal mental processes the behaviorists avoided studying—information processing, thinking, reasoning, and problem solving. **Ulric Neisser** (1928–) gave the new field its name in his 1967 book, *Cognitive Psychology* (Neisser, 1967).

Breakthroughs in computer technology allowed these new cognitive psychologists to use mathematical and computer models to illuminate the mental processes leading to observable behaviors. Alan Newell (1927–1992) and Herbert Simon (1916–2001) wrote groundbreaking artificial intelligence programs using human information processing as their model. The hardware of the computer was viewed as a metaphor for the brain, and its software mirrored the brain's activity. By the 1980s, most university psychology departments were offering courses in cognition. By the 1990s, collaborations between cognitive and biological psychologists led to the new field of cognitive neuroscience, which seeks to identify brain structures and functions involved in processing information. In a later chapter on cognition, language, and intelligence, we will explore more detail about the contributions of cognitive psychologists in more detail.

Ulric Neisser (1928–) contributed the term *cognition* to the emerging field that studied information processing, thinking, reasoning, and problem solving.

To illustrate how the behaviorist and cognitive approaches differ, we can take a look at how each explains language learning by children. Behaviorists like Skinner believed that children acquired language in response to feedback, such as parental approval or being understood. In contrast, linguist Noam Chomsky proposed that human beings are born with innate mechanisms for learning language, which is exactly the type of specialized internal mental processing Skinner rejected. As we will see in our chapters on development and cognition, the cognitive approach to language learning dominates our current understanding.

In contemporary departments of psychology, behaviorist approaches are represented by professors and researchers specializing in learning, who continue to explore the nuances of the effects of experience on behavior. Many of the big questions tackled by behaviorists are now examined through the lens of the cognitive or biological perspective. Behavioral approaches make important contributions to real-world problems, including how best to pay employees and the treatment of psychological disorders and addiction.

Computers were named after the job title of the women who did most computation tasks before the machines were invented and who continued to operate them. Although these early computers were less powerful than your cell phone (not to mention much more expensive), their operation gave psychologists new ideas about how the mind might process information.

Clinical Roots: Freud and the Humanists

With the exception of occasional bursts of insight from the ancient Egyptians and Greeks, the most common view of psychological disorders over the course of history has been the supernatural approach. According to this view, psychological disorders resulted from the actions of evil spirits or other external, magical forces. Although improvements in science and medicine led to more natural than supernatural explanations of psychological disorders, effective treatments were not rapidly forthcoming. Patients in the 17th and 18th centuries were often subjected to bizarre treatments, including being spun around in a chair. As recently as the 1940s, patients with schizophrenia were regularly experimented on. They were subjected to questionable techniques such as "insulin shock therapy,"

Until about 60 years ago, no effective treatments for psychological disorders existed. The application of scientific principles to treatment has finally led to real help.

in which insulin injections led to comas, and were restrained in lukewarm baths. We discuss schizophrenia and its treatment in more detail in our chapters on psychological disorders and therapies.

Between the 17th and 19th centuries, supernatural explanations for psychological disorders began to give way to two scientific approaches: a medical model and a psychological model. The medical model of psychological disorder emphasized physical causes of abnormal behavior and medical treatments, such as medication. The psychological model suggested that abnormal behavior can result from life experiences, leading to fear, anxiety, and other counterproductive emotional responses. Psychological treatments take many forms, from offering support to applying cognitive and behavioral methods to help people think and problem solve in new ways. As we will see in our chapters on psychological disorders and therapies, contemporary psychologists typically combine these approaches to understand disorders and develop effective treatments. For example, we

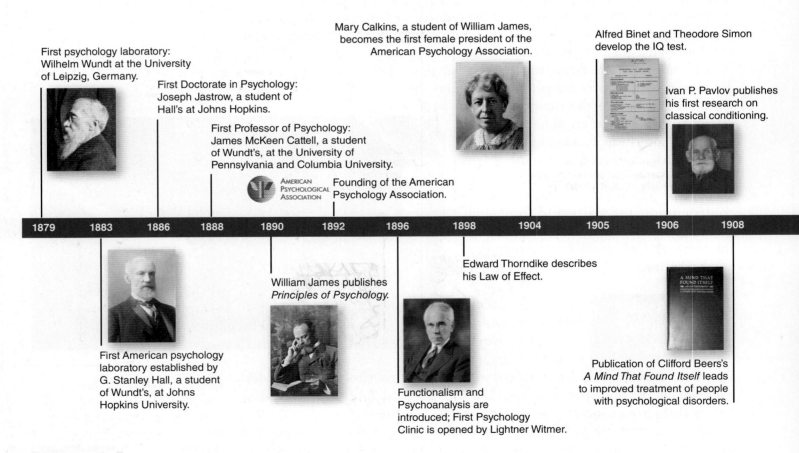

FIGURE 1.7

Milestones in the History of Psychology.

Photos, left to right: © INTERFOTO/Alamy; Library of Congress/Photo Researchers, Inc.; The APA logo is a trademark of the American Psychological Association. Reproduced with permission. No further reproduction or distribution is permitted without written permission from the American Psychological Association; © Mary Evans Picture Library/The Image Works; © Elias Goldensky, University Archives/University of Pennsylvania. Reproduced with permission; Courtesy of the Wellesley College Archives; Courtesy Special Collections & Archives, Truman State University; The Alan Mason Chesney Medical Archives of The Johns Hopkins Medical Institutions; Reproduced with permission of Mental Health America

know that feeling depressed has both physical components (changes in the activity of chemical messengers in the brain) and experiential components (exposure to stressful situations). Treatment for depression often combines medication with efforts to change the way a person thinks about his or her situation.

Sigmund Freud **Sigmund Freud** (1856–1939) built a bridge from his medical training as a physician to his belief in the impact of life experiences on behavior. His *psychodynamic* theory and its applications to the treatment of psychological disorders dominated much of psychological thinking for the first half of the 20th century. Freud managed to combine and communicate ideas about the existence of the unconscious mind, the development of sexuality, dream analysis, and psychological roots of abnormal behavior in such a way that his theories influenced not just psychology but culture. He nearly single-handedly founded the study of personality in psychology,

© Paul Van Scott/Final Score Products

The work of Sigmund Freud (1856–1939) on consciousness, sexuality, abnormal behavior, and psychotherapy played a dominant role in psychology during the first half of the 20th century.

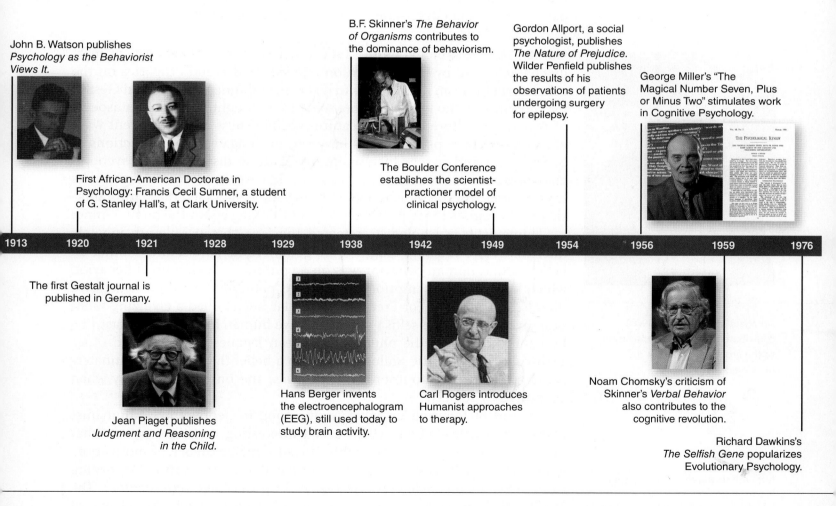

John B. Watson publishes *Psychology as the Behaviorist Views It.*

First African-American Doctorate in Psychology: Francis Cecil Sumner, a student of G. Stanley Hall's, at Clark University.

B.F. Skinner's *The Behavior of Organisms* contributes to the dominance of behaviorism.

The Boulder Conference establishes the scientist-practioner model of clinical psychology.

Gordon Allport, a social psychologist, publishes *The Nature of Prejudice.* Wilder Penfield publishes the results of his observations of patients undergoing surgery for epilepsy.

George Miller's "The Magical Number Seven, Plus or Minus Two" stimulates work in Cognitive Psychology.

| 1913 | 1920 | 1921 | 1928 | 1929 | 1938 | 1942 | 1949 | 1954 | 1956 | 1959 | 1976 |

The first Gestalt journal is published in Germany.

Jean Piaget publishes *Judgment and Reasoning in the Child.*

Hans Berger invents the electroencephalogram (EEG), still used today to study brain activity.

Carl Rogers introduces Humanist approaches to therapy.

Noam Chomsky's criticism of Skinner's *Verbal Behavior* also contributes to the cognitive revolution.

Richard Dawkins's *The Selfish Gene* popularizes Evolutionary Psychology.

Photos, left to right: Ferdinand Hamburger Archives, Sheridan Libraries, John Hopkins University; Courtesy of the Moorland-Spingarn Research Center, Howard University Archives; © Farrell Grehan/CORBIS; © VEM/Photo Researchers, Inc.; © Nina Leen/Time & Life Pictures/Getty Images; © Michael Rougier/Time & Life Pictures/Getty Images; © Jon Roemer; Miller, George A. The magical number seven, plus or minus two: Some limits on our capacity for processing information. *Psychological Review*, 63(2), 81–97. doi: 10.1037/h0043158; © Dennis Van Tine/Retna Ltd./Corbis

In 1920, Francis Cecil Sumner (1895–1954) became the first African American to receive a PhD in psychology for his work on psychoanalysis. Sumner's later work focused on religion and racism.

Abraham Maslow (1908–1970) contributed a theory of motivation to the growing humanism movement.

humanistic psychology An approach to psychology that saw people as inherently good and motivated to learn and improve.

and we will explore his theories more fully within that context. He developed the techniques of psychoanalysis for treating mental disorders, which we discuss in our chapter on therapies. He popularized the use of psychological principles for explaining everyday behavior, and his theories are just as likely to be discussed in your English literature course as they are in a psychology course.

Our enthusiasm for Freud is tempered by a number of valid concerns. As you read and hear about Freud throughout the remainder of this course, keep in mind that he did no real experimentation. His theories are based primarily on his own introspections along with those of his patients, who as primarily upper-class Viennese housewives were not typical of the general population. Freud's theories do not lend themselves to experimentation, an essential requirement for any scientific theory, as we discuss further in our chapter on research methods. For example, how could you possibly design an experiment to demonstrate that dreaming about water indicates you have unconscious concerns about sex? Finally, although psychoanalysis is still used as a therapy technique, it is rarely conducted in the strict Freudian manner. Other techniques, discussed in our chapter on therapies, exceed psychoanalysis in effectiveness and popularity among therapists.

Humanistic Psychology By the 1960s, American psychology was primarily characterized by behaviorism on one side and Freud's theories on the other. Structuralism had fallen into disfavor, and functionalism and Gestalt psychology were no longer distinct schools of thought. Just as other aspects of American culture began to feature rebelliousness against current ways of thinking, some psychologists began to push against the restrictions of behaviorism and psychoanalysis. Many of these disenchanted psychologists had been trained in psychoanalysis, but were not seeing the results they desired. This dissatisfaction with prevailing views led these **humanistic psychologists** to propose new ways of thinking about the human mind.

Humanistic psychologists rejected the idea that people are innately uncivilized and must be taught to be good. Freud, James, and Skinner all believed that human behavior was on a continuum with animal behavior, which led to their assumption that humans naturally shared the aggressive impulses of animals. For Freud in particular, society had a civilizing function on the otherwise selfish and aggressive human being. In contrast, the humanists extended the philosophy of Jean Jacques Rousseau and other 18th-century Romantic philosophers into a belief that people are innately good, are motivated to improve themselves, and only behave badly when corrupted by society.

Instead of focusing on what went wrong in people's lives, humanist **Abraham Maslow** (1908–1970) asked interesting questions about what made a person "good." Maslow introduced a major theory of motivation, which we describe in more detail in our chapter on motivation. According to Maslow, the pinnacle of motivation is the goal of *self-actualization*. The 1990s U.S. Army slogan, "Be all you can be," captures much of the flavor of self-actualization. We will see Maslow's emphasis on what is good about people, as opposed to Freud's focus on what goes wrong with people, reemerge in the form of contemporary positive psychology.

Humanist therapists rebelled against Freudian approaches to treatment. One humanist therapist, **Carl Rogers** (1902–1987), developed a new approach to therapy, *client-centered therapy.* In this type of therapy, the people receiving treatment are referred to as clients rather than patients, reflecting their more equal standing with the therapist and their more active role in the therapy process. Humanistic approaches to therapy have also influenced communication, group process, parenting, and politics. The emphasis on active listening and the use of "I hear what you're saying" reflections have become nearly cliché in courses of leadership training and interpersonal communication. Advice to parents to provide "unconditional" love to their children is a direct application of humanist beliefs, which we discuss in more detail in our chapter on development. Finally, humanistic psychology continues to flavor our political and social domains. When issues such as capital punishment arise, the humanistic contention that there are no bad people, just bad societies, typically appears as part of the debate.

The Freudians and humanists had conflicting views on human nature, with the Freudians believing that we are naturally selfish and aggressive and the humanists believing we are naturally good. These philosophical differences continue to color our discussions of topics. Is the criminal just a "bad" person who was never properly socialized or a "good" person who was corrupted?

Humanist therapists, like Carl Rogers (1902–1987), often rebelled against Freudian approaches to therapy. For example, Rogers (in the white shirt leading a group therapy session) referred to people as "clients" rather than "patients" as Freud did.

When a case of capital punishment occurs, we often read about the prisoner's terrible childhood from one side and the need to protect society from further misdeeds by this person from the other side. Where would the Freudians and humanists line up in this debate?

Summary 1.2

Pioneering Approaches to Psychology

	Foundation of psychology	Things to remember
© INTERFOTO/Alamy **Wilhelm Wundt (1832–1920)**	Structuralism	Behavior can be broken down into its components.
© Bettmann/CORBIS **Max Wertheimer (1880–1943)**	Gestalt psychology	Breaking behavior into components loses meaning.
© Mary Evans Picture Library/The Image Works **William James (1842–1910)**	Functionalism	Behavior is purposeful and contributes to survival.
The Alan Mason Chesney Medical Archives of The Johns Hopkins Medical Institutions **Ivan Pavlov (1849–1936)**	Behaviorism	Experience is the primary source of behavior.
Courtesy of Cornell University **Ulric Neisser (1928–)**	Cognitive revolution	Private mental processing can be studied scientifically.
© Paul Van Scott/Final Score Products **Sigmund Freud (1856–1939)**	Freud's psychodynamic theory	Ideas about the unconscious mind, the role of experience in abnormal behavior, and new approaches to therapy laid a foundation for later study in personality and therapy.
© Ann Kaplan/CORBIS **Abraham Maslow (1908–1970)**	Humanism	People are naturally good and are motivated to improve.

What Are Psychological Perspectives?

Like William James, the behaviorists and Freudians tried to answer the "big questions" of psychology with one single approach. However, it is difficult to build a big theory (which we discuss in our research methods chapter) without a large body of experimental data, and psychology was still a young science. To fill this gap, some psychologists began to pursue an understanding of behavior from more specific points of view, or perspectives. By specializing in only one part of the discipline, as opposed to trying to answer everything at once, these psychologists began to gain an in-depth understanding of the mind.

By the second half of the 20th century, the majority of psychologists were pursuing the perspective approach. Examining psychological phenomena from different perspectives does not imply disagreement, conflict, or a lack of awareness of alternate perspectives. In most cases, a psychologist's perspective simply means that he or she is examining behavior from that point of view. For example, watching a child learn a new vocabulary word will have very different meanings to the biological, developmental, evolutionary, cognitive, social, or behavioral psychologist.

Reflecting the traditional divisions of the field, it is common for psychologists to refer to themselves as social psychologists, developmental psychologists, and so on, indicating their area of specialization and interest. Departments of psychology at universities often continue this organization, and students applying to graduate school in psychology might apply to one particular area of expertise, like choosing an undergraduate major. To illustrate the distinctions among some of the main perspectives, we will consider how each might approach the question of human memory, discussed in detail in a later chapter on memory, as this topic is especially important to students who wish to perform well on their exams.

> The great question that has never been answered and which I have not been able to answer, despite my thirty years of research into the feminine soul, is "What does a woman want?"
>
> —Sigmund Freud

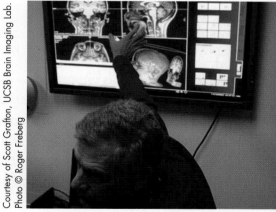

Courtesy of Scott Grafton, UCSB Brain Imaging Lab.
Photo © Roger Freberg

Biological psychologists explore the relationships between the mind, behavior, and their underlying biological processes, often using technology like functional magnetic resonance imaging (fMRI). Scott Grafton of the University of California, Santa Barbara is pointing out the features of the brain of one of your authors.

Seven Perspectives of Psychology

Biological psychology, also referred to as behavioral neuroscience, focuses on the relationships between mind and behavior and their underlying biological processes, including genetics, biochemistry, anatomy, and physiology. In other words, biological psychologists are interested in the physical mechanisms associated with behavior. As we will see in our chapter on biological psychology, technological advances beginning in the 1970s, especially new methods for observing brain activity, initiated an explosion of knowledge about the connections between brain and behavior. Using these new technologies, biological psychologists have approached the question of storage and retrieval of memories in many different ways, ranging from observing changes in communication between nerve cells in slugs to investigating the effects of stress hormones on the ability to form memories. The focus of this perspective is on the mechanisms used to store and retrieve memories, such as changes in the structure of nerve cells or in the biochemical environment of the nervous system.

biological psychology The psychological perspective that focuses on the relationships between mind, behavior, and their underlying biological processes, including genetics, biochemistry, anatomy, and physiology; also known as behavioral neuroscience.

Evolutionary psychologists are interested in how our modern behaviors were shaped by our species' history.

A closely related perspective, **evolutionary psychology,** attempts to answer the question of how our physical structure and behavior have been shaped by their contributions to our species' survival. This perspective should sound familiar to you—it is a modern extension of William James's functionalism, which we discussed previously. Earlier, we also saw evolutionary psychology at work in the shaping of our sensitivity to bitter tastes. The basic principle of evolutionary psychology is that our current behavior exists in its present form because it provided some advantage in survival and reproduction to our ancestors. An evolutionary psychologist might be interested in the fact that we have a very good memory for faces, and particularly for faces of people who have cheated us in the past (Barclay & Lalumière, 2006). In the world of the hunter-gatherer, being cheated out of one's fair share of the hunt was likely to lead to starvation for you and your family, and people who could not keep track of the cheaters were unlikely to survive and reproduce.

Social psychology is important to our understanding of many contemporary problems, including prejudice. In one experiment, some people describing what they heard from other participants about a drawing of a White man threatening a Black man with a razor switched the races of the two men (Allport & Postman, 1945). They now "remembered" hearing about a Black man threatening a White man. Given our judicial system's dependence on eyewitness testimony, understanding these social tendencies provides important guidance.

Cognitive psychology focuses on the process of thinking, or the processing of information. Because our ability to remember plays an integral part in the processing of information, a cognitive psychologist is likely to have a lot to say about the storage and retrieval of memories. A cognitive psychologist might ask why processing seems different when we are trying to remember names and dates while taking a history test compared to remembering how to ride a bicycle. What processes lead to the frustrating experience of "tip of the tongue," in which you remember the first letter or a part of the word you're trying to retrieve but not the whole thing? What strategies can we use to make our memories more efficient? We address these and similar issues in our chapters on memory and cognition.

evolutionary psychology The psychological perspective that investigates how physical structure and behavior have been shaped by their contributions to survival and reproduction.

cognitive psychology The psychological perspective that investigates information processing, thinking, reasoning, and problem solving.

Social psychology describes the effects of the social environment, including **culture,** on the behavior of individuals. Social psychologists recognize that we each construct our own realities and that the social environment influences our thoughts, feelings, and behavior. Early psychologists were limited in their understanding of the mind by their exclusive focus on their own sociocultural contexts. More recently, social psychologists have emphasized the need to explore the influences of sociocultural context and biology on our behavior. Returning to our memory example, the social psychologist might ask how being in the presence of others influences the storage and retrieval of data. When we sit comfortably in our own homes, the answers to *Who Wants to Be a Millionaire* questions come quite easily. In front of millions of viewers, however, we might be lucky to remember our own names.

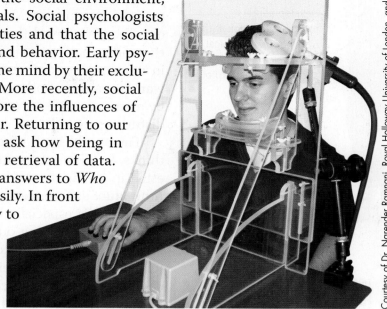

Cognitive psychologists investigate the ways the human mind processes information.

Developmental psychology explores the normal changes in behavior that occur across the lifespan. Using the developmental perspective, a psychologist might look at how memory functions in people of different ages. Three-month-old babies can retain the memory that kicking moves a mobile suspended above their crib for about a month without further practice (Rovee-Collier, 1997). However, most of us have difficulty recalling events that occurred before the age of 3 to 4 years or so. Teens and young adults are able to remember names much faster than are older adults (Bashore, Ridderinkhof, & van der Molen, 1997). We explore these and other age-related changes in memory in our chapter on lifespan development.

Psychologists continue to be interested in what happens when normal behavior breaks down. The **clinical psychology** perspective seeks to explain, define, and treat abnormal behaviors. More recently, clinical and counseling psychologists have expanded their perspective to include the

© Joel Gordon 2001

Social psychologists explore the effects of the social environment on our individual behavior. In this example, the man in the middle is deciding whether or not to conform with the other two men in a simple judgment of line length.

social psychology The psychological perspective that examines the effects of the social environment on the behavior of individuals.

culture The practices, values, and goals shared by groups of people.

developmental psychology The psychological perspective that examines the normal changes in behavior that occur across the lifespan.

clinical psychology The psychological perspective that seeks to explain, define, and treat abnormal behaviors.

Developmental psychologists look at the behavior that is typical for people of certain ages, from infancy to old age.

© StockLite/Shutterstock

individual differences An approach to psychology that investigates variations in behavior from one person to the next.

personality An individual's characteristic way of thinking, feeling, and behaving.

promotion of general well-being, which we describe in a later chapter on positive psychology. Many types of psychological disorders impact memory. Freud believed that traumatizing experiences were more difficult to remember, a process he labeled *repression* (which will be discussed further in our chapters on memory and psychological disorders). In other cases, war veterans and others who have experienced trauma might be troubled by memories that are too good, producing intrusive flashback memories of disturbing events.

Finally, although much of psychology explores how the average person thinks, feels, or acts, some people are not average at all. Psychologists interested in all varieties of behavior, not just the most typical types, pursue an **individual differences** perspective (see ● Figure 1.8). Recognizing individual differences is especially important to psychologists interested in variations in **personality.** Using our example of memory, we can see how individual differences in "need for cognition" can predict memory for verbal material (Cacioppo, Petty, Feinstein, & Jarvis, 1996). People who have a high need for cognition enjoy mental challenges, like solving difficult puzzles. As we'll see in our chapter on social psychology, individuals who are high in need for cognition also respond differently to persuasive messages.

Thinking
Scientifically

Can the Use of a Single Perspective Be Misleading?

We have argued that restricting our thinking about an aspect of mind to the information provided by one perspective can result in an incomplete picture, but can this single-perspective approach actually lead us in the wrong direction?

The answer to that question is a resounding yes. Consider the following example. You are a biological psychologist interested in the effects of amphetamine on aggression. You know from past experience that amphetamine makes individual rhesus monkeys quite a bit more aggressive than usual (we are unlikely to do this study with human beings,

due to ethical concerns discussed in our next chapter; Haber & Barchas, 1983). But you also know that rhesus monkeys are very social animals, so it doesn't make much sense to study them in isolation. Much to your surprise, you find that amphetamine produces no effects at all on the aggressiveness of a colony of rhesus monkeys (Dawe, Davis, Lapworth, & McKetin, 2009).

Your single biological psychology perspective can help explain why the individual monkeys are more aggressive under the influence of amphetamine, but it does not provide much help in explaining why you don't see the same results when you study the

monkeys in a group. However, when you add the insights of social psychology to those of biological psychology, a clearer picture emerges. The social world of the rhesus monkey consists of a strong hierarchy, or pecking order, with each male monkey knowing his position relative to all the others in the colony. Higher ranking monkeys engage in dominance behaviors, including vocalizations and threats, to remind the lower ranking monkeys about who is the boss. Lower ranking monkeys avoid aggression and other signs of dominance by engaging in submissive behaviors designed to prevent aggression, such as imitation (Adams, 1982).

FIGURE 1.8

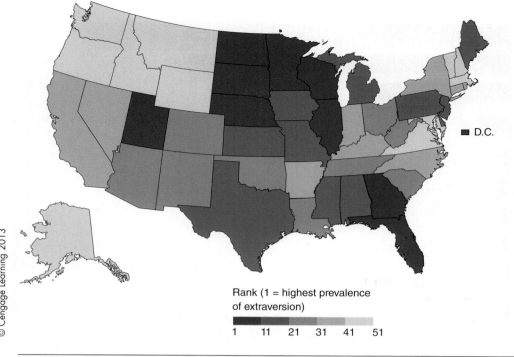

Rank (1 = highest prevalence of extraversion)

1   11   21   31   41   51

■ D.C.

© Cengage Learning 2013

Individual Differences: The Geography of Personality. Where in the United States do you think the most outgoing, extroverted people live? Would you believe that North Dakota has more extroverts than California or New York? Psychologists studying individual differences found that the Midwest has the highest proportion of extroverted people in the country. Why would this be the case? Perhaps the need to develop tight social networks to survive the harsh climate in this part of the United States favored extroverts.

When you take a monkey's rank in the social hierarchy into account (adding the social perspective to the biological one), a clear picture of the results emerges. Amphetamine has different results on aggression that depend on the social status of the animal. Amphetamine increases dominance behavior by dominant monkeys and increases submissive behavior by submissive monkeys. If you just added up all the amphetamine effects for the group, the increases and decreases would cancel each other out, making it look like amphetamine had no effects at all. By adding the social perspective to the question, the discrepancy between the individual and group results can be explained easily. This example illustrates that restricting ourselves to one perspective might cloud our understanding. ✿

© Pete Oxford/Minden Pictures/Getty Images

Studying individual rhesus monkeys will provide useful information, but for these very social animals, incorporating a social perspective helps us understand them more fully.

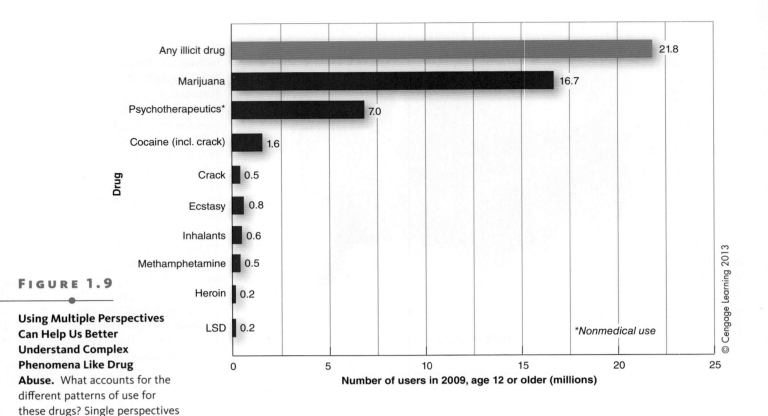

*Nonmedical use

Drug

| | Number of users in 2009, age 12 or older (millions) |

- Any illicit drug — 21.8
- Marijuana — 16.7
- Psychotherapeutics* — 7.0
- Cocaine (incl. crack) — 1.6
- Crack — 0.5
- Ecstasy — 0.8
- Inhalants — 0.6
- Methamphetamine — 0.5
- Heroin — 0.2
- LSD — 0.2

FIGURE 1.9

Using Multiple Perspectives Can Help Us Better Understand Complex Phenomena Like Drug Abuse. What accounts for the different patterns of use for these drugs? Single perspectives can only give us parts of the answer. Combining perspectives can give us the big picture.

Clinical psychologists seek to understand and treat psychological disorders.

A New Connectivity: Integrating Psychology's Seven Perspectives

Entering the 21st century and armed with in-depth research results compiled in the various perspectives, psychologists are returning to the more comprehensive view of the mind envisioned over 100 years ago by William James. Their questions and methods are more likely to blur the lines of the perspectives outlined earlier, often with remarkable results.

Although the 20th-century perspective approach to psychology generated detailed understanding of aspects of behavior and mental processes, it has become more apparent that single perspectives are insufficient for fully describing and explaining psychological phenomena. For example, if we want to understand the phenomenon of drug abuse, many perspectives can contribute to our understanding, but no one specialty offers a complete explanation. Biological psychologists approach drug abuse by tracing pathways in the brain correlated with cravings, developmental and social psychologists consider the family and peer influences, and so on. In each case, we learn something valuable about drug abuse, but understanding the "whole" requires us to zoom out for a more comprehensive perspective (see ● Figure 1.9).

We don't have a crystal ball that will allow us to foresee psychology's future. However, we strongly believe that this future will be one of combining and integrating new and existing perspectives. Many of these new ways of looking at the mind will take advantage of the revolution in techniques for studying the

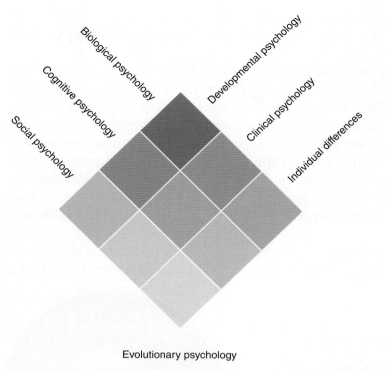

Social psychology

Cognitive psychology

Biological psychology

Developmental psychology

Clinical psychology

Individual differences

Evolutionary psychology

FIGURE 1.10

Contemporary Psychology Integrates Seven Perspectives. Viewing the mind by zooming in using specialized perspectives has led to signi-ficant increases in our understanding, but 21st-century psychology is characterized by efforts to zoom out and integrate multiple perspectives.

brain that began in the 1970s and continues. Already, today's cognitive neuroscientists investigate the brain as an information-processing system and search for the biological basis of topics such as attention, decision making, and memory. Social neuroscientists investigate the biological factors that vary along with people's feelings and experience of social inclusion, rejection, or loneliness. Behavioral neuroscientists pick up previous lines of research on learning, memory, motivation, and sleep and search for connections between these processes and our biology. Clinical and counseling psychologists are more likely today to consider biological processes in their theories about the causes of psychological disorders. By merging our seven perspectives of mind, we stand a much better chance of tackling the remarkable problem of understanding the human mind (see ● Figure 1.10).

What Does It Mean to Be a Psychologist?

In 2006–2007, more than 90,000 students in the United States received bachelor's degrees in psychology (APS Observer, 2010). This amounts to approximately 6% of the 1.5 million bachelor's degrees awarded that year. What are these students likely to be doing in the workforce?

Some students with undergraduate degrees in psychology prefer employment in fields that are directly related to psychology, such as working in research facilities or rehabilitation centers for drug abuse or brain damage. Others are quite successful in a wide variety of "people-oriented" jobs, such as those found in management, sales, service, public affairs, education, human resources, probation, and journalism. This diversity of career pathways reflects once again the "hub" nature of psychology to other fields.

Graduates with master's degrees in psychology, usually requiring one to two years of additional study past the bachelor's degree, can teach at the community college (2-year) level and obtain licensing as therapists in most states, as we discuss further in our chapter on therapies. Many master's level psychologists are employed in health, industry, and education (American Psychological Association [APA], 2009). School psychologists typically work on elementary, middle school, or high school campuses. These psychologists participate in academic and career counseling as well as the identification and remediation of problems that interfere with student success.

Many people working in psychology have earned doctoral degrees, which usually take 2 to 5 years of study beyond the master's level. As shown

Experiencing Psychology

Which Psychology Careers Work for Me?

Please don't assume that we are trying to recruit you to a career in psychology, but just in case you might consider the possibility of becoming a psychologist, you can take the following quiz to help you identify which type of psychology career might fit you best. Obviously, your campus

career counselors offer many additional resources to help you make important choices about your career path, and we recommend that you take advantage of their expertise.

For each question, circle the answer that fits you best.

These questions can be used to divide students' interests into

therapy, applied, and research tracks in psychology. Therapists, as we have described in this chapter, typically work with clients but might also teach. Examples of applied psychology include forensic psychology (application of psychology to the study of crime and the legal system) and sports

1. Do you enjoy working directly with people to help them overcome problems?	Yes	No	Sometimes
2. Do you enjoy solving theoretical problems?	Yes	No	Sometimes
3. Do you enjoy classes that focus on experimental design?	Yes	No	Sometimes
4. Are you good at mathematics and statistics?	Yes	No	Somewhat
5. Do you enjoy working to solve practical, real-world problems?	Yes	No	Somewhat
6. Would you enjoy working with clients in a doctor's office, hospital, or mental health clinic?	Yes	No	Somewhat
7. Is earning a high salary important to you?	Yes	No	Somewhat
8. Are you able to deal with high-stress situations with people who may be psychologically or emotionally unstable?	Yes	No	Possibly

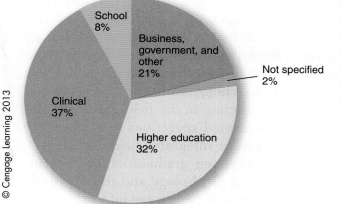

© Cengage Learning 2013

School
8%

Business,
government, and
other
21%

Not specified
2%

Clinical
37%

Higher education
32%

FIGURE 1.11

Where Psychologists Work. Within one year of graduation, individuals earning doctoral degrees between 2008 and 2009 found work in a variety of settings. The majority were employed in clinical and higher education settings, but opportunities for psychologists also exist in schools, businesses, government, and other settings where an understanding of human behavior is helpful. *Source: Data from Michalski et al. (2011).*

in ● Figure 1.11, about 32% of new doctoral level psychologists do what your professor and the authors of your textbook do: teach and conduct research at colleges and universities. About 37% of new doctoral level psychologists work as therapists, either in private practice or in hospitals and clinics. Smaller numbers of new doctoral level psychologists find employment in business and government settings, elementary and secondary schools, and other related fields.

Psychologists entering doctoral programs traditionally identify with one of the major perspectives we discussed earlier, such as social, cognitive,

psychology (working with athletes to optimize performance). Psychologists who teach and conduct research on college and university campuses have pursued the experimental track.

Use the following table to identify which of the tracks is most similar to your answers. Circle your answer for each question and see if you can find a pattern. ✿

© Steven Robertson/iStockphoto

Forensic psychologists attempt to understand the criminal mind and to develop effective treatments for criminal behavior.

Photo courtesy Dr. Vietta Wilson

Sports psychologist Vietta Wilson uses biofeedback to help Canadian biathlete Graham Mater maximize his performance.

Answers

Question number	Therapy	Applied	Experimental
1	Yes	Sometimes	No
2	Sometimes or No	Sometimes or No	Yes
3	Sometimes or No	Sometimes or No	Yes
4	Somewhat or No	Somewhat or No	Yes
5	Yes	Yes	Somewhat or No
6	Yes	Somewhat	No
7	Yes	Yes	Somewhat or No
8	Yes	Possibly	No

or biological. The distribution of new doctoral graduates in psychology by perspective is shown in ● Figure 1.12. Choosing a graduate perspective is similar to choosing an undergraduate major. Although all psychology graduate students might take core courses in research methods and statistics, they typically pursue coursework and research in their particular area of specialization. However, training of psychologists in the 21st century is beginning to reflect the connections occurring in the field itself. Increasingly, students are being trained in combined specialties (e.g., cognitive neuroscience) as psychology becomes a more integrated field of study.

The most rigid distinction occurs between graduate students planning to specialize in clinical or counseling psychology and those who do not. The clinical or counseling "major" includes extensive internships and supervised training prior to government-regulated licensure that usually add at least one year to students' graduate studies. Do not assume that your psychology professors are all therapists. The likelihood is that they are not. It is also important to distinguish between therapists with doctoral degrees in psychology and psychiatrists, who are medical doctors. Currently, the biggest difference between the two professions is that psychiatrists can prescribe medication, but psychologists usually cannot. In New Mexico and Louisiana, however, specially trained psychologists can legally prescribe medications, and this trend might spread to other states. In our chapter on therapies, we will provide more detail about the different types of therapists who treat adjustment problems and psychological disorders.

FIGURE 1.12

Psychological Perspectives.
Students receiving doctoral degrees in 2008–2009 might have identified with one of these major perspectives, but increasingly, doctoral students are choosing to train in multiple or integrated perspectives, such as cognitive neuroscience.
Source: Data from Michalski et al. (2011).

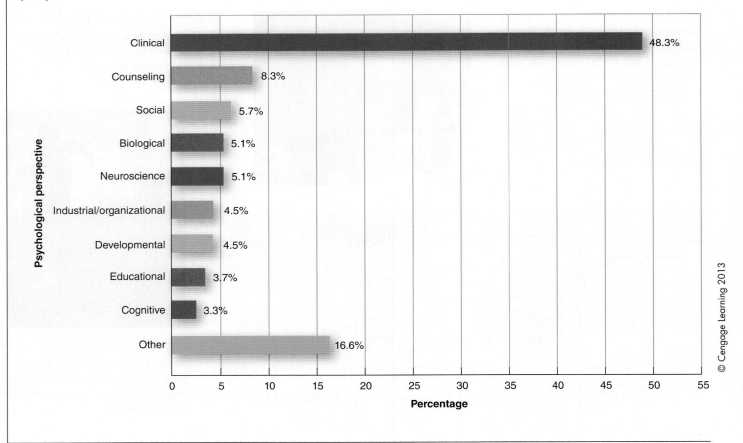

Summary 1.3

Seven Psychological Perspectives

	Perspective	Things to remember
Courtesy of Scott Grafton, UCSB Brain Imaging Lab. Photo © Roger Freberg	Biological psychology	Investigates the connections between the mind, behavior, and biological processes
© Publiphoto/Photo Researchers, Inc. © EPA/Newscom	Evolutionary psychology	Asks how our evolutionary past continues to shape our behavior
Courtesy of Dr. Narender Ramnani, Royal Holloway University of London, and Dr. Joshua Balsters, Trinity College Institute of Neuroscience, Dublin	Cognitive psychology	Investigates mental processes including thinking, problem solving, and information processing
© Joel Gordon 2001	Social psychology	Asks how our behavior is affected by the presence of others
© Stocklite/Shutterstock	Developmental psychology	Investigates the normal changes in behavior that occur across the lifespan
© Alina Solovyova-Vincent/iStockphoto	Clinical psychology	Explains, defines, and treats psychological disorders and promotes general well-being
© Cengage Learning 2013	Individual perspective and personality	Recognizes that behavior varies around averages and that individual differences often interact with environments.

Summary 1.3 (continued)

What Do Psychologists Do?

Typical academic degree	Possible areas of employment
Bachelor's degree	Rehabilitation, research assistance, management, sales, service, public affairs, education, human resources, probation, journalism
Master's degree	Community college teaching, marriage and family counseling, health, education
Doctor of Philosophy (PhD)	University teaching and research, therapy, business, government, education
Medical doctor (MD)*	Psychiatry

*Medical doctors who practice psychiatry are not really "psychologists," as implied by the title of the table, but we think it's important for you to know where they fit in.

Interpersonal Relationships
From the Psychological Perspective

We gave quite a lot of thought to how we might help you, the students reading our book, to see psychology more as an interconnected discipline than as a collection of separate perspectives. The introductory psychology course provides a unique opportunity to see all the perspectives at one time, in contrast to upper division courses that typically focus on one specialty area at a time (personality, social, cognitive, and so on).

One way to connect the dots is to take a single problem and see how the different perspectives represented in the subsequent chapters would address it. We used a mini version of this approach in this chapter when we discussed memory from the vantage point of each perspective. In each chapter, this feature will have more of a perspective flavor, but by the end of the textbook, you will have seen everybody weigh in with different perspectives to give you the whole picture. Because it is most helpful to know something about the perspectives before seeing how they apply, we are saving this feature for the end of each chapter. Ideally, seeing the chapter material in action will make it more memorable for you.

Robert Churchill/Getty Images

The single problem we have chosen to consider this way is one that we know to be on the minds of many of our students: relationships. We are a social species, and the quality of our relationships has a huge impact on our physical and psychological well-being (Cacioppo & Hawkley, 2009). We will see how each of the major perspectives view the question of quality relationships and how the perspectives work together to give us the best understanding possible of this important aspect of life.

By three methods we may learn wisdom:
First, by reflection, which is noblest; second,
by imitation, which is easiest; and third by
experience, which is the bitterest.

—Confucius

Chapter 1
Reflections

© Argosy Publishing, Inc.

This chapter began with a question about why we are so much more sensitive to bitter tastes than to sweet tastes. Initially, this question might have seemed straightforward, best answered by a psychologist who specializes in sensation and perception. We hope that after reading this chapter, you now realize that yes, the specialist has a great deal to say about taste, but we more fully understand psychological questions when we integrate the explanations of specialists working in multiple perspectives.

Just as the Gestalt psychologists that you read about in this chapter believed that perceptions were different than the sum of individual sensations, we believe that our understanding of psychological phenomena benefits from the integration of the contributions of individual specialties. In the case of the bitter tastes, the sensation and perception specialist might emphasize the physical qualities of the taste stimulus, the taste receptors, and the pathways taken by taste information to the brain. Although this is essential and useful information, we gain even more understanding by integrating the specialist's information with input from additional perspectives. The evolutionary perspective highlights the benefits of sensitivity to bitter tastes for avoiding poisons, which of course enhances survival. The developmental perspective reminds us that children are more sensitive to taste than adults, which is probably why the bitter broccoli elicits a strong response from the little boy in the photograph at the beginning of the chapter. Our social connectivity and culture also play important roles, as we eat differently in the presence of others and form likes and dislikes depending on our exposure to certain flavors.

In the remaining chapters, we will continue to emphasize benefits of zooming out periodically to view the whole of psychological phenomena, not just the separate parts contributed by single perspectives. ❮

© Aprilphoto/Shutterstock

KEY TERMS The Language of Psychological Science

Be sure you can define these terms and use them correctly.

behaviorism, p. 18
biological psychology, p. 27
clinical psychology, p. 29
cognitive psychology, p. 28
culture, p. 29
developmental psychology, p. 29
evolutionary psychology, p. 28

functionalism, p. 15
Gestalt psychology, p. 15
humanistic psychology, p. 24
individual differences, p. 30
introspection, p. 5
mind, p. 5
personality, p. 30

philosophy, p. 6
physical science, p. 6
psychology, p. 5
social psychology, p. 29
structuralism, p. 14

MEDIA RESOURCES

Log in to CengageBrain to access the resources your instructor requires. For this book, you can access:

Psychology **CourseMate** brings course concepts to life with interactive learning, study, and exam preparation tools that support the printed textbook. A textbook-specific website, Psychology **CourseMate** includes an integrated interactive eBook and other interactive learning tools including quizzes, flashcards, videos, and more.

WebTUTOR   More than just an interactive study guide, **WebTutor** is an anytime, anywhere customized learning solution with an eBook, keeping you connected to your textbook, instructor, and classmates.

aplia If your professor has assigned **Aplia** homework:
1. Sign in to your account.
2. Complete the corresponding homework exercises as required by your professor.
3. When finished, click "Grade It Now" to see which areas you have mastered, which areas need more work, and detailed explanations of every answer.

Scientific methods, including brain imaging, have allowed researchers to pinpoint structural and functional differences between the brains of fluent speakers and people who stutter.

The Measure of Mind

Methods of Psychology

Learning Objectives

1 Describe the criteria that distinguish scientific observation and reasoning from casual, everyday thinking.

2 Articulate how science uses testable and falsifiable hypotheses, data collection, peer review, and replication to evaluate theories explaining psychological phenomena.

3 Explain the main goal of descriptive research methods and the ways in which case studies, naturalistic observations, and surveys approach this goal.

4 Differentiate the key features, strengths, and limitations of correlational and experimental methods, and apply this distinction in designing a new study or interpreting the results of a study.

5 Compare and contrast cross-sectional versus longitudinal methods for studying change in psychological processes over time.

6 Define reliability and validity, and evaluate a specific operational measure of a variable with respect to these criteria.

7 Differentiate the kind of information conveyed by descriptive versus inferential statistics in describing scientific data, and interpret the meaning of specific statistics (e.g., mean, correlation coefficient).

8 Evaluate specific psychology studies in terms of the ethical guidelines for using human and animal participants in research.

The Oscar-winning film, *The King's Speech*, chronicled the struggles of Great Britain's King George VI as he attempts to overcome his stuttering. Stuttering involves disruptions in normal speech production, such as repeating the starting letter of a word (b-b-b-bird), holding a vowel sound for a long time (ah ah ah), or having difficulty initiating any speech at all. About 5% of the population experience stuttering (Månsson, 2000), with males 2 to 5 times more likely to stutter than females (Craig & Tran, 2005).

Stuttering has been described since the days of the ancient Greeks and occurs across all cultures and ethnicities. Many interesting myths exist regarding its causes and remedies (Kuster, 2005). South African traditions suggest that stuttering results from leaving a baby out in the rain or tickling it too much. A Chinese folk remedy for stuttering was to hit the person in the face when the weather was cloudy. In Iceland, a pregnant woman who drank from a cracked cup was likely to produce a child who stuttered.

Of course, many of us might ask, "How could anybody believe these things?" But at the end of the day, how do we know these are merely myths and not facts? How can we be *so* sure? Instead of dismissing these efforts to explain and predict, think about what might have happened to lead people to these particular conclusions. What is missing from these conclusions is a system for reaching logical, objective results. Science provides us with this system.

What does science have to say about stuttering today? Based on the careful evaluation of stuttering using the methods outlined in this chapter, scientists have concluded that there are multiple causes for stuttering (Kang et al., 2010). Many cases seem to have a basis in genetics, which we discuss in the next chapter. Using scans of brain activity has allowed scientists to zoom in on brain structures and functions that appear to differ between stutterers and fluent speakers, with stutterers showing more activation of the right hemisphere during speech (Gordon, 2002). As we mentioned in our previous chapter, some of the most thorough explanations combine multiple psychological perspectives (Ward, 2006). A complete explanation of stuttering zooms back out to combine a predisposition for the problem, through genetics and biology, with developmental, emotional, and social factors, like feeling embarrassed or anxious about speaking in front of peers.

Although there is no "cure" for stuttering, carefully tested scientific explanations combining input from various perspectives are leading to more effective treatments. In this chapter, you will learn how science provides a system that allows us to construct increasingly realistic models of the world around us. ✹

University of Arizona, Brain Awareness Week 2009.
Courtesy of Dr. Jean-Marc Fellous

Science is a special way of learning about the world through systematic observation and experimentation. These children are learning about the science of the mind during the Dana Foundation's Brain Awareness Week.

What Is Science?

Throughout our history, we human beings have been motivated to understand, predict, and control the world around us. To meet these goals, we need methods for gaining knowledge.

We often take contemporary scientific knowledge for granted, but our ancestors did not enjoy the benefits of science while trying to explain their world. Very early in history, people attempted to understand natural phenomena by applying human characteristics to nature (Cornford, 1957). Skies could look angry or a lake could be calm. Other explanations involved spirits, which were found in humans and all other objects. Earthquakes and illness were viewed as the actions of spirits, and people attempted to influence these spirits through magical rituals.

People often form strong beliefs about their world based on faith, which literally means "trust." Faith is belief that does not depend on logical proof or evidence. We might accept a friend's excuse for being late based on our faith in his or her honesty, without knowing for certain whether our friend is really telling the truth. Science, in contrast to faith, absolutely requires proof and evidence. Our word **science** comes from the Latin *scientia*, which means "knowledge." *Science* doesn't refer to just any type of knowledge but, rather, to a special way of learning about reality through systematic observation and experimentation. The methods we describe in this chapter are designed to supply that evidence.

Science has provided us with explanations for many natural phenomena, like thunder and lightning, that were probably quite frightening for our ancestors.

The Scientific Mind-set

Not all observations are scientific. How does science differ from everyday observations, like the belief that "opposites attract"? As you will learn in our chapter on social psychology, "opposites" do not, in fact, find each other very attractive.

First, science relies on **objectivity** rather than subjectivity. Objectivity means that conclusions are based on facts, without influence from personal emotions or biases. In contrast, subjectivity means that conclusions reflect personal points of view. In the previous chapter, you read about what happened when research participants described what they had heard about photos from memory. Some participants switched the race of a man threatening another person from White (which was the objective fact in the photo) to Black (possibly to fit a biased subjective worldview).

Scientists strive to be objective, but any observation by a human being is, by definition, subjective. Recognizing when you are being subjective can be difficult, so scientists cannot rely on their own introspections to

Science strives to be objective, which means to make judgments that are free from personal emotion or bias. In contrast, people's subjectivity emerged in a classic experiment by Allport and Postman (1945). Some participants remembered hearing that this picture illustrated a Black man threatening another person rather than the objective fact—a White person is doing the threatening.

science A method for learning about reality through systematic observation and experimentation.

objectivity The practice of basing conclusions on facts without influence of personal emotion and bias.

From G. W. Allport & L. J. Postman (1945), "The Basic Psychology of Rumor," in *Transactions of the New York Academy of Sciences, 8,* 61–81.

maintain objectivity. Most of us have had the experience of witnessing an accident in the presence of other people. It can be astonishing to hear the different accounts of what just happened. Didn't we all see the same thing? Of course, we like to believe *our* view of the events is the accurate one. As we discuss in later chapters on memory and cognition, objective facts can be altered easily when processed subjectively by individuals. The scientific methods described in this chapter promote objectivity and help prevent biased, subjective observations from distorting a scientist's work.

© corepics/Shutterstock

We have all had the experience of witnessing an event with other people only to discover that everyone seems to have a different memory of what happened.

Psychology *as a* Hub Science

Testing the Effects of Food Additives on Children's Behavior

How many times have you heard a parent complain about a child's out-of-control behavior and blame it on too much sugar? How would a scientist know if sugar or any other food ingredient affected children's behavior? Scientific discoveries in this area could benefit the fields of nutrition, health, medicine, and child development.

Psychologists have employed the objective, scientific methods needed to provide guidance to both parents and the food industry on this type of topic. So how can scientists objectively test the idea that kids may go "out-of-control" after eating too much sugar? What tools can a scientist use? The "gold standard" for demonstrating the objective effects of any substance, whether a food additive, medication, or recreational drug, is the **double-blind procedure**. This procedure requires a **placebo**, an inactive substance that cannot be distinguished from a real, active substance.

The first "blind" aspect of this procedure is the inability of participants to know whether they have taken a real substance or a placebo. This feature controls for any effects of the partici-

pants' expectations. When we drink coffee, for example, we *expect* to feel more alert, or when we take an aspirin, we *expect* our headache to disappear, so we may "feel" better long before the substance has had time to actually produce any effects. Not letting the subject know whether he or she received the real substance or the placebo helps offset these misleading effects.

The second "blind" is achieved when the researcher does not know if a participant has been given a real substance or placebo until the experiment is over. This aspect ensures that the researcher's own expectations do not tilt or bias his or her observations. If scientists expect participants to act more alert after drinking coffee, for example, this bias could be reflected in their observations and conclusions.

Returning to our question of food additives, what do double-blind,

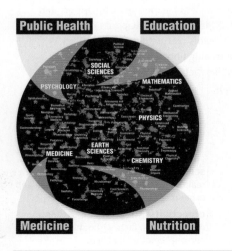

The second important difference between science and everyday observations is the use of systematic observation as opposed to hit-or-miss observation. By "hit or miss," we mean making conclusions based only on whatever is happening around us. If we want to make conclusions about the "human mind," we cannot restrict our observations to our immediate circle of acquaintances, friends and loved ones. Your observations of the people you see frequently are probably quite good. It's just that the people we know represent a small slice of the greater population. We might be surprised to learn that our favorite candidate lost an election, because "everyone we know" voted for him or her.

> Measure what is measurable, and make measurable what is not so.
>
> —Galileo Galilei

Based on observations of their surroundings, college students often believe that drinking alcohol, and even binge drinking (five drinks on one occasion for men, four for women), is a nearly universal behavior for anyone over the age of 18 or so. We can see why a college student might believe this after making hit-or-miss observations. According to the U.S. Department of Justice, 51% of 18- to 21-year-olds reported at least one drinking occasion in the last 30 days, and 37% of this age group reported at least one binge episode during that period (U.S. Department of Justice, 2002). However, this same study showed that 46% of American adults 21 and older do not drink alcohol at all, and another 26% have one drink or less per

double-blind procedure A research design that controls for placebo effects in which neither the participant nor the experimenter observing the participant knows whether the participant was given an active substance or treatment or a placebo.

placebo An inactive substance or treatment that cannot be distinguished from a real, active substance or treatment.

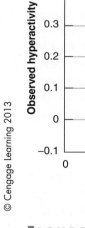

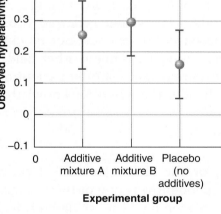

FIGURE 2.1

Hyperactivity and Food Additives. The results obtained by McCann et al. (2007) showed that hyperactivity was higher in children who consumed one of the drinks containing common food additives (the left and middle bars) than in children who consumed the placebo drink containing no additives (the bar on the right).

placebo-controlled studies have to say about their effects on child behavior? In one careful study, young children were given drinks that either had no additives (placebo) or a combination of colorings and preservatives used frequently in packaged foods (McCann et al., 2007). Because it was a double-blind study, the children, of course, did not know which drink they had received, nor did the researchers responsible for observing the children. The outcome of this study showed that general measures of hyperactivity, or unusually large amounts of movement, were higher in the group that had consumed the additives than in the group consuming the placebo. This finding has implications for attention deficit hyperactivity disorder (ADHD), which we discuss in a later chapter on psychological disorders. The ability of these common food additives to make normal children more hyperactive is cause for concern and worthy of further study (see ● Figure 2.1). ✪

Double-blind placebo-controlled studies have provided insight into the relationship between common food additives in fruit drinks and hyperactivity in children.

FIGURE 2.2

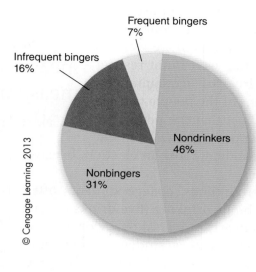

Scientific Observations Are Systematic, Not Hit-or-miss. Science provides ways to make systematic observations. Judgments we make based on the people we know might not apply to larger groups of people. Binge drinking is more common among 18- to 21-year-olds (37% report at least one binge in the last 30 days) compared to adults over 21 (23%). Among adults in general, 46% do not drink at all and another 26% report having one drink per week or less. *Source: Data from U.S. Department of Justice (2002).*

week. An additional 5% drink more than one drink per week, but never four or five on one occasion. As shown in ● Figure 2.2, binge drinkers comprise only about 23% of the adult population (compared to the 37% percent of 18- to 21-year-olds), and only 7% of adults over 21 binge five or more times per month. These numbers, while significant (binge drinkers consume a whopping 76% of the alcohol sold in the United States), hardly support a conclusion that "everybody's doing it."

Finally, science relies on observable, repeatable evidence, whereas everyday observation often ignores evidence, especially when it runs counter to strongly held beliefs. Many people are quite convinced that women talk more than men. We're not certain where that idea came from, and it does not appear to be true. One group of researchers recorded students' talking throughout the day and concluded that "the widespread and highly publicized stereotype about female talkativeness is unfounded" (Mehl, Vazire, Ramírez-Esparza, Slatcher, & Pennebaker, 2007, p. 82). Other studies, in fact, make the argument that in the majority of circumstances, men actually talk more than women (James & Drakich, 1993; Leaper & Ayres, 2007).

Scientific knowledge is both stable and changing. It is a work in progress, not a finished product. The fact that we may learn something new tomorrow should not convince you that today's knowledge is flawed. Most change occurs very slowly on the "cutting edges" of science, not quickly or at the main core of its knowledge base. Unlike with many other fields, we expect science to improve over time. An important feature of scientific literacy is to learn to be comfortable with the idea that scientific knowledge is always open to improvement and will never be considered absolutely certain (American Association for the Advancement of Science, 2009).

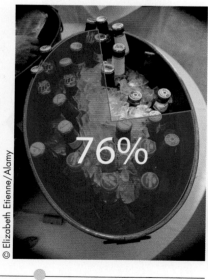

Although binge drinkers make up only 23% of the adult population, they consume an astonishing 76% of all alcohol sold in the United States.

critical thinking The ability to think clearly, rationally, and independently.

The Importance of Critical Thinking

Critical thinking, or the ability to think clearly, rationally, and independently, is one of the foundations of scientific reasoning. The skilled critical thinker can follow logical arguments, identify mistakes in reasoning, prioritize ideas according to their importance, and apply logic to personal attitudes, beliefs, and values.

Critical thinking is not built in but, rather, is a skill people need to learn. You can begin by using five critical thinking questions to evaluate new information you come across in your everyday life, starting with what you read in this textbook (Bernstein, 2011):

1. What am I being asked to believe or accept?
2. What evidence supports this position?

Scientific research results do not support the common stereotype that women talk more than men.

3. Are there other ways this evidence could be interpreted?
4. What other evidence would I need to evaluate these alternatives?
5. What are the most reasonable conclusions?

It is also helpful to recognize the signs that you are not thinking critically (Lau & Chan, 2009):

- Instead of figuring out the answer to a problem yourself, you prefer just being given the answer.
- You prefer to use "gut feelings" about decisions instead of using reason to choose a solution.
- You do not review your mistakes or change your mind if evidence contradicts your original position.
- You resent criticism of your ideas.

Critical thinking is not only essential to good science, but it provides the underpinning of a free society as well. Our abilities to think clearly, rationally, and independently give us the confidence to question the actions of people in authority instead of engaging in blind obedience. We hope you will continue to practice good critical thinking skills long after you complete this textbook.

Fanatic—one who won't change his mind and won't change the subject.

—Winston Churchill

The Scientific Enterprise

Learning scientific facts is not the same as understanding how science works. Science, including psychological science, is more than a collection of facts—it is a process.

Scientific Theories Science seeks to develop **theories**, which are sets of facts and relationships between facts that can be used to explain and predict phenomena (Cacioppo, Semin, & Berntson, 2004). In other words, scientists construct the best possible models of reality based on the facts known to date. Unfortunately, the English language can be the source of considerable confusion regarding the nature of scientific theories. In addition to its use in science, the word *theory* can be used in nonscientific ways to describe a guess, such as "I have a theory about why my professor seems

theory A set of facts and relationships between facts that can explain and predict related phenomena.

unusually cheerful this morning," or a hypothetical situation, as in "that's the theory, but it may not work in practice." Confusion over the multiple meanings of the word *theory* have led people mistakenly to view truly scientific theories, like the theory of evolution, as nothing more than casual guesses or hunches rather than the thoroughly investigated and massively supported principles that they are.

Thinking Scientifically

Using the Five Steps of Critical Thinking to Evaluate Survey Data

Let's see how we might apply the five steps of critical thinking to examine journalists' interpretation of the results of a recent survey. Major news outlets, including the *New York Times*, *The Wall Street Journal*, *USA Today*, and the *Associated Press*, featured stories about one of the interesting outcomes of the U.S. Census Bureau's 2009 American Community Survey. For the first time in recorded U.S. history, fewer 25- to 34-year-olds are married than have never been married. Journalists were quick to blame the economy for this change. Among the headlines were "Saying No to 'I Do' With the Economy in Mind" and "Recession Spurs Young in US to Forgo or Delay Marriage." How do we know whether a bad economy really influences marriage rates?

1. *What am I being asked to believe or accept?* I'm being asked to believe that there is a direct link between the U.S. recession and young adults' decisions to marry.

2. *What evidence supports this position?* The American Community Survey, conducted by the Census Bureau, is an "ongoing survey that provides data every year. . . . Information from the survey generates data that help determine how more than $400 billion in federal and state funds are distributed each year" (U.S. Census Bureau, 2011). The survey includes questions about age, sex, race, family and relationships, income, health insurance, education, veteran status, disabilities, work transportation, and cost of living. Over 2 million respondents representing all geographical locations in the United States participated in the survey by mail, phone, or personal interview. To characterize the economy as a recession, the *USA Today* article cited additional facts from the Census Bureau survey, including a nearly 3% drop in median family income from 2008 to 2009 and the highest number of people living in poverty recorded in the last 51 years (El

Nasser, Overberg, & Thomassie, 2010). As we discuss later in the chapter, the *median* divides the population in half, so the median family income is the point where half of American families have incomes above that point and the other half have incomes below (see ● Figure 2.3).

3. *Are there other ways this evidence could be interpreted?* Economists agree that the United States was experiencing a severe recession when the survey data were being collected, but there are many reasons why people choose to get married. Some, but not all, of these reasons relate to finances. As you will learn in this chapter, these sorts of comparisons (between the population's finances and its marriage rates) are known as correlations, and correlations do not give us the information we need to say "the recession *caused* a drop in marriage rates." All we can say is that marriage rates went down at the same time financial indicators went down.

The best scientific theories not only explain and organize known facts, but they also generate new predictions (see ● Figure 2.4). The word *prediction* comes from the Latin words for "saying before." A scientific prediction is much more than a guess or hunch. It is usually stated in a rigorous, mathematical form that allows the scientist to say that under a certain

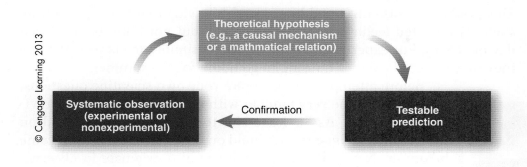

© Cengage Learning 2013

FIGURE 2.4

How to Develop and Test a Theory. Theory building begins with generating hypotheses that are then systematically tested. Hypotheses that are not rejected contribute to the theory and help generate new hypotheses.

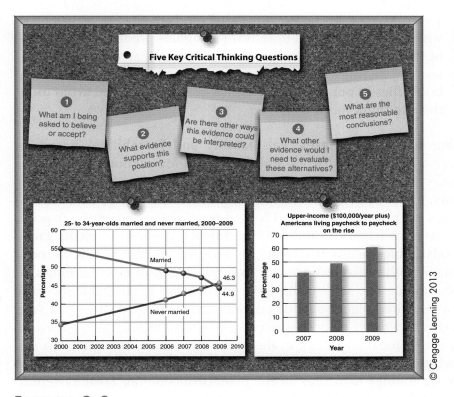

FIGURE 2.3

What Do These Data Really Mean? News headlines were quick to associate a recent drop in marriage rates among young adults with the tough economy. Do the data really support that conclusion? *Sources:* Data from Mather and Lavery (2010); Pisani (2009).

4. *What other evidence would I need to evaluate these alternatives?* Historical data on marriage rates would be helpful. Was the observed drop unique to 2008–2009? Did similar drops occur in previous recessions?

5. *What are the most reasonable conclusions?* Economist Justin Wolfers looked at marriage rates over time, including during periods of economic recession. Based on this analysis, he concluded that the trend for Americans to marry at later ages appears to have had more of an impact than the economy on the observed drop in marriage rates. The median age at first marriage for men has risen from 23 in 1970 to 28 today, and for women from 21 in 1970 to 26 today (Wolfers, 2010). Because of this trend, we would expect to see many fewer married 25- to 34-year-olds today than in 1970, and some of these young adults may eventually marry at later ages. ✿

set of circumstances, the following outcomes are likely to occur (if A, then B). In some cases, a theory's predictions can be quite surprising. For example, you might believe that it's impossible to be happy and sad at the same time. However, one model of emotion, discussed in a later chapter, predicted that it is quite possible to feel happy and sad at the same time (Cacioppo, Berntson, Norris, & Gollan, 2011). This prediction was confirmed by research showing that first-year college students reported feeling either happy or sad, but not both, on a normal day of school, but experienced both emotions simultaneously on the day they moved out of campus housing to go home for the summer.

Before attempting to generate your own scientific questions, it pays to become very familiar with relevant theories and previous discoveries. As Sir Isaac Newton noted, scholars stand on the shoulders of giants—we build on the work of those who came before us. New lines of research can also originate in observation. Scientists are observers not just in the laboratory but in everyday life. Scientific progress often takes a giant leap forward when a gifted observer recognizes a deeper meaningfulness in an everyday occurrence, as when Sir Isaac Newton observed a falling apple and considered its implications for a law of gravity. As we discovered in the previous chapter, Ivan Pavlov realized that when his dogs learned to salivate to signals predicting the arrival of food, something much more significant than slobbering dogs was happening. The learning he observed explains why we get butterflies in our stomach before a performance and avoid foods that we think made us ill.

A contemporary theory of emotion correctly predicted the circumstances for when we might experience mixed emotions of happiness and sadness. Graduation from college is an important accomplishment, but we might feel sad about leaving our friends.

hypothesis A proposed explanation for a situation, usually taking the form "if A happens then B will be the result."

falsifiable A characteristic of a scientific hypothesis meaning that situations in which the hypothesis might be false can be imagined.

testable A feature of a hypothesis that means it can be evaluated using known scientific methods.

Generating Good Hypotheses: Falsifiability and Testability Based on your understanding of past work and theoretical foundations in your area of interest, coupled with your own observations, you can now generate a **hypothesis**, which is a type of inference, or, in other words, an educated guess, based on prior evidence and logical possibilities. Scientific hypotheses must be both falsifiable and testable. Falsifiable does not mean "false." Instead, **falsifiable** means that you can imagine situations that demonstrate your hypothesis to be false. For example, a hypothesis claiming that all planets outside our solar system are uninhabited is falsifiable, because finding an inhabited planet outside our solar system would show that your hypothesis was wrong. Hypotheses can be falsifiable but not necessarily **testable**, which means you can evaluate the hypothesis using known scientific methods. In our example of inhabited planets, we do not have the necessary technology to survey all the planets outside our solar system to determine whether an inhabited one exists. Our hypothesis is falsifiable but not currently testable.

Scientists can never "prove" that their hypotheses are true, because some future experiment, possibly using new technology not currently available, might show the hypothesis to be false after all. All we can do is show when a hypothesis is false. A false hypothesis must always be modified or discarded. As we explore the universe, continued failure to find an inhabited planet does not mean our hypothesis is true. The only outcome of our search that would affect our hypothesis is the discovery of the very first inhabited planet, which would show that our hypothesis is wrong.

Evaluating Hypotheses Once you have a falsifiable and testable hypothesis, you are now ready to collect the data necessary to evaluate it. The existing scientific literature in your area of interest provides considerable guidance regarding your choice of materials, types of data to be collected, and methods for interpreting your data. To explore the many techniques available to psychologists, we will use an ongoing question about whether playing violent video games increases physical aggression. We could benefit from many other studies that specify features of violent video games, measures of physical aggression, and statistical procedures for evaluating this type of question. You do not have to reinvent the wheel. In fact, your results will be given greater consideration if you use methods that are well established and familiar in your area of research. Once we collect our data, our theories help us evaluate the importance and implications of our observations.

Science is a vastly collaborative enterprise. Not only do we "stand on the shoulders of giants" because we benefit from the work that has been done previously, but we depend on many others in the scientific community to help us improve our work and avoid mistakes. Normally this evaluation is done by submitting research to conferences or for publication. During this process, research undergoes **peer review**, in which it is scrutinized by other scientists who are experts in your area. Only if other experts conclude that your research is important, accurate, and explained thoroughly will it be added to the existing body of scientific knowledge. To demonstrate the importance of this peer review, contrast this process to what happens when a person simply decides to transmit a tweet or launch a personal website. The author is solely responsible for the content, and there are no checks at all on the accuracy of that content.

During peer review, research that fits with our existing knowledge is typically accepted more rapidly than work that is less consistent with previous reports. Unconventional findings often undergo **replication**, which means that other scientists independently attempt to reproduce the results of the study in question. If the data are replicated, they will be accepted quickly. If other scientists are unable to replicate the data, their extra effort will have prevented inaccurate results from cluttering the scientific literature. Although this process might slow down the publication of some innovative research, the result—more accuracy—is well worth the effort.

A whopping 80% of Americans believe in a hypothesis suggesting that the government covers up all evidence of extraterrestrial life (CNN, 1997). Is this a falsifiable hypothesis? If you can even imagine the government suddenly placing an alien spaceship on display at the Smithsonian, the hypothesis can be shown to be falsifiable.

Courtesy of NASA

Richard B. Hoover, Ph.D. NASA/Marshall Space Flight Center

Hypotheses must be falsifiable, which means that we can imagine situations that show our hypothesis is false. A hypothesis stating that all planets outside our solar system are uninhabited meets this test, because finding life on another planet would show that the hypothesis was wrong. A NASA scientist, Dr. Richard Hoover, made a controversial claim that alien life similar to this microbe was recovered from a meteorite.

peer review The process of having other experts examine research prior to its publication.

replication Repeating an experiment and producing the same results.

Summary 2.1

Steps to Critical Thinking

Questions for good critical thinking	Questions for detecting poor critical thinking (all answers should be no)
What am I being asked to believe or accept?	Am I accepting another person's conclusion without working out the problem myself?
What evidence supports this position?	Am I using "gut feelings" instead of reason?
Are there other ways this evidence could be interpreted?	Am I forgetting to review my conclusions to check for mistakes?
What other evidence would I need to evaluate these alternatives?	Am I oversensitive to criticism about my conclusions?
What are the most reasonable conclusions?	Am I unwilling to consider alternative explanations?

How Do Psychologists Conduct Research?

Psychologists use a variety of research methods, including descriptive, correlational, and experimental methods. Descriptive methods, including surveys, case studies, and observations, provide a good starting place for a new research question. Correlational methods help psychologists see how two variables of interest, like the marriage rate and economic factors described earlier, relate to one another. Psychologists use experiments to test their hypotheses and to determine the causes of behavior.

In the next sections, we will describe these common research methods used in psychological science and then compare how they might be used to approach a particular question—whether exposure to video game violence increases aggression. Each method—descriptive, correlational, and experimental—provides a different view of the phenomenon in question, and each has its own particular profile of strengths and weaknesses. Each requires different types of statistical analyses, which are described in more depth later in the chapter. Many psychological studies combine several of these methods. When similar outcomes are observed using multiple methods, we have even more confidence in our results.

<table>
<tr><td>

Descriptive Methods

</td><td>

Descriptive methods include case studies, naturalistic observations, and surveys. As we have seen, personal observations and "commonsense" ideas

</td></tr>
</table>

are especially vulnerable to bias, but descriptive methods allow a researcher to make more careful, systematic, real-world observations. Armed with these scientific observations, the researcher will be in a strong position to generate hypotheses.

The Case Study A **case study** provides an in-depth analysis of the behavior of one person or a small number of people. Many fields, including medicine, law, and business, use the case study method. Psychologists often use case studies in situations where large numbers of participants are not available or when a particular participant possesses unique characteristics, as in the case described in this section. Interviews, background records, observation, personality tests, cognitive tests, and brain imaging provide information necessary to evaluate the case.

Photograph of Henry Molaison. Copyright © Suzanne Corkin, used by permission of the Wylie Agency LLC.

One of the most productive case studies in psychology chronicled over 50 years of examinations of Henry Molaison (1926–2008), known in the scientific literature as "the amnesiac patient H.M." In 1953, Molaison underwent brain surgery to control his frequent, severe seizures. Although the surgery may have saved his life, Molaison was left with profound memory deficits, which we describe in our later chapter on memory. Through painstaking testing and evaluation of Molaison, psychologists learned a great deal about the brain structures and processes that support the formation of memories (Corkin, 2002). Even after his death, Molaison continues to contribute to our knowledge. Researchers from MIT, the Massachusetts General Hospital, and the University of California, San Diego are analyzing Molaison's brain at the cellular level.

How could you use the case study method to learn about exposure to video game violence and aggression? You could conduct a case study of Michael Carneal, who was sentenced to life in prison after he began shooting students at his high school, killing three students and seriously wounding five others. Carneal had never shot a real gun before, but he was very fond of playing first-person shooter games like *Doom*. To conduct your case study, you gather background facts about Carneal's case, possibly by interviewing others associated with the case, viewing legal and medical documents, and observing media accounts. You interview Carneal and possibly administer established personality and clinical tests that we discuss in our chapters on personality and therapies.

One of the most famous case studies in psychology is that of Henry Molaison (left), who was known in the literature as "the amnesic patient, H.M." until his death in 2008. For over 50 years, Molaison allowed psychologists to evaluate his memory deficits resulting from brain surgery. After his death, scientists like Jacopo Annese (below) of the University of California, San Diego began a careful examination of Molaison's brain.

© s44/ZUMA Press/Newscom

descriptive method Research methods designed for making careful, systematic observations.

case study An in-depth analysis of the behavior of one person or a small number of people.

What are the advantages of using the case study method to learn about the effects of playing violent video games on aggression? School shooters are thankfully quite rare, and the case study method is well suited to learning about unusual situations. Based on the detailed data you obtain from Carneal's case, you will be better prepared to generate and test hypotheses. A case study can also contribute to science by falsifying a hypothesis. If a hypothesis made a strong prediction that all school shootings are the result of playing violent video games, finding and documenting a case of a school shooter who did not play violent video games would require rejection of the hypothesis.

Michael Carneal is now serving a life sentence in prison after he shot and killed fellow students at his high school in 1997, when he was 14.

Naturalistic Observation If you are interested in learning about larger groups of people than are possible with the case study method, you might pursue a **naturalistic observation**, or an in-depth study of a phenomenon in its natural setting. Compared to the case study method, we are now going to be looking at a much larger group of people, which will strengthen our ability to apply our results to the population in general. We also have the advantage of observing individuals in their natural, everyday circumstances.

A classic example of the method of naturalistic observation is the careful, long-term study of chimpanzees conducted in their habitat by Jane Goodall. In the summer of 1960, the then 26-year-old Goodall began her painstaking observations of chimpanzees living in Gombe National Park in Tanzania. Among her earlier discoveries was the fact that chimpanzees were not vegetarians, as was previously assumed:

> I saw that one of them was holding a pink-looking object from which he was from time to time pulling pieces with his teeth. There was a female and a youngster and they were both reaching out toward the male, their hands actually touching his mouth. Presently the female picked up a piece of the pink thing and put it to her mouth: it was at this moment that I realized the chimps were eating meat. (Goodall, 1971, p. 34)

As a result of Goodall's years spent following the chimpanzees, scientists have a rich, accurate knowledge of the animals' behavior in the field.

Impressed by Goodall's results, you plan to pursue further knowledge about violent video games and aggression by attending LAN (*Local Area Network*) parties, where attendees bring their own computers to a gathering place to play multiplayer, networked video games. You hope that by observing people playing violent video games and watching their subsequent behavior for signs of aggression, you might reach some conclusions about the relationships between video game violence and aggression. As in Goodall's

Jane Goodall used naturalistic observation to illuminate the world of the chimpanzee.

naturalistic observation An in-depth study of a phenomenon in its natural setting.

case, this approach has the advantages of providing insight into more natural, real-world behaviors with larger numbers of participants.

Some naturalistic observations are conducted when people know they are being observed, while others are not. Both situations raise challenges. If we know we are being observed, we might act differently. Your LAN party participants know that aggression is not viewed positively in our culture, so they might act less aggressively when they know they're being watched. Watching people who do not know they're being watched raises ethical issues, which we explore in detail later in this chapter. How would you feel if you discovered you had been an unwitting participant in a study?

The use of naturalistic observation illustrates the importance of choosing a method that is well suited to your research goals. Like the case study method, naturalistic observation can be very helpful for developing hypotheses, but other methods must be used to test them. Most hypotheses in psychology look at the relationships between two or more concepts, like the exposure to violent video games and aggression in our example. Testing a hypothesis would allow you to say whether or not a relationship between exposure to violent video games and aggression actually exists, how strong the relationship is, what direction it is, and so on. It might appear to you that the people you observe are more aggressive following their LAN parties than before, but you have no way to demonstrate your point. People engage in lots of different behaviors during LAN parties. Perhaps eating pizza or staying up all night at LAN parties enhances aggressive tendencies. With only your naturalistic observations to go on, you can't say for sure.

To pursue the question of the effects of violent video games on aggression, you could do a naturalistic observation at a Local Area Network (LAN) party.

The Survey Surveys or questionnaires allow you to ask large numbers of people questions about attitudes and behavior. Surveys provide a great deal of useful information very quickly at relatively little expense.

One of the primary requirements for a good survey is the use of an appropriate **sample**, or subset of a population being studied. Good results require large samples that are typical, or representative, of the population you wish to describe. Major pollsters, like the U.S. Census Bureau discussed earlier, take great pains to recruit survey participants who mirror the characteristics of the public across factors such as gender, age, education, occupation, income, and geographical location.

survey A descriptive method in which participants are asked the same questions.

sample A subset of a population being studied.

People taking surveys might be more interested in pleasing others or appearing "normal" than in answering honestly.

Surveys use self-report, so results can be influenced by people's natural tendency to want to appear socially appropriate (Corbett, 1991). As we will discover in a later chapter on social psychology, people have strong tendencies to conform to the expectations of others. In some surveys, this factor is not a problem. If you ask people if they prefer lattes or mochas, you will probably get a fairly honest answer. However, in cases where people believe that their true attitudes and behaviors will not be viewed favorably by others, they are likely to lie, even when their answers are confidential and anonymous.

Let's see how scientists have used the survey method to explore video game violence. One survey involved 1,254 middle school students attending public schools in South Carolina and Pennsylvania (Olson, 2010). Although the sample did not include children from other geographic locations or children who are homeschooled or attending private schools, it appears to be relatively representative of this age group. Children were asked to respond to 17 motives for playing video games on a 4-point scale from strongly agree to strongly disagree. Like all surveys, this one depends on self-report, which raises the possibility that children would give "the right answer" instead of responding honestly.

What did this scientific survey discover about violent video games? As shown in ● Figure 2.5, a surprising outcome of the survey was the more

FIGURE 2.5

Results From a Real Survey on Video Game Use. Cheryl Olson (2010) asked middle school students why they liked to play violent video games. Over 20% of the boys agreed that the games "help me relax" and "help me get my anger out." *Source: Adapted from Olson (2010).*

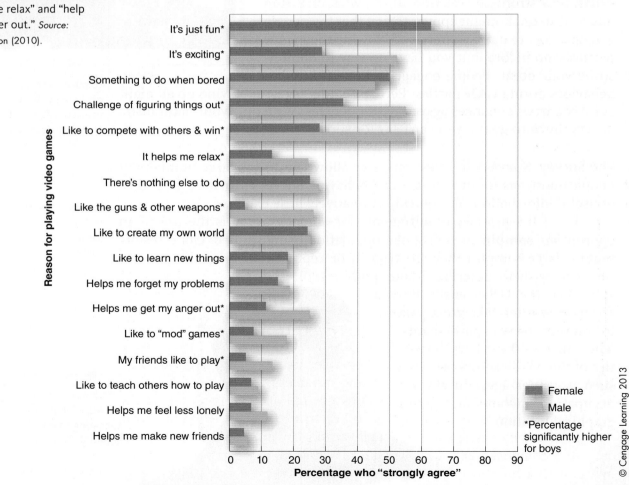

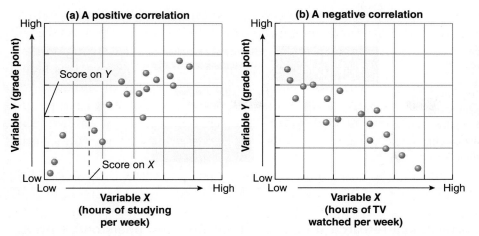

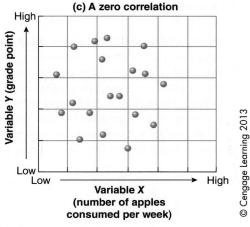

FIGURE 2.6

Correlations Describe the Direction and Strength of Relationships Between Two Variables. (a) In positive correlations, high levels of one variable are associated with high levels of another. (b) In negative correlations, high values of one variable are associated with low levels of the other. (c) In zero correlations, the two variables do not have any relationship with each other at all.

than 20% of boys who reported using violent video games to "help me relax" and "help me get my anger out." You will have the opportunity to take a survey on video games and aggression after you read the next section.

Correlational Methods

Correlations measure the direction and strength of the relationship between two **variables**, or factors that have values that can "vary," like a person's height and weight. Correlations allow psychologists to explore whether hours of sleep are related to student grade point averages (Trockel, Barnes, & Egget, 2000) or if the age of parents is related to the rate of autism among their children (Reichenberg, Gross, Kolevzon, & Susser, 2011). If you're curious about the results of these studies, the first showed that no, sleep and grade point average were not related, and the second showed that yes, age of parents is related to the rate of autism among their children.

We begin our analysis of correlations by measuring our variables. A **measure** answers the simple question of "how much" of a variable you have observed. After we obtain measures of each variable, we compare the values of one variable to those of the other and conduct a statistical analysis of the results. Three possible outcomes from the comparison between our two variables can occur: positive, negative, or zero correlations. In a positive correlation, high levels of one variable are associated with high levels of the other variable. Height and weight usually show this type of relationship. In most cases, people who are taller weigh more than people who are shorter. Two variables can also show a negative correlation, in which high values of one variable are associated with low values of another. For example, high levels of alcohol consumption among college students are usually associated with low grade point averages. The third possible outcome is a zero correlation, in which the two variables do not have any systematic relationship with each other at all. When variables have a zero correlation, knowing the value of one variable does not tell you anything about the value of the other variable (see ● Figure 2.6). In spite of numerous scientific studies to the contrary, emergency room and law enforcement personnel are often convinced that they are busier with emergencies and crime on nights with a full moon. In fact, lunar cycles show zero correlations with either emergency room admissions or arrest rates (Lieber, 1978).

correlation A measure of the direction and strength of the relationship between two variables.

variable A factor that has a range of values.

measure A method for describing a variable's quantity.

FIGURE 2.7

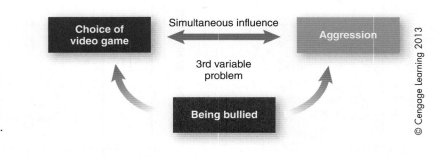

Third Variables and Correlations. Third variables can be responsible for the correlation we observe in two other variables. In our example of video game violence and aggression, being bullied could be a third variable that predicts both choice of violent games and a tendency to be aggressive at school. The possibility of third variables is one reason we must be very careful when we reach conclusions based on correlational data.

Correlational research results are frequently misunderstood. Correlations permit us to discuss the relationships between two variables but tell us nothing about whether one variable *causes* changes in the other. Let us say that we discover a positive correlation between violent video games and aggression: Youth who play the most hours of violent video games have the most reports of physical aggression at school. However, we still cannot say that playing violent video games *causes* physical aggression at school. This conclusion may seem very reasonable to you, and it may actually be true, so why must we abandon it? First, the two variables in a correlation can influence each other simultaneously. Although it may be true that playing violent video games leads to physical aggression at school, youth who experience physical aggression at school may be more attracted to violent video games as an outlet for their frustration. Second, we might be observing a situation in which a **third variable** is responsible for the correlation we see between our two variables of interest. Consider the observation that many school shootings have been perpetrated by people who had been bullied relentlessly by others. Perhaps the experience of having been bullied (the third variable in this case) predisposes both a choice of violent recreation and a tendency to engage in aggressive behavior at school (see ● Figure 2.7).

When you're reading or listening to the news, watch for the use of words like link, association, *or* relationship *used to describe two variables, such as in a headline that states "lack of sleep linked to depression" or "drinking red wine associated with lower rates of heart disease." These key words usually mean that the data are correlational but are often mistaken for causal. Now you know how you should and should not interpret these reports.*

If you cannot make conclusions about causality using correlations, why would you use correlations in the first place? There are a number of circumstances in which correlations are more appropriate than other research methods. For example, it would be totally unethical to ask pregnant women to consume different amounts of alcohol to assess the effects of prenatal alcohol in their infants. Instead, we can ask pregnant women to identify their alcohol intake in diaries, which can then be correlated with various measures of infant functioning. Although this method will not allow us to conclude that drinking during pregnancy causes damage to the fetus, we can correctly identify the strength and direction (positive, negative, or zero) of any relationship between drinks consumed and the infants' outcome measures (see ● Figure 2.8). Using this approach, researchers have shown that heavy maternal alcohol consumption is correlated with abnormal amounts of thickening of the outer layer of the brain (the *cortex,* discussed in a later chapter on biological psychology; Sowell et al., 2008).

third variable A variable that is responsible for a correlation observed between two other variables of interest.

FIGURE 2.8

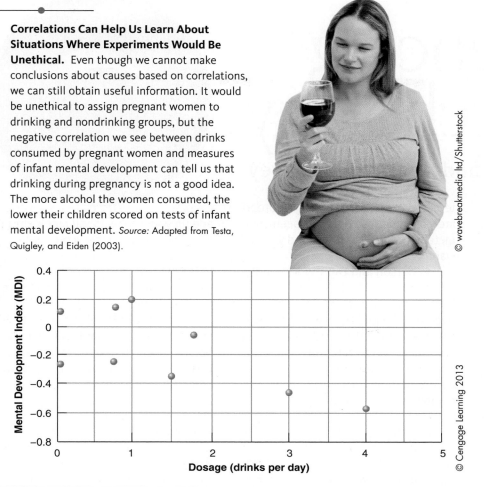

Correlations Can Help Us Learn About Situations Where Experiments Would Be Unethical. Even though we cannot make conclusions about causes based on correlations, we can still obtain useful information. It would be unethical to assign pregnant women to drinking and nondrinking groups, but the negative correlation we see between drinks consumed by pregnant women and measures of infant mental development can tell us that drinking during pregnancy is not a good idea. The more alcohol the women consumed, the lower their children scored on tests of infant mental development. *Source:* Adapted from Testa, Quigley, and Eiden (2003).

Experimental Methods

The scientist's most powerful tool for drawing conclusions about research questions is the formal **experiment**. Unlike cases in which descriptive methods are used, the researcher conducting an experiment has a great deal of control over the situation. Unlike correlational methods, the use of the formal experiment allows us to talk about "cause" (see ● Figure 2.9).

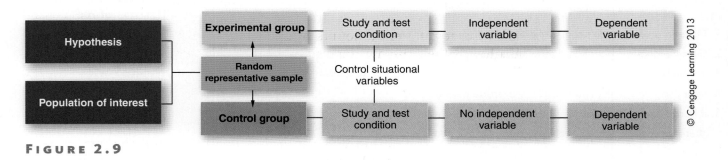

FIGURE 2.9

How to Design an Experiment. A good experimental design features random assignment of participants to groups, appropriate control groups, control of situational variables, and carefully selected independent and dependant variables.

experiment A research method that tests hypotheses and allows researchers to make conclusions about causality.

Experiencing Psychology

Taking a Video Game and Aggression Survey

In addition to using experimental methods, described later in this chapter, to study our question about video games and aggression, Anderson and Dill (2000) compared responses on a standard physical aggression questionnaire (Buss & Perry, 1992) and a video game questionnaire they devised. After you complete your questionnaires, we will tell you how the college students participating in the Anderson and Dill study responded.

As you complete your questionnaires, consider the limitations we raised earlier about the survey method. Physical aggression is a sensitive topic, and we suspect that the Anderson and Dill participants might have been tempted to answer in socially appropriate ways that may not have been completely truthful. See if you find yourself wanting to do the same.

Anderson and Dill's Video Game Questionnaire (Anderson & Dill, 2000) asked students to rate their five most frequently played games. In the interests of time and space, we are asking you to rate only your number 1 most frequently played game. Before reading further, go ahead and complete the two surverys.

Let's add up some scores. To score the Physical Aggression Questionnaire, you first need to reverse question 7 ("I can think of no good reason . . . .") by subtracting your score from 8. Now add up your scores for all nine items. You do not get a single score for the Video Game Questionnaire, but it is helpful to add your scores for a–d to get a measure of "long-term exposure to video games."

The main point of this activity is to get an idea of what it was like to be one of Anderson and Dill's participants. We really cannot make any conclusions about the relationship between video games and physical aggression based on your single scores, but you can compare your results to those reported by Buss and Perry and by Anderson and Dill.

On the Physical Aggression Questionnaire, Buss and Perry

Physical Aggression Questionnaire					
Please rate each of the following items in terms of how characteristic they are of you. Use the following scale for answering these items.					
1 extremely uncharacteristic of me	2	3	4		5 extremely characteristic of me
1. Once in a while I can't control the urge to strike another person.					
2. Given enough provocation, I may hit another person.					
3. If somebody hits me, I hit back.					
4. I get into fights a little more than the average person.					
5. If I have to resort to violence to protect my rights, I will.					
6. There are people who pushed me so far that we came to blows.					
7. I can think of no good reason for ever hitting a person.					
8. I have threatened people I know.					
9. I have become so mad that I have broken things.					

reported that the average score for men was 24.3 and the average score for women was 17.9 out of a possible high of 45. If you're curious, the sex difference in physical aggression was statistically significant, a concept we discuss later in this chapter. This concept means that we believe the sex difference observed by Buss and Perry represents a real difference, not just a chance occurrence.

Comparing your data to that of Anderson and Dill is a bit more difficult, because these researchers actually combined the Buss and Perry questionnaire with another measure of aggression in their analysis of their results. However, they found that this combined Physical Aggression score was positively correlated with long-term exposure to video game violence (a combination of a–d for exposure and e–f for violence) and with amount of recent play time (item a).

Now that you understand correlations, you also know what you can and cannot say about these results. Based on the results of the Anderson and Dill correlations, we still do not know whether (a) having an aggressive personality leads to spending more time playing violent video games, (b) playing violent video games leads to more physical aggression, (c) both of these relationships are true, or (d) some third variable such as experience of being bullied contributes to both physical aggression and choice of violent video games. ✪

Video Game Questionnaire

For the following items, rate your "most played" game:

a. In recent months, how often have you played this game?

1	2	3	4	5	6	7
Rarely			Occasionally			Often

b. During 11th & 12th grades, how often did you play this game?

1	2	3	4	5	6	7
Rarely			Occasionally			Often

c. During 9th & 10th grades, how often did you play this game?

1	2	3	4	5	6	7
Rarely			Occasionally			Often

d. During 7th & 8th grades, how often did you play this game?

1	2	3	4	5	6	7
Rarely			Occasionally			Often

e. How violent is the content of this game?

1	2	3	4	5	6	7
Little or no violent content						Extremely violent content

f. How bloody/gory are the graphics of this game?

1	2	3	4	5	6	7
Little or no blood & gore						Extremely bloody & gory

g. Which of the following categories best describes this game? Check all that apply.

__ Education   __Sports   __ Fantasy   __ Fighting with hands/feet   __ Fighting with weapons   __ Skill

Researchers attempt to reduce the impact of confounding variables on their results. In a test of the effects of aerobic exercise on blood pressure, situational confounding variables, such as (1) traffic outside the building, (2) a noisy treadmill, and (3) a neighbor breathing heavily, can be controlled by holding the environment as constant as possible for all participants. Individual differences, such as (4) an early morning after little sleep or (5) superior fitness, can be controlled by randomly assigning participants to groups.

A researcher begins designing an experiment with a hypothesis, which can be viewed as a highly educated guess based on systematic observations, a review of previous research, or a scientific theory. A hypothesis takes this form: "If I do this, that will happen." To test the hypothesis, the researcher manipulates or modifies one or more variables and observes changes in others. The variable controlled and manipulated by an experimenter ("If I do this . . . .) is known as the **independent variable**. We need some way to evaluate the effects of this manipulation. We use a **dependent variable**, defined as the observed result of the manipulation of the independent variable, to tell us "that will happen" as a result of the independent variable. Like the independent variable, our choice of dependent variable is based on our original hypothesis.

After determining our independent and dependent variables, we still have quite a bit of work to do. In most experiments, we want to know how simply going through the procedures of being in an experiment influences our dependent variable. Perhaps the hassle of going to a laboratory and filling out paperwork changes our behavior. To evaluate these effects, we assign some of our participants to a **control group**, or a group that experiences all experimental procedures with the exception of exposure to the independent variable. The experience of the control group should be as similar as possible to that of the **experimental groups**, who do experience the independent variable.

We want to ensure that our dependent variables reflect the outcomes of our independent variables, instead of individual differences among the participants' personalities, abilities, motivations, and other similar factors. To prevent these individual differences from masking or distorting the effects of our independent variable, we randomly assign participants to experimental or control groups. **Random assignment** means that each participant has an equal chance of being assigned to any group in an experiment. With random assignment, any differences we see between the behavior of one group and that of another is unlikely to be the result of the individual differences among the participants, which tend to cancel each other out.

Individual differences among participants are an example of **confounding variables**, or variables that are irrelevant to the hypothesis being tested that can alter our conclusions. For example, a researcher might want to test

independent variable An experimental variable controlled and manipulated by the experimenter; the "if A happens" part of a hypothesis.

dependent variable A measure that demonstrates the effects of an independent variable; the "result" part of a hypothesis.

control group A group that experiences all experimental procedures with the exception of exposure to the independent variable.

experimental group A group of participants that is exposed to the independent variable.

random assignment The procedure in which each participant has an equal chance of being assigned to any group in an experiment.

confounding variable Variables that are irrelevant to the hypothesis being tested that can alter a researcher's conclusions.

the effects of aerobic exercise on blood pressure. If some of the participants competed in triathlons without the researcher's knowledge, their athletic experience would confound the interpretation of the results. Random assignment to groups typically controls for confounds due to these types of individual differences, but other sources of confound exist. Situational confounds, such as time of day or noise levels in a laboratory, could also affect the interpretation of an experiment. Scientists attempt to run their experiments under the most constant circumstances possible to rule out situational confounding variables.

Let's return to our question about violent video games and aggression, and see how one real experiment addressed the issue. The researchers tested a hypothesis stating that playing a violent video game (the independent variable) would produce higher aggression (the dependent variable) (Anderson & Dill, 2000). The experimental group played a violent game (*Wolfenstein 3D*) while the control group played a nonviolent game (*Myst*). Participants were randomly assigned to groups. You can imagine how the results might be distorted if the experimental group consisted of football players and the control group consisted of members of the chess club. Following their game playing, participants had an opportunity to apply a blast of noise to another person, and the length of the noise blast served as the dependent variable. We're assuming that laboratory conditions were held constant to avoid situational confounds. For example, we know that people feel more aggressive in hot temperatures (Carlsmith & Anderson, 1979). What would happen to our experiment if the air conditioner in the laboratory broke while participants played violent video games, but was fixed right before the next participants played nonviolent games? Results of this carefully controlled experiment confirmed the researchers' hypothesis: Playing the violent game led to the administration of longer noise blasts to another person (see ● Figure 2.10).

FIGURE 2.10

Experimental Method in Action. Anderson and Dill (2000) randomly assigned participants to groups playing violent and nonviolent video games. After playing, each participant was given the opportunity to administer a blast of noise to another person. Keeping conditions in the laboratory as constant as possible would help to reduce the impact of situational variables.

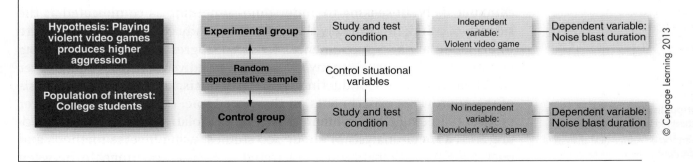

To conduct an experiment, we must carefully operationalize, or define our variables in practical terms. One way to operationalize physical aggression is to measure how often a preschooler has a physical fight with others.

As powerful as it is, the experimental method, like the other methods discussed previously, has some limitations. Experiments can be somewhat artificial. Participants know that they are in a research study, and they may vary their behavior as a result. However, making a laboratory experiment more realistic can raise ethical challenges. In a study conducted in 1962, before current ethical guidelines for research had been adopted, military personnel were led to believe that their lives were really in danger so that experimenters could "realistically" assess the effects of panic on performance (Berkun, Bialek, Kern, & Yagi, 1962). Although the responses of these participants were probably quite representative of "real life," few of us would want to be put in their position. This type of research could not be conducted under today's ethical standards, described later in this chapter.

Artificiality is also a problem in the Anderson and Dill video game study. Our real-world question relates to the likelihood that playing violent video games may elicit real physical violence in real situations. Is a person's willingness to inflict a loud sound on another person in a professor's laboratory truly representative of the type of violence involved in school shootings like Michael Carneal's? It may or may not be, but we need additional research to find out.

Another issue with the experimental method arises from differences in the choices of independent and dependent variables. Independent (controlled) and dependent (measured) variables have to be defined and implemented in some concrete fashion. The process of translating abstract independent and dependent variables into concrete forms is called **operationalization**. There are many ways we can operationalize our variables in practical terms. Anderson and Dill operationalized aggression in terms of how lengthy a sound blast a person was willing to inflict on another person. Other researchers might choose different ways to operationalize aggression, such as frequency of physical fights among preschoolers. As a result, even though there is a large body of work regarding the impact of violent video games on aggression, the methods used are so different that few direct comparisons can be made among the many studies.

Meta-analyses The point of this discussion is not to convince you that scientists don't know what they're talking about, but rather to impress upon you the importance of reviewing research results using your best critical thinking skills. In seeking to understand something as complicated as the science of mind, it is unlikely that any single study could provide complete information about a phenomenon. Instead, progress in our understanding results from the work of many scientists using diverse methods to answer the same question. Conducting a **meta-analysis**, or a statistical analysis of many previous experiments on the same topic, often provides a clearer picture than single experiments observed in isolation. As shown in ● Figure 2.11, a meta-analysis of about 300 studies, using diverse methods and over 54,000 participants, demonstrated a positive relationship between video game violence and aggression (Anderson & Bushman, 2001).

operationalization Defining variables in practical terms.

meta-analysis A statistical analysis of many previous experiments on a single topic.

FIGURE 2.11

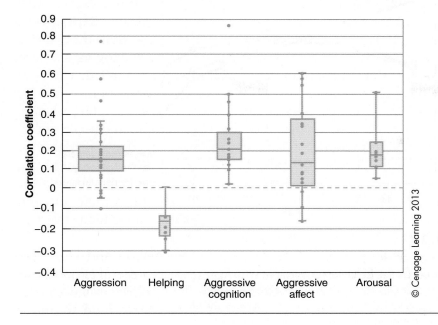

Insights From Meta-analyses.
Combining the findings of over 300 studies representing more than 50,000 participants, Anderson and Bushman (2002) argue that a positive relationship exists between exposure to video game violence and aggression, aggressive cognitions, aggressive affect or mood, and arousal. Video game violence was negatively correlated with helping behaviors. This type of graph is known as a boxplot. The width of each box corresponds to the number of studies of each type. Twenty-five percent of the results fall below the bottom of the box and another 25% are above the top of each box. The line in the middle of a box shows the median, which we define later in this chapter as the point where half of the data are above and half below. *Source: Adapted from Anderson and Bushman (2001).*

© Cengage Learning 2013

The research discussed through the remainder of this textbook has been subjected to considerable skeptical review by the researchers' peers. Most has stood the dual tests of peer review and replication by others. Converging evidence from descriptive, correlational, and experimental research provides us with confidence in our conclusions. Psychology, like any science, has followed its share of wrong turns and dead ends, but the vast majority of the knowledge presented here has been carefully crafted to present the most accurate view possible of behavior and mental processes.

How Do We Study the Effects of Time?

Modifications of the methods discussed previously might be necessary for answering specific questions. Psychological scientists frequently ask questions about normal behaviors related to age. As we will see in our chapter on development, aggression in preschoolers means something different than aggression in a 16-year-old. Considering the impact of video game violence on aggression within the context of age-related change adds a new and useful dimension to our hypothesis, but requires additional attention to the research methods to be used.

Psychologists have three specific techniques for assessing the normal behaviors associated with age: cross-sectional, longitudinal, and mixed longitudinal designs. To do a **cross-sectional study**, we might gather groups of people of varying ages and assess both their exposure to violent video games and their levels of physical aggression. We might be able to plot a

Cross-sectional studies usually show that intelligence scores decrease with age. These results are most likely a cohort effect. Performance on IQ tests has risen approximately 3 points per decade over the past 100 years for reasons that are not fully understood (Flynn, 1984).

cross-sectional study An experimental design for assessing age-related changes in which data are obtained simultaneously from people of differing ages.

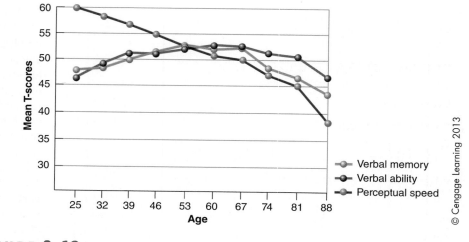

FIGURE 2.12

Special Designs Let Us See Behaviors Associated With Age. Longitudinal designs control for the cohort effects that are often seen in cross-sectional designs. This longitudinal study shows that verbal ability and verbal memory are fairly stable over the lifetime, but that perceptual speed gradually worsens with age. *Source: Adapted from Schaie (1996).*

developmental course for age-related differences in both video game exposure and aggressive behavior. However, the cross-sectional method introduces what we refer to as cohort effects, or the generational effects of having been born at a particular point in history. Being 20 years old in 1950 was very different from being 20 years old in 1980 or in 2010, due to a variety of cultural influences. Today's 10-year-olds, who do not know of a time without the Internet, might respond very differently to violent video games than might today's 40-year-olds for reasons that have nothing to do with age. Any such cohort effects could mask or distort our cross-sectional results.

A method that lessens this dilemma is the **longitudinal study**, in which a group of individuals is observed for a long period (see ● Figure 2.12). One of the longest running longitudinal studies is the Fels Longitudinal Study, currently housed in the Wright State University School of Medicine. This study began in 1929 to observe the effects of the Great Depression on children, but now has enrolled great-grandchildren of the original participants. To use the longitudinal method to answer our question, we could start with a group of infants and carefully plot their exposure to violent video games and their levels of physical aggression into adulthood. The longitudinal approach has few logical drawbacks, but it is expensive and time-consuming to do. Participants drop out of the study due to moves or lack of incentive. Researchers then must worry about whether those who remain in the study still comprise a representative sample.

The third approach, the **mixed longitudinal design**, combines the cross-sectional and longitudinal methods. Participants from a range of ages are observed for a limited period of time, usually about five years. This approach is faster and less expensive than the longitudinal method and avoids some of the cohort effects of the pure cross-sectional method.

longitudinal study An experimental design for assessing age-related changes in which data are obtained from the same individuals at intervals over a long period.

mixed longitudinal design A method for assessing age-related changes that combines the cross-sectional and longitudinal approaches by observing a cross-section of participants over a shorter period than is used typically in longitudinal studies.

Summary 2.2

Principles of Research Methods

Research method	Strengths	Weaknesses
Descriptive methods		
Case study	Can explore new and unusual phenomena; can falsify a hypothesis	Limited generalization
Naturalistic observation	Provides insight into natural, real-world behaviors	Participants act differently when watched; ethical issues
Survey	Provides large amounts of data quickly and inexpensively	Requires large representative sample; people wish to appear socially appropriate and may lie
Correlations © Cengage Learning 2013	Allow us to predict behavior; stimulate development of hypotheses; address some difficult ethical situations	Cannot be used to discuss causality
Experiments © Mary Kate Denny/ PhotoEdit	Control of situations and strong hypothesis testing; allow for judgments of causality	Artificiality, ethical concerns, time-consuming
Assessing the effects of time © Cengage Learning 2013		
Cross-sectional study	Quick and relatively inexpensive	Subject to cohort effects
Longitudinal study	Reduces impact of cohort effects	Expensive, time-consuming; people drop out
Mixed longitudinal study	Less expensive and time-consuming than longitudinal with some control of cohort effects	Still relatively expensive and time-consuming; drop-out problem remains

© PhotoAlto/Alamy

A valid measure actually measures what it is supposed to measure. In this case, your bathroom scale is supposed to tell you how much you really weigh.

How Do We Draw Conclusions From Data?

Asking the right questions and collecting good information are only the beginning of good science. Once we have collected our results, or data, we need to figure out what those data actually mean for our hypotheses and theories. The interpretation of data is not an arbitrary act—scientists follow specific rules when drawing their conclusions.

The Importance of Valid and Reliable Measures

Data are only as good as the measures we use to obtain them. How would we know whether a measure is good or bad? Two standards that any measure must meet are validity and reliability.

Validity means that a measure leads to valid conclusions, or actually measures the concept it is designed to measure. For example, your bathroom scale is supposed to measure how much you weigh. The data obtained from your bathroom scale can lead you to a valid conclusion (this is how much I really weigh) or an invalid conclusion (oh wow, I'm much lighter than the doctor's scale said I am).

How would we determine whether a measure leads to valid conclusions or not? One approach is to see if a measure correlates with other existing, established measures of the same concept. Many universities use the SAT I to help select the best candidates for admission. This test is supposed to measure a student's aptitude for success in college, but some universities have abandoned it in favor of other measures. We could ask which of the following measures—the SAT I, SAT II single subject achievement tests, or high school grade point average—shows the highest positive correlation with first-year college grades. The results of this comparison indicate that the SAT II shows the highest positive correlation with first-year college grades compared to both the SAT I and the high school grade point average (Geiser & Studley, 2001). Thus, we can conclude that the SAT II is the most valid of the three measures for predicting first-year college grades.

Reliability refers to the consistency of a measure. There are several different meanings of reliability in science, including test-retest, inter-rater, inter-method, and internal consistency. The test-retest reliability of the SAT I is quite good, as you might have noticed if you took the test more than once. If you were ill for the first test, or you invested in a preparation course before taking it the second time, your score might change, but otherwise, your scores are very likely to be about the same. Good measures also show high inter-rater reliability, or consistency in the interpretation of a measure across different observers. You can imagine how distressing it would be if one lab identified you as having a fatal disease on the basis of a blood test and another did not. Inter-method reliability describes the positive correlation of several approaches to measure a feature in an individual. Even though we said previously that the SAT II is the most valid predictor of your first-year college grades, it is likely that your SAT I, SAT II, and high school grades are all positively correlated. Finally, internal consistency results from measures within a single test that positively

validity A quality of a measure that leads to valid conclusions (i.e., the measure measures the concept it was designed to measure).

reliability The consistency of a measure, including test-retest, inter-rater, inter-method, and internal consistency.

correlate with each other. Earlier in this chapter, you had the opportunity to complete a survey. Often, students taking tests like this for the first time complain that they are "answering the same question over and over again." In a sense, this is true, because most tests include a number of items related to the same concept to see if the participant answers them in similar ways, which allows the researcher to assess the test's internal consistency.

Reliability is not the same thing as validity. You can obtain a consistent result (reliability) that lacks meaning (validity), but a measure cannot be valid without also being reliable. For example, if you weigh 200 pounds, and your bathroom scale consistently reports that you weigh 150 pounds whether you're looking at the number yourself or your roommate reads it for you, the scale has reliability but not validity. If you get a wildly different number each time you step on the scale, you have neither reliability nor validity. The measure is not consistent (no reliability) and fails to measure the construct—weight in this case—that it is designed to do (no validity).

Descriptive Statistics

Just as we might explore a new research topic using the descriptive research methods outlined earlier, we can use descriptive statistics to explore the characteristics of the data we obtain from our research. **Descriptive statistics** help us organize individual bits of data into meaningful patterns and summaries. For example, research investigating the ability of the SAT I, SAT II, and high school grades to predict college grades in colleges and universities across the country would be overwhelming in the absence of some way of summarizing the individual data points for tens of thousands of students in meaningful ways. Descriptive data tell us only about the sample we have studied. To determine whether the results from our sample apply to larger populations requires additional methods, described in a subsequent section.

We might approach this mass of data first by asking how the scores and grades are distributed. We could arrange SAT I scores from high to low and note how many students obtained each score. The result of our work would be a frequency distribution. We often illustrate frequency distributions with a bar chart, or histogram, like the one shown in ● Figure 2.13.

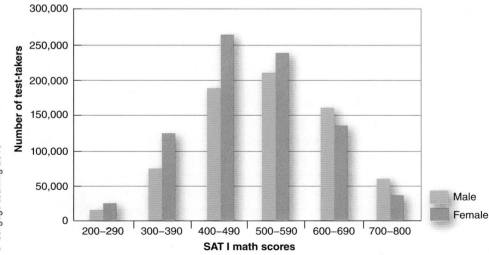

© Cengage Learning 2013

FIGURE 2.13

Frequency Distributions.
Descriptive statistics, such as these frequency distributions of SAT I mathematics scores, allow us to see meaningful patterns and summaries in large sets of data.
Source: Adapted from The College Board (2009).

descriptive statistics Statistical methods that organize data into meaningful patterns and summaries, such as finding the average value.

Central Tendency Frequency distributions are a useful starting place, but we might also be interested in identifying the "average" score on our measures, or the central tendency of our data set. There are three types of measures for central tendency: the mean, median, and mode for each group of scores. The **mean** is the numerical average of a set of scores, computed by adding all scores together and dividing by the number of scores. For all students taking the SAT in 2009, the mean on the critical reading section was 501, the mean on the mathematics section was 515, and the mean on the writing portion was 493.

The **median** represents a halfway mark in the data set, with half of the scores above and half below. The median is far less affected by extreme scores, or outliers, than the mean. In our SAT data, the median scores are quite close to the means: 500 for critical reading, 510 for mathematics, and 490 for writing. Why then, would you ever need to consider a median? In some sets of results, you might find some very extreme scores that could affect the mean. For example, if you asked employees at a small business to report their current annual salaries, you might get the following results: $40,000, $45,000, $47,000, $52,000 and $350,000 (we're assuming this is the boss). The mean in this example would be $106,800, but that figure doesn't really provide a good summary of these numbers. The median, $47,000 in this case, is more representative of your overall results. Take a look at ● Figure 2.14 for another example.

The **mode** refers to the score that occurs most frequently and is easy to determine from looking at a histogram. We do not have exact numbers for modal scores on the SAT, but we can tell you that the most frequent range of scores is between 400 and 490 for all three tests (critical reading,

Many colleges and universities use the SAT or other standardized tests to predict success in college courses. Evaluating the resulting data is easier if we use descriptive statistics to summarize the performances of the many thousands of individual students who take the tests.

FIGURE 2.14

What New Information Can We Learn From a Median?
In many cases, like the SAT data, means and medians are very close together. However, in other cases, like reported lifetime sex partners, these two measures of central tendency provide very different pictures. The average number of sex partners for males is 20, but half of all men report having had 8 or fewer partners. This suggests that the upper half of males have a very large number of partners indeed. *Source: Adapted from ABC News: Primetime (2001).*

mean The numerical average of a set of scores.

median The halfway mark in a set of data, with half of the scores above and half below.

mode The most frequently occurring score in a set of data.

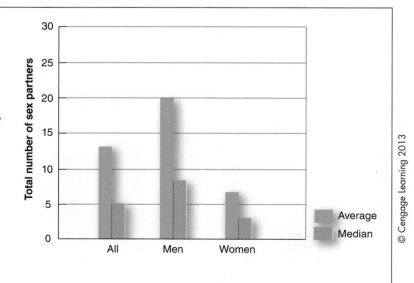

mathematics, and writing). The usefulness of the mode depends on the research question you are asking. In the case of the SAT, the mode doesn't provide very interesting information, so let's return to our drinking data mentioned earlier in the chapter. In this case, the mode among American adults is to drink zero to one drink per week. Seventy-two percent of American adults report this amount of drinking. In response to this finding, the U.S. Department of Justice recommended reducing problem drinking by raising taxes on alcohol (U.S. Department of Justice, 2002). These increased taxes would have little to no effect on nearly three quarters of American adults. The taxes would precisely target those whose behavior the government wants to change (the 23% who are heavy drinkers) while barely inconveniencing the vast majority of the population.

Using the mode is also an advantage over the use of a mean or median when there is more than one mode in a set of data. For example, the mean age of onset for the eating disorder anorexia nervosa, which we discuss in our chapter on motivation, is 17 years of age, but the distribution is bimodal, which means it has two substantial modes. One peak occurs around the age of 14, when many teens struggle with their changing shapes, and another occurs around the age of 18, when many teens leave home and make their own food choices without the watchful eyes of their parents (Halmi, Casper, Eckert, Goldberg, & Davis, 1979). An intervention program designed to coincide with the most likely ages of onset would probably be more effective than one timed to coincide with the mean age of onset (see ● Figure 2.15).

Variability In addition to being curious about central tendency, we might also want to know how clustered our scores are. The traditional way to look at the **variability** of scores is to use a measure known as the **standard deviation**. This measure tells you how tightly clustered a group of scores is

> It is an old maxim of mine that when you have excluded the impossible, whatever remains, however improbable, must be the truth.
>
> —Sir Arthur Conan Doyle (Sherlock Holmes)

FIGURE 2.15

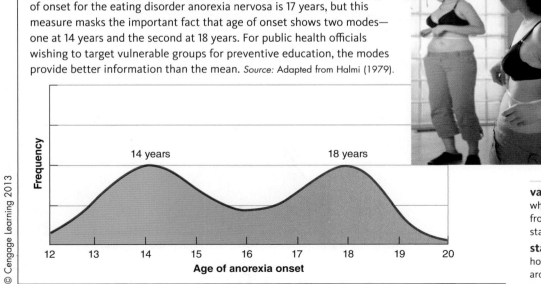

What New Information Can We Learn From a Mode? The average age of onset for the eating disorder anorexia nervosa is 17 years, but this measure masks the important fact that age of onset shows two modes—one at 14 years and the second at 18 years. For public health officials wishing to target vulnerable groups for preventive education, the modes provide better information than the mean. *Source: Adapted from Halmi (1979).*

© Custom Medical Stock Photo/Alamy

variability In statistics, the extent to which scores differ from one another or from their mean; often measured using the standard deviation.

standard deviation A measure of how tightly clustered a group of scores is around their mean.

© Cengage Learning 2013

around the mean. A smaller standard deviation suggests that most of the scores might be found near the mean, whereas a larger standard deviation means that the scores are more spread out away from the mean. Returning to our salary example, we had five salaries with a mean of $106,800. To obtain the standard deviation, which is easy to do with a calculator, you subtract each score from 106,800, square each difference (to eliminate any minus signs), add the squares, divide the total by 5 (the number of scores), and take the square root of the result. In this case, we end up with a standard deviation of 136,021, which means that our average difference between a score and the mean of the scores is 136,021. If we discard our extreme score ($350,000) and find the standard deviation of the remaining 4 scores, it turns out to be much smaller: 4,966.56. These results suggest that the distribution of the first four salaries is tightly clustered, whereas the distribution of all five salaries is more spread out.

The Normal Curve Many measures of interest to psychologists, such as scores on intelligence tests, which we discuss in a later chapter on cognition, appear to form a **normal distribution**, illustrated in ● Figure 2.16. The ideal normal curve in this illustration has several important features. One, it is symmetrical. Equal numbers of scores should occur above and below the mean. Second, its shape indicates that most of the scores occur near the mean, which is where our measure of variability plays a role. In the standard normal curve, shown in (a), 68% of the population falls within one standard deviation of the mean, 95% falls within two standard deviations, and 99% of the population falls within three standard deviations. Instruments for assessing intelligence, discussed in a later chapter on cognition, frequently convert

FIGURE 2.16

The Normal Curve. Many measures of interest to psychologists take the approximate form of a normal distribution. This figure compares a standard normal curve, shown in (a), to the distribution of scores on a standardized test of intelligence, the Wechsler Adult Intelligence Scale (WAIS-IV), shown in (b).

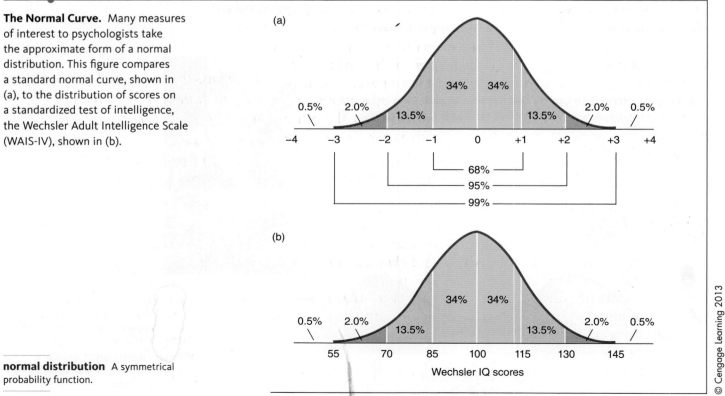

normal distribution A symmetrical probability function.

raw scores earned by many participants to fit a normal distribution having a mean of 100 and a standard deviation of 15. As a result, we would expect 68% of test-takers to receive an IQ score between 85 and 115. Ninety-five percent will score between 70 and 130, leaving only 2.5% to score above 130 and another 2.5% to score below 70.

Descriptive Statistics With Two Variables In our discussion so far, we have been describing single variables, such as number of drinks consumed, salaries, and SAT scores. In psychological research, we often want to describe the relationships between multiple variables.

We can illustrate the relationship between two variables in a scatter plot, like the one shown in ● Figure 2.17. Each dot represents the intersection between scores on two variables of interest. For example, we can compare the distributions of SAT scores as a function of grade point average (GPA). From our scatter plot, it looks like SAT scores and GPAs are systematically related to each other. As one increases, the other does as well, which you should recognize from our earlier discussion as a positive correlation.

Although our scatter plot gives us a sense that GPAs and SAT scores have a systematic relationship, we can compute that relationship exactly using a correlation coefficient. Correlation coefficients can range from +1.00 to −1.00, with a correlation of +1.00 and a correlation of −1.00 being equally strong but differing in the direction of the effect. A zero correlation indicates the two variables have no systematic relationship at all. The farther away a correlation coefficient is from zero, the stronger the relationship between the two variables. When the number is positive, this means that we have a positive correlation; when one factor occurs, the other is very likely to occur, too. Earlier in this chapter, we referred to height and weight as a common example of a positive correlation. In a negative correlation, indicated by a correlation coefficient with a minus sign, as one factor increases, the other decreases. Our previous example of a negative correlation is the amount of alcohol consumed and a student's grade point average (GPA). As alcohol consumption increases, the GPA decreases.

Inferential Statistics Although we can learn a great deal from our descriptive statistics, most of the research described in this textbook features the use of **inferential statistics**, so called because they permit us to draw inferences or conclusions from data. The descriptive statistics described earlier allow us to talk about our sample data, but do not allow us to decide what our sample data might mean more generally. To reach conclusions about how our observations fit the big picture, we use inferential statistics.

On the 2009 SAT I mathematics test, men scored an average of 534 and women scored an average of 499. Does this mean that men perform better

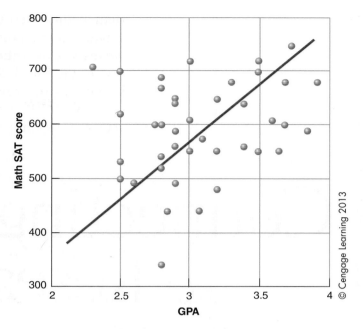

FIGURE 2.17

A Scatter Plot. A scatter plot allows us to visualize the relationship between two variables, such as the math SAT score and high school grade point average (GPA) for one small sample of college students. This relationship should look familiar to you—it is an example of a positive correlation. Source: *Adapted from Young (2011).*

Most universities now publish "25–75" SAT data from their most recently enrolled students. The higher your scores are above the 25% mark, the better your chances of being accepted. The 25% mark on the reading test for Harvard was 690, but only about 3% of all test-takers score 690 or above. You probably need to be in that top 3% or so of test-takers if Harvard is your school of choice.

inferential statistics Statistical methods that allow experimenters to extend conclusions from samples to larger populations.

than women on this test? Or do men and women perform similarly, and this group is just an unusual sample of test-takers? To resolve these questions, we test the hypothesis that men score higher than women on the math portion of the SAT I. Recall that we cannot "prove" a hypothesis to be correct, but we can demonstrate that the hypothesis is false (see ● Figure 2.18).

How do we know when a hypothesis should be rejected? Like most sciences, psychology has accepted odds of 5 out of 100 that an observed

Connecting *to* Research

Do You Believe in ESP?

ESP stands for extrasensory perception, with *extra* in this case meaning "outside" the boundaries of the normal information we obtain from our various senses, such as vision, hearing, and touch. The study of ESP is part of a larger field of *parapsychology*, or the study of psychic phenomena lying outside the typical boundaries of the field of psychology described in our first chapter. Among the abilities grouped as ESP are telepathy (the ability to communicate with other minds without using the usual methods of speaking or writing), clairvoyance (the ability to perceive objects that do not affect the known senses), precognition (knowledge of future events), and premonition (emotional anticipation of future events). In 2005, Gallup pollsters found that 41% of Americans said they believed in ESP, with 25% not sure, and 32% not believing (Gallup poll news service, 2005). Ninety-six percent of the scientists who are members of the National Academy of Sciences do not believe in ESP.

A recent study of ESP (Bem, 2011) has generated considerable

discussion in the scientific community about everything from the statistics we use to the effects of investigator bias. Evaluating this study provides you a good opportunity to practice your critical thinking skills and to apply what you have learned about validity and reliability.

The Question: *Nine experiments involving more than 1,000 participants tested different types of precognition and premonition. We will focus our attention on the first experiment, which tested the following hypothesis: participants should be able to anticipate the position (right side or left*

side of a computer screen) of an erotic photograph (see ● Figure 2.19).

METHODS

One hundred undergraduates (50 men and 50 women) participated. Stimuli, both erotic and nonerotic photographs, were selected from a standard set known as the International Affective Picture System. On each trial, participants saw two curtains on the computer screen and were asked to predict which curtain hid a picture. The sequencing of the erotic and nonerotic pictures and the

Popular shows like *Ghost Hunters* might contribute to the large number of Americans who report a belief in ESP (41%). In contrast, 96% of the members of the National Academy of Sciences do not believe in ESP.

Many populations that are interesting to psychologists are unable to sign informed consent forms legally and require additional ethical protection. In the case of research with infants, parents are required to sign informed consent forms on their child's behalf.

result is due to chance as an acceptable standard for **statistical significance**. We can assess the likelihood of observing a result due to chance by repeating a study, like throwing dice multiple times. We could give the mathematics portion of the SAT to 100 randomly selected samples of male and female college-bound students. If in 5 or more of the 100 samples, men and women score about the same or women score higher than men, we would reject our hypothesis as false.

statistical significance A standard for deciding whether an observed result is due to chance.

---

left-right positions was determined by a random number generator after the participant made his or her selection. This timing was designed to test the precognition of future events (the participants selected a side of the screen before the random number generator selected a location for the picture).

Here is where Bem's methods get a bit murky. The first 40 participants saw 12 erotic pictures, 12 negative pictures (unpleasant images), and 12 neutral pictures. Then for reasons not well explained in the paper, the method was changed for the remaining 60 participants. These participants saw 18 erotic and 18 nonerotic photos, 8 of which were described as "romantic" but not erotic (couple at a wedding, etc.). It is quite unusual for researchers to change their methods in the middle of an experiment and more troubling when there doesn't seem to be a good reason to do so.

RESULTS

Normally, if we have two choices, we have a 50% chance of guessing correctly on each trial. Bem reported that the future position of the erotic images was chosen correctly on 53.1% of the trials, and the future position of the nonerotic images was chosen

Illustration: © Cengage Learning 2013; photo: © Anson0618/Shutterstock

correctly on 49.8% of the trials. Bem reported that his results were statistically significant, or, in other words, very unlikely to happen just due to chance.

CONCLUSIONS

Bem concluded that the choices made by his participants were better than chance, supporting his hypothesis that precognition could be demonstrated.

What do others think of Bem's results? James Alcock, writing for the *Skeptical Inquirer*, concludes that "just about everything that could be done wrong in an experiment occurred

FIGURE 2.19

Evidence of ESP?
Participants in Bem's study were supposed to predict behind which of two curtains a picture would appear.

here" (Alcock, 2011). Among Alcock's concerns were Bem's changing of his method midway through the experiment and his questionable use of statistical analyses.

As we discussed earlier, replication provides an important check on possible researcher bias, and failure to replicate indicates serious flaws in an experiment. So far, the three known replications of Bem's experiments have failed to produce significant results. In spite of the flaws, however, Bem's experiments have contributed to science by stimulating a lively discussion of scientific and statistical methods. ✪

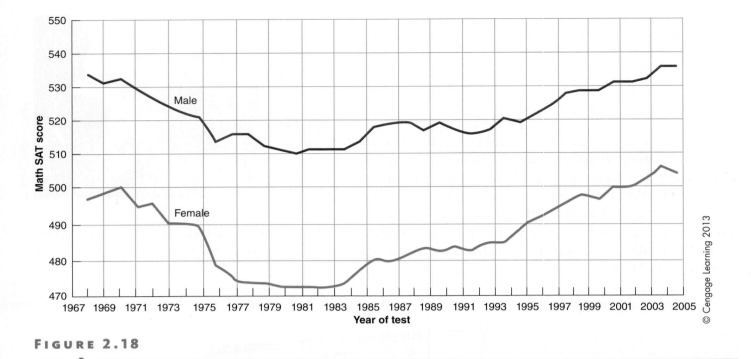

FIGURE 2.18

Are Male and Female Scores on the Math SAT Really Different? Inferential statistics allow us to decide whether the observed differences between the performance of males and females on the math SAT represents a real gender difference or is just due to chance.
Source: Adapted from The College Board (2009).

This type of careful analysis of the SAT data has confirmed that the differences on the mathematics portion of the test between male and female test-takers is, in fact, statistically significant (Halpern et al., 2007). Does this result mean that we should consider this difference when deciding on a major or career? Probably not. Keep in mind that the goal of the SAT is to predict college grades. If you compare the SAT scores of men and women receiving the same letter grade in a mathematics course at the very same school, the women have scored 33 points less on the math SAT than the men (Wainer & Steinberg, 1992). This is just about the same difference that we observed between the mean scores of men and women on the SAT I math test. It appears that for some unknown reason, the SAT might be underestimating women's ability to achieve in college mathematics courses.

How Can We Conduct Ethical Research?

We mentioned earlier that deceiving participants into thinking they were truly in danger raised ethical questions. On what basis do researchers decide what they can and cannot do to their research participants?

Although the vast majority of studies published in psychological journals involve the use of human participants, psychology also has a rich heritage of animal research. Consequently, separate guidelines have been developed for each type of subject. Researchers working in universities and other agencies receiving federal funding must receive the approval of institutional review boards (IRBs) for human participant research and institutional animal care and use committees (IACUCs) before conducting research. The IRBs and IACUCs are guided by federal regulations and research ethics endorsed by professional societies such as the American Psychological Association, the Association for Psychological Science, and the Society for Neuroscience. IRBs and IACUCs must include at least one member of the community outside the university or agency, avoiding the possibility that inappropriate research might be conducted in secret. Note that these procedures currently do not apply to institutions that do not have federal funding, such as private genetics research corporations, although efforts are being made to bring these organizations into compliance with federal standards as well.

> The best scientist is open to experience and begins with romance—the idea that anything is possible.
>
> —Ray Bradbury

As you review the ethical guidelines for both human and animal research participants, keep in mind that the guidelines look much simpler when you read about their provisions than when you try to implement them in the context of real research. This is why the final approval decision lies with a committee as opposed to single individuals.

Human Participants

At the core of ethical standards for human research is the idea that participation is voluntary. No participant should be coerced into participating. Although psychologists are well aware that people who volunteer to participate in research are probably quite different in important ways from those who don't volunteer, we have chosen to give research ethics a higher priority than our ability to generalize research results.

To ensure that a participant is a willing volunteer, researchers must make provisions for reasonable incentives. Incentives, such as pay or extra credit for participation, must not be so extreme that they become the primary motivation for prospective volunteers. To decide whether to volunteer for research, a person must have some knowledge of what the research will entail. Researchers must provide prospective participants with an **informed consent** form, which provides details about the purpose of the study and what types of procedures will occur.

In psychological research, we have the added burden of occasionally dealing with participants who are limited in their abilities to provide informed consent due to the very conditions that make them interesting to study in the first place. Developmental psychologists have an obvious interest in children, but a person cannot sign a legal informed consent until age 18. Can you possibly obtain informed consent from a patient with schizophrenia, who suffers from hallucinations and irrational, delusional beliefs? Or from a person in the later stage of Alzheimer's disease, whose memory and reasoning have deteriorated due to his or her condition? In these cases, legal permission must be obtained from a qualified guardian. The university IRBs play an essential role in evaluating these ethical dilemmas on a case-by-case basis.

Research should also be conducted in a manner that does no irreversible harm to participants. In some cases, to avoid participants' desire to appear "normal" and their tendency to try to "outguess" the research,

informed consent Permission obtained from a research participant after risks and benefits of an experimental procedure have been thoroughly explained.

The Tuskegee syphilis experiment, conducted by the U.S. Public Health Service from 1932 to 1972, involved 400 African American men who had contracted syphilis. Failure to treat or inform these participants about their health led to new regulations to prevent such unethical research from being repeated.

researchers might say they are investigating one factor when they are really interested in another. Most cases of deception are quite mild, as when participants are told that a study is about memory when it is actually a study of some social behavior. When researchers must deceive their participants, extra care must be taken to debrief participants and answer all their questions following the experiment.

Research using human participants should be rigorously private and confidential. Privacy refers to the participants' control over the sharing of their personal information with others, and methods for ensuring privacy are usually stated in the informed consent. For example, some studies involve the use of medical records, which participants' agree to share with the researchers for the purpose of the experiment. Confidentiality refers to the participants' rights to not have their data revealed to others without their permission. Confidentiality is usually maintained by such practices as substituting codes for names and storing data in locked cabinets. Collecting data anonymously, where even the researchers do not know the identity of participants, is the surest way to protect privacy and confidentiality.

Science learns from its past ethical lapses. One of the most egregious examples of unethical research was the Tuskegee syphilis experiment, which lasted from 1932 until 1972. Researchers from the U.S. Public Health Service recruited about 400 impoverished African American men who had contracted syphilis to study the progression of the disease. None of the men was told he had syphilis, and none was treated, even though penicillin became the standard treatment for syphilis in 1947. Many of the federal regulations discussed in this section were developed in response to this research.

While examining the papers of Dr. John Cutler, who led the Tuskegee syphilis study, Wellesley historian Susan Reverby discovered that during the 1940s, U.S. and Guatemalan health officials had deliberately exposed prisoners, soldiers, and mental patients to syphilis and gonorrhea to test the effectiveness of penicillin.

Animal Subjects The topic of using animals in research is guaranteed to stimulate lively, and possibly heated, discussion. Some people are adamantly opposed to animal research of any kind, whereas others accept the concept of using animals as long as certain conditions are met. Currently, about 7 to 8% of published research in psychology journals involves the use of animals as subjects (American Psychological Association [APA], 2005a). Ninety percent of the animals used are rodents and birds, with 5% or fewer studies involving monkeys and other primates. According to the American Psychological Association (APA), the use of dogs and cats in psychological research is rare.

Research using animals must demonstrate a clear purpose, such as benefiting the health of humans or other animals. In addition to serving a clear purpose, animal research requires excellent housing, food, and veterinary care. The most controversial ethical standards relate to minimizing the pain and suffering experienced by animal research subjects. The American Psychological Association provides guidelines for the use of pain, surgery, stress, and deprivation with animal subjects, as well as the termination of an animal's life. The standards approximate the community standards we would expect from local humane societies tasked with euthanizing animals that are not adopted.

© Bill Gallery/Doctor Stock/Getty Images

Ethical guidelines for animal research require having a clear purpose for the experiment, providing excellent care for the animals, and minimizing pain and suffering.

Summary 2.3

Principles of Ethical Research

Human participants	Animal subjects
No coercion	Necessity
Informed consent	Excellent food, housing, veterinary care
No harm	Minimal pain and suffering
Confidentiality and privacy	

National Archives and Records Administration, ARC Identifier 824608

© Bill Gallery/Doctor Stock/Getty Images

Interpersonal Relationships
From a Methodological Perspective

At the end of Chapter 1, we noted that each chapter would feature a discussion of how the chapter's material could be used to talk about relationships. For this chapter on research methods, we ask whether psychological research methods can be used to differentiate between liking and loving another person.

Using the methods described in this chapter, you can probably think of many different ways to approach this question. You could observe friends and compare their behavior to that of romantic partners. You could conduct a survey, asking people to rate certain characteristics of people they love versus those of people they like. Perhaps you could correlate physiological arousal measures, like pupil diameter or heart rate, with ratings of how much a participant likes or loves another person. Conducting an actual experiment might be a bit tricky, though, both in terms of methods and ethics. How could people possibly be randomly assigned to love and like groups?

A fun example of research in this area was contributed by Andreas Bartels and Semir Zeki (2000). These researchers chose to use correlational methods in the form of brain imaging, which we discuss further in our chapter on biological psychology. Brain imaging studies are typically correlational, because we assume that brain activity in particular areas has a relationship with some ongoing behavior. Once again, it is important to recall that we cannot make conclusions about causality based on correlational data.

> No amount of experimentation can ever prove me right, but a single experiment can prove me wrong.
>
> —Albert Einstein

Bartels and Zeki's participants were instructed to supply photographs of people they like and people they love. The photographs were then presented to the participants while their brain activity was observed using functional magnetic resonance imaging, or fMRI. Several differences in brain activity occurred when the participants viewed a lover as opposed to a friend. Not too surprisingly, areas of the brain associated with reward became more active when viewing lovers than when viewing friends. Areas of the brain associated with social judgment, negative emotions, and assessing the intentions and emotions of other people were less active when viewing lovers than when viewing friends. Love, according to these results, appears to be a combination of reward and less social judgment (see ● Figure 2.20).

The results of this scientific research might help us understand some of our everyday experiences with relationships. Of course, we feel rewarded in the presence of a loved one, and we have to admit that we may miss a flaw or two in someone we love. Friends and family members, whose social judgment has not been silenced, do not miss these flaws and often try in vain to alert us to them.

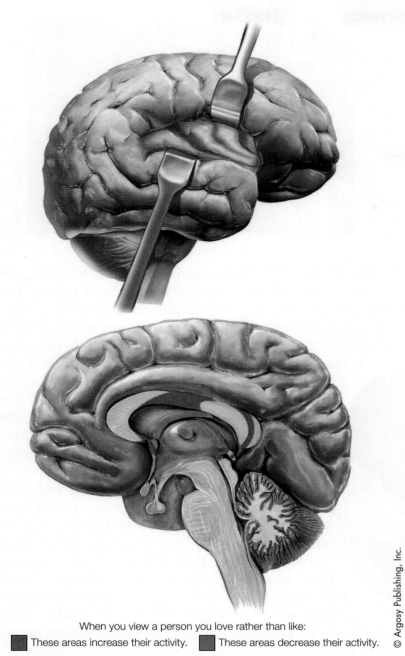

FIGURE 2.20

Imaging Love. When people view a photo of a person they say they "love," brain imaging shows increased activation in reward areas of the brain and decreased activation in areas involved with social judgment.

When you view a person you love rather than like:

◼ These areas increase their activity.   ◼ These areas decrease their activity.

© Argosy Publishing, Inc.

Chapter 2
Reflections

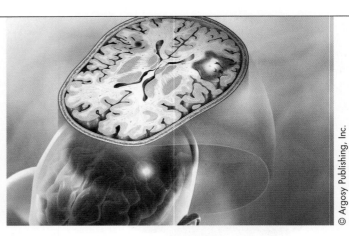

© Argosy Publishing, Inc.

We began our discussion of research methods by asking how we know that stuttering is not caused by tickling a baby or leaving it out in the rain. Before reading this chapter, you probably "knew" these ideas weren't right, but it might have been difficult to say exactly why you felt this way. The brain imaging study demonstrating differences in brain activity between stutterers and non-stutterers probably looked more convincing to you, but it's important to give these types of studies the same scrutiny you would give to the folk myths about stuttering. In other words, practicing critical thinking is important, regardless of how compelling an argument might seem.

This chapter explored the many techniques scientists use to gain knowledge. It should now be much easier for you to identify why you think the scientific approaches to stuttering are more believable than the folk myths, and you know exactly how to test the accuracy of any of the explanations for stuttering. Although we pointed out some of the limitations of these methods, such as the potential artificiality of an experiment, scientists using multiple methods across the perspectives of psychology have compiled an impressive amount of knowledge about the human mind and the behavior it produces. As you read through the remainder of this textbook, we hope you continue to evaluate the results we present using your best critical thinking skills. ❮

© Charity Myers/iStockphoto

Our scientific methods and critical thinking provide powerful tools for discovering the real causes of stuttering.

KEY TERMS The Language of Psychological Science

Be sure you can define these terms and use them correctly.

case study, p. 55
confounding variable, p. 64
control group, p. 64
correlation, p. 59
critical thinking, p. 48
cross-sectional study, p. 67
dependent variable, p. 64
descriptive method, p. 55
descriptive statistics, p. 71
double-blind procedure, p. 47
experiment, p. 61
experimental group, p. 64
falsifiable, p. 52
hypothesis, p. 52
independent variable, p. 64

inferential statistics, p. 75
informed consent, p. 79
longitudinal study, p. 68
mean, p. 72
measure, p. 59
median, p. 72
meta-analysis, p. 66
mixed longitudinal design, p. 68
mode, p. 72
naturalistic observation, p. 56
normal distribution, p. 74
objectivity, p. 45
operationalization, p. 66
peer review, p. 53
placebo, p. 47

random assignment, p. 64
reliability, p. 70
replication, p. 53
sample, p. 57
science, p. 45
standard deviation, p. 73
statistical significance, p. 77
survey, p. 57
testable, p. 52
theory, p. 49
third variable, p. 60
validity, p. 70
variability, p. 73
variable, p. 59

MEDIA RESOURCES

Log in to CengageBrain to access the resources your instructor requires. For this book, you can access:

Psychology **CourseMate** brings course concepts to life with interactive learning, study, and exam preparation tools that support the printed textbook. A textbook-specific website, Psychology **CourseMate** includes an integrated interactive eBook and other interactive learning tools including quizzes, flashcards, videos, and more.

WebTUTOR More than just an interactive study guide, **WebTutor** is an anytime, anywhere customized learning solution with an eBook, keeping you connected to your textbook, instructor, and classmates.

aplia If your professor has assigned **Aplia** homework:
1. Sign in to your account.
2. Complete the corresponding homework exercises as required by your professor.
3. When finished, click "Grade It Now" to see which areas you have mastered, which areas need more work, and detailed explanations of every answer.

Environmental factors such as stress, diet, smoking, and exercise, can influence whether a gene is turned on or off.

The Evolving Mind

3

Nature and Nurture Intertwined

Learning Objectives

1 Analyze the role of genes as the building blocks of human "nature," distinguishing among genotypes, gene expression, and phenotypes.

2 Explain how sexual reproduction increases genetic variation among individuals within a population, even among members of the same family.

3 Assess the importance of heritability estimates and epigenetic analyses in the field of behavioral genetics.

4 Analyze the roles played by mutation, natural selection, migration, and genetic drift as mechanisms of evolution.

5 Articulate the proposal that the human brain is an adaptation, and summarize the evidence supporting this proposal.

6 Evaluate the proposal that altruism is an adaptation, considering the various ways one can benefit by helping another.

7 Explain the mechanisms by which intrasexual and intersexual selection might influence the evolution of human behavior.

8 Explain and illustrate the epigenetic and cultural mechanisms by which nature and nurture can interact to influence human behavior.

© Argosy Publishing, Inc.

We all know that identical twins, like the little boys appearing in the inset photo, are, well, identical. Or are they?

For a long time, scientists were puzzled not by the similarities between identical twins, but by their differences. If two people share the same DNA, as identical twins do, why does one get cancer while the other stays healthy? Why does one become obese while the other remains fit?

When science began to unravel some of the mysteries about genes and how they work, answers to these questions emerged. You have the same DNA in each cell of

© Norbert Schaefer/Photolibrary

your body, yet some cells develop into heart cells, others into brain cells, and so on. How does the same set of DNA know how to make these different types of cells? Genes can be turned on and off. The genes that are not turned off are free to produce the proteins needed to build a particular kind of cell, whether that is a skin cell or a liver cell.

Genes do not just turn on and off as they build a body during development. Your ongoing interactions with the environment can also turn genes on or off. What you eat, whether you smoke or drink, your stress levels, and other environmental factors can influence how your DNA works. Our understanding of these ongoing interactions between genes and the environment is the reason psychologists no longer argue about the separate contributions of nature and nurture. In this chapter, we will explore these interactions in more detail.

Let's zoom in to see what's happening when the environment interacts with DNA. You can see a strand of DNA in the large chapter opener image. In mice, a gene called Agouti produces yellow fur and obesity when it is turned on, but brown fur and normal weight when it is turned off (Dolinoy, Huang, & Jirtle, 2007). Certain environmental factors can influence whether the gene is turned on or off. For example, if pregnant mother mice ate food containing bisphenol-A, or BPA, a chemical found in food and beverage containers, baby bottles, dental sealants, and food cans, their babies were more likely to have yellow fur and be obese than were babies of mice that were not fed BPA. The BPA seems to have turned on the Agouti gene (see ● Figure 3.1).

How does studying the fur color of mice help us understand the differences between identical human twins? The young twins on the previous page have a great deal in common, but as they get older, they are more likely to eat different foods and have different experiences. These environmental influences can change the way their genes are turned on or off,

When pregnant mice are fed a diet containing BPA, found in plastics, their offspring are more likely to have yellow fur and to be obese.

Although they share identical DNA, identical twins become less similar to each other as they age, due to the effects of their different experiences, stress, diet, and habits like smoking on the activity of their DNA. Antonio Nogueira (left) and his identical twin brother Rodrigo (right) both compete in Ultimate Fighting Championship (UFC) bouts, but in different weight classes and with different levels of success. The brothers probably look less similar to each other today than when they were children, reflecting an accumulation of diverse experiences, including injuries.

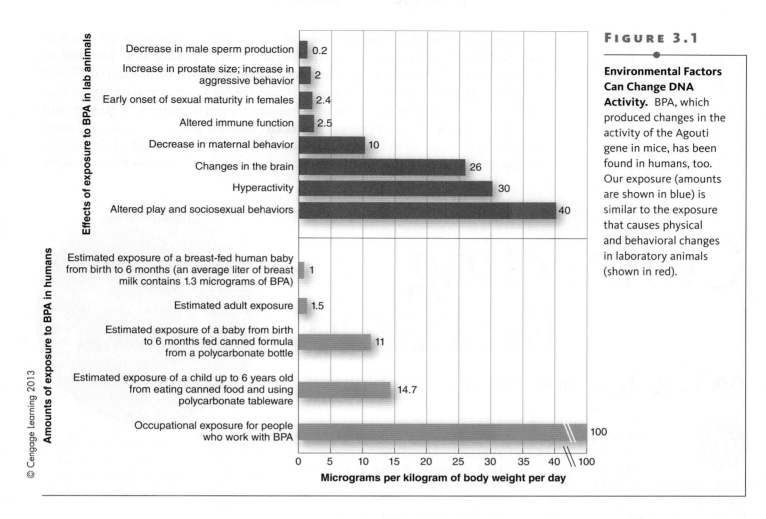

FIGURE 3.1

Environmental Factors Can Change DNA Activity. BPA, which produced changes in the activity of the Agouti gene in mice, has been found in humans, too. Our exposure (amounts are shown in blue) is similar to the exposure that causes physical and behavioral changes in laboratory animals (shown in red).

Effects of exposure to BPA in lab animals

Effect	Value
Decrease in male sperm production	0.2
Increase in prostate size; increase in aggressive behavior	2
Early onset of sexual maturity in females	2.4
Altered immune function	2.5
Decrease in maternal behavior	10
Changes in the brain	26
Hyperactivity	30
Altered play and sociosexual behaviors	40

Amounts of exposure to BPA in humans

Amount	Value
Estimated exposure of a breast-fed human baby from birth to 6 months (an average liter of breast milk contains 1.3 micrograms of BPA)	1
Estimated adult exposure	1.5
Estimated exposure of a baby from birth to 6 months fed canned formula from a polycarbonate bottle	11
Estimated exposure of a child up to 6 years old from eating canned food and using polycarbonate tableware	14.7
Occupational exposure for people who work with BPA	100

0 5 10 15 20 25 30 35 40 100
Micrograms per kilogram of body weight per day

© Cengage Learning 2013

just as the BPA affected the Agouti gene in the mice. These changes accumulate over time, so identical twins become less similar as they age.

In this chapter, we will explore how nature and nurture interact with one another to build the mind across the lifespan, but our own personal experience is not the sole influence on our minds. The interaction between nature and nurture has been shaping the human mind over millennia. ⚙

Why Do We Say Nature and Nurture Are Intertwined?

Along with an understanding of the structures and processes of the brain, which we cover in our upcoming chapter on biological psychology, knowing how our biological history shapes our behavior is an important part of understanding the mind. In our introductory chapter, we explained how contemporary psychologists view the contributions of **nature**, our heredity or innate predispositions, and **nurture**, the results of our experience with the environment, to be closely intertwined as opposed to somehow competing with each other for control over behavior.

nature The contributions of heredity to our physical structure and behaviors.

nurture The contributions of environmental factors and experience to our physical structure and behaviors.

Scholars have not always thought about nature and nurture the way we do today. Instead of viewing the actions of nature and nurture as inseparable, earlier scholars talked in terms of "nature versus nurture" and debated the relative contributions of nature "or" nurture to a particular type of behavior. Credit for describing the contrast between heredity and environment as "nature *versus* nurture" usually goes to Francis Galton (1869), who was also Charles Darwin's cousin. Galton believed that intelligence was largely the result of inheritance, a topic we tackle in a later

Connecting *to* Research

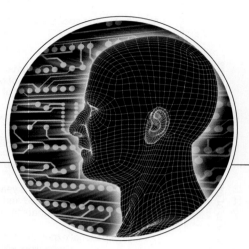

Genes, Bullying, and Emotional Problems

In the introduction to this chapter, you learned about how a mother mouse's diet could influence the fur color and weight of her offspring. We, of course, are not mice, so it is fair to ask if this same type of interaction between genes and experience can happen in human beings. The answer to that question is yes.

Researchers have known for a long time that victims of bullies often, but not always, develop serious emotional problems later in childhood or adolescence. We also know that having a particular genetic profile involving serotonin, one of the chemical messengers we discuss in the biological psychology chapter, can lead to emotional problems, but again, not in all cases. How can we integrate these findings to learn why some children seem at higher risk than others for developing emotional problems after being victimized by bullies? A good answer to this question would allow psychologists to target just the right groups of children for treatment. Karen Sugden and her

colleagues tackled this question by studying bullying and a particular type of serotonin gene in 2,232 children (Sugden et al., 2010).

Fifteen-year-old Phoebe Prince of Massachusetts hanged herself after experiencing months of relentless bullying by female classmates. Even after her death, the bullies showed no remorse but continued to mock her on Facebook. Nine were later charged with a variety of criminal offenses, but no legal proceeding will give Phoebe back her life.

The Republican/Landov

The Question: *Does a particular type of genotype, or individual genetic profile, interact with the experience of bullying to produce a higher risk for emotional problems?*

METHODS

Over 2,000 children enrolled in the British Environmental Risk (E-Risk) study participated in this analysis. The researchers evaluated the children's exposure to bullying during interviews at home when they were 12 years old. Emotional problems were assessed using standard instruments, one to be filled out by parents and the other by teachers. Parents and teachers filled out these instruments twice, once when the child was 5 years old and a second time when the child was 12 years old. Genetic samples were obtained by swabbing the inside of the children's mouths, which is also a standard procedure.

RESULTS

The serotonin gene studied in this research, the serotonin transporter gene, has a long (L) version and a

chapter on cognition, language, and intelligence. Over the next 150 years or so, many thinkers engaged in a highly spirited debate on this question. As we will see in a later chapter on cognition, contemporary psychologists view intelligence as another example of an outcome shaped by both genetic inheritance and environment.

We can say with some certainty that the "either-or" approach to human behavior has produced some of the most contentious discussions in the history of psychology. Our motive for arguing in favor of the "intertwined" approach to nature and nurture is not intended to sidestep difficult questions, but rather to simply support good science. By zooming out to integrate a number of perspectives, both biological and experiential, we reach a more accurate understanding of these questions.

Francis Galton, who was also Charles Darwin's cousin, was the first to use the phrase "nature versus nurture" in his discussion of intelligence.

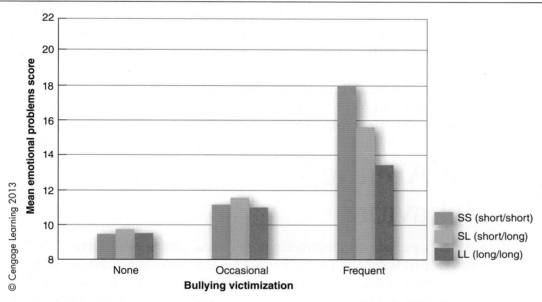

FIGURE 3.2

Interactions Between Genotype and the Experience of Being Bullied. Childhood emotional problems become more common when a child experiences frequent, but not occasional, bullying, especially when the child has the SS genotype for the serotonin transporter gene. *Source: Adapted from Sugden et al. (2010).*

short (S) version, which means that individuals can have one of three genotypes: SS, SL, and LL. These genotypes did not predict emotional problems by themselves, but a history of being victimized by bullies did predict emotional problems.

One of the strengths of this study was its use of a longitudinal design, which we discussed in our chapter on research methods. As you can see in ● Figure 3.2, being bullied not at all or occasionally is not associated with an increase in emotional problems from age 5 to 12, but being

bullied frequently is associated with an increase in emotional problems, especially for children with the SS genotype. Without this longitudinal design, we might not be able to say whether the behavioral problems among the bullied 12-year-olds were related to genotype or to other possibilities, such as stress at home or a greater likelihood of being victimized due to existing emotional problems.

CONCLUSIONS

The results show that being victimized by bullies leads to emotional

problems, but that children with the SS genotype who are bullied frequently are more likely than children with either the SL or LL genotype to experience increased emotional problems at age 12.

These results shed light onto the question of why some bullied children appear to be more negatively affected by the experience than others. The results also allow psychologists to target specific children for treatment, before the emotional problems at age 12 develop into later problems with mental health. ⚙

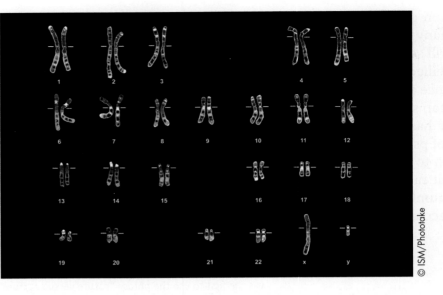

Twenty-three pairs of chromosomes make up the human genotype.

© ISM/Phototake

Ridley (2003) summarizes the need for an integrated nature-nurture approach as follows:

> Genes are not puppet masters or blueprints. Nor are they just the carriers of heredity. They are active during life; they switch each other on and off; they respond to the environment. They may direct the construction of the body and brain in the womb, but then they set about dismantling and rebuilding what they have made almost at once—in response to experience. They are both cause and consequence of our actions. (p. 6)

What Are the Building Blocks of Behavior?

Before we can explore the interactions between nature and nurture that contribute to psychological phenomena, like a person's reactions to being bullied, let's take a look at the genetic mechanisms that help shape the mind.

Every nucleus in the more than 1 trillion cells of your body, with the exception of your red blood cells and sperm or eggs, contains two complete copies of the human genome, a set of instructions for building a human being. Your personal set of instructions is known as a **genotype**, which interacts with the environment to produce observable characteristics known as a **phenotype**. Your genotype might include a gene for blonde hair and another for brown, while your phenotypical, or observable, hair color is light brown.

One copy of your genome was provided by your mother's egg and the other by your father's sperm. Each parent contributes a set of 23 chromosomes, which in turn are composed of many molecules of deoxyribonucleic acid (DNA). Smaller segments of DNA located in particular places on a chromosome are known as **genes**. Each gene contains instructions for making a particular type of protein. **Gene expression** occurs when these genetic instructions are converted into a feature of a living cell. Each cell contains

genotype An individual's profile of alleles.

phenotype Observable characteristics.

gene Small segment of DNA located in a particular place on a chromosome.

gene expression The process in which genetic instructions are converted into a feature of a living cell.

	Father's allele		
Mother's allele	A	B	O
A	AA (Type A blood)	AB (Type AB blood)	AO (Type A blood)
B	AB (Type AB blood)	BB (Type B blood)	BO (Type B blood)
O	AO (Type A blood)	BO (Type B blood)	OO (Type O blood)

Genotypes and Phenotypes of Blood Type. The three possible blood type alleles—A, B, and O—can be combined to produce Type A, Type B, Type O, or Type AB blood.

the instructions for an entire human organism, but only a subset of instructions is expressed at any given time and location. Gene expression in a nerve cell is very different from gene expression in a muscle cell or a skin cell.

Different versions of a gene, or **alleles**, can give rise to different phenotypical traits. Many alleles can occur for a given gene, but a single individual receives only two, one from each parent. For example, alleles for blood type include A, B, and O, but nobody can have all three. Combinations of your two alleles will make your blood Type A (AA or AO), Type B (BB or BO), Type AB (AB), or Type O (OO). See ● Figure 3.3, which illustrates possible blood type combinations.

If both parents contribute the same type of allele, such as a gene for curly hair, the child would be considered **homozygous** for that gene (*homos* means "same" in Greek). If the parents contribute different alleles, such as a gene for curly hair from one parent and a gene for straight hair from the other, the child is **heterozygous** for that gene (*hetero* means "different" in Greek). **Recessive** alleles only determine a phenotype when an individual is homozygous for a particular gene, whereas **dominant** alleles will determine a phenotype in either the homozygous or heterozygous condition. Because alleles for straight hair are recessive and alleles for curly hair are dominant, the only way an individual can have straight hair is if he or she receives two copies of the straight hair allele, one from each parent. An individual receiving one straight hair allele and one curly hair allele will have curly hair (see ● Figure 3.4).

Some genes are characterized by very large numbers of alleles. There are about 500 different alleles for the BRCA1 (Breast Cancer 1) gene, a small number of which are associated with a higher risk for breast and other cancers.

Whether you have straight or curly hair is a very simple example of how dominant and recessive genes interact, but in many human characteristics, one allele does not entirely dominate another. In the research on bullying we discussed previously, we noted that individuals could have SS, SL, or LL genotypes. Neither the S nor L allele dominates the other. As you can see in ● Figure 3.5, The SL group had levels of emotional disturbance that fell between the extremes of the SS and LL groups (Sugden et al., 2010). If either the S or L alleles were dominant, the SL group would behave just like that dominant group instead.

Genetic Variation

If you have siblings, you are very aware of the fact that having the same biological parents does not guarantee similar appearance, personality, and behavior. The development of an egg or sperm cell is like shuffling a deck of cards. In both cases, a large number of possible outcomes may occur. When a

allele One of several different versions of a gene, as in having an A, B, or O blood type allele.

homozygous Having two of the same alleles for a gene.

heterozygous Having two different alleles for a gene.

recessiveness A feature of an allele that will only produce a phenotype in the homozygous condition.

dominance A feature of an allele that will determine a phenotype in either the homozygous or heterozygous condition.

FIGURE 3.4

Effects of Dominant and Recessive Genes. Curly hair (C) is dominant while straight hair (c) is recessive. The only way a child can have straight hair is to inherit two of the recessive straight hair alleles from its parents. In this example, both parents are heterozygous (Cc) with curly hair.

	Father's allele	
Mother's allele	Curly (C)	Straight (c)
Curly (C)	CC (homozygous curly)	Cc (heterozygous curly)
Straight (c)	Cc (heterozygous curly)	cc (homozygous straight)

Experiencing Psychology

Reading a DNA Fingerprint

DNA belonging to different individuals can be compared using autoradiographs. An autoradiograph is formed by labeling DNA fragments with a radioactive marker and then exposing the DNA to X-ray film.

In this case, we are looking at a simple paternity test (PBS, 1998). Four DNA samples have been taken from three people: a mother, her child, and the possible father of the child. The two letters for each segment represent the individual's genotype. For example, in the first autoradiograph on the next page, the mother is an AD, the child is an AC, and the possible father is a BC.

Use the autoradiographs to complete Table 3.1:

TABLE 3.1 Autoradiograph Results

	1 (A, B, C, D)	2 (E, F, G)	3 (H, I, J, K)	4 (L, M, N, O)
Mother		GG		
Child	AC			MO
Possible father			HK	

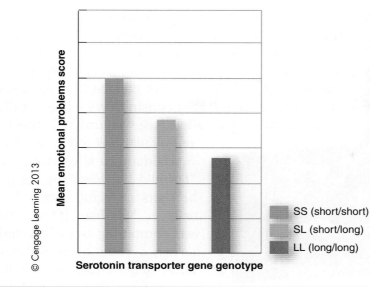

© Cengage Learning 2013

Mean emotional problems score

Serotonin transporter gene genotype

SS (short/short)
SL (short/long)
LL (long/long)

FIGURE 3.5

Some Alleles Do Not Show Dominance.
Neither the S nor the L allele of the serotonin transporter gene dominates the other. Among children who have been bullied frequently, those with the SL genotype (shown in green) experience a level of emotional problems midway between that of those with the SS and LL genotypes. If either the S or the L allele was dominant, we would expect the SL group to behave the same way as the homozygous dominant group. *Source:* Adapted from Sugden et al. (2010).

parent's cell divides to make an egg or sperm cell, each resulting cell contains 23 chromosomes, one chromosome from each of the parent's original 23 chromosome pairs. As a result, a single human can produce eggs or sperm with 2^{23} (8,388,608) different combinations of his or her chromosomes. Add this variability to the different possibilities provided by the other parent, and it may seem surprising that we resemble our relatives as much as we do.

Relatedness   In spite of this potential variability, we remain very similar to our genetic relatives. We will revisit this important point later in the chapter when we discuss the evolution of social behavior. **Relatedness** is defined as the probability that two people share copies of the same allele from a common ancestor. Obviously, if one goes

relatedness The probability that two people share the same allele from a common ancestor.

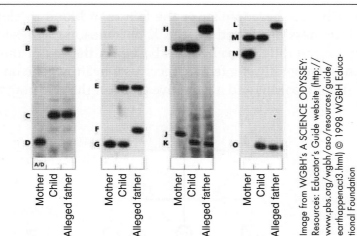

Mother Child Alleged father

A/D

Mother Child Alleged father

Mother Child Alleged father

Mother Child Alleged father

Image from WGBH's A SCIENCE ODYSSEY: Resources: Educator's Guide website (http://www.pbs.org/wgbh/aso/resources/guide/earthappenact3.html) © 1998 WGBH Educational Foundation

To evaluate the likelihood of the possible father's paternity, identify which "letters" the child inherited from its mother and which from its father. The child will receive one allele from each parent, so the child's combinations of alleles must be possible based on the mother's and father's genotypes. For example, if the child had AD in the first column instead of AC, this man would not be the father, as he has neither the A nor the C allele to contribute. Overall, is it possible for this man to have fathered this child?

SOLUTION
Keep in mind that genetic tests never "prove" a relationship. They can only disprove one. In our chapter on research methods, we made this same point about all hypotheses. Based on the evidence in this case, we cannot "prove" the hypothesis that this man is in fact the child's biological parent. All we can do is show that he is not the father. If the child had an AD genotype instead of an AC genotype in the first box, as mentioned earlier, this man could not possibly be the father, as he could not supply either the A or D alleles. Such an "exclusion" result is considered absolute evidence of non-paternity. In contrast, the results of this test suggest that it is very likely that this man is the biological parent of the child. ⚙

WHAT ARE THE BUILDING BLOCKS OF BEHAVIOR?

back in history far enough, we all share common ancestors. Relatedness, however, is usually computed within a limited number of generations.

The chance that you share an allele with one of your parents is one half, as is the chance that you share an allele with a sibling. First cousins have a one-eighth likelihood of sharing an allele (see ● Figure 3.6). These types of calculations led geneticist J. B. S. Haldane to allegedly proclaim, "I would lay down my life for two brothers or eight cousins!" (Connelly & Martlew, 1999). Haldane was computing the likelihood that his genes would be passed down to future generations. As we discuss later in the chapter, evolutionary psychologists suggest that sacrificing yourself for others is much more likely when the "others" are genetically related relatives (see ● Figure 3.7).

Given the fact that each parent can pass along over 8 million different combinations of his or her chromosomes, it might be surprising that family resemblance can be so strong, as it is with the Jonas brothers and with mother-daughter actresses Goldie Hawn and Kate Hudson.

Sex Chromosomes

Twenty-two of the 23 pairs of human chromosomes from each parent are perfectly matched. In other words, a gene appearing on one of a pair of chromosomes, perhaps a gene for hair color or blood type, will have a corresponding gene on its partner. The remaining pair, the X and Y sex chromosomes, does not carry the same genes. Most of the genes located on the Y chromosome are involved with male fertility. The X chromosome contains genes not duplicated on the Y chromosome that influence a wide variety of characteristics, including the clotting of blood and the ability to see the colors red and green.

Genes responsible for hemophilia, or the failure of blood to clot, and red-green colorblindness are found on the X chromosome. These genes are recessive, leading to different outcomes based on the sex of the child receiving the genes. Generally, if a female receives a healthy gene on the X chromosome from one parent and a defective gene on the X chromosome

X chromosome

Y chromosome

FIGURE 3.6

Relatedness. Relatedness refers to the probability that two people share a particular allele from a common ancestor. The chance that you share an allele with one of your parents or a brother or sister is .50, or one half. The chance that you share an allele with a niece or nephew is .25, or one quarter.

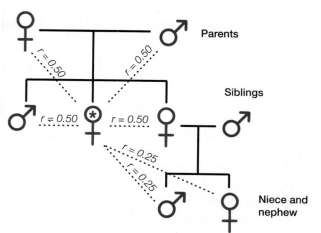

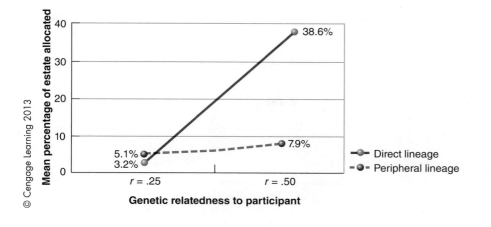

© Cengage Learning 2013

Mean percentage of estate allocated

40 — 38.6%
30
20
10 — 7.9%
5.1%
3.2%
0

r = .25   r = .50

Genetic relatedness to participant

○— Direct lineage
●-- Peripheral lineage

FIGURE 3.7

Relatedness and Inheritance. People leave more of their estates to those who are more closely related. Direct lineage refers to parents, grandparents, or children of the person making the will, whereas peripheral lineage refers to siblings, aunts, uncles, cousins, nieces, and nephews. A sibling has the same relatedness to an individual as a child ($r = .50$), but the child is left much more of the estate.

---

from her other parent, she will be a carrier for the condition but will not experience it herself. In contrast, a male receiving a defective gene on the X chromosome from his mother will have the condition. Because there is no equivalent gene on the Y chromosome to offset the defective recessive gene, it will be expressed. As a result, conditions such as hemophilia and red-green colorblindness are much more frequent among males and are referred to as sex-linked characteristics. Although Queen Victoria of Britain had parents who were not carriers of hemophilia, she, through two of her five daughters (Princess Alice and Princess Beatrice), passed the mutation to various royal houses across the continent. Victoria's son Prince Leopold, Duke of Albany suffered from the disease. For this reason, hemophilia was once popularly called "the royal disease" (see ● Figure 3.8). You can trace hemophilia, or the royal disease, in Queen Victoria's family as illustrated in ● Figure 3.9.

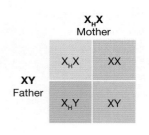

X_HX
Mother

	X_HX	XX
XY Father	X_HY	XY

XY
Father

FIGURE 3.8

Hemophilia Is a Sex-Linked Trait. If a daughter inherits her mother's X chromosome containing the allele for hemophilia (X_H), she will be a carrier but will not have the disease. If a son inherits this X_H chromosome, he will have the disease. Unlike his sister, he does not have a healthy X chromosome to offset the disease allele.

Epigenetics

Having identical genotypes, as is the case with identical twins, does not guarantee identical phenotypes, or observed characteristics. As we explained in the example of the Agouti gene and the fur color and weight of baby mice, different phenotypes can result from the same genotype due to interactions between the organism and its environment. When factors other than the genotype itself

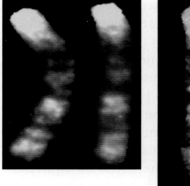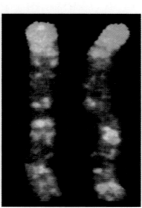

Mario Fraga and his colleagues studied 160 identical twin pairs between the ages of 3 and 74. The two chromosomes on the left belong to 3-year-old twins and those on the right to a pair of 50-year-old twins. Areas of red indicate differences between the two chromosomes related to differences in gene expression. As the twins aged, their gene expression became more different, as indicated by the greater amount of red in the chromosomes from the older twins. Twins who had spent the most time apart showed the greatest epigenetic differences. "Epigenetic differences arise during the lifetime of monozygotic twins," by Mario Fraga et al., in *Proceedings of the National Academy of Sciences* 2005 Jul 102 (30) 10407-8, Fig. 5. © 2005 National Academy of Sciences, U.S.A.

Queen Victoria
(m. Albert of Saxe-Coburg-Gotha)

Victoria   Edward VII   Alfred   Helena   Louise   Arthur

Queen Victoria's mother was not a carrier for hemophilia, and her father did not have the disease. Scientists believe that a mutation occuring in her father's sperm resulted in Victoria's being a carrier.

Alice ⌐ Grand Duke Louis IV of Hesse
├ *Victoria*
├ *Elisabeth*
├ *Irene (m. Henry of Prussia)*
├ *Grand Duke Ernest Louis*
├ *Frederick*
└ *Alix (m. Emperor Nicholas II of Russia)*

One of Alice's two sons had hemophilia, and two of her five daughters were carriers. One daughter, Alix, carried hemophilia into the Russian royal family.

Leopold ⌐ Helena of Waldeck
└ *Alice*

Prince Leopold had the royal disease and his daughter Alice was a carrier.

Beatrice ⌐ Henry of Battenberg
├ *Alexander Mountbatten*
├ *Victoria Eugenie (m. King Alfonso XIII of Spain)*
├ *Leopold*
└ *Maurice*

Two of Beatrice's three sons had the disease. One, Leopold, died during surgery, because hemophilia causes uncontrolled bleeding. Beatrice's daughter, Victoria Eugenie, married into the Spanish royal family and carried the disease with her.

FIGURE 3.9

Hemophilia and European Royalty. Queen Victoria of Great Britain (1819–1901) had nine children. One son (Prince Leopold, Duke of Albany) had hemophilia, and two daughters (Princess Alice and Princess Beatrice) were carriers for the condition. As a result of their marriages to other European royalty, the three children spread the hemophilia gene to the royal families of Germany, Russia, and Spain. For this reason, hemophilia was once popularly called "the royal disease." Illustration: © Cengage Learning 2013; photos, left to right: © Pictorial Press Ltd/Alamy; Mary Evans Picture Library/CHARLOTTE ZEEPVAT; © Mary Evans Picture Library/The Image Works; Mary Evans Picture Library/ CHARLOTTE ZEEPVAT; Background photo: © martan/Shutterstock

produce changes in a phenotype, we say that an **epigenetic** change has occurred. *Epi* is greek for "over" or "above," so "epigenetics" refers to the reversible development of traits by factors that determine how the genes perform. The field of epigenetics explores these gene–environment interactions.

Epigenetic change often works by influencing gene expression, the process by which the DNA forms proteins that contribute to features of living cells. The environment can determine if and when a particular gene is activated. Although many studies in epigenetics examine physical features like fur color, we assume that more complex features of interest to psychologists are also subject to epigenetic influences. In one dramatic example, rats that were licked frequently during infancy by their mothers (the rat equivalent of getting a hug from mom) were calmer than rats licked infrequently when

epigenetics The study of gene–environment interactions in the production of phenotypes.

faced with stress later in life (Champagne, Francis, Mar, & Meaney, 2003). By licking their pups, these mothers had influenced the expression of genes that determined responses to a stress hormone. The nurture provided by the mother had lifelong impact on the offspring's ability to cope with stress. Children exposed to child abuse have been found to have similar long-lasting changes in the expression of genes related to stress hormones (Neigh, Gillespie, & Nemeroff, 2009). Happily, these changes appear to be reversible in children who experience consistent and responsive caregiving by foster parents (Fisher, Van Ryzin, & Gunnar, 2011).

Although the application of epigenetics to psychology is quite recent, it is likely that interest in this approach will continue to grow. Epigenetic change provides a clear example of how the human mind responds to the interplay between nature and nurture.

What Is the Field of Behavioral Genetics?

The field of **behavioral genetics** attempts to identify and understand the links between genetics and behavior. These links can help explain individual differences between human beings as well as the differences we see between our species and others.

Although we can say that all human beings share 100% of their genes, we do not share 100% of our alleles, or variations in each gene, giving each of us a unique version of the genome. In other words, we all share genes that produce eye color of some sort, but our different combinations of alleles result in a wide variety of shades. In fact, there are at least 3 million DNA variations in the human genome, enough for us to differ from one another in nearly every gene (Plomin & Spinath, 2004).

Our species also shares quite a few genes with chimpanzees, mice, fruit flies, yeast, and a weed known as thale cress (see ● Figure 3.10). Behavioral geneticists are less interested in genes we share with other species than in those that make us different from them. For example, recent research points to differences between humans and chimpanzees in a single gene, the *FoxP2* gene, that appears to have had a significant effect on distinctly human behaviors, including spoken language (Konopka et al., 2009).

Behavioral geneticists often speak in terms of the **heritability** of a particular trait, or the statistical likelihood that variations observed across individuals in a population are due to genetics. Heritability is usually presented as a ratio of the amount of variation observed in a population due to genetics relative to the total amount of variation due to both genetic and environmental influences. If genes play no part in producing phenotypical differences between individuals, heritability is zero. For example, genes are responsible for us having hearts, but there is no individual variation

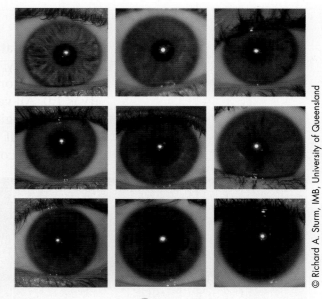

© Richard A. Sturm, IMB, University of Queensland

Our species shares genes for eye color, but combinations of alleles produce many different possible shades.

behavioral genetics The scientific field that attempts to identify and understand links between genetics and behavior.

heritability The statistical likelihood that variations observed in a population are due to genetics.

FIGURE 3.10

Genes Shared With Other Species. Humans share quite a few genes with other species, such as the 18% of genes we share with a weed known as thale cress. However, geneticists are most concerned with the genes that differ from those of other species, like the FoxP2 gene, which appears to be responsible for spoken language. In fact, mutations of this gene cause severe speech and language disorders.

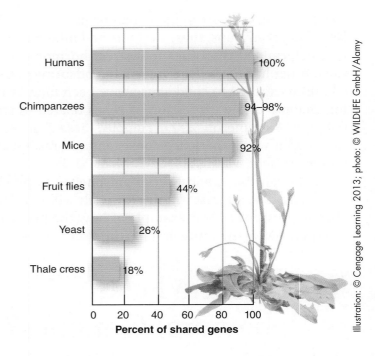

Illustration: © Cengage Learning 2013; photo: © WILDLIFE GmbH/Alamy

in the population in terms of the presence of a heart—we all have one. Consequently, the heritability of having a heart is 0.0. If genes are totally responsible for all phenotypical differences between individuals, heritability is 1.0. All variation in the population in terms of having or not having a fatal neurological condition known as Huntington's disease is entirely due to genetics. If you inherit a Huntington's gene from one parent, you will develop the condition, so the heritability of Huntington's is 1.0. Heritability of most human traits is typically found between these extremes, in the range of 0.30 to 0.60.

Heritability is a concept that is frequently misunderstood. *Heritability always refers to populations, not to individuals.* Saying that a trait such as shyness is 40% heritable does not say that 40% of one individual's shyness is produced by genes and the other 60% by the environment. Instead, a 0.40 heritability ratio suggests that the variations in shyness we see across the population (from very high to very low) are influenced moderately by both genetic and environmental factors (see ● Figure 3.11).

Heritability cannot be assessed without taking the environment into account, which is another source of potential confusion. If the environment is held constant (everybody is treated exactly the same way), the heritability of a trait will appear to be high. For example, if you plant seeds in trays with identical nutrients, water, and sunlight, the height of the resulting plants will be largely due to their genetic differences. In variable environments, heritability will be lower. If you plant seeds in trays receiving different

© Thomas M Perkins/Shutterstock

The environments provided by adoptive parents, like this mother, are more similar to each other than to the environments provided by biological parents. This environmental similarity can exaggerate genetic influences, a result that must be taken into account when investigating heritability using adopted children.

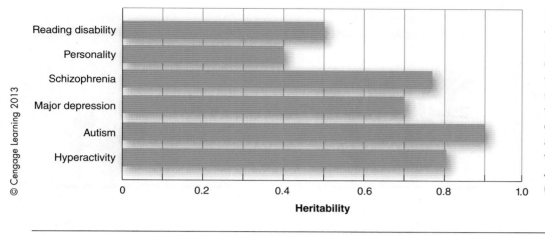

© Cengage Learning 2013

FIGURE 3.11

Heritability of Some Human Conditions. Heritability rates tell us how much of the variability seen in a population can be due to genetics. According to these data, we can say that genes have a greater influence on autism than on reading disabilities. *Source:* Adapted from McGuffin, Riley, and Plomin (2001).

amounts of nutrients, water, and sunlight, the height of the resulting plants will appear to be less influenced by genetics. If you studied the heritability of human intelligence in participants living in extremely wealthy circumstances, genetic influences would be exaggerated, just as they are when you hold the nutrients, water, and sunlight constant for your plants. Researchers assessing heritability of human traits attempt to do so within a "typical" range of environments.

Because of these concerns about the influence of environment on heritability, some researchers question the use of adoption studies for assessing the relative influences of genetics and environment on child development. These studies compare adopted children to their biological and adoptive parents in an effort to assess the relative impact of heritability. Like our plants with constant amounts of nutrients, water, and sunlight, adoptive families share many common features as a result of the screening process they go through before adopting. Consequently, adoptive parents rarely represent as much diversity as the group of biological parents whose children they adopt. If all adoptive families provide a consistent environment, this factor may inflate the apparent heritability of characteristics examined in the adopted children.

An understanding of heritability can help us evaluate some of the contentious arguments in psychology, including issues of group differences in intelligence. Returning once again to our plant example, consider the following (Lewontin, 1970). Grab two handfuls of seeds from the same bag and plant each handful in two different trays. One tray has nutrient-rich soil, and the other has nutrient-poor soil. In all other respects (light, water), the seeds receive the same treatment. The plants growing in either tray share an environment, so the differences between the heights of the plants within a single tray are largely due to genetics. However, the fact that the plants in the nutrient-rich tray are taller than those in the nutrient-poor tray is largely the result of environment. In other words, you can have heritability approaching 1.0 within each group and substantial differences in observed traits between groups, and yet have no genetic differences whatsoever between the two groups (which in our example were drawn randomly from the same bag). Knowing that performance on intelligence tests is heritable does not tell us that observed differences between groups of people are due to differences in genetics (see ● Figure 3.12).

> Historians will have to face the fact that natural selection determined the evolution of cultures in the same manner as it did that of species.
>
> —Konrad Lorenz

FIGURE 3.12

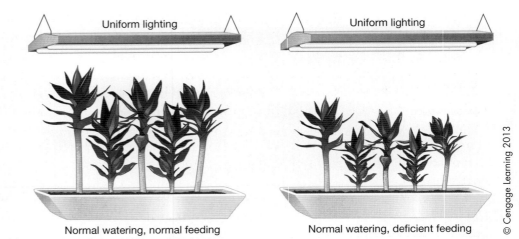

Comparing Heritability Between Groups. In this demonstration by Lewontin, you can have heritability approaching 1.0 within each group and substantial differences in observed traits between groups, and yet have no genetic differences whatsoever between the two groups (the seeds in each tray were drawn from the same bag). Lewontin was attempting to caution scientists wishing to make heritability conclusions regarding observed racial differences in IQ.

Uniform lighting

Uniform lighting

Normal watering, normal feeding

Normal watering, deficient feeding

© Cengage Learning 2013

Psychology *as a* Hub Science

Understanding Risk Taking

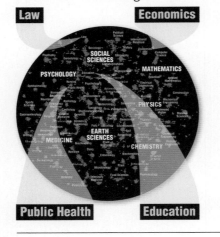

Risk taking is another example of a behavior that demonstrates an interaction between genetic and environmental factors. Risk-taking behavior can lead to a number of outcomes that affect society negatively, including risky financial investments, unprotected sex, accidents, violence, substance abuse, gambling, and victimization. A better understanding of risk taking provides important insights for many fields, including public health, law enforcement, economics, and education.

Researchers have reported that risk taking is significantly heritable (Anokhin, Golosheykin, Grant, & Heath, 2009). However, not only does risk taking vary across the lifespan, with adolescents being notoriously riskier than adults, and between genders (males take more risks than females), but factors such as whether you are a parent, whether you expect to be a parent, your birth order (last-borns are more risky), and how long you expect to live can influence risk-taking behavior (Wang, Kruger, & Wilke, 2009). To give you an idea about how complex risk taking can be, consider the following: in 12-year-olds, heritability in both males and females is modest but significant (28% for males; 17% for females), but at the age of 14, heritability rises to 55% in males and

Another common misunderstanding of behavioral genetics is the belief that we can identify "a gene for" a particular behavior. For instance, the headline of an article written for the popular website WebMD trumpets "Researchers identify alcoholism gene" (Davis, 2004). It is important to remember that genes encode for proteins, not behaviors. Genes build proteins that are used to construct brains, and brains may or may not initiate the behavior of drinking alcohol. Rather than viewing a gene as "causing" a complex behavior, it is much more useful and accurate to view genes as *contributing* to the development and functioning of the nervous system, which in turn generates observable behavior.

Occasionally, it appears that single genes or a small number of genes may have a disproportionately significant effect on behavior. However, most behavioral differences occur due to interactions between the very small effects of large numbers of genes. As we will discuss in a later chapter on psychological disorders, schizophrenia appears to have a moderate genetic basis, but more than 70 different genes have been implicated in the development of the disorder (Mirnics, Middleton, Marquez, Lewis, & Levitt, 2000). Fortunately, methods for analyzing the simultaneous influence of whole sets of genes, as opposed to analyzing one gene at a time, are advancing rapidly. Researchers using these new techniques have identified multiple genes involved with reading disability (Gayan et al., 2005). No one gene can account for reading difficulties, but small differences in clusters of genes can.

becomes nonsignificant for females (Anokhin et al., 2009). Again, when we're discussing heritability, we're describing the role of genetics in the variations we see across a population. So in 14-year-old males, genetics account for 55% of the variations (high to low) we see in risk taking.

Risk taking is not the type of behavior that lends itself to simple explanations. The genetic perspective featured in this chapter provides considerable insight, but if professionals in the fields of public health and education, for example, want to understand the effects of risk taking on rates of unprotected sex or alcohol abuse, a comprehensive exploration of underlying developmental, cognitive, social, and clinical factors will be needed. ✿

Courtesy Kristin Graham

Risk taking is a complex behavior that demonstrates interactions between genetics and the environment that change over the lifespan. Psychologists can contribute to public health, medicine, and education by providing more insight into this type of behavior.

Summary 3.1

Major Concepts in Genetics

Concept	Definition	Example
Genotype © ISM/Phototake	An individual's genetic makeup	A person might have a gene for straight hair and a gene for curly hair.
Phenotype © Richard A. Sturm, IMB, University of Queensland	An individual's observable trait	A person has curly hair.
Gene Fraga et al. (2005). © 2005 National Academy of Sciences, U.S.A.	A sequence of DNA in a specific location on a chromosome that contains the instructions for making a protein.	The serotonin transporter gene is located on chromosome 17.
Gene expression Courtesy Randy L. Jirtle, Ph.D., Jirtle Laboratory at Duke University	Information from a gene is used to produce a protein.	Maternal diet in mice can affect the expression of the Agouti gene.
Allele © Cengage Learning 2013	One of two or more possible variations of a gene	Blood type alleles can be A, B, or O.
Homozygous © Cengage Learning 2013	Having two of the same alleles	Having the SS or LL forms of the serotonin transporter gene
Heterozygous	Having two different alleles	Having the SL form of the serotonin transporter gene
Dominant © Huntstock.com/Shutterstock	An allele that is expressed regardless of whether it is homozygous or heterozygous	The allele for curly hair is dominant.
Recessive	An allele that is expressed only when it is homozygous	The allele for straight hair is recessive.

How Does Evolution Occur?

The human genome is the product of millions of years of **evolution**, defined by modern biologists as "descent with modification from a common ancestor." The study of evolution allows us to trace the family tree of living things.

In his book *The Origin of Species*, Charles Darwin proposed that species evolve or change from one form to the next in an orderly manner (Darwin, 1859). Darwin was well aware of the procedures used by farmers to develop animals and plants with desirable traits by mating particular individuals to each other. A farmer's goal to raise the strongest oxen for pulling a plow might be accomplished by breeding the strongest available oxen to each other. In these cases, the farmer is making the determination of which individuals have the opportunity to produce offspring. Darwin suggested that instead of a farmer choosing which animals would breed and pass their genes along, the pressures of survival and reproduction in the wild would make the choice, a process he named **natural selection**. Organisms that survive long enough to reproduce would pass their traits along to the next generation. Organisms that did not reproduce would not have the opportunity to pass their traits along to future generations. As geneticists often remind us, we have no infertile ancestors.

In the more than 150 years since *The Origin of Species* was first published, our understanding of genetics and the fossil record has expanded exponentially, lending substantial further support for Darwin's views. Surprisingly, Darwin was able to derive his theory without the benefit of a basic understanding of genetics. He was unable to account for the variations he observed in a particular trait. That understanding was provided by Gregor Mendel (1822–1884), who discovered ways to outline and predict the inheritance of particular traits, like the color of flowers, in his research on pea plants (Mendel, 1866). Mendel, in turn, was working without our modern understanding of genes and chromosomes. Combining current understanding of genetics with the natural selection processes proposed by Darwin provides scientists with powerful hypotheses about the progression of species over time.

© Martin Shields/Alamy

Charles Darwin's Theory of Evolution described how species change in an orderly manner.

Darwin understood that breeders could influence the traits of offspring by mating particular individuals. He believed that natural selection operated according to the same principles. The pressures of survival and reproduction in the wild would take the role of the breeder—determining which traits are passed along to the next generation.

© Shannon Stapleton/Reuters/Landov

evolution Descent with modification from a common ancestor.

natural selection The process by which survival and reproduction pressures act to change the frequency of alleles in subsequent generations.

Gregor Mendel (1822–1884) made important discoveries about inheritance at about the same time that Charles Darwin was working on his theory of evolution, but neither scientist was aware of the work of the other, nor did they know about genes and chromosomes. Modern geneticists combine this knowledge to form powerful hypotheses about the nature of living things.

mutation Errors that occur when DNA is replicated.

migration Movement to a new location.

genetic drift Change in a population's genes from one generation to the next due to chance or accident.

Mechanisms of Evolution

In addition to the process of natural selection described by Darwin, evolution can result from mutation, migration, and genetic drift.

Mutations are errors that occur when DNA is replicated. The average human baby is born with about 130 new mutations, but the vast majority have no effect (Zimmer, 2009). Mutant alleles that provide some advantage often spread through the population, but most mutant alleles that result in a disadvantage disappear from future generations. **Migration** occurs when organisms move from one geographical location to the next. Phenotypical traits that are advantageous in one environment might be less so in another. **Genetic drift** produces change from one generation to the next through chance or accident. Type B blood is virtually absent in contemporary populations of Native Americans, most likely due to chance (Halverson & Bolnick, 2008). The handful of ancestors crossing the Bering Strait 10,000 years ago appears to have included no individuals with the Type B allele. If the blood type alleles of the ancestors had been more representative of the entire human population, more of their descendants would have Type B blood.

We can demonstrate the effects of evolutionary processes—mutation, migration, genetic drift, and natural selection—on the history of one allele: the recessive allele for blonde hair. The original appearance of the allele for blonde hair was probably the result of a random mutation that occurred in Northern Europe some 10,000 years ago (Frost, 2006). Migration, or rather the lack of it, might account for the relatively restricted area in Northern Europe populated by blondes until fairly recent times. Geographical barriers of mountain and ocean contained the allele for many centuries. Genetic drift, or changes in the genome due to chance or accident, undoubtedly reduced the global frequency of the blonde allele between 1300 and 1700, as waves of Bubonic plague decimated the European population, which at that time contained nearly everyone carrying the blonde allele. If by chance every single person carrying the blonde allele had died from the plague before reproducing, the allele would have disappeared from the human genome (see ● Figure 3.13).

Has natural selection influenced the blonde gene? Some anthropologists and biologists believe it has. When a person has a choice of mates of equal value, he or she will select the one that "stands out from the crowd" (Frost, 2006). Individuals with blonde hair color, which was different and more rare, might have enjoyed more reproductive success than those with more common, darker hair colors. It is interesting to note that in Germany, with its high percentage of blondes, the trait of blondness is viewed differently than in other countries where blondes are relatively rare. German men report that they would marry a blonde because she is likely to be a good homemaker, but they find women with dark hair more sexually attractive.

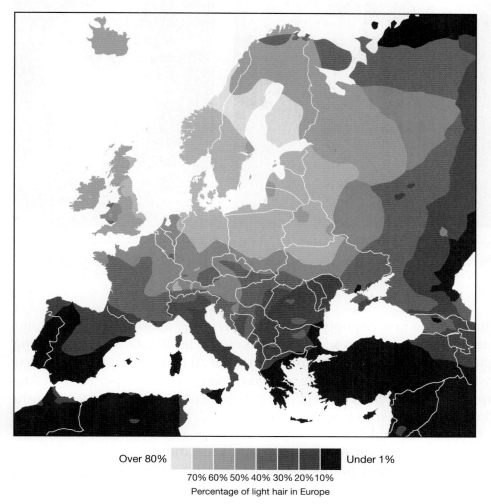

Over 80%   Under 1%

70% 60% 50% 40% 30% 20% 10%

Percentage of light hair in Europe

© Cengage Learning 2013

FIGURE 3.13

Spread of the Blonde Allele.
After the first appearance of the blonde hair allele about 10,000 years ago, its frequency might have been affected by migration, genetic drift, and natural selection.

This finding supports the idea that rare things tend to be viewed as valuable (in this case, attractive; Bem, 2001).

Any consideration of evolution must include the question of what exactly natural selection selects. Natural selection favors the organism with the highest degree of **fitness**, defined as the ability of one genotype to reproduce relative to other genotypes. The concept of fitness includes survival to adulthood, ability to find a mate, and reproduction. Fitness is not some static characteristic, such as being strongest or fastest. Instead, fitness describes the interaction between characteristics and the environment in which they exist. A genotype that succeeds during the Ice Age may be at a significant disadvantage during periods of global warming. Animals in very cold climates tend to have short legs and stocky bodies, which help retain heat, whereas animals in very warm climates have long legs and slim bodies, which release heat. Once again, we see the need to consider nature within the context of nurture.

Adaptation

Adaptation can refer to either the process or the result of change due to natural selection. In other words, a species can respond to an environmental change by adapting, and

fitness The ability of one genotype to reproduce more successfully relative to other genotypes.

adaptation A change due to natural selection.

HOW DOES EVOLUTION OCCUR?   107

Fitness varies across environments. Characteristics like long ears and long legs work in hot, desert climates, but short ears and legs conserve heat in colder climates.

features of the new phenotype may be referred to as adaptations. Adaptations can take many forms. Adaptations can be behaviors, such as jumping higher to better avoid a predator, or anatomical features, such as eyes that can see color. Adaptations do not necessarily produce perfection. Any adaptation that is "good enough" to contribute to the fitness of an organism will carry forward into future generations.

A classic example of very rapid adaptation is the case of the English peppered moth *Biston betularia*. Prior to the Industrial Revolution, the majority of peppered moths found in England were a light gray color, which allowed them to hide against the similar colors of tree bark. Darker moths did occasionally appear beginning in about 1848, but as they were less capable of hiding from predators, they made up only about 1% of the population. With increasing industrialization, tree bark became frequently coated in soot. The once-camouflaged light gray moths now became an easy target for predators against the darker background of the sooty trees. Very rapidly, the darker moths became the norm, reaching frequencies of about 98%. As pollution came under better control, tree bark returned to its original light gray color, and the lighter moths once again became the norm. The peppered moth population successfully adapted to changing environmental circumstances, with color playing the role of an adaptation. The moths did not "decide" to change color. Natural selection, in the form of greater rates of reproductive success on the part of moths with a particular color, changed the frequencies of color genes within the population.

The dark and light coloring of the peppered moth population in Great Britain changed in response to pollution from soot that collected on trees and changed again when pollution controls reduced the soot.

Adaptations often appear to be compromises between costs and benefits. Adult human males have about 10 times as much testosterone as adult human females. Testosterone conveys a reproductive advantage, as men with higher testosterone report having more sex partners and earlier age at intercourse (Lassek & Gaulin, 2009). On the negative side, however, high testosterone levels are correlated with lower immune system functioning, making the high testosterone males more vulnerable to disease.

Adaptation is only one source of evolutionary change. Random events, such as the collision of meteors with Earth and resulting climate changes, are believed to have destroyed some types of life and provided broad opportunities for others. We are also limited in our ability to use adaptation to predict the future. The study of evolution is similar to the study of history. Although we gain insight into wars by studying the causes of World War II, we cannot use our knowledge to predict future wars with any precision. We can be fairly certain that antibiotic-resistant bacteria, global warming, pollution, and reproductive technologies are probably changing the face of the human population as this text goes to press, but where all these changes will lead us remains unknown.

Males with high testosterone report more chances to reproduce, but testosterone also lowers the response of the immune system. Extremely high levels of testosterone, due to the use of performance enhancing drugs, might be contributing to the early deaths of some professional wrestlers, like Curt Hennig.

Evolution of the Human Brain

Our interest as psychologists is in the mind, and the mind and the behavior it produces originate in the structures and processes of the brain and nervous system. A nervous system is a relatively recent invention in the history of life, and one that is enjoyed only by animals. Our species, *Homo sapiens*, which features an especially advanced brain, appeared somewhere between 100,000 and 200,000 years ago.

Anthropologists use the term *hominin* to describe species that walked on two feet, had large brains, and are assumed to be related to modern humans. Over the 7-million-year period of hominin evolution, brains grew very rapidly, suggesting that improved intelligence was quickly translated into substantial advantages in survival. Early tool-using hominins, the *australopithecines*, had brains that were about the same size as those of modern chimpanzees, or about 400 cubic cm. *Homo erectus*, a hominin living about 1.5 million years ago, had a brain of about 700 cubic cm, and the brains of modern humans, or *Homo sapiens*, are about 1,400 cubic cm.

Hominins were not the only creatures who evolved very large brains and considerable intelligence. The other primates, elephants, and whales are not lacking in these areas. Although the challenges of finding food,

Early hominins, like the one on the left, had brains that were about the same size as those of chimpanzees. Very quickly, however, brain size doubled by the time our own species, the modern *Homo sapiens* shown on the right, appeared sometime between 100,000 and 200,000 years ago.

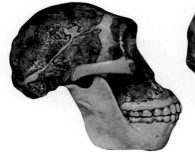
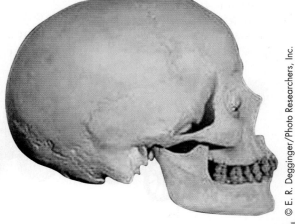

avoiding predators, and navigating through territories require considerable intelligence, these ecological challenges are no match for the complexity of social life faced by the hominins. The major factor distinguishing human intelligence from the intelligence of other species is the richness and complexity of the social behavior supported by the human brain. Managing the abilities to distinguish friend and foe, imitate the behavior of others, use language to communicate, recognize and anticipate the emotions, thoughts, and behavior of others, maintain relationships, and cooperate required the evolution of a special brain indeed (Cacioppo et al., 2002; Hrdy, 2005; Roth & Dicke, 2005). Comparisons of the challenges faced by different species support a stronger role for social complexity than for ecological complexity in building bigger brains (Dunbar & Schultz, 2007).

The Contemporary Human Brain

You surf the Internet, complete your calculus homework, and read this textbook with a brain that is essentially the same size as that of your very early *Homo sapiens* ancestors, who first appeared somewhere between 100,000 and 200,000 years ago.

Although we can understand the advantages of big, intelligent brains to survival, we do not know why advances such as agriculture, literacy, and urbanization have not been accompanied by additional increases in brain size. It is possible that we have reached an equilibrium between our needs for intelligence and the costs of a big brain. Brains are very expensive to run in terms of nutrients. Although the brain comprises only about 2% of the body's weight, it requires about 15% of the body's resources when at rest. In addition, brain size may be limited by the dimensions of the birth canal. Further change may not occur unless we experience a drop in the costs of big brains, a change in nutrients, or additional pressures for greater intelligence.

The fact that brain size has not changed much during *Homo sapiens'* time on Earth does not imply that the evolution of the human brain has ended or that average intelligence has remained the same. Modern genetic techniques allow researchers to "date" changes in a particular gene. Genes involved with brain development appear to have changed as recently as 6,000 years ago (Evans et al., 2004; Evans et al., 2005). As we discuss in a later chapter on cognition, IQ test scores have increased dramatically worldwide over the last 100 years (Flynn, 1999). If brain size has not changed for 100,000 years, let alone during the last 100, how can we account for the observed increase in intellectual performance? It is likely that environmental factors, including nutrition and education, might account for the improvement.

It is somewhat surprising that innovations such as agriculture and transportation are not associated with further increases in human brain size.

Photos, left to right: © Stephen Coburn/Shutterstock; © Rob Wilson/Shutterstock; © gary718/Shutterstock; © bsauter/iStockphoto; © Charlie Hutton/Shutterstock

Summary 3.2

Principles of Evolution

Concept	Definition	Example
Natural selection © Martin Shields/Alamy	A trait's frequency in a population is determined by the survival and reproductive success of the organisms with the trait.	Faster rabbits are more likely to survive and reproduce than slow rabbits, leading to more fast rabbits in subsequent generations.
Mutation © Franck Boston/ Shutterstock	Genetic changes that occur spontaneously or due to external factors like radiation	A mutation about 10,000 years ago led to the appearance of blonde hair.
Migration © Cengage Learning 2013	Populations move from one area to another.	Moving from a cold to a warm climate might change the natural selection of traits in a species.
Genetic drift	Chance events influence the frequency of alleles.	Huntington's disease is much more common than usual among the Afrikaner population of South Africa, because a carrier was among the small number of Dutch immigrants to survive.
Fitness All: © Royalty-free/CORBIS	The ability of one genotype to reproduce relative to other genotypes in a particular environment	The recessive sickle-cell trait has low fitness in general because it can produce disease, but because the trait protects the individual from malaria, it has higher fitness in populations living where malaria is common.
Adaptation © Perennou Nuridsany/ Photo Researchers, Inc. © Michael Willmer Forbes Tweedie/Photo Researchers, Inc.	Evolutionary changes whereby a population becomes better suited to its environment	The moth population changed from primarily light colors to dark colors when the trees they inhabited became darker due to pollution.

How Does Evolution Influence Behavior?

We mentioned in an earlier section that behavior can be adaptive. If an animal that is good at hiding in the bushes is more successful than others of its species in escaping predators, it is likely that the ability to hide will spread through subsequent generations of the population.

Behavior like hiding, however, is unlike the other adaptations we have discussed so far, such as the color of a moth or blonde hair. Color is a physical characteristic, and it is a fairly simple matter to identify the genes associated with these phenotypes. Behavior as a phenotype is considerably more complex. Behavior is not an anatomical structure like a wing or an eye. Can we assume that behavior is shaped by the same evolutionary forces that affect physical traits? Charles Darwin certainly thought so. In his *Descent of Man*, Darwin writes:

> The difference in mind between man and the higher animals, great as it is, certainly is one of degree and not of kind. We have seen that the senses and intuitions, the various emotions and faculties, such as love, memory, attention, curiosity, imitation, reason, etc., of which man boasts, may be found in an incipient, or even sometimes in a well-developed condition in lower animals. (1871, p. 126)

© Mitsuaki Iwago/Minden Pictures/Getty Images

Physical features, like the coloring of an animal that allows it to hide, are well-understood types of adaptations. Evolutionary psychologists attempt to explain how behaviors can be adaptive, too.

evolutionary psychology The psychological perspective that assumes our current behavior exists because it provided survival and reproductive advantages to our ancestors.

The Evolutionary Psychology Perspective

Among the psychological specialties we discussed in our introductory chapter, **evolutionary psychology** is the most relevant to our current discussion of the evolution of behavior. This approach to the mind assumes that our current behavior exists in its present form because it provided some advantage in survival and reproduction to our ancestors (Cosmides & Tooby, 1997).

The evolutionary psychology approach not only owes an obvious debt to Charles Darwin but is also a direct descendant of the functionalism supported by William James. As the term *functionalism* implies, behavior is seen as promoting survival, as opposed to being random and pointless. The goal of evolutionary psychology is to explain how the patterns of behavior we share with other human beings have been shaped by evolution.

Origins of Social Behavior

Reconstructing the evolution of the nervous system is difficult and tracing the origins of individual behavior is even more challenging, but identifying the roots of social behavior might be the most difficult task of all. Occasionally, physical evidence has allowed scientists to determine whether dinosaur parents stayed around to look after their young, but such accounts leave much detail unexplored and unexplained.

A number of factors are believed to influence the social behavior of any particular species, including mating systems, the availability of resources such as food, water, and shelter, the exposure to predators, and competition. We will see how these factors might have shaped the unique social lives of early humans.

Humans as a Social Species In spite of our admiration of the rugged individualist, one of the outstanding features of human beings is our rich and essential social nature, which we explore in more detail in our chapter on social psychology. To understand the evolution of social behavior, we need to explore its advantages for survival and reproduction.

In typical environments, individual animals are likely to come into contact with others, leading to a variety of possible interactions and outcomes. In each case, shown in Table 3.2, Individuals either benefit or not from the interaction, ultimately affecting their survival and reproductive success. Both parties benefit equally if they cooperate. For example, two hunters can work together to bring down an animal that neither could successfully hunt alone. Sharing the resulting meat with the families of both hunters would contribute to their survival and reproductive success. Much social behavior probably originated in these types of situations, where the benefits of cooperation for an individual's survival and reproduction outweighed any disadvantages of cooperating.

Cooperation, however, is not the only way two individuals can interact. One person could steal food from another, allowing the thief's family to survive while the victim's family starves to death. In still other interactions, both participants lose. In some divorce proceedings, the partners are so determined to keep each other from maintaining resources that everything goes to the attorneys. In these cases, the reproductive success of both would be in danger. Finally, in **altruism**, one individual sacrifices himself or herself to benefit another individual.

© Kim Hill/Arizona State University

Although we do not have any cultures today that exist exactly like the hunter-gatherers of our past, the Ache of Paraguay are often used as a model of how that life might have been. Here, the Ache cooperate with each other to fish. Social behaviors like cooperation might have allowed humans, who are not particularly strong individuals, to survive.

	And the second organism:	
The first organism:	Wins	Loses
Wins	Cooperation	Selfishness
Loses	Altruism	Spite

TABLE 3.2 Outcomes of Social Interactions

altruism Sacrifice of one's self for the benefit of another individual.

Altruism is widespread in the animal kingdom. Most of us have experienced a honeybee sting, which is suicidal behavior on the part of the bee in an effort to protect its hive (Wilson, 1975). As we will discuss in greater detail in a later chapter on social psychology, altruism is one of the most challenging social behaviors to explain in evolutionary terms. Charles Darwin himself was puzzled by the apparent sacrifice of some individuals that led to the survival of the group. If altruism results in the destruction of the individual with altruistic genes, why doesn't this behavior disappear? To explain this phenomenon, we return to the concept of relatedness presented earlier in the chapter. Sacrificing your life to save a close blood relative might actually increase the likelihood that your alleles would be passed along to subsequent generations.

At this point, you are probably thinking that you often behave altruistically with people who are not at all related to you. You might have stayed to comfort a friend who just experienced a death in the family, even though you flunked your midterm the next day as a result. How can we explain these behaviors, which are known as **reciprocal altruism** (Trivers & Burt, 1999)? In cases of reciprocal altruism, it is customary to help another individual when you can reasonably expect the other individual to return the favor at some future date. Reciprocal altruism is likely to flourish in situations where individuals are in regular contact with one another. As we will see in a later chapter on social psychology, reciprocal altruism also requires the ability to recognize and remember cheaters.

Altruism can extend to entire social organizations, regardless of the degree of relatedness (Chicago Social Brain Network, 2011). Among the Emperor penguin (*Aptenodytes forsteri*), survival of the chicks in the hostile Antarctic cold depends not only on an individual parent but on the larger huddle formed by other parents. Human survival similarly depends on

© Gherasim Rares/Shutterstock

Altruism, or the sacrifice of yourself for others, is more common among related individuals, but it also occurs when we are in close social contact with others. Honeybees sting to defend their hive, but in doing so, end their own lives.

Cooperation allows human beings to carry out complex behaviors that would be impossible for a single individual to perform successfully.

reciprocal altruism Help you provide another person when you expect the person to return the favor in the future.

© stefanolunardi/Shutterstock

collective abilities, rather than individual success. It might sound counterintuitive, but our altruism might have its roots in the warfare conducted by our hunter-gatherer ancestors (Bowles, 2009). As Darwin observed:

> A tribe including many members who, from possessing in a high degree the spirit of patriotism, fidelity, obedience, courage, and sympathy, were always ready to aid one another, and to sacrifice themselves for the common good would be victorious over most other tribes; and this would be natural selection. (1871, p. 166)

For a gene to survive in subsequent generations, the individual carrying the gene must not only survive, but his or her children must survive to reproduce as well. Because of our long period of dependency in childhood, along with our rather puny fighting equipment in the form of teeth or claws, we humans are especially in need of our social structures for survival. To the extent that genes build structures consistent with social tendencies, they are more likely to survive into future generations.

Genghis Khan may have been the most prolific human male in history. His distinctive Y chromosome has been identified in 16 million living men, or 0.5% of the world's current total.

Sexual Selection

Sexual selection was Darwin's term for the development of traits that help an individual compete for mates (Darwin, 1871). To what extent is human behavior influenced by sexual selection?

Parental Investment Sexual selection is influenced by the different investments in parenting made by males and females (Emlen & Oring, 1977). In many species, including our own, the female bears the majority of the costs of reproduction, from the carrying of the developing organism until birth to the nurturance of the young until adulthood. As a result, human females face much sharper limitations than human males on the number of children they can produce in a lifetime. If the goal is to pass your genes along to subsequent generations, and you are only going to produce one or two children, each child had better be as healthy and well nurtured as possible. The average number of children per woman worldwide dropped dramatically between 1950 and 2005 (United Nations, 2009). Between 1950 and 1955, the number of children per woman was 3.45 in the United States, 5.91 in India, and 6.11 in China. Between 2000 and 2005, those numbers dropped to 2.04, 3.11, and 1.77, respectively (see • Figure 3.14). In contrast, Genghis Khan may have been the most prolific human male in history. His distinctive Y chromosome has been identified in 16 million living men, or 0.5% of the world's current total (Zerjal et al., 2003).

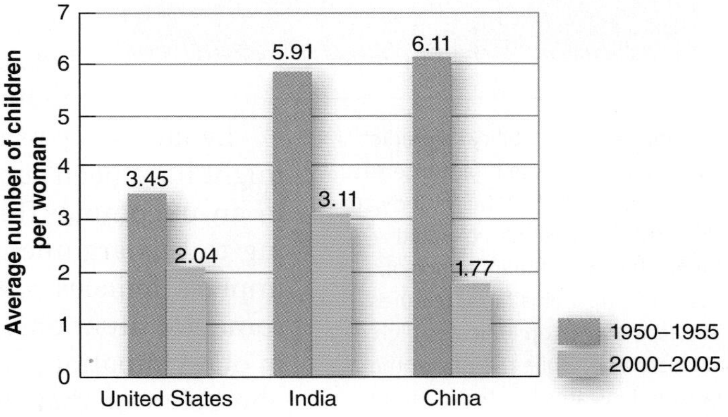

Although Genghis Khan's success in passing his genes to future generations may suggest that the best reproductive strategy for males would be promiscuity, this is not usually the case. In species such as our own, with lengthy and complex development leading to adulthood, a

FIGURE 3.14

The Human Birthrate Is Dropping Rapidly. The average number of children per woman worldwide dropped dramatically between 1950 and 2005. *Source:* Adapted from United Nations (2009, June).

sexual selection The development of traits that help an individual compete for mates.

male that abandons his offspring puts their survival at risk (Gibson, 2008). Even if a man fathers many children, his genes are less likely to make it into the next generation if most or all perish from lack of care.

The mother can maximize her children's chances of survival by choosing a father who will not only pass along healthy genes but will participate in the raising of children. Women have the ability to make very accurate predictions of a man's interest in children, simply by looking at a photograph of his face (Roney, Hanson, Durante, & Maestripieri, 2006). Men with facial features correlated with high testosterone (strong brow ridge, square chin—the Arnold Schwarzenegger look) are viewed as less likely to participate in childrearing than are men with facial features correlated with lower testosterone (a Tom Hanks or Leonardo DiCaprio look). These results suggest that women would be able to determine a man's potential as a father before any reproductive investment occurs.

Traits Possibly Influenced by Sexual Selection Earlier in this chapter, we discussed how blonde hair might have provided a reproductive advantage, because its relative novelty made it an attractive feature. What other types of human traits appear to fit Darwin's ideas about sexual selection?

Sexual selection might occur in two ways. In intrasexual selection (*intra* means "within"), members of one sex compete with each other for access to the other sex. In some species, such as deer, males engage in fights that determine which males are able to mate and which are not. Features like large antlers that assist in winning a fight could become sexually selected. In intersexual selection (*inter* means "between"), characteristics of one sex that attract the other might become sexually selected.

Evolutionary psychologists have argued that a number of human traits might have been subjected to sexual selection, including humor (discussed in an upcoming Thinking Scientifically feature) and vocabulary. According to this argument, human males use humor and their vocabularies to impress females with their intelligence due to intersexual selection. In romantic situations, males use more uncommon, fancy words than they do in other situations (Rosenberg & Tunney, 2008). We can also tell you about one behavior that does *not* successfully attract females—taking unnecessary risks (Wilke, Hutchinson, Todd, & Kruger, 2006). However, risky activities might have more positive outcomes for competition between males than for attracting females.

Detail from F. Moore et al. Figure 1, "Composite male faces constructed to differ in levels of T and C, from the article "Evidence for the stress-linked immunocompetence handicap hypothesis in human male faces," *Proc. R. Soc. B*, March 7, 2011, © The Royal Society 2011.

Women show the ability to predict a man's score on the Infant Interest Questionnaire, which might indicate how involved a father he would be, by detecting the influence of testosterone on his facial features. The face at the top indicates high testosterone, while the one at the bottom indicates low testosterone.

culture Practices, values, and goals shared by groups of people.

Culture Not only are human societies directly influenced by our biological history, but they also bear the stamp of the inventions of the biological brain in the form of **culture**. Cultures provide practices, values, and goals that can be shared by groups of people. Human cultures arise from knowledge that is transmitted socially. Languages, morality, arts, laws, and customs make up a diverse and vibrant part of human social interactions.

Experiences shaped by culture, like other types of experience, interact with survival and reproductive pressures. How might cultural differences have impacted our ancestors' survival? We can gain insight into our species' cultural history by observing contemporary preagricultural societies, such as the Waorani and Yanomamö of the Amazonian Basin. These groups are remarkably warlike. Fights between villages account for 30% of the deaths among Yanomamö males (Chagnon, 1988) and 54% of deaths among Waorani males (Beckerman et al., 2009). These observations suggest that aggression was probably an important part of our ancient past, but we cannot assume this behavior is strictly biological. Instead, cultural traditions in the two groups have led to very different patterns of reproductive success. Aggressive Yanomamö men produce more children than less aggressive Yanomamö, but less aggressive Waorani men have more surviving offspring than aggressive Waorani (Beckerman et al., 2009). A simple cultural distinction—the Yanomamö practice of standing down between raids, which was not a practice shared by the Waorani—appears to account for the differences observed in the impact of aggression on reproductive success.

Our social minds were shaped by the cultures of hunter-gatherer groups until the development of agriculture approximately 10,000 years ago. With improved control of the food supply, less geographical mobility, and larger communities, human beings entered a new era of social interaction. Although we believe that many features found in modern human behavior, such as reciprocal altruism, originated in the hunter-gatherer society, further social adjustments were required as groups became larger and more complex.

The Waorani (left) and Yanomamö (right) of the Amazon basin share very high rates of aggression, yet experience different reproductive outcomes. Reproductive success is higher among the most aggressive Yanomamö and the least aggressive Waorani. A simple cultural distinction—the Yanomamö practice of standing down between raids, which was not a practice shared by the Waorani—appears to account for the differences observed in the impact of aggression on reproductive success.

Agriculture, with its emphasis on land ownership, might have been the origin of patriarchal systems, in which men maintain control of resources, and inheritances follow the male line. Unlike hunter-gatherer societies, which are relatively egalitarian as far as the rights of men and women go, agricultural societies tilted the control of food and important resources in favor of men. Early industrialization merely built upon agricultural systems and, if possible, accentuated the power differential between males and females. More contemporary trends are once again moving in a more egalitarian direction, with women in industrialized countries enjoying considerable financial independence and reproductive choice. These changes will no doubt have further effects on our social environment.

As societies became larger, human beings took advantage of their large brains to devise new cultural systems to maintain group cohesion. Emerging societies shared many of the same types of internal conflict, so we typically find similar moral, religious, and legal systems across diverse cultures that attempt to control marriage, "character" issues such as honesty, and the transfer of precious resources.

The changes that accompanied the move from hunter-gatherer to farmer shaped human culture.

Thinking
Scientifically

The Sexual Selection of Humor

How often have you found yourself roaring with laughter at something the people around you don't find remotely funny? What roles does sexual selection play in a person's sense of humor?

When pairs of female identical or fraternal twins rated various cartoons by Gary Larson (*The Far Side*) on a scale of 0 (a dud) to 10 (the funniest thing you have ever seen), the degree of the women's genetic relatedness did not predict their reaction to the cartoons (Cherkas, Hochberg, MacGregor, Snieder, & Spector, 2000). Unlike many studies that show

greater similarities between identical than fraternal twins, agreement about what is funny was just as likely among the fraternal twins as among the identical twins. According to the researchers, environmental influences, such as peer attitudes and exposure to "Dad's humor," may have dominated the development of each woman's sense of humor.

Although the twins did not show a strong influence of nature in their preferences for humor, this finding does not mean that a sense of humor is purely a result of environmental factors. Significant evidence

points to a very important role for humor in human mate selection. When men and women describe an "ideal date," both sexes indicate that a sense of humor is an important feature, but there is a significant difference in what they mean by that term (Bressler & Balshine, 2006). Men were interested in women who appreciated, rather than produced, humor, while women were interested in men who made them laugh. Women appear to signal their interest in a man by laughing frequently, whereas the frequency of men's

With all the flaws of our groups, whether we're looking at families, communities, or nations, we retain a strong need to belong. As we will see on many occasions in this textbook, human beings do not thrive in isolation. Our dependence on kinship, friendship, and group membership, honed over the course of 100,000 years or more of social living, continues to influence our behavior today.

Human beings have developed a strong need to belong, and develop traditions that enhance a sense of group membership.

laughter appears to be unrelated to their judgment of a woman's attractiveness. Further support for humor's role in mate selection comes from the observation that men and women do not seem to care as much about a sense of humor when selecting a friend as opposed to a lover.

What advantages might a good sense of humor provide that could make it a subject of sexual selection? Producing a good joke requires sophisticated cognitive skills, creativity, and the ability to see situations from more than one point of view, qualities that signal the good intellectual and social functioning preferred by females. ✿

According to evolutionary psychologists, humor might be used by humans to attract mates, because humor indicates intelligence.

Summary 3.3

Evolutionary Influences on Behavior

Concept	Definition	Example
Cooperation © Kim Hill/ Arizona State University	Working together to benefit all parties involved	Hunters working together to kill an animal that individual hunters could not kill on their own
Altruism © Gherasim Rares/Shutterstock	Sacrificing yourself to save another	A young mother threw herself over her infant during a parking lot shootout. She died, but the infant survived.
Reciprocal altruism	Sacrificing when you expect the recipient might do the same for you at some future time	Sharing food with a hungry person thinking that someone might share with you later on
Sexual selection Moore et al. (2011). © The Royal Society 2011.	The evolutionary pressure on traits that help individuals find mates	Women may choose men whose facial appearance is correlated with being a good father.

Interpersonal Relationships
From an Evolutionary Perspective

This chapter emphasized how the human mind has been shaped by its history. Because of the critical role our social behavior played in our species' survival over many thousands of years, it should come as no surprise that the evolutionary perspective has so much to say about important human relationships. However, in its functionality, this evolutionary approach is rarely very romantic.

In our chapter on social psychology, we will argue that "birds of a feather" really do flock together, in that perceived similarities are important to many relationships. We like to believe that our choice of mate is based on factors like physical attractiveness and mutual interests and values. The evolutionary approach, however, suggests that another type of compatibility is important for romantic relationships—a compatibility of genes that contribute to the immune system.

A cluster of genes known as the major histocompatibility complex (MHC) appears to be subject to sexual selection (Wedekind & Füri, 1997). As described in this chapter, this type of sexual selection operates on traits in one sex that influence the choices by the other. A child with a heterozygous set of MHC genes is better prepared to battle infections than is a child with MHC genes that are similar to one another. As a result, our children are more likely to survive if we select a mate that has a different set of MHC genes than we do.

Short of asking potential mates to undergo DNA testing, how are we supposed to accomplish this? Apparently, we do have a method that might have directed the mating choices of our ancestors. Different configurations of the MHC genes produce distinctive body odors that are easily detected and distinguished from one another. When men and women were asked to rate the pleasantness of the odors of T-shirts that had been worn by two women and four men, they preferred smells associated with MHC genotypes that were different from their own. Participants noted that the more "pleasant-smelling" T-shirts often reminded them of an ex. Gender did not play a role—smell preference was not influenced by whether the T-shirt wearer had been of the same or the opposite sex as the perceiver.

We do not want to suggest that this MHC gene cluster is the primary criterion we use for choosing partners, but it does remind us that some of our behavioral tendencies have deep roots in our species' history.

© Shunyu Fan/iStockphoto; © Kathy Puckett/iStockphoto

Although "birds of a feather" usually do "flock together" in human relationships, finding a person with different immune system genes is beneficial for reproductive success.

© Argosy Publishing, Inc.

Chapter 3
Reflections

This chapter began with a story about mice with different fur color and weight, which you might not have expected to see in a textbook about psychology. We hope that this story, and others like it in this chapter, emphasized the need to look at the actions of nature and nurture as inseparable, intertwined influences on the human mind.

Although we discussed the nuts and bolts of the biological influences shaping our mind throughout its history, at no time did we argue that these physical forces act alone. The developmental perspective of psychology reminds us about the immaturity of the newborn human, requiring the long period of nurture that helped shape interactions between men and women. In understanding how nurture can impact nature, we can more clearly see why even identical twins become less alike over the course of their lifespan.

With the help of social psychology and the evolutionary perspective, we gain a greater understanding of ourselves not as "rugged individualists" but, rather, as individuals bound to one another for our very survival as a species. The notion of altruism, of helping others, operates on both the genetic and social levels. We see that the mere action of "helping" can only be fully understood through learning more about how nature and nurture interact.

The mere prospect of going on a date, and whom we choose to date, has deep roots in this nature-nurture relationship as well. Greater knowledge of sexual selection tendencies of males and females might help to explain why you are (or are not) attracted to those around you, or why you sometimes get stuck in the "friend zone"—that unpleasant place where you are viewed as a friend but want to be more. Mysteries like the friend zone may be unraveled with a closer look at how specific facial features, humor, body odor, or the words we use influence such personal relations.

Viewing nature and nurture as interacting influences on our behavior reassures us that we are not somehow helpless captives of our genes. They are certainly an important part of who we are, but our choices and experiences make major contributions to the final product as well. ◄

KEY TERMS The Language of Psychological Science

Be sure you can define these terms and use them correctly.

adaptation, p. 107
allele, p. 93
altruism, p. 113
behavioral genetics, p. 99
culture, p. 116
dominance, p. 93
epigenetics, p. 98
evolution, p. 105
evolutionary psychology, p. 112

fitness, p. 107
gene, p. 92
gene expression, p. 92
genetic drift, p. 106
genotype, p. 92
heritability, p. 99
heterozygous, p. 93
homozygous, p. 93
migration, p. 106

mutation, p. 106
natural selection, p. 105
nature, p. 89
nurture, p. 89
phenotype, p. 92
recessiveness, p. 93
reciprocal altruism, p. 114
relatedness, p. 95
sexual selection, p. 115

MEDIA RESOURCES

Log in to CengageBrain to access the resources your instructor requires. For this book, you can access:

Psychology **CourseMate** brings course concepts to life with interactive learning, study, and exam preparation tools that support the printed textbook. A textbook-specific website, Psychology **CourseMate** includes an integrated interactive eBook and other interactive learning tools including quizzes, flashcards, videos, and more.

Web**TUTOR** More than just an interactive study guide, **WebTutor** is an anytime, anywhere customized learning solution with an eBook, keeping you connected to your textbook, instructor, and classmates.

aplia If your professor has assigned **Aplia** homework:
1. Sign in to your account.
2. Complete the corresponding homework exercises as required by your professor.
3. When finished, click "Grade It Now" to see which areas you have mastered, which areas need more work, and detailed explanations of every answer.

Perceived social isolation or connectedness can produce changes in the cells of our immune system.

The Biological Mind

The Physical Basis of Behavior

Learning Objectives

1 Debate the strengths and limitations of biological psychology as a major psychological perspective, considering the roles of monism, reductionism, and reciprocity between biology and experience.

2 Analyze the implications of advances in methods used to study the brain for our understanding of biological psychology.

3 Explain what it means for a neuron to "fire" an action potential, describing how the neuron's structure makes this possible.

4 Explain the process by which neurons communicate with each other, allowing the nervous system to integrate complex information.

5 Differentiate the roles played by major neurotransmitters in supporting physical functioning and psychological experience.

6 Differentiate the major branches of the nervous system, explaining the core biological function of each branch.

7 Associate key structures in, and regions of, the brain with important aspects of physical and psychological functioning.

8 Explain the process by which hormones influence psychological experience and behavior, differentiating this process from neurotransmission.

Throughout history, human survival has been threatened by the various bacteria and viruses that try to make us their home. The bacteria-driven Black Death decimated Europe between 1346 and 1400, killing an estimated 30 to 60% of the population (Austin Alchon, 2003). Smallpox, measles, and influenza carried by Europeans to the Western Hemisphere killed as many as 90% of the native populations (PBS, 2005). The "Spanish flu" of 1918, which is related to contemporary bird flu strains, killed between 50 and 100 million people worldwide in a period of about one year (Patterson & Pyle, 1991).

We have not been passive bystanders to this devastation. Even though pandemics like the Black Death have caused remarkable destruction, none has killed the entire human population. The survivors often possess some natural, protective resistance to infection, which might then be passed along to their descendants. In some cases, resistance to one type of organism offers protection from completely new organisms. Researchers studying the HIV virus, which causes AIDS, discovered that some people seemed unusually resistant to the virus due to a particular genetic mutation. The mutation is common among northern Europeans, relatively rare in southern Europeans, and completely absent among Asians, Africans, and Native Americans. Some researchers believed surviving the bacterial infection of the Black Death was related to the frequency of the mutation, while others point to surviving smallpox instead (Galvani & Slatkin, 2003).

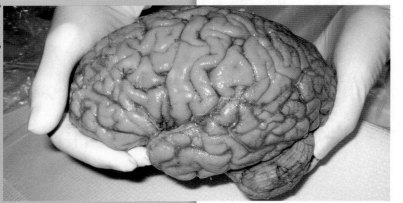

Human brains like this one, carefully held by one of your authors, weigh about three pounds and contain approximately 100 billion neurons. That's about the same number as the stars in our galaxy, the Milky Way.

The discussion so far might sound more like biology or medicine than psychology, but behavior and mental processes have a considerable amount of influence on our abilities to fight bacteria and viruses (Cacioppo & Berntson, 2011). Once again, zooming out to the human social environment and zooming back in again to a much smaller scale gives us a complete and interesting picture.

Human beings, who lack impressive teeth or claws, formed groups to enhance the odds of their survival. Anyone who was socially excluded from these groups experienced a more hostile environment. Social exclusion not only separated a person from the help of others in life-threatening situations, perhaps in fending off a predator, but worse, could lead to outright conflict with others, including combat. Under such hostile circumstances, socially excluded people faced a greater risk from bacterial infections than from viruses. Bacteria enter the body through cuts and scratches, whereas viruses are transmitted through body fluids (e.g., sneezing), so you are most likely to be exposed to them when you are in close contact with other people.

With that background in mind, take a look at the group of people in the image on the preceding page. Do you think the woman on the left is feeling included or excluded? Surprisingly, whether we typically feel socially isolated or socially connected can have serious implications for our health (Cole, Hawkley, Arevalo, & Cacioppo, 2011). If this woman normally feels isolated and often left to fend for herself, she will, like her excluded ancestors, face a greater threat from bacteria than from viruses. In that case, her brain will generate hormonal signals that will tell her immune system (shown in the larger image) to gear up to protect her against bacteria.

In contrast, if she usually feels socially connected to others, her brain will initiate a cascade of hormonal signals that tell her immune cells to prepare to protect her against viruses. This is just one example of how the mind's perceptions of the social environment—whether it is friendly or not, for instance—can impact biological processes that are important to health and survival.

In the previous chapter on nature and nurture, we learned how the challenges of surviving and reproducing in particular physical and social environments could shape a species' biology and behavior. In turn, the resulting biological structures and processes of the mind exert profound influences on our physical and social environments. In this chapter, we will provide a foundation for understanding the biological bases of behavior and mental processes by exploring the structures of the nervous system and the ways that they function. ✪

What Is Biological Psychology?

Many of us find the concept that our "minds" are somehow a result of the activity of nerve cells a bit unsettling. How could our feelings, thoughts, and memories be caused by a bunch of cells? Shouldn't there be more to who I am than something so physical? Such ideas led thinkers like René Descartes to propose a philosophy of dualism, which suggests that "mind" is somehow different and separate from our physical being. If you are more comfortable with thinking about mind this way, go right ahead, as long as you recognize that the field of biological psychology, and the neurosciences in general, embraces the competing philosophy of monism. According to the monistic approach, the mind is what the brain does.

© Dimitri Iundt/TempSport/Corbis

Not only does biology influence behavior, but behavior (thinking about winning and losing in this case) affects biology. Players and even the fans of a winning team experience a temporary increase in testosterone, while the players and fans of the losing team experience a temporary decrease in testosterone.

Biological psychology is a rich, interdisciplinary field of study that combines the methods and theories of psychology with those of biology, physiology, biochemistry, the neurosciences, and other related fields. While investigating a particular behavior, the biological psychologist focuses on links between observed behavior and genetic factors, biochemical factors, and the activity level and structural characteristics of the nervous system. These links do not travel in one direction only, from biological factors to behavior, but are more accurately viewed as reciprocal. For example, we know that if you administer extra testosterone to human males, raising their testosterone to above normal levels, they are likely to behave more aggressively (Pope, Kouri, & Hudson, 2000). In this case, biology (raising testosterone levels) is influencing behavior (aggression). However, we also know that watching his favorite sports team lose lowers a man's testosterone levels (Bernhardt, Dabbs, Fielden, & Lutter, 1998). Here we see the influence of behavior (supporting a particular team and watching the team lose) on biology (testosterone levels).

Early Attempts to Understand Biological Psychology

Advances in the methods we use to observe the structure and function of the nervous system have driven the history of biological psychology. The discovery of contemporary methods, such as the recording and imaging of brain activity, opened whole new areas of inquiry to biological psychologists. Before these methods were available, however, most of our knowledge of the nervous system

biological psychology The interdisciplinary field of study that combines the methods and theories of psychology with those of biology, physiology, biochemistry, the neurosciences, and other related fields.

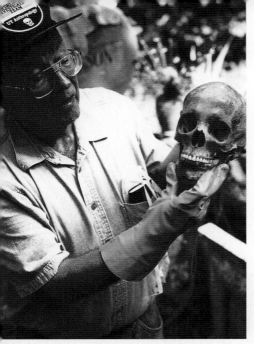

resulted from clinical observations of injured or mentally ill individuals or autopsy, the examination of bodies after death. When used together with contemporary methods, clinical observation and autopsy are quite accurate, but early thinkers lacking contemporary methods often struggled in their attempts to understand the physical basis of mind. They understood many things correctly while making some notable errors. Aristotle, who was accurate on many issues, mistakenly believed that the heart, not the brain, was the source of mental activity.

An interesting historical mistake was phrenology. Toward the end of the 18th century, phrenologists proposed that the pattern of bumps on an individual's skull correlated with his or her personality traits and abilities

Autopsy has been used since 3000 BCE, and it remains a useful source of information, especially in forensics. Dr. Bill Bass, a forensic anthropologist, studies donated bodies as they decompose at the "Body Farm" at the University of Tennessee, Knoxville. The knowledge gained from these investigations makes it possible to determine time of death at crime scenes.

Photo © Jon Jefferson; courtesy of JeffersonBass.com

Thinking Scientifically

When Does Reductionism Work?
When Does It Fail?

Reductionism in science is defined as the explanation of complex things as sums of simpler things. Taking a rather extreme reductionist approach, science fiction often features scenes in which an android reminds a human that they're really not so different after all—the brain is just a computer made up of chemicals, nothing more, nothing less.

In some ways, all modern science is reductionist. Scientists assume that whether you are studying particle physics or human behavior, a single set of fundamental laws explains much of what we observe. We do not need new sets of rules for the features of table salt (sodium chloride) in each context in which it appears. Regardless of whether the chemical

is participating in neural signaling, flavoring our food, contributing to high blood pressure, or making us float more easily when we swim in the ocean, the fundamental principle is the same: salt is salt.

The scientific search for fundamental principles has been fruitful, to say the least, but it does have limitations. Although we can learn a lot by breaking apart complex things to study simple things, we saw some of the risks to this approach in the debates between the structuralists and Gestalt psychologists. Fish swim in schools, geese and ducks fly in a V-formation, ants and bees swarm, cattle form herds, and human beings form societies. We could never understand these more complex phenomena by studying the behav-

ior of an individual member of the group. Nobel laureate physicist P. W. Anderson reminded scientists that large collections of simple things do not always behave the same way that simple things behave in isolation. He wrote that "at each stage (of complexity) entirely new laws, concepts, and generalizations are necessary, requiring inspiration and creativity to just as great a degree as in the previous one. Psychology is not applied biology, nor is biology applied chemistry" (Anderson, 1972, p. 393).

This chapter on the biological foundations of behavior and mental processes relies extensively on reductionist thinking. As you work through the chapter, however, it is important to keep Anderson's cautions in mind. We will begin by analyzing the mind

Phrenologists believed that "reading" the bumps on a person's head, using a bust like this as a reference, could tell them about a person's character.

© Terry Why/Phototake

(Simpson, 2005). The brain supposedly worked like a muscle, getting larger through use, leading frequently used areas of the brain to grow so much that the skull above these areas would bulge. Phrenologists "read" a person's character by locating the bumps on a person's head and identifying the personality traits below each bump according to a map. None of these ideas, of course, was close to being accurate.

Phrenology was especially popular in the United States during the latter half of the 19th century, with employers asking prospective employees to undergo phrenological exams, young lovers seeking exams to ensure compatibility, and even presidential candidates submitting to exams (Stern, 1971). Although the phrenologists were wrong about the significance of bumps on the skull and the effects of activity on the structure of the brain, they did reach one correct conclusion. Their notion that some behavioral functions are localized to certain areas of the brain is one we share today.

at the cellular level by examining nerve cells and their activity. Then our view zooms out from cells to the larger structures of the brain and spinal cord to circuits to systems to beyond the body itself with social interactions among other systems (i.e., other people). As we embark on this journey, it's important for you to remember that some aspects of behavior will continue to be governed by rules that explain the actions of simple things, while others will require the introduction of new rules better suited to more complex combinations and interactions of simple things. ✪

© Fabio Fersa/Shutterstock

Viewing a complex concept as a sum of its simpler parts is not always the best way to understand its full meaning.

© nito/Shutterstock

WHAT IS BIOLOGICAL PSYCHOLOGY?

Contemporary Approaches in Biological Psychology

More modern perspectives of the nervous system emerged from the work of scientists like 19th-century neurologist John Hughlings Jackson (1835–1911). Based on observations of his patients with seizure disorders, Jackson proposed that the nervous system is organized as a hierarchy, with progressively more complicated behaviors being managed by more recently evolved and complex structures (Jackson, 1884).

We can see Jackson's hierarchy at work when we observe people drinking alcohol. Alcohol specifically decreases the activity of parts of the brain involved with judgment and decision making. When a person has had too much to drink, the more complex social controls (such as knowing how close you should stand to a stranger) normally provided by higher level areas of the brain are diminished. Without the influence of these controls, people start doing things that they would not typically do while sober. This change in behavior reflects the now unrestrained influence of the more primitive parts of the brain involved with behaviors such as aggression and sexuality. You might, for example, pick a fight with someone when you normally think fighting is wrong. The aggression and sexuality were there all along, but the normal activity of the higher levels of the nervous system usually restricted their expression to more appropriate circumstances (Siever, 2008).

TABLE
4.1 Research Methods in Biological Psychology

Research method	Description	What questions can we answer?
Skin conductance response (SCR; formerly known as galvanic skin response)	Measurement of electricity passed between two surface electrodes placed on the skin of the hand or finger	What is a person's state of arousal?
Electroencephalogram (EEG)	Measurement of the brain's electrical activity using electrodes placed on the scalp	What is a person's state of arousal?
Evoked potential	Measurement formed by averaging EEG responses to a stimulus, such as a light or tone	Did the person perceive the stimulus?
Single cell recording	Measurement of a single neuron's activity obtained through a surgically implanted electrode	What types of stimulation make this neuron respond?
Magnetoencephalography (MEG)	Recording of the tiny amounts of magnetic output of the brain	What parts of the brain react to this stimulus?
Positron emission tomography (PET)	Uses the accumulation of radioactively tagged glucose or oxygen to identify activity levels in parts of the brain	What parts of the brain are active during a particular task?
Functional magnetic resonance imaging (fMRI)	Identification of active parts of the brain using magnetism to track the flow of oxygen	What parts of the brain are active during a particular task?
Electrical stimulation	Application of small amounts of electricity through a surgically implanted electrode	What behaviors occur if we stimulate this part of the brain?
Transcranial magnetic stimulation	Application of magnetic fields to the brain through an instrument held near the scalp	What behavioral changes occur when magnetism is applied to the brain?
Lesions	Naturally occurring or deliberate damage to the brain	What behavioral changes are correlated with brain damage?

The 20th century saw a burst of knowledge about the nervous system, culminating in the 1990s being designated by the U.S. Congress as the Decade of the Brain. Our understanding of the correlations between brain and behavior leaped forward with continuing improvements in research methods, including many of those found in Table 4.1. In particular, methods that allow scientists to observe the activity of the living brain, including positron emission tomography (PET) and functional magnetic resonance imaging (fMRI), began to answer questions that were impossible to study previously.

Because of these improved methods, today we can talk about how the brain responds differently to images of faces and places (Downing, Chan, Peelen, Dodds, & Kanwisher, 2006), "feels" the pain of social exclusion (Eisenberger, Lieberman, & Williams, 2003; Eisenberger, 2011), and develops abnormally in teens diagnosed with schizophrenia (Thompson et al., 2001), which we discuss in a later chapter on psychological disorders. Moving into the 21st century, the ranks of neuroscientists continue to grow, from 500 members of the Society for Neuroscience in 1969 to more than 40,000 members today (Society for Neuroscience, 2011).

How Do Neurons Communicate?

We begin our exploration of the nervous system by zooming in to see its microscopic building blocks, the nerve cells, or **neurons**. Human brains have about 100 billion neurons. To put this number in perspective, consider the following. If a neuron represented a second, ticking off the neurons in your body alone would take more than 3,170 years! With each neuron forming an average of several thousand connections with other neurons, the connections in the human brain number in the hundreds of trillions. In addition to these large numbers of neurons, the nervous system also contains many supporting cells, known as glia.

Once we are familiar with the structure of neurons and glia, we will turn our attention to the way neurons communicate with one another. Neural communication is a two-step process. The first step takes place within a single neuron and involves the generation of an electrical signal. The second step takes place between two neurons and involves the release of a chemical messenger from one neuron that impacts the activity of the second.

Neurons and Glia

Neurons share many characteristics with other cells found in the body. Like other cells, a neuron has a large central mass, or **cell body**, and within the cell body, a nucleus (see ● Figure 4.1). Most of the typical housekeeping tasks of the cell, such as the translation of genetic codes into the manufacture of proteins, take place in the cell body. Like other cells, neurons feature an outer membrane, which surrounds the neuron and forms a barrier between the fluid outside the cell—the extracellular fluid—and inside the cell—the intracellular fluid. The neural membrane is composed of fatty materials that do not dissolve in water, so even though it is only two molecules thick, it is able to hold the water-based fluids on either side apart. Pores within the membrane act as channels that allow chemicals to move into or out of the cell across the membrane.

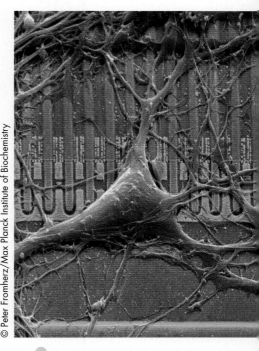

© Peter Fromherz/Max Planck Institute of Biochemistry

This neuron has been grown on a silicon chip, a line of research that might lead to better treatment for people with amputated limbs. Prosthetic devices, like an artificial leg or hand, could possibly communicate directly with the person's nervous system.

neuron A cell of the nervous system that is specialized for sending and receiving neural messages.

cell body The large, central mass of a neuron, containing the nucleus.

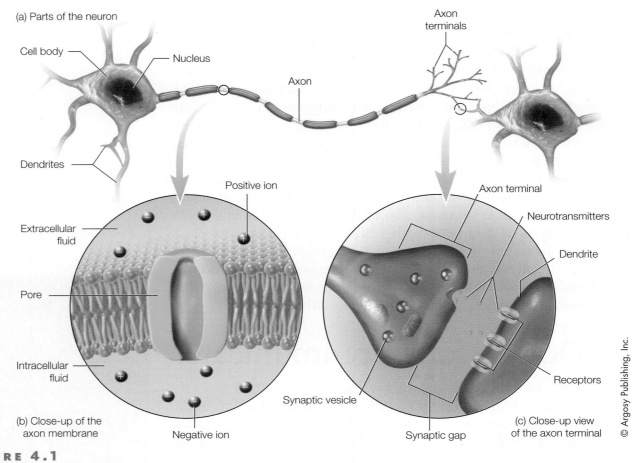

(a) Parts of the neuron

Cell body

Nucleus

Axon terminals

Axon

Dendrites

Positive ion

Extracellular fluid

Pore

Intracellular fluid

(b) Close-up of the axon membrane

Negative ion

Axon terminal

Neurotransmitters

Dendrite

Synaptic vesicle

Receptors

Synaptic gap

(c) Close-up view of the axon terminal

© Argosy Publishing, Inc.

FIGURE 4.1

The Neuron. Neurons share many features with other living cells, but are specialized for the processing of information. **(a) Parts of the Neuron.** Like other types of animal cells, the neuron features a nucleus in its cell body and a fatty membrane that separates the intracellular and extracellular fluids. Unlike most other cells, the neuron has specialized branches, the axon and dendrites, that pass information to and receive information from other cells. **(b) A Close-Up View of the Axon Membrane.** A thin oily membrane separates the intracellular fluid inside the neuron from the extracellular fluid outside the neuron. Pores span the membrane that act as channels, which allow ions to move in or out of the neuron. **(c) A Close-Up View of the Axon Terminal.** Within the axon terminal are synaptic vesicles, which contain chemical messengers called neurotransmitters that transmit signals between neurons. Later in the chapter, we'll see how these neurotransmitters communicate with receptors on the dendrites of other neurons.

axon The branch of a neuron that is usually responsible for transmitting information to other neurons.

dendrite A branch from the neural cell body that usually receives input from other neurons.

Unlike many other types of body cells, neurons have two types of branches that extend from the cell body to allow the neuron to perform its information-processing and communication functions. The branches known as **axons** are responsible for carrying information to other neurons, while the branches known as **dendrites** receive input from other neurons. Although neurons may have many dendrites, they typically have only one axon.

Many axons communicate with immediately adjacent cells and are therefore only small fractions of a millimeter in length, but other axons are quite a bit longer. When you stub your big toe on a rock, the neurons that process this information have cell bodies in your lower back and axons that extend all the way down to your sore toe, a distance of around three feet, depending on your height. At its farthest point from the cell body, an axon bulges to form a terminal. If you look inside an axon terminal with an electron microscope, you can see round, hollow spheres, known as synaptic vesicles, which contain molecules of chemical messengers.

You have probably heard the terms *gray matter* and *white matter* used to describe the brain, but you might not have understood exactly what these terms mean. Now that you understand the structure of neurons, the terms will make more sense. Live neural tissue looks rather pink. When we prepare neural tissue for study using microscopes, the chemicals used to preserve the tissue are absorbed by cell bodies, giving them a pink-gray coloring. In contrast, these chemicals are repelled by the insulating material covering most axons because the insulation has a fatty composition that doesn't mix well with the watery preservatives (we discuss the nature of this insulation shortly). As a result, axons look white, like the fat in a steak. When we examine images of the brain, areas that look gray have a high density of cell bodies, whereas areas that look white consist of large bundles of axons.

If neurons are the stars of the nervous system team, glia are the trainers, coaches, and scorekeepers. They make it possible for the neurons to do their job effectively. Some glia (from the Greek word for "glue") provide a structural matrix for neurons, ensuring that the neurons stay in place (● Figure 4.2). Other glia are mobile, allowing them to move to a location where neurons have been damaged to clean up any debris. Glia form tight connections with the blood vessels serving the nervous system. This forms a blood-brain barrier that prevents many toxins circulating in the blood from exiting into brain tissue where neurons could be harmed. Psychoactive drugs, by definition, are substances capable of penetrating the blood-brain barrier with ease. We discuss psychoactive drugs and the ways in which they act on the nervous system in our chapter on consciousness.

In vertebrates like us, glia wrap around some axons like sausages on strings at a delicatessen, forming an important layer of insulation called **myelin**. Myelin makes neural signaling fast and energy efficient. We will discuss how myelin accomplishes this in a later section on neural signaling. Not all axons in the human nervous system are myelinated. When you hurt yourself, that fast, sharp "ouch" message is

Blood vessel
Neuron
Glia

© Argosy Publishing, Inc.

FIGURE 4.2

The Blood-Brain Barrier. Glia form tight connections with the blood vessels in the nervous system, preventing many toxins from entering the brain. Glia also help hold neurons in place and form the myelin on some axons.

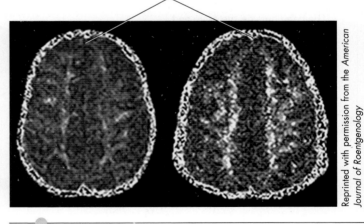

Frontal lobes

The image on the left shows myelin (in white) in the brain of a 2-year-old child. The image on the right shows the much greater amount of myelin in the brain of an 18-year-old. Myelination of the human brain is not complete until a person is in his or her early to mid-20s. The last areas to be completely myelinated are the frontal lobes, which are involved in self-regulation, decision making, and judgment.

myelin The insulating material covering some axons.

carried to the brain by myelinated axons, but the dull, achy message that lasts a lot longer is carried by unmyelinated axons.

One type of glia forms the myelin in the brain and spinal cord and a second type forms the myelin in the remainder of the nervous system (see ● Figure 4.3). These two types of glia behave quite differently from each other when they are damaged. Glia in the brain and spinal cord form scar tissue, inhibiting repair to the damaged nerves. Because of this feature, we consider damage in these parts of the nervous system to be permanent. Obviously, considerable research is under way to figure out how to repair such damage, including work using stem cells to grow bridges across the damaged areas. In contrast, damaged glia in areas of the nervous system outside the brain and spinal cord do not form scar tissue and actually help the damaged axons regrow. As a result, nerve damage in these areas can heal. If this were not so, operations to reattach limbs would be doomed to failure. Nowadays, not only are digits and even limbs that were lost in accidents routinely reattached to their rightful owners but a number of patients whose own hands or faces were damaged beyond repair have undergone successful transplants from cadavers (Clarke & Butler, 2009; Dubernard, Owen, Lanzetta, & Hakim, 2001).

As we explore further in our chapter on development, myelin growth in the human nervous system begins before birth, but it is not completed until early adulthood, possibly as late as the age of 25. The last area of the nervous system to be myelinated is the part of the brain located right behind your eyes, which is involved with judgment and morality (Hayak et al.,

The blood-brain barrier might offer too much protection to the brain in some cases. Many chemotherapy agents used to treat cancer in other parts of the body cannot penetrate the blood-brain barrier, which complicates the treatment of tumors in the brain.

FIGURE 4.3

Glia Form Myelin. One type of glia forms myelin in the brain and spinal cord, and a second type forms myelin in the rest of the nervous system. These types of glia respond differently to nerve damage, making nerve damage outside the brain and spinal cord easier to repair.

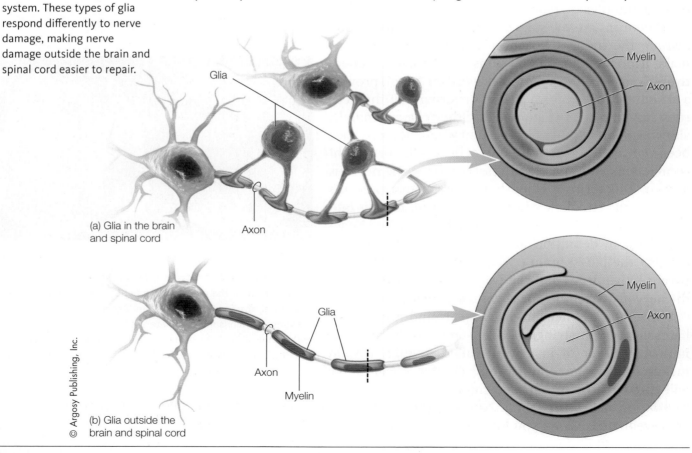

Glia

(a) Glia in the brain and spinal cord

Axon

Myelin

Axon

Axon

Glia

Myelin

Myelin

Axon

© Argosy Publishing, Inc.

(b) Glia outside the brain and spinal cord

2001). Until myelin in this area is mature, these neurons do not work as efficiently, which is one of the possible reasons why teenagers sometimes make different decisions than adults (Baird et al., 1999). You may recall some experiences from your early teens that appear shocking and overly risky to your adult brain. Worse yet, as you move through your 20s, you might find yourself agreeing more frequently with your parents.

© Kai Forsterling/epa/Corbis

Neural Signaling

Now that we have a working knowledge of the structure of neurons, we are ready to talk about how they function. A neuron is a sophisticated communication and information-processing system that receives input, evaluates it, and decides whether to transmit any information to neurons downstream. Its actions are similar to your own when you receive a juicy bit of gossip from a friend, and then decide whether or not to tell somebody else.

As we mentioned earlier, neural communication is a two-step process. In the first step, which takes place in the signaling neuron's axon, the neuron generates an electrical signal known as an **action potential**. This signal travels the length of the axon from its junction with the cell body to its terminal. In the second step, which takes place between two neurons, the arrival of an action potential at the axon terminal of the first neuron signals the release of chemical messengers, which float across the extracellular fluid separating the two neurons. These chemicals influence the likelihood that the second neuron will respond with its own action potential, sending the message along.

© Ivanova Inga/Shutterstock

Courtesy of USGS, Alaska Science Center. Photo by Mayumi Arimitsu.

Electrical Signaling The production of action potentials can be demonstrated using axons dissected from a squid and placed in a tub of seawater, which has a chemical composition similar to the fluid surrounding our body cells (Hodgkin & Huxley, 1952). Of all the possible sources of axons on earth, why choose squid? Axons from a squid can be as much as 1 mm in diameter, large enough to see with the naked eye. The squid axon is also large enough that you can insert a recording electrode into its interior without disrupting its function. The readings from inside the axon can then be compared with readings from a recording electrode placed in the seawater.

When a neuron is not processing information, we say that it is at rest. When a cell is at rest, the difference between the readings from the interior of the axon and the external fluid is known as the **resting potential**. Our recording will show that the interior of the neuron is negatively charged relative to its exterior.

Let's assume that our resting neuron now begins to receive chemical messages from another neuron, a process we discuss in more detail shortly. Neurons can respond to incoming chemical signals by becoming either depolarized or hyperpolarized. The word *polarized* means "far apart," as when political factions disagree. Being depolarized means we have moved

Squid axons are large enough to be seen with the naked eye and will remain active in a bath of seawater for hours. These features make studying neural activity in the squid axon relatively simple.

action potential The electrical signal arising in a neuron's axon.

resting potential The measure of the electrical charge across a neural membrane when the neuron is not processing information.

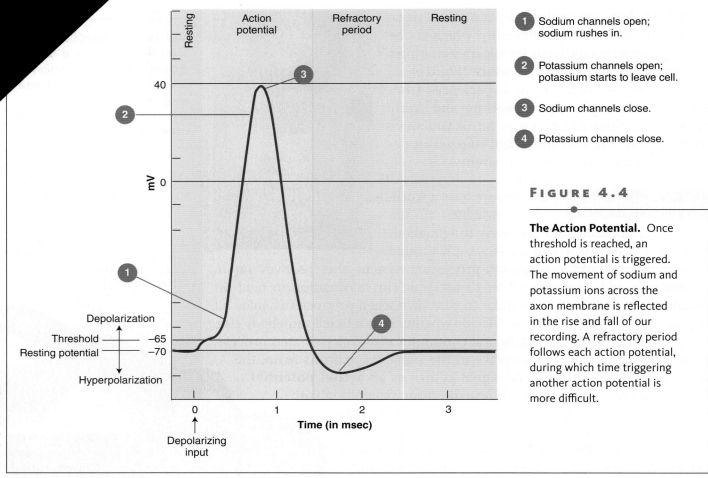

FIGURE 4.4

The Action Potential. Once threshold is reached, an action potential is triggered. The movement of sodium and potassium ions across the axon membrane is reflected in the rise and fall of our recording. A refractory period follows each action potential, during which time triggering another action potential is more difficult.

1 Sodium channels open; sodium rushes in.

2 Potassium channels open; potassium starts to leave cell.

3 Sodium channels close.

4 Potassium channels close.

closer together and being hyperpolarized means we have moved even farther apart than before. In the case of neurons, depolarization means that the difference between the electrical charges of the extracellular and the intracellular recordings is decreasing. Hyperpolarization means that the difference is increasing.

When a neuron is depolarized by sufficient input, it will reach a threshold for producing an action potential. A threshold is the point at which an effect, the action potential in this case, is initiated. Once this threshold is reached, the generation of an action potential is inevitable. Approaching the threshold of a neuron is similar to pulling the trigger of a gun. As you squeeze the trigger, nothing happens until you reach a critical point. Once that critical point is reached, the gun fires, and there is nothing you can do to stop it.

Reaching threshold initiates a sequence of events that reliably produces an action potential (● Figure 4.4). These events involve the opening and closing of pores, or channels, in the neural membrane, which in turn allows certain chemicals to move into or out of the cell. These chemicals are in the form of ions, or electrically charged particles dissolved in water. When threshold is reached, channels open allowing sodium ions to rush into the neuron. Because sodium ions carry a positive electrical charge, we can see their movement reflected in a steep rise in our recording of the difference between the internal and external electrodes. At the peak of the action potential, our recording has

I like nonsense; it wakes up the brain cells.

—Dr. Seuss

completely reversed itself from the resting state. Now the interior of the cell is more positively charged than the outside.

Near the peak of the action potential, channels that allow positively charged potassium ions to move across the membrane begin to open, and potassium begins to leave the cell. As the interior loses these positively charged potassium ions, our recording heads in the negative direction again. Following the production of the action potential, the neuron requires a time-out, or refractory period, during which it returns to its resting state. During this refractory period, the cell is unable or unlikely to respond to further input by producing another action potential.

The size and shape of action potentials are always the same, whether we're recording them in a squid or in a human. You won't see any recordings of short, fat action potentials or tall, skinny ones. Either an action potential occurs, or the cell remains at rest—there is no middle ground. Because of this consistency, we say that action potentials are all-or-none.

Action potentials do not affect the entire axon all at once. The process we have just described takes place first in a very small segment of the axon where the axon connects to the cell body. The next step is propagation, or the duplication of the electrical signal down the length of the axon to the axon terminal, where it will initiate the release of chemical messengers.

We mentioned earlier that myelinated neurons enjoyed some advantages in efficiency and speed, and we are now ready to discuss why that is the case. Propagation takes place differently in myelinated and unmyelinated axons. In an unmyelinated axon, action potentials occur in a step-by-step manner, from one small section of the axon to the next, adjacent section, down the entire length of the axon. In contrast, action potentials in myelinated axons are formed only at the sections of the axon membrane between adjacent segments of myelin, known as nodes of Ranvier. In other words, propagation in myelinated axons can "skip" the sections covered

© Joe Scherschel/National Geographic Stock

Sushi made from puffer fish, known as *fugu*, is a delicacy, but prepared poorly can result in sickness or death. Chefs who prepare *fugu* undergo extensive training and licensing in Japan. The puffer fish toxin blocks the movement of sodium into cells, making electrical signaling impossible. As a result, diners who eat poorly prepared *fugu* can become paralyzed and suffocate to death.

Image provided by Professor Manzoor A. Bhat at the University of North Carolina School of Medicine, Chapel Hill, NC

Node

Node

Paranode

Paranode

Nodes of Ranvier (stained blue) are rich in sodium channels (stained green), which makes the formation of action potentials at the nodes possible. In contrast, there are no channels in the membrane covered by myelin (shown in red).

by myelin. You might think about the difference between propagation in unmyelinated and myelinated axons as being similar to shuffling your feet versus taking long strides. Which covers the most ground faster and more efficiently?

Propagation in unmyelinated axons works well, as evidenced by the wealth of invertebrate life on Earth, from the snails in your garden to the giant squid of the oceans. These animals survive with no myelin at all, but their neural communication is not very fast or energy efficient compared to ours. Forming action potentials at each section down the length of the axon is time-consuming, like taking the local bus that stops at every block. In addition, cleaning up after all these action potentials uses a lot of energy (Swaminathan, Burrows, & McMurray, 1982). The more action potentials it takes to move a signal down the length of the axon, the more energy is expended returning the cell to its resting state.

Propagation in myelinated axons is fast and efficient (● Figure 4.5). After an initial action potential is generated near the cell body, the current flows beneath a segment of myelin until it reaches a node of Ranvier, where another action potential occurs. Like the express bus, the action potentials skip the myelinated sections of the axon, reaching their destination, the axon terminal, about 20 times faster than if the axon were unmyelinated. By covering the same distance with fewer action potentials, the myelinated axon uses less energy returning to the resting potential than an unmyelinated axon would need.

Once the action potential reaches the axon terminal, the neural communication system switches from an electrical signaling system to a chemical signaling one.

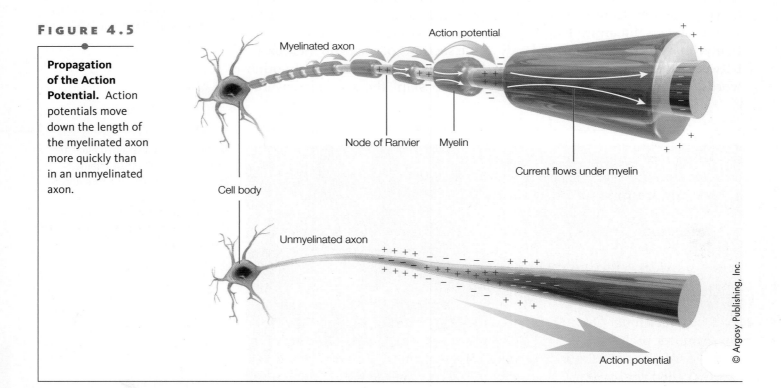

FIGURE 4.5

Propagation of the Action Potential. Action potentials move down the length of the myelinated axon more quickly than in an unmyelinated axon.

Myelinated axon

Action potential

Node of Ranvier   Myelin

Cell body

Current flows under myelin

Unmyelinated axon

Action potential

© Argosy Publishing, Inc.

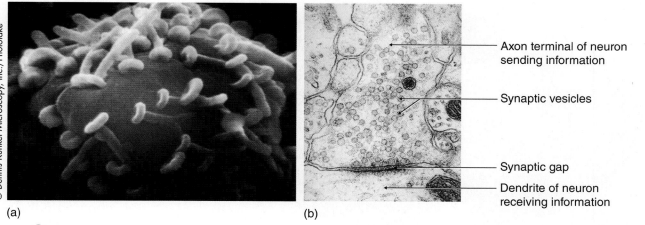

(a)

(b)

- Axon terminal of neuron sending information

- Synaptic vesicles

- Synaptic gap

- Dendrite of neuron receiving information

(a) Axon terminals from many neurons are forming points of communication, known as synapses, on a cell body. (b) We zoom in for an even closer look at the features of a single synapse.

Chemical Signaling The point of communication between two neurons is known as a **synapse**. At the synapse, neurons do not touch each other physically. Instead, they are separated by tiny gaps filled with extracellular fluid. Since electrical signals are unable to jump this gap, neurons send chemical messengers instead. These chemical messengers are called **neurotransmitters** (see Table 4.2).

Figure 4.6 illustrates the sequence of events triggered by the arrival of an action potential at an axon terminal. The neurotransmitters in the axon terminal are contained in synaptic vesicles. The arrival of an action potential releases the vesicles from their protein anchors, much like boats leaving a dock, and the vesicles migrate rapidly to the cell membrane. Because the vesicles are made of the same thin, oily material as the membrane, they easily fuse with the membrane and spill their contents into the synaptic gap. Following release, the vesicles are pinched off the membrane and refilled.

The neurotransmitters released across the synaptic gap come into contact with special channels on the receiving neuron, known as **receptors**. Receptors work with the neurotransmitters like locks and keys. Only a neurotransmitter with the right shape (the key) can attach itself, or bind, to a particular receptor (the lock). Neurotransmitters do not stay bound to receptors very long. Once they pop out of the receptor binding site, neurotransmitter molecules either drift away from the gap, are broken down by enzymes, or return to the axon terminal from which they were released in a process called **reuptake**. In reuptake, special channels in the axon terminal

TABLE 4.2	Important Neurotransmitters
Neurotransmitter	**Behaviors influenced by the neurotransmitter**
Acetylcholine (ACh)	• Movement • Memory • Autonomic nervous system function
Epinephrine (Adrenalin)	• Arousal
Norepinephrine (Noradrenalin)	• Arousal • Vigilance
Dopamine	• Movement • Planning • Reward
Serotonin	• Mood • Appetite • Sleep
Glutamate	• Excitation of brain activity
GABA	• Inhibition of brain activity
Endorphins	• Pain

synapse A point of communication between two neurons.

neurotransmitter A chemical messenger that communicates across a synapse.

receptor A special channel in the membrane of a neuron that interacts with neurotransmitters released by other neurons.

reuptake A process in which molecules of neurotransmitter in the synaptic gap are returned to the axon terminal from which they were released.

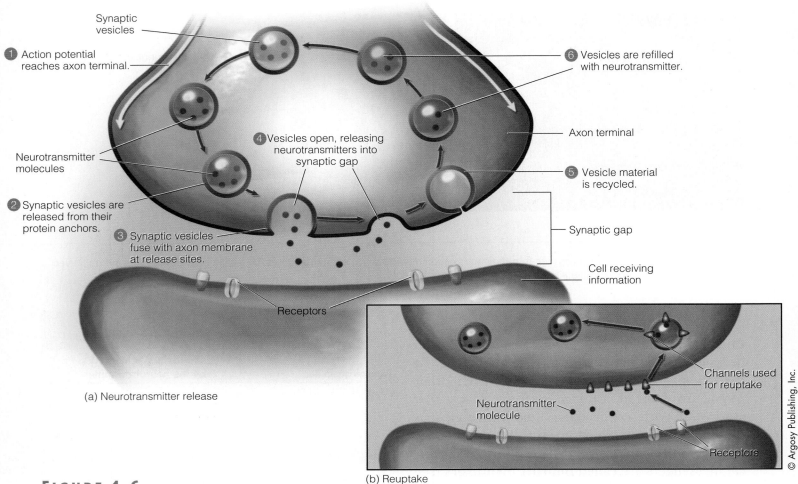

FIGURE 4.6

Chemical Signaling. Because most neurons are separated from each other by extracellular fluid, the action potential cannot jump from one neuron to the next. To cross the gap between neurons, chemical signals are used instead. **(a) Neurotransmitter Release.** The arrival of an action potential at the axon terminal triggers a sequence of events that results in the release of neurotransmitter molecules, which float across the synaptic gap to interact with receptors on the receiving neuron. **(b) Reuptake.** After interacting with receptors, neurotransmitter molecules are often recaptured by the neuron that released them to be recycled and used again later.

The "SSRI" label for some antidepressant medications, including Prozac®, stands for Selective Serotonin Reuptake Inhibitor. People who are depressed often have lower than normal serotonin activity at the synapse. If you inhibit reuptake of serotonin, that means more molecules remain in the synaptic gap longer, where they can continue to interact with receptors. Serotonin activity increases, relieving depression, because we get more "bang for the buck" each time serotonin is released.

membrane allow the neurotransmitters to move back into the releasing neuron, where they are repackaged for later use. Many important drugs, including the antidepressant drug fluoxetine (Prozac®), interfere with or inhibit this reuptake process.

The interaction between neurotransmitters and their receptors can have one of two effects on the receiving neuron: excitation or inhibition. When a neurotransmitter has an excitatory effect, it will slightly depolarize the receiving neuron, increasing the likelihood that the neuron will reach threshold and initiate an action potential. Recall that depolarization reduces the difference between the electrical environments inside and outside the neuron. When a neurotransmitter has an inhibitory effect, it will slightly hyperpolarize the receiving neuron, moving the cell farther from threshold and reducing the likelihood that it will initiate an action potential. Recall that hyperpolarization increases the difference between the electrical environments inside and outside the neuron.

Excitatory messages seem logical. One neuron is telling another to "pass the message along." Inhibitory messages, however, seem somewhat strange at first glance. Why would our nervous systems need a message that says, "Don't pass the message along"? Tetanus, for which you probably have been vaccinated, provides a dramatic example of what can happen when inhibition doesn't work properly. The toxin produced by the bacteria responsible for tetanus selectively damages inhibitory neurons in the parts of the nervous system that control muscle contraction. Normally, excitatory inputs that contract muscles coordinate their activity with inhibitory inputs that tell muscles to relax, allowing for the steady hands we need to put in a contact lens, for example. Without the input of the inhibitory neurons, the system is left with excitation only, and the result is the extreme muscle contraction that gives tetanus its other name—lockjaw.

Synapses usually occur in many locations on the dendrites or cell body of the receiving neuron, and the depolarizing or hyperpolarizing current that results from neurotransmitter activity at these synapses drifts to the junction of the cell body and axon. If there is sufficient depolarization to reach threshold at this junction, the neuron will generate an action potential. If not, it will remain at rest. The neuron's "decision" to generate an action potential or not is referred to as summation; the neuron, in other words, is adding up all incoming messages and making a "decision" based on that information. The neuron's task is not unlike the situation we face when we ask friends and family for advice. We will receive some excitatory advice (Go for it!) along with some inhibitory advice (Don't even think about it!). Our job, like the neuron's, is to sum our input and make a decision. Unlike us, however, the neuron cannot disregard the advice it receives.

© Sue Ford/Photo Researchers, Inc.

Toxins from the bacteria that cause tetanus travel from a wound to the nervous system, where the neurons responsible for inhibiting muscle contraction are selectively damaged. As a result, too much muscle contraction occurs, giving tetanus its alternative name "lockjaw" and causing this affected baby's back to arch. People living in the United States typically receive vaccinations for tetanus, but the disease still strikes many people worldwide.

Types of Neurotransmitters

Researchers have identified more than 50 different chemicals that serve as neurotransmitters at the synapse. Table 4.2 lists some of the neurotransmitters that are particularly interesting to psychologists, and we will highlight a few of these in this section. In our chapter on consciousness, we explore examples of psychoactive drugs, both therapeutic and recreational, that interact with the normal biochemistry of the nervous system.

Acetylcholine (ACh) is a neurotransmitter found in a number of systems important to behavior. ACh is found at the neuromuscular junction, the synapse at which the nervous system commands muscles. Interference with the action of ACh at the muscles can result in paralysis and death, making drugs that act on ACh popular for use as pesticides and as bioweapons. ACh also serves as a key neurotransmitter in the autonomic nervous

© Alison Wright/CORBIS

These residents of the Amazon basin are preparing darts with curare, a chemical derived from plants that causes paralysis by blocking receptors for acetylcholine (ACh) located on muscle fibers. When the receptors are blocked, the muscle is unable to respond to messages from the nervous system, leading to paralysis.

system, discussed later in this chapter, which carries commands from the brain to glands and organs. ACh is also intimately involved in the brain circuits related to learning and memory. These brain circuits are the first to deteriorate in Alzheimer's disease. Not too surprisingly, memory deficits are among the earliest symptoms of Alzheimer's disease to appear. Among the many drugs that act on ACh systems is the nicotine found in tobacco.

Norepinephrine is released in the brain and leads to arousal and vigilance. Consistent with this role in arousal, norepinephrine is also released by the sympathetic division of the autonomic nervous system, discussed later in this chapter. The sympathetic nervous system prepares us to react to emergencies by providing the resources needed for extra activity, like the extra oxygen that is needed to run or throw a punch. Abnormalities in norepinephrine activity have been implicated in a number of psychological conditions that feature disturbances in arousal and vigilance, including bipolar disorder and posttraumatic stress disorder (PTSD), discussed in our chapter on psychological disorders.

Dopamine is a neurotransmitter involved with systems that govern movement, planning, and reward. Parkinson's disease, which makes normal movement very difficult, results when dopamine-releasing neurons in the brain's movement circuits begin to die. In addition, dopamine participates in the brain's reward and pleasure circuits by becoming active whenever we engage in behaviors that promote survival and successful reproduction, such as eating a great meal or having sex. Most drugs that produce addiction, including cocaine and methamphetamine, stimulate increased activity in dopamine circuits. In our chapter on psychological disorders,

Originally used to help children with crossed eyes, Botox is now a popular, but temporary, way to reduce facial wrinkles.

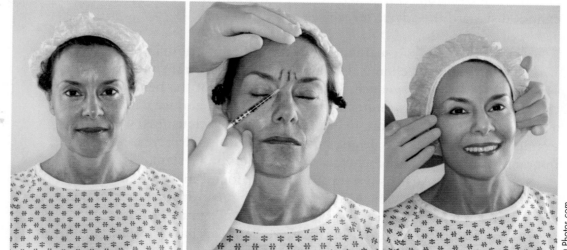

© Photos.com

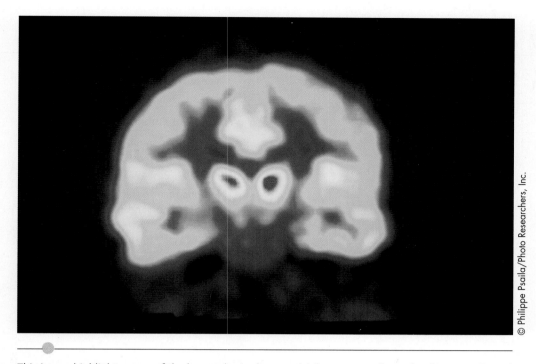

This image highlights areas of the human brain that are rich in receptors for endorphins, our natural opiates. The red areas have the most endorphin receptors, followed by the yellow areas. Opiate drugs, such as heroin or morphine, affect our behavior by interacting with these receptors. The red areas in the center of the image are located in the thalamus.

we will see how disruptions to dopamine circuits have been implicated in schizophrenia and attention deficit hyperactivity disorder (ADHD).

Serotonin is involved with systems regulating sleep, appetite, and mood. Consequently, these three behaviors are tightly linked. As we will see in our chapter on psychological disorders, people who experience depressed mood also show abnormalities in appetite and sleep. Sleep deprivation can result in changes in mood and appetite, even leading to significant overeating (Spiegel, Tasali, Penev, & Van Cauter, 2004).

Endorphins (short for "endogenous morphine," or morphine produced by the body) modify our natural response to pain. In evolutionary terms, it makes a great deal of sense to have a system that will reduce your chances of being disabled by pain during an emergency. All too frequently, however, we underestimate the extent of our injuries until we wake up the next morning feeling very sore indeed. "Runner's high," in which people who regularly engage in endurance sports experience a sense of well-being and reduced sensation of pain, is probably due to the release of endorphins initiated by high levels of activity. Opiate drugs such as morphine, heroin, and Oxycontin© produce their pain-relieving effects by mimicking the action of endorphins at the synapse. In other words, the opiate drugs are so similar in chemical structure to our natural endorphins that the receptors cannot tell them apart and treat the opiates as if they were natural endorphins.

Botox®, which is used to treat muscle spasms or reduce wrinkles, is made from an inactive form of the toxin responsible for botulism, which is produced by bacteria that spoil food. Botox interacts with ACh by preventing its release from the axon terminal. Without the activity of ACh telling a muscle to contract, the muscle remains paralyzed.

Summary 4.1

Neural Communication

	Feature	What to remember
© Peter Fromherz/ Max Planck Institute of Biochemistry	The neuron Cell body Axon Dendrite	• Cell bodies contain the nucleus and carry out most "housekeeping" functions. • Neurons receive information on their dendrites and send information via their axons.
© Argosy Publishing, Inc.	Glia	• Hold neurons in place • Clean up debris • Blood-brain barrier • Formation of myelin
© Cengage Learning 2013	Action potentials	• Without incoming signals, cell has a resting potential. • When cell reaches threshold, an action potential occurs. • Action potentials are followed by refractory periods. • Action potentials are propagated down the axon to the terminal.
© Omikron/Photo Researchers, Inc.	The synapse	• A synapse is a point of communication between two neurons. • When an action potential arrives at a terminal, neurotransmitters are released. • Neurotransmitters interact with receptors in the receiving neuron's membrane. • Neurotransmitters remaining in the synaptic gap are deactivated.
© Philippe Psaila/Photo Researchers, Inc.	Neurotransmitters	• Acetylcholine • Norepinephrine • Dopamine • Serotonin • Endorphins

How Is the Nervous System Organized?

Nervous systems are fairly recent innovations that separate animals from plants. We can place the origin of Earth at 4.5 billion years ago and the first single-celled life forms 1 billion years later, but the first neural nets appeared only 700 million years ago. In these primitive animals, the nerves in the abdomen were just as likely to be important to behavior as the ones in the head. True brains residing in heads did not appear until animals formed skeletons, around 500 million years ago (● Figure 4.7). The first decidedly human brain made its appearance only 7 million years ago, a small blip in the timeline of evolution (Calvin, 2004). The current model of the human brain has only been available for the last 100,000 to 200,000 years.

As neural nets led to true brains, culminating in the modern human brain, capacity for behavior changed accordingly. Just as your cell phone can perform more complex functions than most 20th-century computers, human nervous systems brought a complexity to behavior unimaginable for previous versions. Although a worm's ability to use its neural net to find good things to eat and avoid creatures that consider it good to eat is impressive, we have evolved a nervous system that not only allows you to study this textbook and get an A in your psychology course but also guides you through the maze that is human social life (Cacioppo & Decety, 2011; Dunbar & Schultz, 2007).

We are prepared now to zoom out from the structure and function of the neuron to examine this larger view: the structures and systems constructed from billions of neurons and the behavior they produce. Talking about the connections between the structions of the nervous system and behavior requires a quick word of caution. Just as saying that we have a "gene for" a behavior is overly simplistic and inaccurate, here we want to remind ourselves that saying we have a "center for" a behavior in the brain is equally misleading. Although we can identify structures that participate in certain behaviors, the biology of mind involves intricate and overlapping patterns of activity involving many richly connected structures.

The nervous system can be divided into two major components: the central nervous system (CNS) and the peripheral nervous system (PNS) (● Figure 4.8). The **central nervous system** consists of the brain and the **spinal cord**, which extends from the brain down the back of the body. Although we often see the brain and spinal cord referred to as separate structures, it is important to note that they form one continuous unit of tissue. Nerves branch outward from the CNS to all areas of the body—the lungs, heart, and other organs, the eyes, ears, arms, legs, fingers, and toes. As soon as a nerve branches outward from the CNS, it is

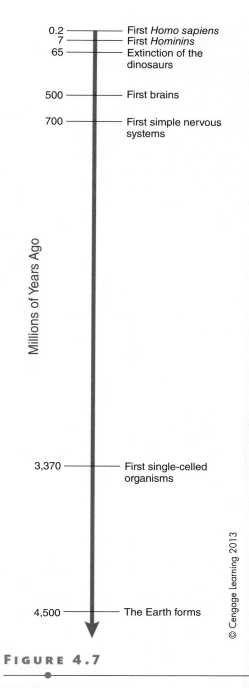

FIGURE 4.7

Timeline of Brain Evolution. Brains are a fairly recent development in the history of evolution, appearing about 500 million years ago or 3 billion years after life first emerged on earth.

central nervous system (CNS) The brain and spinal cord.

spinal cord A long cylinder of neural tissue extending from the medulla of the brain down to the middle of the back; part of the central nervous system.

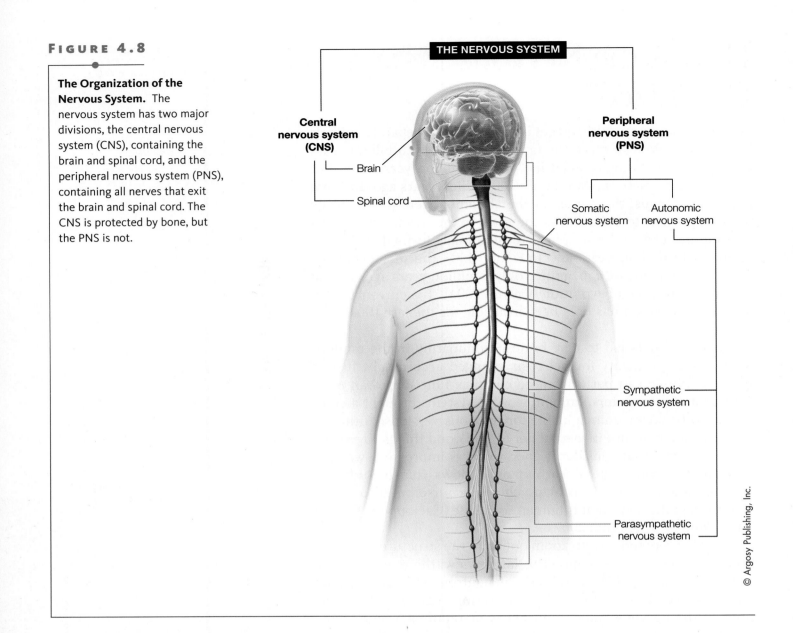

FIGURE 4.8

The Organization of the Nervous System. The nervous system has two major divisions, the central nervous system (CNS), containing the brain and spinal cord, and the peripheral nervous system (PNS), containing all nerves that exit the brain and spinal cord. The CNS is protected by bone, but the PNS is not.

THE NERVOUS SYSTEM

Central nervous system (CNS)

Brain

Spinal cord

Peripheral nervous system (PNS)

Somatic nervous system

Autonomic nervous system

Sympathetic nervous system

Parasympathetic nervous system

© Argosy Publishing, Inc.

considered part of the **peripheral nervous system**. Another way to know you have left the CNS for the PNS is to look for the protection of bone. Nerves of the CNS are encased in bone, but those of the PNS are not.

What Are the Structures and Functions of the Central Nervous System?

The brain and spinal cord are among the best-protected and most well-supplied parts of your body, which is not surprising given their importance for your survival. Although the brain makes up only about 2% of your total

peripheral nervous system (PNS) The nerves exiting the central nervous system that carry sensory and motor information to and from the rest of the body.

body weight, it is the target of about 20% of the blood pumped by the heart. Surrounding the brain and spinal cord are the heavy bones of the skull and spinal vertebrae. Just under these bones, membranes known as meninges provide further protection. Infections of these membranes result in potentially life-threatening cases of meningitis, for which you have likely been vaccinated prior to beginning your college studies.

The brain and spinal cord are further protected by a clear, plasma-like fluid known as cerebrospinal fluid (CSF). CSF seeps out of the lining of hollow spaces in the brain known as the ventricles (● Figure 4.9). Near the base of the skull, openings enable CSF to flow from the ventricles into a space within the meninges, allowing the fluid to flow around the outer surfaces of the brain and spinal cord. Without the cushioning provided by the CSF, a blow to the head would cause considerable damage to the brain. In addition, the CSF "floats" the brain within the skull, preventing any false signals that might result from the weight of some neurons pressing down on others.

To diagnose some medical conditions, it is helpful to obtain a sample of CSF. This is done through a spinal tap, in which a physician removes some of the CSF circulating through the meninges surrounding the spinal cord. CSF is constantly produced, so any blockages in its circulation cause the fluid to build up. The result is hydrocephalus, which means "water on the brain."

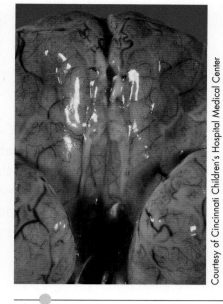

Courtesy of Cincinnati Children's Hospital Medical Center

Meningitis is an infection of the membranes surrounding the central nervous system, or meninges. If you were wondering why your college asked you to obtain a vaccination for meningitis, this is what can happen if you contract the disease.

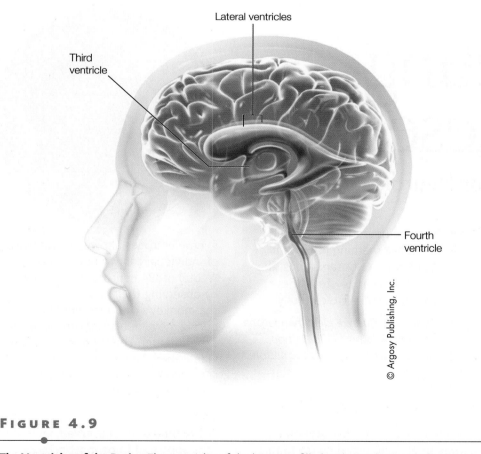

Third ventricle

Lateral ventricles

Fourth ventricle

© Argosy Publishing, Inc.

FIGURE 4.9

The Ventricles of the Brain. The ventricles of the brain are filled with circulating cerebrospinal fluid (CSF), which floats and cushions the brain.

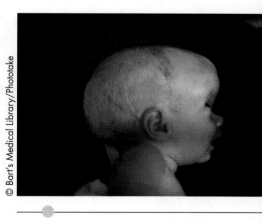

© Bart's Medical Library/Phototake

When blockages occur in the circulation of cerebrospinal fluid, a condition known as hydrocephalus occurs. The word *hydrocephalus* comes from the Greek words for "water" and "head." Before modern treatments became available, babies like this one would usually experience cognitive deficits. These blockages are now identified at birth and can be treated surgically or by installing a shunt to drain off excess fluid, avoiding the damage that would otherwise occur to the brain and preserving the child's intelligence.

The Spinal Cord, Brainstem, and Cerebellum

The spinal cord extends from the lowest part of the brain down into the middle of your back (● Figure 4.10). If you feel the back of your skull where it curves to meet your spine, your fingers will be just below the junction of the spinal cord and the lowest structure of the brain. Although the spinal cord comprises only 2% of the weight of the central nervous system, its functions are vital, as evidenced by the challenges faced by people with spinal damage. The spinal cord serves as a major conduit for information flowing to and from the brain along large bundles of axons, carrying sensory information from the body and delivering commands. Thirty-one pairs of spinal nerves exit the spinal cord to serve the body. These nerves exit and enter the spinal cord between segments of the bony vertebrae in your spine.

When the cushioning disks separating the vertebrae are damaged or the bones are misaligned, the resulting pressure of bone on spinal nerve can produce the excruciating pain of a "pinched" nerve.

A number of important reflexes are initiated by the spinal cord without the assistance of the brain. One type of spinal reflex will make you pull your body away from any source of pain. It doesn't take long for your hand to fly up when you've touched something hot on the stove. When your doctor taps your knee with a hammer during a routine physical, he or she is

Connecting *to* Research

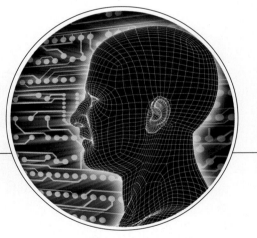

The Discovery of Mirror Neurons

In the early 1990s, a team of Italian scientists led by Giacomo Rizzolatti were busy studying the brain correlates of movement when they noticed something odd (Di Pellegrino, Fadiga, Fogassi, Gallese, & Rizzolatti, 1992). They had observed that certain neurons in a part of a monkey's brain became especially active when the monkey performed certain actions, like reaching for a piece of banana or a peanut. When an experimenter picked up a piece of food to place it within the monkey's reach, some

of the same neurons began to fire. Suspecting something important was behind these observations, the researchers began to study these "mirror neurons" more carefully.

The Question: *Can we identify neurons that respond to a particular action, regardless of who performs the action?*

METHODS

A monkey (*Macaca nemestrina*) served as the research subject. The technique used in this experiment was single cell recording (see Table 4.1), in which surgically inserted

microelectrodes allowed the activity of individual cells to be measured. A total of 184 neurons were tested by observing their activity during the monkey's own movements and during movements performed by an experimenter. The experiments were videotaped. The experimenters also recorded the muscle movements in the monkey's hand and arm.

RESULTS

Thirty-nine of the observed neurons appeared to be most active when either the experimenter or the

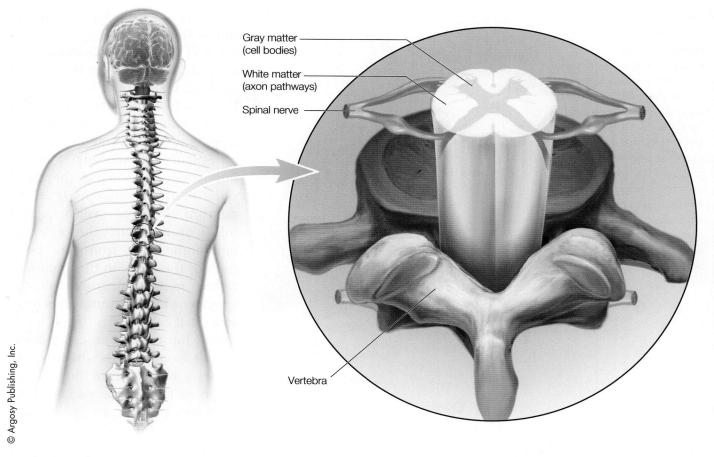

Gray matter (cell bodies)
White matter (axon pathways)
Spinal nerve
Vertebra

© Argosy Publishing, Inc.

FIGURE 4.10

The Spinal Cord and the Spinal Nerves. Thirty-one pairs of spinal nerves exit between the bones of the vertebrae to bring sensory information back to the central nervous system and to carry motor commands to muscles.

monkey performed the same action. The cells' responses were very specific. For example, a cell that became active when the experimenter grasped a piece of food would also become active when the monkey grasped the food, but not when the monkey put food in its mouth. A cell that activated when the experimenter put food in his mouth also activated when the monkey put food in its mouth, but not when the monkey grasped the food.

CONCLUSIONS

The scientists believed they had discovered neurons that provided a mechanism for understanding the

When a monkey reaches for a banana itself or sees someone else reach for the fruit, some of the same neurons in the brain become active. Giacomo Rizzolatti and his colleagues named these "mirror neurons."

actions of others. These cells are now referred to as "mirror neurons" (Caggiano, Rizzolatti, Pomper, Thier, Giese, & Casile, 2011). Although the existence of mirror neurons in humans is still controversial, this discovery stimulated new hypotheses regarding imitation, autism, and empathy. ⚙

© Dan Herrick/Alamy

FIGURE 4.11

Checking Spinal Reflexes. When your physician taps on your knee, your thigh muscle stretches. Information about the stretch is carried to the spinal cord by a sensory nerve. The spinal cord sends a command to the muscle to contract to counteract the stretch, and your foot kicks out. The spinal cord manages this reflex alone. No higher level of processing in the nervous system is necessary for this reflex to occur.

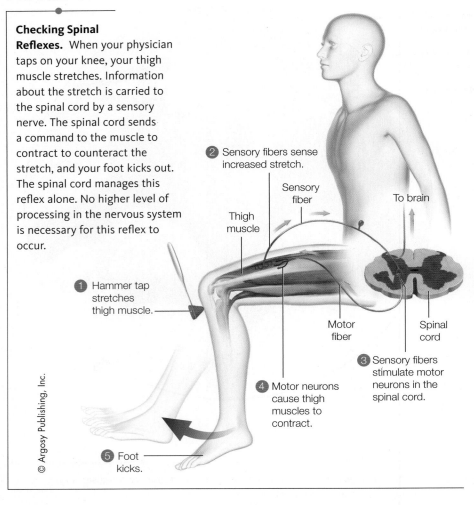

© Argosy Publishing, Inc.

2 Sensory fibers sense increased stretch.

Sensory fiber

Thigh muscle

To brain

1 Hammer tap stretches thigh muscle.

Motor fiber

Spinal cord

3 Sensory fibers stimulate motor neurons in the spinal cord.

4 Motor neurons cause thigh muscles to contract.

5 Foot kicks.

brainstem The part of the brain containing the midbrain, pons, and medulla.

medulla The brainstem structure that lies just above the spinal cord.

checking another type of spinal reflex, the knee-jerk reflex (● Figure 4.11). This reflex is interesting to your doctor, because certain medical conditions, such as diabetes, affect the strength of the reflex. Still other spinal reflexes help us stand and walk.

Spinal reflexes give us an opportunity to look at the functions of three different types of neurons. Sensory neurons carry information from the external environment or from the body back to the CNS. In the knee-jerk reflex, sensory neurons tell the spinal cord that a muscle has been stretched by the tap of the hammer. Motor neurons carry commands from the CNS back to the muscles and glands of the body. In response to information about the stretched muscle, the spinal cord sends a message through motor neurons back to your leg, telling the muscle to contract to counteract the stretch. You know what happens next—your foot kicks as the muscles contract. Neurons that have neither sensory nor motor functions are called interneurons. Inter in this case means "between," as many interneurons form bridges between sensory and motor neurons. The knee-jerk reflex forms a very simple arc between a sensory neuron and a motor neuron and does not require any interneurons. However, interneurons play important roles in more complex reflexes and throughout the nervous system.

Moving up from the spinal cord brings us to the brainstem. Early in prenatal development, the emerging brain forms three bulges. The most forward of these bulges will develop into the two large cerebral hemispheres, which we discuss in a later section. The remaining two bulges form the **brainstem**. If you examine ● Figure 4.12, you can see that the brainstem looks like a stem of a flower, supporting the larger blossom of the cerebral hemispheres. Directly branching from the brainstem are the cranial nerves, which perform the same functions for the head and neck areas that the spinal nerves manage for the remainder of the body. We will discuss the cranial nerves in more depth in a later section on the peripheral nervous system.

The spinal cord merges with our first brainstem structure, the **medulla**. Like the spinal cord, the medulla contains large bundles of axons traveling to and from higher levels of the brain. Because the medulla manages many essential functions, such as heart rate and blood pressure, damage to this structure usually results in quick death.

Just above the medulla is the **pons**, which contains structures involved with the management of sleep, arousal, and facial expressions. *Pons* means "bridge" in Latin. The pons not only serves as a bridge between higher and lower portions of the brain but also connects the **cerebellum** to the rest of the brain. Essential for maintaining balance and motor coordination, the cerebellum is one of the first structures in the brain to be affected by alcohol. As a result, alcohol consumption impairs balance (walking a straight line) and motor coordination (touching your finger to the tip of your nose with your eyes closed). Most sobriety tests are the same tests a neurologist would use to assess the function of the cerebellum.

Because of the cerebellum's position on the brainstem, which is relatively ancient in terms of evolution compared to the cerebral hemispheres, neuroscientists initially underestimated its importance to human behavior. They believed that the cerebellum's activities were restricted to managing the timing and strength of movements. While we still do not know exactly what the cerebellum does, today's scientists believe that it has a broader role in making mental and motor skills more automatic. Damage to the human cerebellum produces subtle deficits in language, cognition, and perception. In autism, a condition that affects language, sensory, and social behaviors, abnormalities in the cerebellum are very common (Courchesne, 1997).

Surprisingly, the cerebellum contains more nerve cells than the rest of the brain combined. Not only does the cerebellum contain huge numbers of neurons, but it is richly connected with the rest of the central nervous system. The cerebellum receives input from approximately 40 million nerve cells located at the highest levels of the brain (Leiner, Leiner, & Dow, 1991). To put that number into perspective, each eye sends input to the brain from only 1 million nerve cells. In turn, the cerebellum sends vast amounts of information back to higher levels of the brain as well as to the pons, medulla, and spinal cord.

FIGURE 4.12

Structures of the Brainstem. The brainstem contains structures responsible for reflexive behaviors, heart rate and breathing, arousal and sleep, preliminary sensory analysis, and balance and movement.

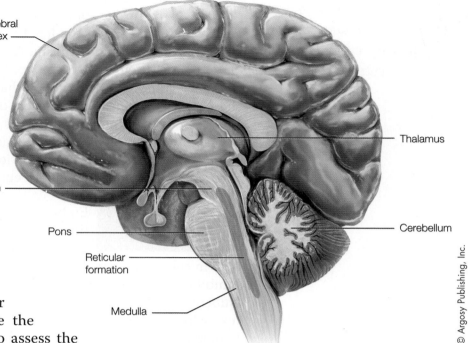

Cerebral cortex

Midbrain

Pons

Reticular formation

Medulla

Thalamus

Cerebellum

© Argosy Publishing, Inc.

© Charlie Neuman/ZUMA Press/Corbis

Most sobriety tests actually assess the function of the cerebellum, which helps us maintain balance and muscle coordination.

pons A part of the brainstem located between the medulla and midbrain.

cerebellum A structure attached to the brainstem that participates in skilled movement and, in humans, complex cognitive processing.

The **midbrain** sits above the pons and contains a number of structures involved in sensory reflexes, movement, and pain. For example, the periaqueductal gray of the midbrain plays an important part in the body's management of pain because it contains receptors for endorphins. When endorphins are present in the periaqueductal gray, they reduce the perception of pain by decreasing the strength of pain messages traveling up the spinal cord to higher levels of the brain.

Opiate painkillers like morphine and Oxycontin® produce some of their analgesic effects by interacting with opiate receptors in periaqueductal gray.

Running the length of the brainstem's core from the upper medulla into the midbrain is the **reticular formation**, which participates in the control of mood, arousal, and sleep, discussed further in our chapter on consciousness. The neurons in these areas are the source of most of the serotonin and norepinephrine in the brain. As a result of the actions of the reticular formation, we are able to respond differently to the world as a function of our state of arousal. The same sound that grabs your attention in a quiet library will be completely ignored while you are sound asleep.

Subcortical Structures

Embedded within the vast tracts of white matter that make up the bulk of the cerebral hemispheres are a number of subcortical structures that participate in self-awareness, learning, emotion, movement, communication, the inhibition of impulses, and the regulation of body states. We call them "subcortical" because they lie *sub*, which means "below," the cerebral cortex, which comprises the wrinkled outermost covering of the cerebral hemispheres.

Early anatomists collected some of these subcortical structures into a limbic system (*limbic* means "border," and these structures form a gentle curve below the cerebral cortex), but this term is losing popularity with contemporary anatomists. You might also have heard the limbic system referred to as "your emotional brain." As you will see in the next few sections, subcortical structures, including some formerly listed in the limbic system, do indeed participate in our emotional life, but they perform many other functions as well. We usually discuss these structures in the singular, as in "thalamus" or "hippocampus," but they actually are paired sets of structures, one on either side of the brain.

midbrain The part of the brainstem that lies between the pons and the cerebral hemispheres.

reticular formation A collection of structures located along the midline of the brainstem that participate in mood, arousal, and sleep.

thalamus A subcortical structure involved with the processing of sensory information, states of arousal, and learning and memory.

basal ganglia A collection of subcortical structures that participate in the control of movement.

hypothalamus A subcortical structure that participates in the regulation of thirst, temperature, hunger, sexual behavior, and aggression.

The Thalamus Just about at the very center of the brain lies the **thalamus**. The thalamus is often referred to as the "gateway to the cortex," as input from most of our sensory systems (vision, hearing, touch, and taste) travels first to the thalamus, which then forwards the information along to the cerebral cortex. The cortex, in turn, forms large numbers of connections with the thalamus. In addition to its role in sensation, the thalamus is involved with memory and states of consciousness. Lesions in the thalamus are associated with profound memory loss (Cipolotti et al., 2008). As you will learn in a later chapter on consciousness, during our deepest stages of sleep, the thalamus coordinates the activity of cortical neurons, "tuning out" the outside world and making it more difficult to be awake. Disturbances in the circuits linking the thalamus and the cortex accompany some seizures.

FIGURE 4.13

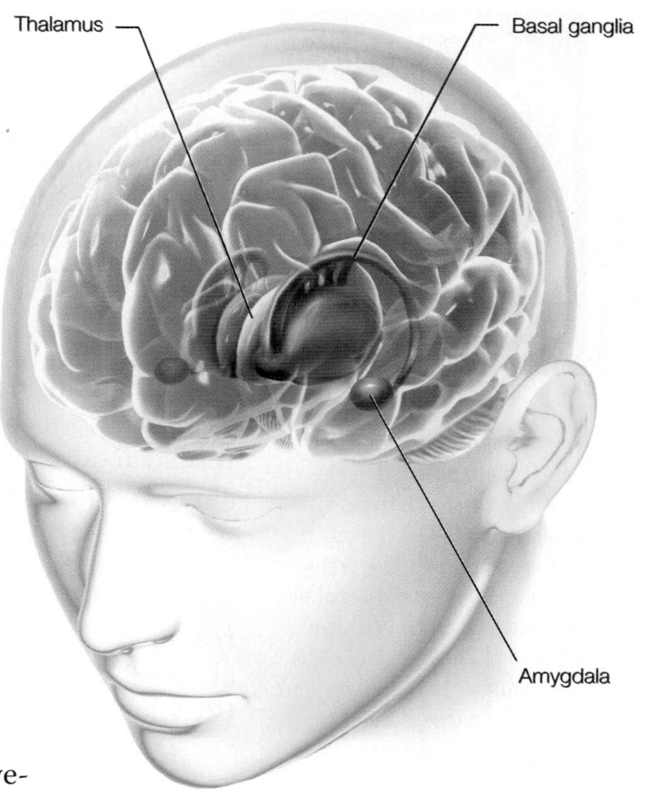

The Thalamus and the Basal Ganglia. Near the very center of the brain, the thalamus receives input from most of our sensory systems and relays the information to the cerebral cortex. Curving around the thalamus are the basal ganglia, which form an important part of our voluntary movement systems.

The Basal Ganglia The **basal ganglia** are a collection of large structures involved with voluntary movement that curve around to cup the thalamus (● Figure 4.13). The basal ganglia receive substantial input from all areas of the cerebral cortex and from motor structures located in the brainstem. In turn, the basal ganglia send information to the cortex.

Degeneration of the basal ganglia occurs in Parkinson's disease, a condition that makes the initiation of voluntary movement extremely difficult. Involvement of the basal ganglia is also suspected in a number of conditions that we will encounter in our later chapter on psychological disorders, including obsessive-compulsive disorder (OCD) and attention deficit hyperactivity disorder (ADHD). These disorders are characterized by inadequate control of voluntary movement. In the case of OCD, patients may endlessly repeat a behavior, such as hand washing, while in ADHD, voluntary movements can be unusually frequent, rapid, and impulsive. Children with the hyperactivity type of attention deficit disorder are often described as "driven by a motor."

The Hypothalamus The **hypothalamus** is a collection of structures involved with motivation and homeostasis, or the regulation of body functions such as temperature, thirst, hunger, biological rhythms, and sexual activities (● Figure 4.14). The hypothalamus is often described as contributing to the "4F" behaviors: feeding, fleeing, fighting, and, well, sex (fornication). The hypothalamus carries out its motivational and homeostatic tasks by directing the autonomic nervous system and the endocrine system and its hormones, which we discuss in detail later in this chapter.

FIGURE 4.14

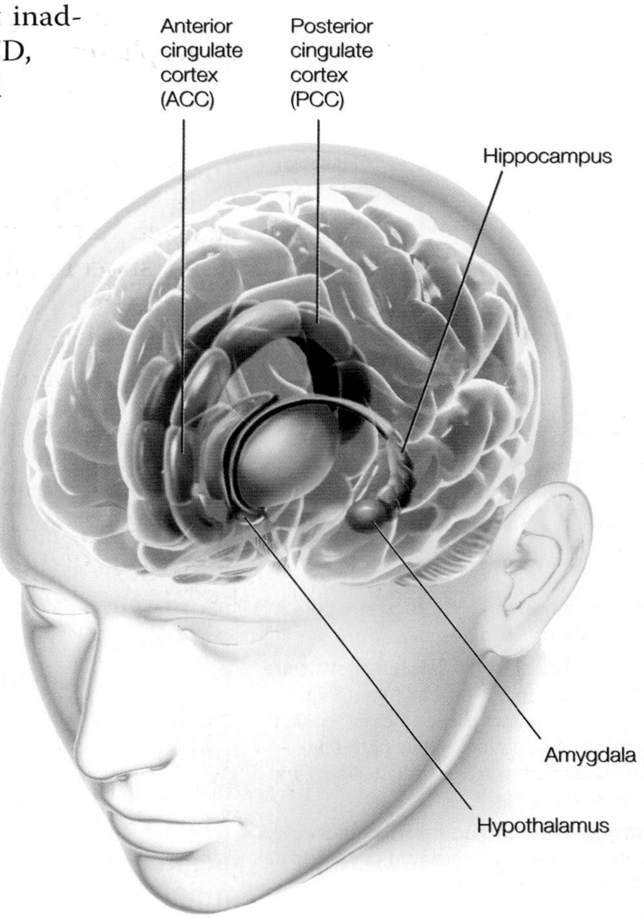

Other Important Subcortical Structures. Subcortical structures located under the cerebral cortex participate in attention, decision making, learning, memory, and emotion.

WHAT ARE THE STRUCTURES AND FUNCTIONS OF THE CENTRAL NERVOUS SYSTEM?

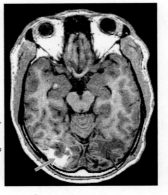

From A. J. Pegna, et al., "Discriminating Emotional Faces Without Primary Visual Cortices Involves the Right Amygdala," in *Nat Neurosci*, Jan. 2005, 8(1): 24–25. © 2005 Nature Publishing Group.

This image is taken from a man who is blind due to damage caused by a stroke to his visual areas, indicated by the red and green arrows. The orange area indicates activation of his amygdala when he is shown a photo of an angry face. This man couldn't tell you if he were looking at a tree, a building, or a face, let alone a happy or angry one, but his amygdala knows and reacts appropriately.

hippocampus A subcortical structure that participates in memory.

cingulate cortex A subcortical structure above the corpus callosum. Its anterior (forward) segment participates in decision making and emotion, and its posterior (rear) segment participates in memory and visual processing.

amygdala A subcortical structure located in the temporal lobe believed to participate in emotional processing.

The Hippocampus The **hippocampus**, named for its shape after the Greek word for *seahorse*, is essential to the formation of long-term memories, which we discuss in more detail in our chapter on memory. Memories are not stored permanently in the hippocampus itself, but it is likely that the hippocampus is involved in the storage and retrieval of memories located elsewhere in the brain. Damage to the hippocampus results in profound impairments in the ability to form new memories, but leaves intelligence, personality, and most memories of events occurring prior to hippocampal damage intact.

The Cingulate Cortex The **cingulate cortex** forms a fold of tissue on the inner surface of each cerebral hemisphere. The forward two-thirds of this structure, known as the anterior cingulate cortex (ACC), participates along with the hypothalamus in the control of the autonomic nervous system, but the ACC has received recent attention from psychologists for its roles in decision making, emotion, anticipation of reward, and empathy. As you will see in our chapter on emotion, the ACC responds similarly to real physical pain and the pain of feeling socially excluded (Eisenberger et al., 2003; Eisenberger, 2011). The rear third, or posterior cingulate cortex (PCC), participates in memory and visual processing.

The Amygdala The **amygdala** gets its name from the Greek word for "almond" due to its shape. One amygdala is deeply embedded in the temporal lobe, the wing of cortex that curves around the side of the brain, in each hemisphere. The amygdala appears to have a role in identifying, remembering, and responding to fear and aggression. Research studies have found that the amygdala becomes more active when people are looking at pictures of fearful facial expressions. The more intense the expression of fear, the more activation is observed in the amygdala (Vuilleumier, Armony, Driver, & Dolan, 2001). Monkeys with damaged amygdalas approached unfamiliar monkeys in a bold and fearless manner, which is very uncharacteristic of these animals (Emery et al., 2001). They also failed to show their species' typical fear of rubber snakes and unfamiliar humans (Mason, Capitanio, Machado, Mendoza, & Amaral, 2006).

Several behavioral deficits have been identified in a patient, known as Patient S.M., who experienced a rare medical condition that damaged the amygdala in both her right and her left hemisphere (Adolphs, Tranel, & Damasio, 1998). Although the patient can identify facial expressions of happiness, sadness, and disgust in photographs, she has a specific difficulty identifying expressions of fear (● Figure 4.15). When researchers exposed Patient S.M. to snakes, spiders, and scary movies, she showed no signs of fear at all (Feinstein, Adolphs, Damasio, & Tranel, 2011). Although Patient S.M. shows no signs of antisocial behavior, other research indicates that people who harm others without feeling any guilt are also impaired in their abilities to perceive fear in facial expressions or voices (Blair et al., 2002; Marsh & Blair, 2008). The condition affecting Patient S.M. does not usually begin until after the age of 10, so having functional amygdalas in childhood might have helped her learn to act in prosocial ways.

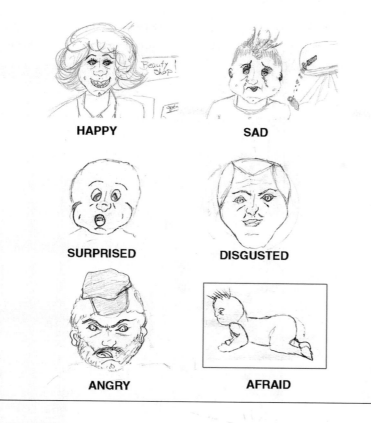

HAPPY **SAD**

SURPRISED **DISGUSTED**

ANGRY **AFRAID**

FIGUR

Results of D
Amygdala. A
damage to bot.
was asked to dr.
representing maj
Her results were c
the exception of he ......ng of
"afraid." *Source:* From R. Adolphs, D.
Tranel, H. Damasio, & A. R. Damasio,
"Fear and the Human Amygdala," in *The
Journal of Neuroscience,* Sept. 1995,
15(9): 5879–5891. Reprinted with
permission of *The Journal of Neuroscience.*

The Nucleus Accumbens The **nucleus accumbens** is an important part of the brain's reward and pleasure circuitry. Whether you are eating, having sex, using addictive drugs, gambling, or simply enjoying a beautiful sunset, this same circuit will come into play (Comings & Blum, 2000). The circuit originates in cell bodies located in the midbrain that form connections with many subcortical structures, and the nucleus accumbens in particular.

The activity of the nucleus accumbens is related to a person's sense of social inclusion. When people who have strong connections to friends and family view a happy social scene, their nucleus accumbens becomes very active. In contrast, when people with weaker social connections view the same happy scenes, their nucleus accumbens shows less activity than those of the socially connected people (Cacioppo, Norris, Decety, Monteleone, & Nusbaum, 2009).

The Cerebral Cortex

Above the brainstem, we find the two large cerebral hemispheres, which are connected by a large bundle of axons known as the **corpus callosum**. The thin layer of cells covering the outer surface of the cerebral hemispheres is the **cerebral cortex** (● Figure 4.16). The cortex, which means "bark" in Latin, covers the cerebral hemispheres like the bark of a tree. Most of the remaining bulk of the hemispheres is made up of white matter, or axon pathways, that connects the cortex with other parts of the nervous system. The average 20-year-old human brain has just around 100,000 miles (162,500 km) of white matter (Marner, Nyengaard, Tang, & Pakkenberg, 2003). The subcortical structures discussed earlier are distributed within this white matter.

nucleus accumbens A subcortical structure that participates in reward and addiction.

corpus callosum A wide band of axons connecting the right and left cerebral hemispheres.

cerebral cortex The thin layer of neurons covering the outer surface of the cerebral hemispheres.

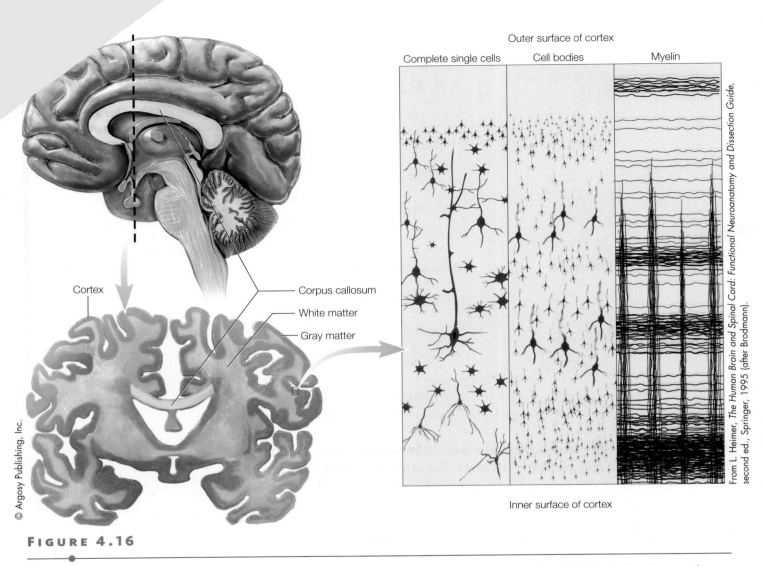

Complete single cells Cell bodies Myelin

Outer surface of cortex

Cortex

Corpus callosum
White matter
Gray matter

© Argosy Publishing, Inc.

Inner surface of cortex

From L. Heimer, *The Human Brain and Spinal Cord: Functional Neuroanatomy and Dissection Guide,* second ed., Springer, 1995 (after Brodmann).

FIGURE 4.16

The Cerebral Cortex. The cerebral cortex (*cortex* means "bark") is a thin layer of cells on the outer surface of the brain. The close-up of the cortex shows different views of the cortex, including the distribution of complete single cells, cell bodies, and myelin.

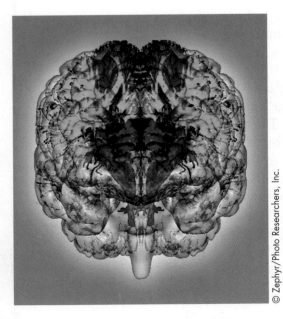

© Zephyr/Photo Researchers, Inc.

If stretched out flat, the human cerebral cortex would cover an area of about 2.5 square feet. To fit within the confines of the skull, the cortex is wrinkled, or convoluted. The degree of cortical convolution positively correlates with the general intellectual capacities of a species. For instance, human brains are more convoluted than sheep brains, which in turn are more convoluted than rat brains (● Figure 4.17).

Each hemisphere of the cerebral cortex may be divided into four lobes, named after the bones of the skull that cover them (● Figure 4.18). Toward the very front of the brain, we find the **frontal lobe**, and directly behind the frontal lobe lies the **parietal lobe**. At the very back of the brain is the **occipital lobe**. Curving around the side of each hemisphere, we find the

Diffusion Tensor Imaging (DTI) highlights the rich connections formed by the white matter in the brain.

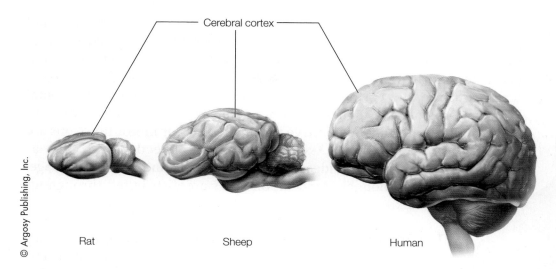

Cerebral cortex

Rat   Sheep   Human

© Argosy Publishing, Inc.

FIGURE 4.17

Degree of the Convolution of the Cortex Predicts Intellect. As species' behavior becomes more complex, we see a corresponding increase in the degree of convolution (wrinkling) of the cerebral cortex. This wrinkling of the brain permits more brain tissue to fit within the skull. As a result, cortical size has increased more quickly over the course of evolution than skull size—an important adaptation given large skulls are difficult to get through the birth canal.

temporal lobe. Because we have two hemispheres, it follows that we have pairs of each type of lobe, usually denoted right or left (e.g., right frontal lobe and left frontal lobe).

Localization of Functions in the Cerebral Cortex As we mentioned earlier in this chapter, the phrenologists were wrong in assuming that behavioral characteristics were reflected in bumps of the skull, but they were correct in suggesting that some functions were localized in particular parts of the brain.

The functions performed by different areas of cerebral cortex within the lobes fall into three categories: sensory, motor, and association. Sensory cortex processes incoming information from the sensory systems, such as vision or smell, which we describe in a later chapter on sensation

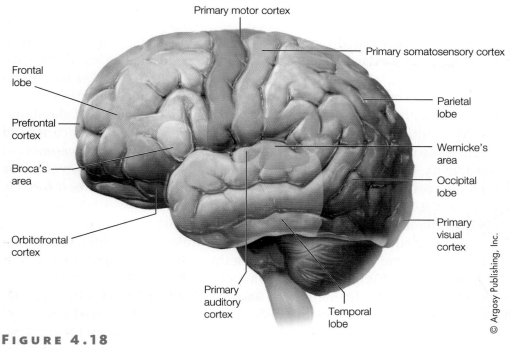

Primary motor cortex

Primary somatosensory cortex

Frontal lobe

Prefrontal cortex

Parietal lobe

Broca's area

Wernicke's area

Occipital lobe

Primary visual cortex

Orbitofrontal cortex

Primary auditory cortex

Temporal lobe

© Argosy Publishing, Inc.

FIGURE 4.18

Lobes of the Cerebral Cortex. The cerebral cortex is traditionally divided into four lobes: frontal, parietal, occipital, and temporal.

frontal lobe The most forward of the four lobes of the cerebral cortex; location of primary motor cortex and areas responsible for some of the most complex cognitive processes.

parietal lobe The lobe of the cerebral cortex that lies at the top of the head between the frontal and occipital lobes; location of primary somatosensory cortex.

occipital lobe The lobe of the cerebral cortex located at the back of the brain; location of primary visual cortex.

temporal lobe The lobe of the cerebral cortex that curves around the side of each hemisphere; location of primary auditory cortex.

and perception. Primary visual cortex is located in the occipital lobe, and primary auditory cortex is located in the temporal lobe. Primary somatosensory cortex ("soma" refers to *body*) is located in the parietal lobe and processes information about touch, pain, body position, and skin temperature. Primary motor cortex is located in the rearmost portion of the frontal lobe and provides the highest level of voluntary control over movement. Areas of the cortex that do not have specific sensory or motor functions are known as association cortex. *Association* means "connection," and association cortex helps us form bridges between sensation and action, language, and abstract thought. Association areas are distributed throughout the cortex.

The Frontal Lobe in addition to being the home of primary motor cortex, the frontal lobe has a number of important, sophisticated cognitive functions. Adjacent to primary motor cortex is Broca's area, named after Paul Broca, who helped identify its functions in the 1860s. Broca's area participates in the production of speech. Consequently, damage to Broca's area caused by a stroke or tumor produces considerable difficulty in speaking, although comprehension of speech remains good. The most forward portion of each frontal lobe, known as the **prefrontal cortex** (*pre* means "before"), is involved with the planning of behavior, attention, and judgment. Abnormalities of frontal lobe activity may account for some of the characteristics of some psychological disorders, including schizophrenia and attention deficit hyperactivity disorder, which we will discuss in detail in our chapter on psychological disorders.

The role of the frontal lobes in the planning of behavior is illustrated by a bizarre condition known as alien hand syndrome, which occurs when connections between the prefrontal cortex and lower areas involved in movement are damaged (Kikkert, Ribbers, & Koudstaal, 2006). This condition has no effect on sensory feedback from the limb, such as touch and position. However, patients with this condition do not seem to have any control over their affected limbs and often remain unaware of the limbs' activities until they are pointed out by another person. For instance, a hand might undo a button or remove clothing without the patient's awareness of the activity. Patients do not recognize the rogue limb as their own and may be seen wrestling it with the other hand in an attempt to control it forcibly or punish it for its activities.

The importance of the frontal lobes is also illustrated by the results of a terrible accident that befell a young railroad worker named Phineas Gage in 1848. While Gage was preparing to blast through some granite, a freak accident sent an iron tamping rod through his head like a bullet, landing about 30 feet away. The rod entered his head under his left cheekbone, passed behind his left eye, and exited out the middle of his forehead. Remarkably, Gage survived his accident, but he was not the same person as before his accident. Although outwardly normal in his intelligence, speech, and movement, Gage was now prone to angry outbursts and unreliability, which made it difficult for him to find and keep employment. As his doctor noted, "His contractors,

prefrontal cortex The most forward part of the frontal lobe of the cerebral cortex.

who regarded him as the most efficient and capable foreman in their employ previous to his injury, considered the change in his mind so marked that they could not give him his place again" (Fleischman, 2002, p. 20).

Gage suffered his accident at a time when modern imaging technologies were nowhere to be seen on the scientific horizon. Today, we know why Gage behaved the way he did as a result of his accident. Scientists recreated the pathway that Gage's tamping rod must have traveled (Damasio, Grabowski, Frank, Galaburda, & Damasio, 1994). The rod missed areas involved in speech, voluntary movement, and the senses of touch, body position, and pain. Thus, Gage had no difficulty speaking or performing complex movements like driving a stagecoach following his accident. The rod did damage areas of the left frontal lobe of Gage's brain (Ratiu & Talos, 2004). Modern patients with damage in this area exhibit many of the same social deficits that Gage demonstrated (Damasio & Anderson, 1993; Damasio, Tranel, & Damasio, 1991; Eslinger & Damasio, 1985). They are impulsive, emotionally unstable, unpredictable, and unable to make reasonable decisions.

Knowing the outcome of the Phineas Gage case, you might be astonished to learn that physicians in the 1940s and 1950s deliberately damaged the frontal lobes of nearly 50,000 American patients in a procedure known as the frontal lobotomy. The intent of the procedure was to reduce fear and anxiety in patients with serious psychological disorders, which it accomplished in many cases, but at great expense to the patient. As you might suspect from reading about Phineas Gage, many were unable to work or live normal lives due to their impulsive, antisocial behavior.

The **orbitofrontal cortex**, a part of the prefrontal cortex located just behind the bony orbits protecting the eyes, plays an important role in our emotional lives (● Figure 4.19). People with damage to the orbitofrontal

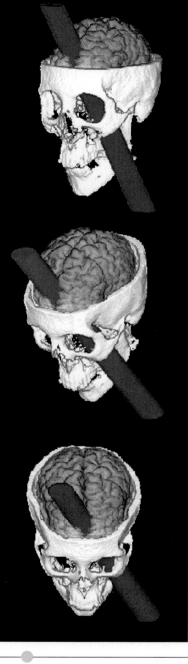

Phineas Gage suffered a terrible injury to his frontal lobes. Modern imaging techniques have allowed scientists to re-create the pathway of Gage's tamping rod through his brain. Remarkably, Gage survived his accident, although his friends described him as a "changed man."

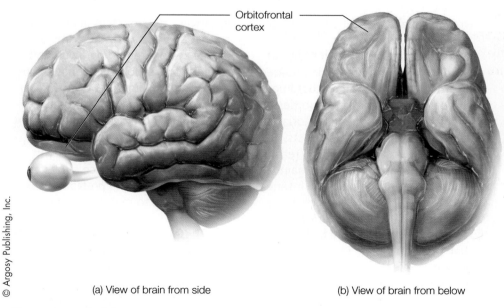

Orbitofrontal cortex

© Argosy Publishing, Inc.

(a) View of brain from side

(b) View of brain from below

FIGURE 4.19

The Orbitofrontal Cortex. People with damage to their orbitofrontal cortex have difficulty controlling impulses and anticipating the negative outcomes of poor decisions. This part of the brain is one of the last areas to mature.

orbitofrontal cortex A part of the prefrontal cortex located right behind the eyes that participates in impulse control.

cortex demonstrate dramatic deficits in their social behavior and experience of emotion, in spite of retaining their intelligence, abilities to learn and remember, language skills, and ability to pay attention (Bechara, Damasio, & Damasio, 2000; Damasio, 1994; Damasio & Anderson, 1993). When faced with a situation that would make most of us blush with embarrassment, people with orbitofrontal cortex damage appear to feel no shame, indeed, no emotion at all. In addition, these patients seem to make very poor decisions. They appear remarkably unable to anticipate the physical and emotional states usually associated with making poor choices. You probably know from personal experience that deciding to break a rule triggers anxiety about the outcomes should you be caught. These emotional states, if strong enough, should help you do the right thing. A person who does not experience this anticipatory anxiety will have no brakes on his or her behavior.

Psychology *as a* Hub Science

Law, Responsibility, and the Brain

In 1843, Daniel M'Naghten was planning to assassinate British Prime Minister Sir Robert Peel, but shot his secretary, Mr. Drummond, instead. M'Naghten told the police that the Tories (Peel's political party) made him do the deed, as they had followed him, persecuted him, and destroyed his peace of mind. In today's psychological terms, we would probably describe M'Naghten's ideas as delusions of persecution, indicating that M'Naghten likely suffered from schizophrenia or a related disorder, which we will discuss in our chapter on psychological disorders. To the outrage of Queen Victoria and many of her British subjects, M'Naghten was acquitted "by reason of insanity" and spent the remainder of his life in hospitals for the insane rather than prison. M'Naghten's legacy in English and American law is the insanity defense, which means that a person can be judged as not responsible for a criminal act if he or she has a mental condition that prevents understanding of the act and/or the wrongfulness of the act (Mobbs, Lau, Jones, & Frith, 2007).

As our understanding of correlations between the brain and behavior improves, psychology is likely to have a great deal to say to the criminal justice system regarding a person's capacity for responsible behavior. In 2005, the U.S. Supreme Court (*Roper v. Simmons*) made it illegal for states to administer the death penalty to an offender whose crime was committed prior to the age of 18, partly in response to neuroscience evidence that showed that the prefrontal cortex continues to mature up to the age of 25.

These issues recently came close to one of our homes, the sleepy little town of San Luis Obispo, California (population 45,000). In 2005, a 13-year-old boy bludgeoned 87-year-old Jerry O'Malley to death with a skateboard, locked up O'Malley's mobile home to delay discovery of the crime, and took O'Malley's car for a

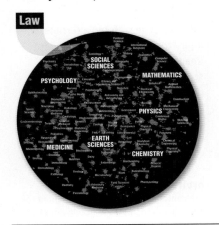

The case of patient E.V.R., who experienced orbitofrontal damage during surgery for a tumor, echoes our discussion of Phineas Gage (Eslinger & Damasio, 1985). Before his surgery, E.V.R. was considered a role model and a respected member of his community. Following his surgery, E.V.R. lost his job, went bankrupt, and divorced his wife to marry a prostitute, whom he divorced two years later. Although he had no difficulties talking about moral dilemmas, he experienced enormous problems when trying to make everyday decisions, such as buying toothpaste or choosing a restaurant.

Researchers are making other connections between abnormalities in the orbitofrontal cortex and antisocial behavior. In a sample of 21 individuals diagnosed with antisocial personality disorder, a condition characterized by rule-breaking and disregard for others which we discuss in our chapter on psychological disorders, the volume of the prefrontal cortex, which includes the orbitofrontal cortex, was about 11% less than in control participants who did not have the condition (Raine, Lencz, Bihrle, LaCasse, & Colletti, 2000). Not only do individuals with antisocial personality disorder or orbitofrontal damage fail to anticipate the emotional consequences of situations but they are unable to delay gratification. They typically choose immediate rewards over long-term benefits, like stealing something now in spite of knowing the long-term benefits of staying out of jail.

> The brain is a wonderful organ; it starts working the moment you get up in the morning and does not stop until you get into the office.
>
> —Robert Frost

joyride. The boy told police, "I knew it was wrong; I just did it." Joseph Wu, director of the Brain Imaging Center at the University of California, Irvine, told the court that the young murderer had "abnormally reduced activity in parts of his brain that govern a person's judgment" (Sneed, 2006, p. B1).

If somebody has evidence of abnormalities in parts of the brain "that govern a person's judgment," does the insanity defense apply? Is this a situation that calls for medical and psychological treatment or incarceration? We do not have answers for these questions today, but further understanding of the brain's structure and function in both law-abiding people and criminals will contribute to the legal system's ability to handle such cases fairly.

If you're curious about the young murderer's outcome, the court

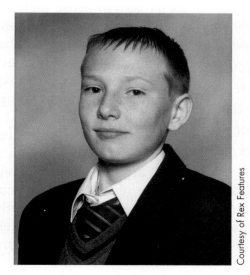

Courtesy of Rex Features

rejected suggestions that he needed treatment instead of incarceration. He was sentenced to a state juvenile corrections facility from which he will be automatically freed at age 25 (Parrilla, 2006). ⚙

How do we respond to youth violence? Fourteen-year-old Martin Dinnegan was stabbed to death by a 16-year-old and a 17-year-old as he got off his London bus in 2007. Perpetrators of crime at these ages are usually treated differently by the criminal justice system, but some are tried as adults. How old should people be before they are held responsible for their actions?

Because the orbitofrontal cortex is one of the last areas of the brain to fully mature (Eshel, Nelson, Blair, Pine, & Ernst, 2007), a relationship between the timing of any damage and the resulting behavior would not be too surprising. It does appear that the impact of orbitofrontal damage on moral behavior is greater the earlier it occurs during the course of development. In one study, two adults who had sustained orbitofrontal damage before the age of 16 months appeared to have been completely unable to acquire moral reasoning or behavior, in spite of their typical middle-class home environments (Anderson, Bechara, Damasio, Tranel, & Damasio, 1999).

The Occipital Lobe The occipital lobe, located at the back of the brain, is home to primary visual cortex. Primary visual cortex begins the process of interpreting input from the eyes by responding to basic information about an image, such as its borders, shading, color, and movement. This amount of processing, by itself, does not allow you to read this page or recognize your professor in the library. Two important pathways link the occipital lobe with the rest of the brain. A pathway connecting the occipital lobe with the temporal lobe allows us to recognize objects we see. The second pathway connects the occipital lobe with the parietal lobe and allows us to process the movement of objects. We discuss these processes further in the next sections.

The Temporal Lobe The temporal lobe also has a number of areas that are specialized for particular functions. The temporal lobe is home to our primary auditory cortex, which allows us to process incoming sounds. As mentioned earlier, the temporal lobe processes some higher visual system tasks, including the recognition of objects and the faces of familiar people. Patients with damage to the temporal lobe are often unable to recognize their loved ones by sight. They have to wait until the person speaks. We discuss this processing of vision and hearing by the temporal lobe in more detail in an upcoming chapter on sensation and perception.

Early scientists discovered that nerves carry only one type of information. When we take a blow to the back of the head, where your primary visual cortex is found, your occipital lobe does not know how to say "ouch." Instead, it responds to the blow as if you saw a flash of light (not necessarily the tweeting birds or stars indicated in cartoons).

We saw earlier how damage to Broca's area in the frontal lobe produced difficulty in speaking. Damage to another language area located in the temporal lobe, Wernicke's area, produces very different results. As we discuss in a later chapter on cognition, language, and intelligence, patients with damage to their Wernicke's area speak quite fluently, but make absolutely no sense. They cannot comprehend speech, but they seem blissfully unaware of their deficits.

The Parietal Lobe The parietal lobe is home to our primary somatosensory cortex, which helps us localize touch, pain, skin temperature, and body position. Damage to the parietal lobe can produce the odd symptoms of neglect syndrome. Patients with this condition have difficulty perceiving a part of their body or part of the visual field.

The parietal lobe processes input about taste and, like the temporal lobe, engages in some complex processing of vision. While the temporal lobe participates in visual recognition, the parietal lobe tells us how quickly something is moving toward us. This can be an essential bit of information when deciding whether or not it is safe to make a left turn in front of oncoming traffic. We discuss these functions of the parietal lobe in depth in our sensation and perception chapter.

Right Brain and Left Brain A special type of localization of function in the cerebral cortex is known as lateralization, or the localization of a function in either the right or left cerebral hemisphere. A basic type of lateralization occurs in the somatosensory and voluntary motor systems in the brain. Movement and sensation on the right side of the body are processed by the left hemisphere, and movement and sensation on the left side of the body by the right hemisphere. If you observe a person who is paralyzed on the right side of the body, you can be fairly certain that this paralysis is a result of motor cortex damage in the left hemisphere. In a similar manner, the visual cortex of the left hemisphere processes all data from the right half of the visual field, while the right hemisphere processes all data from the left half of the visual field. In other words, when you look straight ahead, holding your eyes and head still, everything to the right or left of center will be processed by the opposite hemisphere.

Much of our knowledge of lateralization of the human brain resulted from the careful analysis of a surgical procedure known as a split-brain operation (● Figure 4.20). To treat rare cases of life-threatening epileptic seizures, surgeons in the 1960s cut the patients' corpus callosum and other pathways connecting the right and left cerebral hemispheres (Bogen, Schultz, & Vogel, 1988). Not only did the procedure succeed in reducing or eliminating seizures, but it produced no changes in personality, intelligence, or speech. Only when patients were studied in the laboratory were the consequences of their surgery evident.

In one typical experiment, illustrated in ● Figure 4.21, participants were instructed to fixate on a dot at the center of a screen (Gazzaniga, 1967). The word HE appeared to the left of the dot, while the word ART appeared to the right. As mentioned earlier, this positioning means that the "HE" will be processed by the right hemisphere and the "ART" by the left. Because the corpus callosum and other connections between the two hemispheres were cut in the split-brain procedure, one hemisphere would not know what the other had seen. When asked to indicate the word seen, the participants said "ART." When shown a card with the two words printed on it and instructed to point with the left hand rather than verbalizing the word that was seen,

One patient with neglect syndrome could not recognize his own leg and believed the hospital staff was playing a horrible trick on him by placing a cadaver leg in his bed. Fortunately, the patient's condition improved over time.

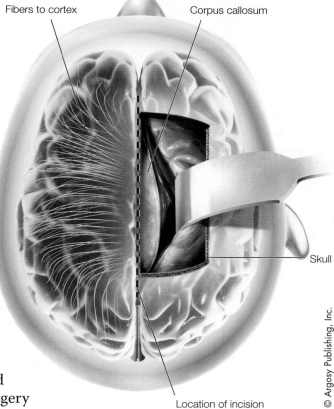

Fibers to cortex

Corpus callosum

Skull

Location of incision

© Argosy Publishing, Inc.

FIGURE 4.20

The Split-Brain Operation. To save patients from life-threatening seizures, physicians cut the corpus callosum, a large band of axons connecting the right and left hemispheres.

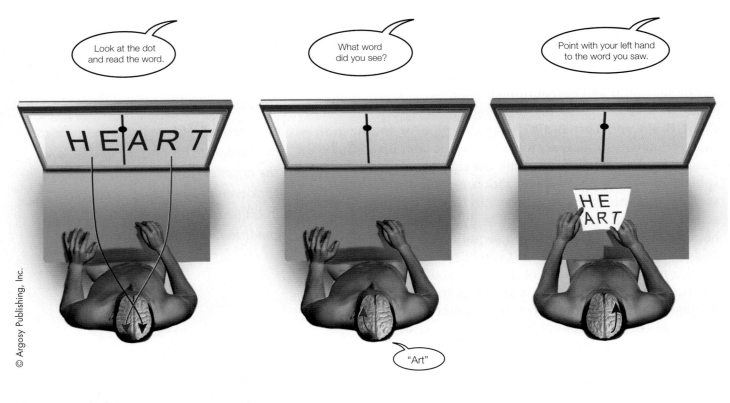

FIGURE 4.21

The Hemispheres Have Different Capacities for Language Functions. When asked verbally what word was seen, participants answered "art," which was seen by the verbal left hemisphere. When asked to point with the left hand (which is controlled by the right hemisphere) to the word that was seen, the participants pointed to "he," which is the word seen by the right hemisphere.

participants pointed to "HE." As mentioned earlier in this section, the right hemisphere provides motor control for the left side of the body, so the left hand was pointing out the word "seen" by the right hemisphere.

Subsequent research indicated that language, for most people, is lateralized to the left hemisphere, although a minority of individuals process language either in the right hemisphere or in both hemispheres (Rasmussen & Milner, 1977). The lateralization of language is correlated, although not completely, with a person's handedness. As shown in a later section, nearly all right-handers lateralize language to the left hemisphere, as do about 70% of people who are left-handed. The remaining individuals process language either in the right hemisphere or in both hemispheres.

Language is not the only cognitive process to show evidence of lateralization. Other suspected lateralized processes include mathematical computation and logical reasoning (left hemisphere) and music, spatial information, intuition, and the visual arts (right hemisphere). Emotional behavior also appears to be lateralized. In most people, activity of the left hemisphere is correlated with positive emotions, whereas activity in the right hemisphere is correlated with negative emotions, providing the cortex with a rough distinction between approaching positive things (left hemisphere activity) and avoiding negative things (right hemisphere activity; Davidson & Irwin, 1999). Anesthetizing the left hemisphere results in temporary feelings of depression, while anesthetizing the right hemisphere produces happiness (Lee et al., 2004).

Right-Left Brain Myths A word of caution is in order here. As noted by Roger Sperry, who won the 1981 Nobel Prize for his investigations of lateralization in the human brain, "The left-right dichotomy in cognitive mode is an idea with which it is very easy to run wild" (Sperry, 1982, p. 1225). Most of us have not undergone a split-brain procedure. Courtesy of our intact corpus callosum and other connections between the two cerebral hemispheres, information passes rapidly from one hemisphere to the other. Suggestions that you can improve your artistic or athletic talent or reduce inattention by "learning to access your right brain" have gained considerable attention in the popular press, but do not hold up to scrutiny in the laboratory. One of the most popular myths about lateralization is the idea that individual differences in artistic talent or logical thinking correlate with one's dominant hemisphere. Hemisphere dominance, as measured by the relative size of the hemispheres and the localization of language and handedness, does not predict occupational choice or artistic talent (Springer & Deutsch, 1998).

The Function of Lateralization What are the advantages of lateralization? Most species of animals show a preference for one "hand" or the other, as when a cat reaches for its prey (Cole, 1955; Holder, 1999).

Lateralization might provide organisms with the ability to multitask (Rogers, 2000). Chicks raised in the dark fail to lateralize visually guided responses normally and are at a disadvantage compared to normal chicks when feeding and watching for predators simultaneously. Success in this type of multitasking has obvious survival advantages. Lateralization in humans may have a more aggressive source. Because left-handedness is relatively uncommon, being left-handed affords an advantage in hand-to-hand combat (and baseball). One hypothesis about the advantage of lefty baseball players is that they see a ball pitched by a right-hander a

© Martin Harvey/Alamy

Human beings are not the only animals to have a preferred hand. However, other primates, like this chimpanzee using a stone to open nuts, are equally likely to be right- or left-handed. In contrast, over 90% of humans are right-handed.

© Yuri Arcurs/Shutterstock

© Anthony Lee/OJO Images Ltd/Alamy

split second faster than a right-handed batter would. Males are about twice as likely to be left-handers as females, and left-handedness becomes even more frequent in societies experiencing sustained conflicts and wars (Faurie & Raymond, 2004).

An alternate hypothesis suggests that human lateralization of brain structures made language possible (Berlim, Mattevi, Belmonte-de-Abreu, & Crow, 2003). This development could have a big price tag, however, as lateralization might also account for our species' vulnerabilities for schizophrenia, discussed in our chapter on psychological disorders. People with schizophrenia show abnormal hemisphere lateralization and are more likely to have ambiguous handedness (Berlim et al., 2003).

Experiencing Psychology

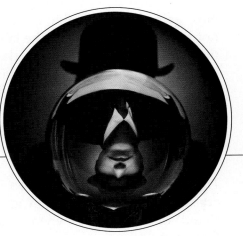

Handedness

Lateralization of language is correlated with handedness. Brenda Milner used the Wada test to determine hemisphere dominance for language, and then correlated these results with people's handedness (Milner, 1974). In the Wada test, usually administered prior to brain surgery, anesthesia is applied to one hemisphere at a time. Once anesthetized in this manner, you will be asked to speak. When the anesthesia wears off, the other hemisphere will be anesthetized, and your language ability will be checked again. When the hemisphere you use to process language is anesthetized, you will be unable to speak or understand language, but you'll do just fine when the other hemisphere is anesthetized. Mixed dominance refers to people who show relatively little lateralization for language and use both

hemispheres approximately equally for this function. These people would have trouble with language when either hemisphere is anesthetized. Milner's results are summarized in Table 4.3.

Handedness represents a continuum, with some people being nearly ambidextrous and others having very strong preferences for using one hand or the other. Although most of us would have no trouble answering a question asking whether we are right- or left-handed, researchers like

Milner must apply systems for determining a person's handedness. One of the frequently used instruments follows:

THE LATERAL PREFERENCE INVENTORY (COREN, 1993)
Simply read each of the questions in Table 4.4. Decide which hand you use for each activity and then circle the answer that describes you the best. If you are unsure of any answer, try to act out the action.

TABLE 4.3 Relationships Between Handedness and Language Localization

Handedness	Language left	Language right	Mixed dominance
Right-handed (90%)	96%	4%	0%
Left-handed (10%)	70%	15%	15%

Although efforts to connect brain lateralization, which is highly correlated with handedness, with occupational choice or artistic talent have not been successful, being in the left-handed minority might provide advantages in sports and in combat. Right-handed pitchers, like Tim Lincecum, are often challenged by left-handed hitters like Adrian Gonzalez.

TABLE 4.4 The Lateral Preference Inventory			
1. With which hand do you draw?	Left	Right	Either
2. Which hand would you use to throw a ball to hit a target?	Left	Right	Either
3. In which hand would you use an eraser on paper?	Left	Right	Either
4. Which hand removes the top card when you are dealing from a deck?	Left	Right	Either
5. With which hand do you normally write?	Left	Right	Either
6. In which hand do you use your racquet for tennis, squash, etc.?	Left	Right	Either
7. With which hand do you use your toothbrush?	Left	Right	Either
8. Which hand holds a knife when you are cutting things?	Left	Right	Either
9. Which hand holds the hammer when you are driving a nail?	Left	Right	Either
10. In which hand would you hold a match to strike it?	Left	Right	Either
11. Which hand holds the thread when you are threading a needle?	Left	Right	Either
12. In which hand would you use a fly swatter?	Left	Right	Either

Source: Coren, S. Bulletin of the Psychonomic Society, 1993, vol. 31, no. 1, pp. 1–3 (16 ref.). Used by permission.

To find your score, count the number of circled "right" answers and subtract the number of circled "left" answers. Ignore any "either" answers. Ambidextrous people will score around zero, very right-handed people will score near +12, and very left-handed people will score near −12.

Although this test can't tell you which hemisphere you use for language (and it's unlikely you'd like to spend your afternoon taking the Wada test), your odds of using your left hemisphere for language if you're very right-handed are quite high. ✪

Summary 4.2

Structures of the Nervous System

	Structure	What to remember
© Argosy Publishing, Inc.	Spinal cord	• Continuous with brainstem • Large axon pathways • Reflexes
© Argosy Publishing, Inc.	Brainstem and cerebellum	• Large axon pathways, arousal, reflexes, and body functions (heart rate, etc.) • Midbrain • Pons • Cerebellum • Medulla • Reticular formation
© Argosy Publishing, Inc.	Subcortical structures	• Embedded in the white matter of the cerebral hemispheres • Thalamus • Basal ganglia • Hypothalamus • Hippocampus • Cingulate cortex • Amygdala • Nucleus Accumbens
© Argosy Publishing, Inc.	Cerebral cortex	• The cortex is a thin layer of gray matter enveloping the hemispheres. • The cortex can be divided into four lobes. • An area of the cortex can have sensory, motor, or association functions. • Some functions are localized and lateralized in the cortex.

What Are the Major Structures and Functions of the Peripheral Nervous System and the Endocrine System?

The brain and spinal cord (the central nervous system) are spectacular processing units, but without input or the ability to implement commands, they would be no different than your computer's CPU without its mouse, keyboard, monitor, printer, and Internet connections. The lights may be on, but not much is going to happen.

In this section, we will explore the structures that provide these essential input and output functions in the body, making observable behavior possible. The peripheral nervous system (PNS) is a major source of connectivity. The PNS can be further separated into two divisions: the somatic nervous system and the autonomic nervous system. The somatic nervous system is comprised of peripheral portions of the sensory and voluntary movement systems. The autonomic nervous system is responsible for homeostasis, or the regulation of important body functions such as temperature and thirst, and our fight-or-flight response to emergencies. The endocrine system (ES) provides a means by which the central nervous system can communicate with the body through the release of chemical messengers into the bloodstream. These systems coordinate their efforts to produce consistent patterns of movement, hormone release, and arousal.

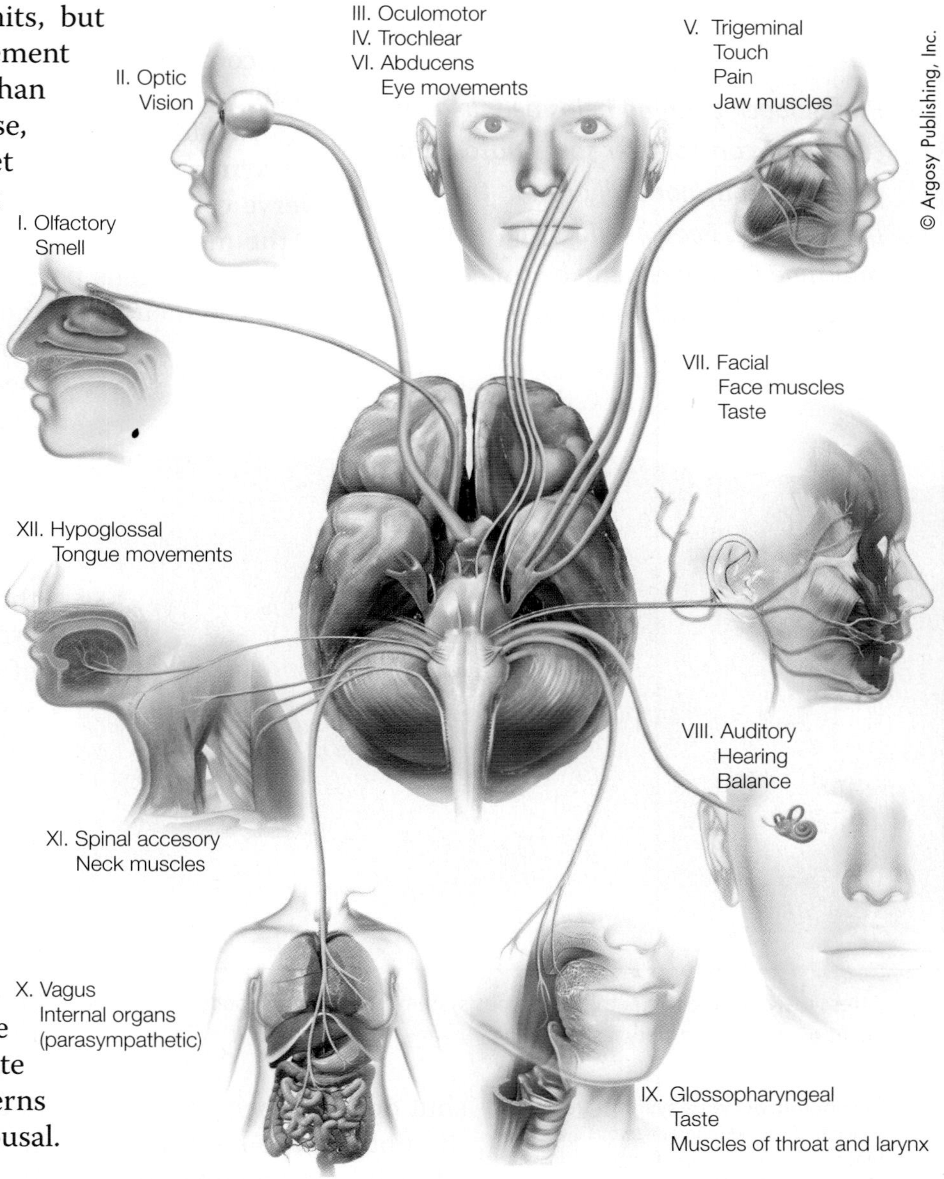

© Argosy Publishing, Inc.

FIGURE 4.22

The Cranial Nerves. Twelve pairs of cranial nerves carry sensory and motor information from the brain to the head, neck, and some internal organs.

- III. Oculomotor
- IV. Trochlear
- VI. Abducens
  Eye movements
- II. Optic
  Vision
- I. Olfactory
  Smell
- V. Trigeminal
  Touch
  Pain
  Jaw muscles
- VII. Facial
  Face muscles
  Taste
- XII. Hypoglossal
  Tongue movements
- VIII. Auditory
  Hearing
  Balance
- XI. Spinal accesory
  Neck muscles
- X. Vagus
  Internal organs
  (parasympathetic)
- IX. Glossopharyngeal
  Taste
  Muscles of throat and larynx

The Somatic Nervous System

The **somatic nervous system** is the part of the peripheral nervous system that transmits commands for voluntary movement from the central nervous system to the muscles and brings sensory input back to the CNS for further processing. These functions are carried out by the 31 pairs of spinal nerves serving the torso and limbs, and the 12 pairs of cranial nerves serving the head, neck, and some internal organs (● Figure 4.22). We will

somatic nervous system The part of the peripheral nervous system that brings sensory information to the central nervous system and transmits commands to the muscles.

discuss the sensory functions of the somatic nerves in more detail in our chapter on sensation and perception.

The Autonomic Nervous System

The function of the **autonomic nervous system** is the control of "tissues other than the skeletal muscle" (Langley, 1921). The term *autonomic* has the same root as the word *autonomy*, or independence. You might think of this system as the "cruise control" of the body, as it ensures that your heart keeps beating and your lungs continue to inhale and exhale without your conscious direction. You wouldn't have much of a social life if you had to consciously issue these commands. This doesn't mean that we are unable to take command of some autonomic functions. When you run, swim, or lift weights, you definitely control your breathing.

Biofeedback training helps people gain conscious control over some autonomic processes that normally run in the background. People who suffer from migraine headaches can be trained to reduce blood flow to the brain.

The autonomic nervous system contains two subdivisions, the **sympathetic division** and the **parasympathetic division**. Nerve cells participating in the sympathetic division are found in the middle regions of the spinal cord in the torso and lower back. Nerve cells participating in the parasympathetic division are located either in the brain or in the lowest segments of the spinal cord. In this sense, the parasympathetic division brackets the sympathetic division, like parentheses.

The two divisions of the autonomic nervous system are active under very different circumstances. The sympathetic division prepares the body for situations requiring the expenditure of energy, while the parasympathetic division directs the storage of energy. You have probably experienced sympathetic arousal, perhaps due to a close call on the highway. In the aroused state produced by the sympathetic division, our hearts race, we breathe rapidly, our faces become pale, and our palms sweat. All these activities are designed to provide the muscles with the nutrients they need for a fight-or-flight reaction. Because so much energy is being expended during arousal, lower priority systems, including your immune system and digestion, are

© Kurt Jones/Ad Stock Images

Stress activates the sympathetic nervous system, preparing the body for fight or flight or, in this case, very fast paddling.

autonomic nervous system The division of the peripheral nervous system that directs the activity of glands, organs, and smooth muscles.

sympathetic nervous system The division of the autonomic nervous system that coordinates arousal.

parasympathetic nervous system The part of the autonomic nervous system associated with rest, repair, and energy storage.

shut down. When your ancestors faced a lion on the Serengeti Plain, they did not need to be using precious resources to fight a disease or to digest a lunch that wouldn't be needed if they failed to survive the attack, so the sympathetic division directed all the body's energy toward running away from the lion (we assume fighting would be less successful in this case). In contrast, the parasympathetic division controls the glands and organs at times of relative calm. Instead of using up energy like the sympathetic division, the parasympathetic division allows you to store nutrients, repair your body, and return the activity of internal organs to baseline levels.

The operation of the internal organs in response to environmental stimuli reflects a sophisticated combination of inputs from both the sympathetic and parasympathetic divisions (Berntson, Cacioppo, & Quigley, 1991). The sympathetic and parasympathetic divisions usually have antagonistic effects on the organs they serve and are designed to alternate their activities (● Figure 4.23). We cannot be simultaneously relaxed and aroused. The sympathetic nervous system dilates the pupils of the eye, whereas

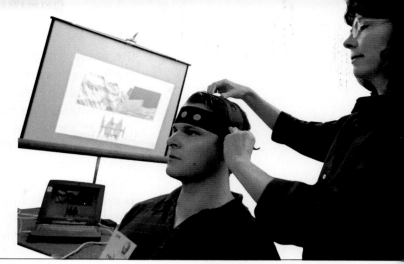

Biofeedback helps people gain control over some otherwise automatic functions, like blood pressure, by changing their thinking, how they are breathing, or the level of muscle tension in their bodies.

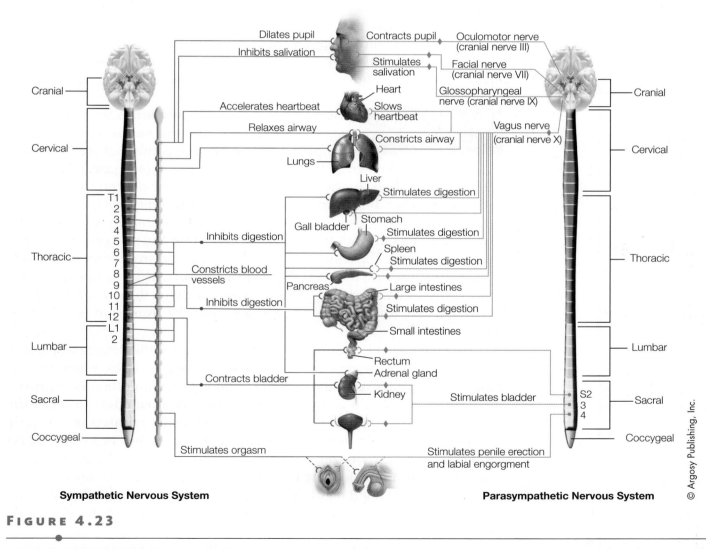

© Argosy Publishing, Inc.

FIGURE 4.23

The Autonomic Nervous System. The sympathetic nervous system (left) usually has the opposite effect on an organ than the parasympathetic nervous system (right). For example, sympathetic input tells the heart to beat faster, while parasympathetic input tells the heart to slow down. However, both systems manage to cooperate during sex.

the parasympathetic division constricts the pupils. The heart responds to sympathetic commands by beating faster, but responds to parasympathetic commands by slowing down. The two divisions do manage, however, to cooperate during sexual activity.

The nature of the autonomic nervous system is important to our understanding of stress. The sympathetic division was designed to deal with emergencies that could be resolved relatively quickly. Our ancestors either escaped that lion or they did not. Worrying about far distant dangers is a luxury that human beings did not have until quite recently. Unfortunately, we now have the opportunity to worry about upcoming exams, next month's rent payment, what to do following graduation, and even if we have sufficient funds for retirement. Whenever you identify something as a significant threat, the sympathetic division goes into action.

Sustained sympathetic activation depletes your body of resources at the same time your parasympathetic division is unable to store new resources. If left unchecked, sympathetic division activity can lead to fatigue and wear and tear on internal organs. Because most modern stress is unavoidable, it is essential that you practice good stress management, such as practicing excellent dietary and sleep habits, exercising regularly, and maintaining strong social networks. We will discuss stress effects on the body and stress management techniques in a later chapter on health.

The Endocrine System

The nervous system communicates by passing messages along nerves, but the **endocrine system** is comprised of a number of glands that release chemical messengers known as hormones into the blood (● Figure 4.24). These chemicals are often identical to the ones used by one neuron to communicate with another, but their action affects more distant cells and can affect many parts of the body in a coordinated fashion. Ultimately, the endocrine system responds to input from the nervous system and from the hypothalamus in particular. The endocrine system is especially involved with arousal, metabolism, growth, and sex. Among the important glands of the endocrine system are the pineal gland, the pituitary gland, the thyroid gland, the adrenal glands, the islets of Langerhans, and the ovaries in females and testes in males.

The pineal gland, and its release of the chemical messenger melatonin, is important in the maintenance of our sleep-waking cycles, which we discuss in our chapter on consciousness. Although not an officially approved medication, melatonin is used by some travelers in an effort to offset the unpleasant effects of jet lag. Melatonin is normally released in the early evening, and it breaks down in the presence of light. Our ancestors had no problems with this, but our modern exposure to artificial light can have negative implications for our health. For example, higher rates of cancer among people working night shifts in hospitals have been attributed to the breakdown of melatonin by light (Dopfel, Schulmeister, & Schernhammer, 2007).

The pituitary gland, located just above the roof of your mouth, is often referred to as the body's master gland, because many of the hormones it releases activate the body's other glands. The pituitary in turn is regulated

endocrine system A system responsible for the release of hormones into the bloodstream.

by the hypothalamus, which lies directly above it. The pituitary hormones form two groups. One group, including oxytocin and vasopressin, is released directly from the pituitary. The second group consists of several hormones that influence the release of hormones by other glands. Oxytocin participates in a number of important functions, including breastfeeding, but is currently getting a lot of attention for its roles in human bonding (Diamond, 2004; Feldman, Weller, Zagoory-Sharon, & Levine, 2007; Gordon et al., 2008). For example, a woman's oxytocin

© R. Gino Santa Maria/Shutterstock

levels in her second month of pregnancy predict maternal bonding behaviors that she will later direct to her infant, such as gazing at the infant, vocalizing, and touching (Feldman et al., 2007). Vasopressin influences water retention by the body, but might also play a role in bonding and parenting behaviors (Kozorovitskiy, Hughes, Lee, & Gould, 2006).

Oxytocin released by the pituitary gland is correlated with human bonding between parent and child and between romantic partners.

Pituitary hormones direct the release of growth hormone, which stimulates growth and regeneration, making it a popular performance-enhancing

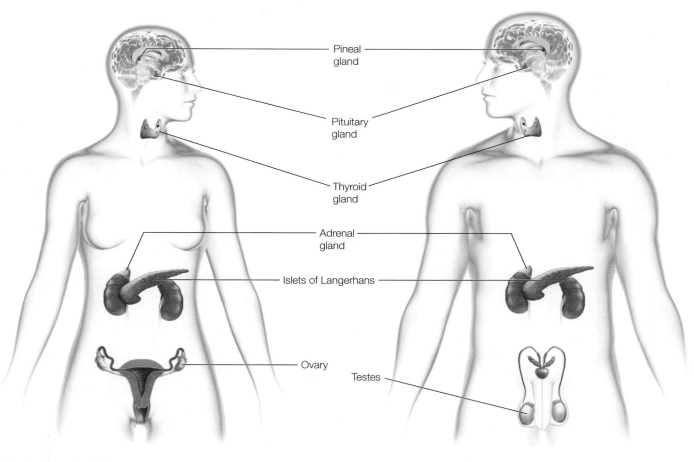

© Argosy Publishing, Inc.

FIGURE 4.24

Glands of the Endocrine System. The endocrine system communicates with other body tissues by releasing hormones from glands into the bloodstream.

© Scott Rovak/UPI/Newscom

Human growth hormone, released normally by the pituitary gland, has become a popular performance-enhancing substance among elite athletes like baseball's Mark McGwire.

substance used illegally by many elite athletes. Other pituitary hormones control the production and release of sex hormones by the ovaries and testes, initiating puberty and maintaining fertility. In response to pituitary hormones, the thyroid gland, located just below your larynx, or voice box, in your throat, raises or lowers your rate of metabolism, or the chemical processes your body needs to sustain life. Low levels of thyroid can mimic the symptoms of depression, described further in our chapter on psychological disorders. The islets of Langerhans, located in the pancreas, produce a number of hormones essential to digestion, including insulin. At times of stress, pituitary hormones activate the adrenal glands, located just above the kidneys in the lower back. In response, the adrenal glands release other hormones, including cortisol, that travel throughout the body and brain to provide a general "wake-up" message.

Summary 4.3

The Peripheral Nervous and Endocrine Systems

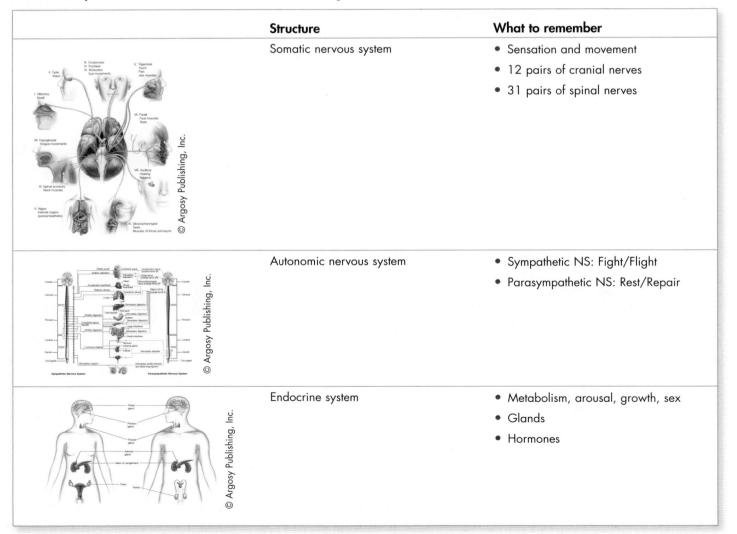

	Structure	What to remember
	Somatic nervous system	• Sensation and movement • 12 pairs of cranial nerves • 31 pairs of spinal nerves
	Autonomic nervous system	• Sympathetic NS: Fight/Flight • Parasympathetic NS: Rest/Repair
	Endocrine system	• Metabolism, arousal, growth, sex • Glands • Hormones

© Argosy Publishing, Inc.

Interpersonal Relationships
From a Biological Perspective

Our species' need to cope with a complex social environment might have pushed the development of our advanced brains. We discussed a number of parts of the brain that are relevant to social functioning. The anterior cingulate cortex responds to social exclusion the same way it responds to physical pain. The amygdala allows us to process fear, a function that seems to be distorted in people who behave in antisocial ways toward others. What else does the biological perspective have to say about social behavior in general and about relationships in particular?

Earlier in the chapter, we described a hormone that seems particularly related to the special type of social behavior that is a close relationship—oxytocin. We described how this hormone relates to mother-infant bonding. Does oxytocin influence romantic relationships as well? The answer appears to be yes. Couples with higher than average oxytocin levels report greater support from their partners and more physical intimacy (Gouin et al., 2010). Hopefully, you are now thinking about a concept you learned from reading our chapter on research methods. These are correlations, right? So we cannot conclude from these data that oxytocin *causes* better relationships. It is possible that people who are just naturally higher in oxytocin activity are better at relationships, or that being in a relationship boosts your oxytocin. Some third variable, perhaps a strong childhood attachment to parents, which we discuss in a later chapter on development, might lead to both higher oxytocin levels and better relationships.

To help us investigate oxytocin and relationships further, we can look at actual experiments in which oxytocin was applied in nasal spray (Ditzen et al., 2009). In one study using this technique, oxytocin nasal spray improved positive communication behaviors in couples engaged in a verbal conflict. There was a bonus, too. Oxytocin also reduced a hormone associated with stress, known as cortisol, which we discuss in a later chapter on health. But here is another interesting twist, once again emphasizing our need to zoom out to consider multiple perspectives of psychology, in this case adding the social perspective to the biological. At least with animals, administration of extra oxytocin reduces stress when animals are in the company of other animals, but not when the animal is alone (Yee et al., 2010). So it is not enough to have a lot of oxytocin on your own—it is most effective in reducing stress when you're with friends.

© Julia Remezova/
Shutterstock

Giving an animal extra oxytocin reduces stress only when it is in the company of other animals. When an animal is alone, extra oxytocin has no effect. Zooming out from the individual to the social perspective gives us a more accurate view of oxytocin's effects.

© WilleeCole/Shutterstock

Chapter 4
Reflections

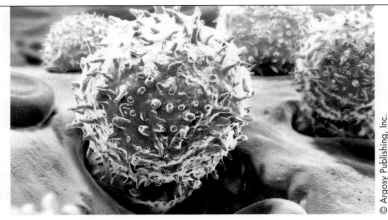

We opened this chapter by examining how the brain anticipates the social environments we encounter in preparation to fight broad categories of disease-causing organisms. The way we look at our social connectedness begins a cascade of biological events that prepare us to battle either viruses (social inclusion) or bacteria (social exclusion). When you began reading this chapter, however, you probably had no idea how the brain could orchestrate such a response without our awareness it was doing so.

To understand a situation like this, psychologists must evaluate the mind across a number of perspectives. The social perspective contributes insight into how and why a person feels isolated from or connected to others. Cognitive psychologists examine the thinking processes leading to an assessment of social inclusion or exclusion. The individual difference perspective explains why one person can feel lonely with a crowd of friends while another person is content with one or two good friends. The developmental perspective points to the periods within our lifespan when this response is particularly likely to occur. The evolutionary perspective reminds us that being alone was dangerous for our ancestors, leading to a motivation to seek the company of others. Cutting across these perspectives, the biological approach provides the mechanism for translating perceptions of inclusion or exclusion into a concrete, proactive response by the immune system.

This chapter examined the components of the biological mind, from the microscopic level of the neuron to the larger structures and systems that make up the central and peripheral nervous systems. An evaluation of our changing social environment, and our place and security within it, requires some of the most sophisticated processing of the cerebral cortex, which in turn communicates to subcortical structures, including the hypothalamus, to implement a response. These subcortical structures activate the endocrine system, leading to the release of hormones that direct the immune system to prepare for bacteria or viruses. An understanding of the physical basis of behavior allows us to explain what might otherwise look like a very mysterious process. ‹

KEY TERMS The Language of Psychological S...

Be sure you can define these terms and use them correctly.

action potential, p.135
amygdala, p. 154
autonomic nervous system, p. 170
axon, p. 132
basal ganglia, p. 152
biological psychology, p. 127
brainstem, p. 150
cell body, p. 131
central nervous system (CNS), p. 145
cerebellum, p. 151
cerebral cortex, p. 155
cingulate cortex, p. 154
corpus callosum, p. 155
dendrite, p. 132
endocrine system (ES), p. 172

frontal lobe, p. 157
hippocampus, p. 154
hypothalamus, p. 152
medulla, p. 150
midbrain, p. 152
myelin, p. 133
neuron, p. 131
neurotransmitter, p. 139
nucleus accumbens, p. 155
occipital lobe, p. 157
orbitofrontal cortex, p. 159
parasympathetic nervous
    system, p. 170
parietal lobe, p. 157

peripheral n...
    p. 146
pons, p. 151
prefrontal co...
receptor, p. 13...
resting potenti...
reticular format... p. 152
reuptake, p. 139
somatic nervous system, p. 169
spinal cord, p. 145
sympathetic nervous system, p. 170
synapse, p. 139
temporal lobe, p. 157
thalamus, p. 152

The rods and cones i...
light energy that...

MEDIA RESOURCES

Log in to CengageBrain to access the resources your instructor requires. For this book, you can access:

Psychology **CourseMate** brings course concepts to life with interactive learning, study, and exam preparation tools that support the printed textbook. A textbook-specific website, Psychology **CourseMate** includes an integrated interactive eBook and other interactive learning tools including quizzes, flashcards, videos, and more.

WebTUTOR   More than just an interactive study guide, **WebTutor** is an anytime, anywhere customized learning solution with an eBook, keeping you connected to your textbook, instructor, and classmates.

aplia If your professor has assigned **Aplia** homework:
1. Sign in to your account.
2. Complete the corresponding homework exercises as required by your professor.
3. When finished, click "Grade It Now" to see which areas you have mastered, which areas need more work, and detailed explanations of every answer.

n the retina begin the process of interpreting the
enters the eye.

The Perceiving Mind

5

Sensation and Perception

Learning Objectives

1 Explain the basic steps of sensation/perception, including transduction of stimuli into neural signals and the distinction between bottom-up and top-down perceptual processing.

2 Classify signal detection outcomes in perception scenarios as hits, misses, false alarms, or correct rejections.

3 Analyze the process by which the physical structures of the eye transduce light waves into neural signals producing the sense of vision.

4 Contrast the trichromacy and opponent process theories of color vision in terms of biological mechanisms and perceptual phenomena explained.

5 Evaluate the evidence for bottom-up and top-down perceptual processing mechanisms in the contexts of object recognition and depth perception.

6 Analyze the process by which physical structures of the ear transduce sound waves into neural signals, producing perception of pitch, loudness, and spatial location in hearing.

7 Summarize the mechanisms by which the somatosensory and chemical sense systems produce perception of body position, touch, temperature, pain, smell, and taste.

8 Analyze the causes of various individual differences in perception (including development and culture) in terms of biology, experience, and their interaction.

We like to think we understand reality. After all, we can see, hear, touch, smell, and taste it, right? We don't live in some science fiction universe where things are not how they appear, or do we?

The human eye can see many different colors, but what does it mean to "see" a color? Is color something that is a fixed quality of an object? Is the sky really blue and is an apple really red? Or does the human mind construct these colors from the light reflected from these objects into the eye? Stop for a moment to look at the "Discovering Psychology" images to the left. In the upper image, the one with many stripes, do the words "Discovering" and "Psychology" look the same? Do the words "Cacioppo" and

"Freberg" look the same? If you're like most people, your answer to these questions will be no. But in the lower image, you can see the words without the stripes in their actual colors. You might think we're being tricky and changing the colors in the upper image, but honestly, we wouldn't do that to you. What makes the words look different in the upper image is the colors surrounding them. The light reflecting from the words into your eye hasn't changed, but the way your mind interprets the information changes because of the words' context. Something happens between the time we zoom in to study the function of the rods and cones of the eye, shown in the larger image, and when we zoom out again to learn how the brain processes vision. Incidentally, this image is an example of the Munker illusion, named after its discoverer (Munker, 1970).

What can we learn from phenomena like the Munker illusion? First, we do believe there is an objective reality out there that follows the laws of physics. At the same time, our experience of that reality is very personal. For example, somewhere between 7 and 10% of men have a type of red-green colorblindness. As you will learn in this chapter, "colorblindness" is really not an accurate term. These men see color, just in a different way than the rest of us. Would being colorblind change the way a person sees the Munker illusion? See for yourself. We can reconstruct how the images would look to a colorblind person (see ● Figure 5.1). The illusion still works to a point, because the colors of "Discovering" and "Psychology" in the striped image look different, and they're not. Is the "reality" seen by a colorblind person different from your reality? We're going to argue that it is not reality that changes but the way the brain views that reality.

As you'll see in this chapter, we carefully construct models of reality from the information we obtain through our senses. We like to think that we are aware of the world around us, and it is somewhat unsettling to realize that the world might actually be quite different from the impressions it forms on the human mind. You will learn how the models built by the human mind have promoted our survival over many generations. Our models are quite different from those built by the minds of other animals, whose survival often depends on obtaining very different types of information from the environment around them.

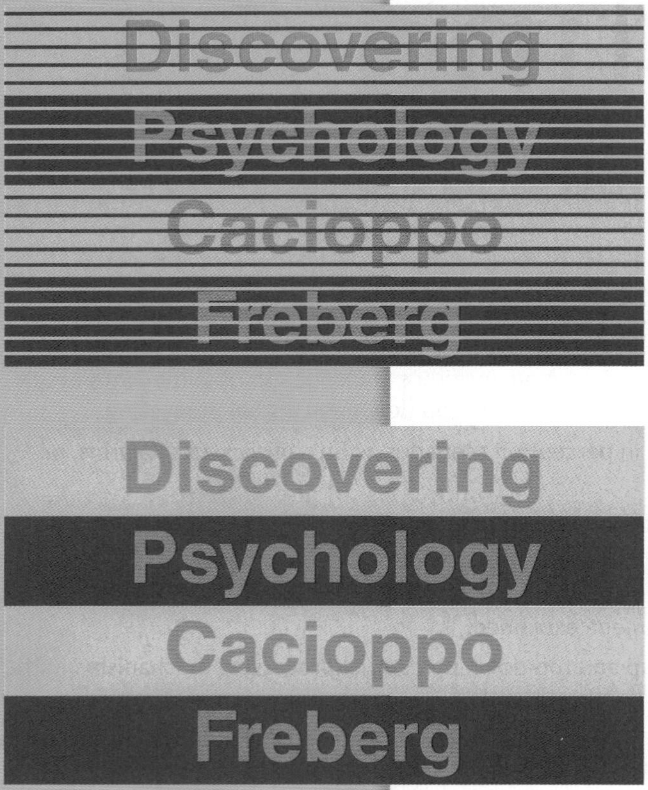

© Cengage Learning 2013

© Cengage Learning 2013

FIGURE 5.1

The Munker Illusion and Colorblindness. Color is constructed by the human mind from light waves that reach the retina, so the experience of color can be intensely personal. Here we see the same images as shown at the beginning of the chapter, but this time they are shown as they would appear to a person with a common form of red-green colorblindness.

How Does Sensation Lead to Perception?

The mind is bombarded with information, whether we are asleep or awake. This information can take many forms, from the electromagnetic energy of the sun to vibrations in the air to molecules dissolved in the saliva on our tongue. The process of **sensation** brings information to the brain that arises in the reality outside our bodies, like a beautiful sunset, or originates from within, like an upset stomach.

Sensory systems have developed through natural selection, described in our chapter on interactions between nature and nurture, to provide information that enhances survival within a particular niche. We sense a uniquely human reality, and one that is not necessarily shared by other animals. Your dog begins howling seconds before you hear the siren from an approaching ambulance, because the dog's hearing is better than yours for these high-pitched sounds. Horses seem to bolt at the slightest provocation, but they may be reacting to the vibration of an approaching car or animal that they sense through their front hoofs, a source of information that is not available to the rider. Some insects, like honeybees, can see ultraviolet light that lies outside the human visible spectrum. Instead of seeing uniformly colored petals of a flower like we do, insects see a "bull's-eye" at the center of the flower, directing them to the nectar and pollen.

The photo on the left shows a Carolina jessamine as we would see it. The photo on the right shows the flower as a honeybee might see it. This photo has been altered to simulate the honeybee's ability to see in the ultraviolet range. The bee's version makes it much easier to find the nectar at the center of the blossom, which of course is much more important to the survival of bees than of humans. Image © Sue Williams and Adrian G. Dyer, from Williams S., Dyer A.G. (2007). A photographic simulation of insect vision. *Journal Ophthalmic Photography 29,* 10–14.

Differences in sensation do occur from person to person, such as the need to wear corrective glasses or not, but they are relatively subtle. However, once we move from the process of sensation to that of **perception,** or the interpretation of sensory input, individual differences become much more evident. Friends voting for different presidential candidates will come to very different conclusions about who won a debate. Everyone present probably sensed similar information from the environment, but each person's perceptions are likely to be unique.

© AP Photo/Roberto Pfeil

We have all had the experience of watching events with others (sensation) and then being shocked by the different interpretations we hear of what just happened (perception).

sensation The process of detecting environmental stimuli or stimuli arising from the body.

perception The process of interpreting sensory information.

FIGURE 5.2

All Species Experience an Adaptive Reality. Human beings see only a small part of the electromagnetic energy emitted from the sun. Some animals see even less. Dogs apparently do just fine seeing blues, yellows, and grays, whereas humans have evolved to see a much more colorful world. Colors that look red to us probably look yellow to a dog, and colors we see as green would look gray or white. The dog's view of the world is simulated in the photo on the right.

© ChristopherCosner.com

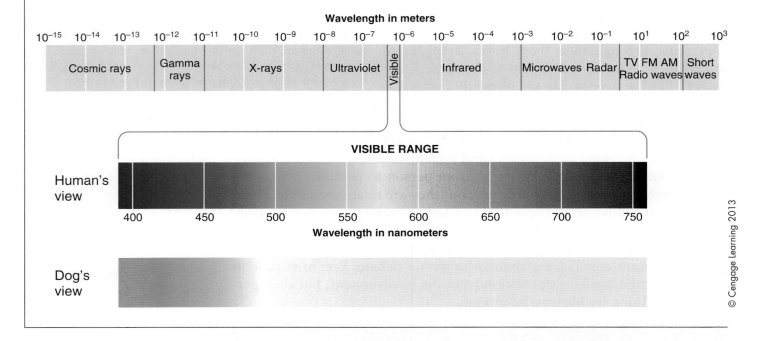

© Cengage Learning 2013

<table>
<tr><td colspan="19" align="center">Wavelength in meters</td></tr>
</table>

| 10^{-15} | 10^{-14} | 10^{-13} | 10^{-12} | 10^{-11} | 10^{-10} | 10^{-9} | 10^{-8} | 10^{-7} | 10^{-6} | 10^{-5} | 10^{-4} | 10^{-3} | 10^{-2} | 10^{-1} | 10^{1} | 10^{2} | 10^{3} |

Cosmic rays | Gamma rays | X-rays | Ultraviolet | Visible | Infrared | Microwaves | Radar | TV FM AM Radio waves | Short waves

VISIBLE RANGE

Human's view

400   450   500   550   600   650   700   750

Wavelength in nanometers

Dog's view

Sensory Information Travels to the Brain

Sensation begins with the interaction between a physical stimulus and our biological sensory systems. A stimulus is anything that can elicit a reaction from our sensory systems. For example, we react to light energy that falls within our visual range, as we will see later in this chapter, but we cannot "see" other types of light energy that fall outside that range, such as the microwaves that cook our dinner or the ultraviolet waves that can harm our skin (see • Figure 5.2).

Before you can use information from your senses, it must be translated into a form the nervous system can understand. This process of translation from stimulus to neural signal is known as **transduction.** You might think of sensory transduction as similar to the processing of information by your computer. Modern computers transduce a variety of inputs, including voice, keyboard, mouse clicks, and touch, into a programming language for further processing.

transduction The translation of incoming sensory information into neural signals.

The Brain Constructs Perceptions From Sensory Information

Once information from the sensory systems has been transduced into neural signals and sent to the brain, the process of perception, or the interpretation of the sensory information, can begin. Perception allows us to organize, recognize, and use the information provided by the senses.

An important gateway to perception is the process of attention, defined as a narrow focus of consciousness. As we discuss in our chapters on consciousness, memory, and thinking, attention often determines which features of the environment influence our subsequent thoughts and behaviors. What types of stimuli are likely to grab our attention? Unfamiliar, changing, or high-intensity stimuli often impact our survival and seem to have a high priority for our attention. Unfamiliar stimuli in our ancestors' environment might have meant a new source of danger (an unknown predator) or a new source of food (an unfamiliar fruit) that warranted additional investigation. Our sensory systems are particularly sensitive to change in the environment. Notice how you pay attention to the sound of your heating system cycling on or off, but pay little attention to the noise it makes while running. This reduced response to an unchanging stimulus is known as **sensory adaptation.** High-intensity stimuli, such as bright lights and loud noises, invariably draw our attention because the situations that produce these stimuli, such as a nearby explosion, can have obvious consequences for our safety.

We rarely have the luxury of paying attention to any single stimulus. In most cases, we experience divided attention, in which we attempt to process multiple sources of sensory information. Many of us try to walk to class without getting run over by a car while texting. These divided attention abilities are limited. We simply cannot process all the information converging simultaneously on our sensory systems. To prioritize input, we use selective attention, or the ability to focus on a subset of available information and exclude the rest.

We refer to the brain's use of incoming signals to construct perceptions as **bottom-up processing.** For example, we construct our visual reality from information about light that is sent from the eye to the brain. However, the brain also imposes its own structure on the incoming information,

We pay attention to unfamiliar, intense, and changing aspects of our environment, as these features often have significance for our survival. Entertainers like Lady Gaga definitely understand how to gain our attention.

© 2010 Jon Kopaloff/Film-Magic./Getty Images

If you think about the most memorable advertisements you have seen lately on television or online, it is likely that they share the features of attention-getting stimuli: novelty (we don't see talking geckos every day), change (rapid movement, use of changing colors, the dreaded pop-up), and intensity (the sound is often louder than the program you're watching).

Although we rarely get to focus on one thing at a time, which means that we can divide our attention, we are not as good at multitasking as we may like to think.

© iofoto/Shutterstock

sensory adaptation The tendency to pay less attention to a nonchanging source of stimulation.

bottom-up processing Perception based on building simple input into more complex perceptions.

Selective attention, or our focus on a subset of input, prioritizes incoming information. However, we can sometimes be so focused that we miss important information. In a classic study by Simons and Chabris (1999), people counting the number of times a basketball was passed in a video completely missed the person in the gorilla suit who walked onstage, faced the camera, and pounded its chest. People who do better on multitasking tend to see the gorilla more often than those who do not. *Source:* From Simons, D.J., & Chabris, C. F. (1999). Gorillas in our midst: Sustained inattentional blindness for dynamic events. *Perception, 28,* 1059–1074. Figure provided by Daniel Simons. © 1999 Daniel J. Simons. Image used with permission.

top-down processing A perceptual process in which memory and other cognitive processes are required for interpreting incoming sensory information.

psychophysics The study of relationships between the physical qualities of stimuli and the subjective responses they produce.

a type of processing known as top-down. In **top-down processing,** we use the knowledge we have gained from prior experience with stimuli to perceive them. For example, a skilled reader has no trouble reading the following sentences, even though the words are jumbled:

> All you hvae to do to mkae a snetnece raedalbe is to mkae srue taht the fisrt and lsat letrtes of ecah wrod saty the smae. Wtih prcatcie, tihs porcses becoems mcuh fsater and esaeir.

How can we explain our ability to read these sentences? Obviously, we require bottom-up processing to bring the sensations of the letter shapes to our brain. From there, however, we use knowledge and experience to recognize individual words. Many students have learned the hard way that proofreading term papers must be done very carefully. Just as in our example, if the brain "expects" to see a particular word, you are very likely to "see" that word, even if it is misspelled, a mistake that is unlikely to be made by the very literal, bottom-up processing of a computer spell-checker.

Can we predict when the mind will use bottom-up or top-down processing? There are no hard and fast rules. Obviously, we always use bottom-up processing, or the information would not be perceived at all. It is possible that we need only bottom-up processing to respond appropriately to very simple stimuli, like indicating whether you saw a flash of light. As stimuli become more complicated, like reading a sentence or recognizing a friend in a crowd, we are more likely to engage in top-down processing in addition to bottom-up.

Measuring Perception Gustav Fechner (1801–1887) developed methods, which he called **psychophysics,** for studying the relationship between stimuli (the physics part) and perception of those stimuli (the psyche or

FIGURE 5.4

Absolute Sensory Thresholds. An absolute threshold is the smallest amount of sensation that can be processed by our sensory systems under ideal conditions. Moving from left to right in this image, we see that (1) the absolute threshold for touch is the equivalent of feeling the wing of a fly fall on your cheek from a distance of 1 cm, (2) the absolute threshold for olfaction is a drop of perfume in the air filling a 6-room apartment, (3) the absolute threshold for sweetness is the equivalent of 1 teaspoon of sugar in 2 gallons of water (but as you already know, the absolute threshold for bitter tastes is even more sensitive), (4) the absolute threshold for hearing is the equivalent of the ticking of an expensive watch 20 feet away, and (6) the absolute threshold for vision is seeing a candle flame 30 miles away on a dark, clear night.

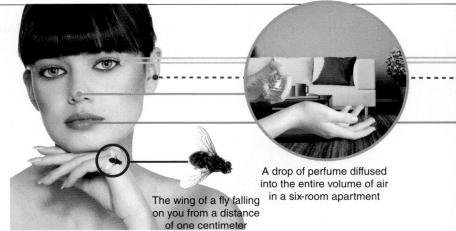

The wing of a fly falling on you from a distance of one centimeter

A drop of perfume diffused into the entire volume of air in a six-room apartment

FIGURE 5.3

Connecting the Physical World and the Mind. Golden rectangles appear in art and architecture dating back to ancient Greece, but why are they attractive? Gustav Fechner made many attempts to link physical realities with human psychological responses. He asked people to choose which rectangles are "most pleasing" or "least pleasing." His results, shown below the rectangles, indicated that the "most pleasing" rectangle was fourth from the right. This rectangle is the closest to having "golden" proportions (1: 1.618). Its sides have a ratio of 13:21.

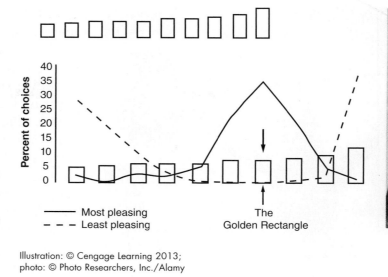

Percent of choices

40
35
30
25
20
15
10
5
0

——— Most pleasing
– – – Least pleasing

The Golden Rectangle

Illustration: © Cengage Learning 2013;
photo: © Photo Researchers, Inc./Alamy

Gustav Fechner

mind part). Fechner's careful methods not only contributed to the establishment of psychology as a true science but are still used in research (see ● Figure 5.3).

The methods of psychophysics allow us to establish the limits of awareness, or thresholds, for each of our sensory systems. The smallest possible stimulus that can be detected is known as the **absolute threshold.** Under ideal circumstances, our senses are surprisingly sensitive (see ● Figure 5.4). For example, you can see the equivalent of a candle flame 30 miles away on a moonless night. We can also establish a **difference threshold,** or the smallest difference between two stimuli that can be detected. The amount of difference that can be detected depends on the size of the stimuli being compared. As stimuli get larger, differences must also become larger to be detected by an observer. For example, it is easier to detect the difference between a 5 lb weight and a 10 lb weight than between a 400 lb weight and a 405 lb weight, even though the absolute difference in weight is the same in both cases.

absolute threshold The smallest amount of stimulus that can be detected.
difference threshold The smallest detectable difference between two stimuli.

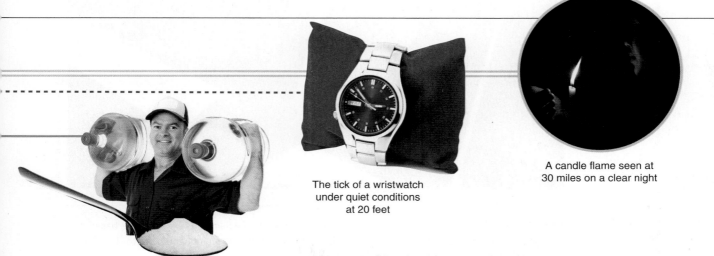

A teaspoon of sugar in two

The tick of a wristwatch under quiet conditions at 20 feet

A candle flame seen at 30 miles on a clear night

Photos, left to right: © drfelice/Shutterstock; © Lisa F. Young/Shutterstock; © chatchai/Shutterstock;
© Karen H. Ilagan/Shutterstock

HOW DOES SENSATION LEAD TO PERCEPTION?

Fechner's work on difference thresholds helps us understand how weightlifters like Eszter Krutzler can perceive the differences between lighter and heavier weights. The difference between 5 and 10 pounds would be much more noticeable, even to an experienced weightlifter, than the difference between 400 and 405 pounds.

Signal Detection Many perceptions involve some uncertainty. Perhaps you're driving rather fast, and you think a distant car behind you might possibly be a police officer. Do you slow down right away? Or do you wait until the car is close enough to know for sure if it's a police officer or not? How do your expectations affect your decision? Maybe you are convinced that as long as you're following another car, you won't get a ticket. How do your personal feelings about making mistakes affect your decision? Would the cost of a ticket ruin your budget?

This type of decision making can have serious implications, such as in the case of decisions made by radiologists after examining the results of mammograms for signs of cancer. Is there reason for concern or not? This situation is different from the thresholds described earlier, because it adds the cognitive process of decision making to the process of sensation. In other words, **signal detection** is a two-step process involving: (1) the actual intensity of the stimulus, which will influence the observer's belief that the stimulus did occur, and (2) the individual observer's criteria for deciding whether the stimulus occurred.

Experiments on signal detection provide insight into this type of decision making. In these experiments, trials with a single, faint stimulus and trials with no stimulus at all are presented randomly. The participant states

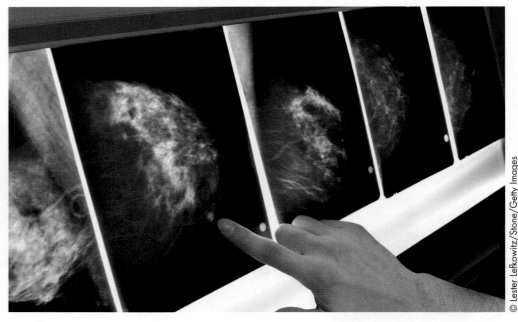

signal detection The analysis of sensory and decision making processes in the detection of faint, uncertain stimuli.

Does the mammogram indicate a woman has cancer or not? Many decisions we make are based on ambiguous stimuli. Signal detection theory helps us understand how an individual doctor balances risks of missing a cancer and alarming a healthy patient.

5.1 Possible Outcomes in Signal Detection

Participant response	Stimulus present	Stimulus absent
Yes	Hit	False alarm
No	Miss	Correct rejection

whether a stimulus was present on each trial. The possible outcomes of this experiment are shown in Table 5.1. In the case of driving fast on the highway, we can use such experiments to help us understand why two people might respond very differently, even if they were sensing the same information. If you are more concerned about correctly identifying patrol cars (maximizing hits), you might use more lenient standards for identifying patrol cars and would end up slowing down frequently (false alarms), but you would get few tickets. In contrast, another person might use stricter criteria for identifying a patrol car than you. He or she would have fewer false alarms but would run the risk of missing real patrol cars (misses), which is likely to be very expensive.

Another example of signal detection is a jury's decision about whether a person is guilty. Based on frequently uncertain and conflicting evidence, jurors must weigh their concerns about convicting an innocent person (false alarm) or letting a real criminal go (miss).

Summary 5.1

Measuring Perception and the Detection of Signals

Concept	Definition	Example
Absolute threshold © Karen H. Ilagan/ Shutterstock	The smallest amount of stimulation that is detectable	Seeing light from a candle flame 30 miles away on a dark night
Difference threshold © Dmitry Kostyu-kov/AFP/Getty Images	The smallest difference between two stimuli that can be detected	Being able to detect the difference between two different weights.
Signal detection © Lester Lefkowitz/ Stone/Getty Images	Correctly identifying when a faint stimulus is or is not present	A radiologist correctly detects cancer in a mammogram.

How Do We See?

Vision, the processing of light reflected from objects, is one of the most important sensory systems in humans. Approximately 50% of our cerebral cortex processes visual information, in comparison to only 3% for hearing and 11% for touch and pain (Kandel & Wurtz, 2000; Sereno & Tootell, 2005). We will begin our exploration of vision with a description of the visual stimulus, and then we will follow the processing of that stimulus by the mind into a meaningful perception.

The Visual Stimulus

Visible light, or the light we can see, is a type of radiation emitted by the sun, other stars, and artificial sources such as the lightbulb. As shown in ● Figure 5.5, light energy moves in waves, like the waves in the ocean. Wavelength, or the distance between successive peaks of waves, is decoded by our visual system as color or shades of gray. The height, or amplitude, of the waves is translated by the visual system into brightness. Large-amplitude waves appear very bright, and low-amplitude waves appear dim.

The human visual world involves only a small part of this light spectrum. Gamma rays, X-rays, ultraviolet rays, infrared rays, microwaves, and radio waves lie outside the capacities of the human eye, but insects can see light in the ultraviolet range, and snakes can see in the infrared range. Each animal's visual world has been shaped by its species' environment and behavior.

The Biology of Vision

Human vision begins with the eye. The eye is roughly sphere-shaped and about the size of a ping-pong ball. Its hard outer covering helps the fluid-filled eyeball retain its shape. Toward the front of the eye, the outer covering becomes clear and forms the **cornea.** The cornea begins the process of bending light to form an image on the back of the eye. Traveling light next enters the **pupil,** which is actually an opening formed by the muscles of the **iris** (see ● Figure 5.6). The iris, which means "rainbow" in Greek, adjusts the opening of the pupil in response to the amount of light present in the environment and to signals from the autonomic nervous system, described in our chapter on biological psychology. Arousal is associated with dilated pupils, while relaxation is associated with more constricted pupils.

Directly behind the pupil and iris is the main optical instrument of the eye, the **lens.** Muscles attached to the lens can change its shape, allowing us to adjust our focus to see near or distant objects. Behind the lens is the main chamber of the eye, and located on the rear surface of this chamber is the **retina,** a thin but complex network of neurons specialized for the processing of light.

Located in the deepest layer of the retina are the specialized receptors, the rods and cones, that transduce the light information. However, before light reaches these receptors, it must pass through numerous blood vessels and neural layers. We normally do not "see" the blood vessels and neural layers due to adaptation. As we mentioned previously in this chapter, adaptation occurs when sensory systems tune out stimuli that never change.

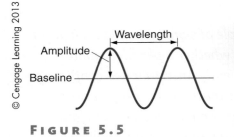

FIGURE 5.5

Light Travels in Waves. The distance between two peaks in a light wave is decoded by the visual system as color, and the height or amplitude of the wave as brightness.

vision The sense that allows us to process reflected light.

cornea The clear surface at the front of the eye that begins the process of directing light to the retina.

pupil An opening formed by the iris.

iris The brightly colored circular muscle surrounding the pupil of the eye.

lens The clear structure behind the pupil that bends light toward the retina.

retina Layers of visual processing cells in the back of the eye.

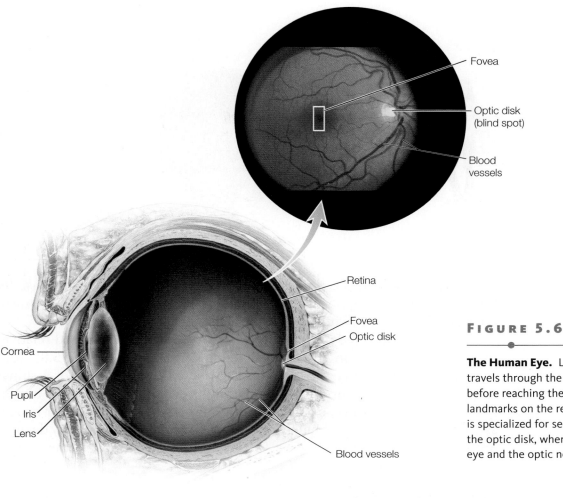

Fovea

Optic disk (blind spot)

Blood vessels

Retina

Fovea

Optic disk

Cornea

Pupil

Iris

Lens

Blood vessels

Illustration: © Argosy Publishing, Inc.; photo: © James P. Gilman, C. R. A./Phototake

FIGURE 5.6

The Human Eye. Light entering the eye travels through the cornea, pupil, and lens before reaching the retina. Among the landmarks on the retina are the fovea, which is specialized for seeing very fine detail, and the optic disk, where blood vessels enter the eye and the optic nerve exits the eye.

Because the blood vessels and neural layers are always in the same place, we see them only under unusual circumstances, such as during certain ophthalmology (eye) tests.

We can identify several landmarks on the surface of the retina. The blood vessels serving the eye and axons that leave the retina to form the optic nerve exit in a place known as the optic disk. Because there are no rods and cones in the optic disk, each eye has a blind spot. Normally, we are unaware of our blind spots because perception "fills in" the missing detail. However, if you follow the directions in ● Figure 5.7, you should be able to experience yours. Toward the middle of the retina is the **fovea,** which is specialized for seeing very fine detail. When we stare directly at an object,

●

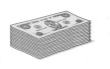

© Cengage Learning 2013

FIGURE 5.7

Now You See It—Now You Don't. There are no photoreceptors in the optic disk, producing a blind spot in each eye. We do not see our blind spots because our brain "fills in the hole." You can demonstrate your blind spot by holding your textbook at arm's length, closing one eye, focusing your other eye on the dot, and moving the book toward you until the stack of money disappears.

fovea An area of the retina that is specialized for highly detailed vision.

FIGURE 5.8

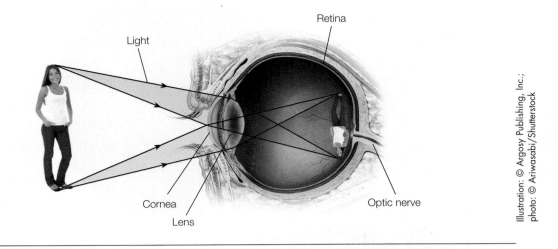

What the Retina "Sees." The image projected on the retina is upside down and reversed, but the brain is able to interpret the image to perceive the correct orientation of an object.

the image of that object is projected onto the fovea. The fovea is responsible for central vision, as opposed to peripheral vision, which is the ability to see objects off to the side while looking straight ahead.

The image projected on the retina is upside down and reversed relative to the actual orientation of the object being viewed (see ● Figure 5.8). You can duplicate this process by looking at yourself in both sides of a shiny spoon. In the convex, or outwardly curving side, you will see your image normally. In the concave, or inwardly curving side, you will see your image as your retina sees it. Fortunately, the visual system has no difficulty decoding this image and providing us with realistic perceptions of the actual orientations of objects.

Rods and Cones **Rods** and **cones** are named after their shapes. The human eye contains about 120 million rods and about 6 million cones.

Rods and cones are responsible for different aspects of vision. The rods are more sensitive to light than the cones and excel at seeing in dim light. As we observed previously, under ideal circumstances, the absolute threshold for human vision is the equivalent of a single candle flame from a distance of 30 miles (Hecht, Shlaer, & Pirenne, 1942). Rods become more common as we move from the fovea to the periphery of the retina, so your peripheral vision does a better job of viewing dim light than your central vision does (see ● Figure 5.9). Before the development of night goggles, soldiers patrolling in the dark were trained to look to the side of a suspected enemy position rather than directly at their target.

This extraordinary sensitivity of rods has costs. Rods do not provide information about color, nor do they provide clear, sharp images. Under starlight, normal human vision is 20/200 rather than the normal daylight 20/20. In other words, an object seen at night from a distance of 20 feet would have the same clarity as an object seen in bright sunlight from a distance of 200 feet. Cones function best under bright light and provide the ability to see both sharp images and color.

rod A photoreceptor specialized to detect dim light.

cone A photoreceptor in the retina that processes color.

Visual Pathways The rods and cones are the only true receptors of the visual system. When they absorb light, they trigger responses in four additional layers of neurons within the retina. Axons from the final layer

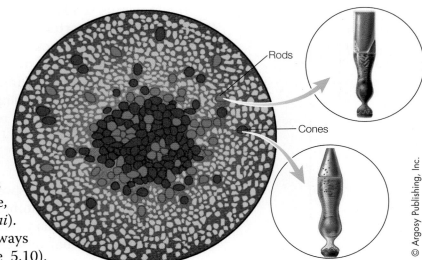

FIGURE 5.9

Distribution of Rods and Cones Across the Retina. In humans, cones (red dots) become less frequent as you move from the fovea to the periphery of the retina. Rods (green dots) and cones are named according to their shapes.

Rods

Cones

© Argosy Publishing, Inc.

of cells leave the back of the eye to form the **optic nerve.** The point at which the optic nerves cross the midline is known as the optic chiasm (named after its X shape, which is similar to the Greek letter *chi*). Beyond the optic chiasm, the visual pathways are known as **optic tracts** (see ● Figure 5.10). About 90% of the axons in the optic tracts will synapse in the thalamus. The remaining fibers connect with the hypothalamus, where their input provides information about light needed to regulate sleep-waking cycles, discussed in our chapter on consciousness, or with the midbrain, which manages a number of visually guided reflexes, such as changing the size of the pupil in response to light conditions.

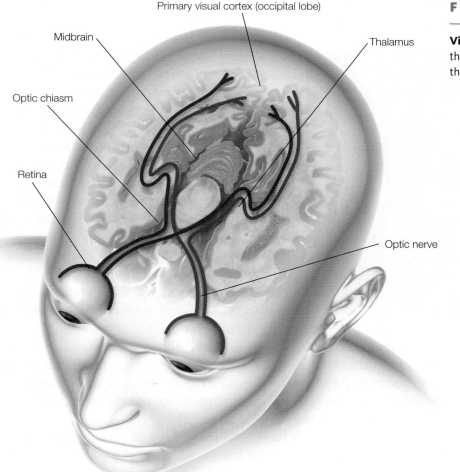

Primary visual cortex (occipital lobe)

Midbrain

Thalamus

Optic chiasm

Retina

Optic nerve

© Argosy Publishing, Inc.

FIGURE 5.10

Visual Pathways. Visual information from the retina travels to the thalamus and then to the primary visual cortex in the occipital lobe.

optic nerve The nerve exiting the retina of the eye.

optic tracts Nerve pathways traveling from the optic chiasm to the thalamus, hypothalamus, and midbrain.

The thalamus sends information about vision to the amygdala and to the primary visual cortex in the occipital lobe. The amygdala uses visual information to make quick emotional judgments, especially about potentially harmful stimuli. As we mentioned in our chapter on biological psychology, monkeys with damaged amygdalas fail to show their species' typical fear in response to seeing a snake. In one fascinating example in a human, a patient with damage to his visual cortex continued to show normal activation of the amygdala in response to images of threatening faces, in spite of his inability to "see" any of the faces at all (Morris, DeGelder, Weiskrantz, & Dolan, 2001).

Primary visual cortex responds to object shape, location, movement, and color (Hubel & Livingstone, 1987; Hubel & Wiesel, 1959; Livingstone & Hubel, 1984). The primary visual cortex begins, but by no means finishes, the processing of visual input. Two major pathways radiating from the occipital cortex into the adjacent temporal and parietal lobes continue the analysis of visual input. The parietal pathway helps us process movement in the visual environment. The temporal pathway responds to shape and color and contributes to our ability to recognize objects and faces.

FIGURE 5.11

Mixing Colored Lights. The primary colors of paint might be red, yellow, and blue, but in the world of light, the primary colors are red, green, and blue.

© Cengage Learning 2013

Visual Perception and Cognition

To actually "see" something requires the brain to interpret the information gathered by the eyes. How do we know our sweater is red or green based on the information sent from the retina to the brain? How do we recognize our grandmother at our front door?

Color Vision Most of us think about colors in terms of the paints and crayons we used in elementary school. Any kindergartner can tell you that mixtures of red and yellow make orange, red and blue make purple, and yellow and blue make green. Mixing them all together produces a lovely muddy brown. Colored lights, however, work somewhat differently (see ● Figure 5.11). The primary colors of light are red, green, and blue, and mixing them together produces white light, like sunlight. If you have ever adjusted the color on your computer monitor or television, you know that these devices also use red, green, and blue as primary colors. Observations supporting the existence of three primary colors of light gave rise to a **trichromacy theory** of color vision.

Trichromacy theory is consistent with the existence of three types of cones in the retina that respond best to short (blue), medium (green), or long (red) wavelengths. Our ultimate experience of color comes not from the response of one type of cone, but from comparisons between the responses of many cones (see ● Figure 5.12).

Very rarely, individuals have either one type of cone or none. To these people, the world appears to be black, white, and gray. Monty Roberts, whose life formed the basis of the film *The Horse Whisperer*, believes that

trichromacy theory A theory of color vision based on the existence of different types of cones for the detection of short, medium, and long wavelengths.

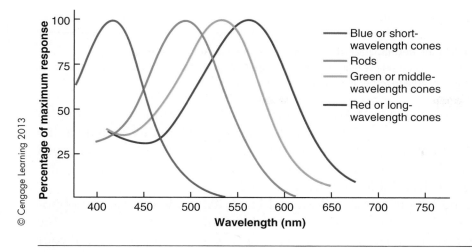

FIGURE 5.12

Responses by Cones to Colored Light. Our perception of color results from a comparison of the responses of the red, green, and blue cones to light. A 550 nm light is perceived as yellow, and produces strong responses in green cones, moderate responses in red cones, and little if any responses in blue cones.

© Cengage Learning 2013

Legend:
- Blue or short-wavelength cones
- Rods
- Green or middle-wavelength cones
- Red or long-wavelength cones

this condition allowed him to study the behavior of herds of horses without distraction (Roberts & Scanlan, 1999). People with two types of cones are often referred to as "colorblind," but as we observed at the beginning of the chapter, this term is really not accurate. With two cone types that will respond differently to the same light, distinctions between colors can be made. Individuals with two types of cones definitely do see color, but they will match color samples differently than the rest of us.

Trichromacy theory does a good job of explaining colorblindness, but it is less successful in accounting for other color vision phenomena, like color afterimages. For example, if you stare at the yellow, green, and black flag in ● Figure 5.13 and then focus on the dot within the white rectangle below, you will "see" an afterimage of the flag in its more traditional colors of red, white, and blue.

An **opponent process theory** of color vision does a better job than trichromacy in explaining these color afterimages. This theory proposes the existence of "opposing" color channels: a red-green channel and a blue-yellow channel. In other words, we cannot see a color like "reddish-green" or "bluish-yellow" because the two colors share the same channel. Opponent process theory gets support from our understanding of the anatomy of the visual system. Groups of cells that process yellow and blue or red and green

© Dan Tuffs/Getty Images

Monty Roberts attributed his ability to observe horses to his lack of color vision, which he thought might be distracting.

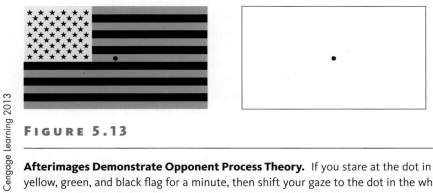

FIGURE 5.13

Afterimages Demonstrate Opponent Process Theory. If you stare at the dot in the center of the yellow, green, and black flag for a minute, then shift your gaze to the dot in the white space below, you should "see" the flag in its traditional red, white, and blue colors.

© Cengage Learning 2013

opponent process theory A theory of color vision that suggests we have a red-green color channel and a blue-yellow color channel in which activation of one color in each pair inhibits the other.

FIGURE 5.14

Color Channels in the Retina. Recordings from cells in the monkey retina support the existence of red-green and yellow-blue channels. Groups of cells that process yellow and blue or red and green are located together in doughnut shapes in the retina.

are located together (see ● Figure 5.14). Stimulation of one color group in each pair, for instance red from the red-green pair, will reduce activity in the cells in the other group, or green in this case. You can't see reddish-green because stimulating the red cells inhibits activity in the green and stimulating the green cells inhibits activity in the red.

Returning to our green, yellow, and black flag, how can we use opponent process theory to explain our experience of the red, white, and blue afterimage? By staring at the flag, you are producing fatigue in some of your visual neurons. Recall that activity in one color group in a channel reduces activity in the other. At the same time, reducing activity in one color group, as we do when we fatigue green by looking at the flag, increases activity in

Psychology
as a Hub Science

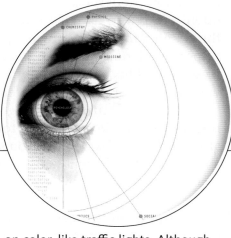

Color and Accessible Web Design

As we have seen in this chapter, people do not perceive color the same way. Between 7 and 10% of males and about 0.4% of females have a form of red-green colorblindness. The reason that males are more affected than females is that the genes for the pigments used by red and green cones

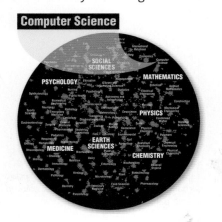

are located on the X chromosome, making red-green colorblindness a sex-linked condition. We discussed this and other sex-linked conditions in our chapter on interactions between nature and nurture. Much smaller numbers of people lack blue cones (0.0011%) or cones altogether (0.00001%). Given the rather common occurrence of colorblindness, making visual materials accessible to people with all types of color vision is a serious concern.

Color can be a very effective tool for designing exciting and engaging websites, but many graphic web designers (who typically have excellent vision themselves) fail to consider how the site might look to a person who is colorblind. One clue for designing an accessible site can be found in other systems based

on color, like traffic lights. Although most of us rely on the color information from the red, yellow, or green lights, the lights also vary in location. In other words, color should never be the only basis for extracting meaning. A second major concern is contrast, which we discuss in the next section. The strong contrast between the black letters on the white pages of this book makes the text easy to read for most people. Colored text against a colored background might add interest, but runs the risk of being harder to read, especially when reds and greens are used. As shown in

● Figure 5.15, various resources exist online that will show how a web page will look to a person with colorblindness, which helps designers maximize accessibility. ⚙

the other group, which in this case will be red. So fatiguing green, black, and yellow causes a rebound effect in each color channel, and your afterimage looks red, white, and blue. (Black and white also share a channel.) If you stare at an image of a real red, white, and blue flag and then look at a white piece of paper, your afterimage will look green, black, and yellow.

Which of these two theories of color vision, trichromacy or opponent processes, is correct? The trichromacy theory provides a helpful framework for the functioning of the three types of cones in the retina. However, as we move from the retina to higher levels of visual analysis in the thalamus and cerebral cortex, the opponent process theory seems to fit observed phenomena neatly. Both theories help us understand color vision, but at different levels of the visual system.

> If only we could pull out our brain and use only our eyes.
>
> —Pablo Picasso

Recognizing Objects

We asked earlier how our brain uses incoming visual signals to recognize our grandmother standing at the front door. One approach to this question assumes that as information moves from the retina to higher levels of visual processing, more complicated responses are built from simpler input. In this hierarchical model, the result would be a "grandmother cell," or a single cell that could combine all previous input and processing to tell you that your grandmother is at the door. This type of hypothetical neuron, capable

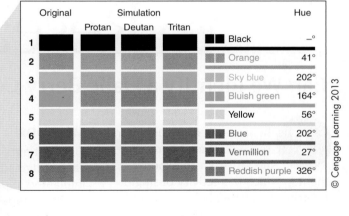

© Paul Dronsfield/Alamy

© Cengage Learning 2013

FIGURE 5.15

Making Websites Accessible. Web designers have found colors that work for people with typical color vision and people who are colorblind. This set of colors shows how different shades would be seen by people with typical vision and by people with three of the most common forms of colorblindness. Even though these colors will be seen differently by the three groups, nobody will mistake one shade for another.

of responding to a very specific stimulus and no others, has been referred to as a **feature detector** (Barlow, 1972).

Although the feature detector model is attractive in many ways, it does not fit perfectly with what we know about the visual system. First of all, we would need a very large number of feature detectors to respond to all the objects and events that we can recognize visually. In addition, a feature detector model is unable to account for the fact that our expectations influence what we see. ● Figure 5.16a may appear to be a random pattern of black dots on a white background. Figure 5.16b may not appear to be a recognizable object of any kind. The sensations produced by these stimuli lead to no meaningful perceptions. However, once we tell you that the first image is a Dalmatian dog, and the second image is a cow, you can instantly pick out their shapes. As a matter of fact, now that you know what the images are, you will probably never see them the way you did initially ever again. Recognizing these objects requires knowledge and memory of what Dalmatians and cows look like. It is unlikely that a single cortical cell acting as a Dalmatian or cow feature detector could incorporate such complex inputs from memory.

If we don't use feature detectors to recognize objects, how else can we accomplish this task? One suggestion is that the visual system may

feature detector A hypothetical cell that responds to only one specific visual stimulus.

Connecting *to* Research

Can We Identify a Halle Berry Cell?

The idea of feature detectors received some interesting support from an experiment in which the activity of single neurons in patients being prepared for neurosurgery was recorded while they viewed faces, landmark buildings, objects, and printed words (Quiroga, Reddy, Kreiman, Koch, & Fried, 2005).

The Question: *Is it possible to identify neurons that preferentially respond to particular faces compared to other faces or stimuli?*

METHODS

Eight patients undergoing presurgical testing had recording electrodes implanted in parts of the brain that might be impacted by their scheduled surgeries. While the participants were lying in bed, images were projected onto a laptop in front of them, and they were supposed to press the "Y" or "N" key to indicate whether the image was a human face. This process ensured that they were paying attention to the images. Images included famous and unfamous faces,

animals, landmarks, and objects. Activity in individual cells was correlated with the image viewed.

RESULTS

The participants did show activity in single cells that correlated with the images they viewed. One participant had a single cell that became significantly more active when he viewed the actress Halle Berry, whether she appeared in photographs, in drawings, or dressed as Catwoman (see

perform a mathematical analysis of the visual field (De Valois & De Valois, 1980). While the hierarchical model implies a reality built out of individual bars and edges, the mathematical approach suggests that we analyze patterns of lines. The simplest patterns of lines are gratings, as shown in ● Figure 5.18. Gratings can vary in two dimensions: frequency and contrast. High-frequency gratings have many bars in a given distance, while low-frequency gratings have relatively few bars.

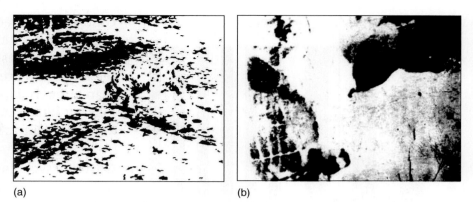

(a)   (b)

FIGURE 5.16

High-contrast gratings have large differences in intensity between adjacent bars, like black next to white. The print you are reading in this textbook is an example of high contrast, as the black letters are quite different from the white page. Low-contrast gratings have more subtle differences in intensity between bars, such as dark gray next to black.

Observing responses to gratings can give us a window into the visual capacities of other species. At a certain point of contrast and frequency, gratings look plain gray. Animals can be trained to make a distinction between gratings and gray circles. For example, if a bird is rewarded with food for pecking at a disk with a grating but not for pecking a uniform gray disk, any performance that is better than 50-50, or chance, indicates that the bird can see the difference between the grating and gray. We can graph the range of gratings that are visible to the observer as a function of their

Can You Figure Out What This Is?
(a) This might look like a splattering of black dots on a white page until you learn that it represents a Dalmatian dog. (b) Top-down processing ensures that once you know this is a photo of a cow, you will be able to pick out its features easily. *Source:* left: From Richard L. Gregory, "The Medawar Lecture 2001 Knowledge for vision: Vision for knowledge," *Phil. Trans. R. Soc. B 2005 360*, 1231–1251, © The Royal Society; right: From K. M. Dallenbach, "A puzzle-picture with a new principle of concealment," from *American Journal of Psychology 64*:3 (July 1951): pp. 431–433. Copyright © 1951 by the Board of Trustees of the University of Illinois. Used with permission of the author and the University of Illinois Press.

● Figure 5.17). The cell activated even when the image consisted of the letters spelling out her name. Another participant had a "Jennifer Aniston" cell that activated when he viewed her photograph, but the cell remained quiet when the photograph included Aniston's ex-husband, Brad Pitt.

CONCLUSIONS
The results of this study support the feature detector approach to perception. However, as the Gestalt psychologists pointed out, there is much more to a "whole" perception than the sum of its parts (activity of single cells). ✪

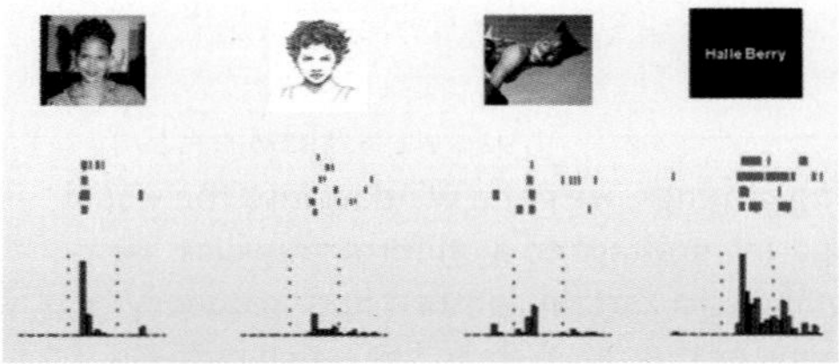

FIGURE 5.17

The Halle Berry Cell. Recordings show that a single cell became active whenever a photo or drawing of actress Halle Berry was presented to the patient. The cell even activated when the patient read Berry's name. *Source:* From R. Quian Quiroga, L. Reddy, G. Kreiman, C. Koch, & I. Fried, Invariant visual representation by single neurons in the human brain, *Nature 435*, 1102–1107 (23 June 2005), doi:10.1038/nature03687

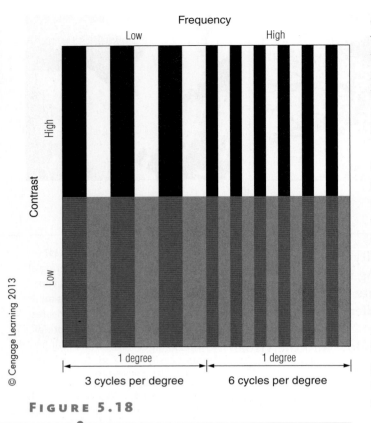

Frequency

Low   High

Contrast — High / Low

1 degree   1 degree

3 cycles per degree   6 cycles per degree

© Cengage Learning 2013

FIGURE 5.18

Gratings Vary in Frequency and Contrast. An alternative to feature detection suggests that the visual system analyzes the visual environment as a collection of patterns, like these gratings. Gratings vary in frequency (number of bars in a given distance) and contrast (the difference in light intensity from one bar to the next).

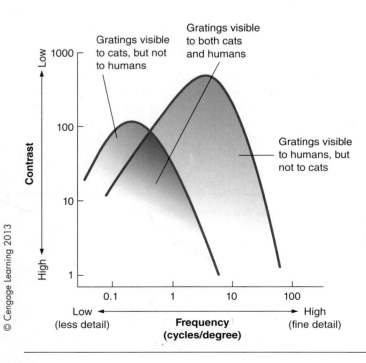

Gratings visible to cats, but not to humans

Gratings visible to both cats and humans

Gratings visible to humans, but not to cats

Contrast — Low / High

Frequency (cycles/degree)

Low (less detail)   High (fine detail)

© Cengage Learning 2013

contrast and frequency. • Figure 5.19 illustrates the visible ranges for human adults and cats. Compared to human adults, cats see less detail. However, cats see large (low-frequency), low-contrast objects better than humans. Large, low-contrast shadows on the wall may get kitty's attention, but not yours. You will think kitty is chasing ghosts again.

Gestalt Psychology As we observed in our introductory chapter, a group of German researchers known as the Gestalt psychologists tackled visual perception with a number of ingenious observations. The word *Gestalt* is derived from the German word for "shape." These psychologists objected to efforts by Wilhelm Wundt and the structuralists to reduce human experience to its building blocks, or elements. Instead, the Gestalt psychologists argued that there are some experiences that lose information and value when divided into parts. The main thesis of the Gestalt psychologists, as stated by Kurt Koffka, maintains, "It is more correct to say that the whole is something else than the sum of its parts" (Koffka, 1935, p. 176).

According to the Gestalt psychologists, we are born with a number of built-in tendencies to organize incoming sensory information in certain ways. This natural ability to organize simplifies the problem of recognizing objects (Biederman, 1987). The first organizing principle suggests that we analyze visual input by dividing a scene into figure and ground. In other words, we identify the main object in the scene (the figure), which stands out from the background. We frequently assume that the figure stands in front of most of the ground, and it seems to have more substance and shape. It is possible to construct ambiguous images, like the one created by the vase on the next page in which the parts of the image seem to switch roles as figure or ground. Although you can switch back and forth between the faces and vase, efforts to see both at once are likely to be frustrating.

FIGURE 5.19

What Do Cats See? Using gratings, we get a window into the visual world of the cat. By comparing gratings to a uniform gray disk, we can learn when a grating having a certain contrast and frequency simply looks gray to humans or the cat. We can see much better detail than kitty, but she sees large shadows that we don't even notice.

A second Gestalt principle is proximity (see ● Figure 5.20). Objects that are close together tend to be grouped together. The dots that make up our Dalmatian are close together, suggesting they belong to the same object. The principle of similarity states that similar stimuli are grouped together. On a close examination of the dog image, the dots that make up the dog are similar to one another and slightly different (more rounded perhaps) than the dots making up the remainder of the image.

The principle of continuity suggests that we assume that points that form smooth lines when connected probably belong together (see ● Figure 5.21). In our dog picture, continuity helps us see the border of the curb or sidewalk and the ring of shadow around the base of the tree. Continuity is perhaps a little less useful in identifying the dog, although we can pick out the lines forming the legs.

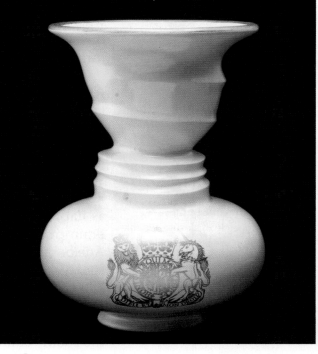

© SSPL/Science Museum/Art Resource, NY

The Gestalt psychologists believed we naturally see the difference between objects and their background, but this figure is designed to make us switch back and forth from vase to background faces. This vase was designed to commemorate an anniversary of Queen Elizabeth of England (face on the right) and her husband, Prince Philip (face on the left).

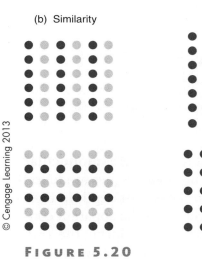

(a) Ambiguous pattern

(b) Similarity   (c) Proximity

FIGURE 5.20

The Gestalt Principles of Proximity and Similarity. The set of dots in (a) do not appear to have any particular relationship with one another, but when we color rows in (b), we suddenly see the dots in columns or rows. Moving two columns or rows very slightly closer to each other in (c) makes us see the array differently, too.

© Cengage Learning 2013

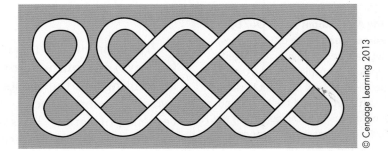

© Cengage Learning 2013

FIGURE 5.21

The Gestalt Principle of Continuity. The Gestalt principle of continuity says that we perceive points forming a smooth line as belonging to the same object. If you follow this knot, you will see that it is actually formed by two objects, but our initial perception is of a single form.

© WWF Registered Trademark. Panda Symbol © 1986 WWF

FIGURE 5.22

The Gestalt Principle of Closure.
Due to the principle of closure, we "fill in the blanks" to see a single object, the World Wildlife logo, although it is really made up of several objects.

Closure occurs when people see a complete, unbroken image even when there are gaps in the lines forming the image (see ● Figure 5.22). We certainly use this approach in viewing the dog when we "fill in the blanks" formed by the white parts of its body.

Finally, the Gestalt psychologists believed in the principle of simplicity, which suggests that we will use the simplest solution to a perceptual problem. This principle may help explain the "fun" in pictures like that of our Dalmatian dog. It is much simpler to assume that this is a random splash of black dots on white background. Finding a hidden picture within the dots is not the simplest solution, which may account for some of our surprise.

Recognizing Depth An image projected onto the retina is two-dimensional, as flat as the sheet of paper on which these words appear. Somehow, the brain manages to construct a three-dimensional image from these data. Adelbert Ames constructed a room that was named in his honor, the Ames room, that illustrated vulnerabilities in our **depth perception** (Ittleson, 1952). When viewed directly from the front, the room appears to be a rectangle. People within the room, shown in ● Figure 5.23, seem to be much larger or smaller than normal. This distortion of perceived size results from the room's ability to confuse our judgment of distance.

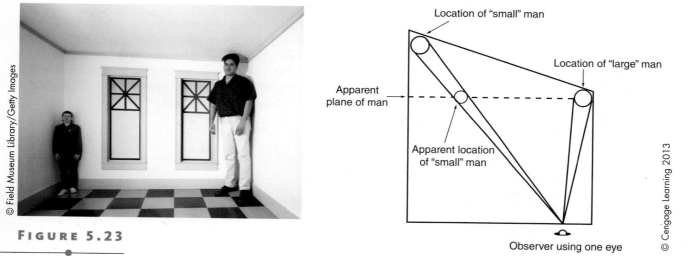

© Field Museum Library/Getty Images

© Cengage Learning 2013

FIGURE 5.23

The Ames Room Tricks Our Depth Perception. Many distance cues, such as the apparently rectangular windows, conspire to make these two people look very different in size. In fact, the person on the right is much closer to us than the person on the left. The diagram shows the actual layout of the Ames Room.

depth perception The ability to use the two-dimensional image projected on the retina to perceive three dimensions.

monocular cue A depth cue that requires the use of only one eye.

binocular cue A depth cue that requires the use of both eyes.

To construct a three-dimensional image, we use both **monocular** (one-eye) and **binocular** (two-eye) **cues.** Many monocular cues are found in paintings, as the artists attempt to provide an illusion of depth in their two-dimensional pieces. The use of linear perspective, or the apparent convergence of parallel lines at the horizon, by Italian artists during the 15th century provided a realism unknown in earlier works. Linear perspective revolutionized the video game and movie industries, beginning humbly with Sega's *Zaxxon* in 1982 and advancing to the ever more realistic environments of *Halo*, Pixar's animated films, and the 2009 film *Avatar*. Other monocular cues include texture gradients and shading. We can see more texture in objects that are close to us, while the texture of distant objects is relatively blurry. Shading and the use of highlights can be used to suggest curved surfaces.

Among the most powerful monocular depth cues is occlusion, or the blocking of images of distant objects by closer objects. We also use relative size to judge the distance of objects, although this method requires that you are familiar with the real size of an object. We know how big people are. When the retinal image of a person is small, we infer that the person is farther away from us than when the retinal image of a person is larger.

Several illusions result from our use of monocular cues to judge depth. The Müller-Lyer illusion, shown in ● Figure 5.24, would not cause us problems were it not for the fact that we perceive the images as corners. In spite of the fact that the main lines project images of equal length on the retina, we tend to see the line with outward-pointing arrowheads as being farther away from our position. The Ponzo illusion, shown in ● Figure 5.25, confounds size and distance judgments in a similar fashion. The parallel lines signal depth, leading us to believe that the upper horizontal line is farther away than the lower line. If both lines project the same image on the retina, the more distant line must be longer.

Relative size also helps to explain the "moon illusion." You may have noticed that the moon appears to be much larger when it is just above the hills on the horizon than when it is straight overhead. In fact, the moon maintains a steady orbit 239,000 miles above Earth. How can we account for the discrepancy in its apparent size? When viewed overhead, the moon is seen without any intervening objects, such as trees and hills, that

Computer graphics make good use of linear perspective to provide a sense of depth in a two-dimensional image.

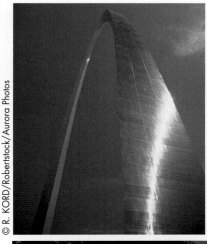

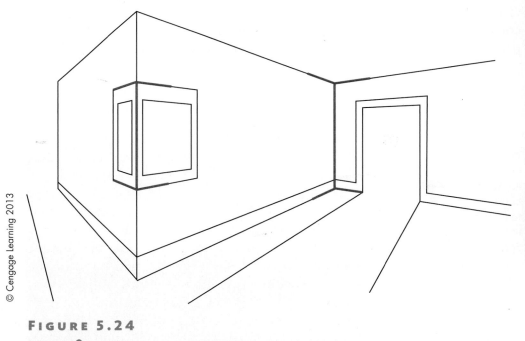

FIGURE 5.24

The Müller-Lyer Illusion. You might find it hard to believe that the two red vertical lines are actually the same length.

Without any relative size cues, it would be difficult to know about how big the St. Louis Arch really is. In the lower photograph, the Arch is shown against the St. Louis skyline, and we see the answer—it is *really* big.

© Cengage Learning 2013

FIGURE 5.25

The Ponzo Illusion. We perceive depth due to linear perspective, which in turn make us see the upper horizontal bar as more distant than the lower bar. Even though they are the same length, the bar perceived as more distant looks longer.

might provide cues about its size and distance. However, when viewed near the horizon, we see the moon against a backdrop of familiar objects whose size we know well. We expect trees and hills to be smaller at the horizon than when they are close to us, and if we group the moon with those objects, we adjust its apparent size as well. The next time you are viewing the full moon as it rises over the hills, form a peephole with your hand, and you will see the moon in its normal small size. Although some researchers argue that atmospheric differences between the two viewpoints may contribute to the illusion, viewing the moon through your hand should demonstrate that the majority of the effect arises from your use of other objects to judge distance.

So far, we have discussed monocular cues that involve a person and a scene that is not moving. The introduction of motion can heighten the impression of depth. As you ride along in a car, focus your gaze at a very distant point. The objects you pass will appear to be moving in the opposite direction of your car, with closer objects appearing to move faster than distant objects. Next, focus on a point about midway between you and the horizon. Now, the closer objects will continue to move in the opposite direction, but more distant objects appear to be traveling with you. This motion parallax has also been used with great effectiveness to enhance the 3-D feeling in video games.

One of our most effective depth cues is **retinal disparity.** Because this cue requires the use of both eyes, we refer to retinal disparity as a binocular cue. Predator species, including ourselves, usually have eyes placed in the front of the head facing forward. As a result of this configuration, the visual scenes observed by the two eyes are different, although they overlap considerably, as shown in ● Figure 5.26. The differences between the images projected onto each eye are referred to as disparities. These disparities do

We all enjoy the view of a large harvest moon appearing over the hills, but the moon is no closer to Earth at the horizon than it is when overhead. The apparent size of the moon results from our use of relative size cues provided by buildings, trees, and hills between us and the moon on the horizon. No such cues are available when we look overhead.

retinal disparity The difference between the images projected onto each eye.

© Christine Churchill

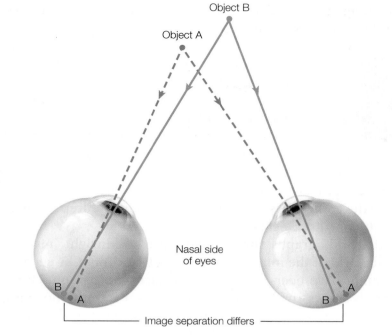

Object B

Object A

Nasal side
of eyes

B

A

B

A

Image separation differs

© Argosy Publishing, Inc.

FIGURE 5.26

Retinal Disparity. The right and left eye see slightly overlapping versions of the visual scene in front of us. We can use the retinal disparity, or discrepancy between the location of two objects on the two retinas, as a very sensitive depth cue.

not tell us exactly how far away an object is. Instead, they provide information about the relative distance between two objects in the visual field. As the distance between the objects increases, disparity increases. To illustrate the sensitivity of this system, you can identify an object as being 1 mm closer than another at a distance of one meter from your body, or a difference of 0.1% (Blake & Sekuler, 2006).

Why would this binocular depth system be an advantage to predators? Most prey species do an excellent job of hiding, often aided by an appearance that blends into the nearby environment. However, retinal disparity allows us to spot tiny variations in the depths of objects in the visual field. This might make an animal stand out against its background, even though it is well camouflaged. Retinal disparity has been used to identify camouflaged military equipment and counterfeit currency. Another favorite application of this binocular cue is the viewing of random-dot stereograms, or magic-eye pictures (Julesz,

© Gene Levine/colorstereo.com

Retinal disparity allows us to pick out a three-dimensional figure in this stereogram. If you have trouble seeing the object, try blurring your focus or focusing on something behind your textbook. The solution is illustrated at the top of the next page.

1971). Infants as young as 4 months can see depth in stereograms, as can monkeys, cats, and falcons (Fox, Aslin, Shea, & Dumais, 1980).

Developmental and Individual Differences in Vision

Although we can't ask human infants what they can or can't see, we can take advantage of the fact that they will gaze longer at patterns than at uniform stimuli, like a patch of a single color. This allows us to construct graphs of the contrasts and frequencies to which children respond similar to those we saw previously for cats. Based on these analyses, we know that human infants can see everything human adults can see, but with less detail. To see well, the infant also needs more contrast than the adult. These findings help explain children's preferences for large, high-contrast objects.

The photographs shown below provide insight into the visual world of the infant. Frequencies that cannot be seen by the infant have been removed from each photograph. Other research shows that infants as young as 4 months not only show binocular disparity as discussed earlier but also show normal adult responses to color (Bornstein, Kessen, & Weiskopf, 1976). Other depth cues discussed previously develop quite early, too. Infants as young as 2 months understand occlusion (Johnson & Aslin, 1995), and the use of the relative size of objects to judge depth appears between the ages of 5 and 7 months (Granrud, Haake, & Yonas, 1985). Infants' abilities to perceive faces also develop quite rapidly, as 2-day-old newborns will spend more time gazing at their mothers' faces than at a stranger's face (Bushnell, 2001).

© Gene Levine/colorstereo.com

This is the object that you should be able to see in the stereogram on the previous page.

Predictable changes occur in other aspects of human vision as we grow older. Accommodation of the lens, which allows us to change focus from near to far objects, becomes slower beginning in middle adulthood. Older adults also respond more slowly to changes in brightness, such as leaving a dark theater into the sunlight. The muscles of the iris begin to lose their elasticity, so pupils remain smaller, further reducing vision by limiting the amount of light that enters the eye. The lens of the eye begins to yellow, which protects the eye from ultraviolet radiation but affects the perception of color.

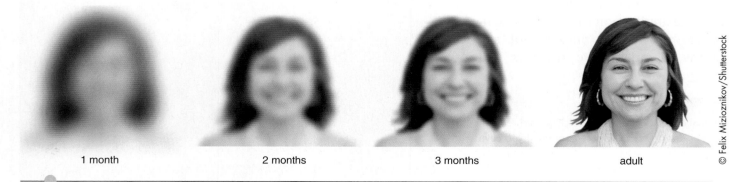

| 1 month | 2 months | 3 months | adult |

© Felix Mizioznikov/Shutterstock

We can filter out the frequencies and contrast that a baby cannot see to simulate what the world looks like to an infant.

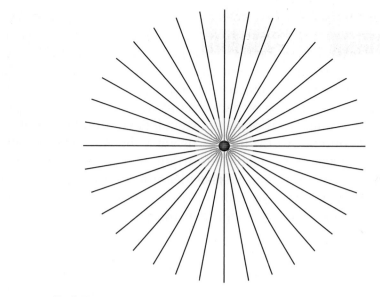

FIGURE 5.27

Astigmatism. If you have astigmatism, which results from an uneven surface in your corneas, some of the spokes of this figure will appear darker than others.

We tend to think that everyone sees the world in the same way we do, that our visual perceptions are like photographs of reality. At this point in the chapter, though, you may be realizing that perception does not work precisely that way, that what you see differs from what other animals see, and that what you see can differ from what other people see. A simple case in point is that people differ in their abilities to see near and far objects, and those who deviate from the average often wear corrective lenses or undergo laser surgery to reshape the cornea. The most common visual problems result from eyeball length, with elongated eyeballs interfering with a person's vision for distant objects (nearsightedness), and shortened eyeballs interfering with vision for close-up objects (farsightedness), as in reading. Vision is also affected by astigmatism, which means that the surface of the cornea is uneven. You can test yourself for astigmatism by looking at ● Figure 5.27.

Sociocultural Influences on Visual Perception

Earlier in the chapter, we explored a number of illusions of depth. There is some evidence that experience plays a role in whether or not these stimuli provoke an illusion. When tested in 1905, residents of Papua, New Guinea, and the Todas of southern India were less likely than Western participants to see the Müller-Lyer illusion (Rivers, 1905). Similar results were found among participants in Africa and the Philippines (Segall, Campbell, & Herskovits, 1966). The Western experience with a "carpentered world" of right angles, rectangles, and straight lines might account for these cultural differences.

In addition, the idea that a figure-ground organization is a built-in aspect of the human condition has been challenged (Chua, Boland, & Nisbett, 2005). Eye movements of American and Chinese college students were recorded as they scanned photographs. As shown in ● Figure 5.28, the American students were more likely to focus quickly on the figure, whereas the Chinese students gave approximately equal viewing time to the figure and to its context or ground. Subsequently, the American students did a better job of identifying which objects they had seen previously, even when the object was shown against a new background. The researchers suggested that some of the differences they observed stem from cultural differences in the importance of context. According to this view, the American emphasis on individualism makes context less important than it might be for the Chinese students, for whom context provides important cues for proper social functioning. Further cross-cultural research would be helpful in determining the universality of perceptual principles.

Thinking Scientifically

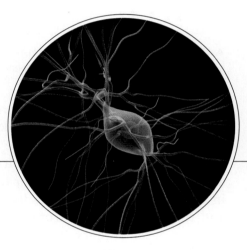

The Roger Shepard Parallelogram Illusion "Turning the Tables"

Anyone can tell, simply by looking, whether or not two tabletops are the same shape, right? For instance, most people would agree that the shapes and sizes of the two tabletops depicted in ● Figure 5.29 are different. One tabletop appears to be rectangular, the other more square. As much as our perceptions may tell us otherwise, these tabletops are identical. (To verify this for yourself, trace one of the tabletops and then rotate it to place it above the other. You will be able to prove for yourself that these tables in fact have identical tops.) It is not our eyes (sensory receptors) that deceive us, it is our brains.

Roger Shepard combined a profound scientific curiosity with a love of mischief. Shepard developed a number of creative visual illusions, including the "Turning the Tables" illustration, which he illustrated himself (Shepard, 1990). The visual illusion produced in this illustration results from our use of a visual system designed to cope with the three dimensions of the physical world on stimuli that have only two dimensions.

In Roger Shepard's own words:

The drawings . . . achieve their effects by means of various visual tricks. But to call them tricks is not to imply that they are without psychological significance. The tricks work by taking advantage of fundamental perceptual principles that have been shaped

by natural selection in a three-dimensional world. Our ability to make pictures, which emerged only recently on an evolutionary time scale, enables us to present the eyes with visual patterns that systematically depart from the patterns that we and our ancestors experienced in nature. In considering the ways pictures can trick the eye, we can gain insight into the nature and ultimate source of the principles of visual perception. (Shepard, 1990, p. 121)

More generally, it is examples like this that underscore the importance of relying on scientific investigation and evidence to unveil how sensation and perception work. ⚙

FIGURE 5.28

Cultural Differences in Viewing Scenes. When viewing this photo of a tiger, American participants spent more time viewing the tiger than the background, whereas Asian participants spent approximately equal amounts of time viewing the tiger and the background. This image shows tracings of eye movements from one representative American participant (left) and one representative Asian participant (right).

© Hannah Faye Chua

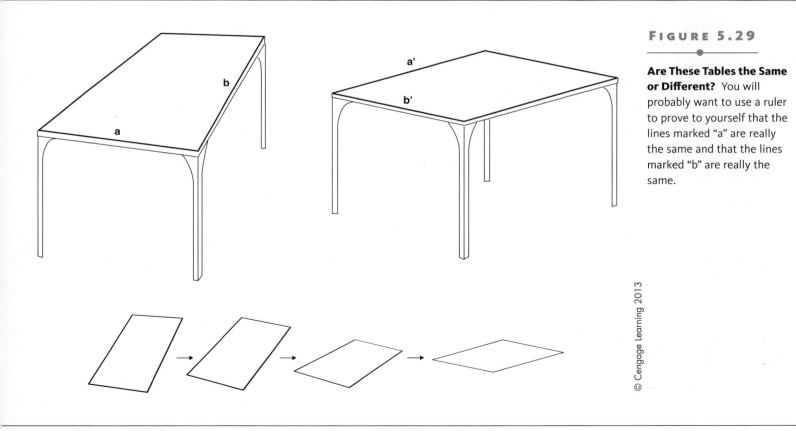

FIGURE 5.29

Are These Tables the Same or Different? You will probably want to use a ruler to prove to yourself that the lines marked "a" are really the same and that the lines marked "b" are really the same.

© Cengage Learning 2013

Summary 5.2

Important Features of the Visual System

Feature	Significance
Cornea 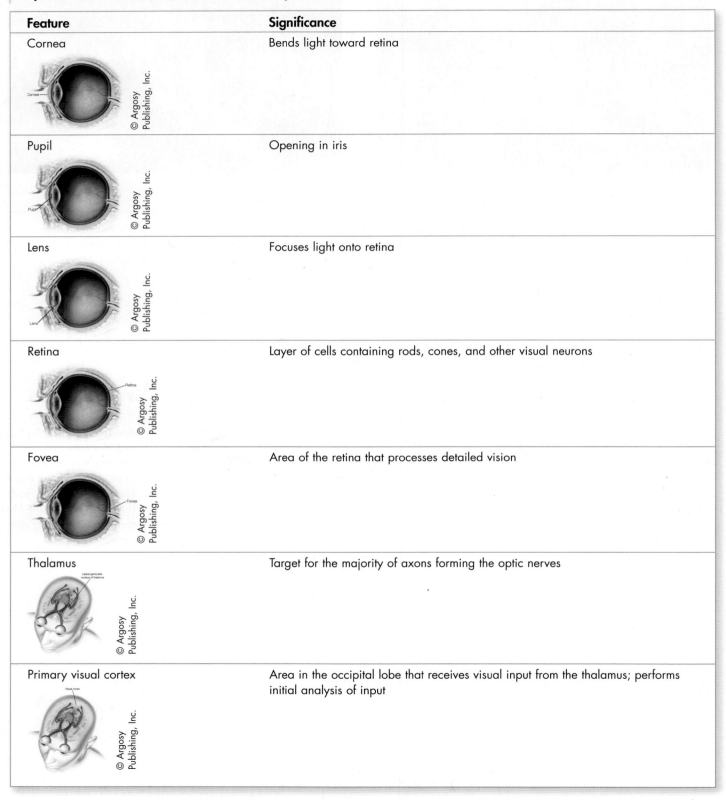	Bends light toward retina
Pupil	Opening in iris
Lens	Focuses light onto retina
Retina	Layer of cells containing rods, cones, and other visual neurons
Fovea	Area of the retina that processes detailed vision
Thalamus	Target for the majority of axons forming the optic nerves
Primary visual cortex	Area in the occipital lobe that receives visual input from the thalamus; performs initial analysis of input

How Do We Hear?

We have spent a considerable amount of time and space on the sense of vision, which might be considered a dominant source of information for human beings. However, when Helen Keller, who was both blind and deaf, was asked which disability affected her the most, she replied that blindness separated her from things, while deafness separated her from people. **Audition,** our sense of hearing, not only allows us to identify objects in the distance, but it plays an especially important role in our ability to communicate with others through language.

The Auditory Stimulus
Sound begins with the movement of an object, setting off waves of vibration in the form of miniature collisions between adjacent molecules in air, liquid, or solids. Because sound waves require this jostling of molecules, sound cannot occur in the vacuum of space, which contains no matter at all. Those explosions we enjoy in *Star Wars* films are great entertainment, but not very good science.

Earlier in this chapter, we described light energy as waves having different amplitudes and frequencies. Sound waves may be described using the same dimensions. However, in the case of sound, the height or amplitude of the wave is encoded as loudness or intensity and the frequency of the wave as pitch. High-amplitude waves are perceived as loud, and low-amplitude waves are perceived as soft. High-frequency waves (many cycles per unit of time) are perceived as high pitched, whereas low-frequency sounds are low pitched. In sound, amplitude is usually measured in units called *decibels* (*dB*), and frequency is measured in cycles per second, or *Hertz* (*Hz*) (see ● Figure 5.30).

Most sounds that we hear are complex combinations of waves. A wave with only one frequency is known as a pure tone, but these rarely occur in nature. The tuning fork used by a piano tuner produces pure tones. A

A "sonic boom" occurs when an airplane is traveling faster than the speed of sound (approximately 756 mph) and gets ahead of the sound waves it is creating. The sound waves left behind by the plane merge into a shock wave that sounds like a "boom" when it reaches our ears.

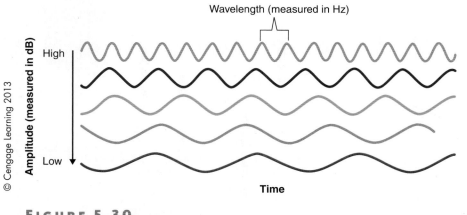

FIGURE 5.30

Features of Sound. Like the light energy we see, sound waves are characterized by frequency and amplitude. We perceive frequency as the pitch of the sound (high or low, measured in Hertz, or Hz) and we perceive amplitude as the loudness of the sound, measured in decibels (dB).

audition The sense of hearing.

complex tone combining multiple waves is perceived as having a characteristic quality, or timbre. The same note played by a piano, clarinet, and violin will sound very different due to each instrument's ability to produce different timbres.

In addition to dizziness and nausea, being exposed to infrasound makes people report feelings of chills down the spine, fear, and revulsion, even though they cannot consciously detect the sound. Some scientists believe that infrasound produced in certain places leads people to conclude the places are "haunted."

As we observed in the case of the light spectrum, parts of the auditory spectrum are outside the range of human hearing. Ultrasound stimuli occur at frequencies above the range of human hearing, beginning at about 20,000 Hz (see ● Figure 5.31). Ultrasound can be used to clean jewelry or your teeth or to produce noninvasive medical images. Infrasound refers to frequencies below the range of human hearing, or less than 20 Hz. Many animals, including elephants and marine mammals, use infrasound for communication. Infrasound is particularly effective in water, as it allows sound to travel for very long distances. In humans, however, infrasound stimuli produce dizziness, nausea, uncontrolled bowel movements, and other unpleasant symptoms and are under study as a possible means of nonlethal crowd control (Vinokur, 2004).

The Biology of Audition

Human audition begins with ears that are located on either side of the head. The components that make up the ear are usually divided into three parts: the outer ear, the middle ear, and the inner ear (see ● Figure 5.32).

The outer ear consists of the structures that are visible outside the body. The pinna, the outer visible structure of the ear, collects and focuses sounds,

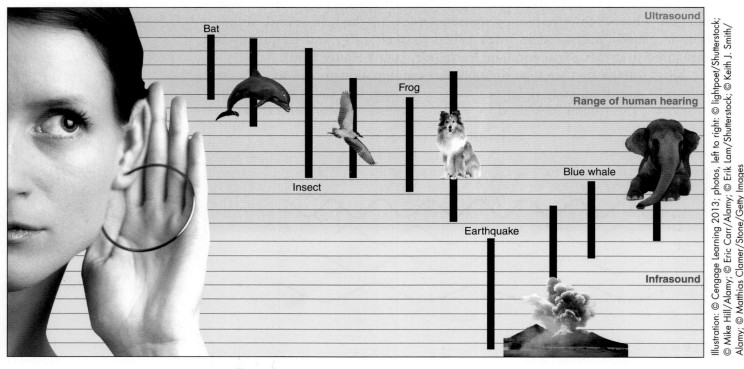

Illustration: © Cengage Learning 2013; photos, left to right: © lightpoet/Shutterstock; © Mike Hill/Alamy; © Eric Carr/Alamy; © Erik Lam/Shutterstock; © Keith J. Smith/ Alamy; © Matthias Clamer/Stone/Getty Images

FIGURE 5.31

Range of Hearing. Ultrasounds are above the range of human hearing, and infrasounds are below the range of human hearing.

like a funnel. In addition, the pinna helps us localize sounds as being above or below the head. Sounds collected by the pinna are channeled through the auditory canal, which ends at the tympanic membrane, or eardrum, at the boundary between the outer and middle ear. The boundary between the middle and inner ear is formed by another membrane, the oval window. The gap between these two membranes is bridged by a series of tiny bones. The purpose of these bones is to transfer sound energy from the air of the outer and middle ear to the fluid found in the inner ear. Sound waves are weakened as they move from air to water. When you try to "talk" to friends underwater, the result is rather garbled. Without the adjustments provided by these small bones, we would lose a large amount of sound energy as the sound waves moved from air to liquid within the ear.

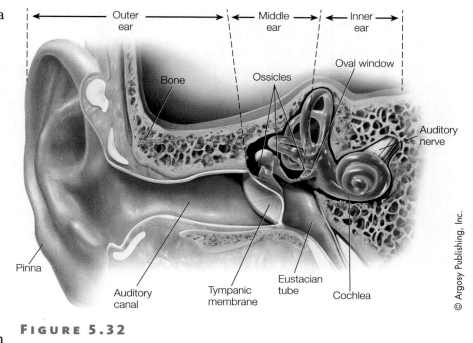

FIGURE 5.32

Parts of the Ear. The human ear is divided into the outer, middle, and inner ear.

The inner ear contains two sets of fluid-filled cavities embedded in the bone of the skull. One set is part of the vestibular system, which we will discuss later in this chapter. The other set is the **cochlea,** from the Greek word for "snail." When rolled up like a snail shell, the human cochlea is about the size of a pea. It contains specialized receptor cells that respond to vibrations transmitted to the inner ear.

The cochlea is a very complex structure, which is better understood if we pretend to unroll it. The cochlea may be divided into three parallel chambers divided from one another by membranes. Two of these chambers, the vestibular canal and the tympanic canal, are connected at the apex of the cochlea, or the point farthest from the oval window. Vibrations transmitted by the bones of the middle ear to the oval window produce waves in the fluid of the vestibular canal that travel around the apex and back through the tympanic canal. Lying between the vestibular and tympanic canals is the cochlear duct. The cochlear duct is separated from the tympanic canal by the **basilar membrane.** Resting on top of the basilar membrane is the **organ of Corti,** which contains many rows of hair cells that transduce sound energy into neural signals. Each human ear has about 15,500 of these hair cells.

The fetus has no bubble of air in the middle ear, having never been exposed to air. Because fluids actually do a better job of transmitting sound waves, there is very good evidence that the fetus can hear outside sounds, such as the voice of a mother, quite well during the final trimester of pregnancy.

As waves travel through the cochlea, the basilar membrane responds with its own wavelike motion, similar to the crack of a whip. The movement of the basilar membrane causes the hair cells of the organ of Corti to move back and forth within the fluid of the cochlear duct. Bending the hair cells stimulates the release of neurotransmitters onto the cells of the

cochlea The structure in the middle ear that contains auditory receptors.

basilar membrane Membrane in the cochlea on which the organ of Corti is located.

organ of Corti A structure located on the basilar membrane that contains auditory receptors.

The movement of tiny hair cells in the inner ear produces neural signals that travel to the brain.

auditory nerve. The basilar membrane needs to move very little before the hair cells are stimulated. If the hairlike structures extending from the top of the hair cells were the size of the Eiffel Tower in Paris, the movement required to produce a neural response would be the equivalent of 1 cm (about 0.4 in.; Hudspeth, 1983).

Auditory Pathways As we mentioned in the previous section, the hair cells stimulate axons forming the auditory nerve. One branch of each auditory nerve cell makes contact with the hair cells while the other branch proceeds to the medulla of the brainstem. From the medulla, sound information is sent to the midbrain, which manages reflexive responses to sound, as in turning toward the source of a loud noise. In addition, the midbrain participates in sound localization, or the identification of a source of sound.

The midbrain passes information along to the thalamus, which in turn sends sound information to the primary auditory cortex, located in the temporal lobe. The primary auditory cortex conducts the first basic analysis of the wavelengths and amplitudes of incoming information (see • Figure 5.33). Surrounding the primary auditory cortex are areas of secondary auditory cortex that respond to complex types of stimuli, like clicks, noise, and sounds having particular patterns.

Auditory Perception and Cognition

Now that we have an understanding of the structures and pathways used to process the sensations that lead to the perception of sound, we turn our attention to the brain's interpretation and organization of these sounds in terms of pitch, loudness, and spatial localization.

Pitch Perception Perception of pitch begins with the basilar membrane of the inner ear (see • Figure 5.34). Place theory suggests that the frequency of a sound is correlated with the part of the basilar membrane showing a peak response. The base of the basilar membrane, closest to the oval win-

FIGURE 5.33

Primary Auditory Cortex. The primary auditory cortex is located in the temporal lobe.

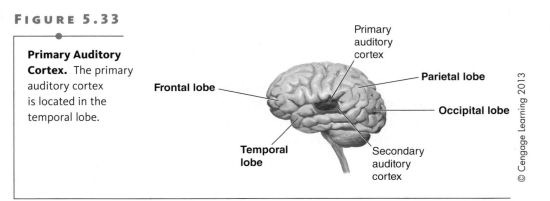

Primary auditory cortex

Parietal lobe

Frontal lobe

Occipital lobe

Temporal lobe

Secondary auditory cortex

© Cengage Learning 2013

auditory nerve Nerve carrying sound information from the cochlea to the brain.

dow, is narrow and stiff. In contrast, at its farthest point near the apex, the basilar membrane is wide and flexible. If you have any familiarity with stringed instruments like a guitar, you know that high tones are produced by striking the taut, small strings and lower tones by striking the wide, floppy strings. The same principle holds for the basilar membrane. High-frequency tones produce the maximum movement of the basilar membrane near the base, while low-frequency tones produce maximum movement near the apex. The hair cells riding above these areas of peak movement will show a maximum response. Place theory works well for sounds above 4000 Hz (which is about the frequency produced by striking the highest key on a piano—C8). Below frequencies of 4000 Hz, the response of the basilar membrane does not allow for precise localization. In these cases, we appear to use another mechanism known as frequency theory, in which patterns of neural firing "match" the actual frequency of a sound.

TABLE 5.2 Loudness of Common Sounds	
Source of sound	Intensity (measured in decibels, or dB)
Threshold of hearing	0 dB
Rustling leaves	10 dB
Whisper	20 dB
Normal conversation	60 dB
Busy street traffic	70 dB
Vacuum cleaner	80 dB
Water at foot of Niagara Falls	90 dB
iPod with standard earbuds	100 dB
Front rows of rock concert	110 dB
Propeller plane at takeoff	120 dB
Threshold of pain/Machine gun fire	130 dB
Military jet takeoff	140 dB
Instant perforation of eardrum	160 dB

Perceiving Loudness Human beings can perceive sounds that vary in intensity by a factor of over 10 billion, from the softest sound we can detect up to the sound made by a jet engine at takeoff (which will also cause pain and structural damage to the ear). Table 5.2 identifies the intensity level of many common stimuli, measured in the logarithmic decibel scale. Our perception of loudness does not change at the same rate as intensity. When the intensity of a sound stimulus is 10 times greater than before, we perceive it as being only twice as loud (Stevens, 1960).

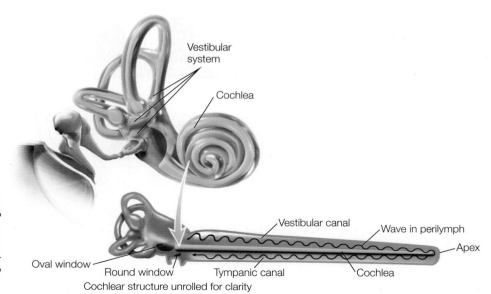

© Argosy Publishing, Inc.

Vestibular system

Cochlea

Oval window
Round window
Tympanic canal
Cochlear structure unrolled for clarity

Vestibular canal
Wave in perilymph
Apex
Cochlea

FIGURE 5.34

Perception of Pitch. Sound waves produce a peak response on the basilar membrane according to their frequencies. Like the strings on a musical instrument, high tones produce the greatest response at the narrow, stiff base of the basilar membrane, while low tones produce the greatest response at the wide, floppy part of the basilar membrane near the apex. Sound waves travel through the cochlea from the oval window, around the apex, and back to the round window. The waves cause movement of tiny hair cells in the cochlear duct, which we perceive as sound.

The frequency of a sound interacts with our perception of its loudness. Human beings are maximally sensitive to sounds that normally fall within the range of human speech, or between 80 and 10,000 Hz (see ● Figure 5.35). Sounds falling outside the range of speech must have higher intensity before we hear them as well. One feature that distinguishes an expensive sound system from a cheaper model is its ability to boost these frequencies that fall outside our most sensitive range.

Localization of Sound The pinna helps us localize sounds in the vertical plane, or in space above or below our head. Our primary method for localizing sound in the horizontal plane (in front, behind, and to the side) is to compare the arrival time of sound at each ear. As illustrated in ● Figure 5.36, the differences in arrival times are quite small, between 0 msec for sounds that are directly in front of or behind you to 0.6 msec for sounds coming from a source perpendicular to your head on either side. Because arrival times for sounds coming from directly in front of or behind you are identical, it is very difficult to distinguish these sources without further information. In addition to arrival times, we judge the differences in intensity of sounds reaching each ear. Because the head blocks some sound waves, a sound "shadow" is cast on the ear farthest away from the source of sound. As a result, a weaker signal is received by this ear.

Just as our visual systems can be "fooled" by certain types of input, our ability to localize sounds is influenced by the interactions between human vision and audition. Even before the invention of surround sound, which

Illustration: © Cengage Learning 2013; photo, top: © RoxyFer/Shutterstock; photo, bottom: © YUYI/Shutterstock

FIGURE 5.35

Human Sensitivity to Sound. These functions plot the results of allowing participants to adjust the intensity of different tones until they sound equally loud. Low frequencies are usually perceived as quieter than high frequencies at the same level of intensity. We are especially sensitive to frequencies found in speech.

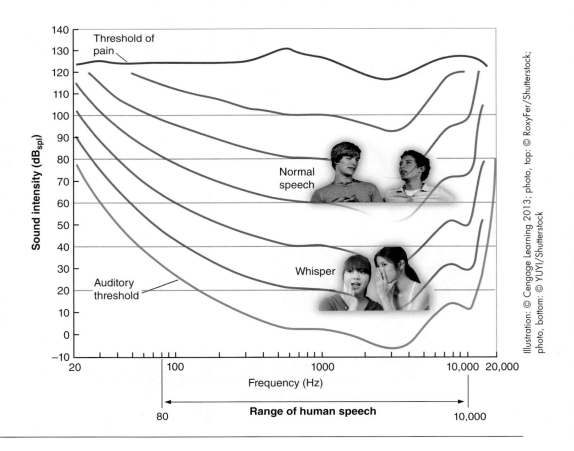

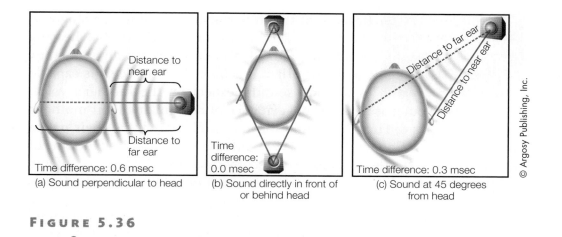

FIGURE 5.36

Where Is That Sound Coming From? We localize sound to the left and right by comparing the differences between the arrival times of the sounds to our two ears.

provides a number of effective sound localization cues, moviegoers perceived sound as originating from the actors' lips, in spite of the fact that the speakers producing the sound are typically above and to the sides of the screen. Our willingness to believe that the sound is coming from the actors' lips probably results from our everyday experiences of watching people speak. In more abstract laboratory conditions, people are more likely to report that a sound moving left to right is actually going in the opposite direction if they see an object going right to left at the same time. Our experience has taught us that objects and the sounds they make usually travel together (Soto-Faraco, Kingstone, & Spence, 2006).

Auditory Groupings In our previous discussion of visual perception, we reviewed the grouping principles developed by Gestalt psychologists. Similar types of grouping occur in audition as well. Sounds from one location are grouped together, as we assume they have the same source, whereas sounds identified as coming from different locations are assumed to have different sources. Sounds that start and stop at the same time are perceived as having the same source, while sounds with different starting and stopping times usually arise from separate sources, like two voices having a conversation or two instruments in a band or ensemble. Grouping plays an especially significant role in the perception of music and speech. In these cases, we see evidence of top-down processing as well, as our expectations for the next note or word influence our perceptions (Pearce, Ruiz, Kapasi, Wiggins, & Bhattacharya, 2010). The similar processing of music and language has led researchers to argue in favor of including more music in school to assist children with language learning (Strait, Kraus, Parbery-Clark, & Ashley, 2010).

We also use vision to localize the source of sounds, which allows us to be pleasantly fooled by talented ventriloquists. Because the dummy's mouth is moving and the ventriloquist's is not, we perceive the sound as coming from the dummy, not the person.

Developmental and Individual Differences in Audition

Because of the importance of audition to language learning, it should not be surprising that hearing begins before birth and develops rapidly in infants. As noted earlier, it is likely that the fetus is capable of hearing sounds, especially the mother's voice. Newborns as young as 2 days show evidence of recognizing their mother's voice (DeCasper & Fifer, 1980) and respond preferentially to their native language (Moon, Cooper, & Fifer, 1993). Infants less than three months of age show strong startle reactions to noise. By the age of six months, infants will turn their heads in the direction of a loud or interesting sound. It is likely that their thresholds for sounds are nearly at adult levels by this age (Olsho, Koch, Halpin, & Carter, 1987). By the age of one year, children should reliably turn around when their name is called.

An important developmental change in audition is the hearing loss that often accompanies aging. Hearing loss tends to occur first at higher frequencies. After the age of 30, most people cannot hear sounds above 15,000 Hz. After the age of 50, most people cannot hear above 12,000 Hz, and people over 70 have difficulty with sounds over 6000 Hz. Because speech normally ranges up to 8000–10,000 Hz, many seniors begin to have difficulty understanding the speech of others, particularly female voices with their higher frequency range.

Among individual differences in hearing is having perfect pitch, which means that you can name a musical tone that you hear. The brains of individuals with perfect pitch appear to be structurally different from those of people who do not have this ability. Areas of the left hemisphere appear to be much larger in musicians with perfect pitch (Schlaug, Jancke, Huang, & Steinmetz, 1995). At the same time, extensive early musical training can shape the structure of the brain (Schlaug et al., 2009).

> If you are distressed by anything external, the pain is not due to the thing itself but to your own estimate of it; and this you have the power to revoke at any moment.
>
> —Marcus Aurelius

Sociocultural Influences on Auditory Perception

Human culture and social life often provide a framework for the interpretation of stimuli. A dramatic example of this type of influence is our reaction to sine wave speech. To produce this stimulus, scientists artificially alter recordings of speech to resemble regular, repeating sine waves, as shown in ● Figure 5.37 (Davis, 2007). When people hear these artificial sounds without any further instructions, they describe them as tweeting birds or other nonlanguage stimuli. However, if people are told the sounds represent speech, they suddenly "hear" language elements (Remez, Rubin, Pisoni, & Carell, 1981).

Sine wave speech shows us how culture in the form of experience with language can shape perception, but in other instances, perception can shape culture. For many people with hearing loss and their families and friends, being deaf means something other than having a disability. Instead, deafness is viewed as a culture, complete with its own set of attitudes, language, and norms. American Sign Language (ASL) is viewed as being quite distinct from signed English and is difficult for signing people in Great Britain and Australia to understand (Mindess, 2006).

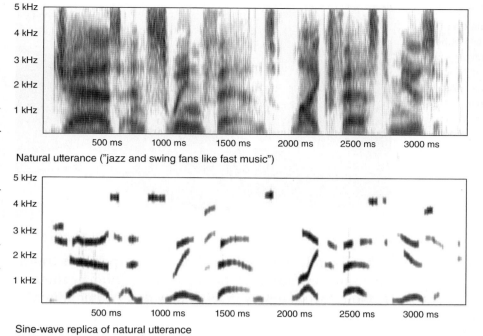

© Remez, R. E. (1998). Sine-wave speech. *Scholarpedia, 3*: 2394.

Natural utterance ("jazz and swing fans like fast music")

Sine-wave replica of natural utterance

FIGURE 5.37

Expectations Influence the Interpretation of Sine Waves. Sine waves are regular and repetitive waveforms, like the ones we included earlier to show how the height and frequency of light and sound waves are interpreted by the mind. Researchers can record speech sounds and transform the recordings into artificial sine waves, like those in this image. If the sounds are played without any information about their source, most people interpret the sounds as "tweeting birds." However, if people are told that the recordings are language, they report "hearing" language, another example of top-down cognitive influences on perception.

How Do We Feel Body Position, Touch, Temperature, and Pain?

Somatosensation (*soma* comes from the Greek word for "body") provides us with information about the position and movement of our bodies, along with touch, skin temperature, and pain. Although these senses may not seem as glamorous as vision and hearing, we are severely disabled by their loss. You might think it would be a blessing to be born without a sense of pain, but people who have impaired pain reception, often die prematurely due to their inability to respond to injury. Although unpleasant, pain tells us to stop and assess our circumstances, which may have promoted the survival of our ancestors.

Somatosensory Stimuli

Unlike the visual and auditory stimuli we have discussed so far in this chapter, somatosensory stimuli arise from within the body itself or make contact with its surface. As a result, these stimuli do not provide an organism much time to react. We can deal with a predator seen or heard from a distance using very different strategies from one that is touching us. Nonetheless, the somatosenses provide essential feedback needed for movement, speech, and safety.

The Biology of the Somatosenses

The transition from walking on four legs to walking on two placed selective pressure on the evolution of primate vision and, to some extent, on audition. By standing up on two legs, primates distanced themselves from many sources of information, like smell. If you don't believe us,

somatosensation The body senses, including body position, touch, skin temperature, and pain.

Eleven-year-old Ashlyn Blocker has a genetic condition that makes it impossible for her to feel pain. Although her parents watch her very carefully, she went several days with a broken ankle before they saw it was swollen and took her to a doctor. She had not complained about any pain. Ashlyn's inability to feel pain also impacts her ability to empathize with other children when they are hurt. This is an aspect of life she just doesn't understand.

try getting down on hands and knees and smelling your carpet. This transition did not place the same evolutionary pressure on the human somatosenses, which work about the same way in us as they do in other animals.

Body Position   To begin our exploration of the somatosensory systems, we return to the inner ear. Adjacent to the structures responsible for encoding sound, we find the sensory structures of the **vestibular system,** which provide us with information about body position and movement. The proximity of these structures to the middle ear, which can become congested due to a head cold, is often responsible for those rather unpleasant feelings of dizziness that accompany an illness. The receptors of the vestibular system provide information about the position of the head relative to the ground, linear acceleration, and rotational movements of the head. We sense linear acceleration when our rate of movement changes, such as when our car pulls away from a stop sign or our airplane takes off.

Like the cochlea, the vestibular receptors contain very sensitive hair cells that are bent back and forth within their surrounding fluid when the head moves. When extensive movement stops suddenly, perhaps at the end of an amusement park ride, these fluids may reverse course. You may have the odd sensation that your head is now moving in the opposite direction, even though you are sitting or standing still. The movement of these hair cells results in the production of signals in the auditory nerve, the same nerve that carries information about sound. These axons form connections in the medulla and in the cerebellum. You may recall from our chapter on biological psychology that the cerebellum participates in balance and motor coordination, functions that are dependent on feedback about movement. In turn, the medulla receives input from the visual system, the cerebellum, and other somatosenses. This arrangement provides an opportunity to coordinate input from the vestibular system with other relevant information. The medulla forms connections directly with the spinal cord, allowing us to adjust our posture in order to keep our balance. Vestibular information travels from the medulla to the thalamus,

The vestibular system helps us maintain a steady view of the world, even when riding the most extreme roller coaster.

vestibular system   The system in the inner ear that provides information about body position and movement.

and then to the primary somatosensory cortex of the parietal lobe and to the primary motor cortex in the frontal lobe. This pathway allows vestibular information to guide voluntary movement.

In human beings particularly, information from the vestibular system is tightly integrated with visual processing. As we move, it is essential that we maintain a stable view of our surroundings. To accomplish this task, any rotation of the head results in a reflexive movement of the eyes in the opposite direction. This action should allow you to maintain a steady view of the world, even on the most extreme rollercoaster.

Touch Touch provides a wealth of information about the objects around us. By simply exploring an object with touch, we are able to determine features such as size, shape, texture, and consistency. These judgments confirm and expand the information we obtain about objects through visual exploration. Touch is not only a means of exploring the environment. Particularly in humans, touch plays a significant role in social communication. Infants who are touched regularly sleep better, remain more alert while awake, and reach cognitive milestones at earlier ages (Ackerman, 1990). We hug our friends and loved ones in order to provide comfort, pat others on the back for a job well done, and shake hands to greet a colleague or conclude a deal. The contributions of the sense of touch to human sexuality are obvious.

Our sense of touch begins with skin, the largest and heaviest organ in the human body. Embedded within the skin are several types of specialized neurons that produce action potentials whenever they are physically bent or stretched. Different types of receptors respond to certain features of a touch stimulus, such as pressure, vibration, or stretch (see • Figure 5.38). In addition to their locations in the skin, receptors may be found in blood vessels, joints, and our internal organs. Unpleasant sensations from a headache or a too-full stomach or bladder originate from some of these receptors. Some receptor fibers wrap themselves around hair follicles and respond whenever a hair is pulled or bent. Others, as we will see later in this section, participate in our senses of pain and temperature.

Information about touch travels from the skin to the spinal cord. Once inside the spinal cord, touch pathways proceed to the thalamus, along with input from the cranial nerves originating in the touch receptors in the skin of the face, the mouth, and the tongue. The thalamus transmits touch information to the primary somatosensory cortex, located in the parietal lobe.

A map of the body's representation in the primary somatosensory cortex, or a sensory homunculus ("little

FIGURE 5.38

Touch Receptors. Different receptors in the skin help us sense pressure, vibration, stretch, or pain.

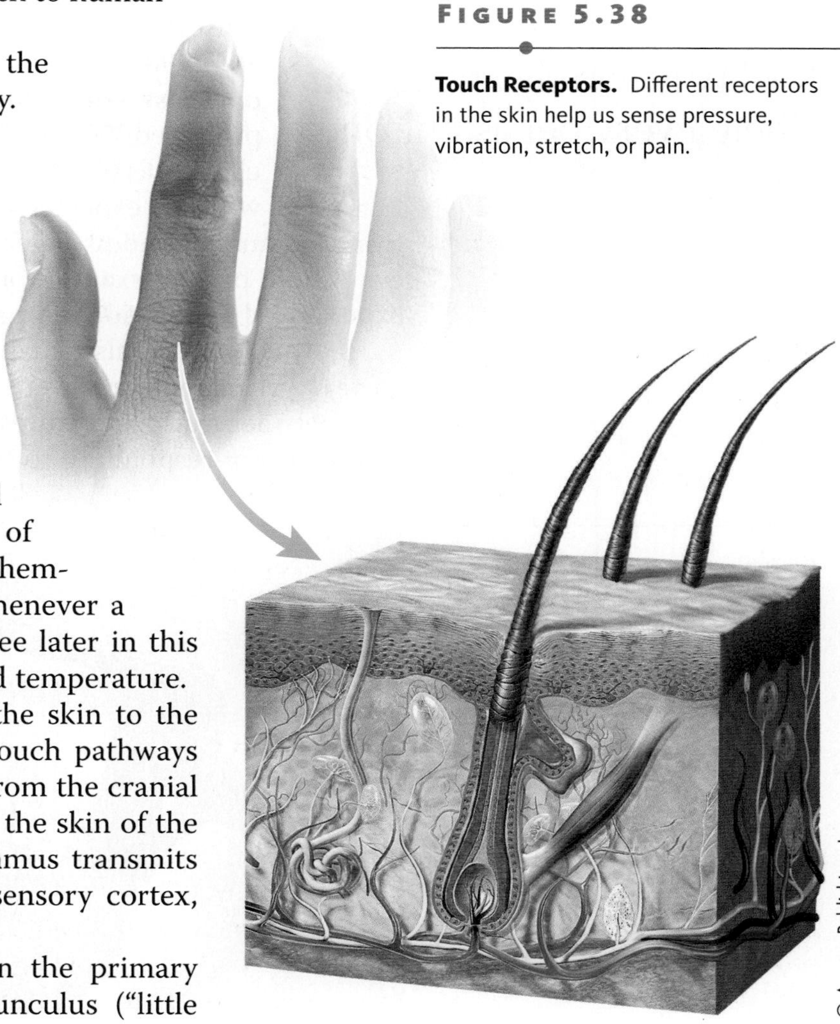

The sensory homunculus ("little man") illustrates the amount of representation each part of the body has in the sensory cortex. The human homunculus emphasizes the hands and face.

> Reality is merely an illusion, albeit a very persistent one.
>
> —Albert Einstein

man") is shown in the statue to the left. As you can see, this odd figure demonstrates that areas of the body are represented on the basis of their sensitivity rather than size. Different species show different patterns of cortical organization for touch. Human beings need sensitive feedback from the lips and hands in order to speak and make skilled hand movements for tool use and other tasks. Rats devote a great deal of cortical real estate to whiskers, whereas lips have a very high priority in squirrels and rabbits.

A notable area that is missing from the homunculus is the brain, which has neither touch receptors nor pain receptors. We can only assume that for much of evolutionary history, any intrusion into the brain itself was likely to be fatal. Consequently, there would be no advantage to "feeling" your brain. Due to the lack of somatosensation in the brain, neurosurgeons are able to work with an alert patient using local anesthesia for the skull and tissues overlying the brain. The surgery itself produces no sensations of pressure or pain.

The representation of touch in the primary sensory cortex is "plastic," which means that it changes in response to increases or decreases in input from a body part. Many individuals who lose a body part experience a phenomenon known as "phantom limb," a term first used by a Civil War physician to describe his patients' experience of "pain" from a missing limb. Phantom sensations can result from the reorganization of the somatosensory cortex following the loss of a body part (Borsook et al., 1998; Ramachandran & Rogers-Ramachandran, 2000). In one case study, touching different parts of the patient's face produced "feelings" from the patient's missing hand. When his cheek was touched, he reported feeling his missing thumb along with the expected cheek, while touching his lip elicited feelings from the missing index finger along with the normal lip sensations. In an even more bizarre example, a patient was embarrassed to report that he experienced a sensation of orgasm in his missing foot.

Increased input also changes the organization of the somatosensory cortex. When monkeys were trained to use specific fingers to discriminate between surface textures in order to obtain food rewards, the areas of the cortex responding to the trained fingertips expanded (Merzenich

The representation of body parts in the primary sensory cortex can change based on the amount of input from a body part. Texting from an early age is likely to result in greater representation for the thumbs.

& Jenkins, 1993). A similar reorganization occurs when blind individuals learn to read braille (Pascual-Leone & Torres, 1993) or when people train extensively on stringed musical instruments (Elbert, Pantev, Weinbruch, Rockstroh, & Taub, 1995). Using your thumbs for text messaging will probably result in adaptations in cortical representation not seen in older generations (Wilton, 2002).

Pain Given the anguish experienced by patients with chronic pain, it is often tempting to think that not having a sense of pain would be wonderful. However, as mentioned earlier, we need pain to remind us to stop when we are injured, to assess the situation before proceeding, and to allow the body time to heal.

Free nerve endings that respond to pain are triggered by a number of stimuli associated with tissue damage. Some pain receptors respond to mechanical damage, such as that caused by a sharp object, while others respond to temperature or chemicals. Among the chemicals that stimulate pain receptors is capsaicin, an ingredient found in hot peppers (Caterina et al., 1997). Information about pain is carried centrally to the brain by two types of fibers. Fast, myelinated axons are responsible for that sharp "ouch" sensation that often accompanies an injury. Slower, unmyelinated axons are responsible for dull, aching sensations. These slower fibers are also responsible for sensations of itch.

In one of the most dramatic examples of how stress can interfere with the perception of pain, Guy Gertsch unknowingly ran the final 19 miles of the 1982 Boston Marathon on a broken leg (Gertsch finished the race with a highly respectable time of 2 hours and 47 minutes).

Pain fibers from the body form synapses with cells in the spinal cord, which in turn sends pain messages to the thalamus. Notice the relatively direct route this information takes, with only one synapse in the spinal cord separating the periphery of the body and the thalamus in the forebrain. This arrangement ensures that pain messages will be received by the brain with great speed. From the thalamus, pain information is sent to the anterior cingulate cortex, which manages the emotional qualities of pain, and to the somatosensory cortex in the parietal lobe.

Pain messages traveling to the brain may be modified by competing incoming sensory signals. Many of us spontaneously rub our elbow after bumping it painfully. A model known as a **gate theory** of pain accounts for this phenomenon (Melzack & Wall, 1965). According to this model, input from touch fibers (reacting to rubbing your elbow) competes with input from pain receptors for activation of cells in the spinal cord (see ● Figure 5.39). Activation of the touch fibers effectively dilutes the amount of pain information reaching the brain.

The perception of pain is affected by the descending influence of higher brain centers. Many forebrain structures form connections with the periaqueductal gray of the midbrain. As we observed in our chapter on biological psychology, this area is rich in receptors for our natural opiates, the endogenous morphines, or *endorphins.* It is likely that the periaqueductal gray is a major target for opiate painkillers, such as morphine. Electrical stimulation of the periaqueductal gray produces a significant reduction in the experience of pain.

Stress provides an example of a higher order cognitive state that influences pain. Survival often depends on the ability to keep moving even in

gate theory The theory that suggests that input from touch fibers competes with input from pain receptors, possibly preventing pain messages from reaching the brain.

FIGURE 5.39

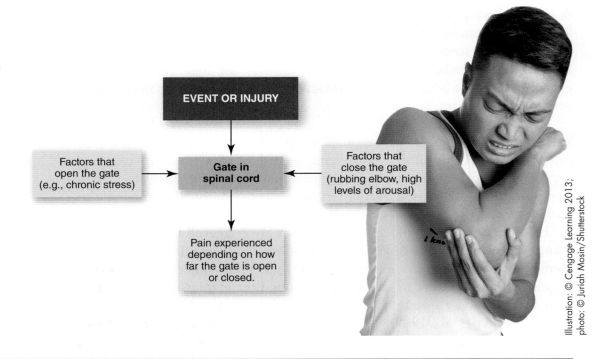

The Gate Theory of Pain. According to the gate theory, incoming pain messages can be influenced by factors like chronic stress (opening the gate wider and producing a greater sensation of pain) or rubbing an injured body part (closing the gate and reducing the sensation of pain).

EVENT OR INJURY

Factors that open the gate (e.g., chronic stress) → Gate in spinal cord ← Factors that close the gate (rubbing elbow, high levels of arousal)

Pain experienced depending on how far the gate is open or closed.

Illustration: © Cengage Learning 2013; photo: © Juriah Mosin/Shutterstock

cases of extreme pain. When levels of arousal are very high, people can be very seriously injured without really being aware of the problem. Another example of cognitive influence on pain perception is the phenomenon of placebo effects. A placebo effect occurs when people experience pain reduction in spite of the fact that they have been exposed to an ineffective substance or treatment, such as a sugar pill instead of an aspirin tablet. Apparently, a person's belief that she or he is being treated for pain may be sufficient to initiate a real decrease in pain sensation.

Sociocultural Influences on the Somatosenses

No other sensory modality is as dramatically affected by culture, context, and experience as our sense of pain. The connection between culture and the experience of pain is vividly illustrated by the "hook-swinging" ritual practiced in India (Melzack & Wall, 1983). This ritual, designed to promote the health of children and crops, involves hanging a male volunteer from steel hooks embedded into the skin and muscles of his back. Instead of suffering excruciating pain, as Westerners might expect, the volunteers appear to be in a state of "exaltation."

Women who have participated in prepared childbirth classes generally report less pain than women who are uninformed regarding the birth process. Although athletes and nonathletes share similar pain thresholds, these groups are quite different in their tolerance of pain (Scott & Gijsbers, 1981). Compared to nonathletes, athletes in contact sports such as boxing,

© Louise Batalla Duran/Alamy

Culture, context, and experience can shape our perception of pain. During a festival dedicated to penance and atonement, Tamil Hindus walk through the streets carrying devices called *kavadis* that hold hooks that are pierced through the skin. Without this cultural context, it is likely that most people would find this experience excruciatingly painful.

rugby, and football appear to tolerate higher levels of pain before identifying a stimulus as painful. Patients who are allowed to self-administer morphine for pain actually require less medication than patients who receive injections from hospital staff. The sense of control may reduce anxiety and the need for pain medication. In treating patients with chronic pain, clearly the psychological aspects of pain management should not be overlooked in favor of a strictly pharmacological approach.

How Do We Process Smells and Tastes?

The famous philosopher Immanuel Kant (1798/1978) considered **olfaction,** or our sense of smell, to be the "most dispensable" sense. Certainly, other species rely much more heavily on olfaction and **gustation,** or the sense of taste, than humans do. Nonetheless, our chemical senses do provide warning of danger, such as smelling smoke from a fire or tasting spoiled food. The chemical senses also contribute a richness to our emotional and social experiences. The smell of perfume or the taste of chocolate may be accompanied by strong emotional reactions. Contrary to Kant's view, people who have lost their sense of smell due to head injury often experience profound depression (Zuscho, 1983). Sharing a meal has a strong effect on bonding for humans and other primates (Brosnan, 2010; Wobber, Wrangham, & Hare, 2010).

Chemical Stimuli Our chemical senses begin with molecules suspended in the air in the case of olfaction and dissolved in saliva in the case of gustation. Olfaction provides more information from a distance, like vision and audition, whereas gustation, like the somatosenses, involves information that is actually in contact with the body.

The Biology of the Chemical Senses Like the somatosenses, the chemical senses are quite ancient in terms of evolution and have not undergone much change over time. However, our sense of smell has been influenced by walking on two feet instead of four. Most olfactory stimuli are relatively heavy and tend to fall to the ground. Consider how your dog puts its nose to the ground when tracking something interesting.

Olfaction Air containing olfactory stimuli is taken in through the nostrils and circulated within the nasal cavities connected to the nostrils, where it interacts with olfactory receptors (see ● Figure 5.40). The receptors are located in a thin layer of cells within the nasal cavity. Unlike most neurons, the olfactory receptors regularly die and are replaced by new receptor cells in cycles lasting 4 to 6 weeks. Cells at the base of the receptors are responsible for producing the mucus surrounding the receptors. One branch of each receptor interacts with molecules dissolved in the mucus. The other

olfaction The sense of smell.
gustation The sense of taste.

FIGURE 5.40

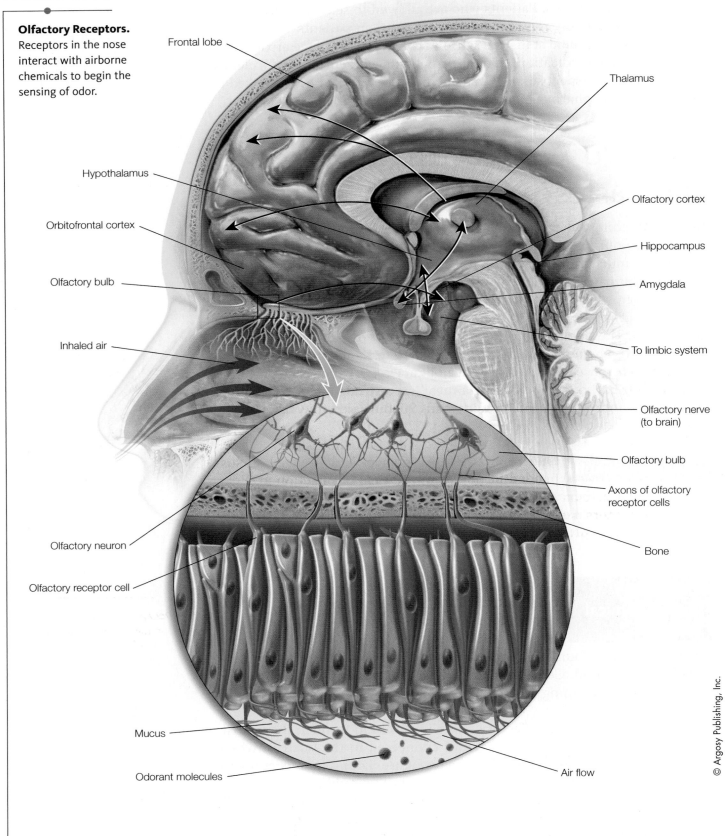

Olfactory Receptors.
Receptors in the nose interact with airborne chemicals to begin the sensing of odor.

Frontal lobe

Thalamus

Hypothalamus

Olfactory cortex

Orbitofrontal cortex

Hippocampus

Olfactory bulb

Amygdala

Inhaled air

To limbic system

Olfactory nerve (to brain)

Olfactory bulb

Axons of olfactory receptor cells

Olfactory neuron

Bone

Olfactory receptor cell

Mucus

Odorant molecules

Air flow

© Argosy Publishing, Inc.

branch carries information back to the central nervous system as part of the **olfactory nerve.** The olfactory nerve fibers synapse in one of the two **olfactory bulbs,** located just below the mass of the frontal lobes.

Unlike most of the other sensory input to the brain, olfactory pathways do not make direct connections with the thalamus before the information reaches the cerebral cortex. Instead, fibers from the olfactory bulbs proceed to the olfactory cortex, located in the lower portions of the frontal lobe, and to the amygdala. Because of the role these areas of the brain play in emotion, which we described in our chapter on biological psychology, these pathways may account for the significant emotional reactions we experience (disgust or pleasure) in response to odor.

Taste The most likely original purpose of our sense of gustation, or taste, was to protect us from eating poisonous or spoiled food and to attract us to foods that boost our chances of survival. Although we seem biased toward detecting negative stimuli (Cacioppo & Gardner, 1999), our attraction to certain tastes also reflects our historical past. Because most of our ancestors were rather constantly facing the threat of famine, we generally find fatty and sugary foods to be especially tasty. Unfortunately, given the current availability of safe and palatable foods, our sense of taste may drive us to eat more than we really need.

Most of us are familiar with four major categories of taste: sweet, sour, salty, and bitter. You may not have heard of the fifth type of taste, known by the Japanese term *umami*, which, roughly translated, means "savory" or "meaty" (Chaudhari, Landlin, & Roper, 2000). In addition, the tongue contains receptors for capsaicin, an active ingredient in hot peppers. These receptors respond to taste and heat. Mice lacking capsaicin receptors happily consumed water containing capsaicin at levels that were rejected by normal mice (Caterina et al., 2000).

Taste receptors are located on the tongue and in other parts of the mouth (see ● Figure 5.41). You are probably aware of the bumpy texture

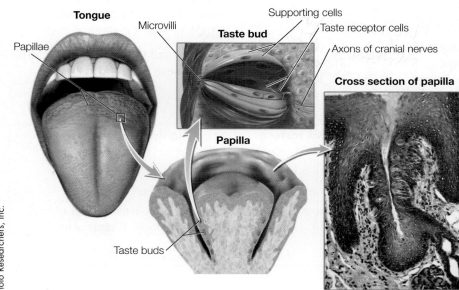

Tongue
Papillae
Microvilli
Supporting cells
Taste receptor cells
Taste bud
Axons of cranial nerves
Cross section of papilla
Papilla
Taste buds

FIGURE 5.41

Taste Receptors. Taste buds are located in the bumps, or papillae, located on the tongue.

olfactory nerve A nerve carrying olfactory information from the olfactory receptors to the olfactory bulbs.

olfactory bulb One of two structures below the frontal lobes of the brain that receive input from the olfactory receptors in the nose.

of your tongue, which results from the presence of **papillae.** Most papillae contain somewhere between 1 and 100 **taste buds.** Each taste bud contains between 50 and 150 receptor cells, which extend tiny hairlike cilia into the saliva that interact with dissolved taste stimuli and transduce the resulting information into neural signals. Like olfactory receptors, taste buds have a limited life before they are replaced. You may have noticed that if you burn your tongue by drinking hot liquid, your taste will be affected for a day or two. However, when the taste buds are replaced, taste should be back to normal.

Information about taste travels from the mouth and tongue to the medulla. The medulla in turn communicates with the thalamus, which sends taste information to the somatosensory cortex of the parietal lobe and to the orbitofrontal cortex where the emotional pleasantness or

papillae Small bumps on the tongue that contain taste buds.

taste bud A structure found in papillae that contains taste receptor cells.

Experiencing Psychology

Are You a Supertaster?

About 25% of the population are supertasters, or people who are extra sensitive to taste, 25% are non-tasters, or people who are relatively insensitive to taste, and the remaining 50% fall between these two extremes. You can use the following exercises to determine your taste category.

1. How does mint taste to you?
Place a mint Life Saver on your tongue and allow it to dissolve (no chewing please). Rate the following qualities of the Life Saver on a scale of 1 to 5 with 1 being "very intense" and 5 being "not intense at all."

Sweetness	1	2	3	4	5
Smell	1	2	3	4	5
Coolness	1	2	3	4	5
"Rush"	1	2	3	4	5

How to interpret your results:
Mint tasters fall into four groups:

Group 1:   Mint is mild, no rush
Group 2:   Mint is moderate, no rush
Group 3:   Mint is moderate, rush
Group 4:   Mint is intense, rush

Here are the further characteristics of these taste groups:

Mildly sensitive tasters (Group 1)	Moderately sensitive tasters (Groups 2 and 3)	Highly sensitive tasters (Group 4)
Weak to undetectable sensation from mint	Moderate to strong sensation from mint	Very strong sensation from mint
The flavor of food is not that important.	The flavor of food is important.	The flavor of food is important.
Many foods liked; few foods disliked; not passionate about food	Many foods liked; few foods disliked; often passionate about food	Great variation in the number of foods liked; often passionate about food

unpleasantness of particular stimuli is processed. As we will see in later chapters, taste information interacts with motivation and learning.

Perception and Cognition in the Chemical Senses

In both olfaction and gustation, we see three interesting perceptual themes: (1) We can easily identify a number of very complex stimuli combining many types of molecules, such as the aroma of coffee, while (2) at the same time, we can detect small differences between similar smells and tastes, and (3) our experience often shapes our perception of an olfactory or gustatory stimulus (Goldstein, 2010). One example of the impact of experience on olfaction is the effect of labeling an odor on people's rating of its pleasantness. If participants smell an onion stimulus labeled "pizza," they not too surprisingly rate the odor as more pleasant than if the identical stimulus is labeled "body odor" (Herz, 2003).

The chemical senses interact to provide the perception of flavor. You have probably noticed that food just doesn't taste very good when your sense of smell is decreased by a bad cold. If you close your eyes and hold your nose, you are unable to distinguish between a slice of apple and a slice of raw potato. Once again, the orbitofrontal cortex plays an important role in the perception of flavor, as the pathways serving olfaction and gustation converge in this part of the brain (Rolls, 2000).

---

2. Count Your Papillae
You will need a gummed reinforcer (sticky white ring for notebooks), a swab, blue food coloring, and a mirror.

Place one reinforcer on the front of your tongue just to the side of midline. Use a swab to apply blue food coloring to the part of your tongue that shows through the center of the reinforcer. The blue food coloring should make your papillae (bumps) more obvious. Count the number of papillae you see in the ring.

How to interpret your results: More than 25 papillae within the reinforcer ring means you're a supertaster. The number of papillae of mild or moderate tasters will be less than 25, but we do not know how to distinguish these two groups based on this factor.

3. Other Eating Habits
Rate the tastes of the following foods and drinks using a 1 to 5 scale with 1 being "dislike strongly" and 5 being "like a great deal."

Broccoli	1	2	3	4	5
Grapefruit	1	2	3	4	5
Coffee (black)	1	2	3	4	5
Dark chocolate	1	2	3	4	5
Red wine	1	2	3	4	5
Sweet white wine	1	2	3	4	5
Dry white wine	1	2	3	4	5

As a child, were you ever described by a parent, teacher, or other adult as a "picky eater"? (circle one)

YES
NO

Can you easily tell the difference between the fat content of milk (for example, between whole and 2% milk, or between 1% and 2% milk)? (circle one)

YES
NO

How to interpret your results: Supertasters tend to dislike bitter foods, so with the exception of sweet white wine, they will have a lot of low numbers. Supertasters are picky eaters as children and are better at detecting differences in fats in foods. ⬡

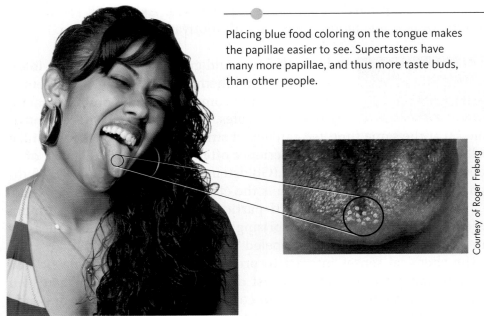

Placing blue food coloring on the tongue makes the papillae easier to see. Supertasters have many more papillae, and thus more taste buds, than other people.

Courtesy of Roger Freberg

© Paul Burns/Blend Images/Alamy

Developmental and Individual Differences in the Chemical Senses

Young children are notorious for putting things in their mouths that adults would quickly reject on the basis of taste, including poisonous substances like drain cleaner. However, this propensity does not mean that children lack a sense of taste. Using facial expressions, researchers have demonstrated that newborns differentiate among sweet, bitter, and sour tastes, but seem relatively oblivious to salty tastes (Rosenstein & Oster, 1988). As we get older, the overall number of taste buds decreases, reducing the intensity of many tastes and providing a possible explanation for why some strong flavors, such as that of broccoli, are enjoyed much more by adults than by children. As we age, our sensitivity to smell also decreases (Cain & Gent, 1991). Because olfaction and taste interact to form the flavor of foods, decreased sensitivity in both senses might affect overall appetite as we age.

Like the other sensory modalities discussed in this chapter, the chemical senses vary from person to person. Females are generally more sensitive to smell than are males (Dorries, 1992; Koelega & Koster, 1974; Ship & Weiffenbach, 1993). The average person has approximately 6,000 taste buds, but this number may vary widely. As we observed previously, supertasters have unusually high numbers of papillae and therefore have more taste buds, too (Bartoshuk, 2000).

Disturbances in the chemical senses are correlated with a number of psychological disorders. Olfaction and the experience of post-traumatic stress disorder (PTSD; see our chapter on psychological disorders) appear to interact in combat veterans. PTSD is often characterized by intrusive, disturbing flashbacks in which the patient essentially relives the traumatic experience. Given the close association between olfaction and memory, researchers hypothesized that some PTSD flashbacks could be initiated by relevant smells. When compared to combat veterans who did not have PTSD, combat veterans with the disorder experienced marked anxiety when exposed to the smell of diesel, accompanied by changes in the activity of the amygdala (Vermetten, Schmahl, Southwick, & Bremner, 2007).

Sociocultural Influences on the Chemical Senses

The sense of smell might seem to play a secondary role to vision and audition in humans, but people have manipulated scent for religious, medicinal, and personal purposes since ancient times. We can speculate that once people learned to control fire, a recognition that some burning things smelled much better than others could not have been far behind, possibly leading to the use of incense in religious rituals. Use of natural materials for medicine and self-adornment provides the historical roots for large, contemporary industries that manufacture scent for a host of consumer products, including perfume, air fresheners, "new car smell" products, and detergents.

Although olfaction often seems to run in the background of our other cognitive processes, it is not immune to the effects of culture and experience. Americans spend millions on products that remove or mask body odor, whereas other cultures do not find such odors offensive. One study compared the categorization of odors by French, American, and Vietnamese participants (Chrea et al., 2004). Although the participants sorted odors similarly into broad categories of floral, sweet, bad, and natural, they differed along more subtle dimensions. The French and American participants quickly sorted odors into fruit or flower categories, but this separation had little relevance to the Vietnamese participants. Exactly how cultural experience contributes to such results remains a mystery.

Experience clearly plays a role in developing an individual's taste preferences. The effects of experience on taste begin in the prenatal environment. Infants whose mothers consumed carrot juice during pregnancy showed stronger preferences for carrot flavor (Mennella & Beauchamp, 1996; Mennella, Jagnow, & Beauchamp, 2001). In terms of survival, this result makes perfect sense. The infant is born with a predisposition to like the safe foods available in his or her environment. Because the food supply historically has varied widely from place to place, delicacies like fruit bat pie are appreciated in Palau but not necessarily in the United States.

© Kristin Graham

Different cultures can prefer very different foods. It is unlikely that you will find fruit bat pie, a delicacy in Palau, in many American restaurants.

Summary 5.3

Important Structures in Audition

Structure	Function
Pinna © Argosy Publishing, Inc.	Collects sound; identifies location of sound as coming from above or below the head
Tympanic membrane © Argosy Publishing, Inc.	Movement begins process of transduction of sound waves to neural signals
Cochlea © Argosy Publishing, Inc.	Contains auditory receptors
Thalamus © Argosy Publishing, Inc.	Receives auditory input from brainstem; connects to primary auditory cortex
Primary auditory cortex © Cengage Learning 2013	Area in temporal lobe that receives auditory input from thalamus; performs initial analysis of input

Interpersonal Relationships
From the Perspective of Sensation and Perception

We mentioned earlier that of the senses we discussed in this chapter, pain was particularly influenced by cognition and context. Can being in a close relationship actually affect the way you feel pain?

The answer appears to be yes. Physical contact with a loved one can impact how the brain processes pain. Women who were expecting an electric shock showed reduced activity in parts of the brain associated with the emotional and arousing aspects of pain when they held their husbands' hands. They even experienced reduced activity, albeit to a lesser degree, when they held the hand of a male they didn't know (Coan, Schaefer, & Davidson, 2006). In addition, the amount of reduction of activity in these pain areas of the brain was correlated with the quality of the marriage—happily married women experienced greater decreases in activity associated with pain than less happily married women.

Perhaps this buffering effect is why you may reach for your partner when frightened during a scary movie. Knowing that such intimacy could literally reduce the pain in a loved one might compel you to make that extra effort to go to the doctor with your partner or make the extra visit to a friend in the hospital. Our understanding of pain in connection with our interpersonal relationships can help us in very tangible ways to create and maintain stronger, healthier relationships.

© Science Photo Library/Alamy

Research shows that physical contact with loved ones actually reduces the sensation of pain.

Chapter 5
Reflections

© Argosy Publishing, Inc.

This chapter began with a question that emerged from psychology's philosophical roots—what is the relationship between the reality "out there" and the mind's construction of that reality? Looking at the Munker illusion reminds us that a feature like the color of a printed word is not a fixed aspect of the environment, but instead is a model of reality assembled by the human mind.

Although the biological processing of sensory information provides the building blocks for creating a model of reality, the product of perception is once again better understood using a combination of perspectives. Top-down processing, which allows us to see a Dalmatian in a scattering of black dots on white, benefits from an understanding provided by the cognitive perspective. The child's preference for bright, high-contrast stimuli is a reflection of the development of our sensory systems. Social psychology contributes to discussions of cultural differences in response to visual illusion or pain. Individual differences occur at the level of sensation, as we saw in the discussion of colorblindness, or in perception, when people observing identical stimuli can still perceive very different realities.

After exploring the different modalities of sensation—vision, audition, position, touch, temperature, pain, olfaction, and taste—a picture emerges of sensory processing that uniquely provides the human mind with exactly those pieces of information that help us survive in our particular niche, a concept consistent with the evolutionary perspective. Yes, we do experience illusions that highlight some of the inner workings of the processes of sensation and perception, but illusions are fun exceptions to processing that works exceedingly well the vast majority of the time. ‹

KEY TERMS The Language of Psychological Science

Be sure you can define these terms and use them correctly.

absolute threshold, p. 185
audition, p. 209
auditory nerve, p. 212
basilar membrane, p. 211
binocular cue, p. 200
bottom-up processing, p. 183
cochlea, p. 211
cone, p. 190
cornea, p. 188
depth perception, p. 200
difference threshold, p. 185
feature detector, p. 196
fovea, p. 189
gate theory, p. 221

gustation, p. 223
iris, p. 188
lens, p. 188
monocular cue, p. 200
olfaction, p. 223
olfactory bulb, p. 225
olfactory nerve, p. 225
opponent process theory, p. 193
optic nerve, p. 191
optic tracts, p. 191
organ of Corti, p. 211
papillae, p. 226
perception, p. 181
psychophysics, p. 184

pupil, p. 188
retina, p. 188
retinal disparity, p. 202
rod, p. 190
sensation, p. 181
sensory adaptation, p. 183
signal detection, p. 186
somatosensation, p. 217
taste bud, p. 226
top-down processing, p. 184
transduction, p. 182
trichromacy theory, p. 192
vestibular system, p. 218
vision, p. 188

MEDIA RESOURCES

Log in to **CengageBrain** to access the resources your instructor requires. For this book, you can access:

Psychology **CourseMate** brings course concepts to life with interactive learning, study, and exam preparation tools that support the printed textbook. A textbook-specific website, Psychology **CourseMate** includes an integrated interactive eBook and other interactive learning tools including quizzes, flashcards, videos, and more.

WebTUTOR More than just an interactive study guide, **WebTutor** is an anytime, anywhere customized learning solution with an eBook, keeping you connected to your textbook, instructor, and classmates.

aplia If your professor has assigned **Aplia** homework:
1. Sign in to your account.
2. Complete the corresponding homework exercises as required by your professor.
3. When finished, click "Grade It Now" to see which areas you have mastered, which areas need more work, and detailed explanations of every answer.

Do we have free will? Transcranial magnetic stimulation switched the hand chosen to carry out a task from right to left, but participants insisted that switching hands was their own idea.

The Aware Mind

Elements of Consciousness

6

Learning Objectives

1 Analyze the meaning of consciousness in terms of alertness, sensory awareness, and self-awareness, and debate whether various nonhuman animals have consciousness.

2 Explain the roles of light and eating in regulating cycles of consciousness, and show how these cycles can be disrupted by technologies of modern life.

3 Differentiate the five stages of sleep in terms of EEG patterns, autonomic nervous system and muscle activity, and possible functions.

4 Compare and contrast several sleep disorders in terms of their symptoms and the type of sleep disturbed.

5 Explain disorders of consciousness in terms of damage or dysfunction in specific areas of the brain.

6 Differentiate the neurochemical mechanisms and effects on consciousness of hallucinogens, stimulants, depressants, and opiates.

7 Evaluate the evidence for hypnosis and meditation as neurologically "real" altered states of consciousness.

What does it mean to have "free will"? This might sound more like a philosophy question than a psychology question at first, but advances in biological and cognitive psychology have allowed psychologists to tackle this question.

Usually, we think of free will as the ability to consciously control our actions and decisions. In the children's game of "rock, paper, scissors," we feel like we are making a conscious decision to choose one of the three options. But how would such a decision be made? What types of processes in the brain correspond to choosing scissors over the other two possibilities?

Research into voluntary movements, like forming your hand into scissors, has shown that the brain makes a commitment to a choice as much as 10 seconds before we become aware of the decision (Soon, Brass, Heinze, & Haynes,

235

© LeventeGyori/Shutterstock© LeventeGyori/Shutterstock

© Argosy Publishing, Inc.

2008). Other research shows that the brain can be manipulated to make an unusual choice without disrupting the individual's sense of free will. Right-handed people normally use their right hands 60% of the time or more when forced to choose to use one hand over the other, but when researchers exposed right-handed subjects' right hemispheres to transcranial magnetic stimulation (TMS), illustrated in the larger image on the previous page, they chose to use their left hands 80% of the time (Ammon & Gandevia, 1990). In spite of making the uncharacteristic choice to use "the wrong hand," the participants in this experiment reported feeling completely in control of their hand movements. If the brain has already committed to a movement, what purpose does a conscious sense of having decided to move serve?

Insight into this question emerged from the study of split-brain patients, described in our chapter on biological psychology. These patients have undergone surgery that severs the connections between their right and left hemispheres, making it possible to expose one hemisphere at a

© Maximilian Weinzierl/Alamy

time to a stimulus. For example, you can show the relatively nonverbal right hemisphere the word "stand," and the patient will usually stand up. However, due to the limitations of the right hemisphere in processing language, the patient will be consciously unaware of having read the word. When asked why they stood up, patients responded by saying they felt the need to stretch. In other words, the mind is building a theory about the behavior that was just performed (Gazzaniga, 2011). This type of observation leads to a view of consciousness as an "interpreter," making sense out of our own actions and the world within and around us. This view helps us understand the observed delay between the brain's commitment to an action and our conscious awareness of that decision—the interpreter needs time to analyze the situation.

In this chapter, we will explore many situations that impact the performance of the interpreter, from the variations found in stages of sleep and wakefulness to the alterations produced by psychoactive drugs and damage to the brain. This journey will require us to zoom in to observe underlying processes in the brain, and then zoom out again to understand the influences of the social context on the phenomenon of conscious awareness. ⚙

Fruit flies living with other fruit flies required more sleep than fruit flies living in isolation, suggesting that one of the possible functions of sleep is to process learning and social experiences. The larger the group of flies, the longer each fly slept each day.

What Does It Mean to Be Conscious?

Our English word "conscious" is derived from the Latin *conscientia*, which means "to know." **Consciousness** refers to "knowing" or being aware of ongoing experiences occurring both internally and in the world around us. We understand that to be "unconscious," perhaps because of a blow to the head, means that we are completely unaware of what is happening within

consciousness A state of awareness.

and around us. However, the term *consciousness* has multiple meanings. Consciousness can refer to a *state* of awareness (alert versus drowsy, for example) or the current *content* of awareness (while reading this page, you hear your neighbor's music). A special type of consciousness, **self-awareness**, occurs when we focus on ourselves as individuals.

Consciousness has been a favorite topic among psychologists for many years. William James (1890) coined the term "stream of consciousness" to capture the moving, seemingly unbroken flow of conscious awareness. Sigmund Freud used the term *consciousness* to refer to aspects of the mind that could be retrieved voluntarily, in contrast to the unconscious parts of the mind that remain hidden to voluntary searches for information. Contemporary cognitive psychologists debate the reasons why some information becomes conscious while other information does not (Baars, 1988).

The Evolution of Consciousness

Most of us would agree that bacteria do not possess consciousness, but people do. This implies that consciousness emerged at some point in the course of evolution. The exact location of that point remains highly debatable. William James maintained that "consciousness grows the more complex and intense the higher we rise in the animal kingdom. That of a man must exceed that of an oyster" (James, 1890, p. 141). If consciousness evolved as suggested by James, what advantages might account for this development?

The question of the emergence of consciousness in animals is complicated by the multiple meanings of *consciousness* described previously. Most, if not all, animals show variations in states of awareness. Even the humble fruit fly takes periods of rest, which are believed to be the fruit fly equivalent of sleep (Shaw, Cirelli, Greenspan, & Giulio Tononi, 2000). Consciousness defined as an awareness of ongoing sensations is probably less common in the animal kingdom. Many animals would survive quite well by simply responding automatically to the world around them ("food" or "predator") without necessarily thinking "I smell food" or "I see a predator." The self-awareness aspect of consciousness—as exemplified in "I" statements—might be the rarest of all among living things, as we will see later in this section.

> Those who have never been brainwashed or addicted to a drug find it hard to understand their fellow men who are driven by such compulsions.
> —Richard Dawkins

Consciousness as Variations in Alertness Varying states of awareness might allow animals to repair their bodies and conserve energy. Food requirements would be much higher if we stayed awake for 24 hours (as you may have noticed while studying for final exams). Another possible benefit of varying states of awareness is maximizing safety. Most animals are specialized for activity in either the light or the dark. Sleeping during the cycle for which an animal is poorly equipped for activity might contribute to its survival. However, being inactive is not a safe thing to do unless you have a safe place to hide (Allison & Cicchetti, 1976). Horses and rabbits are both frequently preyed upon, but horses sleep in the open while rabbits sleep in burrows. Consequently, wild horses sleep as little as 1 to 2 hours per day, while wild rabbits sleep at least 8 hours or more.

self-awareness The special understanding of the self as distinct from other stimuli.

Consciousness as an Awareness of Ongoing Sensations

One possible advantage of being consciously aware of ongoing sensations is the ability to choose responses rather than to respond instinctively (Gazzaniga, 2011). If suddenly faced with a predator, any animal could respond automatically using reflex and instinct, which we discuss in our chapter on learning. Horses are notorious for running whenever the slightest stimulus bothers them. It is unlikely that the horse in these cases is thinking "I hear a mountain lion—I should run." Conscious awareness of sensations provides more options. If a conscious animal hears a sound in the distance that might indicate the presence of a predator, it could choose to continue on, flee, or pause while obtaining further information. This flexibility would be very likely to increase the animal's chances of survival.

Consciousness as Self-Awareness

The self-awareness aspect of consciousness could heighten an animal's drive to survive. Understanding that you are alive is correlated with a heightened meaningfulness of death.

Sleeping habits of different species reflect how likely they are to be preyed upon by other animals and whether or not they have shelter, like a burrow or den, in which to sleep. The lion has few predators and is likely to fall asleep whenever it is convenient. This lion chose to sleep in the shade of a Toyota, trapping the people in the car for several hours.

Psychology *as a* Hub Science

Can Machines Become Conscious?

Hollywood loves to tell the story of the machine that develops consciousness, from *2001: A Space Odyssey*'s Hal to the *Terminator*. Are these scenarios of artificial intelligence remotely possible? How would we judge whether a machine has achieved consciousness? In 1950, Alan Turing devised the "Turing Test" of a machine's ability to think. According to the test, if a human had a conversation with two other beings, one human and one machine, without being able to distinguish between them, then the machine would have passed the test.

Daniel Dennett (1991) suggested that a conscious machine would be impossibly expensive to construct. Instead, Dennett argues that it might be more interesting to set aside the question of consciousness for now and simply build the most human robot possible. Such an effort is currently under way at MIT, where a

robot named "Cog" has been developed (Cog, n.d.). Cog may not have legs yet, but it can see and play in a very human way with a slinky toy. Among the plans for Cog are language abilities, hearing, and touch. Saya, a Japanese robot 15 years in the making, has graduated from receptionist duties to the elementary school classroom, where she calls roll, communicates assignments, and even scolds children for misbehavior. Cog and Saya might not meet our criteria for self-awareness and consciousness, but their behavior is becoming increasingly human. ✪

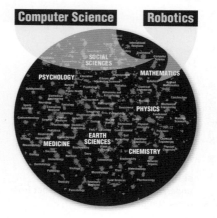

Developmental psychologists have provided a technique for demonstrating self-awareness that can be used with many species. Recognizing one's self in the mirror is believed to be a major developmental milestone in achieving self-awareness. In the so-called rouge test, a dot of rouge or other odorless dye is placed on a child's forehead, and the child is allowed an opportunity to look in a mirror (Lewis & Brooks-Gunn, 1979). Prior to the age of about 18 months, children do not seem to show any indication that they understand the image in the mirror is their own. After that age, they will rub at the spot of rouge or turn their bodies in order to get a better look, thus demonstrating self-awareness.

Chimpanzees "pass" the rouge test by demonstrating behavior similar to that of 18-month-old children (Gallup, 1970). In addition to chimpanzees, orangutans, gorillas raised by humans, bottle-nosed dolphins, Asian elephants, and even parrots have demonstrated self-awareness in this type of experiment (Gallup & Suarez, 1986; Patterson, 1984; Patterson & Cohn, 1994; Plotnik, de Waal, & Reiss, 2006; Povinelli, 1993). Dogs, wild-raised gorillas, and most monkeys do not pass the test.

Other researchers restrict the possibility of self-aware consciousness to species that exhibit complex social behavior. Of what use would self-awareness be if one did not frequently interact with others of the same kind? Social animals must be able to recognize other individuals and respond to them accordingly. Dolphins appear to have special whistles that they seem to use for particular individuals, like names (Janik, Sayigh, & Wells, 2006). Some social animals, including chimpanzees and elephants,

Unlike many other animals, human beings are not restricted by our sensory systems to a particular part of the day. We do face danger, however. Although human beings have their fair share of animal predators, the most common killer of humans is another human. FBI violent crime statistics suggest that the late night and early morning hours, when most of us are safe at home in our beds, are the deadliest (Saskatchewan Learning, 2006).

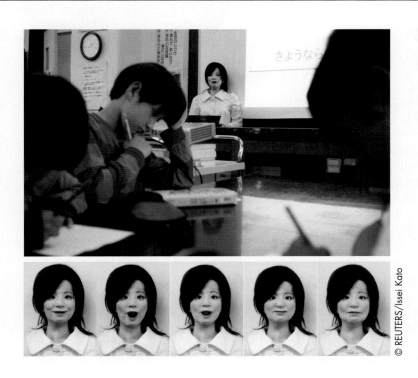

© REUTERS/Issei Kato

Saya the teaching robot controls her classroom by expressing emotions from approval to anger, taking role, and communicating assignments. These abilities do not make her conscious by our definition, but she is remarkably human for a machine.

> The most complicated achievements of thought are possible without the assistance of consciousness.
>
> —Sigmund Freud

show an awareness of death and appear to grieve at the loss of family members. Elephants have been known to remain in the area of a relative's bones for lengthy periods of time (McComb, Baker, & Moss, 2006).

Searching for Consciousness in the Brain

Is it possible to find consciousness in the brain? Consciousness, the mind, and the brain are like a set of nested Russian dolls. The brain, the outside doll, houses the mind but has other functions as well, such as maintaining breathing and body temperature. The mind, the middle doll, houses consciousness, the innermost doll, but also manages unconscious functions such as long-term memory, discussed in our chapter on memory.

In this chapter, we will examine a number of natural, artificial, and pathological circumstances that correlate with variations in consciousness. As a result of these investigations, we can begin to view consciousness as requiring complex interactions between areas of the cerebral cortex and the thalamus, discussed in detail in our chapter on biological psychology.

Thinking Scientifically

What Does "Blindsight" Tell Us About Consciousness?

People who experience damage to the occipital lobes due to stroke or other injuries typically lose the ability to see part of the visual field. The area that is "missing" is known as a scotoma, and its size and location will depend on the location and extent of the brain damage. In the human visual system, about 90% of the fibers leaving the retinas of the eyes travel first to the thalamus, and then on to the primary visual cortex in the occipital lobes. Consequently, we are not surprised that damage to the occipital lobes would be associated with significant loss of vision.

What is surprising is the retention of the ability to perceive stimuli presented in the scotomas of some visually impaired patients, a phenomenon known as blindsight. Blindsight was first described by the Swiss neurologist L. Bard in 1905 and was demonstrated again by Larry Weiskrantz and his colleagues in 1974. Weiskrantz's patients were exposed to flashes of light directed to the area of their scotomas. Subsequently, they were asked to point to the light's origin. Several were able to do so at better than chance rates, but they remained convinced that they were just guessing. In other words, the patients were processing

information without being aware that they were doing so. Blindsight has also been described in monkeys with lesions in their primary visual cortex (Cowey & Stoerig, 1991). Not only did the monkeys correctly identify lights in their scotomas, but they chose a key that meant "no light" to describe their experience.

Even more dramatic is the phenomenon of "affective blindsight" (Hamm et al., 2003; Pegna, Landis, & Khateb, 2008). In these cases, individuals with occipital lobe damage demonstrate normal increases in the activity of the amygdala when shown images of angry or threatening facial expres-

Babies over the age of 18 months are able to recognize themselves in a mirror, which psychologists believe indicates a sense of self-awareness. Happy, a resident of the Bronx Zoo, repeatedly used her trunk to touch a mark that researchers placed above her eye, suggesting that she, too, can recognize her own image in the mirror.

In particular, lesions of the thalamus result in the type of profound unconsciousness typically associated with brain death (Bogen, 1995). We discuss the concept of brain death more fully in a later section of this chapter.

Certain structures in the brain, such as the thalamus, might be necessary, but not sufficient, for consciousness. For example, observing that your television screen no longer produces a picture after you remove a component does not necessarily imply that the sole source of the picture sions. These participants are not consciously "seeing" the faces, but their amygdalas, which we described in our chapter on biological psychology as part of the brain's threat detection systems, are reacting anyway, without the participants' conscious awareness of even having seen a face.

If some aspects of visual processing result in conscious awareness while others do not, what exactly does it mean to be conscious? Is consciousness correlated with brain activity in general, or only with activity in certain parts of the brain? As Weiskrantz reminds us, primary visual cortex may be the largest target for retinal input, but it is one of 10 such targets in the primate brain (Weiskrantz, Barbur, & Shraie, 1995). The phenomenon of blindsight indicates that we can use these other targets, such as the amygdala, to sense light, but we do so with less conscious awareness.

Blindsight reminds us that the study of the mind takes us beyond the borders of normal conscious states and, therefore, beyond the reach of introspection and common sense. ⚙

Damage to the occipital cortex, which contains the primary visual cortex, often produces a characteristic scotoma, or a part of the visual field that cannot be seen.

© Christopher Futcher/iStockphoto

FIGURE 6.1

Brain Structures Associated With Consciousness. Among the brain structures that are believed to participate in consciousness are the cerebral cortex, thalamus, reticular formation, and the complex pathways connecting these parts of the brain. These structures make consciousness possible, because damage to these circuits results in unconsciousness, but they do not determine the content of consciousness.

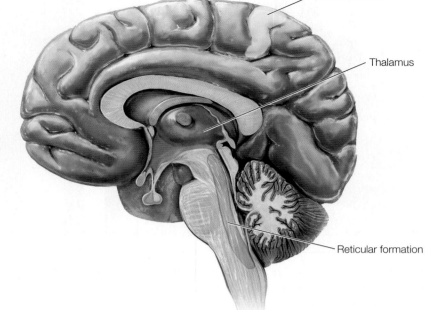

Cerebral cortex

Thalamus

Reticular formation

© Argosy Publishing, Inc.

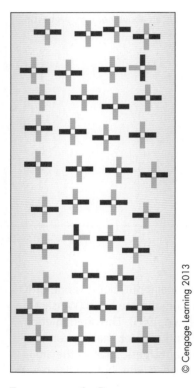

© Cengage Learning 2013

FIGURE 6.2

The Binding Problem. The binding problem refers to the challenge of combining elements of sensation, like color and orientation of lines, and making a unified perception. In this image, see how quickly you can find the two figures that have red vertical bars. This is a difficult task, because all the figures have blue and red elements and horizontal and vertical bars. *Source:* Wolfe et al. (2009). *Sensation & Perception, 2e,* Sinauer, p. 198.

is that particular component; it's likely that other components need to be attached simultaneously and contribute to the creation of the visual image. Likewise, additional brain structures, such as the reticular formation of the brainstem, play an active role in raising or lowering the thresholds of conscious awareness (see ● Figure 6.1). Because of these variations, you are far more likely to hear and respond to a sound while awake than while deeply asleep. Structures such as the thalamus and reticular formation have been described as "enabling" consciousness, but they do not produce its content (Crick & Koch, 2003).

One of the challenges facing psychologists interested in consciousness is how to explain how the brain forms a unified whole out of large quantities of information. This question is known as the "binding problem." For example, as we discussed in the chapter on sensation and perception, different parts of the visual system process features like color, shape, and movement (see ● Figure 6.2). How then, does the brain combine the activity of these different parts to tell you that a baseball is coming toward you?

One suggested solution to the binding problem is that sensory information combines with an individual's past experience to produce expectations for managing a current situation (Lotto & Purves, 2000, 2002; Purves & Lotto, 2002). This integration of sensory input and prior experience becomes part of the "stream of consciousness." The frontal lobes provide working space for this integration, along with opportunities for making decisions. The involvement of learned expectations in the "stream" also provides an attractive explanation for the gradual emergence of consciousness in the developing child. As a child gains more experience, consciousness improves the child's abilities to predict and guide behavior.

Summary 6.1

Definitions of Consciousness

Aspect of consciousness	Definition	Examples
State of awareness © 2011 by Chris Christensen/AmateurTraveler.com	The level of conscious awareness of internal states or surroundings; can be high or low, realistic or distorted	• Asleep or awake • Perceiving realistically or hallucinating • Hypnotized or not • Meditating or not
Content of awareness © Cengage Learning 2013	The ongoing catalog of internal and external stimuli that are the focus of current attention	• Hearing a neighbor's music • Thinking that you're hungry and it's time to eat • Considering the implications of a news report
Self-awareness © Ghislain & Marie David de Lossy/Getty Images	The special understanding of the self as distinct from other stimuli	• I am looking at myself in the mirror. • I know I'm asleep and that this is a dream.

What Happens to Consciousness During Wakefulness and Sleep?

Our first meaning of consciousness involves variations in an animal's state of awareness. Awareness changes dramatically across cycles of **sleep** and **wakefulness**. These cycles follow **circadian**, or daily, **rhythms**. The term *circadian* comes from the Latin words for "about a day."

Circadian Rhythms

Circadian rhythms respond to a combination of internal and external factors. Internal **biological clocks**, controlled by the hypothalamus, provide an approximate schedule for a wide variety of physical processes, including sleep and waking, body temperature, and hunger. These internal biological clocks interact with external stimuli, known as zeitgebers (*zeit* means "time" in German and *geber* means "to give"; hence these stimuli are "time givers").

sleep A normal state of consciousness characterized by reduced awareness of external stimuli.

wakefulness A normal state of consciousness characterized by alertness and awareness of external stimuli.

circadian rhythm A daily biological rhythm.

biological clock An internal mechanism that provides an approximate schedule for a wide variety of physical processes.

Light is one of the most important zeitgebers for human beings. Exposure to the rising sun each day helps to reset the internal biological clocks to the correct "time." In the absence of light, our internal clocks run a few minutes longer than a 24-hour cycle. We become like a wristwatch that is running too slowly. Over time, the distortion adds up, and behavior will only occasionally be synchronized with "normal" cycles of day and night. Totally blind people and sailors on submarines experience longer than normal circadian cycles due to their lack of exposure to natural light (Kelly et al., 1999; Skene, Lockley, & Arendt, 1999).

Eating patterns are also significant zeitgebers, as many midnight snackers already know. Mice normally sleep during the day and feed at night. However, when mice are fed only during the day, they quickly adapt to the new feeding schedule and begin sleeping at night and exploring more during the day (Mieda, Williams, Richardson, Tanaka, & Yanagisawa, 2006).

Modern Challenges for Circadian Rhythms It is very likely that our human ancestors remained awake during daylight and slept throughout the dark of night, and they certainly lacked the technology needed to travel rapidly across time zones. Technology, particularly the invention of artificial light, has shaped our contemporary sleep-waking patterns into something quite different (see ● Figure 6.3). That course we need for graduation is only offered at 7 a.m., or we work until midnight to juggle our work and class schedules. We travel across eight or nine time zones to make an important sales presentation on another continent. These distortions in our natural circadian rhythms can result in problems.

Some occupations, such as hospital and public safety jobs, involve work around the clock, which in turn is correlated with physical and psychological problems. Between 40 and 80% of workers on graveyard shifts (11:00 p.m. to 7:30 a.m.) experience "shift maladaption syndrome," characterized by health, personality, mood, and interpersonal problems (Wagner, 1996). Accident rates in the industrial swing shift (3:00 p.m. to 11:30 p.m.) are higher than in the traditional day shift, and the graveyard shift (11:00 p.m. to 7:30 a.m.) is the most dangerous of all (Hänecke, Tiedemann, Nachreiner, & Grzech-Sukalo, 1998). Not only do shift workers experience more

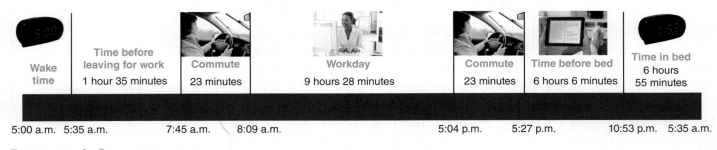

| Wake time | Time before leaving for work
1 hour 35 minutes | Commute
23 minutes | Workday
9 hours 28 minutes | Commute
23 minutes | Time before bed
6 hours 6 minutes | Time in bed
6 hours 55 minutes |

5:00 a.m. 5:35 a.m.　　　　7:45 a.m.　8:09 a.m.　　　　　5:04 p.m.　5:27 p.m.　　　10:53 p.m. 5:35 a.m.

FIGURE 6.3

A Day in the Life of a Typical American Worker. Americans are believed to be somewhat sleep deprived because the average adult spends only 6 hours and 55 minutes in bed, which includes time needed to initiate sleep. Although people try to make up for lost sleep on weekends by sleeping longer, this solution is not very effective. *Source:* Data from 2008 Omnibus Sleep in America Poll, National Sleep Foundation. Illustration: © Cengage Learning 2013; photos (from left to right): © Morgan Lane Photography/Shutterstock; © Martin Novak/Shutterstock; © StockLite/Shutterstock; © Martin Novak/Shutterstock; © Yunus Arakon/iStockphoto; © funkypoodle/iStockphoto

accidents, but they also make more errors. Hospital workers are much more likely to make significant errors during evening shifts than during day shifts (Narumi et al., 1999).

Our modern ability to cross time zones leads to the experience of jet lag, which produces fatigue, irritability, and sleepiness. The travel itself is not to blame, since north-south travel of equal distance does not produce the symptoms of jet lag (Herxheimer & Waterhouse, 2003). Chronic jet lag has even more serious consequences. Flight attendants with four or more years of experience in which time zones were crossed at least once a week had reduced reaction times and made 9% more mistakes on memory tasks than local crews (Cho, Ennaceur, Cole, & Suh, 2000).

As you probably already know from personal experience, some of these challenges to our circadian rhythms are easier to manage than others. Smaller adjustments, such as traveling across one time zone, are easier to make than major adjustments, such as traveling from Los Angeles to the Middle East. It is easier to adjust to time changes when we set the clock to a later point than to an earlier point. For example, let's compare the experiences of two people, one traveling from Los Angeles to New York (setting the clock forward) and the other traveling from New York to Los Angeles (setting the clock back). Let's assume both travelers usually go to bed at 10:00 p.m. and get up at 6:00 a.m. To stay on the same sleep schedule, the LA–NYC traveler must now go to sleep at 7:00 p.m. and wake up at 3:00 a.m.—which will be difficult—whereas the NYC–LA traveler must stay up until 1:00 a.m. but can sleep until 9:00 a.m.—which is easier because it adheres more closely to the normal sleeping arrangement of going to bed in darkness and waking up in daylight (see ● Figure 6.4).

FIGURE 6.4

Jet Lag Is Worse When Traveling East. Traveling eastward is more disruptive than traveling westward. The Los Angeles resident arriving in New York feels like he or she is going to bed 3 hours earlier than usual (7:00 p.m. Los Angeles time) and waking up in the middle of the night (3:00 a.m. Los Angeles time). The New Yorker traveling to Los Angeles has to stay up a little later (1:00 a.m. New York time) but then can sleep later to compensate (9:00 a.m. New York time). Most people find the latter scenario much easier.

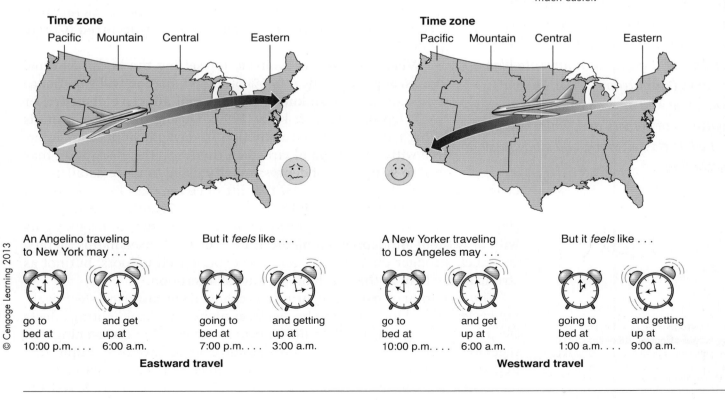

An Angelino traveling to New York may . . . go to bed at 10:00 p.m. . . . and get up at 6:00 a.m.

But it *feels* like . . . going to bed at 7:00 p.m. . . . and getting up at 3:00 a.m.

Eastward travel

A New Yorker traveling to Los Angeles may . . . go to bed at 10:00 p.m. . . . and get up at 6:00 a.m.

But it *feels* like . . . going to bed at 1:00 a.m. . . . and getting up at 9:00 a.m.

Westward travel

© Cengage Learning 2013

FIGURE 6.5

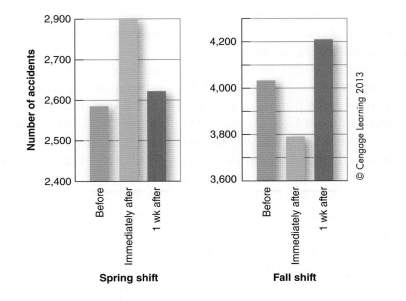

Daylight Saving Time Impacts Rate of Traffic Accidents. An analysis of Canadian traffic accidents showed that accidents increased following the spring shift in daylight saving time, but dropped following the fall shift.

Source: Adapted from Daylight Savings Time and Traffic Accidents by Coren from NEW ENGLAND JOURNAL OF MEDICINE, 1996. Used by permission of Massachusetts Medical Society.

Accommodations to adolescent sleep patterns may be useful. Shifting from a 7:15 a.m. start time to an 8:40 a.m. start time improved both attendance and student grades at Minnesota high schools (Wahlstrom, 2003). Students would be well advised to assess their own patterns of activity and, when possible, schedule classes, work, and study sessions accordingly.

seasonal affective disorder (SAD) A mood disorder in which depression occurs regularly at the same time each year, usually during the winter months.

Daylight saving time offers another opportunity to observe our responses to abrupt changes in our daily schedules. This energy-saving relic from World War I requires the setting of clocks forward one hour in the spring and back one hour in the fall. Even though the shift occurs on a Sunday, behavior the subsequent Monday is still impaired. As shown in ● Figure 6.5, when Canadian traffic accident data were correlated with the two annual daylight saving shifts, the shift back in the fall resulted in a 7% decrease in traffic accidents on the following Monday compared to other fall Mondays. In the spring setting of the clock forward, a comparable 7% increase in traffic accidents occurred (Coren, 1996b).

When less light is available for setting the body's internal clocks, approximately 4 to 6% of the population will experience a type of depression known as **seasonal affective disorder**, or SAD (Jepson, Ernst, & Kelly, 1999). During the winter months at higher latitudes, the reduction in daylight hours may interfere with the setting of circadian rhythms. This disruption may lead to symptoms of depression, discussed in more detail in our chapter on psychological disorders, that lift once the days become longer again. Rates of SAD vary from 1.4% in Florida to 9.7% in New Hampshire (Jepson et al., 1999). SAD is typically treated by exposure to bright lights with or without antidepressant medications. The lights used in this therapy are much stronger than what is normally experienced indoors, but not as strong as the light at the beach on an August afternoon.

The invention of artificial lighting has changed our historical sleep-waking cycles by making it easy to be awake at night. Artificial lighting affects sleep by breaking down melatonin, a hormone released in the evening that regulates sleep cycles. Changes in melatonin release have been implicated in a long list of human diseases, including cancer and heart disease, which are more common among people who work night shifts (Navara & Nelson,

2007). We can't escape artificial lighting, but we can offset some of its negative impact on health by avoiding obesity and tobacco, which also have detrimental effects on melatonin (Schernhammer, Kroenke, Dowsett, Folkerd, & Hankinson, 2006; Schernhammer & Schulmeister, 2004).

© CrackerClips/Shutterstock

Individual Variations in Circadian Rhythms You might believe that the day should start around 2:00 p.m., whereas your roommate pops out of bed smiling at an alarming 6:30 in the morning. What accounts for these individual differences in sleep patterns?

Some individual differences become evident in infancy and remain consistent over the lifespan. "Morning" people have been referred to as "larks" and "night" people have been referred to as "owls" (Akerstedt & Froberg, 1976). Many people fall somewhere between these two extremes and are at their best in the middle of the day. Research on the genetic basis of circadian rhythms suggests that the different patterns may result from different versions of the genes responsible for the activity of our internal clocks (Katzenberg, Young, Finn, Lin, & Mignot, 1998).

Other differences appear to be more age-related. Nearly everyone acts like an owl during adolescence and young adulthood (Carskadon, Wolfson, Acebo, Tzischinsky, & Seifer, 1998). In their mid- to late 20s, many temporary owls will revert to their previous lark or midday state. The exact cause for such a shift during and after adolescence and young adulthood is unclear, but researchers suspect that the shift correlates with a burst of brain development that is initiated at puberty. In fact, some researchers view the return to a previous sleep pattern in young adulthood as a reliable indicator that the brain is now fully mature (Roenneberg et al., 2005).

Courtesy Earth Observatory/NASA

Modern artificial light breaks down the hormone melatonin, which is released only at night. Disruptions caused by the effects of light on melatonin might be responsible for higher rates of disease, and cancer in particular, among employees who work at night in hospitals.

Wakefulness Varying states of awareness can be described using electroencephalogram (EEG) recordings, which provide a general measure of overall brain activity.

During wakefulness, we alternate between two patterns of activity indicated by the recording of **beta** and **alpha waves** in the EEG (see ● Figure 6.6). During beta activity, a person will be actively thinking and very alert.

Regardless of whether they were larks or owls as children, most teens act like owls by naturally staying up late and sleeping in. Usually by the mid-20s, young adults will go back to whichever sleeping pattern they showed prior to puberty, a change that may mark the final maturity of the brain.

beta wave A waveform recorded by EEG that usually indicates alert wakefulness.

alpha wave A waveform recorded by EEG that usually indicates relaxed wakefulness.

© Photos.com

Awake

Alpha waves   Beta waves

© Cengage Learning 2013

FIGURE 6.6

The EEG During Wakefulness. EEG recordings during wakefulness alternate between alpha waves and beta waves. Alpha waves are associated with a relaxed, possibly drowsy state, whereas beta waves are associated with alertness. *Source: Adapted from Horne (1998).*

Beta activity is characterized by rapid (15–20 cycles per second), irregular, low-amplitude waves. A person showing alpha activity is awake but quite relaxed. Alpha waves are slightly slower, larger, and more regular than beta waves, with a frequency of 9–12 cycles per second. One way to reliably produce alpha waves is to close your eyes. Simply reducing the amount of stimulation to the brain normally provided by the visual system is sufficient to produce a downshift into the more relaxed alpha state. Even with the eyes closed, however, you can regain beta activity by engaging in mental calculations.

Daydreaming, or mind wandering, "refers to spontaneous, subjective experiences in a no-task, no-stimulus, no-response situation" (Vaitl et al., 2005, p. 100). Recent research using functional magnetic resonance imaging (fMRI) has found that some parts of the brain become more active during times when we are not faced with particular demands for our attention. As shown in ● Figure 6.7, these brain parts have been described as forming a "default network," which includes the medial prefrontal cortex, the posterior cingulate cortex, and cortex located at the junction of the temporal and parietal lobes (Christoff, Gordon, Smallwood, Smith, & Schooler, 2009; Mason et al., 2007). In contrast, when we are working on a difficult task requiring our undivided attention, we engage an "executive network" that includes the anterior cingulate cortex and the dorsolateral prefrontal cortex. The purpose for having the ability to daydream is unclear. We might daydream simply because we evolved the ability to divide our attention, as described in our chapter on sensation and perception (Mason et al., 2007).

Experiencing Psychology

The Epworth Sleepiness Scale

College students often neglect sleep time to study, work, and socialize. Sixty percent of students reported staying awake for an entire night at least once since coming to college (Thacher, 2008). Poor sleep habits lead to daytime sleepiness, which can affect how much you learn in your classes, how well you work, and your

safety when driving and operating other machinery. How much sleepiness is too much? Try taking the Epworth Sleepiness Scale to see how sleepy you really are (Johns, 1991).

In contrast to just feeling tired, how likely are you to doze off or fall asleep in the following situations? (Even if you have not done some of these things recently, try to work out

how they would have affected you.) Use the scale shown on the facing page to choose the most appropriate number for each situation listed in the chart.

A score greater than 10 indicates excessive daytime sleepiness. If you scored at this level or above, it's time for some lifestyle changes. ✺

Sleep

We spend one third of our lives sleeping. In spite of all that experience, few of us know exactly what is going on during sleep. We know from painful experience that skipping sleep makes us feel terrible, but once again, our introspection into our own personal experience does not provide many answers. By carefully recording and observing the experience of volunteers sleeping in laboratories, psychologists have been able to unravel many of the mysteries of sleep.

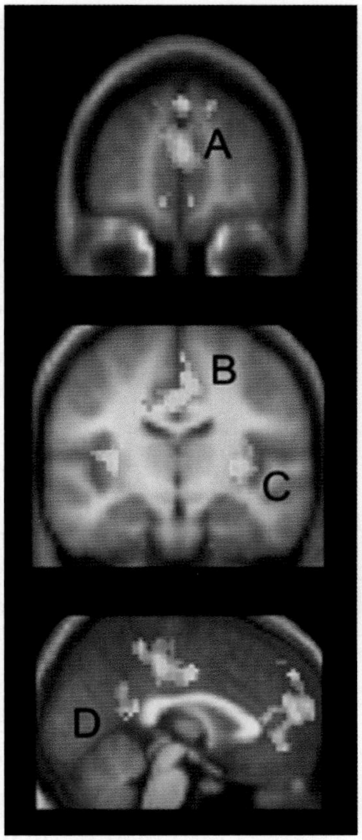

Stages of Sleep On the basis of these observations of sleeping volunteers, we divide sleep into two types: **rapid eye movement**, or **REM, sleep**, and **non-rapid eye movement**, or **N-REM, sleep**. These types of sleep may be differentiated by EEG recordings, muscle tone, autonomic activity, and mental activity (see ● Figure 6.8).

N-REM sleep is divided into four stages. Stage 1 N-REM usually occurs when we first go to sleep. Our examination of the participant's EEG shows patterns that are difficult to distinguish from those of the drowsy, waking volunteer. Some **theta waves** (4–7 cycles per second), which are larger and slower than alpha waves, are observed. At this stage, the person may not be aware that he or she is sleeping. Frequently, we awaken a friend or family member who has fallen asleep in front of the television by turning off the program, only to have the sleeping person deny being asleep.

After 10 to 15 minutes, Stage 1 of N-REM gives way to Stage 2. Now there is no doubt that the person is asleep. Further reductions in heart rate and muscle tension occur, and the EEG begins to show special waveforms

FIGURE 6.7

A "Default" Network Might Produce Daydreaming. These functional magnetic resonance imaging (fMRI) scans show parts of the brain that are active during daydreaming: (A) medial prefrontal cortex, (B) anterior cingulate cortex, (C) insula (the area at the junction of the temporal and parietal lobes), and (D) posterior cingulate cortex. Together, these structures have been described as a "default network" that is active when the brain is awake but relatively at rest. *Source:* From Mason, M. F., et al., Wandering minds: The default network and stimulus-independent thought, *Science, 315,* 393–395. Copyright © 2007 The American Association for the Advancement of Science.

rapid eye movement (REM) sleep The component of sleep characterized by waveforms resembling wakefulness as measured by EEG accompanied by rapid eye movements, muscular paralysis, and autonomic nervous system activation.

non-rapid eye movement (N-REM) sleep The components of sleep characterized by theta and delta wave activity as recorded by EEG and deep physical relaxation.

theta wave A waveform recorded by EEG that is characteristic of lighter stages of N-REM sleep.

Situation	Chance of dozing
Sitting and reading	
Watching TV	
Sitting inactive in a public place (e.g., a theater)	
Riding as a car passenger for an hour without a break	
Lying down to rest in the afternoon	
Sitting and talking to someone	
Sitting quietly after lunch without alcohol	
In a car, while stopping for a few minutes in traffic	
TOTAL SCORE	

0 = Would never doze
1 = Slight chance of dozing
2 = Moderate chance of dozing
3 = High chance of dozing

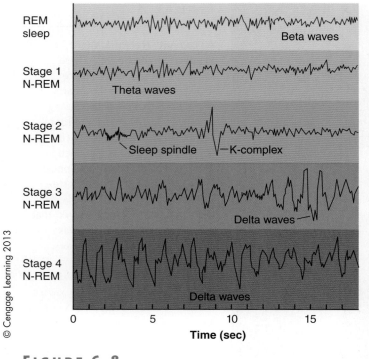

REM sleep — Beta waves

Stage 1 N-REM — Theta waves

Stage 2 N-REM — Sleep spindle — K-complex

Stage 3 N-REM — Delta waves

Stage 4 N-REM — Delta waves

Time (sec)   0   5   10   15

© Cengage Learning 2013

FIGURE 6.8

The EEG During Sleep. Sleep is divided into two components: rapid eye movement (REM) sleep and non-REM sleep. The EEG during REM is very similar to wakefulness. Stages 1 and 2 of N-REM feature theta waves and special waveforms known as sleep spindles and K-complexes, which might represent the brain's attempts to tune out environmental stimuli. Stages 3 and 4 of N-REM feature delta waves and represent the deepest stages of sleep. *Source: Adapted from Horne (1998).*

delta wave A waveform recorded by EEG that usually indicates very deep N-REM sleep.

called K-complexes and sleep spindles that occur only in sleep. These particular types of activity might reflect the brain's efforts to keep us asleep while continuing to monitor the external environment. We usually sleep through familiar stimuli, such as the hum of an air conditioner, while waking in response to unexpected stimuli, such as the sound of a door opening.

After about 15 minutes in Stage 2, we enter Stage 3 and then Stage 4 N-REM sleep. Both of these stages show **delta wave** activity, which is the largest, slowest (1–4 cycles per second) waveform we will observe. Stages 3 and 4 differ primarily in the amount of delta activity that occurs, with Stage 4 having the most. We are very deeply asleep in these stages. Awakening from Stage 4 is difficult, and considerable disorientation may occur before a person becomes fully awake. You may have received a telephone call about an hour after you first go to sleep, when you are likely to be experiencing Stage 4. If you hear the telephone at all, it may take several seconds to locate the phone and wake up enough to have a decent conversation.

The first episode of REM sleep occurs between 90 and 120 minutes after the onset of sleep. This stage is often referred to as paradoxical sleep, reflecting a combination of brain activity resembling wakefulness with the external appearance of deep sleep. During REM, the EEG shows activity very similar to waking activity. The eyes make the periodic movements back and forth that give this stage its name. The autonomic nervous system becomes very active. Heart rate, blood pressure, and breathing become rapid or irregular. Males experience erections, while females experience increased blood flow in the vicinity of the vagina (Hirshkowitz & Moore, 1996). If awakened during this stage, most people will report vivid, story-like dreams, which we discuss in more detail in a later section.

Major postural muscles are completely inactive during REM sleep, effectively paralyzing the sleeper, although smaller muscles in the fingers and toes might twitch. You might have experienced dreams in which something terrible was coming, but you couldn't move. Your dream probably reflects recognition on the part of the brain that you really are paralyzed. This paralysis provides a protective mechanism that prevents you from acting out your dreams. In some cases of sleep disorder, paralysis fails, and people injure themselves or their sleeping partners. In one case study, a man who dreamed of playing football knocked everything off his dresser, hit his head against the wall, and banged his knee on the dresser (Schenck, Bundlie, Ettinger, & Mahowald, 1986).

Because the body is paralyzed during REM sleep, sleepwalking does not happen in this stage. Instead, sleepwalking occurs when a person is in Stage 3 or 4 of N-REM sleep. Sleep-talking, however, usually occurs at the lighter Stages 1 and 2 of N-REM. The talker may be sufficiently aware of the environment to politely wait his or her turn to speak. These phenomena become progressively less common with age.

The cycling between REM and N-REM in humans follows a characteristic pattern over 8 hours of sleep (see ● Figure 6.9). The first half of a night's sleep is characterized by longer periods of N-REM and brief periods of REM. Stages 3 and 4 are especially dominant during these first 4 hours. The second half of the night's sleep switches to a different pattern. REM now dominates sleep, and N-REM remains in the lighter stages. Stages 3 and 4 may be infrequent or absent altogether during the last 4 hours of sleep. As a result of this lighter sleep in the second half of the night, people are easier to awaken than they are during the first half. We usually spend the last half hour or so of the night's sleep in REM and often wake up with the awareness that we have just been dreaming.

The Benefits of Sleep Although we still have many unanswered questions about why we spend one third of our lives sleeping, we do know that lack of sleep can have many negative effects. In a genetic condition known as fatal familial insomnia, middle-aged people gradually lose the ability to sleep. As the name of the disorder implies, the result of this sleep loss is eventual death. The exact cause of death is unknown, although the disorder is associated with damage to the thalamus (Gallassi et al., 1996).

Sleep, and in particular Stages 3 and 4 of N-REM sleep, plays an important role in repairing the body. Sleep deprivation slows the healing of injuries (Murphy et al., 2007), reduces the activity of the immune system (Zager, Andersen, Ruiz, Antunes, & Tufik, 2007) and results in the production of fewer new neurons in adult brains (Guzman-Marin et al., 2003). The vast majority of the release of human growth hormone, which plays important roles in repairing the body, occurs during Stages 3 and 4 of N-REM sleep (Savine & Sönksen, 2000). Another line of evidence supporting the restorative hypothesis of sleep is the behavior of people following intense physical activity. Runners competing in ultramarathons (races that are twice the length of a normal marathon) experience greater amounts of N-REM sleep the night after their performance. It is possible to selectively deprive volunteers in a sleep laboratory of Stages 3 and 4 N-REM sleep. After a night of such deprivation, volunteers typically complain of muscle and joint pain (Moldofsky & Scarisbrick, 1976). Because time spent in N-REM decreases about one half hour per decade after the age of 50 (Van Cauter, Leproult, & Plat, 2000), it is possible that

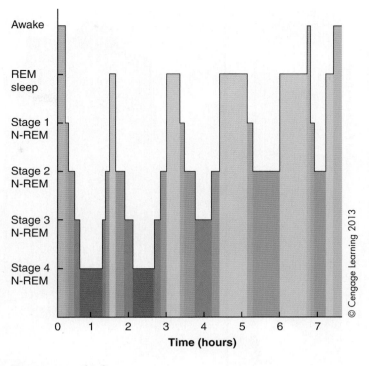

FIGURE 6.9

Nightly Sleep Patterns. Sleep shows a typical progression over the night. The first 4 hours are dominated by N-REM sleep, and the vast majority of Stages 3 and 4 sleep occurs at this time. The second 4 hours feature large amounts of REM sleep. *Source: Adapted from Cartwright (1978).*

Excess sleepiness on the part of decision makers has contributed to many disasters, including the Three Mile Island nuclear meltdown, the Challenger *space shuttle explosion, and the grounding of the oil tanker* Exxon Valdez *(Coren, 1996a). Staying awake for 17 to 19 straight hours produces worse reaction time than being legally drunk (Williamson & Feyer, 2000). It's a good idea to consider these facts before you get in the car to go home after your last final exam.*

Human error, and sleep deprivation in particular, contributed to three of the 20th century's iconic disasters. The 1979 nuclear meltdown at Three Mile Island changed the power industry in the United States. The 1986 explosion of the space shuttle *Challenger*, rattled confidence in the U.S. space program. The 1989 oil spill caused by the running aground of the tanker *Exxon Valdez* energized concerns about environmental protection.

reduced N-REM is the source of some of the muscle and joint aches and pains experienced by older adults (see ● Figure 6.10).

Sleep plays a significant role in the consolidation of memories. Staying up all night results in poor memory performance, and two subsequent nights of normal sleep do not make up for the initial sleep deprivation effects (Stickgold & Walker, 2007). Memories for verbal tasks, emotional material, and procedures are all better following a period of sleep than when followed by wakefulness (Gais & Born, 2004; Wagner, Fischer, & Born, 2002; Wagner, Gais, & Born, 2001). Needless to say, students who wish to retain the material they've studied would be well advised to get a good night's sleep.

The Special Benefits of REM Sleep Birds and mammals are the only creatures to show clear evidence of REM sleep, suggesting that this sleep stage is a fairly recent development in the course of evolution (see ● Figure 6.11).

When volunteers are specifically deprived of REM sleep, they show many of the same symptoms as people who experience an overall lack

FIGURE 6.10

Human Growth Hormone Release. Human growth hormone (HGH) stimulates growth and repair. The vast majority of HGH release occurs during the first 4 hours of sleep each night, primarily during Stages 3 and 4 of N-REM sleep. The drop in time spent in Stages 3 and 4 among older adults might contribute to reduced abilities to heal compared to younger adults. *Source:* Adapted from Coleman (1986).

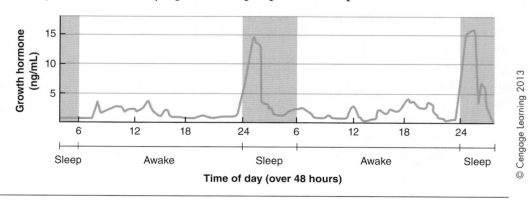

	Total sleep (h)	% REM sleep
 **Cow** *Bos taurus*	4	23
 **Human** *Homo sapiens*	8	31
 **Domestic cat** *Felis sylvestris*	13.2	32
 **Western European hedgehog** *Erinaceus eruopaeus*	10.1	40

FIGURE 6.11

Brainy Animals Need REM. Not only do animals spend different amounts of time overall in sleep, but the percentage of that time spent in REM also varies. Although it looks on the surface like some simpler animals like hedgehogs spend a greater percentage of their sleep time in REM than we do, if researchers control for the brain size of species, it becomes apparent that the more complex the brain, the more time a species spends in REM. This finding is consistent with hypotheses suggesting that REM sleep is important for forming new memories. *Source: Adapted from Lesku et al. (2008). Illustration: © Cengage Learning 2013; photos (top to bottom): © R. Fassbind/Shutterstock; © GeoM/ Shutterstock; © Eric Isselée/Shutterstock; © Vishnevskiy Vasily/Shutterstock*

of sleep, including irritability and difficulty concentrating. In addition, REM-deprived individuals show a phenomenon known as REM rebound (Dement, 1960). When allowed to sleep normally, they spend an unusually large amount of their sleep time in REM. You may have experienced REM rebound during a nap following a night with little sleep. You might be aware of having dreamed vividly during the nap, and you're unlikely to feel very rested. The fact that we seem to make up for lost REM sleep suggests that REM does have a necessary function in the adult brain.

One clue to a possible function of REM is the association of REM with the activity of the immature brain. The proportion of sleep spent in REM is a function of a species' relative maturity at birth (Siegel, 2001). The human infant, born at a very immature stage of brain development relative to other primate species, spends about half of its sleep time in REM (see ● Figure 6.12), compared to the 20% of sleep time spent in REM by adolescents and adults (McCarley, 2007). Premature infants spend up to 80% of their sleep

FIGURE 6.12

REM Over the Lifespan. Infants and young children spend much greater percentages of their sleep time in REM than do adolescents and adults, suggesting that brain activity during REM might help wire the developing brain. *Adapted from Roffwarg et al. (1966).*

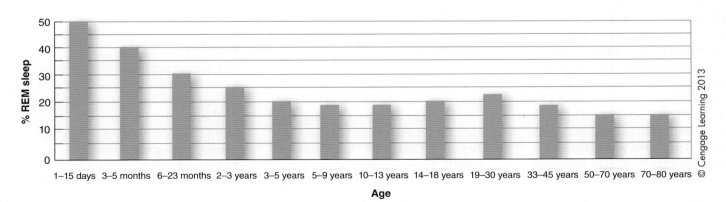

time in REM. REM sleep may provide at least part of the stimulation necessary to correctly "wire" the immature brain (Marks, Shaffery, Oksenberg, Speciale, & Roffwarg, 1995).

REM sleep and mood are tightly interwoven, providing us with a further clue regarding the possible functions of REM. As we will see in our chapter on psychological disorders, individuals with depression experience disruptions in their normal sleep patterns. Without treatment, they enter REM sleep much earlier in the night than typical participants do, and they spend a greater proportion of their sleeping time in REM. One of the possible mechanisms by which antidepressant medications regulate mood is their suppression of REM sleep. Individuals with bipolar disorder, which is characterized by moods that swing from euphoria to depression, also experience sleep abnormalities. Patients show an abnormally low need for sleep. The euphoric manic phase of the disorder can be initiated in some patients by sleep deprivation. Consequently, individuals with a diagnosis of bipolar disorder should take great care to obtain appropriate amounts of sleep.

Connecting *to* Research

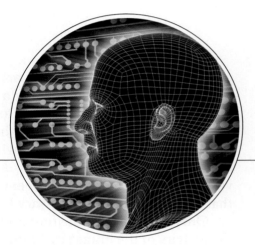

Loneliness Impacts Sleep

Most of us are aware that mood and stress can have negative impacts on our sleep, but it might come as a surprise to you that loneliness can be a problem for good sleep quality, too. Understanding the impact of loneliness on sleep helps explain some of the negative health outcomes associated with feeling socially disconnected. For example, a patient's rating of the statement "I feel lonely" predicted his or her survival up to 5 years following heart surgery (Herlitz et al., 1998). You might think that loneliness affects these patients by making them less likely to follow good health habits, like taking their medication and exercising, but research didn't support this hypothesis. Instead, researchers suspected that loneliness led to poor health by disrupting sleep, which plays an important role in healing the body (Cacioppo et al., 2002).

The Question: *Is sleep quality affected by perceived loneliness?*

METHODS

Sixty-four undergraduates at Ohio State University participated in the study. Their levels of perceived loneliness were assessed using the UCLA-R Loneliness Scale (Russell, Peplau, & Cutrona, 1980). Their sleep quality was measured using a sleep monitor called Nightcap while they spent the night in the campus's Clinical Research Center. Sleep quality measures included sleep onset, sleep duration, number of awakenings, and wake time after onset. The participants' sleep quality was assessed 2 weeks later at home over five consecutive nights.

RESULTS

The participants were divided into high-, medium-, and low-loneliness groups on the basis of their scores on the UCLA-R Loneliness Scale. Sleep quality did vary significantly among these groups, with the high-loneliness group experiencing the lowest sleep quality, and the

These correlations between REM sleep and mood may represent a common underlying biochemical mechanism. Brainstem neurons that release serotonin and norepinephrine are especially quiet during REM, although they are very active during wakefulness and somewhat active during N-REM sleep (Gottesman, 2002). These same neurotransmitters have also been implicated in the regulation of mood states, which helps explain links between REM and mood.

Dreaming

From the earliest times in our history, people have searched for the significance and meaning of their dreams. In ancient Egypt, many people believed that dreams predicted the future. In his classic book, *The Interpretation of Dreams*, Sigmund Freud argued that the unconscious mind expressed itself symbolically through our dreams (Freud, 1900/1953). These are interesting ideas, but what does science have to say about **dreaming**?

The use of EEG technology to track a volunteer's sleep patterns allowed researchers to awaken volunteers and assess a dream experience scientifically for the first time (Aserinsky & Kleitman, 1953; Dement & Kleitman, 1957). Psychologists have made some progress in describing the common features of dreams. Although we generally think of our dreams as being bizarre, most appear to be rather ordinary. According to a classic analysis of the content of thousands of dreams collected from volunteers, most dreams occur in familiar places and involve routine activities. We only participate as characters in our dreams about 15% of the time, and imaginary strangers are more likely to appear than familiar people (Hall,

dreaming A mental state that usually occurs during sleep that features visual imagery.

low-loneliness group experiencing the best sleep quality. The medium-loneliness group had sleep quality scores between these two extremes. In particular, the loneliest participants were more likely to experience restless sleep, as indicated by their spending more time awake during the night after once having fallen asleep.

CONCLUSIONS

The results of this study indicated that lonely people experienced poor quality of sleep. However, there are several ways these results could be explained, as we outlined in our chapter on research methods. First, it is possible that the experience of loneliness causes poor sleep quality. Second, poor sleep quality could interfere with a person's ability to function well socially, leading to loneliness. Third, loneliness and sleep quality could influence each other reciprocally. Finally, some third variable or set of variables could lead to both disruptions of feeling socially connected and of sleep quality. If you're thinking that a likely candidate for one of these third variables is depression, the researchers controlled for this by assessing depression prior to the study and excluding any potential participants who appeared to be depressed.

These results do indicate that the relationships between loneliness and health are more complicated than a simple connection between loneliness and the likelihood that an individual would follow good health practices. ⬡

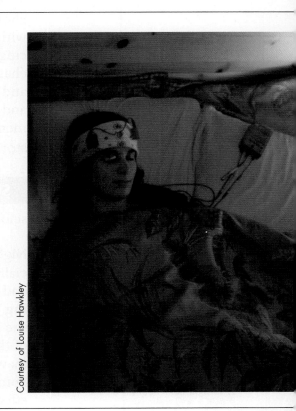

Courtesy of Louise Hawkley

The activation-synthesis theory of dream content suggests that the content of dreams represents the mind's efforts to make sense out of real physical sensations. During REM, the vestibular system of the inner ear is quite active. Because the vestibular system normally informs us about the position and movement of the head, vestibular activity during REM might lead to the commonly experienced dreams of flying or falling.

1951). Perhaps bizarre dreams are remembered more vividly because they are unusual.

An activation-synthesis theory of dreaming suggests that the content of dreams simply reflects ongoing neural activity. For example, dreams of being unable to move in a dangerous situation might accurately mirror the muscle paralysis present during the REM state (Hobson & McCarley, 1977). Common dreams of flying or falling may be caused by the unusual activation of the vestibular system during REM (Hunt, 1989). In our chapter on sensation and perception, we discussed the vestibular system's role in helping us maintain balance. Dreams with sexual content are consistent with the physical sexual arousal that occurs during REM.

According to a more evolutionary view, animals might dream to develop future survival strategies by integrating sensory experience with stored memories when in an "off-line" mode during REM sleep (Winson, 1985). Consistent with this evolutionary approach is the fact that 70% of our dreams involve negative circumstances for which the development of strategies might be helpful (Hall & Van de Castle, 1966). In the weeks following the 1989 earthquake in San Francisco, 40% of students in San Francisco universities reported dreaming about earthquakes, compared to 5% of students in Arizona (Wood, Bootzin, Rosenhan, Nolen-Hoeksema, & Jourden, 1992).

Combining results of brain imaging experiments and cognitive psychology leads to yet another view of dreams. Dreaming behavior correlates with activity in circuits formed by the medial prefrontal cortex, the anterior cingulate cortex, and the basal forebrain (Domhoff, 2003). Simultaneous changes in brainstem activity result in lower sensitivity to outside stimuli, and reduced overall frontal lobe activity might lead to less self-awareness and logical thought. Once the dream state is initiated, the brain draws on memories of general knowledge and personal experience to produce a story line (Foulkes, 1999).

Sleep Disorders

Observing what goes wrong in sleep provides additional insights into the natural variations of consciousness we experience.

Nightmares and Night Terrors When the content of a REM dream is especially upsetting, we refer to the experience as a nightmare. Many adolescents and adults with troubling nightmares benefit from training in **lucid dreaming**. In lucid dreaming, the dreamer becomes aware of the fact that he or she is dreaming and may use this awareness to control or direct the content of the dream. If the lucid dreamer becomes stuck in a nightmare, he or she may have the option of "changing channels" and exiting that line of content. Some researchers report that training in lucid dreaming may serve as an effective treatment for recurring, upsetting nightmares (Zadra & Pihl, 1997).

lucid dreaming A conscious awareness of dreaming accompanied by the ability to control the content of the dream.

Nightmares are often mistaken for **night terrors**, but they are very different phenomena. Nightmares are dreams that occur during REM, while night terrors occur during N-REM sleep, particularly during the first 3 hours of sleep. In night terrors, the usually smooth transition from Stage 4 N-REM sleep upward into REM goes awry. The sleeper becomes acutely distressed, although he or she remains deeply asleep. If awakened, the person shows the disorientation and confusion typically demonstrated when a sleeper is disturbed during very deep N-REM sleep. There is usually no memory of the night terror the next day. There may be a genetic predisposition to night terrors, as 80% of people with this condition report a family history for the behavior (American Psychiatric Association [APA], 2000).

Insomnia After nightmares, the most common sleep problem is **insomnia**, in which a person has difficulty initiating or maintaining sleep. Clearly, there are substantial individual differences in the healthy amount and patterning of sleep. Although most people seem to need about seven to nine hours of sleep per night to function effectively, much wider healthy variations do exist. In one case of "healthy insomnia," an elderly woman slept only 1 hour per night without any apparent detrimental effects (Meddis, Pearson, & Langford, 1973).

Insomnia occurs in one of two forms. In cases of onset insomnia, a person will lie in bed for what seems to be a very long period but be unable to go to sleep. Stress and anxiety are frequent causes of this type of insomnia. Maintenance insomnia occurs when sleep is frequently interrupted or early waking occurs. These cases typically result from stress, substance use, or psychological disorders. Insomnia medications, such as zolpidem (Ambien), have minor effects on sleep, producing sleep 15 minutes faster and lengthening it for about 30 minutes, which might not offset significant side effects, including dependence on the medication, driving or walking while asleep, memory loss, and loss of coordination (Buscemi et al., 2007).

Narcolepsy and Cataplexy Probably the most dramatic sleep disorder is **narcolepsy**. Narcolepsy consists of "sleep attacks," in which REM sleep occurs during wakefulness (Dahl, Holttum, & Trubnick, 1994). Attacks are often instigated by strong emotions. Harriet Tubman, a leader of the Underground Railroad around the time of the American Civil War, was suspected of having narcolepsy. Tubman had a number of close calls as she aided the escape of slaves to the North, as the excitement of the situation brought on frequent attacks.

In addition to sleep attacks, other aspects of REM sleep may intrude into the wakefulness of patients with narcolepsy. Cataplexy occurs when the muscle paralysis normally associated with REM sleep occurs during wakefulness without any loss of consciousness. Unfortunately for those suffering from cataplexy, having sex is a common emotional trigger for the disorder. Many patients with narcolepsy also experience sleep paralysis, or muscle paralysis that either precedes actual sleep or lingers once the person has awakened. Although upsetting, this paralysis is easy to resolve. Simply touching the person is enough to end the paralysis.

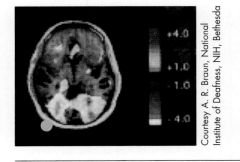

Brain imaging can be used to compare activity during wakefulness with activity during sleep. In this image, areas that are blue or purple are less active during REM sleep than during wakefulness, and areas that are red or yellow are more active during REM sleep than during wakefulness. The bizarre content of dreams occurring during REM sleep might be the result of the lower activity in the frontal lobes (purple) at the top of the image. The visual vividness of dreams might be accounted for by the much higher amount of activity in the visual areas of the occipital lobes toward the bottom of the image (yellow and red).

night terror A sleep disorder occurring in N-REM sleep in which the sleeper wakes suddenly in great distress, but without experiencing the imagery of a nightmare.

insomnia A sleep disorder characterized by an inability to either initiate or maintain normal sleep.

narcolepsy A sleep disorder characterized by the intrusion of REM phenomena into wakefulness.

In spite of her suspected narcolepsy, Harriet Tubman (1820–1913) helped hundreds of slaves escape through the Underground Railroad during the Civil War era. Tubman appears on the left in this photo with some of the former slaves whom she helped. Unfortunately, narcoleptic attacks are often brought on by stress. Tubman had a number of close escapes when she experienced sleep attacks while being pursued by Confederate troops and irate slave owners.

In many cases, narcolepsy appears to be a genetically determined disturbance in the control of REM sleep (Dement, 1974). Researchers have been able to selectively breed for narcolepsy in dogs (Foutz, Mitler, Cavalli-Sforva, & Dement, 1979). The gene suspected of abnormalities in narcolepsy affects the activity of neurotransmitters known as orexins, which we will discuss more fully in our chapter on motivation. Cells in the hypothalamus that normally secrete orexins are missing or damaged in the brains of patients with narcolepsy (Thannickal et al., 2000).

Sleep researcher William Dement is holding Tucker before (left) and after (right) a cataplexy attack. Research on dogs like Tucker showed that narcolepsy is a genetic disorder involving abnormalities in neurotransmitters known as orexins.

The number of deaths from SIDS dropped dramatically when the American Academy of Pediatrics began telling parents in 2003 to put their babies to sleep on their backs instead of on their stomachs. SIDS still occurs, however, so sleeping position is only one of many risk factors, including exposure to cigarette smoke in the home.

Sleep Apnea We take it for granted that automatic functions like breathing will continue uninterrupted during sleep, but this is not the case in **sleep apnea**. In people with sleep apnea, breathing can stop for a minute or two, and the sleeper awakens abruptly gasping for air. Not only does this lack of air disrupt the sleep quality of the person with sleep apnea, but his or her sleeping partner is often disturbed as well. Because most cases of sleep apnea occur in people who are obese and who snore, losing weight and surgical correction of any airway blockages are common treatments. Other cases occur when brainstem neurons responsible for maintaining breathing during sleep malfunction. In these cases, the use of a machine that regulates airflow during sleep is an inconvenient but effective solution.

Sudden Infant Death Syndrome (SIDS) **Sudden infant death syndrome,** or **SIDS**, occurs when a healthy infant simply dies while asleep. Between 1992 and 2003, rates of SIDS in the United States were cut in half when the American Academy of Pediatrics (AAP) began telling parents to put their infants to sleep on their backs instead of on their stomachs (National Institute of Child Health and Human Development [NICHHD], 2003). As we will see in our chapter on development, young infants cannot turn over easily for the first few months of life, making suffocation on blankets and stuffed animals a greater risk. Although some cases might include biological vulnerabilities in serotonin function (Paterson et al., 2006), most affected infants have additional risk factors, such as exposure to tobacco smoke (Ostfeld, Esposito, Perl, & Hegyi, 2010).

Restless Legs Syndrome (RLS) **Restless legs syndrome,** or **RLS**, occurs when one of a person's limbs, usually a leg, experiences a tingling feeling and moves at regular intervals. RLS appears to be quite common, with 15% of a large sample of adults in the United States reporting these symptoms (National Sleep Foundation, 2009). Of special interest to psychologists is the high frequency of RLS among children and adults with attention deficit hyperactivity disorder and the potential genetic links between these two conditions (Schimmelmann et al., 2009).

sleep apnea A sleep disorder in which the person stops breathing while asleep.

sudden infant death syndrome (SIDS) A sleep disorder in which an otherwise healthy infant dies while asleep.

restless legs syndrome (RLS) A disorder characterized by the involuntary movement of an extremity, usually one leg.

Summary 6.2

Features of Wakefulness and Sleep

Stage of wakefulness or sleep		Brain activity recorded by EEG	Observations
Wakefulness *Awake — Alpha waves / Beta waves* © Cengage Learning 2013		Alpha/beta	• Alternating periods of alertness and relaxation • Logical thought • Voluntary movement • Responsive to stimuli
Non-rapid eye movement (N-REM) sleep *Stage 1 N-REM — Theta waves* © Cengage Learning 2013	1	Some theta	• Logical thought • Reduced heart rate and muscle tension • Some responsiveness to stimuli
Stage 2 N-REM — Sleep spindle / K-complex © Cengage Learning 2013	2	Larger amounts of theta	• Less responsiveness to stimuli • Further reductions in heart rate and muscle tension
Stage 3 N-REM — Delta waves © Cengage Learning 2013	3	Some delta	• Further reductions in heart rate and muscle tension
Stage 4 N-REM — Delta waves © Cengage Learning 2013	4	Larger amounts of delta	• Profound reductions in heart rate and muscle tension • Very low responsiveness to stimuli
Rapid eye movement (REM) sleep *REM sleep — Beta waves* © Cengage Learning 2013		Similar to beta, some theta	• Rapid eye movements • Muscle paralysis • Irregular autonomic activity • Vivid dreams

How Is Consciousness Affected by Brain Damage?

If consciousness is a function of the brain, we should be able to identify aspects of consciousness that change reliably when the brain is damaged.

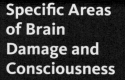

Specific Areas of Brain Damage and Consciousness

In this section, we will explore lessons about consciousness that have emerged from the clinical study of patients with damage to very specific parts of the nervous system.

Among the most striking of these cases are the individuals chronicled by neurologist Oliver Sacks in his book *The Man Who Mistook His Wife for a Hat* (Sacks, 1985). Although Sacks did not always discover the causes of his patients' afflictions, their experiences with changes in consciousness due to nervous system damage remind us of the vast complexity of what we view as consciousness.

Sacks describes the case of Christina, an active, 27-year-old mother of two children, who suddenly developed an inflammation of her somatosensory nerves, which we described in our chapter on sensation and perception. As a result of her condition, Christina no longer had any input about touch and muscle and joint position to tell her where parts of her body were. Consequently, Christina felt as though her body literally disappeared. Using her vision, Christina willed herself to move, but when distracted, she collapsed like a rag doll. Although Christina learned to move, speak, and carry out her normal daily tasks, she remained in a surreal situation in which her body was "blind and deaf to itself . . . . [I]t has no sense of itself" (Sacks, 1985, p. 49). Not only does Christina's dilemma enlighten us as to the importance of sensory feedback for self-awareness, but it also sheds light on what it means to have a "self," which we discuss in a later chapter.

The effects of brain damage on face recognition provide an opportunity to consider how the brain integrates sensory information, memory, and emotion to form a conscious experience. Prosopagnosia is a condition that impacts a person's ability to recognize faces (Bauer, 1984). In one case, a patient was completely unable to identify familiar faces. However, the patient was still able to show differing autonomic responses to familiar versus unfamiliar faces. Separate pathways process the features of faces, emotional responses to faces, and recognition of faces.

In a situation that is reminiscent of many horror film and science fiction classics, patients with Capgras syndrome are convinced that imposters have taken the place of familiar people. In certain tragic instances, patients with Capgras even try to harm the "imposters." This condition appears to be a type of problem opposite that of prosopagnosia. Here the ability to recognize faces remains intact, but the sense of emotion and familiarity is distorted. The damage associated with Capgras is not thoroughly understood, but it is assumed to involve connections between visual areas of the brain and the amygdala (Ramachandran, 1998).

These clinical cases demonstrate the varied aspects of consciousness that contribute to our overall awareness of ourselves and the world around us. When we observe the precise loss of a conscious capacity, such as recognizing your friend's face or even your own body, leaving all other aspects of your awareness intact, we gain an appreciation for the richness of brain activity that must underlie what we call consciousness.

Coma

Our word **coma** comes from the Greek *koma*, which means "deep sleep." Coma produces a profound state of unconsciousness. In a state of coma, a person does not have sleep-waking cycles, cannot be awakened, does not respond to pain or light, and is incapable of any voluntary behavior. Coma results from a wide variety of

Neurologist and author Oliver Sacks has written many case studies that illuminate the relationships between brain damage and changes in consciousness.

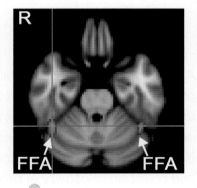

Prosopagnosia results from damage to a part of the temporal lobes on the bottom of the brain known as the Fusiform Face Area (FFA). In this scan using functional magnetic resonance imaging (fMRI), the FFA activity indicates that the person is looking at the image of a face as opposed to a landscape or building. From Timothy J. Andrews et al., Internal and External Features of the Face Are Represented Holistically in Face-Selective Regions of Visual Cortex, *The Journal of Neuroscience*, 2010, *30*(9): 3544–3552; doi:10.1523/ JNEUROSCI.4863-09.2010. Image courtesy Timothy J. Andrews.

coma An abnormal state of deep unconsciousness.

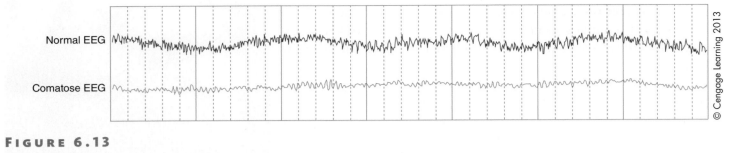

Normal EEG

Comatose EEG

© Cengage Learning 2013

FIGURE 6.13

Normal Versus Comatose EEGs. Even though the patient with the normal EEG recording is drowsy, which should produce a dominant pattern of alpha waves, the normal recording is quite different from the more uniform alpha activity recorded from a patient in a coma.

Agreement about what constitutes consciousness plays an important role in the discussion of brain death. Some neuroscientists argue that consciousness is a function of the cerebral cortex alone, and cessation of activity in this area should constitute brain death. Others argue for a more conservative "whole brain" definition (Howsepian, 1998). Because organ donation decisions are made on the basis of a diagnosis of brain death, it is obviously essential to get this definition right.

persistent vegetative state (PVS) An abnormal state following brain injury featuring wakefulness without consciousness.

medical conditions that impact the nervous system, including traumatic brain injury (TBI) and loss of oxygen. Comas last anywhere from a few days to several weeks. After a period of 2 to 4 weeks, most patients will have recovered, moved on into a vegetative state (described later in this section), or died. Among those who recover, improvement is usually very slow and gradual.

EEG recordings of comatose patients vary depending on the problem that initially resulted in coma. Following resuscitation from cardiac arrest, many patients show a pattern of alpha rhythms, especially in the frontal lobes, or the so-called alpha coma (Chatrian, 1990). These alpha patterns do not change when the patient is exposed to various types of stimulation. Other patterns feature a very low level of overall activity, occasionally interrupted by spikes. None of these patterns are found in the typical, healthy EEG described previously in our section on sleep and waking (see ● Figure 6.13).

Persistent Vegetative State (PVS) Coma can be distinguished from other similar conditions, such as **persistent vegetative state (PVS)** or brain death. PVS often follows a period of coma. PVS is characterized by wakefulness without consciousness. In contrast to the patient with coma, patients with PVS look rather normal. Their eyes open periodically, and they grind their teeth, scream, smile, or cry. Some are responsive to pain. However, most behavior appears to be spontaneous and internally driven as opposed to being elicited by any external stimulus. Medical authorities are divided regarding the possibility of recovering from PVS. Two PVS patients appeared to recover after 5 years of apparent unconsciousness (Avesani, Gambini, & Albertini, 2006). Others dispute these findings and suggest instead that "miraculous recoveries" occur only in patients who were initially misdiagnosed with PVS (see ● Figure 6.14).

Brain Death With the advent of technologies that can artificially maintain certain bodily functions, including respiration and blood circulation, we have been placed in the odd position of requiring a new definition of death. Brain death is now defined as a complete and irreversible lack of measurable brain activity, as evidenced by two flat-line EEG recordings taken 24 hours apart or lack of blood circulation to the brain. (see ● Figure 6.15). In

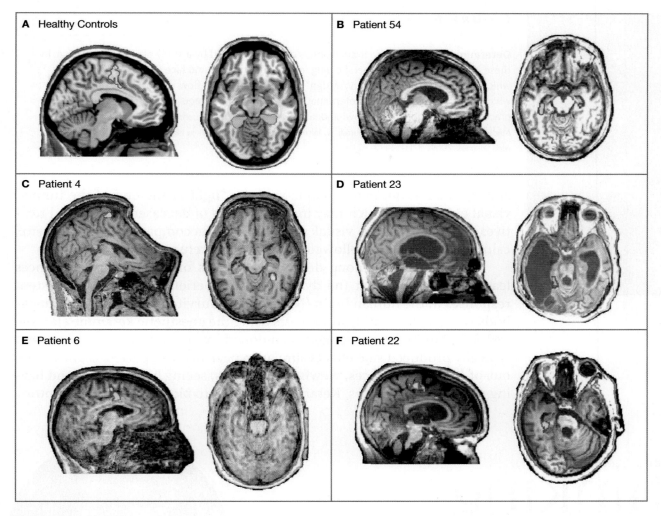

FIGURE 6.14

Is Consciousness Possible in PVS Patients? Using functional magnetic resonance imaging (fMRI), a small number of patients in a persistent vegetative state (PVS) showed brain activation to specific tasks that closely resembled the activation of healthy control participants. The yellow-red areas were active when thinking about movement, and the bluish areas were active when thinking about a spatial task. This research emphasizes the need to develop new ways of assessing the cognitive correlates of brain injuries so that patients can receive the best care possible. *Source:* From Monti, M. M., Vanhaudenhuyse, A., Coleman, M. R., Boly, M., Pickard, J. D., Tshibanda, L., et al. (2010). *Willful modulation of brain activity in disorders of consciousness. New England Journal of Medicine, 362*(7), 579–589. Used by permission of Massachusetts Medical Society.

brain death, the patient shows no responses to external stimuli, including pain, and no reflexes related to the cranial nerves, described in our chapter on biological psychology.

Near-Death Experiences

Once again due to improvements in technology that literally bring people "back to life," over 8 million Americans report having had a **near-death experience** (Mauro, 1992). Patients who recover following a cardiac arrest or some other life-threatening condition often report similar experiences. These experiences typically feature an out-of-body experience, in which the person feels that she is viewing her own body from a floating position

near-death experience An altered state of consciousness reported by people who were close to death due to cardiac or other medical problems that features out-of-body experiences, light at the end of a tunnel perceptions, and a state of calmness.

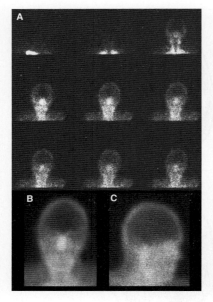

FIGURE 6.15

Determining Brain Death. Brain death is often determined by a study of blood circulation. In these images, blood can be seen flowing into the neck, scalp, and face (particularly the nose, which leads to the phrase "hot nose sign"). However, no blood flow is seen in the brain itself, which remains dark. A careful determination of brain death is required due to the common practice of organ donation following death. *Source:* Reprinted with permission of the Society of Nuclear Medicine from MacDonald, A. and Burrell, S. Infrequently Performed Studies in Nuclear Medicine: Part 2. *J Nucl Med Technol.* 2009: *37*(1), 1–13, Figure 5.

above. In addition, many people report a "light at the end of the tunnel" visual experience, which may include images of deceased friends and relatives or deities. These visual sensations are accompanied by a peaceful, calm emotional state, followed by a reluctant return to the body.

The similarities among documented cases of near-death experiences lead us to assume that the dying-revival experience produces consistent responses in the human brain (Negovsky & Gurvitch, 2004). Strong out-of-body sensations occur in volunteers using the anesthetic ketamine (Jansen, 1996). Ketamine was originally abandoned by anesthesiologists because it typically produced side effects similar to near-death experiences, including out-of-body experiences, viewing loved ones, seeing bright lights, and having mystical experiences. Ketamine is known to block glutamate receptors,

Thinking Scientifically

Can Patients in Vegetative States Communicate?

I t is hard to imagine a more traumatic experience than to be conscious but trapped in an unresponsive body. This is the nightmare that many scientists working with patients with PVS fear might be happening. This fear has led to a search for ways to communicate with the patient.

Following a traffic accident more than 20 years ago, Rom Houben has been in a persistent vegetative state. Doctors attempted to communicate

with Houben by asking him to type with his right index finger, which was not paralyzed. Messages from Houben immediately gained worldwide attention. Unfortunately, follow-up research showed that Houben's speech therapist, who was supposed to be providing support for his hand, was actually responsible for the messages. This "facilitated communication" has often produced similar false results. However, the doctors continue to look for a way to reach Houben, whose brain

appears to be acting only slightly differently than normal in imaging studies (Schnakers et al., 2009).

Using functional MRI, described in our chapter on research methods, other scientists have identified PVS patients whose brains showed reliable and distinct patterns of activity when asked to imagine playing tennis or walking around their own homes (Monti et al., 2010). Using "tennis" for "yes" and "home" for "no," the patients were able to correctly answer

discussed in our chapter on biological psychology. When the brain is damaged, cells typically release large quantities of glutamate. Glutamate, in turn, has further toxic effects on the brain. Consequently, the brain may release its own glutamate blockers in response to damage in an effort to minimize the cell loss produced by excess glutamate release. These glutamate blockers, similar to the artificial ketamine, may be responsible for the reported phenomena of near-death experiences.

Seizures **Seizures** are uncontrolled electrical disturbances in the brain that are often correlated with changes in consciousness, providing further evidence that cortical activity is correlated with consciousness. People with recurring seizures are diagnosed with epilepsy. Seizures frequently occur as a result of brain injury or infection, but can also appear without an obvious cause. Disturbances in the activity of the inhibitory neurotransmitter GABA might account for many seizures. Drugs that inhibit GABA reliably produce seizures, while drugs that enhance GABA activity, like barbiturates, serve to prevent or control seizures. Withdrawal from drugs that boost the activity of GABA, such as alcohol, often stimulates life-threatening seizure activity.

Most seizures may be classified as either partial seizures or generalized seizures. Partial seizures originate in a particular part of the brain, known as the focal area, and are often accompanied by an aura, or a premonition that a seizure is about to occur. Generalized seizures do not arise from a focal area. Instead, these seizures are characterized by the abnormal activation of circuits connecting the cortex and thalamus. Generalized seizures are typically not accompanied by an aura (see ● Figure 6.16).

Partial seizures originating in the temporal lobe often produce distortions of consciousness, leading to the experience of déjà vu (French for "already seen"), a feeling that one is reliving the past, or jamais vu (French for "never seen"), a sense that one's familiar circumstances are suddenly

seizure An abnormal level of brain activation with a sudden onset.

a series of questions, such as "Do you have brothers?" or "Is your father's name Thomas?" In spite of the accuracy of these responses, the patients show no outward signs of consciousness, nor do they show any normal behavioral reactions to stimuli.

Should these patients be shown to have ongoing conscious activity, it is possible that the more radical procedure of implanting electrodes, which has been successful in helping conscious but completely paralyzed patients to communicate by moving computer cursors, might provide them a connection with the outside world. ✪

© REUTERS/Romain Eyckens

After 20 years in an apparent persistent vegetative state (PVS), Rom Houben was able to type with his non-paralyzed finger with the assistance of his speech therapist. Unfortunately, further studies suggested that the therapist was typing, not Houben. However, the appearance of relatively normal patterns of activity in Houben's brain as seen in imaging studies has led physicians to seek other ways to communicate with him.

FIGURE 6.16

Pathways for the Spread of Partial and Generalized Seizures. (a) Partial seizures originate in a focus and spread to cortical and subcortical structures. (b) Generalized seizures do not originate in a focus. Once they begin, generalized seizures spread through the brain symmetrically via connections between the thalamus and cortex.

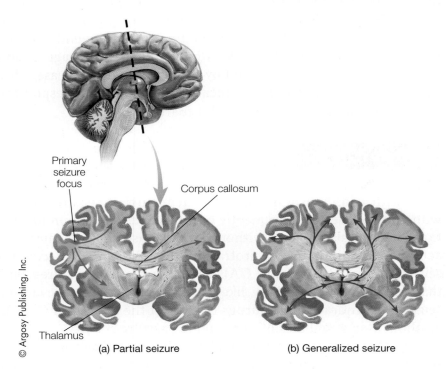

© Argosy Publishing, Inc.

Primary seizure focus

Corpus callosum

Thalamus

(a) Partial seizure

(b) Generalized seizure

foreign or strange. Consciousness is lost completely in generalized seizures. The two major categories of generalized seizure are the tonic-clonic and absence seizures. Tonic-clonic seizures begin with a loss of consciousness, cessation of breathing, and intense muscular contraction. This phase usually gives way to violent, rhythmic contractions that may result in broken bones or other physical injuries. These phases are followed by a period of coma, lasting about five minutes. In an absence seizure, the person briefly loses consciousness and awareness of his or her surroundings, and motor movements are limited to blinking, head turns, and eye movements.

How Do People Intentionally Alter Their States of Consciousness?

Human beings have intentionally altered consciousness in religious, recreational, and healing contexts. Methods may vary dramatically, but we will see that some common themes of these efforts emerge. Individuals who deliberately alter their state of consciousness may be seeking insight, positive emotion (bliss or ecstasy), or a sense of unity or "oneness." The universality of such efforts, which often underlie religious behavior, strongly suggests that these states confer some advantages, although what exactly those advantages may be remains unknown.

<table>
<tr><td>

General Features of Psychoactive Drugs

</td><td>

Historically, human beings have gone to great lengths to obtain **psychoactive drugs,** or substances that alter consciousness. It is no small task, for example, to domesticate a strain of poppy, grow it to

</td></tr>
</table>

maturity, slice its seed case with a sharp instrument, and collect the resulting sap, all for the sake of obtaining opium. In addition, the consequences of the illegal use of psychoactive substances provide further barriers to use.

Human beings may be unique among animals in their willingness to voluntarily seek alterations in consciousness through the deliberate use of psychoactive substances. Most psychoactive substances are quite poisonous (livestock eating tobacco leaves in the field will die) and usually have the bitter taste associated with most poisons. On the rare occasions when nonhuman animals do consume psychoactive substances (cats and catnip or elephants and alcohol), we have no way of knowing whether this consumption is motivated by a desire to alter consciousness.

Before we explore some of the drugs most frequently used to alter consciousness, we will outline several general principles related to the use of drugs, including tolerance, withdrawal, and addiction.

One of the remarkable aspects of human drug use is how much trouble people are willing to go to in order to obtain a drug. Opium poppies are not wild, but must be domesticated. The seed cases of the poppies must be scraped and the resulting sap collected. How this process was discovered remains a mystery.

Tolerance and Withdrawal **Tolerance** occurs when a person must take larger quantities of a drug in order to produce the desired effects. The nervous system is always working to maintain homeostasis, a steady internal balance or equilibrium. When a person takes a drug repeatedly, the nervous system attempts to compensate for the drug's effects. These compensations are both biological and learned (via mechanisms described in more detail in our chapter on learning). Tolerance may occur to some aspects of the drug's effects and not others. For instance, tolerance to the intoxicating effects of barbiturates occurs rapidly, whereas little if any tolerance occurs in the drug's ability to depress breathing. Many deaths due to respiratory failure result when the user boosts his or her dose of barbiturates to maintain the usual level of intoxication.

When some habitually used drugs are no longer available, the user might experience **withdrawal,** a set of behaviors that are the opposite of those produced by the drug. Withdrawing from alcohol, which inhibits the nervous system, produces a rebound effect characterized by so much excess brain activity that life-threatening seizures often occur. Withdrawing from stimulants like caffeine can make the user sluggish and lethargic (see ● Figure 6.17). Although many abused drugs produce significant withdrawal, others do not. Heroin and nicotine produce powerful withdrawal effects, but cocaine usually does not (Coffey, Dansky, Carrigan, & Brady, 2000).

psychoactive drug Any drug with the capability of altering a person's state of consciousness.

tolerance The need to administer greater quantities of a drug to achieve the same subjective effect.

withdrawal Physical responses to the removal of some habitually administered drugs.

addiction A physical or psychological dependence on a substance or activity.

Addiction **Addiction** is traditionally viewed as a physical or psychological dependence on a substance or activity. Although tolerance and withdrawal are two hallmark symptoms of physical dependence on a drug, not all

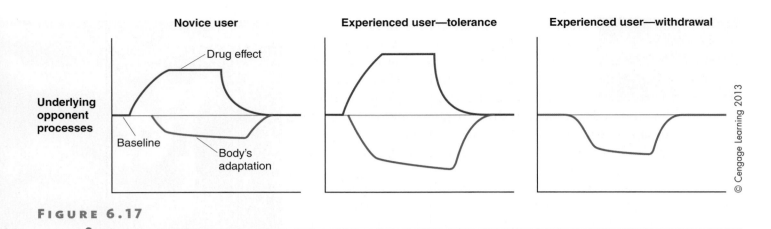

Novice user

Drug effect

Underlying opponent processes

Baseline

Body's adaptation

Experienced user—tolerance

Experienced user—withdrawal

© Cengage Learning 2013

FIGURE 6.17

Tolerance and Withdrawal. Some tolerance and withdrawal effects occur due to the body's efforts to maintain balance, or equilibrium. When a novice uses a drug for the first time, the body does react, but slowly, and the effects of the drug are strong. Tolerance develops when the body's compensations cancel out the drug's effects for the experienced user, who must take larger quantities of the drug to overcome the compensations and achieve the same subjective high. Finally, withdrawal occurs when a habitually used drug is no longer available to balance the body's compensations. As a result, withdrawal symptoms are usually the opposite of the drug's effects—a coffee drinker will feel fatigued without coffee, and an alcoholic might experience seizures due to high levels of brain excitation.

addictive drugs display these features. For example, cocaine is quite addictive in spite of its lack of withdrawal symptoms. The defining features of an addiction are the compulsive repetition of drug use or an activity and the inability to abstain from the addictive behavior in spite of serious negative consequences. Addiction overwhelms normal control of behavior, distorts typical systems of reward, and interferes with the recognition of problems.

Addictive drugs produce a variety of behavioral effects, ranging from stimulation to sedation, but many share the ability to stimulate the release of dopamine in the nucleus accumbens, a brain structure involved with our feelings of reward and pleasure. Researchers have reduced the self-administration of addictive drugs by lab animals by surgically lesioning the animals' nucleus accumbens (Bozarth & Wise, 1986; Zito, Vickers, & Robert, 1985). Does this result mean that lesions of the nucleus accumbens could "cure" human addicts? Quite possibly, but the procedure could not be done without a horrible cost to the patient. Without a functional nucleus accumbens, the ability to feel many types of normal pleasure would be lost.

Although it is true that the nucleus accumbens participates in addiction, higher cognitive and social processes are also intimately involved. As the Vietnam War was winding down in the early 1970s, health providers in the United States were gearing up for what they expected to be an epidemic of heroin addicts returning home. Due to the cheap and ready supply of heroin in Southeast Asia, along with

© Zalmaï/Edit by Getty Images

Should we be concerned about military veterans returning from service in Afghanistan with opium addictions? If the experiences of returning Vietnam veterans are repeated, the answer will be no. Even though heroin was readily available in Vietnam and large numbers of soldiers used heroin while serving, the vast majority quit using upon their return to the United States. These observations remind us that addiction is a complex phenomenon with multiple causes.

the obvious stress of combat, many American soldiers had begun to use the drug overseas. However, their behavior upon returning home took health providers completely by surprise. Less than 3% of the veterans who had tested positive for heroin upon their return to the United States remained "addicted" in a later follow-up test (Robins, Helzer, & Davis, 1975). A clear understanding of addiction includes not only its biological correlates but its social and motivational aspects as well.

Understanding human drug use, therefore, requires us to zoom out to incorporate multiple perspectives. In addition to the biological and social factors, we might ask about the possible adaptations provided by altering human consciousness or why younger people seem more vulnerable to addiction than older adults. Individual differences predict which people are more likely than others to become addicted. Through exploring the different classes of drugs historically used by humans with this more integrated perspective, we gain insight into why the human mind seeks altered states of consciousness in the face of substantial restrictions, consequences, and disapproval.

Hallucinogens

Hallucinogens are psychoactive substances capable of producing hallucinations, or false perceptions, interfering with the normal consciousness of sensory input. Hallucinogens have played an important role in producing religious visions over the ages in many cultures. Modern analyses of written accounts of "potions" used in medieval witchcraft include a number of hallucinogenic substances. Medieval witches didn't fly, but under the influence of the drugs they were using, they apparently believed they could do so (La Barre, 1975). Because of the cultural clash between the mystic qualities of hallucinogens and the decidedly practical and reality-based values of Western culture, hallucinogen use is frowned upon in many Western societies.

Mushrooms Among the most ancient hallucinogens is the fly agaric mushroom, or *Amanita muscaria*. As long as 3,000 years ago, use of *Amanita* was described as turning priests into "living gods" (Wasson, 1968). The *Amanita muscaria* mushroom contains chemicals that interact with GABA and glutamate in the brain to produce hallucination. A New World mushroom, *Psilocybe mexicana*, contains chemicals that boost serotonin activity, leading to vivid visual hallucinations and a psychotic state similar to a first episode of schizophrenia (Vollenweider, Vollenweider-Sherpenhuyzen, Bäbler, Vogel, & Hell, 1998).

Mescaline The green peyote cactus (*Lophophora williamsii*) grows across much of Mexico and the southwestern United States. This plant is a source for mescaline, which was popularized by Aldous Huxley in his book *The Doors of Perception* (Huxley, 1954). Like many hallucinogens, mescaline appears to influence serotonin activity, but its exact mechanism of action is not known.

© Chris Taylor/PictureNature/NHPA/Photoshot

One of the most ancient drugs used to deliberately alter a person's state of consciousness was the *Amanita* mushroom, which produces vivid hallucinations.

hallucinogen A drug that stimulates the experience of false perceptions.

Phencyclidine (PCP)   Phencyclidine (PCP) was originally used as an anesthetic, primarily in veterinary medicine. It is hard to imagine why somebody would purposely take PCP, as the effects are typically unpleasant. In addition to experiencing vivid hallucinations, users become aggressive to the point of being physically violent, and muscular tone becomes either rigid or too flexible. High doses can cause coma or convulsions.

PCP both decreases glutamate activity and increases dopamine activity (Gorelick & Balster, 1995). Because this drug often leads to a psychotic state resembling schizophrenia, researchers are considering the possibility that schizophrenia involves disruptions in normal glutamate and dopamine functioning. We discuss schizophrenia in more detail in our chapter on psychological disorders.

Marijuana   Cannabis, from the *Cannabis sativa* plant, is another drug with a long human history. It was included in the pharmacy written by Chinese Emperor Shen Neng nearly 5,000 years ago. Marijuana, the smoked form of cannabis, remains the most commonly used illegal substance in the United States today. The behavioral effects of cannabis are often so subtle that people may report no changes at all in response to its use. Most individuals experience some excitation, vivid imagery, and mild euphoria. Others respond with depression and social withdrawal. At somewhat higher doses, cannabis produces hallucinations, leading to its formal classification as a hallucinogen. Marijuana uniquely distorts a person's sense of time, distance, and speed, which is why people operating machinery, including automobiles, should not take it (Ramaekers et al., 2006).

Cannabis contains over 60 different psychoactive compounds, known as cannabinoids. The most important of these is tetrahydrocannabinol (THC). THC may produce some of its behavioral effects by interacting with receptors for endogenous cannabinoids, natural substances that are very similar to THC in chemical composition. These receptors are located in parts of the brain involved with pain, appetite, learning, and movement (see ● Figure 6.18). THC has the ability to stimulate dopamine activity, which in turn is usually associated with a potential for physical dependency (Merritt, Martin, Walters, Lichtman, & Damaj, 2008). In addition, a 25-year longitudinal study suggested that heavy and chronic use of marijuana among teens and young adults doubled their risk of developing schizophrenia, discussed further in our chapter on psychological disorders (Fergusson, Horwood, & Ridder, 2005).

LSD   In 1938, a group of Swiss pharmaceutical researchers began investigating potential headache remedies. During the course of the research, one of the scientists, Albert Hoffman, reported some unusual sensations after working with one of the compounds, lysergic acid diethylamide (LSD). Hoffman deliberately ingested some of the chemical and reported vivid, colorful visual hallucinations.

LSD is chemically similar to serotonin, and it interacts with serotonin receptors (Gonzalez-Maeso et al., 2008; Gonzalez-Maeso et al., 2007). LSD's ability to produce hallucination remains poorly

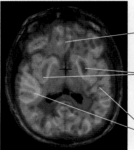

Prefrontal cortex

Basal ganglia

Hippocampus

FIGURE 6.18

Cannabinoid Receptors in the Human Brain. Like our natural opiate receptors that interact with opiate drugs, the brain contains cannabinoid receptors that interact with the major active ingredients found in marijuana. This PET scan shows a high density of cannabinoid receptors (areas of red and yellow) in the prefrontal cortex, the basal ganglia, and the hippocampus. The presence of cannabinoid receptors in the hippocampus and prefrontal cortex is believed to account for marijuana's negative effects on memory. *Source:* Burns et al. (2007).

understood. One of the interesting cognitive outcomes of LSD use is the experience of flashbacks, intrusive and involuntary hallucinations, even after the drug has been discontinued (Halpern & Pope, 2003). Further research will be necessary to identify the mechanisms for this experience.

Stimulants

Stimulants impact consciousness by increasing alertness and mobility, while decreasing reaction time. In contrast to negative attitudes toward hallucinogens, stimulant drugs have been embraced by cultures like our own where the ability to work long and hard is typically valued and rewarded.

Caffeine Caffeine is found in a wide range of sources, including coffee, tea, cola drinks, and many over-the-counter pain relievers (see ● Figure 6.19). Caffeine interferes with the inhibition normally produced by adenosine in the brain. If you keep an inhibitory substance like adenosine from doing its job, the result is increased excitation and alertness.

Caffeine produces dependency, as evidenced by the headaches and fatigue experienced by heavy users when the substance is not available. Some people experience problems with heart rhythms related to caffeine use. Because caffeine crosses the placenta easily and the fetus takes much longer than an adult to clear caffeine from its system, pregnant women are advised to avoid all sources of caffeine (Reznick, 1999). On the positive side, caffeine use is correlated with a lower risk of Parkinson's disease, which causes difficulty moving (Ross & Petrovitch, 2001), Alzheimer's disease, and other forms of dementia (Eskelinen & Kivipelto, 2010). Because these are correlations, we don't know whether the apparent protection against these conditions is due to some specific action of caffeine in the brain or is simply the result of the characteristics of people who enjoy large amounts of caffeine.

The Huichol Indians of Mexico and the American Southwest have traditionally used mescaline from the peyote cactus as an important part of their religious rituals. Huichol artwork reflects the colorful hallucinations that are the typical result of mescaline use and often feature the green peyote cactus, as shown on this beaded prayer bowl.

© J Kevin Foltz/Stellar Stock/Photolibrary
© West1/Dreamstime

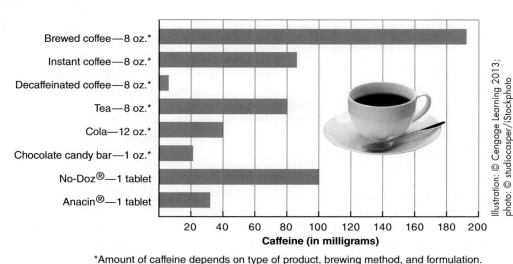

*Amount of caffeine depends on type of product, brewing method, and formulation.

Illustration: © Cengage Learning 2013; photo: © studiocasper/iStockphoto

FIGURE 6.19

Sources of Caffeine. Although most people think immediately of coffee when they hear the word "caffeine," caffeine actually can be found in many different beverages, foods, and over-the-counter medications. *Source: Adapted from Byer and Shainberg (1995).*

stimulant Any drug that increases the activity of the nervous system.

Nicotine After caffeine, the most commonly used stimulant in the United States is nicotine, usually in the form of smoked or chewed tobacco (see ● Figure 6.20). Nicotine mimics the action of the neurotransmitter acetylcholine, increasing heart rate and blood pressure, reducing fatigue, and improving cognitive performance, while at the same time producing muscular relaxation. Normally, when we are mentally alert, our bodies feel somewhat tense, so nicotine's combination of relaxation with alertness is unique.

In spite of repeated warnings of the dangers of using nicotine, it continues to be a very widely used substance. Nicotine use typically begins in adolescence, and adolescents become more rapidly dependent on the substance than adults (Dani & Harris, 2005). Although many social factors contribute to the use of psychoactive substances, nicotine use shows high correlations with later problems with alcohol and other drugs. In addition, people with psychological disorders, schizophrenia and depression in particular, are very likely to use nicotine. Thirty-four percent of all nicotine products sold in the United States is used by the 7% of the population that has a diagnosed psychological disorder (Dani & Harris, 2005). Once again, because these are correlations, we do not know whether nicotine has any causal role in the development of psychological disorders or whether people vulnerable to disorders are simply more likely to enjoy the effects of nicotine.

Cocaine and Amphetamine The behavioral effects of cocaine and amphetamine are quite similar to one another, as both substances boost dopamine activity in the brain. Because of their direct effects on the dopamine

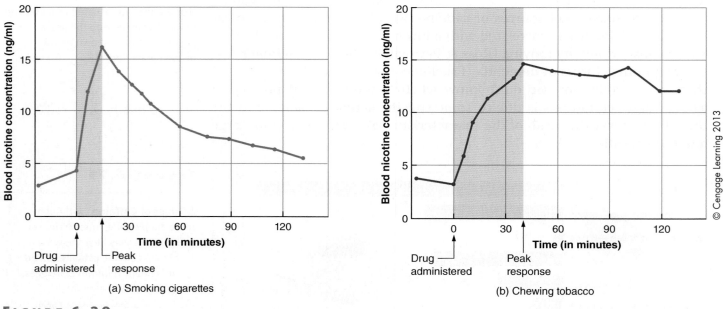

(a) Smoking cigarettes

(b) Chewing tobacco

FIGURE 6.20

© Cengage Learning 2013

Concentration of a Drug in the Blood Supply Depends on the Method of Administration. Drug effects are dependent on the concentration of the drug in the blood supply, and some methods of administration produce effective concentrations faster than others. In the case of nicotine, smoking a cigarette produces a much faster increase in blood nicotine concentration than chewing an equivalent dose of tobacco. However, chewing tobacco produces higher sustained concentrations of nicotine than smoking does. *Source: Adapted from Bennet* (1983).

reward systems of the brain, these drugs are among the most rapidly addictive substances commonly used. At moderate doses, cocaine and amphetamine produce alertness, elevated mood, confidence, and a sense of well-being. At higher doses, these drugs can produce symptoms that are quite similar to schizophrenia. Users experience hallucinations, such as a feeling of bugs running on the skin, and delusional fears that others are trying to harm them. Some users experience repetitive motor behaviors, such as chewing movements or grinding the teeth. Methamphetamine, the current commonly abused form of amphetamine, is particularly likely to lead to symptoms of psychosis (McKetin, McLaren, Lubman, & Hides, 2006).

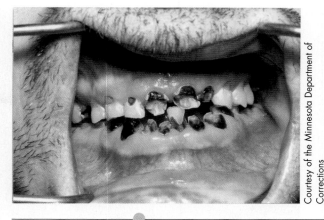

Not only does methamphetamine abuse frequently lead to hallucinations and delusions similar to those caused by schizophrenia, but users experience additional health issues, including a characteristic pattern of dental decay known as "meth mouth." This condition results from the mouth dryness and the clenching and grinding of teeth caused by the drug.

Cocaine, extracted from the leaf of the coca plant, was originally used by the indigenous people of Peru as a mild stimulant and appetite suppressant. Sigmund Freud recommended the use of cocaine in his 1885 book, *Über Coca* (*On Coca*). Freud became disenchanted with the drug when he became aware of its potential for addiction. Historically, cocaine has been added to many popular products, including the original formulation of Coca-Cola. When cocaine was designated a controlled substance, the Coca-Cola Company merely substituted caffeine for cocaine in its highly secret formula.

Amphetamine was originally marketed as a treatment for asthma, and inhalers containing the drug were sold without prescription through the 1940s. It has been widely used by military pilots to ward off fatigue and was sold to 1960s American housewives as a diet aid. Like cocaine, amphetamine's addictive potential led to its being classified a controlled substance.

Methylphenidate (Ritalin) The use of stimulant medications like methylphenidate (Ritalin) for attention problems resulted from an accidental discovery in 1937, when Charles Bradley gave stimulant drugs to a group of children with learning and behavior problems. The children referred to the drugs as their "math pill," because they found it easier to do their math homework while using the medication.

As we will see in our chapter on psychological disorders, children today who are diagnosed with attention deficit hyperactivity disorder (ADHD) are still very likely to take stimulant drugs. The two most common choices are methylphenidate (Ritalin) or a combination of amphetamine salts (Adderall). Both of these drugs boost the activity of dopamine and norepinephrine, which in turn increases users' ability to stay alert and concentrate. At clinical doses, these drugs do not seem to produce dependence, although they affect sleep and appetite. It is a

Prior to World War I, many commercial products contained cocaine. Sigmund Freud originally believed that cocaine was an effective antidepressant. The ability of cocaine to produce rapid addiction eventually changed people's minds about the safety of the drug.

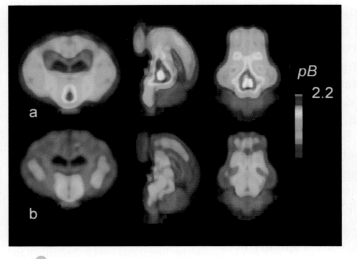

Ethical constraints limit many investigations of drug effects to animals. In this study, researchers observed the effects of MDMA (Ecstasy) use in a pig. The dose of MDMA given to the pig was comparable to doses typical of a chronic recreational human user. (a) These scans indicate the ability of the pigs' brains to bind serotonin, which allows the neurotransmitter to function normally. Red, white, and yellow colors indicate high binding potential, and green, blue, and purple areas indicate less binding potential. (b) Following administration of MDMA, no red, white, or yellow areas remain, showing that the ability to bind serotonin was greatly reduced. From Cumming et al., A PET study of effects of chronic 3, 4-methylenedioxymethamphetamine (MDMA, "ecstasy") on serotonin markers in Göttingen minipig brain. *Synapse*, 2007 Jul, *61*(7), 478–487.

depressant A drug that reduces the overall activity of the nervous system.

common misconception that people will not respond to these drugs with increased concentration unless they have been diagnosed with ADHD. Everybody reacts to these drugs in similar ways, which has led to an increase in their non-prescribed use by college students and others wishing to get a competitive edge in intellectual work.

MDMA (Ecstasy) MDMA (Ecstasy) is a relative of amphetamine and mescaline that increases heart rate, blood pressure, and body temperature. MDMA increases sociability by stimulating the activity of serotonin and oxytocin, a hormone believed to participate in romantic and parental bonding (Thompson, Callaghan, Hunt, Cornish, & McGregor, 2007). Use of MDMA is controversial, with some scientists expressing concern about its apparent detrimental effects on neurons that release serotonin (Capela et al., 2007). Some therapists, however, argue that MDMA might be beneficial to individuals with post-traumatic stress disorder (PTSD), although research evidence for such benefits is lacking (Parrott, 2007).

Depressants

Depressants share the ability to slow down the activity of the nervous system, leading to reductions in alertness and anxiety. Major substances in this category act to boost the activity of the inhibitory neurotransmitter GABA. Because these drugs all converge on the GABA receptor, combining them often results in a fatal level of nervous system inhibition.

Alcohol Alcohol is one of the earliest psychoactive drugs used by humans, dating back into our prehistory. In addition to seeking the relaxation produced by alcohol, early humans might have turned to fermented beverages as a safety precaution against contaminated water supplies, as alcohol has natural antiseptic qualities.

Alcohol's status as a depressant drug might seem confusing in light of its frequent use at parties. Why would anyone take a depressant to have a good time? The answer lies in alcohol's ability to slow down activity in the judgment areas of the cortex, reducing behavioral inhibitions. At low doses, alcohol dilates blood vessels, giving people a warm, flushed feeling. It reduces anxiety, which makes relatively shy people more outgoing at a party. At higher doses, alcohol's inhibition of the higher levels of the brain leads to aggression, risky behaviors, and poor motor coordination. At very high doses, alcohol can produce coma and death, either from suppression of breathing or aspiration of vomit.

As with nicotine, the adverse effects of alcohol do not seem to have much of an impact on its use (see ● Figure 6.21). Not only is alcohol potentially addictive, but it can have devastating effects on the developing fetus, which we discuss further in our chapter on development. Chronic alcoholism can permanently impact the frontal lobes and hippocampus, leading to memory and other cognitive deficits (Harper & Matsumoto, 2005). For

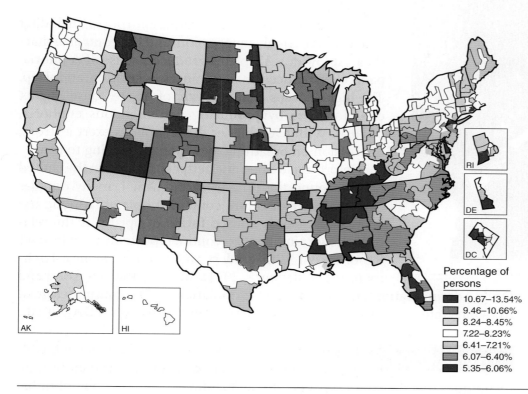

FIGURE 6.21

Alcohol Dependence Varies Geographically. Overall, the rate of alcohol dependence among individuals age 12 and over in the United States is 7.7%. Rates range from 5.4% in southern Utah to 13.5% in south-central Wyoming. Most of the areas with the highest percentage of alcohol dependence are located in the West and Midwest, but reasons for these regional differences are not clear.
Source: Adapted from SAMHSA (2006).

Percentage of persons

- 10.67–13.54%
- 9.46–10.66%
- 8.24–8.45%
- 7.22–8.23%
- 6.41–7.21%
- 6.07–6.40%
- 5.35–6.06%

© Cengage Learning 2013

women with a family history of breast cancer, as little as one-half ounce per day of alcohol (the equivalent of 5 ounces of wine or 12 ounces of beer) can significantly increase the risk of developing cancer (Hulka & Moorman, 2002). Countering these concerns are findings that consuming that same one-half ounce per day or less is correlated with a lower risk of heart disease (Kloner & Rezkalla, 2007).

The social costs of alcohol are just as remarkable as its costs to health. Because of alcohol's action on judgment and impulsivity, this effect might not be surprising. Alcohol is implicated in 68% of murders, 88% of knife attacks, 65% of spousal abuse incidents, and 55% of physical child abuse incidents (Steele & Josephs, 1990). Alcohol is also involved with the majority of suicides.

Benzodiazepines and Barbiturates Like alcohol, benzodiazepines and barbiturates act to increase the inhibition of the nervous system produced by GABA. Also like alcohol, these substances can produce powerful dependence.

Benzodiazepines and barbiturates have legitimate medical uses, such as the reduction of anxiety or the control of seizure activity. At the higher doses associated with nonprescription use, many users experience a sense of euphoria.

Opiates The opium poppy is the source of several natural psychoactive opiates, including morphine and codeine. Heroin can be synthesized through further processing of morphine. These substances are effective because they imitate the action of our natural opiates, or endorphins (which is short for endogenous morphine).

Opiates have legitimate medical purposes, including pain control, cough suppression, and the control of diarrhea. At low doses, opiates produce a sense of euphoria, pain relief, reduced anxiety, muscle relaxation, and sleep. The higher doses characteristic of opiate abuse impact consciousness by producing a tremendous euphoria, or rush. With even higher doses, opiates exert a strong depression on breathing, occasionally leading to death.

Before opiates became better controlled in the United States around the time of World War I, many popular "tonics," like laudanum, contained opiates. Among the current frequently abused forms of opiates is the relatively new painkiller Oxycontin, reportedly used by over 8% of recent 12th graders (Johnston, O'Malley, Bachman, & Schulenberg, 2011). In 2010, the U.S. Food and Drug Administration approved a new formulation of Oxycontin designed to reduce rates of abuse (U.S. Food and Drug Administration [FDA], 2010).

The National Hockey League's Derek Boogaard was found dead in his apartment just before he would have celebrated his 29th birthday. An autopsy indicated that Boogaard died of a combination of alcohol and oxycodone (Oxycontin).

Hypnosis

Hypnosis, another method of deliberately influencing consciousness, has its roots in various healing techniques that date back through human history. Ancient peoples of India, Egypt, and Greece reported techniques that are quite similar to modern inductions of hypnosis. Current interest in hypnosis may be traced to the work of Franz Anton Mesmer (1734–1815), whose name gives us the popular term *mesmerized*. Hypnosis moved into the realm of psychotherapy with the work of Jean-Martin Charcot and his student, Sigmund Freud, whom we discuss in our chapters on personality and therapy. Freud was intrigued by the potential of using hypnosis in psychotherapy, but later abandoned the practice.

How can we define hypnosis? A consensus statement issued by the American Psychological Association (2005b) offers the following definition:

> When using hypnosis, one person (the subject) is guided by another (the hypnotist) to respond to suggestions for changes in subjective experience, alterations in perception, sensation, emotion, thought or behavior.

Psychologists are divided in their opinions about whether hypnosis represents a truly altered state of consciousness. Early research suggested that hypnotized people were more likely to comply with requests to do dangerous things, such as pick up a poisonous snake or throw a beaker of what they believed to be acid into an experimenter's face (Rowland, 1939; Young, 1952). However, later experiments showed that equal compliance could be obtained with participants who were not hypnotized (Orne & Evans, 1965). In these situations, the participants' strong belief that the experimenters would be unwilling to harm them overrode any measurable influence of hypnosis.

Other psychologists firmly believe that hypnosis represents a distinctly altered state of consciousness. When PET scans of hypnotized participants were correlated with self-reports of their hypnotized experience, several

hypnosis An altered state of consciousness characterized by relaxation and increased suggestibility.

structures that play important roles in consciousness, including the anterior cingulate cortex and the thalamus, showed characteristic changes in activity when a person was hypnotized (Rainville, Hofbauer, Bushnell, Duncan, & Price, 2002).

Some of the more grandiose claims on behalf of hypnosis, such as its ability to sharpen perception or improve memory, were discounted to a large degree by the careful experimental analyses conducted by behaviorist Clark Hull (1933). Hull's work demonstrated that hypnosis was not at all related to sleep and that hypnotized participants were very much awake. His work also supported the use of hypnosis for pain relief, which continues to be one of the more useful applications of this procedure.

Individuals are clearly different in their susceptibility to hypnotism, and several scales have been developed to measure these differences. One factor that may account for these individual differences is the likelihood that a person would suspend critical judgment and accept the authority of the hypnotist over his or her own beliefs. This suspension of judgment may accompany changes in brain activity. In one experiment, highly hypnotizable participants were recruited for a study of picture processing (Kosslyn, Thompson, Costantini-Ferrando, Alpert, & Spiegel, 2000). Following hypnotic induction, participants were exposed to color and gray-scale pictures and patterns under the hypnotic suggestion that the stimulus would be presented in color or gray scale. Results revealed that the participants reported seeing a color pattern when they had been told one was being presented whether the pattern that was actually presented was a color or a gray-scale pattern. Similarly, the participants reported seeing a gray-scale pattern when they had been told a gray-scale pattern was being presented whether the pattern that was actually presented was a color or a gray-scale pattern.

Results in which hypnotized individuals have reported what the hypnotist instructed them to feel have been criticized in the past as not producing changes in psychological content or experience but only in producing compliance in terms of what the participants said they saw (Kirsch & Lynn, 1995). However, in the study described in the previous paragraph, the researchers also performed positron emission tomography (PET) scanning during the presentation of the pictures. Results of the PET data indicated that areas of the brain known to respond to color were activated when highly hypnotizable participants were asked to perceive color, whether the participant had actually been shown the color or the gray-scale stimulus, and these brain regions showed decreased activation when the highly hypnotizable participants were told they would see gray-scale, whether they were actually shown the color or gray-scale stimuli (see ● Figure 6.22). In low-hypnotizable participants, on the other hand, changes in brain activation in these regions were greater when color than when gray-scale pictures were presented. Thus, observed changes in subjective experience achieved during hypnosis were reflected by changes in brain function similar to those that occur in perception, supporting the claim that hypnosis can produce actual changes in psychological *experience* in high- but not low-hypnotizable participants.

Although the results of this research are controversial, the scientists argue that their data support the existence of an altered state during

Breath is the bridge which connects life to consciousness, which unites your body to your thoughts.
—Thich Nhat Hanh

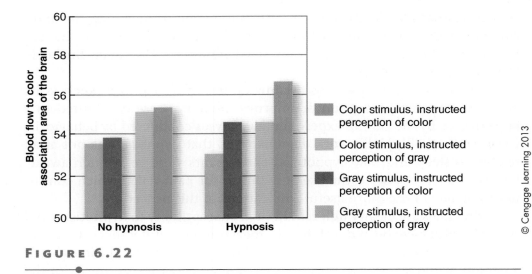

FIGURE 6.22

The Brain Responds to Hypnotic Suggestions to "See" Color. This study compared the blood flow, which is correlated with brain activity, in an area of the brain known to respond to the identification of colors in participants who were either hypnotized or not hypnotized. As you can see in the "no hypnosis" condition, participants' blood flow did not change as a result of the instructions to "see" gray or color. Whether the stimulus was actually gray or a color determined their response, regardless of instructions. However, under hypnosis, we can see that the brain responded to the instructions. In both the gray and color conditions, the hypnotized participants showed more brain activity when they were told they would see color. In fact, hypnotized participants instructed to "see" color showed about the same brain activity as non-hypnotized participants who actually did see color. Adapted from Kosslyn et al. (2000).

(a)   (b)

Red   Blue
Yellow   **Green**
Blue   **Yellow**
Green   Red
Green   **Green**
Yellow   **Blue**
Blue   **Red**

FIGURE 6.23

Hypnosis and the Stroop Test.
Under normal circumstances, participants identify ink colors much faster when (a) the color of the letters matches the word being read (the word *red* appears in a red font) than when (b) it doesn't match (the word *red* appears in a yellow or green font). Highly suggestible hypnotized participants told that they were reading nonsense words instead of real words did not show this typical difference. Their reaction time for naming the ink color was the same whether it matched the color name or not.

hypnosis. They speculate that hypnosis produces dissociation between what is seen and what participants are told should be seen. Such sensory dissociation also supports the use of hypnosis in pain control. In such cases, a burn patient may be told during hypnosis that he or she feels cool and comfortable. If the brain can "color" gray squares on command during hypnosis, it can probably feel coolness instead of burning as well.

Further evidence that behavior under hypnosis is more than social conformity was provided using a task known as the Stroop Test (Raz, Kirsch, Pollard, & Nitkin-Kaner, 2006; Stroop, 1935). In this test, participants are simply asked to respond to the color of the letters they are shown (see ● Figure 6.23). When the ink color and the word are congruent (e.g., the word *red* appears in red ink), reaction time is significantly faster (100–200 msec faster) than when the ink color and the word are incongruent (e.g., the word *red* appears in green ink). Nearly everyone who can read shows a robust Stroop effect, and extensive training does not make the effect go away. This effect is typically explained in terms of a well-practiced skill (reading) taking precedence over a less practiced skill (naming the colors of letters). When instructed to ignore the practiced skill, attention is compromised, and reaction time becomes slower.

Using a posthypnotic suggestion, the researchers told their participants to respond to a cue by viewing the stimuli as gibberish instead of real words. Participants who were rated as having low suggestibility performed in a typical manner on the Stroop Test. In contrast, participants rated as having high suggestibility demonstrated little difference between the amount of time needed to identify the ink colors in the congruent and incongruent conditions. The ability of posthypnotic suggestion to minimize the Stroop effect is remarkable, because other efforts to modulate the effect have all failed. Clearly, hypnotic suggestion has the ability to reorganize cognitive processes, at least in highly suggestible individuals.

In many popular accounts, hypnosis is believed to enhance memory. Controlled laboratory studies indicate that hypnosis does not improve memory performance at all (Kihlstrom, 1997; Kihlstrom & Barnhardt, 1993; Kihlstrom & Eich, 1994). However, as hypnosis researcher John Kihlstrom relates, "There is no question that subjects who receive suggestions for performance enhancement often have the impression that their performance is in fact improved over baseline" (Kihlstrom, 1997, p. 4).

In spite of empirical research to the contrary, websites proudly endorse training in "forensic hypnosis," which promises to solve crimes by improving the memories of witnesses. In many states, however, testimony taken during hypnosis is no longer admissible in a court of law.

The more typical effect of hypnosis on memory is to make it worse. Episodic memories, or memories for events in our personal past, are the most vulnerable to disruption through hypnosis (Kihlstrom, 1997). In addition, hypnosis promotes false recollections. When highly suggestible participants were given the false suggestion during hypnosis that they had awakened to a noise on a particular night, all the participants "remembered" this event following hypnosis, and half of them continued to believe the event even when informed of the nature of the experiment by the researchers (Laurence & Perry, 1983). Unfortunately, hypnosis not only allows false memories to be implanted easily, but it increases the confidence participants have in the accuracy of such memories (Whitehouse, Dinges, Orne, & Orne, 1988). These results support the rejection of hypnosis by the American Psychological Association (APA) as a technique to be used when discussing possible memories of childhood sexual abuse, which we discuss in our chapter on memory.

What, then, can hypnosis actually accomplish? Research supports the use of hypnosis by qualified practitioners for treating pain, depression, anxiety, phobias, stress, habit disorders, postsurgical

The American Psychotherapy Association

hereby awards

Zoe D. Katze, Ph.D.

the designation of

Diplomate

with all the rights, benefits and privileges pertaining thereto, as long as membership requirements are met and the Psychotherapist's Oath of the American Psychotherapy Association is upheld.

Brent McCoy
Chief Association Officer

Michael A. Baer, Ph.D., DAPA
Chair, Executive Advisory Board

Member since
July 27, 2001

Member ID
6568

This certificate is the property of the American Psychotherapy Association, and in the event of its impression, revocation or invalidation for any reason, it must be returned on demand to the American Psychotherapy Association.

APA

AMERICAN PSYCHOTHERAPY ASSOCIATION

© Cengage Learning 2013

Frustrated licensed psychotherapist Steve Eichel demonstrated the lack of regulation of hypnotherapists by managing to acquire a number of impressive looking credentials for Zoe D. Katze, who happens to be Eichel's cat. Zoe's name is a wordplay on the German *die Katze*, which literally means "the cat."

© Sergey Peterman/ Shutterstock

recovery, and many other psychological and medical conditions (American Psychological Association [APA], 2005b). The cautionary note about qualified practitioners arises from the fact that hypnotherapy is largely unregulated in the United States. Therapist Steve Eichel was able to assemble an impressive set of hypnotherapy credentials and professional memberships, complete with the stunning diploma shown in the accompanying photo, on behalf of Zoe D. Katze, who just happened to be Eichel's cat (Eichel, 2002). Zoe D. Katze, or Zoe die Katze, literally translates from German to English as "Zoe the Cat." This exploit does not imply that all hypnotherapists are fakes, but it does suggest that potential clients should do their homework before selecting a therapist.

Meditation

Meditation techniques vary widely and may occur in either religious or nonreligious contexts. When experienced practitioners are asked to describe the subjective experience produced by meditation, they describe a conscious state without thought, accompanied by a blissful emotional state (Travis, 1993).

EEG recordings during meditation feature increased proportions of alpha waves, which we described earlier as being characteristic of an awake but relaxed state. However, these findings are not believed to represent any unique state of consciousness (Vaitl et al., 2005). In participants who had meditated more than three years, increased theta activity, normally found in lighter stages of sleep, was observed over the frontal lobes of the brain (Aftanas & Golocheikine, 2001). Theta activity in the prefrontal areas of the brain has been correlated with positive emotions (Aftanas, Varlamov, Pavlov, Makhnev, & Reva, 2001).

Imaging studies using functional MRI suggest that meditation represents a voluntary regulation of attention and autonomic functions (Lazar et al., 2000). In addition, meditation appears to result in physical changes in the brain. Meditation has been correlated with increased cortical thickness (Lazar et al., 2005) and increased gray matter in the brainstem (Vestergaard-Poulsen et al., 2009). The increased cortical thickness was more noticeable in older participants, suggesting that meditation might offset typical age-related thinning of the cortex (see ● Figure 6.24).

Other Deliberate Changes in Consciousness

A variety of environmental conditions have significant effects on consciousness, including exposure to high altitudes during mountain climbing, underwater conditions in scuba diving, starvation, sleep deprivation, sensory deprivation, twirling, and rhythm-induced trance. These conditions may lead to hallucination and other consistent changes in cognition and emotion.

Several of these environmental factors characterize vision quests, which typically take place within religious contexts. In the traditional Native American vision quest, preparation typically involved 3 to 4 days of starvation and sleep loss. The individual would travel to an isolated location where no shelter could be built. The seeker would then be instructed to concentrate and watch for the appearance of a "guardian." This combination

meditation A voluntary alteration of consciousness characterized by positive emotion and absence of thought.

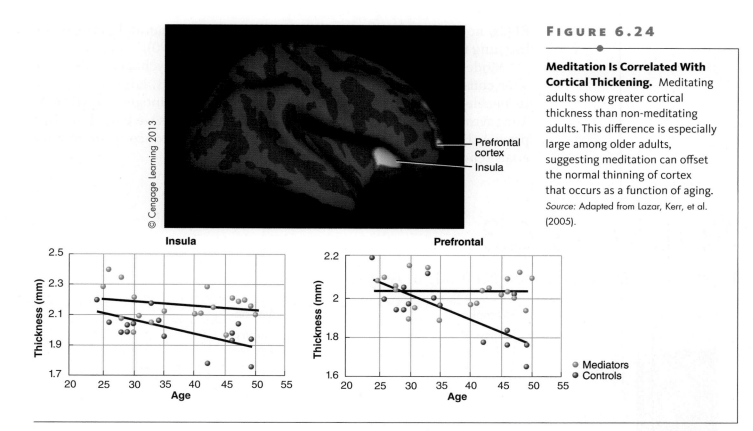

FIGURE 6.24

Meditation Is Correlated With Cortical Thickening. Meditating adults show greater cortical thickness than non-meditating adults. This difference is especially large among older adults, suggesting meditation can offset the normal thinning of cortex that occurs as a function of aging. *Source:* Adapted from Lazar, Kerr, et al. (2005).

of events reliably led seekers to experience the following phenomena: a distorted sense of time, a sensation of "oneness," the appearance of light, the emotion of ecstasy or bliss, and a sense of improved insight (Steiger, 2000). Note the similarities between these experiences and the reported effects of many hallucinogens.

We have all observed young children experiment with their bodies by spinning. Although we do not know the precise reason for such spinning behavior, other than it's just fun, spinning probably represents the child's efforts to alter his or her sensory and cognitive states. Spinning is also used as a meditation-inducing method by the Sufis, a mystic Muslim sect. Sufis may whirl for an hour or more before falling to the ground, where they seek a feeling of oneness with the earth.

It is very likely that dancing has been a part of human cultures for many thousands of years, both for recreational and religious purposes. Accompanied by the equally ancient practice of drumming, dance is capable of initiating trancelike states in the participants (Vaitl et al., 2005). The American Psychiatric Association defines a trance state as an altered state of consciousness accompanied by an unusually narrow focus of attention and movements believed to be beyond the individual's control (APA, 2000). The altered states induced by drumming and dancing include distortion of time, vivid imagery, and strong positive emotions (ecstasy, bliss; Vaitl et al., 2005). Participants listening to rhythmic drumming showed more theta wave activity in their

Sufis belong to a mystic Muslim sect that uses spinning as a means of inducing a state of meditation. Spinning can last an hour or more, after which the Sufi typically falls to the ground and experiences a sense of oneness with the earth.

EEGs, normally associated with light N-REM sleep, than did participants listening to unstructured beat sequences (Maxfield, 1990).

Modern youth are fond of combining dance and psychoactive drugs to alter consciousness, particularly in the context of raves, large parties featuring electronic music, darkness, and the use of hallucinogens or MDMA. The raves feature some themes common to the contexts we have described previously. Unity, or oneness, and positive emotion are once again primary goals reported by the participants.

Summary 6.3

Psychoactive Drugs and Their Methods of Action

Drug class	Examples	Acts on
Hallucinogens © Chris Taylor/ PictureNature/NHPA/ Photoshot	Phencyclidine (PCP) LSD Marijuana	Glutamate Serotonin Endogenous cannabinoids
Stimulants Courtesy of the Minnesota Department of Corrections	Caffeine Nicotine Cocaine, amphetamine Methylphenidate MDMA (Ecstasy)	Adenosine Acetylcholine Dopamine Serotonin, Oxytocin
Depressants © Cengage Learning 2013	Alcohol Benzodiazepines Barbiturates	GABA GABA GABA
Opiates © Scott A. Schneider/Getty Images	Heroin, morphine, codeine, Oxycontin	Endogenous endorphins

Interpersonal Relationships
From a Perspective of Consciousness

We engage in a variety of unconscious behaviors, and not just when we're asleep. Among the unconscious behaviors that have been identified by psychologists is one that is particularly relevant to relationships—the effect of mimicry on liking and feeling close to others (Lakin, Chartrand, & Arkin, 2008). A substantial body of research supports the idea that we unconsciously copy the behavior of others and that when we do copy another person's behavior, he or she likes us better without necessarily knowing why.

Under what circumstances are we most likely to copy the behavior of other people? One possible answer is that we mimic others to avoid or repair social exclusion. Jessica Lakin and her colleagues (2008) made their participants feel socially excluded (temporarily, of course) and then observed that these excluded participants were more likely to mimic another person than were participants who had not been socially excluded. This process extends to group membership as well. Participants excluded by an in-group were subsequently more likely to mimic an in-group member than an out-group member. These results suggest that mimicry developed as an automatic behavior that we could use to respond to threats to our social connectivity, which as we have stated many times previously, could have been a matter of life or death to our hunter-gatherer ancestors.

Because this mimicry is quite automatic and unconscious, we are usually not aware that we are behaving this way. Knowing now that this is an adaptive behavior, look more closely at how you behave when encountering situations in which you feel excluded. It could be a social situation, such as at a party or an organizational event, where you are trying to mingle or initiate a dialogue with others. Or perhaps you observe mimicry when you are around someone you like romantically. Do you feign interest in things you wouldn't necessarily be interested in otherwise? Are you more apt to align yourself with the personality of the person you find interesting? Do you see this kind of behavior in friends or family?

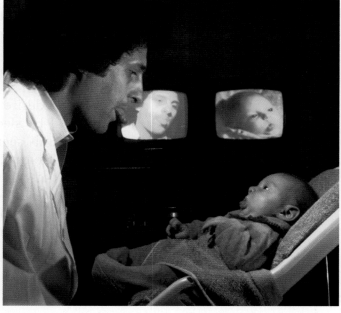

© E. Ferorelli/photo courtesy Andrew Meltzoff, Ph.D.

Babies as young as 2 to 3 weeks imitate the facial expressions of an adult. It is possible that one of the purposes of imitation is to avoid social exclusion. People like us better when we imitate their behavior.

Chapter **6**
Reflections

We introduced this chapter on consciousness by asking a very challenging question: do we or do we not have free will?

It certainly feels like we do, but after reading this chapter, you probably realize that our conscious awareness of the activities of our own mind has its limitations. We mimic others without being aware of doing so and respond correctly to lights and angry faces that we cannot consciously "see." Sometimes, we understand that a nightmare is "just a dream" that we can decide to turn off deliberately, but in other cases, we feel trapped.

Perhaps some of the deliberate attempts people make to change consciousness, such as the use of drugs, drumming, dancing, and meditation, arose from a desire to gain insight into the natural variations in consciousness caused by sleep, wakefulness, coma, and death. These phenomena would certainly seem mysterious prior to the discovery of scientific explanations for their occurrence. The self-awareness accompanying a conscious mind might also have led to a recognition of separateness from others and an associated risk for feeling lonely. These feelings of separateness might have stimulated other deliberate variations in consciousness that share the theme of seeking unity or oneness, which is often associated with positive emotion or bliss. ‹

KEY TERMS The Language of Psychological Science

Be sure you can define these terms and use them correctly.

addiction, p. 267
alpha wave, p. 247
beta wave, p. 247
biological clock, p. 243
circadian rhythm, p. 243
coma, p. 261
consciousness, p. 236
delta wave, p. 250
depressant, p. 274
dreaming, p. 255
hallucinogen, p. 269
hypnosis, p. 276
insomnia, p. 257

lucid dreaming, p. 256
meditation, p. 280
narcolepsy, p. 257
near-death experience, p. 263
night terror, p. 257
non-rapid eye movement (N-REM)
    sleep, p. 249
persistent vegetative state
    (PVS), p. 262
psychoactive drug, p. 267
rapid eye movement (REM)
    sleep, p. 249
restless legs syndrome (RLS), p. 259

seasonal affective disorder
    (SAD), p. 246
seizure, p. 265
self-awareness, p. 237
sleep, p. 243
sleep apnea, p. 259
stimulant, p. 271
sudden infant death syndrome
    (SIDS), p. 259
theta wave, p. 249
tolerance, p. 267
wakefulness, p. 243
withdrawal, p. 267

MEDIA RESOURCES

Log in to CengageBrain to access the resources your instructor requires. For this book, you can access:

Psychology **CourseMate** brings course concepts to life with interactive learning, study, and exam preparation tools that support the printed textbook. A textbook-specific website, Psychology **CourseMate** includes an integrated interactive eBook and other interactive learning tools including quizzes, flashcards, videos, and more.

WebTUTOR   More than just an interactive study guide, **WebTutor** is an anytime, anywhere customized learning solution with an eBook, keeping you connected to your textbook, instructor, and classmates.

aplia If your professor has assigned **Aplia** homework:
1. Sign in to your account.
2. Complete the corresponding homework exercises as required by your professor.
3. When finished, click "Grade It Now" to see which areas you have mastered, which areas need more work, and detailed explanations of every answer.

Axons from the sympathetic nervous system form connections in the gut, contributing to those butterflies we feel at times of excitement.

The Feeling Mind

7

Motivation and Emotion

Learning Objectives

1 Differentiate emotion and motivation, and analyze their relationship to each other.

2 Analyze the physiological and environmental factors that influence hunger and eating.

3 Assess the roles of evolved preferences and physiological and environmental factors in sexual motivation, considering how this motivation varies with gender and over time.

4 Compare and contrast achievement and affiliation motivation in terms of predictors and implication for life outcomes.

5 Associate aspects of emotional responding with activation of central and autonomic nervous system structures.

6 Evaluate the roles of nature, nurture, and their interaction in explaining human communication of emotion, based on research evidence.

7 Differentiate major theories of emotion in terms of the relationship between physical sensations and subjective feelings.

Motivation and emotion, the topics of this chapter, involve neural circuits that often operate below the level of our conscious awareness. We don't decide consciously to feel happy or sad or hungry or thirsty, but instead, we react somewhat automatically to the environment around and within us. We can zoom in to look at these neural circuits, like these sympathetic axons (in blue) forming connections with the gut. We have all had the feeling of butterflies in our stomach when we are excited, and neural pathways like this one are responsible for such feelings.

Zooming out, we can examine motivation and emotion in the larger context of the individual using the example of elite athletes at the Olympic Games. The 2008 Beijing Olympics featured 11,028 athletes who represented the very best in their respective sports, just a tiny fraction of the millions of people who compete in athletics worldwide. To stand out among these elites takes even more

© Michael Steele/Allsport/Getty Images

287

extreme motivation, not to mention talent and hard work. Many athletes competing at this level have focused on their sport to the exclusion of most other activities since they were in elementary school. Yet of the over 11,000 participants, only 1,881 (or 17%) went home with a medal.

Given the odds of obtaining a medal, you would think that any athlete winning one would be absolutely ecstatic, but that is not always the case. As you can see in the photograph on the preceding page of Olympic swimmers on the medal stand, the athletes are showing a range of emotions. Look for a moment at the way the three athletes are holding their flower bouquets. The gold and bronze medalists are holding their bouquets straight up, but the silver medalist is close to dropping his bouquet. His entire demeanor says dejection and disappointment.

Why would a silver medalist be disappointed with such an exceptional achievement? To answer this question, we must zoom out even farther from the individual to consider the social context. Psychologists have found that the reactions of these swimmers are quite typical (McGraw, Mellers, & Tetlock, 2005; Medvec, Madey, & Gilovich, 1995). Apparently, silver medalists are more likely to compare themselves to gold medalists, which leads to disappointment, while bronze medalists are comparing themselves to the fourth-place finishers who do not get a medal at all, which leads to joy.

In this chapter, we will explore the mechanisms responsible for our motivations and emotions, beginning with the underlying physical mechanisms and zooming out to look at individual and, ultimately, social influences on these behaviors. ⚙

© Alan Williams/Axiom/Aurora Photos

Emotions are automatic, spontaneous reactions to the world around us. We do not wake up in the morning and consciously decide to be happy or sad.

emotion A combination of arousal, physical sensations, and subjective feelings that occurs spontaneously in response to environmental stimuli.

How Are Motivation and Emotion Related?

Motivation and emotion are tightly related processes that share the experience of subjective feelings and engage similar processes and structures in the brain. Efforts to differentiate between motivation and emotion can be somewhat frustrating, given their overlapping characteristics and similar definitions.

An **emotion** is defined as a combination of physical sensations, such as a rapid heartbeat, and conscious, subjective feelings, like feeling afraid. Emotions are spontaneous, automatic responses to situations. We do not wake up in the morning and decide to feel happy or sad in the same way we decide which clothes to wear. Instead, our emotional reactions occur automatically in response to our perceptions of surroundings and situations. We often communicate our emotions to others through behaviors such as facial expression, body language, gestures, and tone of voice.

Emotions can be distinguished from moods. A mood is a more general state than an emotion. You can be in a good mood while feeling a variety of specific emotions, such as happiness, pride, or relief. A mood generally lasts a longer time than a single emotion. For example, when we discuss disorders of mood in our chapter on psychological disorders, we note that criteria for depression specify that depressed mood should characterize at least half a day every day for a period of two weeks (American Psychiatric Association [APA], 2000). Because emotions are responses to the ongoing and ever-changing flow of environmental information, it is unlikely that a single emotion would last this long.

Motivation is defined as a process that arouses, maintains, and guides behavior toward a goal. For example, we are motivated to seek a drink of water in response to thirst. The process of motivation is accompanied by distinct emotional states. Thirst is generally quite unpleasant, and taking a drink of water can produce positive emotions like relief and happiness.

Motivation and emotion share the ability to arouse an organism and stimulate behavior, but motivation does so in a more direct and precise fashion than emotions do. People who feel motivated by thirst are likely to do one thing—seek out something to drink. In contrast, experiencing the emotion of sadness stimulates behavior, but that behavior may take many different forms. Some people respond to sadness by crying in a room by themselves, while others will seek out the company of friends.

© Steve Cole/Photodisc./Getty Images

If we are thirsty following a tough workout, we are motivated to seek a drink of water. It is unlikely that a thirsty person would be motivated to find a hamburger instead.

What Does It Mean to Be Motivated?

Animals, including human beings, do not have unlimited time and resources, and a state of arousal is expensive in terms of the energy it requires. Motivational systems allow an animal to be aroused only when necessary, such as when it needs food, and then reduce arousal following the solution of a problem, such as after a meal. Preventing the waste of precious energy resources provides a significant survival advantage. Motivation also provides the benefit of helping an animal prepare to meet future needs. Most animals are motivated to explore their environments, because familiarity with an environment allows them to act more effectively when a need arises.

motivation A process that arouses, maintains, and guides behavior toward a goal.

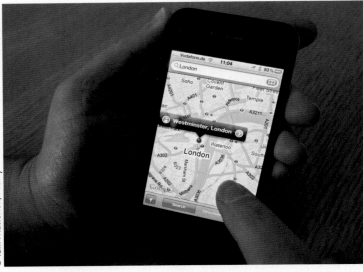

Many animals are motivated to explore their surroundings even when they have no immediate needs, because being familiar with your neighborhood saves time when a need does arise, whether that is food, water, shelter from a storm, or a gas station. Technology to help us deal with unfamiliar places is very popular.

We can think of motivation as a process that maintains **homeostasis**, a term introduced by psychologist Walter Cannon to describe a steady internal balance or equilibrium (Cannon, 1932). To achieve homeostasis, organisms actively defend certain values known as **set points**. Under normal circumstances, we carefully regulate such variables as core body temperature, fluid levels, and body weight around set points. Deviations from these set points stimulate behavior by the organism that is designed to reestablish the original values. You might think about this process as analogous to your home's temperature control. A set point of air temperature is established using your thermostat. If your home's temperature drops below that set point, the furnace is activated until the set point is once again established. If your home's temperature rises above the set point, the air conditioning system is activated until the set point is regained. Similarly, if your core body temperature drops below 98.6° F (37° C), your body initiates a number of processes designed to increase its temperature, such as producing heat by the muscle contractions we know as shivering. If your core body temperature rises above its set point, cooling mechanisms are activated. You sweat, and the evaporating moisture cools your skin. Blood is diverted to the outer parts of the body, leading to a flushed appearance.

Motivation begins with a stimulus, from either the internal or external environment of the organism, that serves as a cue for motivated behavior. Stimuli that are important to survival, such as the presence of a predator or a deficit in body fluids, generate arousal and tension, a state frequently referred to as **drive** (Hull, 1943). Being in a drive state propels the organism into some sort of action related to the stimulus, whether that means running away from the predator to safety or perhaps pulling a bottle of water from a backpack to quench thirst. If actions are successful in regaining equilibrium, we experience **drive reduction**, accompanied by a rewarding feeling of relief.

Drive theories of motivation are often described as "push" theories, as drive is seen as pushing an organism toward a goal. However, not all psychologists agree that motivation requires the "push" of drive. Instead, they suggest that rewards, or **incentives**, have the capacity to "pull" an organism in a particular direction. According to this view, animals are viewed as naturally inclined to act on their environment, rather than waiting passively for a need to arise (Deci & Ryan, 2000). In incentive theories, no reference to unpleasant internal drive states is required to explain motivated behavior.

Incentives or rewards may be intrinsic or extrinsic. **Intrinsic rewards** arise internally, such as feelings of accomplishment when a goal is met. **Extrinsic rewards** come from outside sources, such as money for completing work or praise from a supervisor. These different types of reward can interact in complex ways (see ● Figure 7.1). In some cases, certain extrinsic

homeostasis A steady internal balance, or equilibrium.

set point A value that is defended to maintain homeostasis.

drive A state of tension and arousal triggered by cues important for survival.

drive reduction The state of relief and reward produced by removing the tension and arousal of the drive state.

incentive A reward that pulls an organism's behavior in a particular direction.

intrinsic reward A reward that arises internally.

extrinsic reward A reward from an outside source.

rewards can have negative effects on intrinsic motivation. For example, if a child who enjoys reading suddenly gets paid for each book completed, the child's enjoyment of reading might decrease because the motivation shifts from intrinsic (the love of reading) to extrinsic (the love of reward money; DeCharms, 1968).

Psychologists have studied a wide range of motives, ranging from the mostly physical motives of temperature control and thirst to the much more cognitive and social motives to achieve and affiliate with others. We will explore this range by discussing some specific motives in detail, including hunger, sexuality, achievement, and affiliation. After discussing these examples, we will examine the ways human beings set priorities when faced with competing motives.

FIGURE 7.1

Economist Roland Fryer Asks Whether Incentives Work. Harvard economist Roland Fryer overcame a very tough childhood in Daytona, Florida, to become the youngest tenured African American professor in the history of Harvard University. Drawing on his personal experiences, Fryer experimented with different incentives for a variety of school-related behaviors. His results suggest that the relationships among intrinsic rewards, extrinsic rewards, and behavior can be quite complex. Although previous research has shown that extrinsic rewards can undermine intrinsic motivation, it is important to remember that this result occurs only when behavior is intrinsically motivated in the first place. If children do not intrinsically enjoy reading, Fryer suggests paying them to read might work. Unfortunately, Fryer has been the target of death threats for suggesting this simple solution to illiteracy.

© Sonia Moskowitz-Globe Photos, Inc./Newscom

Location	DALLAS	CHICAGO	WASHINGTON	NEW YORK CITY
What students were paid for	Reading	Grades	Various†	Test scores
Grade level participating	Second-graders	Ninth-graders	Sixth-, seventh-, and eighth-graders	Fourth- and seventh-graders
How much	$2 per book	$50 for A's $35 for B's $20 for C's	Up to $100 every two weeks	$25 (fourth-graders) to $50 (seventh-graders) per test
Average student earned	$13.81	$695.61	$532.85	$139.43 (fourth-graders) $231.55 (seventh-graders)
Study size*	1,780 from 22 schools	4,396 from 20 schools	3,495 from 17 schools	8,320 from 63 schools
Results	**Very Positive** Paying kids to read dramatically boosted reading-comprehension scores.	**Mixed** Kids cut fewer classes and got slightly better grades. Standardized test scores did not change.	**Positive** Rewarding five different actions, including attendance and behavior, seemed to improve reading skills.	**No Effect** Paying kids for higher test scores did not lead to more learning or better grades — or any measureable changes.

© Cengage Learning 2013

*Not including control groups

† A combination of metrics that varied from school to school but always included attendance and behavior

Hunger and Eating

Hunger is a very complex motive. In comparison to the regulation of body temperature through processes like sweating or shivering, the reduction of hunger through eating is much more heavily influenced by emotion, learning, and culture. Human beings take in a remarkable variety of nutrients. The traditional diet of the Inuit people living in Arctic regions contains very little plant material, whereas vegans strictly adhere to a diet that contains no animal material at all.

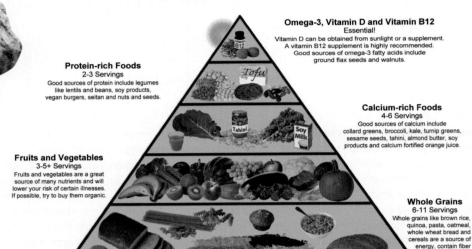

Vegan Food Pyramid

Omega-3, Vitamin D and Vitamin B12
Essential!
Vitamin D can be obtained from sunlight or a supplement. A vitamin B12 supplement is highly recommended. Good sources of omega-3 fatty acids include ground flax seeds and walnuts.

Protein-rich Foods
2-3 Servings
Good sources of protein include legumes like lentils and beans, soy products, vegan burgers, seitan and nuts and seeds.

Calcium-rich Foods
4-6 Servings
Good sources of calcium include collard greens, broccoli, kale, turnip greens, sesame seeds, tahini, almond butter, soy products and calcium fortified orange juice.

Fruits and Vegetables
3-5+ Servings
Fruits and vegetables are a great source of many nutrients and will lower your risk of certain illnesses. If possible, try to buy them organic.

Whole Grains
6-11 Servings
Whole grains like brown rice, quinoa, pasta, oatmeal, whole wheat bread and cereals are a source of energy, contain fiber and many nutrients.

Vegan Food Pyramid © Wanda Embar, www.veganpeace.com. Used with permission.

© dbimages/Alamy

Human beings consume a wide range of diets, from the nearly all-meat diet of the traditional Inuit cultures to the vegan diet.

Thinking Scientifically

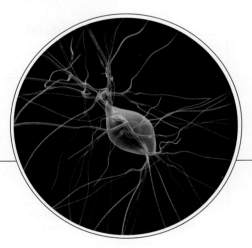

Why Do We Procrastinate?

Most university counseling websites offer advice to students about avoiding procrastination. These sites typically describe procrastination in very negative terms. Procrastinators are seen as less capable, poorly motivated, more anxious, low in self-esteem, and high in anxiety and stress (Ferrari, 1991). At the same time, psychologists report that procrastination is far from rare. About 70% of college students report some procrastination, and 20% procrastinate habitually (Schouwenburg, 1995). In contrast to the negative stereotypes of the procrastinator, better students often report more procrastination, and students who are farther along in their academic careers report more procrastination than students just starting out (Ferrari, 1991). How can we reconcile these divergent views of procrastination in light of our discussion of motivation?

The Sensation of Hunger We respond to combinations of external and internal cues that make us feel hungry. External cues for hunger may include time of day, the sights and smells of favorite foods, admonitions that we should "clean our plates," or the social settings in which food is presented. These external cues may encourage us to eat when our bodies do not need nutrients or to eat more food than we require. Individuals who are relatively less responsive to external cues are less likely to have trouble maintaining a healthy weight.

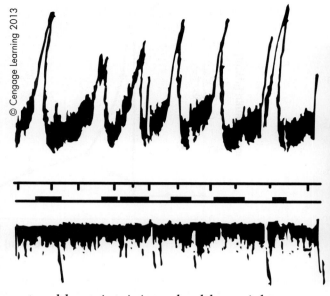

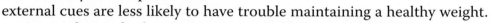

Internal cues for hunger are generated when our bodies are genuinely short on nutrients. Note that "short on nutrients" applies to the maintenance of current, not necessarily ideal weight. A morbidly obese person is likely to feel as hungry as a very thin person when sufficient nutrients are not available to maintain the status quo.

Psychologist Walter Cannon provided an early hypothesis about hunger cues. Cannon believed that stomach contractions were an important component in the detection of hunger. He persuaded his colleague A. L. Washburn to swallow a balloon attached to an air pump (Cannon & Washburn, 1912). The balloon allowed Washburn's stomach contractions to be monitored. Although Washburn's feelings of hunger (as expressed by his pushing a telegraph key, since he couldn't talk with a tube down his throat) correlated with his stomach contractions, these signals do not tell the whole story. Patients who have had their stomachs surgically removed still experience a sense of hunger in the general region where the stomach used to be. Most of us start eating long before our stomachs begin to growl, indicating that additional types of signaling must be at work (see ● Figure 7.2).

FIGURE 7.2

Walter Cannon. Walter Cannon and his assistant, A. L. Washburn, performed one of the earliest experiments on the relationship between stomach contractions and feelings of hunger. The large waves at the top were Cannon's recordings of Washburn's stomach contractions, and the smaller waves at the bottom represent Washburn's key taps indicating hunger. Although these two events are correlated, there is much more to hunger than a growling stomach.

Is it possible that procrastination can be both adaptive and maladaptive? It appears so (Schraw, Wadkins, & Olafson, 2007). Students do report negative consequences of procrastination, particularly on term papers, but also see some advantages. Procrastination may be viewed as a way of prioritizing unrealistic amounts of work. Consequently, the most "successful" procrastinators plan the term's work out carefully in advance.

Working under a tight deadline increases motivation for some people and provides a rationale for forgoing other activities, such as socializing with friends. As stressful as such work may be, completion of a task is followed by immediate relief, which may in turn serve as a potent reward for procrastinating.

In light of these findings, should we continue to try to minimize procrastination? If so, how would we

do this? Part of the answer lies in assessing the reasons students give for procrastinating: managing time (social and work activities take precedence over schoolwork for most students), avoiding boredom, and working more efficiently. It is likely that once procrastination no longer produces the desired results (i.e., the stress becomes too much or performance suffers), the student will be motivated to change. ✪

FIGURE 7.3

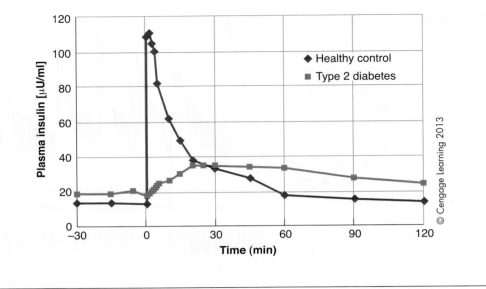

Insulin Release Is Reduced in Type 2 Diabetes. Following a meal (time 0), a healthy person experiences a large spike in insulin levels. In contrast, a person with Type 2 diabetes has a much slower and less dramatic release of insulin. The person with diabetes will not be able to move glucose out of the blood into cells requiring nutrients. The appetite-suppressing action of insulin will be less effective, and the person with diabetes will remain hungry.

A likely candidate for an additional hunger cue is a low level of circulating sugars, particularly **glucose**. Glucose concentrations in the blood are highest just following a meal. As glucose levels drop over time, a person begins to feel hungry again. Glucose levels are intimately connected with levels of the hormone insulin. Insulin, released by the pancreas, moves circulating glucose from the blood into cells awaiting nutrients. Typically, glucose and insulin levels are positively correlated. Right after a meal, both are high. Glucose levels rise as glucose is extracted from the food that has been consumed, and insulin is high because its release is triggered by the anticipation and consumption of food. As time goes by without more food, glucose moves from the blood into other tissues, and insulin is no longer released, leading to lower levels of both substances in the blood. These lower levels of glucose and insulin should signal the need for more food (see ● Figure 7.3).

This is an overly simplistic conclusion, however. You may know people with diabetes mellitus who must check the glucose levels in their blood several times per day, as high levels of circulating glucose can harm many organs. High glucose levels occur in untreated diabetes due to either a lack of insulin production (Type I diabetes) or the body's resistance to insulin (Type II diabetes). Without sufficient insulin activity, circulating glucose is unable to move out of the blood into the cells that need nutrients. If hunger results from low levels of circulating glucose, we would expect people with untreated diabetes to not feel very hungry, but this is definitely not the case. Most patients with high blood sugar report feeling hungry all the time. This makes sense when you consider that their cells are starving due to their inability to obtain glucose from the blood. It is more accurate to say that the amount of glucose that is available to cells is an indicator of hunger (Mayer, 1955). Hunger will result whenever cells are unable to obtain the glucose they require.

Hunger also occurs in response to low levels of stored fats (Kennedy, 1953). If you maintain a healthy weight, you are carrying sufficient body

glucose A type of sugar that plays an important role in hunger levels.

fat to survive five to six weeks of total starvation. Obviously, the heavier the person, the longer he or she can survive without food. One patient survived a total fast of 382 days, during which time his weight dropped from 207 kilograms (455.4 pounds) to 81.6 kilograms (179.5 pounds; Stewart & Fleming, 1973).

The body monitors fat stores by assessing levels of the hormone **leptin**. Leptin, from the Greek word *leptos*, or "thin," is produced and secreted by fat cells (Zhang et al., 1994). Because fat stores and leptin levels are positively correlated, leptin levels provide a measure for the amount of fat that has been stored. Leptin appears to be an important key to feeding behavior. As shown in ● Figure 7.4, leptin levels and their associated fat stores initiate a cascade of events that influence eating behavior. When fat stores and leptin levels are low, brain areas that include the lateral hypothalamus (LH) initiate feeding. When rats' LH is lesioned, the rats fail to eat and die of starvation unless force-fed (Anand & Brobeck, 1951). Stimulation of the LH typically initiates immediate eating.

Low fat stores and leptin levels also activate the parasympathetic division of the autonomic nervous system, enhancing the body's ability to digest and store nutrients. Metabolism, or the chemical reactions required by life, slows down, allowing nutrients to be stored rather than used up right away.

Activation of the parasympathetic nervous system, initiation of feeding behavior, and reduction in metabolic rate allow the animal to find, eat, and store nutrients. As fat stores return to normal, leptin levels increase, and the feeding cycle tapers off. Unfortunately for the person trying to lose weight, the leptin system does a very good job of defending a set point. As the dieter successfully decreases body fat levels, the associated low levels of leptin will initiate a feeding cycle. The dieter will feel constantly hungry, making the maintenance of weight loss often more difficult than the initial loss itself.

Feeding is stimulated by two additional hormones—ghrelin, which is released by the pancreas and the lining of the stomach (Inui et al., 2004), and orexins, produced in the LH (de Lecea et al., 1998; Sakurai et al., 1998). Ghrelin appears to contribute to the rewarding aspects of feeding, while the orexins also participate in sleep, suggesting that they might link feeding, activity levels, and sleep.

FIGURE 7.4

Mechanisms of Hunger.

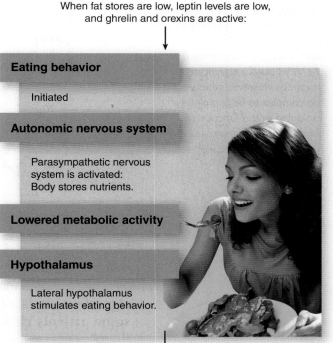

When fat stores are low, leptin levels are low, and ghrelin and orexins are active:

Eating behavior

Initiated

Autonomic nervous system

Parasympathetic nervous system is activated: Body stores nutrients.

Lowered metabolic activity

Hypothalamus

Lateral hypothalamus stimulates eating behavior.

Result: Stored fat levels increase and feeding stops.

Illustration: © Cengage Learning 2013; photo: © kate_sept2004/iStockphoto

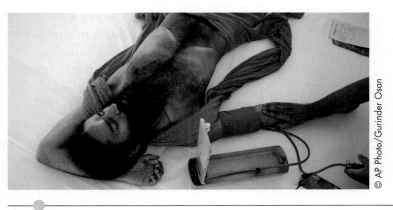

People of normal weight carry enough fat to survive five to six weeks of total starvation, although this is obviously not a good thing to do for one's health. Baba Ramdev, a yoga guru, was hospitalized after losing 12 pounds by the seventh day of a hunger strike against corruption. It is likely that Ramdev was already quite thin at the beginning of his fast.

© AP Photo/Gurinder Osan

leptin A hormone secreted by fat cells that helps the body maintain an appropriate level of stored fat.

FIGURE 7.5

Lesions of the Ventromedial Hypothalamus Lead to Obesity. Following the lesioning of the ventromedial hypothalamus (VMH), rats nearly triple their normal weight, suggesting that the VMH plays a significant role in satiety. However, satiety is too complex to be completely explained as the function of a single part of the brain. *Source:* Adapted from Kurtz, Rozin, and Teitelbaum (1972).

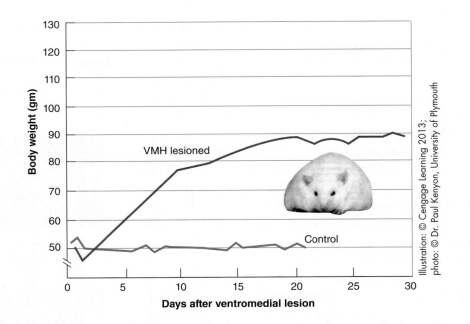

The Sensation of Satiety We reach the point of **satiety**, or fullness, long before the nutrients we have eaten can make their way to waiting cells.

Just as stomach contractions serve as signals for hunger, an obvious sign of satiety is a feeling of stomach fullness. In extreme cases of obesity, some patients choose to have a portion of the stomach stapled or banded in order to produce this feeling of fullness after less food has been eaten. In the brain, the ventromedial hypothalamus (VMH) participates in sensing satiety. As shown in ● Figure 7.5, lesions of the VMH produce a syndrome of large weight gains (Hoebel & Teitelbaum, 1966). Although the VMH plays a significant role in satiety, it is overly simplistic to assume that it works alone and directly. Among the many indirect effects of VMH lesions are boosts in insulin production, which in turn produce low blood glucose levels and hunger.

Other participants in satiety include the gut hormone cholecystokinin (CCK), released by the digestive system in response to the arrival of food, especially fatty foods. CCK appears to contribute to feelings of satiety, although its exact mechanism is unclear (Stacher, 1986). CCK not only acts in the digestive tract but also serves as a chemical messenger in the brain. Drugs that inhibit CCK's action in the brain increase eating behavior, further supporting the hypothesis that CCK normally acts to inhibit further eating (Cooper & Dourish, 1990).

Earlier we observed the cascade of events initiated by low levels of stored fat and leptin that led to feeding and the storage of nutrients. What happens when fat and leptin levels rise again? With increased storage of fat, leptin levels rise. Once again, the assessment of circulating leptin levels by the brain initiates a sequence of events, this time directed at inhibiting feeding (see ● Figure 7.6). The sympathetic division of the autonomic nervous system is activated, leading to the expenditure of energy, metabolic rate increases, and inhibition of feeding. As time without food progresses, fat levels drop, leptin levels drop, and the feeding sequence is initiated again.

Because of leptin's role in satiety, scientists initially believed it might be helpful as a dieting aid. Mice genetically engineered to lack genes that

satiety A sense of feeling full; not requiring further food.

produce leptin are enormously obese. Injections of leptin allow them to lose weight (Halaas et al., 1995). Unfortunately, people in this case do not respond like mice—obese humans actually have very high circulating leptin levels, but appear to become resistant to the satiety messages this state should produce (Friedman & Halaas, 1998). Adding further leptin is unlikely to lead to weight loss.

Keep in mind that our ancestors rarely had to worry about having too much food. Those who lived and reproduced exhibited characteristics best suited for surviving famine. As we will see in the next sections, the same motivational mechanisms that evolved to prevent starvation among hunter-gatherers might not work too well in a society featuring cultural influences on body image and an ample and calorie-rich food supply. Through an examination of the interactions between social and cultural factors with hunger motivation, we gain a better understanding of hunger's mechanisms.

Obesity What exactly do we mean by obesity? Expert opinions regarding ideal weight and the likely impact of obesity on health vary widely, with opinions ranging from doomsday predictions to complaints that the problem has been overstated.

A well-respected approach to body weight is the **body mass index (BMI)**, shown in ● Figure 7.7. The BMI is a simple height-to-weight ratio computed by dividing weight in kilograms by the square of height in meters.

FIGURE 7.6

Mechanisms of Satiety.

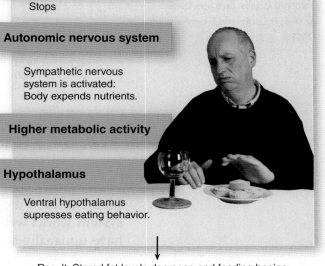

When fat stores are high and leptin levels are high:

Eating behavior

Stops

Autonomic nervous system

Sympathetic nervous system is activated: Body expends nutrients.

Higher metabolic activity

Hypothalamus

Ventral hypothalamus supresses eating behavior.

Result: Stored fat levels decrease and feeding begins.

Illustration: © Cengage Learning 2013; photo: © Christopher Nash/Alamy

FIGURE 7.7

Body Mass Index (BMI).

Height (inches)	80	90	100	110	120	130	140	150	160	170	180	190	200	210	220	230	240	250
80	9	10	11	12	13	14	15	17	18	19	20	21	22	23	24	25	26	28
78	9	10	12	13	14	15	16	17	19	20	21	22	23	24	25	27	28	29
76	10	11	12	13	15	16	17	18	20	21	22	23	24	26	27	28	29	30
74	10	12	12	14	15	17	18	19	21	22	23	24	26	27	28	30	31	32
72	11	12	14	15	16	18	19	20	22	23	24	26	27	28	30	31	33	34
70	12	13	14	16	17	19	20	22	23	24	26	27	29	30	32	33	35	36
68	12	14	15	17	18	20	21	23	24	26	27	29	30	32	34	35	7	38
66	13	15	16	18	19	21	23	24	26	27	29	31	32	34	36	37	39	40
64	14	15	17	19	21	22	24	26	28	29	31	33	34	36	38	40	41	43
62	15	17	18	20	22	24	26	27	29	31	33	35	37	38	40	42	44	46
60	16	17	20	22	23	25	27	25	31	33	35	37	39	41	43	45	47	49
58	17	19	21	23	25	27	29	31	34	36	38	40	42	44	46	48	50	52
56	18	21	22	25	27	29	31	34	36	38	40	43	45	47	49	52	54	56
54	19	22	24	27	29	31	34	36	39	41	43	46	48	51	53	56	58	60
52	21	23	26	29	31	34	36	39	40	44	47	49	52	55	57	60	62	65
50	23	25	28	31	34	37	39	42	45	48	51	53	56	59	62	65	68	70
48	24	28	31	34	37	40	42	46	49	52	55	58	61	64	67	70	73	76

Weight (pounds)

© Cengage Learning 2013

- ☐ BMI under 18.5: Underweight
- ☐ BMI between 18.5–24: Healthy weight
- ☐ BMI between 25–29: Overweight
- ☐ BMI between 30–39: Obese
- ☐ BMI over 40: Severely/morbidly obese

body mass index (BMI) A height-to-weight ratio used to identify healthy weight, underweight, overweight, and obesity.

FIGURE 7.8

The Obesity Epidemic. American rates of obesity have increased dramatically since 1971 in all age groups. Exact reasons for this increase remain unknown, and multiple factors are likely to be involved. *Source: Data from Centers for Disease Control and Prevention (2008a).*

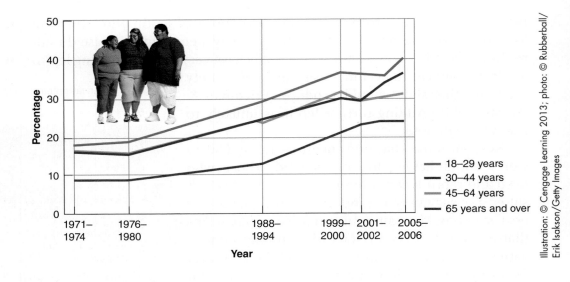

We have converted Figure 7.7 to inches and pounds for convenience. BMI scores between 18.5 and 24.9 are considered healthy. A BMI between 25 and 30 is considered overweight, and a BMI above 30 is considered obese. This system works well for most people, but it does not account for those who have unusually heavy skeletons or musculature. Many elite athletes would score in the overweight or even obese range, in spite of being quite fit.

Using a BMI of 30 or above as a criterion, rates of obesity in the United States nearly tripled from 12% of the adult population in 1991 to 34% in 2008 (Flegal, Carroll, Ogden, & Curtin, 2010). As shown in ● Figure 7.8, obesity rose in all age groups. How can we account for this rapid increase in obesity over the last two decades? It is unlikely that current obesity levels are the result of a single cause. Genetic predispositions, lifestyle issues, and social comparisons all make significant contributions to obesity.

Genes can influence factors such as set point and rate of metabolism, and twin studies indicate that some people are just more likely than others to become obese (Livshits, Kato, Wilson, & Spector, 2007). Although genes are unlikely to have changed dramatically over a few decades, complex interactions between genes and environmental factors, like the BPA in plastic products discussed in our chapter on nature and nurture, could have an impact on current rates of obesity (Dolinoy, Huang, & Jirtle, 2007).

A cultural contribution to obesity is our contemporary, sedentary lifestyle, with many people spending hours sitting in front of televisions or computers. Human beings use energy very efficiently. At rest, we use only 12 kilocalories (kcal; usually described simply as "calories") per pound per day. This means that the average 150-pound couch potato needs only about 1,800 calories of food per day. Even the most demanding activities require a remarkably small investment in resources. Cyclists competing in the challenging Tour de France use an average of 5,900 calories per day (Armstrong & Jenkins, 2000). A single entree at a typical chain

Beginning in the 1800s, in an effort to prevent starvation, initiatives leading to increasing cheap sources of high-calorie foods were adopted worldwide. Currently, global agriculture produces 2,600 calories per person per day, which is expected to rise to 3,000 calories per person per day by 2030 (Caballero, 2007). With such a plentiful food supply, we can see why obesity is becoming a global problem at the same time starvation remains a serious concern in many parts of the world.

restaurant, such as Chili's or The Cheesecake Factory (not counting beverages, appetizers, or dessert), can contain as much as 2,500 calories, the total daily requirement for a person weighing 208 pounds. With such abundant food, it is not too surprising that the American public is getting heavier.

Our natural preferences for sweet, fatty foods coupled with cheap, readily available treats are probably also contributing to our growing size. To avoid starvation, our ancestors developed strong preferences for calorie-rich foods containing sugars and fats. In situations where food supplies are limited, these preferences ensured that human beings would spend the greatest amounts of time and energy seeking these rich sources of calories. Unfortunately, we retain these preferences today and continue to gravitate to sugary, fatty foods when they are available, like our frequenting of popular restaurant food chains with the 2,500-calorie meals or our late-night snacking on pizzas and chips.

Zooming out from individual factors to the larger social context, we see that social factors also contribute to obesity. We apparently "keep track" of how we are doing by comparing our size to that of those in our social circles (see ● Figure 7.9). Having an obese spouse raises your risk of obesity by 37%, and having obese friends raises your risk by 57% (Christakis & Fowler, 2007).

© Trina McManus

The average adult weighing 150 pounds needs only 1,800 calories per day. When a single dessert item like cheesecake provides about 70% of that daily requirement, it becomes easy to see how people eating out frequently could become overweight or obese. It is also likely that before eating the cheesecake, a diner might have an appetizer, salad, entrée, and beverage, too. This doesn't include meals and snacks consumed at other times throughout the day.

Photo: Denise Applewhite/Courtesy Princeton University

Bart Hoebel and his research assistants at Princeton University fed rats equal calories of different kinds of sugars, including high-fructose corn syrup (HFCS). Hoebel reported that "when rats are drinking high-fructose corn syrup at levels well below those in soda pop, they're becoming obese—every single one, across the board. Even when rats are fed a high-fat diet, you don't see this." Concerns about the health effects of HFCS have led the Corn Refiners Association to obtain government permission to refer to HFCS as "corn sugar." According to the organization's website, this name change will "enable consumers to easily identify added sugars in the diet."

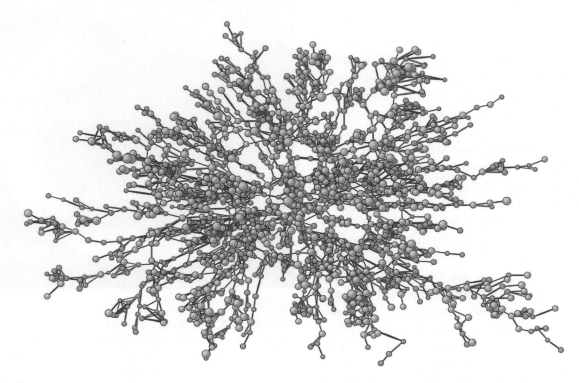

FIGURE 7.9

Is Obesity Catching? Christakis and Fowler (2007) constructed this elaborate model of a social network of over 2,000 people to answer the question of whether our own likelihood of obesity was related to the obesity of our friends and family. Each circle in this image is a person. Yellow circles represent obese people, and green circles represent people who are not obese. An analysis of the network supports the idea that if you have obese family members and friends, you are more likely to be obese. Remember that these are correlations, however, and that the data cannot be interpreted to indicate that having obese friends *causes* you to be heavy. Although Christakis and Fowler argue that social comparisons are important to obesity (I'm doing okay compared to my friends), we must also consider the possibility that "birds of a feather flock together." *Source:* From Christakis, N. A., and Fowler, J. H., The spread of obesity in a large social network over 32 years, *The New England Journal of Medicine.* Copyright © 2007 The Massachusetts Medical Society.

The path to a healthy weight can be difficult. Unfortunately, weight loss for our ancestors usually meant one step closer to death by starvation, and we are well designed to prevent that occurrence. Once a person is obese, a new set point is established and subsequently staunchly defended. Even the surgical removal of fat, or liposuction, does not result in permanent weight loss, as the fat removed by the process is eventually replaced (Dark, Forger, Stern, & Zucker, 1984; Food and Drug Administration [FDA], 2002).

Calorie-reducing diets do work, but dietary changes cannot be viewed as something to do just until a goal weight is reached. If the dieter returns to his or her previous eating habits, the lost weight is quickly regained. Successful diets should be viewed as lifestyle changes that are sustainable for an individual. For example, removing one sugared soft drink per day should result in about a 10-pound weight loss over the next year. It is essential for the dieter to avoid triggering mechanisms designed to prevent starvation, like lowering metabolic rates. By keeping activity levels up and restricting weight loss to a pound or two per week at most, it is possible to slide weight loss under the radar of our vigilant weight maintenance systems.

Efforts to use chemicals to control weight have been discouraging. Most medications used to reduce weight do so by suppressing appetite. During the 1950s and 1960s, it was not uncommon for American doctors to prescribe amphetamines for weight loss. Although amphetamines do suppress appetite, their psychoactive and addictive properties make this approach less than desirable. Currently approved chemical approaches for treating obesity include orlistat (Xenical), which reduces the absorption of fats by the digestive tract, and sibutramine, which is similar to amphetamine. Unfortunately, taking these drugs produces modest weight loss of 5–10 pounds per year, which might not be enough to offset diarrhea and other side effects in the minds of dieters (Rucker, Padwal, Li, Curioni, & Lau, 2007).

Some individuals who become discouraged with diets and medication have begun to turn instead to surgical interventions, including stomach stapling and gastric bypass procedures, which literally reduce the amount of nutrients that can be consumed or processed. While the weight loss resulting from these procedures can be dramatic (the average bypass patient loses 90 pounds within three months of surgery; Maggard et al., 2005), these procedures represent major surgery, often result in complications, and should be considered very carefully.

Although it is feasible that current research into brain mechanisms for hunger and satiety may eventually lead to better treatments for obesity, lifestyle changes leading to healthier eating and exercise habits remain the most reliable approach.

Anorexia Nervosa and Bulimia Nervosa Coexisting with our ongoing obesity epidemic are eating disorders characterized by unusual patterns of restricted eating and distortions of a person's body image. Normally, we have a fairly accurate view of what we look like. People with distorted body image can be convinced that they are obese when in fact they are in danger of starvation.

Traditionally, eating disorders have been viewed as a problem for women, but much less typically for men. However, contemporary research suggests that increasing numbers of men are experiencing eating disorders (Hudson, Hiripi, Pope, & Kessler, 2007) and body dissatisfaction (Pope, Katz, & Hudson, 1993). As many as 25% of individuals with eating disorders today are male. Rates of eating disorder are about 6 times higher among homosexual and bisexual men compared to heterosexual men, although sexual orientation does not seem to be associated with any additional risks for eating disorder among women (Feldman & Meyer, 2007). In addition, some men appear to suffer from muscle dysmorphia, a body distortion problem in which they see themselves as 90-pound weaklings even though they spend hours each day developing muscle at the gym (Chung,

© Drew D. Saur

Contrary to popular opinion, many people do lose weight by dieting and are successful in maintaining their weight loss for years. The National Weight Control Registry tracks over 5,000 case studies of successful maintainers, including Drew Saur. Drew lost over 150 pounds and has maintained his loss since 2005. He began by counting the calories he was consuming and was astonished to find that he was eating about 5,000 calories per day, not surprising given his starting weight of 325 pounds. By gradually reducing calories and waiting to eat until he felt hungry, Drew lost about two to three pounds per week. He began walking, and when his weight loss permitted more activity, he switched to running. Successful dieters/maintainers like Drew do not view dieting as something drastic to do before a wedding or class reunion, but as a gradual lifestyle change that is livable.

We have defined healthy weight as a BMI between 18.5 and 24.9, yet the typical runway model held up as a cultural standard for beauty has an average BMI of only 16.5. In response to a number of deaths of ultrathin models, some European countries now require models to maintain a minimum BMI of 18.5. The United States has not followed suit, and American designers have complained that this standard would require a 6-foot-tall model to "balloon" to 136 pounds. In contrast, a 6-foot-tall model with a 16.5 BMI would weigh a scant 121 pounds. It is not surprising that young women exposed to these standards of beauty occasionally develop distorted images of their own bodies.

2001). These men are more likely to experiment with anabolic steroids in order to increase muscle mass (Rohman, 2009).

Anorexia nervosa is characterized by the maintenance of unusually low body weight and a distorted view of the body as obese. *Anorexia* literally means "loss of appetite." Anorexia nervosa is dramatic, but rare, affecting about 1% of women and 0.3% of men (Hudson et al., 2007). Anorexia nervosa is one of the few psychological disorders that can actually kill, with up to 10% of patients eventually dying from the condition (APA, 2000). Other symptoms include interruption of normal menstruation, very dry and yellow skin, fine downy hair (lanugo) on the face and other parts of the body, increased sensitivity to cold, and cardiovascular and gastrointestinal problems.

Bulimia nervosa is characterized by cycles of binge eating, in which unusually large amounts of food are consumed, and purging through the use of vomiting or laxatives. Bingeing is often followed by feelings of depression, disgust, and a sense of lost control. Bulimia is somewhat more common than anorexia, affecting 1.5% of women and 0.5% of men (Hudson et al., 2007). Binge eating disorder, or binge eating without the other symptoms of bulimia, occurs in about 3.5% of women and 2% of men (Hudson et al., 2007) and is under consideration as a separate category of psychological disorder. About 20% of patients with anorexia also engage in bouts of binge eating and about 8 to 9% follow this bingeing with efforts to purge (Garfinkel et al., 1996). Fatalities among patients with bulimia alone are rare, but do occur in patients with overlapping anorexia and bulimia.

Environmental factors, especially cultural attitudes toward beauty, can play a significant role in the development of both anorexia and bulimia. Anne Becker and her colleagues were observing eating patterns in the Fiji Islands when American television became available for the first time in 1995 (Becker, Burwell, Herzog, Hamburg, & Gilman, 2002). Prior to this time, Becker reported that dieting was unknown in this culture, which valued a "robust, well-muscled body" for both men and women. The Fijian language has a term for "going thin" that is used to express concern about someone who may be losing weight due to health problems. In the United States, people may say, "Have you lost weight? You look great!" In Fiji, a person is more likely to say, "Are you okay? You look like you're going thin."

These cultural norms underwent nearly overnight change with the introduction of American television, with its frequent images of glamorous, ultrathin actresses. Suddenly, 74% of the adolescent girls in Becker's study reported themselves as being "too big or too fat." Teens began to report dieting with the same frequency as their American counterparts,

anorexia nervosa An eating disorder characterized by the maintenance of unusually low body weight and a distorted body image.

bulimia nervosa An eating disorder characterized by bingeing, purging, and having feelings of depression, disgust, and lost control.

a radical shift from Becker's observations since 1988. Because Becker's data are correlational, we cannot conclude that watching TV produced disordered eating in Fiji. However, her results are suggestive of strong cultural influences on patterns of disordered eating.

Evidence from twin studies indicates that people do have a significant genetic vulnerability to disordered eating, but not toward a specific type of disorder (Bulik et al., 2010). It is likely that general personality characteristics that increase a person's risk for eating disorders may be inherited, not the disorders themselves (Hsu, Chesler, & Santhouse, 1990).

Once an eating disorder is established, biological factors contribute to maintaining abnormal patterns of eating. Even after patients with anorexia nervosa regain normal weight, some still show evidence of elevated levels of hormones that typically raise metabolism and inhibit feeding (Stanley et al., 2003). The binge-purge cycling of bulimia involves processes similar to those of addiction (Hoebel, Patten, Colantuoni, & Rada, 2000). When food-deprived rats are given access to sugar water, they tend to binge by consuming larger than normal amounts. Subsequently, if the bingeing rats are given naloxone, a chemical that blocks the action of opiate drugs (discussed in our chapter on consciousness), they respond as if they had been addicted to opiates. For both bingeing and addicted rats, naloxone produces anxiety, agitation, and chattering teeth. People who fast and then binge on sweets may set up a similar addictive process that is difficult to stop.

Effective treatments exist for anorexia nervosa and bulimia. Treating anorexia nervosa can be challenging, as the therapist is frequently facing a patient who is terrified of gaining weight. The first priority, of course, is keeping the patient alive, and this effort typically involves hospitalization and careful monitoring of food intake. Cognitive-behavioral therapy may be used to address distortions of body image (see our chapter on therapy), but no known medications are effective in treating anorexia (Johnson, Tsoh, & Vanrado, 1996). About 50% of patients with anorexia will make a full recovery, but nearly 20% fail to respond at all. Treating bulimia is somewhat more encouraging. Antidepressant medications, particularly selective serotonin reuptake inhibitors (SSRIs), are usually quite effective, especially when combined with cognitive-behavioral treatment (Johnson et al., 1996).

© Michael DeFreitas/Photoshot

© Tom Cockrem/Lonely Planet Images

Prior to the introduction of American television programming to the islands of Fiji in 1995, the cultural ideal for both men and women was a "robust, well-muscled body," as evidenced by this traditional dancer. Dieting and eating disorders were completely unknown. A very short time after American television was available, however, Fijian rates of dieting and eating disorders grew to match American rates, and ideal beauties became slimmer.

Sexual Motivation

Although sexual behavior is essential for the survival of a species, unlike eating, it is not essential to the survival of an individual organism. However, individuals' sexual behavior appears to be maintained by processes similar to the life-sustaining motivations we have already discussed.

The evolutionary psychology perspective maintains that the goal of a species' sexual behavior is to produce offspring who will in turn reproduce. According to this approach, males and females experience different pressures that shape their reproductive behaviors. Compared to females, males are able to produce many more offspring during a lifetime. Supplying sperm

Although reports about unfaithful men, like Arnold Schwarzenegger, seem to outnumber those about women in celebrity tabloids, recent research shows that powerful women are about as likely to cheat on their mates as powerful men are.

takes much less time than a pregnancy. In addition, women typically have the greater responsibility for child-rearing tasks, which last many years.

According to evolutionary psychologists, these differences in reproductive opportunities and amount of parental investment are responsible for more selectivity in mate choice by women compared to men. Because women can produce fewer children and must invest heavily in their care, the best reproductive strategy for women would be to ensure their children's health by choosing the partner with the healthiest genes. In contrast, a man's best reproductive strategy might be promiscuity. However, there is no point in producing a large number of children who fail to survive, so any "natural" tendency toward promiscuity would be offset by the many advantages a father provides his children, such as protection and the encouragement of exploration. Current cross-cultural data continue to show an overwhelming majority of monogamous human relationships worldwide (UNdata, 2008).

Cross-cultural data comparing the importance of different characteristics in a mate also show sex differences (Buss, 1989). Both men and women from 37 cultures worldwide agreed that kindness, emotional stability, dependability, and a pleasant disposition were valuable characteristics in a mate. However, as shown in ● Figure 7.10, women were more influenced by the financial prospects of their potential mates, whereas men were more influenced by physical attractiveness. Even in the United States, where it is

Thinking Scientifically

The Impact of Pro-Ana Websites

Freedom of speech is a cherished right, especially in the United States, and we decide to restrict access to data very reluctantly, as in the case of movie and video game rating systems. In spite of these strong values, many health professionals cringe

when viewing so-called pro-ana sites online. Some of these communities are designed to actually help people with eating disorders, but many are unabashedly in favor of promoting thinness at any cost.

One example, prothinspo.com, is written by a self-described former

model, who says that the purpose of the site is to "help us meet our goals," which are to achieve "perfection." The author further states that "thinspiration is not a negative part of today's society" (Jodee, 2010). The site features links for "Fasting Help

more feasible for women to support themselves than in most of the cultures included in the study, most women still prefer a mate whose earning power exceeds their own.

Sexuality is an extremely complex aspect of human behavior. In this chapter, we will focus on the more physical aspects of sexual motivation. In a later chapter on social psychology, we will discuss phenomena related to attraction and maintaining relationships, and in our chapter on development, we will explore sexuality across the lifespan.

Hormones and Sexual Motivation The females of many mammalian species, including cats and dogs, undergo estrus, a period of hours or days during which the female is receptive, or willing to have sex. In these species, hormone levels and sexual behavior are tightly linked. In humans and Old World primates, menstrual cycles replace periods of estrus. The sexual behavior of these non-estrus species is quite different (Rushton, 2001).

Human females show receptivity throughout the menstrual cycle. Some women report feeling slightly more interest in sex around the time of ovulation, a situation that has obvious advantages for the reproduction of the species, as this is the time when sexual behavior is most likely to lead to pregnancy (Slob, Bax, Hop,

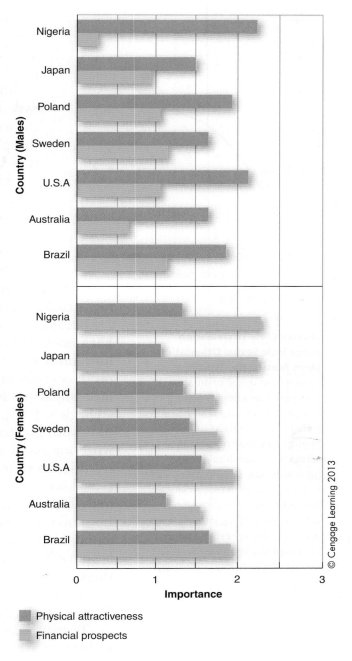

FIGURE 7.10

Cross-Cultural Surveys Show Gender Differences in Mate Preferences. Using a scale from 0 = unimportant to 3 = indispensable, men and women in 37 countries rated characteristics they preferred in a mate. A mate's financial prospects were more important to women than to men, and a mate's physical attractiveness was more important to men than to women. *Source:* Data from Buss (1989).

and Answers," "purging tips," and "pro-ana tips," along with "thinspiration" photos of painfully thin celebrities, actresses, and models. The site is typically first to show up on a Google search for pro-ana sites and reports thousands of hits per day.

What do we know about the influence of these sites? Teens already diagnosed with eating disorders visit pro-ana sites regularly, and very few of their parents were aware either of the existence of these sites or their teens' use of the site (Wilson, Peebles, Hardy, & Litt, 2006). Individuals with eating disorders who frequent pro-ana sites show more disturbed body image and eating habits than patients who view medical information sites about their disorders (Harper, Sperry, & Thompson, 2008).

Further research would be helpful in finding out how the use of these sites influences the recovery of patients with eating disorders. In the meantime, raising awareness among parents, peers, and health advisors of the existence and content of these sites might increase our ability to help those who have eating disorders. ☺

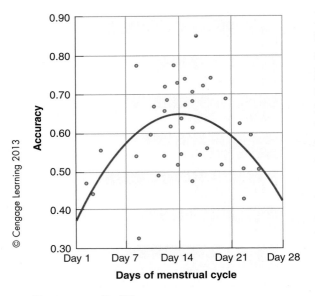

FIGURE 7.11

Women Close to Ovulation Judge Male Sexual Orientation More Accurately. Women asked to judge the sexual orientation of men based on a brief presentation of a photograph of a man's face were most accurate at their approximate time of ovulation within their menstrual cycles (approximately Day 14). This study suggests that even though women are receptive to sex throughout the menstrual cycle, interest in sex is likely to be highest at a time of increased fertility. *Source: Adapted from Rule, Rosen, Slepian, and Ambady (2011).*

Because most oral contraceptives prevent ovulation, women using this form of birth control do not show the characteristic changes in dress and voice observed in ovulating women.

testosterone A male hormone.

Rowland, & van der Werff ten Bosch, 1996). As shown in ● Figure 7.11, women who are near ovulation make more accurate assessments of the sexual orientation of men, but show no comparable change in their ability to identify the sexual orientation of other women (Rule, Rosen, Slepian, & Ambady, 2011). Accuracy improved even more when the experimenters manipulated the women to think romantic thoughts, reminding us that while the physical aspects of sexual motivation can be significant, they always interact with social and cognitive influences.

Around ovulation, women provide subtle cues about their fertility. Participants can accurately identify women who were near ovulation based on how "attractively" they were dressed (Haselton, Mortezaie, Pillsworth, Bleske-Rechek, & Frederick, 2006). The ovulating women showed more attention to detail regarding dress, hair, and makeup. Women also speak in higher, more feminine tones when they are ovulating than at other times of the menstrual cycle, especially in social situations (Bryant & Haselton, 2009).

Because women's behavior around ovulation reflects the activity of hormones responsible for the menstrual cycle, it is surprising that these hormones appear to have little influence on sexual interest. Menopause produces substantial changes in a woman's female hormone levels, but has little impact on her sexual interest and activity (Galyer, Conaglen, Hare, & Conaglen, 1999). If anything, women often respond to this change in fertility with greater interest in sexual activity, due to the relief of no longer worrying about unplanned pregnancy.

If levels of female hormones do not correlate with a woman's level of sexual interest, are there other biological factors that do? Perhaps surprisingly, female sexual interest and activity is correlated with levels of the male hormone, **testosterone**. Women typically produce about one tenth the amount of testosterone that males produce. Medical conditions that reduce a woman's testosterone production often lead to sexual dysfunction. When these women are treated with low doses of testosterone provided through a skin patch, they report having sex more frequently and enjoying it more (Shifren et al., 2000).

Testosterone is also correlated with sexual interest in males. However, as long as a man's testosterone falls within a normal range, it does not provide a strong predictor of an individual's sexual frequency (Gray et al., 2005; Mazur & Booth, 1998). Below normal levels of testosterone, as in castration, are usually accompanied by very low sexual desire and activity.

Male testosterone levels fluctuate over the course of a day and are influenced not only by a man's biology but by a number of environmental factors, notably competition. Male collegiate athletes experience increases in testosterone in anticipation of competition. Following a competition, testosterone continues to rise among the winners and temporarily decreases in the losers (Booth, Shelley, Mazur, Tharp, & Kittok, 1989). Simply observing a competition may influence testosterone levels. Men cheering for the successful Brazilian soccer team at the 1994 World Cup experienced increased testosterone levels, whereas men supporting the losing Italian team experienced a decrease (Bernhardt, Dabbs, Fielden, & Lutter, 1998). These fluctuations are more dramatic when taking the location of the venue into account. Losing at home produces a more dramatic decrease in testosterone than losing a game as the visiting team. This response to losing a competition at home may represent a remnant of our ancestors' need to defend their territory. We can assume that losing a battle is catastrophic in any circumstances, but losing near your family and home makes them especially vulnerable to destruction.

Human beings show wide variations in sexual satisfaction (see ● Figure 7.12). Cross-cultural studies show that subjective sexual satisfaction depends on a number of factors, including relative equality between men and women, mental and physical health, and the importance of sexual behavior for an individual (Laumann et al., 2006). The stability of relationships, which also impacts sexual satisfaction in a positive way, is related to hormone levels. Men in stable, long-term relationships have lower testosterone levels than single men or men who are within a few years of divorce (Mazur & Michalek, 1998). These correlations do not allow us to make judgments about causality, as we explained in our chapter on research methods. It is possible that the competition for mates that single men experience produces this increase, as we noted previously that competition is linked with increased testosterone. Conversely, it is also possible that men with higher testosterone levels are not as successful at maintaining stable relationships. Evidence supporting this second hypothesis was provided by a long-term study in which partnering and unpartnering did not impact men's testosterone levels (van Anders & Watson, 2006). In other words, if a man's testosterone was fluctuating as a result of competition, as suggested in the first hypothesis, this study should have provided evidence for changes in testosterone as a function of relationship status, but none was observed. For both men and women, individuals with the lowest testosterone levels

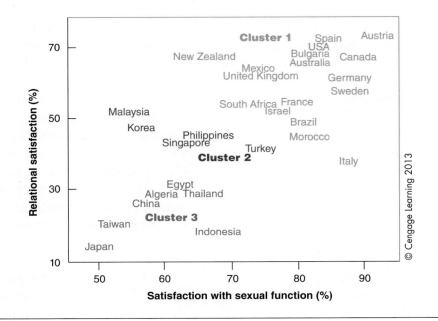

© Cengage Learning 2013

FIGURE 7.12

A Cross-Cultural Comparison of Relational and Sexual Satisfaction. A survey of nearly 30,000 participants in 29 countries showed wide variations in sexual satisfaction. In most countries, there was a strong correlation between relational satisfaction (defined as a combination of physical pleasure with a partner and emotional satisfaction with a partner) and sexual satisfaction. Gender differences in satisfaction with sexual function were the smallest in Cluster 1 countries. *Source:* Adapted from Laumann et al. (2006).

were more likely to be in monogamous, committed relationships. Single individuals had higher levels of testosterone, and individuals with multiple, committed relationships (such as married men with long-term mistresses) had the highest testosterone levels of all (van Anders, Hamilton, & Watson, 2007).

An important feature of human social behavior across our evolutionary history has been the importance of forming families to provide supportive, reproductive, and nurturant advantages. Although the resulting cultural values have often linked sexual desire and romantic love, these two functions represent distinct biological and emotional states. Romantic love involves the establishment of long-term relationships, whereas sexual desire promotes mating and reproduction. It is possible to experience sexual desire without romantic love, just as it is possible to experience romantic love without sexual desire (Diamond, 2004).

We have seen how sexual desire or interest is correlated with testosterone for both men and women, but romantic love is associated with two other hormones, oxytocin and vasopressin (see ● Figure 7.13). In human beings, both hormones are active in the brain, but vasopressin is expressed more by males and oxytocin by females (Ishunina & Swaab, 1999; van Londen et al., 1997). In both sexes, oxytocin enhances bonding. Women release oxytocin during breast-feeding and even respond to a brief hug from their partners with a spike in oxytocin release (Light, Grewen, & Amico, 2005). Oxytocin is released at orgasm in both sexes. However, due to the greater overall expression of oxytocin in the brains of females along with the 10 times higher testosterone levels in men, it does appear that women are more likely than men to equate sexual desire with feelings of romantic love (Diamond, 2004). We do not mean to imply that men do not bond, because of course they do, but high testosterone levels are likely to make sexual activity highly salient for young men, with or without the bonding associated with oxytocin release.

In light of these sex differences, it is not too surprising to learn that college women report a preference for interacting with men sexually through traditional, planned dates with an expectation for further contact, while college men report a preference for interacting sexually with women through "no strings attached" hookups (Bradshaw, Kahn, & Saville, 2010). Complicating contemporary relationships still further is the fact that oxytocin release can be classically conditioned, a process we describe in a later chapter on learning. With each successive sexual encounter with a person, that individual becomes a stronger learned signal for oxytocin release, which in turn facilitates bonding (Witt, Carter, Lederhendler, & Kirkpatrick, 1997). Women intending to hook up might find themselves bonding with their partners instead. Counselors in university health centers are well aware that women often seek counseling following a hookup, but men typically do not (Grossman, 2007).

Sexual Orientation Individual differences in human sexuality are substantial and normal. One of the ways individuals vary is in their **sexual orientation,** which refers to a stable pattern of attraction to members

sexual orientation A stable pattern of attraction to members of a particular sex.

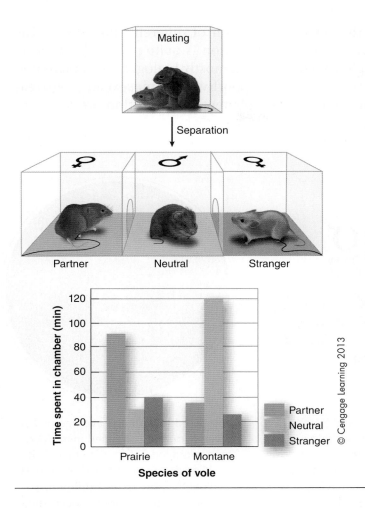

FIGURE 7.13

Oxytocin, Vasopressin, and Two Species of Voles. The discovery of the importance of oxytocin and vasopressin to bonding originated in the study of two types of rodents—the prairie vole and the montane vole. Although very similar in many ways, the two types of vole differed in both their bonding to a partner and their parenting behaviors. Prairie voles are monogamous for life, but montane voles are not. Prairie voles share parenting duties, but montane voles do not. Differences between the two types of vole in oxytocin and vasopressin were closely associated with the behavioral differences, with the prairie voles showing higher levels of both hormones than the montane voles. In one type of study, voles are allowed to mate, and then they are placed in a test box. On either side of the male, who can move freely, are two females—a stranger and the partner—who are tethered in their boxes and can't move. The chart shows how much time the average male prairie vole and montane vole spend with the partner, with the stranger, or alone. As you can see, the prairie voles prefer to be with their partners, but the montane voles prefer to be alone.

of a particular sex. Orientation is not synonymous with behavior. Many people engage in same-sex behavior and fantasy while maintaining a strong heterosexual orientation. In the Sambia tribal culture of New Guinea, all adolescent males are expected to engage in same-sex behavior prior to marrying women (Stoller & Herdt, 1985). The adult sexual orientation of these men remained overwhelmingly heterosexual.

It is difficult to determine the number of individuals who are homosexual (Savin-Williams, 2006). Among adults in the United States, 4% of women and 9% of men report having engaged in homosexual behavior, and 1% of women and 2% of men identify themselves as homosexual. The exact determinants of sexual orientation remain unknown, and it is possible that different

A homosexual orientation is carefully defined as a stable pattern of attraction to people of your own gender. Homosexual behavior can occur with or without a homosexual orientation. Among the Sambian people of New Guinea, young males are separated from their mothers and expected to engage in homosexual behavior with older males. The Sambian people believe that obtaining semen in this manner transforms them into powerful warriors (Herdt, 1987). After marriage, the now adult man no longer engages in homosexual behavior.

factors contribute to the sexual orientation of different individuals. The discussion of the causes of sexual orientation is quite politically charged, however, because people who believe in a mostly biological explanation of sexual orientation are typically more supportive of homosexuality, whereas people who believe in a mostly environmental explanation are less supportive (Tygart, 2000).

Experiencing Psychology

The Revised Sociosexual Orientation Inventory (SOI-R)

This short questionnaire measures an individual's tendency to engage in sexual relationships without deep emotional commitment (Penke & Asendorpf, 2008).

Follow these directions to score your questionnaire. You will have four scores. For the first one, score items 1, 2, and 3 as follows: 0 = 1, 1 = 2, 2 = 3, 3 = 4, 4 = 5, 5 or 6 = 6, 7–9 = 7, 10–19 = 8, and 20 or more = 9. Add scores for these three items. Second, subtract your answer for item 6 from 10, then add the result to your answers to

items 4 and 5. Third, add items 7–9 together. Finally, add all three composite scores together.

What do the scores mean? The first scale measures behavior, or what people actually report doing. In a sample of German participants, Penke and Asendorpf (2008) found that men scored an average of 2.76 and women an average of 2.65 on this scale. The second scale measures attitudes. In the same sample, men scored an average of 6.42 and women scored 5.41. The third score measures desire, and men reported an average of 5.62

compared to women's average of 3.96. Overall, on the combined instrument, men averaged 4.93 and women 4.01.

Consistent with the evolutionary perspective, the largest difference between men and women occurred in the desire scale. Penke and Asendorpf (2008) reported that the desire scores interacted with relationship status. Desire was reduced in people who were currently in a committed relationship and was negatively correlated with measures of relationship quality, commitment, and fidelity. ⚙

Please respond honestly to the following questions:								
1. With how many different partners have you had sex within the past 12 months?								
❑ 0	❑ 1	❑ 2	❑ 3	❑ 4	❑ 5–6	❑ 7–9	❑ 10–19	❑ 20 or more
2. With how many different partners have you had sexual intercourse on *one and only one* occasion?								
❑ 0	❑ 1	❑ 2	❑ 3	❑ 4	❑ 5–6	❑ 7–9	❑ 10–19	❑ 20 or more
3. With how many different partners have you had sexual intercourse without having an interest in a long-term committed relationship with this person?								
❑ 0	❑ 1	❑ 2	❑ 3	❑ 4	❑ 5–6	❑ 7–9	❑ 10–19	❑ 20 or more

Genetics appears to influence sexual orientation, although the exact mechanisms are not well understood and are likely to be quite complex. Like most human behaviors, sexual orientation is likely to be the result of an interaction between genetic factors and other aspects of the individual's experience, which can include prenatal factors. To assess the genetic contribution to sexual orientation, researchers have compared rates of homosexuality in twins. If one identical male twin is homosexual, his twin has about a 50% chance of also being homosexual (Kirk, Bailey, & Martin, 2000).

Among the other possible biological variables affecting sexual orientation are levels of prenatal, but not adult, sex hormones. Women with a condition known as congenital adrenal hyperplasia (CAH) experienced high levels of circulating male hormones as fetuses. Consequently, they are often born with masculinized external genitalia, are more likely to describe

4. Sex without love is OK.								
❑ 1 Strongly disagree	❑ 2	❑ 3	❑ 4	❑ 5	❑ 6	❑ 7	❑ 8	❑ 9 Strongly agree

5. I can imagine myself being comfortable and enjoying "casual" sex with different partners.								
❑ 1 Strongly disagree	❑ 2	❑ 3	❑ 4	❑ 5	❑ 6	❑ 7	❑ 8	❑ 9 Strongly agree

6. I do *not* want to have sex with a person until I am sure that we will have a long-term, serious relationship.								
❑ 1 Strongly disagree	❑ 2	❑ 3	❑ 4	❑ 5	❑ 6	❑ 7	❑ 8	❑ 9 Strongly agree

7. How often do you have fantasies about having sex with someone you are *not* in a committed romantic relationship with?

❑ 1 – never	❑ 4 – about once a month	❑ 7 – several times per week
❑ 2 – very seldom	❑ 5 – about once every two weeks	❑ 8 – nearly every day
❑ 3 – about once every two or three months	❑ 6 – about once a week	❑ 9 – at least once a day

8. How often do you experience sexual arousal when you are in contact with someone you are *not* in a committed romantic relationship with?

❑ 1 – never	❑ 4 – about once a month	❑ 7 – several times per week
❑ 2 – very seldom	❑ 5 – about once every two weeks	❑ 8 – nearly every day
❑ 3 – about once every two or three months	❑ 6 – about once a week	❑ 9 – at least once a day

9. In everyday life, how often do you have spontaneous fantasies about having sex with someone you have just met?

❑ 1 – never	❑ 4 – about once a month	❑ 7 – several times per week
❑ 2 – very seldom	❑ 5 – about once every two weeks	❑ 8 – nearly every day
❑ 3 – about once every two or three months	❑ 6 – about once a week	❑ 9 – at least once a day

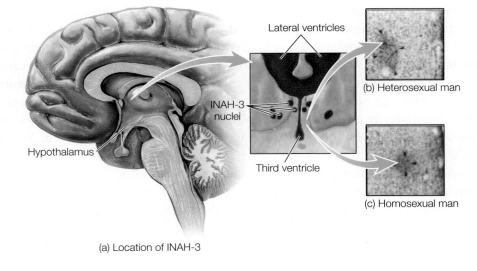

Lateral ventricles

(b) Heterosexual man

Hypothalamus

INAH-3 nuclei

Third ventricle

(c) Homosexual man

(a) Location of INAH-3

© Argosy Publishing, Inc.

FIGURE 7.14

Some Brain Differences May Correlate With Sexual Orientation. Simon LeVay reported that an area of the hypothalamus known as INAH-3 differs between heterosexual and homosexual men. If you compare the samples in (b) and (c), you can see that INAH-3, outlined by the four dark arrows, appears to be larger in the heterosexual male sample than in the homosexual male sample. The impact of this size difference on adult sexual behavior or sexual orientation remains unknown, however, as these are correlational data. *Source: Adapted from LeVay, S. (1991).*

themselves as "tomboys," and are more likely to engage in lesbian or bisexual behavior (Meyer-Bahlburg, Dolezal, Baker, & New, 2008). However, the majority of women with CAH are heterosexual, just as the vast majority of lesbian and bisexual women do not have a history of CAH or similar conditions.

An interesting clue to the origin of sexual orientation arises from the observation that birth order influences the odds that a man is homosexual. Men who have older brothers are more likely to be gay than men who have no siblings, younger siblings only, or older sisters (Blanchard, 1997). Theoretically, carrying a male fetus could provoke a mother's immune response, which would become stronger with each successive male fetus she carries. Her immune response could influence the development of her fetus by altering significant hormonal processes. Additional research is needed to identify the ways an immune system response of the mother could change the structure of her fetus's developing brain (James, 2006).

Several structures in the brain are known to be different in males and females and also seem to differ between homosexual and heterosexual males. Among these is a small cluster of neurons located in the hypothalamus known as INAH (see ● Figure 7.14). There are four separate nuclei in INAH. Two of these, INAH-2 and INAH-3, are notably larger in males than in females (Allen, Hines, Shryne, & Gorski, 1989). The exact function of these nuclei is unknown, although it is likely that they participate in sexual behavior. Building on this research about differences between the brains of men and women, Simon LeVay asked whether INAH-3 might be different in heterosexual and homosexual males. After examining the brains of over 40 individuals, LeVay (1991) concluded that INAH-3 in homosexual men was about 2–3 times smaller than in heterosexual men, or about the same size as typically found in women.

LeVay was quite cautious in his interpretation of his results. The homosexual individuals in his sample had all died from AIDS. Otherwise, there would be little reason to note sexual orientation on a person's medical records. Although it is unlikely that AIDS would produce this type of change in the brain, LeVay could not rule out that possibility based on his data. LeVay also raised the possibility that engaging in homosexual behavior might influence INAH-3, even in the adult, although he gave little credence to that possibility.

Due to the difficulties arising from this type of research in humans, others have investigated the correlations between brain structure and sexual behavior in animals. Among domestic sheep, 6 to 8% of rams (males) mate exclusively with other males. The sheep equivalent of INAH-3 is about the same size in ewes (females) as in the rams that mated with other rams. This structure is larger in rams that mated with ewes (Roselli, Larkin, Resko, Stellflug, & Stormshak, 2004).

> All women do have a different sense of sexuality, or sense of fun, or sense of like what's sexy or cool or tough.
>
> —Angelina Jolie

Cognitive and Social Motives

So far, our discussion has focused on motivational behavior that is central to maintaining life. In addition, human beings experience a wide range of complex cognitive and social motives. A lengthy list of these types of complex motives published in 1938 included achievement, affiliation, autonomy, nurturance, dominance, play, and order (Murray, 1938). More recent work focuses on needs for competence and relatedness (Deci & Ryan, 2000). Although some psychologists retain strong distinctions between biological and psychological motives, the dividing line is surely blurred. When an individual's need for affiliation is not met, the consequences of the resulting loneliness definitely include biological factors, such as increased rates of illness and death (Hawkley, Masi, Berry, & Cacioppo, 2006).

Achievement Motivation Psychologist David McClelland has devoted much of his career to the study of **achievement**, which is usually defined as a desire to excel or outperform others (McClelland, 1953, 1985; McClelland & Boyatzis, 1982). Environmental circumstances such as learning may influence a person's desire to succeed. However, overall achievement motivation appears to behave more like a personality trait, which we discuss in more detail in our chapter on personality, than the types of motivation we have discussed so far.

High achievers insist on excellent performance in every task they undertake. People with high levels of achievement motivation share a cluster of characteristics. They prefer very clear feedback. A high-achieving student accustomed to judging performance on the basis of his or her GPA may find the working world, with its more ambiguous employment reviews, somewhat frustrating. Other benchmarks, such as salary level or

achievement A desire to excel or outperform others.

having the corner office, may take on the function previously performed by grades.

Does high achievement motivation provide advantages to those who have it? To answer this question, we need to be able to assess an individual's level of achievement motivation. Using measures of individual achievement motivation, we can see that people who are high in achievement motivation seek out and typically succeed in competitive, entrepreneurial occupations (McClelland, 1985). One of the important factors predicting the success of high achievers in business is the amount of control they have over their work environment (Winter, 2010). In other situations, such as politics, control is harder to maintain, which can frustrate high achievers. A corporate CEO has an easier time implementing decisions than a political leader, who must convince many others that a decision is correct. Under these conditions of lower personal control, individual achievement motivation fails to predict success.

People with high achievement motivation demand excellence and prefer clear feedback. There is no question about who did or did not win this race.

Psychology as a Hub Science

Children of Lesbian and Gay Parents

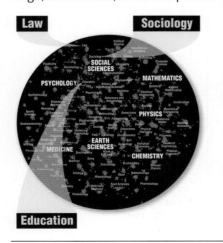

Debate currently rages in many communities regarding same-sex marriage, civil unions, domestic partnerships, and the adoption and foster care of children by lesbian and gay adults. Psychology cannot provide all the answers to these debates, but it can shed some scientific light on the implications for children of having a lesbian or gay parent. A scientific understanding of these issues can better inform legal adoption and foster care decisions as well as provide those who work with children and families a realistic perspective.

Among the outcomes of family type explored by researchers have been children's gender development, sexual orientation, and social relationships (Patterson, 2009; Wainright & Patterson, 2008). As we will see in our chapter on development, gender identity refers to the person's sense of being male or female. Related aspects of gender development include gendered behavior, which means that a child conforms to social norms regarding masculine and feminine behavior, and sexual orientation. Research with very young children has shown few differences in gender identity or gendered behavior between children living with same-sex or opposite-sex parents (Patterson, 2009). Peer relationships among adolescents being raised by female same-sex couples were not different in quantity or quality from those

The Motivation to Affiliate Human beings are a social species. When people are asked to identify which pleasures are most important to their happiness, the overwhelming majority rate love, intimacy, and social **affiliation** above wealth, fame, and even physical health (Cacioppo & Patrick, 2008).

Not only do people value affiliation, but a perceived lack of connection with others can have devastating effects. Solitary confinement is viewed as one of the worst punishments human beings inflict on one another. The effects of social isolation can be as detrimental to good health as high blood pressure, lack of exercise, obesity, or smoking (House, Landis, & Umberson, 1988). Not all behaviors associated with feeling isolated or rejected are self-destructive. In some cases, feeling isolated can result in outwardly hostile behavior (see ● Figure 7.15). Students told in an experiment that a personality test had shown that they were "the type likely to end up alone later in life" showed less empathy and more aggression toward other students than did students told that they would enjoy "rewarding relationships throughout life" (Twenge,

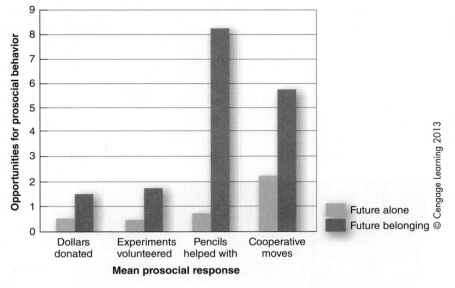

FIGURE 7.15

Effects of Social Exclusion on Helping Behaviors. Participants who were told that a personality test indicated they were likely to spend their future alone, without significant relationships, were far less helpful across different types of tasks than participants who were told that they were likely to have a future featuring acceptance and belongingness. *Source:* Adapted from Twenge, Baumeister, Tice, and Stucke (2007).

affiliation Being associated with other people.

among adolescents with opposite-sex parents (Wainright & Patterson, 2008). The results of research into the sexual orientation of those raised by same-sex or opposite-sex parents are inconclusive. Some researchers report no differences, while others showed that about 9% of boys raised by gay fathers, compared to the 2% of adult males in the general population that we mentioned earlier, identify themselves as gay (Patterson, 2009). In general, the research evidence shows little if any differences in outcomes for children raised by heterosexual or homosexual parents. ○

According to the 2010 U.S. Census, about one third of lesbians are parents and about one fifth of gay men are parents. Homosexual parents are raising children from prior heterosexual relationships, children born through assisted reproduction, or adopted children.

Baumeister, Tice, & Stucke, 2001). It is probably not an accident that most individuals responsible for school shootings are described as "outcasts" or "loners."

The experience of loneliness appears to serve as an aversive signal that, like hunger, thirst, and pain, evolved to warn human beings that they are facing a threat to their survival and that their social connections are in need of repair (Cacioppo & Patrick, 2008). Social connections are especially important to the survival of human beings. Compared to other species, human beings require the greatest amount of parenting to survive to adulthood and reproduce. In addition, as we discuss in a later chapter on social psychology, human beings are not well equipped to survive in isolation. Our ancestors formed hunter-gatherer groups because the cooperative sharing of responsibilities enhanced the survival of all.

Individuals differ in the amount of social connection they desire. Early work on affiliation by Henry Murray (1938) and David McClelland (1985) viewed the need for others as similar to a personality trait, as we discuss further in our chapter on personality. Some people are relatively happy working in a cubicle for hours on end, while this lack of social contact would be intolerable for others. Still others might feel lonely even when surrounded by large numbers of caring friends and family members. We appear to have a set point for social activity that operates similarly to the set points we mentioned in our discussion of hunger. When we sense a gap between our actual social connectivity and what we desire, we experience the unpleasant state of loneliness, which in turn motivates us to seek out more social experiences. Twin studies show that this set point, like the others we have discussed, is influenced by our genetics (Boomsma, Willemsen, Dolan, Hawkley, & Cacioppo, 2005). Knowing one identical twin's need for affiliation helps predict the other twin's need as well.

Individual predispositions interact with a person's situation to predict his or her desire for affiliation. We frequently join others to share good events, whether that means a birthday, a wedding, a promotion, or simply the end of another round of final exams. We have all enjoyed the camaraderie of staying in the stands long after our team has won an important game, celebrating with nearby fans and exchanging high fives.

Affiliation is not just for good times, however. People often find the company of others to be stress reducing. In a classic series of experiments, Stanley Schachter (1959) showed that people expecting to be given a painful electric shock were more likely to seek out the company of other participants than wait for their shock alone. Not all stressful situations are equally likely to produce affiliation, however. In one study, participants were told that they would be performing very embarrassing behaviors, such as sucking on large pacifiers (Sarnoff & Zimbardo, 1961). Needless to say, these

People affiliate not only to share happy occasions, like the wedding of Prince William and Kate Middleton, but also to reduce stress in sad times. These family members of victims of the September 11 terrorist attacks have gathered to throw flowers in the memorial pools at Ground Zero.

participants made very different choices than the participants expecting shock in the previous study. They definitely preferred to be alone.

Exactly what does the company of other people contribute to reducing stress? It appears that we appreciate the company of others when we expect them to reduce our stress. In many cases, other people can reduce our stress by providing information. Hospital patients awaiting dangerous surgeries preferred roommates who had already been through the procedure to those who had not yet had surgery (Kulik, Mahler, & Moore, 1996).

Motivational Priorities

We have discussed a number of different motivations, from hunger to sex to achievement to affiliation. If faced simultaneously with a number of drives and demands, how do we decide which motivations to follow first?

An early effort to provide a model for how motivations could be prioritized was contributed by Abraham Maslow in 1943. Maslow viewed motivation as a hierarchy of needs, in which lower levels must be satisfied before the individual has the time and energy to pursue higher level needs. As shown in ● Figure 7.16, Maslow's model is typically illustrated as a pyramid.

At the lowest level of the pyramid, we find "physiological needs," including food, water, and shelter. These basic needs must be met on a daily basis, or life will be threatened. Consequently, if meeting these needs is a challenge for a person, Maslow predicted that the person is unlikely to care about needs appearing at higher levels of the hierarchy. In a classic study of caloric restriction, young healthy men were given approximately 1,500 calories per day for 6 months, which resulted in a loss of about 25% of their normal body weight (Keys, Brozek, Henschel, Mickelsen, & Taylor, 1950). Not only did the men become obsessed with food, but their interest in sex declined dramatically.

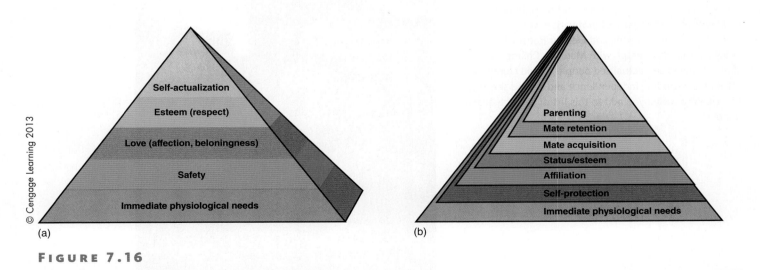

© Cengage Learning 2013

(a)

(b)

FIGURE 7.16

Classic and Contemporary Hierarchies of Needs. Maslow's classic pyramid depicting his hierarchy of needs is shown in (a). Douglas Kenrick and his colleagues (2010) have proposed an updated version of the pyramid (b) that incorporates developmental and evolutionary perspectives. *Source: Adapted from Kenrick, Griskevicius, Neuberg, and Schaller (2010).*

Once physiological needs are generally met, Maslow suggests that we turn our attention to safety, and then to belongingness, represented by the love and affection of others. For Maslow, these three lower categories are essential to human life. Unfortunately, one doesn't need to look too far in the daily news to read about large numbers of the world's population who do not attain these basic needs.

Schoolteachers often face students who come to school hungry or sick due to poverty or neglect. According to Maslow, it will be difficult for the teacher to interest these children, whose basic needs are unmet, in learning about long division.

Freed from the challenges of meeting basic needs, we begin to seek esteem, or the respect we receive from other members of the community. At the pinnacle of human striving, however, is the goal of **self-actualization**, according to Maslow. A person seeking self-actualization desires to fully meet his or her potential, as suggested by the Army slogan "Be all you can be." Cultures differ dramatically in their emphasis on self-actualization, with individualistic nations like the United States embracing this value more than collectivist nations in Southeast Asia, where harmony and belongingness are highly valued (Hofstede, 1984).

Maslow's classic theory received a recent modification that retained the overall hierarchical organization but added three new perspectives: the evolutionary functions of motives, the development of motives over the lifespan, and the cognitive priorities assigned to motives in response to environmental stimuli (Kenrick, Griskevicius, Neuberg, & Schaller, 2010). This modified pyramid, illustrated in Figure 7.16, replaces self-actualization with mate acquisition, mate retention, and parenting. The authors of the revision noted that self-actualization was interesting, but they could not find an evolutionary explanation for why we would seek to reach this level. Many of the activities described by Maslow as helping people to reach self-actualization, such as art and poetry, might be better explained as efforts to gain status, which in turn would attract mates.

Abraham Maslow did not believe that everyone achieved self-actualization. Among the select few he believed had reached this pinnacle of motivation were Abraham Lincoln, Mahatma Gandhi, and Eleanor Roosevelt, shown in this photograph with Madame Chiang Kai-shek. Maslow's self-actualized people shared common attributes, including independence and a good sense of humor. Who would you add to this list of self-actualized people?

© AP Photo

self-actualization A state of having fulfilled your potential.

Summary 7.1

Important Concepts in Motivation

Term		Meaning	Example
Motivation © Michael Steele/ Allsport/Getty Images		A process that arouses, maintains, and guides behavior to a goal	Being thirsty leads you to seek out a drinking fountain and get a drink of water.
Homeostasis © Steve Cole/Photodisc/ Getty Images		A steady internal balance or equilibrium	We are motivated to maintain a constant internal temperature. If we feel cold, we shiver and put on more clothing.
Set point © Drew D. Saur		A value actively defended to maintain homeostasis	It is hard to lose weight because we actively defend our previous weight by slowing down metabolism when fewer calories are consumed.
Drive © AP Photo/Gur- inder Osan		A state of arousal or tension resulting from stimuli that are important to survival	Being hungry is unpleasant.
Drive reduction © dbimages/Alamy		The feelings of relief and reward following a return to equilibrium	Quenching your thirst on a very hot day is very rewarding.
Incentives © Sonia Moskowitz- Globe Photos, Inc./ Newscom		Rewards that motivate behavior without the experience of any unpleasant drive state	We enjoy throwing a great surprise party for a friend's birthday.

Why Are We Emotional?

Whether we're experiencing happiness or sadness, anger or disgust, an emotion combines a physical sensation, such as a rapid heartbeat, and a conscious, subjective feeling, like fear or sadness.

Emotional behavior is not unique to human beings. Charles Darwin (1872) made a careful study of the facial expressions produced by humans and other primates. He concluded that all primates form facial expressions using the same muscles, which in turn led him to state that emotional facial expression must have evolved. Although we are frequently cautioned about anthropomorphism, or the attributing of human qualities to other animals, it is easy to identify with the anger of a mother bear defending her cubs or the fear of a gazelle trying to outrun a cheetah.

The evolution of a behavior implies that it makes survival more likely. The survival benefits of motivation are rather obvious, but what about those of emotion? A major advantage provided by emotion is the ability to produce arousal. The word *emotion* is derived from the Latin word meaning "to move." The arousal produced by an emotion stimulates action, which might be life-saving. According to the **Yerkes-Dodson law**, the ideal amount of arousal interacts with the complexity of a task (Yerkes & Dodson, 1908). For simple tasks, such as outrunning a predator, greater arousal leads to greater performance. For more complex tasks, like taking a difficult exam, arousal levels that are too high can begin to interfere with performance (see ● Figure 7.17). We have all had the experience of "choking," or performing badly because of too much arousal. In addition to providing general arousal, each emotion is associated with a positive or negative quality, which "moves" us in the direction of either approach or avoidance

Wellcome Library, London

Fig 18. Chimpanzee disappointed and sulky. Drawn from life by Mr. Wood.

© Sergey Lavrentev/123rf

Charles Darwin discovered that humans and other primates use the same facial muscles to produce emotional expressions, leading him to hypothesize that emotions evolved. Can you figure out what emotion is being expressed by both the chimpanzee and the man? Try imitating the expression yourself and think about how you feel. Still no luck? The emotion being expressed is disappointment.

Yerkes-Dodson law A description of the relationships between task complexity, arousal, and performance.

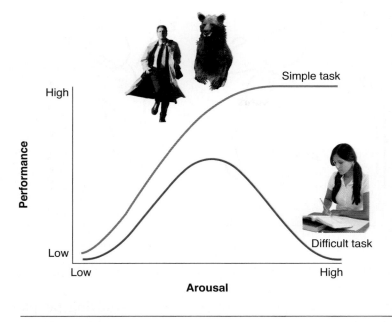

FIGURE 7.17

The Effects of Arousal on Performance. The Yerkes-Dodson law predicts that the complexity of a task interacts with an organism's arousal level to determine the quality of performance. For simple tasks, like running to escape a predator, greater arousal leads to a relatively steady improvement in performance. For difficult tasks, like completing an exam, moderate amounts of arousal lead to the best performance, and very high arousal can lead to weaker performance. Illustration: © Cengage Learning 2013; photos: © Tetra Images/Alamy; © Cathy Hart Photography/Alaska Stock/Alamy; © mocker_bat/iStockphoto

(Davidson & Irwin, 1999). The negative emotion of disgust tells us to avoid rotting food, and positive feelings of happiness cement our social bonds.

In addition to producing beneficial arousal, emotions enhance survival by providing an important means of communication. Nonverbal forms of communication such as facial expression, calls, and body language were used to provide information to others long before humans began using the spoken word (see ●Figure 7.18). If one person assumes a body posture indicating fear, the emotion ripples through a crowd to its edges in a very short amount of time (de Gelder, Snyder, Greve, Gerard, & Hadjikhani, 2004). Human infants manage to communicate a wide range of needs to their parents before developing the ability to speak. You have no difficulty whatsoever interpreting the facial expressions, body language, and gestures of the driver behind you, who obviously didn't approve of your lane change technique.

An additional and welcome benefit of having emotions is our ability to enjoy the arts. Evidence for a coordinated development of language and emotional communication remains in our contemporary brain, which uses the same pathways for language and for the perception and appreciation of music (Schön, et al., 2010). Without the capacity to feel, we would find it difficult to appreciate a Picasso or the moving strains of "Yesterday" by the Beatles. We wouldn't enjoy a good cry at the end of *Pride and Prejudice* or jump out of our seats while watching *Saw*. The universal nature of human responses to many poems, pieces of music, and other artistic accomplishments points to shared underlying mechanisms, shaped through our evolutionary past. Shared enjoyment of the arts contributes greatly to social bonding in human societies. When we dance together, sing together, or watch plays

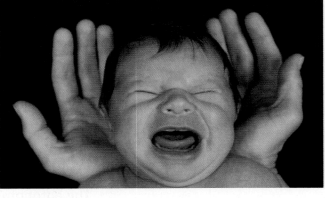

Long before infants learn to speak, they are able to communicate with adults by using facial expressions.

WHY ARE WE EMOTIONAL?

321

FIGURE 7.18

Body Language. One of the advantages of emotions is the ability to communicate nonverbally. Even with these simple stick figures, it is easy to interpret how each character feels.

and other visual displays of art, shared emotional responses contribute to feelings of community and closeness.

We can also identify the advantages of emotion by studying people whose emotional lives have been impacted by brain damage. In our chapter on biological psychology, we reviewed the case of Phineas Gage, whose frontal lobe damage changed him from a responsible, well-liked member of the community to an impulsive, indecisive, and emotionally volatile individual who had difficulty keeping a job. More recently, the case of a young man named Eliot, who had frontal lobe surgery to remove a tumor, was described by Antonio Damasio (1994). Like Gage, Eliot maintained his intelligence and other skills after his surgery, with the notable exception of his ability to establish priorities. Damasio hypothesizes that emotions provide a bridge to past experiences that can be used to set priorities like approach and avoidance. In the absence of normal feedback from the body that can be used to identify emotional states (my heart is beating fast so I must be scared), Eliot can no longer use these past experiences to guide his current decisions.

The Biology of Emotion

In our chapter on biological psychology, we identified a number of nervous system structures that participate in our emotional lives.

The autonomic nervous system, which controls many activities of our glands and organs, participates in the general arousal associated with emotional states. In particular, activity of the sympathetic division of the autonomic nervous system is correlated with our "fight-flight" response to perceived danger. The autonomic nervous system is under the immediate control of the hypothalamus, a structure that plays an important role in most motivated behavior.

Researchers have asked if specific patterns of autonomic activity occur during particular emotional states. In an analysis of a large number of studies conducted over the past 50 years, autonomic measures did not reliably predict particular emotional states, such as happiness or sadness (Cacioppo, Berntson, Larsen, Poehlmann, & Ito, 2000). However, the analysis indicated that the autonomic responses associated with negative emotions generally appear to be stronger than those associated with positive emotions. Fear, with its rapid heartbeat and sweaty palms, provokes a much more dramatic set of physical reactions than feelings of happiness.

It is interesting to note that we seem to place a general priority on negative emotions, probably because they signal more serious threats to survival than positive emotions, at least in the short term. When an event results in a positive emotion, little change in behavior is required, but when an event results in a negative emotion, action can be more important to survival (Cacioppo, Berntson, Norris, & Gollan, 2011).

In addition to the hypothalamus, several other subcortical structures, described in our chapter on biological psychology, appear to participate in the regulation of emotion. Among these, the amygdala, the cingulate cortex, and the insula appear to play particularly important roles in our emotional lives. Other areas that play major roles in emotion include the basal ganglia and, of course, the cerebral cortex.

The mind's priority for processing negative events has been described in earlier chapters. For example, in our introductory and sensation and perception chapters, we discussed the fact that we are far more sensitive to bitter tastes, because these are often associated with poisons, than we are to sweet tastes, which are rarely life threatening.

The Amygdala and the Insula The amygdala and the **insula**, regions located within the fold at the junction of the frontal and temporal lobes, play important roles in the identification of emotional stimuli and the initiation of arousal in response to the perception of these stimuli.

One of the first clues to the importance of the amygdala to emotion resulted from an experiment conducted in 1939 in which researchers removed both temporal lobes, which include the amygdala, from rhesus monkeys (Klüver & Bucy, 1939). After recovery, the normally hard-to-handle adult rhesus monkeys became much tamer, and their emotions were much less intense. They allowed themselves to be picked up and stroked and appeared to be relatively oblivious to stimuli that normally elicit intense fear, such as snakes. They made fewer fear-related grimaces and vocalizations.

Subsequent research has refined our understanding of the role of the amygdala. This structure acts to evaluate environmental stimuli for potential danger and coordinate appropriate responses (Schumann, Bauman, Machado, & Amaral, 2006). The activity of the amygdala changes when participants look at faces expressing happiness or fear (Williams et al., 2006). As fearful expressions become more intense, activity in the amygdala increases as well (see ● Figure 7.19). If the amygdala is damaged, animals typically respond inappropriately to danger. Rats with damaged amygdalas fail to learn to fear a tone or other stimulus that reliably predicts the onset of electric shock (LeDoux, Cicchetti, Xagoraris, & Romanski, 1990). Rhesus monkeys with lesioned amygdalas show less fear of rubber snakes or restraint around unfamiliar monkeys, a potentially dangerous way of behaving in a species that enforces very strict social hierarchies (Emery et al., 2001; Mason, Capitanio, Machado, Mendoza, & Amaral, 2006).

Insight into the role of the amygdala in human beings has been provided by case studies in which disease has damaged this structure (see ● Figure 7.20). Patient S.M. experienced damage to both amygdalas due to a rare disease (Adolphs, Tranel, Damasio, & Damasio, 1994). Although S.M. can recognize the emotions of happiness, sadness, and disgust portrayed in

insula Regions of cortex located at the junction of the frontal and temporal lobes.

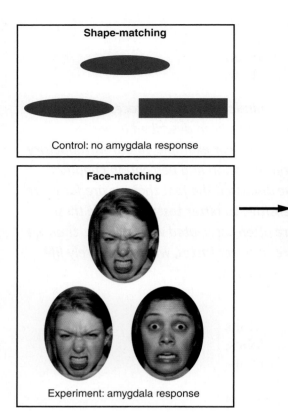

Shape-matching

Control: no amygdala response

Face-matching

Experiment: amygdala response

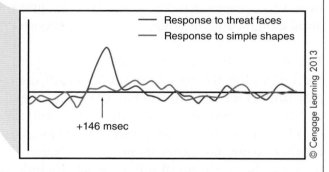

FIGURE 7.19

The Amygdala Responds to Fear and Threat. A combination of functional magnetic resonance imaging (fMRI) and recordings taken of the magnetic output of the brain (magnetoencephalography) allowed researchers not only to localize the reaction of the brain to threatening or frightened faces to the amygdala but also to measure the timing of the response. It takes a bit over one tenth of a second for the amygdala to process these negative emotions. The geometric shapes were used as a control condition, and as you can see, they did not initiate any reactions in the amygdala. From Cornwell et al., Evoked amygdala responses to negative faces revealed by adaptive MEG beamformers, *Brain Research,* 2008 Dec. 9; 1244: 103–112.

Response to threat faces
Response to simple shapes

+146 msec

© Cengage Learning 2013

FIGURE 7.20

Patient S.M. Does Not Perceive Negative Emotion in Music. Patient S.M., whose amygdalas have been damaged by a rare condition called Urbach-Weithe disease, was asked to rate pieces of music according to how scary, peaceful, happy, or sad they sounded to her. As comparisons, 16 patients who had undergone temporal lobe surgery that had damaged their amygdalas and 20 healthy control participants were asked to perform the same task. Consistent with other findings about Patient S.M., her detection of "scary" was significantly less than that of the control subjects, as were the performances on this task by the patients whose surgery had damaged their amygdalas. Differences in emotional judgments along the other three dimensions did not differ among the participants. *Source:* Adapted from Gosselin et al. (2007).

Patient S.M.
Post-surgical patients
Controls

© Cengage Learning 2013

photographs, she has selective difficulty identifying fear correctly (Adolphs et al., 1994; Adolphs, Tranel, Damasio, & Damasio, 1995). Patient S.M. has particular difficulty using information from the eye region of the face in judging emotion, although when she was instructed to pay attention to eyes, her performance improved (Adolphs et al., 2005; Adolphs, 2007). Individuals with autism, discussed in our chapter on psychological disorders, share Patient S.M.'s reluctance to make eye contact and difficulties identifying other people's emotions, especially fear. One of the most consistent biological correlates of autism is abnormal development of the amygdala (Amaral, Schumann, & Nordahl, 2008) (see ● Figure 7.21). These findings suggest that the amygdala participates in both the active exploration of the social environment and the interpretation of the results of that exploration (Adolphs, 2007).

When the amygdala perceives danger, it initiates a hormonal cascade involving the pituitary gland and the adrenal glands that produces an increased release of neurotransmitters in the brain, leading to an increase in overall arousal. We will discuss this process in greater detail in our chapter on stress and coping.

The amygdala is part of a tightly connected circuit that includes the frontal lobes of the cortex, the cingulate cortex (discussed in the next section), and the insula (see ● Figure 7.22). This circuit plays an important role in the identification and classification of emotional stimuli. The role of the insula in emotion was illustrated by an experiment in which patients with damage to the insula were asked to rate pictures on a scale from very pleasant to very unpleasant and to indicate how arousing each picture was (Berntson et al., 2011). These participants showed an overall decrease both in their ratings of positivity or negativity and in their arousal ratings when compared to control participants. In contrast, patients with damage to their amygdalas did not show any deficits in assessing positivity and negativity. However, the patients with damage to the amygdala indicated much less arousal in response to unpleasant pictures. These results suggest that the amygdala plays an important role in initiating arousal, particularly to negative stimuli, while the insula more broadly helps us make the important distinction between positive and negative stimuli.

The Cingulate Cortex and the Basal Ganglia

The cingulate cortex, shown in ● Figure 7.23, serves as a major gateway between the amygdala and other subcortical structures and the frontal areas of the cortex.

The cingulate cortex is the target of a number of pathways communicating information about physical pain. The emotional quality of pain probably results from its processing at this level of the brain. In addition to physical pain, the cingulate cortex participates in the processing of social pain, as in the negative feelings associated with being

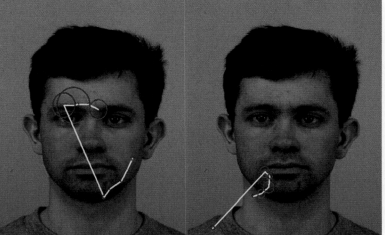

Image courtesy of Brendon Nacewicz, University of Wisconsin-Madison

FIGURE 7.21

Eye Contact and Detecting Emotion. Eyetracking technology allows researchers to identify where people look when they view a stimulus. Fixation points for healthy participants are shown on the left, and fixation points for participants with autism are shown on the right. Participants with autism do not look at eyes as much as healthy participants do.

FIGURE 7.22

The Insula.

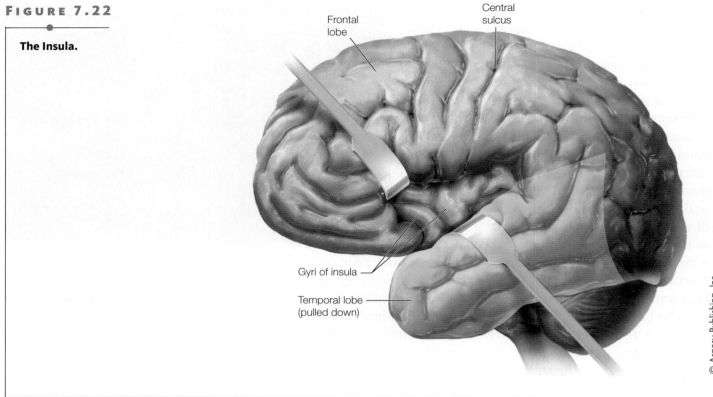

Frontal lobe

Central sulcus

Gyri of insula

Temporal lobe (pulled down)

© Argosy Publishing, Inc.

FIGURE 7.23

The Cingulate Cortex and Basal Ganglia. The cingulate cortex forms circuits with the frontal cortex, the amygdala, and other subcortical structures involved with emotional processing. This structure shows similar activation when you experience physical pain, like stubbing your toe, and when you experience the pain of social exclusion. The basal ganglia are part of the brain's voluntary movement systems and help coordinate movement in response to assessments of emotion. The basal ganglia show particularly strong activation that correlates with the emotion of disgust.

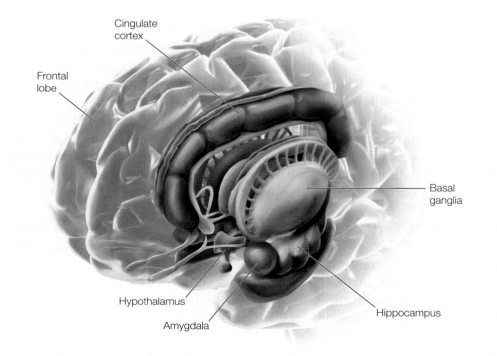

Cingulate cortex

Frontal lobe

Basal ganglia

Hypothalamus

Amygdala

Hippocampus

© Argosy Publishing, Inc.

The results of this study suggest that the participants were not very good at discriminating the physical sensations associated with fear and sexual arousal. We can assume that the attractiveness of the female would be constant, suggesting that the setting in which she was seen largely accounted for the differences in sexual content in interviews and the likelihood of seeking further contact with her. One might speculate that similar mistakes underlie the popularity of horror films and amusement parks with impossibly high roller coasters as dating activities. Scare your date to death, and he or she may interpret feelings of fear as love. These results suggest that in some circumstances, we might not be as good at interpreting our physical sensations as predicted by the James-Lange theory.

The Cannon-Bard Theory of Emotion Walter Cannon disagreed with the James-Lange theory and proposed his own theory, which was later modified by Philip Bard (Bard, 1934; Cannon, 1927). The product of these two men's work is known as the **Cannon-Bard theory**. The James-Lange theory proposes a sequence of events, from physical sensations to subjective feeling, but the Cannon-Bard theory proposes that both factors occur simultaneously and independently (see ● Figure 7.30).

How are these theories different? Let's assume that you are innocently reading your textbook in your room when a bear walks in the door. For James-Lange, the sight of the bear would immediately set off physical sensations that you would then cognitively interpret as fear. For Cannon-Bard, the sight of the bear would immediately and simultaneously trigger a subjective feeling of fear (oh no, there's a bear in my room) and physical sensations (probably the autonomic nervous system's fight-flight response in this example). Unlike James-Lange, the Cannon-Bard theory does not assume that the experience of a subjective feeling is dependent on any physical sensations.

The Cannon-Bard theory fares somewhat better in explaining the Capilano Canyon results. Cannon and Bard would be very comfortable with the notion that fear and sexual arousal would produce similar physical sensations, and the participants may simply have erred in their cognitive assessment of the situation. Instead of saying, "I'm really scared because I'm on this bridge," the participants would say, "I think this interviewer is very attractive." According to this model, a person's cognitive assessments of an emotional situation work independently of any physical sensations that might occur.

John Stibbard, son of the owner of the Capilano Suspension Bridge, poses on the bridge with the Olympic Torch after completing his leg of the torch run in preparation for the 2010 Winter Olympics in Vancouver, Canada.

© AP Photo/Matt Dunham

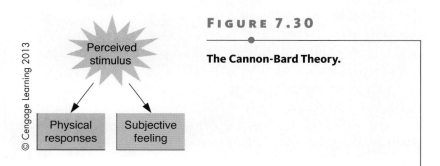

FIGURE 7.30

The Cannon-Bard Theory.

© Cengage Learning 2013

Cannon-Bard theory A theory of emotion featuring the simultaneous and independent occurrence of physical sensations and subjective feelings during an emotional experience.

The Schachter-Singer Two-Factor Theory Stanley Schachter and Jerome Singer proposed a two-factor theory of emotion (see ● Figure 7.32). Schachter and Singer (1962) believed that each emotional experience begins with an assessment of our physical sensations. Because these reactions can be similar among emotional states (fear and sexual arousal on

Connecting *to* Research

Botox and the Ability to Read the Emotions of Others

Botox, a deactivated form of the same toxin that causes botulism poisoning from spoiled food, helps people with neurological disorders of movement, but it is more commonly used for cosmetic purposes. Botox reduces wrinkling by paralyzing the small muscles that are used in facial expressions. The ability of Botox to prevent facial movement provides an interesting test for the James-Lange theory. Without feedback from our facial expressions, can we identify our own emotions? Without the ability to

imitate the facial expressions of others, can we still identify how they're feeling? These questions were scientifically investigated by Neal and Chartrand (2011).

The Question: How would increasing and decreasing the ability to move facial muscles impact participants' judgments of the emotions of others?

METHODS

In a first experiment, 31 female participants were recruited from cosmetic surgery clinics. Sixteen participants had been treated with Botox, and

the other 15 had been treated with a dermal filler material, which does not restrict the movement of facial muscles. Participants viewed photographs of eyes and the surrounding area and were asked to choose which of four emotional adjectives (happy, sad, and so on) best fit the expression they saw (see ● Figure 7.31). In a second experiment, a gel that made facial movement difficult was placed on the faces of half of a group of 95 participants and on the arms of the other half. Participants completed the same test of identification of emotion as before, along with two control

Several actresses from the *Real Housewives of Beverly Hills* television series have admitted to using Botox. One prominent Beverly Hills plastic surgeon has told his celebrity clients that Botox might actually hurt their acting careers as it makes facial expression more difficult. Botox not only immobilizes the face but also has been shown to decrease empathy. Research has indicated that being unable to imitate the expressions of another person reduces the accuracy of judgments of that individual's feelings.

Photo by: Casey Rodgers/Bravo/NBCU Photo Bank via AP Images

the Capilano bridge), they suggested that interpreting these states requires another step. Any emotional arousal signals us to make a conscious, cognitive appraisal of our circumstances, which then allows us to identify the emotion we're experiencing. Physical sensations may lead to several different interpretations, based on the way an individual assesses a situation.

Returning to our example of the bear entering your room, we can see how the **Schachter-Singer two-factor theory** differs from James-Lange and Cannon-Bard. For Schachter and Singer, the sight of the bear would initiate a general state of arousal. To identify the source of your arousal, you would assess your situation, attribute your arousal to the presence of a bear in your room, and identify your feelings as fear (with considerable accuracy, we would assume.)

Schachter-Singer two-factor theory A theory of emotion in which general arousal leads to assessment, which in turn leads to subjective feelings.

tests—identifying emotion in voices, which is unlikely to be affected by facial expression, and a set of arithmetic questions.

RESULTS

In experiment 1, the Botox group performed significantly more poorly on the identification of emotions task than the control group that had received the dermal filler instead of Botox. In experiment 2, participants with the restricting gel placed on the face performed better than those with the gel on their arms.

CONCLUSIONS

Both experiments support the idea that feedback from facial expressions of emotion influences the ability to identify emotional states in other people. The participants in the first experiment who used Botox had less facial mobility than the participants who had used the dermal filler. The lack of facial mobility caused by Botox appears to have interfered with the participants' ability to accurately assess another person's emotional state as indicated by a facial expression. In the second experiment, making the muscles work harder to imitate a facial expression by applying a restrictive gel actually improved the participants' ability to identify the facial expressions of others. These results are quite consistent with the James-Lange theory's emphasis on feedback from the body as important to the subjective identification of emotion, not just in ourselves but in other people. These results suggest that an important side effect of Botox might be a reduction in social competence and empathy due to an inability to read the emotions of other people correctly. ⚙

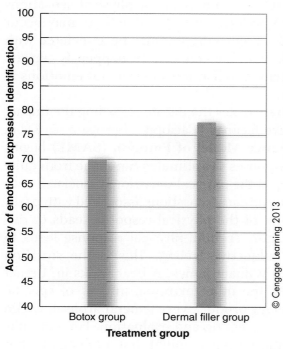

FIGURE 7.31

Botox Reduces the Ability to Identify Facial Expressions in Others. Following treatment for wrinkles with either Botox or an injected dermal filler (Restylane), participants were asked to identify the emotional expression of faces presented on a computer screen. The dermal filler group was significantly better than the Botox group at correctly identifying the emotions. This result suggests that by reducing the ability to imitate another person's facial expressions, Botox limits a person's perception of the emotions of other people. *Source:* Adapted from Neal and Chartrand (2011).

© Cengage Learning 2013

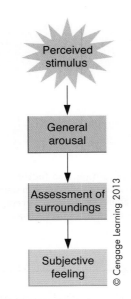

FIGURE 7.32

The Schachter-Singer Two-Factor Theory.

Somatovisceral Afference Model of Emotion (SAME) A model of emotion in which a range of physical sensations from precise to general requires varying degrees of cognitive processing prior to subjective feelings.

Schachter and Singer (1962) directly tested this approach by injecting volunteers with epinephrine (adrenalin), which causes a high level of arousal. The participants had been told that they were getting an injection of a vitamin and that their vision would be tested as soon as another volunteer arrived to participate in the experiment. The second volunteer was actually an actor employed by the researchers. In half of the trials, the actor behaved in a happy, silly manner, while in the other half, he acted angry and stomped out of the room. The results supported a role for cognitive assessment of the environment in the identification of emotion. Participants who were exposed to the happy actor rated themselves as feeling happy, while participants exposed to the angry actor felt more negative. Importantly, when the participants were accurately informed that they were getting a drug that produced arousal instead of a vitamin, the behavior of the actor did not influence their assessment of the situation. Instead, they attributed their feelings to the drug.

A later attempt to replicate Schachter and Singer's study did not succeed (Marshall & Zimbardo, 1979). As we discussed in our chapter on research methods, a failure to replicate a study casts very serious doubts on the results. Nonetheless, Schachter and Singer's theory has provided considerable insight into how we identify our subjective feelings. Schachter and Singer account easily for the Capilano bridge study. Once aroused by being on the scary bridge, the male subjects assessed their circumstances and attributed their feelings to sexual attraction. Additional support is provided by research that demonstrates that arousal produced by one emotion can transfer to and intensify a second emotion. People who have just exercised (producing physiological arousal) are more likely to become angry or sexually aroused when exposed to relevant stimuli (Reisenzein, 1983).

Contemporary Approaches Each of these theories offers important insights into our experience of emotion, yet none definitively resolves our original question regarding the relationship between physical sensations and subjective feelings. The same patterns of physical activity may occur during a variety of emotions, and a single emotion may be associated with a variety of physical states. That mistakes can and do happen is certain. Nonetheless, we seem to manage quite well at interpreting our emotions in the majority of situations.

A more contemporary model reconciles the debate regarding the impact of physical sensations on subjective feelings (Cacioppo, Berntson, & Klein, 1992). The **Somatovisceral Afference Model of Emotion (SAME)** begins with a recognition that physical responses to a stimulus can range from quite specific to quite general. For example, the physical sensations associated with disgust can be more precise than the physical sensations associated with pride.

The initial degree of specificity of the physical response leads to different cognitive processing. A highly specific physical response leads to unambiguous recognition of a subjective feeling. This is the situation that appeared most interesting to William James. A bear walks in, I react physically, I know I'm scared. At the other extreme, instead of specific physical responses, a situation might produce very general arousal, which will require significant cognitive processing and evaluation. For example, a valedictorian giving a graduation speech might not understand her arousal until she sees her parents and other members of the audience clapping and realizes the emotion she is feeling is pride. This scenario is closest to that proposed by Schachter and Singer (1962).

SAME provides for middle ground between James-Lange and Schachter and Singer. If a physical response is only partially specific, an ambiguous message is sent forward that is clarified by the presence of additional cues or information (see ● Figure 7.33). The model correctly predicts that emotional responses range from immediate to delayed, based on the amount of cognitive processing that is required. Emotions that are associated with a precise set of physical responses, like fear, occur very quickly, but emotions that are associated with more general arousal, like pride, occur relatively slowly.

Contemporary cognitive approaches to emotion place little emphasis on the physical correlates that are featured so prominently in the classical theories. Instead, these approaches emphasize the role of appraisals, or interpretations, of stimuli in eliciting emotion. For example, Ellsworth (1994) expresses some frustration with the approach taken by William James when she says, "Bears do not automatically cause us to run or tremble." Instead, the interpretation of the stimulus, the bear in this case, forms the starting point for the emotional cascade. Appraisal theories further assume that interpretation requires a sequence of judgments, rather than a single decision about a stimulus (Ellsworth, 1991). For example, attention may be aroused by some change in the environment. No recognizable emotion has yet occurred, and if the appraisal of the stimulus determines it to be of no significance, arousal will return to baseline. However, if the stimulus is found to have positive or negative value (a source of food or a predator, for instance), feelings and physiological responses change yet again.

An emphasis on appraisal as a starting point for emotion may help us account for the vast range of emotional reactions that individuals might have to the same event. One person may view material wealth as essential to happiness, whereas another will view successful relationships with others as a primary goal. These different cognitive patterns may be expected to produce different emotional responses to the same event. A letter to an advice columnist described a situation in which a man's wife had wrecked his very expensive antique automobile in a serious accident ("Dear Abby," 2006). Our first person, who values money, is likely to respond with dismay at the loss of the expensive car. Our second person, who values relationships, is likely to be very happy that his beloved wife survived the accident in one piece.

A variation of the appraisal approach to emotion suggests that emotions frequently occur in response to an individual's progress toward a goal (Carver & Scheier, 1990). According to this view, failure to reach a desired goal in the anticipated amount of time will lead to negative emotions. For example, a sprinter competing in a 100-meter event may be distressed when she is passed by another runner, even though she is on pace to a new personal best.

© Ian Paterson/Alamy

FIGURE 7.33

The Somatovisceral Afference Model of Emotion (SAME). This ambiguous image (you should find yourself alternating between seeing a young woman and an old woman) can serve as a model for how the mind processes a range of emotional situations, from very simple to very complex. If we look at a very simple image, we need very little cognitive assessment to respond appropriately. As images become more complex, we require increasing amounts of cognitive assessment before we respond. Processing the simple emotion of fear is similar to processing an unambiguous image. Processing more complex, ambiguous emotions, like pride, requires more cognitive assessment, just like viewing this ambiguous image does.

Summary 7.2

Theories of Emotion

Name of theory	Major features
James-Lange 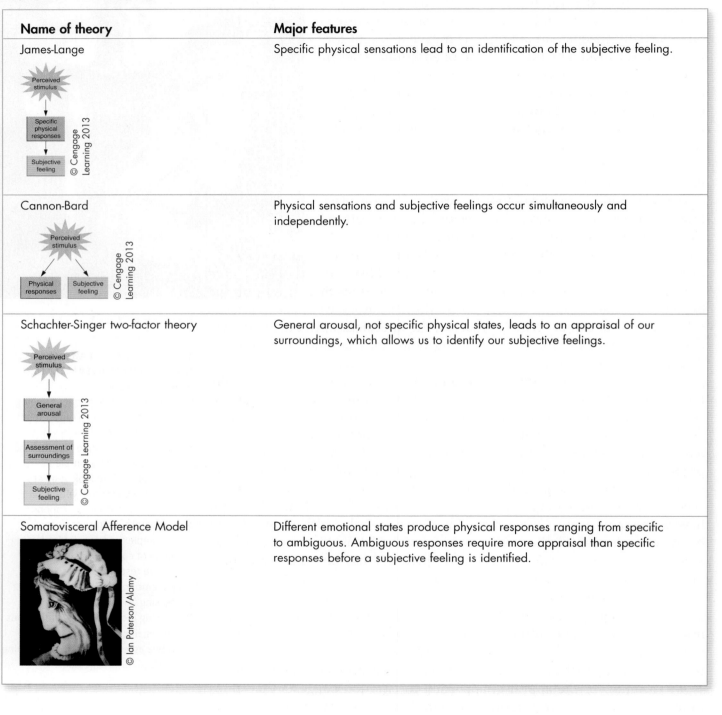	Specific physical sensations lead to an identification of the subjective feeling.
Cannon-Bard	Physical sensations and subjective feelings occur simultaneously and independently.
Schachter-Singer two-factor theory	General arousal, not specific physical states, leads to an appraisal of our surroundings, which allows us to identify our subjective feelings.
Somatovisceral Afference Model	Different emotional states produce physical responses ranging from specific to ambiguous. Ambiguous responses require more appraisal than specific responses before a subjective feeling is identified.

Interpersonal Relationships
From the Perspective of Emotion

The idea that good relationships are characterized by positive emotional interactions and that bad relationships feature many negative emotions sounds obvious. However, it is unrealistic to think that happy couples never experience any conflict. They do, but the way they fight can have a big influence on the likelihood they will stay together.

Psychologist John Gottman uses a combination of heart rate, facial expression, and an analysis of the way people talk about their relationships to each other and to others to predict whether a relationship will last (Gottman, 2011). He is correct over 90% of the time. One of Gottman's key observations is the ratio of positive to negative comments in a couple's discussion of a problem. Happy couples make 5 times more positive comments about each other and their relationship during these discussions (e.g., we laugh a lot versus we never have any fun).

In several places in this textbook, we have emphasized how the human mind is skewed toward the negative, like noticing bitter tastes over sweet. This slant suggests that it is all too easy to focus on your partner's negative qualities, which will lead to negative emotions and conflict. If we put our relationships on evolutionary cruise control, the ratio of positive to negative comments might drop to a point where the relationship is in danger. Maintaining a more positive outlook on your partner requires attention and work.

Try observing how people you know talk about their significant others (or watch your own behavior, if you're brave enough). Are you achieving Gottman's 5:1 ratio of positive to negative?

© image100/Alamy

Research by John Gottman shows that happy couples do experience negative emotions with each other. However, for every negative incident, they tend to experience 5 times as many positive emotional interactions with each other.

Chapter 7
Reflections

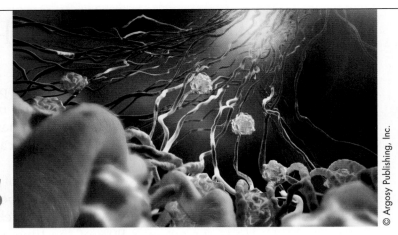

© Argosy Publishing, Inc.

Before reading this chapter, you might have believed that motivation and emotion were primarily private, individual sets of behaviors. We often feel that others really can't get inside our heads well enough to understand us. Now, however, we hope you see that although motivations and emotions might begin at the individual level, these behaviors are stimulated and shaped by the social world around us.

Our Olympic silver medalists, described at the beginning of the chapter, would probably feel quite elated to win such a prestigious award if motivation and emotion were purely individual experiences. After all, very few of us ever reach a level of achievement that allows us to be second in the world out of nearly 7 billion people. The fact that the silver medalists did not feel elation at all, but instead experienced a quite negative state of disappointment, only occurs because of social comparisons. Because they are comparing themselves with the gold medal winners instead of the many other athletes they beat, they feel the pain of defeat. The bronze medal winners do feel happy, and once again, we need to zoom out to the social perspective to see why. We might say that they're happy because they beat a lot of other athletes, but we've already seen that this explanation is not sufficient in the case of the silver medalists, so it is unlikely to work here. Instead, by comparing themselves with the "might have been" of going home without a medal, like the unfortunate fourth-place finishers, the bronze medalists become very happy indeed.

Motivation and emotion originate in the less voluntary, less conscious aspects of the mind and usually proceed in a bottom-up fashion to influence behavior. Athletes continually hear about the importance of displaying good character and being a gracious loser, but these cognitive values are not enough to help our silver medalist accept defeat with grace. At the same time, however, the cognitive abilities of the human mind can exert top-down influence on emotion and motivation, like William James's attempts to remedy his depression by "sitting up cheerfully." ◄

© AP Photo/The Canadian Press/Jonathan Hayward

KEY TERMS The Language of Psychological Science

Be sure you can define these terms and use them correctly.

achievement, p. 313
affiliation, p. 315
anorexia nervosa, p. 302
body mass index (BMI), p. 297
bulimia nervosa, p. 302
Cannon-Bard theory, p. 337
catharsis, p. 334
display rule, p. 330
drive, p. 290
drive reduction, p. 290

emotion, p. 288
extrinsic reward, p. 290
glucose, p. 294
homeostasis, p. 290
incentive, p. 290
insula, p. 323
intrinsic reward, p. 290
James-Lange theory, p. 333
leptin, p. 295
motivation, p. 289

satiety, p. 296
Schachter-Singer two-factor theory, p. 339
self-actualization, p. 318
set point, p. 290
sexual orientation, p. 308
Somatovisceral Afference Model of Emotion (SAME), p. 340
testosterone, p. 306
Yerkes-Dodson law, p. 320

MEDIA RESOURCES

Log in to CengageBrain to access the resources your instructor requires. For this book, you can access:

Psychology **CourseMate** brings course concepts to life with interactive learning, study, and exam preparation tools that support the printed textbook. A textbook-specific website, Psychology **CourseMate** includes an integrated interactive eBook and other interactive learning tools including quizzes, flashcards, videos, and more.

WebTUTOR More than just an interactive study guide, **WebTutor** is an anytime, anywhere customized learning solution with an eBook, keeping you connected to your textbook, instructor, and classmates.

aplia If your professor has assigned **Aplia** homework:
1. Sign in to your account.
2. Complete the corresponding homework exercises as required by your professor.
3. When finished, click "Grade It Now" to see which areas you have mastered, which areas need more work, and detailed explanations of every answer.

Learning something new produces structural
changes in neurons.

The Adaptive Mind

8

Learning

Learning Objectives

1 Compare and contrast reflexes, instincts, and learned behaviors in terms of complexity, flexibility, and the effects of experience.

2 Analyze the components of a classical conditioning experiment, identifying the unconditioned stimulus, conditioned stimulus, unconditioned response, and conditioned response.

3 Evaluate whether a classical conditioning scenario has the features needed to produce acquisition of a conditioned response, extinction, spontaneous recovery, conditioned inhibition, generalization versus discrimination, and/or latent inhibition.

4 Differentiate operant conditioning from classical conditioning and implement operant conditioning principles in real-life learning scenarios (e.g., training a pet or child).

5 Compare and contrast positive reinforcement, negative reinforcement, positive punishment, and negative punishment in terms of learning process and effects on behavior.

6 Analyze the ways in which animals' evolved instincts appeared to constrain learning in some studies of classical and operant conditioning (e.g., Garcia & Koelling, 1966; Breland & Breland, 1961).

7 Analyze the classic "Bobo Doll" study and other examples of observational learning, identifying the cognitive processes necessary to produce learning and differentiating observational learning from operant conditioning.

8 Apply learning principles and terminology to analyzing problems with interpersonal relationships, phobias, addiction, and other behaviors.

Although you may not have had an opportunity to learn to surf, we're assuming that in your role as a student you are very familiar with the process of learning. Knowing how to learn, however, is different from understanding how and why learning occurs. What is going on in the minds of these people as they learn to do something new?

A behavior like learning to surf is very complicated, so scientists interested in learning have often begun their examinations using animals that are much simpler than humans as they learn to do much more simple behaviors than surfing. Scientists have zoomed in to observe changes that happen in single neurons, like the image at the beginning of this chapter, found in simple animals like the sea slug *Aplysia californica*. The sea slug is capable of learning to anticipate an electric shock that happens every time it is touched, and it demonstrates this knowledge by protectively withdrawing its body in response to touch before the shock is administered. Because the slug has such a simple nervous system compared to ours, scientists have been able to identify which neurons are involved in this learning and to describe what changes take place in the neuron's functioning that make new behaviors—like withdrawing prior to shock—possible.

Is it possible that human learning shares anything in common with learning in slugs? The answer to this question is yes and no. Some types of learning are common across animals with vastly different evolutionary histories and complexities, like humans and sea slugs. In other cases, we see interactions between nature and nurture. Experience, or nurture, frequently interacts with the nature of the organism exposed to the experience. You can talk to your kitten and to an infant, but only the infant will respond to this experience by learning to understand what you're saying and how to reply. Each species brings its own unique and innate building blocks of learning, accumulated over many generations, to any given situation. Zooming out still farther, we will see how learning in groups can often be different from learning as an individual. Even the lowly sea slug learns differently when alone than when in a group of fellow slugs. Slugs in isolation seem to have a terrible time learning to stop trying to eat food that is too tough to swallow (Schwarz & Susswein, 1992), but they learn this task easily when in the presence of other slugs (Susswein, Schwarz, & Feldman, 1986). Apparently, the slugs can communicate with each other using pheromones, and the presence or absence of these chemicals has a powerful effect on their ability to learn (Schwarz, Blumberg, & Susswein, 1998). The people on the previous page who are learning to surf in a group might have a very different experience if they were taking individual lessons. ⊙

Animals, like this "ferocious" kitten, use reflexive piloerection to make themselves look bigger, the evolutionary purpose of which is to appear so menacing that they can avoid conflict altogether.

How Do Animals Use Reflexes, Instincts, and Learning to Respond to the Environment?

Animals, including ourselves, behave in response to the environment. Behavior can take the form of either externally observable actions or internal processes, such as emotions, thoughts, and physiological responses. These behaviors fall into three broad categories: reflexes, instincts, and learned behaviors. Each type of behavior has its role in helping us survive but differs dramatically in its ability to adapt to a changing world.

Reflexes are inevitable, involuntary responses to stimuli. In casual conversations, we sometimes attribute a baseball player's high batting average or our ability to step on the brake in time to avoid an automobile accident to great reflexes, but in fact, these examples involve learned behaviors that have become very fast and automatic as a result of lots of practice. Nobody is born knowing how to hit baseballs or use the brakes of a car, so these behaviors do not meet our definition of a reflex.

In human beings, most reflexes are controlled by nervous system circuits located in the spinal cord and brainstem, described in our chapter on biological psychology. Your physician checks one of these reflexes by tapping your knee with a hammer. The tap stretches your leg muscles, and the stretch is sensed by neurons in the spinal cord. Motor neurons in the spinal cord tell your thigh muscle to contract to compensate for the stretching, and your foot kicks out. No experience with knee-tapping is necessary to produce this behavior, nor can you voluntarily prevent it. By the time your brain realizes your knee was tapped, you have already reacted. Other reflexes pull our bodies away from painful stimuli, as when we step on a tack or piece of glass or touch a hot stove, turn our heads in the direction of loud sounds, and help us stand upright and walk.

Reflexes produce very fast, very reliable responses that serve to promote your welfare. If you've ever touched a hot stovetop and found yourself pulling your hand back seemingly before you even knew what you had done, you know at least one benefit of reflexes.

© David Trood/Getty Images; © Tyler Olson/Shutterstock

Goose bumps are what is left of piloerection in humans. These signals of arousal are remnants of a time when we had enough hair to make this an easily noticeable response.

Reflexes have the disadvantages of being inflexible and not very adaptable to change, however. For example, we respond to stress or cold by forming goose bumps, or bumps on the skin. This reflex appears to be a leftover from a time in which our species had more body hair. Goose bumps raise each strand of hair, which in times of stress makes an individual look larger, scaring off predators or competitors, and in response to cold, traps more insulating air near the skin. As humans lost most of their body hair over time, the advantages of this reflex decreased, but we still retain the behavior.

Instincts, also referred to as fixed action patterns, are inborn patterns of behavior elicited by environmental stimuli. Instincts share the reflex's reliability and lack of dependence on experience, but the resulting behaviors are much more complex, requiring many more neurons than the number involved in a reflexive kick of your foot. Instinctive behaviors occur in the mating and parenting behaviors of many species (Tinbergen, 1951). For example, a mother dog will instinctively lick clean her very first litter of

reflex Inevitable, involuntary response to stimuli.

instinct An inborn pattern of behavior elicited by environmental stimuli. Also known as a fixed action pattern.

pups immediately after birth. An example of a human instinct is contagious yawning, or yawning in response to seeing others yawn (Provine, 1986). Although yawning has multiple functions, including cooling the brain, contagious yawning might be related to empathy, helping to synchronize the arousal state of whole groups. Children with autism, a psychological disorder in which empathy is distinctly impaired, fail to show contagious yawning (Senju et al., 2007).

Psychologists define **learning** as a relatively permanent change in behavior (or the capacity for behavior) due to experience. The core of this definition is "change in behavior." After learning, we can do something new that we couldn't do before, providing us with enormous advantages in surviving a changing world. Not all changes in behavior are due to learning, however. Our behavior changes as we mature from infancy through adulthood, as we will see in our chapter on development. Behavior can be changed by brain damage or by having a psychological disorder. So our definition of learning limits the changes we consider to be learned to those that result from experience. The other qualification in our definition, "relatively permanent," prevents the labeling of brief or unstable changes—such as when we experience different moods or suffer from an illness—as learning. Exactly how permanent learning is will be discussed in our chapter on memory.

Twentieth-century psychology was dominated by the beliefs that compared to other animals, human beings have relatively few reflexes and instincts and that most human behavior results from learning. William James actually argued that human beings have more instincts than other animals, although we are usually unaware of them (James, 1887). According to James, our behavior simply *appears* more complex and thoughtful because we often face the need to choose between competing instincts. Animals with fewer instincts experience fewer conflicts, so their behavior appears to be more automatic and less thoughtful.

James's approach to instinct and learning is echoed in the writings of contemporary evolutionary psychologists, who argue for an innate learning instinct that prepares human beings to learn certain things in particular ways based on our evolutionary history (Cosmides & Tooby, 1997). Cognitive psychologists also revive the flavor of James by suggesting that learned behavior resulting from experience can look very automatic and instinctive (Bargh & Chartrand, 1999). For example, prejudice toward a group of people requires learning, but prejudiced behavior often occurs without much conscious awareness, as we explore further in a later chapter on social psychology. People who consciously believe that they are without prejudice toward members of a minority group will nonetheless sit farther away from an individual from that group than from members of the majority (Dovidio & Gaertner, 2005).

The interactions between instinct and learning also provide an explanation for another observation: experience has different effects at different

Instinctive contagious yawning might provide survival advantages by synchronizing the arousal state and behaviors of groups.

© SERDAR/Alamy

learning A relatively permanent change in behavior or the capacity for behavior due to experience.

Imprinting, in which a young organism bonds with adults, provides an example of how experience has different effects at different times in the lifespan. These baby swans are following their parents because the parents were the first things they saw when they hatched. After a very short delay of a day or two, exposure to the parents would not lead to following. If the baby swans saw a human experimenter instead of their parents upon hatching, they would follow the human instead.

Organisms usually show imprinting by the time they are mobile, which for swans means the first day of life, but for human children means closer to one year. Because these children have imprinted on their primary caregivers instead of their preschool teacher, the teacher needs a bit of technological help to encourage his charges to follow him on a walk.

times in an organism's lifespan, as we discuss further in our chapter on development. We do not attempt to teach philosophy to 2-year-old children because they are not yet capable of learning this material. Imprinting, the tendency of young animals to bond with and follow an adult, is very dependent on timing. Birds that see a human immediately upon hatching follow that person everywhere, but birds who first see a human after having been hooded for their first few days out of the shell attempt to flee in terror (James, 1887).

What Are the Three Main Types of Learning?

Learning is traditionally divided into three categories: associative, nonassociative, and observational. More than one type of learning can operate simultaneously in the same situation.

Associative learning occurs when we form associations, or connections, among stimuli and/or behaviors. Associative learning helps us to predict the future based on past experience. In other words, if A happens, then B is likely to follow. The ability to anticipate the future provides enormous survival advantages, as animals gain time to prepare. Psychologists who

associative learning The formation of associations or connections among stimuli and behaviors.

It is likely that the first time this dog's owner attempted to dress it up the dog was a bit upset. After repeated experiences of being dressed up, however, the dog probably has habituated, which means that it has learned that no harm results from the process. Now it remains calm.

© treasure dragon/Shutterstock

Many universities offer special programs for students who are the first in their extended families to attend college, in recognition of the need to level the playing field with students who enter college having already learned a great deal about college life from observing their college-educated family members.

classical conditioning A type of learning in which associations are formed between two stimuli that occur sequentially in time.

operant conditioning A type of learning in which associations are formed between behaviors and their outcomes.

nonassociative learning Learning that involves changes in the magnitude of responses to a stimulus.

habituation A simple form of learning in which reactions to repeated stimuli that are unchanging and harmless decrease.

sensitization An increased reaction to many stimuli following exposure to one very strong stimulus.

observational learning Learning that occurs when an organism watches the actions of another. Also known as social learning or modeling.

study learning describe two types of associative learning: classical conditioning and operant conditioning. In **classical conditioning**, we form associations between pairs of stimuli that occur sequentially in time. If a child sees a bee for the first time and then gets stung, the child will form a connection between seeing bees and the pain of being stung. The next time a bee flies by, the child is likely to feel quite frightened. In **operant conditioning**, we form associations between behaviors and their consequences. If you study hard, you will get good grades. We will discuss each of these forms of associative learning in more detail in later sections.

Nonassociative learning involves changes in the magnitude of responses to a single stimulus rather than the formation of connections between stimuli. Two important types of nonassociative learning are habituation and sensitization. **Habituation** reduces our reactions to repeated experiences that have already been evaluated and found to be unchanging and harmless. For example, you might sleep much better the second night than the first in the same hotel, because you have adapted to the new noises in that environment. Sometimes, we habituate to things that we should, ideally, still be noticing. A major concern about exposing children to violent media is the possibility that their emotional responses to violent images will habituate, leading to higher tolerance for violent behavior (Gunter, 1994).

In contrast to habituation, **sensitization** *increases* our reactions to a wide range of stimuli following exposure to one strong stimulus. Following an earthquake, people often experience exaggerated responses to movement, light, or noise. If you are awakened by a loud crash, even if you figure out it's just your roommate coming home late at night, it might be harder to get back to sleep due to your suddenly increased state of arousal. Every little sound now seems magnified.

© Vitalij Lang/Shutterstock

Following an earthquake, this little boy is likely to be extra jumpy for awhile in response to other stimuli, like loud noises, due to sensitization.

Why would we show habituation to some stimuli and sensitization to others? In general, habituation occurs in response to milder stimuli, whereas sensitization occurs in response to stronger stimuli. Habituation ensures that we do not waste precious resources monitoring low-priority stimuli. Sensitization is particularly useful in dangerous situations. After detecting one harmful stimulus, raising our overall level of responsiveness should improve reaction time should other dangers arise.

Observational learning (also known as social learning or modeling), occurs when an organism learns by watching the actions of another. If your knowledge of table manners does not extend to the many forks, knives, and spoons at a very fancy dinner, you might want to watch what others do before diving into your own food. Observational learning provides the advantage of transmitting information across generations within families and cultures.

© Blend Images/Alamy

Watching others is a very efficient way to learn new skills, like dancing. Imagine for a moment how difficult it would be to write a description of how this dance should be performed. Watching others is also a very useful way to learn what is harmful to do.

Summary 8.1

Types of Learning

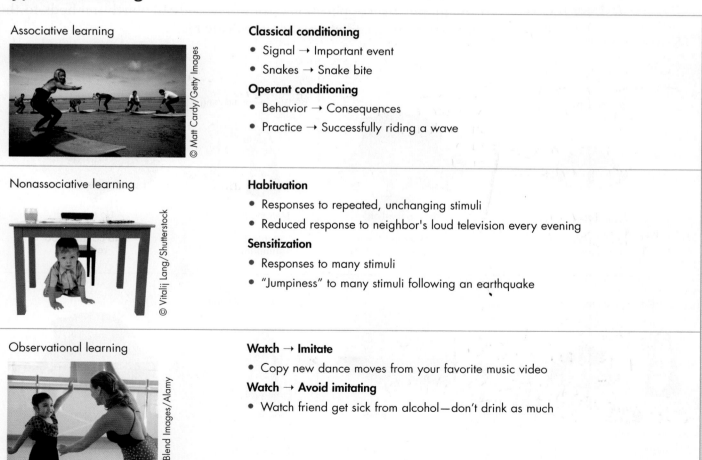

Associative learning	Classical conditioning
© Matt Cardy/Getty Images	• Signal → Important event
	• Snakes → Snake bite
	Operant conditioning
	• Behavior → Consequences
	• Practice → Successfully riding a wave

Nonassociative learning	Habituation
© Vitalij Lang/Shutterstock	• Responses to repeated, unchanging stimuli
	• Reduced response to neighbor's loud television every evening
	Sensitization
	• Responses to many stimuli
	• "Jumpiness" to many stimuli following an earthquake

Observational learning	Watch → Imitate
© Blend Images/Alamy	• Copy new dance moves from your favorite music video
	Watch → Avoid imitating
	• Watch friend get sick from alcohol—don't drink as much

What Is Classical Conditioning?

FIGURE 8.1

Classical Conditioning Terminology. 1 and 2. Before conditioning, food (unconditioned stimulus—UCS) reliably produces salivation (unconditioned response—UCR) and the sound of the metronome produces no reliable responding. 3. During conditioning, the sound of the metronome is followed by the food (UCS), which again produces salivation (UCR). 4. After conditioning, the sound of the metronome (conditioned stimulus—CS) by itself is sufficient to produce salivation (conditioned response—CR). Learning has occurred.

As we discussed in our introductory chapter, Ivan Petrovich Pavlov (1849–1936) is so tightly connected to the study of classical conditioning that the phenomenon is frequently referred to as Pavlovian conditioning. Pavlov switched his interests from the study of digestion to the study of learning after noticing that his dogs had learned to anticipate the arrival of food. Instead of salivating when presented with food, Pavlov's dogs began to salivate as soon as the lab assistant retrieved them from the kennel or strapped them into their experimental harnesses in the laboratory. Most people would probably not have noticed the differences in the dogs' behavior. Pavlov not only noticed but realized the full significance of his observations: the dogs had formed an association between stimuli preceding the food and the arrival of the food itself. In other words, the dogs had learned that certain stimuli served as signals for the eventual appearance of food (see ● Figure 8.1).

If you are like most people reading about classical conditioning for the first time, you are probably wondering why we are spending so much time and effort discussing salivating dogs. If classical conditioning were that limited in its scope, it probably wouldn't warrant more than a small footnote in the history of psychology. Instead, classical conditioning explains many of our learned emotional responses to our environment. It forms the basis for many practical applications from prepared childbirth methods to the treatment of drug addiction and unrealistic fears.

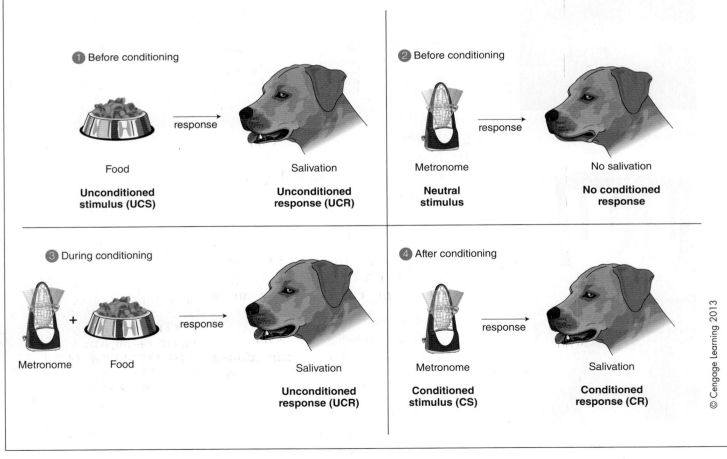

① Before conditioning

response

Food
Unconditioned stimulus (UCS)

Salivation
Unconditioned response (UCR)

② Before conditioning

response

Metronome
Neutral stimulus

No salivation
No conditioned response

③ During conditioning

Metronome + Food

response

Salivation
Unconditioned response (UCR)

④ After conditioning

Metronome
Conditioned stimulus (CS)

response

Salivation
Conditioned response (CR)

© Cengage Learning 2013

Classical Conditioning Terminology

In describing the process of classical conditioning, Pavlov distinguished between *conditioned* and *unconditioned* stimuli and responses. "Conditioned" refers to something that must be learned, while "unconditioned" refers to factors that are reflexive or that occur without any learning. Therefore, a **conditioned stimulus (CS)** refers to an environmental event whose significance is learned, while an **unconditioned stimulus (UCS)** has innate, built-in meaning to the organism. In a typical experiment by Pavlov, dogs heard the sound of a ticking metronome just before food appeared through a small door. The ticking sound was the conditioned stimulus, while the food was the unconditioned stimulus. Dogs do not have an innate response to the sound of ticking metronomes, but they generally are born knowing what to do with food. An unconditioned stimulus (UCS) may be pleasant, like food, but it may also be unpleasant, like electric shock. The important features of a UCS are its innate biological significance and its reliable ability to elicit a response without prior exposure. Just as our dog didn't require training in order to salivate in response to meat powder, few of us need any experience with electric shock before we respond with fear and other negative emotions.

Conditioned responses (CRs) are learned reactions, while **unconditioned responses (UCRs)** don't need to be learned; they appear without prior experience with a stimulus. Salivating when food is put in your mouth is unconditioned, because we do this reflexively without any prior experience, but salivating to ticking metronomes only occurs as a result of experience. Our definition of learning requires behavior to change, so the appearance of conditioned responding tells us learning has occurred. Once learning has taken place, the organism now responds to conditioned stimuli that reliably predict the arrival of the unconditioned stimulus. This ability to anticipate future stimuli provides significant advantages to an organism in the struggle for survival.

As we'll see in this section, understanding classical conditioning will illuminate a wide range of behaviors you might have seen in yourself or others, from the avoidance of foods that you associate with feeling sick to the butterflies you feel in your stomach before a big performance to the development of social prejudices.

> Learning without thinking is useless. Thinking without learning is dangerous.
> —Confucius

Classical Conditioning Phenomena

Pavlov and those following in his footsteps have extended the usefulness of classical conditioning by exploring its features and development in more detail.

Acquisition **Acquisition** refers to the development of a conditioned response. Pavlov argued that acquisition requires contiguity, or close proximity in time between the conditioned stimulus (CS) and the unconditioned stimulus (UCS). If the CS occurs long before the UCS, the organism may not view the two stimuli as related. A CS that occurs simultaneously with a UCS or, worse yet, following a UCS, is obviously not a very useful signal.

conditioned stimulus (CS) An environmental event whose significance is learned through classical conditioning.

unconditioned stimulus (UCS) A stimulus that elicits a response without any prior experience.

conditioned response (CR) A response learned through classical conditioning.

unconditioned response (UCR) A response to an unconditioned stimulus that requires no previous experience.

acquisition The development of a learned response.

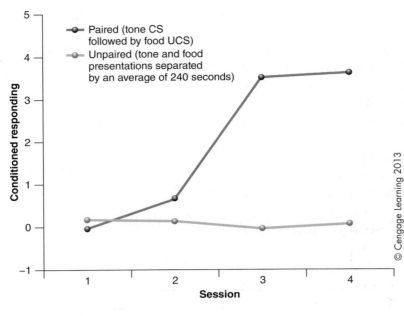

FIGURE 8.2

Acquisition of Conditioned Responses. With each pairing of the conditioned stimulus (CS) and unconditioned stimulus (UCS), conditioned responses (CRs) become more likely.

© Cengage Learning 2013

A dinner bell sounded after food has been served is not very helpful (see ● Figure 8.2).

Acquisition also requires contingency, or a correlation between the conditioned stimulus (CS) and unconditioned stimulus (UCS). Learning about a reliable signal is easier than learning about a signal that only occurs some of the time. To demonstrate the contingency factor, Robert Rescorla (1968) exposed rats to sound followed by a mild electric shock, which quickly produced fear of the sound. For some rats, a shock was administered only after a sound, while for other rats, shocks were administered following the sound on some occasions and without any sound on others. All the rats had the same number of contiguous sound-shock pairings. They differed in the correlation between sound and shock. Sound signaled shock 100% of the time for some rats, while others experienced some unsignaled shocks (i.e., shocks without being paired with a sound). Learning was faster for rats experiencing signaled shocks 100% of the time. As the percentage of signaled shocks decreased, learning about the signal slowed. If your migraine headaches are always preceded by exposure to bright light, you are much more likely to fear bright lights in the future than if your headaches follow exposure to bright lights only once in awhile (see ● Figure 8.3).

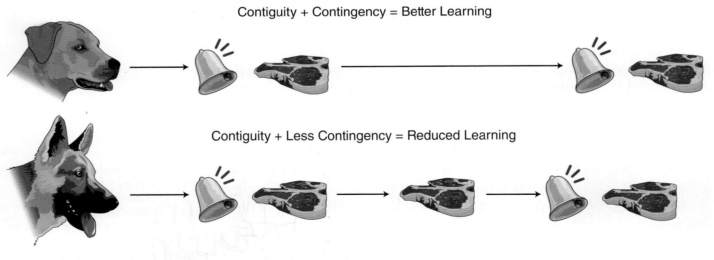

Contiguity + Contingency = Better Learning

Contiguity + Less Contingency = Reduced Learning

© Cengage Learning 2013

FIGURE 8.3

Contingency Predicts Conditioning. Imagine the experience of the two dogs in this experiment. Food (unconditioned stimulus—UCS) *always* follows hearing the bell (conditioned stimulus—CS) for both dogs, which demonstrates contiguity. However, the first dog *only* receives food after the bell, while the food is not always signaled by the bell for the second dog. Robert Rescorla predicted correctly that the dog in the first line would learn the association between bell and food faster than the dog in the second line, because the first dog's bell is a more reliable signal for food (contingency).

Extinction and Spontaneous Recovery Conditioned responses will disappear, or undergo **extinction**, if the association between the conditioned stimulus (CS) and the unconditioned stimulus (UCS) is broken. When Pavlov continued to expose his dogs to the ticking of the metronome without providing any food, the dogs eventually stopped salivating in response to the sound of the metronome (see ● Figure 8.4).

Pavlov believed that extinction is not the same thing as forgetting but is actually new learning that overrides old learning. As evidence for this belief, Pavlov pointed to the occurrence of **spontaneous recovery**, or the reappearance of conditioned responses (CRs) following periods of rest between sessions of extinction training. Even if a dog has completely stopped salivating to the sound of the metronome by the end of an extinction session, conditioned salivation will reappear at the beginning of the next session. In other words, the conditioned responding is decreasing during a session of extinction training not because the dog is forgetting the relationship between ticking and food, but because the dog is now learning that ticking no longer predicts food, and it may take several sessions for this new learning to completely replace the old. The phenomenon of spontaneous recovery is consistent with our definition of learning as a relatively permanent type of change.

Without the ability to extinguish conditioned responses, adjusting to further changes in the environment would be difficult, if not impossible. We would not be able to learn to enjoy dogs again after being bitten by one. An addict whose associations between needles and the effects of using heroin never extinguished would have an even harder time overcoming addiction.

Inhibition learning helps an organism behave adaptively when they've learned that something important will *not* occur. These zebras may have learned that when lions act a certain way, they are already full and unlikely to hunt again. These inhibitory signals tell the zebras that they can drink in safety, at least for a little while.

extinction The reduction of a learned response. In classical conditioning, extinction occurs when the unconditioned stimulus no longer follows the conditioned stimulus. In operant conditioning, extinction occurs when the consequence no longer follows the learned behavior.

spontaneous recovery During extinction training, the reappearance of conditioned responses after periods of rest.

Inhibition So far, we have been discussing examples of excitatory classical conditioning, in which the organism learns that a conditioned stimulus (CS) predicts the occurrence of an unconditioned stimulus (UCS).

FIGURE 8.4

Extinction and Spontaneous Recovery. Addiction often involves the association of conditioned stimuli (CSs), such as the syringe, with the unconditioned stimulus (UCS) of a drug. Recovering addicts can be exposed to extinction—viewing the syringe (CS) without receiving the drug (UCS). This process reduces any conditioned responses (CRs) that might be contributing to cravings for the drug. However, extinction typically requires multiple sessions. When the recovering addict returns for the next extinction training session after a period of rest, he or she is likely to show CRs again. Eventually, with enough training, extinction will be complete and no further spontaneous recovery will be observed.

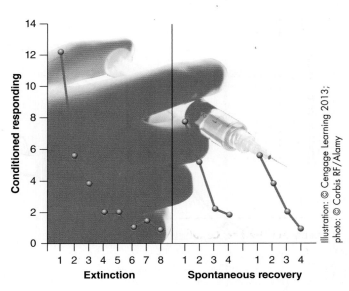

Pavlov was also quite interested in the classical conditioning of **inhibition**, in which a conditioned stimulus (CS) predicts the nonoccurrence of an unconditioned stimulus (UCS) (Pavlov, 1927). To demonstrate inhibition, we can begin by establishing excitatory conditioning by pairing a signal—a light—with shock. After some experience with this pairing, a rat will have learned to fear the light. Now we continue to present light-shock pairings, but we add other training trials that include the inhibitory CS—a sound—by presenting the light and sound together followed by no shock. Even though the light is present, the rat learns that it is not going to be shocked in the presence of the sound, and it shows no fear.

For a vulnerable animal in the wild, it is important to know not only that a predator at a water hole is in hunting mode (the sight of the prowling predator is an excitatory CS signaling fear) but also that a predator relaxing after a recent kill is unlikely to kill again soon (the sight of a predator calmly drinking water is an inhibitory CS that tells the animal that the predator is unlikely to attack soon and that it is safe). For drug addicts, establishing inhibitory conditioned stimuli (CSs) associated with the lack of an expected drug effect might provide a more powerful method for rehabilitation (Kearns, Weiss, Schindler, & Panlilio, 2005). If an addict learns that drugs are never available in the presence of a certain signal, turning the signal on whenever the addict's resolve is weak might help prevent a relapse.

Generalization and Discrimination Once a conditioned response is successfully acquired, organisms often show a tendency to respond to stimuli that are similar to the conditioned stimulus. For example, the child who learned to be afraid of bees after being stung might also begin to fear wasps and yellow jackets, a process that Pavlov referred to as **generalization**.

Generalization has obvious survival value. If our ancestors had one bad experience with a lion, it would make sense to avoid all lions, as well as other animals with lion-like characteristics. If you felt sick after eating chocolate bacon at the fair, it probably would be a good idea to avoid other weird chocolate-covered foods, at least for a while. Unfortunately, our tendency to generalize can have negative outcomes. For example, a soldier traumatized in combat might react with unnecessary fear to sounds that are similar to gunfire on the battlefield, such as the backfiring of a car back at home.

Counteracting our tendency to generalize is another learning process known as **discrimination**, which allows us to make fine distinctions between the implications of stimuli. In the laboratory, if you present food following a high tone but never following a low tone, a dog will initially learn to salivate following both tones due to generalization. As learning progresses, the dog eventually learns to discriminate, or differentiate, between the abilities of the two stimuli to predict food. As a result, salivation to the high tone will continue, but salivation to the low tone will stop (see ● Figure 8.5). If

inhibition A feature of classical conditioning in which a conditioned stimulus actually predicts the nonoccurrence of an unconditioned stimulus.

generalization The tendency to respond to stimuli that are similar to an original conditioned stimulus.

discrimination A learned ability to distinguish between stimuli.

FIGURE 8.5

Generalization and Discrimination. The dog is receiving food after the high tone, but receives nothing after the low tone. Early in training, the dog salivates after both tones due to generalization. Further along in training, the dog learns to discriminate between the abilities of the two tones to signal food and now salivates only after the high tone.

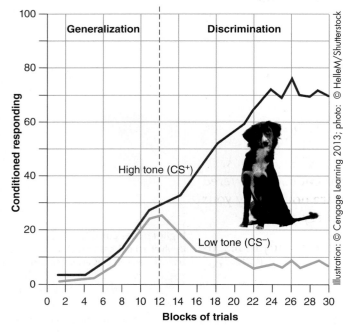

Illustration: © Cengage Learning 2013; photo: © HelleM/Shutterstock

generalization had led the soldier to react with fear to the sound of a backfiring car, further experience with the sound would help distinguish it from real gunfire in combat. Because the sound of a backfiring car is not followed by any fear-producing unconditioned stimuli, it will eventually lose its ability to elicit fear.

Higher Order Conditioning We have seen how conditioned responding spreads to similar stimuli through generalization. In addition, conditioned responding can occur in response to stimuli that predict the conditioned stimulus (CS), a process known as higher order conditioning. **Higher order conditioning** allows us to make even more distant predictions about the occurrence of significant events. A person who was bitten by a dog might show fear the next time the dog is seen, since the sight of the dog (conditioned stimulus—CS) is now associated with the pain of the bite (unconditioned stimulus—UCS). Subsequently, the sight of the dog (conditioned stimulus—CS) might begin to act more like an unconditioned stimulus (UCS), producing fear in response to other stimuli (the sight of the dog's yard or doghouse, the dog's barking) that might signal the appearance of the dog.

Higher order conditioning occurs when stimuli associated with a conditioned stimulus (CS) gain the ability to elicit conditioned responses (CRs) on their own. If a child has learned to fear dogs (CS) because of a previous bite (unconditioned stimulus—UCS), anything that signals "dog" might now produce fear, too, including the sight of a doghouse, a dog's feeding bowl, or a chew toy.

Latent Inhibition In most of the research we have reviewed so far, the stimuli used as conditioned stimuli (CSs) are unfamiliar. Pavlov's dogs had probably never heard a metronome before participating in his experiments. What happens when you are already familiar with a conditioned stimulus (CS)? The answer is you will take a longer amount of time learning to respond to it. It takes more time to learn about a *familiar* conditioned stimulus (CS) than about an *unfamiliar* conditioned stimulus (CS), a phenomenon known as **latent inhibition** (Lubow & Moore, 1959). The phenomenon is *latent* in the sense that its effects are not seen right away (when the stimuli are first presented) but emerge later when the rate of learning is examined. The *inhibition* part of the term refers to the relatively poor learning that occurs in response to familiar stimuli.

If you have eaten lots of pizzas over time (familiar conditioned stimulus), but get sick after eating one, you are not very likely to associate the pizza with feeling ill. It is more likely that you would need to be sick many times after eating pizza before you learned to connect eating pizza with being ill. In contrast, if you get sick the first time you eat chocolate covered ants (unfamiliar conditioned stimulus), assuming these are not already your favorite treat, you'll associate eating ants with feeling ill very quickly.

Cognitive and Biological Influences on Classical Conditioning

Early behaviorists concentrated their study of learning on external behaviors that they could observe directly. As new technologies became available, such as brain imaging methods and more powerful computers used to model thinking and reasoning, psychologists interested in learning began to explore

higher order conditioning Learning in which stimuli associated with a conditioned stimulus also elicit conditioned responding.

latent inhibition The slower learning that occurs when a conditioned stimulus is already familiar compared to when the conditioned stimulus is unfamiliar.

Due to latent inhibition, classical conditioning proceeds more slowly when a new conditioned stimulus is familiar than when it is unfamiliar. If you got sick after eating a familiar food (perhaps pizza), you are less likely to associate your illness with the food than if you got sick after eating an unfamiliar food, like these insect-containing lollipops.

internal processes, leading to revolutionary advances in our understanding of cognition and biology.

Early behaviorists also limited most of their studies to simple animals rather than humans. This restriction resulted from strong beliefs that behavior followed the same general rules in all organisms, which meant that it was safe to apply experimental results from studies using rats to the behavior of humans and that having more control over your experimental subjects (food, housing, etc.) led to better science. Although the latter may be true, psychologists discovered that treating the learning animal as some kind of interchangeable black box was overly simplistic. Some learning processes have clearly been conserved over the course of evolution, allowing us to make conclusions relevant to humans about the changes at a synapse that accompany classical conditioning in the sea slug *Aplysia californica* (Carew & Kandel, 1973). In other cases, species bring their unique biology into the learning situation, as we will see in a later section on taste aversion learning. Psychologists have learned to be cautious about generalizing their conclusions across species.

The Element of Surprise In our earlier discussion of the acquisition of classically conditioned responses, we talked about the contributions of contiguity (closeness in time) and contingency (the correlation between the conditioned and unconditioned stimuli). It should be easy to learn about a signal that both precedes and is predictive of an important event. The bell on your microwave both precedes and predicts the availability of food, and we would not be surprised if your mouth started watering a bit whenever you hear it.

What happens, however, if you already possess one really good signal but add another one that also precedes and predicts an unconditioned stimulus (UCS)? Based on past experience, you have learned that if your computer monitor suddenly goes dark (conditioned stimulus—CS), something terrible (unconditioned stimulus—UCS) has happened to your computer. Whenever you see a dark screen, you feel extremely stressed (conditioned response—CR). Let's assume that the next time a dark screen appears, the computer also emits a funny sound. Even though the sound both precedes and predicts a hard drive crash, it's unlikely that you will learn much about the sound and its relationship with hard drive crashes. We don't bother to learn much about new signals that provide no additional information, even if they meet our requirements for contiguity and contingency (Kamin, 1968, 1969).

How can we account for this failure to learn under circumstances that should produce strong learning? Robert Rescorla and Allan Wagner (1972) proposed a model of classical conditioning in which learning will occur as a function of how *surprising* the association between the conditioned stimulus (CS) and unconditioned stimulus (UCS) appears. If you already know that eating peanuts makes you sick, you would not be surprised to learn that a protein bar that made you sick contained peanuts. You don't need to

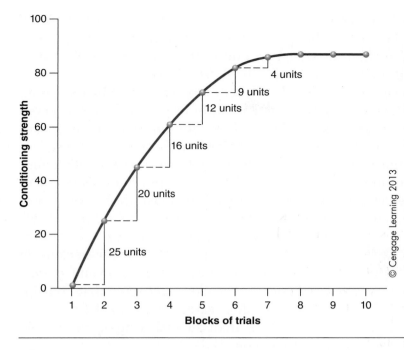

FIGURE 8.6

The Rescorla-Wagner Model. According to the Rescorla-Wagner Model, the rate of learning about a conditioned stimulus (CS) depends on how new or surprising the association between the CS and the unconditioned stimulus (UCS) appears to be. Early in training, learning proceeds rapidly (25 units per block or set of trials) because the association is new and surprising. Later in training, gains in conditioning strength (measured by how often a conditioned response or CR occurs) level off, because the association between CS and UCS is now familiar and no longer surprising (4 units per block of trials).

learn anything new about protein bars, because peanuts already work perfectly well as a signal for illness. It is likely that you will check protein bar ingredient labels more carefully for peanuts in the future, but you haven't been conditioned to feel nauseated while eating protein bars that do not contain peanuts (see ● Figure 8.6).

We can't imagine early behaviorists using terms like *expect*, *surprise*, and *predict*, as these represent internal states they believed were impossible to investigate scientifically. But today, it seems unreasonable to discuss some aspects of learning without using this vocabulary.

Taste Aversion We have already used some examples of classical conditioning involving food that you really dislike because you got sick after eating it. These classically conditioned taste aversions result when the sight, smell, or flavor of the food (conditioned stimulus—CS) has been paired in the past with illness (unconditioned stimulus—UCS). Dislike of the food is the resulting conditioned response (CR).

Taste aversion isn't just another interesting example of classical conditioning. Its demonstration led to a substantial rethinking not only of classical conditioning but of behaviorism in general. Pavlov believed that any stimuli that met the criteria for conditioned or unconditioned stimuli could be successfully paired to produce classical conditioning. He made no provisions in his theory for any special interactions between particular types of stimuli. John Garcia, who had a background not only in psychology but also in biology, did not believe that stimuli were so interchangeable. In what became known as a classic taste aversion study, Garcia and Koelling (1966) demonstrated that the types of stimuli used as conditioned and unconditioned stimuli do matter and that some combinations are learned much faster than others. Garcia and Koelling presented groups of rats with either saccharin-flavored water ("tasty water") or plain water. When the rats consumed the plain water, their drinking triggered a light and a clicking sound, which the researchers referred to as "bright-noisy water." After drinking either tasty or bright-noisy water, half the rats were given an injection of lithium chloride, which produces strong sensations of nausea, and the other half received an electric shock (see Table 8.1).

This type of experiment should look very familiar to you by now as an example of classical conditioning. Tasty water or bright-noisy water served as conditioned stimuli (CSs) while shock or lithium chloride served as unconditioned stimuli (UCSs). Garcia and Koelling subsequently presented tasty and bright-noisy water to see if either would be avoided, with avoidance serving as an indication of the conditioned response of disgust with or dislike of the water. Rats immediately learned associations between tasty water and subsequent illness, but had difficulty learning to use the bright-noisy water as a signal for illness. Conversely, bright-noisy water, but not tasty water, became an effective signal for shock. After all, if you feel sick, you are much more likely to decide that your illness was a result of eating "mystery" leftovers for breakfast rather than the flickering of the fluorescent lights in your classroom.

This experiment had far-ranging implications. Not only did these findings challenge Pavlov's views of the relative interchangeability of stimuli, but they prompted a renewed interest in the biological predispositions of organisms, or their "preparedness" to learn certain things. Although rats readily formed associations between taste and illness but not between visual stimuli and illness, birds easily formed associations between visual stimuli and illness but not between taste and illness. Rats see very poorly, so they usually are dependent on taste and smell for identifying food. Birds have excellent vision and typically identify food sources using visual cues, such as the markings of particular species of butterfly.

The willingness of behaviorists to treat organisms as interchangeable black boxes with irrelevant internal features was severely challenged by this work, paving the way to an abandonment of the rigid behaviorism that had dominated psychology for most of the 20th century. Many learning theorists closed down their rat and pigeon labs and turned their attention to emerging cognitive, biological, and evolutionary approaches.

TABLE 8.1	The Experimental Design Used by Garcia and Koelling (1966)	
	Conditioned stimuli (CSs)	
Unconditioned stimuli	Bright-noisy water	Tasty water
Lithium chloride	Weak learning	Strong learning
Shock	Strong Learning	Weak learning

© UF/IFAS photo by Thomas Wright

Garcia and Koelling's work on taste aversion helped to explain why butterflies have evolved to mimic the coloring of species that taste bad to birds. If the bird has become ill after eating a butterfly with a certain appearance, it will avoid eating butterflies that look the same way. Note that the taste of food was important to the rat, which doesn't see well, but the sight of the food is important for birds, which have excellent sight and whose sense of smell is not particularly useful when they are flying high above potential prey.

Applying Classical Conditioning

Although strict behaviorism no longer dominates research in psychology as it did for the first half of the 20th century, it still provides powerful explanations of human behavior and very effective therapeutic tools for producing change. The pervasiveness of classical conditioning in everyday life is quite remarkable. When your palms get sweaty and you feel butterflies in your stomach before a big exam, awaken just before your alarm clock goes off, or feel more awake just because you smell coffee brewing, you can blame your responses on classical conditioning. If you are a clinician working with a traumatized combat veteran who is frightened by the smell of diesel fuel or a coach working with an athlete to overcome "choking" in big games, classical conditioning gives you some of the answers you need to produce positive change.

Understanding classical conditioning provides insight into many situations where our emotional responses seem to be triggered by the environment. Following a poor performance, an athlete and a coach might be able to figure out how to avoid the same mistakes in the next big competition.

Overcoming Fear In 1920, John Watson and Rosalie Raynor conducted an experiment with an 9-month-old infant named Albert. By today's standards, this experiment hardly appears well designed or ethical, but the results of the experiment led to research that shed a great deal of light onto human fear. While Albert played with a tame, white laboratory rat (conditioned stimulus—CS), Watson and Raynor made a loud noise (unconditioned stimulus—UCS) by hitting a steel bar with a hammer. Albert was quite frightened by this noise (unconditioned response—UCR). A week later, Albert was once again offered the rat, but this time he was afraid (conditioned response—CR). His fear generalized to other white, furry objects, including a rabbit, a dog, a fur coat, and a Santa Claus mask. Watson and Raynor had successfully demonstrated that fears could result from classical conditioning.

Although Albert left Watson and Raynor's laboratory without any treatment for his fear, one of Watson's students, Mary Cover Jones, demonstrated how classical conditioning procedures could be used to reduce learned fears. Her experiment featured a 3-year-old named Peter, who had a serious phobia, or intense, unrealistic fear, of rabbits (Jones, 1924). Could classical conditioning provide a way to reduce Peter's fears? One possible approach would be to use extinction. As we mentioned previously, conditioned responding will extinguish if the conditioned stimulus is presented alone, without the unconditioned stimulus. Treating phobias by exposing people to fear-producing stimuli in a manner that is safe until they no longer respond (i.e., extinction)

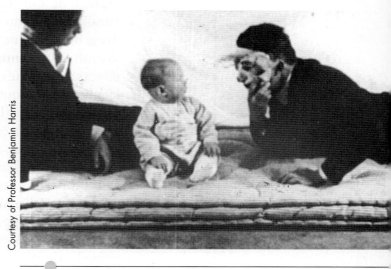

John Watson and Rosalie Raynor observe Little Albert's generalization to a bunny mask worn by Watson. The mask is similar to the original conditioned stimulus (CS) in their experiment—a white laboratory rat—which stimulated Albert's conditioned fear.

is known as flooding. Although flooding works, it is often traumatic. Being exposed to a stimulus you find very frightening until you are no longer afraid is not fun. Imagine forcing a person afraid of heights to bungee jump until the fear of heights is gone.

Instead of using extinction/flooding, Mary Cover Jones treated Peter with counterconditioning, or the substitution of one conditioned response for another, opposite response. Jones associated food, a new unconditioned stimulus (UCS), with the presence of a rabbit (conditioned stimulus—CS). Eventually, Peter was able to stroke the rabbit while eating. While not particularly hygienic, this achievement represented a big improvement in Peter's life.

Counterconditioning has many useful applications. Aversion therapy can be used to replace inappropriate positive reactions to a stimulus with negative reactions. For example, a compound containing silver interacts with nicotine to make a tobacco cigarette taste terrible. Substituting a negative outcome for a positive outcome of smoking helps some smokers quit more easily (Rose, Behm, Murugesan, & McClernon, 2010).

A variation of counterconditioning used to treat fear is known as **systematic desensitization**. Associations between a phobic stimulus and fear are replaced by associations between the phobic stimulus and relaxation. The person undergoing treatment is first trained to achieve a state of physical and mental relaxation, usually by tensing and relaxing muscle groups from head to toe. Once relaxation is achieved, the fear stimulus is gradually introduced, either in physical form or through guided imagery in which the person is asked to imagine the stimulus. If relaxation falters at any point, the person retreats to an earlier stage of exposure to the fear stimulus until he or she can relax again.

Addiction in addition to the influences on addiction discussed in our chapter on consciousness, classical conditioning can contribute to dependence on a drug or behavior. Stimuli associated with drug use often become conditioned stimuli for the effects of a drug. For example, peak caffeine levels occur about 45 minutes after drinking a cup of coffee (Liguori, Hughes, & Grass, 1997), yet most coffee drinkers report feeling more awake as soon as they take that first sip in the morning, or possibly even smell the coffee brewing.

One of the challenges faced by people recovering from addiction to substances is the fact that environmental cues (conditioned stimuli—CSs) associated with the effects of substance use (unconditioned stimuli—UCS) continue to elicit craving (conditioned response—CR) for the drug of

systematic desensitization A type of counterconditioning in which people relax while being exposed to stimuli that elicit fear.

© imageegami/Shutterstock

choice. Note that most treatments for substance abuse involve simply abstaining from a drug as opposed to extinction or counterconditioning. There is nothing about avoiding the use of a drug that substantially weakens the previously formed associations surrounding its use. Consequently, being exposed to previously established conditioned stimuli (CSs), including the people with whom one did the drugs previously or the context in which one used the drugs, often leads to a former addict's relapse (Chaudhri, Sahuque, & Janak, 2008). The sight, smell, or taste of a recovering alcoholic's favorite drink or even a visit to a favorite bar is often enough to undermine the person's abstinence from drinking. Reducing these associations can help the addict continue to abstain.

Attitudes and Prejudice Classical conditioning contributes to the formation and change of attitudes (Cacioppo & Berntson, 2001). After all, advertisers have been using classical conditioning for years to influence consumer attitudes about products. By forming associations between the products and other stimuli we value, like celebrities, advertisers hope that our opinions of their product will improve. Consider all the product placements in movies. If Tony Stark of *Iron Man* drives an Audi, that brand takes on a whole new level of glamour.

> Human beings, who are almost unique in having the ability to learn from the experience of others, are also remarkable for their apparent disinclination to do so.
>
> —Douglas Adams

© New Line Cinema/The Kobal Collection/Art Resource, NY

Marketers hope that associations between their products and images of glamorous celebrities will boost their sales by making their products appear more valuable.

Prejudice, which is discussed further in our chapter on social psychology, is a negative attitude about a group of people. Like other attitudes, prejudice is influenced by classical conditioning, although it has many other roots as well. In particular, latent inhibition can contribute to the development of negative attitudes (Cacioppo, Marshall-Goodell, Tassinary, & Petty, 1992). Consider the following. Because of latent inhibition, if a child has grown up with little exposure to people outside his or her own race, people of the child's own race are more familiar, and learning to associate their race with other attributes should be slow. In contrast, the child will have had much less pre-exposure to people of other races. Latent inhibition effects would predict that children exposed to news reports about crime would form stronger associations between people of unfamiliar races and crime than between people of their own race and crime.

Psychology *as a* Hub Science

Classical Conditioning Informs Medicine

While reading about Pavlov's experiments with salivating dogs, it might be difficult to grasp the full significance of Pavlov's results, but there were some very good reasons why his laboratory continued to receive considerable resources during difficult times of war and revolution (Gantt, 1928).

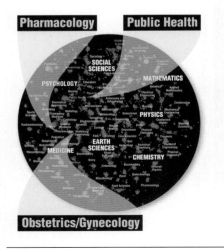

Pavlov himself understood many of the possible applications of his work.

Pavlov was the first to describe conditioned placebo effects. A placebo is a sham treatment, like a sugar pill, and a placebo effect occurs when administering a placebo actually seems to produce an improvement in health. After receiving the opiate painkiller morphine in a particular laboratory, Pavlov's dogs began to show effects of the drug whenever they returned to the room. Simply entering the room (a placebo condition) was enough to reduce pain. This response should look familiar to you by now. The laboratory had taken on the ability to signal (conditioned stimulus—CS) the eventual administration of the drug (unconditioned stimulus—UCS) and the pain relief produced by the drug (unconditioned response—UCR).

Exactly why placebos work remains the subject of debate (Eccles, 2002). In human patients, the cognitive expectation that taking a medicine will make you feel better probably plays a strong role. However, classical conditioning has its part to play as well. If a patient with a bad cold is mistakenly prescribed an antibiotic, which is not effective against the viruses responsible for the cold, eventually the patient will recover. On subsequent occasions, taking an antibiotic might actually make the patient feel better right away, due to expectations of improvement and the development of the antibiotic as a conditioned stimulus for improved health. This "trap" might account for the deliberate use of placebos by physicians, the demand for ineffective treatments by patients, and the trends to overprescribe certain medications (Dixon & Sweeney, 2000).

Creativity and Schizophrenia Due to latent inhibition, most of us form associations with unfamiliar stimuli faster than we do with familiar stimuli. This quality helps us focus our energy toward dealing effectively with novelty and change in our environments.

Less latent inhibition is seen in very creative people and in people diagnosed with schizophrenia than is seen in the general public (Baruch, Hemsley, & Gray, 1988a, 1988b; Lubow, Ingberg-Sachs, Salstein-Orda, & Gewirtz, 1992). This difference means that creative people and people with schizophrenia form new associations with familiar stimuli faster than most people do. They make connections under circumstances in which most of us would not. Reduced latent inhibition might account for the creative person's ability to see familiar things in new ways, which is a positive outcome, but it also might lead to the tendency of people with schizophrenia to make odd, inappropriate connections among ideas. In our chapter on psychological disorders, we will refer to this tendency as a "loosening of associations." For example, a person with schizophrenia might suggest that a painting has a headache. Needless to say, this is not the type of association between stimuli that most people would make.

Pavlov's research also forms the basis for prepared childbirth techniques. In 1951, a French physician named Fernand Lamaze was invited to tour medical facilities in the Soviet Union, where he was exposed to methods for reducing pain during childbirth using Pavlovian concepts. In most cases, pain is an important signal for injury, and as such, most of us respond to pain with fear and anxiety. Counterconditioning can be used to help mothers respond to painful contractions, not with fear and anxiety, which heighten the sense of pain, but with a sense of calm produced by progressive muscle relaxation.

Although Lamaze's claims for pain-free childbirth have not been confirmed (the vast majority of women request anesthetics during childbirth whether trained or not), women who receive training prior to giving birth report somewhat lower pain scores, making training a useful addition to other medical techniques (Melzack, Taenzer, Feldman, & Kinch, 1981). ✪

Prepared childbirth is an example of counterconditioning, in which women are trained to respond to contractions with relaxation rather than with fear and anxiety.

© Ruth Jenkinson/Dorling Kindersley/Getty Images

Summary 8.2

Classical Conditioning Phenomena

Classical conditioning phenomenon	Description	Example
Acquisition	Gradual development of conditioned responding	Pavlov's dog salivates on a higher percentage of trials as training progresses.
Extinction	Reduction of conditioned responding when a CS is presented without being followed by a UCS	If the metronome is no longer followed by food, the dog stops salivating to the metronome.
Spontaneous recovery	Reappearance of conditioned responding following periods of rest between extinction training sessions	The dog shows no salivation at the end of the day's extinction training, but after a night of rest in the kennel, the dog salivates at the beginning of the next extinction session.
Inhibition	CS predicts the nonoccurrence of the UCS	As long as a gauge is "in the green," your equipment will not explode. You do not feel fear.
Generalization	Responding to stimuli that resemble the CS	Little Albert's fear of white rats generalized to a Santa Claus beard.
Discrimination	Responding to the CS but not to similar stimuli that have not been paired with the UCS	A combat veteran learns to distinguish between the sound of gunfire and the backfire from a car.
Higher order conditioning	Conditioned responding to stimuli that predict the occurrence of a CS	A child who has been bitten by a dog begins to fear the street where the dog lives.
Latent inhibition	Acquisition is slower to a familiar CS.	An American forms a taste aversion faster to fruit bat pie than to hamburgers.

What Is Operant Conditioning?

In our discussion of behaviorism in our introductory chapter, we introduced you to Edward Thorndike and his Law of Effect. To recap, Thorndike had observed the learning that took place when a cat tried to escape one of his "puzzle boxes." According to Thorndike, the cats learned to escape by repeating actions that produced desirable outcomes and by eliminating behaviors that produced what he called "annoying" outcomes, or outcomes featuring either no useful effects or negative effects. Consequently, the Law of Effect states that a behavior will be "stamped into" an organism's repertoire depending on the consequences of the behavior.

The association between a behavior and its consequences is referred to as operant or instrumental conditioning. In this type of learning, organisms *operate* on their environment, and their behavior is often *instrumental* in producing an outcome. B. F. Skinner extended Thorndike's findings using an apparatus that bears his name—the Skinner box, a modified cage containing levers or buttons that can be pressed or pecked by animals.

Operant conditioning differs from classical conditioning along several dimensions. By definition, classical conditioning is based on an association between two stimuli, whereas operant conditioning occurs when a behavior is associated with its consequences. Classical conditioning generally works best with relatively involuntary behaviors, such as fear or salivation, whereas operant conditioning involves voluntary behaviors, like walking to class or waving to a friend.

Types of Consequences

As we all know from experience, some types of consequences increase behaviors and some types decrease behaviors. Skinner divided consequences into four classes: positive reinforcement, negative reinforcement, positive punishment, and negative punishment. Both types of reinforcement increase their associated behaviors, whereas both types of punishment decrease associated behaviors (see Table 8.2).

We all have our own unique set of effective reinforcers and punishers. You might think that getting an A in a course is very reinforcing, making all those extra hours spent studying worthwhile, but top grades may be less meaningful to the student sitting next to you who came to college for the social life. A parent might spank a child believing that spanking is an effective form of punishment, only to be surprised to find that the child's unwanted behavior is actually becoming more rather than less frequent. For some children, the reward of getting the parent's attention overrides the discomfort of the spanking part of the interaction. In other words, the identity of a reinforcer or punisher is defined by its effects on behavior, not by some intrinsic quality of the consequence itself. The only accurate way to determine the impact of a consequence is to check your results. If you think

TABLE 8.2 Types of Consequences

	Add stimulus to environment	Remove stimulus from environment
Increase behavior	Positive reinforcement	Negative reinforcement
Decrease behavior	Positive punishment	Negative punishment

you're reinforcing or punishing a behavior, but the frequency of the behavior is not changing in the direction you expect, try something else.

Positive Reinforcement

By definition, a positive reinforcement increases the frequency of its associated behavior by providing a desired outcome. Once again, it is important to note that each individual has his or her own menu of effective reinforcements. In a common application of operant conditioning, children with autism are taught language, with candy serving as the positive reinforcement. Benjamin Lahey tells of his experience trying to teach a child with autism to say the syllable "ba" to obtain an M&M candy (Lahey, 1995). After 4 hours without progress, Lahey turned to the child's mother in frustration, asking her what she thought might be the problem. The mother calmly replied that her son didn't like M&Ms. Lahey switched to the child's preferred treat, chopped carrots, and the child quickly began emitting "ba's." Chopped carrot is probably not the first reinforcer you would try with a 4-year-old boy, but in this case, it made all the difference.

The Premack Principle can help you maintain good time management. If you prefer socializing to studying, use the opportunity to socialize as a reward for meeting your evening's study goals.

Thinking Scientifically

Why Do People Deliberately Injure Themselves?

Thorndike's Law of Effect stipulates that behaviors followed by positive consequences are more likely to be repeated in the future, and behaviors followed by negative consequences are less likely to be repeated. Why then, do large numbers of people, particularly in adolescence, engage in self-injury, or deliberate physical damage without suicidal intent (Klonsky & Muehlenkamp, 2007)? In one study, an astonishing 46% of 9th and 10th graders reported a self-injury in the previous year (Lloyd-Richardson, Perrine, Dierker, & Kelley, 2007).

As we will learn in this chapter, reward and punishment are in the eye of the beholder. The first challenge we face in our analysis of self-injury is the assumption that pain is always a negative consequence. For most of us, it is. However, adolescents who engage in self-injury report feelings of relief or calm, in spite of the obvious pain they inflict on themselves. Such feelings probably serve to reinforce further bouts of self-injury. Self-injury often occurs in response to feelings of anger, anxiety, and frustration, and as we will see, alleviation of these negative feelings might also reward

the injurious behavior (Klonsky, 2007; Klonsky & Muehlenkamp, 2007). Finally, injury is associated with the release of endorphins, our bodies' natural opiates. The positive feelings associated with endorphin release also might serve to reinforce the behavior.

Self-injury frequently but not always occurs in people diagnosed with psychological disorders, such as depression, anxiety disorders, eating disorders, or substance abuse, which we discuss further in our chapters on motivation and emotion and psychological disorders. Others engag-

If everyone has a different set of effective reinforcers, how do we know what to use? A very simple technique for predicting what a particular animal or person will find reinforcing is the Premack Principle, which states that whatever behavior an organism spends the most time and energy doing is likely to be a very important behavior to that organism (Premack, 1965). It is possible, therefore, to rank a person's free time activities according to his or her priorities. If Dr. Lahey had been able to observe his young client's eating habits before starting training, it is unlikely that he would have made the mistake of offering M&Ms as reinforcers. The opportunity to engage in a higher priority activity is always capable of rewarding a lower priority activity. Your grandmother may never have heard of David Premack, but she knows that telling you to eat your broccoli to get an ice cream generally works.

Both Thorndike and Skinner agreed that positive reinforcement is a very powerful tool for managing behavior. In fact, in our later discussion of punishment, we will argue that the effects of positive reinforcement are much more powerful than the effects of punishment. Unfortunately, in Western culture, we tend to provide relatively little positive reinforcement. We are more likely to hear about our mistakes from our boss than to hear about all the things we've done correctly. Much of our time and effort go into controlling unwanted behaviors with punishment. It is possible that we

According to the Premack Principle, a preferred activity can be used to reinforce a less preferred activity. Most children are likely to prefer candy over carrots, so rewarding a child with candy for eating carrots will often increase carrot consumption. One little boy with autism, however, preferred carrots to M&Ms, and his training proceeded much more smoothly when carrot rewards were substituted for candy rewards.

© M. Itani / Alamy

© Carolyn Jenkins/ Alamy

ing in the behavior have a history of sexual abuse. Observations that captive animals in zoos and laboratories are often prone to self-injury might provide additional insight into the causes of this behavior (Jones & Barraclough, 1978).Treatment usually consists of therapy for any underlying psychological disorders along with avoidance, in which the person is encouraged to engage in behaviors that are incompatible with self-harm. To assist these individuals further, we need to be able to see reward and punishment from their perspective, not just our own. ○

If the consequences of a behavior influence how likely a person is to repeat the behavior in the future, how can we explain the prevalence of self-injury? Why don't the painful consequences of this behavior make people stop? In situations like this, operant conditioning tells us that we need to look for possible reinforcers for the behavior that override any of the painful outcomes. In the case of self-injury, people report feeling "calm" and "relief." To treat such behaviors effectively, psychologists need to understand what advantages they provide from the perspective of the person doing the behavior.

© Rusig/Alamy

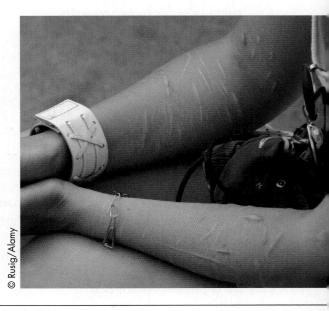

Actress Natalie Portman "loves" her Oscar, not because of its intrinsic value (you can't eat it, etc.), but because the award has become a conditioned reinforcer.

Many superstitious behaviors, like wearing your "lucky socks," can be learned through operant conditioning. Operant conditioning does not require a behavior to "cause" a positive outcome in order to be strengthened. All that is required is that a behavior be followed by a positive outcome. Unless you suddenly have a string of bad performances while wearing the lucky socks, you are unlikely to have an opportunity to unlearn your superstition.

conditioned reinforcer A reinforcer that gains value from being associated with other things that are valued. Also known as a secondary reinforcer.

negative reinforcement A method for increasing behaviors that allow an organism to escape or avoid an unpleasant consequence.

feel entitled to good treatment from others and therefore feel we should not have to provide any reward for reasonably expected behaviors. The problem with this approach is that extinction occurs in operant as well as in classical conditioning. A behavior that is no longer reinforced will drop in frequency. By ignoring other people's desirable behaviors instead of reinforcing them, perhaps with a simple thank you, we risk reducing their frequency.

Some reinforcers, known as primary reinforcers, are effective due to their natural roles in survival, such as food. Others must be learned. We are not born valuing money, grades, or gold medals. These are examples of **conditioned**, or secondary, **reinforcers** that gain their value and ability to influence behavior from being associated with other things we value. Here we see an intersection between classical and operant conditioning. If you always say "good dog" before you provide your pet with a treat, saying "good dog" becomes a conditioned stimulus (CS) for food (unconditioned stimulus—UCS) that can now be used to reinforce compliance with commands to come, sit, or heel (operant behaviors). Classical conditioning establishes the value of "good dog," and operant conditioning describes the use of "good dog" to reinforce the dog's voluntary behavior.

Human beings are capable of generating long chains of conditioned reinforcers extending far into the future. We might ask you why you are studying this textbook right now, at this moment. A learning psychologist might answer that you are studying now because studying will be reinforced by a good grade at the end of the term, which in turn will be reinforced by a diploma at the end of your college education, which in turn will be reinforced by a good job after graduation, which in turn will be reinforced by a good salary, which will allow you to live in a nice house, drive a nice car, wear nice clothes, eat good food, and provide the same for your family in the coming years.

Negative Reinforcement

Negative reinforcement, which sounds contradictory, involves the use of unpleasant consequences to increase the frequency of an associated behavior. Negative reinforcement increases the frequency of behaviors that allow an organism to avoid, turn off, or postpone an unpleasant consequence, or so-called escape and avoidance behaviors. Let's look at a laboratory example of negative reinforcement before tackling real-world examples. If a hungry rat in a Skinner box learns that pressing a bar produces food, a positive consequence, we would expect the frequency of bar pressing to increase. This would be an instance of positive reinforcement. On the other hand, if pressing the bar turns off or delays the administration of an electric shock, we would still expect the frequency of bar pressing to increase. This would be an instance of negative reinforcement.

Be careful to avoid confusing negative reinforcement with punishment, which we cover in the next section. By definition, a punishment

decreases the behaviors it follows, whereas both positive and negative reinforcers *increase* the frequency of the behaviors they follow. Returning to our Skinner box example, the rat's bar pressing will increase following both positive reinforcement (food) and negative reinforcement (turning off a shock). If we shocked the rat every time it pressed the bar (punishment), it would stop pressing the bar very quickly.

Many everyday behaviors are maintained by negative reinforcement. We buckle up in our cars to turn off annoying beeps, open umbrellas to avoid getting wet, scratch an insect bite to relieve the itch, take an aspirin to escape a headache, apply sunscreen to avoid a sunburn or skin cancer, and apologize to avoid further misunderstandings with a friend.

In many real-world cases, positive and negative reinforcement act on behavior simultaneously. A heroin addict uses the drug to obtain a state of euphoria (positive reinforcer), but also to eliminate the unpleasant symptoms of withdrawal (negative reinforcer). You might study hard to achieve high grades (positive reinforcers), while also being motivated by the need to avoid low grades (negative reinforcers).

Putting up an umbrella to avoid getting wet from the rain is an example of a negatively reinforced behavior.

Punishment

A **punishment** is any consequence that reduces the frequency of an associated behavior. **Positive punishment** refers to applying an aversive consequence that reduces the frequency of or eliminates a behavior. As we observed previously, we can demonstrate that a rat will quickly stop bar pressing if each press results in an electric shock. **Negative punishment** involves the removal of something desirable. In the Skinner box, we can change the rules for a rat that has learned previously to bar press for food. Now, food is made available *unless* the rat presses the bar. Under these conditions, the rat will also stop bar pressing quickly (see ● Figure 8.7).

Both Thorndike and Skinner were in agreement about the relative weakness of punishment as a means of controlling behavior. Part of the weakness of punishment effects observed by these and other psychologists arises from the difficulties of applying punishment effectively in real contexts. Three conditions must be met for punishment to have any observable effects on behavior: significance, immediacy, and consistency (Schwartz, 1984).

As we observed with reinforcement, consequences have to matter to the person or animal receiving them (i.e., *significance*). If we use a punisher that is too mild for a particular individual, there is little incentive for that person to change his or her behavior. College campuses usually charge a fairly significant amount of money for parking illegally. However, there will typically be some students for whom that particular punishment is not

punishment A consequence that eliminates or reduces the frequency of a behavior.

positive punishment A consequence that eliminates or reduces the frequency of a behavior by applying an aversive stimulus.

negative punishment A method for reducing behavior by removing something desirable whenever the target behavior occurs.

FIGURE 8.7

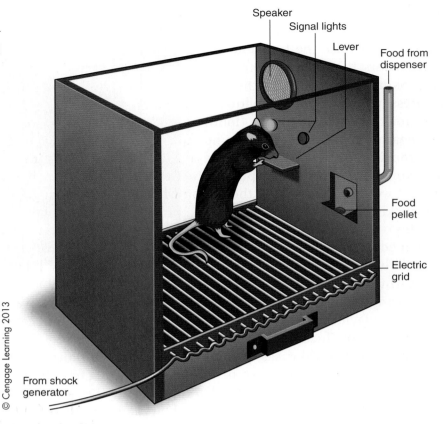

The Skinner Box. A specially adapted cage called a Skinner box, after behaviorist B. F. Skinner, allows researchers to investigate the results of reinforcement and punishment on the likelihood that the rat will press the bar.

The likelihood of getting a ticket influences drivers' behavior. At an intersection with cameras, drivers are very unlikely to run a red light, but at other intersections, behavior might be determined by whether or not a police officer is nearby.

sufficient to ensure that they will park legally. How high would a parking fee have to be to gain complete compliance on the part of the university community? What if you risked the death penalty for parking illegally? We can be fairly certain that most people would leave their cars at home altogether rather than risk that particular consequence. The point is that punishment can work if a sufficiently severe consequence is selected, but using the amount of force needed to produce results is rarely considered practical and ethical. Free societies have long-standing social prohibitions against cruel and unusual punishments, and these conventions are incompatible with using the force that may be needed to change the behavior of some individuals.

Immediate punishment is much more effective than delayed punishment (i.e., *immediacy*). For the rat in the Skinner box, delays of just 10 seconds can reduce the effectiveness of electric shock as a punisher. Human beings, of course, are much more capable than rats at bridging long intervals. Nonetheless, the same principle holds true. Delayed punishment is much less effective than immediate punishment. We should not be too surprised that the months or years that are required to try and convict a serious criminal may greatly reduce the impact of imprisonment on his or her subsequent behavior.

Our final requirement for effective punishment is its uniform application (i.e., *consistency*). College students are a prosocial, law-abiding group as a whole, yet many confess to determining their highway speed based on the presence or absence of a police car in their rearview mirrors. The experience of exceeding the speed limit without consequence weakens the ability of the possibility of tickets and fines to influence behavior. On the other hand, at intersections known to be controlled by cameras, compliance is generally quite high. If you are absolutely certain that running a red light will result in an expensive ticket, it would be very foolish indeed to test the system.

Skinner recommended extinction as an alternative to punishment (Skinner, 1953). In our discussion of classical conditioning, we used the term *extinction* to refer to the disappearance of conditioned responding that occurs when the conditioned stimulus (CS) no longer signals the arrival of an unconditioned stimulus (UCS). Extinction in operant conditioning has a similar meaning. Learned behaviors stop when they are no longer followed by a reinforcing consequence. Obviously, parents and teachers cannot look the other way when one child is being physically aggressive toward another, but in many other instances, Skinner's approach is quite successful in reducing the frequency of unwanted behaviors (Brown & Elliot, 1965). Although ignoring a child's tantrums can be embarrassing for many parents, this can be an effective strategy for reducing their frequency.

Schedules of Reinforcement

Reinforcing a behavior every time it occurs is known as continuous reinforcement. Although it is highly desirable to use continuous reinforcement when a new behavior is being learned, it is obviously inconvenient to do so forever. Most employers expect workers to show up every day, but do not want to pay them more than once or twice per month. Once we deviate from continuous reinforcement, however, the manner in which we do so may have a dramatic impact on the target behavior. To obtain the results we want, it is helpful to understand what happens when we use **partial reinforcement**, or the reinforcement of the desired behavior on some occasions but not others.

Psychologists have identified many ways to apply partial reinforcement, but we will concentrate on two variations: ratio schedules and interval schedules. In a ratio schedule of partial reinforcement, reinforcement depends on the number of times a behavior occurs. In an interval schedule of partial reinforcement, reinforcement depends on the passage of a certain amount of time. Either type of schedule, ratio or interval, can be fixed or variable. In fixed schedules, the requirements for reinforcement never vary. In variable schedules, the requirements for reinforcement are allowed to fluctuate from trial to trial, averaging a certain amount over the course of a learning session.

Concerns about the effects of piecework on worker well-being contributed to the Fair Labor Standards Act of 1938, which included a provision for a minimum hourly wage.

Fixed Ratio Schedules A **fixed ratio (FR) schedule** requires that a behavior occur a set number of times for each reinforcer. Continuous reinforcement, discussed earlier, is equivalent to a fixed ratio (FR) of 1. If we now raise our requirement to two behaviors per reinforcer, we have a schedule of FR 2, and so on. Using the Skinner box, we can investigate the influence of fixed ratio schedules on the rate at which a rat will press a bar for food. To do so, we will track cumulative responses as a function of time. Fixed ratio schedules produce a characteristic pattern of responding. In general, responses are fairly steady, with a significant pause following each reward.

partial reinforcement The reinforcement of a desired behavior on some occasions but not others.

fixed ratio (FR) schedule A schedule of reinforcement in which reinforcement occurs following a set number of behaviors.

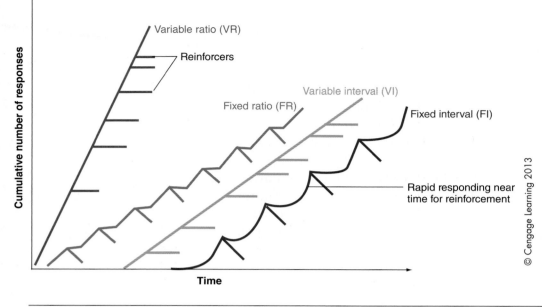

FIGURE 8.8

Schedules of Reinforcement.
The schedule used to deliver reinforcement has a big impact on resulting behavior. In general, the variable schedules produce higher rates of responding than do their fixed counterparts. The fixed interval (FI) schedule produces a characteristic pattern of low rates of responding at the beginning of the interval and accelerated responding as the end of the interval approaches. We see this same pattern of response in the rate with which Congress passes bills in a session.

© Cengage Learning 2013

© SCPhotos/Alamy

Workers in the garment industry are often paid "by the piece," or with a set amount of money for each finished garment. This compensation system is an example of a fixed ratio schedule. Because workers cannot make money when their equipment breaks down and they tend to view lunch and other breaks as costing them money, this schedule is not considered to be fair to workers.

variable ratio (VR) schedule A schedule of reinforcement in which reinforcement occurs following some variable number of behaviors.

As the amount of work for each reward is raised, responding becomes slower (see ● Figure 8.8).

In early industrial settings, workers were often paid "by the piece," a real-world example of the use of a fixed ratio schedule. In other words, a worker would be paid a fixed amount every time he or she produced a certain number of products or parts on an assembly line. Most workers find this system less than ideal. If equipment malfunctions, the worker cannot earn any money. Lunch breaks would also then be viewed as loss of income rather than a helpful time of rest. Some examples of piecework remain today, including the work of most physicians, who get paid by the procedure, and building contractors, who get paid for constructing a fixed number of homes in a new development.

Variable Ratio Schedules As in fixed ratio schedules, **variable ratio (VR) schedules** also involve counting the number of times a behavior occurs. However, this time the required number of behaviors is allowed to fluctuate around some average amount.

In the Skinner box, we might set our variable ratio (VR) schedule to 10 for a one-hour session. This means that over the course of the session, the rat must press an average of 10 times for each food pellet. However, this schedule may mean that only one press will deliver food on one trial, but 30 presses will be required on the next. The rat is unable to predict when reinforcement is likely to occur, leading to a high, very steady rate of responding in our cumulative record. We do not see the characteristic pausing observed following reinforcement in the fixed ratio (FR) schedule because the rat cannot predict when the next reward will occur.

One of the most dramatic real-world examples of the variable ratio schedule is the programming of slot machines in casinos. Slot machines are human versions of Skinner boxes that use variable rate (VR) schedules. The casino sets the machine to pay off after some average number of plays, but the player doesn't know if a payoff will occur after one coin is inserted or after thousands. You don't have to observe the behavior of people playing slot machines very long in order to see a demonstration of the high, steady responding that characterizes the variable rate (VR) schedule. The programming of slot machines can be very sophisticated. Slot machines that are located in places where people are unlikely to return (airports, bus stations) pay off less frequently than those in places people are more likely to play regularly.

Fixed Interval Schedules Unlike the ratio schedules, reinforcement in interval schedules depends on the passage of time rather than the number of responses produced. In a **fixed interval (FI) schedule**, the time that must pass before reinforcement becomes available following a single response is set at a certain amount. In the Skinner box, a rat's first bar press starts a timer. Any responses that occur before the timer counts down will not be reinforced. In a sense, the interval serves as a time-out, or a period during which reinforcement is not available. As soon as the timer counts down to zero, the rat's next bar press is reinforced, and the timer starts counting down again. In the fixed interval (FI) schedule, the interval is the same from trial to trial. Animals and people have a good general sense of the passage of time, leading to a very characteristic pattern of responding in fixed interval (FI) situations. Reinforcement is followed by a long, postreinforcement pause. As the end of the interval is anticipated, responding increases sharply. A graph of the number of bills passed by Congress as a function of time looks very similar to the rat's performance on an FI schedule in the Skinner box (Weisberg & Waldrop, 1972). Very few bills are passed at the beginning of a session, but many are passed just at the end.

Most casinos feature a large number of slot machines, which are essentially Skinner boxes for people. The slot machine is programmed on a variable ratio (VR) schedule, which means that the player cannot predict how many plays it will take to win. In response, players exhibit the same high, steady rate of responding that we observe in rats working on VR schedules in the laboratory.

Variable Interval Schedules As you may have already guessed, the **variable interval (VI) schedule** is characterized by an interval that is allowed to fluctuate around some average amount over the course of a session. This time, our bar-pressing rat will experience intervals that range around some average amount, say, 2 minutes. On one trial, the rat may obtain reinforcement after only 30 seconds, whereas the next trial may involve an interval of 5 minutes. Over the session, the average of all the intervals will be 2 minutes. As in the variable ratio situation, we see a high, steady rate of responding.

You are probably quite familiar with variable interval (VI) schedules in the form of pop quizzes administered by your professors. Your professor might tell you that there will be five quizzes given during the term, but the timing of the quizzes remains a surprise. You might have the first two only

fixed interval (FI) schedule A schedule of reinforcement in which the first response following a specified interval will be reinforced.

variable interval (VI) schedule A schedule of reinforcement in which the first response following a varying period of time is reinforced.

Fishing works according to a variable interval (VI) schedule of reinforcement. Fish (the reinforcers) are caught after periods of time-out that vary in length. As in laboratory demonstrations of the VI schedule, fishing usually produces a steady rate of responding.

© holbox/Shutterstock

one day apart, followed by a two-week interval before the next quiz. Your best strategy, like the rat in the Skinner box on a variable interval (VI) schedule, is to emit a high, steady rate of studying behavior.

Partial Reinforcement Effect in Extinction Many a parent has regretted the day that he or she unintentionally put an unwanted behavior on a partial reinforcement schedule by uttering the words, "Okay, just this once." Perhaps the parent is strongly opposed to buying candy for a child at the supermarket checkout counter (where, of course, thanks to John Watson and his applications of psychology to advertising, candy is displayed conveniently at child-eye height). Then comes a fateful day when the parent is late coming home from work, the child is hungry because dinner is delayed, and, unintentionally, the parent gives in "just this once," putting begging-for-candy on a variable schedule. Subsequently, when the parent returns to his or her previous refusal to buy candy, a high, steady rate of begging behavior will occur before it once again extinguishes.

Back in the laboratory once more, we compare the behavior of two rats in Skinner boxes. One is working on a continuous, or fixed ratio (FR 1), schedule of reinforcement. The other is working on a partial schedule of reinforcement, perhaps a variable ratio (VR 3). After several sessions of training, we now stop reinforcement altogether for both. It may come as a surprise to you that the rat working on the continuous schedule will stop pressing long before the rat accustomed to the variable ratio (VR 3). In other words, extinction occurs more rapidly following continuous reinforcement than following partial schedules. This outcome is known as the **partial reinforcement effect in extinction**.

> Repetition is the mother of learning.
>
> —White Mountain Apache Indians

The partial reinforcement effect is probably due to one of two factors or a combination of both. First, the transition from continuous reinforcement to extinction is more obvious than the transition from a partial schedule to extinction. If you are accustomed to being paid for a babysitting job every time you work, you will definitely notice any of your employer's failures to pay. In contrast, if your neighbor typically pays you about once a month for raking his yard, you might not notice right away that he hasn't paid you for awhile. Second, partial schedules teach organisms to persist in the face of nonreinforcement. In a sense, partial schedules teach us to work through periods in which reinforcement does not occur. Consequently, we might view extinction as just another case where continuing to perform might eventually produce reinforcement. In cases where positive behavior is occurring, such as working on your senior thesis regularly in spite of a

partial reinforcement effect in extinction The more rapid extinction observed following continuous reinforcement than following partial reinforcement.

much-delayed grade, persistence is an enormous advantage. On the other hand, as shown in our earlier example of begging for candy, placing an undesirable behavior on partial reinforcement will make it much more difficult to eventually extinguish.

Comparing Schedules What happens if you are exposed to two or more schedules of reinforcement at the same time? This scenario is realistic, as we face these types of choices every day. Which is a more rewarding use of my time—studying for my midterm or making some extra money by working overtime? In making choices, animals and people follow the matching law, which states that the relative frequency of responding to one alternative will match the relative reinforcement for responses on that alternative (Herrnstein & Heyman, 1979). The law powerfully accounts for the effects on behavior of frequency, magnitude, and delays in reward.

Time spent playing online video games provides an interesting example of the effects of simultaneous schedules of reinforcement. The millions of users of massively multiplayer online role-playing games (MMORPGs), such as Everquest and Star Wars Galaxies, spend an average of 22 hours per week on their games (Yee, 2006). What could possibly compel these people to make such a lopsided choice between online interactions and real-life social experience? One clue to this choice is the fact that substantial numbers of players report that "the most rewarding or satisfying experience" they had over the last 7 or 30 days took place while gaming. We would assume that if the frequency and magnitude of rewards available in gaming were higher than those in real life socializing, the person would choose to spend his or her time accordingly.

Children are not born with terrific table manners, and parents would wait a long time to see perfect table manners to reinforce. Instead, we can use shaping, or the method of successive approximations, to gently move behaviors in the desired direction.

Shaping: The Method of Successive Approximations

So far, our discussion of operant conditioning has centered on increasing or decreasing the frequency of a particular behavior. What happens if you want to increase the frequency of a behavior that rarely or never occurs? Most parents would like to teach their children to use good table manners, but you could wait a long time for the opportunity to reward young children for using the correct utensil to eat their food.

Fortunately, we have a method for increasing the frequency of behaviors that never or rarely occur. Using **shaping**, or the **method of successive approximations**, we begin by reinforcing spontaneous behaviors that are somewhat similar to the target behavior we want to train. As training continues, we use gradually more stringent requirements for reinforcement until the exact behavior we want occurs. You can think of shaping as a funnel. We start out with generous criteria for reinforcement (thank you for picking up the spoon) and gradually narrow our criteria (thank you for putting the spoon in the food) until we are reinforcing only the target behavior (thank you for using the spoon

© Shmel/Shutterstock

shaping/method of successive approximations A method for increasing the frequency of behaviors that never or rarely occur.

to eat your applesauce). One of the most positive features about the shaping process is that we don't have to be perfect before we obtain reinforcement.

The rats in Skinner boxes that have been described in this chapter did not spontaneously start pressing levers. Somebody had to teach them to do so. We begin by making sure the hungry rat understands that food is available in the Skinner box. Using a remote control, we activate the food dispenser a few times. Quickly, the rat forms a classically conditioned association between the sound of the food dispenser and the arrival of food in the cup. If we continue to feed the rat in this manner, it is unlikely that it will ever learn to bar press. There is no reason for it to do so, as it already is obtaining the food it needs. So, we narrow our criteria for obtaining food from simply existing in the box to standing in the corner of the box that contains the bar. If we press our remote control every time the rat is in the correct corner, it will begin to stay there most of the time. Now we want the rat to rear on its back feet so that it is likely to hit the bar with its front feet on the way down. If we begin to reinforce the rat less frequently for staying in the corner, it will begin to explore. Eventually, the rat is likely to hit the bar with its front feet while exploring, producing a bar press. Now it will begin to press on its own. In the hands of an experienced trainer, this process takes about half an hour.

Shaping involves a very delicate tightrope walk between too much and too little reinforcement. If we reinforce too generously, learning stops, because there is no incentive for change. If your music teacher always tells you that your performances are perfect, you will stop trying to improve them. On the other hand, if we don't reinforce frequently enough, the learner becomes discouraged. Reinforcement provides very important feedback to the learner, so insufficient reinforcement may slow down or stop the learning process.

Teaching more complex behaviors requires chaining, or the breaking down of the complex behavior into manageable steps. Chaining can be done in a forward direction, such as teaching the letters of the alphabet from A to Z, or in a backward direction, such as teaching the last step in a sequence, then the next to the last, and so on. Chaining can be very useful when training new skills, such as working independently on academic projects, to children with special needs (Pelios, MacDuff, & Axelrod, 2003). Backward chaining is used by most trainers of animals used in entertainment. For example, dogs have been taught to perform the Macarena (Burch & Bailey, 1999). The trainer uses a verbal, gestural, or clicker cue while shaping the last step in the dance. When the dog performs this last step reliably, the trainer adds the next-to-the-last step, and so on until the entire complex sequence is mastered.

Learning is not child's play.
We cannot learn without pain.

—Aristotle

Cognitive, Biological, and Social Influences on Operant Conditioning

Even the most radical behaviorists, including B. F. Skinner, did not deny the existence of cognitive, social, or biological influences on learning (Jensen & Burgess, 1997). Instead, behaviorists believed that internal processes followed the same rules as externally observable behavior. Skinner wrote, "We need not suppose that events which take place within an organism's skin have special properties. . . . A private event may be distinguished by its limited accessibility but not, so far as we know, by any special nature or structure" (Skinner, 1953, p. 257). However, as we saw in the case of classical conditioning, the results of some operant conditioning experiments stimulated greater interest in the cognitive, social, and biological processes involved in learning.

Cognitive Influences on Operant Conditioning

One of the important principles of operant conditioning is that consequences are required for learning to occur. Edward Tolman challenged this notion by allowing his rats to explore mazes without any food reinforcement (Tolman, 1948). Subsequently, when food was placed in the goal boxes of the mazes, the previously unreinforced rats performed as well as rats that had been reinforced all along. Tolman referred to the rats' ability to learn in the absence of reinforcement as **latent learning**. He argued that the rats had indeed learned while just exploring, but they did not demonstrate their learning until motivated by the food reward to do so. We usually judge whether learning has occurred by observing outward behavior. Tolman's rats remind us that there is a difference between what has been learned and what is performed. Students are all too familiar with the experience of performing poorly on exams in spite of having learned a great deal about the material.

In addition to challenging the role of reinforcement in learning, Tolman also disputed traditional behaviorist explanations of the nature of the learning that occurred in mazes. Tolman believed that instead of learning a simple operant "turn right for food" association, rats learned "this is where I can find food" (Tolman, 1948, 1959). After training rats to follow a path in a maze to find food, Tolman blocked the path, and the rats were allowed to choose from a number of additional paths. If the rats had learned a simple turn–get food response, they should have chosen the paths that were more similar to the training path. In fact, they showed evidence of choosing paths that required them to turn in a very different direction compared to their previously trained path (Tolman, Richie, & Kalish, 1946) (see ● Figure 8.9).

To account for his results, Tolman suggested that the rats had formed cognitive maps, or mental representations of the mazes. Map formation was viewed as a unique, nonassociative learning process that didn't follow the previously established rules of associative learning (O'Keefe & Nadel, 1978). For example, in contrast to the gradual acquisition of learning that usually occurs in classical and operant conditioning, cognitive maps are instantly updated when new information becomes available.

Chimpanzees show considerable abilities in forming cognitive maps (Menzel, 1978). After being carried around a circuitous route in their one-acre compound as nine vegetables and nine fruits were placed in 18 locations,

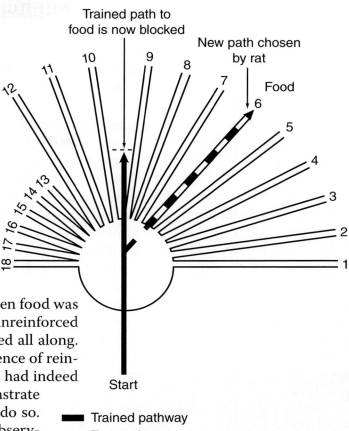

© Cengage Learning 2013

FIGURE 8.9

Tolman's Maze. Tolman did not believe that rats wandering around a maze learned "turn right for food" in the way that early behaviorists believed they did. Instead, Tolman believed the rats were learning a more cognitive map for where they can find food. Tolman provided evidence for his approach by blocking a learned pathway to food. If the behaviorists were right, the rats should choose the path most similar to the trained one. However, the rats did not do that. They showed evidence of having formed cognitive maps and were willing to turn in a very different direction if that led to food.

latent learning Learning that occurs in the absence of reinforcement.

chimpanzees were released in the center of the compound. They not only navigated to each food location using the shortest pathways, but, given their preference for fruit over vegetables, they visited the spots containing fruit first. They showed no indication that they were attempting to retrace the pathway over which they were carried as the food was put in place.

Biological Influences on Operant Conditioning Just as the work of Garcia and Koelling highlighted the need to consider biological limitations on classical conditioning, biological boundaries in operant conditioning were described by Keller and Marion Breland, two of B. F. Skinner's former students. In their 1961 book, *The Misbehavior of Organisms* (a wordplay on Skinner's classic book, *The Behavior of Organisms*), the Brelands outlined some of the challenges they encountered while using operant conditioning to train animals for entertainment.

In one instance, the researchers described how they sought to train a pig to pick up large wooden coins and to deposit the coins in a large wooden "piggy bank." Initially, all went well. The pig would quickly learn to deposit four or five coins (an example of a fixed ratio schedule) for each food reward. Eventually, however, the pig began to work slower and slower, to the point where it couldn't obtain enough food for the day. Instead of taking the coins to the piggy bank, the pig would repeatedly toss them in the air and sniff around to find them. Raccoons trained with the coins ultimately tried to wash them instead of depositing them in the bank. The animals' natural approach to food, the rooting by the pigs and the washing by the raccoons, began to interfere with their handling of the coins. You may already have suspected that the coins had become the object of some higher order conditioning due to their relationship with food. The Brelands concluded "that these animals are trapped by strong instinctive behaviors, and clearly we have here a demonstration of the prepotency of such behavior patterns over those which have been conditioned. We have termed this phenomenon 'instinctive drift.'" (Breland & Breland, 1961, p. 683).

Keller and Marian Breland watch one of their star pupils from their I. Q. Zoo attraction. Unfortunately, the intrusion of animals' instinctive behaviors often interfered with the behaviors they had acquired through operant conditioning, and they could no longer perform. The Brelands referred to this phenomenon as "instinctive drift."

Courtesy of Bob Bailey/Animal Behavior Enterprises

Social Influences on Operant Conditioning So far in our discussion of classical and operant conditioning, we have focused on the individual in isolation. Learning can certainly take place when people or animals are alone, but it often occurs in the presence of others, especially in a species as social as ours. As we will see in a later section, people are particularly likely to learn by observing others. What do we know about the impact of others on our operant learning?

The presence of others may not just promote learning, it may be necessary for learning. Human infants learn more about language when they are listening to another person face-to-face than when they are watching a person speak on television (Kuhl, 2007; Meltzoff, Kuhl, Movellan, & Sejnowski, 2009). Although operant conditioning alone cannot account for language learning, as we discuss in our chapters on development and cognition, these results emphasize the importance of social interaction in producing the arousal, focus, and motivation that contribute to effective learning.

Experienced whale trainer Dawn Brancheau was killed by one of her favorite killer whales during a 2010 show at Sea World in Orlando, Florida. Animal experts believed that the whale had simply reverted to normal whale behavior, similar to the instinctive drift observed by the Brelands.

As we mentioned previously in our discussion of cognitive maps, learning and the performance of learned behavior are not always identical. Our performance of learned behaviors varies depending on an interaction between the presence of others and the complexity of the learned task. For very simple tasks, like pedaling a bicycle or reeling in a fishing line, the presence of others makes us perform faster, a phenomenon known as social facilitation (Triplett, 1898). In complex tasks, such as taking a difficult college entrance exam, the presence of others can make us perform slower and more poorly. Once again, this effect is not restricted to complex organisms like ourselves, as the same results can be observed in the lowly cockroach (Zajonc, 1965). In a straight maze leading to food, cockroaches with an audience of other cockroaches ran faster. In a more complex maze involving several turns, the cockroaches responded to an audience by running more slowly.

Applying Operant Conditioning

Important applications of operant conditioning may be found in contemporary approaches to psychotherapy, education, advertising, politics, and many other domains.

Quite possibly one of the oddest applications was B. F. Skinner's secret World War II defense project code-named Project Pigeon. Lagging well behind the Nazis in the area of guided missile technology, the United States invested $25,000 (worth about $400,000 in today's dollars) in Skinner's "organic homing device" (Capshew, 1993). Skinner, who had considerable experience training pigeons to peck at visual stimuli in his laboratory, now trained them to peck at a projected image of a missile's target. Riding in a chamber within the missile, the pigeon's pecks would be translated into updated commands for correcting the path of the bomb. Unfortunately for Skinner (but fortunately for his pigeons), Project Pigeon elicited laughter from military officers instead of approvals (Skinner, 1960). Although never implemented, Project Pigeon stimulated Skinner and his intellectual descendents to look outside the laboratory for useful extensions of their work on learning.

B. F. Skinner's Project Pigeon was one of the more bizarre applications of operant conditioning research. Pigeons enclosed in this capsule were trained to peck at projected images of bomb targets. Although Skinner's device was superior to other World War II missile guidance systems, it was never implemented.

Token economies can be very effective ways of managing behavior. Tokens, including money, can be traded for a valued reinforcement of the worker's choice. This woman's purchase might motivate her work, but another worker might use the same paycheck to buy a motorcycle or go on vacation.

token economy An application of operant conditioning in which tokens that can be exchanged for other reinforcers are used to increase the frequency of desirable behaviors.

Token Economies A widely used application of operant learning is the **token economy**. Money, in the form of coins, bills, or bank statements, is fairly useless. You can't eat it, wear it, or shelter in it. Nonetheless, people do value it because it takes on secondary reinforcing qualities due to its history of association with other things that have intrinsic value. The use of money to buy things of personal value is an example of a token economy. You earn money for doing certain things, and then you have the opportunity to trade the money you earned for items of value to you. This system meets the best practices criteria we described for positive reinforcement. Each person can obtain reinforcement that has unique personal value. One friend may spend all of his discretionary money on going out to dinner, while another invests in the stock market. Both find money reinforcing for doing work.

An informed approach to compensating employees should include consideration of learning principles. "Menu" approaches to employee benefits provide an excellent example of this application. Historically, employers offered a set program of health, retirement, and other benefits to their entire workforce regardless of individual needs. We would expect this approach to be minimally reinforcing, as it does not match reinforcers to worker priorities. Catering a benefits

Experiencing Psychology

How Do I Break a Bad Habit?

We all have behaviors that could use some improvement. Maybe we eat poorly, drink too much, smoke, or lash out angrily at others. An understanding of the processes of learning provides us with powerful tools for changing behavior. Let's assume that your eating habits, like those of many students, do not exactly meet the "my mom would approve" standard. Yet you are learning in your psychology course that good health habits are essential tools for managing stress. How do we bring about the necessary changes?

Before doing anything to produce change, we need to understand your current behavior. Many people have a very poor understanding of what they actually eat during a day, so we will start by keeping a diary. What foods and how much do you eat? What else is going on when you eat well or poorly? What possible reinforcers or punishers are influencing your eating patterns? For the sake of example, let's say that you observe a tendency to eat high-calorie snacks late at night while studying, even when you are not hungry. Your goal, then, is to eliminate these late-night

snacks. Your baseline shows that your snacking is a social behavior. You only consume these extra foods when studying with a group. The social camaraderie and good taste of the food serve as powerful reinforcers for the behavior.

Now that we have a better understanding of our problem behavior, we are in a good position to construct a plan. Some people might say that we should depend on willpower to avoid late-night snacks by just saying that we won't have any. Unfortunately, we appear to have limited

package to individual needs is much more sensible. A young worker in good health might be more motivated by a benefits package that includes childcare, while a more mature worker may worry about long-term care in the event of a disability. By allowing workers to select their benefits from a menu, everybody can find something worth earning.

All of us respond positively to token economies, but they are especially useful in educational and institutional settings. Teachers provide frequent rewards in the form of checks, stars, or tickets that can be exchanged later for popcorn parties or a night without homework. The key to an effective token economy is to offer ultimate rewards that are truly valuable to the people you wish to motivate. If students don't care about popcorn parties, offering these will have little effect. Token economies are equally useful in prison settings and in institutions serving people with intellectual disability or mental illness.

© Ellen B. Senisi

An important application of operant conditioning principles is their use in behavior therapies for conditions like autism. Operant conditioning can be used to increase the frequency of language use and socially appropriate behaviors, like eye contact.

Behavior Therapies As we will see in our chapter on psychological therapies, learning theories have also been applied successfully to the clinical setting in the form of behavior therapies. After all, our formal definition of learning states that it involves a change in behavior, and changing behavior is precisely what therapists seek to do. In addition to the extinction and counterconditioning applications of classical conditioning, behavior therapies make use of operant conditioning concepts such as extinction, reward, and, on rare occasions, punishment. Coupled with cognitive methods designed to address the way people think about their circumstances, these methods comprise the most popular and effective means for treating many types of disorder, from substance abuse to depression. One of the most dramatic applications of behavior therapy is the treatment for autism pioneered by Ivar Lovaas (Lovaas, 1996; Lovaas et al., 1966). Autism is a lifetime condition characterized by severe language and social deficits. Although behavior therapy doesn't cure autism, behavioral interventions, like the use of chaining described previously, typically improve an individual's level of functioning.

quantities of willpower, and using some up temporarily reduces our supply for use on subsequent decisions (Gailliot et al., 2007). Given the fact that the average person makes a stunning 200–250 food-related decisions per day, many requiring willpower, anything we can do to lessen the load should be helpful (Wansink & Sobal, 2007). Consequently, engineering our environment to reduce the need to make choices and to use some of our limited supply of willpower would be helpful. This goal could be accomplished by scheduling group study sessions for earlier times in the day, ensuring that you no longer keep high-calorie snacks in your room, substituting healthy food items for high-calorie snacks, or using evening socialization time to engage in activities that do not provide much opportunity for snacking, such as sports.

Our next step is to agree on appropriate consequences for our behavior. Once again, it is essential that we design consequences that are meaningful to each individual. As we have argued in this chapter, positive reinforcement has many advantages over punishment. We might try placing the money we're saving on junk food in a designated jar to buy a special (nonfood) treat at the end of a successful week or allow ourselves an extra study break each night we meet our goals. If you are convinced that the only way you will change is through punishment, we could take an alternate approach. One of the most successful stop-smoking programs in the country punishes its clients by collecting money from them in advance, then making sizable donations to a political candidate the client loathes for each cigarette smoked.

As you implement your program, track your progress and make any modifications that seem necessary. In addition to the improvement of your target behavior, a very beneficial side effect of applying learning methods to your behavior is the knowledge that given the right tools, you can be in control of your behavior. ✪

Summary 8.3

Schedules of Reinforcement

Schedule	Features	In the lab	Everyday example
Fixed ratio © SCPhotos/Alamy	Reinforcement occurs after a set number of responses.	A rat presses 3 times for each food pellet.	A garment worker is paid for finishing 10 shirts.
Variable ratio © Tetra Images/Photoshot	Reinforcement occurs after a variable number of responses, which average a set number for a session.	A rat is fed on average after 3 responses, but the number of responses required for obtaining food varies between 1 and 15.	People play slot machines and win sometimes on the first play and other times after thousands of plays, on a schedule determined by the casino.
Fixed interval © Cengage Learning 2013	Each response begins an interval during which no reinforcement is available. The first response after the interval will be reinforced.	A rat's first press after each 1 min interval has timed out will be reinforced.	Students study more hours right before finals than during the beginning of the term (although unlike in the rat's case, this behavior does actually contribute to reinforcement).
Variable interval © holbox/Shutterstock	Each response begins an interval of varying length, with an average length for the session set by the experimenter.	A rat's first press after an interval will be reinforced. The interval will average 1 min over the session, but reinforcement could be obtained after intervals ranging between 10 sec and 3 min.	A fisherman trails his line behind the boat, and at various intervals of time, a fish will be caught.

What Is Observational Learning?

The ability to learn by watching others, known as observational learning, provides considerable advantages, especially in a social species like our own. Learning occurs without personally experiencing negative consequences. This ability to learn from observing others greatly expands our learning capacity, especially when we then generalize from these concrete examples (watching successful students) to produce effective rules (good time management is important to being a successful student). Observational learning can also have a dark side, as we will see in our later discussion of the pioneering work by Albert Bandura (1965) on the modeling of aggression by children.

Not only do we learn by observing others, but it appears that observational learning can override other influences on behavior, possibly due to our being such a social species. Parents learn, often the hard way, that children are much more likely to pattern their own behavior after what they observe their parents doing than what they hear their parents say.

Babies learned more Chinese when listening to a person face-to-face than while watching the same person speak on a television monitor.

A wide variety of behaviors, both positive and negative, appear to be influenced by observation, including aggression, achievement motivation, language development, phobias, cognitive development, moral judgment, and suicidal behavior. People benefit greatly from exposure to positive role models, especially those with whom they can identify. We worry about the relatively small number of women in university math and science faculties not only because of the possibility of discrimination but also because seeing women in these positions might inspire young girls to follow in their footsteps. On the other hand, the use of steroids by sports heroes might lead to role modeling of a different sort by young people.

It is easy to find examples of observational learning in our daily lives. New college students identify successful, more experienced students in their classes and copy their behavior. Stumped by your new computer

Observational learning can provide a quick and easy way to learn without having to go through individual trial and error.

software, not to mention the manual that came with it, you watch as a tech-savvy friend shows you how to make it work. Young athletes pore over films of superstars to perfect their technique. Popular cooking shows on television teach you to prepare a special meal. Cross-generational cycles of domestic violence persist as children continue the patterns of aggressive behavior they observe in their parents and grandparents. Our task in this section is to identify the circumstances in which this type of learning occurs and the variables that affect its outcomes.

Albert Bandura and Aggression

Albert Bandura's work on the observational learning of aggression provides one of the strongest arguments against exposing children to violent media (Bandura, 1965). Bandura was interested in **imitation**, which is defined as the copying of behavior that is unlikely to occur naturally and spontaneously (Thorpe, 1963).

In a series of classic studies of the imitation of aggression in children, Bandura observed children's interactions with a toy known as a Bobo doll. This is an inflatable toy clown with sand in the bottom, allowing it to rock back and forth when pushed. Bandura showed three groups of 4-year-olds a film in which one of his female students physically and verbally assaulted an unfortunate Bobo doll. The adult yelled, "Pow, right in the nose!" when punching the doll in the face, "Sockeroo, stay down!" when hitting the doll with a mallet, and "Bang!" when throwing a ball at the doll. The first group of children saw the adult being rewarded for aggression with candy and soda. A second group of children saw the adult being verbally reprimanded. The third group did not see any consequences for the adult's actions. Subsequently, when the children were allowed an opportunity to play with a Bobo doll, they displayed a significant amount of aggression. In all cases, boys were more likely to behave aggressively than girls. The group that witnessed the reprimand of the adult model showed slightly less aggression.

Bandura identified four necessary cognitive processes in the modeling of others' behavior: attention, retention, reproduction, and motivation.

imitation The copying of behavior that is unlikely to occur naturally and spontaneously.

After watching an adult model assault the Bobo doll, young children copied the adult's movements and verbalizations. Children who did not see an adult attack the doll did not show spontaneous aggressive behavior when given a chance to play with the doll.

© Albert Bandura/Stanford University

Models that get our *attention* are more likely to elicit imitation. A person must *retain* a memory of what the model did. We must be able to *reproduce* the behavior. Many of us enjoy watching elite athletes perform, but no matter how long and often we watch Maria Sharapova or Lebron James, few of us have the talent to duplicate their movements. If you happen to play tennis or basketball, however, you can learn to improve your game if you carefully observe these superstars. Finally, a person must have a *motivation* for imitating the behavior. Either past or anticipated reinforcement will encourage us to model another person's behavior. In *vicarious reinforcement*, witnessing somebody else getting reinforced for a behavior raises the likelihood that we will imitate the behavior. At the same time, witnessing the other person getting punished for the behavior should reduce the likelihood that you will copy it.

Imitation

Imitation is not limited to the copying of aggression. It occurs frequently in the animal world, which suggests that this behavior provides some adaptive advantages. When rats have observed another rat bar-pressing for food, it takes them less time to learn to bar-press themselves (Del Russo, 1971). Laboratory-raised monkeys quickly learn to fear snakes when exposed to a wild monkey who reacts to snakes with fear (Mineka & Cook, 1988). Imitation of gestures occurs in a number of species in addition to our own, including chimpanzees (Custance, Whiten, & Bard, 1995), dolphins (Harley, Xitco, Roitblat, & Herman, 1998), octopuses (Fiorito & Scotto, 1992), and parrots (Moore, 1992).

As we mentioned in our chapter on motivation and emotion, imitation of facial expressions might serve as a building block on the road to achieving empathy (Iacoboni & Dapretto, 2006; Iacoboni & Mazziotta, 2007). Individuals with autism do not participate in the back-and-forth imitation of gestures and facial expressions typically found in infants (Dapretto et al., 2006). Later in life, these individuals usually experience severe deficits in empathy and social skills (Williams, 2008).

Mirror Neurons

Imitation in monkeys and humans involves special neurons known as mirror neurons, which we discussed in our chapter on biological psychology. Mirror neurons in monkeys show similar patterns of activity when the individual performs an action or watches another individual perform the same action (Rizzolatti, Fadiga, Gallese, & Fogassi, 1996; Ruby & Decety, 2001). Identification of mirror neurons in humans has been complicated by ethical concerns about the methods used. In monkeys, mirror neurons were observed through surgically implanted electrodes, as we described in our *Connecting to Research* feature in the chapter on biological psychology. Obviously, this type of invasive procedure would be difficult to do in humans. However, recent recordings taken while patients were undergoing surgical treatment for seizures provided researchers with an opportunity to investigate the existence of mirror neurons in humans. This investigation led to the conclusion that mirror neurons do, in fact, exist in humans as well as in monkeys (Keysers & Gazzola, 2010).

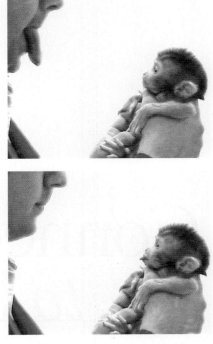

© Pier Francesco Ferrari, University of Parma, from PLoS Biology, Sept. 2006, Vol. 4, Issue 9

Imitation forms the basis of much observational learning. A remaining question is whether imitation involves mirror neurons that activate whether you perform a behavior or see another perform the same behavior.

What purposes might be served by mirror neurons? One suggestion is that mirror neurons would help us predict the actions of others, allowing us to understand intentions (Fogassi et al., 2005). Once again, the ability to predict future circumstances would contribute significantly to the survival of an organism. Mirror neurons might also form the basis of empathy. Individuals who appear to be high in empathy show stronger activation than other people in identified mirror systems in the human brain (Gazzola, Aziz-Zadeh, & Keysers, 2006; Jabbi, Swart, & Keysers, 2007).

Children use gestures, like pointing at a cookie jar to indicate "I want a cookie," long before they learn to use words to convey the same meaning. It is likely that preverbal hominins also used gestures to communicate. Mirror neurons might have played a role in the development of language, both for our species and for individual learners (Ramachandran, 2006). Consistent with this argument, mirror neurons in monkeys are located in a part of the brain that is quite similar to the human Broca's area of the frontal lobe (Petrides, Cadoret, & Mackey, 2005). As we discussed in our chapter on biological psychology, activation in Broca's area is correlated with the production of speech.

Because individuals with autism do not show typical imitative behaviors in childhood, a natural extension would be to look for possible correlates in the mirror neuron systems in autism. Some researchers have presented evidence that mirror neuron function is disturbed in individuals with autism, especially when they are engaged in emotional or social tasks (Perkins, Stokes, McGillivray, & Bittar, 2010). Others argue that a "broken mirror"

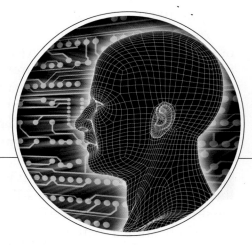

Connecting *to* Research

Why Do Children Over-Imitate?

We have seen that imitation occurs in many species and might have special advantages for human children. To quickly absorb the benefits of culture, children can watch adults use objects and tools and then replicate those actions. This tendency is so strong that children across many different cultural settings have been shown to "over-imitate." In other words, they copy movements performed by adults that are not required to carry out a task successfully (Nielsen & Tomaselli, 2010).

The Question: Why would children over-imitate adults? Do they trust adults so much that they copy everything adults do? Or are they over-imitating in order to build stronger relationships and be better liked by adults? This second explanation is consistent with other research suggesting that we like people who imitate us, discussed *previously in our chapter on consciousness (Lakin, Chartrand, & Arkin, 2008).*

METHODS

Thirty-six children between the ages of 4 and 5 years participated in the study. They observed two adults open a box to obtain a toy. One adult would open the box using only the movements that were completely necessary, while the other adult would

explanation for the social deficits observed in individuals with autism is overly simplistic and that further research is necessary before making strong conclusions about mirror neuron function in this population (Fan, Decety, Yang, Liu, & Cheng, 2010).

Cultural Transmission of Learning

An individual's learning may serve him or her well throughout a lifetime, but the invention of culture provides opportunities to pass the benefits of experience along for many generations. A society is a group of people living together. Culture, in contrast, consists of all the socially transmitted information used by the group of people, including ideas, concepts, and skills. Observational learning in particular provides a powerful tool for transmitting this information over time.

Richard Dawkins (1976) envisioned a way to break culture down into observable parts. He referred to the basic unit of cultural transmission as a meme. Memes, he said, are transmitted by observational learning from one person to another and can take the form of ideas, symbols, or practices. Melodies, religious beliefs, catch-phrases, and the technology for building arches are examples of memes. Dawkins viewed memes as the cultural equivalents of genes—they replicate from one person to the next, and they respond to selection pressure. Memes that provide an advantage, such as knowledge of the use of fire, are likely to continue. Those that do not confer much advantage, such as some fads, are likely to die out quickly. Still others, such as pagers, are abandoned when more effective replacements (cell phones) emerge.

> The beautiful thing about learning is that no one can take it away from you.
>
> —B. B. King

Among the most social of memes are the Internet memes, which are "inside jokes" passed along to others using technologies such as social networking sites and e-mail. Special websites that chronicle Internet memes allow viewers to provide updates of their favorite memes, which, of course, contributes to their popularity. In 2008, teachers grading student essays

open the box after performing some irrelevant actions, such as tapping the right side of the box three times or swiping the top of the lid. After the demonstration, one adult would leave the room, and the other adult would tell the child, "Now it's your turn."

RESULTS

All the children were able to open the box. If the adult who remained with the child was the one who opened the box without any unnecessary movements, the child was very unlikely to demonstrate the unnecessary movements. If the adult who remained was the one who had

performed the unnecessary movements, however, the child was very likely to over-imitate and reproduce the unnecessary movements, too.

CONCLUSIONS

The results of this study support the social affiliation explanation of over-imitation. Children only showed over-imitation when the adult remaining with them in the room was the one who had performed the unnecessary actions. The researchers suggest that imitation in humans is not just about learning new skills efficiently—imitation promotes shared experience with other people and builds rapport.

Over-imitation has been recently observed in chimpanzees (Price, Lambeth, Schapiro, & Whiten, 2009). Chimpanzees that watched videos of another chimpanzee assembling a tool out of two parts to reach a food reward were more likely than chimpanzees that did not see the video to assemble the tool themselves, even when the tool was unnecessary for obtaining food. We need more research to identify whether the same motives for over-imitation observed in children also apply to the chimpanzees. ⚙

from the Advanced Placement English literature exam were puzzled by insertions of the defiant phrase "This is Sparta!" (from the movie *300*) in many of the essays. In each case, the students had written the phrase, then carefully crossed it out with a single line (students are instructed that AP readers will ignore anything that is crossed out). The source of the prank was a 30,000-member-strong group on Facebook dedicated to inserting a bit of humor into the dreaded testing situation. As Dawkins would predict, the Sparta meme self-replicated. To urge the 1,100 weary teachers to finish their essays on the last day of readings, the AP Chief Reader pumped his fist and shouted "This is Sparta!"

Summary 8.4

Features Promoting Observational Learning and Imitation

Feature	Description	Example
Attention	We are more likely to model the behavior of people who get our attention.	Children wear the jerseys of the best players in the sport.
Memory	We must retain a memory of the behavior to be imitated.	A student re-creates from memory a math proof demonstrated earlier that day by a professor.
Reproduction	We must have the ability to reproduce the behavior.	An athlete works on her technique after watching films of an elite athlete in her sport.
Motivation	Past or anticipated reinforcement for the behavior will motivate us to perform it.	One student received extra credit for participating in an experiment, so his friends also signed up to participate.

Interpersonal Relationships
From the Learning Perspective

Knowledge of the way we learn can actually improve your social life and possibly even your love life. Operant conditioning can help you decrease unwanted behaviors and increase desired behaviors toward you by people with whom you interact. Your behavior influences the way others behave toward you. If you are regularly finding that you are treated poorly in relationships, understanding the learning perspective provides powerful tools for change.

In this chapter, we have recommended an emphasis on regularly noticing and rewarding desired behaviors. It is easy to fall into the trap of feeling entitled to good behavior from the people who are close to us, which can lead to these behaviors being taken for granted and ignored. Without positive reinforcement, these good behaviors might be extinguished. It takes very little time and energy to thank people for the nice things they do for us, and this simple courtesy can increase the frequency of positive interactions in the future.

> If you hold a cat by the tail, you learn things you cannot learn any other way.
>
> —Mark Twain

When the inevitable undesirable behaviors occur, many people turn to punishment. Skinner believed that part of the love affair we have with punishment is due to the reinforcing properties of punishment to the punisher. Skinner (1971) stated, "We 'instinctively' attack anyone whose behavior displeases us—perhaps not in physical assault, but with criticism, disapproval, blame, or ridicule" (p. 190). Punishing a partner for bad behavior might make you feel better, but at a significant cost. These behaviors are not exactly endearing, and frequent use of them is likely to end relationships.

If punishment is out, what then do we recommend you do when you experience negative behavior from a partner? If possible, try to ignore negative behaviors, putting them on extinction. Unfortunately, some people would rather have negative attention from you than no attention at all and will prefer punishment from you to being ignored. This is particularly likely to be the case if you have forgotten to reinforce positive behaviors. If you combine positive reinforcement of good behavior and extinction of negative behavior, you should notice quite an improvement. Obviously, some behaviors like aggression cannot be ignored and require either a complete end to the relationship or professional counseling.

Thoughtfully observing the way you treat other people and their reactions to your behavior, using the learning principles described in this chapter, should provide you with the understanding you need to improve your relationships.

Chapter 8
Reflections

© Argosy Publishing, Inc.

This chapter explored the mind's ability to adapt to its environment as a result of its experience with that environment. This ability to adapt spans the range of animal life from the simple sea slug we examined in the introduction to this chapter to the remarkable ability of the human mind to tackle the most complex academic subject matter. In some cases, we use the same processes to learn as the sea slug (you hopefully by now recognize that the learning described at the beginning of the chapter was an example of classical conditioning). Also like the sea slug, our ability to learn varies with our social circumstances. We learn differently in isolation than we do in groups, or differently when interacting with another person face-to-face than when watching that person on a television screen. In other instances, our learning is quite different from that of the sea slug. We often use learning processes like imitation that are not found in many other animals.

The different types of adaptation described in this chapter began with relatively unconscious, nonassociative processes such as habituation, sensitization, and classical conditioning and proceeded to the more conscious control of behavior through operant conditioning and the use of observation to adapt. In each case, these adaptations have served us well by promoting our chances for survival. Because learning is all about changes in behavior, understanding these processes provides us with powerful tools for further adapting our behavior to meet our needs. ‹

Some types of learning, such as nonassociative learning and classical conditioning, characterize most living things, from the simple sea slug to human beings. Other types of learning, such as operant conditioning and observational learning, are restricted to species with more complex nervous systems.

© Daniel Gottshall/Visuals Unlimited

KEY TERMS The Language of Psychological Science

Be sure you can define these terms and use them correctly.

acquisition, p. 355
associative learning, p. 351
classical conditioning, p. 352
conditioned reinforcer, p. 372
conditioned response (CR), p. 355
conditioned stimulus (CS), p. 355
discrimination, p. 358
extinction, p. 357
fixed interval (FI) schedule, p. 377
fixed ratio (FR) schedule, p. 375
generalization, p. 358
habituation, p. 352
higher order conditioning, p. 359
imitation, p. 388

inhibition, p. 358
instinct, p. 349
latent inhibition, p. 359
latent learning, p. 381
learning, p. 350
negative punishment, p. 373
negative reinforcement, p. 372
nonassociative learning, p. 352
observational learning, p. 352
operant conditioning, p. 352
partial reinforcement effect in
    extinction, p. 378
partial reinforcement, p. 375
positive punishment, p. 373

punishment, p. 373
reflex, p. 349
sensitization, p. 352
shaping/method of successive
    approximations, p. 379
spontaneous recovery, p. 357
systematic desensitization, p. 364
token economy, p. 384
unconditioned response (UCR),
    p. 355
unconditioned stimulus (UCS), p. 355
variable interval (VI) schedule, p. 377
variable ratio (VR) schedule, p. 376

MEDIA RESOURCES

Log in to CengageBrain to access the resources your instructor requires. For this book, you can access:

Psychology **CourseMate** brings course concepts to life with interactive learning, study, and exam preparation tools that support the printed textbook. A textbook-specific website, Psychology **CourseMate** includes an integrated interactive eBook and other interactive learning tools including quizzes, flashcards, videos, and more.

WebTUTOR More than just an interactive study guide, **WebTutor** is an anytime, anywhere customized learning solution with an eBook, keeping you connected to your textbook, instructor, and classmates.

aplia If your professor has assigned **Aplia** homework:
1. Sign in to your account.
2. Complete the corresponding homework exercises as required by your professor.
3. When finished, click "Grade It Now" to see which areas you have mastered, which areas need more work, and detailed explanations of every answer.

The hippocampus, a seahorse-shaped region of the brain, plays an important role in memory. In the case of Henry Molaison, discussed in this chapter, surgical removal of a large part of the hippocampus reduced his seizures, but left him with serious memory deficits.

The Knowing Mind

Memory

Learning Objectives

1 Describe the importance of attention to memory.

2 Define encoding, storage, and retrieval.

3 Differentiate between sensory memory, working memory, and long-term memory.

4 Describe the subtypes of long-term memory, including procedural, declarative, episodic, and semantic memories.

5 Explain the models describing the organization of long-term memories.

6 Summarize the variables influencing retrieval from short- and long-term memory.

7 Describe forgetting, decay, interference, motivated forgetting, and confabulation.

8 Summarize the biological correlates of memory.

In our chapter on research methods, we introduced you to one of the most famous case studies in psychology—the case of Henry Molaison (1926–2008), known in the scientific literature as "the amnesic patient H.M." To reduce Molaison's severe seizures, possibly resulting from a minor head injury caused by a childhood accident, his neurosurgeons carried out an experimental procedure that would be considered radical today but was even more so in 1953. They removed the majority of Molaison's hippocampus in both hemispheres, along with some of the surrounding neural tissue. As a result, Molaison's memory functions declined dramatically, although his personality and intellect remained intact.

What made Molaison and his famous brain so important to our understanding of memory? Psychologists have learned a great deal from people with brain damage, from the unfortunate Phineas Gage to contemporary patients with Alzheimer's disease or damage from strokes. In most of these cases, however, correlating observed damage with observations of behavior is difficult.

Photograph of Henry Molaison. Copyright © Suzanne Corkin, used by permission of the Wylie Agency LLC.

Accidents, disease, and stroke are messy and do not leave behind neat areas of damage on both sides of the brain. Molaison's case, in contrast, featured the precision that would characterize a planned experiment, which of course it was not. The areas of damage were exact and symmetrical on both sides of the brain, which has now been confirmed by brain imaging and the study of Molaison's dissected brain.

Zooming in to view the results of this type of surgery, we can ask what scientists learned from their study of Molaison. Brenda Milner, followed by her student Suzanne Corkin, studied Molaison for more than four decades. His case produced a string of surprises, which we discuss in more detail later in this chapter. Certain structures in the brain are important for memory, but more so for some types of memories than for others. Some tasks we can perform automatically; that is, we can remember how to do something without remembering that we know how to do it. This ability supports our observations of a range of consciousness, which we discussed in our chapter on consciousness. As scientists at MIT, the Massachusetts General Hospital, and the University of California, San Diego, continue to study Molaison's brain, it is likely that further surprises are in store.

The careful slicing of Molaison's preserved brain took over 53 straight hours and was broadcast live on the Internet.

Zooming out to Molaison the individual, we can see that his story is more extensive than the study of his brain. According to people who knew him, he was a really nice man who loved animals, watching trains, and doing crossword puzzles. His favorite television show was the 1970s hit *All in the Family,* which ironically featured a main character, Archie Bunker, who was unable to adapt to the changing world around him. In spite of Molaison's being the subject of decades of study, many questions about him remain. Why did he seem less affected by pain than other people? Why could he eat two complete dinners in a row, as long as they were presented a few minutes apart, without feeling too full? Why could he accurately rate the intensity of an odor but be unable to tell the difference between a rose and something rotten? Although his ability to learn new facts following his surgery was remarkably impaired, why did he know scattered facts from the following decade—that a president was assassinated in Dallas or that "Bob Dylan" was the correct way to complete "Bob Dy—"? Which of these observations shows the effects of his surgery? Of his accident? Of his seizures?

Zooming out still farther, we ask ourselves how our social interactions would be affected by being unable to remember new people we have met. Molaison remembered people, like his surgeon, whom he had met prior to his surgery, but never learned to recognize Brenda Milner, Suzanne Corkin, or other scientists who met him later, even though he saw them regularly for decades. He retained a genuine concern for other people and took great pride in the fact that his case was helping science, but it is hard to imagine that his life was not somewhat lonely and socially isolated. During a 1969 interview, Molaison told a scientist, "Right now, I'm wondering, have I done or said something amiss? You see, at this moment, everything looks clear to me, but what happened just before? That's what worries me. It's like waking from a dream" (Milner, Corkin, & Teuber, 1968, p. 217).

We often think of memory as something we need to succeed on exams, but in this chapter, you will be learning that memory means much, much more to our human experience. It is our memories that allow us to form new connections with people, places, and things; to experience a new acquaintance, over time, becoming an old friend; to experience the continuity of time rather than living one's life, again and again, as a single, isolated moment. ⊙

What Are the Advantages of Memory?

Memory is defined as the ability to retain knowledge. The problems encountered by Henry Molaison provide us with a glimpse of how our lives would be altered without certain memory abilities, but can we make more general conclusions about how memory helps animals adapt and survive?

Memory and the Continuum of Information Processing

Memory does not exist in isolation. Instead, cognitive psychologists see memory as part of a continuum of **information processing** that begins with attention, sensation, perception, and learning, which we explored in previous chapters, and progresses to the use of stored information in thinking, problem solving, language, and intelligent behavior, which we discuss in our next chapter (see ● Figure 9.1). Information flows in both directions along this continuum, leading to the bottom-up and top-down processing we observed in our chapter on sensation and perception. Memories of the characteristics of Dalmatian dogs helped you identify the photograph of one in our chapter on sensation and perception and should also help you interact with one appropriately (thinking and problem solving).

Memory can be divided into three steps: encoding, storage, and retrieval. In today's digital environment, it is common for psychologists to illustrate these processes by comparing the way the brain and computers process information. In both the brain and the computer, encoding of incoming information must occur before the information can be processed further. **Encoding** refers to the process of acquiring information and transferring it into memory. The computer acquires data entered as strokes on a keyboard, touches on a screen, recorded sounds, or mouse clicks, and translates this information into the zeros and ones that the computer can process and store. In our chapter on sensation and perception, we described how the sensory systems translate or transduce electromagnetic energy, sound waves, pressure,

Problem solving

Thinking

MEMORY

Learning

Perception

Sensation

Attention

FIGURE 9.1

The Information Processing Continuum. Memory is located on a continuum of information processing that flows both from the bottom up and from the top down. We use our memories of Dalmatian dogs to recognize one in an ambiguous photograph and interact with a new one you happen to meet. Illustration: © Cengage Learning 2013; photos, top to bottom: from Richard L. Gregory, "The Medawar Lecture 2001 Knowledge for vision: vision for knowledge," *Phil. Trans. R. Soc. B* 2005 360, 1231–1251, © The Royal Society; © AnetaPics/ Shutterstock; © Steve Smith/Taxi/Getty Images

Take a minute and write down the five most important things you need to remember today. How would your life be affected if you couldn't remember these things?

memory The ability to retain knowledge.
information processing A continuum including attention, sensation, perception, learning, memory, and cognition.
encoding The transformation of information from one form to another.

and chemical stimulation into action potentials that can be processed by the nervous system.

Both computer and brain must store incoming data. In both systems, **storage**, or the retention of information, can vary in time from very brief traces to essentially permanent storage (if you know where to look). As we will see later in this chapter, storage of memories in the brain can last anywhere from fractions of a second (sensory memory) to several seconds (short-term and working memory) to indefinitely (long-term memory). However, storage in a computer and storage in the mind differ in one very important respect. Computers store encoded information in very reliable and unvarying ways, like putting socks in a drawer or papers in a file. What you retrieve is essentially identical to what was stored. In contrast, human memory does not generate such exact records. Instead, bits of information are stored that are later reconstructed into usable memories. Although this process typically results in a useful memory, errors and distortions can occur. We will explore these variations in later sections of this chapter.

The culmination of the memory process for both brain and computer is the **retrieval** of stored information. As you have no doubt experienced in using both your computer and brain, storing information is no guarantee that you can find the information again when you need it. Later in this chapter, we will discuss the many ways that memory retrieval can fail. Two of the most common causes of retrieval failure are interference and stress. For example, we seem to know all the

Information processing for both brain and computer begins with encoding, in which data are acquired and transferred to memory. Just as computers can encode information from many sources, including touch, keystrokes, mouse, and voice, the brain encodes information from different sensory channels, including vision, hearing, touch, taste, and smell.

Both brains and computers feature the ability to store memories, with one critical difference. The computer stores exact copies of data, but the brain does not. Instead, the brain stores bits of data that are reconstructed later for use. This photo shows the high-security computer memory storage at the Swedish Bahnhof, a facility located 100 feet underground in a concrete bunker. The facility manages servers for many secretive organizations, including WikiLeaks.

storage The retention of information.
retrieval The recovery of stored information.

answers when watching *Who Wants to Be a Millionaire* in the safety of our own homes, but when actually put on the spot, we might be lucky to remember our own names. Fortunately, understanding the strengths and weaknesses of the brain's memory functions may be one of the more practical topics for students that we cover in psychology. Once you understand what can go wrong, you will have an easier time ensuring that your study habits will maximize your performance in school.

Memory Provides an Adaptive Advantage

Evolutionary psychologists view memory as "a component of a neural machine designed to use information acquired in the past to coordinate an organism's behavior in the present" (Klein, Cosmides, & Tooby, 2002, p. 308). The evolution of memory allowed animals to use information from the past to respond quickly to immediate challenges, a monumental advance in the ability to survive. Instead of reacting to each predator or source of food as an entirely new experience, an animal with the ability to remember past encounters with similar situations would save precious reaction time.

Encoding and storing memories do not guarantee that they can be retrieved when you need them. Stress can make retrieving even the simplest of memories surprisingly difficult.

As we discussed in our chapter on nature and nurture intertwined, useful adaptations often come with a price, like the unwieldy antlers of the male deer that require energy to build yet help the deer fight successfully for mates. The development of a memory system is no exception to this rule. Forming memories requires energy. For memory systems to flourish within the animal kingdom, the survival advantages needed to outweigh the energy costs. Given the 81 years or so of human life expectancy, it would be difficult to demonstrate the energy costs of memory in people, but we can observe the costs in a simpler organism, the fruit fly (*Drosophila*), which has a life expectancy of only 10 to 18 days. Fruit flies are capable of learning classically conditioned associations between odors and electric shock. After experiencing pairings of odor and shock, the flies will fly away from the odor 24 hours later (Mery & Kawecki, 2005). However, to form memories about odor and shock, the flies must use more energy than they use for activities that do not require memory. When deprived of food and water, the flies that remembered how to avoid shock died about 4 hours faster than flies that did not form memories. The fact that nearly all animals have the capability of forming memories in spite of the high energy costs is a testament to memory's benefits to survival.

Even though processing memory requires energy, the benefits to survival far outweigh the costs. Without memory, this squirrel would be unable to retrieve the acorns stored weeks ago.

How Are Memories Processed?

Psychologists have proposed a number of models to try to describe how memory works. One of the most influential models of memory was proposed by Atkinson and Shiffrin (1968, 1971). According to this classic model, information flows through a series of separate stages of memory (see ● Figure 9.2). The idea of memory stages paralleled the development of computers, where distinctions between an active window on the desktop and the information saved on a hard drive or other media provided models for memory storage areas that differ in capacity and duration. The

FIGURE 9.2

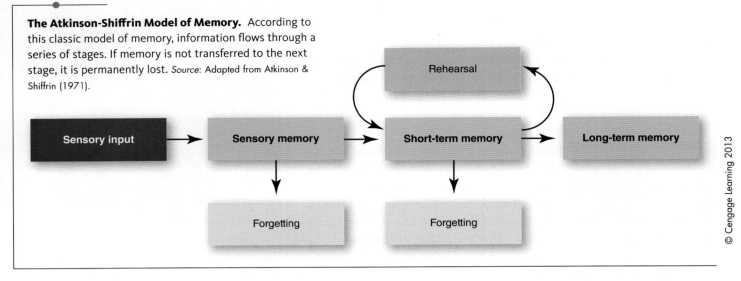

The Atkinson-Shiffrin Model of Memory. According to this classic model of memory, information flows through a series of stages. If memory is not transferred to the next stage, it is permanently lost. *Source:* Adapted from Atkinson & Shiffrin (1971).

Rehearsal

Sensory input → Sensory memory → Short-term memory → Long-term memory

Forgetting

Forgetting

© Cengage Learning 2013

model also included control processes, a person's active interventions that influence memory. For example, you might use certain strategies, like repeating a bit of information, that help you remember it later. We will consider these stages and control processes in detail in this section.

Contemporary cognitive psychologists have continued to modify this original model, while retaining the basic ideas that memories can be stored for very different periods of time and that control processes influence the system.

To illustrate the flow of information in this model, let's consider what happens when you use your memory to complete a specific task—remembering a phone number provided to you by a new acquaintance.

Sensory Memory While settling into your seat before class, you are having a nice conversation with one of your classmates about getting together to study for an upcoming exam. Your classmate gives you her cell phone number so you can arrange a good time to meet. This incoming information, the auditory signals of your classmate's voice in this case, is processed in a first stage, the **sensory memory**. This stage holds enormous amounts of sensory data, possibly all information that impacts the sensory receptors. However, the data remain for very brief periods of time, usually a second or less, or as long as the neural activity produced by a sensation continues. The information held in sensory memory has been compared to a rapidly fading "echo" of the real input. You can demonstrate the duration and "fade" of sensory memory information by rapidly flapping your hand back and forth in front of your eyes. When you do this, you can "see" where your fingers were at a previous point in time.

Sensory input is translated, or transduced, into several types of code or representation. A representation of a memory refers to a mental model of a bit of information that exists even when the information is no longer available. Visual codes are used for the temporary storage of information about visual images (Baddeley, Eysenck, & Anderson, 2009). Haptic codes are used to process touch and other body senses. Acoustic codes represent

sensory memory The first stage of the Atkinson-Shiffrin model that holds large amounts of incoming data for very brief amounts of time.

sound and words. Psychologists believe that input from different sensory systems remains separate in sensory memory, and although these different sensory streams are processed fairly similarly, there are some differences. Acoustic codes, also known as echoic memories, last somewhat longer than visual codes, also known as iconic memories, possibly to meet our needs to hear entire words and phrases before we can begin to understand spoken language.

George Sperling demonstrated the duration of iconic memories by testing recall for briefly presented matrices of 12 to 16 letters. Participants were usually able to identify four or five. However, the process of verbally instructing participants to do this task takes time, during which the sensory memory for the matrix fades rapidly. If different tones were used to signal a row of the matrix to be recalled instead of verbally asking for a response, participants demonstrated recall for as many as 12 of the original 16 items (Averbach & Sperling, 1961; Sperling, 1960). If the tone was sounded less than a quarter of a second after presentation of the matrix, participants could usually recall all four letters in a row. After a quarter of a second delay or more, recall fell to one letter (see ● Figure 9.3).

Why do we have a sensory memory? Only a very small subset of this incoming data will be processed by the next stage. It is likely that we need to collect incoming data until it makes enough sense to process further. The first number in your classmate's phone number might be very simple (two), but it still contains two speech sounds (the "t" and "oo") that must be combined to make sense.

Our ability to "see" what we have written with a sparkler results from the remaining traces in our sensory memories. The actual light is long gone.

Short-Term Memory A tiny amount of information in the sensory memory will move to the next stage, **short-term memory (STM)**, for further processing. When you focus on your new friend's phone number, the information will move from sensory memory to short-term memory. Consider all the other information that might be processed by your sensory memory

short-term memory (STM) The second stage of the Atkinson-Shiffrin model that holds a small amount of information for a limited time.

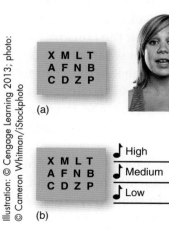

(a)

(b)

X M L T
A F N B
C D Z P

X F
D Z
C

X M L T
A F N B
C D Z P

♩ High
♩ Medium
♩ Low

P
D Z
C

Illustration: © Cengage Learning 2013; photo: © Cameron Whitman/iStockphoto

FIGURE 9.3

Sperling's Demonstration of the Duration of Sensory Memory. George Sperling briefly presented a matrix of letters to participants. When asked to recall the whole matrix (a), most participants could remember about four or five letters. However, when tones instead of verbal commands were used to signal which row to remember (b), participants were able to recall whole rows at a time, which implies they could remember more than four or five items. Sperling concluded that they could "see" the entire matrix in sensory memory for a very brief time, which allowed them to respond correctly. *Source:* Adapted from Sperling (1960).

Because our short-term memory holds a limited amount of information for a short time, we often rely on creative solutions, like this To-Do tattoo, to maintain the information we need.

at the same time. Perhaps you are aware that the professor's PowerPoint has just appeared on the screen or that the heater in the classroom just cycled on or that your stomach growled because you didn't have time for breakfast. None of these bits of information will be processed in short-term memory unless you pay attention to them. If you are distracted by one of these, it is likely that you will need to ask your friend to repeat her number.

Like sensory memory, short-term memories feature different types of representations. Acoustic codes, representing sounds, and visual codes, representing images, occur in short-term memory along with semantic codes, which represent the meaning of words.

We can demonstrate the existence of separate types of codes by examining the errors people make when retrieving information from memory. Many errors are based on sound (acoustic codes) rather than on other sensory features (Conrad, 1964). For example, if an experimenter shows a participant a card with the letters *B R X T* and asks the participant to recall the last letter, errors are most likely to involve letters that sound like "tee" when pronounced, such as *C, D,* or *P.* Note that none of these letters looks anything alike. These error analyses suggest that part of the encoding process involves the immediate translation of some sensory experiences into the sounds of language. However, visual codes in short-term memory are easily demonstrated by asking participants to recall features of maps (Kosslyn, 1980). Other experiments demonstrate the influence of word meanings in encoding. For example, when participants were presented with lists of words with similar meanings (such as *big, huge, large, wide, tall*) or lists without this type of similar meanings (*dog, light, peace, apple, shirt*), their memory for the similar lists was best (Baddeley, 1966).

Short-term memory, like the sensory memory that precedes it, appears to have remarkable limitations in duration. Without additional processing, information in short-term memory usually lasts 30 seconds at most (Ellis & Hunt, 1983). In a classic experiment, participants were shown stimuli consisting of three consonants, such as *RBP* (Peterson & Peterson, 1959). After seeing one of these triplets, participants counted backward by threes for periods of zero to 18 seconds to prevent their processing the consonant triplet further. As shown in ●Figure 9.4, accuracy dropped rapidly. It is very likely that the Petersons' task actually overestimates the length of time material may be stored in short-term memory. The Petersons' participants were aware in advance that they would be tested on the items, and in spite of the distraction of counting backward, they may have been able to engage in deliberate efforts to retain the triplets in memory.

You are probably thinking right now that you know exactly what to do to prevent this loss of information. If you repeat the information over and over, a process known as **rehearsal**, information stays in short-term memory indefinitely as long as you are not asked to think about anything else. During rehearsal, data are easily displaced by new, incoming bits of data.

rehearsal Repetition of information.

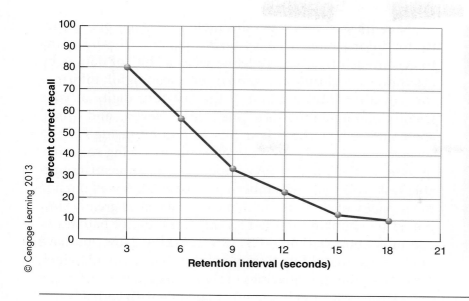

FIGURE 9.4

The Duration of Short-Term Memory. In a classic study by Peterson and Peterson (1959), participants were given triplets of letters, like XPJ or BTP, to recall. Their ability to remember the letters decreased as the time between presentation and recall increased. These results led the Petersons to propose that short-term memory might last up to 18 seconds, but more contemporary scientists using different methods think that it lasts as little as 2 seconds.

While you are getting ready to program your classmate's number into your phone, you can rehearse the number in your short-term memory. However, if your attention is diverted from rehearsing the number when the professor calls on you, the phone number will be gone. The incoming information of the professor's question seems to push the previous data out of the system. If rehearsing the information has been insufficient for moving it into the next stage, long-term memory, the data will be lost.

In addition to limitations of duration, short-term memory is characterized by severe limitations in capacity. George Miller argued that we can process somewhere between five and nine items or "bits" (digits, letters, words, etc.) in short-term memory simultaneously, or in his words, "the magic number 7 plus or minus 2" (Miller, 1956). More recently, other psychologists have set the limit at about four items (Cowan, 2000). Obviously, memory capacities do vary from individual to individual, and memory tasks appear prominently in standardized tests of intelligence, discussed in a later chapter. People who enjoy larger than average short-term memory capacity excel at a number of cognitive tasks, including reading (Baddeley, Logie, Nimmo-Smith, & Brereton, 1985).

> I wish I could take credit for it [a good memory] but it's just my genes, I think.
> —Brenda Milner

You might be wondering how short-term memory could be useful, given these limitations. However, it is exactly these limitations that make short-term memory an ideal solution for the tasks we ask it to complete. Most tasks for which we use short-term memory require us to search its contents to find the right information. If short-term memory were capable of holding dozens of pieces of information instead of nine or fewer, this search process would be lengthy and difficult. The brief duration of short-term memories ensures that room will be freed up regularly for incoming information. It is also convenient to have a mechanism that allows you to use information and then discard it. You may not wish to devote precious room in your memory banks to the telephone number of a plumber you need only once or twice. Short-term memory allows us to use information without overburdening our storage capacities.

© Andre Jenny/Alamy

Chase and Simon (1973) presented images of chess pieces on chessboards for only 5 seconds to chess masters and people who didn't play chess. When the images were from real games, the chess masters recalled the placement of the pieces much better than the nonplayers, because they were able to use their knowledge of chess to chunk the images of the pieces' locations in short-term memory. When the pieces were placed randomly on the boards, however, the chess masters were unable to use chunking and performed no better than the nonplayers.

Nonetheless, it is often desirable to expand our capacity for information in short-term memory. The best way to accomplish this is to redefine what a "bit" of data is by grouping, or **chunking,** similar or meaningful information together (Miller, 1956). If the last four digits of your friend's phone number are "one," "five," "seven," and "nine," she could reduce these four bits to two by saying "fifteen seventy-nine." Trying to remember the following sequence of letters—FBIIRSCIAEPA—appears to be an insurmountable task. After all, remembering 12 letters lies well outside the capacity of short-term memory. The task is greatly simplified by chunking the letters into meaningful batches of common abbreviations—FBI IRS CIA EPA. Now you have only 4 meaningful bits to remember rather than 12, which is safely within the capacities of short-term memory. Failure to use chunking as a strategy occurs frequently in people with verbal learning disabilities (Koeda, Seki, Uchiyama, & Sadato, 2011). In the absence of chunking, each item to be remembered is processed as a single, unrelated bit of information, which rapidly overwhelms the capacity of short-term memory.

Working Memory The classic description of short-term memory viewed this stage as a place to store information for immediate use. As investigations into memory advanced, researchers proposed an adaptation of this model called **working memory,** shown in ● Figure 9.5 (Baddeley & Hitch, 1974). Short-term memory and working memory differed in two ways. First, short-term memory involves the passive storage of information, while working memory involves an active manipulation of information. Second,

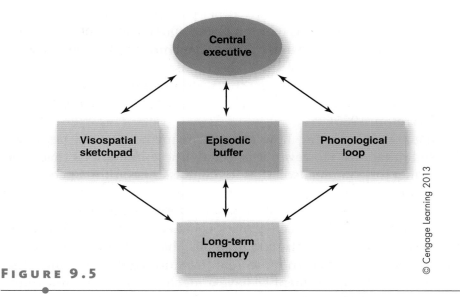
© Cengage Learning 2013

FIGURE 9.5

chunking The process of grouping similar or meaningful information together.

working memory An extension of the concept of short-term memory that includes the active manipulation of multiple types of information simultaneously.

Working Memory. Baddeley's model of working memory differs from short-term memory in two important ways: (1) information in working memory can be actively manipulated, whereas short-term memory passively stores memory, and (2) working memory can manage multiple types of information simultaneously, whereas short-term memory cannot.

short-term memory was viewed as managing a single process at a time, whereas working memory was more complex, allowing multiple processes to occur simultaneously.

To illustrate the difference between a passive and active memory system, we might consider the following exchange between you and your new friend:

You: "So we can meet to study on Tuesday and Thursday night next week?"

Your friend: "No, Tuesday doesn't work for me. Can we meet on Wednesday instead?"

Passively storing the two sentences that you heard your friend say without actively thinking about them together would not allow you to process their meaning accurately. You need to combine "Tuesday doesn't work" with "meet on Wednesday instead" to understand the meaning of this conversation. Passively storing "meet on Wednesday instead" would not help you understand whether Wednesday was a substitution for Tuesday or Thursday or possibly both.

The idea that working memory could manage more than one process at a time resulted from observations that participants could manage two short-term memory tasks at the same time (Baddeley & Hitch, 1974). For example, participants could read a list of numbers followed by reading a paragraph. This task should quickly overwhelm the limited capacity of short-term memory, as reading the paragraph should displace the earlier list of numbers. However, this outcome was not what the researchers observed. Participants had no difficulty remembering the numbers, suggesting that the numbers were stored separately from the words in the paragraph.

After further exploration of the types of information that could be maintained separately in short-term memory, four components were proposed (Baddeley et al., 2009): a phonological loop, a visuospatial sketch pad, a central executive, and an episodic buffer.

The phonological loop is the working memory component responsible for verbal and auditory information. As you repeat your friend's phone number (maintenance rehearsal) while reaching for your phone, you are using your phonological loop. The visuospatial sketch pad holds visual and spatial information. When you describe the route from your friend's dorm to your favorite coffee shop, where you plan to hold your study session, you use your visuospatial sketch pad to help you describe the way. The central executive manages the work of the other components by directing attention to particular tasks (Baddeley, 1996). Divided attention, which we discussed in our chapter on sensation and perception, requires the skills of the central executive. While discussing the route to the coffee shop with your friend (phonological loop), you visualize the route (visuospatial sketch pad), and your central executive parcels out just the right amount of attention to allow you to do both tasks well.

The episodic buffer provides a mechanism for combining information stored in long-term memory, which we discuss in the next section, with

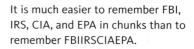

It is much easier to remember FBI, IRS, CIA, and EPA in chunks than to remember FBIIRSCIAEPA.

the active processing taking place in working memory. This component helps explain why chunking the string of letters earlier (FBI IRS CIA EPA) is easier than remembering the letters as individual bits of information—FBIIRSCIAEPA. Without information from long-term memory about what FBI and the other abbreviations mean, making these chunks would not provide any advantage.

Scientists have made progress in their search for brain activity that correlates with working memory. Parts of the prefrontal cortex, along with the anterior cingulate cortex (ACC), appear to be responsible for the functions of the central executive (Kaneda & Osaka, 2008). Activity in the ACC might explain some individual differences in working memory abilities. People with large working memory capacities show more ACC activation during memory tasks than people with smaller working memory capacities (Osaka et al., 2003).

© Doug Goodman/Photo Researchers, Inc.

Observations of patients with brain damage also support a role for the prefrontal cortex as the central executive (Barceló & Knight, 2002). Patients with prefrontal damage can learn to sort playing cards according to a rule, such as "put all the cards having the same color (red or black) together." However, when they are asked to switch to a new rule, such as "sort the cards by number (aces together, twos together, and so on)," they experience a great deal of difficulty and continue to sort according to the original rule instead of switching their attention to the new one.

Maturation of the prefrontal lobes in human infants is correlated with their development of object permanence, a task that requires working memory. Prior to the age of 8 months or so, infants will stop looking for an object when it is hidden from view, suggesting that they are unable to retain memory of the object. A few weeks later, the infant will actively search for the object.

Further support for the importance of the prefrontal cortex in working memory comes from observations of the development of memory in infants. The appearance of object permanence, which we discuss further in our chapter on development, coincides with increased maturity of the frontal lobes in human infants (Diamond & Goldman-Rakic, 1989). Prior to the age of 8 months or so, human infants will not search for a toy that is hidden from them while they watch. This behavior is definitely a case of "out of sight, out of mind." After the age of 8 months, however, human infants will immediately search for the hidden toy, indicating that they have formed a mental representation of the object in memory. Monkeys with prefrontal lesions perform like the younger human infants and do not show a sense of object permanence (Diamond & Goldman-Rakic, 1989).

Long-Term Memory

The final stage of memory processing is **long-term memory (LTM)**. Unlike sensory, short-term, and working memory, long-term memory seems to have few, if any, limitations in either capacity or duration. We do not appear to run out of room in long-term memory for new data, and information can last a lifetime. The oldest person alive can still recall significant childhood memories and learn new things. Although old memories may become

long-term memory (LTM) The final stage of the Atkinson-Shiffrin model that is the location of permanent memories.

more difficult to retrieve, this process is much different from losing them altogether simply because of the passage of time.

Moving Information Into Long-Term Memory In most cases, information moves from short-term or working memory to long-term memory through rehearsal. You might find that after you see your new friend's number several times as you text her, you have somehow memorized it without trying to do so. Rehearsal can be divided into maintenance rehearsal, which means simple repetition of the material, and elaborative rehearsal, which involves linking the new material to things you already know.

Of the two types of rehearsal, elaborative rehearsal is a more effective way to move information into more permanent storage. The benefits of elaborative rehearsal can be explained using a **levels of processing** theory (Craik & Lockhart, 1972). When we look at written words we want to remember, we can attend to many "levels" of detail: the visual appearance of the word (font, all caps, number of letters, etc.), the sound of the word, the meaning of the word, or the personal relevance of the word. These characteristics may be placed along a continuum of depth of processing from shallow to deep, with the encoding of the appearance of a word requiring less processing and effort than the encoding of the sound of a word, which in turn requires less processing and effort than the encoding of the meaning or personal relevance of a word, and so on. According to the levels of processing theory, words encoded according to meaning would be easier to remember than words encoded according to their visual appearance, because encoding meaningfulness produces a deeper level of attention and processing (Craik & Tulving, 1975).

In one study designed to test the levels of processing theory, participants recalled more words when their instructions elicited the encoding of word meanings than when they were instructed to determine more surface features of each word, such as whether it appeared in capital letters

The accumulated knowledge of a long life, like this Australian aborigine tribal elder's familiarity with his harsh surroundings, probably meant the difference between life and death for many of our ancestors. There is no evidence that very old people are unable to add new information to their long-term memories or necessarily lose information they have known a very long time.

Repeated exposure to information does not guarantee good memory. We use many familiar objects on a daily basis, like the $20 bill below, yet few of us can accurately describe their features.

levels of processing The depth (shallow to deep) of processing applied to information that predicts its ease of retrieval.

Our ATM machines usually deliver our cash in $20 bills, but handling these on a regular basis does not mean that we remember exactly what they look like. Which president is pictured on the bill? Whose signature as Secretary of the Treasury appears on the bill? Are the fonts used for all the 20s the same or different? Most people can't answer these questions from memory.

FIGURE 9.6

Levels of Processing Theory. Craik and Tulving (1975) tested the levels of processing theory by investigating their participants' recognition of words they had seen only briefly (about one fifth of a second) following one of three types of questions. The three types of questions focused the participants' attention on aspects of the word they were about to see. The questions pointed to very surface features (Is the word in capital letters or not?), acoustic features (Does the word rhyme with another word or not?), or semantic features (Does the word make sense in this sentence or not?). Theoretically, deciding that a word is in capital letters or not takes less processing than deciding whether it rhymes with another word, which in turn takes less processing than thinking about its meaning to answer the sentence question. The results supported the levels of processing theory. Recognition of words preceded by a semantic question was better than for words preceded by a rhyme question, which were recognized better than words preceded by a font question. *Source: Adapted from Craik and Tulving (1975).*

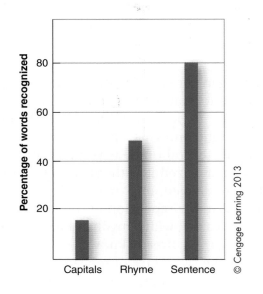

(see ● Figure 9.6; Craik & Tulving, 1975). In another study, deeper levels of processing were accompanied by more subvocal speech (reminiscent of "talking to yourself"), indicated by measurements of tiny activities in the muscles of speech (Cacioppo & Petty, 1981). However, the levels of processing theory is not very specific about the meaning of "deep" or "shallow" processing. How would we apply this approach to evaluate participants' recall for music, touch, or visual images? Further work on this theory needs to identify exactly what determines "depth" of processing during encoding.

Differences Between Working and Long-Term Memory In addition to not sharing limitations of duration and capacity with working memory, long-term memory appears to be unique in other ways. Given the enormous amount of data stored in long-term memory, we cannot retrieve information by using the item-by-item search strategies that we use in working memory. Instead, we have a system of associations or cues that we use to locate data, like your computer uses folders to organize separate files. We will discuss the organization of long-term memory in more detail in later sections of this chapter.

Differences between working and long-term memories can be seen in classic experiments demonstrating the serial position effect. This phenomenon can be observed when participants are asked to learn a list of words and recall them in any order they choose. As shown in ● Figure 9.7, recall of items takes on a U-shaped appearance when retrieval is plotted as a function of an item's position in a list during presentation (Murdoch, 1962).

The superior recall for the first items on a list is known as the primacy effect, which is believed to result from the storage of these items in long-term memory. Using a typical list of 20 words, participants would have the most rehearsal time for the first word, a bit less for the second, and so on through the list. Because rehearsal can move information from working to long-term memory, the earlier words with their greater share of rehearsal

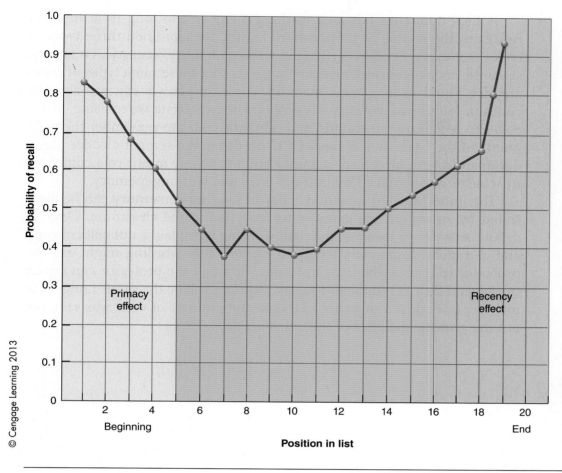

FIGURE 9.7

The Serial Position Effect. When participants are given a list of words to remember, and they can recall the items in any order, the likelihood that a word on the list will be remembered depends on its position in the list. The primacy effect refers to the superior recall for the first words on the list, and the recency effect refers to the superior recall for the last words on the list. The primacy effect probably occurs because participants have had more time to place these items in long-term memory. The recency effect probably occurs because these last words still remain in working memory at the time of retrieval. A delay in retrieval erases the recency effect, but not the primacy effect.

© Cengage Learning 2013

would be more likely to be stored in long-term memory than the later words on the list, which probably were not rehearsed much at all.

The superior recall for the last words on the list is known as the recency effect, which probably occurs because these items remain in working memory at the time of recall. The recency effect, but not the primacy effect, disappears if recall is delayed by 30 seconds (Glanzer & Cunitz, 1966). After 30 seconds, items in long-term memory will still be available for recall, but items in working memory will be long gone.

One of the strongest arguments in favor of the separation of working and long-term memory is the occurrence of clinical cases in which one capacity is damaged, while the other remains intact. Henry Molaison (the amnesic patient H.M.), whom we met at the beginning of this chapter, was able to remember a small amount of information for a few seconds but experienced enormous difficulties when trying to store new information in his long-term memory. In another case study, a patient with brain damage appeared to have the opposite problem. Patient K.F. had normal long-term memory, as indicated by his ability to form new memories. However, his working memory was seriously impaired (Shallice & Warrington, 1970). When asked to recall a list of digits (a typical working memory task), he could remember only one or two digits at a time, a big deviation from the typical ability to recall five to nine digits.

A final difference between working memory and long-term memory relates to the coding of information. Earlier, we identified three types of codes that occur in short-term and working memory: acoustic, visual, and semantic codes. Research evidence suggests that these same types of codes are also found in long-term memory. For example, we can use acoustic codes in long-term memory to recognize the ringtone we're using, visual codes to recognize our friends, and semantic codes to remember the main points of the page we just read. Of these three, the semantic codes play a dominant role in long-term memory but a relatively minor role compared to acoustic and visual codes in short-term and working memory.

The importance of semantic codes in long-term memory can be illustrated by an experience many of us have had in the classroom. Once in awhile, a professor uses just the right wording to explain a difficult concept, and a student desperately trying to capture that wording might ask the professor to repeat what was just said. Although the professor can repeat the general idea, it is unlikely that the wording will be the same. Long-term memory has taken a snapshot of the meaningfulness of what was said, but not the acoustic qualities of the exact words.

Summary 9.1

Types of Memory

Type of memory	Major features
Sensory memory © moomsabuy/Shutterstock	• Large capacity • Brief duration • Separate channels for different sensory types (acoustic, visual, etc.)
Short-term memory/working memory © Fred & Friends/www.fredandfriends.com	• Limited capacity (5–9 bits) • Limited duration (30 sec maximum) • Expansion of capacity through chunking • Expansion of duration through rehearsal • Central executive, visuospatial scratchpad, episodic buffer, phonological loop
Long-term memory © Susie Bennett/Alamy	• Very large capacity • Very long duration

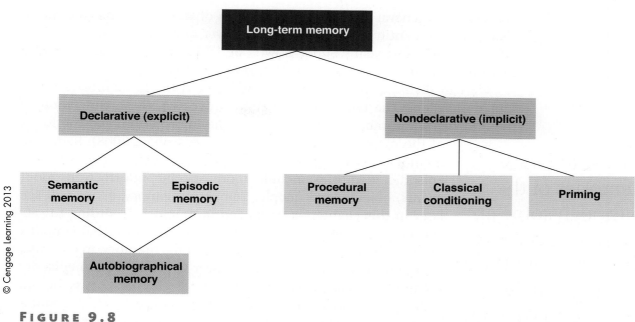

FIGURE 9.8

Types of Long-Term Memory. Long-term memory can be divided into several different categories, beginning with a distinction between declarative, or explicit, conscious, memories and nondeclarative, or implicit, unconscious, memories. Declarative memories are further divided into semantic and episodic memories, which are combined when we use autobiographical memories. Examples of nondeclarative memories are procedural memories, classical conditioning, and priming.

What Are the Different Types of Long-Term Memory?

Long-term memory can be divided into several different categories (see ● Figure 9.8). These categories not only help us describe memory more precisely but also represent the activities of different parts of the brain.

Long-term memory can be divided into declarative or conscious memories and nondeclarative or unconscious memories. **Declarative memories** are easy to "declare," or discuss verbally. Declarative memories are also referred to as **explicit memories** because they are typically accessed in a very conscious, direct, and effortful manner. In contrast to declarative memories, **nondeclarative memories** are difficult to discuss. For example, classical conditioning, which we examined in our chapter on learning, produces nondeclarative memories. We might find it difficult to explain to another person why we get nervous right before an exam or dislike a food we ate once before becoming ill. Nondeclarative memories are also known as **implicit memories** because they affect our behavior in subconscious, indirect, and effortless ways. We are aware of their outcomes—"I don't want to eat that food"—but we are usually consciously unaware of the information processing that led to that outcome.

declarative memory Consciously retrieved memories that are easy to verbalize, which include semantic, episodic, and autobiographical information; also known as explicit memories.

explicit memory A conscious memory; also known as a declarative memory.

nondeclarative memory Unconsciously and effortlessly retrieved memories that are difficult to verbalize, including memories for classical conditioning, procedural learning, and priming; also known as implicit memories.

implicit memory An unconscious memory; also known as a nondeclarative memory.

semantic memory A general knowledge memory.

Declarative Memories

Declarative, or explicit, memories are further divided into semantic and episodic memories (Tulving, 1972, 1985, 1995). **Semantic memory** contains your store of general knowledge in the form of word meanings and facts. Using your semantic memory, you can answer questions such as "Which NFL team won last year's Super Bowl?" or "What is a churro?" **Episodic memory** is a more personal account of past experiences.

We can distinguish between semantic and episodic memories along four dimensions: the type of information processed, the organization of the information in memory, the source of the information, and the focus of the memory (Williams, Conway, & Cohen, 2008). Semantic memory contains general knowledge about the world, whereas episodic memories include more specific information about events, objects, and people. Semantic memory, as we will see later in this chapter, is organized in memory according to categories. For example, we have a category for birds that contains our semantic knowledge of birds. Episodic memory, in contrast, is organized as a timeline. To answer a question from episodic memory, we often use time as a cue—"When I was in the eighth grade, my family took a vacation at the beach." Semantic knowledge originates from others, like your professors, or from repeated experience—"The ocean is colder in California than in Florida, because every time I've gone to the beach in either location, this is what I have observed." Episodic memories can result from a single, personal experience. Finally, the two types of memories serve different purposes. Semantic memory provides us with an objective understanding of our world, whereas episodic memory provides a reference point for our subjective experience of the self.

In spite of the differences just outlined, semantic and episodic memories often overlap. You could form an episodic memory of where you were when you stored a specific semantic memory. A colleague was introduced to a student's parents as follows: "Mom, Dad, this is Professor Jones. He's the one I told you about who taught us that rats can't barf." Not only did the student retain a semantic memory about rat behavior (which incidentally is true and is relevant to understanding the classical conditioning of taste aversion in rats), but the student correctly retained an episodic memory of when and where the fact was learned.

We can see that semantic and episodic memories usually interact dynamically to provide a complete picture of the past. Our semantic knowledge of the relative temperatures of the Pacific and Atlantic Oceans depends on the personal experiences of either hearing the fact in a geology classroom or vacationing on both coasts of the United States. At the same time, we use our semantic knowledge to interpret our episodic memories. Without semantic knowledge of *ocean*, *temperature*, *Atlantic*, and *Pacific*, we would be unable to organize our experience into a coherent conclusion—the ocean is colder in California than in Florida.

This type of blending of semantic and episodic memories characterizes **autobiographical memories** (Williams et al., 2008). Autobiographical memories can contain factual, semantic aspects of personal experience without any episodic aspects. You might know you were born in Pasadena, California, but of course, you would not have any memory of being born. On the other hand, your autobiographical memories of Pasadena might

> I've never tried to block out the memories of the past, even though some are painful. I don't understand people who hide from their past. Everything you live through helps to make you the person you are now.
>
> —Sophia Loren

episodic memory A memory for personal experience.

autobiographical memory Semantic or episodic memories that reference the self.

also include episodic memories of attending the Rose Parade on New Year's Day as a child, complete with images of the sights, sounds, and emotions of that experience.

Autobiographical memories appear to be accessed from two points of view. In some cases, we "relive" an experience very vividly, viewing our memory of an experience from a personal vantage point. In other cases, we seem to be seeing our life's history as if we were watching a highlights reel, from the vantage point of an observer rather than a participant. Newer memories are more likely to be viewed from the personal perspective, whereas older memories are viewed from the observer perspective (Robinson & Swanson, 1993).

Cognitive psychologists are curious about the functions of an autobiographical memory. Unlike storage of semantic memories about coursework, we do not seem to store autobiographical memories intentionally. We work hard to memorize facts about our world, but the process of storing autobiographical information seems effortless. What do we accomplish by storing our experience in this very personal way? Like other memories, autobiographical memories help us organize our experience in ways that help us respond to current challenges. If you can recall what you did to solve a problem successfully in the past, you know what to do when you see that problem again. Having an autobiographical memory also provides a sense of continuity or consistency in the self, which we explore in more detail in a later chapter (Bluck, Alea, Haberman, & Rubin, 2005).

Finally, and perhaps most importantly, an autobiographical memory helps us build social bonds with others throughout our lifespan. Think for a moment about the conversations you have with people you just met. What do you talk about? We might start a conversation with very general topics, such as the weather, but to achieve greater intimacy, people eventually begin to disclose more personal information (Robinson & Swanson, 1990). The source of that information is usually your autobiographical memory.

Nondeclarative Memories

Earlier, we defined nondeclarative, or implicit, memories as unconscious memories. In other words, nondeclarative memories influence our behavior without our conscious awareness of having used a memory. You might have

You might have semantic memories that tell you about the characteristics of Labrador retrievers, and episodic memories about the day you chose your first puppy. Your autobiographical memories combine these two elements to give you an account of your own life. A semantic element of your autobiographical memory might be the fact that your dog's parents were champions. The episodic elements of your autobiographical memory for the event might include memories of your puppy's warmth and the happy way you felt that day.

© martin phelps/Alamy

© Karina Wallton/Shutterstock

© age fotostock/SuperStock

It might have been years since this grandfather last put on a pair of ice skates, but to help his granddaughter learn to skate, he's willing to get back out on the ice. He might be a little wobbly at first, but procedural memories for skilled movement are very persistent. He'll quickly be skating as if he'd done it every day.

The distinction between nondeclarative procedural memories and declarative memories is one reason why it is so challenging to be a computer help desk technician who must talk users through a repair procedure over the telephone. It would be much easier to demonstrate how to fix the computer, which is why some software companies prefer to have the technician take over the computer remotely and apply the needed fixes as opposed to verbalizing procedures for the user. It also explains why few star athletes go on to be good coaches. Performing a task is not the same as talking about it.

procedural memory An implicit memory for how to carry out skilled movement.

priming A change in a response to a stimulus as a result of exposure to a previous stimulus.

had the experience of just being able to do something, like using roller blades for the first time in many years, without really knowing how you are doing it (Tulving, 1985). We also described nondeclarative memories as being difficult to describe in words (Smith & Grossman, 2008).

Cognitive psychologists have studied three types of nondeclarative memories in detail: classical conditioning, which we discussed in our chapter on learning, procedural memories, and priming. **Procedural memories** are also referred to as "skill memories," because they contain information about how to carry out a skilled movement, like driving a car. **Priming** occurs when exposure to a stimulus changes a response to a subsequent stimulus. For example, people who listened to rude words were more likely to interrupt a researcher than those who listened to polite words (Bargh, Chen, & Burrows, 1996). Hearing the rude words had primed these individuals to respond rudely to the investigator.

Classical Conditioning Classical conditioning results when we learn that a stimulus signals an important upcoming event. As we discussed in our chapter on learning, classical conditioning probably accounts for many of the involuntary and unconscious emotional responses we have to the world around us, such as feeling tense or fearful when we enter a dentist's waiting room. We experience these emotions without deliberately remembering our previous visits to the dentist, and it is likely that we would find it difficult to explain why we feel this way (unless we remember the information we learned about classical conditioning in our introductory psychology course).

Procedural Memories Procedural memories, which are memories for how to carry out motor skills and procedures, are especially difficult to describe in words. Imagine for a moment having to write an essay about how to use scissors for a person who had never seen a pair of scissors. In contrast, few of us experience any difficulties demonstrating procedures (Squire, 1987). Consider the differences between showing somebody how to use scissors (procedural memory) and writing an essay about how to use scissors (semantic and episodic memory). Which would be faster and easier?

One great advantage of procedural memories is their ability to automate our performance. When a novice driver first learns to operate a car with a manual transmission, a great deal of conscious effort must go into the correct sequence of procedures—clutch, gas, shift. Once the skill is well learned, it is doubtful that the driver is aware of this sequence; the person "just drives." When procedures become automatic, we are free to direct our limited capacities for divided attention to other aspects of the task. A musician who has mastered the procedure of playing a difficult piece can direct attention to the finer points of expression. Unfortunately, if a procedure is learned incorrectly, like a bad golf swing, considerable effort must be expended to think about fixing the swing, which will slow down performance. The golfer must put in sufficient practice time to make the new, correct swing automatic again.

Priming Priming, or the change in our response to a stimulus due to pre-exposure to related stimuli, explains many everyday effects of familiarity. We may believe very strongly that our behavior is unaffected by exposure to advertising. However, people rate advertisements they have seen more positively than those that they have not seen, even if they can't consciously remember having seen any of the advertisements before (Perfect & Askew, 1994). We agree that the unconscious way our attitudes can be manipulated is a bit unsettling.

Priming can influence our responses to stimuli that are perceptually related (two visual stimuli, for example) or conceptually related (two words having a related meaning). For example, researchers investigated the effects of perceptual priming on participants' responses to both possible figures (shapes that could exist in the real world) and impossible figures (shapes that could not physically exist; Soldan, Mangels, & Cooper, 2008). Previous exposure to the possible shapes did show a priming effect, but exposure to the impossible shapes did not (see ● Figure 9.9).

Conceptual priming is often studied using a technique called the lexical decision task (see ● Figure 9.10). In this task, a participant views two rapidly presented stimuli and must decide whether the stimuli are both real words (such as "roof")

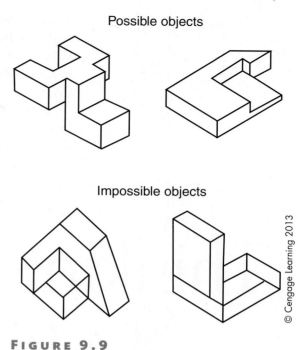

FIGURE 9.9

Perceptual Priming. Priming occurs when stimuli are related perceptually or conceptually. In this experiment demonstrating perceptual priming, prior exposure to a possible object (one that could really exist) increased memory for the object later. However, no priming effects were seen among impossible objects (those that could not really exist). *Source:* Adapted from Soldan, Mangels, and Cooper (2008).

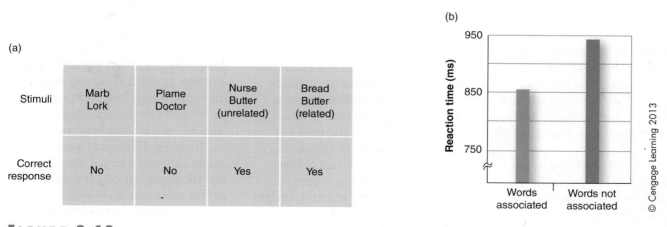

FIGURE 9.10

Conceptual Priming. Conceptual priming can be investigated within the lexical decision task, in which participants were asked to judge whether two words appearing together were both real words or not. Some examples of real and non-real words can be seen in (a). Non-real words are made by switching one letter from a real word, like *flame* and *plame* or *fork* and *lork*. Pairs of real words were either related to each other by meaning or not. The participants' reaction time in this task, shown in (b), demonstrates that participants responded faster to related word pairs (*bread–butter*) than to unrelated word pairs (*nurse–butter*). These results support the idea that we organize items in long-term memory based on their meaning.

or not (such as "loof"). Reaction time, in the form of hitting one key for real words and another for nonwords, serves as the dependent variable. When the two stimuli are related words (e.g., doctor–nurse), reaction time is faster than when the stimuli are unrelated words (e.g., butter–nurse) (Meyer & Schvanevelt, 1971).

Priming not only explains many of our unconscious daily responses to familiar stimuli but has contributed to our understanding of how information is organized in long-term memory, which we discuss in a later section. In addition, priming experiments have been helpful in identifying the ways the brain manages different aspects of long-term memory, which we turn to in the next section.

Thinking Scientifically

Can Subliminal Messages Influence Our Behavior?

If we can process some types of information implicitly, or without conscious awareness, is it possible to sell us a product or change our behavior without our knowledge? The idea of subliminal messages suggests that information can enter the memory system below the threshold of conscious awareness and influence the behavior of the unsuspecting recipient of the message. The word *subliminal* means "below threshold," and in this case, the term refers to the threshold for conscious awareness of a stimulus.

In 1956, social psychologist James Vicary claimed that he could boost sales of popcorn and Coca-Cola by flashing the messages "Eat Popcorn" and "Drink Coke" for a third of a millisecond (a millisecond is 1/1000th of a second) at five-second intervals during a film, which is too short an exposure to be seen consciously. In the ensuing uproar, several nations passed laws banning subliminal advertising. By 1962, Vicary confessed in an interview that he had made up the whole thing. Controlled, independent research found no increase in sales using Vicary's technique (Pratkanis, 1992). Nonetheless, controversies continue regarding the use or suspected use of subliminal messages to influence people's behavior without their awareness. From the $50 million per year subliminal recording industry, which claims its products can help you lose weight, improve your memory, or become an extrovert, to claims about the ability of "backward masking" in popular music to influence behavior, this concern has not been laid to rest easily.

To provide some scientific insight into this question, psychologists distinguish between subjective and objective thresholds of awareness (Vokey, 2002). In our sensation and perception chapter, we defined a threshold as the smallest amount of a stimulus that can be detected reliably. Any stimulus below the objective threshold is so weak that a person is not able to guess about its occurrence above a chance level. Above the objective threshold, we see a continuum of stimuli intensity that will be detected with increasing accuracy and conscious awareness. The subjective threshold is reached when detection becomes better than chance, yet participants still believe they are "just guessing" about whether an event occurred. At a further point along the continuum, the participants consciously detect the stimulus and no longer believe they are guessing. Subliminal messages would be located above the subjective threshold but below the threshold for conscious awareness.

Considerable evidence suggests that stimuli occurring below a person's objective threshold have no effect on behavior at all. In contrast, stimuli falling between the subjective threshold and the point where stimuli become clearly conscious do indeed appear to have the ability to

Through the careful observation of patients with brain damage along with brain imaging studies in healthy participants, scientists have discovered correlations between activity in parts of the brain and specific components of long-term memory. These discoveries support the distinctions made by cognitive psychologists between declarative and nondeclarative memories based on observations of behavior.

Declarative Memories and the Hippocampus In our chapter on biological psychology, we described the important role played by the hippocampus in memory. The hippocampus itself is unlikely to serve as a storage location for memories, but it clearly participates in the consolidation of information into long-term memory.

Now that we are familiar with some of the distinctions between declarative and nondeclarative memories, we can examine the case study of Henry Molaison (the amnesic patient H.M.) in more detail. Molaison's extensive loss of tissue in the inner part of both temporal lobes included

influence behavior. These findings are a far cry from the claims made for subliminal recordings, however. No empirical studies have been able to demonstrate any effectiveness for these products. Participants who were told they were using a "self-esteem" recording, when they had actually been given an "improve your memory" recording, nonetheless rated their self-esteem as having improved (Greenwald, Spangenberg, Pratkanis, & Eskenazi, 1991). This result is probably another example of a placebo effect, which we discussed in our chapter on research methods. Our expectations for many treatments (I'm taking an aspirin so my headache will disappear) often influence our cognitive assessment of the results.

Psychologists have also attempted to clarify the possible impact of backward messages (backmasking) inserted into popular music. Backward messages can be produced by reversing a sound recording, which is very easy to do with today's digital recording software. Backward messages have been viewed by some people as

subliminal, although there is a strong likelihood that any words in a backward message fall below our objective thresholds.

Careful analyses of backward messages in rock and roll songs concluded that some were coincidental (backward speech still sounds like speech), while others were inserted by artists like the Beatles as obvious jokes or artistic statements (Poundstone, 1983). Backmasking has been featured in recordings ranging from Britney Spears to Pokemon Rap to

© Splash News/Newscom

Bloodhound Gang to Missy Elliott (Backmaskonline.com, 2011).

Regardless of the heavy weight of scientific evidence against the effectiveness of subliminal messages in influencing behavior, several lawsuits have alleged that subliminal messages in music led to suicide. The group Judas Priest was the target of a wrongful death suit for the group's use of backward lyrics. Expert testimony failed to demonstrate any evidence that listening to subliminal messages actually affected any subsequent behavior, and the suit was unsuccessful (Moore, 1996). ⚙

The Beatles were one of the first groups to use deliberate backmasking of both instruments and vocals in their 1966 album *Revolver*. With the use of digital recording, the process of backmasking has become very simple and has been used by a diverse set of more recent recording artists including Missy Elliott and Bloodhound Gang. Because we cannot perceive the backmasked messages consciously as words, it is very unlikely such messages could influence behavior.

the hippocampus and amygdala in both hemispheres (Corkin, Amaral, Gonzalez, Johnson, & Hyman, 1997). In follow-up observations of Molaison, Brenda Milner discovered that not all his memories were equally affected by his surgery (Milner, 1966, 2005). Molaison retained most of his memory for events leading up to his surgery, but his ability to form new memories was profoundly reduced. The inability to form new memories is known as anterograde amnesia. Remarkably, Molaison was unable to transfer any new information about people, places, events, and numbers to long-term memory. For example, he failed to remember having met anyone he encountered following his surgery even though he might interact with them repeatedly. His working memory was sufficient for holding normal conversations, as long as there were no large delays between responses. Much to Milner's surprise, Molaison learned a new procedural task, mirror tracing, as well as typical control participants did. In one of these tasks, Molaison was asked to draw the shape of a star while looking at a sample star and his own hand in a mirror. After three days, Molaison mastered the task. However, if asked, he would deny ever having performed the task. His procedural memories were intact, but his declarative memories for the details of the task were nonexistent (see ● Figure 9.11).

Circuits connecting the hippocampus and adjacent temporal lobe memory areas with the cortex (see ● Figure 9.12) are believed to participate

© Cengage Learning 2013

FIGURE 9.11

Separating Declarative and Nondeclarative Memories.
The mirror-tracing task requires a participant to trace a five-pointed star, which is mounted on a wooden board that blocks the participant's view of the star and his or her hand. The participant must view the star and his or her hand in a mirror. This task is especially challenging because the mirror reverses the image, so if you want the pencil to trace around the star away from your body, you have to move your pencil toward your body instead. Brenda Milner was surprised to observe that Henry Molaison learned the mirror-tracing task at a normal rate, even though he didn't remember the details of the task. This outcome suggested to Milner that nondeclarative, procedural memories like the mirror-tracing task were not managed by the brain the same way as declarative memories.

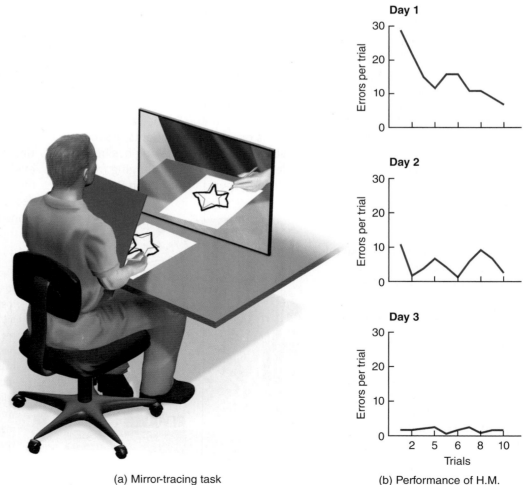

(a) Mirror-tracing task

(b) Performance of H.M.

in long-term memory consolidation. Damage to these structures or their connections typically results in anterograde amnesia similar to that experienced by Henry Molaison.

Declarative Memories and the Cerebral Cortex

Semantic, episodic, and autobiographical memories involve the participation of the cerebral cortex.

Semantic memories appear to be widely distributed across the cerebral cortex (see ●Figure 9.13). Using brain imaging, researchers can observe which parts of the cerebral cortex are active when a person is thinking about particular memories. Naming animals is associated with activity in the occipital lobes, suggesting that visualizing an animal's appearance might be helpful in this task (Martin, Wiggs, Ungerleider, & Haxby, 1996). Naming tools activated areas of the frontal and parietal lobes normally associated with movements and action words. To name a hammer, for example, we might consider the hand movements associated with using hammers and words such as *pound* or *hit*.

Episodic memories are affected by damage to the prefrontal cortex. Damage in this area can produce a condition known as source amnesia. Patients with source amnesia maintain their semantic knowledge, but do not recall how they acquired it. A patient who experienced damage to his prefrontal cortex as the result of a traffic accident retained his semantic and procedural knowledge of the game of chess, but he could not remember how old he was when he learned or who taught him to play the game (Tulving, 1989).

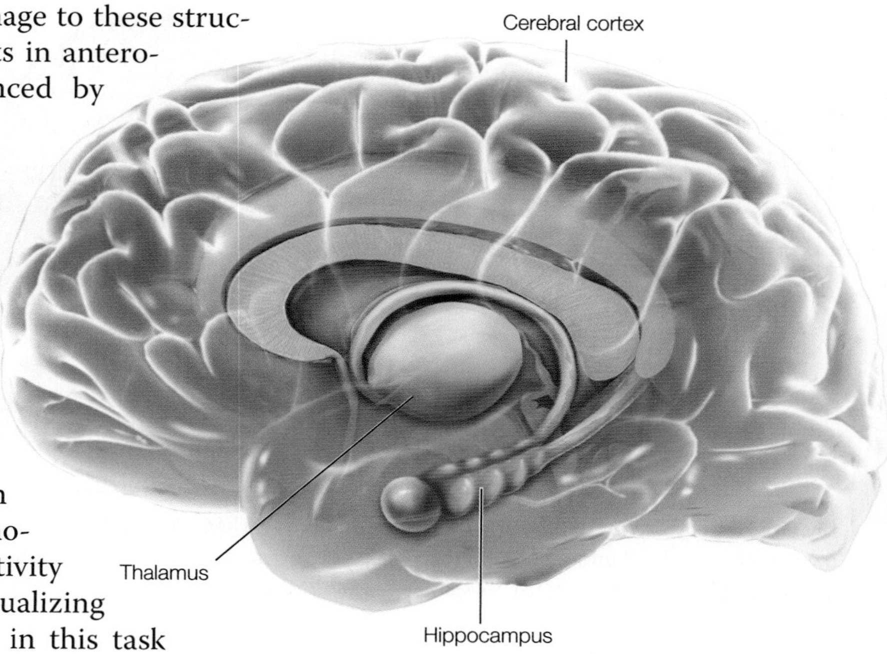

Cerebral cortex

Thalamus

Hippocampus

© Argosy Publishing, Inc.

FIGURE 9.12

The Hippocampus and Memory. Damage to the hippocampus or to the pathways connecting it to the cerebral cortex frequently produce the type of declarative memory problems experienced by Henry Molaison.

FIGURE 9.13

Semantic Memories Are Widely Distributed in the Brain. Different patterns of activity in the cerebral cortex are correlated with various types of semantic memories. Naming animals (a) is associated with activity in the visual cortex of the occipital lobe, suggesting that we think about what an animal looks like in order to name it. Naming tools (b) activates areas associated with hand movements, suggesting that we think about how we would use a hammer or saw in order to name one.

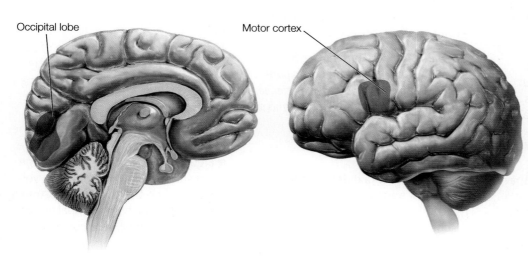

Occipital lobe

Motor cortex

© Argosy Publishing, Inc.

(a) Naming animals, but not tools

(b) Naming tools, but not animals

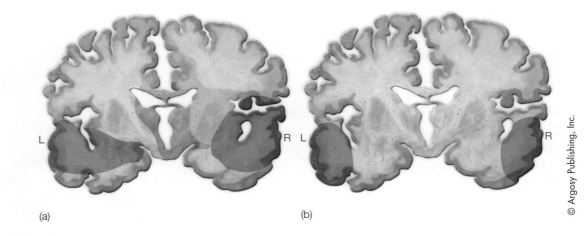

Changes in activity

- Large increase
- Medium increase
- Small increase
- No increase

L   R L   R

© Argosy Publishing, Inc.

(a)   (b)

FIGURE 9.14

My Life History or Yours? The brain responds differently when you're listening to your own autobiographical information (a) than when you're listening to another person's autobiographical information (b). *Source:* Adapted from Fink et al. (1996).

Connecting *to* Research

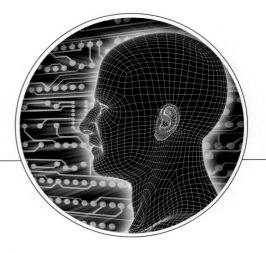

What Does Driving a Cab in London Do to Your Brain?

In addition to its role in the consolidation of new long-term declarative memories, the hippocampus participates in another important memory function—the maintenance of spatial maps for navigation. Finding your way around your environment is a problem common to most animals, including human beings (especially in the many thousands of years before GPS and Mapquest).

Animal research suggested that the hippocampus can change in response to navigation experience, but similar research had not been done with human participants. The researchers believed that London cab drivers, because of their extensive use of navigation, would be an interesting group to observe.

The Question: *Will differences be observed between human participants with extensive navigational experience (London cab drivers) and others who do not have this experience?*

METHODS

Sixteen London taxi drivers and 50 control participants were analyzed using structural magnetic resonance imaging (MRI), which allowed researchers to compare the volume of different parts of the brain between the two groups.

RESULTS

The posterior, or rear, portion of the hippocampus had significantly larger volume in the taxi drivers than in the controls, and the anterior, or front, portion of the hippocampus had significantly larger volume in the controls than in the taxi drivers (see ● Figure 9.16). No other parts of the brain showed any differences in volume between the two groups. Among the taxi drivers, hippocampal volume in the right hemisphere correlated significantly with years of experience

Autobiographical memories are perhaps the most widely distributed of all types of memory in the cerebral cortex (Svoboda, McKinnon, & Levine, 2006). Because these memories capture perceptual, factual, and emotional details of past experience, we find activation not only in the prefrontal areas associated with episodic memories but also in the relevant areas of cerebral cortex associated with perception and movement. Can we distinguish between episodic memories and autobiographical memories? People do show different patterns of brain activity when listening to their own autobiographical stories than when they listen to the autobiographical stories of other people (see ● Figure 9.14; Fink et al., 1996).

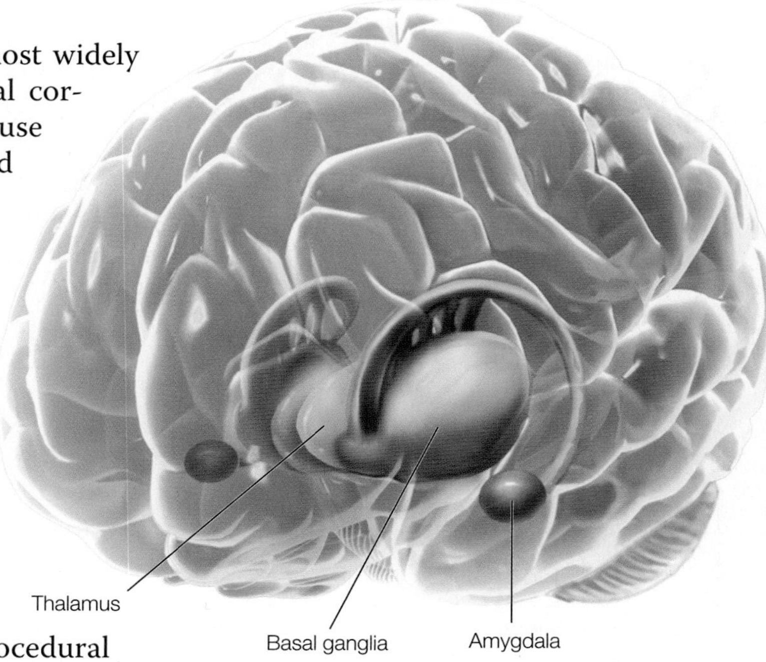

Procedural Memories and the Basal Ganglia Procedural memories are correlated with activation of the basal ganglia, forebrain structures that are part of the brain's motor systems (see ● Figure 9.15). Patients with Huntington's disease and with Parkinson's disease, both of which produce degeneration in the basal ganglia, typically experience great difficulty with learning new procedures (Knowlton et al., 1996; Krebs, Hogan, Hening, Adamovich, & Poizner, 2001). In contrast, their declarative memories remain relatively intact. Recall that Henry Molaison experienced the opposite outcome. His procedural memory abilities were intact, but his declarative memory abilities were severely impaired.

Thalamus

Basal ganglia   Amygdala

© Argosy Publishing, Inc.

FIGURE 9.15

The Basal Ganglia and Procedural Memories. Procedural memories are correlated with activity in the basal ganglia, which are part of the brain's system for managing voluntary movement.

driving a taxi. As we discussed in our biological psychology chapter, right hemisphere activity appears to be correlated with spatial thinking.

CONCLUSIONS

The researchers were able to determine that extensive use of navigational abilities changed the structure of the hippocampus. Their results were consistent with previous reports relating navigation to the hippocampus in rodents, monkeys, patients with hippocampal damage, and imaging studies. The researchers' analysis did not allow them to make any conclusions about how the hippocampus had actually changed at the microscopic level, although it is likely that they were observing the results of adult neurogenesis, or the production of new neurons. ✪

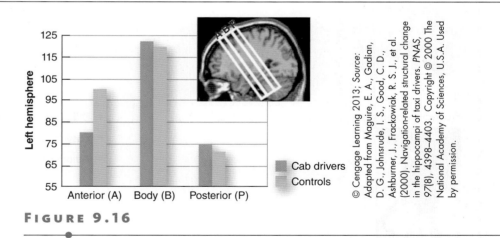

FIGURE 9.16

© Cengage Learning 2013; Source: Adapted from Maguire, E. A., Gadian, D. G., Johnsrude, I. S., Good, C. D., Ashburner, J., Frackowiak, R. S. J., et al. (2000). Navigation-related structural change in the hippocampi of taxi drivers. PNAS, 97(8), 4398–4403. Copyright © 2000 The National Academy of Sciences, U.S.A. Used by permission.

Experience Changes the Hippocampus. To navigate successfully across the complex city of London, cab drivers must form spatial maps. Considerable evidence shows that the hippocampus plays an important role in forming spatial memories in many species, including humans. What was surprising about the results found by Maguire et al. (2000) was that the navigation experience seemed to have changed the structure of the cab drivers' hippocampus compared to those of control participants. Cab drivers had more volume in the posterior hippocampus than did controls, and controls had more volume in the anterior hippocampus than did cab drivers. No differences between the groups were observed in the body of the hippocampus.

Summary 9.2

Types of Long-Term Memory

Memory type	Declarative/explicit or Nondeclarative/ implicit?	Features	Correlated brain structures
Semantic memory © martin phelps/Alamy	Declarative, explicit	• General knowledge • Organized by category	Sensory and motor cortex
Episodic memory © Karina Wallton/Shutterstock	Declarative, explicit	• Personal history • Organized chronologically	Prefrontal cortex
Autobiographical memory © Argosy Publishing, Inc.	Declarative, explicit	• Combines semantic and episodic memories • References self	Combination of prefrontal, sensory, and motor cortex
Procedural memory © age fotostock/ SuperStock	Nondeclarative, implicit	• Difficult to verbalize • Easy to demonstrate • Automated skills	Basal ganglia

How Is Long-Term Memory Organized?

Little research exists regarding the organization of nondeclarative memories in long-term memory, but significant efforts have been made to understand the organization of declarative memories. Within the category of declarative memories, far more is known about semantic than about episodic organization. However, both types of memory appear to follow some of the same basic principles. Memories that share characteristics appear to be more closely linked than memories that show very little overlap between their various features.

For example, let's assume that over the past weekend, you attended a basketball game on campus, made a trip to the library to work on a term paper, and went hiking with friends. These experiences have some elements in common (you may have used your car on all three occasions or some of the same people may have been present) and other elements that are quite different (the level of enjoyment you experienced or whether you were indoors or outdoors). Theoretically, the experiences that have more overlapping features are likely to be more closely associated in your memory than are the experiences that are quite different from one another.

> The difference between false memories and true ones is the same as for jewels; it is always the false ones that look the most real, the most brilliant.
>
> —Salvador Dali

Connectionist Theories

More formal explanations have evolved to account for this tendency to group memories that share overlapping features. These explanations fall under the heading of connectionism, or the view of the mind as an interconnected network made up of simpler units.

A doctoral dissertation in computer science by Ross Quillian, later refined with cognitive psychologist Allan Collins, was one of the first efforts to apply a connectionist approach to memory (Collins & Quillian, 1969; Quillian, 1966). Quillian was actually attempting to program a computer to recognize language, and in so doing, described the organization of semantic memory as a hierarchy of concepts, or categories. For example, a hierarchy of concepts about living animals could include "bird" and "fish." These categories in turn include "canary" and "ostrich" and "shark" and "salmon," respectively. Concepts are also linked to relevant specific properties, such as "has wings" or "has fins." The model is "connectionist" because it suggests that thinking about one concept will automatically lead to thinking about related concepts and their properties.

Collins, along with Elizabeth Loftus, modified the original Collins and Quillian model to produce a **spreading activation model** (Collins & Loftus, 1975). The spreading activation model recognized that we do not organize concepts according to strict hierarchies and that people form their own organizations in memory based on their personal experiences (see ● Figure 9.17). For example, if you ask people to report the first words that come to mind when they see the word *red*, you are likely to get many different sets of answers.

spreading activation model A connectionist theory proposing that people organize general knowledge based on their individual experiences.

FIGURE 9.17

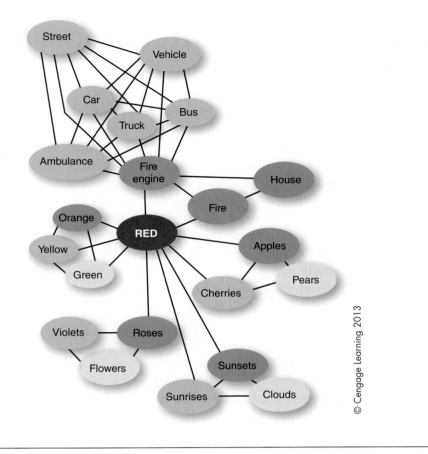

Spreading Activation.
According to the spreading activation theory, thinking about "red" will activate nearby concepts ("orange," "green," and "fire") faster than more distant concepts ("sunsets," "roses"). This network suggests that a person would answer the question "Is a bus a vehicle?" faster than the question "Is an ambulance a vehicle?" *Source: Adapted from Collins and Loftus (1975).*

© Cengage Learning 2013

The spreading activation model also suggests that concepts and properties differ in the strength of their connections. For example, even though avocados and oranges are both examples of the concept "fruit," it is likely that most people have a closer link in their memories between "orange" and "fruit" than between "avocado" and "fruit." If asked whether an avocado or an orange is a fruit, we would assume that reaction time to the second statement would be much faster.

The spreading activation model does an excellent job of accounting for the results of the lexical decision experiments demonstrating priming that we described earlier. Using the spreading activation model, we could assume that seeing the first word activates a concept. This activation would spread to connected concepts and properties. For closely related concepts like "doctor" and "nurse," activating the "doctor" concept would lead to activation of the "nurse" concept even before the participant actually sees the word *nurse*, allowing for a very quick decision to be made as soon as the word appears. In contrast, with unrelated words like *butter* and *nurse*, the "nurse" concept would not be activated until the word actually appears, resulting in a relatively slower decision.

Inferences: Using Schemas

As early as 1932, psychologist Frederic Bartlett observed that memory does not work like a video recording of events (1932/1967). Bartlett read long, involved stories to his participants, and then asked them to recall the stories 20 hours later. Not too surprisingly, the recalled stories were shorter and had less detail than the original story. Somewhat more surprisingly, participants added features to the recalled stories that had not actually appeared in the original. These additions were not random. In most cases, the details added by participants fit the theme or meaning of the story.

Bartlett concluded that memory storage does not occur in a vacuum. When we encounter new information, we attempt to fit the new information into an existing **schema**, or set of expectations about objects and situations. Details that are consistent with our schemas are more likely to be retained, whereas inconsistent details are more likely to be left out. Details may be added in memory if they make a story more consistent and coherent. For example, you are more likely to recall having seen books in a photograph of a professor's office than in a photograph of a farmer working in the fields. Even if no books appeared in the professor's office, you might recall seeing some anyway, as most professors have offices filled with books. In a later chapter, we will explore the development of schemas and the formation of concepts during childhood.

Schemas appear to be very important in the process of memory storage, as demonstrated by a clever experiment in which participants were asked to read the following passage:

© keith morris/Alamy

We are more likely to remember details that are consistent with our schemas than those that are not. We will remember books in the professor's office and brushes and canvases in the artist's studio.

> The procedure is actually quite simple. First you arrange things into different groups depending on their makeup. Of course, one pile may be sufficient depending on how much there is to do. If you have to go somewhere else due to lack of facilities that is the next step, otherwise you are pretty well set. It is important not to overdo any particular endeavor. That is, it is better to do too few things at once than too many. In the short run this may not seem important, but complications from doing too many can easily arise. A mistake can be expensive as well. The manipulation of the appropriate mechanisms should be self-explanatory, and we need not dwell on it here. At first the whole procedure will seem complicated. Soon, however, it will become just another facet of life. It is difficult to foresee any end to the necessity for this task in the immediate future, but then one never can tell. (Bransford & Johnson, 1972, p. 722)

© Jose AS Reyes/Shutterstock

The "self" is one of the most important schemas we have for organizing our thinking. If you can think about how the material you study is reflected in your own experience, it will be much easier to remember.

schema Set of expectations about objects and situations.

At this point, you are probably scratching your head in confusion. Reading this passage is bad enough, and remembering much of it later seems impossible. However, what if we tell you that the passage is about doing your laundry? With the laundry schema in mind, try rereading the passage. It is likely to make a lot more sense than when you read it the first time, and you will remember much more of what you read.

How Do We Retrieve Memories?

Storing information, whether in memory or on the hard drive of a computer, does us little good unless we can locate and retrieve the information when we need it. Without a system of retrieval, our stored memories would be no more useful to us than a library in which books were placed on shelves at random. You might get lucky sometimes and find what you are looking for, but in most cases, the search would take so long that the information would no longer be needed.

Retrieval systems help us find the information we need, whether we are searching online, looking for a book, or trying to remember something important. Organized information is always easier to find than disorganized information.

Retrieval From Short-Term Memory

Imagine that you were told to remember the following letters for a subsequent test:

c a f h k

During the test, you are shown a series of letters one at a time. If the letter you are shown matches one on your list, you pull the "yes" lever as quickly as possible. If the letter is not on your list, you pull the "no" lever. This is exactly the type of procedure used by Saul Sternberg (1966, 1967, 1969) to investigate recall from short-term memory.

Because of the small number of items that we can hold in short-term memory, it is tempting to assume that we can bring them all up simultaneously to perform Sternberg's task correctly. However, this probably is not the way memory works. Sternberg varied the length of the lists of letters from one to five and found that reaction time on his task increased a consistent 38 msec for each additional item added to the list. In other words, if you were asked to say whether or not "h" was on your list, you would first consider "c," then "a," then "f," and so on until you reached the target letter.

Experiencing Psychology

Schemas and False Memories

Bartlett observed that using schemas to frame our memories can result in our adding details that improve a memory's consistency and coherence. In other words, we can "remember" things that did not actually occur because they fit our schemas. We can demonstrate this "fill in the blank" tendency in memory by asking you to memorize some word lists.

Step 1: Read through both lists of words in order, and try to remember as many as you can.

List One: sheets, pillow, mattress, blanket, comfortable, room, dream, lay, chair, rest, tired, night, dark, time

List Two: door, tree, eye, song, pillow, juice, orange, radio, rain, car, sleep, cat, dream, eat

Sternberg's results suggest that we search through short-term memory one item at a time rather than retrieving its contents all at once.

Retrieval From Long-Term Memory

The popularity of games like *Trivial Pursuit*, crossword puzzles, and television game shows highlights an interesting aspect of memory retrieval. It feels really good when you can remember something. At the same time, most students are all too familiar with the intense feelings of frustration that accompany the inability to retrieve information. You know the answer, but it just isn't coming to mind.

The Role of Cues Students are quite familiar with the impact of cues on the ability to retrieve information. A **cue** is any stimulus that helps you access target information. Most students find recognition tasks, such as true-false or matching exam items, relatively easy. These tasks provide very complete cues (the correct information is right on the page in front of you). All you need to do is make a judgment about how well the presented information matches what is stored in memory. Compared to recognition tasks, recall tasks, such as essay exams, require an additional step. Information must be retrieved from memory and then recognized as correct. Recall tasks provide many fewer cues than recognition tasks and are typically more difficult as a result.

In addition to the amount of information provided, what makes a stimulus an effective cue for recalling a particular bit of information? The most effective cues are those we generate ourselves, a finding that provides a practical application to student life. In one experiment, one group of students wrote down three words of their choosing for every one of 600 words they were expected to learn while another group studied the same 600 words accompanied by three words for each term selected by another person (Mäntylä & Nilsson, 1988). Although recall in the second group was an excellent 55%, the students who selected their own retrieval cues remembered a remarkable 90% of the words. In a later section on improving your memory, we will emphasize the benefits of incorporating your

© STOCK4B/Photoshot

The popularity of memory games, like *Trivial Pursuit*, probably results from the rewarding feeling we get when we retrieve a sought-after memory.

cue A stimulus that aids retrieval.

Step 2: Without looking back at the list, write down as many words as possible from List One in any order.

Analysis: Check your list of recalled words for any that did not appear in List One. "Pillow" and "dream" appear in both lists, but "sleep" appears in List Two only. Many people insert "sleep" into their List One responses (a false memory) because so many of the words on List One fit the sleep schema. It is unlikely that you will insert words into your recalled list that are not related to the schema of sleep. See if you can construct some lists on your own that produce other "false memories." We return to the issue of false memories and retrieval later in this chapter. ⚙

own experience when forming new memories. If you are able to put concepts to be learned in your own words and associate them with personal experiences, it is very likely that they will be easier to remember.

Why are cues helpful? Cues might work due to a process known as **encoding specificity** (Flexser & Tulving, 1978; Tulving, 1983; Tulving & Thomson, 1973). Each time you form a long-term memory, bits of information are encoded along with other important bits that were present at the same time. As a result, each memory is processed in a unique and specific way, as this exact same combination of bits is unlikely to occur together again. Any stimulus that was present and noticed during this encoding process could serve as a cue for retrieving the target memory. Because greater numbers of cues aid retrieval, the more similar your retrieval circumstances are to your encoding circumstances, the more likely you are to successfully retrieve the target memory. We know from experience that if we have forgotten something, retracing our steps is the fastest way to remember what we forgot. By returning to the situation where we last processed the target information, we surround ourselves with cues that should lead to successful retrieval.

Among the bits of information that get encoded along with target memories are features of the surrounding environment, leading to context-dependent memory. You are probably familiar with advice about studying in a well-lit, quiet, professional environment in order to perform your best on exams. Duplicating your testing situation when you study should provide the greatest number of retrieval cues. When participants were asked to learn lists of words in one of two distinctive rooms while either standing or sitting, recall was best when participants were tested in the same room and position as when they learned the information (Greenspoon & Ranyard, 1957). As shown in ● Figure 9.18, scuba divers who learned words

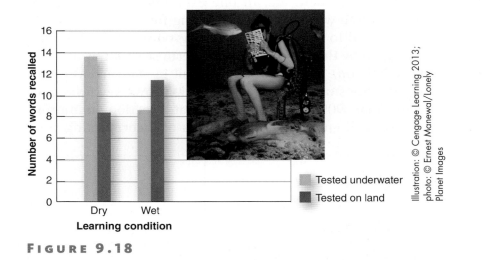

FIGURE 9.18

Our Surroundings Are Encoded in Context-Dependent Memories. Features of our environment get encoded along with target memories. Participants learning lists of words either on land or while underwater recalled more words when tested in the same context compared to when they were tested in the opposite context. This diver might find it more difficult to retrieve information about the types of fish if tested on dry land instead of underwater. *Source: Adapted from Godden and Baddeley* (1975).

encoding specificity Memories incorporate unique combinations of information when encoded.

either on land or underwater retrieved the most words when their encoding and testing circumstances were the same (Godden & Baddeley, 1975). Although these effects are small, it is still a good idea to study in a quiet classroom-like environment, which may help explain why studying in the library has remained popular through the years.

Context-dependent memory not only is relevant to retrieving declarative memories but also explains some of the advantages of simulation in learning new procedures, such as flying a helicopter or driving a tank. The goal of simulation technologies is to produce the most realistic training experience possible. The more similar the simulation environment is to the real thing, the more transfer of learning we might expect to see.

Context-dependent memory can extend beyond a person's physical environment and body position to include cues from internal physiological states. The most dramatic of these instances of state-dependent memory occur in response to drugs. Participants were asked to learn word lists after smoking either marijuana or a placebo cigarette (Eich, Weingartner, Stillman, & Gillan, 1975). As we discussed in our chapter on research methods, a placebo is an inactive substance that cannot be distinguished from an active substance. Once again, participants experiencing the same conditions during encoding and retrieval (marijuana–marijuana or placebo–placebo) performed the best. This finding is especially surprising given the fact that the marijuana–marijuana group outperformed the marijuana–placebo group.

In addition to drug-related internal states, mood can serve as an encoding cue. In one creative study, patients with bipolar disorder (described in our chapter on psychological disorders), whose moods swing from mania to depression, learned words in one state (mania or depression) and tried to retrieve them in either the same state (mania–mania or depression–depression) or the opposite one (mania–depression or depression–mania) (Weingartner, Miller, & Murphy, 1977). The participants were most successful when learning and retrieving occurred in the same state, whether that was mania or depression. College students were able to recall more happy events from their diaries when they were already in a happy mood (Bower, 1981). It should not be too surprising, therefore, that once people are feeling depressed, they tend to focus on their more negative memories, further reinforcing their negative moods.

The ability of a cognitive state to serve as a retrieval cue has been demonstrated by clever experiments using bilingual speakers. Russian immigrants to the United States showed better recall for episodic memories when the language used to recall the memories was the same as the language used when the memories were encoded (Marian & Neisser, 2000). Another cognitive cue, achievement motivation, has also shown context-dependent effects (Woike, Lavezzary, & Barsky, 2001). If you read stories with achievement motivation cues, your recall will be best when your own state of achievement motivation matches that of the story.

Drugs, including the caffeine in coffee, can produce strong state-dependent effects on memory. If you study while drinking coffee, taking a test without coffee is likely to make retrieval more difficult.

It may be tempting to blame state-dependent memory for the experience of alcohol-related "blackouts," but these are more likely to result from alcohol's active interference with the formation of long-term memories (Lisman, 1974). There is no evidence that getting drunk again will make it easier to recall what happened the last time a person got drunk.

Tip-of-the-Tongue Retrieval is not an all-or-none phenomenon. Instead, retrieval proceeds in a step-by-step manner, with each new step bringing you closer to the target. This incomplete retrieval is best illustrated by the Tip-of-the-Tongue (TOT) phenomenon. TOT is probably a very familiar experience for you. You are trying to remember a word or name, and you might retrieve another word that either starts with the same letter or has the same meaning. You know that the retrieved word is not the one you're looking for, but you're close.

© andrej pol/Shutterstock

Tip-of-the-tongue (TOT) experiences were elicited in volunteers by describing rare words in English. One of the items was the name of this weird-looking instrument this naval cadet is learning to use. Participants often are able to retrieve the first letter of the word (*s*) and the number of syllables (two) without necessarily retrieving the whole word (*sextant*), which demonstrates retrieval is not all-or-none.

In a classic series of experiments, more than 200 TOT experiences were induced in research participants by presenting definitions of relatively rare English words (Brown & McNeill, 1966). For example, participants were asked to supply a word for "a navigational instrument used in measuring angular distances, especially the altitude of the sun, moon and the stars at sea." You may be picturing the object right now, or thinking about a movie of an old salt using this instrument . . . it starts with an *s* . . . but most of you will have difficulty retrieving the word *sextant*.

Participants in these studies showed considerable evidence of partial recall during their TOT experiences. They were able to identify words that they recognized instantly, as opposed to words they did not know. Many were able to identify the first letter and the number of syllables in the target word. Incorrect words that were retrieved frequently sounded like the target, although their meanings were usually quite different. In some cases, retrieving the incorrect word appeared to block the retrieval of the correct item, but in other cases, the incorrect word served as an additional cue.

Reconstruction During Retrieval What exactly is happening when we retrieve a bit of stored information?

When retrieved, information to be used flows from long-term memory back into working memory. The computer analogy of memory sees this process as similar to opening a saved document stored on the hard drive of your computer in the active window on your desktop. However, there are some big differences between opening a file on a computer and retrieving a memory. As we mentioned previously, instead of storing and retrieving accurate files like a computer, the mind **reconstructs** a memory out of the stored bits. The mind accomplishes this task by blending retrieved information with new content currently present in working memory (Bartlett, 1932/1967). When you retrieve the target information, you are reconstructing something sensible to fit the occasion, as opposed to simply reproducing some memory trace.

In the case of either the computer or the mind, memories are prone to change. As you probably know from your own experience, any document that is currently active on the desktop can be modified. When the modified document is then saved under the same filename, future retrievals will bring up the modified file, not the original one. Memory might possibly work in the same way. Once a memory is activated for use, it will interact

reconstruction The rebuilding of a memory out of stored elements.

with all other data currently in working memory. Any changes that result during this activation will then be re-encoded as a new long-term memory.

As a storyteller begins, he or she discovers that certain aspects of the story provoke more of a reaction from the audience. These aspects are emphasized and perhaps exaggerated for even greater effect, and the new, more exciting story replaces the original version in long-term memory. Fish become larger, vacations are more exciting, and heroes become more heroic. When participants were asked to repeat a complicated story on several occasions, they had a tendency to simplify the story, highlight some aspects more than others, and adjust the story to fit their own world-views (Bartlett, 1932/1967). Such alterations probably form the basis of mythology. In the retelling of the adventures of Odysseus or King Arthur, accounts of the original true events are lost or hopelessly distorted.

Most of us would like to believe that our memories, especially for important life events, are relatively accurate. Elizabeth Loftus set out to evaluate the reliability of eyewitness testimony in courtroom settings and discovered that memories are rather flexible. In one experiment, participants watched a video of an automobile accident and answered a number of questions about what they had seen (Loftus & Palmer, 1974). One group heard the question "How fast was the white sports car going while traveling along the country road?" while the other group heard the same question with a slight addition—"How fast was the white sports car going *when it passed the barn* while traveling along the country road?" There was no barn in the video, but when participants were asked one week later if they had seen a barn, 20% of those who had heard the barn question answered yes, while fewer than 5% of the other participants did so. One must assume that skilled attorneys are quite aware of this feature of memory and could certainly use such leading questions to the advantage of their clients (see ● Figure 9.19).

> Memory, of all the powers of the mind, is the most delicate and frail.
>
> —Ben Jonson

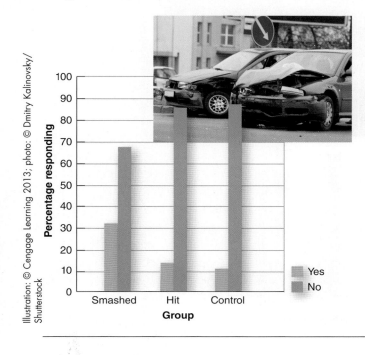

Illustration: © Cengage Learning 2013; photo: © Dmitry Kalinovsky/Shutterstock

FIGURE 9.19

Memory Reconstruction. After participants viewed a short video of an automobile accident, Loftus and Palmer (1974) asked one group, "About how fast were the cars going when they *hit* each other?" while a second group was asked, "About how fast were the cars going when they *smashed* each other?" One week later, both groups were asked if they recalled seeing glass on the road after the accident. There was no glass on the road in the video, so the correct answer was no. Hearing the word *smashed* instead of *hit* increased the likelihood that a participant would "remember" glass on the road and answer yes. *Source: Adapted from Loftus and Palmer (1974).*

These findings raise two possible explanations, but do not inform us about which is more likely. The first explanation suggests we might overwrite the old memory (no barn) with the new (barn), effectively erasing the original. The second explanation suggests we simply form a new memory (barn) that coexists with the old, original memory (no barn). However, deliberate efforts to change memories and then retrieve the original have been unsuccessful (Bekerian & Bowers, 1983). This does not, of course, mean that it can't be done, but simply that it has not yet been done. However, these unsuccessful efforts to retrieve original memories may shift our opinion more to the overwriting hypothesis.

If you began this psychology course believing, like many people do, that memory works like a video of life, it might surprise you to learn that this is definitely not the case. It may be quite unsettling to realize that memories are open to change and revision, and that those distinct and confident childhood memories we cherish may be somewhat inaccurate or even flat out wrong. However, it also doesn't make sense to think that we would evolve a system of memory that was usually wrong. Instead, fuzzy trace theory suggests that we use precious resources to form different types of memories based on our needs, ranging from "verbatim," or exact, accounts to "gist," which means we retain the general idea of events (Reyna, 2008). We use gist in situations where a relatively vague level of information is sufficient, because this is a more efficient use of resources. We use the more energy-intensive verbatim memories for situations that require very detailed, accurate recall, such as remembering the periodic table of the elements in your chemistry class. This system works well for us most of the time, but later in this chapter, we will see how relying on gist instead of retrieving verbatim information can lead to false memories (see ● Figure 9.20).

FIGURE 9.20

The Use of Gist Increases With Age.
Older children, with their improved language skills, use gist more effectively than younger children (Odegard, Cooper, Lampinen, Reyna, & Brainerd, 2009). When children attended birthday parties with a theme (e.g., Harry Potter or SpongeBob Squarepants), older children appeared to be able to use the theme of the party to provide gist, leading to their successful recall of more events. Younger children, however, could not remember theme-related events (magic potions at Hermione's party) any better than generic birthday party events (blowing out candles on a cake), suggesting that forming a theme gist was not helpful. Source: Adapted from Odegard, Cooper, Lampinen, Reyna, and Brainerd (2009).

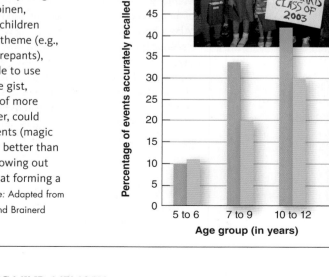

Illustration: © Cengage Learning 2013; photo: © Randall Hyman Photography

A checkpoint for the accuracy of our memories results from source monitoring (Johnson, Hashtroudi, & Lindsay, 1993). Under normal circumstances, we do a good job of distinguishing between external and internal sources of information, as in "I said that" or "I thought about saying that." Once again, this system works well for us most of the time, but it can produce false memories when we attribute a memory to the wrong source. For example, you might think you told your roommate you would be coming in late, but you may have only mentally reminded yourself to do so. You have mistaken an internal source of information (I thought that) with an external source (that happened).

We can also use our memories to make distinctions between fantasy and reality. When participants were asked to imagine having a conversation with either former president George W. Bush or Cinderella, different patterns of brain activation occurred (Abraham, von Cramon, & Schubotz, 2008). While considering a realistic possibility (talking to George Bush), the prefrontal cortex areas associated with episodic memory processing became more active. When considering fantasy (talking to Cinderella), areas of the brain that participate in semantic processing became more active. Semantic memories are important for determining if something is logically possible. Some false memories might involve confusion between these patterns of activation, allowing the fantasy to seem real.

Retrieval of Emotional Events

Take a moment and write down the most important five events in your life last year. Do these events have anything in common with each other? We're willing to guess that each of the events on your list is associated with strong emotions. From an evolutionary perspective, this makes good sense. In our chapter on emotion, we argued that emotions provide quick guidance for approach and avoidance decisions. Many of our emotional experiences, while not all life-threatening, do have significance for us, and forming strong memories of these events will help us respond effectively to similar situations in the future.

Emotions, and negative emotions in particular, do not have a simple relationship with memory retrieval. In some cases, we seem to have difficulty remembering negative events, which we discuss in a later section on motivated forgetting. Some individuals report that they can recall few if any of the details of having been sexually molested as children. In other cases, memories for negative events seem much more vivid and intrusive than other types of memories. Most adults in the United States seem to have formed a **flashbulb memory** of the terrorist attacks of 9/11, or an especially vivid memory including details of where they were and what they were doing when they first heard the news. Individuals diagnosed with post-traumatic stress disorder (PTSD) often experience intrusive flashbacks of the events that originally traumatized them. How do we reconcile these differences in retrieval for emotional events?

© Viviane Moos/Corbis

People often report especially vivid episodic memories about where they were and what they were doing when they first heard news that evoked a strong emotional response, although research evidence suggests that these memories are not always as accurate as we think they are.

flashbulb memory An especially vivid and detailed memory of an emotional event.

To answer this question, we need to consider what happens to the hippocampus and to the amygdala during a negative emotional experience. As we have mentioned previously, the hippocampus plays an essential role in the formation of new declarative memories, whereas the amygdala helps us assess emotional situations, and negative situations in particular. The independence of these two structures in memory formation can be demonstrated by a case in which a man nearly died from being buried in the sand (Diamond, Campbell, Park, Halonen, & Zoladz, 2007). Following his rescue, the man reported feeling constantly fearful during the day and troubled by nightmares at night, but he had no idea why. His fear had been processed by his amygdala, but lack of oxygen during the event had produced damage to his hippocampus, making it impossible for him to process the declarative details of his experience. The opposite result occurs in patients with an intact hippocampus but a damaged amygdala (Cahill, Babinsky, Markowitsch, & McGaugh, 1995; Hurlemann et al., 2007). These patients show good memory for nonemotional details of a story, but do not show the typical enhanced memory for negative events in a story.

In most emotional situations, the hippocampus and amygdala will work in tandem to produce a memory that has both declarative and emotional detail. Flashbulb memories might seem extra vivid because the amygdala is even more active during memory formation than usual. Although people tend to be overconfident in the accuracy of their flashbulb memories, and even flashbulb memories appear to fade over time, retrieval of these memories continues to be more accurate than other, less emotional, everyday events that occurred at about the same time (Davidson, 2008).

We start to see extremes in retrieval, such as complete failure to recall an emotional event or an intrusive, overly vivid amount of recall, when an event has been encoded during unusually high levels of stress.

Scientists are experimenting with chemicals that either block the formation of or erase existing traumatic memories (Cao et al., 2008; Pitman et al., 2002). What are the ethical implications of using these techniques with people?

Researchers have demonstrated that sudden stress produces a decrease in activity in the prefrontal cortex, which in turn impairs working memory function (Qin, Hermans, van Marle, Luo, & Fernández, 2009). High stress also initiates the release of cortisol into the blood circulation, which produces a general arousal but also specifically increases the activity of the amygdala (LeDoux, 1996). Very high levels of cortisol are correlated with the reporting of more false memories (Payne et al., 2007). A further understanding of the coordinated processing of declarative and emotional aspects of memory should help us gain a better understanding of the retrieval of emotional memories.

Why Do We Forget?

Now that we understand the processes involved with the formation, storage, and retrieval of memories, we can turn our attention to the troublesome topic of forgetting. For students, whose job description involves committing large amounts of information to memory, an understanding of the processes leading to forgetting is the source of much practical advice for improving memory and avoiding memory failure.

For the purposes of our discussion, we define **forgetting** as a decrease in the ability to remember a previously formed memory. The key here is that to "forget," a memory has to have been formed in the first place. This definition excludes a number of instances that we have discussed previously. For example, many students maintain that they "forgot" information needed for an exam, when in fact they were daydreaming during the lecture covering the material and never learned it in the first place. This example is better understood in terms of lack of attention and encoding failure than as an example of forgetting. Using our definition, you can't forget something you never learned. When forgetting is the result of brain injury or disease, we usually refer to the loss of information as amnesia.

If we were never able to forget where we parked all the previous times we used this lot, finding our car today would be extremely difficult.

Understanding forgetting is complicated by the fact that we measure memory indirectly by looking at performance. As most students are all too aware, actual memory for a topic can be quite different than performance on an exam. Stress, illness, time pressure, and distractions can temporarily reduce our ability to recall information. When we discuss true forgetting, we are not considering the effects of these temporary difficulties. It would be very handy for both students and instructors if some sort of modern imaging technology would allow us to "see" whether introductory psychology had been adequately stored in the brain, but alas, this is not currently possible.

Although forgetting can be frustrating, it also has its adaptive benefits. Forgetting might provide a way to prioritize the things we should remember. For example, we are often asked to change our computer passwords to maintain security. At first, this can lead to annoying competition in memory between the old and new passwords. Over time, however, the strength of the old password weakens. Functional MRI studies have shown that prefrontal areas of the brain appear to actively suppress memories that are used less frequently (Kuhl, Dudukovic, Kahn, & Wagner, 2007). By suppressing these lower-priority memories, we can avoid confusion and reduce the amount of work we have to do to recall higher-priority memories.

Decay

Decay occurs when our ability to retrieve information we do not use fades over time. Imagine taking last term's final exams today. How would you do? It might seem to you that the material you learned last term is gone forever, but just because you can't retrieve something doesn't mean the memories are lost.

A classic method of measuring the retention of material in long-term memory over time is the method of savings. This method compares the rate of learning material the first time to the rate of learning the same material a second time. It might take you 50 practice trials to learn the periodic table of elements for your chemistry class. Perhaps you don't study chemistry again for a year or two. In a subsequent course, you once again need to memorize the table. This time, it only takes you 20 trials. The greater speed

forgetting A decrease in the ability to remember a previously formed memory.

decay Reduction in ability to retrieve rarely used information over time.

It's likely that the people attending this high school reunion might have forgotten the names of some of their classmates whom they hadn't seen for 60 years.

of learning the table the second time indicates that you retained, or "saved," some prior memories of the table. Using this technique, we can demonstrate that people who studied high school Spanish, but never used it later on, retained most of their memories for Spanish vocabulary words 50 years later (Bahrick, 1984). Instead of a large amount of "forgetting" due to the passage of time, we usually see that most of the material we learn is actually retained nearly indefinitely.

Although the idea of decay fits our everyday experience of "forgetting" quite well, most contemporary psychologists believe that the simple passage of time does not do a very good job of predicting memories that are easy or difficult to retrieve (Berman, 2009). It is likely that forgetting occurs due to a combination of factors, which may or may not include decay.

Interference

A significant factor in forgetting is **interference**, or the competition between new and older information in the memory system. The brain requires a measurable amount of time to consolidate a memory, or to produce a physical representation. In the window of time in which memories are being processed but not yet fully consolidated, they may be subject to distortion, loss, or replacement by interference from other bits of information.

How long is this window? Synaptic consolidation, the physical changes related to memory that occur at the level of the synapse, might take minutes or hours. Memory loss usually occurs when this consolidation is interrupted. Individuals who experience unconsciousness as a result of a head injury rarely remember much about the immediate circumstances leading to the injury. Procedures such as general anesthesia or electroconvulsive shock therapy (ECT, described in our chapter on therapies) often produce slight memory deficits spanning a period of hours or possibly a day or two before and after treatment. Storage of memories in the cerebral cortex, might take years, during which time information can be lost or distorted (Dudai, 2004).

Interference can be demonstrated by comparing performance in a list-learning task. The more lists a participant must learn, the more difficult it becomes for the participant to remember words on the first list (Tulving & Psotka, 1971). In other words, learning new lists of words interfered with memory for the first list.

Does this mean that the first list is somehow erased from memory by the incoming information? To test this hypothesis, researchers gave participants in one experiment a little help in the form of memory cues. The lists all contained categories of items, such as types of buildings (e.g., house, barn, garage, hut). If the experimenters provided their participants with a cue in the form of the category (types of buildings), the effects of having learned additional lists were quite small. It appears that the words on the first list were maintained in memory, but that learning additional lists made them hard to retrieve.

interference Competition between newer and older information in memory.

To make matters worse, interference can work in two directions (Underwood, 1957) (see ●Figure 9.21). Let's assume your foreign language class is assigned one list of vocabulary words to study each night. You have procrastinated a bit on your homework, and to catch up for a quiz the next day, you now have three lists of vocabulary words to study instead of the usual single list. Our interest will be on how well you can remember the second of the three lists. If we compare your memories for the second list to those of students who studied the first list when it was assigned, we find that your performance is relatively poor. In other words, learning the first list on the same night as the second list produces proactive interference for the second list. Proactive interference refers to reduced memory for target information as a result of earlier learning.

At the same time, we can compare your memories for the second list to the performance of your classmates who studied the third list the night after they studied the second list. Again, your performance is likely to be worse. Reduced memory for target information due to subsequent learning is known as retroactive interference. This is the type of interference that was demonstrated in the multiple lists study we discussed previously (which you may recall unless too much retroactive interference has occurred).

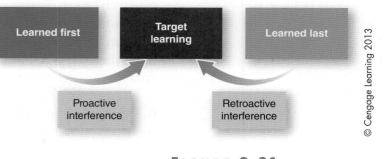

FIGURE 9.21

Proactive and Retroactive Interference. If we measure recall of a target list of words, we find that it is worse both when preceded by learning another list (proactive interference) and when followed by learning another list (retroactive interference).

Motivated Forgetting

The Internal Revenue Service reports that many more people who owe money fail to sign their tax returns than those who are due a refund. Assuming that the failure to sign the return is not a conscious act of defiance, how can we account for this lapse in memory?

Theories of **motivated forgetting**, or the failure to remember or retrieve unpleasant or threatening information, suggest that the nonsigners are protecting themselves from further unpleasantness by "forgetting" to sign their tax forms.

Memory is a servant to our overarching goals. Retrieval, for better or worse, is often influenced by our motivations, and our motivations can distort the memories we retrieve. While not exactly forgetting in the sense of our earlier definition, motivated distortions of memory can be so extreme that the original information is essentially lost during the process.

In one example of the influence of motivation on recall, participants were presented with a list of choices, such as between two internships, roommates, or cars for sale, with equal numbers of corresponding positive and negative features (high resale value or some rust in the case of the cars). Subsequently, they remembered the positive features associated with their ultimate choices better than the negative features (Henkel & Mather, 2007). When they were deceived into thinking they had actually chosen the other option instead (due to a friendly "reminder" from the experimenter), they continued to remember the false choice more positively. In related

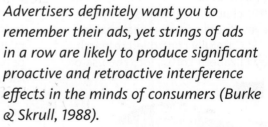

Advertisers definitely want you to remember their ads, yet strings of ads in a row are likely to produce significant proactive and retroactive interference effects in the minds of consumers (Burke & Skrull, 1988).

motivated forgetting Failure to retrieve negative memories.

research, participants conveniently demonstrated less recall for ethical rules after they had been given an opportunity to cheat (Shu, Gino, & Bazerman, 2011). In our later chapter on social psychology, we will explore how these types of discrepancies between behavior and attitudes can change the attitudes themselves, not just the memories for them.

Identifying the presence of motivated forgetting can have serious practical implications. Beginning in the 1970s, largely due to greater public recognition that incest was more common than previously believed, many adults began to report having been a victim of sexual abuse during childhood. These cases represented a range of possible motivated forgetting, from suppression, in which the individual consciously remembered the incidents but had not reported them to parents or other authorities, to repression, in which the individual reported no conscious memory of the incidents until the memories were suddenly recovered during therapy or while reading a news report of a child molestation case.

Psychology
as a Hub Science

How Reliable Are Eyewitnesses?

Our legal system relies very heavily on the testimony of eyewitnesses, especially those who have nothing to gain by telling a lie. Given the flexible nature of human memory as discussed in this chapter, is the trust we place in eyewitness accounts reasonable?

Carefully controlled research by Elizabeth Loftus into the use of eyewitness testimony (Loftus, 1979; Loftus & Palmer, 1974), along with the development of forensic DNA testing in the 1990s, seriously compromised trust in eyewitness testimony. Out of all cases in which an innocent person has been cleared of a crime due to DNA evidence, about 75% involved mistaken identification of the perpetrator by an eyewitness (Wells, Memon, & Penrod, 2006).

Psychologists have used research on eyewitness behavior to make scientifically based recommendations to law enforcement officials. For example, the manner in which photograph lineups of possible suspects are shown to witnesses affects the likelihood of mistaken identification. In the typical procedure, witnesses view lineup photographs simultaneously, which allows them to compare all the people and choose the person who looks most similar to their memories of the perpetrator. Unfortunately, this procedure makes mistaken identification more likely in the event that the real suspect does not appear in the lineup. The witness will simply choose the person who looks most like the remembered perpetrator. If a sequential procedure is used, in which the witness must respond "yes" or "no" to each picture before moving on to the next, mistaken identifications occur less frequently (Steblay, Dysart, Fulero, & Lindsay, 2001).

Perhaps juries could evaluate eyewitness testimony more accurately if they took the witness's apparent confidence into account. In other words, a person who seems very confident about identifying a suspect might be expected to be

A number of psychologists studying memory suspected that not all reports of recovered memories of child abuse were true and that some might represent confabulation, or a confusion between imagined and true memories. As we mentioned earlier in this chapter, our source monitoring abilities usually prevent us from mistaking false for true memories, but the system does not perform perfectly. Under the right set of circumstances, it is relatively easy for people to believe very strongly in a memory that is simply not true.

We demonstrated in an earlier section on schemas that false recall for verbal stimuli can be produced by presenting words that are associated by meaningfulness (e.g., bed, rest, awake). In this case, most participants form a false memory for the presentation of the word *sleep* (Deese, 1959). Perhaps you are thinking that memorizing strings of words in a laboratory has little relevance to the experience of traumatized victims of child abuse. Elizabeth Loftus, whom we met earlier in our discussion of memory reconstruction, addressed that concern by demonstrating that much more complex false memories were rather easy to implant in her participants. Loftus (2003) described how imagining an event had happened or even just reading the testimonials of witnesses could increase a person's confidence that a false event had actually occurred. Most persuasive of all is the use of photographs. When a real family photo was superimposed on a hot air balloon, 50% of participants

Elizabeth Loftus (2003) demonstrated that it was relatively easy to implant a false memory in her participants of having taken a hot air balloon ride during childhood.

more accurate than a witness with less confidence. Unfortunately, such an appealing idea has major flaws. Even witnesses who express a 95% confidence in their judgment (expecting to be wrong only 5% of the time) are correct only 70 to 75% of the time (Brewer, Keast, & Rishworth, 2002). In addition, witness confidence can be easily manipulated by feedback that confirms an identification. Simply telling witnesses, "Good, you identified the suspect," retroactively changes the witnesses' recollections of how confident they were about an original identification, how good a view they had of the perpetrator and events, and how much attention they paid to the suspect's face during the crime (Wells & Bradfield, 1998).

Special consideration must be given to cases in which the eyewitness is a child. An understanding of children's memory development is critical for evaluating the child's ability to serve as a witness to a crime. Some data indicate that children's memories for significant events, like a trip to an emergency room, are quite reliable as long as four to five years later (Peterson & Whalen, 2001). On the other hand, young children are accustomed to pleasing adults with their answers and are more suggestible than adolescents and adults. Fortunately, understanding the strengths and limitations of children's memory systems has allowed experts to develop methods for obtaining the most accurate reports possible from child witnesses (Bruck & Ceci, 2009).

Further improvements should accompany the development of new, more reliable measures of recognition, such as brain imaging, reaction time, rapid presentation of faces, and analyses of eyewitness eye movements (Wells et al., 2006). ✿

The traditional lineup used in the criminal justice system is very likely to produce a mistaken identification when the real perpetrator is not included. The witness simply picks the most similar person. Psychologists have shown that giving "yes" or "no" answers to one photo at a time reduces the risk of a mistaken identification.

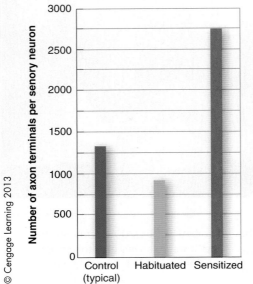

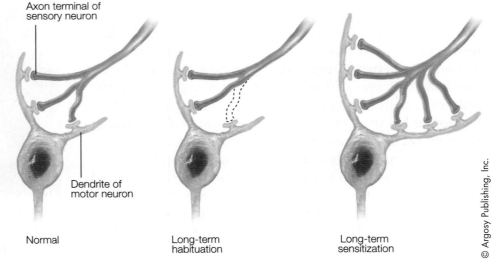

Axon terminal of
sensory neuron

Dendrite of
motor neuron

Normal

Long-term
habituation

Long-term
sensitization

© Argosy Publishing, Inc.

© Cengage Learning 2013

FIGURE 9.22

Learning Changes Neural Structure. Neurons have smaller numbers of axon terminals following habituation, but larger numbers following sensitization (Bailey & Chen, 1983).

"remembered" the ride, including details about how old they had been at the time and the fact that the photo was taken by a particular person.

Until we understand more about the nature of confabulation, a cautious approach to repressed memories is probably the best course of action. We can neither prove nor disprove these memories without additional evidence, so any therapy should be aimed at relieving distressing symptoms without reference to their source.

What Is the Biology of Memory?

In our previous discussions of working and long-term memory, we outlined some of the brain areas believed to coordinate those processes. In this section, we will zoom in for a closer look to see how the brain in general appears to manage memory at the cellular and biochemical levels.

Memory at the Level of the Synapse

Forming new memories requires changes in the connections neurons make with one another at the synapse, or synaptic consolidation. You might find it strange to think that such a process is going on in your own brain as you read this chapter.

Eric Kandel and his colleagues have demonstrated persistent changes in the strength of synapses responsible for several types of learning in the sea slug, including classical conditioning (Antonov, Antonova, Kandel, & Hawkins, 2003; Brunelli, Castellucci, & Kandel, 1976; Carew & Kandel, 1973). In addition to changes in synaptic strength, it appears that learning stimulates a cascade of gene expression, which in turn produces the long-term structural changes in neurons that represent memories. The number of axon terminals increases following sensitization and decreases following habituation (Bailey & Chen, 1983). These observations are consistent with the behavior observed in each case—lower levels of responses to stimuli in habituation and higher levels of responses to stimuli in sensitization (see ● Figure 9.22).

One of the major processes responsible for change at the synaptic level during learning is **long-term potentiation**, or **LTP**, which enhances

long-term potentiation (LTP) The enhancement of communication between two neurons resulting from their synchronous activation.

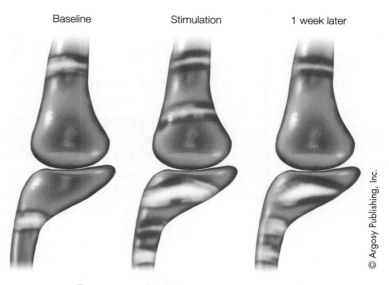

© Argosy Publishing, Inc.

FIGURE 9.23

communication between two neurons. This phenomenon can be demonstrated experimentally by applying a rapid series of electric pulses to one area of the nervous system and observing the increased reactions of cells receiving input from that area (Bliss & Lømo, 1973) (see ● Figure 9.23). Results from demonstrations of LTP suggest that the relatively simultaneous activation of a neuron sending information and the neuron receiving this information produces changes that make the synapse more efficient. LTP shares many features with memory, which makes it an attractive candidate for being one of the processes underlying memory phenomena. LTP lasts a very long time, possibly indefinitely, which is similar to our thinking about long-term memories. Second, both memories and LTP can be formed after only very brief exposure to stimuli.

Long-Term Potentiation (LTP). Long-term potentiation (LTP) can be demonstrated by applying a series of electrical pulses (center) and observing the increased reactions of cells receiving input (right) compared to their previous baseline (left). LTP shares many features with memory, such as being long-lasting and formed after a very brief exposure to stimuli.

Biochemistry and Memory

Psychologists have long suspected that the neurotransmitter acetylcholine (ACh), discussed in our chapter on biological psychology, plays an important role in memory and attention. Evidence for acetylcholine's role in memory takes many different and interesting forms.

Drugs that inhibit systems using ACh as a major neurotransmitter typically interfere with memory formation (Atri et al., 2004). Patients with Alzheimer's disease, which is characterized by severe memory deficits, typically show degeneration of neural circuits that use ACh. Medications prescribed to reduce the symptoms of Alzheimer's disease typically boost ACh activity (Holzgrabe, Kapkova, Alptuzun, Scheiber, & Kugelmann, 2007). Elderly rats that performed well in a maze had higher levels of ACh synthesis than their less capable peers (Zyzak, Otto, Eichenbaum, & Gallagher, 1995). Finally, honeybees treated with drugs that interfere with the breakdown of ACh learn faster than untreated bees (Shapira, Thompson, Soreq, & Robinson, 2001) (see ● Figure 9.24).

Researchers are also interested in the role of the neurotransmitter glutamate in memory formation. One type of glutamate receptor, known as the NMDA receptor, is a prime candidate for learning-related changes such as those observed in long-term potentiation (LTP) (Qiu & Knopfel, 2007). Not too surprisingly, chemicals that enhance the activity of glutamate receptors have been shown to boost memory formation in rats (Balschuna, Zuschrattera, & Wetzel, 2006). Similar compounds are being tested for possible use in treating Alzheimer's disease.

Acetylcholine

FIGURE 9.24

Illustration: © Cengage Learning 2013; photo: © Eric1513/ Dreamstime

Acetylcholine and Memory. Research on honeybees has implicated the neurotransmitter acetylcholine (ACh) in the formation of new memories. Honeybees that were allowed to forage (forming new memories about the location of food) and those trapped in a hive yet given drugs that promote ACh activity showed the same amount of structural growth in their nervous systems (Weinberger, 2006).

How Can We Improve Memory?

Most college students by definition have very good memory skills—this is an essential component of academic success, and those who lack these skills generally do not end up in higher education. However, we can always improve, and the observations made by psychologists studying memory provide many practical suggestions.

We have already discussed several lines of research that have practical implications for improved memory. The structure of long-term memory implies that organized material will be easier to remember than disorganized material. Elaborative rehearsal, especially when you can connect material to your own experience, anchors new material in your existing memory stores and makes it easier to retrieve. The effects of state, mood, and context on retrieval suggest that studying in circumstances that are most similar to those where you will retrieve your memories will give you the best outcome.

In addition to these basic suggestions, we would like to offer a few more tips that might be especially useful, both during and after your college experience.

Distribute Practice Over Time

Psychology professors will never give up trying to convince students that cramming is a terrible memory strategy. Persistent faith in cramming is surprising, given that we all know that concert pianists and basketball players are better off practicing an hour a day each day for a week than practicing six hours straight the night before a performance. The mind works in similar ways whether it learns to play basketball or whether it learns the periodic table of elements, so the same learning strategies should work in either case.

Nearly all forms of learning show evidence of an advantage of distributed practice (practice spread out over time) as opposed to massed practice

Most of us realize that the best way to improve our music or athletic skills is to practice every day (distributed practice). We would think it very odd if an athlete or musician crammed practice in the night before a game or performance (massed practice). The same advantage of distributed over massed practice holds for academic work, too, but unfortunately, that fact does not deter some students from cramming for exams.

(practice condensed to a short period of time) (Russo & Mammarella, 2002). In other words, spacing the input of information to the brain over time produces better memory than cramming. Whether we are discussing the learning of classically conditioned responses by sea slugs or the learning of complex semantic information by college students, the advantage of distributing learning over time is a constant. By giving the brain more time to consolidate each memory, less is likely to be lost to interference.

Take Tests

We usually think about tests as measuring a student's ability to retrieve memories, but test-taking is actually a powerful tool for forming memories, too (Roediger & Butler, 2011). In fact, research demonstrates that test-taking produces superior long-term memory when compared with repeated studying of material. In addition, test-taking improved participants' ability to think about learned material with greater flexibility and to apply material to new situations.

We are not advocating that you abandon reviewing your textbook and lecture notes, but we do hope you will take advantage of the online testing opportunities that accompany this textbook.

> The memory is sometimes so retentive, so serviceable, so obedient—at others, so bewildered and so weak—and at others again, so tyrannic and beyond control.
>
> —Jane Austen

Sleep

Initially, many psychologists believed that the positive role of sleep in memory formation resulted from a lack of interference. If you learned something right before going to sleep, no further information would enter the system to cause interference. More sophisticated research, however, has demonstrated that sleep plays an active role in the consolidation of memories. Changes related to memory that occur in the brain during sleep might be different than the changes that occur when we learn something while awake. Wakeful learning might serve to strengthen new connections, but sleep-related processing might reorganize existing memories to accommodate new information (Stickgold & Walker, 2007).

Declarative and procedural memories appear to be stronger following a period of non-rapid eye movement sleep (N-REM; see our chapter on consciousness) (Gais & Born, 2004; Smith & Fazekas, 1997). Other research has indicated that rapid eye movement (REM) sleep benefits the retention of highly emotional material (Wagner, Fischer, & Born, 2002; Wagner, Gais, & Born, 2001). Further research is needed to provide a clearer picture of the relationship between different phases of sleep and the formation of different types of memories. Nonetheless, we can say with confidence that students who pull "all-nighters" are not doing their memory systems a favor. In one experiment, staying up all night produced very poor memory for a previous task, and two additional nights of adequate sleep did not compensate for the original deprivation (Stickgold, James, & Hobson, 2000).

Recite

Most students recognize that a certain number of rehearsals of reading and lecture notes are required for success on exams. One of the traps in a dependence on rehearsal is that we can easily mistake the ease with which we cover familiar material for

© Tetra Images / Alamy

Putting information you need to remember in your own words is a very effective memory strategy. Recitation takes advantage of our tendency to remember things better when they're associated with the self. If they are your words, you will remember them.

actually knowing the material. Just because you can read something doesn't mean you "know" it.

A somewhat more efficient method is recitation, or the verbalizing of the material to be learned in your own words. Recitation takes advantage of a general superiority for self-referential information. Participants who processed words in reference to themselves (e.g., "Does the word 'honest' describe you?") are more likely to remember the word *honest* than are participants who processed the definition of the words (e.g., "Does 'honest' mean the same thing as 'trustworthy'?") (Rogers, Kuiper, & Kirker, 1977). This result has obvious relevance for students wishing to improve their memories. If you can think about the information you are trying to learn in self-referential ways ("This example of episodic memories in my textbook reminds me of something that happened to me the other day"), your memory for the information will be enhanced. By putting information in your own words, you make it more relevant to yourself.

Recitation is still used as a classroom technique in very small classes, but you can duplicate this process on your own. After you have a reasonable grasp of the material, try talking about it. The most significant benefit of recitation is that you quickly realize what you do *not* understand when you try to explain the material to someone else. Most of us with classroom teaching experience are well aware of this phenomenon. You can think that you understand something, but when you try to explain it, it just doesn't come out right. This is a signal that more work on the topic is needed.

Use Mnemonics The early Greeks devised a number of methods, known as **mnemonics**, for improving memory. Mnemonic devices expand memory capacity by linking the material to be remembered to information that is relatively effortless to retrieve. The "first letter" approach takes advantage of chunking. You condense a large amount of information into an acronym. For example, the four types of processes in working memory start with the letters P, V, C, and E, for phonological, visuospatial, control, and episodic.

Even more effective is the use of first letters to make some type of phrase or sentence. This approach allows you to recall lists of items that must be in a correct order.

For example, it is easy to remember the 12 pairs of cranial nerves in the proper order if you use this sentence: *On old Olympus' towering top a Fin and German viewed some hops* (*o*lfactory, *o*ptic, *o*cculomotor, *t*rochlear, *t*rigeminal, *a*bducens, *f*acial, *v*estibulocochlear, *g*lossopharyngeal, *v*agus,

mnemonics Memory aids that link new information to well-known information.

spinal accessory, and *h*ypoglossal). Perhaps *easy* is not the correct word, but at least recall should be easier. Many similar mnemonic devices take advantage of the ease of remembering rhymes ("one is a bun, two is a shoe") or even use your body (counting on your fingers).

One of the classic Greek techniques was the method of loci, or places. This technique is particularly handy when you are trying to memorize a list of items in order, such as the planets in our solar system or the cranial nerves. The method takes advantage of the fact that we form excellent representations of visual images in memory. You begin by imagining a familiar place, perhaps your childhood home. As you imagine yourself walking through your home, you visualize each item in a particular location. If you wish to remember your grocery list (although writing the items down is probably much easier), you might imagine a carton of eggs on the little table in your entry, a loaf of bread on the sofa, a box of cereal on the television, and so on. To recall your list, all you need to do is to take another imaginary walk through your house, recalling the items you placed as you go. If all goes well, you should remember all your items in the correct order.

This technique may sound like a lot of work, but it can be very effective. One of us had a colleague in graduate school who performed so perfectly on her neuroanatomy exams that her professors actually accused her of cheating. She related to them how she had been taught the method of loci as a childhood game and had practiced the technique throughout her academic career. After they posed several difficult lists to her, all of which she recalled perfectly, they were convinced of her honesty.

The ancient Greek mnemonic device, the method of loci, takes advantage of our superior memory for visual images of familiar places. Although the method involves consciously imagining things in a particular place, we often use location as a memory aid less consciously. You are probably familiar with the layout of your favorite grocery store and use that mental image to guide your memories for the food you need to purchase. If the store reorganizes its layout between trips, you might forget something.

Summary 9.3

Types of Forgetting

Type of forgetting	Features	Assessment
Decay © Steve Skjold/ Alamy	Reduced ability to retrieve infrequently used material over time	Assessed using savings technique
Interference © Cengage Learning 2013	Competition between newer and older information in the memory system	Assessed by comparing performance in a list-learning task
Motivated forgetting © pasphotography/ Shutterstock	Failure to retrieve negative information	Comparison of recall for memories associated with positive or negative emotions

Interpersonal Relationships
From the Perspective of Memory

Shared memories are a characteristic of close relationships. You may know people in close relationships who seem to know intuitively what the other is thinking, perhaps even finishing the partner's sentences. According to a theory of transactive memory, couples in long-term relationships also develop a division of labor in regard to memory, where each partner knows certain things, but also knows what information can be retrieved from the partner if needed (Wegner, 1986; Wegner, Giuliano, & Hertel, 1985). For example, one partner might not keep track of where candles are stored in the house, but knows that the other partner does know where the candles are and can be called upon to provide that knowledge in the event of an emergency.

How do couples develop systems like this? Three major strategies have been identified (Wegner, Erber, & Raymond, 1991). First, one partner can explicitly agree to take on an area of expertise, such as managing the household finances. Second, as people get to know each other better through self-disclosure, they also learn about each other's relative areas of

People in close relationships form transactive memories, or a division of labor for remembering certain things. She might remember how to do certain home repair tasks, and he might remember others. Together, they have access to far more information than either individual could manage separately.

knowledge and expertise. One partner might have an interest in computer science, while the other thinks that computers work by magic. If something goes wrong, the second person will turn to the first. Finally, couples learn about their partner's access to information. If you know that your partner discussed holiday plans with your families, you are likely to assume that your partner knows more about your holiday options than you do.

From an evolutionary standpoint, what are the advantages of working out this division of memory labor? One major advantage of this type of transactive memory is that a couple working well together has access to far more knowledge than either individual could manage separately. We can also assume that the convenience of these systems, in contrast to managing knowledge individually, would contribute to further bonding. Transactive memory is negotiated over long periods of time between each couple in ways that are unique and not interchangeable with others.

More recently, the concept of transactive memory has been extended from intimate couples to larger groups (Peltokorpi, 2008). In the context of larger groups, transactive memory contributes to group cognition, or information processing that differs from individual cognition. As in the case of intimate couples, transactive memory contributes to the group's ability to manage more information than any one individual could be expected to do in an efficient manner based on the relevant specialties of the individuals making up the group.

Whether transactive memory takes place at the couple or large organizational level, it takes time to develop. People beginning a new relationship can expect some miscommunications and misunderstandings (and overdue bills and lost candles) until their transactive memory system begins to take shape.

Chapter 9
Reflections

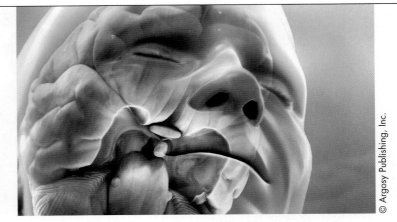

At the beginning of this chapter, we argued that memory meant so much more than the ability to succeed on exams. The people you have met in this chapter with various memory deficits have illustrated some of the memory functions we usually take for granted. Henry Molaison was trapped in time, unable to learn much of anything that occurred in his life after his surgery when he was 27 years old. Patient K.F. has good long-term memories, but cannot remember more than one or two digits at a time. The man who was nearly buried alive in sand experiences nearly constant fear, but cannot remember the accident that made him feel that way. Patients with prefrontal cortex damage can learn how to sort cards according to a rule, but have tremendous difficulty switching to a new rule. Still other patients with Huntington's disease and Parkinson's disease, both of which damage the basal ganglia, struggle to learn new skills and procedures. More globally, patients with Alzheimer's disease experience a progressive decline in all memory functions, to the point where they no longer recognize their loved ones and possibly even themselves.

As we have zoomed in for a close-up look at the structures of the brain correlated with memory functions, even to the level of a single synapse, and back out again to individual memory capacities and farther still to group cognition, we have seen how memory connects time, general knowledge, skilled patterns of behavior, emotion, and a sense of self to provide us with the remarkable advantage of being able to use the past to understand the present and predict the future. ‹

KEY TERMS The Language of Psychological Science

Be sure you can define these terms and use them correctly.

autobiographical memory, p. 414
chunking, p. 406
cue, p. 429
decay, p. 437
declarative memory, p. 413
encoding, p. 399
encoding specificity, p. 430
episodic memory, p. 414
explicit memory, p. 413
flashbulb memory, p. 435
forgetting, p. 437

implicit memory, p. 413
information processing, p. 399
interference, p. 438
levels of processing, p. 409
long-term memory (LTM), p. 408
long-term potentiation (LTP), p. 442
memory, p. 399
mnemonics, p. 446
motivated forgetting, p. 439
nondeclarative memory, p. 413
priming, p. 416

procedural memory, p. 416
reconstruction, p. 432
rehearsal, p. 404
retrieval, p. 400
schema, p. 427
semantic memory, p. 413
sensory memory, p. 402
short-term memory (STM), p. 403
spreading activation model, p. 425
storage, p. 400
working memory, p. 406

MEDIA RESOURCES

Log in to CengageBrain to access the resources your instructor requires. For this book, you can access:

Psychology **CourseMate** brings course concepts to life with interactive learning, study, and exam preparation tools that support the printed textbook. A textbook-specific website, Psychology CourseMate includes an integrated interactive eBook and other interactive learning tools including quizzes, flashcards, videos, and more.

WebTUTOR   More than just an interactive study guide, **WebTutor** is an anytime, anywhere customized learning solution with an eBook, keeping you connected to your textbook, instructor, and classmates.

aplia If your professor has assigned **Aplia** homework:
1. Sign in to your account.
2. Complete the corresponding homework exercises as required by your professor.
3. When finished, click "Grade It Now" to see which areas you have mastered, which areas need more work, and detailed explanations of every answer.

Observing brain activity while a person watches a movie is helping filmmakers produce more effective movie trailers.

10

The Thinking Mind

Thinking, Language, and Intelligence

Learning Objectives

1 Explain the role of mental representations in thinking, and differentiate the feature detection, prototype, theory-building, and schema models of concept formation.

2 Summarize the four steps of problem solving, incorporating existing research on how to approach each step successfully, and apply to a problem.

3 Analyze the building blocks of language, and debate whether nonhuman animals have language.

4 Associate key brain regions with specific decision-making and language processes.

5 Analyze the interacting roles of nature/instinct and nurture/learning in human language, using evidence from children's language development and variations in language processing.

6 Define general intelligence, and evaluate the evidence for multiple intelligence subtypes.

7 Analyze the interactions between nature/genes and nurture/environment in explaining individual differences in intelligence.

Daily life is full of decisions—some big and some small.

How does the mind reach a decision?

Psychologists have learned a great deal about the processes involved in reaching a decision and have identified many steps we can take to improve our decision making. Zooming in, we can use imaging technologies to observe how the brain reacts to a number of different choices. Do you really want to see that movie based on its trailer?

Film producers are now using brain imaging to edit movie trailers to elicit the reactions they want from an audience (MindSign Neuromarketing, 2011). They have only a few seconds to convince the audience to decide to see their film. Assuming that the ability of a film to elicit emotion drives the decision to see it, filmmakers take out the parts of a trailer that produce a neutral emotional response and splice together the most dramatic parts. Is such a practice scientifically valid? It may be useful in some cases. In our chapter on motivation and emotion, we discussed how emotions can range along a continuum. Some emotions are associated with very precise physical responses, as in the case of fear, while others are associated with more vague physical responses, as in the case of pride. It is likely that you could develop a movie trailer that would evoke great fear in viewers, but eliciting other, more complex emotions might be more difficult.

Zooming out to the moviegoers' decision to see a movie, what other factors, aside from seeing an emotional trailer, might influence their choice? Individual differences very likely play a key role. One person might really enjoy horror films, while another does not. Using the social perspective to zoom out still farther, we can see that people often respond to horror films based on their beliefs about the expectations of others. You might think that males are predisposed to like horror films and females to like "chick flicks," but psychology is rarely that simple. Instead, a person's reaction to horror films is strongly determined by her social attitudes and how she thinks her same- and opposite-sex peers would respond to the film (Mundorf, Weaver, & Zillmann, 1989).

In this chapter, we will explore how we use the tools of language and intelligence to think, which in turn guides our behavior. Beginning with the parts of the brain that process information, we will zoom out to the individual differences of personality and experience and farther still to the social and larger cultural contexts that shape the very way we think. ⊙

What Do We Think About?

The word **cognition**, as in the term *cognitive psychology*, is derived from the Latin *cogito*, which literally means "to think." Thinking allows us to manipulate information internally to construct models of the world, plan our interactions with that world, and regulate ourselves to meet our goals. Given the extent of these concepts, it should come as no surprise that cognitive psychology covers a broad area of topics. In addition to perception, learning, and memory, which we discussed in previous chapters, cognitive psychology addresses questions of thinking, language, and intelligence.

We think about what we know. In the broadest sense of the word, knowledge is the entire body of information acquired through study, investigation, observation, and experience. To manage this large collection of knowledge, the mind often uses symbols, or mental representations, to signify information. For example, an icon on your computer desktop represents Microsoft Word, and a profile photograph on Facebook represents your best friend.

The most familiar uses of mental representations are found in language, both written and spoken. Depending on the language you choose, you could represent the animal coming toward you on the sidewalk as a *hund* (German), *chien* (French), *gau* (Chinese), *perro* (Spanish), or *dog* (English). Representations can be visual, too. For instance, imagine that you snap a photo of a dog using your cell phone or you sketch a picture of the dog. Despite

© Facebook

© 2011 Twitter

Courtesy of Google

© Yelp.com

The mind uses symbols, or mental representations, to signify information, just as websites have icons that link to some of your favorite social-based networks, representing Facebook, Twitter, Google+, and Yelp.

cognition Internal mental processes including information processing, thinking, reasoning, and problem solving.

the differences in these two visual representations, the dog to which each refers is the same. We can view the representation of the dog (the sound or appearance of the word used, the patterns of light in your photo or drawing) as a vehicle for carrying information about the content of our knowledge of this dog (it seems to be a friendly, young Golden Retriever).

Our interest in this chapter is in the ability of minds to form mental representations and manipulate them to make sense of the world. What forms can representations take? What are the relationships between representations and the content they symbolize?

Thought as Images

Temple Grandin, a college professor with autism spectrum disorder, describes her way of thinking as "thinking in pictures" (Grandin, 2010). Albert Einstein is also widely quoted as relying on mental visualization in the early stages of his thinking and only later putting his ideas into words (Einstein, 1945). To what extent do the rest of us share their ability to think in mental images? By *mental image*, we are referring to a representation of any sensory experience that is stored in memory and can be retrieved for use later. For example, you can call up a visual image of your first car, picture the letters of your name, or silently hum the first bars of "Happy Birthday to You" to yourself quite easily.

People appear to treat mental images much like they would a real object (Kosslyn, 1978, 1980, 1994). We can turn visual mental images around in our minds, zoom in or out, and identify their features (see ● Figure 10.1). If you were to think about a map of the United States (assuming you have a good grasp of geography), it would take you longer to mentally count

Temple Grandin, a college professor with autism spectrum disorder, is shown here with actress Claire Danes, who portrayed her in a recent made-for-television movie. Grandin has described her cognitive experience as "thinking in pictures." It is likely that young children depend on a similar approach to thinking, but learning language provides a whole new dimension to our ability to think.

FIGURE 10.1

Forming Mental Maps. A person familiar with New York City could follow a mental route between these buildings, zoom in or out, and identify important features like landmarks and a favorite place to have coffee.

© REUTERS/Chip East

London-based artist Stephen Wiltshire, who like Temple Grandin has autism spectrum disorder, has been described as "a human camera." Stephen can fly over a major city like New York in a helicopter for about one hour and then re-create highly accurate and detailed drawings of the city. Stephen's talent is an extreme and unusual form of the use of visual imagery.

the major cities between Los Angeles and New York than those between Chicago and New York, just as it would if you were looking at a real map.

Children are particularly likely to use visual images in their thinking. In one study, between 2 and 15% of elementary school children experienced long-lasting and detailed visual images of a complex picture they had seen previously for a short interval (Haber & Haber, 1964). The children described the scene using the present tense, suggesting that they were scanning a mental replica. Except for rare cases like Temple Grandin, few adults can do this. It is possible that language becomes an increasingly important way to organize thinking during childhood and might actually begin to overwrite or interfere with the ability to directly access visual images.

Regardless of the exact form taken by mental representations, our knowledge would be useless to us unless we imposed some type of organization on all the bits we know. To supply this organization, we extract special, organizing ideas known as **concepts** from the specific instances and occurrences we experience.

Thought as Concepts

Concept formation is not unique to humans. Non-human animals as diverse as pigeons and monkeys demonstrate concept formation (Herrnstein, 1979). In one study, pigeons learned to peck at projected images of water with fish to obtain food rewards, but to withhold pecking at images of water without fish (Herrnstein & de Villiers, 1980). Subsequently, an entirely new set of slides was presented. The pigeons successfully distinguished between the fish and non-fish slides, even though they had never seen these particular images during their prior training. The pigeons appeared to have extracted a "fish" concept from their experience. What exactly does it mean to have a "fish" or any other type of concept? How are we (and the pigeons) able to construct a new concept?

Pigeons appear to be able to form concepts, such as people and non-people. If their pecking is reinforced with food in the presence of an image containing people, but not in the presence of images of scenes without people, they will learn to peck only when the people images are present. The experimenters used hundreds of "people" images, varying in number, distance from the camera, age, ethnicity, and other variables, but the pigeons still responded appropriately.

Pigeon in Skinner box

Left: Courtesy William Palya, Jacksonville State University; right: Courtesy of Will Vaughan

Examples of nonhuman and human stimuli for concept formation experiment

concept An organizing principle derived from experience.

TABLE

10.1 Approaches to Concept Formation

Approach	Application to dog category	Disadvantages
Dictionary definition	A dog is a domesticated carnivorous mammal (*Canis familiaris*) related to the foxes and wolves and raised in a wide variety of breeds.	More information than you need to classify a dog correctly
Common features	Dogs are furry animals with four legs that bark and wag their tails.	Too many exceptions (e.g., Chihuahuas are not "furry")
Overlapping features	Compare features of suspected dog with features of dog concept.	Most categories lack precise boundaries (e.g., "tastes good" might be a category feature for dogs in some cultures but not in others).
Prototype	Average of all members of dog category	Does not provide a good way to think about a category's variability
Exemplar	A specific instance of a category used as a model	Excludes some category members that are too dissimilar to model

You already "know" what a dog is. If you were asked to feed your neighbor's dog while your neighbor goes on vacation, it is likely that you could locate the correct animal, provide dog food instead of cat food, and exercise appropriate caution if your neighbor's dog happens to be unfriendly. This activity sounds very simple, but what if you found yourself trying to recruit an alien from another planet to help you with your task? What information about dogs would the alien need to know in order to succeed? Essentially, what you must convey to your alien friend is the concept of "dog" (see ● Table 10.1).

You might start the discussion with a dictionary definition of "dog." In the dictionary, however, you find that a dog is "a domesticated carnivorous mammal (*Canis familiaris*) related to the foxes and wolves and raised in a wide variety of breeds." This definition seems rather remote from what we "know" to be a dog. You really don't need to know what dogs eat and who their nearest relatives are to identify one correctly.

Perhaps we can find some common features of dogs that would allow us to distinguish between dog and non-dog. We could tell our alien friend that dogs are furry animals with four legs that bark and wag their tails. Unfortunately, there is a major logical flaw in this system (Wittgenstein, 1953). No matter how careful your definitions, even for the simplest of concepts, somebody will be able to think of an exception. Although we can agree that all dogs are animals, this feature alone is insufficient for distinguishing dogs from cats and raccoons. Having fur does not describe the Chihuahua, and Basenjis don't bark. A dog that has lost a leg in an accident no longer has four legs. Most dogs we know do wag

Although correct, this dictionary definition of a dog might not help you figure out if an animal standing in front of you is a dog or not.

dog
[dawg, dog]
noun, verb, dogged, dog-ging.
-noun
A domesticated carnivorous mammal (*Canis familiaris*) related to the foxes and wolves and raised in a wide variety of breeds.

© Dmitry Kalinovsky/Shutterstock

their tails, but there may be an abused dog that keeps its tail perpetually between its legs, as well as dogs that have tails too stubby to wag at all.

To resolve this dilemma, we can make our definition more flexible. Instead of being rigidly defined by a checklist of features, a concept could describe a group of instances that share overlapping features. This approach is similar to a feature detection model (Smith, Shoben, & Rips, 1974). According to this type of model, people determine the truthfulness of statements like "a canary is a bird" by considering overlapping features (wings, beak, flies, chirps). Using this approach, the alien could compare the features of an animal suspected of being a dog with a checklist of dog features. There are several problems with this approach, too. Some categories are quite clear, like triangles, but others do not have precise enough boundaries for the checklist approach to work. People in some cultures would list "taste good" as a feature of dogs, but Americans probably would not. In addition, the feature checklist approach just doesn't seem to match our personal experience with thinking. When you think about a dog, do you really access a mental checklist of dog features?

Prototypes and Exemplars An alternate approach to thinking about concepts is to consider some type of "standard" dog, or a **prototype** that represents your entire category (Rosch, 1973, 1983). The prototype results from an averaging of all the members of your category, and it may not even resemble any real instance (Posner & Keele, 1970). For example, the prototypical dog will have average size, an average tail, average ears, average coloring, and so on. When thinking about a category, we might also retrieve a specific instance of a concept, or an **exemplar.** This could be the dog you raised during your childhood or a dog featured in your favorite movie.

The processes in which prototypes and exemplars are used are quite similar. Whichever standard you choose, you compare new instances to it to get a sense of "fit." The more similar the new objects are to the standard, the more likely you are to include them in your concept. Both approaches are also able to account for the tendency of people to rate apples as more typical fruits than avocados, or robins as more typical birds than penguins (Malt & Smith, 1984). Apples are not only closer to the "average" fruit than avocados are, but they are also much more likely to be chosen as an exemplar fruit due to the extensive experience most people have with apples, at least in the United States.

Using common features to identify dogs, such as "has hair" or "has four legs," would exclude these two: a dog with three legs and an American hairless terrier.

Apples are more likely than avocados to be a person's exemplar fruit, due to the extensive experience we have with apples in the United States.

prototype A representation of a category formed by averaging all members of the category.

exemplar A specific member of a category used to represent the category.

In spite of the similarities between the prototype and exemplar approaches, exemplars do have some advantages. Compared to prototypes, exemplars provide a better way of thinking about the variability of a category (Rips & Collins, 1993). Averages, which characterize prototypes, do not provide much information about the range of features that can be found in a category. For example, imagine that you were just introduced to a young man named Christian Cantwell, who tells you that he is an athlete. Judging from Cantwell's imposing physical appearance (he is 6'5" and weighs 300 pounds), he seems more similar to your prototypical NFL football player than what he actually is—a star track-and-field athlete. In contrast, while your personal exemplar for a track-and-field athlete might be a sprinter or distance runner instead of a shot-putter like Cantwell, the individual instances you know can help you comprehend the variability found within the concept.

Just when we are feeling comfortable about using prototypes and exemplars to solve our alien's dog problem, we run into an additional dilemma. The use of prototypes and exemplars rests on similarity. Similar objects will be included in a concept, and dissimilar objects will be excluded. What if our new friend comes across a lifelike dog robot? In many ways, the robot looks and acts like our prototype and exemplar dogs, yet we know it is not a dog. What if we find an unfortunate dog that has been killed on the highway? It hardly retains much similarity to the prototype and exemplar dogs, yet nobody, except perhaps the alien, would question its identity as a dog. Clearly, we need more than prototypes and exemplars to solve our problem.

Concepts as Theories It might be useful to view concept formation as a type of theory building. In our chapter on research methods, we defined theories as "sets of facts and relationships between facts that can be used to explain and predict phenomena." This definition can also apply to a concept. Like theories, concepts can guide our thinking and be continually tested for

© Image of Sport Photos/Newscom

You might mistakenly put Olympic shot-putter Christian Cantwell in your category of NFL football player because of his appearance, which is closer to the prototypical football player than it is to the prototypical track-and-field athlete. Using exemplars to guide the use of concepts helps us think about the variability of a category.

Even when a prototype is well understood, like the signs and symptoms of a disease, evidence suggests that exemplars might work better. Physicians diagnosing cancer who had recently seen similar cases (exemplars) made more accurate diagnoses than those who had not (Brooks, 1990; Brooks, Norman, & Allen, 1991).

© jeremy sutton-hibbert/Alamy

Prototypes and exemplars depend on similarity, which can result in similar items, like this robotic dog, being included in our dog category.

accuracy against new, incoming information. Also like theories, our concepts do not exist in isolation. As we mentioned in our chapter on memory, concepts can be viewed as part of a vast, interconnected network of memories.

Thinking about concepts as theories provides insight into the problem of judging category membership, such as deciding whether an avocado is a fruit. Prototypes and exemplars provide a useful starting place for judging category membership. We test our theory that the new item (avocado) fits the category by comparing it to the prototypes (average fruit) and exemplars (apple) of a concept (fruit). We might make the occasional mistake, such as including bats or excluding ostriches in a concept of "bird," but most of the time, we will be successful and fast.

This approach also has the advantage of being consistent with observations of how children acquire new concepts, which we explore in more detail in our chapter on development. A child might start with a prototype or exemplar dog based on the family pet, possibly overapplying the concept to other four-legged animals at the zoo and failing to apply it to dogs of different breeds. With the help of feedback from others (no, that's a tiger, not a dog; or yes, a Chihuahua really is a dog), the concept becomes more refined. Our alien friend is likely to need the same type of feedback from us as he attempts to apply his newly learned concept of dog to the variety of animals he encounters.

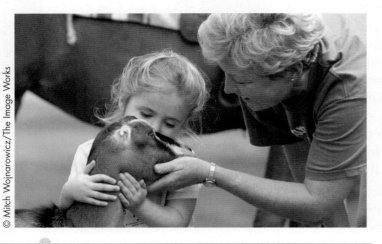

It is unlikely that this toddler has a vocabulary word for many of the animals seen for the first time in a petting zoo. Theories of what kind of animal this really is will be shaped with the help of her parents.

Concepts and Schemas Our dog concept is embedded in a rich, complex set of beliefs and expectations about dogs, animals, nature, and personal experience known as a schema, which we discussed in our chapter on memory. This type of schema not only shapes memory storage and retrieval of information relevant to dogs but it also allows us to predict new facts about them. If our schema includes "likes to play ball," we know that playing ball with a friend's new dog is likely to be successful.

Under what circumstances do people apply a schema to new information? Once again, comparisons to "typical" members of a category appear to play a role. People who are told a new fact about a very typical instance of a category are more willing to extend the new fact to all members of a category, whereas a new fact about an atypical category member is less likely to be widely applied (Rips, 1975). For example, if you learn about a new fruit disease found in apples (an exemplar fruit for many people), you are more likely to think other fruits are vulnerable than if you learn that the disease targets a less typical member of the fruit category, such as olives or avocados.

Concepts and the Brain Can we find brain activity that correlates with thinking about a particular concept or category of things? In our chapter on memory, we described imaging studies that identified different patterns of brain activity when people thought about animals or tools (Martin, Wiggs, Ungerleider, & Haxby, 1996). When asked to name animals, the participants showed activation in the visual cortex, suggesting that you need to think about what a zebra looks like to name it correctly. Naming tools, in contrast, was accompanied by activation in frontal and parietal lobe areas associated with movement, implying that it is helpful to think about what you do with a screwdriver when you are attempting to name it correctly.

This specialization in the brain for processing different types of categories is supported by observations of patients with brain damage. A small number of patients have been identified who have specific difficulties naming pictures of animals, although they can successfully name other living things (fruits and vegetables) and nonliving things (tools and furniture; Mahon & Caramazza, 2009). Not only do these patients have difficulty naming animals, but they also struggle to answer questions about animals, such as "Does a whale have legs?" Similar questions about nonliving things do not cause any difficulty.

In our chapters on learning and memory, we have emphasized the important role played by experience in building up our knowledge. Similarly, our discussion so far on concept formation has also stressed experience. However, it appears that this experience interacts with existing structures in the brain that help to organize our incoming information. For example, the vast majority of patients with specific deficits in processing categories perform differently from control participants in one domain—animals versus nonliving things (see ● Figure 10.2; Mahon & Caramazza, 2011). This observation might indicate that our brains are predisposed to make this distinction between the two categories. If forming concepts helps to organize appropriate responses, our ancestors' ability to form types of categories very quickly might have conferred a significant survival advantage.

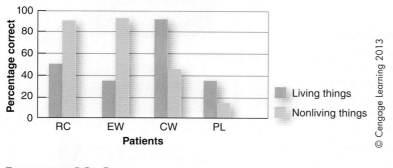

© Cengage Learning 2013

FIGURE 10.2

Some Categories Might Be Hard-Wired in the Brain. Some individuals with brain damage have difficulty processing certain types of semantic information. The pattern of these deficits varies depending on the location of the damage. For example, Patient C.W. can name living things better than nonliving things, while Patient R.C. names nonliving things better than living things. However, the categories that are affected in this way are relatively few: animals, fruits and vegetables, nonliving things, and members of our own species. This suggests that our brains have been shaped through natural selection to form certain types of categories. *Source: Adapted from Mahon & Caramazza (2011).*

How Do We Solve Problems?

One of the primary purposes of thinking is to guide behavior. In particular, thinking helps us deal with the many types of problems we face daily. Whether you are figuring out how to cope with a busy schedule, help a friend who is feeling blue, or complete your calculus homework, a **problem** exists whenever there is a difference between where you are and where you would like to be (Newell & Simon, 1972). For example, when you step on the bathroom scale after days of feasting and indulging around the holidays, the weight shown on the scale might be quite different from the weight you know to be ideal for your health and appearance; you now have a problem. In addition, referring to a situation as a "problem" implies that obstacles exist. Returning to a healthy weight can be challenging for many people.

Problem solving is defined as the use of information to meet a specific goal (Lovett, 2002). As shown in ● Figure 10.3, problem solving begins with recognizing a problem exists (you now weigh too much) followed by the development and use of strategies that solve it (you go on a diet) and the evaluation of the success of those strategies (you have either lost the holiday weight or not).

Effective problem solving puts thinking processes to work in a systematic way. Because good problem-solving skills are so important to psychological well-being, we will examine the process in detail using these four steps (Polya, 1957):

1. Understand the problem.
2. Make a plan.
3. Carry out the plan.
4. Look back.

FIGURE 10.3

Problem-Solving Flow Chart.
Effective problem solving can be achieved by following a system proposed by Polya (1957). If you reach step 4 and the problem is solved, you can exit the system. If the problem is not solved, you return to step 1 and try again.

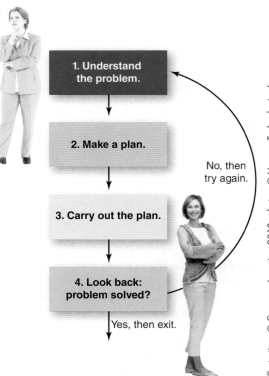

problem A situation in which a current state is separated from an ideal state by obstacles.

problem solving The use of information to meet a specific goal.

Illustration: © Cengage Learning 2013; photos: © Hemera Technologies/Photos.com; © Jacob Wackerhausen/Photos.com

Given the close relationship between cognitive psychology and computer science, we should not be too surprised to see this problem-solving process as a type of looping computer program. If we reach step 4 and our solution has taken us to where we want to go, we stop. If we reach step 4 and our problem still exists, we return to earlier steps to try another solution or to generate new solutions. This looping of steps, reminiscent of looping statements in computer programs, continues until the problem is resolved, as we might see when we learn by trial and error.

Understand the Problem

Although carefully formulating a problem takes time, this is generally time well spent. All relevant data should be collected, analyzed, and organized. What do we know? What information do we need that is missing? How does all this information fit together?

An important part of this step is to represent or frame the problem in a useful way (Lovett, 2002). What does it mean to represent a problem? In our chapter on memory, we talked about forming mental representations of experiences that subsequently can be manipulated by the mind. In the case of problem solving, the mental representations we form relate to how we see the problem. For example, you might represent your weight problem as the result of your holiday splurge or as the result of a broken bathroom scale. Your representation of the problem in these two different ways clearly leads to separate solutions, and in many cases, your representation will determine how successful you will be at solving the problem.

A big problem, like world hunger, seems insurmountable at first glance, but by breaking it into smaller, intermediate problems, much progress can be made toward an eventual solution.

Psychologists have identified a number of helpful suggestions for making the most useful representations of problems and for avoiding some common mistakes that frequently lead to failure. For example, big, long-term problems are easier to solve if they are broken down into components, or intermediate goals. Your primary goal in college is to obtain a degree, but it is useful to consider how you plan to meet intermediate goals such as completing your general education courses, your major courses, and electives.

The representation of a problem can be improved by recognizing any personal bias you might have toward particular solutions. In our weight example, your reluctance to cut back on treats might lead you to conclude that the bathroom scale is at fault instead of your own behavior. Your amount of self-efficacy, or belief in your abilities to succeed, might also influence the way you conceive a problem (Bandura, 2001). You might believe that your attempts to diet never work, so there is no point in even trying. By recognizing these biases, you can approach your problem with a more open and fair mind.

Careful formulation of a problem also helps us avoid distractions from irrelevant information. For example, consider the following (Sternberg, 1986):

> Fifteen percent of the people in Topeka have unlisted telephone numbers. You select 200 names at random from the Topeka phone book. How many of these people can be expected to have unlisted phone numbers?

FIGURE 10.4

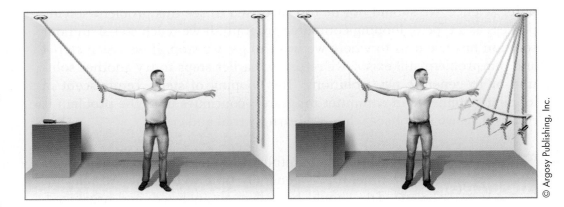

© Argosy Publishing, Inc.

Functional Fixedness.
Functional fixedness, or our tendency to think about a concept in only one way, can interfere with problem solving. In this classic problem, the person's task is to grab both ropes simultaneously. The only tool available is a screwdriver, which can be tied to one rope and used to make the rope swing within reach. If you only think about the screwdriver one way, as a tool used to turn screws, you cannot solve this problem.

If you immediately set to work computing relationships between 200 names and 15%, you are fairly typical. Most people assume the numbers in this problem are significant, when in fact, they are completely irrelevant. The correct answer is zero, because unlisted numbers by definition do not appear in public phone directories.

Another pitfall that interferes with a useful representation of a problem is known as **functional fixedness**, or a person's tendency to think about a concept in its most typical form and no others. For example, in the string problem illustrated in ● Figure 10.4, most people fail to see the potential of the screwdriver as a weight. Instead, they tend to think about the screwdriver in terms of its typical use as a tool to turn screws (Maier, 1931).

Make a Plan   Making a plan to solve your problem requires you to first generate possible solutions and then choose the best one to implement.

When aggressive children are asked how to solve social problems, such as persuading another child to share a desirable toy, they generate fewer solutions than more prosocial children. Eventually, most children will generate an aggressive solution (grab the doll and run), but perceiving additional options (trading a piece of candy for the toy, arguing that "sharing is nice") might make it less likely that the prosocial child will use the aggressive solution.

functional fixedness A possible barrier to successful problem solving in which a concept is considered only in its most typical form.

© Warren Goldswain/Shutterstock

Recipes are examples of algorithms. If you follow the recipe step-by-step, you should be able to produce the cookies you want every time.

Chocolate chip cookies

Ingredients
1/2 cup unsalted butter
3/4 cup packed dark brown sugar
3/4 cup sugar
2 large eggs
1 teaspoon pure vanilla extract
1 bag semisweet chocolate chips
2 1/4 cups all-purpose flour
3/4 teaspoon baking soda
1 teaspoon fine salt

Generating Solutions Generating possible solutions obviously involves some creativity, but most importantly, it requires time. People who spend the most time on a problem typically generate the most diverse solutions. Generating the most solutions raises your chances of finding one that will work.

A number of factors can interfere with finding appropriate solutions. You might be so upset about the numbers on the bathroom scale that you refuse to consider any efforts to lose weight. Some people dislike risk so intensely that they fail to consider a full range of alternative solutions. To escape the chaos and ambiguity involved with facing a problem, people can rush to find a solution, overlooking more appropriate courses of action. Judging and discarding solutions too early in the process also leads to failure. Generating impractical solutions requiring resources we don't have is not useful. An expensive stay at a weight reduction spa might work, but it probably doesn't fit a student budget. Understanding that we have these weaknesses in our approach to problem solving should help us avoid them in the future.

Some types of problems lend themselves to precise, step-by-step rules for reaching a particular solution, known as **algorithms**. Algorithms have the advantage of producing an accurate solution reliably. Let's assume you have a three-number combination lock on your bicycle, but you have forgotten the combination. You can start with using 001 for the first input, then 002, until you reach the correct solution for unlocking your bike. Algorithms are efficient when run by a computer, but their cost in time when used by the human brain can be very high. You could be very, very late to your next class by the time you unlock your bike.

The importance of generating multiple solutions to a problem is highlighted by what happens when people fail to do this. One of the consistent differences between violent and nonviolent youth is the ability of the nonviolent individuals to generate multiple solutions for common problems (Cook, Williams, Guerra, Kim, & Sadek, 2010). If violent youth perceive a problem, a violent solution is often the only one that occurs to them. Improving problem-solving abilities is a focus of many contemporary treatments for violent youth (Greene, 2010).

algorithm A precise, step-by-step set of rules that will reliably generate a solution to a problem.

Because of the time needed to use algorithms, we often substitute "rules of thumb," or shortcuts to problem solving, known as **heuristics**. Because heuristics do not go through the exhaustive evaluation of solutions required by algorithms, they are faster. Another advantage of heuristics is that they typically require far less information than algorithms do. However, unlike algorithms, heuristics do not guarantee a solution.

Not only can heuristics fail to find a solution, they can lead us in the wrong direction. Amos Tversky and Daniel Kahneman identified several heuristics that seem to produce faulty decisions (1973, 1974). The first type, the **availability heuristic**, is used when people predict that events that are easy to think about will be more frequent. For example, dramatic and memorable media reports make people think shark attacks are much more common than they really are. If we asked which is more common, being killed by a shark or by falling airplane parts, which would you choose (see ● Figure 10.5)? You actually have 30 times the risk of being killed by falling airplane parts than by sharks (Plous, 1993). In the aftermath of 9/11, with its vivid media imagery of airplanes crashing, more Americans chose to drive rather than fly. The extra traffic that resulted from fear of flying led to an estimated 9% increase in automobile fatalities, compared to typical rates, in the three months following the attacks (University of Michigan Transportation Research Institute, 2004).

As we mentioned earlier in this chapter, people often form prototypes, or average examples, when thinking about a category. These prototypes then "represent" the category when we are deciding which new examples might also fit the category. Tversky and Kahneman's second type of heuristic, the

FIGURE 10.5

The Availability Heuristic. Which is more likely? Being hit by an airplane part or being attacked by a shark? The availability heuristic leads us to believe that events that are easy to think about are more frequent. Because of the frequent media coverage of shark attacks, such as Rodney Fox's close call with a great white in Australia, people think shark attacks are common. You might be very surprised to learn that you are 30 times more likely to be killed by falling airplane parts, like this turbine engine that fell from the sky onto a car in Brazil, than by a shark (Plous, 1993).

heuristic A shortcut to problem solving; also known as a "rule of thumb."

availability heuristic A rule of thumb in which the frequency of an event's occurrence is predicted by the ease with which the event is brought to mind.

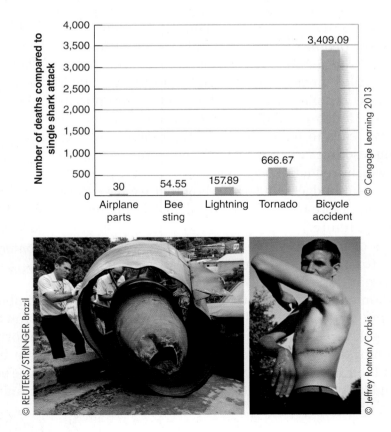

© Cengage Learning 2013

© REUTERS/STRINGER Brazil

© Jeffrey Rotman/Corbis

representativeness heuristic, leads people to estimate that stimuli which are similar to a prototype are more likely to fit the category than are stimuli which are different from the prototype. To illustrate this heuristic, Tversky and Kahneman asked participants whether Thomas, who is short, slim, and loves poetry, is more likely to be an Ivy League classics professor or a truck driver. Most people assumed that Thomas would be a classics professor, as his description is closer to that of a prototypical professor than a prototypical truck driver. However, this conclusion is statistically quite unlikely. There are very few Ivy League classics professors, and even if most fit Thomas's description, the numbers would still be quite low. In contrast, there are thousands of truck drivers in the United States. Even if a very small proportion of them shared Thomas's characteristics, the numbers would be large. Consequently, the odds are that Thomas is a truck driver.

Heuristics are most likely to fail when a correct solution requires a relatively sophisticated understanding of probability. Many sports fans (and coaches) believe that players have "streaks" or "hot hands," but statistical support for such a belief is lacking. Most people simply do not understand that chance sequences can look very systematic. If you toss a coin 20 times, there is a 25% chance that you will get five heads in a row. Records of free throw attempts by members of the Philadelphia 76ers showed that players had about a 75% chance of making a second shot, regardless of whether the first shot went in (Gilovich, Vallone, & Tversky, 1985). No evidence of any "streaks" was apparent, but the truth is not always easy to sell. When asked about the results of streak research, former Texas Tech basketball coach Bobby Knight commented, "There are so many variables involved in shooting a basketball that a paper like this really doesn't mean anything" (Gilovich, 1993, p. 17).

Although some of these examples make it sound like heuristics lead to bad decisions, it is likely that the ability to use heuristics to make quick, effective, and efficient decisions was a significant adaptive advantage for our ancestors (Haselton et al., 2009). An example of a very effective heuristic is the **recognition heuristic** (see ● Figure 10.6), which predicts that people will place a higher value on the more easily recognized alternative (Gigerenzer, 2008). In one study, American college students were asked which of two cities was larger. In making size decisions about German cities, such as Hamburg and Munich, students tended to choose the city they recognized most (Goldstein & Gigerenzer, 2002). They were correct about 73% of the time (Hamburg has about 1.8 million residents compared to Munich's 1.3 million). The recognition heuristic has been shown to beat other, more conventional means of selecting stocks. Companies whose names were recognized by the most people also had stocks that performed better than the overall markets (Reips & Orth, 2006).

Decide on a Solution Once we have generated a set of solutions, we now decide which one to try first. How is this decision reached?

The **affect heuristic** is particularly relevant to the way people make important choices (Slovic, Finucane, Peters, & MacGregor, 2002). According to this approach, we use our emotional responses to each choice to guide our decisions. Based on our past experience with similar choices, we

© National News & Pictures

The representativeness heuristic makes us believe that stimuli similar to a prototype are more likely than stimuli that are dissimilar. Corporal Katrina Hodge, a former Miss England referred to in the press as "Combat Barbie," may not fit your prototype for decorated wartime soldier. However, there are many more soldiers than beauty queens, so the likelihood that a beautiful woman is a soldier is actually higher than the likelihood that she is a beauty queen.

representativeness heuristic A rule of thumb in which stimuli similar to a prototype are believed to be more likely than stimuli that are dissimilar to a prototype.

recognition heuristic A rule of thumb in which a higher value is placed on the more easily recognized alternative.

affect heuristic A rule of thumb in which we choose between alternatives based on emotional or "gut" reactions to stimuli.

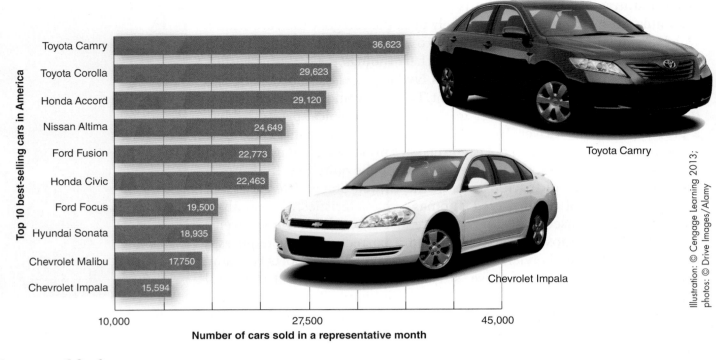

Top 10 best-selling cars in America

Car	Number
Toyota Camry	36,623
Toyota Corolla	29,623
Honda Accord	29,120
Nissan Altima	24,649
Ford Fusion	22,773
Honda Civic	22,463
Ford Focus	19,500
Hyundai Sonata	18,935
Chevrolet Malibu	17,750
Chevrolet Impala	15,594

10,000   27,500   45,000

Number of cars sold in a representative month

Toyota Camry

Chevrolet Impala

FIGURE 10.6

The Recognition Heuristic. The recognition heuristic predicts that if you think the Toyota Camry looks more familiar than the Chevy Impala, you will correctly judge the Toyota as having better sales in the United States (number 1 seller) than the Impala (number 10 seller).

literally develop a "gut" reaction to our options, pushing us toward alternatives we expect to produce desirable outcomes and away from alternatives we expect to produce undesirable outcomes. Our decision making is also affected by the need to avoid the complex emotion of regret (Connolly & Zeelenberg, 2002). By considering ways to explain and justify the reasons for their decisions in advance, people are able to live more comfortably with the decisions they have made.

An alternate approach to decision making, the utility theory, is also popular in economics. According to this theory, we compute the expected outcomes of our choices and select the best likely one. The expected outcome is computed by multiplying measures of the usefulness of the outcome by its expected probability. For example, to choose an elective course for your next term, you might consider a course that provides positive outcomes, like being interesting and satisfying a graduation requirement. At the same time, you wish to avoid negative outcomes, such as getting a poor grade or spending a lot of money on materials. If you weight each outcome according

Even though we might carefully weigh the pros and cons of buying one laptop over another, the affect heuristic suggests that we use our emotional or "gut" responses to make decisions, too.

to its probability and add up the results, you will end up with your own mini cost-benefit analysis.

You might find that applying utility theory is a useful exercise when faced with an important decision, like whether to accept a job offer with modest pay in your hometown or one with higher pay in another state. It is clear, however, that we rarely make decisions by solving equations. Even when utility is held constant, people show a preference for one solution or the other based on how the solutions are framed. People rate basketball players who are described as making 75% of their free throws higher than those who are described as missing 25% of the time, even though the math is identical in both cases. Medical treatments that are described as effective 80% of the time are viewed more positively than those that fail 20% of the time. Tversky and Kahneman (1987) illustrated the importance of framing in decision making using an Asian Disease Problem. Even though the outcome in both situations is that 400 people will die, the alternative framed using the word "saved" was preferred by 72%. In contrast, the alternative framed using "will die" was preferred by only 28% (see ● Figure 10.7). As we mentioned earlier, the way a problem is represented or framed can have a large effect on whether or not it will be solved. Framing can impact the choice of a solution through its interaction with a person's willingness to select risky solutions. When a problem is framed in terms of losses, as in the "will die" framing of the Asian Disease Problem, people are more comfortable choosing the risky solution. In contrast, when a problem is framed in terms of gains, as in the "saved" frame of the Asian Disease Problem, people generally become more cautious. If we have already "saved" 200 people, we don't want to risk saving fewer.

Good decision making is a skill that can be taught (Baron & Brown, 1991), and those who have received formal training in decision making make better real-world choices (Larrick, Nisbett, & Morgan, 1993). Psychologists have identified skills that seem quite powerful in their ability to predict decision-making competence, such as a good understanding of probability (Parker & Fischhoff, 2005). How well do these decision-making skills predict behavior in the real world? When participants' performance on the identified skills was compared with real-life decision making, such as having bought new clothes or shoes they never wore, strong correlations were observed between their abilities on the skills and the quality of their real-world decision making (Bruine de Bruin, Parker, & Fischhoff, 2007).

Carry Out the Plan   Your belief that you can implement a particular solution will determine whether you decide to pursue that solution or look for another solution. Once you have decided on a solution, it is time to try it out.

FIGURE 10.7

Framing Effects. Tversky and Kahneman's classic "Asian disease problem" asks people to choose one of two solutions to the following problem: "If a disease was coming to the U.S., and 600 people were expected to die, what should the president do?" Both solutions resulted in the deaths of the same number of people (200), but one was phrased positively (400 will be saved) and the other was phrased negatively (200 will die). When the question was framed negatively, people were much more likely to choose the riskier alternative.

Measures of decision-making skills, such as a person's understanding of probability, are negatively correlated with poor real-world decision making, such as the number of times you buy things you never use.

At this point, one of the most critical elements in successfully implementing your solution is planning. Solutions that might otherwise succeed can fail when people do not anticipate the time and resources needed for implementation. It is one thing to decide that you need to exercise more to lose your holiday weight, but without further planning, this solution might not work. How much exercise will you need? What activities should you do?

Experiencing Psychology

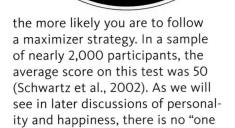

Are You a Maximizer or a Satisficer?

Many variables influence an individual's approach to decision making. Classic research suggests that some people are "maximizers," which means that their decision making is aimed at reaching the "best" outcome. Other people, the "satisficers," are more willing to choose outcomes that are merely acceptable (Simon, 1957). This instrument was designed to identify which type of style you use (Schwartz et al., 2002).

Add up all of your answers. Your score can range from a high of 91 to a low of 13. The higher your score, the more likely you are to follow a maximizer strategy. In a sample of nearly 2,000 participants, the average score on this test was 50 (Schwartz et al., 2002). As we will see in later discussions of personality and happiness, there is no "one

Indicate how much you agree with each of the following by circling the appropriate number:						
1. No matter how satisfied I am with my job, it's only right for me to be on the lookout for better opportunities.						
1 Completely Disagree	2	3	4	5	6	7 Completely Agree
2. When I am in the car listening to the radio, I often check other stations to see if something better is playing, even if I am relatively satisfied with what I'm listening to.						
1 Completely Disagree	2	3	4	5	6	7 Completely Agree
3. When I watch TV, I channel surf, often scanning through the available options even while attempting to watch one program.						
1 Completely Disagree	2	3	4	5	6	7 Completely Agree
4. I treat relationships like clothing: I expect to try a lot on before finding the perfect fit.						
1 Completely Disagree	2	3	4	5	6	7 Completely Agree
5. I often find it difficult to shop for a gift for a friend.						
1 Completely Disagree	2	3	4	5	6	7 Completely Agree
6. Renting videos is really difficult. I'm always struggling to pick the best one.						
1 Completely Disagree	2	3	4	5	6	7 Completely Agree

FIGURE 10.8

Gantt Charts. Good organization can help you carry out your plan successfully. A Gantt chart is a classic way to break plans into manageable pieces and schedule the time needed for each piece. The chart shows the starting and ending point for each part of the plan.

When? Where? Is your solution practical? If you are a couch potato, thinking you will implement your exercise solution by training for next month's marathon might not be realistic. If time management is not your strongest skill, you might consider using a Gantt chart, such as the one shown in ● Figure 10.8, to help you set aside the time you need for each part of your solution.

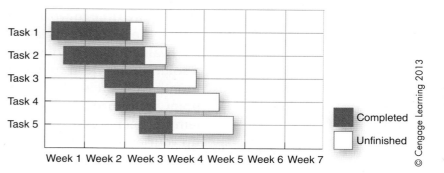

© Cengage Learning 2013

size fits all" approach to psychological well-being. We will caution you, however, that people with very high maximizer scores tend to be less happy and more prone to depression (Schwartz et al., 2002). If your score is very high, we are not suggesting that you lower your standards. However, you might review upcoming decisions with your score in mind to see if your perfectionist approach is giving you the best overall outcomes. ☯

© mangostock/Shutterstock

7. When shopping, I have a hard time finding clothing that I really love.						
1 Completely Disagree	2	3	4	5	6	7 Completely Agree

8. I'm a big fan of lists that attempt to rank things (the best movies, the best singers, the best athletes, the best novels, etc.).						
1 Completely Disagree	2	3	4	5	6	7 Completely Agree

9. I find that writing is very difficult, even if it's just writing a letter to a friend, because it's so hard to word things just right. I often do several drafts of even simple things.						
1 Completely Disagree	2	3	4	5	6	7 Completely Agree

10. I never settle for second best.						
1 Completely Disagree	2	3	4	5	6	7 Completely Agree

11. Whenever I'm faced with a choice, I try to imagine what all the other possibilities are, even ones that aren't present at the moment.						
1 Completely Disagree	2	3	4	5	6	7 Completely Agree

12. I often fantasize about living in ways that are quite different from my actual life.						
1 Completely Disagree	2	3	4	5	6	7 Completely Agree

13. No matter what I do, I have the highest standards for myself.						
1 Completely Disagree	2	3	4	5	6	7 Completely Agree

As you implement your solution, you will need to know if it is bringing you closer to your goal, which usually means that you need some type of measurement of success. In the example of our holiday weight gain, the logical way to assess progress is to get back on the scale at regular intervals. At the same time, solutions usually require time to work, and a failure to make immediate progress should not be the basis for discarding a promising solution.

Evaluation is an ongoing process, but it is especially important once a solution has been fully implemented. You might have predicted that six months of exercise should return you to your goal weight. At the six-month point, we return to the original problem. Does it still exist? If not, the problem has been solved, and we can move on to other issues (although keeping up your exercise program is always a good idea). If the problem still exists, we return to the make-a-plan step and try again. Maybe this time, we need to combine exercise with counting calories.

People have a reasonably effective "commonsense" approach to making decisions, but once again, careful psychological research can point out where we are vulnerable to poor decision making. If you find yourself unhappy with some of the outcomes of your previous decisions, following the steps in this section on future occasions might help you find better solutions.

The Biological Psychology of Decision Making

What processes can we observe in the brain during decision making? As we have seen on previous occasions in this textbook, observing the effects of brain damage on a behavior can illuminate the contributions of particular parts of the brain to that behavior. Damage to the orbitofrontal cortex, as in the case of the unfortunate Phineas Gage described in our chapter on biological psychology, reliably produces impulsivity and poor judgment. Patients with this type of damage often begin to gamble obsessively, turn their personal lives upside down, and become unemployable.

If damage to the orbitofrontal cortex reduces an individual's ability to make sound decisions, how exactly does the orbitofrontal cortex contribute to decision making under normal circumstances? The orbitofrontal cortex helps us think about the relative value of particular choices. Single neurons within the orbitofrontal cortex of rhesus monkeys appear to encode the relative values of choices between two different types of fruit juice (Padoa-Schioppa & Assad, 2006). Choices varied according to value (monkeys prefer grape to apple) and quantity (4 drops of juice were preferred to 1 drop of juice). A sample neuron might behave as follows. If the value chosen was low (1 drop of grape juice or 3 drops of apple juice), the activity of the neuron was also low. The same neuron may have responded with somewhat higher activity when the monkey chose 2 drops of grape or 6 drops of apple juice, a slightly higher value outcome. The greatest amount of activity would occur whenever the monkey chose a highly valued option, such as 3 drops of grape or 10 drops of apple juice (see ● Figure 10.9).

> Language is, in effect, the vehicle for concepts and ideas that belong to everyone, and it reinforces individual thinking with a vast system of collective concepts.
>
> —Jean Piaget

FIGURE 10.9

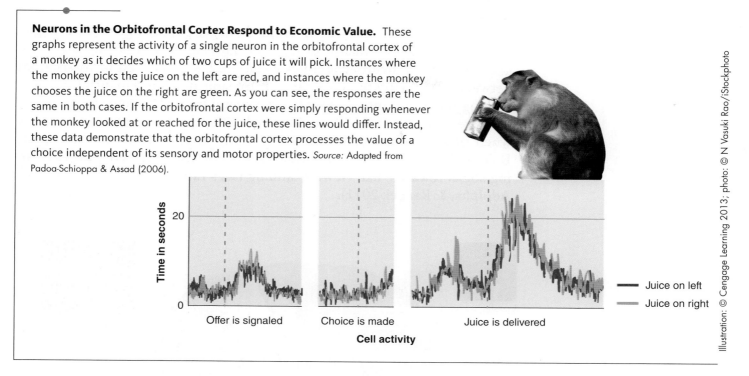

Neurons in the Orbitofrontal Cortex Respond to Economic Value. These graphs represent the activity of a single neuron in the orbitofrontal cortex of a monkey as it decides which of two cups of juice it will pick. Instances where the monkey picks the juice on the left are red, and instances where the monkey chooses the juice on the right are green. As you can see, the responses are the same in both cases. If the orbitofrontal cortex were simply responding whenever the monkey looked at or reached for the juice, these lines would differ. Instead, these data demonstrate that the orbitofrontal cortex processes the value of a choice independent of its sensory and motor properties. *Source:* Adapted from Padoa-Schioppa & Assad (2006).

Time in seconds — 20 — 0

Offer is signaled   Choice is made   Juice is delivered

Cell activity

— Juice on left
— Juice on right

Illustration: © Cengage Learning 2013; photo: © N Vasuki Rao/iStockphoto

The anterior cingulate cortex participates in a wide variety of cognitive functions, and you will be reading about this structure in several different chapters of this text. In general, activity in the anterior cingulate cortex fluctuates regularly during tasks that involve motivation, attention, and deciding among several alternatives. The role of the anterior cingulate cortex in decision making can be illustrated by observing its activity in individuals with obsessive-compulsive disorder (OCD), which we discuss further in our chapter on psychological disorders. Some individuals with this disorder hoard, or keep everything—newspapers, magazines, old clothes, and other items most people would consider trash. Apparently, simple decisions about what to keep and what to throw away become overwhelming in these cases. Abnormally low activity in the anterior cingulate cortex accompanies the hoarding behavior shown by these individuals (Saxena et al., 2004). This finding suggests that a minimum amount of activity in the anterior cingulate cortex is necessary for carrying out everyday decision making.

Damage to the amygdala, which normally helps us anticipate threat or danger, reduces a person's "loss aversion." Throughout this textbook, we observe many instances in which organisms give a priority to avoiding bad consequences over approaching good ones, as in our superior sensitivity to the bitter tastes that might signify poison over sweet tastes. In decision making, animals and people prioritize the avoidance of loss, even when a larger reward might be possible later. In this case, the adage "a bird in the hand is better than two in the bush" is actually supported by careful research. However, individuals with damage to the amygdala show typical responses to changes in the size of a reward, but are remarkably insensitive to the potential of loss (De Martino, Camerer, & Adolphs, 2010). The

© WR Publishing/Alamy

Making simple decisions about what to keep and what to throw away can be very difficult for some individuals. Hoarding behavior is correlated with unusually low levels of activity in the anterior cingulate cortex (Saxena et al., 2004).

amygdala appears to inhibit our making choices that are likely to have negative consequences.

Along with the analysis of brain damage, psychologists have begun to look for brain correlates of decision making using imaging technologies. The field of neuroeconomics is particularly interested in correlations between brain activity and financial decision making. Financial decision making might tap into a more basic, general reward system. As shown in ● Figure 10.10, brain structures involved with processing rewards are active when people expect to win or lose money (Breiter, Aharon, Kahneman, Dale, & Shizgal, 2001). These same areas are also involved with evaluating social rewards, like viewing smiling faces rather than angry faces (Lin, Adolphs, & Rangel, 2011).

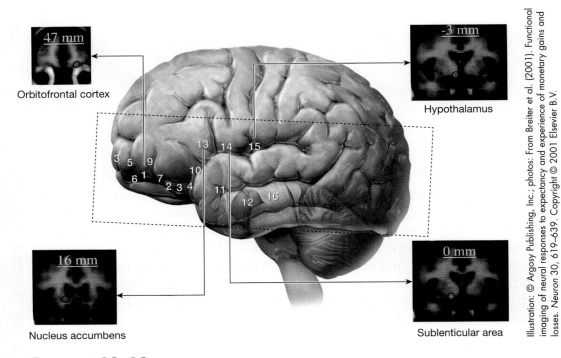

Illustration: © Argosy Publishing, Inc.; photos: From Breiter et al. (2001). Functional imaging of neural responses to expectancy and experience of monetary gains and losses. *Neuron* 30, 619–639. Copyright © 2001 Elsevier B.V.

FIGURE 10.10

The Same Areas of the Brain Respond to Reward and to the Expectation of Winning or Losing Money. Using functional magnetic resonance imaging (fMRI), researchers found similar activity in 16 different areas, including (1) the orbitofrontal cortex, (13) the nucleus accumbens, (14) the sublenticular area, and (15) the hypothalamus, when participants anticipated either winning or losing money. These same structures might participate in a general reward network in the brain.
Source: Adapted from Breiter et al. (2001).

Summary 10.1

Heuristics

Type of heuristic	Definition	Example
Availability © REUTERS/ STRINGER Brazil	Events that are easy to think about are more likely.	In spite of news and missing child reports that make kidnappings appear to be common, fewer than 100 children per year are abducted by strangers in the United States.
Representativeness © National News & Pictures	Stimuli that are similar to a prototype are more likely than stimuli that are different from the prototype.	A big, muscular student at Ohio State is probably a football player (in spite of the fact that fewer than 100 out of Ohio State's 60,000-plus students are on the football team).
Recognition © Drive Images/ Alamy	A more recognizable stimulus has a higher value.	Wine labeled as "California wine" is rated higher than the very same wine labeled "North Dakota wine."
Affect © Alex Segre/ Alamy	We use an emotional response ("gut feeling") to choose one alternative over another.	Choosing to eat dessert instead of staying on your diet.

Psychology *as a* Hub Science

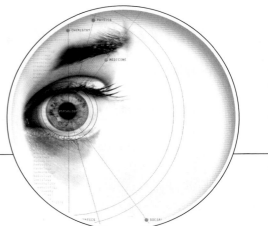

Influencing Decisions With Neuropolitics

Neuroeconomics is an area of research that explores correlations between financial decision making and brain activity, usually measured using fMRI (Camerer, 2008). Neuromarketing takes this process a step farther by attempting to modify persuasive messages to elicit the most positive response to everything from logos to package designs to advertisements in print or video. Movie trailers, as we saw at the beginning of this chapter, movie costumes, and even software interfaces are being modified in response to patterns of brain activa-

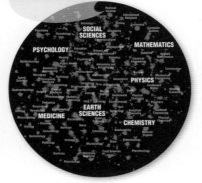

tion. Brain activation in response to one product can be compared directly to the response elicited by a competitor's product.

One of the first studies to explore the application of brain imaging to marketing compared participants' responses to Coke and Pepsi (McClure et al., 2004). When participants did not know which cola they were drinking, both brands (which are nearly identical in chemical composition) elicited an identical response in both brain activity and preference. When participants were told which brand they were drinking, however, both their subjective preferences and brain activity changed. People appeared to use their memories and other cognitive functions to react to a particular brand, resulting in a strong preference for one or the other (see ● Figure 10.11).

We are all accustomed to being bombarded with persuasive messages, which we explore further in a chapter on social psychology. Using technology to develop more engaging products and advertising is simply good business sense. This application

of technology gets especially interesting, however, when it is applied to politics. One provider's website features political services under the heading "Pennsylvania Avenue." The service promises to help develop political advertisements and even speeches that target "each and every demographic and political affiliation" (MindSign Neuromarketing, 2010). One has to wonder what Abraham Lincoln's Gettysburg Address might have become with this input.

The marketing of these services, however, implies that we know a great deal more about how the brain responds to effective and ineffective messages than we currently do. Suggestions that "brain activation" occurs during a "good" message and "deactivation" occurs during a "weak" message are hopelessly vague and possibly misleading. Brain activation is just as likely to occur when you hate a message as when you like it. However, this result does not rule out the possibility that technology will be able to provide precise feedback in the very near future. ⚙

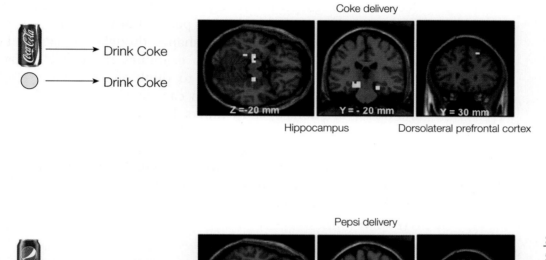

FIGURE 10.11

Coke or Pepsi? Groups of participants show equal preference for Coke and Pepsi in blind taste tests. When scanned during tasting, participants showed activity in the dorsolateral prefrontal cortex that corresponded with their personal preferences for the drinks. This activity probably correlates with their processing of the sensory experience. However, seeing an image of a Coke can prior to drinking a sample produced greater activity in the hippocampus as well as the dorsolateral prefrontal cortex relative to when the drink was preceded by a flash of yellow light (a control stimulus). This result suggests that memory of the Coke brand, processed by the hippocampus, is contributing to the response. In contrast, no such change in brain activity occurred when the Pepsi can was used as a signal. It appears that Pepsi is losing the advertising battle with Coke. *Source:* Adapted from McClure et al. (2004). Neural correlates of behavioral preference for culturally familiar drinks. *Neuron* 44(2), 379–387. Copyright © 2004 Elsevier B.V.

How Does Language Influence Behavior?

Language has been defined as a system for communicating thoughts and feelings using arbitrary signals, such as voice sounds, gestures, or written symbols. As we discussed previously, language provides us with powerful tools for organizing and manipulating our thinking, problem solving, and decision making. Although thoughts can be represented visually as well as verbally, language extends our thinking abilities to abstract concepts like truth and beauty that would be difficult to visualize. Above all, language connects us with others. Not only can we communicate with people in our immediate vicinity, but language spans time and distance, allowing us to share the thoughts of people living long ago and in very distant places. Because of language, the thoughts we record today might reach into the future to influence the thinking of people not yet born.

Language both reflects and shapes thought. Benjamin Lee Whorf's hypothesis of linguistic relativity examines the effect of having a rich vocabulary on a person's ability to think about a topic (Whorf, 1956). According to Whorf, a skier who can name and identify powder, slush, and other variations of snow thinks differently about the snow than does a person born and raised in a tropical climate. Whorf's theory predicts that the use of gender-free words such as *server* instead of *waiter* or *waitress* or *flight attendant* instead of *stewardess* would have a real impact on behavior. Researchers have shown that the use of *he* or *him* as opposed to *she, her,* or *they* in a sentence prompt leads children to produce stories about males (Hyde, 1984).

Left: © National Snow and Ice Data Center/Photo Researchers, Inc.; right: © iofoto/Shutterstock

language A system for communicating thoughts and feelings using arbitrary signals.

According to Benjamin Lee Whorf, a skier who knows what "early sintering" means is able to think differently about snow than a person who is unfamiliar with the term. Sintering occurs when snow crystals break down and fuse into larger crystals.

The Evolution of Human Language

To fix the emergence of human languages in time, we can assume that certain complex social behaviors would be difficult to conduct without the ability to speak. Elaborate tool use and cooperation would be much easier to accomplish using language. Because our version of the human species, *Homo sapiens*, appeared between 100,000 and 200,000 years ago, most anthropologists are convinced that human language existed at that time, if not earlier. A critical gene mutation in the *FOXP-2* gene occurring around 100,000 years ago possibly marked the start of modern language as we know it (Corballis, 2004). Regardless of timing, the enormous advantages of language to human culture and cooperation would ensure its continuity.

Much evidence points to Africa as the source of the first human languages. Some anthropologists suggest that it would be difficult for early humans to migrate successfully to other continents without the cooperation provided by language. Taking a very different approach, an analysis of over 500 contemporary languages has demonstrated that the number of speech sounds in a language decreases systematically with the culture's distance from Africa along migration routes (Atkinson, 2011). Many African languages feature over 100 speech sounds, compared to 45 in English and 13 in Hawaiian (see ● Figure 10.12).

Languages are living entities, under constant pressure to change. A report on endangered languages states that nearly half the world's spoken languages may soon be lost. Following assimilation into larger cultures, speakers might stop using their native languages or fail to transmit them to their children (Malone, 2006). With each language lost goes an opportunity for scientists to understand the unique local knowledge of a culture, along with the historical and cognitive implications of the language.

Language is intimately connected to cultural values. For example, the English language contains a large number of words that signify the passage of time. In contrast, the Hopi Native American tribes have only two words relevant to time, loosely translated as "sooner" and "later" (Le Lionnais, 1960). What does this difference tell you about the two cultures?

The Basic Building Blocks of Language

Language works like a set of building blocks, beginning with basic speech sounds (phonemes), which are combined into meaningful units (morphemes), and then combined in meaningful strings according to the rules of grammar.

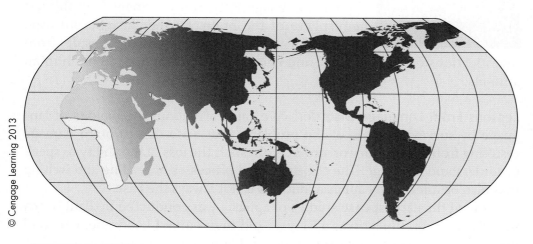

© Cengage Learning 2013

FIGURE 10.12

Phoneme Diversity Shows the Path of Language. The number of phonemes, or speech sounds, per language decreases with the distance of the culture using the language (indicated by shades of red) along migration routes from the western coast of Africa. Many African languages feature over 100 speech sounds, compared to 45 in English and 13 in Hawaiian. *Source:* Adapted from Atkinson, Q. D. (2011). Phonemic Diversity Supports a Serial Founder Effect Model of Language Expansion from Africa. *Science 332*(6027), 346–349. Copyright © 2011 The American Association for the Advancement of Science.

Click languages include sounds made by clicking the tongue, and might be among the very earliest forms of language used by human beings.

Human beings produce over 500 different **phonemes**, or speech sounds like the "c" in *cat*. The number and types of phonemes are limited only by the physical features of the human vocal apparatus. Not all phonemes appear in all languages. Individual world languages vary from as few as 11 phonemes to over 140 (Holt, Lotto, & Kluender, 1998). English features about 45 different phonemes, which we represent visually using the 26 letters of the alphabet either singly (*s*) or in combination (*sh*). Most written languages attempt to match visual symbols to phonemes, although many new readers of English struggle with the different pronunciations represented by the same letters, as in the *ough* in *through, rough, trough, slough,* or *thought*.

Phonemes are combined into **morphemes**, which are defined as the smallest components of speech that carry meaning. Most morphemes are words, but word prefixes (as in *pre*school and *sub*urban) and word endings (as in dog*s* and walk*ed*) also qualify as morphemes, as they change the meaning of the root word. English contains approximately 100,000 morphemes, which can be used to produce more than a million words. The average high school graduate in the United States knows approximately 80,000 words, but vocabulary continues to increase steadily with years of higher education (Miller & Gildea, 1987).

Morphemes are combined into phrases and sentences according to rules of grammar. For example, different languages have their own rules about the meaningful ordering of nouns and adjectives. In English, you can say "the brown dog," but not "the dog brown," while the reverse is true in Spanish. This type of natural grammar is usually learned early in childhood by interacting with other speakers, in contrast to the formal grammar instruction featured in schools.

The Biological Psychology of Language

As we discussed in our chapter on biological psychology, language is typically managed by the left hemisphere of the brain. Further insights into the localization of language processing result from investigations of brain damage and efforts to teach language to nonhuman animals.

Lessons From Language Disorders We can learn about the biology of language by surveying some of the problems that arise due to brain damage resulting from head injury or stroke. **Aphasia** is the loss of the ability to speak or understand language. The closely related processes of reading and writing may also be affected by aphasia, but this is not always the case.

One of the earliest case studies of aphasia was conducted by Paul Broca in 1861. Broca's subject was a 51-year-old man named Leborgne, who had been institutionalized for over 20 years. Leborgne came to be referred to

phoneme A speech sound.
morpheme The smallest component of speech that carries meaning.
aphasia The loss of the ability to speak or understand language.

as "Tan," because when questioned, "tan" was one of a very few syllables Leborgne could produce. Leborgne entered the hospital after several months of being unable to speak. He apparently understood much of what was said to him and retained his ability to answer numerical questions by raising an appropriate number of fingers on his left hand (Herrnstein & Boring, 1965). Leborgne died shortly after Broca's examination of him, and Broca performed an autopsy on his patient's brain. Broca found significant damage to the patient's left frontal lobe, possibly due to a stroke. The damaged area is now referred to as Broca's area, in honor of Paul Broca's discovery (see ● Figure 10.13).

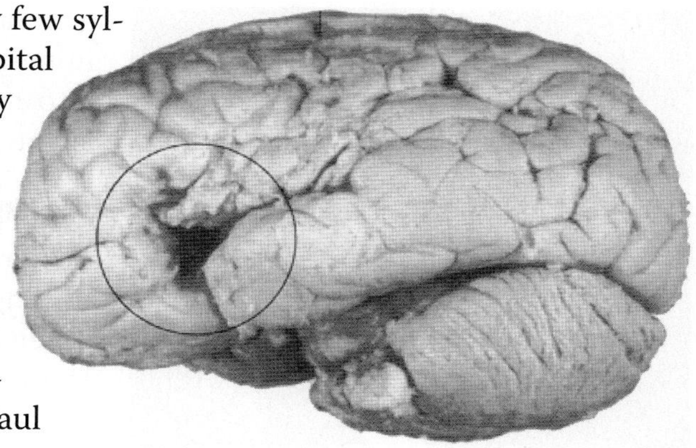

Today, Leborgne would be diagnosed with Broca's aphasia. This condition is characterized by difficulty producing speech. The speech that the patient manages to produce is slow and very effortful, but it generally makes sense. In some cases, patients retain the ability to curse, as in Tan's "Sacre nom de Dieu!" (In the name of God), which he uttered in frustration when unable to make himself understood with gestures. A contemporary patient with Broca's aphasia described his condition by saying, "Speech . . . can't say . . . talk, you see" (Gardner, 1976, p. 61).

About 13 years after Paul Broca presented his revolutionary work on patient Tan, Carl Wernicke published his observations on another type of language deficit (Wernicke, 1874). In honor of his contributions, this syndrome is now referred to as Wernicke's aphasia, and the affected area of the brain is known as Wernicke's area. Wernicke's area is located near the primary auditory cortex, located in the temporal lobe.

The symptoms of Wernicke's aphasia could hardly be more different than those of Broca's aphasia. Where Broca's aphasia affects the production of speech, Wernicke's aphasia affects its comprehension. In Broca's aphasia, speech is slow and laborious, but generally meaningful. In Wernicke's aphasia, the opposite is true. Speech is rapid and fluent, but virtually meaningless. A contemporary patient with Wernicke's aphasia said,

> Oh sure, go ahead, any old think you want. If I could I would. Oh, I'm taking the word the wrong way to say, all of the barbers here whenever they stop you it's going around and around, if you known what I mean, that is typing and tying for repucer, repuceration, well we were trying the best that we could while another time it was with the beds over the same thing. (Gardner, 1976, p. 68)

If you don't pay attention to the meaning, the speech of patients with Wernicke's aphasia sounds rather normal, if slightly fast. Grammar is

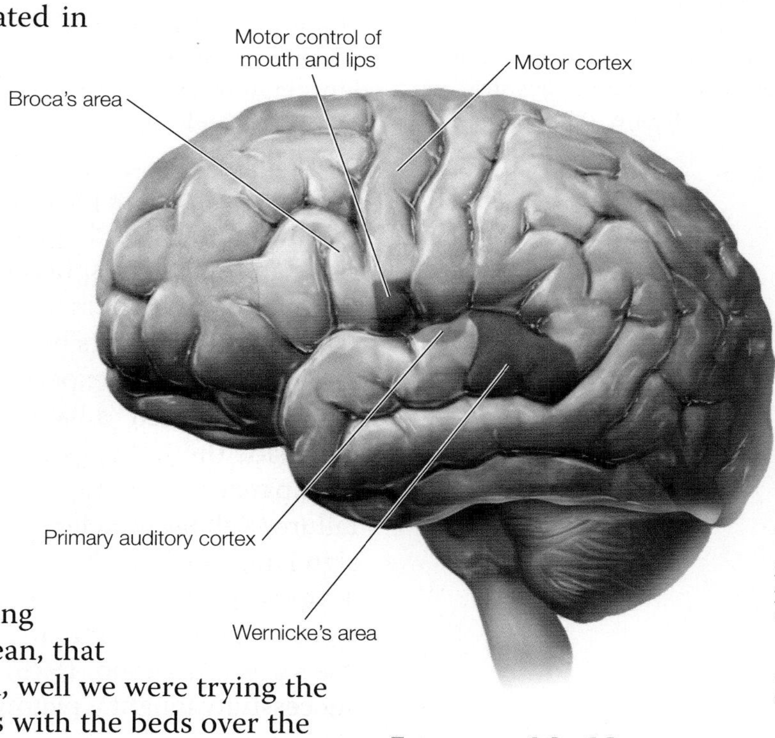

When Patient Tan died, Paul Broca performed an autopsy and discovered severe damage in a region now known as Broca's area, which is involved with the production of speech. From Corsi, P., ed., *The Enchanted Loom*, New York: Oxford University Press, 1991. Musée Dupuytren, Paris. Photo by Dr. Jean-Louis Signoret.

Motor control of mouth and lips

Motor cortex

Broca's area

Primary auditory cortex

Wernicke's area

© Argosy Publishing, Inc.

FIGURE 10.13

The Major Brain Structures Participating in Language.

© Dimension Films/Photofest

The soundtracks of horror films, adventure films, dramas, and war films use sound features that characterize animal distress calls to heighten viewer arousal. It is likely that these sounds add to the fear produced by the visual images (Blumstein, Davitian, & Kaye, 2010).

generally correct. On further examination, we find that meaningfulness is completely lacking. These patients are completely locked into a world without social connection, yet they do not seem overly aware of their circumstances nor are they in any apparent distress.

It is overly simplistic to assume that the brain has only two main language "centers," Broca's and Wernicke's areas. Instead, contemporary research has identified complex pathways for processing language that connect Broca's and Wernicke's areas to other cortical areas involved in cognition (Dronkers, Pinker, & Damasio, 2000).

Are Nonhuman Animals Capable of Real Language? Later in this chapter, we discuss several approaches to learning language. The evolutionary approach suggests that language results from some innate capacity shaped by natural selection. This view implies that we might be able to find precursors of human language in the behavior of other animals.

Many animals communicate with each other, often in complex ways. All forms of communication, however, do not involve the flexibility and creativity we see in language. We can identify three major patterns of animal communication (Dronkers et al., 2000). Some animals have a fairly inflexible group of calls used for functions such as signaling danger and identifying territories. A second set contains signals that communicate magnitude, as in the case of bee dances that indicate the location of food. Finally, other animals communicate through sequences of behavior, as in the case of birdsong. The extent to which these animal forms of communication may have acted as precursors for human language in an evolutionary sense is speculative at this point.

To search for animal precursors to human language capability, the most logical place to start is with the great apes. Chimpanzees, bonobos, and gorillas have a part of the brain analogous to the human Broca's area. In both humans and apes, this area shows a difference in size between the right and left hemispheres that might be correlated with language ability (Cantalupo & Hopkins, 2001).

Many researchers have attempted to teach human languages to apes. In one of the earliest experiments in ape language, Winthrop N. Kellogg and his wife "adopted" a baby chimpanzee named Gua in 1931. Gua was raised alongside the Kelloggs' son, Donald. However, due to the limitations of the chimpanzee vocal apparatus, efforts to teach Gua to talk were doomed to failure (Kellogg & Kellogg, 1933). In 1969, Allen and Beatrice Gardner taught sign language to a chimp named Washoe (Gardner & Gardner, 1969). After 4 years of work, Washoe had mastered 132 signs. The Gardners' efforts were followed by Francine Patterson, who trained a gorilla named Koko to use signs (Patterson, 1978). Sue Savage-Rumbaugh and her colleagues have successfully taught a pygmy chimpanzee named Kanzi to associate geometric symbols with words (Savage-Rumbaugh, Shanker, & Taylor, 1998). Even before his own training began, Kanzi appeared to have learned 10 symbols simply by observing his mother's training sessions. Kanzi also seems to be able to understand some human speech. When given 660 verbal requests, such as "Put the collar in the water," Kanzi behaved correctly 72% of the time.

In addition to investigations of language behavior in apes and monkeys, Irene Pepperberg makes a strong case for her African grey parrots (Pepperberg, 1990). While we often use the term "to parrot" to indicate mindless mimicry, Pepperberg argues that her parrots actually demonstrate complex cognitions related to language. Additional debate has also occurred regarding the language abilities of dolphins and whales, dogs, and prairie dogs (Bloom, 2004; Caldwell & Caldwell, 1976; Janik, Sayigh, & Wells, 2006; Lilly, 1967; Slobodchikoff, Perla, & Verdoli, 2009).

Whether efforts to communicate with animals demonstrate real language abilities is the subject of ongoing debate. Although children build vocabularies spontaneously, critics point out that ape language must be taught laboriously (Terrace, 1979). Word order does not seem to matter too much to apes, although it has an essential role in human language. Trainers of the apes might be making biased observations. When Washoe signed "water-bird" while observing a swan, the Gardners concluded that she was making a new, creative observation, but Washoe may simply have noticed a "bird" sitting on the "water."

Whether we believe that animals have true language or not, we are left with an enormous respect for both the complexity and intelligence of animal behavior and the remarkable sophistication of human language.

Sue Savage-Rumbaugh of Georgia State University taught Panbanisha, a bonobo chimpanzee, to point to symbols to produce grammatical sentences. Although apes can be taught to use symbols, linguists disagree about whether such behavior truly represents language.

How Do We Learn Language?

Historically, the topic of language learning has been characterized by the type of splintered, either/or, nature/nurture type of thinking that is rejected by an integrative view of psychology. Several psychological perspectives provide important input into the question of language learning, and no one perspective explains all our observations of the process.

Learning language proceeds differently than do many types of learning. No specific instruction is needed, as it is for the related skills of reading and writing. A typical child exposed to language will learn language. The type and extent of exposure, however, is very important in determining how well an individual child will learn. Social interaction is an essential component of this process, and two-way interaction in the form of conversation produces maximum results. Conversing with children produces greater language competence than simply reading to them (Zimmerman et al., 2009). Even when exposure is one-way, as when a child is listening to a speaker, more language learning will occur when a real person is speaking with the child face-to-face than when a child is listening to the same speaker on television (Kuhl, 2007; Meltzoff, Kuhl, Movellan, & Sejnowski, 2009). This finding implies that parents using passive television or computer videos to enhance their child's language learning are likely to be very disappointed in the outcomes.

Irene Pepperberg's African gray parrots have demonstrated sophisticated language-like behaviors. For example, when shown an object, Alex could correctly state its color, shape, and material. After only 6 repetitions, he correctly referred to himself as "gray" when asked his color.

Behaviorists, including B. F. Skinner, argued that children learn language through operant conditioning, which we described in our chapter on learning (Skinner, 1970). Using a word correctly is reinforced when it produces a desired outcome. This approach might explain your success in learning key terms for your psychology exams, but there is much more to learning language than memorizing vocabulary words and their definitions. The types of mechanisms proposed by the behaviorists simply do not seem to match up well with observations of children in the process of learning language. Parents responding to children's sentences are much more likely to attend to the meaning of a sentence than to its grammatical structure. When the child says, "We goed to the store today," the parent is likely to respond, "Oh no, that's not right. We went to the store yesterday." The parent is modeling the correct use of the past tense (*went* instead of *goed*), but shows much more interest in shaping truthfulness.

Several observations, including the speed and ease with which very young infants can learn complicated language tasks, have led to the assumption by many, including linguists Noam Chomsky (1957) and Steven Pinker (1994), that human beings have an inborn capacity for learning language. No human culture on Earth exists without language. Language acquisition follows a common course, regardless of the native language being learned. Whether a child is exposed to English or Cantonese, similar language structures appear at just about the same point in development. For example, children all over the world go through a stage in which they overapply language rules. Instead of saying, "She went to the store," the child will say "She goed to the store." Eventually, the older child will switch to the correct forms, long before any formal instruction. In addition, human brain structure is correlated with language. As we discussed in our chapter on biological psychology, most people process language in the left hemisphere of the brain. Damage to these left hemisphere language areas due to stroke or other brain injury produces specific types of language deficits.

Assuming an inborn capacity for learning language further implies that language has a basis in our genes. Several genetic conditions appear to selectively impact individuals' language learning abilities. For several generations, members of a family known as the KE family have been studied extensively by researchers interested in the genetics of language. Many, but not all, KE family members have very severe difficulties with the production of language accompanied by a mutation in a single gene (Lai, Fisher, Hurst, Vargha-Khadem, & Monaco, 2001). The KE family mutation occurred in the *FOXP-2* gene, the same gene suspected of mutating about 100,000 years ago, making human language possible in the first place (see ● Figure 10.14).

Another condition affecting language, Williams syndrome, results from a rare genetic mutation and produces a moderate level of intellectual disability. We discuss intellectual disability later in this chapter. In most cases, individuals with intellectual disability experience difficulties with language, but individuals with Williams syndrome are fluent speakers with very large

Two-way interaction in the form of conversation produces the fastest language learning, reinforcing the very social nature of this behavior.

© Flashon Studio/Shutterstock

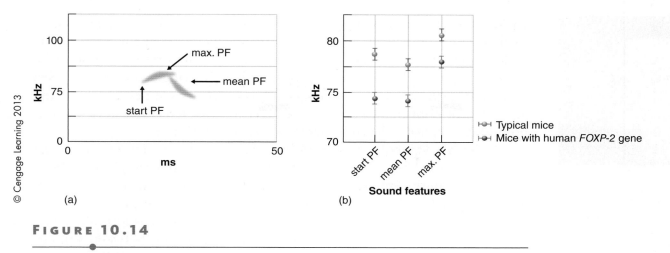

(a)

(b)

FIGURE 10.14

***FOXP-2* and Mice With Lower Voices.** Although it is an inaccurate exaggeration to call the *FOXP-2* gene "the language gene," research evidence suggests that this gene plays an important role in vocalization. When the human version of the *FOXP-2* gene is inserted into mice, they do not start talking of course, but they do show differences compared to typical mice in their ultrasonic vocalizations (above the range of human hearing). In (a), a typical ultrasonic recording is shown with the starting peak frequency (PF), the maximum PF, and the average or mean PF. In (b), you can see that typical mice are higher in all three aspects as well as in the slope of the sound recording compared to the mice with the human FOXP-2 gene. *Source:* Adapted from Enard et al. (2009).

vocabularies. Williams syndrome and another genetic disorder, Down syndrome, produce a similar level of intellectual disability, but language use in these two groups is quite different (Bellugi, Wang, & Jernigan, 1994). When asked to name all the animals he knew, a child with Down syndrome replied, "Horsie, dog, ice cream." A child of the same age and IQ with Williams syndrome answered, "Weasel, newt, salamander, ibex, yak."

Although a person's ability to use language is usually consistent with his or her intelligence, we have just seen that this is not the case in Williams syndrome. On the other end of the intelligence scale, it is not unusual for a person of normal to high intelligence to have significant difficulties learning language (Tallal, Ross, & Curtiss, 1989). Very accomplished people who have been diagnosed with verbal learning disabilities or suspected of having learning disabilities include such notables as Albert Einstein, Sir Winston Churchill, Leonardo da Vinci, Thomas Edison, and even psychology's own William James.

Variations in Language Processing

Language learning and use can vary widely, and these variations provide us with a richer understanding of how human beings can communicate. We examine three variations of particular interest here. Why do some children have such a hard time learning to read? What happens when people learn more than one language? How does American Sign Language, which uses movement instead of sound, compare with more conventional spoken languages?

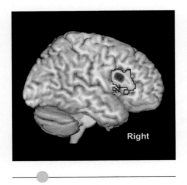

Activity in the right prefrontal cortex during a rhyming task, which requires the ability to discriminate among phonemes, accurately predicted gains in reading skill over the next few years by children with dyslexia. *Source:* From Hoeft et al., "Neural systems predicting long-term outcome in dyslexia," in *Proceedings of the National Academy of Sciences,* January 4, 2011, vol.108, no.1, 361–366, Fig. 2.

Dyslexia Individuals with dyslexia experience difficulties in learning to read in spite of typical intelligence and exposure to adequate teaching methods (Shaywitz, Morris, & Shaywitz, 2008). The first description of a dyslexic patient, Percy F., was published by W. Pringle Morgan in 1896 (Shaywitz, 1996). Percy F. was described by Morgan as "quick at games, and in no way inferior to others of his age. His great difficulty has been—and is now—his inability to learn to read" (Shaywitz, 1996, p. 98).

Dyslexia is strongly influenced by genetic factors, which in turn result in differences in the symmetry of the cerebral hemispheres (Beaton, 1997; Gilger, Hanebuth, Smith, & Pennington, 1996). People with dyslexia are more likely to be left-handed or ambidextrous than people without dyslexia (Eglinton & Annett, 1994). In addition to these differences in brain structure, people with dyslexia have difficulty distinguishing between similar-sounding phonemes, or basic speech sounds, such as *m* or *n* (Merzenich et al., 1996). Compared to typical readers, their brains show different patterns of activation during rhyming tasks, which are based on the sound of words (Frith & Frith, 1996).

Because reading most languages depends on matching phonemes to the letters that represent them, people with dyslexia show evidence of using a "workaround" when they read. Brain activity has been recorded while university students with and without dyslexia were reading (Shaywitz et al., 1998). Compared to typical readers, readers with dyslexia showed less

Carol Greider, a Nobel Prize–winning professor of molecular biology and genetics, struggled with dyslexia from elementary school through graduate school. Although the condition was challenging, Greider states, "Perhaps my ability to pull more information out of context and to put together different ideas may have been affected by what I learned to do from dyslexia."

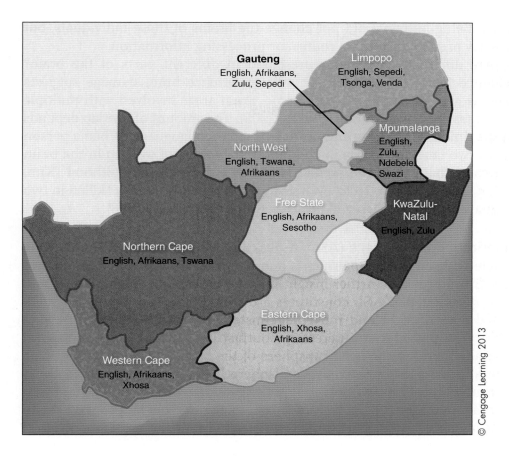

Gauteng
English, Afrikaans, Zulu, Sepedi

Limpopo
English, Sepedi, Tsonga, Venda

Mpumalanga
English, Zulu, Ndebele, Swazi

North West
English, Tswana, Afrikaans

Free State
English, Afrikaans, Sesotho

KwaZulu-Natal
English, Zulu

Northern Cape
English, Afrikaans, Tswana

Eastern Cape
English, Xhosa, Afrikaans

Western Cape
English, Afrikaans, Xhosa

© Cengage Learning 2013

FIGURE 10.15

Many People Speak Multiple Languages. Eleven different languages are recognized in South Africa, and each province recognizes at least two different languages. The most commonly spoken home language (23.8%) is Zulu. Many South Africans speak two or more languages.

activity in a pathway connecting visual cortex in the occipital lobe to Wernicke's area in the temporal lobe. Instead, the readers with dyslexia showed greater activation of Broca's area, which participates in speech production.

Multilingualism More than half the world's population is **bilingual**, or proficient in at least two languages (Chertkow et al., 2010; Kavé, Eyal, Shorek, & Cohen-Mansfield, 2008) (see ● Figure 10.15). In comparison to the learning of a single language, learning two or more languages takes time. Children learning two languages simultaneously can master approximately the same number of vocabulary items as children learning a single language, but this total must be divided between the two languages. A typical 10-year-old knows about 40,000 words. For the single-language learner, these 40,000 words are obviously all in the same language. For the bilingual learner, the 40,000 words will be divided between the two languages (Pearson, Fernandez, & Oller, 1993; Umbel, Pearson, Fernandez, & Oller, 1992). This characteristic may produce the appearance of vocabulary delay in the bilingual learner in childhood. By adulthood, any remaining discrepancies in vocabulary size are likely to be small and insignificant. Any disadvantages in total vocabulary might be offset by other advantages. Older adults who were bilingual seemed to experience a delayed onset of symptoms of Alzheimer's disease compared to monolingual older adults (Craik, Bialystock, & Freedman, 2011; Chertkow et al.,

Relying on Broca's area while reading is like reading out loud to yourself, which will slow down reading speed. If you have ever read a bedtime story to a child, you are aware of how much slower reading out loud is compared to reading silently.

bilingual Proficient in two languages.

2010). Being bilingual did not change the brains of these individuals, but possibly provided alternate routes for processing information.

Are different languages represented in different parts of the brain? Evidence from bilingual people who experience brain damage suggests that the answer to this question is no. Brain areas involved with multiple languages appear to overlap (Pearce, 2005). The amount of overlap depends on the timing of learning and proficiency in each language. When a person learns two languages early in childhood, the extent of overlap in the brain is greater than when the second language is learned in adulthood (Kim, Relkin, Lee, & Hirsch, 1998). When a person is nearly equally skilled in two languages, more overlap will occur as well (Perani et al., 1998).

American Sign Language (ASL) American Sign Language (ASL), used by people with hearing impairments and people who wish to communicate with them, provides further insight into the processing of language. There is no question that ASL constitutes a distinct language, although it uses spatial cues of sight and movement instead of sound (Klima & Bellugi, 1979). ASL provides an interesting contrast between language functions, generally found in the left hemisphere of the brain, and spatial functions, generally managed by the right hemisphere.

Both clinical observation and imaging studies support the notion that the brain manages ASL in the same way it manages other languages, in spite of its obvious spatial characteristics. Prior to brain surgery, surgeons first identify which functions are processed by each hemisphere in an individual patient's brain by anesthetizing one hemisphere at a time. When the left hemisphere of an English-speaking patient proficient in ASL was anesthetized, she made errors in both spoken English and ASL signing. Neither anesthetizing the right hemisphere nor the subsequent surgery on her right hemisphere produced deficits in either language (Damasio, Bellugi, Damasio, Poizner, & Gilder, 1986). In spite of the spatial nature of ASL, this case suggests that a language is still a language, and the left hemisphere is the likely place for that language to be processed. These clinical observations have been confirmed by imaging studies. The same areas of the brain are activated during language tasks regardless of whether the subject uses spoken English or ASL (Neville et al., 1998).

American Sign Language (ASL) is a distinct language based on sight and movement rather than sound.

Summary 10.2

Aphasia

Type of aphasia	Location of damage	Symptoms
Broca's aphasia	Broca's area (left frontal lobe in most people)	Slow, effortful speaking combined with good comprehension
Wernicke's aphasia	Wernicke's area (left temporal lobe in most people)	Fluent, meaningless speech without comprehension

What Is Intelligence?

Intelligence refers to an individual's "ability to understand complex ideas, to adapt effectively to the environment, to learn from experience, to engage in various forms of reasoning, and to overcome obstacles" (Neisser et al., 1996, p. 77).

Assessing Intelligence

The assessment, or testing, of intelligence represents an attempt to assign a number to an individual's abilities, allowing him or her to be compared with others.

Formal intelligence testing began in 1904, when Alfred Binet was instructed by the French government to devise an objective means of identifying schoolchildren who needed additional help to succeed. Binet and his colleague, Théodore Simon, assumed that relatively bright children behaved cognitively like older children, while less intelligent children would behave like younger children. They devised items that they believed would indicate children's "mental age," relative to their peers. In this system, children who successfully completed an item at an earlier age than most of their peers would have a higher mental age, while those who were not able to complete an item until they were older would have a lower mental age.

Stanford University professor Lewis Terman adapted Binet's test for use in the United States and named his revised version the Stanford-Binet Intelligence Scales (Terman, 1916). Terman began using the **intelligence quotient (IQ)**, which is computed by dividing children's mental age by their chronological age and, for convenience, multiplying by 100. For example,

Along with Théodore Simon, Alfred Binet devised a test aimed at identifying schoolchildren who were intellectually disabled. Binet and Simon's test laid the groundwork for today's intelligence testing.

intelligence The ability to understand complex ideas, adapt effectively to the environment, learn from experience, engage in reasoning, and overcome obstacles.

intelligence quotient (IQ) A measure of individual intelligence relative to a statistically normal curve.

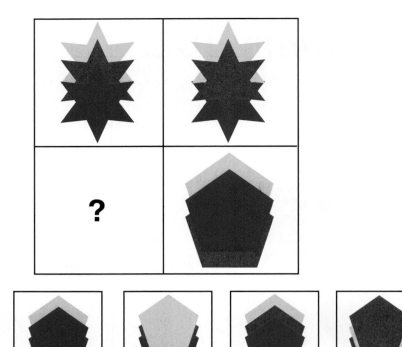

FIGURE 10.16

IQ Testing. One of the most frequently used IQ tests today is the WISC-IV, which is used on children between the ages of 7 and 16. In addition to items that assess vocabulary and verbal reasoning, the test includes items for working memory, processing speed, and perceptual reasoning. To complete this matrix reasoning item, children must select the one out of five options that fits best. *Source:* Adapted from Wechsler Intelligence Scale for Children, Fourth Edition (WISC-IV). Copyright © 2003 NCS Pearson, Inc. Reproduced with permission. All rights reserved. "Wechsler Intelligence Scale for Children" and "WISC" are trademarks, in the U.S. and/or other countries, of Pearson Education, Inc. or its affiliate(s).

a bright child with a mental age of 15 and a chronological age of 12 would have an IQ of 125 (15/12 = 1.25; 1.25 = 100 = 125).

The most frequently used intelligence tests today include the Stanford-Binet Intelligence Scales and the Wechsler Adult Intelligence Scale (WAIS). A sample item from the children's version of the Wechsler test is shown in ● Figure 10.16. These tests no longer use the concept of mental age. Instead, contemporary tests place individual performance on a statistically normal curve, described in our chapter on research methods. Contemporary tests also incorporate new features designed to more accurately assess people of extremely low or high intellect, the elderly, and individuals with language difficulties.

As we discuss in our chapters on research methods and personality, constructing a good test can be difficult. A good test must demonstrate both reliability and validity. In short, the test should provide consistent results that correlate with other measures of the same construct. Although no test is perfect, most IQ tests show relatively good reliability and validity (Kaplan & Saccuzzo, 2001). It is important to keep in mind, however, that the intent of IQ tests is to predict school performance as opposed to the complex construct of "intelligence" described at the beginning of this section. Consequently, it is not surprising to find that correlations between IQ and performance in mathematics and verbal skills, which are essential for success in contemporary education, are relatively high, but are much lower for performance in art and design (Deary, Strand, Smith, & Fernandes, 2007).

We do not identify people as "athletically disabled" or "musically disabled" for purposes of special education, but clearly, such people exist. Our views of intellectual disability are intimately connected to the capabilities valued by our systems of education.

General and Specific Abilities

In discussions of intelligence, some psychologists focus on an individual's overall abilities, while others focus on particular types of abilities.

Using the statistical technique of factor analysis, which he helped develop, Charles Spearman distinguished between a **general intelligence** (**g**) factor and specific factors that apply to single tasks (Spearman, 1904). For example, Spearman argued that *g* was important for learning Latin, but not for distinguishing between two musical tones.

General intelligence can be divided into **fluid intelligence** and **crystallized intelligence** (Cattell, 1971). Fluid intelligence refers to the ability to think logically without needing previously learned knowledge, like seeing patterns in a visual stimulus, while crystallized intelligence requires specific, learned knowledge, like vocabulary or the multiplication tables. A person needs pattern recognition, a type of fluid intelligence, to play chess or Sudoku well, but understanding the rules of the game requires crystallized intelligence. Fluid intelligence peaks in young adulthood and then declines (although it declines slowly in individuals who continue to actively use fluid intelligence), while crystallized intelligence remains more stable through adulthood (see ● Figure 10.17).

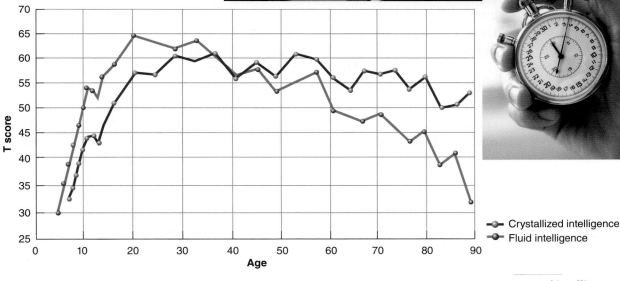

- Crystallized intelligence
- Fluid intelligence

Illustration: © Cengage Learning 2013; photos: (top) © Carlo Allegri/Getty Images for LAPA; (bottom) © acilo/iStockphoto

FIGURE 10.17

Fluid and Crystallized Intelligence Across the Lifespan. Fluid intelligence, like reaction time, includes abilities that do not require acquired knowledge. Fluid intelligence peaks in young adulthood and then gradually declines over the remaining lifespan. In contrast, crystallized intelligence, which does require acquired knowledge, remains fairly stable throughout adulthood. Composer John Williams has contributed memorable soundtracks (*Jaws, Star Wars*, the Harry Potter films) in a career spanning more than six decades. *Source:* Adapted from Li et al. (2004).

general intelligence (*g*) A measure of an individual's overall intelligence as opposed to specific abilities.

fluid intelligence The ability to think logically without the need to use learned knowledge.

crystallized intelligence The ability to think logically using specific learned knowledge.

Individuals with Williams syndrome provide examples of how general intellect can diverge from other abilities and talents. Gloria Lenhoff, shown here with her parents, has a tested IQ of 55, but has performed as a lyric soprano and has played her accordion with Aerosmith.

General intelligence theories do not provide us a way to explain splinter skills, or islands of ability that occur against an overall background of lower functioning. Gloria Lenhoff, who has Williams syndrome and an IQ of about 55, cannot make change for a dollar or subtract 3 from 5, but has performed as a lyric soprano with the San Diego Master Chorale and with Aerosmith (Maher, 2001). Leslie Lemke, who is both intellectually disabled and blind, listened one time to Tchaikovsky's Piano Concerto No. 1. Hours later, Lemke sat down at the piano, which he had never studied, and played the entire composition without error (Treffert & Wallace, 2002). Professional musicians are unlikely to be able to duplicate this feat.

The separability of "intelligences" in these exceptional cases suggests that intelligence is a combination of factors rather than one single thing, like the processing speed of your computer. Howard Gardner interprets these and similar findings to mean that we have multiple, independent types of intelligence (Gardner, 1983, 1999). Gardner proposed no less than eight different types of intelligence. Robert Sternberg proposed a triarchic theory of intelligence, in which a combination of analytical, creative, and practical abilities allows people to achieve success (Sternberg, 1985; Sternberg & Salter, 1982). He argues that it is possible to be gifted in one aspect without being gifted in others.

Both general and specific approaches to intelligence can be useful. We can assume that people have separate strengths and abilities, like those outlined by Gardner and Sternberg. Among these diverse abilities, purely cognitive abilities, such as verbal, mathematical, spatial, and logical skills, show strong positive correlations with one another, supporting an argument for general intelligence, or *g*. At the same time, abilities involving sensory, motor, and personality factors are much less likely to show strong correlations, supporting an argument for multiple intelligences in these domains (Visser, Ashton, & Vernon, 2006).

Emotional and Social Intelligence

Traditional views of intelligence focused on education-related skills, but emotional and social skills are important to successful adaptation, too. Building on arguments in favor of multiple intelligences, and in recognition that previous work on intelligence seemed to neglect social skills, models of emotional and social intelligence were proposed (Goleman, 2006; Mayer & Salovey, 1993). Social and emotional intelligence allows people to manage emotions and reason about the mental states of others.

Clinical cases involving individuals with brain damage, psychological disorders, and intellectual disability provide evidence for social and emotional abilities that are separate from cognitive abilities. In our chapter on motivation and emotion, we discussed roles for the prefrontal cortex, amygdala, and insula in emotion. Patients with damage to connections between these structures performed very poorly on a standard measure of emotional and social intelligence, in spite of their having normal IQ and no evidence of other psychological disorders (Bar-On, Tranel, Denburg, & Bechara, 2003). Individuals with autism spectrum disorder often display cognitive abilities that are superior to their social abilities. Individuals with Down syndrome, which produces moderate intellectual disability, display relatively strong social skills (Fidler, Most, Booth-LaForce, & Kelly, 2008).

Some psychologists view social and emotional intelligence as different from "school-based" intelligence and equally if not more important for success. In a classic study, children were given a single marshmallow with instructions to not eat it when an experimenter left the room. They were told that if they did not eat it, they would receive two marshmallows when the experimenter returned. When the children were tracked down 12 years later, the two-thirds who had been able to delay gratification (they didn't eat the marshmallow) were less stressed and more confident than the one-third who had not been able to delay gratification (Mischel, Ebbesen, & Raskoff Zeiss, 1972).

Biological Influences on Intelligence

Because the mind is the outcome of the brain, investigations of the brain have been undertaken in search of associations between its structure and activity and an individual's intelligence. For the purposes of this type of research, standardized tests are used as the measure of intelligence.

Brain Structure, Brain Activity, and Intelligence Brain imaging studies demonstrate that standard measures of intelligence positively correlate with overall brain volume (Deary, Penke, & Johnson, 2010; McDaniel, 2000; Pol et al., 2006). More precisely, intelligence measures are positively correlated with the thickness of the cerebral cortex, particularly in the prefrontal cortex and temporal lobes (Deary et al., 2010). Because intelligence is such a broad concept, it is unlikely that we have "intelligence centers" in the brain. Instead, scientists have suggested that intelligent brains enjoy quick, efficient communication of information from one area to another along axon pathways. This possibility has led to studies investigating white matter health, which also shows positive correlations with measures of intelligence (Achard, Salvador, Whitcher, Suckling, & Bullmore, 2006). Studies of people with brain damage indicate that fluid intelligence, but not crystallized intelligence, is negatively affected by damage to the frontal lobes. These observations are complemented by studies showing high levels of frontal lobe activity during diverse tests believed to demonstrate fluid intelligence (Gray & Thompson, 2004).

Different brain architectures may underlie intelligence in men and women (Haier, Jung, Yeo, Head, & Alkire, 2005). In men, IQ was most strongly correlated with the amount of gray matter located in both frontal lobes and the left parietal lobe. In women, IQ was highly correlated with the volume of gray matter in the right frontal lobe and Broca's area and with the volume of white matter throughout the brain. According to these researchers, general intelligence was more likely linked to gray matter in men, but white matter in women. These structural differences help to explain why males and females differ in brain size and structure, but do not differ significantly in measures of general intelligence (Deary, et al., 2010). Apparently, males and females follow different paths to intelligent behavior, which reinforces the complexity of this topic.

Measures of brain activity during tasks requiring intelligence have also demonstrated individual differences. The brains of people with high scores on standard intelligence measures do not have to work as hard as the brains of people with lower scores to solve the same problem (Haier et al., 1992). This research supports the view of intelligence as processing information quickly and efficiently (see ● Figure 10.18).

Intelligence also seems to be related to the timing of brain development. As children approach puberty, the gray matter of the brain experiences a period of growth that slows down again later in adolescence. Children with average IQ scores showed a peak thickening of cortical gray matter around the age of 8, but children with superior IQ scores experienced a much later peak thickening at around age 13 (Shaw et al., 2006).

Connecting *to* Research

What Is Collective Intelligence?

We have been discussing the concept of a general intelligence that characterizes an individual, but is it possible for the same sort of measure to describe the abilities of groups of people? Such a measure might be quite useful to organizations using teams.

The Question: *Do groups of people have a "collective intelligence" that predicts their performance? If so, what factors contribute to a group's collective intelligence?*

METHODS

Nearly 700 people completed individual intelligence tests and then were randomly assigned to work groups of 2 to 5 individuals (Woolley, Chabris, Pentland, Hashmi, & Malone, 2010). Each group was assigned several tasks to complete that varied in the amount of coordinated activity required for success, including solving visual puzzles, brainstorming, making collective moral judgments, and negotiating the allocation of limited resources. Some groups finished their session by playing checkers against a computerized opponent, while others completed an architectural design task. Additional measures were taken of factors believed to be related to group performance, including motivation, satisfaction, group cohesion, social sensitivity, and distribution of speaking turns.

RESULTS

Evidence suggested that a group or collective intelligence did emerge. For each group, performance across the different tasks was highly and positively correlated. Further statistical analyses ruled out the average individual intelligence of the group or the maximum individual intelligence of individuals in the group as significant predictors of group performance, leaving collective intelligence as a single, strong predictor of group performance (see ● Figure 10.19).

What was the basis of this collective intelligence? Surprisingly, typical group features such as motivation, satisfaction, or group cohesion failed to predict group performance. Individual

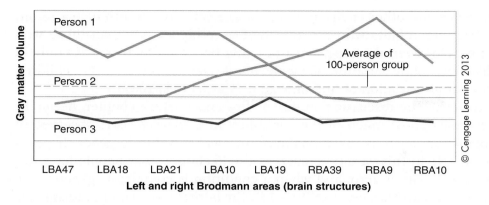

FIGURE 10.18

Correlations Between Brain Structure and IQ Show Multiple Patterns. The relationships between brain structure and IQ are complex. The individual depicted with the blue line had the highest IQ score out of 100 participants, and in each area of the brain believed to correlate with IQ, he showed much higher than average cortical thickening. Person 2 and Person 3 had identical scores on an IQ test, but their patterns of cortical thickening were quite different from one another. Further research might help psychologists better understand the relationships between observed differences in brain structure and intelligence. *Source:* Adapted from "What Does a Smart Brain Look Like?" by Richard J. Haier, from *Scientific American MIND,* November/December 2009. Reproduced with permission. Copyright © 2009 Scientific American, Inc. All rights reserved.

Genetics and Intelligence As we observed in our chapter on the interactions between nature and nurture, simple either/or thinking about nature and nurture is rarely correct when considering human behavior, including intelligence. The influences of heredity (nature) interact intimately with

features, such as the individual intelligence of the members, also failed to predict group performance. Instead, the members' scores on the social sensitivity instrument, called the "Reading the Mind in the Eyes" test, and how evenly speaking turns were distributed had a large impact on the group's collective intelligence.

CONCLUSIONS

Most students have had significant experience with group projects, and you might have had an opportunity to observe the collective intelligence of your groups. This research shows that bringing together the most intelligent people might not guarantee the best results. Instead, members who are more empathic and do not dominate the conversation might have the greatest success in completing the group's work. ✪

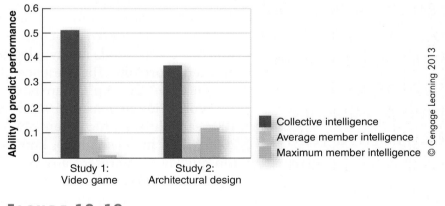

FIGURE 10.19

Collective Intelligence. A group's performance on a variety of tasks, from playing video games to constructing a complex architectural design, was predicted better by the group's "collective intelligence" than by the average intelligence of the group's members or by the highest IQ among the group's members. *Source:* Adapted from "Evidence for a collective intelligence factor in the performance of human groups" by Woolley, A. W., Chabris, C. F., Pentland, A., Hashmi, N., & Malone, T. W. from *Science 330*(2010), 686–688. Reprinted by permission of AAAS.

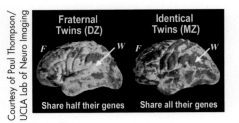

Fraternal Twins (DZ) — F ... W — Share half their genes

Identical Twins (MZ) — F ... W — Share all their genes

A comparison of the amount of gray matter in the brains of identical and fraternal twins showed that the identical twins were more similar to each other, as indicated by red and yellow coloring, especially in areas where gray matter thickness is correlated with IQ.

There are painters who transform the sun to a yellow spot, but there are others who with the help of their art and their intelligence, transform a yellow spot into the sun.

—Pablo Picasso

experience and other environmental factors (nurture) to produce a result. For example, infants who are breastfed have higher IQs than those who are not. However, the experience of being breastfed increases IQ only in children with one variation of a gene, but it has no effect on IQ in children with another variation of the same gene (Caspi et al., 2007).

To recap the discussion in our nature and nurture chapter, heritability estimates how much of the variability in a characteristic observed in a population, such as variations in adult height, is due to genes. If genes play no role in this variation, such as the likelihood that people have tattoos, heritability is zero, and when a condition is completely genetic, like Huntington's disease, heritability is 1.0. The heritability of adult intelligence as measured by IQ tests is usually reported to be about .75 (Neisser et al., 1996). When we say that the heritability of intelligence is .75, we are saying that 75% of the variance in intelligence observed in the population can be attributed to genetics, not that 75% of an individual's intelligence is due to his or her genes.

As we observed in an earlier section, both overall brain size and the proportion of gray matter are correlated with intelligence, and both are approximately 85% heritable, based on comparisons of identical and fraternal twins (Gray & Thompson, 2004). Although many genes are known to influence brain development, none has been conclusively linked to high IQ performance. It is very likely that a very large number of genes, each having a small impact and interacting with the individual's environment, contribute to the development of the brain.

The fact that a trait demonstrates high heritability does not imply that change or improvement is impossible. A case in point is the highly heritable condition of phenylketonuria (PKU), in which a person cannot properly metabolize a particular amino acid found in many foods. Left unchecked, the condition leads to intellectual disability, discussed in a later section of this chapter. However, if a child with PKU is given an appropriate diet in which problem foods are avoided until maturity, intellectual development proceeds normally. The presence of data showing that IQ is heritable does not mean we "give up" on anybody's intellectual development.

Worldwide increases in IQ of about 3 points per decade over the last 100 years illustrate the potential for change (Dickens & Flynn, 2001; Flynn, 2006). This increase in IQ, known as the Flynn Effect, has occurred far too quickly to represent any genetic changes. Instead, the Flynn Effect is much more likely to have resulted from environmental change, particularly improvements in health. Using information from the World Health Organization, researchers have identified strong correlations between a nation's freedom from serious infectious diseases and its citizens' average IQ (Eppig, Fincher, & Thornhill, 2010). As nations become wealthier and more capable of battling disease, their citizens' IQs increase (see ● Figure 10.20).

Psychologists have produced long lists of environmental factors that influence intellectual development, including nutrition and exposure to mentally stimulating activities. Most of these environmental advantages are not cheap. Consequently, it is not surprising to find that socioeconomic status, a measure of family income, education, and other "class" factors, is positively correlated with IQ (Turkheimer, Haley, Waldron, D'Onofrio, &

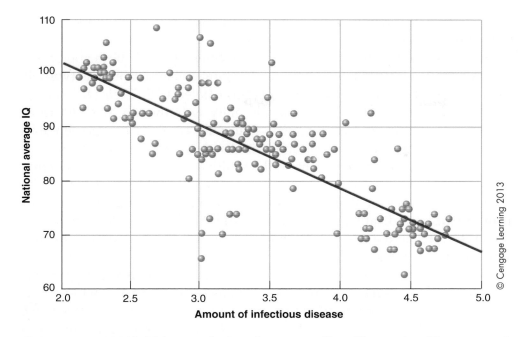

© Cengage Learning 2013

FIGURE 10.20

Relationships Between IQ and Infectious Disease. Worldwide, a nation's overall average IQ has a negative correlation with its rate of infectious disease. This finding raises the possibility that as we improve health, we will also improve IQ. *Source: Adapted from "Parasite prevalence and the worldwide distribution of cognitive ability" by Eppig, C., Fincher, C. L., & Thornhill, R., from Proceedings of the Royal Society B: Biological Sciences* (2010). Used by permission.

Gottesman, 2003). This correlation does not tell us if more intelligent people enjoy higher socioeconomic status, if higher socioeconomic status provides means to optimize intelligence, if some unknown third factor produces both high intelligence and high socioeconomic status, or if some combination of these factors occurs. Nonetheless, poverty continues to be a significant risk for low IQ.

Extremes of Intelligence

Assuming that IQs are normally distributed, with an average of 100 and a standard deviation of 15, about 68% of the population should fall within one standard deviation (85–115), and 95% of the population should fall within two standard deviations (70–130). The remaining 5% is divided between the two tails of the distribution, either above 130 or below 70 (see ● Figure 10.21).

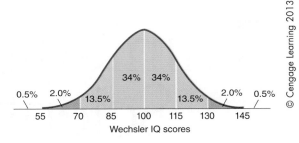

© Cengage Learning 2013

FIGURE 10.21

IQ Distribution. IQ test results form an approximately normal distribution, which means that about 68% of the population falls between IQs of 85 and 115. Ninety-five percent of the population falls between IQs of 70 and 130, with the remaining 5% divided between the two tails.

Intellectual Disability Approximately 1 to 3% of the population will score 70 or below on a standardized IQ test (Szymanski & King, 1999). Although such a score is the starting point for a diagnosis of **intellectual disability**, other factors must be considered. In addition to an IQ below 70, individuals with intellectual disability demonstrate problems with adaptive behaviors, or life skills. These behaviors might include the ability to balance a checkbook, receive correct change from a cashier, read a bus schedule, buy groceries, maintain personal hygiene, and other skills required for independent living.

Intellectual disability is usually divided into categories of mild, moderate, severe, and profound based on IQ scores and level of adaptive functioning (American Psychiatric Association [APA], 2000). Mild intellectual disability is typically accompanied by IQ scores of 55 to 70, or between 2 and 3 standard deviations from the mean of 100. With proper intervention, individuals in this group will be able to master the sixth-grade curriculum, although it will typically take them until age 18 to do so. Most

intellectual disability A condition diagnosed in individuals with IQ scores below 70 and poor adaptive behaviors; also referred to as mental retardation.

Mental retardation *is the term used by the current edition of the* Diagnostic and Statistical Manual, *but it is likely that the next edition will use the term* intellectual disability *instead. Given the importance of intelligence measures in diagnosing this condition, the new term seems more accurate and possibly less stigmatizing.*

individuals in this group will live independently, and many work, marry, and have families.

The causal factors for mild intellectual disability provide both good news and bad news. The good news is that mild intellectual disability is typically not the result of genetic or medical problems (Zigler, 1967; Zigler & Hodapp, 1986). As a result, mild intellectual disability is frequently referred to as familial retardation, recognizing that it usually results from preventable, environmental causes. Poverty is an obvious risk factor for this condition, as poor parents may be unable to obtain the health care and diet and other environmental benefits needed to produce healthy children (see ● Figure 10.22).

IQ scores between 40 and 55, or between 3 and 4 standard deviations from the mean, indicate moderate intellectual disability. Unlike mild cases, moderate intellectual disability typically results from genetic or medical conditions rather than familial factors. Genetic conditions such as trisomy 21, or Down syndrome, are very likely to produce disability in this range. The academic attainment of most individuals in this category will be limited to the second-grade curriculum, and once again, most will not achieve this level until about the age of 18 years. Most of these individuals will need some type of assisted living, although the type and extent of needed services vary widely among affected individuals.

Severe intellectual disability is diagnosed in individuals with IQ scores between 25 and 40, or 4 to 5 standard deviations below the mean, while

Thinking Scientifically

Can Children's IQs Be Increased With Special Baby Videos?

In spite of advice from the American Academy of Pediatrics telling parents that children under the age of 2 should have zero screen time (television or computers), the market for electronic media designed to make babies smarter is booming (Committee on Public Education, 2001). Sporting names like *Baby Einstein*, *Brainy Baby*, and *Baby Genius*, these materials make their intent very clear to consumers. The popularity of these

programs does indicate that today's parents take the need for nurture very seriously.

Surprisingly little scientific research has been done on the use of these products with very young children. Research on the television show *Sesame Street* showed beneficial effects on outcomes such as vocabulary and school readiness. *Sesame Street* has long-term effects as well, boosting adolescent grades in English, math, and science and overall

GPA (Anderson, Huston, Schmitt, Linebarger, & Wright, 2001; Huston, Anderson, Wright, Linebarger, & Schmitt, 2001). However, the *Sesame Street* studies were conducted with preschoolers, not babies.

One study found that watching baby videos actually had a detrimental effect on young children's language acquisition. Infants below the age of 16 months and exposed to the videos understood from 6 to 8 fewer words for each hour of exposure

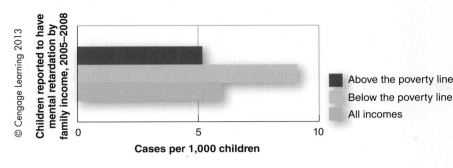

© Cengage Learning 2013

Children reported to have mental retardation by family income, 2005–2008

Cases per 1,000 children

- Above the poverty line
- Below the poverty line
- All incomes

FIGURE 10.22

Poverty Is a Risk Factor for Intellectual Disability.
Mild forms of intellectual disability, leading to IQs between 55 and 70, are also known as "familial retardation," because these cases are not due to medical or genetic problems. Poverty is a large risk factor for this level of intellectual disability. A little more than 5 out of 1,000 children living above the poverty line have intellectual disability, but this number jumps to 9 out of 1,000 among children living below the poverty line.

profound intellectual disability is diagnosed in individuals with IQ scores below 25. Both severe and profound intellectual disability generally result from serious medical conditions and are identified at birth or very early in infancy. Individuals with severe intellectual disability can learn a few high-priority words, such as "stop" or "hot." Individuals with profound intellectual disability can learn some basic self-care skills, such as feeding themselves or washing their hands. Depending on the nature of the medical problems, these individuals will require significant assistance and supervision.

Individuals with intellectual disability face a number of common problems. Many children with intellectual disability form insecure attachments with their caregivers, described in detail in our chapter on development (Clegg & Sheard, 2002). Ideally, children form a secure attachment, characterized by demonstrating

© Charles Lewis/The Buffalo News

Sujeet Desai, who has Down syndrome, plays six instruments and is a graduate of the Berkshire Hills Music Academy in Massachusetts. Desai travels extensively as an advocate for people with disabilities.

compared to nonexposed infants (Frederick, Dimitri, & Andrew, 2007). Needless to say, this finding generated quite a discussion in the nearly $5 billion children's educational media industry.

Earlier in this chapter, we described research demonstrating that young children learn language from a speaker in the room, but not from the same speaker being televised. This research suggests that the concerns about language learning and very young children's media use are worth exploring further. In the meantime, we hope that young parents can sit back, relax, play with, and enjoy their children, who grow up all too quickly anyway. ☼

© Niamh Baldock/Alamy

In spite of expert opinions from the American Academy of Pediatrics recommending that children under the age of 2 years spend no time at all watching television or computer screens, the market for special baby videos is booming.

WHAT IS INTELLIGENCE?   **499**

Photo by Bob Elbert, Iowa State University

Mattias Gassman (right), shown with his parents, graduated summa cum laude with two bachelor's degrees from Iowa State University at the age of 18. His degrees are in biophysics and German and classical studies, and he completed a minor in history. He was scheduled to begin his graduate studies in classics at the University of Minnesota in preparation for becoming a college professor, which he could do by the time he is 23. Like many gifted children, Mattias was an early reader, poring through the family encyclopedia at the age of 6.

giftedness An extreme of intelligence defined as having an IQ score of 130 or above.

a clear preference for a caregiver over strangers, protesting when the caregiver leaves, and indicating a willingness to explore the environment (Ainsworth & Bowlby, 1965).

Depending on the severity of the intellectual disability, language skills are typically impacted (Chapman, 1995). Children with intellectual disability have problems expressing themselves clearly, although they may understand a great deal that is said to them. In conjunction with typically poor social skills, these language deficits may result in peer rejection. Consequently, successful intervention programs address language and social skills in addition to academic and life skill work.

Between 10 and 40% of individuals with intellectual disability experience some type of emotional or behavioral disorder (McGaw, Shaw, & Beckley, 2007). Anxiety, impulsiveness, and mood disorders are the most common disorders seen in this population. When intellectual disability is more severe, individuals may engage in pica, or the eating of nonedibles, or self-injurious behaviors, such as banging the head against the floor or wall.

Giftedness and Genius

Just as variations occur on the low side of the IQ distribution, so they do on the upper tail. Intellectually **gifted** individuals, who make up approximately 1 to 3% of the population, score 2 or more standard deviations above the mean, or more than 130 on a standardized IQ test. Genius combines unusually high intelligence with creativity and achievement (Renzulli & Delcourt, 1986).

Having a high IQ provides some significant advantages to individuals in many aspects of life. One of the longest running studies in psychology is a longitudinal examination of gifted children initiated in 1921 (Terman, 1925; Terman & Oden, 1959). The original participants were children who were selected because of their very high IQs, averaging 150. Through adulthood, the gifted participants not only maintained their high IQs but also enjoyed better physical health, emotional stability, occupational attainment, and social satisfaction throughout their adult lives.

High intellect, particularly as measured by an IQ score, does not capture completely what we mean by genius. In spite of their successes, the gifted participants in the longitudinal study just cited did not produce "genius" work. Nor do all remarkable thinkers possess particularly high IQs. Nobel laureate Richard Feynman was disappointed to learn that his IQ was "only" 124 (Gleick, 1992).

Like individuals on the lower extreme of IQ scores, children with unusually high IQ scores benefit from educational opportunities tailored to their abilities. Unfortunately, the structure of public education in the United States, with its emphasis on grade levels based on age, rarely provides optimum learning for gifted children. A report by the U.S. Department of Education noted that children with IQs of 140 or above typically know at least half of a grade's curriculum even before the school year begins, and those with IQs of 170 or above know virtually all of it (U.S. Department of Education Office of Educational Research and Improvement, 1993). Their time in school is subsequently wasted, and the material is so easy that it encourages poor learning habits ill-suited to later educational challenges. Ideally, we could begin to offer education targeted to an individual's intellectual strengths and weaknesses.

Summary 10.3

Types of Intelligence

Type of intelligence	Description	Example
General intelligence (*g*) Copyright © 2003 NCS Pearson, Inc. Reproduced with permission.	A single measure of an individual's intellectual ability that predicts most of his or her intellectual performance	Verbal, mathematical, spatial, and logical skills show high positive correlations within an individual.
Fluid intelligence © acilo/iStock-photo	A type of general intelligence that allows logical thinking without needing learned knowledge	Recognizing relationships between geometric shapes.
Crystallized intelligence © Carlo Allegri/ Getty Images for LAPA	A type of general intelligence that requires learned knowledge	Using your knowledge of the multiplication tables to figure out interest on a new car loan.
Multiple intelligences © Katie Orlinsky	Single skills that tend to show relatively low correlations with each other and with general intelligence	Strong musical abilities in people with Williams syndrome, which results in a lower than normal IQ.
Emotional and social intelligence © Bill Aron/ PhotoEdit	The ability to manage emotions and reason about other people's states of mind	Managing anger appropriately and showing empathy for others.
Collective intelligence © Cengage Learning 2013	A quality of group process independent of individual group members' intelligence that predicts group performance	A team featuring good social sensitivity and conversation sharing completes a task successfully.

Interpersonal Relationships
From the Cognitive Perspective

Earlier in this chapter, you had an opportunity to take the Maximizer/Satisficer test (Schwartz et al., 2002). A very high score on this test predicts that you will be quite a perfectionist in your decision making. You might need to evaluate all your choices before you can settle on one, so you are unlikely to be known for making quick decisions. Because maximizers tend to feel more regret when a decision doesn't work out well, they have a tendency to avoid making decisions at all. Although they may experience better outcomes than satisficers on many occasions, maximizers might still feel worse. Satisficers are more likely to see their glass of life as half full, whereas maximizers are more likely to see their glass as half empty.

What does this distinction mean for interpersonal relationships? Finding a romantic partner and making a long-term commitment to that person involve some very important decisions. Romance is consistently ranked among the top regrets in life for most people (Roese & Summerville, 2005). These facts suggest that maximizers might run into some predictable obstacles within the realm of relationships. Either they will let

Faced with a large array of choices, satisficers will pick one that works, but maximizers will evaluate all the options to find the perfect choice. We're guessing that most of these candies taste very good.

opportunities pass by, because they are still looking for that perfect person, or they will avoid making a commitment for fear of regretting it later. Their perfectionist standards might make it impossible for them to appreciate a partner who is actually a good match, perhaps because he or she does not look like a supermodel or squeezes the toothpaste tube the wrong way.

Does this mean maximizers are doomed in relationships? Not at all. Recognizing that our automatic ways of behaving will not always lead us to our goals can help us identify areas where we need to take conscious, systematic control. Many maximizers blame their partners for a failed romance (the partner just didn't measure up) instead of taking a hard look at their own contributions to the relationship. If you know your maximizing tendencies are leading you in the wrong directions, you can use the steps to effective problem-solving outlined earlier in this chapter to supply alternatives that might work better.

Chapter 10
Reflections

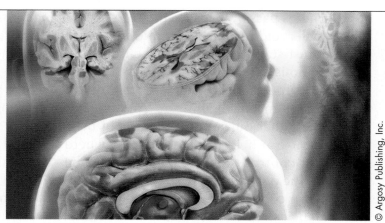

© Argosy Publishing, Inc.

The mental processes explored in this chapter eluded scientific study until rather recently, as our inner life of thought only expresses itself indirectly in our outwardly observable language and behavior. People who literally say "whatever is on their mind" usually end up with very few friends. Somehow, our individual intelligence and learning abilities help us express our thoughts through language and behavior that are well adapted to the complex social and physical world around us.

Psychologists have made great progress by zooming in to identify the underlying physical processes that are correlated with many of these mental processes, from the decision to buy Coke or Pepsi to the way people with dyslexia read to the contributions of healthy white matter to individual intelligence. Zooming back out again, we can see how our language abilities not only help us organize our thoughts but possibly make an even larger contribution to our abilities to work in groups. One of the important characteristics of the groups with the highest collective intelligence was their "fair" distribution of talking time. Individuals with high intelligence, verbal skills, and knowledge can accomplish a great deal on their own, but they can offer so much more when these attributes are combined with good social intelligence. ‹

© Leontura/iStockphoto

One of the prominent features of the groups with high collective intelligence was the fair distribution of talking time. No one person dominated the conversation.

KEY TERMS The Language of Psychological Science

Be sure you can define these terms and use them correctly.

affect heuristic, p. 467
algorithm, p. 465
aphasia, p. 480
availability heuristic, p. 466
bilingual, p. 487
cognition, p. 454
concept, p. 456
crystallized intelligence, p. 491
exemplar, p. 458

fluid intelligence, p. 491
functional fixedness, p. 464
general intelligence (*g*), p. 491
giftedness, p. 500
heuristic, p. 466
intellectual disability, p. 497
intelligence, p. 489
intelligence quotient (IQ), p. 489
language, p. 478

morpheme, p. 480
phoneme, p. 480
problem, p. 462
problem solving, p. 462
prototype, p. 458
recognition heuristic, p. 467
representativeness heuristic, p. 467

MEDIA RESOURCES

Log in to CengageBrain to access the resources your instructor requires. For this book, you can access:

Psychology **CourseMate** brings course concepts to life with interactive learning, study, and exam preparation tools that support the printed textbook. A textbook-specific website, Psychology CourseMate includes an integrated interactive eBook and other interactive learning tools including quizzes, flashcards, videos, and more.

WebTUTOR More than just an interactive study guide, WebTutor is an anytime, anywhere customized learning solution with an eBook, keeping you connected to your textbook, instructor, and classmates.

aplia If your professor has assigned Aplia homework:
1. Sign in to your account
2. Complete the corresponding homework exercises as required by your professor.
3. When finished, click "Grade It Now" to see which areas you have mastered, which areas need more work, and detailed explanations of every answer.

Around the age of 3 years, fiber pathways connecting the frontal lobes with the rest of the brain are developing rapidly, making changes in decision making and memory possible.

The Developing Mind

11

Life-Span Development

Learning Objectives

1 Evaluate the evidence for innate sensory capacities, preferences, and reflexes in newborn infants.

2 Construct a timeline of major physical, cognitive, and social/emotional changes that take place during the prenatal period, infancy, childhood, adolescence, and adulthood, and give examples of ways in which these three trajectories influence each other.

3 Differentiate Piaget's four stages of cognitive development (sensorimotor, pre-operational, concrete operational, formal operational), and critique Piaget's theory using research from alternate approaches.

4 Debate the adaptive function of infant attachment, and analyze the roles of temperament, culture, and parenting in driving individual attachment styles.

5 Illustrate the importance of nature/nurture interaction in development, using specific examples of epigenetic processes, critical/sensitive periods, and the impact of experience on biological development.

6 Debate the research evidence for continuity versus discontinuity in the trajectories of physical, cognitive, and social/emotional development.

What is your earliest memory? A birthday party? A new puppy? We are guessing that your earliest autobiographical memories, which we discussed in our chapter on memory, probably date to when you were between 3 and 5 years old. Why this age period and not another?

Zooming in, we can see that one of the factors driving memory abilities is the development of the brain during childhood. As you will see in this chapter, changes taking place in the hippocampus and frontal lobes somewhere during the third year of life give children a boost in their abilities to form long-term memories, particularly about the sequences of events that make up our autobiographical memories. But there are other parts to this story.

To form an autobiographical memory, children must have a sense of self. As we discussed in our chapter on consciousness, babies as young as 18 months can recognize themselves in a mirror. In this chapter, you will learn about the further development of self-awareness as children gradually separate from their parents and family and move into adult roles in the community.

Zooming out still farther, we find that cultures can influence the formation and timing of autobiographical memories. When White American adults are compared with Chinese adults, the White Americans access more autobiographical memories from earlier ages and provide more episodic details of these memories (Wang, 2008). Wang believes that this difference observed in adults originates earlier in childhood, when White American children show more "emotion knowledge," or an understanding of how situations can lead to emotions, than Chinese children (see ● Figure 11.1). Emotion knowledge is assessed by asking children such questions as "What makes people happy?" Cultures can influence emotion knowledge development by focusing on information relevant to the self versus more general aspects of information.

To understand the development of autobiographical memory, psychologists must explore the biological, individual, developmental, social, and cultural contributions to this ability. At the same time, the development of an autobiographical memory capability forms reciprocal influences with these other aspects of the individual's behavior. In this chapter, we will explore many examples of how the normal changes that occur across the life span interact with our behavior and mental processing. ⚙

A major milestone in children's development of a sense of self is the ability to recognize themselves in a mirror by the age of 18 months.

What Does It Mean to Develop?

In our earlier chapter on learning, we defined learning as a "relatively permanent change in behavior due to experience." In this chapter, we will explore an additional force for changes in behavior—changes that unfold with the passage of time. The study of human development considers changes in behavior that correlate with growth or maturation.

New Ideas About Development

The ways psychologists think about human development have changed over the years. Early students of human development were very quick to pronounce age-related changes complete at some specified age. Sigmund Freud, whom we will discuss in our chapter on personality, and Jean Piaget, whom we will meet later in this chapter, believed that many of the important developmental changes had already occurred once an individual reached puberty.

More contemporary views of development expand the examination of age-related changes from childhood and adolescence to cover the entire

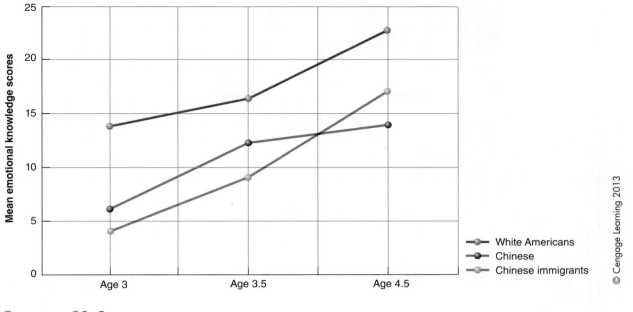

FIGURE 11.1

Cultural Influences on Emotion Knowledge. White American adults recall more childhood autobiographical memories in greater detail than Chinese adults. These differences may have their roots in much earlier cultural influences on emotional knowledge, or an understanding of how a situation can lead to emotions. When asked to describe situations that would make a person happy, sad, fearful or angry, White American children provided more information than Chinese or Chinese immigrant children. Emotional knowledge increases when a person focuses on information relevant to the self rather than more general information. *Source:* Adapted from Wang, Q. (2008). *Emotion knowledge and autobiographical memory across the preschool years: A cross-cultural longitudinal investigation. Cognition, 108*(1), 117–135. Used by permission of Elsevier.

life span. Young adults, their younger siblings, their middle-aged parents, and their elderly grandparents differ from each other in substantive ways. Today, we know that the brain is not a finished product until a person's mid-20s (Thompson et al., 2000), a far cry from the earlier notion that cognition was mature around puberty. Even after the mid-20s, the brain can develop small numbers of new neurons, which may participate in learning, and is able to form new connections until the end of life (Gage, 2000; Gould, Reeves, Graziano, & Gross, 1999).

We have also changed the way we view interactions between biology and experience in the development of a human being. Early thinkers believed that babies brought few organizing principles with them at birth and that they were quite dependent on experience to help them sort out the world around them. William James described the world of the infant as follows: "The baby, assailed by eyes, ears, nose, skin, and entrails at once, feels it all as one great blooming, buzzing confusion" (James, 1890, p. 488). As you will discover later in this chapter, contemporary psychologists believe that human infants are born with a long list of capabilities, including ways to organize their sensory experiences, learn language, and develop a personality. While these systems might take years to complete, human infants are not as dependent on experience as earlier thinkers believed them to be.

Early developmental psychologists described normal age-related changes up through childhood to puberty, but not beyond. Today, we know that the ages represented in these four generations bring their own set of characteristic behaviors.

As we explore the normal changes that occur at different stages of life, we will concentrate on three interwoven threads: physical development, cognitive development, and social and emotional development. Although we discuss each separately, they are constantly interacting. For example, moving independently by crawling or walking produces a more rapidly changing and interesting environment, which spurs an infant's cognitive growth. At the same time, a mobile infant is likely to elicit different reactions from parents or caretakers than one that is stationary, stimulating further social and emotional development.

In addition to documenting these three types of change over time, the study of development highlights several major questions that stretch across the entire life span. How does nature interact with nurture? Is development gradual and continuous or abrupt and discontinuous? How much of human development is universal across the human species or dependent upon a person's culture?

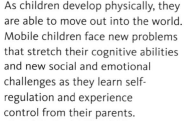

© Jerry Arcieri/Corbis

As children develop physically, they are able to move out into the world. Mobile children face new problems that stretch their cognitive abilities and new social and emotional challenges as they learn self-regulation and experience control from their parents.

Nature and Nurture Intertwined Although we will be discussing the genetic heritage of individuals as well as environmental influences on their development, we will be emphasizing the interactions between nature and nurture that predict developmental outcomes.

Significant progress has been made in the understanding of how genes and the environment interact. As we discussed in our chapter on nature and nurture, we now understand that the underlying DNA that makes up our genes is turned on or off by the surrounding chemical tags (the epigenome) that accumulate through life. The study of this process is known as epigenetics. Among the external environmental factors that can chemically "tag" our DNA are diet, nurture, and stress.

This epigenetic process is not constant across the life span, just as an individual's physical, cognitive, and social and emotional behaviors change. In prenatal development, most of the chemical tags that influence gene expression come from within the developing organism, with some external influence from the mother's diet and her stress hormones. After birth, internal signals continue to be important in driving physical growth, but the child is now exposed to a wider array of environmental influences, including diet, social interactions, and physical activity. Throughout the remaining life span, epigenetic tags continue to accumulate in response to ongoing experience. This process leads to the divergence in appearance and health seen in older identical twins that we noted in our chapter on nature and nurture.

These outcomes mean that epigenetics plays an increasingly dominant role over the life span. Because younger children have had less time for epigenetic interactions between their genes and experience to take place, they have more in common with each other at any particular age than do older adults, whose decades of experience have caused their epigenetic paths to lead them in many different directions. A group of 8-year-olds is much more consistent in its physical characteristics and behaviors than

a group of 20-year-olds, who still have more in common with each other than any group of 65-year-olds. This contrast between children and adults might have led earlier psychologists to the mistaken belief that development "stopped" at some point in childhood or adolescence, when all they were seeing was a transition point where internal influences were becoming overshadowed by external ones.

Continuity or Discontinuity Another major question asks whether development proceeds gradually and smoothly over time (continuity) or changes more abruptly from one stage to the next (discontinuity). The gradual approach might be visualized as a rainbow, with one color (stage) gradually merging into the next, with no bold line separating the two. In contrast, the discontinuity approach views development as a staircase to be climbed. The behavior on one step is qualitatively different from the step that preceded it, and the change from one step to the other is abrupt (see ● Figure 11.2).

As in the case of nature and nurture, the continuity-discontinuity debate does not have a "right answer." Some features appear to be more continuous in their developmental course, such as the gradual development of infant temperament into later personality. Other features do seem to appear seemingly out of nowhere. In our previous chapter on memory, we noted how infants around the age of 8 months develop a sense of object permanence,

Epigenetic influences accumulate over the life span. Groups of 8-year-olds will have more in common than groups of 20-year-olds, who will have more in common than groups of older adults. The contrast between the degree of similarity seen in children compared to adults might have lead early developmental psychologists to the mistaken conclusion that development "stopped."

FIGURE 11.2

Continuity Versus Discontinuity in Development. Development can appear as a gradual, continuous process, such as the acorn growing into a mighty oak tree, or as a sudden, discontinuous process, such as the butterfly emerging from a chrysalis.

or the ability to form a mental representation of an object that they can no longer see. This milestone probably occurs when an infant reaches a level of maturation in the prefrontal cortex that supports this new behavior. Babies do not gradually show object permanence—it is completely absent one day and is present the next, but the underlying cortical development is very likely to be more continuous than the observable behavior.

Universal or Ecological Development Psychologists taking the universal approach to development look for age-related behaviors that are found across the entire human species, whereas psychologists taking an ecological view ask questions about the impact of culture and environment on development.

Which approach is correct? Both universal and ecological approaches improve our understanding. Although we will see universals of development in this chapter, such as the age at which most children begin walking unassisted, we will also see that children growing up in cultures where early walking is encouraged walk at slightly younger ages than children growing up in cultures where restricting infant movement is the norm. Although a consideration of human universals is useful, most contemporary psychologists would be unwilling to consider many behaviors outside their context of social relationships and culture.

The universal approach sees development as common to all people, whereas the ecological approach emphasizes the influences of environment and culture on development. In the United States, we tend to look at child soldiers, some as young as 10 years old, as being a product of the poverty and lack of opportunity in their environments. However, some universal aspects of being a preteen or young teen, such as an immature sense of morality and greater obedience to adults, might apply equally to very young violent gang members in the United States.

How Do We Change Prenatally?

Now that we have explored some of the major themes of development, we are ready to apply them to development beginning with conception, or the merger of the mother's egg with the father's sperm. As we discussed in our chapter on nature and nurture, this merger combines the genetic material from each parent that will begin to orchestrate development.

The 9 months between conception and birth are full of growth and activity. For the first 2 weeks following conception, the developing organism is known as a **zygote**. During the second week, the zygote typically completes its journey through the mother's fallopian tube to the uterus, where it implants in the lining. During weeks 3 through 8 following conception, we use the term **embryo**, and for the remainder of the pregnancy, we use the term **fetus**.

zygote The term used to describe a developing organism immediately following conception until the embryo stage, or the first 2 weeks following conception in humans.

embryo The term used to describe a developing organism between the zygote and fetus stages, or between 3 and 8 weeks following conception in humans.

fetus The term used to describe a developing organism between the embryo stage and birth, or between 8 and approximately 40 weeks following conception in humans.

The nervous system has a very high priority in human prenatal development. During the first week following conception, the zygote differentiates into three germ layers—the *ectoderm, mesoderm,* and *endoderm* (see ● Figure 11.3). The ectoderm develops into nerve tissue and skin, while the mesoderm will give rise to muscle and bone. The endoderm is the source of much of the body's soft tissue, such as the organs of the digestive tract. By the fourth week following conception, the nervous system has differentiated into forebrain, midbrain, hindbrain, and spinal cord. During the seventh week, cells that will form the cerebral cortex begin a carefully orchestrated journey from the lining of the neural tube to their ultimate destinations. By the seventh month of pregnancy, the majority of the brain's cells have been formed (Rakic, 2000).

(a)

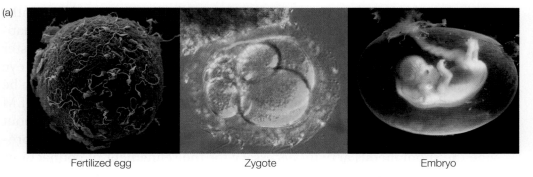

Fertilized egg   Zygote   Embryo

(b) Developing nervous system

Ectoderm

Mesoderm

FIGURE 11.3

Prenatal Development.
(a) For the first 2 weeks after conception, the developing organism is known as a zygote. Cell division continues at a very rapid pace as the zygote travels down the mother's fallopian tube, reaching the uterus during its second week. The embryo stage lasts from week 3 through week 8 following conception.
(b) During the zygote stage, cells begin to differentiate into three types: the ectoderm, which is the source of cells making up the nervous system, the mesoderm, which develops into muscle and skeleton, and the endoderm, which will form internal organs.
Illustration: © Argosy Publishing, Inc.; photos: © Eye of Science/Photo Researchers, Inc.; © K. H. Kjeldsen/ Photo Researchers, Inc.; © Dr. G. Moscoso/Photo Researchers, Inc.

Other systems, while perhaps not as dramatic as the nervous system, also begin to differentiate and develop during the embryonic stage. The heart, stomach, liver, and other organs are formed during this period, and the initial differentiation between male and female internal sex organs occurs. As we transition from embryo to fetus 2 months after conception, the fetus is about 1 inch long, weighs about 1 gram (0.04 ounces), and looks decidedly human.

The remainder of the pregnancy involves continued growth and maturation of the systems that are now in place (see ● Figure 11.4). New neurons are born in large numbers and begin the process of forming connections

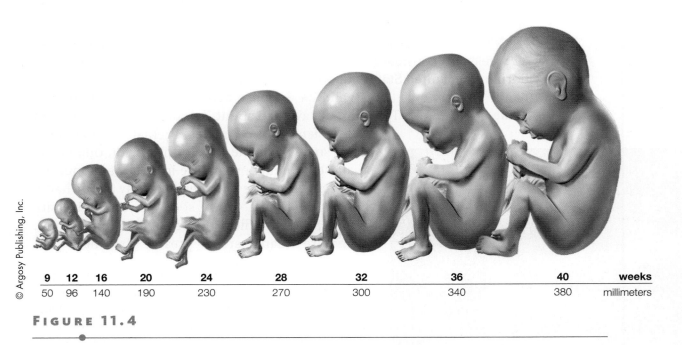

9	12	16	20	24	28	32	36	40	weeks
50	96	140	190	230	270	300	340	380	millimeters

© Argosy Publishing, Inc.

FIGURE 11.4

Fetal Development. During the fetal stage, from 8 to approximately 40 weeks following conception, considerable growth and maturation of organs and tissues prepare the fetus for birth.

with each other. Myelination of the nervous system begins about six months following conception (Rivkin et al., 1995). As you may recall from our chapter on biological psychology, myelin allows neurons to communicate faster and more efficiently. During the seventh month of the pregnancy, rapid eye movement sleep (REM; described in our chapter on consciousness) can be recorded for the first time (Inoue et al., 1986). In children and adults, REM sleep corresponds with vivid dreaming, but we can merely speculate about the quality of the REM experience in the fetus. Fetal REM sleep might provide the spontaneous activity necessary for the refinement of connections in the nervous system.

You may be under the impression that the fetus resides in a rather isolated, self-contained environment in the womb, but this is not the case. As we observed in our previous discussions of hearing and language, the fetus's ability to hear noises outside the mother's body is quite good during the last few months of pregnancy (Birnholz & Benacerraf, 1983). Newborn babies show an immediate preference for their mother's voice (DeCasper & Fifer, 1980). When pregnant mothers read the Dr. Seuss classic *The Cat in the Hat* out loud twice a day, their infants later preferred to listen to tapes of their mothers, but not others, reading this story (DeCasper & Spence, 1986). This preference has obvious advantages in the attachment and bonding that occurs between mother and newborn.

We also begin learning food preferences before birth. When pregnant women consumed carrot juice, their infants subsequently chose to eat more cereal prepared with carrot juice than did infants whose mothers did not consume any carrot juice during pregnancy. The infants exposed prenatally to carrot juice also appeared to enjoy the carrot juice cereal more than infants who were not exposed prenatally (Mennella, Jagnow, & Beauchamp, 2001). Once again, this type of learning appears quite adaptive. Children may be born with a familiarity and preference for the safe and available foods in their environment.

Most pregnancies last about 40 weeks, and babies born between 37 and 42 weeks are considered typical, or "term," births. Just over 12% of babies born in the United States are born prematurely, or before 37 weeks of pregnancy (Martin et al., 2008) and 2% are born before 32 weeks of pregnancy (Cole et al., 2011). Term infants average about 7 pounds at birth, with an average length of 20 inches. Premature infants are much smaller. At the time of her birth, one of the smallest surviving premature infants was about the size of a cell phone and weighed only about half a pound, less than a can of soda (Loyola University Health System Office of Media Relations, 2005). Premature infants are at greater risk than term

Compared to a typical baby born at around 40 weeks following conception, who is typically about 20 inches long and weighs about 7 pounds, little Rumaisa Rahman was born only 25 weeks following conception. Rumaisa was about 8 inches long and weighed a little over half a pound. Her twin sister, Hiba, was a little larger, weighing 1 pound, 4 ounces at birth.

infants for a number of conditions that can affect lifetime health and development, including disorders of the lungs, vision, and the development of the brain (Cole et al., 2011).

Genetic Risks to Development

In the vast majority of cases, prenatal development proceeds according to plan. As we observed in our chapter on nature and nurture, genetic abnormalities that have adverse effects are rarely passed along in large numbers. The more common genetic abnormalities seen in children are those that become more likely when their parents are older.

Older parents, and particularly mothers, have an increased probability of errors in the development of eggs and sperm. A woman's eggs are first formed when she is in her own prenatal period. Each of these immature eggs contains a complete set of 46 chromosomes, only half of which (23) will be passed along to her child. The child's other 23 chromosomes will be contributed by the father through fertilization. The final division of a woman's immature egg into a mature ovum, leaving only 23 chromosomes, does not occur until just before ovulation. Before they make this last crucial division, a 40-year-old woman's eggs have been exposed to 40 years of environmental influences, possibly including harmful factors such as X-rays, which raise the probability that something will go wrong as they divide. In contrast, it takes a little over two months for a man to produce a sperm cell, which reduces the chances of the cell's exposure to harmful influences.

Down syndrome, or trisomy 21, results from the child's receiving three copies of the 21st chromosome instead of the usual two, usually due to faulty cell division during the production of the mature ovum (see ● Figure 11.5). Down syndrome results in intellectual disability, a pattern of mild physical abnormalities, and a probable life span of only 40 to 50 years. A woman's chances of giving birth to a child with Down syndrome are only about 1 out of 2,000 at age 18, but rise to 1 out of 30 at age 45.

The vast majority of genetic abnormalities in an embryo will result in spontaneous abortion, or miscarriage, often before the woman has any

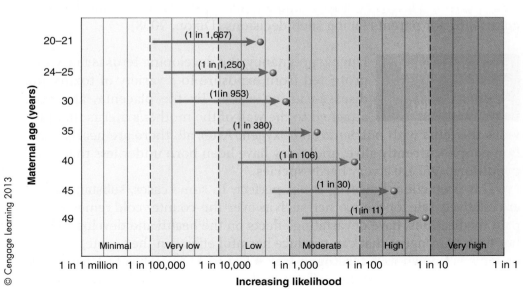

© Cengage Learning 2013

FIGURE 11.5

Risk of Down Syndrome and Maternal Age. Many genetic disorders, such as Down syndrome, are more common as the age of the mother increases. Errors in the final cell division forming the mother's egg immediately prior to ovulation become more likely over time as a woman is exposed to more potentially harmful environmental influences, such as radiation.

FIGURE 11.6

Risks From Teratogens.
The yellow bars indicate when particular systems are most vulnerable to disrupted development due to teratogens.

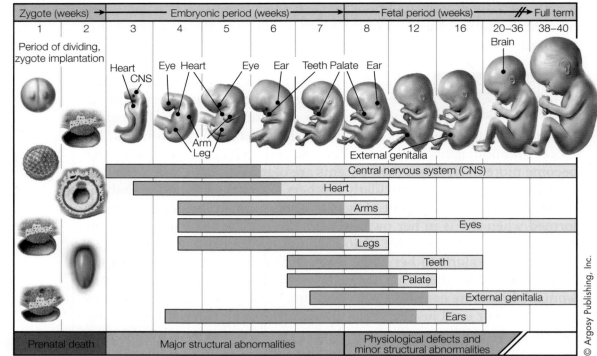

According to one expert in medical ethics, today's technology makes it possible to screen embryos for every known disease-causing mutation in the human genome (Leroi, 2006). What would be the benefits and costs of this practice?

idea she was pregnant at all. In addition, advances in the ability to screen for genetic disorders have led to a sharp reduction in births of individuals with many genetic conditions. Parents who are known carriers of genetic disorders might choose to use assisted reproductive technologies to screen embryos prior to implantation (Petrou, 2009). Other technologies alert parents that a fetus has a genetic disorder, providing them with the choice to terminate the pregnancy. Approximately 30% of fetuses with Down syndrome in the United States are aborted, which is low compared to the 85% of fetuses with Down syndrome aborted in France (Leroi, 2006). These practices raise significant ethical questions about how "perfect" a fetus needs to be and emphasize the need for expert genetic counseling for parents facing such decisions (Dixon, 2008).

Environmental Risks to Development

During pregnancy, the developing fetus is fairly well protected from exposure to a variety of toxins and disease-causing agents by the placenta, an organ attached to the wall of the mother's uterus that provides the fetus with nutrients and oxygen. After all, there are nearly 7 billion people currently alive, and many have been born under less than ideal conditions. We are a very hardy species.

This protection, however, is not perfect. In some cases, substances that are relatively safe for the mother, such as over-the-counter cold remedies and pain medications, have devastating effects on the health and development of her fetus. Any agent that can produce harmful effects in the zygote, embryo, or fetus is known as a **teratogen** (see ● Figure 11.6). Table 11.1 lists some common teratogens and their effects. A dramatic example of a teratogen was

teratogen A chemical agent that can harm the zygote, embryo, or fetus.

the medication thalidomide. During the 1960s, thalidomide was prescribed to many women in Europe to prevent morning sickness. However, the drug was associated with frequent fetal abnormalities of the arms and legs, so it was not approved for use in the United States. Commonly used antidepressant medications, discussed in more detail in our chapter on therapies, easily cross the placenta to the fetus, resulting in dosages in the fetus that are about the same as that of the mother (Kendall-Tackett & Hale, 2010). Exposure to these medications has been linked to higher rates of premature birth and other complications. Because even the most safe and routine substances are capable of acting as teratogens, pregnant women are well advised to consult with health care providers before taking any type of medication.

Recreational drugs consumed by the mother are the most common and preventable sources of adverse effects in the developing fetus. In spite of widely publicized medical advice about the necessity of abstaining from recreational drugs during pregnancy, significant numbers of women are unable or unwilling to do so. Infants born to women who use tobacco are at risk for premature birth and being underweight, circumstances that are major risk factors for numerous physical and psychological problems later on in the child's life (Centers for Disease Control [CDC], 2010e).

There are no known safe levels of alcohol consumption for pregnant women, leading to strongly worded advice to completely abstain from alcohol. You might be thinking, "My mother drank when she was pregnant with me, and I'm okay," but until we have more information, it is just not worth the risk. The intricate programming of nervous system development in the fetus appears to be especially vulnerable to interruption by alcohol consumed by the mother during pregnancy (Haycock, 2009). Alcohol

TABLE

11.1 Examples of Some Common Teratogens and Their Effects

Teratogen	Type	Effects on the child
Alcohol	Recreational drug	• Small stature • Facial abnormalities • Hyperactivity • Intellectual disability
Phenytoin (Dilantin)	Prescription medication for epilepsy	• Heart defects • Intellectual disability • Cleft palate • Slow growth
Varicella (chicken pox)	Viral infection	• Scars • Small head size • Blindness • Seizures • Malformed and paralyzed limbs
Aspirin	Over-the-counter pain medication	• Heart defects • Intellectual disability • Slow growth

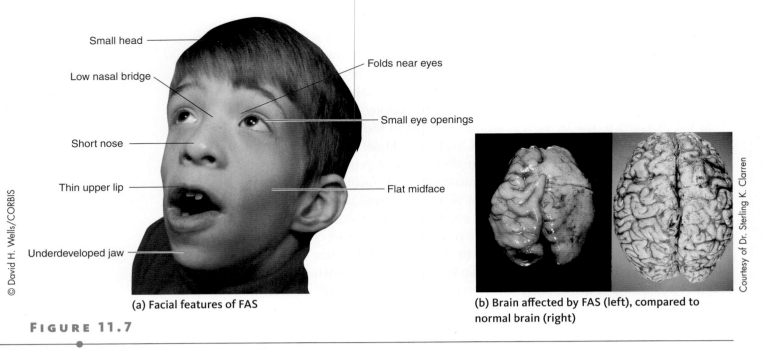

Small head

Low nasal bridge

Short nose

Thin upper lip

Underdeveloped jaw

Folds near eyes

Small eye openings

Flat midface

© David H. Wells/CORBIS

Courtesy of Dr. Sterling K. Clarren

(a) Facial features of FAS

(b) Brain affected by FAS (left), compared to normal brain (right)

FIGURE 11.7

Fetal Alcohol Syndrome (FAS). No known amount of alcohol consumption is considered safe during pregnancy, yet 1 out of every 12 pregnant women in the United States drinks during pregnancy, and 1 out of 30 binge drinks (has 5 or more drinks at one time; CDC, 2009). Drinking during pregnancy can result in fetal alcohol syndrome (FAS), which produces characteristic facial features, reduced brain volume, and attentional and other behavioral problems in children.

consumption by a pregnant woman can result in a condition known as **fetal alcohol syndrome (FAS)**. As shown in ● Figure 11.7, FAS produces a number of physical abnormalities, including growth retardation, skin folds at the corners of the eyes, nose and mouth abnormalities, and small head circumference, as well as cognitive and behavioral problems, including reduced IQ, attention problems, and poor impulse control (Streissguth et al., 1991).

Mothers who drink alcohol during pregnancy are often malnourished and have other health problems that indirectly affect their developing fetus (Steinhausen, Willms, & Spohr, 1993). They are more likely to smoke or use other psychoactive drugs, which produce their own sets of problems for the fetus. A mother's use of alcohol, tobacco, marijuana, or cocaine during pregnancy significantly reduces the volume of gray matter of her child's brain, but combinations of two or more of these drugs produce even more dramatic reductions. As we mentioned in our chapter on biological psychology, gray matter refers to areas populated by neural cell bodies, and the thickness of cortical gray matter is correlated with measures of intelligence. These are not short-term effects, as children exposed prenatally to multiple drugs show reduced gray matter thickness and head circumference at 10 to 13 years of age (Rivkin et al., 2008).

In addition to following a typically balanced, nutritious diet, pregnant women need additional nutrients to meet the needs of the growing fetus. Folic acid, found in fortified wheat products, green leafy vegetables, citrus, eggs, and chickpeas, reduces the likelihood of spina bifida, in which the early development of the spinal cord is disrupted, leading to movement disorders. DHA omega-3, found in oily fish, is important for proper development of the fetus's brain and retina of the eye (see ● Figure 11.8). However,

fetal alcohol syndrome (FAS)
A condition resulting from alcohol consumption by the mother during pregnancy that produces physical abnormalities and cognitive and behavioral problems in her child.

because most oily fishes also contain mercury, which is very harmful to brain development, pregnant women should be cautious about choosing a source for this nutrient. Even with a healthy diet, many pregnant women need supplements of Vitamin D, calcium, and iron.

A pregnant woman can be exposed to viruses that can trigger conditions that occur immediately or later in the child's life (Cannon, Kendell, Susser, & Jones, 2003). Women who contract rubella, or German measles, during pregnancy may give birth to children with a wide variety of problems, including heart disease, blindness, deafness, and intellectual disability. One of the most significant viral risks to the fetus today is the mother's infection with HIV, which can be passed from mother to child during pregnancy, birth, or breast-feeding. Worldwide, mothers transmit HIV to nearly 500,000 babies per year. Fortunately, an infected mother can significantly reduce her offspring's chances of contracting HIV by using medications that slow down the reproduction of the virus (Mofenson, 2010). Women with HIV might also be advised to deliver via cesarean section and to avoid breast-feeding to reduce the chances of passing the virus to their children.

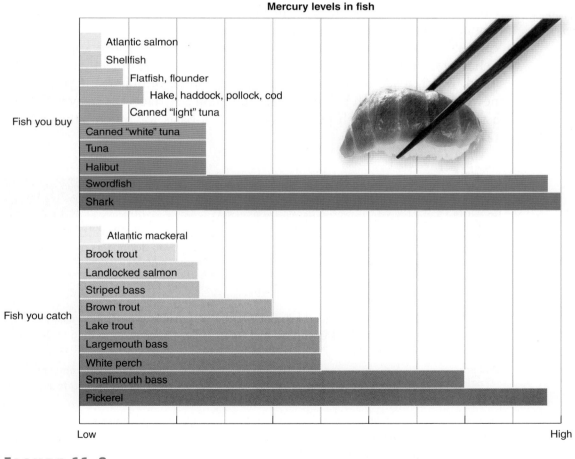

Mercury levels in fish

Fish you buy
- Atlantic salmon
- Shellfish
- Flatfish, flounder
- Hake, haddock, pollock, cod
- Canned "light" tuna
- Canned "white" tuna
- Tuna
- Halibut
- Swordfish
- Shark

Fish you catch
- Atlantic mackeral
- Brook trout
- Landlocked salmon
- Striped bass
- Brown trout
- Lake trout
- Largemouth bass
- White perch
- Smallmouth bass
- Pickerel

Low — High

FIGURE 11.8

Avoiding Environmental Toxins While Pregnant. Pregnant women are advised to eat seafood to obtain beneficial amounts of DHA omega-3, which is important for the development of the brain and retina, but at the same time should avoid seafood tainted with mercury, which can have adverse effects on brain development.

What Can Newborns Do?

Human development is characterized by a much longer period of dependency than in other primates, including chimpanzees and gorillas. Physical abilities present at birth in other primates, such as independent movement, require about one year to develop in human infants (Walker & Shipman, 1996). Dependency in human cultures means much more than being unable to move independently. Human adults house, feed, clothe, protect, and educate their young for the better part of two decades, if not longer. However, even though human newborns are much less mature than primate infants of other species, they still come into the world with a number of useful capacities.

Newborn babies will grasp anything placed in their hand, including a parent's finger.

The Newborn's Reflexes

According to medical definitions, the "newborn" stage of life begins officially at birth and lasts for 28 days. Newborns have a number of reflexive behaviors that begin to operate immediately (see Table 11.2). A baby immediately turns its head to the source of a touch, opens its mouth, and searches for the mother's nipple. This rooting reflex obviously assists the newborn with the essential process of feeding. If an object is placed in the baby's mouth, it begins to suck reflexively, which also leads to effective feeding. Other reflexes form the basis for the later development of more sophisticated behaviors. Very young babies will reflexively grasp any object placed in the hand, which leads to the later voluntary grasping of objects. If you hold a newborn upright with his or her feet touching a surface, the baby will show a stepping reflex, which possibly serves as a basis for much later walking (Zelazo, 1998).

TABLE 11.2 Newborn Reflexes

Reflex name	Action	Possible purpose
Babinski	Stroking the baby's foot causes toes to spread out.	Unknown; disappears as nervous system matures
Blink	Eye closes in response to strong stimuli.	Protects eyes
Moro	If the baby's head falls backward, the arms first spread out and then "hug."	A possible evolutionary remnant allowing primates to cling to an adult
Palmar	Placing an object in the hand produces reflexive grasping.	A possible evolutionary remnant allowing primates to cling to an adult's fur
Rooting	Stroking a baby's cheek results in the baby's turning toward the touch and opening its mouth.	Helps the baby nurse
Stepping	Placing the baby's feet on a flat surface initiates stepping.	Possible precursor to walking
Sucking	The baby sucks anything that touches the roof of the mouth.	Helps the baby nurse

The Newborn's Activity

Newborns spend up to 16 to 18 hours per day sleeping. As we mentioned in our chapter on consciousness, a large proportion of this time is spent in REM sleep, which might participate in the wiring of the newborn's brain.

During times of wakefulness, the baby alternates between periods of alert looking about and periods of physical movement of the arms and legs. Unfortunately for parents, most newborns also spend about two to three hours per day either crying or being close to tears. As upsetting as this crying may be, it represents the infant's first efforts at communicating with the parents. Babies generally cry for a reason, such as hunger or pain, and most parents are stimulated by the crying to find ways to make their infant more comfortable.

The Newborn's Senses

Newborns have significant, although immature, sensory capacities. Because babies obviously can't talk, researchers have had to be fairly creative in assessing their sensory capacities (see ● Figure 11.9). Measures of heart rate, facial expression, and head movements may correlate with distinctions between stimuli. Researchers also take advantage of habituation, the type of learning in which we reduce responding to repeated stimuli. Because of habituation, babies will gaze longer at a new stimulus than at one they have seen previously. When the baby spends equal time looking at two stimuli, we can assume he or she cannot tell the difference between them.

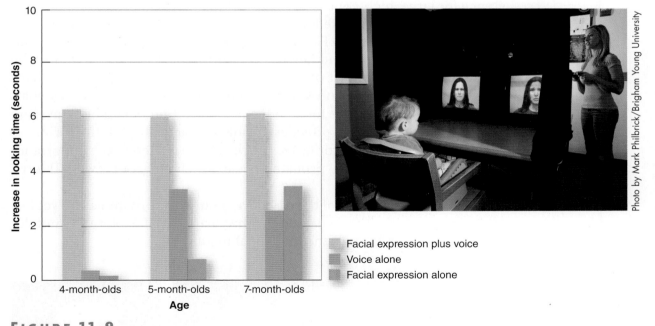

Facial expression plus voice
Voice alone
Facial expression alone

FIGURE 11.9

Studying Infants Requires Clever Experimental Methods. By studying the amount of time infants will look at a new stimulus after habituation, such as the face of a person, Ross Flom and Lorraine Bahrick were able to demonstrate that infants as young as 4 months could correctly perceive emotional expression if they both saw and heard the same expression simultaneously. The ability to perceive emotion using voice alone appeared around the age of 5 months, and the ability to perceive emotion from facial expression alone appeared around 7 months. *Source: Adapted from Flom & Bahrick (2007).*

Newborns show considerable sensitivity to smells and respond differently to pleasant smells (chocolate, honey) than to unpleasant smells (rotten eggs) (Maurer & Maurer, 1988). They are also capable of recognizing their mother by smell, which has obvious survival advantages. Babies even recognize their mother's favorite brand of perfume (Porter, Makin, Davis, & Christensen, 1991). Infants are quite sensitive to taste and can respond differentially to the major taste qualities of sweet, sour, bitter, and salty. They apparently have a sweet tooth and will nurse longer when their breast-feeding mother has consumed sweet-tasting foods (Mennella & Beauchamp, 1996).

The fetus can hear quite well beginning in the seventh month of pregnancy, but improvement in hearing continues after birth. We might tiptoe around a sleeping newborn, but older children and adults have superior hearing for very quiet sounds. The infant's ability to hear is best for sounds found in the range of frequencies that normally occur in human speech. This ability allows infants to begin the process of learning language.

Infant vision can be tested by measuring the amount of time the child spends viewing a pattern rather than a uniform screen. Using this technique, we can demonstrate that young infants do not see detail at a distance as well as adults do. In addition, infants need more contrast than adults in order to see well. As we discussed in our chapter on sensation and perception, contrast refers to differences in intensity between adjacent stimuli. The black letters on this white page are an example of high contrast, whereas dark gray letters on a black background would be an example of low contrast. These features of infant vision probably explain babies' preference for large, high-contrast, colorful objects.

Newborns demonstrate an innate preference for looking at faces (Pascalis & Kelly, 2009) (see ● Figure 11.10). This capacity has obvious advantages in social behavior and language learning. We know that infants who refuse to make eye contact often develop social and language impairments later on (Knickmeyer, Baron-Cohen, Raggatt, & Taylor, 2005; Mundy et al., 2007). An early preference for viewing faces is not unique to humans, suggesting that this behavior provides an adaptive advantage. Other primates show similar preferences for faces, which may be related to the importance of social relationships in primate species, including our own (Thierry, 1994).

The emerging picture of the newborn infant is one of immature yet formidable capacities. The remainder of this chapter will explore the unfolding of these capabilities as the individual matures.

FIGURE 11.10

Newborns Show a Preference for Face-like Stimuli. Newborns looked at the stimulus on the left for about 16 seconds longer than the less face-like stimulus on the right. Looking time has been used as one measure of preference for infants. *Source:* Adapted from Turati, C., Simion, F., Milani, I., & Umiltà, C. (2002). Newborns' preference for faces: What is crucial? *Developmental Psychology, 38*(6), 875–882. Used by permission of American Psychological Association.

© Cengage Learning 2013

Summary 11.1

Milestones of Prenatal and Newborn Development

Stage	Timing	Highlights
Zygote 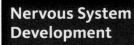 © K. H. Kjeldsen/Photo Researchers, Inc.	1–2 weeks postconception	• Differentiation into germ layers
Embryo © Dr. G. Moscoso/Photo Researchers, Inc.	3–8 weeks postconception	• Nervous system and organs form • Sex organs differentiate in males and females
Fetus © Argosy Publishing, Inc.	Week 9 postconception through remainder of pregnancy	• Growth and maturation of existing organs • REM sleep in seventh month of pregnancy • Good hearing from seventh month of pregnancy
Newborn © Tony Wear/Shutterstock	First 28 days of life	• Reflexive movement • Large amounts of sleep • Improving sensory capacities • Preference for faces

What Physical Changes Occur in Infancy and Childhood?

Physical development in infancy and childhood features very rapid growth, particularly during the first year of life, when the child triples his or her birth weight (see ● Figure 11.11). This growth requires significant nutrition. The infant is likely to enjoy the best health if he or she is breast-fed for one year, with a gradual introduction of solid foods after the first six months of life (Rebhan et al., 2009).

Nervous System Development In the latter months of pregnancy and for the first 18 months of life, the human brain shows rapid growth in gray matter, or collections of neural cell bodies, which we discussed in our chapter on biological psychology. Following this

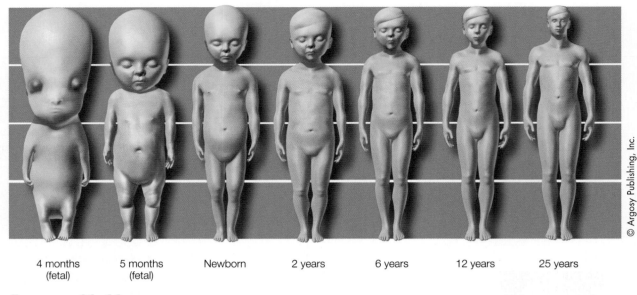

| 4 months (fetal) | 5 months (fetal) | Newborn | 2 years | 6 years | 12 years | 25 years |

© Argosy Publishing, Inc.

FIGURE 11.11

Physical Growth Is Very Rapid in Childhood. Infants grow very rapidly, tripling their birth weight during the first year alone. As they grow, their proportions also change significantly. The newborn's head takes up approximately one quarter of his or her height, whereas the adult's head is about one seventh to one eighth of his or her height. In contrast, the ratio of the trunk to overall height remains the same over the life span at about three eighths. *Source: Adapted from Kail and Cavanaugh (2010).*

If a child's rate of growth during the first year of life continued, a 10-year-old would be about the size of a jumbo jet (McCall, 1979).

burst of brain growth, cells and connections that are not useful are systematically deleted. In other words, we produce more neurons and synapses than we will eventually need, then keep only those that are working well for us (see ● Figure 11.12).

What does it mean to have neurons and synapses that are working well? The nervous system develops according to a "use it or lose it" principle, which emphasizes the important role of experience in wiring the brain. Children who are raised in a stimulating and enriched environment, with many things

FIGURE 11.12

Synapse Formation and Experience. Synaptic growth occurs at different times in brain systems involved with sensation, language, and higher cognitive functions (judgment, reasoning). We produce many more synapses than we need, then retain only those that are used, in a "use it or lose it" fashion. Exposing children to stimulating environments helps them reach their maximum intellectual potential. *Source: Adapted from Nelson (2000).*

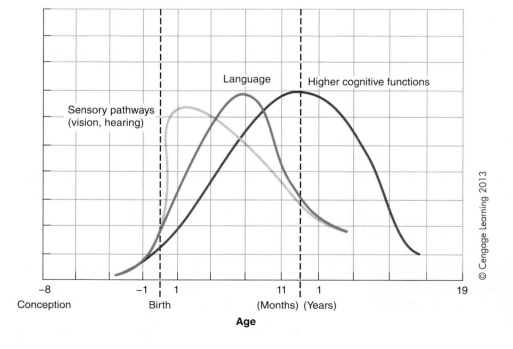

© Cengage Learning 2013

to explore, are likely to have the best outcomes. Children living in intellectually impoverished circumstances may retain too few connections, which may lead to mild forms of intellectual disability.

Myelination, the growth in white matter that begins about six months after conception, continues to develop at a fairly regular rate throughout childhood and adolescence (see ● Figure 11.13). An interesting spurt in myelination occurs between the ages of 6 and 13 years in parts of the brain associated with language and spatial relations (Thompson et al., 2000). The rather sudden end of this white matter growth coincides with the ending of a sensitive period for language development. Bilingual individuals who learn language after the age of 10 or so process their second languages differently than native language speakers (van Hell & Tokowicz, 2010). Unfortunately, most students in the United States begin foreign language study after this age.

FIGURE 11.13

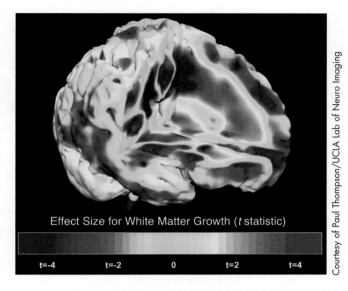

Myelination Increases During Childhood. Imaging technologies have captured the progress of myelination (white matter growth) in childhood. Red and yellow areas show the largest changes. Myelinated systems are much faster and more efficient than unmyelinated systems.

Effect Size for White Matter Growth (*t* statistic)

t=-4   t=-2   0   t=2   t=4

Courtesy of Paul Thompson/UCLA Lab of Neuro Imaging

Motor Development

As we mentioned earlier, newborn human infants are relatively helpless compared to their chimpanzee and gorilla counterparts. The newborn human's mobility is handicapped by her proportions. One quarter of her length is made up by her head. In contrast, adults' heads make up approximately one seventh to one eighth of their height. Motor development, or change in the individual's ability to move and perform physical skills, is largely driven by our human genetic blueprint. Identical twins typically reach motor milestones such as walking with more similar timing than fraternal twins or non-twin siblings (Fox, Hershberger, & Bouchard, 1996). Because identical twins share more genes in common than fraternal twins, reaching milestones at the same time indicates an important role for genetics in early motor development.

Motor development in childhood proceeds simultaneously in two directions. First, we see development in the head-to-toe direction. Controlling the muscles of the neck and shoulders allows the 2-month-old infant to raise his or her head to look around. This achievement is followed by development of the muscles of the torso at about 3 months of age, which are necessary for rolling and sitting. Between 6 and 9 months, the baby begins to crawl, although some happily skip this stage. Finally, around the first birthday, the muscles of the legs are developed sufficiently to support the weight of the child when standing or walking. Well into middle childhood, children continue to improve their movement and coordination, demonstrated by the abilities to skip rope, hop on one foot, and combine movements, such as throwing a ball while running (see ● Figure 11.14).

The second direction of motor development begins at the midline, an imaginary line dividing our bodies in equal halves, and proceeds outward. Infants can bat at toys suspended above their cribs (3 months) before they are able to grasp any objects (5 months). In other words, accurately directing

Parents in most cultures attempt to teach toileting practices when children are about 2 years old. Not coincidentally, the motor systems required to achieve sphincter control are generally myelinated somewhere around 21 months of age (Largo, Molinari, von Siebenthal, & Wolfensberger, 1996).

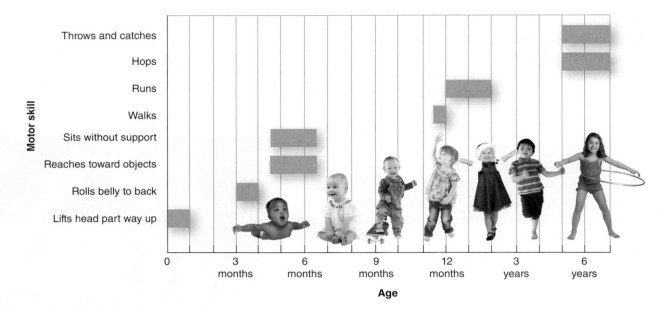

FIGURE 11.14

Motor Milestones. These motor milestones emerge at predictable times over the course of childhood, but can range significantly from child to child. The ages in this chart represent the average time at which children reach a milestone.

Illustration: © Cengage Learning 2013; photos, left to right: © Flashon Studio/Shutterstock; © NADKI/Shutterstock; © Max Topchii/Shutterstock; © Tom Viggars/Shutterstock; © Nadia Virronen/Shutterstock; © Jaimie Duplass/Shutterstock; © Andre Blais/Shutterstock

the arms precedes the ability to direct the hands and fingers. Incidentally, infants learn to grasp objects before they learn to release them, a fact parents may wish to consider before wearing long hair or dangling earrings. Well into elementary school, children are continuing to master control over the fine muscle movements of the hands and fingers required for writing. Perhaps you recall the rather large-lined paper you used in first grade and the challenges of coloring "within the lines." Females enjoy a slight advantage in developing fine motor skills (Hampson, 1990; Hampson & Kimura, 1988; McEwen, 2001). In contrast, boys enter kindergarten with significantly more muscle mass than girls of the same age and often prefer large-scale movements such as running, climbing, and jumping (Wang et al., 1999).

We can predict with some certainty the average age at which each motor milestone will be reached. However, we must be cautious when measuring the progress of any one child against the average age. Around these average ages is a wide range of normal development. Although the majority of children might walk unassisted around their first birthday, some children walk as early as 9 or 10 months of age, while still others do not take their first steps alone until about 18 months of age.

Although early motor milestones are driven largely by biology, they do respond to experience. It is possible to slow down motor milestones by restricting movement. Some cultures, out of safety concerns, restrict the movement opportunities of young children, which slightly delays motor milestones such as walking alone (Kaplan & Dove, 1987). In other cases,

© Robin Moore/National Geographic Stock

Kenyan parents often encourage early walking in their children. Compared to American children, whose average age of walking unassisted is about one year, Kenyan children observed by Super (1976) walked between the ages of 7 and 11 months. In contrast, practices such as swaddling young infants are associated with slightly later attainment of motor milestones.

motor milestones may be reached slightly earlier by providing specific practice in sitting, standing, and walking (Super, 1976). These changes in the developmental timeline are usually slight, because myelination of motor nerves usually just precedes the achievement of a new skill. Once the relevant parts of the nervous system are sufficiently mature, new skills develop rapidly with little practice.

How Does Cognition Change During Infancy and Childhood?

Interacting with brain development and the child's ability to move and explore the environment are changes in the way children process information and solve problems. Even when children are exposed to the same information as adults, their thinking often leads them to very different conclusions. When asked why clouds move across the sky, a 4-year-old might suggest that the clouds are pulled by airplanes, but an adult is unlikely to come to this conclusion. Both child and adult have observed clouds and airplanes moving across the sky, but viewing these occurrences as related is something that only a small child would do. To understand these differences, we need to examine how cognition changes as a function of age and experience.

One of the classic theories about the development of cognition was proposed by Swiss psychologist Jean Piaget (1896–1980). While working with Théodore Simon, who along with Alfred Binet developed some of the first intelligence tests, Piaget became more interested in the errors made by the children rather than their correct responses. He believed that these errors were representative of growth in the child's ability to reason. Later, Piaget's views were challenged and revised by psychologists who believed that he underestimated the capabilities of children at particular ages. We will explore these contemporary approaches after we look more carefully at Piaget.

A preschool child might believe that airplanes pull clouds across the sky, but an adult is unlikely to come to the same conclusion, even though they are watching the same events.

Jean Piaget

Stage	Approximate age	Highlights
Sensorimotor stage	Birth to age 2	• "Here and now" rather than past and future • Exploration through moving and sensing • Object permanence
Preoperational stage	2–6 years	• Language acquisition • Egocentrism • Illogical reasoning
Concrete operational stage	6–12 years	• Logical reasoning • Mastery of conservation problems • "Learn by doing"
Formal operational stage	12 years and above	• Abstract reasoning • Idealism • Improved problem solving

TABLE 11.3 Piaget's Theory of Cognitive Development

If a child can learn about robins without making changes to his or her schema of "bird," assimilation will occur. In contrast, learning about kiwis might require changes in the bird schema, and accommodation will occur.

assimilation The incorporation of new learning into an existing schema, without the need to revise the schema.

accommodation The incorporation of new learning into an existing schema that requires revision of the schema.

sensorimotor stage Piaget's stage of development beginning at birth and ending at the age of 2 years and characterized by active exploration of the environment.

Piaget's Theory of Cognitive Development

According to Piaget's theory, cognitive abilities develop through regular stages, making Piaget's work a classic example of the discontinuity approach discussed earlier in this chapter. Cognition matures as the child increasingly uses concepts and organizing schemas to think. We discussed concepts and schemas in our earlier chapter on cognition.

Two types of adjustments can be made to a schema, depending on the nature of any discrepancies between new information and the existing category. Assume that a child has a rather well-developed schema for birds, which includes features such as "has wings," "has feathers," and "can fly." If the child then learns about a new species of bird, such as a hawk, the child can *assimilate* the new information into the existing bird schema. Hawks definitely have wings and feathers and the ability to fly. In **assimilation**, no changes to the existing schema are required in order to add the new instance. However, let's now assume that the child meets a kiwi, a small, flightless bird from New Zealand. The kiwi doesn't fit neatly at all into the existing schema, which assumes that all birds can fly. The schema must be adapted to fit the new information, a process Piaget referred to as **accommodation**. Through accommodation, the child now understands that although most birds can fly, some exceptions occur.

In addition to his interest in the development and refinement of schemas, Piaget made many other observations about cognition at different ages. We will now explore the particular characteristics found in each of Piaget's four stages (see Table 11.3).

The Sensorimotor Stage Piaget's first stage, the **sensorimotor stage**, begins at birth and lasts until the child's second birthday. The name of this stage reflects the infant's existence in the here and now. The child at the sensorimotor stage does not think extensively in terms of past and future.

Sensations immediately evoke motor responses. As soon as they can crawl, infants work their way (usually quite rapidly) through the environment, exploring new objects by interacting with them physically, particularly by putting them in their mouths. Infants do not seem particularly deterred by features such as taste and are very likely to sample the drain cleaner under the sink unless parents take appropriate precautions to "baby-proof" their homes.

One of the major milestones that occur during the sensorimotor stage is the achievement of **object permanence**. As we discussed in our chapter on memory, infants under the age of 8 months or so do not seem to be able to form clear memories, or mental representations, for objects once they are removed from the immediate present. Piaget, being Swiss, carried a rather beautiful gold pocket watch, which of course was quite attractive to young children. If Piaget covered the watch with his beret while an infant watched, the infant would not show any signs of searching for the now missing watch. Around the age of 8 months or so, infants become more persistent. If you hide the pocket watch now, they will look for it. Object permanence coincides with achieving sufficient growth in the prefrontal cortex, as discussed in our chapter on memory (Diamond & Goldman-Rakic, 1989).

During the sensorimotor period, the child's language abilities are developing rapidly. By the age of 18 months, children usually have a working vocabulary of 10 to 50 words, and by the age of 2 years, they are beginning to combine words into short but meaningful sentences, such as "Want cookie" or "Go bye-bye". These new ways of thinking symbolically lead the child into the subsequent preoperational stage.

The Preoperational Stage Piaget's **preoperational stage** lasts from approximately age 2 to age 6, or the child's preschool years. While significant advances in cognitive and language abilities occur during this stage, thinking is still relatively immature. The stage gets its name from the notion that children are still incapable of engaging in internal mental operations or manipulations, such as following the transformation of objects from one form to another.

Piaget used a variety of creative tasks to demonstrate the characteristics of the reasoning of the preoperational child. **Conservation** tasks require the child to recognize that changing the form or appearance of an object does not change its quantity. One of the observations that led Piaget to consider cognitive development as occurring in stages is the rather abrupt way in which conservation tasks are often solved. Children who could not solve the problem a few weeks earlier suddenly look at the adult experimenter with pity, as if to say, "This may be the world's stupidest grown-up."

In addition to difficulty with transitions, preoperational children have limited abilities to understand points of view other than their own, a characteristic described by Piaget as **egocentrism**. One kindergarten teacher

Preoperational children are unlikely to recognize that pouring liquid from one glass to another of a different size and shape does not change the amount of liquid. They usually believe that the glass that is "higher" holds more. The abruptness with which children master conservation tasks led Piaget to suggest that cognitive development proceeds in stages, but other psychologists believe changes occur more gradually.

object permanence The ability to form mental representations of objects that are no longer present.

preoperational stage Piaget's stage of development beginning at the age of 2 years and ending at the age of 6 years and characterized by use of symbols, egocentrism, and limits on the ability to reason logically.

conservation The ability to understand that changing the form or appearance of an object does not change its quantity.

egocentrism Limitations on the ability to understand the point of view of other people.

asked his class where the sun went at night and received an enthusiastic response of "Yuba City" (which is located in northern California) from one of the students. As it turned out, the young student had moved recently from Yuba City to his current home in San Luis Obispo. Because these were the only two places on earth the child knew, if he was in one place and the sun wasn't there, there was only one other logical place for the sun to be. You guessed it—Yuba City.

Preoperational thinking is also limited by beliefs that appearances are real. While older children understand that movies feature real people dressed up and acting like superheroes, the younger child might believe that not only is the superhero real, but he can really fly.

One of Piaget's legacies to early childhood education is his emphasis on hands-on learning. Colorful objects, or "manipulatives," have replaced endless worksheets used to teach math concepts such as sorting to older generations of students.

The Concrete Operational Stage Piaget referred to the stage between the ages of 6 and 12 as the **concrete operational stage**. Rather suddenly, problems of conservation are easily solved, and thinking becomes more logical. The only remaining limitation is an inability to handle abstract concepts, which will not be resolved until the next and final stage.

Piaget used the term *concrete operations* for this stage because he observed that children reasoned best when allowed to engage in "hands-on" learning. This observation of Piaget's has had an enormous impact on the way early childhood education is conducted in many nations. Endless paper-and-pencil worksheets requiring students to regurgitate math facts have given way to colorful boxes of manipulatives, which allow children to count and sort real things. Children's museums, petting zoos, interactive websites, and other opportunities for experiential learning have become commonplace.

The Formal Operational Stage For Piaget, cognitive development matures in the **formal operational stage**, which begins around the age of 12. The final piece to be added to the child's cognitive skill set is the ability to handle abstract concepts. Abstract concepts usually involve "what if" types of questions and form the heart of scientific inquiry. If you were to ask a group of sixth graders what would happen if everyone on earth became blind tomorrow, they would likely struggle to come up with a reasonable answer. A group of high school students, however, would readily reply that people who were already blind would become instant leaders, as they would have existing skills for coping with blindness.

Accompanying the ability to think abstractly is a big improvement in problem solving. Younger children tend to approach problems by trying things out and seeing what happens, a rather inefficient trial-and-error approach. Teens are more likely to think through several alternatives in a more systematic manner. Abstract thinking ability also appears to stimulate a burst of idealism. What if we could solve world hunger? These are the

concrete operational stage Piaget's stage of development beginning at the age of 6 years and ending at the age of 12 years and characterized by logical but not abstract reasoning.

formal operational stage Piaget's stage of development beginning at age 12 and extending through adulthood and characterized by mature reasoning capabilities.

types of questions teens begin to ask, and they are not always content with the more practical and less idealistic responses of older adults.

Criticisms of Piaget Piaget's classic theories set the standard for his time, but more contemporary developmental psychologists argue that some aspects of his view of cognitive development need updating and revising.

Piaget's strong interest in biology led him to look at human development from a species perspective, which in turn reduced his interest in individual differences. Other psychologists point out that individual cognitive development can be quite variable. Some adults fail to achieve the ability to reason abstractly, or do so only on some problems and not others. This variability makes cognitive development look much more gradual and continuous than stage-like as suggested by Piaget.

> True terror is to wake up one morning and discover that your high school class is running the country.
>
> —Kurt Vonnegut

Piaget did not specify any mechanisms responsible for moving from one stage to the next. Today, using brain imaging methods, we can explain some of these changes, such as the achievement of object permanence and frontal lobe development. Other transitions, such as the relatively sudden mastery of conservation problems, are not so easily explained.

Many psychologists believe that Piaget underestimated the capabilities of young children. At the same time, he might have overestimated the cognitive abilities of adolescents. As we discussed in our biological psychology chapter, the human brain is not fully mature until a person's early 20s, so we would not expect fully adult cognition in an adolescent. For example, adolescents perceive risk as well as adults do, but unlike adults, adolescents are likely to be enticed by a large reward into selecting a very risky alternative (Reyna et al., 2011).

Finally, Piaget has been criticized for viewing the developing child in relative isolation from his or her family, community, and culture. These criticisms have formed the basis for extensions to Piaget's approach, described in the next section.

Alternative Approaches to Cognitive Development Although Piaget provides a useful starting place for the evaluation of cognitive development, not all researchers agree with his conclusions. In the next sections, we will explore some of these alternatives to Piaget's classic approaches to cognitive development.

Vygotsky An alternative to Piaget's approach was proposed by Soviet psychologist Lev Vygotsky (1896–1934). Piaget and Vygotsky illustrate the theme of universal versus ecological development introduced at the beginning of the chapter. Unlike Piaget, whose interest viewed human development as universal across cultures, Vygotsky (1934/1962) stressed the role of culture and cultural differences in the development of the child. For Vygotsky, cultures teach children not only what to think but how to think.

Piaget's developing individual learns to understand the world by actively exploring it, like a miniature scientist, whereas Vygotsky's individual gains knowledge of the world by interacting socially and collaboratively with parents, teachers, and other members of the community (see ● Figure 11.15). Language was a particularly important aspect of cognitive development for Vygotsky. Children first use language to initiate social contact and opportunities to learn. Later, self-directed talk, such as "I need to finish my game before dinner," aids in problem-solving and, in the older child, forms *inner speech.*

Information Processing An information processing model of cognitive development provides important extensions to Piaget's theory (Kail & Bisanz, 1992).

The overall rate of processing information, analogous to your computer's CPU speed, increases during childhood (Cerella & Hale, 1994). In tasks that require judgment, such as deciding which of two numbers is larger, adults are three times faster than 4- and 5-year-olds and twice as fast as 8- and 9-year-olds (Kail & Bisanz, 1992). Surprisingly, by the time children enter elementary school, their performance on tasks requiring focused attention and disregard of distracters reaches adult levels (McKay, Halperin, Schwartz, & Sharma, 1994). In contrast, the ability to sustain attention over time remains very limited until the age of 11 years. Around this age, attention span begins to lengthen significantly each year until adulthood.

Children's memory abilities change dramatically following their second year of life (Bauer, Larkina, & Deocampo, 2011; Bauer & Lukowski, 2010). These changes are likely due to maturation of brain structures related to memory. The amygdala and most of the hippocampus are relatively mature

FIGURE 11.15

Vygotsky's Zone of Proximal Development. Unlike Piaget, Lev Vygotsky viewed development as taking place within the social and cultural environments. His "zone of proximal development" included tasks that the child could learn to do with the assistance of parents, teachers, or other adults or peers. Vygotsky's advice is to provide children with activities that are within reach, but neither too easy nor too hard.

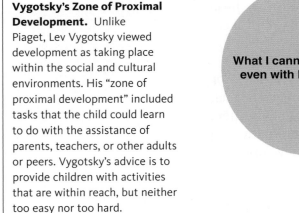

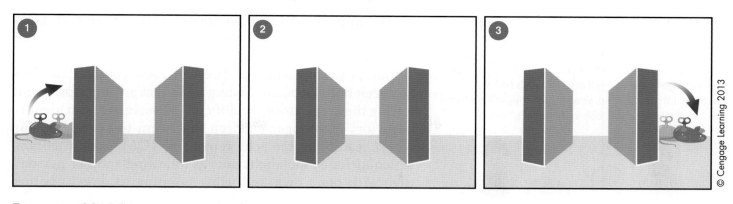

FIGURE 11.16

Children Possess Naïve Theories. Many contemporary psychologists believe that Piaget underestimated the reasoning abilities of young children. Children as young as 2-1/2 months of age looked longer at this impossible situation (the mouse toy, which is moved from left to right behind the blocks, should have been visible as it passed between the two blocks). *Source:* Adapted from Baillargeon, Gertner, and Wu (2011).

at a very early age, around 6 months, but changes in the frontal lobe and hippocampus during the third year of life allow children to form more long-term memories, particularly for sequences of events. Improved memory and a growing sense of self combine to produce some of the first autobiographical memories between the ages of 3 and 5 years (Wang, 2008).

Naïve Theories Piaget suggested that children's abilities to understand objects in their world develop slowly over time. Contemporary developmental psychologists believe that Piaget's assertion was wrong. Instead, very young children seem to understand a great deal about objects and how they work, even before they have had much experience interacting with them (Baillargeon, Li, Gertner, & Wu, 2011). For example, infants as young as 2-1/2 months old looked longer at an impossible situation (a toy mouse that should have been seen moving between two blocks did not appear), as shown in ● Figure 11.16.

Theory of Mind Piaget used the concept of egocentrism to describe the young child's relative lack of awareness of the viewpoints of others. An elaboration of this concept, **theory of mind (TOM)**, has emerged as an important tool in tracking typical and abnormal development. Theory of mind occurs when a person understands that others have beliefs, desires, and intentions that are different from his or her own (Premack & Woodruff, 1978). The classic procedure for demonstrating TOM is the *false belief task*, often referred to as the "Sally–Anne" task (Wimmer & Perner, 1983). Imagine that one doll, Sally, places her ball in a basket and then leaves the room. Another doll, Anne, enters the room, moves the ball from the basket to a box, and then leaves. If Sally comes back, where will she look for her ball? Children who have developed a theory of mind understand that their personal knowledge of where the ball is located is different than the knowledge of Sally, who was absent when the ball was moved. They will correctly decide that Sally will look in the basket (see ● Figure 11.17).

theory of mind (TOM) The understanding that others have thoughts that are different from one's own.

FIGURE 11.17

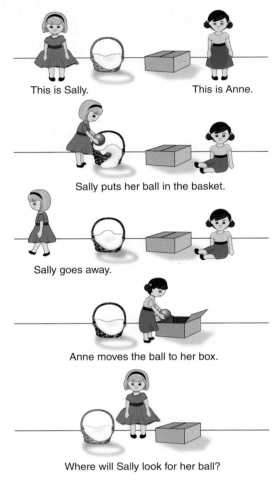

Testing Theory of Mind (TOM). Children who have achieved theory of mind recognize that their personal knowledge of the whereabouts of Sally's ball is different from Sally's knowledge, and they will predict correctly that she will look in the basket.

This is Sally.   This is Anne.

Sally puts her ball in the basket.

Sally goes away.

Anne moves the ball to her box.

Where will Sally look for her ball?

© Cengage Learning 2013

Developmental psychologists generally agree that TOM emerges in children around the age of 3 to 4 years, somewhat earlier than the end of Piaget's preoperational period. Although the presence of TOM in even younger children has been hotly debated, finding tasks that are appropriate for testing these age groups is difficult. However, we can identify behaviors in younger children that seem to act as building blocks leading to the achievement of TOM. Joint attention, which includes such behaviors as following another person's gaze with one's own and using pointing to direct another person's attention to something in the environment, emerges in the first year of life (Barresi & Moore, 1996). Others mention the ability of young children to distinguish between living and nonliving objects as another important step in the development of TOM. Finally, young children appear to make distinctions between intentional and unintentional behaviors, as 3-year-olds will imitate the former, but not the latter (Williamson, Jaswal, & Meltzoff, 2010).

Regardless of the age at which we decide children have TOM, its existence appears critical to further social development, the topic of our next section. A failure to develop a typical TOM has been linked to the development of autism, a disorder characterized by extreme social difficulties which we discuss in more detail in our chapter on psychological disorders (Gopnik, Capps, & Meltzoff, 2000).

How Do Social and Emotional Behaviors Change During Infancy and Childhood?

In contrast to the writings of philosophers such as John Locke and strict behaviorists such as John Watson, developmental psychologists believe that children do not begin life as a tabula rasa, or blank slate. Their personal characteristics, many of which are influenced by genetics, immediately predispose them to certain patterns of experience and elicit different reactions from other people. The bold, adventurous, noisy child will seek out different activities than the shy, cautious, quiet child, contributing to a very different set of experiences in life. Parents, teachers, and peers are likely to respond very differently to these two individuals, further shaping their experience, opportunities, and behavior. These interactions between predispositions, the responses the predispositions elicit in others, and the experiences selected as a result converge to produce the adult personality, which we explore in a later chapter.

Temperament

A child's temperament reflects his or her prevailing patterns of mood, activity, and emotional responsiveness.

Alexander Thomas and Stella Chess proposed that children showed evidence of different temperaments within the first few months of life (Thomas & Chess, 1977, 1989). The nine separate temperament traits proposed by Thomas and Chess were distilled more recently by Mary Rothbart (2007) and her colleagues into three categories: surgency or extroversion (happy, active, vocal, social), negative affect or mood (angry, fearful, shy, frustrated), and effortful control (the ability to pay attention and inhibit behavior). Differences along these initial dimensions predict adult personality. Because these individual differences emerge so early in life, it is likely that they represent genetic differences, a topic we revisit in our chapter on personality. In addition, temperaments are predictive of later psychological disorders. Children who are fearful and shy are at greater risk for anxiety disorders and depression, while children who are frequently angry are at greater risk for externalizing disorders, or problems with aggression and self-control (Rothbart, 2007).

Thomas and Chess reminded us that children do not develop within a vacuum. While temperament may predispose a child to interact with the environment in certain ways and definitely will have an impact on the behavior elicited from caregivers and others, the environment in which the child finds himself or herself will also have an impact. Thomas and Chess refer to this concept as "goodness of fit." Rothbart came to the same conclusion. For example, fearful children with gentle parents developed a stronger internal sense of right and wrong than fearful children with punitive parents (Rothbart, 2007). Similar interactions between temperament and parenting have also been reported in rhesus monkeys, emphasizing the possible biological and evolutionary contributions to these outcomes (Suomi, 2006). Rhesus infants with a particular genotype were unusually aggressive, but only if they were raised by their mothers (see ● Figure 11.18).

FIGURE 11.18

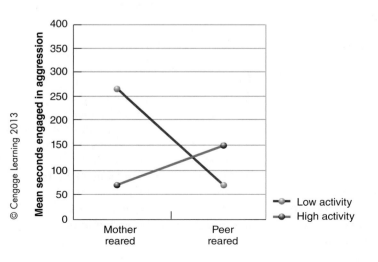

Parenting and Temperament Interact. In rhesus monkeys, variations in a gene called MAOA are related to aggressive behavior. Monkeys with the low-activity variant are typically more aggressive and attain higher rankings within the monkeys' dominance hierarchy than monkeys with the high-activity variant of the gene. This relationship is seen when the monkeys are raised normally with their mothers. However, when monkeys are raised in peer groups without contact with their mothers, the relationship is reversed. The monkeys with the high-activity version are more aggressive. This research supports the "goodness of fit" interactions between child temperament and parenting style proposed by Thomas and Chess and by Rothbart. *Source:* Adapted from Newman, T. K., Syagailo, Y. V., Barr, C. S., Wendland, J. R., Champoux, M., Graessle, M., et al. (2005). Monoamine oxidase: A gene promoter variation and rearing experience influences aggressive behavior in rhesus monkeys. *Biological Psychiatry, 57*(2), 167–172. Reprinted by permission of Elsevier.

Temperament interacts not only with the socialization provided by parents but also with the larger-scale socialization provided by culture. In the United States, but not in China, children with higher effortful control showed lower levels of negative affect, such as anger. In China, but not in the United States, higher effortful control was correlated with less surgency/extroversion (Ahadi, Rothbart, & Ye, 1993).

Attachment

Because of the physical dependency of the human infant on the adult caregiver, maintaining closeness is a high priority. Infants engage in a number of behaviors, such as smiling, cooing, and crying, that are very effective in ensuring adult attention.

Attachment between parent and offspring is not unique to humans. Harry Harlow was interested in identifying the behaviors that led to attachment between mothers and infants, and investigated attachment in rhesus monkeys (Harlow, 1958). Freudian theories still popular in Harlow's day suggested that the pleasure obtained through feeding formed the basis of the bond. Behavioral approaches suggested that the infant was positively reinforced with food for staying near the mother. Harlow was not convinced by either of these arguments and set out to contrast

attachment Emotional bonding between an infant and a parent or caregiver.

Connecting *to* Research

The Evolution of Attachment Behavior

There is a big difference between a newly hatched goose following its mother due to imprinting and the two-way interactions that promote attachment between human mothers and their newborns, including body contact, mutual gaze, and exaggerated facial expressions. Are these more sophisticated interactions exclusively human? Research evidence suggests that the answer to this question is no. Rhesus monkeys also show complex mutual behaviors between mothers and their newborns (Ferrari, Paukner, Ionica, & Suomi, 2009).

The Question: *Do rhesus monkeys have behaviors that are the equivalent of human mother-infant behaviors that promote bonding?*

METHODS

Fourteen mother-infant rhesus monkey pairs were observed while they were living among social groups housed in indoor-outdoor enclosures. Six additional pairs were observed in a more naturalistic setting. For the first two months of the infants' lives, the researchers filmed and recorded the frequencies of mutual gaze (infants and mothers making eye

contact) and lipsmacking (an important rhesus social behavior).

RESULTS

The rhesus infant-mother pairs engaged in frequent mutual gaze and lipsmacking behaviors. The infants spent much more time gazing at their mothers than at other individuals, and this time increased with the age of the infant. Lipsmacking behavior was also a frequently observed method for mothers and infants to interact with each other. This behavior is never observed between adults,

Harry Harlow (1905–1981) studied infant attachment by removing baby rhesus monkeys from their mothers at birth and providing them with a wire mother, such as the one shown here, and a similar mother covered with carpet. Regardless of which "mother" provided food, the infant monkeys spent more time cuddling with the cloth mother than the wire one. Harlow concluded that "contact comfort" provided by the mother was more important to attachment than the food she provided.

the mother's ability to provide food with her ability to provide comfort, security, and safety.

To observe this distinction between the mother's provision of food and comfort, Harlow removed newborn rhesus monkeys from their biological mothers. The infant monkeys were presented with two surrogate mothers, one made of wire and the other of cloth. Either surrogate could be rigged with a milk bottle, allowing Harlow to investigate all combinations of comfort and feeding. Regardless of which "mother" provided food, infant monkeys spent most of their time clinging to the cloth mother and ran to her immediately when threatened by a novel toy. The wire mothers were visited only if they provided food, and then for only as long as the infant was feeding. Based on his observations, Harlow concluded that the Freudian and behavioral emphasis on feeding was wrong. Instead, the mother's ability to provide contact comfort was critical in forming a strong attachment on the part of her infant.

A key factor in predicting the timing of attachment appears to be mobility. Young birds that are mobile upon hatching need to form immediate attachments to a protective adult. Human infants, who are not particularly mobile until the second half of their first year of life, have more time to bond with a caregiver. About the same time infants begin to crawl, usually between 6 and 8 months, they also begin to show evidence of having

so it is exclusive to interactions with infants.

Mutual gaze and lipsmacking both appear to be sensitive to the age of the infant. By the time the infant is in its second month of life, it is spending considerable time outside the mother's vicinity, much as a human child might do when it attends day care or preschool. As the infant physically separates more frequently from the mother, the frequency of the mutual gaze and lipsmacking behaviors also decreases. The behaviors observed in the enclosed area were confirmed by observations in the more naturalistic setting.

CONCLUSIONS

Rhesus monkeys show some of the same types of mother-infant interactions, believed to enhance bonding, that have been observed in humans. This finding suggests that behaviors that set the stage for social interactions in humans are not unique to our species but, rather, have their roots in the evolutionary past. ⊙

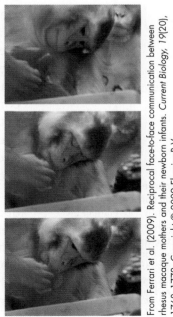

From Ferrari et al. (2009). Reciprocal face-to-face communication between rhesus macaque mothers and their newborn infants. *Current Biology*, 19(20), 1768–1772. Copyright © 2009 Elsevier B.V.

Rhesus monkey mothers and infants show many of the same types of behavior that enhance bonding in human mothers and infants, including mutual gaze.

Secure attachment results from responsive parenting that teaches the child that the parent is there for him or her. Unresponsive parenting teaches children that their needs may or may not be met, so their best strategy is to make regular, frequent, and persistent demands for the parent's attention.

secure attachment A pattern of infant-caregiver bonding in which children explore confidently and return to the parent or caregiver for reassurance.

insecure attachment A pattern of infant-caregiver bonding that can take several different forms but is generally characterized as less desirable for the child's outcomes than secure attachment.

bonded with particular people in the form of separation anxiety (Bowlby, 1969/1982, 1973/1999a, 1973/1999b). Prior to this stage, infants tolerate being handed around to admiring relatives and babysitters without much protest. Once children demonstrate stranger anxiety, however, they will respond to unfamiliar people with crying and distress.

Although stranger anxiety may be a nuisance for parents hiring a new sitter or an insult to visiting relatives, it is an important step forward in the infant's social development. The child now recognizes who does and, more importantly, who does not belong in his or her social world. Infants who do not make this distinction put themselves at greater risk, as they may venture too far from parents or go off quietly in the company of strangers. As we mentioned in our chapter on motivation and emotion, the timing of separation anxiety appears to be constant across many cultures, which implies that it is an example of a human universal pattern with its roots in biology (Kagan, Kearsley, & Zelazo, 1978).

Several different patterns of attachment between infant and caregiver were demonstrated in classic research by Mary Ainsworth and her colleagues (Ainsworth, Blehar, Waters, & Wall, 1978). Young children in a laboratory playroom were observed through a two-way mirror as their mothers or a friendly stranger left or entered the room. Based on the children's reactions to these separations and reunions, their attachment to their mothers was classified as either secure or insecure. Children who demonstrated **secure attachment** played happily and interacted positively with the stranger as long as their mothers were present. However, when the mother left, the child responded by searching for her, crying, and showing other signs of distress. Efforts by a stranger to comfort the child were rejected. When the mother returned, she was greeted warmly, and the child returned to his or her play.

The remaining children demonstrated different patterns of **insecure attachment**. Two of these, avoidant and anxious-ambivalent attachment, were identified by Ainsworth, and a fourth, disorganized attachment, was identified in later work (Main & Solomon, 1986). Children with avoidant attachment did not react to their mother's leaving with distress and allowed themselves to be comforted by the stranger. When the mother returned, the child with an avoidant attachment did not immediately approach her. Children who showed anxious-ambivalent attachment never seemed very comfortable, even when their mother was present. Her leaving was greeted with great distress, and the child was alternately clingy and rejecting when she returned. Children with disorganized attachment seemed confused and not well attached at all. Such children showed contradictory behavior, such as approaching the mother walking backward.

The child's temperament type, discussed previously, interacts with the quality of his or her attachment to caregivers. Avoidant or anxious-ambivalent attachment is more common in children with high negative affect (Vaughn & Bost, 1999). Because of the challenging aspects of their strong negative emotions, these children might elicit less warm and nurturant behavior on the part of a caregiver. In response to little attention from the caregiver, the infant forms a weaker attachment, and the cycle continues.

Mary Ainsworth used the "strange situation" to assess the quality of children's attachment to their mothers. While watched through a two-way mirror, the child's mother first leaves and then returns. Using a careful grading scale, researchers rate children as having a secure attachment or one of several variations of insecure attachments.

Cultural influences on parenting behaviors also influence attachment. Psychologists have compared the frequencies of Ainsworth's three attachment types in the United States to frequencies in Japan and Germany (Cole, 1999). The Japanese sample had about the same proportion of securely attached infants as reported by Ainsworth but had higher proportions of anxious-ambivalent attachments and absolutely zero cases of avoidant attachment. In Germany, the number of anxious-ambivalent infants was about the same as in the United States, but many more had avoidant attachments. The exact features of each culture's norms responsible for these differences remain to be explored.

What types of parenting behavior might foster secure attachment? When you are in public places, such as parks and malls, take a minute to watch parents interact with their children. Some parents are sensitive and responsive to their children's needs (Cox, Owen, Henderson, & Margand, 1992). The responsive parents are teaching their children that the world is a predictable place in which their parents are there for them when needed. Consequently, these children feel free to explore their environment, knowing that if an emergency arises, they will be able to quickly and reliably obtain assistance from their parents. Small securely attached children have a relatively short radius of exploration, which lengthens gradually as they get older.

In contrast, unresponsive or inconsistent parents are teaching their children that the world is an unpredictable place and that the parent may or may not be there for them when needed. In response to such insecure circumstances, children do not venture very far from the parent. As suggested by the results of partial reinforcement experiments discussed in our chapter on learning, children with unresponsive or inconsistent parents make regular, frequent, and persistent demands for attention, because they know that only a small subset of these demands will be met. It might seem counterintuitive, but ignoring children results in clinginess and constant demands for attention, whereas meeting children's needs promptly and reliably fosters independence.

Although American psychologists view a secure attachment to be ideal, attachment might be better viewed with an ecological approach than with a universal approach. Secure attachment is a good model for relatively safe societies (Belsky, 1999). In a safe society, parents have the time and resources to be attentive to children, and the child's exploration is unlikely to put him or her in much danger. In contrast, secure attachments in dangerous societies might actually be maladaptive. If the environment is dangerous, parents have less opportunity to be responsive to their children, and exploration might put the child in great danger. The message that the world is an unpredictable place in which we may or may not be able to help you so stay close might be more realistic under these circumstances.

Parenting Styles We rarely face a task as difficult as parenting with so little training or information. We get more guidance about setting up a computer than about being a good parent. Most parents simply re-create aspects of their own experience, with the more thoughtful parents making a conscious effort to change things that they disliked. If you generally like the way you were parented, chances are that you will feel rather comfortable taking on the parental role yourself. On the other hand, if you do not feel that you were treated well by your parents, you might feel somewhat lost when it comes to finding an approach that suits you.

Thinking
Scientifically

Do Parents Make a Difference?

In 1998, the publication of Judith Rich Harris's *The Nurture Assumption* challenged many of the basic beliefs psychologists held previously regarding the impact of parenting, such as the effects of the parenting styles discussed earlier (Harris, 1998). Most psychologists viewed factors such as parenting style as environmental, but Harris suggested instead that correlations between parenting style and child outcome were due to genetics. For example, children of authoritative parents are just as

likely to experiment with alcohol as teenagers as are children of indulgent parents, but children of indulgent parents are much more likely to become binge drinkers (Bahr & Hoffmann, 2010). The environmental approach would say that this outcome was probably due to differences between the two types of parents in their willingness to limit their children's behavior. In Harris's view, these outcomes are more influenced by genetics. In other words, if you have a certain genetic makeup, you are more likely to parent indulgently

and produce children who binge drink.

You might expect Harris to be criticized by those who believe she takes the "nature" side of the argument too far, but in fact, she has been criticized for not taking the genetic argument even farther. Harris argued that any remaining variation among children that cannot be accounted for by parental genes is the result of peer influence and that peer influence is an environmental variable. Other research confirmed

TABLE
11.4 Parenting Styles

	High support	Low support
High behavioral regulation	Authoritative	Authoritarian
Low behavioral regulation	Indulgent	Uninvolved

Parenting styles can be divided into four categories. These four parenting styles vary along two dimensions: support and behavioral regulation (Baumrind, 1975; Maccoby & Martin, 1983). Parental support takes the form of empathy and recognition of the child's perspective. Behavioral regulation involves supervision of the child's behavior accompanied by consistent discipline and clear expectations (Luyckx et al., 2011).

If we look in the upper left-hand box of Table 11.4, we find the authoritative parenting style, a cross between high support and high regulation. This is the ideal style for parents, as evidenced by the superior outcomes among children raised by parents using this style (Milevsky, Schlechter, Netter, & Keehn, 2007; Simons & Conger, 2007). The authoritative parent is a teacher who disciplines the child with an eye toward making that child a productive, prosocial member of the community. Limits are appropriate for the age and stage of the child's development, and consequences are educational, not punitive. For example, a teen who abuses the privilege of using the family car might lose that privilege for a reasonable time. Because of the emphasis on teaching, these parents tend to use little or no physical punishment. They are consistent and firm but also warm and reasonable. They communicate their standards and invite feedback, but there is no question as to who is running the show.

The upper right-hand box contains the cross between low support and high regulation, or the authoritarian parenting style. The high regulation

Harris's belief in the importance of peer influence on child outcomes, but peer choice appears to be affected by genes, too (Plomin, 1999). We can even see how some aspects of peer influence are more genetic than others. For example, a teen's choice of peers who are similarly motivated to attend college is more influenced by genetics than is his or her choice of associating with delinquent peers (Iervolino et al., 2002).

In practical terms, what does Harris's work offer to young parents? As we stated in our discussion of intelligence in a previous chapter, the fact that something is influenced by genetics does not mean that we cannot or should not intervene to improve the situation. We do not ignore children with genetic conditions that are known to impact intellect, nor should parents interpret Harris as giving them permission to kick back and put their parental duties on cruise control. Regardless of any genetic predispositions to parent in a certain way, we can strive thoughtfully and intelligently to use the authoritative parenting style. ✪

Photo by Nomi L. Harris

Judith Rich Harris

© Gail Albert Halaban/Corbis Outline

In her 2011 book *Battle Hymn of the Tiger Mother*, Amy Chua described her initial efforts to raise her daughters in a "strict, Chinese" fashion instead of a Western style emphasizing self-esteem over achievement, followed by adjustments she made in response to her older daughter's rebelliousness at age 13. How do Chua's experiences fit with our discussion of parenting styles?

provided by these parents prepares children for the limits they inevitably meet in the community from other authority figures such as teachers and law enforcement personnel, but this is considered a less-than-ideal approach in most contemporary environments due to lower levels of warmth and support (Luyckx et al., 2011). Authoritarian parents have a greater tendency than authoritative parents to use harsh punishments, including physical punishment. This behavior can prompt some rebelliousness in the child that is not seen as frequently in response to authoritative parents.

Cross-cultural research has found that the impact of authoritarian parenting does not differ between collectivist cultures and individualistic cultures (Sorkhabi, 2005). Authoritarian parenting in China, Egypt, Australia, and the United States is viewed quite similarly by the children exposed to it, and the outcomes for children of authoritarian parents vary little across these cultures. These children tend to have few problems with externalizing ("acting out") behaviors, such as drug use. However, compared to children raised in authoritative homes, the children of authoritarian parents have more internalizing symptoms, such as depression (Luyckx et al., 2011).

In the lower left-hand box, we find the indulgent parenting style, produced by crossing high support with low regulation. These are very warm, loving parents, but they simply do not want to be the ones who tell their children the dreadful word "no." They are much more comfortable letting others, such as teachers, neighbors, and law enforcement, be the ones to establish any rules. Children of indulgent parents are monitored much less than children of authoritative and authoritarian parents and show a much higher level of cigarette and alcohol use and antisocial behavior (Luyckx et al., 2011).

The lower right-hand box represents the cross between low support and low regulation, or the uninvolved parenting style. This style generally does not occur unless there is something seriously wrong with the family situation. Illness, marital discord, psychopathology, or substance abuse can prevent the parent from carrying out his or her duties in regard to children. As a result of the incapacity of the parent, the children are basically ignored. In extreme cases, neglect may require the intervention of social services in order to maintain the health and safety of the child. By the 12th grade, children of uninvolved parents drink and smoke nearly twice as much as children of authoritarian or authoritative parents, and sons of uninvolved parents are at a very high risk of antisocial behavior (Luyckx et al., 2011; see ● Figure 11.19).

Does a parent consistently stay in the same box? The answer to that question is no. Life circumstances can radically change a parent's style. A very competent parent can be thrown off balance by loss of a job, poor health, divorce, or other disruptions. Once the challenging circumstances are resolved, we would expect that parent to get back on track. What if a person's parents each use a different style? Although this does happen on occasion, the vast majority of couples share a common style of parenting (Milevsky et al., 2007). If the parents do have differing styles, the presence of one authoritative parent can protect the children from the negative outcomes associated with other styles (Milevsky et al., 2007).

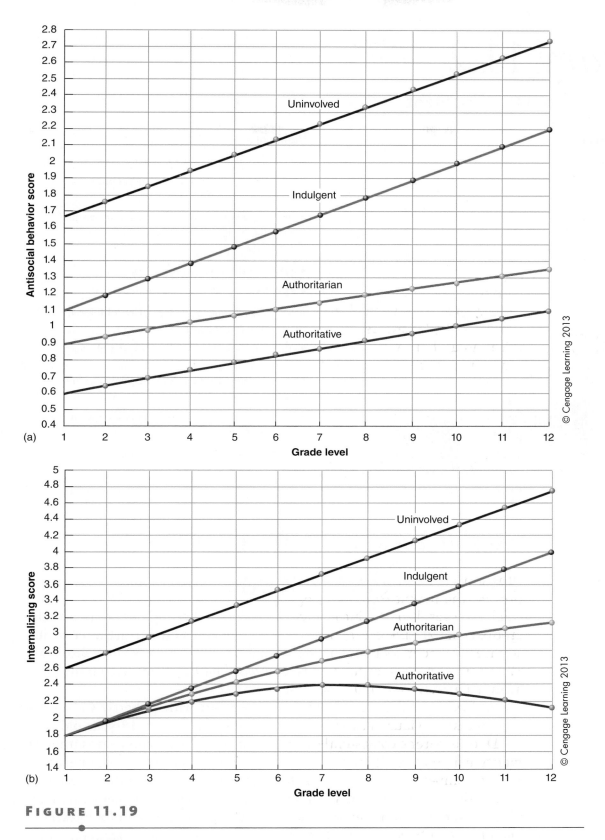

FIGURE 11.19

Parenting Style and Child Outcomes. Authoritative and authoritarian parenting styles are associated with lower rates of antisocial behavior in children than the indulgent or uninvolved parenting styles. However, children with authoritarian parents begin to show progressively higher rates of internalizing problems (feeling depressed and withdrawn) over the course of adolescence compared to children with authoritative parents. *Source:* Adapted from Luyckx et al. (2011).

Summary 11.2

Highlights of Childhood Development

Aspect of development	Highlights
Physical development  © Robin Moore/ National Geographic Stock	• Height and weight increase rapidly. • Both gray and white matter in the brain increase. • Motor control improves from head to toe and from the midline outward to the periphery of the body.
Cognitive development  © Lindsey Parnaby/epa/ Corbis	• Children demonstrate naïve theories. • Children learn language rapidly. • Assimilation and accommodation of information build better concepts. • Thought becomes more logical and abstract.
Social/emotional development  Footage from www .davidsonfilms.com	• Temperament shapes initial responses to the environment. • Children form secure and insecure attachments to caregivers. • Parenting styles interact with temperament.

What Does It Mean to Be an Adolescent?

Adolescence is an artificial, arbitrary period of development that is a relatively recent phenomenon in human experience. In hunter-gatherer societies, sexual maturity at puberty signaled the young person's entry into adult roles, privileges, and expectations. Our word *puberty* comes from the Latin word for "adult."

Although adolescence is assumed to begin with puberty, we do not have much consensus regarding its endpoint. Legally, an 18-year-old is an adult in the United States. However, we restrict legal alcohol consumption to those over 21, and rental car companies rarely rent cars to young adults under the age of 25. Lifestyle factors associated with adulthood, such as financial independence from parents, separate living arrangements, marriage, and parenthood, are far more descriptive of the end of adolescence than age.

Two factors have resulted in an extended period of adolescence in modern, industrial societies, such that it starts earlier and ends later than in the past. One is the dramatic decrease in the age at which **puberty** occurs. Over the last 100 years, the average age of puberty in the United States

adolescence A period of development beginning at puberty and ending at young adulthood.

puberty A period of physical changes leading to sexual maturity.

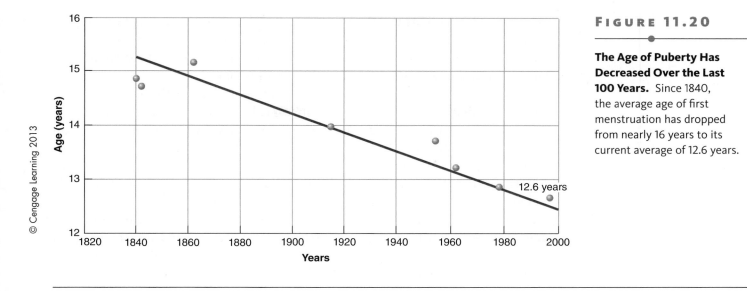

FIGURE 11.20

The Age of Puberty Has Decreased Over the Last 100 Years. Since 1840, the average age of first menstruation has dropped from nearly 16 years to its current average of 12.6 years.

has dropped from about age 16 to around age 12 (Frisch, 1983; (see ● Figure 11.20). For people living 100 years ago, taking on adult roles around the age of puberty was much more realistic than it would be today. Recent evidence shows that this trend is ongoing. We do not know exactly why puberty is occurring earlier. A second factor contributing to the length of modern adolescence is the extended period of education and training needed in technological societies. Youth at puberty are simply not prepared to assume adult roles in most modern cultures.

Physical Changes in Adolescence

Physical changes in adolescence provide individuals with their final preparation for taking on adult roles. Among the most striking physical changes in this period are those related to sexual maturity and brain development.

The physical growth that accompanies the onset of adolescence does not happen to everyone at the same time. Middle school students show a wide range of physical maturity.

Sex and the Adolescent The onset of puberty is marked by a cascade of hormone release, culminating in the maturity of reproductive organs and the development of **secondary sex characteristics**. Males experience muscular development, maturity of the external genitalia, growth of facial hair, and enlargement of the larynx, which leads to a deeper voice. Females experience breast growth, maturity of the external genitalia, maturity of the uterus, and changes in fat distribution and quantity. Menarche, or the first menstrual cycle, occurs relatively late in the puberty process for girls. In response to the same hormones, skeletal growth for both boys and girls begins to slow down. Individuals experiencing early puberty will stop growing at an earlier age.

The obvious evolutionary purpose of puberty is to prepare an individual for sex, so not too surprisingly, teens respond to the physical changes of puberty with a dramatic increase in sex drive. For the hunter-gatherer, no

secondary sex characteristics
Physical changes occurring at puberty associated with sexual maturity.

WHAT DOES IT MEAN TO BE AN ADOLESCENT?   **545**

conflicts occurred, as the assumption of adult roles, including adult sexual relationships, coincided with these feelings. With modern children experiencing puberty as young as 7 or 8 years old, however, we face challenges that are relatively new in our evolutionary history.

Sexual maturation during the teen years parallels further development in gender identity, the assumption of sex-role behaviors, and sexual orientation. As we discussed in our chapter on motivation, sexual orientation refers to a stable pattern of attraction to people of a certain sex, independent of gender identity, sex-role behavior, and sexual experiences. Gender identity refers to a person's sense of being male or female, and sex-role behavior refers to a pattern of traditionally male or female behavior. Many variations in combinations of these variables occur. People with a homosexual orientation typically demonstrate a gender identity consistent with their biological sex, while showing the same range of variation in sex-role behaviors, from traditionally masculine to traditionally feminine, as people with a heterosexual orientation.

The Adolescent Brain Early developmental psychologists, including Piaget, argued that cognition is rather mature at puberty, which in turn implies that the brain is mature. In some aspects this conclusion is correct. By the teens, areas of the brain that process language, spatial relations, hearing, and other sensory processes appear complete. However, much additional work remains to be done before we can consider the brain to be fully adult. Far from considering the brain complete at puberty, today's psychologists are viewing the early teen years as being a second critical period of growth (the first being prenatally up to age 18 months) (Kuhn, 2008).

The onset of puberty is accompanied by substantial gray matter growth, which peaks between the ages of 11 and 12 years. Following this burst of growth, the gray matter normally thins somewhat over the remainder of the teen years (see ● Figure 11.21). Abnormalities in this process may be associated with the onset of schizophrenia, described in our chapter on

FIGURE 11.21

Brain Growth in Adolescence.
In contrast to early developmental theories such as Piaget's that viewed the mind as mature at the outset of adolescence, gray matter growth continues into early adulthood, although the pace slows and the cortex actually thins in some areas. Areas shown in red and yellow are experiencing the greatest rates of growth. Courtesy of Paul Thompson/UCLA Lab of Neuro Imaging

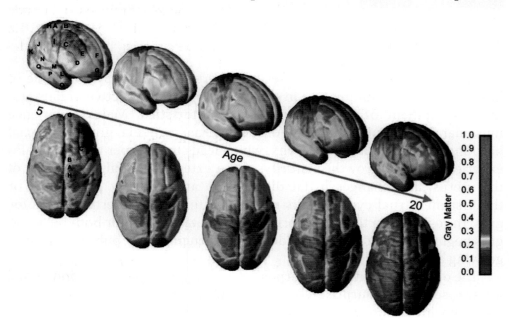

psychological disorders. Youth with early-onset forms of this disorder show four times more loss of gray matter in the frontal lobes than is usually seen in teens of the same age (Rapoport et al., 1999). On the other hand, white matter, or myelin, continues to mature through the teen years and into young adulthood. Myelination of the frontal lobes is much greater in adults aged 23 to 30 than in youth between the ages of 12 and 16. Unfortunately, the adolescent's white matter is more susceptible than an adult's to damage from binge drinking (McQueeny et al., 2009).

Structural differences between the brains of teens and adults affect their interpretations of the emotions of other people. Functional magnetic resonance imaging (fMRI) has been used to observe brain activity in adolescents and young adults while they react to photographs of facial expressions of emotion (Thomas, De Bellis, Graham, & LaBar, 2007; Yurgelun-Todd, 2007). Adults identified the expressed emotions accurately, but teens frequently misunderstood the emotions being displayed. The amygdala, which provides a quick, subconscious assessment of emotion, showed the same pattern of activity in adults and teens. However, the adults showed more activity in the frontal lobes than the teens did, which might account for the adults' superior judgment of emotional expression.

> The old believe everything; the middle-aged suspect everything; the young know everything.
>
> —Oscar Wilde

The earlier maturation of the emotional parts of the brain, such as the amygdala, relative to the logical frontal lobes might account for some of the "risky" behaviors that characterize the teen years, such as reckless and drunk driving, driving without seatbelts, experimenting with drugs, and having unprotected sex. Risky behavior does not result from the teen's inability to judge what is risky or not. If anything, teens actually view life as more risky than it really is and vastly overestimate their personal risks for becoming crime victims or dying in the near future (Fischhoff, de Bruin, Parker, Millstein, & Halpern-Felsher, 2010). At the same time, teens typically believe that they are somehow immune from the consequences of risky behavior—for example, that drunk driving accidents happen to *other* people (Reyna & Farley, 2006). The teen brain also responds more vigorously to pleasure than the adult brain, which means that the immediate pleasurable consequences of a risky behavior can overwhelm the teen's "better judgment" (Galvan, Hare, Voss, Glover, & Casey, 2007).

Cognitive and Moral Development in Adolescence Continuing maturity of the nervous system, interacting with the expanding physical and social environment of the adolescent, leads to more adult ways of thinking and reasoning.

Adolescent Cognition During adolescence, both working memory and reaction time reach adult levels. Teens' problem solving abilities continue to improve. While we all use heuristics, or "rules of thumb" that provide shortcuts to a solution, the adolescent begins to think more logically or analytically (Kokis, Macpherson, Toplak, West, & Stanovich, 2002). For example, children often use their personal experience as a heuristic—the teacher didn't catch my friend cheating on the test, so it's safe for me to

Adolescence is a time when youths apply their new executive strategies to problems and build their knowledge base for specific subjects. Teen film student Jonesha Willis was recognized for her work with The Young Oscar Reel Dreams Award in Hollywood, California.

cheat, too—instead of the more logical, statistical reasoning of the teen—my friend might have had a lucky break, but this teacher is extra good at catching cheaters, so my odds of getting caught remain high, in spite of my friend's experience.

Teens are hard at work acquiring data, and as they build up their knowledge bases, their ability to use executive processes such as strategies improves (Peverly, Brobst, & Morris, 2002). As we mentioned in our chapter on memory, the more you know about a subject, the easier it becomes to learn new things about it. You acquire skills specific to a subject, such as how to solve statistics problems or prepare for a final covering thousands of pages of reading in your literature course.

Moral Reasoning Our human history and literature are filled with heroes and villains, and we are fascinated by their development. How does one child grow to be Mother Teresa, and another to be Adolf Hitler?

Lawrence Kohlberg, a student of Piaget's, attempted to extend Piaget's theory of cognition to explain the development of moral reasoning (Kohlberg, 1981, 1984). To assess changes in moral reasoning, Kohlberg presented children, adolescents, and adults with a number of ethical dilemmas. He was not so interested in the choice the participant would make in response to the dilemma as he was in the reasoning the participant provided for his or her choice. Consider the following dilemma and imagine the choices you might make.

> In Europe, a woman was near death from a very bad disease, a special kind of cancer. There was one drug that the doctors thought might save her. It was a form of radium that a druggist in the same town had recently discovered. The drug was expensive to make, but the druggist was charging 10 times what the drug cost him to make. He paid $200 for the radium and charged $2,000 for a small dose of the drug. The sick woman's husband, Heinz, went to everyone he knew to borrow the money, but he could get together only about $1,000, which was half of what it cost. He told the druggist that his wife was dying and asked him to sell it cheaper or let him pay later. But the druggist said, "No, I discovered the drug and I'm going to make money from it." Heinz got desperate and broke into the man's store to steal the drug for his wife.

Based on the participants' responses, Kohlberg identified three major stages in moral reasoning, shown in Table 11.5. Children and young adolescents are typically in the **preconventional** stage of moral development. In this stage, children will make moral choices based on their expectations of reward and punishment. Their advice to Heinz might be to steal the drug, because letting your wife die is bad, or to avoid stealing because he might be punished for it. Needless to say, some individuals never progress beyond this stage. Stealing or cheating is okay as long as you don't get caught.

Kohlberg believed that during adolescence, the majority of the population moves to the next stage, **conventional morality,** and stays there. In this stage, rules are seen as governing moral behavior and are therefore to be followed. Conventionally moral people are also sensitive to public

preconventional morality Kohlberg's stage at which moral choices are made according to expectations of reward or punishment.

conventional morality Kohlberg's stage of moral development in which moral choices are made according to law or public opinion.

TABLE 11.5	Kohlberg's Stages of Moral Development
Stage	**Features**
Preconventional	Uses probability of rewards and punishments to guide behavior
Conventional	Maintains reputation and follows the law
Postconventional	Follows self-chosen ethical principles

opinion. They want to do the right thing so that others will approve of their behavior. Heinz might be advised to steal the drug or not based on how others would view his behavior. Although conventional morality adds to the stability of a society, it runs the risk of being arbitrary and rigid. In addition, history is full of situations in which local public opinion was supportive of morally abhorrent activities, such as genocide or slavery.

The final step of moral development for Kohlberg was **postconventional morality**. Relatively few people, according to Kohlberg, attain this stage. In conjunction with the abstract reasoning of formal operations, the individual now recognizes that rules are made by human beings and can therefore be flawed. Consequently, personal standards are used as reference points. Obviously, if everybody used postconventional reasoning to select a driving speed on the highway, chaos would ensue. However, the postconventional thinker is likely to evaluate laws and rules critically before complying with them. In the case of Heinz, the legal aspects of theft would be given much less attention than the morality of the druggist's request for compensation and Heinz's request for special consideration for his wife.

Kohlberg is not without his critics. Postconventional reasoning has been criticized as characteristic of males in Europe and the United States, rather than representing a universal stage of moral development (Murphy, Gilligan, & Puka, 1994). Children and adults living in the United States give responses to Kohlberg's dilemmas consistent with the culture's emphasis on personal justice and individual rights. Other cultures place a higher priority on interpersonal factors, such as duty and responsibility to others, and these values can lead to different responses to ethical dilemmas (Miller & Bersoff, 1992).

Social and Emotional Development in Adolescence

As the teen prepares to transition to adulthood, questions emerge about what kind of adult to be. The focus of social activity begins to shift from the family to the peer group, which of course is where most adult interaction will be taking place.

Identity Formation in Adolescence We pick up social development in adolescence by introducing Erik Erikson, a student of Sigmund Freud who outlined stages of social development beginning in infancy, shown in

postconventional morality Kohlberg's stage at which moral choices are made according to personal standards and reason.

11.6 Erikson's Psychosocial Stages

Stage	Challenge	Description
Birth to 18 months	Trust versus mistrust	The child views the world as a safe, dependable place.
18 months to 3 years	Autonomy versus shame and doubt	The child begins to explore.
3 to 6 years	Initiative versus guilt	The child begins to act on the world.
6 to 12 years	Industry versus inferiority	The child develops self-confidence.
Adolescence	Identity versus role confusion	Teens begin to form an identity by asking "Who am I?" Failure to achieve a stable identity leads to role confusion and problems with subsequent stages.
Young adulthood	Intimacy versus isolation	Young adults with clear identities form stable, intimate relationships, while others experience feelings of loneliness and isolation.
Midlife	Generativity versus stagnation	Midlife adults who find value in their lives, even if they have not met all their earlier goals, experience generativity. They are likely to "put back" energy into family, work, and community.
Late adulthood	Integrity versus despair	Toward the end of life, adults who feel that they have lived fully experience a sense of integrity and calm.

Table 11.6. Erikson made significant contributions to our understanding of **identity**, or a unified, consistent sense of self (Erikson, 1968). For Erikson, social development proceeds in stages, with each stage characterized by a fork in the road between a positive outcome and a less than desirable outcome. Adolescence challenges teens to develop a sense of identity (the positive outcome). If they fail, the result is role confusion (obviously, the less desirable outcome).

Teens begin the process of identity formation by asking such questions as "Who am I?" and "What kind of person do I want to be?" These are profound questions indeed, made possible by the newly developed abstract reasoning skills of the teen. The answers are not immediately apparent. Considerable exploration may be necessary before the teen discovers a direction. Many teens may try on a number of different identities, from jock to nerd to goth, before finding one that works.

Many teens explore questions of identity by trying on different roles and affiliating with different groups.

© Image Source/Alamy

Because this process may be somewhat unpleasant, teens may be tempted to short-circuit the process. One technique for prematurely adopting an identity is to assume the identity of a group (Erikson, 1968). By affiliating with a particular club, clique, or gang, teens take on a preformed identity and avoid the challenges of finding their own individual identities. A second approach is the adoption of ready-made identities provided by parents or other mentors. Although parents may have valuable advice regarding choice of college major and career, these are highly individual choices with significant implications. In one

identity A consistent, unified sense of self.

tragic instance, a young man was told from an early age that he should be a physician. He was provided with a Halloween costume of a doctor and was introduced to friends and family members as "our future MD." When the young man began to fail his first semester pre-med courses, he attempted suicide to avoid facing his disappointed parents. Fortunately, the attempt was unsuccessful. In subsequent counseling, therapists helped him identify his special talent for helping troubled youth. The young man obtained his teaching credential and has achieved notable success in working with inner-city youth.

The Benefits of Ethnic Identity For many adolescents, ethnic identity, or how an individual feels about being a member of a particular ethnic or racial group, is a major part of their overall identity (see • Figure 11.22). As we will see in a later chapter on social psychology, having an ethnic identity boosts the overall self-esteem of adolescents and young adults.

An ethnic identity is usually the outcome of an adolescent's exploration of what it means to be a part of the group and a sense of belonging to that group. Many environmental factors contribute to this experience, including family attitudes and the extent of exposure to same-ethnic peers (Kiang, Witkow, Baldelomar, & Fuligni, 2010). Ethnic identities differ in centrality, or the degree to which an individual feels pride in and connection with a group (Charmaraman & Grossman, 2010).

A growing number of individuals identify with more than one ethnic or racial group. Psychologists are investigating this multiethnic experience to see what changes might be required in their theories of ethnic identity development (Shih & Sanchez, 2009).

Family Influences Running parallel to the search for identity is a tendency on the part of teens to spend more time with peers and less with family. Although this preference can be upsetting for the parents, especially if the peers are not to their liking, it may be viewed as a natural step in teen development. After all, most significant social relationships in adulthood

FIGURE 11.22

Ethnic Identity May Lead to Higher Self-Esteem. Identifying with an ethnic group appears to boost the overall self-esteem of African American and Hispanic teens during adolescence and young adulthood. *Source:* Adapted from Erol and Orth (2011).

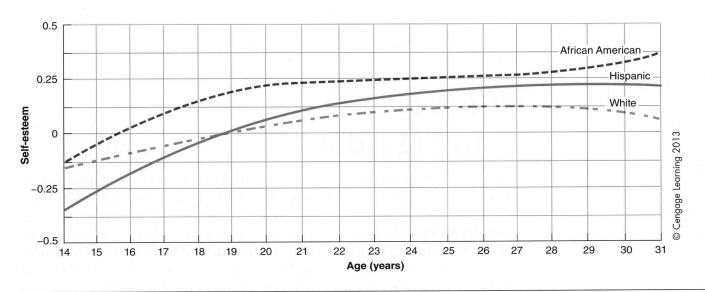

© Cengage Learning 2013

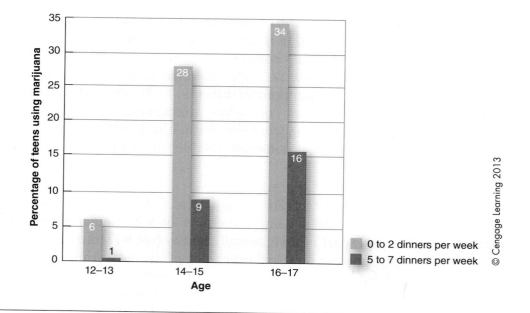

FIGURE 11.23

Family Remains Important in Adolescence. As teens begin to spend more time in the company of peers, balancing that experience with time spent with family is associated with lower risk for substance abuse and other common teen problems. In 2007, 59% of teens reported having at least five dinners per week with their families.

will be with age peers, rather than individuals who are years older or younger. This affiliation with peers can be taken too far, however, as there is evidence that teens who continue to interact regularly with their parents, such as having regular dinners together, are more likely than teens who don't interact much with parents to avoid pitfalls of substance abuse (see • Figure 11.23) and promiscuity (Fulkerson et al., 2006). A healthy balance between family and peer influences appears to produce the best outcomes.

In contrast to popular press accounts of the "stormy" teen years, most teens (and their parents) navigate their passage to adulthood with no more than a few bumps and bruises (Steinberg & Levine, 1997). "Generation gaps" may occur, but teens typically do not deviate too far from their parents' values. Research indicates that most teens love their parents, feel loved by their parents in return, share many of their parents' values, and turn to them regularly for advice (Steinberg & Levine, 1997). Even the "rebellious" teen rarely goes in the opposite direction from his or her parents. Very few of the student radicals of the 1960s were the offspring of conservative parents (Troll, Neugarten, & Kraines, 1969). Instead, these young people were slightly more to the left of their already left-leaning parents.

What Is It Like to Be a Young Adult?

As we mentioned previously, defining the exact point when a person becomes an adult is not easy. In developing nations, marriage remains the dominant marker for adulthood, but in industrialized nations, numerous roles are considered, including the completion of education, full-time employment, independent living, marriage, and parenthood. People do not usually assume all these roles simultaneously, leading to a gradual emergence of adulthood over a period of several years, often extending into the mid-20s.

The timing of many of these milestones has changed over time. In 1970, the average age of a first-time mother in the United States was 21, but this rose to 25 by 2006 (Mathews & Hamilton, 2009). If you reacted to this statistic by thinking, "Oh, that's still too young," it is likely that you are responding to a social clock, or your sense of the "right" time for taking on a role. Compared to their parents' generation, contemporary young adults believe that adult roles should be assumed at later ages and that the social clock is more flexible (Peterson, 1996).

Physical Status The young adult has reached the pinnacle of physical development. If you are in this age group, you are as tall, strong, and fit as you're ever likely to be. Your brain is completely mature, and your senses and reaction time are in excellent shape.

Unfortunately, nothing lasts forever. Age-related loss of muscle mass typically begins as early as 25 years of age, and about 3 to 5% of muscle mass is lost in each subsequent decade of life (Nair, 1995). Not too surprisingly, relatively few over-40 football players remain in the NFL. It is not too early for young adults to consider how to best maintain their physical health. Through childhood and adolescence, we have seen that physical development often follows a blueprint that is strongly genetic. In adulthood, however, lifestyle factors begin to play a greater role in a person's outcomes. In a longitudinal study of over 20,000 adults, following four simple steps added 14 years to life: eating fruits and vegetables, not smoking, drinking alcohol moderately if at all (fewer than two drinks per day for men, fewer than one for women), and exercising (defined in the study as one hour per week; Khaw et al., 2008).

Cognition in Young Adulthood: Postformal Thought In your college experience, you might have seen a professor become very annoyed by a student's inquiry about "the right answer." The search for a single answer, however, is characteristic of formal operations as described by Piaget. At this stage of cognitive development, the teen can follow a logical course of steps to solve a problem (Guignard & Lubart, 2006; Wu & Chiou, 2008). Any lack of agreement with the solution is viewed by the formal operational thinker as a sign that the solution is incorrect.

Although many questions we face in college have right answers, such as an element's atomic weight or whether or not a hypothesis was shown to be incorrect, many more are open to debate. The professor's frustration with your fellow student's interest in only one right answer reflects a difference in adolescent versus adult thinking, or postformal thought. Postformal thought recognizes that the "right answer" is often "it depends" and that many important questions are complex and ambiguous (King & Kitchener, 2002). Adolescents are much more likely to think in absolutes and defer to authorities, such as professors (Perry, 1970). Efforts to move adolescents toward independent, postformal thought are often described as "critical thinking" exercises.

Why is it important to embrace postformal ways of thinking? In our chapter on research methods, we discussed the importance of generating

Photos by Andrew Crowley/The Telegraph

Becoming a parent is no longer restricted to young adulthood. In 1970, the average age of a first-time mother in the United States was 21, and few women became mothers for the first time after the age of 35. These three mothers were 41, 44, and 45 when they gave birth to their first children.

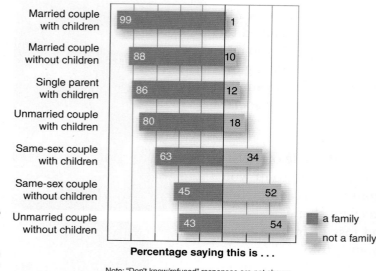

Married couple with children — 99 | 1
Married couple without children — 88 | 10
Single parent with children — 86 | 12
Unmarried couple with children — 80 | 18
Same-sex couple with children — 63 | 34
Same-sex couple without children — 45 | 52
Unmarried couple without children — 43 | 54

a family
not a family

Percentage saying this is . . .

Note: "Don't know/refused" responses are not shown.

Question wording: "As I read you a list of different arrangements, please tell me whether you consider each to be a family or not."

© Cengage Learning 2013

FIGURE 11.24

What Is a Family? American attitudes about what constitutes a "family," a term once restricted to two parents living with their biological children, continue to change and expand to recognize diverse approaches to intimacy. *Source:* Adapted from "The Decline of Marriage and Rise of New Families" from http://www.pewsocialtrends.org/2010/11/18/the-decline-of-marriage-and-rise-of-new-families/. Used by permission of Pew, Social & Demographic Trends.

and testing new hypotheses to move science forward. Using formal operations, a student can evaluate a hypothesis and conclude whether or not it needs to be rejected. However, postformal thinking is an integral part of creativity, in science or in any other field (Guignard & Lubart, 2006). Scientists who are unable to look beyond the "right answers" already existing in their fields are unlikely to make creative contributions that stretch that knowledge.

Relationships in Young Adulthood

As teens enter young adulthood, Erickson suggests that they confront a new challenge: intimacy versus isolation. Frequently, the search for intimacy concludes with marriage and the establishment of a family. Those who fail to find the level of intimacy they seek might experience feelings of loneliness, which in turn can elicit behaviors that are more likely to alienate others instead of promoting intimacy (Cacioppo & Hawkley, 2005). One key to successful intimacy, according to Erikson, is to have established a solid identity in adolescence. If you still don't know who you are, it is unlikely that you will make good judgments about the type of person who will make you happy.

Current trends in the United States include diverse approaches to intimacy and family. In addition to forming traditional families that include two biological parents and their children, large numbers of people are choosing to remain single, live together without being married, be single parents, have children without being married, divorce, and remarry. Along with these changes, public attitudes regarding the question, "What is a family?" continue to change. In the United States, 80% of the public consider an unmarried couple with children to be a family (see ● Figure 11.24), although only 43% consider an unmarried couple without children to constitute a family (Pew Research Center, 2010).

For those who do choose to have children, the experience of being parents often dominates much of their adult lives. Although most parents are quite happy with their choice to take on this role, many young couples experience a drop in marital satisfaction as they adjust to new responsibilities (Demo, 1992). After all, it's rather difficult to feel attractive for your partner with peanut butter and jelly in your hair. Marital satisfaction decreases when children are quite young (see ● Figure 11.25), and rebounds when children become more independent. Couples who describe their relationships as successful experience milder impacts from having children.

What Happens During Midlife?

Just as our criteria for leaving adolescence for young adulthood were somewhat vague, we do not have a set of reliable characteristics that signal

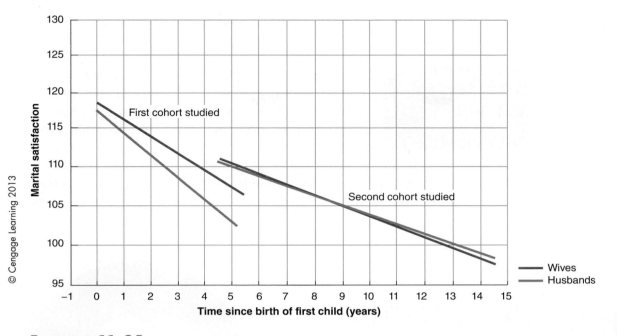

FIGURE 11.25

Marital Satisfaction Drops During Parenting. Couples typically experience a drop in marital satisfaction after the birth of a first child. In this longitudinal study that followed two groups or cohorts of participants, marital satisfaction continued to drop up to the first child's 15th birthday. Couples whose marital satisfaction was higher as newlyweds are much more likely to weather these challenges than couples whose relationship was rocky from the outset. *Source:* Adapted from Lawrence, E., Rothman, A. D., Cobb, R. J., Rothman, M. T., & Bradbury, T. N. (2008). Marital satisfaction across the transition to parenthood. *Journal of Family Psychology, 22*(1), 41–50. doi:10.1037/0893-3200.22.1.41

the transition between young and middle adulthood. Some people view a specific age, such as 40, as a starting point for midlife. Psychologists often point to physical changes, such as graying hair or menopause in women, as signposts for this new transition. Others suggest that a person's growing sense of mortality, possibly boosted by the death of a parent, leads to a feeling of being closer to death than to birth (Jaques, 1965).

As with the urban myths about the "storm" of adolescence, you have probably heard popular accounts assuming that we all have some "midlife crisis" (Levinson, Darrow, Klein, Levinson, & McKee, 1976). For most people, this is simply not true (Rosenberg, Rosenberg, & Farrell, 1999). Middle adulthood is not without its challenges, as many adults find themselves simultaneously caring for children and aging parents, working to meet their career and financial goals, and dealing with physical and possibly marital changes.

With increasing life expectancies on one side and later parenthood on the other, many contemporary midlife adults find themselves "sandwiched," or caring for their aging parents and growing children at the same time.

However, there appears to be no evidence for a large-scale crisis associated with any one age.

<table>
<tr><td>**Physical and Cognitive Aspects of Midlife**</td><td>The major theme of physical and cognitive development in midlife is stability. Assuming that people maintain good health, any changes in the physical and cognitive domains tend to be mild and gradual.</td></tr>
</table>

menopause The complete cessation of a woman's menstrual cycles.

The most significant physical change in midlife for women is the end of their ability to reproduce. **Menopause** is the point where menstruation stops. For most women, menopause is complete in their early 50s, but loss

Experiencing Psychology

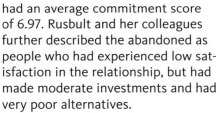

How Committed Are You?

According to an influential model of relationships, the persistence of a relationship is a direct result of the partners' commitment, which in turn is determined by the partners' satisfaction with the relationship, the quality of their alternatives, and the amount of investment they have already put into their relationship (Rusbult, Martz, & Agnew, 1998). In this section, you will have an opportunity to take the commitment test used by Rusbult and her colleagues. If you are not currently in a relationship, you might think about a previous one or perhaps the relationship of someone you know well.

To obtain your total score, add your responses to questions 1, 2, 5, 6, and 7. Add the scores for questions 3

and 4 and subtract this total from 18. Add both subtotals together. Among college participants who indicated that they had been involved in a dating relationship for an average of nearly 20 months, the average overall score on the test was 43.5 out of a possible 56. Rusbult and her colleagues found that this commitment score was a strong predictor of the breakup of relationships, which they assessed by calling their participants later. Those who remained in the relationship had an average score of 6.79 on the commitment items (you can divide your total commitment score by 7 to get a comparable score). People who initiated the breakup of the relationship had an average commitment score of 4.36, and people who were abandoned by the partner

had an average commitment score of 6.97. Rusbult and her colleagues further described the abandoned as people who had experienced low satisfaction in the relationship, but had made moderate investments and had very poor alternatives.

As with any pencil and paper test you take, the results of this one (especially if you ask your partner to take it, too) should not form the basis of life-changing decisions. As you can imagine, this test is subject to large social desirability effects when the results are not confidential, as they were in the real study. Most people are going to give the answers they are expected to give. ⊙

of fertility is a very gradual process beginning many years earlier. Menstrual cycles may become irregular in a woman's 40s as her sex hormone levels that regulate the cycles begin to drop. During the period of transition between the start of irregular periods and the final disappearance of menstruation, women can experience a number of physical and psychological symptoms. Hot flashes, night sweats, headaches, joint pain, mood swings, and sleep disturbances are common complaints, and the severity of these issues can range from barely noticeable to nearly disabling. Hormone treatments to offset these symptoms are used quite cautiously, as they can also increase a woman's risk of stroke, heart attack, breast cancer, and later dementia (Banks & Canfell, 2009).

Men experience much more gradual changes in their reproductive status through the remainder of their lives. Sperm quantity may be reduced, but men in their 80s remain half as fertile as men who are 25. Most men experience little if any decreases in testosterone over the course of the midlife years, although other conditions, such as diabetes, can interfere with the maintenance of an active sex life. For both men and women in midlife, the availability of a partner is much more predictive of sexual activity than any health issues (Karraker, DeLamater, & Schwartz, 2011).

To complete the test, circle the appropriate number:							
1. I want our relationship to last for a very long time.							
1 Do Not Agree At All	2	3	4	5	6	7	8 Agree Completely
2. I am committed to maintaining my relationship with my partner.							
1 Do Not Agree At All	2	3	4	5	6	7	8 Agree Completely
3. I would not feel very upset if our relationship were to end in the near future.							
1 Do Not Agree At All	2	3	4	5	6	7	8 Agree Completely
4 It is likely that I will date someone other than my partner within the next year.							
1 Do Not Agree At All	2	3	4	5	6	7	8 Agree Completely
5. I feel very attached to our relationship—very strongly linked to my partner.							
1 Do Not Agree At All	2	3	4	5	6	7	8 Agree Completely
6. I want our relationship to last forever.							
1 Do Not Agree At All	2	3	4	5	6	7	8 Agree Completely
7. I am oriented toward the long-term future of my relationship (for example, I imagine being with my partner several years from now).							
1 Do Not Agree At All	2	3	4	5	6	7	8 Agree Completely

Social Changes in Midlife

In contrast to the relative stability in the physical and cognitive domains during midlife, this period of life is characterized by significant changes in social and work roles.

Children grow up and move out. If you are the youngest child in your family, you may have noticed that your parents are beginning to feel somewhat more relaxed. For many parents, the "empty nest" period following their last child leaving home is actually accompanied by an improvement in marital satisfaction (Birchler, 1992). Your parents no doubt love you, but they're also relieved to have many of the responsibilities of parenting behind them. However, as ● Figure 11.26 shows, the likelihood that negative emotions will accompany an empty nest varies from culture to culture (Mitchell & Lovegreen, 2009).

Adults in midlife continue to pursue their careers, becoming more expert, or they might initiate a new career that was not previously compatible with the financial and social responsibilities of raising a family. Recent economic and social changes have made midlife work much less stable than it has been for previous generations. At a time when midlife workers want to stay employed longer than previous groups (at least until age 65), some are experiencing downward mobility by taking jobs below their levels of skill and experience or early withdrawal from employment altogether (Elman, 2011).

During midlife, Erikson suggests that adults experience either generativity or stagnation. Many people, particularly during adolescence, set a number of goals for themselves. You may want to win a Nobel Prize or the Olympics, or simply help others have a better life. Whatever your goals, by the time you reach midlife, you will have a rather good idea about whether or not these goals will be met. In many cases, we find that progress has been made toward our goals, although we perhaps didn't meet them completely. Wherever an adult finds himself or herself at midlife, the question

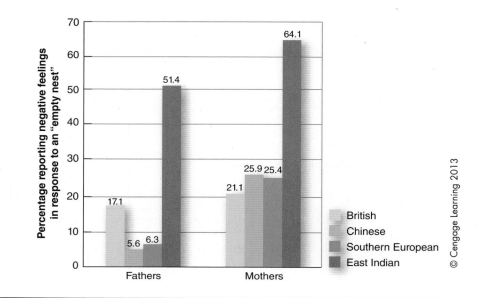

FIGURE 11.26

Responses to the "Empty Nest" Vary Across Cultures. Although most Americans report positive reactions to their last child leaving home, reactions do vary across cultures. Among Canadians of different ethnic groups, being an "empty nest" parent has different meanings. Parents from Chinese and Southern European cultures are less likely to report negative responses to their last child leaving home than are parents with a British background. Parents from India experienced the most negative response of all the groups studied. *Source:* Adapted from Mitchell and Lovegreen (2009).

© Cengage Learning 2013

posed by Erikson is whether or not value exists. If people feel that their lives have had value, even if they are short of their goals, they experience generativity. Adults experiencing stagnation, in contrast, have not found much satisfaction in their lives.

What Is Late Adulthood Like?

As we have seen in our discussion of previous stages of development, the starting point of late adulthood is rather vague. You might think of age 65, a common retirement age, as a starting point, but many of today's older adults are living and working longer than ever before and so are conceiving of "old age" differently than in the past. For example, the baby boomers, or individuals born between 1945 and 1964, are more likely than other age groups to choose 72 as the start of old age (Cohn & Taylor, 2010). Current life expectancy in the United States is 77.9 years (Centers for Disease Control and Prevention [CDC], 2011a).

Physical Changes in Late Adulthood

Assuming good health, the effects of aging on an adult's physical status are gradual and rather mild. Nonetheless, some physical change is inevitable, and understanding the nature of these changes provides guidance for coping with them.

The brain reaches maturity at about age 25, and few further changes occur until about the age of 45. At that time, the weight of the brain begins to decrease, leading to about a 5% decrease by the age of 80 (Anderton,

© REUTERS/David Bebber/BEB/ASA/ACM

Fauja Singh, born in 1911, competes in marathons worldwide as part of the Sikhs in the City team, a group of four runners whose combined age is over 330 years. Running marathons isn't necessary to prevent cognitive decline, but people who participate in 20 minutes or more per day of physical activity have the lowest rates of dementia.

1997). However, this decrease is not accompanied by dramatic cognitive and behavioral changes. Results from the Baltimore Longitudinal Study of Aging (2000) show that healthy aging is accompanied by very mild changes in the speed of learning and problem solving and that most of these observable changes occur very late in life. As with other physical changes, age-related changes in sensory abilities are gradual, and their effects can be offset by the use of technologies, such as eyeglasses and hearing aids.

Cognition in Late Adulthood

Intelligence remains relatively stable during adulthood, as long as general health remains good. Although many people erroneously believe that aging is inevitably accompanied by loss of intellect, only about 6.4% of the population over the age of 60 experiences dementia, such as Alzheimer's disease (Ferri et al., 2005). Cardiovascular disease, including strokes, may have a negative effect on intellect by reducing blood flow to the brain.

Certain types of intelligence change more due to aging than others. As we discussed in our previous chapter on cognition, crystallized intelligence, or the use of accumulated knowledge, changes less than fluid intelligence, or a person's basic information processing skills (Horn & Hofer, 1992). Fluid intelligence correlates with speed of processing, whereas crys-

Psychology
as a Hub Science

Entertainment and the Aging Brain

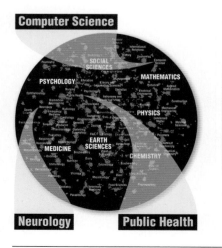

Computer Science

Neurology   **Public Health**

According to the U.S. Centers for Disease Control and Prevention, the number of Americans over the age of 65 has increased from only 3 million to more than 36 million during the last 100 years (Centers for Disease Control and Prevention [CDC], 2007). Over the next 25 years, this group will balloon to over 75 million with the addition of the baby boomers. Not only are the overall numbers of older adults growing, but expectations for an improved quality of life

have increased. Today's seniors want to remain independent, active, and healthy.

Scientists have identified a number of lifestyle factors, especially physical exercise in midlife and later adulthood, that seem to protect people from developing dementia (Geda et al., 2010). But what about commercial technologies that claim to improve cognitive functioning? A number of high-profile technology firms, including Nintendo and

tallized intelligence might be viewed as wisdom, or the ability to draw on past knowledge and experience to solve problems.

Many people maintain high levels of intellectual functioning well into their senior years. Early studies of scientific, scholarly, and artistic accomplishments as a function of age demonstrated a peak in a person's 40s (Dennis, 1966). However, more recent studies show a relatively constant level of professional output. Among professors, research output was far more related to pressure to publish than to a professor's rank or age (Stroebe, 2010).

Old age isn't so bad when you consider the alternative.

—Maurice Chevalier

Social and Emotional Aspects of Late Adulthood

In later adulthood, Erikson suggests that people experience either integrity or despair. Older people who are happy with their life's experiences generally experience integrity (Sneed, Whitbourne, & Culang, 2006; Vaillant & Koury, 1993). They met their goals for the most part and had a rather fun time doing it. In contrast, people who reach their senior years feeling that life passed them by are likely to experience a sense of despair.

You might hold a common stereotype about older adults being sad and lonely. If so, you will probably be surprised to learn that psychological research has found that depression is higher in young people than in healthy, older adults (see ● Figure 11.27) and that older adults report higher subjective well-being overall than young adults (Carstensen, Isaacowitz, & Charles, 1999). Given the frequent challenges of aging, including physical and cognitive changes, what could possibly account for this increase in emotional well-being? Part of the explanation lies in the way people look at the time they have remaining in life (Carstensen, Fung, & Charles, 2003; Carstensen et al., 2010). When people see a long stretch of time remaining

MindWeaver, are marketing "games" designed not just to avoid cognitive decline but to actually improve mental functioning. Nintendo's Brain Training system even quantifies the improvement in terms of "brain age."

Do these systems actually work? Nintendo's system is based on "learning therapy," developed by Ryuta Kawashima. Kawashima and his colleagues have published studies that investigate the usefulness of activities such as reading out loud and performing arithmetic for patients who already have been diagnosed with dementia (Kawashima et al., 2005; Sekiguchi & Kawashima, 2007). Further research is necessary to establish the usefulness of these activities for preventing cognitive decline in healthy adults. In the meantime, if you find these games fun, that is probably a good enough reason to play them. ⊛

FIGURE 11.27

Depression Rates Decrease Over the Life Span. In contrast to stereotypes about sad, older adults, depression rates are actually highest in late adolescence and young adulthood and decrease gradually over the life span. *Source:* Adapted from Kessler et al. (2003).

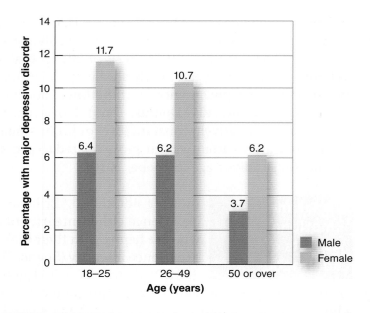

in their lives, they pursue achievement, possibly at the expense of meeting their social and emotional needs. In contrast, when older adults are looking at a much shorter period of remaining life, their goals are refocused toward seeking positive emotional experiences.

One thing that doesn't change during our journey through the life span is the need for social connection. Older adults show significant benefits from their friendships, but they have fewer of them than younger adults and are less likely than younger adults to form new ones (Rawlins, 2004). Relationships with siblings can be especially meaningful for older adults (Connidis, 1992).

Relationships with grown children and grandchildren also form a significant part of the social life of older adults. Traditionally, many parents entered the role of grandparent during midlife, but with more young adults postponing parenting, the grandparent role is occurring later as

Grown children and grandchildren play an important part in the social life of many older adults. Unlike other primates, human beings live long past their reproductive years, suggesting that grandparents may have historically contributed to the survival of their extended families.

© hanhanpeggy/iStockphoto

well. Human beings are somewhat unusual among primates in their length of life span beyond their productive years, a phenomenon known as the "grandmother effect." A healthy woman might live 40 or 50 years past her age at menopause. It is possible that her contributions to the care of her grandchildren, freeing her children for other tasks, might have provided an adaptive advantage over the course of evolution (Herndon, 2010).

Marriage in late adulthood is typically seen as making an important contribution to continued good health. In married older adults, interacting with the spouse contributes to happiness by buffering the individual from stress (Waldinger & Schulz, 2010). Seniors who have remained married to the same person for decades have seen many changes in their relationships over the years. We observed earlier that parents of young children experience a drop in marital satisfaction, which improves as children leave the home as young adults. Long-term marriage partners show more similarities with each other due to a lifetime spent in each other's company, along with a characteristic lack of attention to past negative events and personality traits (O'Rourke & Cappeliez, 2005). In other words, they believe their relationship has been more positive than it actually was. These couples also show an interesting pattern of conflict avoidance, which contributes to higher levels of marital satisfaction.

both: © Ross Parry Agency Ltd

Ralph and Phyllis Tarrant, ages 107 and 101, respectively, have been married 77 years and still live independently as of 2011. Mrs. Tarrant says that the secret of their long-lasting marriage is "getting on with each other, a good diet, exercise, avoiding cigarettes— and a tot of whisky each night."

Summary 11.3

Highlights of Adolescent and Adult Development

Aspect of development	Highlights
Physical change Daily Mail/Rex/Alamy	• Adolescents mature sexually and reach adult height and weight. • The brain continues to grow through adolescence and into young adulthood. • Menopause is a major transition for women in midlife. • Among healthy older adults, physical changes are gradual.
Cognition Arnold Turner/WireImage/Getty Images	• Working memory and reaction time reach adult levels during adolescence. • Thinking becomes more logical during adolescence and more independent in young adulthood. • Moral reasoning in adults is usually conventional or postconventional. • Intelligence remains relatively stable in healthy adults.
Social/emotional life Image Source/Alamy	• Adolescents seek to develop identity. • Relationships might lead to marriage and parenting in young adulthood. • Midlife adults may experience changes in family and work domains. • Older adults show significant benefits from social connections.

Interpersonal Relationships
From the Developmental Perspective

Getting married and being married can mean very different things at different stages in life. Very young couples (marrying under the age of 21) are at higher risk for later divorce. The stability of marriages rises steadily through the 20s and levels off in the early 30s (Lehrer, 2006). In other words, couples marrying at later ages have the same chance of divorce as a couple in their late 20s or early 30s.

The desire to marry also varies as a function of age (Mahay & Lewin, 2007). The proportion of single people expressing no desire to marry is highest in young adults between the ages of 18 and 24 and also among older adults between the ages of 55 and 69. In contrast, only 3 to 4% of single people between the ages of 24 and 54 express no desire to marry. It is possible that the lack of desire to marry among single older adults is due to their beliefs about the potential benefits of getting married relative to the costs. For example, having children reduces desire to marry in older singles, suggesting that they view a new marriage as somehow interfering with that aspect of their lives (Mahay & Lewin, 2007).

One of the more interesting age-related changes in marriage is the impact of similar personalities on a couple's marital satisfaction throughout the life span (Shiota & Levenson, 2007). You have heard us on several occasions in this textbook repeat the saying "Birds of a feather flock together," and overall that is quite true. So it is surprising to note that some similarities in personality are predictive of reduced marital satisfaction, and more so at some life stages than at others. Early in marriage, personality similarities can promote bonding and intimacy. At midlife, however, the focus of the couple often turns to more practical than romantic tasks, such as raising children, advancing careers, and running a household. In this new environment, similarities in the personality trait of conscientiousness are associated with less marital satisfaction (Shiota & Levenson, 2007). The interaction between the highly conscientious person's drive to finish tasks and the midlife tendency to be a bit less flexible in routine suggests that putting two such individuals under the same roof is likely to produce substantial conflict. We might also speculate that two very non-conscientious partners might be overwhelmed by the midlife workload, and the stress resulting from constantly playing catch-up on tasks might take a toll on the relationship. Fortunately, as the family workload diminishes later in life, the married couple's focus returns to intimacy, and the negative effects of similar personality recede again.

Chapter 11 Reflections

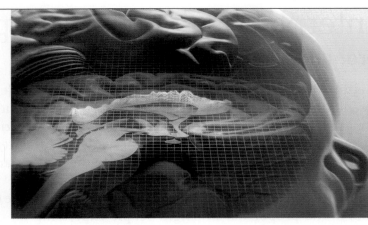

© Argosy Publishing, Inc.

Although the developmental perspective has contributed significantly to psychology on its own, we have seen how a combination of perspectives adds richness to our understanding of the life span.

We began our chapter with a discussion of autobiographical memories, which are usually our earliest memories from childhood. To understand the timing of these memories (between ages 3 and 5 years) and their features (typically memories for highly emotional events), we needed to zoom in to explore the physical development of the child's mind. Growth of the brain and nervous system has not only provided the structure needed to form long-term memories by these ages but also made possible a sense of self. Without the ability to distinguish between self and other, we might have early autobiographical memories about a birthday party, but those memories would lack the meaningfulness of "my" birthday party.

Understanding the formation of an autobiographical memory for one individual child does not explain why White American adults remember more autobiographical memories and in greater detail than do their Chinese counterparts. Zooming farther out, we see how experiencing one's culture can have a large impact on which memories are retained. According to Wang (2008), Chinese preschools explicitly try to focus the preschoolers' attention on their group identity and duty. Wang argues that by doing so, the schools produce the unintentional effect of reducing the vividness of memories anchored to the self.

Across the life span, similar interactions among our evolutionary history, biology, personality, cognition, and social experience help to shape the many facets of age-related behavior described in this chapter. ◄

KEY TERMS The Language of Psychological Science

Be sure you can define these terms and use them correctly.

accommodation, p. 528
adolescence, p. 544
assimilation, p. 528
attachment, p. 536
concrete operational stage, p. 530
conservation, p. 529
conventional morality, p. 548
egocentrism, p. 529
embryo, p. 512

fetal alcohol syndrome (FAS), p. 518
fetus, p. 512
formal operational stage, p. 530
identity, p. 550
insecure attachment, p. 538
menopause, p. 556
object permanence, p. 529
postconventional morality, p. 549
preconventional morality, p. 548

preoperational stage, p. 529
puberty, p. 544
secondary sex characteristics, p. 545
secure attachment, p. 538
sensorimotor stage, p. 528
teratogen, p. 516
theory of mind (TOM), p. 533
zygote, p. 512

MEDIA RESOURCES

Log in to CengageBrain to access the resources your instructor requires. For this book, you can access:

Psychology **CourseMate** brings course concepts to life with interactive learning, study, and exam preparation tools that support the printed textbook. A textbook-specific website, Psychology CourseMate includes an integrated interactive eBook and other interactive learning tools including quizzes, flashcards, videos, and more.

WebTUTOR More than just an interactive study guide, WebTutor is an anytime, anywhere customized learning solution with an eBook, keeping you connected to your textbook, instructor, and classmates.

aplia If your professor has assigned Aplia homework:
1. Sign in to your account
2. Complete the corresponding homework exercises as required by your professor.
3. When finished, click "Grade It Now" to see which areas you have mastered, which areas need more work, and detailed explanations of every answer.

Different versions of the serotonin transporter gene are not equally distributed throughout the world.

The Individual Mind

12

Mind

Personality and the Self

Learning Objectives

1 Compare and contrast the psychodynamic, humanist, trait/Big Five, and social-cognitive theories of personality in terms of the specific individual differences that are emphasized and how these differences are explained.

2 Debate the validity of self-report inventories versus projective tests as measures of personality, considering the strengths and limitations of each.

3 Differentiate and illustrate several distinct aspects of "self" (self-concept, self-awareness, self-esteem, self-regulation) in terms of their content, sources, and implications.

4 Analyze evidence for the biological bases of personality and the self, using studies of identical versus fraternal twins and of correlations with brain region volumes and activity.

5 Distinguish between the personal and interpersonal self, and relate these to cultural differences in individualistic versus collectivistic aspects of self-concept.

Although you might be comfortable with the idea that a trait like a moth's color can make it better adapted to one environment over another, how do you feel about your personality as an adaptation? Are there some types of personalities that thrive in some circumstances better than others? Can a culture shape personality? Can the personalities of a group of people shape their culture?

In our chapter on nature and nurture, we introduced you to a very interesting variation in the serotonin transporter gene, which can come in two versions, or alleles: short (S) and long (L). Children with two short alleles (SS) were more likely than children with either a combination of alleles (SL) or two long alleles (LL) to react negatively to the experience of being bullied (Sugden et al., 2010). Zooming out to the map of the world, you can see that these genotypes are not equally distributed worldwide. Yellow areas have very low frequencies of the S allele, and red areas have very high frequencies. South Africa has a relatively small number of people with the S allele (28%) compared to the United States, Australia, and Great Britain (about 40 to 45%), which in turn is much less than China (about 80%).

Besides having different distributions of the serotonin transporter gene, what else do you know about these cultures? If you thought about

Asians have a much higher probability of having the S allele of the serotonin transporter gene than people living in many other parts of the world.

© Glow Asia RF/Alamy

these cultures as differing in their emphasis on individualism versus collectivism, you are exactly right. Although a number of cultures with lower frequencies of the S allele have more collectivistic cultures than the United States, there is a positive correlation between the percentage of S allele carriers and a culture's rating on a scale from individualistic to collectivistic (Chiao & Blizinsky, 2010). Why would this be the case? Like all correlations, multiple relationships are possible. A population with a certain genetic mix might be more likely to form a particular type of culture, a culture might shape the reproductive success of its members, some outside variable could influence both the genetic mix and form of the culture, or some combination of these factors could influence each other simultaneously (see ● Figure 12.1).

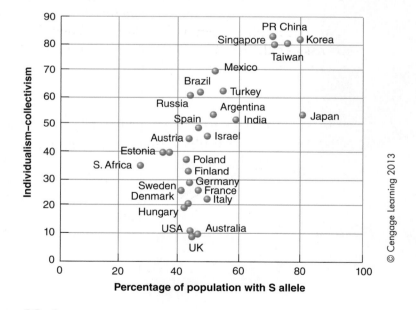

© Cengage Learning 2013

FIGURE 12.1

The Distribution of the S Allele as a Function of Culture Type. The percentage of people carrying the S allele varies according to a culture's position on the continuum from individualism to collectivism. Only about 40% of people in highly individualistic cultures such as the United States, Australia, and the United Kingdom carry the S allele compared to nearly 80% in highly collectivistic cultures such as China, Japan, and Korea. *Source: Adapted from Chiao and Blizinsky (2010).*

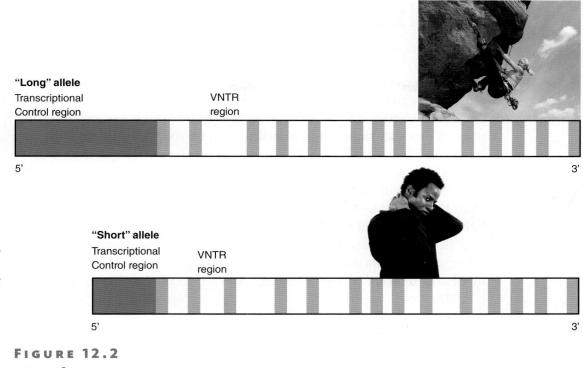

"Long" allele

Transcriptional Control region

VNTR region

5'   3'

"Short" allele

Transcriptional Control region

VNTR region

5'   3'

FIGURE 12.2

The Serotonin Transporter Gene. The serotonin transporter gene comes in two versions, or alleles. People with a copy of the short (S) allele tend to be more anxious and cautious, whereas people with a copy of the long (L) allele are prone to greater risk-taking and creativity.

Zooming in to the level of the individual, we find that people carrying the S allele are especially attentive to negative information, like words and pictures that produce negative emotions (Beevers, Gibb, McGeary, & Miller, 2007; Osinsky et al., 2008). This focus on negativity might assist a person to cope well within a collectivistic environment, as it could lead to a heightened sensitivity to another person's anger or fear. Early recognition of impending negative interactions might give people a chance to smooth things over before they escalate. The L allele, on the other hand, is associated with more attention to positive stimuli, greater risk-taking, and creativity (Fredrickson, 2001; Isen, Daubman, & Nowicki, 1987), which are probably better suited to the individualistic cultural environment. The person carrying the S allele might be too cautious for the individualistic cultural environment, whereas the person carrying the L allele might act like a bull in a china cabinet in the collectivistic cultural environment (see ● Figure 12.2).

It is interesting to note that although the S allele is a risk factor for depression, China has a much lower rate of depression than the United States in spite of the much higher frequency of the S allele in the Chinese population (Chiao & Blizinsky, 2010). The collectivistic cultural environment might buffer an individual with the S allele from the stress that can lead to depression. As you will see in this chapter, individual differences are an important aspect of behavior and mental processing, but must be viewed within the larger contexts of the social and cultural environment. ◎

What Is Personality?

Suppose you were given the following feedback about your personality:

You have a need for other people to like and admire you and yet you tend to be critical of yourself. Although you have some weaknesses, you are generally able to compensate for them. You have considerable unused capacity that you have not turned to your advantage, however. Disciplined and self-controlled on the outside, you tend to be worrisome and insecure on the inside. At times you have serious doubts as to whether you have made the right decision or done the right thing. You prefer a certain amount of change and variety and become dissatisfied when hemmed in by restrictions and limitations. You also pride yourself as an independent thinker and do not accept other's statements without satisfactory proof. But you have found it unwise to be too frank in revealing yourself to others. (Forer, 1949, p. 120)

How well does this description fit your own beliefs about your personality? You might be impressed by how this paragraph presents such specific and personalized information about you. Ironically, most of you probably can relate to this description because it applies to nearly everyone. So the question is: If our personalities are so unique, how can we all be so easily described in a few brief sentences?

The science of **personality** explores characteristic patterns of thinking, feeling, and behaving. To what extent is a person's personality truly unique and to what extent is personality based on some general characteristics that describe nearly everyone? That is, how much do our personalities overlap with those of others? How consistent or inconsistent is our behavior across time and across different situations? How much of a role does biology or experience play in developing our personalities? Is the basic nature of human beings good or bad?

Our understanding of personality has progressed a great deal over the past century. The study of personality for the first half of the 20th century was dominated by the psychodynamic approaches of Sigmund Freud and his followers, who regarded personality as shaped by early childhood experiences. Some theorists, notably the humanists, actively rebelled against Freud and his psychodynamic approach. Others reflected a growing interest in other perspectives of psychology, such as behaviorism, cognition, and biological psychology.

Personality theories represent far more than simple curiosity about human behavior. These theories are intimately bound to our views of normal and abnormal behavior, which we will discuss in a later chapter on psychological disorders. Many of the psychologists who tackled personality theory also contributed influential ideas to the treatment of psychological disorders.

Personality is our characteristic way of thinking, feeling, and behaving. How unique are we? How much do our personalities overlap with the personalities of other people?

personality Characteristic patterns of thinking, feeling, and behaving.

How Do Psychodynamic Theories View Personality?

The term *psychodynamic* was first used in a publication by Ernst von Brücke in 1874 (von Brücke, 1881). Von Brücke used the term as an extension of the first law of thermodynamics, which states that energy in a closed system can change from one form to another, but cannot be created or destroyed. You may not have heard of von Brücke before, but it is much safer to assume you are familiar with one of his students, Sigmund Freud (1856–1939), who made psychodynamics the foundation of his theory of personality.

Freud's Psychodynamic Theory

As a young physician practicing neurology, Freud became known for his success in treating patients with hysteria, a condition characterized by physical symptoms without medical cause that is known today as somatoform or somatic symptom disorder. Freud sought to incorporate his observations and interactions with his patients into a new, unifying theory of psychology. His treatment approach, which we cover in a later chapter on psychotherapy, was known as **psychoanalysis**.

Freud's Model of the Structure of Personality Personality was viewed by Freud as a closed energy system, in which "psychic" or instinctive energy moves among three compartments: the id, ego, and superego (see ● Figure 12.3).

Superego

Id

Ego

Illustration: © Cengage Learning 2013; photos, clockwise from top left: © lukaszfuz/Shutterstock; © hartphotography/Shutterstock; © IKO/Shutterstock

FIGURE 12.3

The Id, Ego, and Superego. Freud viewed the mind as a closed system in which energy flows from one compartment to the next. It is the job of the ego, or self, to balance the pleasure-seeking impulses of the id with the morality imposed by the superego.

psychodynamic A theory put forward by Sigmund Freud in which psychic energy moves among the compartments of the personality: id, ego, and superego.

psychoanalysis Sigmund Freud's treatment approach based on his psychodynamic theory.

Freud proposed that the **id**, which literally means "it" in Latin, is present at birth and contains the primitive drives that serve as a source of energy for the personality, such as hunger, thirst, and sex. According to Freud, the id operates according to the pleasure principle, in which it seeks immediate gratification and relief. As a child begins to interact with parents and other social influences, the ego and superego begin to control the id.

The **ego** is the component of the personality that is readily seen by others, so it acts as the person's "self." Its task is to coordinate the needs of the id with reality. The **superego** develops when a child begins to internalize his or her society's rules for right and wrong, forming what we normally refer to as a "conscience."

In healthy personality development, energy in these three compartments remains balanced. Many cartoons, from Donald Duck to Bart Simpson, have made use of this balance motif. The id, in the form of a devil version of the character, fights with the superego, an angel version of the character, over the course of action to be taken by the character's ego, or self. Imbalances among the components can be the source of unhealthy behavior. An overly dominant id can lead to antisocial behavior, or an overactive superego produces too much guilt.

Levels of Awareness Freud likened the mind to an iceberg, with about one tenth of the mind being conscious and the remaining nine tenths **unconscious** (Freud, 1953). Freud believed that we can retrieve information voluntarily from the conscious but not the unconscious mind—a notion that predated contemporary research on implicit and explicit memories, which we discussed in our chapter on memory. Material that could move at any time into the conscious state, but is not there presently, is preconscious (see ● Figure 12.4). Your conscious mind might be concentrating on understanding Freud right now, but your preconscious mind might contain a thought about how nice it would be to stop for a break and get a slice of pizza.

According to Freud, unacceptable and threatening ideas maintained in the unconscious mind are actively repressed, or blocked from entering consciousness. Repressed ideas can leak into consciousness in the form of anxiety symptoms, dreams, and verbal errors we now refer to as "Freudian slips."

Defense Mechanisms Threats to the balance between the id, ego, and superego can result in anxiety, or the sense that danger is just around the corner. When the ego is faced with anxiety, it engages in a variety of protective behaviors referred to as **defense mechanisms**. Freud defines 9 primary defense mechanisms, shown in Table 12.1: repression, sublimation, rationalization, displacement, reaction formation, projection, denial, regression, and identification. According to Freud, each of these mechanisms helps us channel potentially self-destructive or painful psychic energy into more constructive or manageable behaviors. Freud noted, though, that each mechanism has its limits; if a person continually uses a particular defense mechanism or even defense mechanisms in general, she risks doing damage to the self as well.

> I celebrate myself, and sing myself, / And what I assume you shall assume, / For every atom belonging to me as good belongs to you.
>
> —Walt Whitman

id The component of Freud's personality theory containing primitive drives present at birth.

ego The component of Freud's personality theory that is the self that others see.

superego The component of Freud's personality theory that internalizes society's rules for right and wrong, or the conscience.

unconscious mind The part of mental activity that cannot be voluntarily retrieved.

defense mechanism In Freud's personality theory, a protective behavior that reduces anxiety.

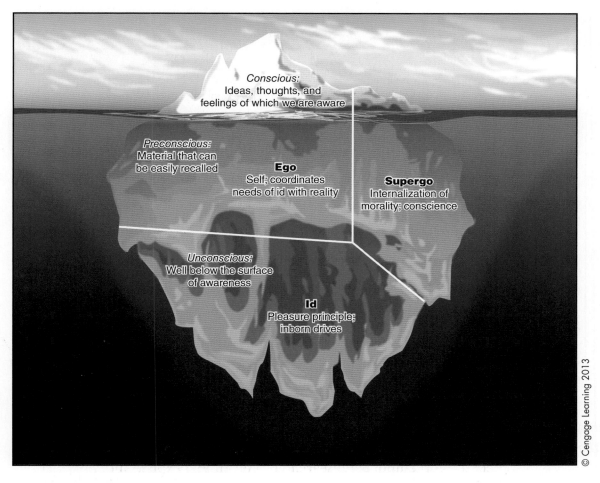

FIGURE 12.4

Freud's Levels of Conscious Awareness. According to Freud, we are consciously aware of only a small percentage of the mind's activities. Some information is located in the preconscious mind and can become conscious at any moment. Information in the unconscious mind can affect our behavior without our awareness.

Stages of Psychosexual Development For Freud, the development of the personality is critical to the remainder of his theories and to the therapeutic process of psychoanalysis. When treating patients for various problems, Freud assumed that the origins of the problems could be found in his patients' developmental past, not in their present circumstances.

As the name *psychosexual* implies, Freud was interested in how the developing personality would deal with the sexual impulses of the id. It is important to note that Freud's use of the word *sexual* was closer to our word *sensual*, referring to all sources of physical pleasure. For the infant, simple touch or

Freud believed that sublimation could redirect psychic energy into more prosocial activities. Organizers of the modern Olympics hoped that nations would compete in sports rather than fight wars.

TABLE

12.1 Freud's Defense Mechanisms

Defense mechanism	Definition	Example
Repression	Anxiety-producing information is returned to the unconscious mind.	A person "forgets" about an embarrassing incident from middle school.
Sublimation	Unacceptable urges are redirected into more prosocial channels.	Aggressive youth take martial arts classes.
Rationalization	Excuses are made for anxiety-producing behavior.	An athlete using performance enhancing drugs says that "everybody is doing it."
Displacement	Negative emotions are redirected from the real source to another target.	You yell at your roommate because your boss yelled at you at work.
Reaction formation	Behavior is opposite to your true feelings.	A guilty partner who is planning to end a relationship sends flowers.
Projection	Anxiety-producing characteristics or behaviors of the self are attributed to others.	A person who cheats on a partner checks his or her partner's cell phone and e-mail for possible cheating.
Denial	Failure to process anxiety-producing information	A student who flunks out of college doesn't move home.
Regression	Reverting to immature behavior to relieve anxiety	A person bursts into tears whenever his or her partner wants to talk about relationship problems.
Identification	Resolving anxiety by taking on the characteristics of others	A small child reassures a teddy bear about fear of the dark.

In an exchange with Albert Einstein regarding the best way to achieve world peace, Freud argued that we should broaden identification, one of his defense mechanisms, by seeking common ground with others. Freud repeated the quote, "Thou shalt love thy neighbor as thyself."

nursing might provide what Freud would refer to as sexual pleasure. Freud proposed five **psychosexual stages** of personality development: oral, anal, phallic, latency, and genital. Like several of the theorists whose work we explored in our chapter on development, Freud believed that the person developed in a stagelike fashion and that successful passage through each stage contributed to the psychic health of the person. Table 12.2 lists Freud's stages and their main characteristics.

Freud believed that an important milestone, the Oedipus complex, occurred during the phallic stage of development. Freud applied the *Oedipus complex* term to both boys and girls, but his followers restricted the term to boys' development and added the concept of an Electra complex for girls. Freud's Oedipus complex begins with the idea that the child's first love object is the parent of the opposite sex. The child competes with the same-sex parent for attention from the opposite-sex parent. Freud argues that the Oedipus complex will be resolved when the child reduces conflict through identification with the same-sex parent. As part of this identification process, the values of the parents are internalized by the child.

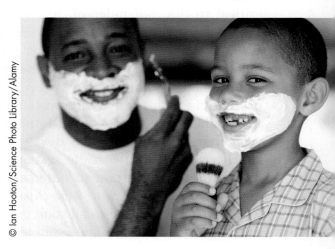

© Ian Hooton/Science Photo Library/Alamy

According to Freud, children reduce conflict arising from the Oedipus complex by identifying with their same-sex parent.

psychosexual stage A stage in Freud's theory of the developing personality.

TABLE
12.2   Freud's Psychosexual Stages of Development

Stage	Approximate ages	Main characteristics
Oral stage	Birth to 1 year	Pleasure obtained by sucking
Anal stage	1 to 3 years	Conflict between child's ability to eliminate wastes at will versus societal expectations of toilet training
Phallic stage	3 to 6 years	Oedipus and Electra complexes lead to identification with same-sex parent
Latency stage	6 to 12 years	Focus on internalization of society's rules
Genital stage	12 years and above	Focus on adult sexual interests and behaviors

For Freud, personality is the product of conflict occurring during the psychosexual stages. Personality characteristics emerge as the id, ego, and superego resolve their conflicts and struggle for balance. Freud believed that a failure to resolve a particular conflict, such as weaning, toilet training, or finding a sexual identity, resulted in fixation. If fixation occurs, the person maintains childlike behaviors that are related to the conflict and stage in which problems occurred. For example, a child who does not receive adequate stimulation in the oral stage may experience an oral fixation. According to Freud, this person may continue to pursue oral gratification, in the form of overeating, smoking, or drinking, throughout adulthood.

Fixations could lead to the development of a neurosis, Freud's term for what is now referred to as an anxiety disorder, which we discuss in our chapter on psychological disorders. A neurosis for Freud represents a continuing conflict between the ego and the id, superego, or both. Should the conflict become so great as to produce a conflict between the ego and reality, psychosis (including abnormal behaviors characteristic of schizophrenia and other serious disorders) might occur (Freud, 1938).

Sigmund Freud has become a mainstay in popular culture.

Contemporary Views of Freud Although there is no question regarding the tremendous influence Sigmund Freud has had on modern thinking, his legacy today is considered mixed. Freud's approach to development contrasts sharply with the scientific theories of development we explored in the preceding chapter, and most psychologists today do not adhere to Freud's theory. But his work remains important in that it had such a profound influence in psychology and popular culture. Instead of viewing children as miniature adults, Freud saw them as having different needs at different ages, which revolutionized many aspects of parenting and child care. We continue to be vastly entertained and intellectually challenged by plays, novels, and other art featuring characters who are driven by unconscious conflicts to behave in ways they don't understand.

A few Freudian constructs appear to be supported by scientific investigation, even though the

Freud and the Arts: Freud's theories often find their way into books, plays, and movies, as characters are driven by unconscious conflicts they don't understand.

Freud's approach to child development was popularized in the United States by Dr. Benjamin Spock, whose Book of Baby and Child Care *graced the bookshelves of 24 million American families between 1940 and 1970 (Bach, 2006).*

theoretical mechanisms he proposed have been refuted. The notion of defense mechanisms, the distinction between conscious and unconscious processes, and descriptions of some types of adult personalities remain topics of research in psychological science (Kline, 1981). On the other hand, contemporary scientists point out that Freud's ideas rarely lend themselves to scientific investigation. For example, how would you design an experiment to study the Oedipus complex? Some of his other ideas, such as women's penis envy, are viewed as remarkably sexist (Sprengnether, 1990). Additional criticisms center around the effectiveness of psychoanalysis, which we discuss in more detail in our later chapter on psychotherapy.

The Neo-Freudians

No theory as influential as Freud's is likely to be left alone without revision. A number of Freud's followers began to diverge from his approach to construct their own psychodynamic theories. We refer to these as "neo" or "new" Freudians. A common feature of the **neo-Freudian** theories was a substitution of social competence for sexuality and pleasure as the major motivation for human behavior. These theorists brought the psychodynamic approach closer to contemporary views of human beings as social animals, a theme we discuss throughout this textbook. Unfortunately, the theories put forward by the neo-Freudians share one of Freud's greatest weaknesses—the proposal of constructs that do not lend themselves to scientific investigation. We will highlight a few of the notable contributions of this group.

Alfred Adler Alfred Adler (1870–1937) contributed the notion of an inferiority complex to psychodynamic thought (Adler, 1956). According to Adler, an inferiority complex, or overwhelming feelings of inferiority, can lead to overcompensation, usually in the form of seeking the appearance of superiority rather than the substance. For example, a person might overcompensate for feelings of inferiority with peers by purchasing a fancy, expensive automobile. Adler was also one of the first psychologists to suggest that siblings, along with parents, could have an influence on development, leading to investigations of the effects of birth order (Adler, 1956).

Alfred Adler suggested that an inferiority complex can lead to overcompensation in the form of seeking the appearance of superiority. "Man heels" that add at least 2 inches of height have become increasingly popular and are worn frequently by Hollywood stars.

Imaginechina via AP Images

neo-Freudian A theorist who attempted to update and modify Freud's original theory of personality.

Carl Jung Carl Jung (1875–1961), a Swiss psychiatrist, divided the unconscious mind into two components. The personal unconscious remained the same as Freud's unconscious mind. Jung added a deeper level, the collective unconscious, comprised of our common psychological predispositions as human beings passed from generation to generation (Jung, 1928). After observing common themes in cultures around the world during his extensive travels, Jung argued that generations of experience with concepts such as darkness, power, death, and parents would lead to characteristic ways of unconsciously thinking about such topics. Jung's ideas are echoed in today's evolutionary approach to psychology, which views the mind as having adapted over the course of evolution (Walters, 1994).

This Tibetan mandala represents unity formed out of the four elements of earth, wind, water, and fire, a theme that Carl Jung believed was universal in the human collective unconscious.

In addition to his expansion of the concept of the unconscious, Jung deviated from Freud by providing more specific information about differences in individual personality. In particular, Jung's concepts of the personality characteristics of extroversion (outgoing) and introversion (relatively less outgoing) are still very much alive in current discussions of personality. Jung's personality characteristics form the basis for several currently popular personality tests, such as the Myers-Briggs Type Indicator (MBTI).

Karen Horney Karen Horney (1885–1952; pronounced "horn–eye") was one of the first female psychiatrists. Horney rejected many of Freud's ideas to concentrate on aspects of the culture that contributed to women's feelings of inferiority. Simultaneously, while treating male patients, Horney became convinced that men envied women's ability to become pregnant and be mothers. Her emphasis on the impact of a male-dominated society on women helped set the stage for many subsequent feminist scholars (Horney, 1923–1937/1967).

How Do Humanists Approach Personality?

Until the 1960s, American psychology was dominated by two perspectives—behaviorism and the psychodynamic approach. At that time, some psychologists began to consider other ways of approaching psychology in general, and personality specifically. One alternative approach, initially referred to as "third-force" psychology (behaviorism and psychodynamic theory were forces one and two), later became known as humanistic psychology.

Humanistic psychology differed from behaviorism and the psychodynamic approach in distinctive ways. Humanists were convinced that human beings are unique, and they argued that the animal research favored by behaviorists was irrelevant. The humanists' belief that human nature is

Karen Horney was one of the first female psychiatrists, and although considered a neo-Freudian, she rejected many of Freud's ideas to concentrate on the sources of women's feelings of inferiority.

basically good contrasts dramatically with the darker view of human nature put forward by Freud and other psychodynamic theorists. The humanists believed that psychodynamic theories placed too much emphasis on abnormal behavior. Instead, they advocated studying exceptional people to see why they succeeded, a tactic continued by contemporary positive psychology approaches, discussed in a later chapter on health psychology.

One of the leading humanists, Abraham Maslow, was primarily interested in human motivation, and we discussed his contributions to this area in our chapter on motivation. He did not attempt a full-fledged theory of personality, although he made some interesting conclusions about the characteristics of exceptional people. After reviewing biographies of people like Albert Einstein, Jane Addams, William James, and Abraham Lincoln, Maslow observed that exceptional people had a number of common traits (Maslow, 1950). In addition to the expected characteristics, such as creativity, realistic thinking, and concern for others, Maslow's exceptional people had some surprising qualities. They had few friends, well-developed senses of humor, and periodic mystic or peak experiences.

Carl Rogers, another notable humanist, put forward a theory of personality based on his experience as a therapist (Rogers, 1951, 1980). We discuss Rogers's approach to therapy in our later chapter on psychotherapy. Rogers, like Maslow, believed that humans strive toward self-actualization, or maximizing their individual potential. For Rogers, people who follow the path laid out by their feelings will lead productive, healthy lives. They will experience congruence, or similarity, between their real selves and their ideal selves. Congruence is most likely to occur in response to unconditional positive regard, or a nonjudgmental appreciation for a person's true nature. Being treated judgmentally makes people act in ways that are incongruent, or inconsistent, with their ideal selves, which might lead to disordered behaviors (see ● Figure 12.5).

As we observed in the case of psychodynamic theories, it is somewhat difficult to move from the humanists' description of personality to our original definition of personality as consisting of stable and consistent patterns of behavior. The humanists are more interested in the process by which personality develops than in the actual characteristics that emerge. Like the psychodynamic theories they rejected, the humanists are subject to criticisms of being unscientific in their methods (Child, 1973). We will return to the humanists' contributions to therapy in a later chapter.

FIGURE 12.5

Carl Rogers's Humanistic Theory of Personality. Carl Rogers, like other humanists, believed that people were striving for self-actualization, or the ability to maximize their potential. Achieving that goal depended on the response of other people (family, friends, society) to the self. If a person receives unconditional positive regard, or nonjudgmental acceptance, he or she can reach self-actualization. On the other hand, if a person's acceptance is conditional on whether or not he or she pleases others, the result is "self-discrepancies" that can lead to depression, anxiety, and other negative outcomes. *Source:* Adapted from Bernstein (2011).

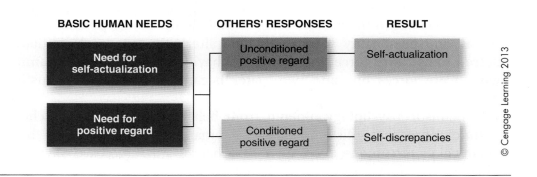

© Cengage Learning 2013

How Do Trait Theories Explain Personality?

Following a discussion of psychodynamic and humanist approaches to personality, the trait approach seems relatively simple. A **trait** is a stable personality characteristic.

Psychologists were hard at work testing personality traits, using methods described later in this chapter, long before they derived coherent theories to explain their findings. They realized intuitively that traits often clustered together. An outgoing person might also be expected to be brave and cheerful. However, these approaches lacked the precision required by a true theory of personality. Statistical methods of correlation and factor analysis came to the rescue (see ● Figure 12.6). As we discussed in our chapter on research methods, correlations allow us to see if two variables have some systematic relationship with each other, such as height and weight or speed and strength. Factor analysis allows a researcher to compare large numbers of correlations simultaneously, which makes the technique perfectly suited to the study of clustered personality traits (Spearman, 1904).

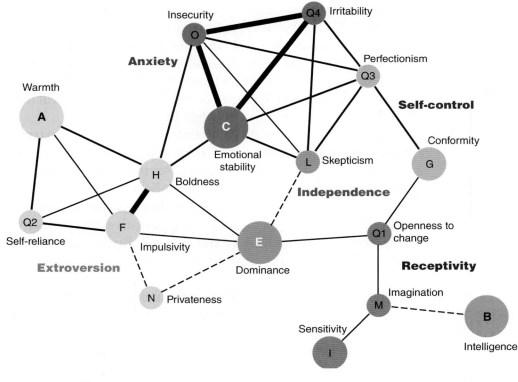

© Cengage Learning 2013

FIGURE 12.6

Factor Analysis Identifies Clusters of Personality Traits. The statistical technique of factor analysis allows psychologists to identify factors that positively correlate or cluster together as well as the strengths of those relationships. Raymond Cattell identified 16 personality factors that formed five clusters (extroversion, anxiety, self-control, independence, and receptivity) that are similar to the factors in the Big Five theory proposed later by McCrae and Costa (1985). The darker lines represent stronger statistical relationships.

trait A stable personality characteristic.

FIGURE 12.7

The Big Five Theory of Personality.

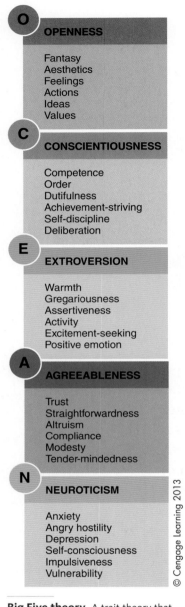

O OPENNESS

Fantasy
Aesthetics
Feelings
Actions
Ideas
Values

C CONSCIENTIOUSNESS

Competence
Order
Dutifulness
Achievement-striving
Self-discipline
Deliberation

E EXTROVERSION

Warmth
Gregariousness
Assertiveness
Activity
Excitement-seeking
Positive emotion

A AGREEABLENESS

Trust
Straightforwardness
Altruism
Compliance
Modesty
Tender-mindedness

N NEUROTICISM

Anxiety
Angry hostility
Depression
Self-consciousness
Impulsiveness
Vulnerability

© Cengage Learning 2013

Big Five theory A trait theory that identifies five main characteristics that account for the majority of individual differences in personality.

extroversion One of the Big Five traits (opposite to *introversion*) characterized by warmth, gregariousness, assertiveness, activity, excitement-seeking, and positive emotion.

introversion One of the Big Five traits (opposite to *extroversion*) characterized by coolness, reserve, passivity, inactivity, caution, and negative emotion.

neuroticism A Big Five personality trait characterized by anxiety, angry hostility, depression, self-consciousness, impulsivity, and vulnerability.

Early Trait Theories

One of the earliest efforts to identify personality traits began with the selection of 4,500 words that described observable traits out of a dictionary (Allport & Odbert, 1936). Some of these terms were defined as central traits, or those characteristics that most clearly define and differentiate a person (Allport, 1937). These are the types of terms you might use when trying to describe someone you know: smart, hard-working, and outgoing.

Emerging computer technologies in the 1940s allowed psychologists to refine lists of traits further (Cattell, 1946/1969). Using factor analysis, the original list of 4,500 words was reduced to 16 major personality traits. Each trait took the form of a continuum between opposites. For example, the trait of suspiciousness would range from "trusting" at one extreme to "suspicious" at the other. The basic methods and elements for trait theories were now in place.

The Big Five Theory

A common theme found in the work of early trait theorists is that relatively few traits are required to accurately describe and predict an individual's behavior. Based on this work, a **Big Five theory** identified five core traits: openness to experience, conscientiousness, surgency (extroversion), agreeableness, and neuroticism (McCrae & Costa, 1985, 1987; Norman, 1963). To remember the Big Five traits, use the acronym OCEAN. The development of a personality test to measure the five traits has made it possible for many investigators to explore Big Five theory scientifically (see ● Figure 12.7). The current version of the test is known as the NEO-PI-R (Costa & McCrae, 2011). You will have an opportunity to take a short version of this test in this chapter.

Each of the Big Five traits consists of a continuum from one extreme to the other. **Extroversion** (opposite of *introversion*) is characterized by warmth, gregariousness, assertiveness, activity, excitement-seeking, and positive emotion, although extroverts also tend to be a bit insensitive and overbearing. **Introversion** is characterized by coolness, reserve, passivity, and caution, although introverts also tend to be sensitive and reflective. Extroverts tend to seek out social activity and find it invigorating, whereas introverts are more likely to want time to themselves to recharge their batteries.

The second characteristic, **neuroticism**, combines anxiety, angry hostility, depression, self-consciousness, impulsivity, and vulnerability. The opposite trait could be described as emotional stability. Although scoring high on neuroticism sounds quite unpleasant, this trait does appear to have survival advantages (Zhang, Chrétien, Meaney, & Gratton, 2005). In threatening and impoverished environments, high neuroticism may be precisely what is required to increase one's chances of surviving to reproduce. We observed a similar argument in our chapter on development, in which a child's insecure attachment to the parents was shown to have potential benefits for survival in a dangerous environment (Belsky, 1999). Whether considering a personality trait or attachment, the anxious, clinging child is more likely to stay near protection, enhancing survival in dangerous situations.

Openness to experience involves fantasy, feelings, actions, ideas, values, and aesthetics (an appreciation for the arts). People who score high on openness are curious, unconventional, and imaginative. They are more likely to be interested in exploring aspects of life that are different from their own, whether this means trying new foods, traveling to exotic locations, or studying other religions. People who score low on openness are more likely to be practical, traditional, and conforming. They prefer the familiar over the new, choosing a chain restaurant in a new city rather than experimenting with the local cuisine.

Agreeableness includes trustworthiness, altruism, trust, compliance, modesty, and tender-mindedness. People who score low on this trait tend to be cynical, uncooperative, and rude. Once again, we face the challenge of finding any advantages for a negative-sounding trait like disagreeableness. At least in employment settings, disagreeable people seem more capable of making "tough decisions," whereas their more agreeable colleagues might find it more difficult to supervise others (Rust, 1999). In one study, men who scored below the mean on measures of agreeableness earned 18% more than men who were more agreeable (Judge, Livingston, & Hurst, 2012).

Finally, **conscientiousness** incorporates competence, order, dutifulness, achievement striving, self-discipline, and deliberation. People scoring high on this trait are reliable, are hardworking, and complete tasks on time. People scoring low on this trait are unreliable, somewhat lazy, and undependable. It might be frustrating to work on group projects with people who are low in conscientiousness, but under some circumstances, they do make valuable contributions. For example, they might help by identifying unnecessary steps in a process, reducing the time pressure felt by a group, or even promoting some forms of "outside the box" thinking and problem solving.

In the years following the development of the Big Five theory, the traits it outlines have provided a valuable framework for investigating job performance (Barrick & Mount, 1991), parenting style (Prinzie, Stams, Deković, Reijntjes, & Belsky, 2009), psychological disorders and substance abuse (Kotov, Gamez, Schmidt, & Watson, 2010), happiness (DeNeve & Cooper, 1998), academic performance (Komarraju, Karau, & Schmeck, 2009), and many other domain-specific outcomes. Evidence across diverse cultures, including the United States, Japan, Korea, Germany, Portugal, Israel, and China, suggests that these personality traits represent a universal human characteristic (McCrae & Costa, 1997).

People who score high on the trait of openness are curious, unconventional, and imaginative.

Across a wide range of professional, skilled, and unskilled job descriptions, the conscientiousness variable had the greatest positive correlation with success (Barrick & Mount, 1991). Surprisingly, the same meta-analysis found little relationship between agreeableness and job performance.

Out of the Big Five characteristics, conscientiousness shows the highest positive correlation with work-related success, whether a person is employed in a professional, skilled, or unskilled job.

openness A Big Five personality trait characterized by an appreciation for fantasy, feelings, actions, ideas, values, and aesthetics.

agreeableness A Big Five personality trait characterized by trustworthiness, altruism, trust, compliance, modesty, and tender-mindedness.

conscientiousness A Big Five personality trait characterized by competence, order, dutifulness, achievement striving, self-discipline, and deliberation.

Experiencing Psychology

A Short Version of the Big Five Inventory

The full version of one of the tests frequently used to measure Big Five traits, the Big Five Inventory (BFI), contains 44 items. The following 10-item version has served as a reasonable substitute for the full test for research purposes when time is limited (Rammstedt & John, 2007). If reading about the different Big Five traits has left you wondering about your own personality, this is your chance to get an idea of where you stack up on each of these factors.

To take the test, just circle the number that represents your best answer for each item. At the end, we'll tell you how to add up your scores. A self-report test like this is only as good as you make it by answering honestly. Wanting to appear socially desirable by downplaying your negative characteristics might make you feel better, but this approach will reduce the validity of the test results. At the same time, no paper-and-pencil test is perfect, and if a result does not fit the way you and others honestly view your personality, feel free to disagree with the results. ✪

The BFI-10 Personality Test				
1. I see myself as someone who is reserved.				
1 Disagree strongly	2 Disagree a little	3 Neither agree nor disagree	4 Agree a little	5 Agree strongly
2. I see myself as someone who is generally trusting.				
1 Disagree strongly	2 Disagree a little	3 Neither agree nor disagree	4 Agree a little	5 Agree strongly
3. I see myself as someone who tends to be lazy.				
1 Disagree strongly	2 Disagree a little	3 Neither agree nor disagree	4 Agree a little	5 Agree strongly
4. I see myself as someone who is relaxed, handles stress well.				
1 Disagree strongly	2 Disagree a little	3 Neither agree nor disagree	4 Agree a little	5 Agree strongly
5. I see myself as someone who has few artistic interests.				
1 Disagree strongly	2 Disagree a little	3 Neither agree nor disagree	4 Agree a little	5 Agree strongly

6. I see myself as someone who is outgoing, sociable.				
1 Disagree strongly	2 Disagree a little	3 Neither agree nor disagree	4 Agree a little	5 Agree strongly

7. I see myself as someone who tends to find fault with others.				
1 Disagree strongly	2 Disagree a little	3 Neither agree nor disagree	4 Agree a little	5 Agree strongly

8. I see myself as someone who does a thorough job.				
1 Disagree strongly	2 Disagree a little	3 Neither agree nor disagree	4 Agree a little	5 Agree strongly

9. I see myself as someone who gets nervous easily.				
1 Disagree strongly	2 Disagree a little	3 Neither agree nor disagree	4 Agree a little	5 Agree strongly

10. I see myself as someone who has an active imagination.				
1 Disagree strongly	2 Disagree a little	3 Neither agree nor disagree	4 Agree a little	5 Agree strongly

Here is how you should score your results. To ensure that you don't just pick the same number for each item, half of the questions "reverse" the scale. Follow the directions below carefully so that you obtain a correct score. Scores can range from 1 to 5 on each trait.

Extroversion: Q1R (Reverse) and Q6

Subtract your answer to Q1 from 6 and add to your answer to Q6. Divide by 2.
Scores of 1 or 2 are introverted, scores of 4 and 5 are extroverted, and a score of 3 is neutral.

Agreeableness: Q2 and Q7R (Reverse)

Add your response to Q2 to (6 minus score on Q7) and divide sum by 2.
Scores of 1 or 2 are disagreeable, scores of 4 and 5 are agreeable, and a score of 3 is neutral.

Conscientiousness: Q3R (Reverse) and Q8

Add (6 minus score on Q3) to Q8 and divide sum by 2.
Scores of 1 or 2 are low conscientiousness, scores of 4 and 5 are high conscientiousness, and a score of 3 is neutral.

Neuroticism: Q4R (Reverse) and Q9

Add (6 minus score on Q4) to Q9 and divide sum by 2.
Scores of 1 or 2 are low neuroticism, scores of 4 and 5 are high neuroticism, and a score of 3 is neutral.

Openness: Q5R (Reverse) and Q10

Add (6 minus score on Q5) to Q10 and divide sum by 2.
Scores of 1 or 2 are low openness, scores of 4 and 5 are high openness, and a score of 3 is neutral.

How Do Situations Affect Personality?

Not all psychologists were convinced by the argument that personality originated in stable traits that produce consistent patterns of behavior across different situations. Research showing that situations could exert a stronger influence on people's behavior than any individual predispositions highlighted limits to the general trait approach. We discuss a number of these situations in our chapter on social psychology. For example, studies of obedience or conformity might be better understood by evaluating the situations people encounter rather than any predispositions or traits they bring to the laboratory (Asch, 1951; Milgram, 1963).

Consistent with their emphasis on experience, learning theorists attempted to capture the effects of circumstances and situations on personality development. Early behavioral learning approaches gave way to social-cognitive learning theories that emphasized the importance of social rewards, such as approval, and internal processes, such as expectations, in shaping personality.

Are these people helping to free a car from the snow because of their individual personality traits? Or do situational variables do a better job than personality traits at predicting our behavior?

Classic Behavioral Approaches to Personality

Behaviorist approaches to personality emphasized learning as an important influence on personality development. Because learning is a lifetime process, behaviorists expected to see more change and variability than would trait theorists in personalities observed over time.

According to behaviorist B. F. Skinner, the principles of operant conditioning, discussed in our chapter on learning, would lead to the development of stable "response tendencies" that might appear to others as "traits." For example, if your parents were very strict about enforcing rules at home, like finishing chores, you might look like a very conscientious person who always finishes assigned tasks on time.

Compared to personality traits, Skinner's response tendencies were more flexible and subject to change. If a person experienced something new, his or her ways of responding would change to reflect that new interaction with the environment. If you now move away from home to college, and you no longer have your parents to reward or punish you based on your completion of tasks, you might not be conscientious at all about finishing your homework on time.

Social-Cognitive Learning Theories of Personality

Midway in the 20th century, some behaviorists began to think in more cognitive terms and believed that learning theories of personality had neglected motivations, emotions, and cognitions. These behaviorists recognized the importance of personality in social contexts, where your behavior is shaped and rewarded by interactions with other people. The resulting **social-cognitive learning theories** are consistent with our observations that single perspectives in psychology do not always capture the whole story.

Locus of Control One influential social-cognitive learning theory popularized a type of cognitive expectancy known as **locus of control** (Rotter, 1966). If you have an external locus of control (*locus* means "place"), you expect that most of the things that happen to you occur due to chance or luck or factors beyond your control. On the other hand, if you have an internal locus of control, you believe that most of your outcomes are due to your own efforts.

Due in large part to cultural norms in the United States emphasizing independence, many American psychologists see having an internal locus of control as an advantage. People with an internal locus of control manage stress more effectively, floss their teeth more regularly, seek shelter in response to tornado warnings, use their seat belts while driving, and practice effective birth control (Wallston, 2005). On the other hand, people with an internal locus of control tend to be less sympathetic with the plight of others, viewing their troubles as due to their choices and behavior as opposed to outside forces they can't control (Lane, 2001).

People with an internal locus of control believe that most of our outcomes are due to our own efforts, while people with an external locus of control believe that our outcomes are more often due to factors beyond our control. Although people with an internal locus of control experience less stress, they tend to be less sympathetic with the plight of others. The person with an internal locus of control might believe this woman needs to try harder to escape homelessness, while the person with an external locus of control might believe this woman just needs help and better opportunities.

Reciprocal Determinism and Self-Efficacy Albert Bandura, whom we met in our chapter on learning, attempted to capture a balance between external, environmental factors and internal traits in his theory of **reciprocal determinism** (Bandura, 1990, 1993). Like other social-cognitive learning theorists, Bandura rejected the strict behaviorism of Skinner as applied to personality. He agreed with Skinner that the environment can determine behavior, but reciprocally, as people influence the environment through both their internal cognitions and their behavior.

Bandura believed that observation of others' behavior played an important role in the development of personality. Although much of his work centered on aggression, Bandura believed that many other characteristics were learned in this same manner. He was particularly interested in self-efficacy (Bandura, 1990, 1993, 1995). This characteristic refers to a person's level of confidence in her or his own abilities to gain reinforcement. If your self-efficacy is high, you have strong expectations that positive outcomes are within reach. If you study hard and get good grades, you expect to obtain a good job in your chosen career. On the other hand, if your self-efficacy is low, you might doubt your abilities to reach your goals. Self-efficacy can be situation specific. You might be confident in your abilities in science but less so in rock climbing. A person's self-efficacy influences his or her environment and experiences. A confident job candidate is probably more likely to be hired than an applicant who appears insecure.

social-cognitive learning theory
A theory of personality that features cognition and learning, especially from the social environment, as important sources of individual differences in personality.

locus of control A cognitive expectancy featured in social-cognitive learning theories of personality about the source of individual outcomes; an external locus of control sees outcomes as resulting from luck or chance, while an internal locus of control sees outcomes as the result of individual effort.

reciprocal determinism A social-cognitive learning theory of personality that features the mutual influence of the person and situation on each other.

If-Then Relationships Walter Mischel argued that trait theories could not explain the variation in an individual's behavior across situations (Mischel, 1968). For example, when 51 boys at a summer camp were observed, their extroversion–introversion scores could not predict the extent of their extroverted or introverted behaviors across 21 different situations (Newcombe, 1929). Instead of focusing on traits alone, Mischel argued that the stability we expect in a person's behavior arises from her or his characteristic way of interpreting situations (Mischel, 2004).

To illustrate this process, consider two children who both score "high" on some measure of aggression. Trait theorists would expect the children to be consistently more aggressive than their low-scoring peers, regardless of circumstances, yet these are precisely the results that Mischel finds lacking in actual studies (Mischel, 1968). Instead, an individual child's behavior can be predicted by considering "if-then" relationships between situations and behavior (Mischel & Shoda, 1995). One child may be aggressive when approached by peers, but will respond passively to an adult's efforts to apply discipline, while another might show the opposite pattern. In other words, *if* the child experiences a particular situation (interacting with peers or adults), he or she will *then* respond with a unique, stable set of behaviors (aggressive or passive). These if-then patterns will be characteristic of an individual, leading to the stable characteristics we think of as personality.

Self-efficacy is the belief that you can handle a challenging situation and obtain future rewards.

What Are the Biological Bases of Personality?

Biological theories of personality attempt to build bridges between observed traits and their underlying biological correlates. Among the biological variables theorists have attempted to connect to personality are temperament, genetic predispositions, and brain structure.

Temperament and Personality

We introduced the concept of **temperament**, or a child's pattern of mood, activity, or emotional responsiveness, in our chapter on life-span development. Contemporary psychologists believe that temperament is biological in origin (Rothbart, 2011) but quickly begins to interact with the social and physical environments. Not only does a bold, fearless child select different activities, but he or she will be treated differently than a quiet, cautious child by peers, parents, and teachers.

Two dimensions of temperament appear particularly important for adult personality: reactivity and self-regulation (Ahadi & Rothbart, 1994; Rothbart & Derryberry, 1981; Rothbart, Ahadi, & Evans, 2000). Reactivity describes differences in people's responses to novel or challenging stimuli. People's responses may vary in terms of both intensity and timing. Some people respond to such stimuli immediately with highly intense

temperament A child's pattern of mood, activity, or emotional responsiveness linked to later personality.

anxiety, others more slowly, and some barely notice the stimuli at all. Self-regulation involves the ability to control attention and inhibit responding to perceived stimuli. These dimensions of temperament appear to be related to the Big Five traits. Higher reactivity is characteristic of introversion and neuroticism (Aron et al., 2010), while self-regulation is associated with later conscientiousness (Rothbart, Sheese, Rueda, & Posner, 2011).

Genetics and Personality

The early emergence of temperament in life suggests a possible genetic origin for personality.

Most efforts to study the effects of genetics on personality use the twin study method, such as the Minnesota Study of Twins Reared Apart (Bouchard, 1994; Bouchard, Lykken, McGue, Segal, & Tellegen, 1990). In this ongoing research, Thomas Bouchard and his colleagues have studied 59 pairs of identical twins and 47 pairs of fraternal twins who had been raised in separate families, as well as a larger number of twins raised in the same home. The pairs of identical twins were quite similar, regardless of whether they were raised together. Some characteristics showed stronger positive correlations between identical twins, such as their scores on an occupational interest scale. Other characteristics showed relatively weaker positive correlations, such as nonreligious social attitudes. The critical finding was that the identical twins raised apart and together were very similar to one another, whether the overall positive correlation for a particular characteristic was strong or weak (see ● Figure 12.8).

Differences in the temperament dimension of reactivity predict children's responses to novel or challenging stimuli. Children with high reactivity often display high introversion and neuroticism later in life.

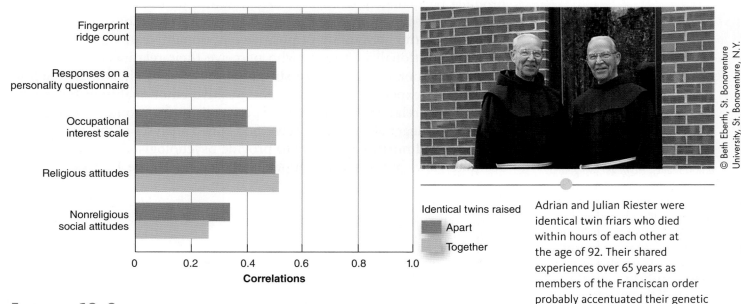

Identical twins raised
Apart
Together

FIGURE 12.8

Adrian and Julian Riester were identical twin friars who died within hours of each other at the age of 92. Their shared experiences over 65 years as members of the Franciscan order probably accentuated their genetic similarities.

Comparisons Between Identical Twins Raised Together or Apart. Some characteristics, such as the number of ridges you have in your fingerprints, are much more strongly influenced by genetics than other characteristics, such as your nonreligious social attitudes. Regardless of how much genetic influence a trait might have, identical twins show considerable similarity, whether they grow up in the same household or not.

The Big Five personality traits show an approximate heritability of .50 in humans (Bouchard & Loehlin, 2001). As we discussed in our chapter on nature and nurture, heritability always refers to populations rather than individuals. Saying that a trait such as shyness has a heritability of .40 does not mean that 40% of a person's shyness is produced by genes and the other 60% by the environment. Instead, a .40 heritability ratio suggests that across the human population, the variations we see in shyness from high to low are influenced moderately by both genetics and environmental factors.

If genetics accounts for about half of the variability seen in the population's personality, what is the source of the other half? Environmental influences take the form of shared experiences, which affect all members of a family, and non-shared experiences, which affect single individuals. For example, you and your siblings might have the shared experience of attending the same elementary school and always having Thanksgiving dinner with the extended family, but the non-shared experiences of studying different musical instruments, having different friends, or playing different sports.

Knowing about the heritability, or variation across the population, for a trait like extroversion does not tell us much about the development of an individual's personality. Our general heritability estimates are similar to knowing the overall average annual temperature in North America. Although this information could be useful for the study of global warming trends, it doesn't tell us much about whether California is likely to have more wildfires or if the skiing industry in Colorado will have a good year. We know that the population heritability for a factor such as positive emotionality is between .46 and .52, but this fact doesn't tell us much about how heritability interacts with shared and non-shared environments to produce particular outcomes (Krueger, South, Johnson, & Iacono, 2008). For example, depending on a teenager's perceived relationship with his or her parents, the heritability of positive emotionality can vary widely. The positive emotionality of teens who perceive their relationship with their parents as poor is much more strongly predicted by their individual, or non-shared, experiences, whereas the positive emotionality of teens who enjoy strong relationships with their parents is more strongly predicted by genetics (Krueger et al., 2008). These fine-tuned analyses of the interactions of nature and nurture are likely to provide psychologists with much more accurate views of the sources of personality (see ● Figure 12.9).

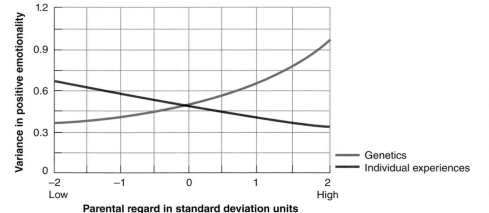

FIGURE 12.9

Genetics and Teen's Relationships With Parents Interact to Predict Positive Emotion. Without taking environment into account, genetics explains between 46% and 52% of the variability we see in positive emotionality. However, we gain a much better understanding of positive emotions when we also consider environments, such as a teen's relationship with his or her parents. When teens report a positive relationship with their parents, most of the variation we see in their positive emotionality is genetic, but when their relationship with their parents is poor, their positive emotionality is better predicted by their individual experiences than by their genetics.
Adapted from Krueger, South, Johnson, and Iacono (2008).

© Cengage Learning 2013

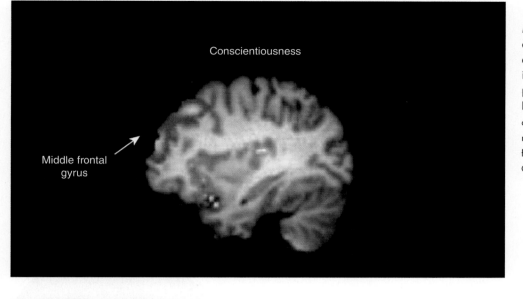

Conscientiousness

Middle frontal gyrus

Measures of the Big Five trait of conscientiousness are positively correlated with the volume of areas in the prefrontal cortex involved with planning and the voluntary control of behavior. *Source:* From DeYoung, C. G., et al. (2010). Testing predictions from personality neuroscience: brain structure and the big five. *Psychological Science, 21*(6), 820–828. Copyright © 2010 Sage Publications.

Personality and Brain Structure

Given the evidence of genetic influence on personality, and the very early emergence of temperament in life, it is reasonable to assume that some individual differences in personality are reflected in the structures of the brain. Early efforts to link personality and biology examined correlations between extroversion and neuroticism and the activities of the autonomic nervous system and reticular formation, structures involved with levels of arousal discussed further in our chapter on biological psychology (Eysenck, 1967).

Researchers have identified structural correlates in adults for four of the Big Five personality traits: extroversion, agreeableness, neuroticism, and conscientiousness (Canli, 2009; DeYoung et al., 2010). The differences in structure appear to occur in logical places. For example, people who differ in neuroticism show different volumes of areas of the prefrontal cortex, anterior cingulate cortex, and hippocampus, areas that have been implicated in sensitivity to threat and stress. People with different levels of conscientiousness had different volumes in areas of the prefrontal cortex involved with planning and the voluntary control of behavior (DeYoung et al., 2010). These relationships are correlational, which means that we do not know if they are responsible for personality, the result of personality, or due to some unknown additional variables.

The Evolution of Personality

If we accept the idea that personality characteristics can be influenced by genetic factors, an interesting question arises. How might differences in personality have evolved? Some evolutionary psychologists argue that characteristics such as the Big Five are present across a variety of cultures because these are the characteristics that affect survival in our social species (Buss, 1996, 1999).

To bolster the evolutionary approach, it would be useful to identify "personality" in other species and observe its development. Ivan Pavlov, discussed in our chapter on learning, noticed that individual dogs

Courtesy of Jennifer Mather/University of Lethbridge and Roland Anderson/Seattle Aquarium. University of Lethbridge photograph

After noticing that staff at the Seattle Aquarium had been naming their octopuses based on their behavior (from shy Emily Dickinson to destructive Lucretia McEvil), Jennifer Mather tested 44 octopuses systematically for their responses to stimuli such as being touched with a brush. The octopuses seemed to have unique and stable responses, similar to having a "personality."

responded differently to frustration: Some responded "cheerfully," others with "anger," some went to sleep, and the last group appeared to have a nervous breakdown (Pavlov, 1906). Using a modified human personality questionnaire to evaluate animals, extroversion and neuroticism have been identified in hyenas, octopuses, guppies, rats, pigs, dogs, cats, donkeys, monkeys, gorillas, and chimpanzees (Gosling, Mollaghan, & Van Lange, 2006). Agreeableness, which might form the basis for cooperative behavior, has been observed to vary in nonhuman primates (Adams, 2011). However, the only species identified as showing variations in conscientiousness were human beings and chimpanzees (Gosling et al., 2006).

Thinking Scientifically

Does Personality Predict Political Orientation?

Groucho Marx is quoted as saying, "All people are born alike—except Republicans and Democrats." We usually like to think that our political views represent carefully thought out analyses of current issues and history. Is it possible that our personalities predispose us to a particular political worldview?

In a meta-analysis of 88 studies with over 22,000 participants, some characteristic personality differences between conservatives and liberals did emerge (Jost, Glaser, Kruglanski, & Sulloway, 2003). Conservatives scored higher than liberals on conscientiousness, while liberals scored higher than conservatives on openness to experience. Locus of control also seems to vary according to political persuasion. Conservatives are more likely to believe that a person's outcomes reflect his or her personal efforts (an internal locus of control), while liberals are more likely to believe that external factors, like the opportunities one is given in life, determine a person's outcomes (Taylor, 2008).

As we discussed previously, genetics are believed to play a role in the Big Five personality traits. Because of findings that traits vary between liberals and conservatives, some psychologists have taken this result a step farther by suggesting that political persuasion might also be influenced by genetics (see ● Figure 12.10). For example, one study suggested that novelty-seeking behavior, or the tendency to actively seek out new experiences, is close enough to openness to expect it to vary with political persuasion (Settle, Dawes, Christakis, & Fowler, 2010). Novelty-seeking is correlated with one of three variations, known as 7R, in a gene related to dopamine function. These researchers reported an interesting interaction between the gene variant and adolescent friendships. Having the 7R allele or not did not predict a teen's number of friends or political affiliation. However, people with the 7R allele who also had many friends in adolescence were more likely to be liberal than people with the 7R allele who had fewer friends. People with no 7R alleles showed no relationship between number of friends and political ideology.

How do these findings compare with your own political views? What about your friends and family members? Are there third variables, such as the political attitudes of your parents, that might account for these relationships between personality and political views? How seriously should we take these conclusions? ⚙

How Can We Assess Personality?

Personality is assessed, or tested, for a variety of reasons, including the refinement of personality theories, the construction of a correct diagnosis of a psychological disorder, or the selection of an ideal employee.

In everyday life, we make assessments of other people's personalities by listening to them and watching their behavior. Observation remains one of the most reliable means of making judgments about other people (Leichtman, 1995). On the other hand, observation takes precious time and can be biased, as we will discuss in a later chapter on social psychology. In addition to observation, we rely on interviews. When you meet a person for the first time, you ask questions to see "what kind of person" he or she might be. Although a skilled interviewer might be able to obtain reliable information, it is also easy for the person being interviewed to conceal some aspects of personality.

To avoid the pitfalls of observation and interview, many psychologists turn to standardized tests of personality. We discussed some of the features of standardized testing in our research methods section. In our chapter on research methods, we noted that good tests require validity and reliability.

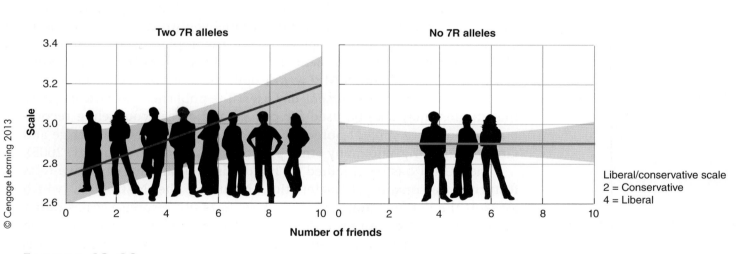

FIGURE 12.10

Friends, Alleles, and Political Points of View. According to Settle et al. (2010), genes and the number of friends you have can influence your choice of political affiliation. People with two copies of the 7R variant of the D4 dopamine transporter gene, which is related to novelty-seeking behavior, tend to be liberal if they have many friends but more conservative if they have fewer friends. For people with alleles other than the 7R variant, the number of friends does not make a difference in their political beliefs. Having the 7R variant did not predict either political persuasion or the number of friends people have. Only when both genetic influences and number of friends were taken into account simultaneously were the authors able to predict political viewpoints. *Source: Adapted from Settle et al. (2010).*

A valid test literally does the job it is advertised to do. For example, if you constructed a test of creativity, people with high scores on your test should demonstrate more creativity than people who have lower scores. A reliable test returns similar results when it is interpreted by different observers or is taken repeatedly.

Personality Inventories

Personality inventories are objective tests, often using numbered scales or multiple choice, like the short Big Five test that you took earlier in the chapter. These tests have some obvious advantages over more subjective measures, such as interviews or observation. Large numbers of people can be assessed quickly and inexpensively. Many of the tests appear to perform quite well in terms of reliability and validity (McCrae, Kurtz, Yamagata, & Terracciano, 2011). On the other hand, the results of personality inventories are based on self-report and might be influenced by a person's need to appear socially appropriate. An individual who is applying for a job in sales is unlikely to admit to being shy. Further, answers on a questionnaire may indicate a person's beliefs but have relatively less to say about how a person would actually behave. Claiming to be honest on a questionnaire says little about whether a cashier will steal money from the cash register or provide free food for groups of friends, as we will explore in a chapter on social psychology.

One of the most frequently used personality inventories is the Minnesota Multiphasic Personality Inventory, or MMPI, published in the early 1940s and most recently revised in 2001. This test compares the responses of typical people and those hospitalized for a psychological disorder to a number of true-false items (Hathaway & McKinley, 1940, 1943) (see ● Figure 12.11). For example, responses to the question "I usually feel that life is worthwhile and interesting" might differentiate between people who either are or are not depressed. People with schizophrenia, but not others, are likely to agree with the statement "I seem to hear things that other people can't hear." Although the MMPI was designed to assist with clinical diagnosis, this is only one of its present-day uses. The publisher's website suggests that the test may also be used for college and career counseling recommendations, screening of potential public safety employees, marriage and family counseling, and many other purposes (Pearson Assessments, 2005).

The MMPI has been joined by hundreds of additional objective tests featuring personality characteristics, including the NEO-PI-R, which assesses the Big Five traits. Most of these tests use response scales rather than the true-false options of the MMPI. These numbered scales are often referred to as Likert scales, after one of their earliest proponents, Rensis Likert (Likert, 1932). For example, you might be asked to select the number that best describes you:

Outgoing	7	6	5	4	3	2	1	Withdrawn

Projective Tests

Projective tests are derived directly from the Freudian defense mechanism of projection, discussed earlier in the chapter. According to the psychodynamic approach, we supposedly can access the unconscious mind by providing an ambiguous

personality inventory An objective test, often using numbered scales or multiple choice, used to assess personality.

projective test A test of personality based on Freudian theory that provides an ambiguous stimulus onto which the test-taker "projects" his or her personality.

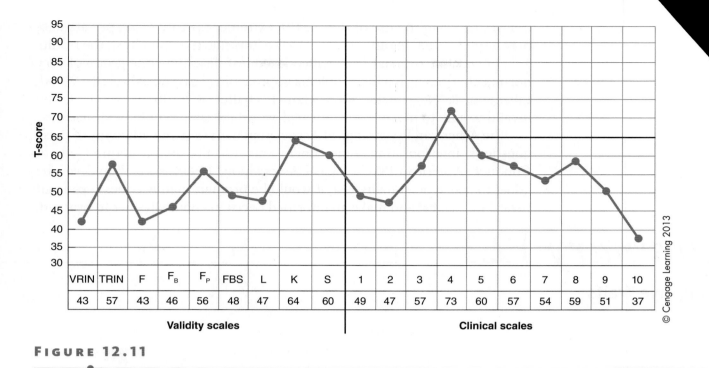

	VRIN	TRIN	F	F_B	F_P	FBS	L	K	S	1	2	3	4	5	6	7	8	9	10
	43	57	43	46	56	48	47	64	60	49	47	57	73	60	57	54	59	51	37

Validity scales **Clinical scales**

© Cengage Learning 2013

FIGURE 12.11

The Minnesota Multiphasic Personality Inventory (MMPI). The Minnesota Multiphasic Personality Inventory (MMPI) compares a participant's responses along a number of dimensions to people with diagnosed psychological conditions. Scores above 65 are cause for concern. In this case, the individual scores normally with the exception of his score on scale 4, which is the Psychopathic Deviate scale. This scale measures conflict, struggle, anger, and respect for society's rules. This person might be diagnosed with Antisocial Personality Disorder, which we discuss in a later chapter on psychological disorders.

stimulus, onto which the participants "project" their personalities as they describe the object.

One of the most famous projective tests is the Rorschach Inkblot Test, which contains 10 different inkblots, some in color and others in black and white (Rorschach, 1921). The job of the participants is to describe what each inkblot looks like to them. These responses are written down by the examiner and scored according to a manual. For instance, the examiner might note that a participant talked about a part of the inkblot instead of the entire image. This response would be scored as an indication of the participant's concrete, rather than abstract, way of thinking. In spite of serious questions about its reliability and validity (Wood, Nezworski, & Lilienfeld, 2003), the Rorschach Inkblot Test remains more widely used than the MMPI. Out of a randomly selected group of 1,000 therapist members of the American Psychological Association (APA), 82% reported using the Rorschach at least "occasionally," and 43% use it "frequently" or "always" (Watkins, Campbell, & Nieberding, 1995).

The Ethics of Personality Testing

Personality tests are widely used by therapists, potential employers, judges, and attorneys (Newitz, 2000). These applications of personality assessment raise important ethical concerns. Who gets to see these data? How are they stored? For what purposes may they be used? Is the examiner trained in the administration and evaluation of tests? In many

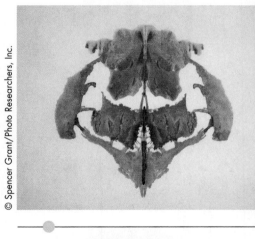

© Spencer Grant/Photo Researchers, Inc.

Swiss psychologist Hermann Rorschach (1884–1922), the son of an artist, was nicknamed "Klecks," or "inkblot," by his high school classmates because of his hobby of making inkblot pictures. After becoming a psychiatrist, he became curious about why people saw the inkblots very differently, and he began analyzing their responses. In spite of very poor validity and reliability, the Rorschach Inkblot Test continues to be used widely.

cases, such as in the use of the MMPI, extremely sensitive and private data may be generated. In other cases, like the Rorschach Inkblot Test, the results are at best controversial. This widely used test described one group of very normal children as having problems approaching "psychosis" (Garb, Wood, Lilienfeld, & Nezworski, 2005; Hamel, Shaffer, & Erdberg, 2000). Using invalid results to make important real-world decisions could be disastrous.

The American Psychological Association has wrestled with many of these questions, incorporating some conclusions into the organization's Code of Conduct (American Psychological Association, 1996/2007). Should you be asked to take a personality test, it would be prudent to fully educate yourself regarding the test and make an informed decision about whether to proceed.

Summary 12.1

The Big Five Traits

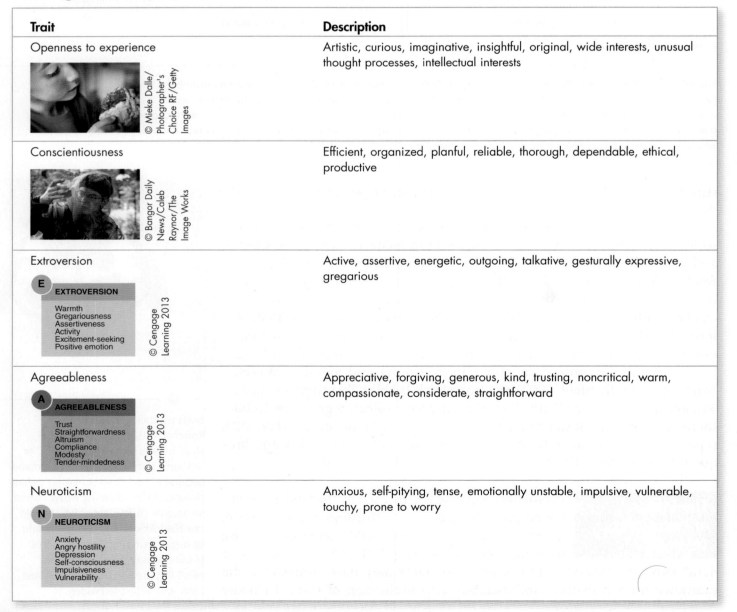

Trait	Description
Openness to experience	Artistic, curious, imaginative, insightful, original, wide interests, unusual thought processes, intellectual interests
Conscientiousness	Efficient, organized, planful, reliable, thorough, dependable, ethical, productive
Extroversion	Active, assertive, energetic, outgoing, talkative, gesturally expressive, gregarious
Agreeableness	Appreciative, forgiving, generous, kind, trusting, noncritical, warm, compassionate, considerate, straightforward
Neuroticism	Anxious, self-pitying, tense, emotionally unstable, impulsive, vulnerable, touchy, prone to worry

What Does It Mean to Have a Self?

One of the most fundamental psychological distinctions we make is the distinction between our self and others. William James argued in favor of "the belief in a distinct principle of selfhood" and believed that such a principle could be studied scientifically (James, 1890, Vol. I, p. 330). Knowing something about the personalities of others makes it easier for us to anticipate what others will feel, think, or do and, therefore, to interact more effectively with them. But what about the patterns of thought, feelings, and actions we see in ourselves? When we think about this personal knowledge, we are thinking about the **self**. Scientists have explored a number of questions about the self. What factors influence the development of the self? What are the advantages of a sense of self? Can the sense of self be correlated with brain activity?

Defining the Self

Psychologists approach the study of the self by examining the *ABC*'s: affect, behavior, and cognition. The affective, or emotional, components of the self include our evaluation of the self, or level of self-esteem, which we discuss in greater detail later in this chapter. Behavior and self-concept form reciprocal relationships. We gain self-knowledge by observing our behavior, and our concepts of the type of people we are influence our behavior. Cognitive processes help us organize information and think about the self.

The self does not exist in a vacuum. It both shapes and is shaped by our social environment. Our development of a self sets the stage for our understanding of the behavior of others. Early in infancy, as children begin to recognize themselves as separate beings, they begin to form hypotheses about why others behave in certain ways. This social perception is subject to many of the same strengths and weaknesses that we find in a person's knowledge of the self.

Self-Concept

Just for the moment, set this text aside, grab a pencil and a piece of scratch paper, and write a list of 10 things that complete the sentence "I am _____."

If you are like most college students, this description of your **self-concept** will include references to demographic factors, such as age, sex, or student status (first-year, psychology major, etc.); personality features, such as outgoing or shy; relationships with others (friend, lover, daughter, son, sister, brother); physical attributes (pretty, tall, brown-eyed); and various other roles (athlete, club member, Texan).

We use **self-schema** to think about these many aspects of the self (Markus, 1977). As we discussed in our chapters on cognition and development, schemas provide cognitive structures for organizing information. The structure provided by a self-schema will influence not only the way you view yourself but also how you view and interact with others.

A major implication of having a self-schema is the suggestion that we may process self-relevant information differently than the same type of

Courtesy of Laura Freberg

Courtesy of John Cacioppo

Our self-concept captures the way we see ourselves, which we often portray through our choice of social networking profile pictures. Here are your authors' current profile pictures on Facebook. What do your profile pictures say to others about you?

---

self Patterns of thought, feelings, and actions we perceive in our own minds.

self-concept A person's description of his or her own characteristics.

self-schema A cognitive organization that helps us think about the self and process self-relevant information.

FIGURE 12.12

Using a Self-Schema Improves Recall for Words. Participants in this experiment were asked if a word was in larger font (structural), rhymed with another word (phonemic), meant the same thing as another word (semantic), or described the participant (self-reference). As you can see from these results, when participants used their self-schemas to consider a word, later recall for the word was much better than when the word was considered structurally, phonemically, or semantically. These results suggest that your memory for material you are studying will be improved by thinking about how it relates to your own life. Adapted from Rogers, Kuiper, and Kirker (1977).

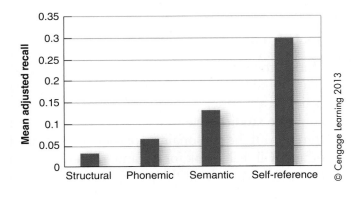

information about others. For example, we might think about our own brown hair in different ways than we think about our neighbor's brown hair. In one of the earliest studies on this self-reference effect (SRE), four groups of participants were given lists of adjectives to memorize with different instructions (Rogers, Kuiper, & Kirker, 1977). The first group judged the size of letters making up the word, the second group judged whether the word rhymed with another word, the third group judged whether the word had the same meaning as another word, and the last group judged whether or not the word described them. The fourth group's recall for the words was subsequently superior to recall by the other groups (see ● Figure 12.12). These results implied that the self provided "a superordinate schema" (Rogers et al., 1977, p. 685).

Questions remain, however, as to the true cause of the observed SRE. Is there something special about self-schemas, or is the SRE simply a result of general memory processes, such as depth of processing or elaboration, which we discussed in our chapter on memory? For example, memory enhancement also occurred in a group that judged whether or not words described the participants' mothers (Bower & Gilligan, 1979). We may remember self-relevant information simply because we know a lot about the subject—ourselves.

Self-Awareness

When answering the questions posed in the previous section, how do you know what to say? To know yourself requires you to make the self an object to be examined. Just as you try to figure out what kind of people your classmates and instructor are, you have the capacity to turn this analysis inward to the self. **Self-awareness**, or knowledge of your own internal traits, feelings, roles, and memories, is the result of this self-study. In addition, self-awareness allows us to establish boundaries between the self and other people. When we talk about ourselves, look at ourselves in a mirror, watch a video of ourselves, or "stand out from the crowd" in some way, we become much more self-aware than usual. This state of heightened self-awareness is typically quite unpleasant for most people. Many people experience negative mood when they look in a mirror (Fejfar & Hoyle, 2000).

self-awareness Knowledge of personal traits, feelings, roles, and memories.

Related to this negative self-awareness is the concept of self-consciousness, our awareness of our own characteristics and the way the self is perceived by others. In many cases, we overestimate how much attention others pay to our behavior, a phenomenon known as the spotlight effect. When student participants wearing an embarrassing T-shirt featuring '70s pop singer Barry Manilow entered a room full of other students, they expected at least half of their fellow students to notice (Gilovich, Medvec, & Savitsky, 2000). In fact, only 23% of the students paid any attention to the T-shirts. The particularly active spotlight effect that often accompanies puberty is responsible for much of the pain of adolescence (Elkind, 1967; Elkind & Bowen, 1979). As a result, teens are typically convinced that every flaw and blemish they possess will be scrutinized by others. How reassuring it would be to understand that other teens are so worried about the imaginary audience's reactions to their own flaws and blemishes that they scarcely have time to notice the flaws of others.

Self-consciousness might be unpleasant, but it makes people behave more ethically. When children were instructed to "take only one Halloween candy," they were more likely to comply when they could see their image in a mirror (Beaman, Klentz, Diener, & Svanum, 1979). In a similar study, an "honor system" coffee bar featured either a poster showing a pair of eyes or a poster showing a bouquet of flowers (Bateson, Nettle, & Roberts, 2006). People were much more likely to put money in the box to pay for their coffee when they saw the poster of the eyes (see ● Figure 12.13).

Sources of Self-Knowledge How do we obtain self-knowledge? An obvious source of self-awareness is the process of introspection, or the direct observation of one's own thoughts and feelings. After all, who is in a better position to know what goes on inside our heads than we are? Unfortunately, as we discussed in our chapter on research methods, introspection as a scientific method is not considered very reliable.

Perhaps we could bypass any analysis of mental states altogether and focus instead on our observable behavior. People seem to use their

Barry Manilow might have sold millions of records in the 1970s, but students in 2000 thought wearing this shirt would be embarrassing. We tend to overestimate how much attention others pay to us, though, and only 23% of participants noticed the T-shirt at all.

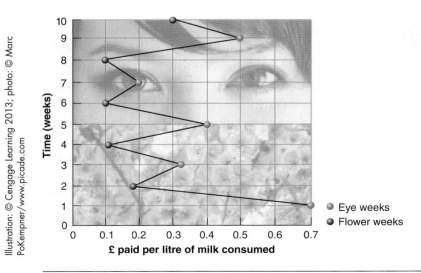

FIGURE 12.13

Self-Consciousness and Honesty. The amount of money collected in a college department "honor system" coffee bar relative to consumption was measured by tracking milk consumption (this study was conducted in the United Kingdom, where coffee apparently is rarely consumed "black"). Donations increased when a poster of eyes appeared above the bar and decreased when a poster of flowers appeared above the bar. Self-consciousness, perhaps from feeling "watched" by the photograph of eyes, typically results in more ethical behavior. Whether or not we are responding similarly to the large numbers of surveillance cameras in our environments remains to be demonstrated through future research. *Source:* Adapted from Bateson, Nettle, and Roberts (2006).

© AP Photo

Because of the importance of the self in organizing our memories, the past is often viewed as if we were the "leading player." John Dean's memories of Watergate weren't factually wrong, but made him look more central than he really was.

behavior as a clue to their characteristics, just as any other observer does (Bem, 1972). If I see myself behaving in a kindly and respectful way toward others, maybe I am a kindly and respectful person. In support of this approach, participants who were gently encouraged to provide flattering descriptions of themselves scored higher on a subsequent test of self-esteem (Jones, Rhodewalt, Berglas, & Skelton, 1981). In other words, if I observe myself providing a positive self-analysis, it must be true.

The people around us also contribute to our self-knowledge. We use the reactions of other people like a mirror to "see" our own characteristics, developing a looking-glass self. We also incorporate the opinions of significant others about us into our self-concept. If our parents viewed us as brilliant, it is likely that we would view ourselves as brilliant, too. Unfortunately, using the reactions of others works better when defining some characteristics than others. If our parents inaccurately view us as brilliant, we soon learn the truth at school. If they unfairly think we're lazy, though, it is more difficult to figure out they're wrong.

An obvious component of self-knowledge arises from autobiographical and episodic memories, described in our chapter on memory. Who we are today is intimately linked with the self from the past that we remember. While providing valuable information about "who we are," episodic and autobiographical memories can provide a partial, incomplete, and occasionally inaccurate picture. As one psychologist noted, "The past is remembered as if it were a drama in which the self was the leading player" (Greenwald, 1980, p. 604). For example, a comparison of the testimony during the Watergate scandal given by John Dean, President Richard Nixon's legal counsel, and the taped versions of the meetings he described showed that Dean captured most of the meaningfulness of the events that transpired (Neisser, 1981). However, Dean's testimony presented his role as having been much more important and central than it really was.

Self-Esteem

Not only do we form a self-concept, but we judge its value. This personal report card is known as **self-esteem**. Self-esteem may be global, based on our overall self-worth, or specific, relating to particular characteristics such as appearance or intelligence. Self-esteem introduces an emotional aspect to our self-concept. Not only do we judge ourselves, but we experience emotional responses to that judgment.

These judgments of the self are not necessarily accurate. Most people experience "positive illusions," which lead them to judge themselves more positively and less negatively than they judge others (Taylor & Brown, 1988). In spite of inaccuracies, people who experience positive illusions typically enjoy a heightened sense of well-being.

People with high and low self-esteem respond quite differently to failure. The low self-esteem person tends to overgeneralize from failure

self-esteem A judgment of the value of the self.

(Brown & Mankowski, 1993). In other words, people with low self-esteem who fail one exam might assume that they are going to fail all their classes. This tendency to overgeneralize may explain why people with low self-esteem are more prone to depression, discussed further in our chapter on psychological disorders. In contrast, people with high self-esteem respond to failure in one domain by exaggerating their abilities in other domains (Brown & Smart, 1991). If a person with high self-esteem fails an exam, she is more likely to remind others about how great she is in sports, appearance, or dating.

Sources of Self-Esteem Because of the importance of self-esteem to psychological well-being, psychologists have looked at the origins of self-esteem very carefully.

Many psychologists believe that the process of developing self-esteem begins very early in childhood. Long before the child has a working model of the self, he or she is experiencing the emotional consequences of acceptance and rejection (Erikson, 1963; Sroufe, Carlson, & Levy, 2003). As we discussed in our chapter on development, children form a variety of attachments with their primary caregivers (Ainsworth, Blehar, Waters, & Wall, 1978; Bowlby, 1969). A child's pattern of attachment in infancy predicted his or her self-esteem at age 6 years (Cassidy, 1988). Self-esteem does not appear to change much over the lifespan (Block & Robins, 1993; Trzesniewski, Donnellan, & Robins, 2003). Early differences in self-esteem seem to be magnified and reinforced over time, as having high or low self-esteem influences both the selection of activities and the reactions of others to the self.

Self-esteem is also influenced by social comparisons, or the judgments we make of our own worth relative to those around us (Festinger, 1954). The impact of social comparisons on self-esteem was demonstrated in an experiment in which researchers placed an advertisement for a research assistant (Morse & Gergen, 1970). Prospective employees found themselves in a waiting room with another candidate, who was actually an actor working for the experimenters. The actor took either the role of "Mr. Clean" or "Mr. Dirty." Participants waiting with Mr. Clean experienced

Reproduced with kind permission of Unilever PLC and group companies.

Dove, a division of Unilever that produces skin and hair care products, lists its "social mission" as building women's self-esteem. The company reports that only 4% of women worldwide consider themselves "beautiful." To combat the influence of upward social comparisons, in which girls and women judge their attractiveness against the impossibly beautiful images of women in the media, Dove produced a video featuring the transformation of a model's real photograph (before on the left) into the photoshopped product on a billboard (after on the right).

drops in self-esteem, whereas the self-esteem of participants waiting with Mr. Dirty rose.

Once again, we see divergent patterns of behavior by those with high and low self-esteem. People with high self-esteem tend to make downward comparisons, in which they compare themselves to those they consider less worthy on a particular dimension. For example, a beautiful woman with high self-esteem is more likely to congratulate herself on how much better looking she is than her friends, but is unlikely to compare herself with the current crop of Hollywood beauties. In contrast, people with low self-esteem are likely to do just the opposite. A beautiful woman with low self-esteem will engage in upward comparisons, chastising herself because she doesn't measure up to the most beautiful women in the world.

Regardless of self-esteem, we all seem to engage in a reassuring type of downward comparison when viewing our own pasts (Wilson & Ross, 2000). Most of us look back in time with a sense that we have improved. Our virtues are greater today than they used to be, and our faults are less.

Gender, Race, and Culture and Self-Esteem Given the influence of social comparisons on self-esteem, we might suspect that belonging to certain social groups would affect an individual's self-esteem. If you are a member of a privileged group in society, for example, shouldn't you have higher self-esteem than people who have experienced prejudice and discrimination?

Higher rates of depression among women, discussed further in our chapter on psychological disorders, might predict that females would have lower self-esteem than males. In a very large meta-analysis representing thousands of participants, males had a very small advantage over females in self-esteem (Kling, Hyde, Showers, & Buswell, 1999). This advantage is larger in adolescence and early adulthood, but dissipates with age.

Similar meta-analyses of self-esteem demonstrated differences based on race and ethnicity in the United States (Twenge & Crocker, 2002; Erol & Orth, 2011). As we noted in our chapter on development, beginning in adolescence, Black Americans score higher than White Americans in measures of self-esteem. However, Americans identifying themselves as Asian, or Native American scored below White Americans in measures of self-esteem. Hispanic adolescents had lower self-esteem than White teens, but reported higher self-esteem at age 30 than White Americans (Erol & Orth, 2011).

Cultural differences between groups might account for some of these results. As we mentioned previously, people in more collectivistic cultures might avoid "standing out" from the group by giving themselves highly positive ratings (see ● Figure 12.14). Results from tests that tap into implicit attitudes by asking participants to associate themselves with either positive words (glorious, happy, laughter) or negative words (agony, horrible, nasty) suggest that Asian Americans have about the same level of self-esteem as White Americans, but that cultural values of modesty usually override their outward expression of that self-esteem (Greenwald & Farnham, 2000).

> Personality is the glitter that sends your little gleam across the footlights and the orchestra pit into that big black space where the audience is.
>
> —Mae West

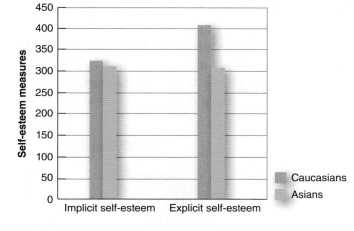

FIGURE 12.14

Cultural Differences in Explicit and Implicit Measures of Self-Esteem. Apparent cultural differences in self-esteem must be evaluated carefully. Using explicit measures of self-esteem, it appears that White Americans have higher self-esteem than Asian Americans. However, when implicit measures of self-esteem are used, this difference disappears, suggesting that the observed difference is probably due to cultural norms related to modesty. *Source:* Adapted from Greenwald and Farnham (2000).

Using Self-Enhancement to Protect Self-Esteem The good news is that most of us feel rather positively about ourselves. The bad news is that we are just a wee bit unrealistic. In fact, people who actually perform most poorly are the most likely to engage in self-enhancement by inflating their opinions of themselves. College students who performed in the bottom 12% on tests of logic, grammar, and humor guessed that they actually performed better than 62% of their peers (Kruger & Dunning, 1999). As student performance increased, the amount of inflation decreased.

Some people begin protecting their self-esteem long before a performance takes place. In self-handicapping, a person begins to build an excuse in advance, just in case she or he does fail (Berglas & Jones, 1978). People use a number of self-handicapping strategies, including taking drugs, failing to practice or do homework, commenting on poor health or stress, or sandbagging. Sandbagging occurs when you let everyone know how bad you are at something. By lowering expectations of your performance, nobody will notice much when you fail. Although self-handicapping may protect your self-esteem, it does not make you popular with others (Rhodewalt, Sandonmatsu, Tschanz, Feick, & Waller, 1995).

Another protective method for self-enhancement is to associate with others you admire. This approach has been labeled the "bask in reflected glory (BIRG)" effect (Cialdini et al., 1976). On the Monday following a football game, university students are more likely to wear sweatshirts with their school's name if their team won than if it lost. We are equally quick to distance ourselves from failure. Many an athlete or performer has been surprised at how many "friends" they have during successful times, and how very quickly those friends disappear when times are tough.

Self-enhancement may serve to protect self-esteem, but it can have a number of unwanted effects. Primary among these negative side effects is being disliked by others. People who engage in self-enhancement typically make good first impressions, but these impressions do not last (Paulhus, 1998).

The "bask in reflected glory (BIRG)" effect predicts that sales of apparel featuring a winning team are likely to be much higher than those for a losing team. Associating with those we admire can produce self-enhancement.

The **Advantages of Self-Esteem** Having high self-esteem provides a number of benefits both to the individual and to groups to which the individual with high self-esteem belongs. Among the advantages of high self-esteem to the individual are happiness and persistence (Baumeister et al., 2003). These outcomes occur because high self-esteem acts as a "buffer." When faced with bad news, people with high self-esteem are

Psychology *as a* Hub Science

Self-Esteem, Academic Performance, and Juvenile Delinquency

The claims made on behalf of self-esteem are often dramatic. The California Task Force on Self-Esteem and Personal and Social Responsibility published a report that declared "many, if not most, of the major problems plaguing society have roots in the low self-esteem of many of the people who make up society" (Mecca, Smelser, & Vasconcellos, 1989). Teachers, parents, and therapists express similar beliefs and actively work to increase the self-esteem of others. These approaches mirror a commonsense attitude toward self-esteem.

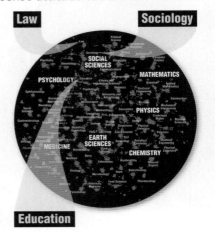

High self-esteem obviously seems more desirable than low self-esteem, and interventions designed to raise self-esteem appear on the surface to be a good thing. How accurate are these views of self-esteem?

Self-esteem and school grades are positively correlated, although the effects are not large (Hansford & Hattie, 1982). The important question, however, is whether self-esteem *causes* various outcomes or whether it *results* from those outcomes instead. As we discussed in our chapter on research methods, it is not possible to use correlational data to determine causal factors. Consider the example of a student who achieves very high grades. Does the student's success reflect the impact of high self-esteem, or does the achievement of high grades make the student feel more positively about himself or herself? Or like many correlations, is an unidentified third factor such as intelligence or social class responsible for the observed correlation?

Explicit efforts to identify the causal relationships between self-esteem and school performance have

failed to support the commonsense hypothesis that high self-esteem produces good performance. A sample of 1,600 young males in the 10th grade was followed for an additional 8 years (Bachman & O'Malley, 1977). No evidence for a causal role for self-esteem in school performance was discovered. Instead, third factors, including socioeconomic status, IQ, and early school performance,

Although many people believe that raising children's self-esteem is a good thing, research suggests that self-esteem is more likely to be the outcome rather than the cause of behavior. Providing "feel-good" messages that are not based in real achievement can actually backfire (Forsyth & Kerr, 1999).

Douglas Pulsipher / Alamy

You will find a good paying job.

Law

Sociology

SOCIAL SCIENCES

MATHEMATICS

PSYCHOLOGY

PHYSICS

EARTH SCIENCES

MEDICINE

CHEMISTRY

Education

more likely to weather the storm than are people with low self-esteem. In addition, high self-esteem enhances social dominance within a peer group (Juvonen, 2005).

Self-esteem contributes to belongingness, or the maintenance of good social relationships (Baumeister & Leary, 1995; Leary, 2004; Leary & Downs, 1995; Leary, Tambor, Terdal, & Downs, 1995). Because social rejection could have such devastating effects on survival in our evolutionary past, self-esteem could have emerged as a way of estimating the likelihood of rejection. Self-esteem drops following the experience of social exclusion (Leary et al., 1995). A drop in self-esteem serves as an early warning signal that rejection by the group is imminent and that behavior designed to regain the favor of the group should be initiated (see ● Figure 12.15).

appeared to be responsible for the correlation between self-esteem and school performance. Among studies that have reported a causal relationship between self-esteem and school performance, the direction of the relationship is not consistent with the commonsense hypothesis. High self-esteem is more likely to be a result of good grades, not vice versa (Rosenberg, Schooler, & Schoenbach, 1989).

What do these findings mean for efforts like the California Task Force, which sought to raise achievement by improving self-esteem? Unfortunately, interventions intended to boost self-esteem may backfire. When students receiving poor grades on a midterm were sent an e-mail message designed to boost their self-worth, they performed significantly worse on the next exams than students in control groups (Forsyth & Kerr, 1999). This study provides an important lesson for those who wish to raise self-esteem. Providing indiscriminate "feel-good" messages that are not anchored in real achievement may actually result in lower achievement.

If relationships between school achievement and self-esteem are much weaker than many believe, what about the relationships between self-esteem and social problems such as aggression? Once again, our com-

monsense hypotheses fail us. We have heard parents, teachers, and legislators lament that many social problems would dissipate if only we could raise self-esteem. Bullies, we were told, were especially likely to suffer from low self-esteem. This commonsense notion was challenged by Roy Baumeister and his colleagues, who discovered that very aggressive people were much more likely to have positive, and frequently inflated, views of their self-worth (Baumeister, Campbell, Krueger, & Vohs, 2003; Baumeister, Smart, & Boden, 1996).

Not only are bullies unlikely to suffer from low self-esteem, they are less anxious, less depressed, and less lonely than prosocial youth who do not participate in bullying (Juvonen, 2005). Even more disturbing is the finding that middle school students rate their bullying peers as "the coolest kids in their classes" (Juvonen, 2005, p. 37). Instead of raising the self-esteem of bullies, which might make things worse, school-based programs could try to reduce the reinforcing admiration bullies receive from their peers. ⚙

Contrary to many stereotypes, bullies typically do not suffer from low self-esteem. They actually experience less depression, less anxiety, and less loneliness than prosocial youth and are likely to be considered by peers "the coolest kids in their classes" (Juvonen, 2005).

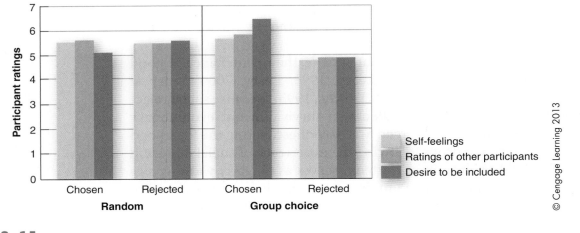

FIGURE 12.15

Self-Esteem as a Signal for Social Rejection. Participants who believed they had been rejected as group project members by peers experienced reduced self-feelings (self-esteem), rated the other participants more negatively, and expressed a lower desire to be included than participants who were either chosen by the group or who believed group membership had been randomly assigned. Believing that you were chosen by the group, however, did not improve self-esteem. These results suggest that feelings of low self-esteem might have developed over the course of human history as a warning signal for social rejection. *Source:* Adapted from Leary, Tambor, Terdal, and Downs (1995).

A terror management theory suggests that self-esteem works together with a cultural worldview to buffer our fear of death (Greenberg, Pyszczynski, & Solomon, 1986; Pyszczynski, Greenberg, & Solomon, 1991). Cultural worldviews can include shared beliefs that allow us to attain feelings of immortality, whether through producing children, writing books, or holding religious beliefs in an afterlife. By conforming to these cultural worldviews, people enjoy enhanced self-esteem that reduces their anxiety related to death.

Having members with high self-esteem is an advantage to groups in several respects. People with high self-esteem are more likely to speak out critically in groups (LePine & Van Dyne, 1998). Groups that do not have members who are willing to question group decisions might fall prey to poor decision making, discussed further in a later chapter on social

Terror management theory suggests that self-esteem serves as a protection against our fear of death. When people are reminded of their own mortality, self-esteem can increase. Ironically, new federally mandated warnings about death from smoking scheduled to appear on cigarette packages beginning in 2012 might have the unintended consequence of increasing favorable attitudes toward smoking on the part of some smokers, particularly those who already equate smoking with improving their image and self-esteem (Hansen, Winzeler, & Topolinski, 2009).

psychology. People with high self-esteem not only value themselves but also value the groups to which they belong (Aberson, Healy, & Robero, 2000). People with low self-esteem do not show this favoritism. If a group is highly valued by its members, its overall success is likely to be enhanced, which in turn will benefit its members.

Self-Regulation To meet the expectations we have for ourselves, we often engage in self-regulation, also known as self-control, or conscious executive efforts to control our thoughts, motives, feelings, and behaviors (Carver & Scheier, 2000). Failures to regulate behavior frequently lead to some of the most perplexing problems facing society, including drug abuse, domestic violence, and binge eating. In addition, deficits in self-regulation characterize a number of psychological disorders we discuss in a later chapter, including schizophrenia, attention deficit hyperactivity disorder (ADHD), and obsessive-compulsive disorder.

We do not enjoy unlimited supplies of self-control (Muraven & Baumeister, 2000). Once we "use up" our personal supply, we are temporarily more vulnerable to temptation. In an experiment that shouldn't surprise anyone who has been on a diet, female dieting participants watched a documentary in the presence of snacks that were either within reach or across the room (Vohs & Heatherton, 2000). Subsequently, the participants were given the opportunity to "test" as much ice cream as they'd like. The participants who had watched the documentary with snacks right in front of them ate more ice cream than the previously less-tempted participants. The implications of this experiment suggest that dieters and others who wish to change habits would be served well by limiting their exposure to temptation, thus saving their self-regulatory energy reserves (see ● Figure 12.16).

FIGURE 12.16

Self-Control Is a Limited Resource. People who resisted eating chocolate in favor of eating healthier but less appetizing radishes gave up much faster than people who chose to eat chocolate or those who were not exposed to either food when subsequently asked to perform a frustrating task. These data suggest that we do have willpower, or the ability to self-regulate, but we do not have it in unlimited quantities. You might have noticed that sticking to a plan becomes more difficult as the day progresses. *Source:* Adapted from Baumeister, Vohs, and Tice (2007).

Even worse, the harder we think about *not* doing something, the more likely we are to do it (Wegner, 1994). Try, for example, to avoid thinking about a white bear for the next 30 seconds. If you are like most people, your thoughts were suddenly dominated by images of white bears. We can explain this phenomenon as follows. When you try to control your behavior, you simultaneously activate a concern about failing. In an effort to avoid failure, you automatically pay more attention to the item or behavior to be avoided. "What exactly is this white bear thing I should avoid?" Because of this attention, we end up doing exactly what we hoped to avoid doing.

The Brain and the Self

If the mind is the product of the activity of the nervous system, is it possible to locate the self within these patterns of activity? This question suggests that information about the self is processed in unique and special ways by the nervous system (Gillihan & Farah, 2005). As we have seen so far in this chapter, the concept of self can mean many things. Brain correlates have been found for our knowledge of our own bodies—their configuration, appearance, and location—as well as for our memories of personal experiences, our interpersonal connections, and our use of a first-person perspective.

An important aspect of the self is the recognition of our own faces. The right hemisphere appears to play a special role in distinguishing our own faces from those of other people. When participants viewed a photograph combining one half of their face with the half-face of a famous person, they recognized themselves when the left hemisphere was anesthetized but reported seeing the famous person when the right hemisphere was anesthetized (Keenan, Nelson, O'Connor, & Pascual-Leone, 2001) (see ● Figure 12.17).

In addition to playing an important role in recognizing our own faces, the right hemisphere could be necessary for the construction of our stable traits and attitudes. The location of patients' brain damage due to a type of age-related dementia (right hemisphere only, left hemisphere only, or both hemispheres) can be correlated with observed changes in personal characteristics that usually show little change over time, such as political views and religious beliefs (Miller et al., 2001). Only the patients with right hemisphere damage alone showed changes in these normally stable characteristics.

Schizophrenia, which we discuss more fully in our chapter on psychological disorders, often produces distortions in a patient's sense of self (Feinberg, 1978). One common symptom is a delusion of control, or the sense that some external agent is either monitoring or influencing one's behavior. This delusion is highly relevant to our current discussion, as it represents confusion over the behavior produced by the self or by others. For example, patients with this symptom might describe their behavior as controlled by others through implants in their brains. A comparison of brain activity during such delusions and after they recede indicated that the delusions of control were correlated with excess activity in the right hemisphere (Spence et al., 1997).

> Psychological freedom, a firm sense of self-esteem, is the most powerful weapon against the long night of physical slavery.
>
> —Martin Luther King Jr.

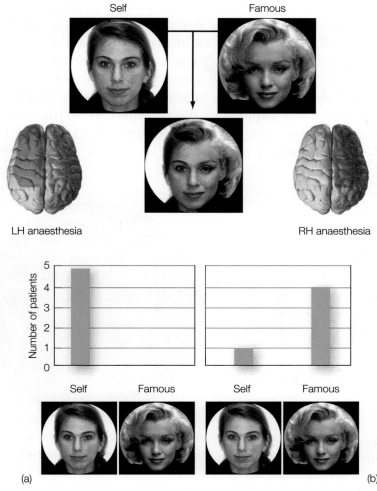

Illustration: © Argosy Publishing, Inc.; photo (Marilyn): © Alfred Eisenstaedt/Time & Life Pictures/Getty Images

FIGURE 12.17

Recognizing Your Own Face. Participants in this experiment viewed blended faces made from one half of their own photograph and the photograph of a famous person. When the participants' left hemispheres were anesthetized, leaving the right hemisphere active, they believed the photo was their own (a). When their right hemispheres were anesthetized, leaving the left hemisphere active, most believed the photo showed the famous person (b). These results suggest that for many people, the right hemisphere plays a role in recognizing our own faces. *Source:* Adapted from Keenan, Nelson, O'Connor, and Pascual-Leone (2001).

Psychologists have searched for biological correlates of our unique first-person perspective of the world. People often report a sense of "losing themselves" when engaged in certain tasks, such as concentrating hard on a problem, watching a movie, or having sex. Self-awareness is frequently correlated with activity in the frontal areas of the brain (David et al., 2006; Heatherton et al., 2006; Ochsner et al., 2005; Ochsner et al., 2004). However, given the large number of different aspects of the self discussed in this chapter, it should not be surprising that a widely distributed network of brain structures participates in the processing of the self (Cacioppo & Decety, 2011).

The Social Self The self we have discussed so far represents the personal self, or the attributes that differentiate an individual's self from all others (Brewer & Gardner, 1996). This self both shapes and is shaped by interactions with others. Just who those others are and how they interact with the self has been the subject of significant psychological inquiry.

The Interpersonal Self William James remarked that an individual has "as many different social selves as there are distinct groups of persons about whose opinion he cares" (James, 1890, p. 294). In other words, in addition to having a personal self, we experience an **interpersonal self**. In current psychological discussions of the self, influences on the interpersonal self fall into two categories—a person's significant others and the social groups to which the person belongs. Significant others include family members, friends, coworkers, and others with whom the self interacts, in the present or in the past. As we interact with significant others, we experience the relational self (Brewer & Gardner, 1996; Chen, Boucher, & Tapias, 2006).

interpersonal self The self we are in the presence of other people.

Connecting *to* Research

Effects of Culture on the Self Can Be Modified

Our discussion of culture and the self has assumed that individualistic and collectivistic values are socially transmitted to people growing up in a culture and that these values in turn result in a stable and relatively unchanging view of the self. However, we can also assume that regardless of culture, all human beings share both a need for independence and a need to belong. If this is the case, is it possible to show that a person's situation can modify his or her emphasis on individualistic and collectivistic values (Gardner, Gabriel, & Lee, 1999)?

The Question: Can cultural influences on the self be modified by a person's situation?

METHODS

Seventy-five White American college students and 82 Chinese students attending the University of Hong Kong participated in this study. Thinking about independence versus interdependence was manipulated

by reading a story about a general choosing a warrior to send to the king. The stories differed in the warrior chosen (the best individual for the job versus a member of the family) and in the benefits of the choice (benefits to the general versus benefits to his family). A control group did not hear any story at all.

The effects of the two stories were assessed by asking each participant to complete a values inventory that measures how obligated a person feels to help others.

RESULTS

Participants hearing the independence version of the warrior story, regardless of culture, produced more individualistic responses to the values survey than collectivistic responses. Participants hearing the interdependence version of the warrior story, again regardless of culture, produced more collectivistic responses to the values survey than individualistic responses. Participants

who heard a story that was consistent with their cultural norms (independence for U.S. participants and interdependence for Chinese participants) did not differ in their responses to the values survey from the control groups from their respective cultures.

DISCUSSION

Although we tend to think of culture influencing the self, this experiment demonstrated that views of the self as independent or interdependent can be changed by a person's immediate situation (such as hearing a story that emphasizes one aspect or the other). This result supports the ideas that both the need for independence and the need to belong are human universals and that the relative dominance of one over the other is modifiable through experience and situational variables (see ● Figure 12.19). ✪

A widely distributed network of brain structures participates in processing the different aspects of self. Self-referential processing, or the processing of information relevant to ourselves but not others, can occur in our emotional, facial, memory, motor, social, spatial, and verbal domains.

The influence of the larger groups to which we belong provides our collective self (Brewer & Gardner, 1996).

The concept of the interpersonal self implies that an individual's self is more flexible and complex than it would be on the basis of a personal self alone. This flexibility is illustrated by the suggestion that we have a relational self when we are with a particular person, such as the "me when I'm with mom" (Chen et al., 2006, p. 153). It is likely that a great deal of overlap occurs among the many interpersonal selves we experience, but recognizing that we may not be completely consistent across all social situations is important. The differences we experience echo the discussion earlier in the chapter about personality traits and situations.

▲ Emotional domain: self > nonself
▽ Facial domain: self > nonself
◻ Memory domain: self > nonself
◆ Motor domain: self > nonself
◁ Social domain: self ∩ other
● Social domain: self > other
✚ Spatial domain: self > nonself
▶ Verbal domain: self > nonself

From Northoff, G., et al. (2006). Self-referential processing in our brain—A meta-analysis of imaging studies on the self. *Neuroimage, 31*(1), 440–457. Copyright © 2006 Elsevier B.V.

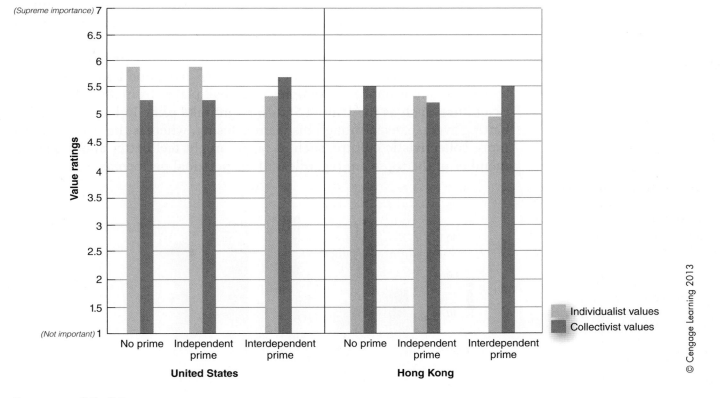

FIGURE 12.19

Individualism and Collectivism Are Modifiable. Listening to a story that emphasized individualistic or collectivistic values elicited congruent responses from participants, regardless of whether they lived in an individualistic culture (United States) or a collectivistic culture (Hong Kong). These results suggest that both independent and interdependent views of the self are human universals and that the relative dominance of one over the other is modifiable by a person's experience and situation. *Source:* Adapted from Gardner, Gabriel, and Lee (1999).

When we interact with significant others, such as family members, we experience the relational self. When we interact with larger groups, such as the residents and tourists enjoying New York City, we are experiencing the collective self.

Cultural Influences on the Self Given the interpersonal dimensions of the self described in the previous section, it should come as no surprise that the concept of the self means different things in different cultures.

One aspect of cultural differences that is particularly relevant to the study of the self is the distinction between individualism and collectivism (see ● Figure 12.18). Individualism is characterized by an emphasis on independence and self-reliance. In contrast, core values of collectivism include interdependence, cooperation, and lack of conflict. As we discussed in the introduction to this chapter, these relative weightings of self and others tend to characterize entire nations. The United States, Australia, Great Britain, Canada, and the Netherlands appear to be the most individualistic, while Venezuela, Colombia, Pakistan, Peru, Taiwan, and China appear to be the most collectivistic (Hofstede, 1980).

Two major differences occur between highly individualistic cultures and more collectivistic cultures (Markus & Kitayama, 1991). The first difference predicts a person's source of satisfaction. People in individualistic cultures feel best about themselves when they experience personal achievement, whereas people in collectivistic cultures feel good about belonging to a successful group. For example, a baseball player from an individualistic culture, such as the United States, might take pride in having a terrific batting average, even though his team is losing, whereas the player from a more collectivistic culture, such as Japan, might feel better about being a member of the top team regardless of his personal performance.

FIGURE 12.18

Individualism and Collectivism. Geert Hofstede compared cultures on five different dimensions related to a continuum of individualism, which features self-reliance, and collectivism, which features interdependence. Compared to the Japanese, Americans are less tolerant of an unequal distribution of power, much more likely to expect self-reliance, less assertive and competitive, less tolerant of ambiguity and lack of structure, and less likely to be thrifty and persistent. *Source:* Adapted from http://www.geert-hofstede.com/hofstede_dimensions. php?culture1=14&culture2=95

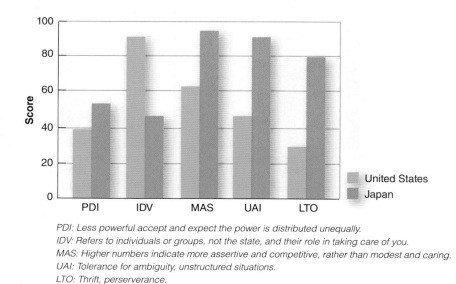

PDI: Less powerful accept and expect the power is distributed unequally.
IDV: Refers to individuals or groups, not the state, and their role in taking care of you.
MAS: Higher numbers indicate more assertive and competitive, rather than modest and caring.
UAI: Tolerance for ambiguity, unstructured situations.
LTO: Thrift, perserverance.

The second difference predicts a person's sense of being similar to other group members. In individualistic cultures, people are more likely to see themselves as unique. In collectivistic cultures, conformity and appearing similar to others are more highly valued. White American and Korean participants were offered the gift of a pen, which they were to choose from a group of three or four pens of the same color and one pen with a unique color. Seventy-four percent of the White Americans chose the uniquely colored pen, while 76% of the Koreans chose a pen with the more common color (Kim & Markus, 1999).

Summary 12.2

Some Important "Self" Terms

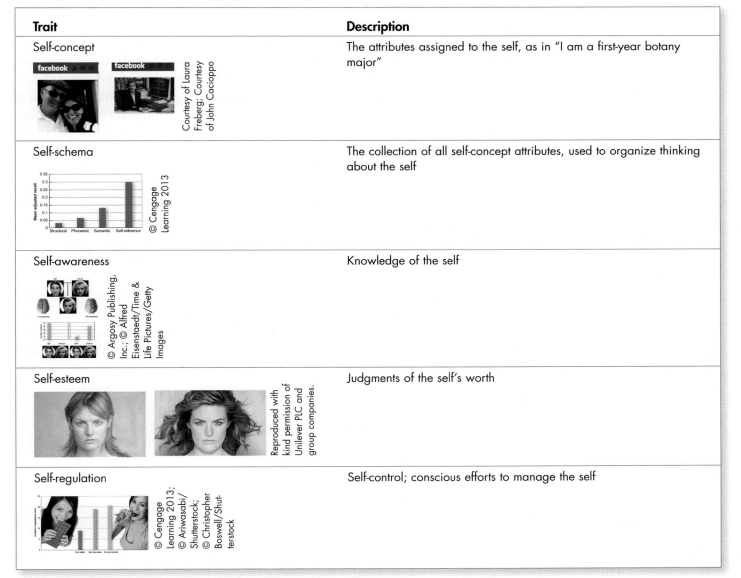

Trait	Description
Self-concept	The attributes assigned to the self, as in "I am a first-year botany major"
Self-schema	The collection of all self-concept attributes, used to organize thinking about the self
Self-awareness	Knowledge of the self
Self-esteem	Judgments of the self's worth
Self-regulation	Self-control; conscious efforts to manage the self

Courtesy of Laura Freberg; Courtesy of John Cacioppo

© Cengage Learning 2013

© Argosy Publishing, Inc.; © Alfred Eisenstaedt/Time & Life Pictures/Getty Images

Reproduced with kind permission of Unilever PLC and group companies.

© Cengage Learning 2013; © Ariwasabi/Shutterstock; © Christopher Boswell/Shutterstock

Interpersonal Relationships
From the Personality Perspective

Personality provides a perfect opportunity to revisit the "birds of a feather flock together" theme that we have discussed on many occasions in this textbook. Is it true that people who have similar personalities are attracted to each other?

In our previous chapter on development, we discussed research that showed that people in long-term relationships who have similar personalities experienced different levels of satisfaction at different stages in their relationships (Shiota & Levenson, 2007). Early in a relationship, similarity was particularly important to promoting bonding and intimacy. But what happens when we take one more step backward in time to look at the effects of similarity when people first meet each other?

In one study, pairs of heterosexual, opposite sex college students were left in a waiting room while a researcher ran an "errand" (Cuperman & Ickes, 2009). Without their knowledge, the pairs' interactions were filmed. As predicted by "birds of a feather," pairs of introverts and pairs of extroverts reported having a better conversation and liking their partner more (see ● Figure 12.20). However, similarity in agreeableness was not so important. Obviously, leaving two disagreeable people together did not result in a very pleasant conversation. Surprisingly, though, having at least one agreeable person produced the same quality of interaction as having two agreeable people. Apparently, agreeable people know how to produce a good interaction whether or not their partner is equally capable.

You might be wondering how personality similarities and differences stack up next to other factors when people first meet, and the answer is not well, at least in the context of a speed dating session for college students (Luo & Zhang, 2009). Under these circumstances, the overwhelming determinant of attraction for both men and women was physical appearance. No similarity in attitudes and Big Five characteristics was able to significantly predict attraction. This outcome might be one of the reasons why we are cautioned to "get to know each other better" before becoming involved in a serious relationship. If similarity plays an important role in long-term satisfaction, even with the bumps and bruises of middle age described by Shiota and Levenson (2007), it appears that we need more time than the speed dating situation provides to make important relationship decisions.

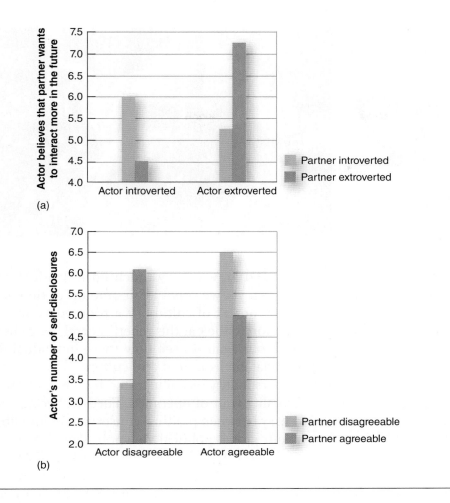

(a)

(b)

© Cengage Learning 2013

FIGURE 12.20

Do Opposites Attract? Introverts conversing with other introverts and extroverts conversing with other extroverts were more likely to believe their partner would want to interact in the future than pairs in which one person was introverted and the other was extroverted. When agreeableness was investigated, one disagreeable person having a conversation with another disagreeable person was not very positive, but as long as one of the partners was agreeable, the conversation went well. *Source:* Adapted from Cuperman and Ickes (2009).

Chapter 12
Reflections

© Argosy Publishing, Inc.

The focus in this chapter was very much on individuals in the form of personality and the self, yet we spent a fair amount of time talking about the much larger social context of culture. We zoomed in on several occasions during this discussion to look at the genetic correlates of personality, and then zoomed back out again to see how these individual differences interacted with the social environment and culture.

The role of genetics in personality was illustrated by the correlation of the 7R allele and the personality trait of openness. Further, because openness has been reported to vary between political conservatives and liberals, it is possible that some of our global political viewpoints might have their roots in our biological past. However, the 7R allele by itself did not predict liberalism or conservatism. Instead, researchers noted that only when the social environment was taken into account, in the form of a person's reported number of adolescent friendships, did the allele seem to make a difference. Having the combination of the 7R allele and many teen friendships made it more likely for a person to be a political liberal.

We also saw that the S and L alleles for the serotonin transporter gene were not equally distributed around the world and that cultures with higher numbers of S allele carriers were more likely to be collectivistic, while cultures with higher numbers of L allele carriers were more likely to be individualistic. At the same time, the impact of carrying the S allele is quite different across cultures. Carrying the S allele can be a risk for depression, but China has a lower rate of depression than the United States in spite of China's much higher proportion of S allele carriers.

Although we can talk about personality as a stable set of characteristics, it is clear that the ability to predict and understand another person's behavior depends on taking individual, situational, social, and cultural influences simultaneously into account. ❮

KEY TERMS The Language of Psychological Science

Be sure you can define these terms and use them correctly.

agreeableness, p. 583
Big Five theory, p. 582
conscientiousness, p. 583
defense mechanism, p. 574
ego, p. 574
extroversion, p. 582
id, p. 574
interpersonal self, p. 610
introversion, p. 582
locus of control, p. 587
neo-Freudian, p. 578

neuroticism, p. 582
openness, p. 583
personality, p. 572
personality inventory, p. 594
projective test, p. 594
psychoanalysis, p. 573
psychodynamic, p. 573
psychosexual stage, p. 576
reciprocal determinism, p. 587
self, p. 597
self-awareness, p. 598

self-concept, p. 597
self-esteem, p. 600
self-schema, p. 597
social-cognitive learning
    theory, p. 587
superego, p. 574
temperament, p. 588
trait, p. 581
unconscious mind, p. 574

MEDIA RESOURCES

Log in to CengageBrain to access the resources your instructor requires. For this book, you can access:

Psychology **CourseMate** brings course concepts to life with interactive learning, study, and exam preparation tools that support the printed textbook. A textbook-specific website, Psychology **CourseMate** includes an integrated interactive eBook and other interactive learning tools including quizzes, flashcards, videos, and more.

WebTUTOR More than just an interactive study guide, **WebTutor** is an anytime, anywhere customized learning solution with an eBook, keeping you connected to your textbook, instructor, and classmates.

aplia If your professor has assigned **Aplia** homework:
1. Sign in to your account.
2. Complete the corresponding homework exercises as required by your professor.
3. When finished, click "Grade It Now" to see which areas you have mastered, which areas need more work, and detailed explanations of every answer.

Genes on Chromosome 6 not only influence a person's immune system, but also determine a detectable body odor that affects our choice of a partner.

The Connected Mind

Social Psychology

13

Learning Objectives

1 Distinguish dispositional and situational attributions, identifying attributional biases in the correspondence bias, self-serving bias, and just-world belief.

2 Differentiate prejudice, stereotyping, and discrimination, and explain stereotypes in terms of concept formation processes.

3 Define "attitude," relate attitude development to learning principles, and contrast cognitive dissonance and the central versus peripheral routes to persuasion as mechanisms of attitude change.

4 Distinguish conformity, compliance, and obedience, and evaluate classic social influence studies in terms of ethical conduct of research.

5 Evaluate whether groups enhance or impair performance, using research on the social facilitation effect, social loafing, deindividuation, group polarization, and groupthink.

6 Summarize research on the mechanisms of attraction, relationship building, and relationship maintenance, and apply these principles to new scenarios.

7 Analyze the biological, situational, personality, and cultural factors that predict cooperation or competition in social interactions.

8 Summarize the interactions between nature and nurture in human aggression, and apply these principles to the problem of violence prevention.

Much of our success as a species can be attributed to our social nature. But as we all know from personal experience, the social world can be very challenging; consider, if you can, some of the truly embarrassing memories you have about social mistakes you've made. In fact, our need to understand our complex social environment was one of the driving forces that shaped the development of our very large human brains (Cacioppo & Decety, 2011).

Among the social environments with the largest minefields is the connection we make with others in intimate, romantic relationships. The two people in the photograph on the preceding page obviously find each other attractive, and they are engaged in behaviors—both variable and choreographed—designed to further their relationship. Looking at the developing relationship, psychologists can see a number of processes at work, such as first impressions and the effects of perceived similarities, that we discuss in detail in this chapter.

Zooming in, however, we see an entirely different set of processes at work. Although most of us believe that we choose romantic partners on the basis of perceived attractiveness and compatibility, there really is some "chemistry" at work here, too. The highlighted genes in the larger image help determine a person's immune system response. Further, the presence of different variations of these genes, or alleles, is associated with different detectable body odors (Wedekind & Füri, 1997). As attractive and compatible as these individuals seem to each other, one might reject the other in response to this odor. Our evolutionary history has left us with the ability to detect a genetic compatibility in a partner as well as more surface compatibilities.

Zooming out from our couple, we see that their romance takes place within a much larger social context. What will their families and friends think of their relationship? How do cultural attitudes and biases shape the likelihood of their success? To what extent will they feel comfortable conforming to these cultural expectations or rejecting them? All of these external factors can also help determine the course of their relationship. ⊗

Individual human beings are not very imposing predators, but cooperating in groups makes our species much more formidable.

Why Are Human Beings So Social?

Human beings depend on each other. We sit in houses and offices built by contractors and laborers, work on computers designed and built by armies of engineers and technicians, eat food grown and transported by others, wear clothes made by people living halfway around the globe, and look forward to the next text message from a friend.

As far back as the historical record goes, we have evidence that human beings lived in groups. What advantages might cooperative living have provided to our early ancestors? As predators or fighters, individual human beings have rather modest equipment relative to other species. Our teeth and nails are not particularly frightening, and we are frequently outmatched in speed and strength. It is our human abilities to think and to use tools, to employ and detect deceit, and to communicate, work together, and form alliances that make us such a formidable species.

Early evolutionary pressures favored humans who chose to affiliate, or associate with others, and by doing so, sculpted much of the social behavior we observe today. Social interaction is not just a helpful option but

Including the third player   Excluding the third player

FIGURE 13.1

Eliciting Feelings of Exclusion. Psychologists have many ways to make participants feel socially excluded for short periods so they can evaluate the effects social exclusion has on everything from brain activity to sharing cookies. Many experiments use this Cyberball game, developed by Kip Williams of Purdue University. The participant, represented by the little hand in the foreground, is initially included in the game of catch with the other two players, who are really just part of a computer program. Midway through the game, the other players throw the ball between themselves, excluding the participant, whose little hand is left with nothing to do.

a basic human need, which can be even more powerful than other basic needs such as hunger, which we addressed in our chapter on motivation (Baumeister & Leary, 1995; Cacioppo, Berntson, Sheridan, & McClintock, 2000). A mother's ability to comfort her infant through touch has a greater impact on the infant's attachment to her than her ability to provide food (Harlow & Harlow, 1973). Participants expecting a painful electric shock prefer the company of strangers to facing their fears alone (Schachter, 1959). We depend on today's mobile technologies that allow us to carry our social networks wherever we go (Taylor, 2002).

Not only do we need social contact, but we react negatively when social support is withdrawn (see ●Figure 13.1). Social isolation shares similar risks of death with high blood pressure, obesity, and a sedentary lifestyle and is positively correlated with risk of suicide (House, Landis, & Umberson, 1988; Trout, 1980). Disruptions of social connections through divorce, bereavement, separation, or ridicule are known to be among the most stressful experiences people may face (Williams, 2007). Perceived isolation, or loneliness, can initiate a cascade of negative interactions that further separate the individual from the social contact he or she needs and wants, interfere with the quality of sleep, increase feelings of negative mood and hostility, and lead to a heightened sensitivity to threat and attack (Cacioppo, Hawkley, & Thisted, 2010; Hawkley & Cacioppo, 2010). The isolated person begins to behave in ways that are self-protective but that paradoxically push people away and promote further rejection and isolation.

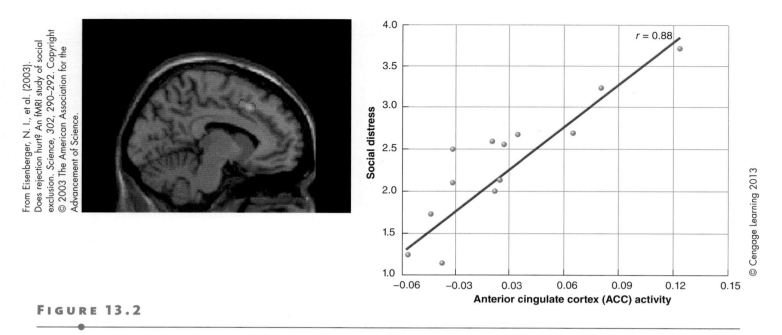

From Eisenberger, N. I., et al. (2003). Does rejection hurt? An fMRI study of social exclusion. *Science, 302,* 290–292. Copyright © 2003 The American Association for the Advancement of Science.

© Cengage Learning 2013

FIGURE 13.2

Rejection Hurts. Increased social distress caused by exclusion in the Cyberball game is strongly and positively correlated with higher levels of activity in the anterior cingulate cortex (ACC). The red and yellow colors indicate greater activity during exclusion compared to inclusion in the Cyberball game. This pattern of brain activity is very similar to the activity observed when participants are experiencing genuine physical pain from having their fingers pinched. *Source: Adapted from Eisenberger, Lieberman, and Williams (2003).*

Evidence that this need for social contact has been incorporated into our genetic heritage can be found in our development and biology. As we discussed in our chapters on development and on motivation and emotion, the age at which children experience distress due to separation from caregivers peaks at around 18 months across a diverse set of cultures (Kagan, Kearsley, & Zelazo, 1978). In our chapter on biological psychology, we discussed how the same parts of the brain are activated when a participant experiences physical pain and the pain of social exclusion (Eisenberger, Lieberman, & Williams, 2003; Kross, Berman, Mischel, Smith, & Wager, 2011) (see ● Figure 13.2). The ability to feel "pain" as a result of social exclusion might have reinforced social behaviors in early humans. As Naomi Eisenberger points out, "If it hurts to be separated from other people, then it will prevent us from straying too far from the social group" (CBSNews.com, October 9, 2003).

How Accurate Are First Impressions?

Our success in the social world begins with our ability to perceive the characteristics and intentions of others. What was your immediate reaction to your psychology professor on your first day of class? If you're like most people, you came to some very quick conclusions that are likely to last a long time. We form rapid and enduring first impressions of other people.

Speed dating, in which people have a very limited time to decide whether they would like any further contact with another person, takes advantage of the very rapid assessments we make of one another. After only 30 seconds of contact, people make enduring evaluations of other people.

When we say first impressions are formed "rapidly," we are not talking about months, weeks, days, or hours, but in some cases, less than a minute. In a meta-analysis of research using "thin slices of behavior" (exposure lasting less than 30 seconds), initial impressions did not change much after longer periods of exposure (Ambady & Rosenthal, 1993). Speed-dating provides an interesting environment for observing these "thin slice" impressions. Researchers asked men and women to participate in 3-minute social exchanges, followed by their rating each potential partner as date, friend, or no contact (Wilson, Cousins, & Fink, 2006). After only 3 minutes of observation, people accurately predicted their compatibility with a potential partner as measured by a reliable instrument called the Compatibility Quotient (CQ).

We make quick assessments of others by focusing on a subset of traits and behaviors, rather than trying to sum up an entire person. Halo effects occur when one or a small number of characteristics have a large impact on overall perception. If people see characteristics they value or dislike, they tend to make simple "thumbs up" or "thumbs down" assessments. One person might be attracted to blue eyes, and another turned off by tattoos. In one study, students hearing a professor described as "warm" instead of "cold" were willing to say after a very brief encounter that he was a more effective teacher, less ruthless, and more humorous (Widmeyer & Loy, 1988).

First impressions are not only fast but persistent. Once we have reached a conclusion about a person, even after a brief social exchange in a speed-dating experiment, we tend to stick with that assessment for a long time, even in the face of contradictory information. Most of us have formed a false first impression of others, either overly positive or overly negative, that breaks down only after extensive further exposure, if at all.

Even if we form the occasionally faulty first impression, the fact that we construct first impressions so readily implies that they offer some value to us. In particular, people are very likely to use faces to form impressions. Although the tendency to make these judgments may be characteristic of all human beings, our abilities to shape accurate first impressions also interact with culture. As shown in ● Figure 13.3, Japanese and American participants successfully used their first impressions to predict which

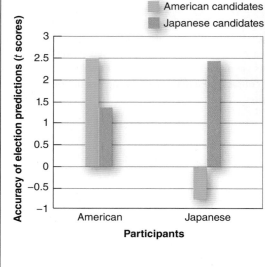

FIGURE 13.3

Judging Winners and Losers Across Cultures. Can you pick which of these candidates won or lost their elections?* Apparently, participants can do this quite well, but only within their own cultures. Based on viewing the photos of candidates' faces, without recognizing the candidate or even knowing the person was running for office, Americans did a good job of predicting the outcome of an election for unfamiliar American candidates for the U.S. Senate, but did not do very well when predicting the outcome for Japanese candidates for the *shugi-in* (the Japanese equivalent of the House of Representatives). Japanese participants predicted the success of Japanese candidates, but most of the American candidates they expected to win ended up losing. *Source:* Adapted from Rule et al. (2010).

*The two to the left won; the two to the right lost.

political candidates would win an upcoming election, but only for candidates from their own cultures (Rule et al., 2010).

Why Did That Just Happen?

We not only "size up" other people very quickly in terms of their personal characteristics, but we also ask "why" they behave the way they do. Being able to predict the behavior of others has significant survival value. Our answers to these questions about why others behave in certain ways are **attributions**, or judgments about the causes of other people's behavior.

Behavior can be seen as resulting from some combination of internal (**dispositional**) factors and external (**situational**) factors (Heider, 1958). For example, if your friend just flunked an important exam, you could try to answer the question "Why?" by considering your friend's personal characteristics and circumstances. In considering your friend's disposition, you might recall that he is very anxious (being anxious is dispositional), which might have interfered with his performance on a stressful test. In considering your friend's situation, you remember that he just broke up with his girlfriend of several years, which was very depressing and distracting for him as he prepared for his test (breaking up is situational).

Thinking that disposition and situation act in an either/or fashion instead of interacting to produce an outcome is not any more helpful to our understanding of behavior than to use either/or thinking in considering nature and nurture (Funder, 2009; Johnson, 2009). However, as we will see in the next section, the weight placed on dispositional and situational variables as explanations for behavior can vary dramatically from one case to the next. Although our attributions typically guide us in the right direction,

attribution A judgment about the cause of a person's behavior.

dispositional attribution A judgment assigning the cause of a person's behavior to his or her personal qualities or characteristics.

situational attribution A judgment assigning the cause of a person's behavior to his or her environment.

we do make errors. We are not able to read minds, so we must make a logical leap from what we observe in a person's behavior to the internal state of mind that produced it. Sometimes that leap takes us in the wrong direction.

The Correspondence Bias

When you hear about a person flunking a test, you are likely to start making conclusions about his or her disposition (she is a lazy student or he is not very smart), even though you are well aware that the person's professor has a reputation for writing brutal exams. This willingness to infer a person's disposition from his or her observed behavior, even when strong situational factors are obvious, is known as the **correspondence bias** (Gilbert & Jones, 1986; Gilbert & Malone, 1995). In other words, we usually expect people's behavior to *correspond* to their dispositions, even when the situation may be having a powerful effect.

Are the famous Walmart Greeters really friendly people? Or are they just doing their jobs? Because of the correspondence bias, we tend to view Walmart Greeters as very friendly people, even though we fully understand that their jobs require them to act this way.

Given the importance of making accurate attributions to our survival and social relationships, why would such an error ever occur? Psychologists are still debating the reasons for this error. One possibility might be the genuine stability of personality traits, discussed in our previous chapter on personality. Although traits interact with situations to produce behavior, people often believe the "you did it because that is the kind of person you are" explanation is accurate. There is some obvious truth to these beliefs, which is why they persist. But at the same time, our discussion of personality showed that situations make important contributions to behavior. We might consider ourselves helpful people, but we might ignore someone with a flat tire when we're late for class or work.

Other factors that contribute to the correspondence bias include a lack of awareness of the power of the situation and unrealistic beliefs about how situations should affect people (Gilbert & Malone, 1995). In many everyday instances, we simply do not have enough information about somebody's circumstances to consider situational variables in our attributions. A grumpy, unenthusiastic professor might be having health or personal problems of which students in the classroom are completely unaware. By default, students will believe that the professor is characteristically grumpy and unenthusiastic. In other cases, we seem to misjudge the likelihood that typical people will respond to a situation in a certain way. Later in this chapter, you will learn how a majority of individuals were willing to electrocute another participant simply because they were told to do so by an experimenter. You might think, "I would never respond to the situation like that," which might lead to your misjudging the power of the situation completely.

Classic research proposed a global neglect of situational variables in making attributions, a concept labeled as the fundamental attribution error (FAE; Ross, 1977). According to this view, the correspondence bias occurs because people completely failed to consider situational variables at all, leading by default to an overestimation of dispositional contributions to

correspondence bias The tendency to view behavior as the result of disposition even when the behavior can be completely explained by the situation in which it occurs.

the resulting observed behavior. Although this might seem to be the case on some occasions, we have already seen that the correspondence bias can arise from multiple causes. In addition, research evidence for a consistent neglect of observed situational variables is lacking (Gawronski, 2004). For example, in the study mentioned above about administering shock, how do you think people view the minority of participants who did not comply? If we globally ignore situational variables, we should attribute the behavior of these individuals to their strong moral character (disposition), but this is not what usually happens (Gilbert & Malone, 1995). Instead, most people

Experiencing Psychology

What Is Your Attributional Style?

 Ways of assigning causality are often so stable and characteristic of individuals that they have been referred to as attributional "styles," and questionnaires have been devised to identify a person's style (Seligman, Abramson, & Semmel, 1979). The following is an adapted, shortened version of the Attributional Style Questionnaire (Peterson et al., 1982).

Instructions: Please try to vividly imagine yourself in the situations that follow. If such a situation happened to you, what would you feel would have caused it? While events may have many causes, we want you to pick only one—the major cause if this event happened to you. Please write this cause in the blank provided after each event. Next, we want you to answer some questions about the cause and a final question about the situation.

Situation 1: You become very rich.

1. Write down the *one* major cause _____

2. Is the cause of your becoming rich due to something about you or to something about other people or circumstances? (circle one number)

1 Totally due to other people or circumstances	2	3	4	5	6	7 Totally due to me

3. In the future, will this cause again be present? (circle one number)

1 Will never again be present	2	3	4	5	6	7 Will always be present

4. Is the cause something that just influences becoming rich or does it also influence other areas of your life? (circle one number)

1 Influences just this particular situation	2	3	4	5	6	7 Influences all situations in my life

attribute the minority's behavior to simply responding to the situation "the way people ought to do." Psychologists are continuing to explore the basis of the correspondence bias.

Defensive Attributions

The correspondence bias is not the only flaw in our judgments of behavior. When our personal needs and motives enter the picture, additional errors can occur.

Classic studies suggested that an *actor-observer bias* occurs when we use situational variables to explain our own behavior while continuing to use dispositional variables to explain the behavior of others (Jones &

© Franck Robichon/EPA/Newscom

Olympic figure skater Rachael Flatt told a newspaper, "I was ultimately responsible for my work, no one else! No excuses! And, that is true in daily training. I am responsible for my own work, no one else." Elite athletes like Rachael rarely indulge in the *self-serving bias*, in which we attribute our successes to dispositional qualities (I'm a talented athlete) and our failures to situations (the judging wasn't fair or the ice wasn't prepared properly). By avoiding this bias, athletes can learn from their mistakes and continue to improve their performances.

Situation 2: You have been looking for a job unsuccessfully for some time.						
1. Write down the *one* major cause _____						
2. Is the cause of your unsuccessful job search due to something about you or to something about other people or circumstances? (circle one number)						
1 Totally due to other people or circumstances	2	3	4	5	6	7 Totally due to me
3. In the future when looking for a job, will this cause again be present? (circle one number)						
1 Will never again be present	2	3	4	5	6	7 Will always be present
4. Is the cause something that just influences looking for a job or does it also influence other areas of your life? (circle one number)						
1 Influences just this particular situation	2	3	4	5	6	7 Influences all situations in my life

Interpreting your scores: There are 12 situations in the complete questionnaire, and we have provided just a quick sample, so you are cautioned to not take your results too seriously.

The first situation is an example of a "good" situation, and the second situation is an example of a "bad situation." People often make different attributions in these types of situations, as we discussed in our section on the self-serving bias. Add up your scores on questions 2–4 for each situation and divide by 3 to get your "composite" score. Are these the same or different for the two situations? Higher scores indicate you attribute the situation more to yourself than to your circumstances.

Each question 2 indicates your tendency to form internal attributions (dispositional). Each question 3 indicates the stability of your attributions (these same reasons are usually present), and each question 4 indicates the globality of your attributions (these reasons affect most situations I'm in).

Attribution style questionnaires have been used widely to assess people with psychological disorders such as depression and potential job applicants. For example, people often view their successes as internal (dispositional) and stable, whereas they view their failures as external (e.g., situational) and unstable. Depressed people, in contrast, view their successes as external and unstable, and their failures as the result of internal, stable, and global factors (Seligman et al., 1979). ☼

© Marmaduke St. John/Alamy

A just-world belief leads people to expect that good things happen to good people and that bad things happen to bad people. A strong just-world belief might lead people to "blame the victim" thinking, making them less sympathetic to the poor and the sick.

just-world belief The assumption that good things happen to good people and bad things happen to bad people.

Nisbett, 1972). If my friend and I both flunked a test, I flunked because I was sick, but my friend flunked because he's not a very hard worker. Although this suggestion has some intuitive appeal, a more recent meta-analysis suggested that people judge their own behavior very similarly to the behavior of others (Malle, 2006).

Because of a self-serving bias, we view our successes differently than our failures (Miller & Ross, 1975). When we succeed, we are more likely to attribute our success to dispositional variables. For example, if you get an A in this course, you are likely to congratulate yourself on the basis of your brains and hard work. In contrast, if you fail the course, your failure is due to situational factors, such as the professor's asking unfair questions on the final exam. The self-serving bias can make you feel better, but it can also make it harder to learn from experience. Elite athletes, for example, are much less likely than less successful athletes to use situational variables to "excuse" poor performance, such as blaming the weather when they lose a game (Roesch & Amirkhan, 1997). By considering their own contributions to failure, the elite athletes can make the adjustments necessary for future success.

Similar attribution errors occur at the group level (Forsyth & Schlenker, 1977). In a group-serving bias, an organization will tend to attribute success to its dispositional characteristics, but will attribute failures to the situation. If a sports team wins, most of the members attribute the victory to team disposition, such as talent, good preparation, or sheer will. If a team loses, the members are unlikely to blame the loss on team dispositional factors (Sherman & Kim, 2005). By failing to consider dispositional factors that might be remedied in the future, a group might miss opportunities to correct its course of action.

In addition to the self-serving bias, we frequently engage in other types of defensive reasoning. It is a short step from "your behavior reflects your disposition" to causal judgments about the outcomes of behavior, such as "you get what you deserve." Through the **just-world belief**, people assume that good things happen to good people and bad things happen to bad people (Lerner & Miller, 1978). When you see something bad happen to a good person, you might reduce your anxiety by thinking the person must have done something to deserve the bad outcome, and you can avoid that outcome by behaving differently. However, this reduction in personal anxiety can come at the expense of the victim, who is being blamed unfairly. Strong just-world beliefs have been positively correlated with negative attitudes toward the poor, people with HIV/AIDS, the elderly, and the unemployed (Sutton & Douglas, 2005).

Cultural Influences on Attribution

There are subtle differences in attribution between cultures that value individualism and cultures that value collectivism. Individualistic cultures, including the United States and many other Western nations, stress individual achievement and competition. Collectivist cultures, including people in many Asian nations, traditionally have valued cooperation as a means of attaining family and work group goals.

Members of collectivist cultures tend to place more emphasis on situations rather than dispositions (Choi, Nisbett, & Norenzayan, 1999; Ho & Fung, 2011). For example, in the United States, murder is viewed as resulting from the disposition of the murderer, whereas in China, murder is often described in terms of the histories of the people involved and the situation in which the murder occurred (Morris & Peng, 1994). As a result, members of individualistic cultures are more likely to demonstrate the correspondence bias.

These cultural differences in attribution may have their roots in the tendency for people in Eastern cultures to focus on context or situations and relationships, while people in Western cultures are more likely to focus on objects than situations (Masuda & Nisbett, 2001). As we mentioned earlier, we tend to attribute behavior to the factors we perceive. If being raised in a particular culture leads you to focus on different features of the environment, the attributions that are made will vary accordingly (see ● Figure 13.4).

Because of the importance placed on individual achievement in individualistic societies, members of these societies are more likely to use defensive attributions, such as the self-serving bias (Leung, Kim, Zhang, Tam, & Chiu, 2011). Members of more collectivist cultures show an interesting group-serving bias, in which they attribute more success to the group than it deserves and less of its failures than it deserves (Leung et al., 2011). That

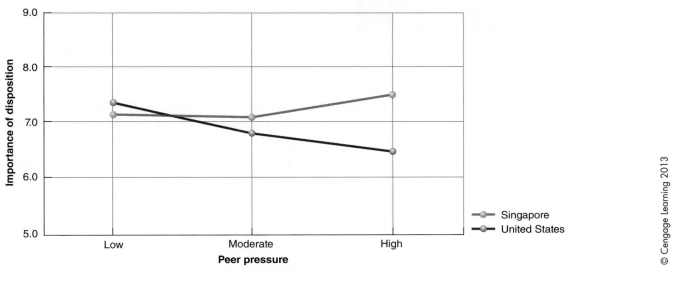

© Cengage Learning 2013

FIGURE 13.4

Situational Attributions and Punishment Across Cultures. In the individualist United States culture, but not in collectivist Singapore, recognition of peer pressure leading to crime (a situational variable) reduces the attribution of the crime to a person's disposition. An American criminal who commits a crime due to peer pressure is not seen to be as "bad" as a person who acts without such pressure. As a result, "extenuating circumstances" usually lead to reduced sentences in the United States. Even though collectivist nations like Singapore place a higher emphasis on situational variables when making attributions overall, they do not view peer pressure as a reason to reduce punishment of an individual. If anything, the individual will be blamed for associating with the wrong peer group. *Source:* Adapted from Tetlock, Self, and Singh (2010).

is, if you were raised in a collectivist culture, you would show the same attributional biases about your in-group as an individual raised in an individualistic culture would show about herself or himself.

Why Are We Prejudiced?

Among the most damaging perceptions we form about other people are those that are based on their group memberships, which can include (but are not limited to) factors such as race, gender, age, socioeconomic status, height, weight, disabilities, attractiveness, sexual orientation, and religion.

When a person makes a negative assessment of another person on the basis of his or her membership in a group, the person is showing **prejudice**. The term *prejudice* literally means "to prejudge." Prejudice is usually accompanied by **stereotypes**, or a simplified set of traits that are associated with group membership, such as all blondes are dumb or women have no interest in videogames or football. **Discrimination** is behavior based on prejudice and stereotyping. Hiring practices, housing, educational opportunities, and many other facets of modern living can be conducted in discriminatory ways. Discrimination usually occurs when a decision maker uses a group stereotype to judge an individual, such as using gender stereotypes as the basis for hiring only male computer programmers or female elementary school teachers.

Sources of Prejudice

In our earlier chapter on cognition, we observed that human beings organize information and experience into categories or concepts, which is generally useful. Our concepts are associated with a variety of characteristics, such as "birds have feathers." We frequently have exemplars, or best examples, of each category. If you think of the word *bird*, you are probably more likely to imagine a canary than an ostrich. Finally, we generalize from our known concepts when faced with new information. If we know that birds peck at objects placed before them, we are less likely to stick our fingers near the beak of a new type of bird. In other words, based on our past experience with birds, we are prejudging the behavior of a new, unfamiliar type of bird. This process of categorizing information enables us to make rapid decisions about new situations and objects, similar to the rules of thumb, or heuristics, we discussed in our chapter on cognition.

Effective concepts are inclusive, recognizing a full range of associated characteristics. When our categories are oversimplified, we are left with stereotypes. Although it's true that most birds fly, it is inaccurate to oversimplify the matter by saying "birds fly," as ostriches certainly do not. Stereotypes often contain an element of truth, but become inaccurate due to the information they exclude. More importantly, stereotypes conflict with our valid desires to be viewed and treated as individuals.

If stereotypes can lead us astray, why are they so pervasive and persistent? People tend to misjudge correlations between groups and their stereotypical behaviors. They might overestimate the percentage of Asian students who excel in math and science or underestimate the number of

People often have negative stereotypes about overweight people as a group. In one online survey, over 75% of respondents believed that overweight people should either buy a second seat or pay a "fat tax" to travel on airplanes (Siegfried, 2010). Comedian Kevin Smith, ejected from a Southwest Airlines flight for "infringing on a portion of the next seat," tweeted that he "broke no regulation, offered no 'safety risk' (what, was I going to roll over a fellow passenger?)."

prejudice A prejudgment, usually negative, of another person on the basis of his or her membership in a group.

stereotype A simplified set of traits associated with membership in a group or category.

discrimination Unfair behavior based on stereotyping and prejudice.

White athletes who play professional basketball. Attributions, discussed earlier, also contribute to continued stereotyping. If you see an exception to your stereotype, perhaps a female who is running faster than her male friend, you might view her success as the result of situational variables. Perhaps the man is letting her win to be nice. This type of thinking allows us to maintain a "women are weaker" stereotype.

You have probably noticed that people's prejudice toward a group often conflicts with their behaviors toward individual members of that group. Someone might express dramatically prejudiced opinions about a group, yet treat members of that group very well. Individuals can be viewed as being "different" or "exceptions," allowing people to retain their stereotypes in the face of conflicting observations. Instead of rethinking a stereotype about truck drivers and country music, you view your truck driving friend who enjoys opera to be one of a kind. Finally, stereotypes are often maintained by people's expectations. In one experiment, students listening to a basketball game were informed that a certain player was either Black or White. After the game, students who believed the athlete was Black expressed their stereotypes by rating the player as being more athletic, while those who believed the athlete was White gave him praise for his intelligence and hustle (Stone, Perry, & Darley, 1997).

Prejudice can result from direct experience (I had one boring history professor, so all history professors must be bad) or indirectly absorbed from the social world of peers, parents, community, and media. Human prejudice based on group membership, however, might have deeper roots in our evolutionary past. Recognizing and reacting to individuals based on group affiliation was probably a very important skill for early hunter-gatherers, whose survival often depended on quickly identifying others as potential trading partners or foes. This pressure could have led to a tendency to distinguish between in-groups, or the group to which we belong, and out-groups, or everybody else (see ● Figure 13.5). This categorization

© Jennie Hart/Alamy

Oversimplified categories, such as "girl toys" or "boy toys," can lead to stereotypes.

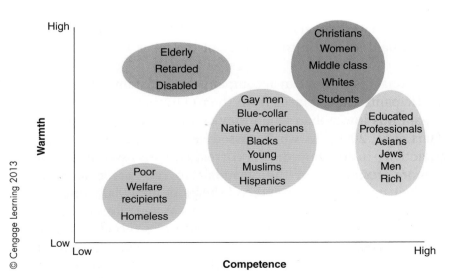
© Cengage Learning 2013

FIGURE 13.5

American Perceptions of Out-groups. Out-groups often elicit mixed reactions. Some out-groups (rich people) are respected for their perceived competence but disliked for lack of warmth. Elderly people and the disabled are viewed as low in competence, but they are viewed warmly due to the lack of threat they pose. Groups such as the poor are viewed most harshly as a result of having both low status and representing a threat of exploiting the in-group. *Source:* Adapted from Fiske, Cuddy, Glick, and Xu (2002).

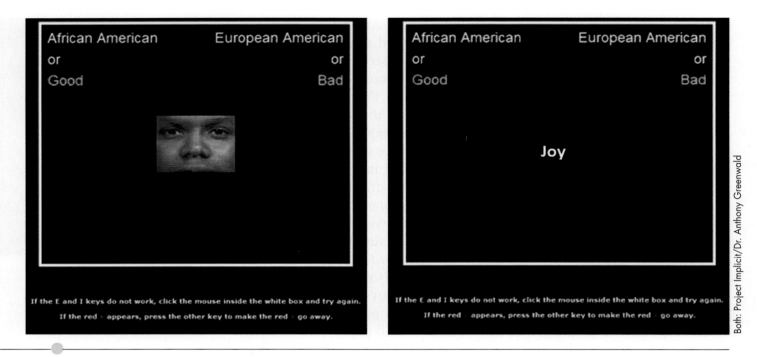

The Implicit Association Test (IAT) measures reaction time to assess people's unconscious attitudes. In this version of the test, either a face (African American or European American) or a word will appear at the center of the screen. In these examples, the participant would push a specified key on a computer for the face (African American) and then again for the word (joy is good). Later in the test, the combinations at the top of the screen are switched to African American or Bad and European American or Good. An implicit bias in favor of African Americans would be shown if reaction time in the first condition (African American or Good) is faster than in the second condition (African American or Bad).

was made primarily on the basis of physical appearance, and people still instantly and often unconsciously categorize others on the basis of physically observable features, including age, gender, and race (Fiske, 1998).

This type of categorization was demonstrated by recording participants' brain activity as they viewed photographs of faces and made judgments of either race or gender (Ito & Urland, 2003). Participants reacted very quickly to both race and gender information, even when the information was irrelevant to their task. In other words, a participant who was asked to differentiate between male and female faces still showed evidence of having paid attention to the race of the faces without being asked to do so.

Different emotional responses can accompany these instant categorizations. When participants viewed faces from their own racial group, activity in the amygdala was lower than when they viewed faces from another racial group (Hart et al., 2000). As we discussed in our chapter on biological psychology, activity in the amygdala is correlated with assessments of threat. Furthermore, responses of the amygdala to race are correlated with several implicit measures of prejudice (Phelps et al., 2000). Implicit measures are designed to demonstrate subconscious associations between concepts (literature and math, for example) and attitudes (good and bad, for example) (Nosek, 2007). White participants who showed the greatest differences in amygdala activity while viewing Black and White faces were also more likely to associate positive words such as *joy*, *love*, and *peace* with Whites and negative words such as *cancer*, *bomb*, and *devil* with Blacks. The amygdala activity in response to viewing Black faces might reflect the fear and other negative assessments made by these participants based on racial stereotypes.

Understanding that biological and evolutionary processes are involved with in-group–out-group differentiation does not make prejudice inevitable or acceptable. By understanding why we develop prejudice, we can better identify ways to reduce it. As we will see later in this section, prejudice can change.

Outcomes of Prejudice

Prejudice, whether subtle or overt, can lead to discriminatory behavior in a number of ways. Not only are African Americans convicted of murder more likely than Whites to be given the death penalty in the United States but perceptions of "Blackness" are also predictive of a murderer's being sentenced to death (Eberhardt, Davies, Purdie-Vaughns, & Johnson, 2006). Researchers presented photographs of African American defendants to participants without telling them that the men depicted had been convicted of murder. The participants ranked the photographs on the basis of stereotypical "Black features," such as broad nose, dark skin, and thick lips. The ratings were highly predictive of the men's sentences when the victim was White. Men who appeared more stereotypically African American were over twice as likely to be given the death sentence as men whose physical appearance was less stereotypical. This difference disappeared, however, when the victim was also African American (see ● Figure 13.6).

Prejudice affects not only the way we view others but also the way we view our own behavior. Raising awareness of a negative stereotype about a group to which we belong has the ability to reduce our performance, a phenomenon known as stereotype threat (Steele, 1997; Steele & Aronson, 1995). Anxiety about confirming a negative stereotype attributed to your group can prevent you from doing your best work.

FIGURE 13.6

Implications of Stereotyping. Participants' ratings of stereotypical "Black features" predicted the men's likelihood of being sentenced for murder with the death penalty, but only when the victim was described as White. The men in these photographs have no criminal records but are examples provided by the authors for individuals who were viewed as less stereotypical (left) and more stereotypical (right). *Source:* From Eberhardt, J. L., et al. (2006). Looking deathworthy: Perceived stereotypicality of black defendants predicts capital-sentencing outcomes, *Psychological Science 17*(5), 383–386. Copyright © 2006 Association for Psychological Science.

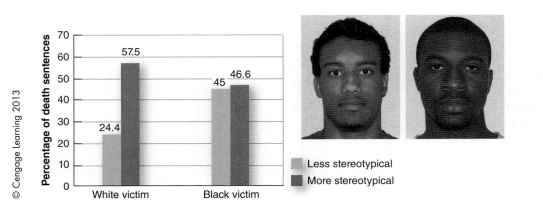

© Cengage Learning 2013

In a set of studies demonstrating this effect, researchers asked Stanford undergraduate students to complete difficult items taken from the verbal portion of the Graduate Record Exam (GRE), used as part of the admissions process for some graduate programs (Steele & Aronson, 1995). One group of students, the stereotype threat group, was told that the test accurately assessed their cognitive abilities, a statement that was designed to stimulate thinking about possible racial stereotypes about intelligence. The other group was told that the test was a routine laboratory procedure. Subsequently, the performance of Black and White students on the test was compared. In the stereotype threat condition, the Black students performed more poorly than White students with equal verbal abilities, as measured earlier by their entrance scores on the similar Scholastic Aptitude Test (SAT). In contrast, in the nonthreatening condition, Blacks and Whites with equal SAT scores performed similarly on the GRE items, which is the result we would expect due to the tests' reliability and validity, which we discussed in our chapter on research methods (see ● Figure 13.7).

Reducing Prejudice

Although we would prefer a world in which prejudice didn't occur in the first place, psychologists have gained insight into how prejudice can be reduced.

Increased contact can reduce prejudice (Farley, 2000). However, not just any contact will have this effect. To be effective in reducing prejudice, contact must occur under certain circumstances. For example, contact between people of equal standing is more effective in reducing prejudice. If people are from very different socioeconomic groups, greater contact may actually increase rather than decrease between-group resentment.

Contact is particularly beneficial in reducing prejudice when groups participate in cooperative activities (see ● Figure 13.8). In a study using two groups of boys at a summer camp, negative feelings between the groups decreased after the boys cooperated to solve false "emergencies," such as interruptions to the camp's water supply (Sherif, Harvey, White, Hood, & Sherif, 1961). Another classic example of the effectiveness of cooperation in

FIGURE 13.7

Stereotype Threat. When Black students at Stanford University were told that a verbal test measured their true abilities (stereotype threat), their subsequent performance was less than when they were told that the test was being used to understand the "psychological factors involved in solving verbal problems" (no stereotype threat). The different instructions did not affect the performance of the White students. *Source: Adapted from Steele and Aronson (1995).*

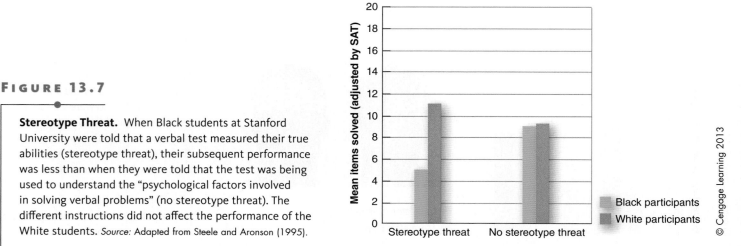

© Cengage Learning 2013

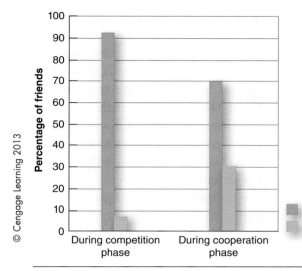

© Cengage Learning 2013

FIGURE 13.8

The Reduction of In-group and Out-group Bias Through Cooperation. After arbitrarily dividing campers into two groups, the Rattlers and the Eagles, Sherif and his colleagues observed considerable in-group–out-group bias between the groups. During this phase, few of the campers reported having friends from the out-group. To resolve the resulting discord, the researchers set up "false" emergencies, such as a problem with the camp's water supply, that required the boys to cooperate. After cooperating, many of their previous biases were no longer present, and more boys reported having friends among the out-group. *Source:* Adapted from Sherif, Harvey, White, Hood, and Sherif (1961).

■ Choice of friends from in-group
■ Choice of friends from out-group

reducing prejudice is the "jigsaw classroom," designed to reduce racial tensions in newly desegregated school districts in the 1970s (Aronson, 2011). Children in cooperative groups were assigned a part of the "answer" that their group needed to learn, leading to interdependence among the group members. Rather than competing for the teacher's approval, the children in the jigsaw task helped their teammates by listening and teaching. Outcome research indicated that students in jigsaw classrooms mastered the material better, liked their group members better, were absent less frequently, and showed evidence of more empathy and higher self-esteem (Aronson, 2011). This type of cooperative contact is used in deliberate efforts to reduce prejudice in about 80% of elementary schools in the United States (Paluck & Green, 2009).

Illustration: © Cengage Learning 2013; photo: © Monkey Business Images/Shutterstock

Cooperative learning programs similar to Aronson's jigsaw classroom are used in the vast majority of public schools in the United States today.

Because so much prejudice originates in categorizing people and then engaging in "in-group–out-group" thinking, another strategy for reducing prejudice is to expand the definition of the in-group. For example, if a White female and an Asian female concentrate on the similarities they share as women, they should experience fewer feelings of bias toward one another on the basis of race (Deschamps & Doise, 1978). Although this effect is not always seen in the laboratory (Vescio, Judd, & Kwan, 2004), when combined with "real-world" extended contact, the strategy seems to be promising (Eller, Abrams, Viki, & Imara, 2007). Perhaps if we stop focusing on our group identities, we can consider ourselves members of the human race or residents of the planet. If we cooperate to solve problems of hunger, sickness, poverty, and degradation of the environment, the result could be a reduction in prejudice.

Summary 13.1

Sources of Attribution Error

Type of error	Definition	Example
Correspondence bias © AP Photo/The Janesville Gazette, Dan Lassiter	Overestimating the dispositional causes of a person's behavior	My friend flunked his exam because he's not very bright.
Self-serving bias © Franck Robichon/EPA/Newscom	Attributing personal success to dispositional causes while attributing personal failure to situational causes	I got an A on one test because I'm smart, but I flunked the other test because it was unfair.
Group-serving bias	Attributing group success to dispositional causes while attributing group failures to situational causes	Our team won its first game because we're really talented and skilled, but lost the second because the referees were biased.
Just-world thinking © Marmaduke St. John/Alamy	Assuming that people get what they deserve	That rape victim should have dressed more modestly.

How Are Our Attitudes Influenced by Others?

To survive, all animals must make appropriate approach or avoidance responses to stimuli. The reflexes, fixed action patterns, and unconditioned responses discussed in our chapter on learning provide some guidance in simple situations, such as seeing a predator. To respond to more complex situations, human beings form **attitudes**, or favorable or unfavorable evaluations that predispose behavior (Petty & Cacioppo, 1986b).

Attitudes are pervasive. We form positive and negative attitudes about everything from world events to celebrities to brands of peanut butter, and attitudes provide an efficient means of communicating with others. If a friend asks you for a recommendation for a movie, restaurant, or class, a simple attitude statement ("I liked my psychology class!") can serve as a quick and efficient summary for a wide set of beliefs, behavioral experiences, and emotions. Decision making is simpler, faster, and less stressful when attitudes exist to serve as a guide. Attitudes can influence behavior, which is why the advertising industry spends billions of dollars each year in an attempt to shape your attitudes toward various products.

Because we depend on our attitudes to guide our behavior, we want to make sure they are "correct" (Festinger, 1950). Imagine what would happen if you woke up one day to discover that your attitudes about people, objects, and issues were all wrong. Suddenly, your closest friends would really dislike you, your major would be a poor match for your interests and abilities, and your entire collection of music would sound dreadful. Occasional mistakes happen, but holding accurate attitudes makes it easier for us to maneuver through the environment successfully.

Attitudes share three basic elements (the ABCs): affect (emotion), behavior, and cognition. For example, how might your attitudes about your college major be affected by hearing a news report about the job market for new college graduates? The affective aspect of an attitude addresses emotional responses to the object. Information about your future job prospects could make you feel quite helpless, frightened, or angry. Behavior reflects the way people respond to the object. After hearing the news, you might schedule an appointment with your advisor to discuss the ways you can pursue the subjects you love and still have a great career. The cognitive aspect of an attitude includes beliefs about the object. In response to the news, you might believe that you have chosen the wrong major.

Photo by Joi Ito licensed under a Creative Commons Attribution License

If you have any doubt whether or not people are emotional about their attitudes, just ask some friends if they prefer Apple (represented by the late Steve Jobs, left) or PC (represented by Bill Gates, right). Be prepared to duck for cover.

Attitude Formation

We form many attitudes on the basis of our personal experiences. You like a flavor of ice cream after sampling it, and you dislike the parking situation at your school because you can never find a spot near your classes. In other cases,

attitude Positive or negative evaluations that predispose behavior toward an object, person, or situation.

Some of our attitudes result from personal experience, but others are quickly absorbed from the world around us, especially through peers and the media.

Cognitive dissonance helps explain why hazing, or requiring an unpleasant initiation in order to become a member of a group, increases the value of the group (Aronson & Mills, 1959). If you choose to endure so much to join, the group must be something very special.

cognitive dissonance The uncomfortable state that occurs when behavior and attitudes do not match and that can be resolved through attitude change.

we absorb attitudes from our contacts with peers, parents and other family members, religious leaders, teachers, and the media.

We often adopt the attitudes of those around us to strengthen our chances of being socially included. As a result, many people prefer to stay on the "winning side" by forming attitudes based on how frequently they hear an opinion expressed by others and in the media (Noelle-Neumann, 1984). Later in this chapter, we explore how fear of social rejection can lead to conformity and strict adherence to social norms or values.

The principles explored in our chapter on learning play important roles in the development of attitudes. Operant conditioning suggests that approval or disapproval will shape a person's attitudes. An opinion expressed in class that is followed by nods and claps will be repeated in the future more than one that is met with horror and disgust. Because of classical conditioning, you are likely to form positive attitudes toward stimuli associated with positive outcomes. If a song is popular at a happy time of your life, it is likely that your subsequent attitude toward the song will be positive, too. Observational learning can also be a powerful mechanism for learning attitudes. Children who are exposed to particular attitudes in their homes, communities, and media duplicate them, especially if they observe the person expressing the attitude being rewarded.

Identical twins who were adopted by different families at birth, making it unlikely that they were exposed to the same attitudes, still show a surprising amount of similarity among their attitudes as adults (Bouchard, Lykken, McGue, Segal, & Tellegen, 1990). In other studies utilizing twin data, genetics appeared to influence the likelihood a person would hold liberal or conservative attitudes (Alford, Funk, & Hibbing, 2005). Obviously, we do not have Republican or Democratic genes and people do change their minds, but we possibly have genetic predispositions that influence our adoption of certain attitudes.

Cognitive Dissonance

Although our attitudes typically guide us well, attitude change is often desirable. After all, we are sometimes just flat out wrong! Addiction, for example, includes attitudes and preferences that are not in the best interests of anybody concerned. The addict by definition cannot easily change these attitudes and preferences, however. Similarly, people who are unable to change their attitudes in the face of new evidence can be quite handicapped. Understanding the circumstances in which attitude change takes place gives us additional insight into the formation of our attitudes and their role in guiding our behavior.

Cognitive dissonance provides a powerful tool for producing attitude change (Festinger, 1957). Cognitive dissonance is an uncomfortable state that occurs when our outward behavior doesn't match our attitudes. For example, you might have been accepted by several colleges and universities, but you can choose to attend only one (the behavior). Thinking about the positive features of the schools you reject causes dissonance (I like these schools but I didn't choose them), which could be resolved either by becoming a "superfan" of your chosen school or by forming negative attitudes toward the schools that you reject. How could you even consider making another choice? Who would want to go to those other schools anyway?

Cognitive dissonance appears to change attitudes by producing an unpleasant state of arousal, caused by a person's feeling responsible for helping to bring about a negative event (Cooper, 2011). Adolescent participants who evidenced online gaming addictions first rated a new online game and then followed directions to tell peers that the game "really wasn't fun." When asked to rate the game a second time, they gave it more negative rankings than they had prior to their expressing a negative opinion about it (Wan & Chiou, 2010). In the case of the online gamers, they might believe that their false statements about the game's quality could deprive fellow gamers of the pleasure of playing the game or damage the reputation and income of the company making the game. The resulting negative emotions can be reduced by bringing attitudes more into line with their behavior.

Brain imaging studies provide substantial support for cognitive dissonance (see ● Figure 13.9). Participants undergoing functional MRI were asked to describe the somewhat unpleasant scanner experience as actually pleasant (van Veen, Krug, Schooler, & Carter, 2009). Many people find

Choosing to smoke in spite of constant warning messages can produce cognitive dissonance. To reduce dissonance, this smoker may start to believe that the warnings are not believable and that smoking isn't really that bad for you.

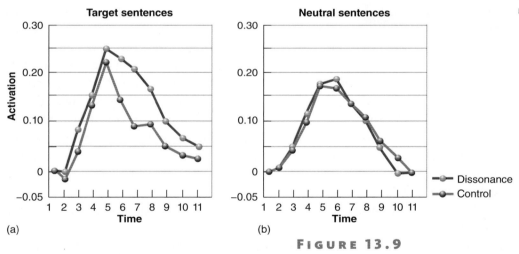

(a)   (b)

FIGURE 13.9

Cognitive Dissonance and the Anterior Cingulate Cortex. Participants undergoing functional magnetic brain imaging (fMRI) were divided into two groups: a dissonance group that was asked to tell the next participant how pleasant the rather unpleasant scanning experience was, and a control group that did not have this experience. Both groups responded to target sentences, such as "I feel calm, peaceful in the scanner," or neutral sentences, which did not involve attitudes toward the scanner experience. (a) The dissonance group responded to the target sentences with more activation in several parts of the brain, including the anterior cingulate cortex (ACC) and the insula (located at the junction of the temporal and frontal lobes), compared to the control group. (b) The groups did not show any differences in response to the neutral sentences. (c) The yellow-orange areas are more active during the dissonance situation (dissonant group—target sentences) than during the other situations (dissonant group—neutral sentences; control group—target and neutral sentences).

Source: Adapted from van Veen, Krug, Schooler, and Carter (2009).

(c)

being confined in the scanner tube and the loud banging of the magnets to be unpleasant rather than "pleasant." Levels of activity in a participant's anterior cingulate cortex (ACC) and insula were higher when she or he made dissonant statements about how pleasant the fMRI experience was compared to neutral statements. A greater difference in activation seen during the production of dissonant and neutral sentences predicted a participant's amount of attitude change. In other words, the more activity observed in a participant's ACC and insula during dissonant sentences compared to neutral sentences, the more positively the participant later rated the fMRI experience.

Why Does Persuasion Happen?

Cognitive dissonance produces attitude change, but not in response to a direct effort by another person. When we change our attitudes in response to information provided by others, **persuasion** occurs. Knowing how to persuade others and understanding the efforts of others to persuade you are important life skills.

The Elaboration Likelihood Model (ELM)

The **Elaboration Likelihood Model (ELM)** organizes and predicts our responses to persuasive messages by recognizing two major pathways leading to changes in attitudes (Cacioppo & Petty, 1984; Petty & Cacioppo, 1981). The first, known as the central route to persuasion, occurs when a person considers persuasive arguments carefully and thoughtfully. The second, known as the peripheral route to persuasion, occurs when a person responds to peripheral cues, which we describe in the following section, without considering the quality of the argument carefully. Importantly, attitudes achieved through the central route are more enduring, more resistant to counter-persuasion, and more predictive of behavior than are attitudes achieved through the peripheral route (Petty & Cacioppo, 1986a).

Why do we need two systems for responding to persuasive messages? Ideally, we would use the central route to consider all messages that we encounter. However, given our limited time, knowledge, and cognitive resources, a thorough evaluation of all the messages we perceive is not practical. Using the peripheral route allows us to use heuristics, or rules of thumb (described in our chapter on cognition), to react promptly to many situations. If you feel overwhelmed by the large number of candidates on your ballot, you might use the heuristic of voting along party lines or voting like your friends.

Routes to Persuasion

What determines whether we use the central or peripheral route? According to the ELM, a person's motivation influences which route he or she uses to evaluate a particular argument. When students are highly motivated to take time out of their busy schedules to attend a presentation by a guest speaker on campus because they know and care about the topic of the lecture, they

persuasion A change in attitudes in response to information provided by another person.

Elaboration Likelihood Model (ELM) A model that predicts responses to persuasive messages by distinguishing between the central and peripheral routes to persuasion.

are likely to use the central route and evaluate the speaker's points carefully.

People are also likely to use the central route to persuasion when they are well educated about a topic. However, even people who are very knowledgeable will occasionally take the peripheral rather than the central route. If you know about a topic but do not have the time to think about it or don't care about it, you might find the shortcuts provided by the peripheral route more useful. In addition, because using the central route requires so many cognitive resources, including attention, we are less likely to process persuasive messages this way when we are distracted by other information or activities. As you concentrate on driving down a busy highway, you do not have the cognitive resources to evaluate the messages on billboards very carefully.

These international experts on cosmetics technology are likely to use the central route to persuasion while evaluating the speaker's message. They will concentrate on the logic of the message and will be relatively unimpressed by peripheral cues, such as the speaker's attractiveness or use of emotion.

If a person is using the peripheral route to persuasion, what cues might influence the amount of attitude change that occurs? Peripheral cues usually apply to the persuasive message itself (e.g., the number of arguments), the manner in which the message is presented (e.g., speed of speech, accent), or the characteristics of the speaker (e.g., credibility or celebrity).

Emotional appeals can influence people using the peripheral route. Both positive and negative emotions can enhance persuasion. Students asked to read persuasive messages about topics such as curing cancer and the state of military forces were more likely to agree with the statement they read while happily snacking on Pepsi and peanuts (Dabbs & Janis, 1965). Efforts to persuade using negative emotions are especially common. We hear daily warnings about the dangers of drinking too much, not using our seatbelts, engaging in risky sex practices, riding a bicycle without a helmet, eating trans fats, and so on (Leventhal & Watts, 1966; Robberson & Rogers, 1988).

Arousing negative emotions, such as fear, can be risky. If people are too frightened by a message, they tend to go into a state of denial. "It's really not

Driving down a busy highway requires your full attention, making it unlikely that you will have the resources you need to evaluate persuasive messages using the central route. Instead, the billboards you pass hope to influence you in just a few seconds to think better of the product or message they display.

that bad," they will say, or "That can't happen here." Denial is most likely to occur if the audience is not given an action step they can use to reduce their anxiety. It is fine to scare smokers to death about the appearance of their lungs, as long as you include a message that tells them where to get help to quit smoking. Having a sense of control over their response will reduce the fear and make the message more persuasive (Ajzen, 1991).

A positive response to the speaker can enhance a message's persuasion. In spite of the commonsense warning that "beauty is only skin deep," people have a deep-seated stereotype that what is beautiful is good (Dion, Berscheid, & Walster, 1972). Student evaluations of their professors are heavily influenced by the perceived attractiveness of the professor (Hamermesh & Parker, 2003). People are more likely to be persuaded by people they like and with whom they share some similarity (Cialdini, 2001; Van Knippenberg & Wilke, 1992). Similarities need not be very substantial to produce this effect; participants who shared a first name or birthday with the supposed author of a persuasive essay were more likely to agree with the essay (Silvia, 2005).

A credible speaker is usually more persuasive, especially when traveling the peripheral route (see ● Figure 13.10). Credibility in turn is based on the

Psychology *as a* Hub Science

Social Media and Influence

The Internet is providing new ways to communicate, from the use of webcams, video, and live chat to Twitter, Facebook, Google⁺, and blogs. Many of these new technologies have

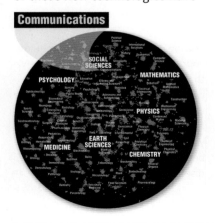

Communications

advantages in providing immediacy and collaboration. To the extent that they duplicate the advantages of face-to-face communication, we would expect them to provide effective means of persuading others.

Not only does the Internet provide a new medium for communicating persuasive messages, but it challenges the status of the credible, expert speaker as well. Historically, persuasive messages from traditional news outlets such as newspapers, magazines, radio, and television were more of a one-way street. However, in an environment in which everybody with a computer can produce information, receivers of information can be influencers as well by sharing and commenting on mes-

sages in blogs and on social networking sites. Initial research in this area suggests that user-generated content in the form of blogs, uploaded videos, comments, and reviews is considered as credible and accurate as formal news reports prepared by professional journalists (Lee, Park, Lee, & Cameron, 2010). In addition, knowing that content is "popular" with other users significantly raises a message's impact (Steyn, Wallstrom, & Pitt, 2010).

Once again, we see the power of the social group in shaping our ideas (see ● Figure 13.11). Emerging interactions between new social media and credibility are likely to continue changing the landscape of persuasion. ⚙

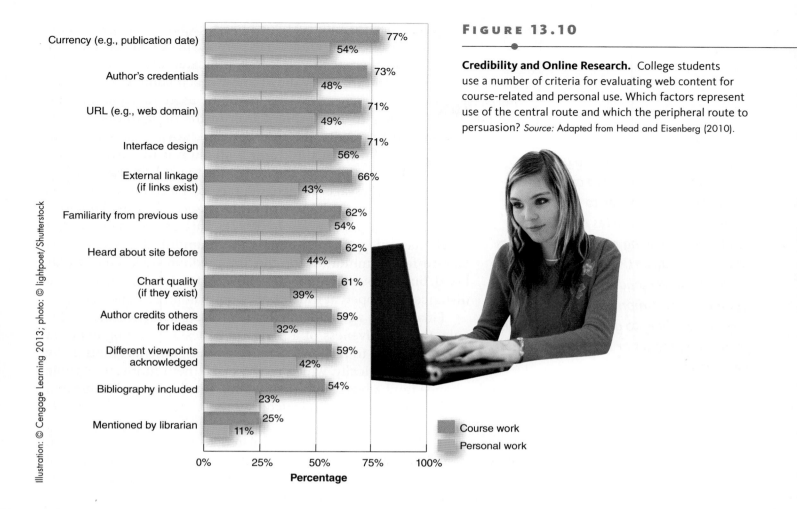

Criteria	Course work	Personal work
Currency (e.g., publication date)	77%	54%
Author's credentials	73%	48%
URL (e.g., web domain)	71%	49%
Interface design	71%	56%
External linkage (if links exist)	66%	43%
Familiarity from previous use	62%	54%
Heard about site before	62%	44%
Chart quality (if they exist)	61%	39%
Author credits others for ideas	59%	32%
Different viewpoints acknowledged	59%	42%
Bibliography included	54%	23%
Mentioned by librarian	25%	11%

Percentage (0% 25% 50% 75% 100%)

- ■ Course work
- ■ Personal work

FIGURE 13.10

Credibility and Online Research. College students use a number of criteria for evaluating web content for course-related and personal use. Which factors represent use of the central route and which the peripheral route to persuasion? *Source:* Adapted from Head and Eisenberg (2010).

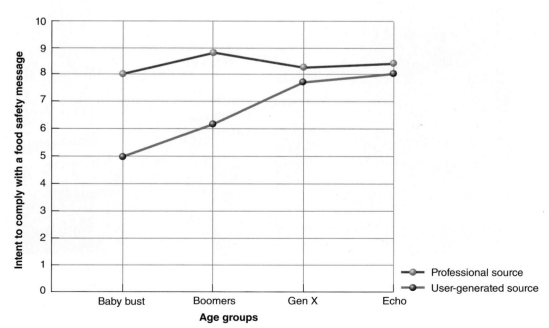

Age groups: Baby bust, Boomers, Gen X, Echo

Intent to comply with a food safety message (y-axis: 0–10)

- ● Professional source
- ● User-generated source

FIGURE 13.11

Responses to User-Generated Messages by Age Group. Social media, with their ability to make users into spokespersons, raise new issues for our understanding of speaker credibility in persuasion. Different age groups have embraced user-generated content, such as blogs, tweets, and articles shared on Facebook, to different degrees. Younger age groups are as likely to say they would comply with a food recall message posted on their Facebook wall by a friend (user-generated message) as they are to an official notice from the Centers for Disease Control and Prevention (professional message), but older age groups are less likely to say they would comply with the user-generated messages. *Source:* Adapted from Freberg (2011).

WHY DOES PERSUASION HAPPEN?

speaker's perceived expertise and trustworthiness. Expertise is often established by a person's history and credentials. We suspect your psychology professors would look different to you if they indicated that their degrees were in other subjects and that they didn't know much about psychology.

Persuasion is also influenced by the medium used to communicate a message, from the face-to-face presentation of the door-to-door salesperson to print media, the Internet, and movies and television. Typically, we find that the closer a medium is to a live interaction with another person, the more effective it is in transmitting a persuasive message. In general, face-to-face contact remains more effective than the use of other media (Bavelas, Hutchinson, Kenwood, & Matheson, 1997). This arrangement is the most "natural" way for humans to communicate. Not only is face-to-face communication the first medium we learn in childhood, but various technologies allowing for communication at a distance developed at much later points in human history.

Finally, the age and intelligence of an audience can influence the effectiveness of a persuasive message. Young children are more likely to respond to persuasive arguments emotionally rather than logically, which might make them more susceptible to attitude change (and advertising) than adults. Intelligent, well-educated audiences are more difficult to persuade in most situations (Rhodes & Wood, 1992).

Once again, the influences of cues related to the message, speaker, medium, or audience are greatest when people are using the peripheral route to persuasion. When people are using the central route, their focus will remain on the quality of the arguments being presented.

The less a speaker stands to gain by persuading you, the more credibility the speaker will appear to have. We understand that athletes and other celebrities are being paid large amounts of money to advertise particular products, so we tend to discount their opinions. A testimonial by someone who has nothing to gain by speaking in favor of a product or issue is much more persuasive.

Children are more likely than adults to respond to persuasive messages emotionally rather than logically, making them much more susceptible to persuasion. Threatened with lawsuits from public interest groups, several major U.S. food companies agreed to reduce their marketing to children and to make products that appeal to children more healthy.

Why Do We Go Along With the Group?

When acceptance by a group is important to us, we are motivated to behave in ways that increase the likelihood of gaining the group's approval and avoiding rejection. Groups typically have rules for behavior, known as **social norms**. Social norms can be explicit, or conscious, like wearing shoes into a restaurant; they can also be implicit, or unconscious, like moving to the back of an elevator and turning to face the doors.

We often conform to social norms without being asked to do so. In contrast, compliance and obedience lead us to fulfill a request from another person. In compliance, the person making the request has no authority over us, but in obedience, the request is coming from an authority figure.

Conformity

Matching your behavior and appearance to the perceived social norms of a group constitutes **conformity**.

In a classic study of conformity by Solomon Asch (1951), participants were asked to match a reference line to one of three comparison lines. As you can see in ● Figure 13.12, the lines are sufficiently different that solving this task was not exactly rocket science. In the conformity condition, one real participant was placed among a group of confederates ("fake" participants who are employed by the investigator). Before the real participant gave his answer, the confederates provided some wrong answers. Would the real participant tell the truth or conform to the answer given by the confederates? In about one third of the trials, the participants conformed by deliberately choosing a response they knew was wrong. About three quarters of the participants conformed on at least one trial.

Conformity to expectations associated with roles was investigated in the Stanford Prison Study (Haney, Banks, & Zimbardo, 1973). In a very

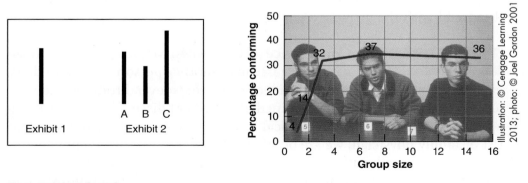

FIGURE 13.12

Conformity. When a lone participant was asked to match the "Exhibit 1" line to Line A, B, or C, the person obviously chose the correct line, A. However, when placed in a group of confederates told to pick another line, participants became more likely to "go along." Conformity reached its peak in groups of three to four people and did not increase as the group became larger. *Source: Adapted from Asch (1951).*

social norms Usually unwritten or unspoken rules for behavior in social settings.

conformity Matching behavior and appearance to perceived social norms.

In 2001, Stephen Reicher and Alexander Haslam re-created aspects of the classic Stanford Prison Study, which was conducted by Philip Zimbardo and his colleagues in the 1970s. Zimbardo argued that the roles of guard or prisoner overwhelmed individuality, but Reicher and Haslam believe that the participants were simply responding to Zimbardo's instructions. Scientists do not always agree with each other, and their debates bring us closer to realistic representations of our world.

short time, young men who had been randomly assigned to prisoner or guard roles quickly adopted behaviors consistent with those roles, leading to such inappropriate behavior that the study was stopped after only 6 days instead of the planned 14 days. More recently, a similar prison experiment was conducted for BBC television with somewhat different results. The British prison experiment differed from the Stanford Prison Study in the amount of direction provided to the participants from the investigators, and much less conformity to roles of guard and prisoner was observed.

Why do people conform? Conformity can be useful in ambiguous situations. If you are uncertain about what to do, such as how to dress at work, observing the behavior of others and conforming to it can be very helpful. In a computer simulation comparing the effectiveness of social learning strategies, which includes imitation of others, to nonsocial learning strategies, such as trial-and-error, the social strategies proved far more successful (Rendell et al., 2010). The availability of others to copy might contribute to the overall success of group over independent living.

Conformity also reduces the risk of rejection by a social group, a situation that would have greatly threatened the survival of our human ancestors. In a study demonstrating the rejection of nonconformists, participants were asked to debate the fate of an imaginary juvenile delinquent named Johnny Rocco (Schachter, 1951). Three members of the group were confederates. One was instructed to agree with the group consistently, another to disagree with the group consistently, and the third to switch positions from disagreeing to agreeing with the group. When the real participants rated how well they liked other members of the group, members who agreed with the majority were all well liked, and the confederate who changed position was liked best of all. The participants were unanimous in their intense dislike of the confederate who disagreed with the group.

Compliance

Compliance occurs when we simply agree to do something because another person asks us to do it, even if that person has no authority over us whatsoever. From messages on junk mail that tell us to "Open immediately. Do not discard" and advertising appeals to "Buy now" to the medical instructions we receive from our dentist or family physician, we are bombarded with requests for compliance.

Complying with authority figures such as teachers or police officers can provide considerable advantages to society. It is more difficult, however, to explain why people would develop the tendency to comply with requests made by strangers who have no authority. It appears that our natural tendency to affiliate leads us to behave in ways that encourage the development of relationships, including being compliant.

Compliance is higher when factors that normally lead to the formation of relationships are present, such as perceived similarity and physical

compliance Agreement with a request from a person with no perceived authority.

attraction. For example, we are more likely to comply with requests presented by physically attractive people (Lynn & Simons, 2000; McCall, 1997). This behavior provides yet another example of the "beauty is good" stereotype that influences persuasion in general. People are more likely to comply with a request from a person who shares some similarity, even when the similarity represents irrelevant dimensions, such as a shared birthday (Burger, Messian, Patel, del Prado, & Anderson, 2004).

Many seemingly simple yet sophisticated sales techniques exploit our natural tendencies to comply in response to perceiving a social tie with another person (Cialdini & Goldstein, 2004). Once a sense of relationship is established, powerful norms of reciprocation are brought into play. Reciprocation, in which we feel obligated to give something back to people who have given something to us, is one of the most powerful tools of social influence (Gouldner, 1960). The importance of reciprocation to the cohesion of early human groups can probably not be overestimated. If somebody shared food with you, and you reciprocated by sharing yours, a powerful bond would be formed.

Reciprocation has been used to explain compliance in the **door-in-the-face** scenario, in which a large, unreasonable demand is followed by a smaller request, which is really the one the requester expects to work (Cialdini et al., 1975). For example, you might be asked to donate a very large amount to an organization, followed by a request to "give what you can afford." By lowering the initial demand, the salesperson has made a concession. The rules of reciprocation now suggest that you have an obligation to that person and should respond to this concession with one of your own—you send a donation (see ● Figure 13.13).

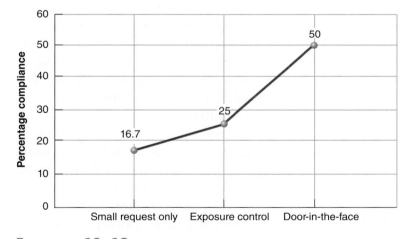

© Cengage Learning 2013

FIGURE 13.13

Door-in-the-Face. In a study by Cialdini et al. (1975), participants in the door-in-the-face condition were first asked to volunteer for 2 hours per week for 2 years as a "big brother/big sister" at a local juvenile detention center. None agreed. Subsequently, they were asked to spend 2 hours chaperoning a group of delinquents to a local zoo, and half agreed. In comparison, only 16.7% of the participants hearing only the zoo request agreed, and 25% of people asked if they would choose one of the two activities agreed to the zoo request. It is possible that feeling guilty for turning down the first request makes people more likely to agree to a second, smaller request. *Source:* Adapted from Cialdini et al. (1975).

door-in-the-face A persuasive technique in which compliance with a target request is preceded by a large, unreasonable request.

According to the foot-in-the-door technique, agreeing with a small request, such as clicking the "Like" button on Facebook, makes it more likely that you will agree with larger requests, like buying products from a company.

In addition to reciprocity, the need to appear consistent may also drive considerable compliance. The **foot-in-the-door** technique, in which a small request is followed up by a larger request, is especially effective in gaining compliance. "Liking" an organization on Facebook (a small request) can lead to more purchases and brand loyalty (larger requests). Another technique based on the need to appear consistent is the low-balling strategy, in which an initially favorable deal is revised upward once the buyer appears committed (Cialdini, Cacioppo, Bassett, & Miller, 1978). Once you have made a commitment to buy a car, the salesperson leaves to "check" the deal with a supervisor. Invariably, he or she returns with just a few more charges to make the deal "work." The salesperson is counting on you to agree to the higher price, because you have already made a public commitment to buy the car. If you stand up at this point and prepare to leave, it is likely those extra charges will quickly disappear.

Obedience

Obedience is defined as compliance with the request of an authority figure. When you take an exam from a professor or show your driver's license to a police officer, you are being obedient.

In a series of classic experiments, Stanley Milgram demonstrated that when personal ethics come into conflict with demands from an authority, the authority usually wins (Milgram, 1974). Milgram's participants entered his laboratory at Yale University believing that they were to take part in a study of the effects of punishment on learning. The other "participant" present was in fact a confederate, and the situation was rigged so that the real participant would take the role of "teacher" while the confederate took the role of "learner." The punishment for failing to learn pairs of words was an electric shock, to be administered by the teacher to the learner using an intimidating piece of equipment. The learner/confederate actually received no shocks at all, and his verbal responses to shocks were prerecorded.

In most cases, Milgram's experiment began uneventfully. The first challenge to the teacher occurred, however, at 75 volts, at which time the learner's first recorded protest could be heard. When faced with this situation, many of Milgram's participants looked to the experimenter in the room for guidance. The experimenter assured the participant that "the experiment must continue" and "you have no choice." Although most participants showed signs of stress and verbally stated their concerns about the procedure, all of Milgram's original 40 participants went as far as 300 volts, and 26 out of the 40 (65%) fully complied by administering the maximum shocks (450 volts). Milgram followed up his original scenario by modifying variables that might have influenced the large number of people willing to comply. No differences in outcome were observed when the experiment was conducted in an off-campus office or with participants of different ages and occupations.

Among the variables that did seem to influence Milgram's results was proximity, both between the teacher and learner and between the teacher

foot-in-the-door A persuasive technique in which compliance with a small request is followed by compliance with a larger request that might otherwise have been rejected.

obedience Compliance with a request from an authority figure.

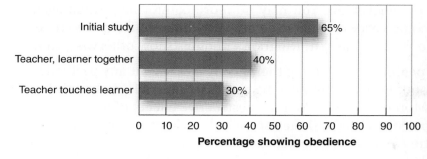

From the film Obedience © 1968 by Stanley Milgram, © renewed 1993 by Alexandra Milgram, and distributed by Penn State Media Sales. Permission granted by Alexandra Milgram.

FIGURE 13.14

Circumstances Affecting Obedience. After his initial study, in which the teacher could hear but not see the learner, Milgram varied the experimental circumstances to see what variables influenced the amount of obedience his participants displayed. The "teacher, learner together" condition took place with both people in the same room. In the "teacher touches learner" condition, the teacher had to hold the learner's hand down on a shock device. As the teacher and learner came into more contact, obedience dropped, but remained surprisingly high overall.

and the experimenter. The proximity between teacher and learner ranged from complete separation, in which the two people could neither see nor hear one another, to very close, in which the teacher was instructed to physically hold the learner's hand on a shock grid. As proximity between teacher and learner increased, rates of obedience dropped to about 30% (see ● Figure 13.14). The implications of this result for modern war technologies are clear. People are more likely to press a button that harms a person they can neither see nor hear than they are to harm a person whose pain is apparent. The proximity of the teacher and experimenter was also quite influential. The experimenter communicated with the teacher while in the room, by telephone, or by tape recording. Obedience dropped dramatically as interaction with the experimenter, who represented authority, became more remote.

Obedience varies across cultures, but none is immune. Milgram's data suggest that about 65% of the American general population, with equal numbers of men and women, would fully comply in his basic experiment (Milgram, 1963). The highest rates of obedience are found in the general publics of the Netherlands (92%; Meeus & Raaijmakers, 1995), Austria (80%; Schurz, 1985), and Germany (85%; Mantell, 1971). Australia reports some of the lowest levels of obedience, along with one of the few notable gender differences reported in the obedience literature. Forty percent of Australian male students were obedient, and only 16% of Australian female students were obedient (Kilham & Mann, 1974).

Milgram's original goal was to illuminate some of the most troubling behavior of modern times, the killing of millions of innocent people in the Holocaust, so it is no surprise that his results are among the most disturbing in modern psychology. Milgram clearly demonstrated the power of authority to gain compliance. But did he meet his goal of modeling Nazi obedience? He believed so. You may be more comfortable thinking that people who could carry out genocide are very different from the students sitting next to you in class. But Milgram's findings show otherwise, that

> ordinary people, simply doing their jobs, and without any particular hostility on their part, can become agents in a terrible destructive process. Moreover, even when the destructive effects of their work become patently clear, and they are asked to carry out actions incompatible with fundamental standards of morality, relatively few people have the resources needed to resist authority. (Milgram, 1974, p. 6)

You might be thinking optimistically that people today are different from Milgram's participants in the 1960s. Between the 1920s and 1980s, parents in the United States shifted their preferences for their children's outcomes from obedience to autonomy (Alwin, 1988). We can begin to evaluate the impact of this parenting change, because Milgram's experiment has been partially replicated fairly recently (Burger, 2009). By "partially replicated," we mean that Burger made procedural changes for the purposes of meeting ethical requirements, such as informing participants that they could leave if they felt uncomfortable. In spite of these changes, Burger's results were similar to Milgram's (82.5% of Milgram's participants obeyed under the same circumstances in which 66.7% of Burger's male participants obeyed).

> Whenever you find yourself on the side of the majority, it is time to pause and reflect.
>
> —Mark Twain

No society can exist without any obedience at all. If everyone drove a car according to his or her own ideas, chaos, not to mention a large number of accidents, would no doubt result. As much as we value truth and independence, we also value our relationships with others. In cases where these values conflict, many people apparently give their social relationships the top priority. Risking rejection just to be "right" might directly oppose your need to remain affiliated with a group (Moscovici, 1976).

However, history is full of instances where blindly following orders leads people into highly unethical behavior. Even on a daily basis, obedience to authority can overwhelm individual judgment. In one chilling obedience experiment, 22 nurses were telephoned by a doctor they didn't know and instructed to administer a drug not listed on a patient's chart in double its normal dose (Hofling, Brotzman, Dalrymple, Graves, & Pierce, 1966). Astonishingly, 21 of the 22 nurses indicated they would be willing to comply. One could argue that it is desirable for nurses to carry out the directions of physicians, but at what point do we want people to question authority?

The Power of One

Our discussion of conformity, compliance, and obedience would be incomplete without considering the circumstances in which an individual or small group can influence a larger group. Asch provided a clue to the necessary conditions when he noted that conformity was greatest when a person faced a unanimous group. A single individual's willingness to take an opposing view may encourage others to also resist the pressure to conform to a misguided action, or at least to reconsider their original position.

To successfully influence the majority, a minority voice must display consistency and confidence. In a study designed to determine the factors that enabled a minority to influence a majority, people occasionally agreed with an individual who consistently stated that blue slides were green, but never agreed with an individual who judged blue to be green only part of the time (Moscovici, Lage, & Naffrechoux, 1969). Individual voices that are raised confidently, as in the case of Gandhi or Martin Luther King Jr., are more likely to influence the majority than are more tentative efforts.

The anonymous Tank Man of the 1989 Tiananmen Square protests in Beijing, China, created a minutes-long standoff by maintaining his position in front of a column of tanks. Single individuals disagreeing with a majority with confidence and consistency can stimulate others to reconsider their positions. We do not know the fate of Tank Man today.

How Do Groups Work Together?

We have explored many instances in which situations seem to have a large impact on people's behavior. Given the sociability of our species, it should not be surprising to learn that one of the most powerful situational influences on our behavior is the presence of other people. How is our behavior different when we are with others compared to when we are alone?

Social Facilitation

Social facilitation occurs when the presence of other people changes individual performance. In 1898, Norman Triplett reported that cyclists riding in pairs rode faster than cyclists riding alone (Triplett, 1898). Social facilitation is not limited to cycling. Children spinning fishing reels did so faster when in groups than when they were alone.

We have all seen skilled performers "choke" in front of an important audience. Why does performance improve in front of audiences in some situations and become worse in others? Psychologists noticed that well-practiced skills, like riding a bicycle, improved with an audience, but when people were still learning a new skill, they performed badly (Zajonc, 1965; Zajonc & Sales, 1966). When we're performing a well-practiced skill, most

For a dominant pattern of behavior, such as the well-practiced routines of these professional dancers, social facilitation due to the presence of others should increase performance.

social facilitation The presence of other people changes performance.

of what we do is correct, but when we are learning something new, most of the things we do are actually wrong. The presence of the audience appears to enhance whichever patterns of behavior are currently dominant—the right moves in a well-practiced skill and the wrong moves in a new skill. The moral of this story is to make sure you practice thoroughly before you perform in front of an audience.

If you're bothered by social loafing in your group projects, it can be reduced by reestablishing individual accountability, such as allowing group members to grade each other on their contributions (Aggarwal & O'Brien, 2008). In contrast, providing a single group grade without acknowledgment of individual contributions is almost guaranteed to produce some level of social loafing.

The complexity of a task can also interact with the presence of an audience to produce either improved or impaired performance (Bond & Titus, 1983). This result implies that one of the functions of the audience is to increase the performer's level of arousal. The Yerkes-Dodson Law, discussed previously in our chapter on motivation and emotion, states that performance on simple tasks improves steadily with arousal, but performance on complex tasks first improves and then becomes impaired as arousal continues to grow (Yerkes & Dodson, 1908). Improvements in performance are more likely to occur when people are engaged in simple, well-practiced activities, such as riding a bicycle, as opposed to highly complex, novel activities, such as memorizing a difficult list of words.

Although each of these children seems to be working very hard, social loafing predicts that for each child added to a side, the effort by each individual child will be reduced.

Social Loafing

While working on group projects, you have probably had opportunities to observe **social loafing**, or the reduced motivation and effort shown by individuals working in a group as opposed to working alone. When engaged in a tug-of-war game at a picnic, members of a team will exert less individual effort with each additional person added to their side (Kravitz & Martin, 1986). Individuals will cheer less loudly in a large group than they will in a smaller group (Latané, Williams, & Harkins, 1979).

Individual, gender, cultural, and task variables interact to produce social loafing. Women are somewhat less likely to demonstrate social loafing than men, and participants from Eastern cultures are less likely to loaf than those from the West (Karau & Williams, 1993). Simple physical tasks, such as screwing and unscrewing nuts and bolts, reliably produce social loafing in most people (Petty, Cacioppo, & Kasmer, 1988). Task complexity interacts with need for cognition, or the motivation to engage in and enjoy effortful cognitive endeavors (Cacioppo, Petty, & Kao, 1984). People with a low need for cognition show social loafing during both a physical task and a brainstorming task, in which they are asked to generate a list of possible uses for an object (Cacioppo, Petty, Feinstein, & Jarvis, 1996). In contrast, individuals who demonstrate a high need for cognition take pleasure in difficult mental tasks, and although they show social loafing on the simple physical task, they do not socially loaf during the more intellectually demanding brainstorming task. Individuals appear to be less likely to take the opportunity to socially loaf on tasks that are intrinsically enjoyable to perform.

social loafing Reduced motivation and effort shown by individuals working in a group.

© Ladi Kirn/Alamy

Deindividuation

Deindividuation refers to the immersion of the individual within a group, which makes the individual relatively anonymous. Deindividuation can lead normally law-abiding people to commit uncharacteristic atrocities, including riots and lynchings.

Why would people go along with the negative behavior of a surrounding group, especially if they are unlikely to behave this way on their own? One possibility is that anonymous people feel less accountable for their actions. In an experiment using a paradigm similar to Milgram's obedience experiments described earlier, participants dressed in hoods and oversized lab coats administered longer shocks than control participants who were dressed in normal clothing with name tags (Zimbardo, 1969). Other psychologists suggest that you do not necessarily "lose yourself" in a group, but that your attention shifts from a personal identity to the identity of the surrounding group (Lea & Spears, 1991). If that surrounding group begins to act in antisocial ways, the personal controls normally present within yourself might not be enough to resist going along.

Deindividuation, or the loss of personal identity within a crowd, can lead people to do things that they would not do on their own.

Group Polarization

Common sense suggests that discussion with others who express different opinions should produce more moderate attitudes for everyone in the group. Surprisingly, this is not always the case. In **group polarization**, a period of discussion actually pushes group members to take more extreme positions in the direction they were already inclined (Moscovici & Zavalloni, 1969). Group polarization does not reverse the direction of attitudes but, rather, accentuates the attitudes held at the outset (see ● Figure 13.15). If group members began mildly favorable on gun control, their attitudes will be more favorable after discussion, whereas if group members began mildly unfavorable on gun control, their attitudes will be more unfavorable after discussion.

Two pressures appear to push individuals to take more extreme positions following a group discussion. First, conformity and the desire for affiliation contribute to group polarization. If the majority of a group is leaning in a particular direction, what could be a better way of "fitting in" than agreeing with that majority, and maybe even taking their argument one step farther? There is also a tendency for like-minded people to affiliate with each other, which can provide reinforcement for existing opinions, increase people's confidence in those opinions, lead to the discovery of new reasons for those opinions and counterarguments to opposing views, and reduce exposure to conflicting ideas. Second, exposure to discussion on a topic introduces new reasons for holding an attitude. If you are already opposed to gun control, and you listen to additional arguments supporting your position, you might end up much more opposed than you were originally.

Group polarization is frequently studied in the context of the behaviors of juries. Following deliberations, final sentencing decisions by mock juries are typically more severe or more lenient than the original opinions expressed by individual group members (Bray & Noble, 1978). Group

If you participate in online discussions, you might notice a difference in the way people relate on platforms such as Facebook compared to "anonymous" platforms such as some message boards and chat rooms. Deindividuation would predict that anonymous message boards would feature less inhibition, such as less civil discussion, than would platforms where individual identity is obvious.

deindividuation Immersion of an individual within a group, leading to anonymity.

group polarization The intensifying of an attitude following discussion.

FIGURE 13.15

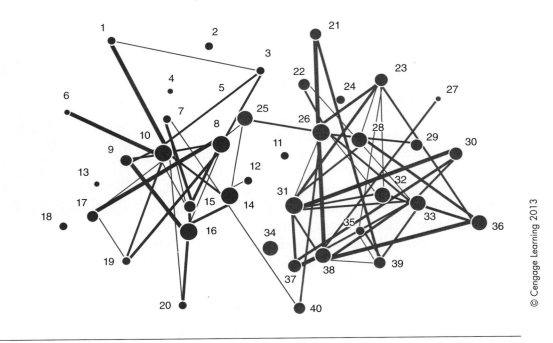

Group Polarization in the Blogosphere. Forty leading blogs, 20 conservative (red) and 20 liberal (blue), were analyzed for mutual citations to each other's posts. As this diagram indicates, there are relatively few conversations between the groups. Group polarization would suggest that these conversations might result in even more extreme opinions for both groups.
Source: Adapted from Adamic and Glance (2005).

© Cengage Learning 2013

© Richard Koci Hernandez KRT/Newscom

Smart, experienced groups of people can make some not-so-smart decisions due to groupthink. In 2001, Yahoo! had the opportunity to buy a company called Google, started by Stanford graduates Sergey Brin (left) and Larry Page (right). The Yahoo! executives hesitated, and the opportunity passed.

groupthink A type of flawed decision making in which a group does not question its decisions critically.

polarization appears to be even more powerful in online discussions, where people are exposed to many more arguments on issues than they might generate on their own (Sia, Tan, & Wei, 2002).

Groupthink

As we discovered in our discussion of conformity, the presence of others can influence the process of decision making. In Solomon Asch's experiments, individuals appeared to make a choice in favor of group harmony over accuracy. If group members suppress dissenting opinions in the interests of group cohesion, the group may fall into a state of **groupthink**.

This type of flawed decision making might account for a number of unfortunate group decisions throughout history (Janis, 1971). The individuals comprising the groups that decided to launch the *Challenger* space shuttle over the objections voiced by engineers, leading to its explosion shortly after takeoff, were not stupid or inexperienced. Instead, their decision making process could have led them in the wrong direction. More recently, psychologists have identified groupthink as a possible precursor to decisions by the United States and Great Britain to launch a preemptive strike in Iraq, based on their conviction at the time that Saddam Hussein had weapons of mass destruction (Houghton, 2008).

Groupthink is especially likely in cohesive groups with high morale whose members already share similar attitudes (Baron, 2005). Members of cohesive groups are less likely to consider risks or alternatives associated with their chosen plan of action. In many cases, the group is far from unanimous, but individuals are unwilling to step forward in dissent, just as many of Asch's participants preferred to go along rather than rock the boat. This illusion of a unanimous group further stifles serious consideration of alternatives prior to making a decision.

Summary 13.2

Group Processes

Group process	Definition	Example
Social facilitation © Tristram Kenton/Lebrecht Music & Arts	Individual performance is influenced by the presence of others.	A jogger runs faster with a buddy than when running alone.
Social loafing © Ladi Kirn/ Alamy	Working in a group decreases individual effort.	A student puts less effort into a group project than into an individual term paper.
Deindividuation © REUTERS/ Darren Staples	Behavior differs when in a group from when alone and identifiable.	A normally law-abiding citizen loots a store during a riot.
Group polarization © Cengage Learning 2013	Attitudes become more intense following discussion.	After a late-night debate with like-minded friends, a student holds more extreme views about an issue than before.
Groupthink © Richard Koci Hernandez KRT/ Newscom	Flawed group decision making that fails to consider dissenting views.	A group of friends decide to engage in a risky behavior that seems very dumb in hindsight.

How Well Do We Get Along With Others?

If you think about the people with whom you interact regularly, from friends and family to roommates to classmates to coworkers to professors, it is obvious that our relationships with others are not all the same. Learning to get along well with different people, or gaining so-called social skills, is one of the most important tasks we face, and one that can influence important outcomes throughout life. Psychologists have discovered a number of underlying themes that affect this important part of life.

Part of our heritage as a social species involves the need to not only affiliate with a group but also form important social relationships with individual people. These relationships can be between family members, peers, coworkers, neighbors, or romantic partners.

Attraction and Liking

Attraction refers to our attitudes about other people and can vary along a continuum from strong liking to strong dislike. Attraction varies in quality as well as strength, which in turn helps to determine the type of relationship we form with another person. We are attracted to our romantic partners in stronger and more physical ways than we are attracted to our friends and acquaintances. We certainly know what attraction to another person feels like, but it is more difficult to identify the variables that predict our attraction to a particular person.

Before you can be attracted to a person, you need to have some contact with that person. Contact becomes more likely when people work, live, or spend leisure time in proximity to, or near, one another. In an early exploration of this concept, 5,000 marriage licenses in which one or both partners lived in Philadelphia were examined (Bossard, 1932). In about one third of the marriages, the partners had lived five blocks or less from one another prior to marrying. As distance between homes increased, the number of couples decreased. In the contemporary era of online dating, proximity obviously can take forms other than physical closeness.

Musicians recognize the advantages of the mere exposure effect. Hearing a song frequently will make it more likeable. Placement of a song in a television show or movie is virtually guaranteed to boost sales of the artist's work.

Proximity is important to relationships because simple contact can increase liking. In contrast to the proverb that states "familiarity breeds contempt," regular exposure to neutral or positive stimuli generally leads to increased liking, a principle known as the **mere exposure effect** (see ● Figure 13.16). In one example of this effect, participants who viewed nonsense words described as "Turkish" words and Chinese-like symbols reported liking them better than those they had not viewed before (Zajonc, 1968). The mere exposure effect applies to people, too (Swap, 1977). From an evolutionary point of view, the mere exposure effect might have led people to avoid unfamiliar, and possibly dangerous, stimuli (Young & Claypool, 2010). Unfortunately, having an inclination to make more negative responses to unfamiliar people might also contribute to prejudice.

To what extent do similarities and differences influence our friendships and romantic relationships? In one experiment, college students read the results of an attitude survey supposedly filled out by another student (Byrne, 1961). As the attitudes expressed became closer to the students' own attitudes, the students reported that the anonymous person was better liked, more intelligent, and better informed about current events. Apparently, assuming we like ourselves, we find it easy to like people with whom we are similar. People tend to choose friends and romantic partners who are similar in race, ethnicity, religion, values, education, and age (Buss, 1985; Kandel, 1978). However, the number of interracial couples in the United States has grown dramatically since 1960 (Joyner & Kao, 2005; Lee, 2010).

Although people may be initially attracted to those with whom they share similar characteristics, being attracted to another person also increases similarity, a process known as attitude alignment. Attitudes of

mere exposure effect Repeated exposure increases liking.

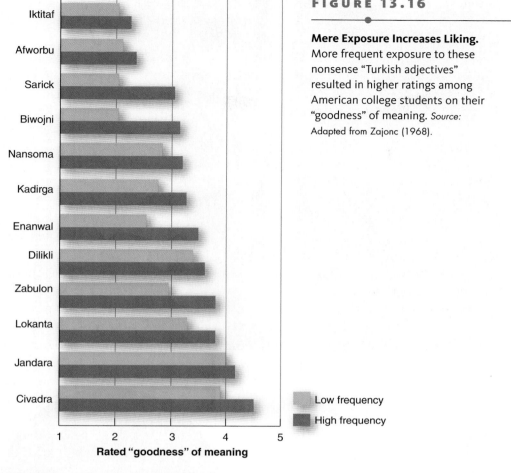

FIGURE 13.16

Mere Exposure Increases Liking. More frequent exposure to these nonsense "Turkish adjectives" resulted in higher ratings among American college students on their "goodness" of meaning. *Source:* Adapted from Zajonc (1968).

dating partners grow closer together in a gradual process (Davis & Rusbult, 2001). At the same time, partners in stable relationships often overestimate the similarity of their attitudes (Murray, Holmes, Gellavia, Griffin, & Dolderman, 2002).

Physical appearance is a dominant factor in romantic attraction. After completing questionnaires assessing personality and academic achievement, participants were randomly paired for a "Computer Dance." Male participants were subsequently asked if they would ask their partner for a second date. The only significant variable out of all the personality and other data collected that predicted the likelihood of a second date was the woman's physical attractiveness (Walster, Aronson, & Abrahams, 1966).

Cultures frequently have their own definitions of physical beauty, but we appear to have some underlying, biological preferences. Beauty serves as a marker for health and fertility. By choosing a beautiful mate, you may be enhancing your abilities to produce healthy children with a strong chance of survival. Preferences for faces rated as beautiful by adults can be demonstrated in infants as young as 3 months of age (Langlois, Roggman, & Rieser-Danner, 1990). Subjective judgments of beauty are heavily influenced by symmetry, or the degree of similarity between one half of the body or face and the other. Symmetrical bodies are more likely to be healthy bodies, and so are highly sought out in prospective mates

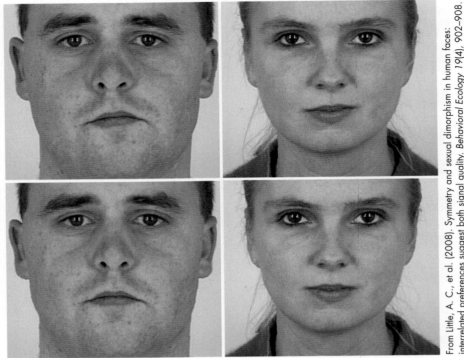

People show strong preferences for symmetrical faces (bottom row) compared to the less symmetrical versions of the same faces (top row). Symmetry may serve as an outward sign of genetic health (Little et al., 2008).

From Little, A. C., et al. (2008). Symmetry and sexual dimorphism in human faces: interrelated preferences suggest both signal quality. *Behavioral Ecology* 19(4), 902–908. Copyright © 2008 Oxford University Press.

Thinking Scientifically

Is Physical Attractiveness More Important to Men Than to Women?

Some of the research about attraction that we have discussed might leave you with the idea that men care more about physical attractiveness in their partners than women do. Many studies in which you *ask* men and women what they desire in a partner show this difference (Buss, 1989; Walster et al., 1966). However, psychologists began to notice that sex differences in the priority assigned to physical attractiveness did not occur when researchers asked participants to evaluate live human beings as poten-

tial partners instead of just asking them what they valued most in a partner (Eastwick & Finkel, 2008). Also, if we have a general "beauty is good" bias and physical attractiveness is positively correlated with health, why would there be a gender difference in the importance of appearance in a partner (see ● Figure 13.17)?

Insight into this question emerged from a study that directly compared explicit, or conscious, judgments with implicit, or unconscious, judgments of the importance

of physical attractiveness (Eastwick, Eagly, Finkel, & Johnson, 2011). These researchers compared the results of an explicit questionnaire (what is important to you in a partner) with results of an implicit procedure, which used reaction time to compare a participant's categorization of items, such as "I like" and "sexy, gorgeous, attractive." Consistent with previous research, men expressed more interest in physical attractiveness than women did using the explicit instrument, but there were no gender differences in the impor-

(Thornhill & Gangestad, 1994). As further evidence of the importance of symmetry in mate choice, symmetry of faces was more important in opposite-sex judgments of attractiveness than in same-sex judgments of attractiveness (Little, Jones, DeBruine, & Feinberg, 2008).

Across many cultures, men prefer female figures in which the circumference of the waist is about 70% of the circumference of the hips, or the so-called 0.7 waist-to-hip ratio, which also predicts high fertility (Singh, 1993; Singh, Dixson, Jessop, Morgan, & Dixson, 2010).The argument for a "magic" waist-to-hip ratio has been challenged by researchers who argue that instead, men base their preferences for female figures on body mass index (BMI), a commonly used ratio of height and weight discussed in our chapter on motivation. Worldwide, men consistently preferred female figures representing a BMI of 20 (the equivalent of a 5'4" woman who weighs about 117 pounds) over thinner or heavier shapes (Tovée, Reinhardt, Emery, & Cornelissen, 1998).

Most romantic couples share a common level of physical attractiveness, a concept known as the matching hypothesis. Couples who were most similar in terms of physical attractiveness were more likely to be together nine months later (White, 1980). However, when longer-lasting relationships are examined, female partners tend to be rated as slightly more attractive than their male partners (McNulty, Neff, & Karney, 2008).

Most long-term couples share an approximately equal level of attractiveness and may even look alike, as do Sting and Trudie Styler.

Although Playboy *centerfolds and Miss America winners became up to 16 pounds thinner between 1940 and 1990, they maintained the same 0.7 waist-to-hip ratio (Singh, 1993). Such diverse figures as the more voluptuous ancient Greek statue of Venus de Milo or actress Marilyn Monroe as well as the skinnier, more waiflike models Twiggy and Kate Moss show the 0.7 ratio, despite the obvious differences in weight among these women.*

© Valerie Macon/Getty Images

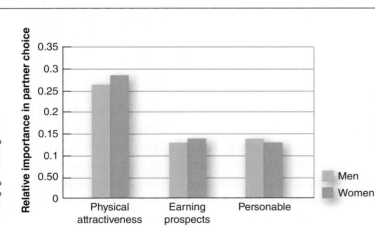

© Cengage Learning 2013

FIGURE 13.17

Men and Women Make Similar Evaluations of Potential Partners. In contrast to studies that ask men and women what they look for in a partner, when faced with real choices in person, men and women do not differ in the emphasis they place on physical attractiveness, earning prospects, and how "personable" a potential partner is. *Source:* Eastwick and Finkel (2008).

tance of physical attractiveness using implicit measures.

These results make a certain amount of sense. Much of our attraction to others seems to operate at the implicit, unconscious level. In fact, many people have had the experience of finding a partner who seems so "right" according to explicit values (held by the person and often his or her family and friends as well), yet the relationship somehow lacks an undefinable "chemistry." Our further understanding of the role played by these implicit values should help us navigate the important realm of relationships more successfully. ☺

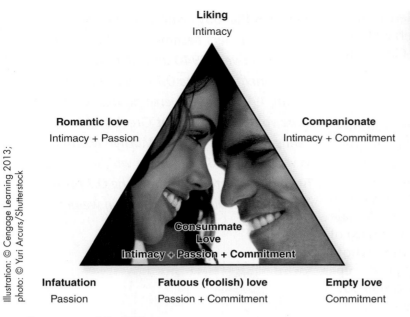

Liking
Intimacy

Romantic love
Intimacy + Passion

Companionate
Intimacy + Commitment

Consummate
Love
Intimacy + Passion + Commitment

Infatuation
Passion

Fatuous (foolish) love
Passion + Commitment

Empty love
Commitment

FIGURE 13.18

Sternberg's Triangular Model of Love. According to Robert Sternberg, close relationships vary along the dimensions of intimacy, passion, and commitment. Consummate love combines all three.

Building Relationships

Self-disclosure, or sharing personal information about yourself, follows a regular progression as people become more intimate with each other (Taylor & Altman, 1987). Acquaintances talk about general topics other than themselves. New friends might discuss their personal abilities and attitudes whereas close friends move on to consider dreams and goals. Intimate friends might share fears and negative past behaviors.

Intimacy is highest when falling in love, but what does love look like under the microscope? Sternberg's triangular model of love distinguishes between the building of different types of relationships along dimensions of intimacy, passion, and commitment (Sternberg, 2004). Intimacy refers to the closeness or bonding we experience with another person, passion includes sexual attraction and romance, and commitment describes the intent to maintain the relationship over time. Intimacy without passion or commitment is characteristic of most friendships. Passion by itself characterizes an infatuation or "love at first sight." Commitment alone could describe the situation in which a person remains loyal to a partner whose health makes intimacy and passion no longer possible, as in the case of dementia (see ● Figure 13.18).

Combinations of intimacy and passion describe romantic love. Without the addition of commitment, this type of love can fade quickly. Intimacy and commitment occur together as companionate love. This love exists without passion in deep friendships, family relationships, and long-term partnerships in which sexuality no longer plays a significant role. A combination of passion and commitment can occur in an impulsive "whirlwind" relationship, in which insufficient time has elapsed for the development of true intimacy. Finally, people who are lucky enough to find all three components in the same relationship experience consummate love.

Maintaining Relationships

What factors keep people together? Some strategies seem particularly important to many types of relationships, including friendships, family relationships, and romantic relationships. People continue to use openness and self-disclosure as relationships mature, along with participation in joint activities, provision of reassurance, and communication (Berscheid, Snyder, & Omoto, 2004; Canary, Stafford, Hause, & Wallace, 1993).

Maintaining a relationship may become easier over time. As couples spend more time together, they build up a shared history, which provides them a stronger basis for understanding each other. Couples who have been together for many years appear to have the ability to communicate a thought or emotion with a single look to each other (Schober & Carstensen, 2010). Long-term relationships can also become boring, however. Aron and colleagues have found that couples who continue to engage in novel and exciting activities also have higher relationship satisfaction (Aron, Norman, Aron, McKenna, & Heyman, 2000).

Ending Relationships

As you are no doubt well aware, real life does not typically follow the scripts of fairy tales, in which the lovers ride off into the sunset to live "happily ever after." Maintaining relationships takes time and effort, and sometimes people are just wrong for one another. A sense of inequity or unfairness in a relationship may cause it to end. Equity in a relationship suggests that the costs, such as curtailed freedom and less time to oneself, are offset by benefits, such as companionship and security. In general, more equitable romantic relationships are stable, enjoyable, and sexually intimate.

Most couples experience their share of ups and downs, but the relative number of their positive and negative experiences is related to the likelihood the relationship will survive or end (Gottman, Swanson, & Swanson, 2002). Couples appear to need about five positive interactions to offset one negative interaction. As the ratio of positive to negative interactions slips toward 1:1, the likelihood that the relationship will end increases. Couples with a lot of apparent conflict might still stay together, as long as their conflict is offset by a larger amount of positive times together.

Infidelity often contributes to the ending of a romantic relationship. Data describing how frequently romantic partners cheat on each other are difficult to obtain and show wide variations, as in the 33 to 75% of men and 26 to 70% of women reported to cheat on their partners in one review of the literature (Buss & Schmitt, 1993). Men and women also appear to respond to different aspects of cheating behavior (see ● Figure 13.19). Males become jealous of sexual infidelity, whereas females are more distressed by emotional infidelity (Buss, Larsen, & Westen, 1992). In other words, a woman would be less distressed if her partner had a one-night stand while drunk than if he had an ongoing relationship with a mistress whom he supported financially. In any case, relationship jealousy can have dangerous implications. Over a quarter of homicides in the United States are estimated to involve jealousy (Goldsmith & Zimmerman, 2001).

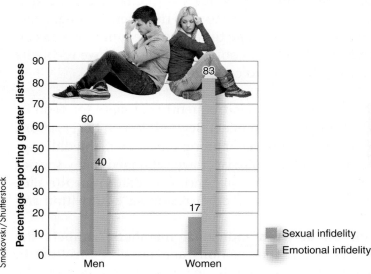

Illustration: © Cengage Learning 2013; photo: © Ljupco Smokovski/Shutterstock

FIGURE 13.19

Gender Differences in Response to Partner Infidelity. When asked which would cause greater distress, your partner cheating on you sexually or becoming deeply emotionally involved with a rival, men reported greater distress from sexual infidelity whereas women reported greater distress from emotional infidelity. *Source:* Adapted from Buss, Larsen, and Westen (1992).

Summary 13.3

Sternberg's Three Types of Love

Type of love	Combines	Excludes
Romantic love	Intimacy + passion	Commitment
Companionate love	Intimacy + commitment.	Passion
Consummate love	Intimacy + commitment + passion	

Illustration: © Cengage Learning 2013; photo: © Yuri Arcurs/Shutterstock

Why Do We Cooperate in Some Situations and Compete in Others?

The advantages of cooperation can be illustrated by a real-life tale of two 1864 shipwrecks in the South Pacific. Members of one crew worked cooperatively with one another as equals, while members of the other maintained their formal command structure. After one year, the first crew managed to build a boat and get rescued, while the second was decimated by cold, hunger, and cannibalism (Druett, 2007).

Our social interactions with each other can feature cooperation, or working together toward common goals, or competition, where we struggle with each other to obtain limited resources.

Both cooperation and competition have a long history in shaping our behavior. In our chapter on the interactions between nature and nurture, we described natural selection as an ongoing race between organisms competing for scarce resources and opportunities to reproduce (Darwin, 1859). The stakes in this race are very high. Individuals with characteristics that give them an advantage over others are able to pass their genes along, while losers fail to reproduce or die. At the same time, because human beings do not live alone, our survival depends on cooperation. How do we reconcile tendencies to compete with the need to cooperate?

Competition and Cooperation in Animals

Individual animals frequently compete for food or opportunities to mate. Beginning with observations of "pecking order" among chickens (Schjedlderup-Ebbe, 1922), biologists have cataloged many species that use competition, usually in the form of fighting, to determine the allocation of mating opportunities, food, and other resources both within and between groups.

Too much competition between individual members hampers the cohesion of a group, breaking it into factions and possibly resulting in injuries among its members. Consequently, many animals minimize the extent of within-group conflict by displaying clear signals of dominance, or high status. The mandrill, a type of baboon, not only uses facial expressions and gestures to signify its position in a dominance hierarchy, but the coloring of the face, rump, and genitalia is also reflective of individual fighting abilities (Setchell & Wickings, 2005).

Do humans have analogous signals of dominance? It appears that the male of the species does (Mazur & Mueller, 1996). Dominant human male faces are handsome and muscular, featuring strong chins, deep-set eyes, and prominent brows. In contrast, "baby-faced" males are rated by observers as being more submissive (McArthur & Berry, 1987). Humans obviously have the advantage of augmenting their natural signals of status by purchasing and displaying expensive automobiles, homes, and jewelry.

Animals minimize the damage caused by competing for dominance by displaying clear signals of submission. The dog on its back is letting the other dog know that its dominance has been recognized.

Individual Differences in Cooperation and Competition

Individuals vary in their predisposition to cooperation or competition. In one experiment, groups of participants were given the opportunity to compete (by keeping tokens) or cooperate (by sharing tokens) while they observed the decisions made by their group members (Kurzban & Houser, 2005). Three different "types" of dispositions emerged: Seventeen percent of the participants were "cooperators," who gave their tokens freely without paying much attention to the behavior of other group members; 20% were "free riders," who didn't give up any of their tokens; and 63% of the participants were "reciprocators," who cooperated only after seeing others do so. Even though the cooperators were in the minority, their behavior is very important to group survival. By contributing selflessly, they encourage the majority of the group to cooperate, too.

The Influence of Culture on Competition and Cooperation

Members of successful groups are more likely to survive and reproduce than members of unsuccessful groups. Because it is in our best interest to belong to effective groups, we cooperate with other group members and are quick to conform to their norms and judgments. Cooperation becomes ingrained in the group's culture and is passed along to new members.

Cooperation is essential to successful group behavior.

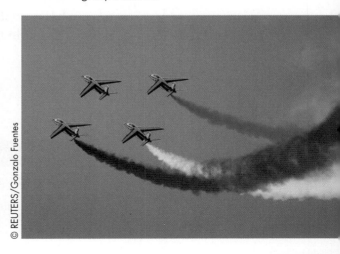

Why is cooperation so essential to successful group behavior? Without cooperation, there would be no basis for gathering diverse areas of individual expertise into a meaningful, useful whole. Under the influence of culture, human beings have progressed from simple divisions of labor to highly specialized areas of expertise. Individuals might spend their entire academic careers exploring the structure of the frog retina or the surface characteristics of one of Saturn's moons. At the same time, no single person working alone would be able to put human beings on the Moon or produce all the special effects expected by contemporary movie audiences. Few fans would pay to see an individual football player demonstrate his skills on an otherwise empty field on Sunday afternoon. Cooperation is the glue that holds productive groups together, from the operating room of a hospital to the baseball stadium.

The importance of group membership to survival is reflected in the remarkable loyalty human beings show to their culturally defined groups. Fans of a particular sports team may be every bit as loyal to their group (and as potentially violent) as our early hunter-gatherer ancestors were to their tribe or clan. Unfortunately, the same loyalty and cultural distinctiveness that bind us to our groups may lead us into conflict with other groups, discussed later in this chapter.

Choosing Between Cooperation and Competition

How do people decide when to compete and when to cooperate?

A classic model of competition and cooperation within groups is known as the prisoner's dilemma (Poundstone, 1992). Assume that you and another person have been arrested for a crime, but the police have limited evidence against you. Without being able to communicate with your partner, you are given the choice to confess (defect from your partner) or to remain silent (cooperate with your partner). If you both remain silent, you will each be sentenced to 1 year. If you both confess, you will each receive 10 years. However, if one confesses and the other remains silent, the prisoner who confesses will be set free, and the silent prisoner will receive a 20-year sentence. The "dilemma" arises from the fact that the best individual strategy is to confess or defect from your partner, but if both of you figure this out and subsequently confess, your outcome is much worse than if you both remained silent (see ● Figure 13.20). In the prisoner's dilemma, cooperation is moderately rewarded (a 1-year sentence) while defection is punished (10 years). If only one of you confesses, however, the confessor is highly rewarded (freedom) while the other person is severely punished (20 years).

For real people, computers, and even animals, the most successful strategy in the prisoner's dilemma situation is the "tit-for-tat (TFT)" (Axelrod & Hamilton, 1981). In TFT, you make cooperation your first move and then repeat your partner's successive moves. The success of the TFT strategy has been attributed to three aspects: It is nice (one begins with cooperation), it is able to retaliate and punish uncooperative behavior (defection by the

FIGURE 13.20

The Prisoner's Dilemma.

Prisoner A	Prisoner B	
	Prisoner B stays silent.	Prisoner B confesses.
Prisoner A stays silent.	A and B both serve 1 year each.	A serves 20 years. B goes free.
Prisoner A confesses.	A goes free. B serves 20 years.	A and B both serve 10 years each.

© Cengage Learning 2013

partner is followed by one's own defection), and it is forgiving (one returns immediately to cooperation following cooperation on the part of the partner; Brembs, 1996).

The research on individual differences in cooperation discussed earlier found that the majority of the human participants were reciprocators, whose behavior is most similar to the TFT strategy (Kurzban & Houser, 2005). The prevalence of this "type" might reflect its typical success. If most people are reciprocators, how can we explain the existence of the other "types"? Free riders clearly benefit from their selfish behavior, but what advantages might increase the chances of the cooperators' survival? It is much easier to be generous when one is well off, so acting like a cooperator might make people believe you have lots of resources, improving your chances of attracting a mate (Milinski, Semmann, & Jrambeck, 2002). A person's reputation is also a powerful motivator for cooperation. In ongoing prisoner's dilemma games, participants use other people's record of cooperation (or lack thereof) to determine whether or not to cooperate with them (Milinski et al., 2002). In small hunter-gatherer bands or basketball teams, having a reputation for selfishness is not likely to make you successful.

Culture can shape a person's choice of competition and cooperation. When two people from different countries played the prisoner's dilemma game, less cooperation and more competition occurred than when two people from the same country participated with each other (Matsumoto & Hwang, 2011). Further, the bigger the difference between the native countries of the participants along the dimension of individualism or collectivism, the less cooperation occurred. This finding reflects the in-group bias we mentioned earlier in the chapter.

Contributing to our cooperative abilities is a deep-seated, possibly biological sense of fair play that is shared with other species in the animal kingdom. Capuchin monkeys will happily trade pebbles for slices of

Capuchin monkeys refuse to exchange pebbles for a slice of cucumber after seeing another monkey receive a more highly valued grape for its pebble, suggesting that nonhuman primates have a sense of fairness.

© Fiona Deaton/Shutterstock

cucumber until they see another monkey receiving a more preferred grape for its pebbles. After seeing the "unfairness" of their situation, they are no longer willing to work for cucumber slices (Brosnan & De Waal, 2003). When people playing a prisoner's dilemma game were observed with fMRI, viewing the faces of cooperators produced activation in brain areas normally linked to reward (Singer, Kiebel, Winston, Dolan, & Frith, 2004). In contrast, when people were treated unfairly, activation occurred in parts of the brain associated with anger, disgust, and pain (Sanfey, Rilling, Aronson, Nystrom, & Cohen, 2003).

Connecting *to* Research

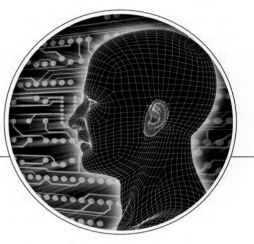

Trust and the Amygdala

Although we have not yet used the word *trust* in our discussion of cooperation, the development of cooperative relationships depends at least in part on the reasonable expectation that if we treat others well, they will return the favor. We know when to withhold trust following a betrayal. Without the ability to figure out whom to trust, we would be incapable of following any "tit for tat" strategies. From our previous discussions of the amygdala's role in perceiving threat, this is a logical structure to investigate as a biological correlate for monitoring trustworthiness.

The Question: *Can we discover what types of brain activity help us determine which people can be trusted?*

METHODS

Adult participants with amygdala damage (32 people), with comparable damage that did not include the amygdala (48 people), and no

brain damage (59 people) played a computerized version of a standard Trust Game (Koscik & Tranel, 2011). In this version of the Trust Game, the participant starts with $20, which he or she can keep or share with a partner. Any money given to the partner is tripled, and then the partner can keep the total or share any amount with the first participant. Then a new round begins with $20 again. So if I give you $10 out of my $20, you now have $30, which you can share or not with me and so on. Participants are made aware of all decisions by their partners, so they know if their generosity is being matched or not. Although participants were told they were engaging with "another player," they were, in fact playing with a computer.

RESULTS

The healthy control participants exhibited a tit-for-tat strategy. They led with generosity, and then responded reciprocally to their

partners. If the partners were generous, the participants continued with this strategy, but if the partners were selfish, the participants would become selfish, too.

Participants with damage to structures other than the amygdala were more variable in their responding, which is not surprising given the variation in the locations of their brain damage. However, the group with amygdala damage remained unfailingly trusting (see ● Figure 13.21). In other words, even when faced with a partner who was completely selfish, the amygdala group continued to be generous. They were unable to assess the trustworthiness of their partner or respond appropriately to selfishness.

DISCUSSION

These results add a new dimension to our understanding of the functions of the amygdala. Prior research, discussed in our chapters on biological

Altruism and Helping

We have all read stories about soldiers, fire fighters, and others who have sacrificed their own lives to save the lives of others. These instances are examples of **altruism**, or helping behavior that either fails to reward or actually harms the person who performs it. If behavior usually leads to improved survival and reproduction, how can we account for altruism? Charles Darwin suggested that "[a] tribe including many members who . . . were always ready to give aid to each other and sacrifice themselves for the common good, would be victorious over most other tribes; and this would be natural selection" (Darwin, 1871, p. 166). Although this suggestion is attractive, it suffers from a major flaw in logic. The system suggested by Darwin would produce free riders who were not altruistic themselves but who would benefit from the altruistic behaviors of the members of their group (Dawkins, 1976). These individuals, since they would undoubtedly live to reproduce, should eventually swamp the group with "selfish" genes.

altruism Helping others without personal gain or with personal costs.

psychology and on motivation and emotion, pointed to the amygdala as a structure that helps us perceive threat, whether that threat comes in the form of snakes, dominant members of our species, or facial expressions and voices. Especially interesting about this study is that the amygdala in this case is not responding to visual cues from faces or auditory cues from a person's tone of voice. Responding appropriately to the trustworthiness of a partner (in this case a computer program) is a highly complex cognitive process, yet successfully assessing danger in this process still requires an intact, functioning amygdala. ✦

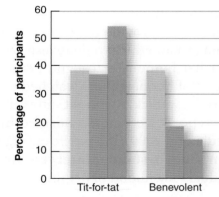

❶ Tit-for-tat reciprocity refers to participants' change in money sent to the other player that mirror the changes in the amount sent from the other players.

❷ Benevolent reciprocity refers to the cases where the amount of money sent by the participant increases in response to a decrease or no change in the amount of money sent by the other player.

AMG (amygdala damage)
BDC (brain damage control – not amygdala)
NC (normal control participants)

© Cengage Learning 2013

FIGURE 13.21

The Amygdala and Trust. The typical strategy in the Trust Game, adopted by the normal control participants in this study, is tit-for-tat. Relatively few participants in the normal control group responded with any of the other strategies. Although many in the group with amygdala damage also followed tit-for-tat, a significant percentage used the benevolent strategy, which meant that they increased the amount of money they gave a partner when the partner either decreased his or her contribution or didn't change it. This outcome suggests that the participants with amygdala damage were trusting when trust was not in their best interest. *Source:* Adapted from Koscik and Tranel (2011).

Several different evolutionary mechanisms have been proposed that account for the continuation of cooperative, altruistic behavior (Nowak, 2006). One researcher has proposed that "altruistic" genes will survive as long as the cost to the altruist is associated with a large enough benefit to relatives (Hamilton, 1964). Japanese macaque monkeys are much more likely to defend close relatives from attack than unrelated monkeys (Kurland, 1977). People are more likely to help their relatives than strangers, as in helping to raise their children. Altruism is also maintained by expectations that a favor might someday be returned by those you have helped, a process known as reciprocal altruism (Trivers, 1971). Vampire bats often regurgitate blood to share with bats who did not hunt successfully; bats are more likely to share with those who had shared with them recently (Wilkinson, 1984, 1990).

Selfishness might be limited by punishment administered by other group members. Participants who had the opportunity to punish those who had not cooperated activated reward circuits in the brain, lending credence to the phrase "revenge is sweet" (Fehr & Rockenbach, 2004). Unfortunately, the willingness to pay a big price in order to carry out revenge against those who seem "unfair" might also lead to irrational acts, such as suicide bombings.

There are other instances of altruism, however, that do not fit these models. People adopt children who are totally unrelated to themselves. Arland Williams, a passenger on an airplane that crashed into the freezing Potomac River in 1982, passed lifelines to other passengers before disappearing beneath the water himself. These altruistic acts represent psychological altruism, or conscious efforts to help. This type of altruism can be transmitted by a culture through learning (Dawkins, 1976). In fact, the tendency to feel pleasure when helping others is quite low in children and gradually increases into adulthood (Cialdini, Kenrick, & Baumann, 1981).

If cooperation confers so many benefits to individuals and groups, how can we explain the failure of some individuals to provide help when it is desperately needed? In 1964, a young woman named Kitty Genovese was murdered on a New York City street near her home late at night. Sensational news reports at the time stated that 38 of her neighbors watched for over half an hour while Kitty struggled with her attacker without intervening or calling the police. Although these reports were not confirmed by later court testimony in the case (onthemedia.org, 2009), the public outrage they stimulated led to a series of experiments into **bystander intervention**. This research demonstrated that an individual's likelihood of helping drops as the number of other observers grows. In a typical experiment investigating this phenomenon, college students filled out a questionnaire as their room filled with smoke (Latané & Darley, 1968). The researchers were interested in how frequently and quickly the students reported the smoke. When the college students were alone, nearly 80% sought help within 6 minutes. When three participants were tested together, only 40% reported the "emergency" within 6 minutes.

The effect of the number of observers on the likelihood of intervention is probably influenced by a sense of individual responsibility. When you are the only person available to help, your responsibility is clear. When a crowd

Sensational accounts of the murder of Kitty Genovese stimulated research in bystander intervention, which asked questions about why people seem to help in some situations and not in others.

bystander intervention The study of situational variables related to helping a stranger, most notably the decreased likelihood of helping as the number of bystanders increases.

of people is gathered around the scene of an accident, it is much easier [to] assume that others have already called 911 or that a physician or nurse who is better qualified to help will be present. People also fail to act due to fears of appearing foolish as a result of misinterpreting a situation. Emergencies can be ambiguous. What sounds like a case of domestic violence next door might actually be a loud movie or video game, or actors practicing a scene for a play. People who feel anonymous are less likely to help, which is consistent with our previous observations of how anonymity can lead to less socially desirable behavior. Finally, people are more likely to help when it is safe and convenient for them to do so. If you are heading for your car at the end of the day when you notice a classmate with a flat tire, you are likely to lend a hand. On the other hand, if you are late for work or a final exam, you may conveniently assume that someone else will take care of the situation as you continue on your way.

Why Are We Aggressive?

Aggression is the conscious intent to harm others, and it can take several forms. Instrumental aggression is the intentional harm, usually physical, done to others to obtain a goal, such as attacking a person to steal a wallet or purse. Relational aggression harms another person's social standing through behaviors such as ignoring, exclusion, and gossip. Other types of aggression include defensive aggression, in which the person may do harm to others in self-defense, and maternal aggression, a rather common phenomenon in the animal world (and occasionally among humans) in which sickly or unwanted offspring are killed.

Like most of the behaviors we discuss in this textbook, factors leading to human aggression form complex interactions. Efforts to find simple correlations between violence and single variables such as economic growth, population trends, illegal drug trade, availability of guns, and domestic violence versus stranger violence do not tell the whole story. We can capture the flavor of this complexity by examining homicide rates across cultures. The average homicide rate worldwide is about 10 per 100,000 residents, or twice the number killed in war (United Nations Office on Drugs and Crime, 2001). Colombia has a murder rate of 62 homicides per 100,000 residents per year, compared to the rate in the United States of just under 5 per 100,000 people (United Nations Office on Drugs and Crime, 2001). Rates in large cities within the United States vary substantially, from Washington, D.C.'s 45 homicides per 100,000 to Honolulu's 2 (U.S. Department of Justice, 2006).

> Prejudices are what fools use for reason.
>
> —Voltaire

The Biological Psychology of Aggression

Is a capacity for aggression simply part of being human? Biological explanations of aggression point to several possible sources of human aggression: genetics, biochemistry, and nervous system structure and activity.

aggression The conscious intent to harm another.

Aggression is clearly a disposition that can be selectively bred in animals, as evidenced by the development of the famous fighting bulls of Spain and hyperaggressive laboratory mice (Lagerspetz & Lagerspetz, 1983). Human twin and adoption studies imply that aggressive tendencies in human beings are at least partly influenced by genetics (Rushton, Fulker, Neale, Nias, & Eysenck, 1986). As we have seen so frequently in this textbook, genes associated with aggressive behavior interact with nurture or experience. Among children who were abused, those with one version of a gene linked to aggression in animals were very likely to behave aggressively, while those with the other form rarely did so, even when the abuse they experienced was severe (Craig, 2007).

Both naturally occurring chemicals and recreational drugs can influence aggression. Among the naturally occurring chemicals implicated in aggression are the androgens, or male hormones such as testosterone (see ● Figure 13.22). Prenatal exposure to high levels of androgens, which can occur naturally or due to medications occasionally given to pregnant women, increases the aggressive play of both male and female preschoolers (Reinisch, Ziemba-Davis, & Sanders, 1991). Adult men with higher levels of prenatal testosterone exposure score higher on standardized questionnaires of aggression (Bailey & Hurd, 2005; Burton, Henninger, Hafetz, & Cofer, 2009). Testosterone levels on the high end of the typical range in teen and adult males are positively correlated with delinquency, drug abuse, and aggression (Dabbs & Morris, 1990). Testosterone levels for both male and female criminals correlate with the violent nature of the crimes for which they were sentenced as well as the dominance and violence they demonstrate while in prison (Dabbs, Frady, Carr, & Besch, 1987; Dabbs & Hargrove, 1997). Testosterone appears to affect aggressive behavior by increasing the sensitivity of the amygdala to threatening stimuli, such as angry faces (Derntl et al., 2009). When feeling threatened, a person might engage in more aggressive behavior as a pre-emptive strike.

Many psychoactive substances affect the likelihood that a person will behave aggressively. For instance, alcohol has been implicated in between 57 and 85% of violent crimes (Boles & Miotto, 2003; Pernanen, 1991). In addition, many suicides are committed under the influence of alcohol (Sher, 2006). The most likely mode of action for alcohol in stimulating aggression is its general disinhibiting effects on behavior. As we discussed in our chapter on biological psychology, alcohol silences higher cortical

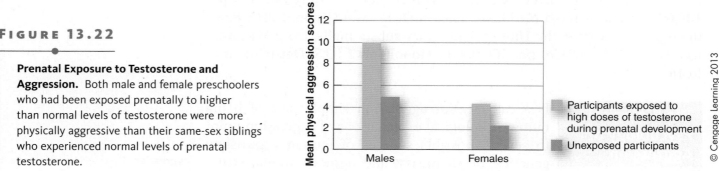

FIGURE 13.22

Prenatal Exposure to Testosterone and Aggression. Both male and female preschoolers who had been exposed prenatally to higher than normal levels of testosterone were more physically aggressive than their same-sex siblings who experienced normal levels of prenatal testosterone.

Participants exposed to high doses of testosterone during prenatal development

Unexposed participants

© Cengage Learning 2013

areas responsible for impulse control, often leading to behavior that is normally actively suppressed, including aggression.

Keeping in mind the complexity of human aggression, we can point to variations in brain structure and function that are correlated with senseless violence. Antisocial, violent behavior is correlated with some types of brain damage, although these findings interact with experience in ways similar to the genetics studies discussed earlier (Davidson, Putnam, & Larson, 2000). The diversity of patterns of brain activity leading to aggression was demonstrated in a study comparing brain activity in murderers who had experienced neglect, poverty, physical abuse, or sexual abuse and murderers who had experienced none of these social deficits (Raine, Stoddard, Bihrle, & Buchsbaum, 1998). The brain activity of the neglected and abused murderers was quite similar to the nonviolent control participants. In contrast, the brain activity of the non-abused murderers was quite different, suggesting that their violent behavior had very different roots compared to the murderers with a history of child abuse. The non-abused individuals showed an unusually reduced level of activity in the frontal lobes. Given the essential role of the frontal lobes in higher order judgment and impulse control, this lower level of activity might help account for their inability to control their aggression.

Learning and Aggression

Although it is probably safe to say that our human heritage contains a capacity for aggression, the actual expression of aggression is elicited by environmental factors and modified by experience.

As we discussed in our chapter on learning, Albert Bandura provided compelling evidence that children who observe aggression are likely to behave aggressively themselves (Bandura, 1973). In Bandura's classic demonstration of social learning, preschoolers who observed an adult attack an inflatable Bobo doll toy mimicked not just the adult's violent actions but also his or her yells of "sock him in the nose," "knock him down," and "kick him."

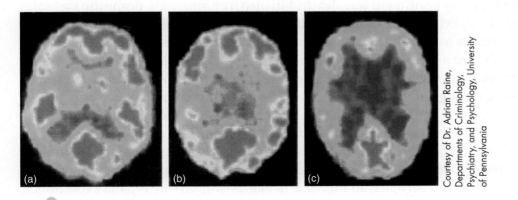

Courtesy of Dr. Adrian Raine, Departments of Criminology, Psychiatry, and Psychology, University of Pennsylvania

(a) (b) (c)

These brain images were taken from (a) a person with no history of criminal behavior, (b) a person who was convicted of murder and had a strong history of childhood abuse and neglect, and (c) a person who was convicted of murder and had no history of childhood abuse or neglect. The murderer who had been abused and neglected shows activity that is not distinguishable from that of the person without a criminal history. The murderer with no history of abuse or neglect shows very little activity in the frontal lobes (toward the top of the image) or in the middle parts of the brain that usually respond to emotional stimuli.

Opportunities to observe violence are plentiful. Within the family, children who are disciplined with screaming, slapping, and beating are more likely to be physically aggressive with their peers at school (Patterson, Chamberlain, & Reid, 1982). Even when the parents are violent toward each other, without involving the child directly, the child's level of violent behavior may be impacted. In a study of over 2,000 violent children and teens, a recent exposure to violence in the home was a useful predictor for the child's violent behavior outside the home (Singer, Miller, Guo, Slovak, & Frierson, 1998).

Additional opportunities to observe violence are provided by media. By the age of 18, the average American has seen an estimated 200,000 acts of violence on television alone (Strasburger, 2007). Sixty-one percent of television programming includes violence, with only 4% featuring an antiviolence theme (Federman, 1998). Children and youth are exposed to increasingly violent and graphic images and ideas through films, video games, and music lyrics. As we discussed in our chapter on research methods, however, care must be taken to avoid misinterpretation of the research results showing correlations between media exposure and aggression.

Preventing Aggression

The human species loses a smaller percentage of the population to war today than in the time of our hunter-gatherer ancestors (LeBlanc, 2003), but we still have a long way to go.

As in the case of reducing prejudice, redefining the boundaries of the "in-group" might be contributing to this improvement. Instead of hunter-gatherer clans of 100 or so individuals fighting with their neighboring clans, we have nations of millions that cooperate as units. Increasing economic dependencies among nations further reduce the advantages of between-group violence. Damage to one nation's critical infrastructure, such as its ability to produce or process oil, is likely to have adverse effects for all nations, including the attacker. In spite of this progress, we remain plagued not only by continued war deaths but also by homicides, domestic violence, rape, bullying, and other destructive aggressive behaviors. Psychologists continue to search for effective ways to reduce aggression.

There are no simple solutions to the problem of aggression. You might think that we could take advantage of catharsis, or the reduction of an emotion through its expression, but the research results do not support this approach. Catharsis theories of aggression are common but suffer from the same weaknesses shown by catharsis explanations of emotion discussed in our chapter on motivation and emotion. Just as expressing an emotion typically heightens rather than decreases a feeling, people who engage in aggression experience an increase in aggression. In one typical experiment, participants first were "angered" by a person who criticized essays they had written (Bushman, 2002). Subsequently, the participants who were given opportunities to hit a punching bag while thinking about the critic administered louder sound blasts to the critic when given the opportunity to retaliate than did participants in control groups. Despite the intuitive appeal of the notion of catharsis, when it comes to aggression catharsis is generally ineffective.

We cannot do great things on this Earth, only small things with great love.

—Mother Teresa

© Andy Aitchison/In Pictures/Corbis

Homicides among the Turkana of Kenya are quite rare, in spite of the fact that children are explicitly encouraged to be aggressive to each other, under the watchful eyes of adults. However, the Turkana are exceedingly aggressive toward their neighbors. Over human history, the trait of aggression has probably been valued when turned against other groups, but not when it is turned inward.

Another frequent suggestion for reducing aggression that has failed to gain research support is an active teaching approach in which children are rewarded for sensitivity and cooperation. Cross-cultural data show that homicide rates are often high in cultures that feature a loving socialization of children and aversion to interpersonal conflict, such as the Inuit, !Kung Bushmen, and Gebusi of New Zealand, yet very low among cultures where children are explicitly taught to fight, like the Turkana of Kenya (Dyson-Hudson & Dyson-Hudson, 1999 ; Dyson-Hudson & Dyson-Hudson, 1995).

Much of the research we have discussed so far focuses on individual variables, whether that is a person's genetic makeup or socialization. To truly understand aggression, we need to zoom out to see this behavior within the social context. For example, we know that if groups rarely interact, they are more likely to fight than to cooperate. In contrast, if groups interact regularly and anticipate future interactions, they may still compete, but they tend to do so in more prosocial ways.

The social environment can also determine whether aggressiveness escalates to actual violence. In a study using surveillance footage of public places, researchers observed actual fighting behavior (Levine, Taylor, & Best, 2011). In many cases, one or more third parties (usually friends of the combatants) intervened to stop the fight. In an interesting contrast with the helping behavior observed in the bystander intervention literature discussed previously, third parties are more likely, not less likely, to intervene in a fight when the number of bystanders is larger. Perhaps the implications of the aggression spreading to include the whole group makes stopping the fight a very high priority for members of the group.

Research using surveillance camera footage shows that third parties often intervene in an effort to de-escalate violence (Levine, Taylor, & Best, 2011). Unlike most of the laboratory studies of bystander intervention, third parties in the filmed incidents were more, not less, likely to intervene as groups of onlookers became larger. Further research should help clarify the exact conditions leading to helping behavior.

Image courtesy of Mark Levine, Department of Psychology, Exeter University

Summary 13.4

Cooperation and Competition

	What is it?	Influential factors
Cooperation © REUTERS/Gonzalo Fuentes	Working together to reach a goal	• Individual differences • Tit-for-tat strategy • Culture • Innate sense of fair play
Competition © Paul Wayne Wilson/PhotoStock-File/Alamy	A contest for resources	• Availability of resources • Signals for dominance and submission
Altruism The New York Times Photo Archive	Helping others without personal gain or with personal cost	• Number of potential helpers available • Relatedness to person needing help • Punishment for selfishness • Expectation of future reciprocation • Conscious desire to help • Sense of personal responsibility to help
Aggression Image courtesy of Mark Levine, Department of Psychology, Exeter University	The conscious intent to harm another	• Interactions between genetics and child maltreatment • Use of alcohol and other drugs • Testosterone levels • Brain structure and activity • Observational learning

Interpersonal Relationships
From the Social Perspective

The social perspective has a great deal to say on the topic of interpersonal relationships, much of which we have already discussed in this chapter. One aspect of relationships, however, can use further explanation—the social rejection we experience in our intimate relationships. Our previous discussion of the "ending" of relationships was practical, but perhaps did not capture the strong emotions that usually accompany this life event for most people.

Why does it hurt so much to "break up"? We know that social exclusion in general can activate parts of the brain, especially the anterior cingulate cortex (ACC), that also are activated by the sensations of physical pain (Eisenberger et al., 2003). Psychologists believe that the ACC processes the emotional components of pain, but not necessarily the physical sensations of the pain itself (see ● Figure 13.23).

As hurtful as it may be to be snubbed by a group of mean girls in a high school cafeteria, common experiences such as this do not have the personal significance of being rejected by a lover. Most of the previous research on social exclusion models the snubbing type of peer rejection. It turns out that if, instead, you expose participants to photographs of their ex-partners who rejected them, the experience not only produces activation in the ACC but also recruits areas of the somatosensory cortex that directly respond to the sensation of pain (Kross et al., 2011).

This extension of our understanding of the biological correlates of social rejection might help us to explain why some individuals respond to rejection by developing chronic pain disorders, such as the somatoform disorders we discuss further in our chapter on psychological disorders. These disorders produce physical symptoms, including aches and pains, that do not have an obvious origin in tissue damage.

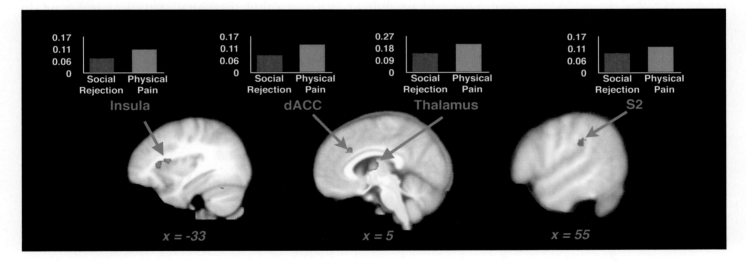

FIGURE 13.23

Viewing an Ex Who Rejected You Is Extremely Painful. Earlier in the chapter, you saw how being excluded from a computerized game of catch produced activity in the anterior cingulate cortex (ACC) that was similar to the activity observed during physical pain. In this experiment, similar outcomes were observed when participants viewed the photo of a person who rejected them recently after a serious relationship. Areas showing similar increases in activity while viewing a former rejecting partner or experiencing physical pain included the insula, ACC, thalamus, and secondary somatosensory cortex. Rejection does indeed hurt. *Source:* From Kross, E., et al. (2011). Social rejection shares somatosensory representations with physical pain. *Proc Natl Acad Sci, 108*(15), 6270–6275. Copyright © 2011 The National Academy of Sciences.

Chapter 13
Reflections

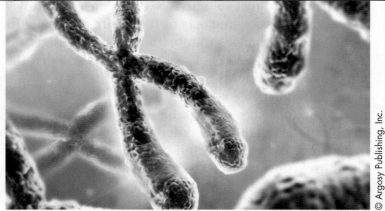

© Argosy Publishing, Inc.

We began this chapter with an examination of a couple at the beginning stage of a romantic relationship.

Using the explanations presented in this chapter, we could zoom in to look at the specifics of their situation, from the very microscopic level of gene compatibility to their extrinsic and intrinsic responses to each other's physical attractiveness to measures of similarity. We could zoom out much farther to see the impact of the larger social environment and culture on their relationship. To what extent might this couple be influenced by stereotyping and prejudice? What are their personal attitudes, and how do those influence their behavior? How susceptible are they to conformity pressures or more overt demands from family and friends?

We'd like to think that our couple will form a strong, cooperative relationship leading to a state of consummate love, but as you now know, fairy tale endings might happen in the movies, but successful real relationships require work and commitment. ‹

KEY TERMS The Language of Psychological Science

Be sure you can define these terms and use them correctly.

aggression, p. 669
altruism, p. 667
attitude, p. 637
attribution, p. 624
bystander intervention, p. 668
cognitive dissonance, p. 638
compliance, p. 646
conformity, p. 645
correspondence bias, p. 625
deindividuation, p. 653

discrimination, p. 630
dispositional attribution, p. 624
door-in-the-face, p. 647
Elaboration Likelihood Model
   (ELM), p. 640
foot-in-the-door, p. 648
group polarization, p. 653
groupthink, p. 654
just-world belief, p. 628
mere exposure effect, p. 656

obedience, p. 648
persuasion, p. 640
prejudice, p. 630
situational attribution, p. 624
social facilitation, p. 651
social loafing, p. 652
social norms, p. 645
stereotype, p. 630

MEDIA RESOURCES

Log in to CengageBrain to access the resources your instructor requires. For this book, you can access:

Psychology **CourseMate** brings course concepts to life with interactive learning, study, and exam preparation tools that support the printed textbook. A textbook-specific website, Psychology **CourseMate** includes an integrated interactive eBook and other interactive learning tools including quizzes, flashcards, videos, and more.

WebTUTOR   More than just an interactive study guide, **WebTutor** is an anytime, anywhere customized learning solution with an eBook, keeping you connected to your textbook, instructor, and classmates.

aplia If your professor has assigned **Aplia** homework:
1. Sign in to your account.
2. Complete the corresponding homework exercises as required by your professor.
3. When finished, click "Grade It Now" to see which areas you have mastered, which areas need more work, and detailed explanations of every answer.

An interactome between genes implicated in autism with other cellular proteins confirmed links between autism and several related conditions and identified new genes that warranted further study.

The Troubled Mind

14

Psychological Disorders

Learning Objectives

1 Critique the general definition of psychological "disorder" and its application in the *Diagnostic and Statistical Manual (DSM)*.

2 Analyze the roles of biology, cognition, and experience in the major psychological disorders, demonstrating how these factors interact to produce symptoms.

3 Identify common and differentiating symptoms of the anxiety disorders (GAD, panic disorder, phobia, OCD, and PTSD), and use your analysis as a basis for diagnosis.

4 Differentiate clinical depression and mania from normal sadness and good mood, linking these diagnostic criteria to the general definition of disorder.

5 Distinguish the symptoms of schizophrenia from those of dissociative and somatoform disorders, and debate the link between schizophrenic symptoms and creative thinking.

6 Assess the psychological mechanisms that may support behavioral symptoms of antisocial and borderline personality disorders.

7 Debate the diagnostic criteria for autism and ADHD, considering ways to distinguish symptoms of these disorders from normal childhood behavior.

Of all the reasons to study psychology, finding ways to improve the lives of people with psychological disorders might be one of the most rewarding. This process begins with understanding the features and possible causes of a disorder.

Identifying the causes of psychological disorders requires us to pull together multiple threads leading from the genetic, biological, cognitive, developmental, and social aspects of being human. These causal factors interact with one another in complex ways, so the same disorder might look one way in one individual and quite different in another. We do not know what caused this small child to develop the symptoms of autism, but we at least know where to start looking.

We have cautioned you on several occasions in this textbook to avoid the idea that we have "genes for" this trait or the next, because the reality is much more complex. As we zoom in to analyze the genetic contributions to autism, you will see that we have zoomed way past the traditional array of 46 human chromosomes featured in our chapter on nature and nurture. Instead, we are looking at a visual representation of something biologists call an "interactome," which is a map of all the interactions between proteins in a cell. In this particular case, the researchers were attempting to identify the relationships between 539 proteins that formed interactions with proteins produced by 26 genes already implicated in autism. The resulting map not only confirmed links between autism and several related conditions but also identified genetic relationships that warranted further study.

What does an interactome mean for this child? Understanding more about the sources of autism has not yet, unfortunately, led to improved treatments. As we mentioned in our chapter on learning, the only effective treatment for autism today is the use of behavioral therapies. But such discoveries do have the potential to improve the lives of individuals with autism down the road, or to provide information eventually that will help us prevent further cases.

To fully understand this child's experience requires us to zoom out to consider his overall development. Psychologists point out that we say "a person with autism" instead of an "autistic person" for very good reasons. People are not their disorders, and much is happening in this child's life that has nothing to do with autism. We could consider the impact of his parents, whose age might have been a risk factor for his autism, or study their abilities to manage his behavior and help him reach his potential. Zooming even farther out, we can investigate the effects of autism on the social connectedness this child experiences as he ventures out into the world.

In this chapter, you will discover a number of different types of psychological disorders, each with a unique history and set of characteristics. In our following chapter, we will explore the treatments and therapies that psychologists have developed to address the challenges to well-being posed by these disorders. ⚙

© Jeffrey L. Rotman/Peter Arnold/Getty Images

We refer to "people with autism" instead of "autistic person" because there is so much more to people than their disorders. To fully understand a child with autism, we need to consider the impact of his environment. This young boy is obviously enjoying his "dolphin therapy."

	NORMAL	MILD
Emotions	Good alertness and positive emotional state.	Feeling sad or down temorarily, but not for long.
Cognitions	"I'm not getting the grades I want this semester, but I'll keep trying to do my best."	"I'm struggling at school this semester. I wish I could study better, or I'll fail."
Behaviors	Going to classes and studying for the next round of tests. Talking to professors.	Going to classes with some trouble studying. Less contact with others.

What Does It Mean to Have a Psychological Disorder?

Mental health experts define a psychological disorder as "a clinically significant behavioral or psychological syndrome or pattern that occurs in an individual and that is associated with present distress (e.g., a painful symptom) or disability (i.e., impairment in one or more important areas of functioning) or with a significantly increased risk of suffering death, pain, disability, or an important loss of freedom" (American Psychiatric Association [APA], 2000, p. xxi). What does this definition really mean?

The study of psychological disorders is referred to as abnormal psychology. It is surprisingly difficult but absolutely necessary for psychologists to agree on the differences between typical and abnormal behaviors, because deciding that an individual's behaviors and mental processes are abnormal is the first step toward labeling that person with a psychological disorder and providing treatment (see ● Figure 14.1).

We can start with the literal meaning of the word *abnormal*. In Latin, the prefix *ab* means "away from" and *norma* means "the rule." In other words, abnormal behavior is literally behavior that is not typical, usual, or regular. This meaning implies a statistical definition of abnormality. By this definition, behaviors that most people do are normal, whereas behaviors that characterize a minority of people are abnormal.

This statistical approach has the advantage of being very clear (see ● Figure 14.2). For example, mental retardation (intellectual disability) is one of the categories in the *Diagnostic and Statistical Manual of Mental Disorders,* a handbook for diagnosis that we discuss in more detail later in the chapter. The diagnosis of mental retardation relies heavily on statistics. A score of 70 or below on a standard IQ test is the typical cutoff for identifying an individual with mental retardation (APA, 2000). Even in this relatively clear situation, however, the statistical approach represents merely a starting point. A diagnosis of mental retardation also requires an individual to demonstrate difficulties with adaptive skills, which include factors such as communication, self-care, safety, and use of community resources.

Many behaviors considered abnormal are actually quite similar to normal behaviors. We all know what it feels like to be depressed, so how is that different from having a mood disorder? This chapter will help you understand the distinctions, but because those distinctions can be subtle, we also caution you against "First-Year Medical Student's Disease," or the sense that you have all the disorders you are studying.

FIGURE 14.1

A Continuum From Normal to Psychological Disorder. Psychological disorders can be understood both categorically, which means that they each have their own set of distinct characteristics used for diagnosis, and as part of a continuum from normal behavior to severely disordered behavior. The diagnostic criteria we discuss in this chapter guide psychologists in their identification of the types and severity of disorders their patients and clients might have. *Source: Adapted from Kearney and Trull (2012).*

MODERATE	PSYCHOLOGICAL DISORDER—LESS SEVERE	PSYCHOLOGICAL DISORDER—MORE SEVERE
Feeling sad, but a strong positive experience such as a good grade could lift mood.	Intense sadness most of the day with some trouble concentrating and some loss of appetite.	Extreme sadness all of the time with great trouble concentrating and complete loss of appetite.
"These bad grades really hurt. This may set me back for a while. I'm really worried."	"I'm so worried about these grades that my stomach hurts. I don't know what to do."	"These bad grades just show what a failure I am at everything. There's no hope; I'm not doing anything today."
Skipping a few classes and feeling somewhat unmotivated to study. Avoiding contact with professors and classmates.	Skipping most classes and unable to maintain eye contact with others. Strong lack of motivation.	Unable to get out of bed, eat, or leave the house. Lack of energy and frequent crying.

© Cengage Learning 2013

FIGURE 14.2

Statistical Abnormality. The word *abnormal* literally means "away from the rule." Both intellectually gifted individuals, usually defined as having IQs over 130, and individuals with mental retardation/intellectual disability, usually defined as having an IQ below 70, are equally "abnormal" in this statistical sense of the word. Academy Award–winning producer Quentin Tarantino (*Pulp Fiction, Kill Bill, Django Unchained*) has an IQ of 160. Although neither he nor his films are "typical," we are unlikely to refer to Tarantino as "abnormal." Statistics alone do not capture what we mean by abnormal behavior.

0.13% 2.14% 13.59% 34.13% 34.13% 13.59% 2.14% 0.13%

55 70 85 100 115 130 145

Illustration: © Cengage Learning 2013; photo: © a. berti/MARKA/Alamy

© Peter Horree/Alamy

Defining abnormal behavior as a deviation from what is considered ideal immediately runs into problems of cultural specificity. Behaviors like hearing voices that others cannot hear might be considered less than ideal in Western cultures, but might be considered a gift in others. The ability to hear voices was considered an advantage for shamans, like the one represented transforming into his jaguar spirit companion in this Costa Rican piece from 1000–1500 CE.

A purely statistical approach, however, has several major drawbacks. First, it implies a cultural specificity that we would like to avoid. Because most members of one culture may behave in ways very different from those of people in another, the purely statistical approach to abnormality might result in very different definitions of psychological disorder from one culture to the next. Second, a statistical definition fails to capture the distress that often accompanies a psychological disorder, both for the person experiencing the disorder and for those interacting with that person.

To address these concerns, we might suggest that abnormal behavior deviates from some ideal manner of behaving. This approach succeeds in capturing the general distress most of us experience when observing or experiencing abnormal behavior. Unfortunately, this approach does nothing to avoid cross-cultural differences in defining disordered behavior. Different cultures are often characterized by very diverse ideals. In Western nations, hearing voices that others cannot hear is generally considered abnormal. In other cultures, hearing voices may be viewed more positively as a sign of religious giftedness (Al-Issa, 1977; Kurihara, Kato, Sakamoto, Reverger, & Kitamura, 2000). More troublesome is the simple fact that it is very difficult, if not impossible, to reach consensus regarding what constitutes ideal behavior. People, including experts in psychology, have deeply divided value judgments regarding sexual conduct, recreational drug use, and a whole host of other activities.

A simple modification of this "deviation from the ideal" approach can help us to achieve some consensus. Behaviors that cause harm to others are viewed as less than ideal. Unless the person is acting defensively, few of us would disagree that such behavior is negative and undesirable. We are also sympathetic to those who have conditions that produce harm to themselves. We can combine the best aspects of each of these approaches to construct a formal definition of abnormal behavior: *Abnormal behavior is unusual, distressing, and harmful to self or others.*

We don't really know how many people have psychological disorders. It is not uncommon for a single individual to be diagnosed with **comorbid** disorders, which means more than one disorder occurs at the same time, so simply adding up the rates for each type of disorder is not a solution. Statistics can look very different for different time-frames. Estimates of the number of people who experience a psychological disorder during the previous year are around 26% (Kessler, Chiu, Demler, & Walters, 2005), but estimates of the number of people experiencing a disorder as least once during their lifetimes are as high as 65% (Moffitt et al., 2010).

Our tolerance for people engaging in acts that are harmful to themselves is variable. Most states in the United States have prohibitions against committing suicide (the irony in prosecuting such laws appears to have been lost on the legislators).

Although college students have the same rates of psychological disorders as their age peers who are not attending college, as shown in ● Figure 14.3, rates of psychological disorders in young adults are higher than in the general population and appear to be increasing (Hunt & Eisenberg, 2010). Nearly half of young adults under the age of 24 met criteria for at least one psychological disorder in the previous year, including 18% for a personality disorder, 12% for an anxiety disorder, and 11% for a mood disorder (Blanco et al., 2008). We discuss each of these categories in more detail in this chapter.

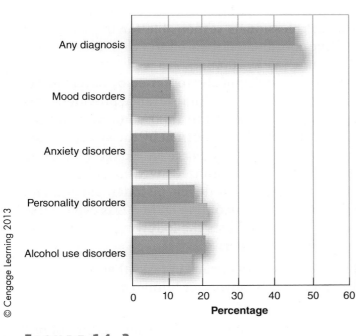

© Stockbyte/Photos.com

© Cengage Learning 2013

FIGURE 14.3

Rates of Psychological Disorders in College Students. Based on face-to-face interviews, college students and their same-age peers who do not attend college have a very high rate (nearly 50%) of meeting the criteria for at least one psychological disorder over the past 12 months. College students and age-peers not in college did not differ significantly in their rates of psychological disorder, with the exception of alcohol use disorders, which were higher among those attending college. *Source:* Adapted from Blanco et al. (2008).

comorbidity The presence of two or more disorders in the same individual.

How Are Psychological Disorders Diagnosed?

The first official effort in the United States to gather data on psychological disorders was the recording of a single category, "idiocy/insanity," in the 1840 census (APA, 2000).

The *Diagnostic and Statistical Manual of Mental Disorders (DSM)* has undergone a number of revisions since its first edition in 1952. Over its history, the DSM has become less Freudian and more sensitive to cross-cultural issues. The DSM is published by the American Psychiatric Association.

Diagnostic and Statistical Manual of Mental Disorders (DSM) A system for classification of psychological disorders published by the American Psychiatric Association (APA).

When you visit your physician or student health center complaining of a sore throat, your health care provider makes note of your symptoms, compares them to known categories of illness, swabs your throat for a sample, and determines your diagnosis. You have strep throat. Based on that diagnosis, you are given a prescription for an antibiotic. Unlike medical illnesses, however, psychological disorders are diagnosed purely on the basis of observable behaviors. There are no blood tests, scans, or other medical diagnostic procedures that can be used to determine if a person has a psychological disorder.

To promote consistency in the diagnosis of psychological disorders, mental health professionals typically refer to the ***Diagnostic and Statistical Manual of Mental Disorders (DSM)***, first published by the American Psychiatric Association (APA) in 1952. The current edition is known as DSM-IV-Text Revision, or DSM-IV-TR (2000), and DSM 5 is slated for publication in May 2013 (American Psychiatric Association [APA], 2011a, 2011b). A second classification system in wide use is the *International Statistical Classification of Diseases and Related Health Problems* (ICD-10), which was published by the World Health Organization (WHO) in 1992. An updated 11th edition is due to be published in 2015 (World Health Organization [WHO], 2011). Professionals responsible for the DSM and ICD classification systems have coordinated their efforts to reduce the differences between the two systems (APA, 2000).

Although the DSM is the standard diagnostic tool used by psychiatrists and psychologists, and is required by most health insurance providers, it is not without its critics. Beginning with DSM-III in 1980, some very normal behaviors seem to have been categorized as abnormal by the system. Allen Frances, a psychiatrist who chaired the Task Force in charge of writing the DSM-IV, expressed concern that the committee's well-meaning efforts had led to three "false epidemics" (attention deficit disorder, autism, and childhood bipolar disorder) and that the upcoming DSM 5 was even worse (Frances, 2010). For example, DSM-IV-TR lists the following as a criterion for Attention-Deficit Hyperactivity Disorder:

> often avoids, dislikes, or is reluctant to engage in tasks that require sustained mental effort (such as schoolwork or homework). (APA, 2000, p. 92)

It is hard to imagine how this criterion fits the "unusual" aspect of our definition of abnormality. Controversial proposals for the most recent revision extend the abnormal category of depression to include grieving for a loved one and classify some rapes as the result of "paraphilic coercive disorder" instead of simply being criminal, aggressive behaviors.

In spite of its flaws, the DSM remains the best and most frequently used tool for the diagnosis of psychological disorders. Our discussion of different types of psychological disorders is therefore grounded in the DSM system.

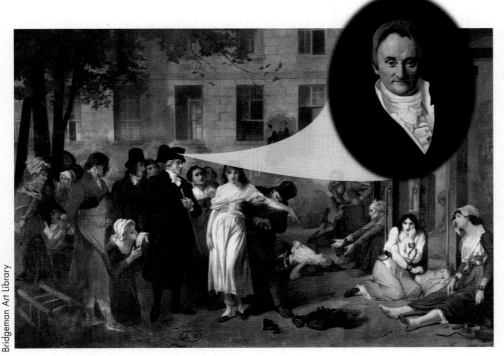

Philippe Pinel (1745–1826) is often referred to as "the father of modern psychiatry." After observing the more humane treatment of inmates by a former patient turned employee named Jean-Baptiste Pussin at Bicêtre Hospital outside Paris, Pinel followed Pussin's example by removing the patients' iron shackles. Instead of the usual "treatments" of the day— bleeding, purging, and blistering— Pinel made a practice of conversing with the patients regularly.

What Do the Psychological Perspectives Tell Us About Disorders?

We have seen many examples in this textbook of behaviors that are best understood when viewed from multiple perspectives. The study of psychological disorder provides yet another example of how an integration of multiple perspectives can be very useful. This is particularly the case when considering the possible causes for abnormal behaviors.

Historically, the most common approach to understanding abnormal behavior has been through the use of supernatural explanations. People who behaved in ways that were unusual and frightening were viewed as being possessed by devils, which of course led to some very unenlightened "treatments," including being burned at the stake. As science progressed, the supernatural explanations gave way to two major approaches still very much in evidence: a biological approach and a more psychological approach.

The traditional biological approach to psychological disorders searched for the causes of abnormal behavior in physical disease or damage. We see this approach today in discussions of genetic predispositions to disorders, references to depression as the result of chemical imbalances in the brain, or suggestions that attention deficit disorder is the outcome of brain immaturity. The traditional psychological approach, in contrast, put a greater emphasis on experience, learning, and other environmental factors. The behaviorist, Freudian, and social psychology perspectives historically fell into this category of explanation.

Although considerable progress toward helping people with their disorders was made by psychologists working within one of these single perspectives, combining perspectives is a more useful way to proceed. The disorders themselves do not share similar relevance to biological and psychological factors, making a one-size-fits-all approach inappropriate. Some of the disorders we discuss in this chapter have much more to do with biology than others. To insist on applying the same type of explanation for all disorders distorts this causal diversity. The contrast between biology and psychology in explaining psychological disorder contributed to the false either/or approach to nature and nurture that we have argued against throughout this textbook. Deciding which aspects of a factor such as stress are biological or psychological is not consistent with our current thinking that mind and body are not separate entities.

What might an integrated approach to psychological disorder look like? First, we propose that the various perspectives discussed in this textbook (evolutionary, biological, learning, developmental, cognitive, individual, and social) all have a great deal to say about disorders, but each will have more to say about some disorders than about others. By considering the contributions of factors from multiple perspectives, we should have a greater appreciation of the complex interactions that occur among perspectives.

In addition, an integrated perspective helps us understand the reciprocal relationships between factors leading to psychological disorder. Just as a person who is diagnosed with depression might show low levels of serotonin activity in the brain, being in a leadership position boosts a person's serotonin levels. A simple biological explanation suggesting that chemical imbalances lead to depression or a simple psychological explanation stating that people who feel powerless are more likely to be depressed misses the nuances of these reciprocal relationships.

The richer understanding of the causal factors leading to a psychological disorder pays off in the development of more effective treatments. Single-perspective thinking usually leads to single-perspective treatments. If you believe that depression is purely the result of chemical imbalances of the brain, then a simple prescription should do the trick. If you believe that hearing voices others can't hear is the result of childhood communication patterns, you will miss the opportunity to provide medication that can very effectively end these troubling symptoms. Inclusive models describing the entire range of causal factors are much more likely to result in effective treatments tailored to the needs of individuals.

Keeping these perspectives in mind, we will now explore a sampling of the major categories of psychological disorder.

© Jed Jacobsohn/Getty Images

Being in a position of leadership, like team captain Matt Barkley of the USC Trojans, has been shown to correlate with higher levels of serotonin activity, while being diagnosed with depression is correlated with lower levels of serotonin activity. Are leaders chosen because of their high serotonin? Or does serotonin increase when we perceive ourselves as respected by our peers? Simple explanations that view depression as a result of either chemical imbalances or feelings of powerlessness do not capture the rich interactions among our biology and cognitions.

What Is an Anxiety Disorder?

Anxiety disorders take many forms, but all share the core characteristic of unrealistic and counterproductive levels of anxiety. Anxiety has two major components: (1) strong negative emotions and (2) physical tension due to the anticipation of danger (Barlow, 1988). It is the anticipation of danger that separates anxiety from the closely related emotion of fear. When we are afraid, usually something is happening in the present that is producing that feeling, whereas anxiety occurs when we are worried about the future. **Anxiety disorders** represent an exaggeration of what is normally a useful response. Normal levels of anxiety protect us from engaging in risky activities, such as running up debts, driving recklessly, or failing to prepare for work or school, but excessive anxiety can cause a person to withdraw from positive life experiences and interpersonal relationships.

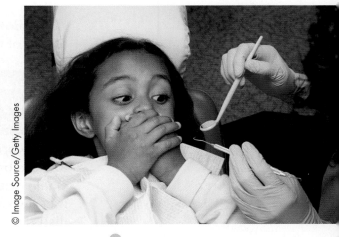

Anxiety is the anticipation of danger. Normal levels of anxiety remind us about the risks of engaging in dangerous activities, but disordered anxiety can prevent people from engaging in everyday activities.

Nearly 30% of all Americans experience one or more anxiety disorders during their lifetime, although not all seek treatment (Kessler et al., 2005). People appear to have genetic vulnerabilities to anxiety disorders in general, but not for specific types of anxiety disorder (Andrews, Steward, Allen, & Henderson, 1990; DiLalla, Kagan, & Reznick, 1994). As we will see later in this chapter, families with members who are diagnosed with anxiety disorders are also likely to have members diagnosed with depression, as these types of problems appear to share an underlying genetic basis (Weissman, Warner, Wickramaratne, Moreau, & Olfson, 1997). Anxiety disorders differ across gender and ethnicity for reasons that are not currently well understood. Women are more likely to be diagnosed with anxiety disorders than are men, and African Americans and Hispanics living in the United States are less likely to be diagnosed with anxiety disorders than are White Americans (Kessler et al., 2005).

Evidence of a predisposition to anxiety appears early in life (Biederman et al., 1990; Schwartz, Snidman, & Kagan, 1999). As we observed in our chapters on development and on personality, children's initial temperament and reactivity can predispose them to anxiety. Young infants show consistent levels of response to novel stimuli, such as the smell of cotton swabs dipped in alcohol (Kagan, 1997). Twenty percent of the infants in this study were classified as "high reactives" to these stimuli, due to their increased activity and distress when novel stimuli were presented. When the high-reactive children were placed in a novel laboratory environment at the ages of 4 to 5 years, they still showed heightened levels of fear compared to their peers.

Unlike most other types of psychological disorders, anxiety disorders do not impair a person's ability to think realistically. In most cases, adult patients with anxiety disorders recognize that their circumstances do not warrant their extremely anxious responses, but they feel unable to control them. A person looking out the window of a skyscraper is well aware that the likelihood of falling is quite low, but feelings of fear and anxiety persist.

anxiety disorder A disorder featuring anxiety that is not proportional to a person's circumstances.

Young children with anxiety disorders are usually less aware that their feelings are unrealistic.

As we transition from DSM-IV-TR to DSM 5, many of these disorders will no longer be clustered as "anxiety disorders," but instead will be in stand-alone categories. Nonetheless, anxiety continues to be an important aspect of the experiences of people with these disorders.

Generalized Anxiety Disorder

Generalized anxiety disorder (GAD) is diagnosed when a person has experienced excessive anxiety and worry for 6 months that is not correlated with particular objects or situations (APA, 2000). In other words, the person experiences a great deal of worry, but the worry is focused on life in general, not upcoming midterms or spiders. GAD is associated with physical complaints, including headache, stomachache, and muscle tension. GAD is often comorbid, or coexisting, with other anxiety disorders, substance abuse, and depression (APA, 2000).

Biological Explanations of GAD To explain psychological disorders like GAD, the biological perspective considers underlying genetics, biochemistry, and structure. Like all anxiety disorders, GAD does show evidence of genetic predisposition (Kendler et al., 1995; Molina et al., 2011). A reasonable place to start looking for correlates of anxiety in brain structure and function is the fear circuit involving the amygdala, which we discussed in our chapters on biological psychology and on motivation and emotion. The amygdala is particularly rich in receptors for GABA, a neurotransmitter that inhibits brain activity. As discussed in our chapter on consciousness, drugs such as alcohol and the benzodiazepine tranquilizers (e.g., Valium) have their main anxiety-reducing effects at these GABA receptors. Not too surprisingly, then, people often self-medicate with alcohol and tranquilizers to reduce their anxiety levels, leaving them vulnerable to substance abuse disorders.

The amygdala forms complex connections with the prefrontal areas of the frontal lobe. As we observed in our discussion of aggression in a previous chapter, the prefrontal cortex coordinates our decisions based on potential dangers identified by the amygdala. For example, if you see a driver's angry face in your rearview mirror, your amygdala will alert the prefrontal cortex about a potential threat or danger, and your prefrontal cortex will use memories of similar past experiences and reasoning to decide to pull over safely to the slower lane to let the angry driver go by. It is possible that this circuit is not responding typically in cases of GAD. Participants with GAD showed greater prefrontal activity in response to angry faces when compared to participants with no anxiety disorders, suggesting that the prefrontal cortex had to work "harder" to control the danger messages, and thus the fear response, sent forward by the amygdalas of people with GAD (Monk et al., 2008).

Cognitive Explanations of GAD Several cognitive models of GAD have been proposed (Beck, 1985). As we discussed in our chapters on development and on cognition, we often organize our thinking about the world into

A circuit connecting the amygdala, which appears to respond to threat, with the prefrontal cortex might not work in a typical way in people with generalized anxiety disorder (GAD). Participants with GAD showed more prefrontal activity than typical participants without any psychological disorders when viewing angry faces. This finding suggests that the prefrontal cortex had to "work harder" to control incoming danger signals from the amygdala (Monk et al., 2008).

generalized anxiety disorder (GAD) A disorder characterized by excessive anxiety and worry that is not correlated with particular objects or situations.

schemas, or systems of belief. If a high-reactive child develops a schema that says "the world is a dangerous place," even very safe experiences begin to look dangerous through this filter. A different cognitive approach suggests that worrying can become a person's coping strategy for anxiety. By examining "what-ifs," the person might believe that he or she is coping, but so many situations are capable of triggering the coping response that the result is nearly constant worry (Wells, 2006). Bill Murray's character in the 1991 film *What About Bob?* expresses this type of worry when he asks his psychiatrist, "What if my bladder explodes?"

Social Explanations of GAD Social perspectives also add to our understanding of GAD. Individuals in lower socioeconomic classes in the United States are about twice as likely to be diagnosed with GAD than people in middle or upper socioeconomic classes (Kessler et al., 2005). Disruptions in social connectivity due to divorce, separation, death of a spouse, or loss of a job are also associated with higher rates of GAD (Wittchen & Hoyer, 2001).

Integrating the Perspectives Pulling these perspectives together into an integrated model, we might predict that GAD is most likely to occur in individuals with a high-reactive temperament, possibly due to their genetic background, who subsequently develop schemas and other cognitive patterns that maintain high levels of worry. When these individuals experience unusual amounts of stress due to socioeconomic factors and disruption of social networks, their risk for developing GAD is likely to be even higher.

Actress Emma Stone needed a stunt double during recent filming because she experienced a panic attack on the set. Stone also told *Glamour* magazine that she was in treatment for "borderline agoraphobia" and couldn't leave her mother's side. Panic and agoraphobia often occur together. Having an occasional panic attack is quite common and does not mean that a person has panic disorder, which is characterized by repeated attacks and fear of future attacks.

Panic Disorder The DSM distinguishes between the experience of a single **panic attack**, characterized by intense fear and autonomic arousal, and **panic disorder**, which features repeated panic attacks and fear of future attacks (APA, 2000). How does panic differ from the anxiety that characterized GAD? Anxiety seems to relate to more distant threats, like final exams from the perspective of the first day of the term. In contrast, panic is associated with nearby, imminent threats (Mobbs et al., 2007).

Having a panic attack does not mean that you should be diagnosed with panic disorder. It is not at all unusual for a person to experience one or two panic attacks in her or his lifetime. One quarter to one third of college students report having had at least one panic attack in the previous year (Asmundson & Norton, 1993; Brown & Cash, 1990). However, panic disorder is much less common, affecting 2.7% of the population in any given year (Kessler et al., 2005). Women are more likely to experience panic attacks and panic disorder than are men. More than half of patients with panic disorder have also been diagnosed with depression or another type of anxiety disorder (Kearney, Albano, Eisen, Allan, & Barlow, 1997). Panic attacks begin to occur in adolescence and young adulthood (Robins & Regier, 1991).

By all reports, panic attacks are extremely unpleasant. Symptoms typically last about 10 minutes. Feelings of intense fear or discomfort are accompanied by both physical and cognitive symptoms. Strong arousal of the sympathetic nervous system leads to the experience of a pounding

panic attack The experience of intense fear and autonomic arousal in the absence of real threat.

panic disorder A disorder characterized by repeated panic attacks and fear of future attacks.

heart, sweating, trembling, shortness of breath, chest pain, nausea, and dizziness or faintness. Not too surprisingly, people experiencing such symptoms may believe they are dying or going crazy. For some individuals, panic attacks may be brought on by identifiable stimuli, such as being swept along in a crowd. For others, the attacks seem to come out of nowhere. In either case, many people experiencing repeated attacks may begin to fear leaving their homes, a condition known as agoraphobia, a type of phobia that we will discuss in a later section.

Biological Explanations of Panic A clue to the biological origin of panic attacks comes from the fact that they can be produced artificially in patients with panic disorder, but not in people who do not have panic disorder, by administering an injection of sodium lactate (Papp et al., 1993; Pitts & McClure, 1967).Researchers have suggested that the sodium lactate interacts with orexins, chemical messengers we discussed in our chapters on consciousness and on motivation and emotion. Orexins, which are released by cells in the hypothalamus, play important roles in wakefulness, vigilance, and appetite. People with panic disorder have larger quantities of orexins than people without the disorder (Johnson et al., 2010). It is possible that disturbances involving the orexins might lead to panic attacks.

Cognitive Explanations of Panic Cognitive theories of panic attacks suggest that the interpretation of body symptoms, such as an increased heart rate, could lead to increasing anxiety and, ultimately, to panic (Bakker, Spinhoven, van Balkom, & van Dyck, 2002; Harvey, Watkins, Mansell, & Shafran, 2004). A person might interpret increased heart rate and rapid breathing as a heart attack instead of the result of having walked briskly from a parking lot. Concern about having a heart attack leads to further physiological arousal, which leads to more anxiety, until a full state of panic is reached. Unfortunately for such theories, panic surprisingly does not increase levels of the stress hormone cortisol, which suggests that there is more to a panic attack than just responding to the stress of thinking you are ill (Hollander et al., 1989).

Social Explanations of Panic Social influences can be seen in the symptoms related by patients with panic disorder. Many patients worry about appearing "weird" or "crazy" to other people, which can lead to increased anxiety and more panic attacks (Hicks et al., 2005). Culture appears to play an important role in how panic attacks are interpreted. Although the underlying physical characteristics remain similar from country to country, interesting variations have been observed. For example, dizziness is an important aspect of panic attacks in China, constipation and shortness of breath are common complaints in Rwanda, and gastrointestinal symptoms signal panic for patients in Thailand (Hinton & Good, 2009). Social factors also influence the development of panic disorder. Panic disorder is more common in children who have experienced parental loss or separation and in adults who have recently experienced significant, stressful life events (Klauke, Deckert, Reif, Pauli, & Domschke, 2010).

> I can do comedy, so people want me to do that, but the other side of comedy is depression . . . to be funny you have to have that other side.
> —Parker Posey

Integrating the Perspectives A combination of the factors just discussed is likely to provide the best explanation for the development and experience of panic disorder. A panic attack could occur as a result of a chain of events: (1) A person with a biological predisposition to panic, possibly involving the orexin systems of the brain, is also (2) exposed to social stressors in the form of parental loss or separation or significant life stressors, and then (3) interprets physical symptoms of arousal as threatening or embarrassing, and finally (4) has cognitions leading to panic that are modulated by his or her cultural expectations.

Phobias

Phobias are diagnosed when a person experiences unrealistic fear. Unlike cases of generalized anxiety disorder discussed previously, people with phobias know exactly what object or situation triggers their fear and anxiety. Avoidance of the fear stimulus is a typical method of coping. This avoidance is often quite inconvenient. A person who is afraid of heights and elevators might book a vacation hotel reservation years in advance, simply to ensure that a room on the second floor will be available.

Phobias are divided into three categories in the DSM-IV-TR: agoraphobia, social phobia, and specific phobia (APA, 2000). However, proposals for DSM 5 list agoraphobia and social phobia (relabeled as social anxiety disorder) as separate disorders (APA, 2011a).

Agoraphobia is the fear of open spaces and is named after the ancient Greek *agora,* or marketplace. As we mentioned previously, agoraphobia is a common outcome of panic disorder. When a person becomes afraid of the embarrassment of having panic attacks in public, he or she might opt to simply stay at home. Fear can occur in a number of different situations, including being outside the home alone, while using public transportation, being in open spaces such as parking lots, being in shops, or standing in line or in a crowd. Agoraphobia often prevents working or engaging in normal social activities (Kessler et al., 2005).

Social phobia (renamed social anxiety disorder in DSM 5) is the fear of being scrutinized and criticized by others, particularly during public speaking and when meeting new people. Many of us are a little uneasy in these situations, but for people with social phobia, the fear and anxiety caused by these situations are out of proportion for the particular situation. In other words, the person with social phobia feels crippling anxiety while doing things that most people take in stride, like introducing yourself to others at a party. In most cases, social phobia begins during adolescence. As we discussed in our chapter on development, adolescents often experience a "spotlight effect," or belief that others are scrutinizing them. For an anxious teen, this spotlight effect might be exaggerated, leading to social phobia.

Cultural variables appear to be particularly significant in the development of social anxiety. Social anxiety is more prevalent in collectivistic cultures, with their emphasis on shame and the opinions of other people,

© Ivan Franco/EPA/Newscom

Hamburg striker Paolo Guerrero has an extreme fear of flying, and like many people with phobias, his first response is to avoid the fear stimulus. He had to board a plane five times before he could manage to stay on. For an international athlete, this could be a very inconvenient phobia. Guerrero is receiving treatment and is reported to be making good progress.

phobia Unrealistic fear of an object or situation.

agoraphobia Unrealistic fear of open spaces, being outside the home alone, or being in a crowd.

social phobia/social anxiety A disorder characterized by an unrealistic fear of being scrutinized and criticized by others.

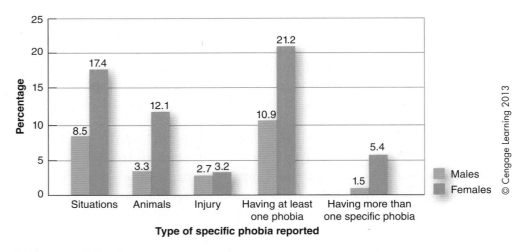

Morita Masatake (1874–1938) founded the Morita Therapy for the treatment of anxiety disorders, including the culture-bound syndrome taijin kyofusho, which affects 10 to 20% of the Japanese population. This condition, recognized in the DSM, is characterized by fear of offending others, by blushing or having an offensive appearance or body odor. Morita recommended treating anxiety by accepting your feelings, knowing your purpose, and doing what needs doing. His therapy continues to be used today.

In Japan, some people experience taijin kyofusho, *which is a fear of offending or embarrassing other people with their odor, eye contact, or appearance (Tarumi, Ichimiya, Yamada, Umesue, & Kuroki, 2004). This condition is significantly different from the emphasis on a person's own embarrassment that is typical in social anxiety as experienced in Western cultures.*

specific phobia Fears of objects other than those associated with agoraphobia or social phobia/social anxiety.

than in individualistic cultures. Asian American college students were more likely than White American students to report negative emotions in social situations (Lee, Okazaki, & Yoo, 2006).

Specific phobias are fears of objects or situations other than those associated with agoraphobia and social phobia (see ● Figure 14.4). These fear stimuli may be animals, natural phenomena (water or earthquakes), blood and injury, or situations (flying, heights, bridges, and so on). Note that people do not ordinarily form phobias for harmless objects such as coffee cups and keys (Mineka, Sutton, Craske, Hermans, & Vansteenwegen, 2006).

The evolutionary perspective suggests that phobias might be exaggerations of an otherwise useful sense of caution. The items that become fear stimuli do have some realistic potential for harm, such as snakes, spiders, and the sight of blood. As we noted in our chapter on learning, the connections formed in phobias can arise from classical conditioning. A stimulus (conditioned stimulus, or CS) becomes associated with a negative experience (unconditioned stimulus, or UCS) that results in fear (unconditioned response, or UCR), giving the CS the ability to elicit fear (conditioned response, or CR). We might be biologically prepared to form connections between certain stimuli and feelings of fear (Seligman, 1971). Learning can also influence the development of phobias through imitation and observation, as when a child sees a parent scream when a spider walks across the room.

Cognitions influence phobias. In spite of the fact that a spider in your house or garden is simply minding its own business while doing spider things, people with spider phobias tend to believe that the spider is

FIGURE 14.4

Prevalence of Different Types of Specific Phobias. In a large random sample of adults, 21.2% of women and 10.9% of men reported having at least one phobia, as defined by the DSM. Gender differences were seen in the prevalence of situational phobias (lightning, enclosed spaces, darkness, flying, and heights) and animal phobias (primarily spiders and snakes). However, no gender differences occurred in injury phobias (injections, dentists, injuries). More than one type of specific phobia was reported by 5.4% of the women and 1.5% of the men. *Source: Adapted from Fredrikson, Annas, Fischer, and Wik (1996).*

intending to attack them or move toward them (Riskind, Moore, & Bowley, 1995). People who have height phobias misjudge real physical heights, believing that they are higher up than they really are (Stefanucci & Proffitt, 2009).

Some people with obsessive-compulsive disorder must arrange their possessions in particular ways, or they will experience overwhelming anxiety.

Obsessive-Compulsive Disorder (OCD)	

Obsessive-compulsive disorder (OCD) is one of the more dramatic disorders and will have its own category outside the anxiety disorder category in DSM 5. Individuals with this disorder are haunted by distressing, intrusive thoughts (**obsessions**) and/or the need to engage in repetitive, ritualistic behaviors (**compulsions**). About 1% of the U.S. population reports experiencing OCD each year (Kessler et al., 2005).

Obsessions are distinct from everyday worries, which usually focus on real-life problems. Common obsessions include concerns about contamination (catching diseases from shaking hands), repeated doubts (wondering if you have hurt somebody), ordering (needing things arranged in a particular order or configuration), inappropriate impulses (hurting somebody else or shouting obscenities at a funeral), and sexual imagery (APA, 2000).

Compulsions appear to be efforts to ward off the anxiety produced by obsessions or some other feared event. For example, people troubled by obsessions about contamination may engage in compulsive hand washing hundreds of times per day. Other common compulsions include checking (for locked windows, faucets turned off), counting, ordering objects, and requesting or demanding assurances. Although obsessions and compulsions may have some logical connection, such as fear of germs and hand washing, this is not always the case. As you may have seen on television reality shows that exploit these cases, some people compulsively hoard things and are unable to discard junk, which can result in living quarters featuring narrow paths through tall piles of papers and other possessions.

The childhood rhyme "don't step on a crack or you'll break your mother's back" captures the ineffectiveness of obsessive-compulsive thinking.

Biological Explanations of OCD The biological perspective has made important contributions to our understanding of the causes of OCD. Twin studies suggest a strong genetic vulnerability for the disorder, with concordance rates between identical twins of 63 to 87% (Menzies et al., 2008). A concordance rate is a measure of agreement. If one identical twin is diagnosed with a disorder, the concordance rate provides the likelihood the other twin will also be diagnosed with the disorder. It is probable that significant interactions between this genetic vulnerability and the environment can occur. Symptoms of OCD may arise following head trauma, the brain inflammation caused by encephalitis, and seizure disorder (Grisham, Anderson, & Sachdev, 2008). Young children who experienced birth complications or streptococcal infections (e.g., strep throat) may be more likely to develop the disorder later in life (Swedo et al., 1997).

Imaging studies provide insight into the patterns of brain activity that accompany obsessions and compulsions (see ● Figure 14.5). Several

obsessive-compulsive disorder (OCD) A disorder associated with intrusive obsessions and compulsions.

obsession An intrusive, distressing thought.

compulsion Repetitive, ritualistic behavior associated with high anxiety.

© Randal Pfizenmaier/Alamy

FIGURE 14.5

OCD and the Orbitofrontal Cortex. When compared to healthy control participants, patients with OCD have greater gray matter density in the areas shown in red. When patients with OCD experience symptoms, the areas in yellow become especially active. Areas of the orbitofrontal cortex, shown in orange, are anatomically different from healthy controls and are activated during OCD symptoms, suggesting an important role for the orbitofrontal cortex in OCD. *Source:* Adapted from Rotge, J.-Y., et al. (2010). Anatomical alterations and symptom-related functional activity in obsessive-compulsive disorder are correlated in the lateral orbitofrontal cortex. *Biological Psychiatry, 67*(7), e37–e38. Copyright © 2010 Elsevier.

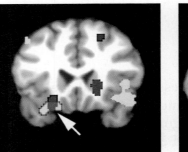
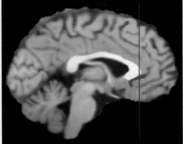

Orbitofrontal cortex

structures, including the orbitofrontal cortex, prefrontal cortex, the anterior cingulate gyrus, and the caudate nucleus of the basal ganglia, appear to be more active than usual in patients with OCD (Saxena, 2003; Szeszko et al., 2004). Individuals with OCD appear to have lower than normal amounts of serotonin activity, and individuals with the lowest levels of serotonin activity experience the most severe obsessions and compulsions (Piacentini & Graae, 1997).

The evolutionary perspective suggests that OCD might have its roots in normal grooming and territoriality behaviors that somehow become overly exaggerated in some cases (Rapoport, 1989). Human beings who anticipated threats like disease from dirty hands or threats from the perimeters of their territories probably benefited from proactive strategies like hand washing and checking (Brune, 2006). Disordered behavior similar to OCD does occur elsewhere in the animal kingdom. Dogs may lick and chew their front paws to the point of causing extensive tissue damage, which can be prevented by giving the dogs the same medications used to treat humans with OCD (Seksel & Lindeman, 2001).

Learning Explanations for OCD Learning explanations of OCD focus on the rewarding aspects of compulsions. As we pointed out in our discussion of operant conditioning, any behavior that produces a positive outcome (reducing anxiety associated with an obsession) is likely to be repeated in the future. For example, if hand washing reduced anxiety about germs and disease, hand washing might become progressively more frequent, to the point where it would be considered abnormal. The DSM specifies that engaging in compulsive behavior for more than one hour per day is considered abnormal (APA, 2000).

Social Explanations for OCD Culture plays a role in how frequently OCD occurs and what obsessions and compulsions are more likely. Anthropologists have identified interesting parallels between cultural rituals and OCD. For example, many normal cultural rituals involve elements similar to OCD, including washing, special colors, stereotyped actions, and rigid

694   Chapter 14 | THE TROUBLED MIND: PSYCHOLOGICAL DISORDERS

rules (Dulaney & Fiske, 1994). Like the evolutionary perspective, this cultural view suggests that OCD might represent an exaggerated version of normal behaviors.

Post-traumatic Stress Disorder (PTSD)

Post-traumatic stress disorder (PTSD) is the current term used to describe a condition formerly known as "shell shock" or "battle fatigue." PTSD is unique among disorders listed in the DSM, as it is the only one with a specified cause: To be diagnosed with PTSD, you must have experienced trauma (APA, 2000). Although combat, especially hand-to-hand combat, is still recognized as one of the most likely experiences leading to PTSD, we now understand that other types of trauma may produce the same results (Insel, 2007). PTSD may follow automobile accidents, assaults, abuse, and the experience of natural disasters.

© REUTERS/Asahi Shimbun

Although combat remains the most frequent cause of post-traumatic stress disorder (PTSD), people who experience natural disasters, like the 2011 Japanese earthquake and tsunami, are also at risk for the disorder.

PTSD symptoms include hypervigilance; avoidance of stimuli associated with the trauma; emotional numbing; and repetitive, intrusive thoughts, flashbacks, and dreams about the traumatic event. Obviously, the last thing a person in this situation wants to do is to "relive" the traumatic event, so these symptoms can be very upsetting. Children with PTSD tend to reenact the traumatic event in their play (Cohen, Chazan, Lerner, & Maimon, 2010). In other words, they may play "terrorist attack," "car crash," or "tsunami," possibly in an effort to reduce their fear. This reenactment play can have either positive or negative effects on the child (Cohen et al., 2010). Children whose play included a reworking of the traumatic event (revenge or a happy ending) were less disturbed than children whose play was repetitive without any resolution.

PTSD affects between 3 and 4% of the adult population in the United States every year (Kessler et al., 2007). After large-scale traumatic events, health workers typically expect about 10% of the population to develop PTSD (Kessler, Sonnega, Bromet, Hughes, & Nelson, 1996). For example, more than 12% of lower Manhattan residents developed PTSD following the terrorist attacks of 9/11 (DiGrande et al., 2008). Children appear to be more vulnerable than adults, with 25% developing PTSD following automobile accidents in which they were injured, compared to 15% of their parents (de Vries et al., 1999). Between 8.5 and 14% of combat soldiers serving in Iraq and Afghanistan experienced severe impairment due to symptoms of PTSD after returning home, and up to 31% experienced some impairment (Thomas et al., 2010).

Biological Explanations for PTSD Biological explanations for PTSD focus on the hippocampus, a structure we have discussed previously in the context of the biology of memory formation. Brain imaging studies consistently show that PTSD is correlated with smaller hippocampal volume (Bossini et al., 2008; Bremner et al., 1995). This leaves us with two competing hypotheses: Are people with a naturally smaller hippocampus more vulnerable to PTSD? Or is there something about the experience of trauma that is toxic to the hippocampus? Both hypotheses seem reasonable. As we

post-traumatic stress disorder (PTSD) A disorder caused by the experience of trauma, which leads to flashbacks, dreams, hypervigilance, and avoidance of stimuli associated with the traumatic event.

observed in our chapter on motivation and emotion, stress increases the release of cortisol, which in turn may have toxic effects on the hippocampus (Sapolsky, Krey, & McEwen, 1985). Identical twins with combat-related PTSD had about the same hippocampal volume as their twin brothers who had not experienced combat, but had smaller hippocampal volume than veterans without PTSD (see ● Figure 14.6). This outcome suggests that having a small hippocampus might represent a preexisting vulnerability to developing PTSD if the person is exposed to trauma (Gilbertson et al., 2002). However, it remains likely that some structural features produce greater vulnerability to PTSD at the same time PTSD produces structural changes (Robinson & Shergill, 2011).

PTSD is correlated with lower levels of naturally occurring benzodiazepine activity in the frontal cortex (Bremner et al., 2002; Geuze et al., 2008). Extra benzodiazepines can be administered in the form of major tranquilizers, such as Valium, which produce relaxation and lack of anxiety. If naturally occurring benzodiazepine activity was low, anxiety would be the logical result. Lower levels of natural benzodiazepine activity might also explain the unfortunate tendency for people to self-medicate for PTSD with alcohol (Jakupcak et al., 2010). Alcohol reduces anxiety using biological mechanisms similar to those of the benzodiazepines.

Learning Explanations for PTSD Learning, and classical conditioning in particular, contributes to the symptoms of PTSD. Individuals with PTSD show conditioned responses to stimuli associated with the traumatic event. Combat veterans with PTSD seem particularly sensitive to smells, such as burning rubber and diesel (Rothbaum, Rizzo, & Difede, 2010). Needless to say, most people actively avoid any stimuli that remind them of the traumatic event.

FIGURE 14.6

Hippocampal Volume and Vulnerability to PTSD. In a study of identical twins in which one member of each twin pair experienced combat, the severity of PTSD symptoms was negatively correlated with hippocampal volume. The hippocampal volume of the twins who were not exposed to combat was similar to that of their brothers, indicating that hippocampal volume could be a preexisting vulnerability for the development of PTSD. *Source:* Adapted from Gilbertson et al. (2002).

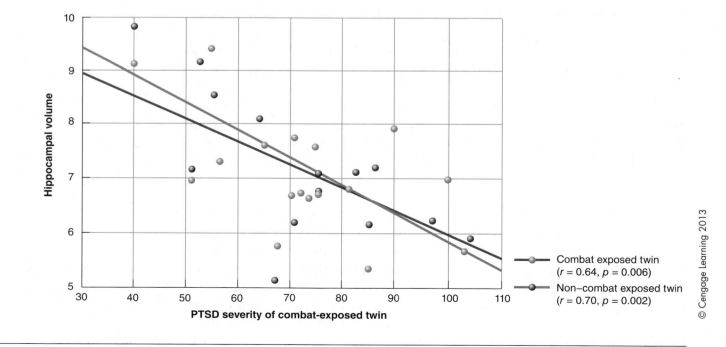

© Cengage Learning 2013

Social and Cultural Explanations for PTSD Social and cultural factors play significant roles in the development of PTSD. People reporting low social support in the six months prior to 9/11 were twice as likely to be diagnosed with PTSD as people who reported strong social support during this period (Galea et al., 2002). Cultural factors also influence the likelihood of PTSD. Following 9/11, PTSD was more common in New York City residents of some ethnicities than others, affecting 13.4% of Hispanics, 9.3% of Black Americans, 6.5% of White Americans, and 3.2% of Asian Americans (Galea et al., 2002).

Summary 14.1

Major Types of Anxiety Disorders

Disorder	Symptoms	Possible causal factors under investigation
Generalized anxiety disorder © wavebreakmedia ltd/Shutterstock	Excessive anxiety for 6 months that is not correlated with objects or situations	• Genetic predisposition • Stress • Fearful schemas • Low socioeconomic status • Disruptions in social connectivity
Panic disorder © Russ Einhorn/Splash News/Newscom	Repeated panic attacks accompanied by excessive worry about having panic attacks	• Possible abnormality in orexin function • Cognitions regarding symptoms • Expectations and embarrassment • Cultural influences
Phobia © Ivan Franco/EPA/Newscom	Excessive fear of an object or situation	• Exaggeration of normal caution • Classical conditioning • Cognitions about fear stimulus • Collectivist cultures emphasizing shame
Obsessive-compulsive disorder © Randal Pfizenmaier/Alamy	Intrusive, repetitious, and anxiety-producing thoughts and behaviors	• Genetic predisposition • Low serotonin activity • Prefrontal and basal ganglia activity • Extension of grooming and territorial behaviors • Rewarding aspects of compulsions • Extension of cultural rituals
Post-traumatic stress disorder © REUTERS/Asahi Shimbun	Exposure to traumatic event, following by flashbacks, hypervigilance, nightmares	• Hippocampus and prefrontal cortex • Benzodiazepine receptors • Classical conditioning • Social support

What Are Mood Disorders?

Mood disorders, also known as affective disorders, fall into two major categories: **major depressive disorder** and **bipolar disorder**. Major depressive disorder is characterized by lengthy, uninterrupted periods of depressed mood and loss of pleasure in normal activities. Because mood is disordered in only one direction, major depressive disorder is also referred to as unipolar disorder. In bipolar disorder, mood is disordered in two directions. Periods of depression alternate with periods of **mania**, in which the person experiences unrealistically elevated moods. Although both types of disorder include depression, these are unique disorders with separate causes and treatments. These mood disorders feature numerous subtypes in the DSM, primarily reflecting differences in the timing and severity of symptoms, but we will restrict our description to a summary of their major features.

Major Depressive Disorder

Although most of us experience the occasional "blues," these feelings are usually not as severe or chronic as the depressed feelings that characterize a mood disorder. According to the DSM, major depressive disorder is characterized by depressed mood most of the day, nearly every day, for a period of at least two weeks. Patients with depression complain about feeling sad and empty, and periods of tearfulness are common. The DSM also notes that depression can produce anhedonia, or loss of pleasure. You are probably already familiar with the term *hedonist*, which refers to a person who is a pleasure seeker. Anhedonia refers to a person's *dis*interest in activities that previously provided pleasure, such as sex, eating, or social activities.

To be diagnosed with major depressive disorder, a person must show at least five symptoms, one of which must be either depressed mood or anhedonia. The remaining symptoms can be divided into physical and cognitive groups. The physical symptoms of major depressive disorder are related to disturbances in autonomic function typically found in the presence of high levels of stress, described in our later chapter on stress and coping. Appetite and sleep may be disturbed. Some patients experience a loss of appetite whereas others begin to eat too much. As we observed in our chapter on consciousness, many patients with depression experience frequent wakefulness whereas others experience oversleeping (more than nine hours per night). Fatigue or restlessness may occur. Among the cognitive symptoms of depression are difficulty concentrating, feelings of hopelessness and worthlessness, and, in some cases, thoughts of suicide (APA, 2000, 2011a).

Prevalence of Major Depressive Disorder Major depressive disorder is one of the most frequently diagnosed psychological disorders. Although reported prevalence rates vary widely, typical estimates suggest that as many as 5% of men and 13% of women may experience depression during their lifetimes (Hasin, Goodwin, Stinson, & Grant, 2005). Depression decreases with age, with people over 50 being about half as likely as people between the ages of 18 and 25 years to be diagnosed with depression.

major depressive disorder (unipolar disorder) A disorder characterized by lengthy periods of depressed mood, loss of pleasure in normal activities, disturbances in sleep and appetite, difficulty concentrating, feelings of hopelessness, and possible thoughts of suicide.

bipolar disorder A mood disorder characterized by alternating periods of mania and depression.

mania A period of unrealistically elevated mood.

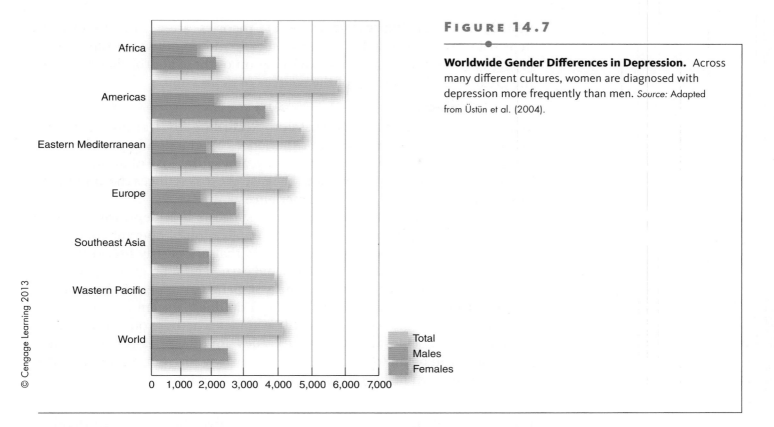

FIGURE 14.7

Worldwide Gender Differences in Depression. Across many different cultures, women are diagnosed with depression more frequently than men. *Source:* Adapted from Üstün et al. (2004).

© Cengage Learning 2013

Women experience depression more frequently than men do. This discrepancy between rates of depression in men and women has been observed to be independent of race, ethnicity, social class, and country of residence (Strickland, 1992; Üstün, Ayuso-Mateos, Chatterji, Mathers, & Murray, 2004) (see ● Figure 14.7). It is possible that female hormones may participate in mood through some currently unknown mechanism. Mood disturbances can be associated with hormonal changes in women, including postpartum depression and mood changes accompanying menopause (Rapkin, Mikacich, Moatakef-Imani, & Rasgon, 2002). However, it is also possible that women are more likely than men to admit feeling depressed to others and to seek help with depression. Men may mask or cover their depressed mood by engaging in activities such as drinking alcohol.

The equal rates of depression among Amish men and women in Pennsylvania provide interesting insights into the role of gender in this disorder (Egeland & Hostetter, 1983). Amish men do not drink, so it is unlikely that masked depression affects their depression rates. Amish women, like men, are expected to work outside the home, making the "sick" role difficult to maintain and possibly keeping their rates of reported depression low. These results support the idea that gender differences in depression may be less biological and more likely due to situational factors such as alcohol use and employment outside the home.

In the general population of the United States, women make up about two thirds of all cases of major depressive disorder. In contrast, rates of depression among the Amish are equal for men and women. Psychologists have suggested that because Amish men do not drink alcohol, their depression would not be masked. The workloads of Amish women might keep their rates of reported depression lower than in the general population.

© Images-USA/Alamy

Causes of Major Depressive Disorder Theories attempting to explain depression range from the learning, social, and cognitive to the strictly biological. It is likely that some combination of these approaches provides the greatest understanding of the sources of depression.

Learning Explanations of Depression According to learning theories, depression occurs when a person experiences a reduction in positive reinforcement or an increase in negative outcomes. The loss of an important relationship can lead to depression, because the loss reduces the amount of positive reinforcement a person experiences.

A variation of the learning approach suggests that depression results from **learned helplessness**, which is an application of operant conditioning. Instead of experiencing consequences that are clearly linked to your previous behavior (I studied very hard and earned an A on my test), learned helplessness occurs when consequences of behavior appear to be random or uncontrolled (the amount of studying I do doesn't seem to make a difference in my test grades). If you get low grades whether you study hard or not, you might begin to believe that grades are outcomes that cannot be controlled. You begin to feel helpless in preparing for your exams, and this belief in your own helplessness can lead to depression.

Cognitive Explanations of Depression Cognitive theories frame depression as the result of a combination of negative thoughts about the self, the world, and the future (Beck, 1975). For example, students failing an exam might respond by doubting their academic abilities (self), assuming that they will fail the course (future), and deciding they hate the class anyway (world). The resulting dysfunctional beliefs would result in depression. Beck's view of the development of depression led directly to the use of cognitive therapies for depression, which we discuss in our next chapter.

Another cognitive process that contributes to the development and maintenance of depressed mood is rumination (Nolen-Hoeksema, 2003). Susan Nolen-Hoeksema describes rumination in depression as "repetitively focusing on the fact that one is depressed; on one's symptoms of depression; and on the causes, meanings, and consequences of symptoms of depression" (Nolen-Hoeksema, 1991, p. 569). Rumination can arise from attempts to gain insight into one's problems, but too much rumination actually interferes with problem solving (Watkins & Brown, 2002). When rumination is encouraged by asking participants to focus on their moods, they find it difficult to solve several different types of problems (see ● Figure 14.8). When participants are distracted from this inward focus by thinking about neutral topics (such as "think about the Statue of Liberty"), their problem-solving abilities improve immediately. Typically, rumination is correlated with negative outcomes, including delaying recovery from depression during treatment (Siegle, Sagratti, & Crawford, 1999), predicting depression following the death of a loved one (Nolen-Hoeksema & Girgus, 1994), and increasing a person's likelihood to abuse alcohol (Nolen-Hoeksema, 2003).

Insanity: doing the same thing over and over again and expecting different results.
—Albert Einstein

learned helplessness A state in which experiencing random or uncontrolled consequences leads to feelings of helplessness and possibly depression.

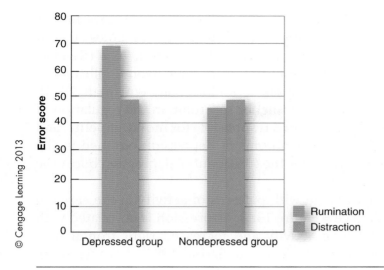

© Cengage Learning 2013

FIGURE 14.8

Rumination and Problem-Solving. Rumination and distraction were induced in depressed and nondepressed participants, who then completed a problem-solving task. To induce rumination, participants were instructed to think about "what your feelings mean." To induce distraction, participants were asked to think about "the shape of a large black umbrella." Subsequently, all participants were asked to complete a problem-solving task. More errors occurred in the depressed ruminating group than in the other groups. These results suggest that rumination competes with other cognitive processes, possibly contributing to the problems with concentration experienced by people with depression. *Source: Adapted from Watkins and Brown (2002).*

Depression might be influenced by the types of attributions a person makes (Abramson, Seligman, & Teasdale, 1978). As we mentioned in our chapter on social psychology, an attribution is a belief about causality. Attributions can vary along several dimensions (internal–external, stable–unstable, global–specific), and making some types of attributions might predispose a person to depression. The internal–external dimension, which is similar to the locus of control discussed in our personality chapter, represents beliefs that outcomes are due to personal effort or due to luck or chance. The stable–unstable dimension captures beliefs about whether circumstances can change. People make global attributions (I'm stupid) or more specific attributions (I'm not great in algebra, but I'm very good at geometry). Overall, people who make internal, stable, and global attributions (what happens to me is my fault, circumstances never change, and I'm always this way) are more prone to depression. People with this attributional style earn lower grades in college, perform more poorly as sales representatives, and experience worse health (Seligman, 1987).

Rates of both depression and rumination drop in middle adulthood. Young adults often find it frustrating when they are trying to ruminate about problems with their parents, only to have their parents immediately shift into problem-solving mode. The young adult might not feel "ready" to fix the problem yet.

Social Explanations of Depression Depression reflects feeling generally sad, whereas loneliness is a more social process that reflects feeling badly about the state of one's relationships with others. The two states are related, yet can occur independently. In older adults, loneliness increased depressive symptoms, but depression itself did not increase loneliness (Cacioppo, Hawkley, & Thisted, 2010). Social and evolutionary theories of depression and loneliness suggest that these states might actually promote an individual's survival by promoting better relationships with others (Allen & Badcock, 2003; Cacioppo et al., 2006). Expressions of depression, such as sad facial expressions and crying, can serve as a safe call to others for connection and comforting responses in what the person may feel is a threatening social context. The response of others to these signals may foster the repair of frayed or broken social connections (Allen & Badcock, 2003; Cacioppo et al., 2006). Even when others do not respond, the symptoms of depression may protect people from additional negative interactions by reducing their social activities.

Biological Explanations of Depression The biological perspective identifies a number of factors contributing to depression. Twin studies suggest that the heritability of major depressive disorder is about 33% (Kendler et al., 1995; Wurtman, 2005). A number of genes have been implicated in depression, including genes affecting serotonin function (Wurtman, 2005). A large body of research points to a role for serotonin in the regulation of mood. Serotonin's role in brain systems responsible for mood, appetite, and sleep corresponds closely to the symptoms of depression outlined in the DSM. Most effective medications for the treatment of depression boost the activity of serotonin at the synapse.

Depressed mood is correlated with patterns of activity in the cerebral hemispheres of the brain (see ● Figure 14.9). Depression is correlated with both reduced left frontal lobe activity and increased right frontal lobe activity (Hecht, 2010; Schaffer, Davidson, & Saron, 1983). Because these data are correlational, we cannot make a judgment regarding cause and effect. People who have a tendency to show a particular pattern of brain activity, possibly due to genetic factors, may be more vulnerable to depression. On the other hand, it is equally logical to propose that the experience of depression may produce different patterns of brain activity.

Depression might be part of a larger disturbance in daily, or circadian, rhythms (Soria et al., 2010). The DSM criteria for depression include sleeping either less than or more than normal (7 to 9 hours per night; APA, 2000, 2011a). People who are depressed spend too much time in rapid eye movement (REM) sleep, and most medications that are used to treat

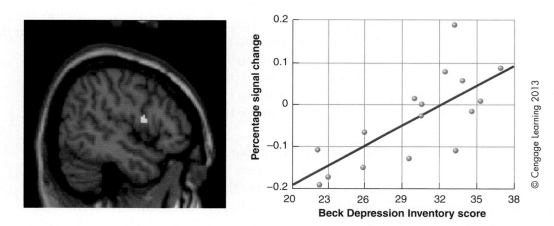

FIGURE 14.9

Right Hemisphere Activity and Depression. Imaging studies typically show unusually high levels of activity in the right prefrontal cortex of patients with depression, particularly in the area shown in yellow (the dorsolateral prefrontal cortex). In this experiment, the amount of activity observed in this area during an emotional picture judging task was positively correlated with the patients' scores on the Beck Depression Inventory, a standard questionnaire used to assess severity of depressive symptoms. In other words, the more severe the person's symptoms of depression, the more extreme right hemisphere activity he or she displayed. *Source:* Adapted from Grimm, S., et al. (2008). Imbalance between left and right dorsolateral prefrontal cortex in major depression is linked to negative emotional judgment: An fMRI study in severe major depressive disorder. *Biological Psychiatry, 63*(4), 369–376. Copyright © 2008 Elsevier.

depression reduce REM sleep (Rijnbeek, de Visser, Franson, Cohen, & van Gerven, 2003).

Stress and Depression The experience of severe stress, whether arising from the death of a loved one, illness, or frustration of major life goals, frequently occurs immediately before the onset of a depressive episode (Brown & Harris, 1989; Mazure, 1998). However, the majority of people exposed to such stressors do not respond by becoming depressed, reinforcing the complexity of the development of this disorder. The physical and cognitive responses to high levels of stress, such as difficulty sleeping or concentrating, are quite similar to the symptoms of depression. Depression provides an example of a **diathesis-stress model**, which suggests that biological vulnerabilities for a disorder interact with a person's experience with stress (Zubin & Spring, 1977).

Integration of Perspectives The picture emerging from this discussion of causal factors in depression is complex. It is likely that underlying biological predispositions interact with cognitive patterns and life events to produce the disorder. For example, the serotonin transporter gene, which we have discussed previously in the contexts of personality and responses to bullying, does little by itself to help us predict a person's risk for depression. However, among people experiencing significant stress, those with one or two copies of the short version of the gene were much more likely than those with two copies of the long version to develop depression (Caspi et al., 2003).

A biological bridge between the experience of stress, circadian rhythms, and the development of depression is formed by hormones released at times of stress, including cortisol. Cortisol levels follow circadian patterns, with the greatest cortisol release in the early morning followed by a gradual drop throughout the day and evening. However, cortisol is also released at times of stress and helps prepare the body for "fight or flight." Feedback loops involving the hippocampus usually prevent too great a release of cortisol. It is possible that in cases of depression, this feedback loop is not working correctly, and cortisol levels remain high (Stokes, 1995). The body simply cannot maintain high levels of arousal indefinitely, and depression may result.

Bipolar Disorder In bipolar disorder, periods of depression alternate with periods of mania. The DSM does not differentiate between the symptoms of depression that occur in major depressive, or unipolar, disorder and in bipolar disorder. What makes bipolar different from major depressive disorder is the addition of a manic phase.

A manic phase is characterized by abnormally elevated mood, accompanied by a number of additional symptoms (APA, 2000, 2011a). Patients may

Illustration: © Cengage Learning 2013; photo: © vita khorzhevska/Shutterstock

In bipolar disorder, periods of mania alternate with periods of depression.

diathesis-stress model A model that suggests that the experience of stress interacts with an individual's biological predisposition to produce a psychological disorder.

demonstrate grandiosity, in which they feel unrealistically special or important. The person's behavior, characterized by little need for sleep, rapid speech, difficulty concentrating, and rapidly shifting ideas, seems to be running at an abnormally high speed. Unlike many other disorders, however, mania actually increases productive, goal-directed behavior. However, due to the person's tendency to meet the DSM criterion for "excessive involvement in pleasurable activities that have a high potential for painful consequences," hospitalization is often necessary for the patient's

Connecting *to* Research

Recognition of Facial Expression by People With Depression

How does the world look to a person who is depressed? Does the experience of depression affect a person's attention to negative stimuli? As we mentioned in our chapter on motivation and emotion, positive and negative emotions often serve as guides to approach and avoidance behaviors (Davidson & Irwin, 1999). Because it is usually more important to survival that we avoid predators and other dangers than it is to miss approaching something positive such as a tasty food, we have a bias toward noticing the negative. If we're experiencing ongoing negative mood, does that have an effect on our sensitivities to positive and negative stimuli?

Among the important types of positive and negative stimuli we need to process are facial expressions, as these are our clues to successfully navigating the social environment. Few of us would miss dramatic facial expressions, but the subtle ones

require more attention (Gollan, McCloskey, Hoxha, & Coccaro, 2010).

The Question: *How do people with depression compare to control participants in their ability to detect subtle facial expressions of emotion?*

METHODS
Eighty-eight participants, half of whom had been diagnosed with major depressive disorder but were not treated with medication, observed photographs of facial expressions on a computer screen. The photographs depicted four basic emotions: happiness, surprise, sadness, and "harsh" (a category that combined photos showing disgust, fear, and anger). The photos were morphed to present a range of intensity from mostly neutral to very intense (see ● Figure 14.10). Two hundred photos were presented for only one-half second each. The participants pushed one of six

keys to identify the emotion being expressed.

RESULTS
The participants with depression were more sensitive to sad faces than the control participants, especially when the emotion was expressed at a lower intensity. The groups were equally accurate in identifying the positive emotions (happiness, surprise) and the harsh emotions (fear, anger, and disgust). The severity of the participants' depression was positively correlated with their accuracy in recognizing sad faces, but not with their accuracy in recognizing other emotional expressions.

CONCLUSIONS
The participants with depression were not only more sensitive to very subtle expressions of sadness than the healthy control participants but also more likely to misidentify other emotional facial expressions as sad.

protection (APA, 2000, p. 357). Classic cases of bipolar disorder combine a one-week period of mania with two weeks of depression. However, many variations occur in the timing and severity of these phases. Children and youth with bipolar disorder tend to experience more rapid cycling, with several mood swings occurring within the same day or even overlapping (Geller et al., 1995).

Bipolar disorder occurs far less frequently than major depressive disorder (between 0.4 and 1.2% of the population as opposed to 5 to 13% for major depressive disorder; Lewinsohn, Klein, & Seeley, 1995). The two mood disorders also differ in their relationships to gender. Unlike major depressive disorder, which affects more women than men, bipolar disorder is found in approximately equal numbers of men and women The median age of onset for bipolar disorder is between 19 and 23 years of age, and the number of youth diagnosed with bipolar has risen dramatically in the last 20 years (Moreno et al., 2007) (see ● Figure 14.11).

In contrast, they were equally likely as control participants to misidentify happy, surprised, or harsh facial expressions. These findings indicate that people with depression not only are more likely to be attending to more sad stimuli but also might misinterpret neutral stimuli as sad. These tendencies might add to the challenges faced by the person with depression in the social environment. ✪

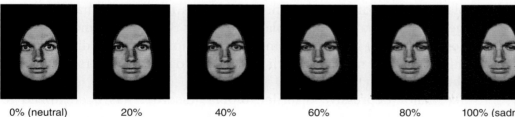

0% (neutral)   20%   40%   60%   80%   100% (sadness)

Emil F. Coccaro, M.D. at the University of Chicago

FIGURE 14.10

Heightened Sensitivity to Sad Expressions in Depression. Participants see one photo for only one-half second and must determine which of six emotions (happiness, surprise, sadness, disgust, fear, or anger) is being displayed. Morphed images are made by combining neutral (0%) and high (100%) intensity images. Each emotion is easier to identify as its intensity increases. Participants with depression needed to see the same amount of intensity as healthy control participants before correctly identifying happy, surprised, or "harsh" facial expressions, but needed to see less intensity than control participants before correctly identifying sad faces. This heightened sensitivity to the sad moods of others might reinforce the negative feelings of the person with depression.
Source: Adapted from Gollan et al. (2010).

© Cengage Learning 2013

Mean accuracy / Intensity of sad expression

Depressed
Control

FIGURE 14.11

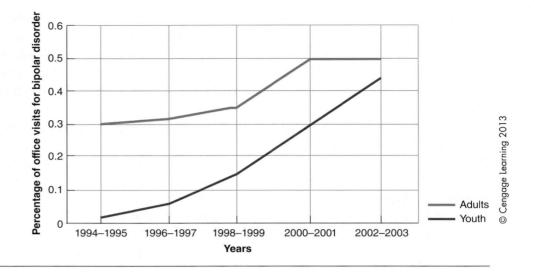

Actors (such as Russell Brand), actresses, poets, painters, and musicians seem to have a disproportionate risk for bipolar disorder compared to people in other occupations. We do not know if having bipolar disorder allows these creative people to express emotion more effectively in their art, or whether the arts are simply more welcoming to those who have mood disorders than the corporate boardroom.

Genetic predispositions play a greater role in bipolar disorder than in major depressive disorder. Concordance rates among identical twins for bipolar disorder are commonly reported to be as high as 85%, in contrast to the 30 to 40% concordance rate for major depressive disorder (Kieseppä, Partonen, Haukka, Kaprio, & Lönnqvist, 2004). Adoption studies also support a powerful role for genetics (Taylor, Faraone, & Tsuang, 2002). There is considerable overlap between the genes believed to play a role in bipolar disorder and those implicated in schizophrenia, which we discuss later in this chapter (Kikuchi et al., 2003). In spite of the differences between unipolar and bipolar disorder, these disorders might also share overlapping genetic vulnerabilities. Bipolar disorder is 3 to 4 times more likely in families that have at least one member with major depressive disorder than in families with no members with any psychological disorders (Dubovsky & Dubovsky, 2002).

Like major depressive disorder, bipolar disorder has been linked to imbalances in serotonin activity. Both conditions produce disturbances in sleep, which is closely related to serotonin activity. Bipolar disorder not only involves a decreased need for sleep, but manic episodes can be triggered in vulnerable individuals by sleep deprivation (Kasper & Wehr, 1992).

Among the many possible environmental factors that could interact with genes associated with bipolar disorder is diet. Omega-3 fatty acids, generally found in fish, may provide some protection from bipolar disorder (Noaghiul & Hibbeln, 2003). As shown in ● Figure 14.12, prevalence rates for bipolar disorder are highest in countries where fish is rarely consumed (such as Germany) and lowest in countries where fish is an important diet staple (such as Iceland). However, attempts to improve symptoms in patients with bipolar disorder by administering omega-3 supplements have produced weak results (Stahl, Begg, Weisinger, & Sinclair, 2008). The impact of omega-3 fatty acids on a person's vulnerability for bipolar disorder might be more important during prenatal development than later on in life.

Many unanswered questions regarding the development of this condition remain. Bipolar disorder may be overrepresented in groups of people with artistic and creative talent (Jamison, 1993, 1995). Based on

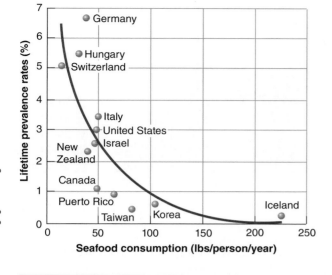

FIGURE 14.12

Bipolar Rates Are Lower in Nations With High Seafood Consumption. Rates of bipolar disorder are negatively correlated with a nation's consumption of seafood, suggesting that the omega-3 fatty acids contained in seafood might help prevent bipolar disorder. *Source:* Adapted from Noaghiul and Hibbeln (2003).

biographical accounts, the poet William Blake, composers Handel and Mahler, and visual artists van Gogh and Michelangelo might have had bipolar disorder. Many noted actors and actresses, including Carrie Fisher (*Star Wars*) and Vivien Leigh (*Gone with the Wind*), have been diagnosed with bipolar disorder. Comparisons of people with bipolar disorder and major depressive disorder with healthy people in creative and noncreative professions support this hypothesis. The patients with bipolar disorder scored similarly on tests of creativity to healthy people in creative occupations and higher than people with major depression and healthy people in noncreative occupations (Santosa et al., 2007). While it is possible that the dramatic mood swings that characterize bipolar disorder might enhance creative activities, it is also possible that the arts provide a more comfortable environment for those who are emotionally volatile. It is hard to imagine a person with bipolar disorder working comfortably within a rigid corporate organization, while artistic organizations frequently embrace people who are different.

Suicide

Suicide, or the intentional taking of one's own life, does not have a separate category in the DSM. Among the most frequent psychological disorders associated with suicide are depression, alcoholism, and schizophrenia (Bryan & Rudd, 2006) (see ● Figure 14.13). Suicide is a leading cause of death, accounting for approximately 34,000 deaths per year in the United States (Centers for Disease Control and Prevention [CDC], 2011b). It is possible that the real number of suicides could be much higher, as many events assumed to be accidents, such as single car crashes and drownings, might be intentional.

Suicide rates show complex variations across age, gender, socioeconomic status, religious affiliation, marital status, and ethnicity (Centers for Disease Control and Prevention [CDC], 2010c). Suicide is the 11th leading cause of death in the United States for all ages, but is the second leading

Russell Armstrong, husband of Taylor Armstrong of *Real Housewives of Beverly Hills*, committed suicide after his wife filed for divorce. In addition to his divorce, Russell faced a $1.5 million debt he had hidden from his wife.

FIGURE 14.13

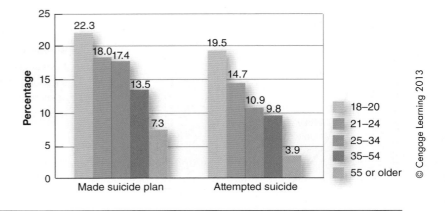

Depression Carries a High Risk of Suicidal Thinking and Suicide Attempts. Among individuals experiencing at least one depressive episode in the past year, thinking seriously about suicide and actually making a suicide attempt happened very frequently.

cause of death among young adults ages 25 to 34 and the third leading cause of death among 15- to 24-year-olds. Males account for 79% of all suicides in the United States, although women attempt suicide 2 to 3 times more often than men. Men tend to use more lethal means, such as guns, in committing suicide, whereas women tend to use drug overdose. Native Americans have the highest suicide rate in the United States, followed by White Americans, Hispanic Americans, African Americans, and Asian Americans. Married adults are less likely to commit suicide than single, divorced, or widowed adults (Luoma & Pearson, 2002).

Thinking Scientifically

What Should We Do When We Think Somebody Might Commit Suicide?

Approximately 1,100 college students in the United States die in suicides each year, making suicide the second leading cause of death in this population (Wilcox et al., 2010).

These statistics raise the possibility that as a college student, you may become aware of another person's risk for suicide. According to the American Foundation of Suicide Prevention, we can make ourselves aware of risk factors and take action that might save a life (American Foundation for Suicide Prevention [AFSP], 2007). Among these risk factors are evidence of a psychological disorder (particularly depression), alcohol and other substance use, a past history of suicide attempts, being male (males

have a 3 to 5 times higher completion rate than females), and impulsivity. More immediately, the occurrence of a traumatic event (job loss, ending of an important relationship) might increase a person's risk.

Approximately 75% of individuals who attempt suicide show prior evidence of their intent (AFSP, 2007). People might say things like "my fam-

The biological perspective suggests that low levels of cholesterol and disturbances in serotonin function are predictive of suicide attempts (Asellus, Nordström, & Jokinen, 2010). The implication of low serotonin levels in suicide helps to explain why depression is typically present when people attempt suicide. People who choose violent methods, such as firearms, over less violent methods, such as overdosing on pills, have lower levels of serotonin activity in the prefrontal cortex (Carballo et al., 2009). Biological vulnerabilities frequently interact with the use of substances. One third of people who commit suicide used alcohol at the time of death, and 20% used opiates, including heroin and prescription pain killers (CDC, 2010). Impulsiveness is often a characteristic of suicides, so the use of these substances can be tragic because they lessen people's ability to control impulsive behavior.

Not all people with low levels of serotonin activity and depression attempt or commit suicide, suggesting that we must once again consult additional perspectives for an explanation. Exposure to childhood trauma appears to interact with low serotonin levels to make suicide more likely (Moberg, Nordström, Kristiansson, & Jokinen, 2011). A person's cognitions about the future seem to play a very important role in his or her risk for suicide. When patients with a history of suicidal thoughts but no attempts were followed over a 10-year period, the patients that did commit suicide differed with the other patients in their degree of hopelessness, but not in the severity of their overall depression or the frequency of their thinking about suicide (Beck, Emery, & Greenberg, 2005). The social psychology perspective reminds us that people who feel lonely, ostracized, or disconnected from others are more likely to commit suicide (Alcántara & Gone, 2008; Rojas & Stenberg, 2010). Understanding the interactions of biological, cognitive, and social correlates of suicide can help mental health professionals construct more effective prevention programs.

© Picture Partners/Alamy

Understanding that the combination of depression, impulsivity, alcohol or substance use, a past history of suicide attempts, and a recent breakup or other traumatic event may increase the risk of suicide can help us offer support to a person who exhibits these characteristics.

ily would be better off without me," or speak in ways that indicate they are saying good-bye. Purchasing a gun or putting one's affairs in order (giving away prized possessions like a computer) are signs of risk. Hopelessness, rage, or increased use of drugs and alcohol are also common responses to feeling suicidal (AFSP, 2007).

In the event that you do suspect someone of being suicidal, experts advise you to take the situation very seriously. Yes, it may be true that some people "cry wolf," but with a life at stake, who wants to take that chance? Be a good listener, and reassure the person that depression can be treated, that he or she is not alone, and that you care. If possible, take

your friend to a place where professional help is available, whether that is your campus health center or a local emergency room. Do not leave the person alone, and remove any possible means of self-harm (drugs, weapons, etc.). If such steps are not possible, call the National Suicide Prevention Lifeline at 1-800-273-TALK or 911. ◉

What Are Dissociative Disorders?

Dissociative disorders feature disruptions in a person's identity, memory, or consciousness.

Dissociative disorders can take several forms. Dissociative amnesia occurs when a person forgets important information about specific events, often following a frightening or traumatic event. In dissociative fugue, people become confused over their identity and often combine this loss of identity with sudden travel and the assumption of a new identity. These situations typically last a few hours or days, but not longer periods (Kopelman, 2002).

Depersonalization/derealization disorder occurs when a person experiences strong feelings of unreality about either the self or the surrounding environment (APA, 2000, 2011a). People might feel as though they are watching their behavior from outside their bodies or that the world is dreamlike. However, they retain their abilities to understand that their feelings are not realistic. In other words, they feel as if they're outside their bodies, but they don't really believe this is actually happening.

Possibly the most controversial of the dissociative disorders is dissociative identity disorder, which was previously known as multiple personality disorder. According to the DSM, dissociative identity disorder (DID) is characterized by the experience of two distinct "personality states" or an "experience of possession" that is not consistent with a person's religious or cultural beliefs (APA, 2000, 2011a).

Dissociative identity disorder experienced a spike in popularity as a diagnosis in the mid-1990s, but has since dropped in frequency. Media attention might have contributed to the frequency with which this disorder was diagnosed. Prior to the popularization of patients named Sybil and Eve

Heisman Trophy winner, NFL star, and MMA fighter Herschel Walker has spoken about his experience with dissociative identity disorder (DID) to encourage military veterans to seek help for psychological disorders.

dissociative disorder A disorder characterized by disruptions in a person's identity, memory, or consciousness.

in books and films during the 1970s, very few cases of dissociative identity disorder had ever been described in the scientific literature. Following this media interest, thousands of cases were diagnosed, but primarily in the United States and Canada. Responses to extreme stress frequently include detachment, numbness, or altered memory and cognitions, but this is quite different from the development of additional identities. It is possible that well-meaning therapists can misinterpret these stress symptoms as dissociative identity disorder, and worse yet, suggest this possibility to their clients. People diagnosed with dissociative identity disorder, like those with other dissociative disorders, score very high on tests of suggestibility that predict a person's susceptibility to hypnosis and in measures of being likely to fantasize (Giesbrecht, Lynn, Lilienfeld, & Merckelbach, 2010). These findings imply that patients may have difficulty distinguishing between reality and fantasy and might accept a therapist's suggestion without considering it critically.

What Are Somatoform Disorders?

Historically, **somatoform disorders** involved physical symptoms that do not have an underlying medical cause (APA, 2000). However, in recognition of the mind-body dualism represented in this traditional view, the category will be reorganized in the DSM 5 and renamed "somatic symptom disorders" (APA, 2011a).

To the patient, the somatoform symptoms appear quite serious and often disabling. Among the different symptoms are vague pain complaints, gastrointestinal upset, sexual problems, amnesia, breathing problems, or unexplained sensory or motor problems. Patients with somatoform symptoms usually visit physicians very frequently, report high numbers of

Pop entertainer Michael Jackson was described by his mother as "addicted" to plastic surgery. She related that during adolescence, her son became obsessed with his perceived physical "flaws." Although Jackson was never formally diagnosed with body dysmorphic disorder (BDD), many people with BDD engage in similar types of behavior.

somatoform disorder/somatic symptom disorder A disorder characterized by physical symptoms that do not have an underlying medical cause.

physical complaints, and are at risk of becoming dependent on pain medications. They can become preoccupied with their health and often insist on unnecessary medical tests and procedures.

One of the former somatoform disorders, body dysmorphic disorder, has been recognized as a poor fit for this category and instead will be classified along with obsessive-compulsive disorder in DSM 5 (APA, 2011a). This disorder is characterized by the unrealistic perception of physical flaws. Many people with this condition undergo numerous cosmetic surgeries. Others continually try to "perfect" their bodies through bodybuilding activities and other strategies.

Unlike the somatoform disorders, body dysmorphic disorder shows a significant influence of heredity (Feusner, Neziroglu, Wilhelm, Mancusi, & Bohon, 2010). In addition, people with this disorder might not be as out of touch with reality as you might think. Their visual perception of subtle facial distortions appears to be much better than normal, so they may indeed be noticing "flaws" that the rest of us cannot see (Reese, McNally, & Wilhelm, 2010).

What Is Schizophrenia?

Schizophrenia is not the most common type of disorder, affecting approximately 1% of the human population worldwide (Kessler et al., 2007), but it is certainly one of the most dramatic. This condition influences and distorts a broad range of behaviors, including perception, cognition, movement, and emotion.

Symptoms of Schizophrenia

Among the symptoms of schizophrenia are delusions, hallucinations, disorganized thought and speech, and disorders of movement (APA, 2000, 2011a). The experience of these symptoms together constitutes psychosis. **Delusions** are defined as false, illogical beliefs. These may take a number of different forms, including delusions of persecution by others (paranoia) or grandiosity, a feeling of unrealistic power or importance.

Hallucinations are false perceptions. Although hallucinations may occur in several sensory modalities, most hallucinations in schizophrenia are auditory (Tien, 1991). Patients often report hearing voices, which can be accusatory or otherwise unpleasant, contributing to the distress associated with the disorder. Auditory hallucinations are not imaginary, but are real sensations correlated with increased activity in the primary auditory cortex of the temporal lobe (Dierks et al., 1999). Simply asking patients to remember or imagine sounds did not produce the type of activity in the auditory cortex seen during an auditory hallucination, indicating that the hallucination experience is different from simple memory or imagination.

A third symptom of schizophrenia involves disorganized patterns of thought and speech. The patient jumps inexplicably from one topic to the next. People with schizophrenia appear to have difficulty inhibiting secondary meanings for some words (Titone, Levy, & Holzman, 2000). For example,

Zelda Fitzgerald, wife of *The Great Gatsby* author F. Scott Fitzgerald, lived a flamboyant celebrity life. Fitzgerald patterned aspects of some of his fictional heroines after Zelda's erratic behavior. After being diagnosed with schizophrenia at the age of 30, she spent most of the remainder of her life in and out of psychiatric hospitals.

© Everett Collection Inc/Alamy; *The Great Gatsby.* Cover design by Francis Cugat. New York: Charles Scribner's Sons, 1925. First Edition Facsimile published by Collectors Reprints, Inc., New York, 1988.

schizophrenia A disorder characterized by hallucinations, delusions, disorganized thought and speech, disorders of movement, restricted affect, and avolition/asociality.

delusion A false, illogical belief.

hallucination A false perception.

the word *jam* can refer to either a fruit spread for toast or an impromptu musical session. Most people would use context (a conversation about food or music) to decide which meaning was appropriate. Patients with schizophrenia might not experience this filtering, leading their thoughts to jump from food to jazz and on to other atypical connections.

This "loosening of associations" between ideas might be due to the reduced latent inhibition in patients with schizophrenia, which we discussed in our chapter on learning. According to this argument, latent inhibition typically results in fewer associations being made to familiar stimuli. If you have had a lot of experience connecting jam and food, you are unlikely to consider other uses of the word *jam*. The person with schizophrenia, however, would be less inhibited in the connections he or she might make, leading to trains of thought that seem bizarre to the rest of us.

Schizophrenia also features "grossly abnormal psychomotor behavior." Patients with schizophrenia often demonstrate unusual patterns of movement. In some cases, the person may be unusually active, while others barely move throughout an entire day. Unusual behaviors occur, including grimaces and gestures. The maintenance of awkward or unusual body positions for hours at a time is referred to as catatonia. These patients appear aware of their surroundings, but they don't move. Most of us would find it difficult to sit for a few minutes without shifting position, let alone hours at a time.

Some patients with schizophrenia experience "catatonia," which means that they maintain awkward or unusual body positions for hours at a time.

In addition, schizophrenia can produce negative symptoms, or behaviors that are seen in healthy people but not in patients. These symptoms include "restricted affect and avolition/asociality" (APA, 2011a). A person with restricted affect does not show typical outward signs of emotion, such as facial expressions and tone of voice, in situations where an emotional response is expected. Avolition/asociality (the *a-* means "lack of") refers to a patient's lack of goal-oriented behavior and to his or her social withdrawal.

The Causes of Schizophrenia

Like many other types of psychological disorders, it is likely that schizophrenia has multiple sources of causality. No one factor by itself is likely to be sufficient to produce the disorder.

Biological Factors in Schizophrenia Significant evidence points to a genetic vulnerability for schizophrenia. People with close family members who have been diagnosed with schizophrenia are more likely to develop the disorder themselves (Gottesman, 1991). If one identical twin is diagnosed with the disorder, his or her twin has about a 50% lifetime risk of developing the disorder (see ● Figure 14.14). Comparisons of adopted children with their biological and adoptive parents also support a role for genetics (Kety, Rosenthal, Wender, & Schulsinger, 1968). A large number of different genes have been implicated in the development of schizophrenia and appear to overlap with those involved with bipolar disorder (Owen, Craddock, & Jablensky, 2007). In one case of identical triplets, two of the triplets were diagnosed with schizophrenia and the third was diagnosed with bipolar disorder (McGuffin, Reveley, & Holland, 1982).

FIGURE 14.14

Genetics and Schizophrenia.
A person's lifetime risk of developing schizophrenia increases when closely related family members have been diagnosed with the disorder, suggesting that genes play a significant role. The fact that having a spouse with schizophrenia doubles the risk (from 1 to 2%) probably reflects the tendency for people to marry others with whom they share similarities.

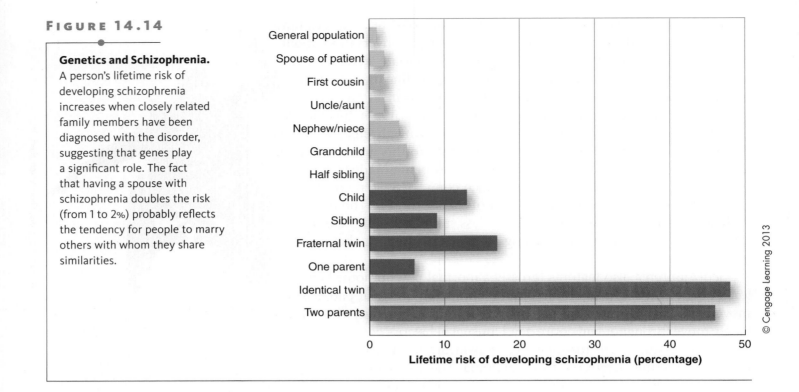

© Cengage Learning 2013

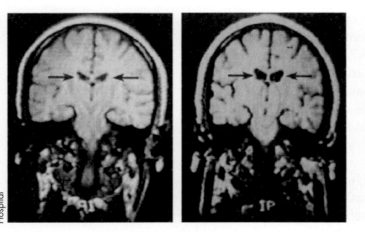

Courtesy D. R. Weinberger, NIMH, St. Elizabeth's Hospital

MRI images of the brains of a pair of identical twins show the differences in the size of the lateral ventricles (see arrows) found in healthy people (left) and people with schizophrenia (right). The ventricles are fluid-filled spaces and enlarge whenever significant numbers of nearby neurons have died.

A number of structural and biochemical features accompany schizophrenia. One reliable correlate of schizophrenia is the presence of enlarged ventricles (Yotsutsuji et al., 2003). As we discussed in our chapter on biological psychology, the ventricles are fluid-filled spaces in the brain that are not responsible for any particular behavior. The ventricles will enlarge in response to any condition resulting in a loss of neural tissue in adjacent areas, so we can assume that schizophrenia is associated with neural degeneration.

Most patients with schizophrenia also demonstrate a lower level of frontal lobe activity than healthy control participants, both at rest and during effortful cognitive tasks (Berman, Torrey, Daniel, & Weinberger, 1992). The importance of the frontal lobes to higher cognitive processes and attention suggests that this difference would have significant influences on behavior. In addition, pathways in the brain that manage olfaction, or the sense of smell, travel through the frontal lobe. Lower overall frontal lobe activity might account for some of the difficulties patients with schizophrenia experience with their sense of smell.

Schizophrenia might involve abnormal brain development during adolescence. Teens typically experience a burst of cortical gray matter growth at puberty followed by a wave of gray matter loss extending into their early 20s. Healthy teens experience very little loss of gray matter, whereas teens diagnosed with schizophrenia experience a loss that has been likened to a "forest fire" (Thompson et al., 2001).

Abnormalities in dopamine activity might be the major biochemical culprit in schizophrenia. Drugs that boost dopamine activity, such as amphetamine and the Parkinson's disease treatment l-dopa, can produce hallucinations and paranoid delusions (Goetz, Leurgans, Pappert, Raman, & Stemer, 2001). Medications that block dopamine activity are usually quite effective in reducing these same symptoms.

However, this dopamine hypothesis of schizophrenia is not perfect. About one fourth of patients with schizophrenia do not respond favorably to drugs that reduce dopamine activity (Kane & Freeman, 1994). In particular, the negative symptoms, such as restricted affect, are not improved at all by these drugs (Goff & Evins, 1998). In addition, medications that influence neurotransmitters other than dopamine may also be effective (Syvalahti, 1994). Finally, phencyclidine (PCP, or angel dust) produces a syndrome that is quite similar to schizophrenia, despite the fact that PCP acts on synapses using glutamate, not dopamine, as their neurotransmitter (Mössner et al., 2008). Although it seems certain that dopamine does play a role in schizophrenia, the nature and scope of that role remain unclear.

Psychological Factors and Schizophrenia The 50% concordance rate for schizophrenia in identical twins indicates a role for genetics in the development of the disorder. On the other hand, 50% is not 100%, and we need to account for the remaining factors.

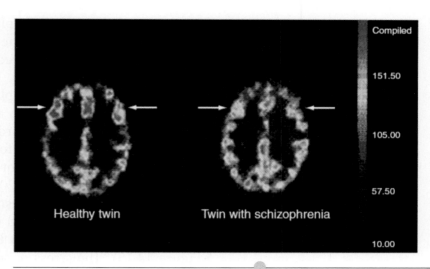

When the brain activity of these identical twins is observed through brain imaging, the frontal lobes (arrows) appear to be more active in the healthy twin on the left than in the twin with schizophrenia on the right. Red and yellow areas indicate greater activity, while green and dark areas are relatively inactive. From Daniel Weinberger, M.D., E. Fuller Torrey, M.D. (formerly of NIMH), Karen Berman, M.D. NIMH Clinical Brain Disorders Branch Division of Intramural Research Programs, NIMH 1990

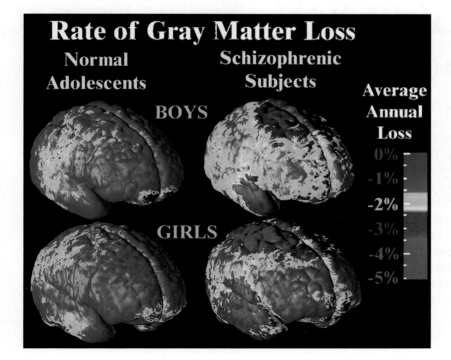

Teens typically experience a burst of gray matter growth at puberty followed by a wave of gray matter thinning that extends into the early 20s. Compared with their healthy peers, teens diagnosed with schizophrenia experience much greater gray matter loss. Areas colored purple and red indicate the greatest amount of loss, followed by areas colored yellow and green (Thompson et al., 2001). From Thompson, P. M., et. al. (2001). Mapping adolescent brain changes reveals dynamic wave of accelerated gray matter loss in very early-onset schizophrenia. *Proc Natl Acad Sci, 98*(20), 11650–11655. Courtesy of Paul Thompson/UCLA Lab of Neuro Imaging.

Extreme stress seems to play a role in the appearance and severity of schizophrenia among genetically vulnerable people. Schizophrenia appears nearly 5 times more frequently in members of lower than of higher socioeconomic groups (Keith, Regier, & Rae, 1991). The stress of living in poverty may trigger schizophrenia in vulnerable individuals. However, others argue that people who are susceptible to schizophrenia "drift" to lower paying jobs. In other words, the disorder reduces the patients' socioeconomic status, accounting for the higher rates of the disorder among the poor. Other stresses might accompany a person's minority status in a community (Boydell et al., 2001). African immigrants living in London neighborhoods with the lowest proportions of African immigrants were twice as likely to be diagnosed with schizophrenia as African immigrants living in neighborhoods with the highest proportion of minorities (see •Figure 14.15). The stress of social isolation due to minority status may have contributed to higher rates of schizophrenia.

When we talk about environmental influences, factors such as stress come to mind. However, environmental influences also include biological variables such as the prenatal environment, including the pregnant woman's exposure to viral illness. Another environmental variable that might trigger schizophrenia in genetically vulnerable individuals is marijuana use

Experiencing Psychology

The Remote Associates Test (RAT)

The thinking of people with schizophrenia shares a feature with the thinking of unusually creative people—more data than usual are viewed as being relevant to a particular problem. The Remote Associates Test (RAT) provides a measure of this type of thinking that correlates with other measures of creativity. Although people diagnosed with schizophrenia tend to do more poorly on the RAT than people without any disorders,

people described as "psychosis-prone" who possess strong coping skills score quite high on this test (Fodor, 1995).

The RAT presents you with sets of three words, and your task is to find a single word that makes sense when paired with the other three words. For example, "star" is the solution for the group of "falling," "actor," and "dust." The following list is a small sample of the RAT, which typically contains more than 60 items.

How did you do? If you did very well, it is likely that you excel in other creative activities. Do you have to worry now about being diagnosed with schizophrenia? Absolutely not. Schizophrenia and creativity are definitely not the same thing, but analyzing these overlapping characteristics might help us understand schizophrenia better. ✪

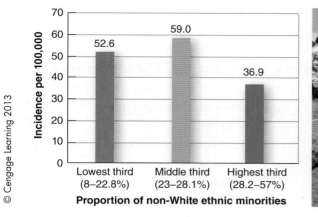

FIGURE 14.15

Stress and Schizophrenia. African immigrants living in South London were more likely to be diagnosed with schizophrenia if they lived in a predominantly White neighborhood (lowest and middle thirds of non-White ethnic minority populations) than if they lived in a primarily non-White neighborhood. An explanation based on self-selection (people choosing to live in each type of neighborhood) is unlikely in this case, as nearly all the participants were assigned to public housing units rather than having a choice of where to live. These findings suggest that the stress of minority status might contribute to higher risk for schizophrenia. *Source:* Adapted from Boydell et al. (2001).

(Ho, Wassink, Ziebell, & Andreasen, 2011). A 25-year longitudinal study concluded that cannabis use nearly doubled the risk of schizophrenia (Fergusson, Horwood, & Ridder, 2005). As we mentioned in our chapter on development, adolescence is a time of brain growth, and heavy marijuana use during this period produces a reduction in white matter volume in the frontal lobes that might interact with a person's genetic vulnerabilities for schizophrenia (Ho et al., 2011).

Problem terms	Solution (Write this in now, and then view the answers below.)	Percentage of people who solve the problem
1. Broken Clear Eye		80
2. Cracker Union Rabbit		65
3. Room Blood Salts		60
4. Chocolate Fortune Tin		45
5. Hall Car Swimming		40
6. Note Dive Chair		30
7. Shopping Washer Picture		25
8. Sore Shoulder Sweat		10

Answers: 1. Glass, 2. Jack, 3. Bath, 4. Cookie, 5. Pool, 6. High, 7. Window, 8. Cold

Summary 14.2

Mood Disorders, Dissociative Disorders, Somatoform Disorders, and Schizophrenia

Disorder	Symptoms	Possible causal factors under investigation
Major depressive disorder Grimm et al. (2008)	• Chronic depressed mood • Lack of pleasure • Sleep disturbances • Appetite disturbances • Difficulty concentrating • Hopelessness • Possible suicidal thoughts	• Loss of positive reinforcement • Learned helplessness • Negative cognitions • Rumination • Attributions • Stress • Genetics • Reduced serotonin activity • Patterns of brain activity • Circadian rhythms
Bipolar disorder © vita khorzhevska/ Shutterstock	• Depression alternating with: • Elevated mood • Grandiosity • Little need for sleep • Rapid speech • Difficulty concentrating	• Genetics • Serotonin disturbances • Diet
Dissociative disorders © Esther Lin/ Zuffa LLC/ Getty Images	• Memory disturbance (amnesia) • Stress or trauma • Identity disturbance (fugue) • Depersonalization • Experience of two distinct personality states (dissociative identity disorder)	• Stress or trauma
Somatoform disorders/Somatic symptom disorders © Ron Galella/WireImage/Getty Images; © AP Photo/Arne Dedert; © Carlo Allegri/Getty Images	• Pain • Gastrointestinal upset • Sexual problems • Amnesia • Breathing problems • Unexplained sensory or motor problems	• Unknown
Schizophrenia © Everett Collection Inc/Alamy; *The Great Gatsby.* Cover design by Francis Cugat. New York: Charles Scribner's Sons, 1925. First Edition Facsimile published by Collectors Reprints, Inc., New York, 1988.	• Delusions • Hallucinations • Disorganized thought and speech • Movement disorders • Restricted affect • Avolition/asociality	• Genetics • Reduced frontal lobe activity • Disruption of brain development • Dopamine and glutamate abnormalities • Stress • Prenatal environment • Marijuana use

What Are Personality Disorders?

Several different types of **personality disorder** are recognized in the DSM (APA, 2000, 2011a). A personality disorder is characterized by impairments in identity, in personality traits, and in the establishment of empathy or intimacy. Personality disorders cannot be diagnosed in people under the age of 18. To illustrate this category of disorders, we will look at two of the personality disorders in greater detail: antisocial personality disorder, which is more common in males, and borderline personality disorder, which is more common in females.

Antisocial Personality Disorder

Antisocial personality disorder (APD) is characterized by an unusual lack of remorse and empathy. Individuals with this disorder have little regard for normal social rules and conventions. Their behavior is frequently risky and irresponsible, and they form shallow, fleeting relationships with others.

APD is quite similar to the term *psychopath*, which has not been used by the DSM system since its third edition was published in 1980. Criteria for APD in DSM-III and DSM-IV focused on a person's behaviors, especially criminal behaviors, whereas the term psychopath implies flaws in the person's consistent traits or character (APA, 2000; Hare, 2006). As a result of this difference, APD as defined by the DSM criteria was believed to be about twice as common as psychopathy. Estimates of antisocial personality disorder ranged around 2% in the United States, with 3% of men and 1% of women meeting the DSM criteria (APA, 2000). Hare (2006) has estimated the number of psychopaths in the United States as approximately 1%. As you can see in Table 14.1, the DSM 5 criteria for APD have become more similar to definitions of psychopathy.

personality disorder A disorder characterized by impairments in identity, in personality traits, and in the establishment of empathy or intimacy.

antisocial personality disorder (APD) A disorder characterized by an unusual lack of remorse, empathy, or regard for normal social rules and conventions.

TABLE 14.1 Antisocial Personality Disorder (APD) and Psychopathy

APD in DSM-IV TR (APA, 2000)	APD in DSM 5 (APA, 2011a)	Psychopathy (Hare, 2006)
• Repeatedly performs acts that are grounds for arrest	• Ego-centrism	• Ego-centrism
• Deceitfulness	• Does not conform to lawful or ethical behavior	• Superficial
• Impulsivity	• Lack of empathy	• Lack of remorse
• Irritability and aggressiveness	• Incapable of intimate relationships	• Lack of empathy
• Disregard for others' safety	• Manipulative	• Deceitful
• Irresponsibility	• Deceitful	• Manipulative
• Lack of remorse	• Callous	• Shallow emotions
• Onset before age 15	• Hostile	• Impulsive
	• Irresponsible	• Poor self-control
	• Impulsive	• Needs excitement
	• Takes risks	• Irresponsible
		• Early behavior problems
		• Adult antisocial behavior

Anders Behring Breivik killed 8 people with a bomb before shooting another 69 people at a nearby youth camp on July 22, 2011. Police told reporters that during a reenactment of the shootings, Breivik "didn't show any remorse." Although we don't know whether Breivik will be diagnosed with antisocial personality disorder, a callous lack of empathy and remorse is typical of people with this diagnosis.

© Jon Are Berg Jacobsen/Aftenposte/EPA/Newscom

Another potential source of confusion about this category is its relationship to criminal behavior. Not too surprisingly, given the emphasis on criminal behavior in the DSM-III and DSM-IV descriptions of APD, 47% of male prisoners and 21% of female prisoners were found to have APD (Fazel & Danesh, 2002). In contrast, only about 7.7% of male prisoners and 1.9% of female prisoners appear to be true psychopaths (Coid et al., 2009). The distinction is important, because criminal psychopaths frequently show different patterns of criminal behavior than criminals who are not psychopaths. Ninety-three percent of homicides committed by criminal psychopaths were premeditated, or carried out "in cold blood." In contrast, only 48.4% of homicides committed by nonpsychopathic criminals took this form (Woodworth & Porter, 2002). Instead, these criminals were more likely to murder impulsively.

It is very important to note that most individuals with APD or psychopathy do not engage in outright criminal behavior, and not all criminals have APD or psychopathy. Noncriminal individuals with APD were easily recruited by placing a newspaper ad calling for "charming, aggressive, carefree people who are impulsively irresponsible but are good at handling people and at looking after number one" (Widom, 1978, p. 72).

Causes of Antisocial Personality Disorder Research on individuals with antisocial parents suggests a genetic contribution to this disorder. Related traits such as fearless dominance, impulsive antisociality, and callousness show substantial heritability rates between .46 and .67 (Blair, Colledge, Murray, & Mitchell, 2001). Children adopted at birth who have antisocial biological parents are much more likely to engage in antisocial behavior (Cadoret & Cain, 1981). When children of biological parents who are not antisocial are adopted by antisocial parents, they are less likely to engage in antisocial behavior than children with biological parents who are antisocial (Mednick & Kandel, 1988). As we have mentioned previously in this textbook, child maltreatment interacts with a genetic predisposition to violent antisocial behavior (Caspi et al., 2003).

A genetic influence on a trait usually implies that the trait provides some advantage, but how can this be the case for a tendency toward antisocial behavior? One suggestion is that fearlessness characterizes both heroes and people with antisocial behavior (Lykken, 1982). Having heroic people in your population might offset the negative impact of having some antisocial people. To test his hypothesis about the similarities between these two groups, Lykken devised an "Activity Preference Questionnaire," which asks respondents to choose between a frightening or embarrassing situation and one that is simply unpleasant. For example, would you prefer to wash a car or drive a car 95 miles per hour? People who either engage in antisocial behavior or who have behaved heroically typically choose the risky alternative (driving fast) over a chore (washing car), whereas cautious people typically choose the chore over the risky alternative.

A relative lack of response to emotions, especially those of others, might also contribute to antisocial behavior disorder. While undergoing brain imaging, people with APD, unlike the control participants, showed

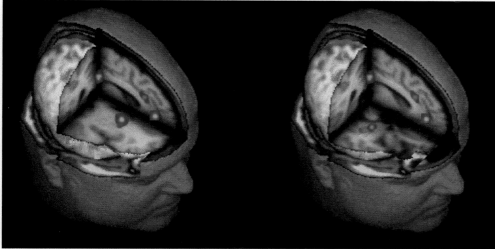

(a)   (b)

The areas marked in blue showed less activity in criminal psychopaths than in noncriminal control participants during the processing of negative emotional words like "rape" or "torture." These areas are associated with emotional processing and include (a) the cingulate cortex and the basal ganglia and (b) the hippocampus and amygdala. The failure of negative emotional stimuli to produce normal levels of arousal might allow the psychopath to engage in harmful behaviors without experiencing normal remorse or empathy (Kiehl et al., 2001).

little activation of parts of the brain that are usually active during emotional processing when listening to words such as "torture," "rape," or "cancer" (Hare, 2006; Kiehl et al., 2001). Participants were also shown neutral scenes and rather gruesome images of murder scenes. Once again, the people with APD showed different patterns of brain activation than the typical control participants. In particular, the amygdalas of people with APD showed relatively little activity. As we discussed in our chapters on biological psychology and on motivation and emotion, the amygdala normally participates in recognition of fear and other negative emotions in others. Other research indicates that children with antisocial tendencies are impaired in their ability to identify expressions of sadness and fear in others, a finding that is consistent with lower activity in the amygdala (Blair et al., 2001; Stevens, Charman, & Blair, 2001).

Antisocial behavior is associated with abnormalities of the orbitofrontal cortex. Orbitofrontal abnormalities occur at higher rates among murderers and those diagnosed with APD (Davidson, Putnam, & Larson, 2000). As we observed in our chapter on biological psychology, damage to the frontal areas of the cortex often leads to poor judgment and impulsivity. In one representative case, two adults who had been raised in stable, middle-class homes but who had experienced damage to the orbitofrontal cortex in infancy both showed a profound inability to understand the consequences of their negative behavior (Anderson, Bechara, Damasio, Tranel, & Damasio, 1999). They engaged in stealing, lying, and aggressive behavior and were very poor parents.

Borderline Personality Disorder

The term **borderline personality disorder** originated from the idea that the characteristics of this disorder fell on the "border" between anxiety and psychosis.

According to the DSM, borderline personality disorder is characterized by instability in interpersonal relationships, self-image, and emotion. Individuals with this disorder may engage in "frantic efforts" to avoid abandonment, either real or imagined, and may behave in impulsive, self-destructive

borderline personality disorder
A disorder characterized by instability in interpersonal relationships, self-image, and emotion.

ways (see ● Figure 14.16). Suicide and self-mutilating behaviors, which we discussed in our learning chapter, are quite common. Relationships are often initially very intense and idealized, but if the individual perceives any slight rejection, "love" can turn to anger very quickly.

Borderline personality disorder affects about 2% of the population, with women outnumbering men by a factor of 3 to 1 (Skodol & Bender, 2003). People with borderline personality disorder appear to be vulnerable to a number of additional disorders, including bipolar disorder, substance abuse, eating disorders, and other personality disorders.

Causes of Borderline Personality Disorder Borderline personality disorder is 5 times more common among close relatives with the disorder than among the general population, suggesting a biological predisposition (APA, 2000). However, as many as 70% of individuals with this diagnosis have histories of abandonment, neglect, and physical and/or sexual abuse (Hunt, 2007). These findings suggest that traumatic experiences interact with a possible genetic predisposition to produce disordered behavior.

Psychology *as a* Hub Science

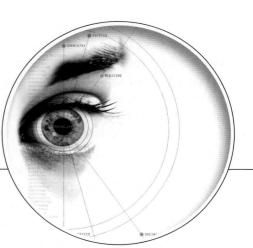

The "Dark Side" of Leadership

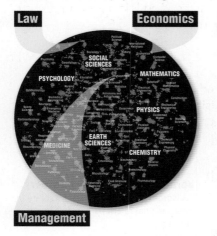

At a 2002 convention of law enforcement officers in Canada, psychologist Rob- ert Hare made a startling suggestion (Hare, 2002). With slides in the background depicting convicted World-Com CEO Bernard Ebbers and Enron CFO Andrew Fastow, Hare asked his audience why law enforcement personnel are screened for psychopathy, but not executives responsible for millions of dollars of people's savings and retirement funds.

When we hear the term *psychopath*, most of us think of characters like Hannibal Lecter of *The Silence of the Lambs*. However, Hare and other psychologists suggest that psychopaths are more likely to be the people next door, your coworkers, and maybe even your friends and relatives. Not only are psychopaths relatively common (around 1% of the population) but their characteristics might also allow them to be disturbingly successful. When profiles of 39 top British executives were compared to those of criminals and psychiatric patients, the executives were found to be more charming, egotistical, manipulative, and lacking in empathy (Board & Fritzon, 2005). Consequently, researchers began to refer to the executives as "successful" psychopaths, whereas the criminals and patients were "unsuccessful" psychopaths. Hare and his

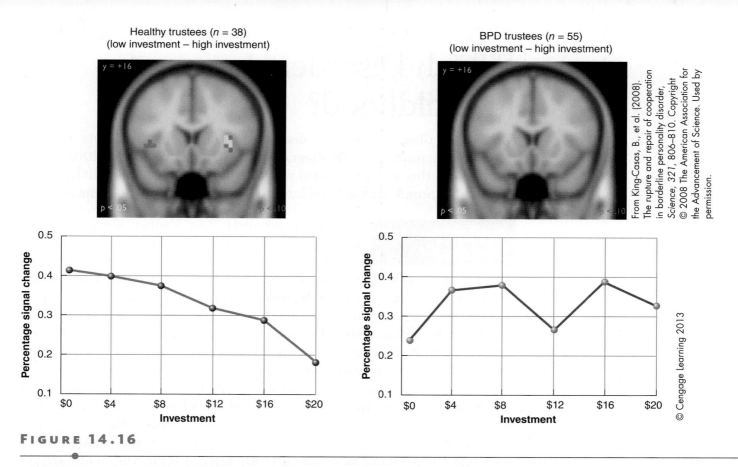

Healthy trustees (n = 38)
(low investment – high investment)

BPD trustees (n = 55)
(low investment – high investment)

© Cengage Learning 2013

FIGURE 14.16

Abnormal Responses to Trust in Borderline Personality Disorder. Not only do people with borderline personality disorder (BPD) perform differently than healthy controls in experimental activities measuring trust, but their brain activity during a trust game is also different. In the healthy participants, activity in the anterior insula decreases when an offer is higher, or more fair. In the participants with BPD, insula activity did not correspond well with the offers they received. This inability to respond to trust normally might explain some of the difficulties these patients experience in building healthy relationships with others.

colleague Paul Babiak would agree. Using scales they hope to market to corporations wishing to avoid hiring the next Andrew Fastow, these researchers have shown that corporate psychopaths score very high on items measuring the "selfish, callous, and remorseless use of others" (Babiak & Hare, 2006). Unlike criminal psychopaths, however, the corporate psychopaths did not show patterns of instability and social deviance.

Unfortunately, rapid and uncertain change in the business environment may provide fertile ground for corporate psychopaths to rise to the top. In a world of downsizing, an executive like Sunbeam's "Chainsaw" Al Dunlap, who fired half the corporation's workforce, might actually look like just the right person for the job. Dunlap had also been divorced by his first wife for "extreme cruelty," had thrown a chair at one of his executives, allegedly altered Sunbeam's financial records to make his performance look better, and demanded additional severance pay when he was fired for cause.

Modern corporations often find it difficult to distinguish between the behavior of the corporate psychopath and the person who is a genuinely visionary leader. Leaders such as Bill Gates and the late Steve Jobs may seem insensitive to others' feelings, according to leadership experts, but they turn their grandiosity toward making their organizations great rather than plundering them for personal gain (Maccoby, 2003). ⬡

Psychologists Paul Babiak and Robert Hare have suggested that it might be difficult to distinguish between tough corporate leaders and true psychopaths. Although corporate psychopaths score very high on measures of selfishness, callousness, and the remorseless use of others, they did not show patterns of instability and social deviance found in criminal psychopaths.

WHAT ARE PERSONALITY DISORDERS?

Which Disorders Emerge in Childhood?

Most of the disorders we have discussed so far might have roots in childhood but are more typically diagnosed in adolescence and adulthood. The disorders in this section, autism and attention deficit hyperactivity disorder, are diagnosed in childhood but often continue throughout the lifespan.

Autism Spectrum Disorder

In 1943, psychiatrist Leo Kanner identified three major areas of disturbance in a group of children: social relatedness, communication, and ritualistic behavior. Kanner's observations form the basis of our current diagnostic criteria for **autism spectrum disorder** (APA, 2000, 2011a). Autism represents a spectrum because the severity of the observed deficits can vary widely from individual to individual. Adjustment can range from relatively normal, allowing independent living, to intellectual disability, requiring living with parents or in institutional settings.

Rates of autism have been increasing rapidly over the last two decades (see ● Figure 14.17). Approximately 1 child out of every 110 in the United States now has autism spectrum disorder (Rice, 2009). Rates of autism in California jumped 273% between 1987 and 1998 (Shute, 2000, June 5). Although the presence of some currently unknown environmental trigger has not been completely ruled out, it is also possible that rising prevalence rates are the result of increased awareness of the disorder among parents and health care providers, relaxed applications of the diagnostic criteria, and the increased availability of services for children with the disorder (Barbaresi, Katusic, Colligan, Weaver, & Jacobsen, 2005). Males are far more likely to be diagnosed with autism than females, possibly by a factor of 4 to 1.

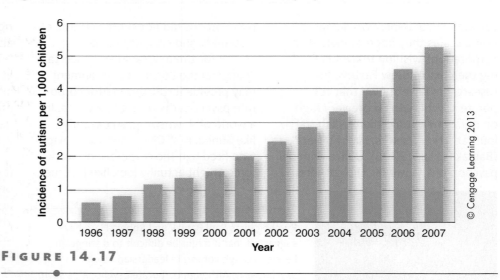

© Cengage Learning 2013

FIGURE 14.17

autism spectrum disorder A disorder characterized by deficits in social relatedness and communication skills that are often accompanied by repetitive, ritualistic behavior.

The Prevalence of Autism Appears to Be Increasing. It is clear that rates of autism spectrum disorders have increased over the last two decades, but the reasons for this increase remain a source of debate in the scientific community. It is possible that the rates are truly increasing, but increased awareness among parents and health care providers, relaxed applications of the diagnostic criteria, and increased availability of services might also be contributing to the observed increases.

Problems with social relatedness are at the core of this disorder, regardless of the individual's level of intelligence and adjustment. Beginning in infancy, most children with autism do not make eye contact or take pleasure in reciprocal games like "peek-a-boo." Insight into the thoughts and points of view of others is particularly lacking. As we discussed in our chapter on development, children develop a theory of mind by the time they are 3 to 4 years of age. Many researchers believe that a failure to develop a normal theory of mind is responsible for many of the social deficits observed in autism (Baron-Cohen, 1991; Senju, Southgate, White, & Frith, 2009). Language skills of individuals with autism can vary widely, from having no language abilities at all to delayed acquisition of language to normal skills (Ellis Weismer, Lord, & Esler, 2010). Even when language skills are relatively normal, individuals with autism spectrum disorder usually experience difficulty maintaining conversation with others because of their deficits in social skills.

Individuals with autism often object strenuously to changes in the environment and show a high level of repetitive, routine behavior. Rituals may include repetitive movements, such as rocking, hand-flapping, head-banging, and twirling. Other individuals may engage in extremely limited preoccupations, such as learning all models of cars ever made by Ford. One possible source of this ritualistic behavior is a general dysfunction in sensory networks. Most individuals with autism show unusually increased or decreased sensitivity to stimuli (Lane, Young, Baker, & Angley, 2010). They may be relatively insensitive to pain or cold, but very distressed by normal sound levels (see ● Figure 14.18). Ritualistic behavior may serve to control or override these disparate sensations.

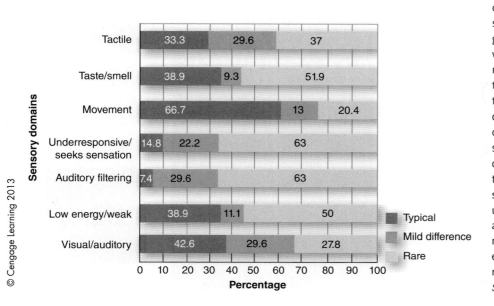

© Cengage Learning 2013

FIGURE 14.18

Sensory Sensitivity Is Different in Autism. Children with autism often show differences from healthy children in their sensitivity to environmental stimuli. This graph shows the percentage of children with autism whose scores on an instrument measuring sensitivity were the same as typical children, mildly different from typical children (between 1 and 2 standard deviations from the mean), and rare compared to typical children (more than 2 standard deviations from the mean). The domains measured included sensitivity to touch (tactile), sensitivity to taste and smell, sensitivity to movement (e.g., fear of falling), underresponsiveness (e.g., touches people), auditory filtering (e.g., failure to respond to name when called), low energy (e.g., tires easily), and visual/auditory (e.g., responds negatively to loud noises or bright lights). *Source:* Adapted from Lane et al. (2010).

Causes of Autism

Although the causes of autism remain somewhat mysterious, and probably show variable patterns from case to case, scientists are making progress. Parental age appears to provide one risk factor, with older parents more likely than younger parents to give birth to a child with autism (Grether, Anderson, Croen, Smith, & Windham, 2009). Given the postponement of parenting we discussed in our chapter on development, this finding has implications for understanding the increasing rates of autism.

Family and twin studies provide strong evidence that autism is influenced by genetics (Le Courteur et al., 1996). The concordance rate between identical twins may be as high as 90% and possibly more. Very large numbers of genes are involved, and recent research attention is being focused on the expression of these genes during brain development (Sakai et al., 2011; Yang & Gill, 2007). Autopsies of the brains of people with autism and people with no history of psychological disorder show dramatic differences (Voineagu et al., 2011). In the typical control brains, 174 genes were expressed differently in the frontal lobes compared to the temporal lobes, but in the brains of people with autism, no gene showed evidence of being expressed differently in the two areas.

Abnormalities in cortical development might lead to unusual minicolumns, vertical arrays of neurons perpendicular to the surface of the cerebral cortex that represent the smallest processing units of the brain. Individuals with autism have narrower and more numerous minicolumns than healthy individuals (Casanova et al., 2006; Peters, 2010).

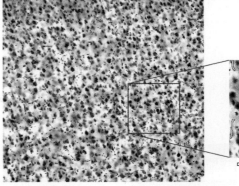

(a) Healthy controls

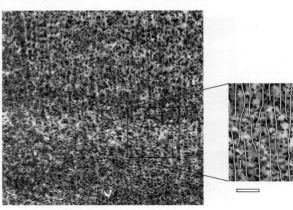

(b) Individuals with autism

Minicolumns in the cerebral cortex function like the microprocessors in modern computers by serving as the basic unit that receives input, processes it, and responds. Individuals with autism (lower image) have smaller minicolumns than healthy controls (top image). What does this difference mean for information processing? Smaller minicolumns favor the process of discrimination, described in our learning chapter as distinguishing between stimuli, while larger minicolumns favor generalization, or applying a response to similar stimuli. Behavioral domains that are difficult for people with autism, such as language, face recognition, and following another person's gaze, require more generalization than discrimination.

Environmental factors undoubtedly play a part in autism. Environmental factors are likely to interact with genetics, especially during sensitive periods of prenatal brain development (Engel & Daniels, 2011). For example, researchers found an increased rate of autism in the children of mothers with a particular genetic profile who reported taking no prenatal vitamins prior to their third month of pregnancy (Schmidt et al., 2011). Standard prenatal vitamins appeared to contain substances that offset some of the impact of having genes associated with risk for autism.

One of the unfortunate consequences of the uncertainty surrounding the causes of autism has been the vulnerability of concerned parents seeking answers. In a paper later retracted by the British medical journal *Lancet,* unsubstantiated claims that the routine measles/mumps/rubella vaccination caused autism were published. Similar controversies in the United States about a type of mercury preservative in vaccinations ensued, promoted by well-known figures such as model Jenny McCarthy and members of Congress.

The weight of the scientific evidence shows that vaccinations play *no* part in the development of autism (Schechter & Grether, 2008) (see ● Figure 14.19). Despite the clear data and reassurances from medical experts, worried parents have withheld vaccinations from their children, leading to increasing numbers of cases of life-threatening,

Narrow minicolumns similar to those found in the brains of people with autism were observed in the brains of three distinguished scientists, none of whom had autism symptoms, who donated their brains for scientific study. These similarities suggest that the minicolumn structure might account for the extreme focus of interests typical in autism (Casanova, Switala, Trippe, & Fitzgerald, 2007). Outstanding scientists, like people with autism, have been known to study minute details for very long periods.

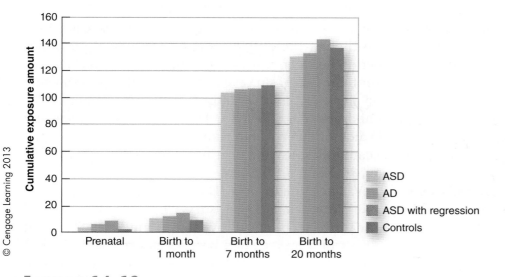

© Cengage Learning 2013

FIGURE 14.19

Scientific Evidence Does Not Support a Role for Vaccinations in the Development of Autism. Cumulative exposure to thimerosal, a mercury-containing preservative that has been used in vaccines, was the same for children diagnosed with an autism spectrum disorder (ASD), a narrower classification of autism (AD), autism spectrum disorder with regression (ASD with Regression, in which the child makes normal progress, then develops symptoms), and healthy controls. In spite of clear scientific evidence to the contrary, many people have been influenced by celebrities such as model Jenny McCarthy and have withheld vaccinations from their children. As a result, communities are facing epidemics of clearly avoidable and disabling diseases, such as measles.

preventable diseases that had previously been believed to be under control. For example, in the first half of 2008, measles cases in the United States doubled compared to the rates observed between 2000 and 2007, and all cases involved unvaccinated school children (Centers for Disease Control and Prevention [CDC], 2008b).

All children can be active and noisy, but most usually learn quickly to restrict those behaviors to the right times and places. Children with attention deficit hyperactivity disorder often struggle to sit quietly in class or wait in line.

Attention Deficit Hyperactivity Disorder (ADHD)

Attention deficit hyperactivity disorder (ADHD) is perhaps one of the most contentious categories described in the DSM. The criteria for the disorder are difficult to distinguish from the behaviors of many typical young children. Because most children diagnosed with ADHD will be treated with medication, the stakes for accurately diagnosing the condition are high indeed.

ADHD involves inattention and hyperactivity. Some individuals show both inattention and hyperactivity, but a large number of inattentive people show no hyperactivity at all (APA, 2011a). The core feature of inattention is the inability to maintain sustained attention, or on-task behavior, for an age-appropriate length of time. This problem is evidenced in the diagnostic criteria for inattention, such as difficulties in following instructions, in organizing and completing work, and in avoiding careless mistakes. Children with hyperactivity express a high level of motor activity and find engaging in structured activities, such as waiting in line or sitting quietly in class, very challenging. These children are noisy, active, and boisterous, and often appear to take action without thinking it through. Even as adults, individuals who were diagnosed with ADHD as children have more traffic accidents than people without the disorder (Barkley, 2004; Barkley & Cox, 2007).

Many of these behaviors are seen in children who do not have any psychological disorders. Although the DSM attempts to provide guidelines about making a distinction between normal and abnormal inattentiveness and hyperactivity, fewer than 40% of surveyed pediatricians reported using the DSM criteria to evaluate cases of ADHD (Wasserman et al., 1999). More than half the children in a very large sample who were receiving medication for ADHD did not meet even relaxed diagnostic criteria for the disorder, let alone the carefully constructed criteria spelled out in the DSM (Angold, Erkanli, Egger, & Costello, 2000).

One of the DSM criteria for ADHD is "often fidgets with hands or feet or squirms in seat." If you have visited an elementary school classroom lately, you might have noticed that most children are very active. At what point does squirming become a psychological disorder requiring medication?

Estimates of the prevalence rate for ADHD range widely in both childhood and adulthood (Kessler et al., 2011). A survey of parents conducted by the Centers for Disease Control and Prevention found that 7.74% of children between the ages of 4 and 17 had been diagnosed with ADHD (Centers for Disease Control and Prevention [CDC], 2005). About 57% of these children had been treated with medication. This amounts to 4.4 million children in the United States diagnosed with ADHD, with some 2.5 million receiving medication (see ● Figure 14.20).

attention deficit hyperactivity disorder (ADHD) A disorder characterized by either unusual inattentiveness, hyperactivity with impulsivity, or both.

Causes of ADHD

The National Institutes of Health (NIH, 2009) concluded that "scientists are not sure what causes ADHD." However, twin and adoption studies support a significant role for genetics in the development of ADHD. Heritability may be as high as 76% (Franke, Neale, & Faraone, 2009).

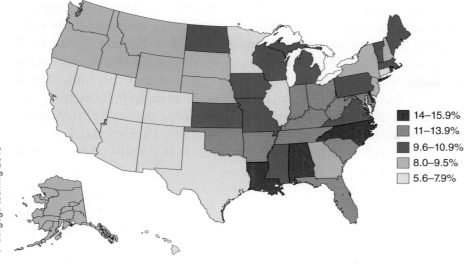

Diagnoses of ADHD in the United States. The number of children diagnosed with ADHD in a 2007 report from the Centers for Disease Control and Prevention (CDC) varies dramatically by region in the United States, from a low of 5.6 to 7.9% in the Southwest to 11 to 15.9% in parts of the Midwest and Southeast. Reasons for these regional discrepancies are not clear, although low socioeconomic status is considered a risk factor for ADHD. The differences might also represent variations in how the diagnostic criteria are applied by local health care providers.

- 14–15.9%
- 11–13.9%
- 9.6–10.9%
- 8.0–9.5%
- 5.6–7.9%

© Cengage Learning 2013

The frontal lobes may be underactive in cases of ADHD (Barkley, 1997). Because the frontal lobes inhibit unwanted behavior, lower activity in this part of the brain may lead to hyperactivity and impulsivity. The frontal lobes, and the prefrontal areas in particular, appear to mature more slowly in children with ADHD than in healthy controls (Shaw et al., 2007). Peak cortical thickness, a measure of brain maturity, occurred in healthy controls around the age of 7.5 years, but not until the age of 10.5 years in children with ADHD. The caudate nucleus, part of the basal ganglia that we described in our chapter on biological psychology, also shows delayed development in ADHD (Krain & Castellanos, 2006). White matter circuits connecting the basal ganglia and the frontal lobes appear to mature differently in people with and without ADHD (Helpern et al., 2011).

The parts of the brain implicated in ADHD, such as the prefrontal cortex and the basal ganglia, feature large amounts of dopamine activity. As we will see in our chapter on therapies, most of the medications used to treat ADHD, such as Ritalin or Adderall, act by boosting the activity of dopamine, suggesting that dopamine activity might be lower than usual in cases of ADHD (Volkow et al., 2009).

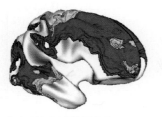

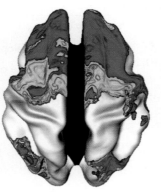

- Greater than 2 years' delay
- 0–2 years' delay

Among the many differences observed in the brains of children with ADHD compared to those of healthy controls is the rate of brain maturity, as measured by cortical thickening. These images demonstrate areas of the brain that developed later in children with ADHD than in healthy controls. Peak cortical thickness occurred around the age of 7.5 years in healthy children, but was not seen in children with ADHD until an average age of 10.5 years. This finding implies that children with ADHD can be expected to lag behind their age-peers in some tasks, but will eventually experience improvement (Shaw et al., 2007). From Shaw, P., et al. (2007). Attention-deficit/hyperactivity disorder is characterized by a delay in cortical maturation. *Proceedings of the National Academy of Sciences (PNAS), 104*(49), 19649–19654. Copyright © 2007 National Academy of Sciences, U.S.A.

WHICH DISORDERS EMERGE IN CHILDHOOD?

As in autism, myths about the causes of ADHD are common. Sugar is often blamed for hyperactive behavior, but evidence from carefully controlled studies does not support this belief (Milich & Pelham, 1986; Wolraich, Wilson, & White, 1996). However, as we discussed in our chapter on research methods, a well-controlled study suggested that combinations of common food additives made normal children demonstrate more hyperactivity (McCann et al., 2007). It is unlikely that "poor parenting" is responsible for these symptoms (Schroeder & Kelley, 2009). Parents can, however, learn new behavioral management techniques that greatly improve their child's behavior.

Summary 14.3

Personality Disorders, Autism Spectrum Disorder, and Attention Deficit Hyperactivity Disorder

Disorder	Symptoms	Possible causal factors under investigation
Antisocial personality disorder © Jon Are Berg Jacobsen/ Aftenposte/EPA/ Newscom	• Lack of remorse • Lack of empathy • Disregard for social norms	• Genetics • Orbitofrontal cortex abnormalities
Borderline personality disorder King-Casas et al. (2008).	• Instability in personal relationships • Unstable self-image • Unstable emotion	• Genetics • Abandonment • Neglect • Physical or sexual abuse
Autism spectrum disorder © Manuel F. Casanova, M.D., Department of Psychiatry and Behavioral Sciences, University of Louisville	• Problems with social relatedness • Problems with communication • Ritualistic behavior	• Genetics • Parental age • Disruptions in brain development • Unknown environmental influences
Attention deficit hyperactivity disorder © Ellen B. Senisi/The Image Works	• Inattentiveness • Hyperactivity	• Genetics • Brain development • Frontal lobe activity • Food additives

Interpersonal Relationships
From the Clinical Perspective

There are hidden costs in war. Soldiers, most of whom are about the same ages as those of you reading this textbook, are permanently changed by their experiences in ways that are often difficult for those of us who have not shared those experiences to understand. They have faced the fear of death and the realities of injury, held dying friends in their arms, and felt guilty that their lives were spared. They know that death really does smell like rotten apricots and that no matter what your religious training has been to the contrary, it's not that hard to take another person's life when a gun is pointing at you. You might not notice veterans in your classes, but if you watch carefully, they will seldom select a seat with its back to a big window, and they carefully size up each person entering the room.

Some cope with these challenges better than others. As we stated previously, between 8.5 and 14% of U.S. veterans serving in Iraq and Afghanistan experience severe PTSD, and up to 31% experience some impairment (Thomas et al., 2010). Veterans usually come home to loved ones and families, who are also affected by their soldiers' combat experiences in what has been called "secondary traumatization" (Galovski & Lyons, 2004). Although not directly threatened, the soldiers' families have had challenges of their own as they cope with their helpless fear of loss. Understanding that bad news comes to the front door in the person of a military chaplain makes each FedEx delivery or visit by a neighbor a heart-pounding experience. The spouses who have learned over the course of a year to run households independently and balance the checkbook might not want to return some of these tasks to their returning partners.

Among the biggest challenges for veterans with PTSD and their families are the results of having symptoms of hyperarousal, emotional numbing, and stimulus avoidance (Monson, Taft, & Fredman, 2009). Although veterans without PTSD have the same rates of intimate aggression as the general population, the risk of intimate aggression is much higher in those with PTSD, and the severity of symptoms predicts the likelihood of aggression. Because of the emotional numbing and avoidance symptoms of PTSD, a returning veteran does not engage in much self-disclosure, or discussion of his or her thoughts, feelings, and experiences. As we discussed in our chapter on social psychology, self-disclosure is an important component of intimacy.

A soldier's existing level of social support is one of the strongest protections against the initial development of PTSD (Brewin, Andrews, & Valentine, 2000). After trauma, a person with PTSD recovers more quickly with strong social support. Unfortunately, with ongoing PTSD, that social support tends to diminish, as the symptoms of PTSD take their toll on relationships (Kaniasty & Norris, 2008).

By recognizing the importance of the larger social network to PTSD, psychologists can begin to develop more effective preventions and interventions that take the entire social system into account, not just the individual with PTSD symptoms.

Both soldiers and their families are changed by war, and their reunions, while happy, are not always smooth. Strong social support is a critical variable in the development and course of post-traumatic stress disorder (PTSD) resulting from combat.

Chapter 14
Reflections

© Argosy Publishing, Inc.

We began this chapter by zooming in to look at an interactome based on genes associated with autism. In many of the disorders we discussed in this chapter, we found evidence for a "genetic predisposition." In none of the disorders, however, did genes play a solo role.

Instead, as in so many other aspects of behavior, our genes interact with many other biological, developmental, cognitive, and social factors to produce the final organism, whether that is a healthy person or a person with a psychological disorder. Those other factors might take many different forms, from the possibility of prenatal viral infection in schizophrenia to food additives in ADHD to feeling connected with others or not in depression. These factors not only interact in complex ways in a single disorder but also have different magnitudes of effect in one case compared to another. And as we discuss in the next chapter, many of these disorders can be effectively treated to improve people's lives and the lives of those with whom they live and interact.

Just as in medicine, the development of effective treatments is promoted by the accurate characterization and diagnosis of mental health problems. Research over the past century has led to tremendous advances in our understanding and diagnosis of different psychological disorders, and research promises to continue to change and improve both. Having said this, the complexity among causal factors and the way they interact in individual cases makes the task of our next chapter, therapies, all the more challenging, as we attempt to find the most effective ways to help people with psychological disorders. ‹

KEY TERMS The Language of Psychological Science

Be sure you can define these terms and use them correctly.

agoraphobia, p. 691
antisocial personality disorder (APD),
   p. 719
anxiety disorder, p. 687
attention deficit hyperactivity
   disorder (ADHD), p. 728
autism spectrum disorder, p. 724
bipolar disorder, p. 698
borderline personality disorder, p. 721
comorbidity, p. 683
compulsion, p. 693
delusion, p. 712
*Diagnostic and Statistical Manual of
   Mental Disorders (DSM)*, p. 684

diathesis-stress model, p. 703
dissociative disorder, p. 710
generalized anxiety disorder (GAD),
   p. 688
hallucination, p. 712
learned helplessness, p. 700
major depressive disorder (unipolar
   disorder), p. 698
mania, p. 698
obsession, p. 693
obsessive-compulsive disorder
   (OCD), p. 693
panic attack, p. 689
panic disorder, p. 689

personality disorder, p. 719
phobia, p. 691
post-traumatic stress disorder
   (PTSD), p. 695
schizophrenia, p. 712
social phobia/social anxiety, p. 691
somatoform disorder/somatic
   symptom disorder, p. 711
specific phobia, p. 692

MEDIA RESOURCES

Log in to CengageBrain to access the resources your instructor requires. For this book, you can access:

Psychology **CourseMate** brings course concepts to life with interactive learning, study, and exam preparation tools that support the printed textbook. A textbook-specific website, Psychology **CourseMate** includes an integrated interactive eBook and other interactive learning tools including quizzes, flashcards, videos, and more.

WebTUTOR More than just an interactive study guide, **WebTutor** is an anytime, anywhere customized learning solution with an eBook, keeping you connected to your textbook, instructor, and classmates.

aplia If your professor has assigned **Aplia** homework:
1. Sign in to your account.
2. Complete the corresponding homework exercises as required by your professor.
3. When finished, click "Grade It Now" to see which areas you have mastered, which areas need more work, and detailed explanations of every answer.

Both medication and behavioral treatments reduce abnormal activity in the basal ganglia associated with obsessive-compulsive disorder.

Healing the Troubled Mind

Therapy

Learning Objectives

1 Summarize the core principle and steps of evidence-based practice in psychotherapy, and apply the steps to an example case.

2 Differentiate the training/licensure required for, and types of care offered by, psychiatrists, clinical psychologists, counselors, hypnotherapists, and life coaches.

3 Analyze the key principles of psychoanalytic, humanistic, behavioral, and cognitive psychotherapy techniques, and link these principles to major movements in the history of psychology research.

4 Explain the biological mechanisms by which medication, electroconvulsive therapy (ECT), psychosurgery, deep brain stimulation, and bio/neurofeedback are thought to alleviate symptoms of disorder.

5 Integrate biological and psychotherapeutic approaches to treating anxiety, mood, dissociative, somatoform, schizophrenic, personality, and childhood disorders, explaining how they work together in the context of a particular disorder.

We have all been told how important it is to wash our hands to avoid illness, especially during flu season. But people with obsessive-compulsive disorder (OCD) might wash their hands several hundred times each day.

Why do people with OCD behave this way? In our previous chapter, we highlighted some of the possible causes of OCD, including a genetic vulnerability and the presence of too much activity in several brain structures, including the basal ganglia. In this chapter, we will talk about how psychotherapists can improve the situations of people with OCD and the other disorders we discussed in the previous chapter.

Zooming in, we can see what happens to a person's brain by using a PET scan following therapy for OCD. A PET scan provides a measure of brain activity. The red and yellow areas are considerably more active than the green, blue, and dark areas. The most common approach to treating OCD is to prescribe medications. When a person is medicated for OCD, we observe a reduction in the activity of the basal ganglia. (The basal ganglia are involved in motor control, including actions over which you are not exerting conscious control.) Some people do not respond well to medication, and we must find other ways to help those individuals.

The patients who do not respond well to medication can benefit from behavioral therapies, based on the principles of classical and operant conditioning we discussed in our learning chapter. In the case of OCD, a woman with hand washing compulsions could be trained to anticipate when she might feel like washing her hands inappropriately. Then she would engage in some competing activity, perhaps going out to her garden to pull some weeds or pick some flowers. Finally, she would reward herself for resisting the temptation to wash her hands too much.

Is it possible to show any differences in brain activity resulting from behavioral treatments? The answer is yes (Baxter et al., 1992). When patients with OCD who have been treated with behavioral methods are compared to patients using medication, their PET scans show the same type of decrease in activity in the basal ganglia.

In this chapter, we will be exploring a wide number of approaches that have been used to improve the situations of people with psychological disorders. Some take the form of medication and other biological treatments, while others represent a variety of psychological treatments, like the behavioral approach to OCD discussed here. The effects of these treatments might have more in common than you think, as in the case of the changes in brain activity that result from the biological and psychological treatments of OCD. Just as we have argued for the advantages of integrating psychological perspectives to understand behavior and mental processes, the field of clinical psychology is recognizing the benefits of applying multiple perspectives to the treatment of psychological disorders. ⚙

How Do Psychologists Provide Therapy?

Our previous chapter on psychological disorders explored a diverse range of problems that can contribute to personal and interpersonal distress. Once considered virtually untreatable, many of these disorders respond very positively to the treatments available today. Unfortunately, many people with disorders still do not seek help, possibly due to some of the stigma related to having a psychological problem or a lack of awareness that effective help is now available (see ● Figure 15.1). Sixty years ago, many people diagnosed with schizophrenia faced a discouraging future of institutionalization and

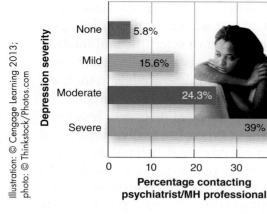

FIGURE 15.1

Many People With Psychological Disorders Do Not Receive Care. As symptoms of depression become more severe, people are more likely to obtain treatment from a psychiatrist or mental health professional, which would include clinical psychologists. It is difficult to tell whether the remaining individuals receive no care at all or are seen by their family physicians or other health care providers. *Source: Adapted from Pratt and Brody (2008).*

little, if any, improvement (see ● Figure 15.2). Today, although about 30% of patients with schizophrenia do not seem to respond to available treatments, the other 70% experience some relief from their troubling symptoms (Bobo & Meltzer, 2010; Wiersma, Nienhuis, Slooff, & Giel, 1998).

Approaches to Treatment Biological treatments, such as the medications described in more detail in later sections of this chapter, are often combined with psychological treatments, or **psychotherapies**, which generally involve a conversation between the professional providing the therapy and the person seeking help. For example, a person who is terrified of being part of a crowd might benefit from a combination of medication for anxiety and psychotherapy. As we will see in this chapter, different combinations of methods can be tailored to different types of problems and to the individuals being treated.

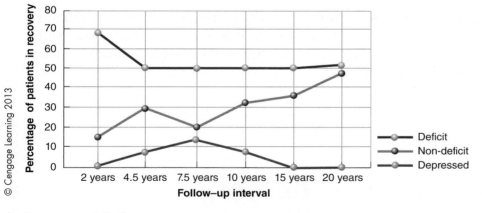

FIGURE 15.2

Recovery in Schizophrenia. Scientists are making progress in identifying which patients with schizophrenia are more responsive to current treatments. A "deficit" group of patients differed from a "non-deficit" group primarily in their having more emotional disturbances. "Recovery" was defined very strictly in this study as no psychiatric hospitalizations, no major symptoms, and at least half-time work or the equivalent level of functioning. In a 20-year study of the patients' outcomes, using a group of patients diagnosed with depression as a comparison group, the non-deficit group made more progress than the deficit group. Identifying which patients respond to existing treatments will help researchers and health care providers develop more effective treatment plans for each individual. *Source: Adapted from Strauss, Harrow, Grossman, and Rosen (2010).*

psychotherapy Treatment designed to improve symptoms of psychological disorder through conversation between the therapist and patient or client.

HOW DO PSYCHOLOGISTS PROVIDE THERAPY?

Illustration: © Cengage Learning 2013; photo: © Thinkstock/Photos.com

© Cengage Learning 2013

Biological Approaches Biological approaches to treatment have their roots in our understanding of the biological factors that contribute to psychological disorders. Along with the overall burst of scientific and medical knowledge beginning in the 18th century, scientists began to learn more about psychological disorders and their causes. This knowledge, in turn, set the stage for the discoveries of more effective biological treatments.

Improved medical knowledge made psychological disorders less mysterious. When untreated, syphilis (a common type of sexually transmitted disease) can produce a characteristic set of abnormal behaviors, including hallucinations, delusions, and changes in mood and personality. As we noted in our previous chapter, these behaviors are characteristic of a number of psychological disorders, including schizophrenia. The discovery that behaviors like hallucinations could have a biological cause (syphilis is caused by a bacterial infection) led to the recognition that abnormal behavior can result from infection or other medical conditions. In these cases, the abnormal behaviors should disappear when the underlying medical condition is treated.

The use of one biological approach to treatment, medication, revolutionized the care of people with some psychological disorders. In 1949, an Australian psychiatrist named John Cade discovered that lithium salts could produce remarkable improvements in the behavior of patients with bipolar disorder. Cade's discovery was followed quickly by breakthroughs in the use of medication to treat schizophrenia. Bolstered by these successes with some of the most troubling psychological conditions, the pharmaceutical industry quickly introduced medications for depression and anxiety. These successes not only led to better outcomes for many patients but also strengthened the credibility of using biological approaches to treat abnormal behaviors.

Psychological Approaches Running parallel to the successes of scientists engaged in biological approaches to disorders were significant contributions from those who focused on the psychological and emotional underpinnings of disorders.

Australian psychiatrist John Cade searched for alternatives to the electroconvulsive therapy, lobotomies, and psychoanalysis that were commonly used in the 1940s. After observing that lithium salts had a sedating effect on guinea pigs, he tried lithium on himself to test for side effects. He then tried lithium on his patients, and noticed that those with bipolar disorder appeared to respond favorably. Lithium is an element, so could not be patented, providing little financial incentive for the pharmaceutical industry. However, lithium was approved for use in the United States in 1970. Lithium salts continue to be used extensively to treat bipolar disorder, although we now understand that this treatment does have serious side effects.

Mouse: © Eric Isselée/Shutterstock; Periodic table: © Ron Dale/Shutterstock

During the 19th century, psychologists and psychiatrists were very interested in "hysteria," a condition that would be diagnosed today as a somatoform, or somatic symptom, disorder. Hysteria did not seem to have any biological basis and did not respond to the medical treatments of the day. Among the first efforts to treat hysteria through nonmedical means was the use of hypnosis by Franz Anton Mesmer (1734–1815), whose name gives us the alternate term for being hypnotized—"mesmerized." Mesmer attempted to treat hysteria by inducing a hypnotic state, described further in our chapter on consciousness. In many cases, people with hysteria no longer experienced their symptoms under hypnosis and, following Mesmer's suggestions made during hypnosis, continued to be symptom-free even after they left the hypnotic state.

Despite skepticism regarding Mesmer and his techniques, other scientists continued to explore hypnosis, suggestion, and hysteria. When positive outcomes were reported by the noted French neurologist Jean-Martin Charcot (1825–1893), hypnosis and suggestion took on a new legitimacy in the scientific community. Among admirers of Charcot and his work were Josef Breuer (1842–1925) and his more famous colleague, Sigmund Freud (1856–1939). As we will see later in this chapter, Freud eventually abandoned his interest in hypnosis in favor of other approaches, which eventually gave rise to psychoanalysis. Instead of hypnotizing people, Freud encouraged them to speak freely about whatever came to mind.

During the 20th century, psychological approaches to treatment reflected the rise of the behavioral and humanist perspectives, described in our introductory, learning, and personality chapters. The behaviorist perspective, unlike the biological and Freudian approaches, focused exclusively on observable behavior and approached the treatment of abnormal behaviors using the principles of classical conditioning, operant conditioning, and observational learning, described in our chapter on learning. The cognitive revolution of the second half of the 20th century added a recognition of the role of cognitions in abnormal behavior. Later in this chapter, we will explore the use of cognitive-behavioral treatments for disorders such as phobias and depression.

The rise of humanistic psychology in the second half of the 20th century also led to new **humanistic therapies**. As we discussed in our introductory chapter, the humanists specifically rebelled against psychodynamic thinking and the practice of psychoanalysis. Humanist therapist Carl Rogers wished to separate his procedures, described in greater detail later in this chapter, from the more traditional Freudian psychotherapies of his time by referring to treatment as **counseling** rather than psychotherapy or psychoanalysis (Rogers, 1942). Today's field of counseling psychology mirrors the more positive view of human nature held by the humanists by focusing on personal strengths and development.

Photo Researchers, Inc.

Franz Anton Mesmer (1734–1815), whose name gives us the term *mesmerized*, attempted to use hypnosis to treat people with "hysteria," which would now fall under the somatoform or somatic symptom disorders. Mesmer's practices inspired Sigmund Freud to use hypnosis, although he eventually abandoned the technique in favor of other approaches.

Mesmer's methods for using hypnosis to treat hysteria were quite theatrical and were denounced as fraudulent by none other than Benjamin Franklin, who was serving as the U.S. ambassador to France at the time.

© Roger Ressmeyer/CORBIS

Carl Rogers and the humanists rebelled against the practices of psychoanalysis and established new approaches of counseling psychology.

humanistic therapy A therapy approach patterned after the theories proposed by humanistic psychologists.

counseling Treatment originally proposed by humanistic therapists that includes a focus on personal strengths and development; now used to refer to treatment for adjustment problems as opposed to severe psychological disorders.

FIGURE 15.3

Evidence-Based Practice. Evidence-based practice (EBP) began in medicine and spread to psychotherapy and other helping professions. EBP combines the personal experience of the clinician, the best scientific evidence, and a consideration of patient values and expectations to tailor scientifically valid treatments to the individual.

Evidence-Based Practice (EBP) The beginning of the 21st century has featured greater demands to tie clinical practice to research on the outcomes of treatment. As shown in ● Figure 15.3, evidence-based practice (EBP) combines research evidence, clinical expertise, and patient values to provide the best outcome for a patient (Straus, Richardson, Glasziou, & Haynes, 2011). The movement toward EBP began in medicine, but has since spread throughout the helping professions, including psychology.

EBP combines five steps (Thyer, 2004). The first step is to construct an answerable question, such as "Which treatments produce the best outcomes in cases of post-traumatic stress disorder?" Next, the clinician conducts a search of the most current scientific literature related to the question. In other words, doing something "because I've always done it this way in my practice" is no longer an option. Third, the clinician critically evaluates the relevant literature, using the standards for good science that we discussed in our research methods chapter. This information is then integrated with data regarding a particular case, including the patient's values and circumstances. Finally, the clinician evaluates his or her performance based on the patient's outcomes and makes necessary adjustments.

If you think these EBP steps sound like the problem-solving system we introduced in our chapter on cognitive psychology, you're exactly right. You might have assumed that your health care provider would take this approach automatically, but many historically have been convinced that science can do little to assist them with an individual case and that clinical practice was more art than science. Large numbers of clinicians have traditionally valued their "clinical expertise" over the body of knowledge represented by science (Baker, McFall, & Shoham, 2008). Given the demanding financial realities of health care in the 21st century, however, a logical, scientific evidence–based approach to the delivery of health care services is not just the most effective approach but also the necessary thing to do.

Clinical Assessment Before a therapist can provide any type of useful treatment, he or she needs to understand the problems presented by the person to be treated. The choice of assessment methods will be guided by the training and experience of the clinician, but it usually includes the methods we described in our chapter on personality: interviews, observations, and some set of standardized tests (Groth-Marnat, 2009).

The Therapists

A wide range of professionals, including general medical practitioners, psychiatrists, psychologists, social workers, nurses, and religious leaders, provide counseling and psychotherapy. Licensing of these professionals to provide treatment for psychological disorders is administered by state governments in the United States and provincial governments in Canada. Requirements for licensing can vary widely from state to state and can result in a bewildering array of titles. For example, the simple term *therapist* is not regulated consistently across the United States. We will use the term **psychotherapist** for any of the many types of licensed professionals described in this section who provide psychotherapy.

Psychiatrists first obtain a standard MD (Medical Doctor) degree, and then spend an additional three to four years specializing in psychiatry. Because of their training and licensure as physicians, psychiatrists are allowed to perform the medical procedures we review later in this chapter, particularly the prescribing of medication. It is difficult to generalize across the entire profession, but psychiatrists are somewhat more likely to look for the causes of disorder in biological factors than in learned or environmental factors and to assume a biological treatment such as medication will be most effective. In addition, the medical model does not see treatment as taking place within a relationship of equals. Instead, expertise is simply transmitted from the doctor to the patient, and little input is expected from the patient. We will see alternatives to this model in the procedures conducted by other types of therapist.

The word *psychologist* is used to describe professionals who have completed advanced degrees in psychology, including those who become psychotherapists. Most psychologists, including the professors teaching your introductory course, earn the traditional academic Doctor of Philosophy (PhD) degree in psychology, but not all choose career paths as licensed psychotherapists. Clinical psychology is the path taken by psychology graduate students who wish to study, teach, or practice psychotherapy. In addition to completing the academic requirements for a PhD, clinical psychology students must spend an additional year providing treatment in a supervised internship.

Beginning in the 1970s, an alternate route to becoming a clinical psychologist arose from suggestions that the practice of psychology could be modeled after dental and medical schools (Norcross & Castle, 2002). The

Dr. Benjamin Rush (1749–1813), "the father of American psychiatry," believed that psychological disorders were caused by the "irritation" of the blood vessels in the brain. He invented the "tranquilizer chair" for patients and wrote a textbook published in 1812, *Medical Inquiries and Observations Upon Diseases of the Mind*, that was the standard in the field for the next 50 years.

psychotherapist A licensed professional who provides psychotherapy.

psychiatrist A medical doctor who specializes in psychiatry and can use medical procedures, such as the prescribing of medication, to treat psychological disorders.

Doctor of Psychology (PsyD) degree was developed to train students to provide services without undergoing the extensive training in research methods that characterizes the PhD degree.

Both PhD and PsyD programs can earn accreditation by the American Psychological Association. PsyD programs are becoming increasingly popular with students (see ● Figure 15.4). However, the lack of emphasis on research characteristic of the PsyD degree has led to concerns about the ability of these graduates to think scientifically about their choice of methods (Baker et al., 2008). For example, without a solid background in science, objective evaluation of and adherence to the evidence-based practice model could be quite difficult. Sixty-five percent of the faculty in institutions granting the traditional PhD teach scientifically supported cognitive-behavioral techniques (Norcross & Castle, 2002). In contrast, only about 30% of faculty in PsyD programs teach cognitive-behavioral techniques.

How do clinical psychologists and psychiatrists differ, other than that they earn different degrees? One of the traditional distinctions has been psychiatrists' ability to prescribe medication, but that difference is gradually disappearing. In 2002, New Mexico became the first state to allow select psychologists to prescribe medication, followed by Louisiana in 2004 (Daly, 2006). The requirements for already licensed clinical psychologists to gain prescription privileges are quite rigorous. Psychologists wishing

Experiencing Psychology

Self-Hypnosis

As you can see from the previous discussion, administering therapies for psychological disorders and problems with adjustment is typically the domain of highly trained professionals. However, there are a few activities people can do safely on their own to reduce stress and change habits. In our chapter on learning, we outlined a method you could use to change unwanted habits based on behavioral therapies. In this section, we review simple relaxation techniques used in self-hypnosis,

not unlike those that are used in prepared childbirth and meditation. Hypnosis, as we mentioned in our chapter on consciousness, does affect people differently, so some people will achieve greater relaxation using these techniques than will others. If you do not feel more relaxed on your first attempt, more practice might be helpful.

In addition to bringing about a very relaxed state, self-hypnosis uses affirmations, or positive suggestions, related to your goals. For example, you might be feeling stressed about

an upcoming job interview or exam. You can prepare a short list of affirmations prior to your self-hypnosis session that counter any doubts or negative thinking about your upcoming event. The best affirmations are specific, emotional, and in the present tense: "I am very well qualified for this job" or "I truly believe I have mastered the content of this course."

The next step is to put on some comfortable clothes and find a private, quiet place to sit down. Begin your session with relaxation.

FIGURE 15.4

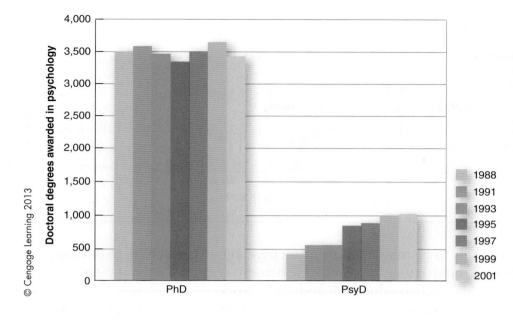

© Cengage Learning 2013

PsyD Degrees Are Becoming More Common. While PhD degrees awarded in psychology have remained constant, the number of PsyD degrees awarded between 1988 and 2001 grew 169%, a trend that continues. By 2006, PsyD degrees accounted for 30% of all doctorates in psychology and 42% of the clinical/counseling degrees. *Source:* Salazar & Frincke, 2005.

to prescribe medication in these states must go through an additional 450 classroom hours of neuroscience study, 80 hours of clinical practicum, and 400 physician-supervised hours of care with at least 100 patients.

In addition to treating people with diagnosed psychological disorders, clinical psychologists often provide marriage and family counseling, substance abuse counseling, vocational counseling, grief counseling, rehabilitation counseling, and prison counseling. However, these types of service are also provided by counselors, who typically do not provide services for psychological disorders such as schizophrenia. In other words, a couple experiencing marital conflict might seek out either a counselor or a clinical psychologist, whereas a person experiencing hallucinations and delusions

With each breath, imagine waves of relaxation running from your head downward. Say to yourself, "I am feeling relaxed. With each breath, I am becoming more relaxed." Some people prefer the more traditional "I am feeling sleepy. My arms and legs are beginning to feel heavy." Once you are feeling completely relaxed, begin to alternate your affirmations with your relaxation statements. Some people prefer to record their affirmations and play them back during a session. Do this for 15 to 20 minutes or so, and see how you feel.

If your efforts are not providing the results you want, you might choose to invest in commercial recordings that are designed to help you achieve a relaxed state. You do not need to worry about being helplessly hypnotized in your home and unable to wake up—stories like this make good Hollywood entertainment, but are not realistic. ✪

If you find it difficult to relax by following the instructions in this section, the use of progressive relaxation methods might help. In this approach to relaxation, you tense and relax muscle groups from head to toe. With a bit of practice, you should be able to more easily achieve a state of relaxation when you want to do so.

© Anan Kaewkhammul/Shutterstock

FIGURE 15.5

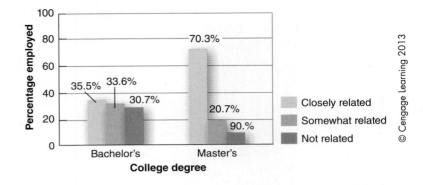

Job Opportunities for Workers With Bachelor's or Master's Degrees in Psychology More workers with master's degrees in psychology are employed in degree-relevant fields than workers with bachelor's degrees. Closely related fields include substance abuse counselor and applied behavior analysis therapist. Somewhat related fields include human resources administrator and nonprofit organization program coordinator. *Source:* Salazar & Frincke, 2005.

© Cengage Learning 2013

is more likely to be treated by a clinical psychologist or psychiatrist. Counselors can hold either master's or doctoral degrees in psychology and related fields, such as education and social work.

Students pursuing undergraduate psychology degrees frequently ask if they can do anything in the mental health field without a graduate degree. About one-third of undergraduates in psychology obtain jobs that are closely related to the field (see ● Figure 15.5).Students completing an undergraduate degree in psychology often work in group homes and camps for troubled youth, or in hospital or outpatient settings under supervision. Many others seek work in "people" related professions, including human resources, sales, and teaching.

In recognition of the historical role of religious leaders in providing counseling to members of their congregations, most states allow religious leaders to provide this service without further licensure. The Master of Divinity (MDiv) degree typically includes human development and counseling courses taught within schools of divinity. In a fairly new development, some universities are offering MDiv degrees that prepare students to be either religious leaders or counselors in the outside community.

Among the least frequently regulated practitioners are hypnotherapists. Only two states (Florida and Texas) require that a person using hypnotherapy be a licensed psychotherapist. Three states (Indiana, New Mexico, and Washington) insist that hypnotherapists register with the state. As we mentioned in our chapter on consciousness, there are many legitimate uses of hypnosis in therapy, and there are many legitimate therapists who use the technique. We also recounted the adventures of Zoe D. Katze, who is a hypnotherapist certified by the National Guild of Hypnotists, the American Board of Hypnotherapy, and the International Medical and Dental Hypnotherapy Association. She is a Professional Member of the American Association of Professional Hypnotherapists. Zoe also happens to be a cat, owned by a real psychotherapist named Steve Eichel (Eichel, 2002).

Another unregulated area in the provision of psychological services is the field of life coaching, which requires no licensing. According to the International Coach Federation (ICF), "Professional coaches provide an ongoing partnership designed to help clients produce fulfilling results in their personal and professional lives. Coaches help people improve their performances and enhance the quality of their lives" (International Coach Federation [ICF],

© Erich Schlegel/Corbis

Donald Asher writes and speaks about career hunting, college applications, and resume building, topics often presented by "life coaches." Although unlicensed, coaches also do many of the same tasks as psychotherapists. Licensed psychotherapists have found that referring to themselves as "coaches" rather than "therapists" reduces some of the stigma their clients might feel in using their services.

2006). Substitute *psychotherapist* for *coach* in this definition, and few would disagree with the resulting statements. Coaches seem to perform the same duties as psychotherapists. In fact, some psychotherapists have found that referring to themselves as "coaches" expands their practices, possibly because of the lower stigma of seeing a "coach" rather than a "therapist" in the minds of some clients. Few studies have attempted to evaluate the effectiveness of coaching, but those that have done so note that clients are very satisfied with the services (Grant, 2003). Life coaching provides the advantage of being more appealing to men, who generally seek more traditional psychotherapy in much smaller numbers than do women (McKelley & Rochlen, 2007).

Although licensure provides significant protection for the public, any consumer of psychological services must thoroughly investigate prospective psychotherapists. Zoe D. Katze may be an extreme example, but we suspect she is not alone.

Credentials are not always what they seem. For example, the author of the 1992 best seller *Men Are From Mars, Women Are From Venus*, lists himself as "John Gray, PhD" (MarsVenus.com, 2007). Gray's resume includes 9 years as a monk under the leadership of Beatles guru Maharishi Mahesh Yogi, a bachelor's and a master's degree in the Science of Creative Intelligence from the Maharishi European Research Institute in Switzerland, and a PhD from the now-defunct Columbia Pacific University (CPU) in California, which was described by the state government as a "diploma mill."

So far, we have focused our discussion on credentialing practices in the United States. Worldwide, an even greater variety of professionals perform psychotherapy and counseling under diverse licensure and oversight practices. The United Kingdom, Australia, and Canada provide systems that are similar to those in the United States for delivering psychotherapy (Priebe, 2006). In these countries, psychotherapy is conducted by a number of different professionals, including physicians, psychologists, social workers, nurses, and others in similar professions. In each case, performing psychotherapy requires training beyond that needed to simply obtain the appropriate professional degree. Some European countries are more restrictive. Germany and Russia are particularly strict in their accreditation rules. Because of the prevalence of state-run health systems in Europe, assessments of treatment outcomes are regularly conducted (Priebe, 2006). In the United States, treatment outcomes are a question of interest to academic researchers, but are rarely assessed as comprehensively as in many other nations, although that circumstance is likely to change with further government involvement in health care.

Popular television celebrity "Dr. Phil" McGraw was criticized heavily for a 2008 visit to hospitalized Britney Spears, after which he told the press that Spears needed both psychological and medical treatment. Dr. McGraw had allowed his licensure as a psychologist to expire in the state of Texas and has never obtained a license in the state of California, where he tapes his show and visited Spears. In 2002, the California Board of Psychology determined that McGraw did not need a license, because he was "doing more entertainment than psychology." However, his statement about Spears appeared to cross the professional line for many health care professionals.

Delivering Psychotherapy

Many people imagining a session of psychotherapy will think of a stereotypical Freudian scenario. The patient reclines on a couch, while a bearded man sitting in a chair scribbles copious notes. Although some therapy continues to take place using such a setting, many more options are available.

Variations in Length of Treatment Most psychotherapy occurs in the form of individual therapy, involving face-to-face, hour-long meetings between the therapist and the patient or client (as we will see in a subsequent

Many people thinking about psychotherapy imagine a bearded man scribbling notes next to a patient reclining on a couch, but this stereotype is usually far from the truth.

section, terminology varies among practitioners). In traditional psychoanalysis, such meetings are quite frequent (four to five times per week) and take place over the course of years. In cognitive-behavioral therapies, described in detail in a later section, sessions might occur once per week for about six weeks. Given the approximate rates of up to $150 per hour for individual therapy, insurance providers are pressuring psychotherapists to find faster, more efficient ways to provide treatment. Many insurance plans limit psychotherapy sessions to 10 per calendar year.

Brief therapy, advocated by Milton Erickson and others, specifically avoids spending long periods searching for the historical basis of a person's problems. Instead, therapists using this approach focus on "solution-building rather than problem-solving" (Iveson, 2002). Consequently, practitioners argue that only three to five sessions are necessary. Many brief therapy interventions involve only one session, and no cases require more than eight.

Alternatives to Individual Therapy In addition to individual sessions, psychotherapy can take place with groups of patients or clients in **group therapy**.

It is important to note that group therapy does not imply particular types of treatment approaches. Although some treatment approaches seem better suited for group work than others, therapists of all persuasions are known to utilize groups in their work. The groups formed by the therapist can be homogeneous, in the sense that the group members share a common problem, or heterogeneous, in which the group members have diverse diagnoses. In most cases, groups are limited to between 6 and 12 individuals. People with severe conditions, such as psychotic, suicidal, or antisocial tendencies, are usually excluded from groups until they progress sufficiently to act as good group members.

brief therapy Psychotherapy provided in a very short time frame, usually between three and five sessions.

group therapy Psychotherapy conducted with a group of patients or clients rather than individually.

People participating in group therapy benefit from reduced feelings of isolation. Seeing the progress of others with the same condition raises hope and provides opportunities to model successful strategies.

Although many groups are organized and supervised by a licensed psychotherapist, leaderless self-help groups are also quite popular. Weight Watchers, Alcoholics Anonymous (AA), and other groups modeled after AA have become very popular sources of support and self-improvement. These groups often operate with a member-leader who is not a psychotherapist, and they function outside the realm of government licensure and supervision.

In addition to the obvious cost-effectiveness of having a group split the therapist's fee, group therapy offers a number of advantages (Yalom, 1995). For example, group therapy offers hope to members, who benefit from seeing others who have made more progress with their condition. Group members also benefit from knowing that others share their condition, decreasing their sense of isolation. Although practitioners generally believe that group therapy is effective, research on group therapy outcomes is very difficult to conduct because of the large number of variables that must be considered. The need to control for such factors as different disorders and previous treatment history make this area very challenging for researchers.

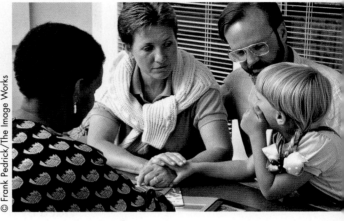

© Frank Pedrick/The Image Works

Family therapy combines individual sessions with sessions that include some combination of family members, like these parents and their young daughter.

Family therapy, in which various family members participate in therapy individually and in combination with other family members, is another alternative to the purely individual provision of treatment. **Couples therapy** is a type of family therapy that focuses on intimate relationships. Family therapy is frequently used when a child or teen is experiencing problems, as these problems typically impact and are affected by the behavior of other family members. Family therapists face a number of significant challenges. In some cases, the member who seems to need treatment the most refuses to participate. In others, maintaining the confidentiality of all participants can be difficult. Teens might disclose information that will help the parents do their job much better, but sharing this information with the parents could interrupt the trust the therapist has built up with the teen.

Innovative Delivery Systems An emerging delivery system for psychotherapy is online therapy. When "online therapy" is used as a Google search term, over 139 million results are returned. The benefits of privacy, engaging in therapy from home, and the ability to choose a suitable therapist regardless of location provide significant advantages for some clients. In its early days, online therapy was conducted through e-mail or chat. Because the written word conveys less information than a therapist obtains face-to-face, this method could be viewed as a disadvantage. However, many online therapists have taken advantage of Skype and other voice and video technologies. Online delivery of cognitive-behavioral therapy (CBT) has been shown to be as effective as face-to-face CBT (Ruwaard, Lange, Schrieken, & Emmelkamp, 2011).

Other technologies have influenced the delivery of psychotherapy. Therapists can buy products such as Wiley's Thera*Scribe*, a computer program that includes over 2,500 prewritten interventions, goals, objectives, and suggested diagnoses. The program generates reports catering

family therapy A type of therapy in which family members participate individually and in combination with other family members.

couples therapy A type of family therapy that focuses on intimate relationships.

The benefits of privacy, engaging in therapy from home, frequent 24-7 coverage, video interactions using Skype or similar technologies, and the ability to choose a suitable therapist regardless of location provide significant advantages for some clients. Online delivery of cognitive-behavioral therapy (CBT) has been shown to be as effective as face-to-face delivery (Ruwaard et al., 2011).

Courtesy of Mountain Employee Assistance Program

to Medicare and other managed care organizations. The time savings provided by these technologies can be useful in controlling costs, but receiving a prewritten evaluation might seem somewhat impersonal to individuals seeking therapy. If you receive a treatment plan from your campus health center that is nearly identical to a friend's, you might not feel the counselor really cared much about you.

Contemporary Challenges in Treatment

Providing treatment for psychological disorders has changed dramatically since the days of Sigmund Freud. Originally, therapy was provided by individual professionals in small private practices. In the latter part of the 20th century, however, this model became increasingly rare as psychological treatments became more likely to be managed by large organizations, including insurance companies. Many of the concerns about these new models of managed psychological treatment echo similar complaints from the medical community regarding contemporary medical treatment. Decisions formerly made by the therapist about the types of disorders that warranted treatment and the length, frequency, and type of treatment to be offered are now more likely to be made by insurance company personnel without medical or psychological training (Baker et al., 2008).

In addition to the need to adapt to the managed care of psychological disorders, psychotherapy faces many of the same challenges as medicine in providing scientifically valid treatments. Just as we would expect our physician to provide a scientifically supported treatment for cancer, we should expect a psychotherapist to provide equally well-documented treatments for depression. In our earlier section on evidence-based practice (EBP), we joined most research clinical psychologists and psychiatrists in endorsing the use of science in selecting, implementing, and evaluating psychological treatments. However, as we saw in our discussion of the Rorschach Inkblot Test in our chapter on personality, a lack of scientific support does not always prevent an approach from being widely used.

Frustration over the lack of emphasis on science in psychotherapy has led to considerable debate. Currently, the American Psychological Association (APA) has the primary responsibility for accrediting programs that train clinical psychologists with either PhD or PsyD degrees. This system has been challenged by a new accreditation body, the Psychological Clinical Science Accreditation System (PCSAS; 2011), which specifically aims to increase the scientific basis of clinical treatment and research literacy among clinical psychologists. Time will tell if PCSAS will be able to nudge the clinical psychology community into a greater reliance on research-based methods.

Summary 15.1

The Psychotherapists

Title	Degrees	Specialties
Psychiatrist Stock Montage/ Getty Images	MD	• Treats psychological disorders • Prescribes medication
Clinical psychologist © Frank Pedrick/ The Image Works	PhD or PsyD	• Treats psychological disorders and problems with adjustment • If specially licensed, prescribes medication
Counselor © Roger Ressmeyer/ CORBIS	PhD, PsyD, EdD, or various master's degrees	• Specializes in problems with adjustment

What Different Types of Psychotherapies Are Used?

Because Sigmund Freud is typically credited with being the first person to use "talking therapy" in his efforts to improve his patients' psychological symptoms, we begin our discussion of specific treatment approaches with **psychoanalysis**. A psychotherapist who uses psychoanalysis is typically known as a psychoanalyst. Psychoanalysis has not fared well in scientific studies of its effectiveness, although supporters continue to argue in its favor (Lichtenberg, Lachmann, & Fosshage, 2010; Leichsenring &

psychoanalysis The treatment approach developed by Freud and practiced by those who believe psychodynamic theories.

Freud's study featured not only the famous couch but also Persian rugs and a sample of Freud's collection of antiquities.

Freud called his slips "faulty actions." For example, a man texting his partner "I wish you were her" instead of "I wish you were here" would have a great deal of explaining to do. Modern cognitive psychologists are more likely to blame slips on conflicts between grammar sequences than between the unconscious and conscious minds.

Rabung, 2008). The absence of strong evidence for its efficacy has led to a decline in its use. However, psychoanalysis served as an important step to contemporary treatments.

Psychoanalysis Sigmund Freud's approach to psychotherapy reflected several key themes from his theory of personality. In particular, Freud emphasized the importance of conflict between the self (ego), the aggressive energy of the id, and the restrictions supplied by society (superego). Freud's view of the ability of the unconscious mind to affect behavior is also central to his therapeutic approach. Because of Freud's training as a physician, the psychoanalyst takes a directive role, which means that he or she is definitely in charge of the session. Like your physician, the psychoanalyst does not expect any contributions from you other than information about your symptoms.

Freud's psychoanalysis is a classic example of an **insight therapy**. Insight therapies assume that people will improve once they understand their problems. For Freud, many psychological disorders arose from problems that resided in the unconscious mind, out of conscious awareness. Although the person might not be consciously aware of these continuing conflicts, the conflicts exert their influence on behavior and through dreams. For example, a patient might arrive at the therapist's office complaining about her inability to enjoy a satisfactory sex life with a beloved spouse. Although many different factors could obviously contribute to such problems, the psychoanalyst is likely to suspect the influence of some traumatic experience that is relatively unavailable to the patient's conscious thoughts. Perhaps the patient is the victim of childhood sexual abuse, or she might be experiencing a conflict between the ultra-strict morality she learned from her parents and her current desire to have a fulfilling relationship with her partner. For the psychoanalyst, the "cure" lies in uncovering the unconscious contributions to the patient's problems. Once she understands the source of her problems (the insight), her situation should improve.

How does one go about uncovering unconscious material? Although Freud experimented with the use of hypnosis to access the unconscious mind, he became dissatisfied with the results and abandoned the procedure. Instead, Freud decided to use the technique of **free association**. Free association occurs when a person says whatever comes to mind. As we mature, most of us become aware that we do not literally "speak our mind" out of consideration for our fellow humans. Although small children might tell a person, "You're fat," such comments, although they may be true, are not the type that most adults consider polite. We learn to think before we speak. To engage in free association, this self-censor must be turned off, allowing the patient to verbalize those thoughts that are typically withheld. Without the self-censor, the famous "Freudian slips" might occur and are assumed to reflect unconscious wishes.

insight therapy A therapy that improves symptoms of psychological disorder by building the patient's or client's understanding of his or her situation.

free association The psychoanalytic technique of encouraging a patient to say whatever comes to mind without attempting to censor the content.

© Cengage Learning 2013; courtesy of damnyouautocorrect.com

We're not certain how Freud would analyze the often embarrassing mistakes people experience as a result of the autocorrect feature on their phones.

Not all psychoanalysts engage in dream analysis, but it is likely that therapists interested in dream analysis are psychoanalysts. For Freud, dreaming represented a censored reflection of unconscious wishes and, therefore, a potential source of much useful insight into the unconscious mind. If the patient is undergoing dream analysis, he or she is taught to awaken following a dream in order to jot some notes that can later be reviewed with the therapist, who will attempt to interpret the dream's symbolic meanings.

In addition to reviewing the content of free association, dreams, and Freudian slips, the analyst looks for signs of transference and resistance. **Transference** occurs when a patient uses an earlier relationship, usually with a parent or other authority figure, as a prototype for a current relationship, such as that between the patient and therapist. If the patient begins yelling at the therapist, the therapist might infer that the patient reacted similarly to parents and others in authority under similar circumstances in the past. **Resistance** occurs when the patient is getting closer to insight. Freud believed that we have unconscious wishes to maintain infantile fantasies and avoid punishment, and efforts to uncover this material will be resisted by the patient. Resistance, for the psychoanalyst, can be expressed in many forms. When a patient changes the subject, disagrees with the analyst's interpretation, or even misses an appointment because of a flat tire, the analyst might suspect he or she is getting closer to the uncomfortable truth.

In recent years, psychoanalysis has changed in the length and frequency of treatment. Driven by demands from insurance providers, psychoanalysts have developed new, briefer treatments. These briefer approaches tend to be less past-oriented as well. In other words, the psychoanalyst might ask about a person's recent experiences at work rather than his or her experiences as a toddler.

Does psychoanalysis work? Some published meta-analyses suggest that psychoanalysis produces better results than no treatment and occasionally produces results comparable to more modern approaches to therapy (Leichsenring, 2005; Leichsenring & Rabung, 2010; Shedler, 2010). However, these studies have been criticized on the basis of their methods, such as including Rorschach Inkblot results as measures of patient improvement (McKay, 2011).

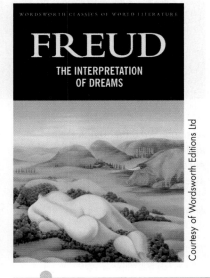

Courtesy of Wordsworth Editions Ltd

The Interpretation of Dreams by Sigmund Freud was originally published in German in 1900. The 600 copies of the first edition sold slowly, and the publisher did not issue a second edition until 1909. Nonetheless, this book is considered one of Freud's most influential.

transference A psychoanalytic technique in which the therapist uses the responses of the patient to the therapist to understand the patient's approach to authority figures in general.

resistance A psychoanalytic technique in which the patient's reluctance to accept the interpretations of the therapist indicate that the interpretations are correct.

Humanistic Therapies

As we mentioned in our chapter on personality, humanistic approaches developed in direct opposition to the theories and techniques of Freud and his followers. Where Freud believed that human beings are inherently selfish and aggressive, the humanists believed that human beings are inherently good, possessing natural drives to grow and improve. Society for Freud had a beneficial effect on behavior by providing controls on our selfish and aggressive tendencies. For the humanists, society can interfere with growth by providing judgmental feedback.

Not too surprisingly, this conflict in theory led to an equal opposition in treatment approaches. As we mentioned previously, the psychoanalyst takes a very powerful, directive role reminiscent of a medical doctor. The individual seeking therapy is identified as a patient. As in the medical setting, the therapist identifies the nature of the patient's problems and prescribes a course of action. Other than supplying information, the patient has a relatively passive role in the process. In contrast, the humanistic therapist is nondirective and treats the person seeking therapy, referred to as a "client" instead of as a patient, as more of an equal in the process. The client is expected to take an active role in helping to identify his or her problems and a positive course of action.

Although we think that dressing and sitting like your client is not necessary to demonstrate empathy, attempting to see situations through the client's eyes is an important part of humanistic therapies.

Primary among the humanistic approaches to treatment is the **person-centered therapy** of Carl Rogers (1942). In place of the psychoanalytic goal of uncovering unconscious sources of problems, person-centered therapy aims to achieve congruence, which we discussed in our chapter on personality. For Rogers, discrepancies between the ideal and real selves, as in the case where we fail to live up to our ideals, can lead to psychological disorders. Therapy techniques that bring the selves into alignment should effectively treat the disorders.

Among the techniques used to achieve this congruence are empathy, unconditional positive regard, and the reflection and clarification of feelings. The empathic therapist attempts to see the world through the eyes of the client, as opposed to imposing his or her worldview. Allowing the client to feel understood in this manner contributes to the establishment of a safe, supportive environment where natural growth can occur. Unconditional positive regard, discussed in our chapter on personality, also contributes to the safety of the therapeutic setting. Rogers believed that much human unhappiness resulted from conditional regard, in which children learn they have value only when their behavior is pleasing

person-centered therapy A humanistic therapy approach developed by Carl Rogers to help clients achieve congruence.

According to the humanists, people who learn they have value only when their behavior is pleasing to authority figures can benefit from a therapy setting that features unconditional positive regard.

© wincott/Shutterstock

to an authority figure. The nonjudgmental, unconditional positive regard of the therapy setting is designed to compensate for those earlier, potentially damaging experiences.

Reflection techniques consist of the therapist restating some of the client's comments in a way that conveys understanding. As such, reflection contributes to empathy and the client's sense of being fully understood. For example, a client might state that he felt very helpless when his boss reprimanded him for losing an important account. The therapist might simply comment, "You sound like you were very angry and frustrated when your boss yelled at you." Clarification allows the therapist to point out important insights the client might have reached. The therapist might clarify the situation with the boss by pointing out its similarities with the feelings we have as children when we are corrected by an adult.

Even when psychotherapists use therapy techniques other than a person-centered approach, they frequently incorporate some or all of Rogers's communication strategies, such as reflection. These strategies have also become quite popular in programs designed to improve interpersonal communication and group process. For example, it is not uncommon for teens to stomp into the house and declare that they "hate" their parents. The typical response of the parent at that point is to become hurt and angry. The argument escalates as the parent retaliates with a hurtful statement, perhaps "I wish you were never born!" Rogers suggests that such immature battles are easily avoided. Instead of retaliating, the parent might say, "I know it makes you very angry when I restrict your privileges, but we had a deal, you broke it, and that means there will be consequences." Reflecting another's emotions in this way may increase the chances of defusing needless hostility and of coming to a mutual understanding, since the person will know more concretely that he or she is "being heard."

Reflecting feelings takes practice to avoid sounding silly or reverting to the cliché "I hear what you're saying," but you might give it a try the next time someone confronts you. Reflecting the other person's feelings instead of focusing on your own helps you stay calm, and it's hard to carry on a one-sided argument with a calm person.

Like psychoanalysis, humanistic approaches to therapy work better in some instances than in others. Rogers referred to his approach as "counseling," and his techniques are probably better suited to problems of adjustment than cases of serious disorders, such as schizophrenia. Efforts to assess the outcomes of humanistic therapy scientifically have been rejected by its followers. For example, one group of proponents argued that "natural science methodology should not be privileged over human science methodology" (Bohart, O'Hara, & Leitner, 1998, p. 141). By now, you probably understand that we would reject this suggestion and argue instead that science is science, regardless of the phenomenon being examined.

Behavioral Therapies

Freud's psychodynamic theory, humanistic theory, and behaviorism were among the most dominant influences in psychology during the 20th century. We have seen how psychodynamic and humanistic theories were applied to psychotherapy in the form of psychoanalysis and Rogers's person-centered therapy, so it should come as no surprise to find that behaviorism has similar applications. Given our formal definition of learning as "a relatively permanent change in behavior due to experience," it seems logical to use

The subject of Freud's famous case study of "Little Hans" was actually named Herbert Graf. Graf grew up to be a successful opera producer at New York's Metropolitan Opera and the Salzburg Festival in Austria. He is shown here directing the great Marion Anderson as she rehearses for her operatic debut in Verdi's "Masked Ball" in 1954.

learning as a way to increase the frequency of desirable behaviors and decrease unwanted behaviors in the therapy setting.

Behavior therapies represent applications of classical and operant conditioning to problems of adjustment and psychological disorders. These techniques have proved helpful in both reducing unwanted behaviors and increasing the frequency of desirable behaviors over a wide range of psychological conditions, including autism and schizophrenia. The first book to use the term behavior modification in its title was Leonard Ullman and Leonard Krasner's *Case Studies in Behavior Modification*, published in 1965. The public initially distrusted behavioral treatment methods, because they were based on animal research and assumed human behavior was relatively simple. The mysticism of the psychoanalysts' unconscious drives and impulses seemed far more romantic. However, when behavior modification produced successful results in cases that were previously considered untreatable, such as autism, respect for the approach grew.

Like behaviorism in general, behavior modification focuses on what can be observed and makes few if any assumptions about such unseen factors as an unconscious mind. We can contrast the way Freud and a therapist using behavior modification might approach Freud's case of Little Hans, a 5-year-old boy who had a phobia of horses (Freud, 1909/1976). For Freud, Hans's phobia resulted from the Oedipus complex issues that were supposedly at their height at his age. Horses, Freud argued, symbolized Hans's father. The boy had noted that he was especially frightened of horses with black bits in their mouths, which Freud suggested represented the father's moustache. Freud concluded that Hans's fear of horses resulted from his unconscious fear of retaliation by the father for sexual fantasies about his mother and would disappear with the resolution of Hans's Oedipus complex.

Now it is the behaviorist's turn. According to classical conditioning theory, phobias can result from conditioned fears. In Hans's day, horses were the most frequently used means of transportation, especially in large cities. Accidents involving horses were frequent and quite serious. Hans related that he was frightened of horses falling, and with good reason, as it

Behavioral treatments for phobias have been improved with the development of virtual reality for exposing clients to fear-producing stimuli. Researchers at the University of Washington have developed "Spiderworld" and successfully demonstrated that participants could reduce their fear of real spiders after undergoing three treatment sessions.

behavior therapy Applications of classical and operant conditioning principles to the treatment of symptoms of psychological disorder and adjustment problems.

most significant gains, and the effects of the treatment seemed to diminish with the increasing age of the child. Today, it is common practice to begin behavioral treatment for autism as early as possible. The team also realized that generalization, which we discussed in our chapter on learning, was very important. They achieved the best results when they began to train parents to continue their methods at home, rather than relying just on the treatment provided by the clinics during occasional visits. Finally, they were able to streamline their very complicated techniques, although even today, the delivery of behavioral therapy in autism is an extremely time-consuming process taking place during most of the child's waking hours each day. ☻

One of Lovaas's earliest patients was Pamela. She eventually learned to read, but when left alone, she reverted to her self-stimulation behaviors. After working with older children like Pamela, Lovaas realized that his treatment would be more effective if it were begun at a very early stage of development.

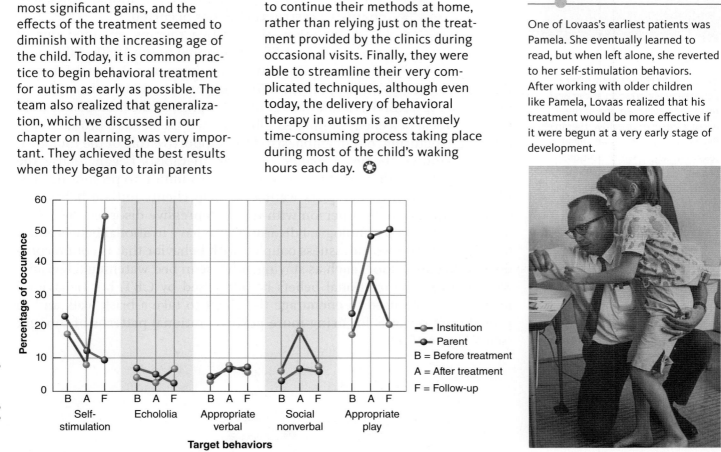

© Cengage Learning 2013

FIGURE 15.6

Behavior Modification and Autism. In this early study, Lovaas, Schreibman, and Koegel (1974) demonstrated that their behavioral techniques reduced unwanted behaviors (self-stimulation and echolalia) while increasing desirable behaviors (appropriate verbalizations, social nonverbal communication, and appropriate play) in children with autism. However, gains were quickly lost in children who were discharged from treatment to institutions rather than to their parents. From these early studies, Lovaas learned that the timing of his treatments was very important, because the younger children responded better to therapy. *Source: Adapted from Lovaas, Schreibman, and Koegel (1974).*

Aaron Beck (1921–), shown here addressing a workshop at the Beck Institute, developed one of the earliest types of cognitive therapies. Beck's approach featured cognitive restructuring, in which irrational beliefs, such as "everyone must love me or I can't be happy," are replaced with more rational beliefs, such as "I can be happy because I have some people who love me."

important aspect of the therapy process occurs when the therapist attempts to change the irrational beliefs of the client. For example, let's assume a therapist is trying to help a student with test anxiety. The student has an irrational belief that she is going to flunk out of school, despite her adequate GPA. To help the student realize that her belief is irrational, the therapist might ask her to provide evidence of the likelihood of flunking out or to identify the worst possible outcome of giving up the belief. Faced with logic, the student begins to substitute a new, rational belief for the old, irrational belief, and **cognitive restructuring** has occurred.

A variation of cognitive therapy emerged out of work by Albert Ellis, beginning in the 1950s. Ellis's version of cognitive therapy is known as Rational Emotive Behavioral Therapy (REBT; Ellis, 1975). Compared to many other types of psychotherapy, REBT is somewhat confrontational, as the therapist is more openly critical of a client's thinking. Ellis retained the need to produce cognitive restructuring, but deemphasized the supportive role of the therapist.

As cognitive therapy expanded further, therapists began to use the term **cognitive-behavioral therapy (CBT)**. In addition to promoting cognitive restructuring, therapists wanted to help clients initiate behavioral changes. For example, a person with major depressive disorder, described in our chapter on psychological disorders, can have irrational beliefs about hopelessness and worthlessness coupled with behavior that is counterproductive to good mood, such as staying at home in bed watching television. Not only can the irrational beliefs be addressed by CBT, but behavioral methods can be used to encourage the client to take a brisk walk and to provide self-rewards for using more positive, rational patterns of thought (see ● Figure 15.7).

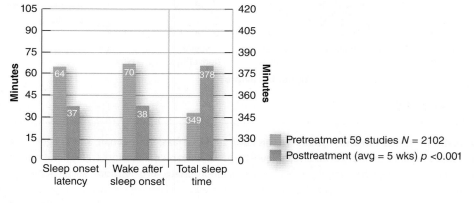

cognitive restructuring A technique used in cognitive therapies in which new, rational beliefs replace earlier, irrational beliefs held by the client.

cognitive-behavioral therapy (CBT) A combination of cognitive restructuring with behavioral treatments that has been shown to be effective in reducing symptoms of many psychological disorders.

FIGURE 15.7

Cognitive-Behavioral Therapy (CBT) Produces Clear, Long-Lasting Improvements in Many Conditions. The use of cognitive-behavioral therapy (CBT) is best understood in the treatment of major depressive disorder, but CBT can improve many conditions, including insomnia. In this experiment, CBT produced improvements in the amount of time needed to get to sleep (sleep onset latency), the amount of wakeful time after the onset of sleep, and total sleep time. *Source: Adapted from Morin et al. (1994).*

Cognitive-behavioral therapy has an excellent record of success, particularly in the treatment of major depressive disorder (Roth & Fonagy, 1996; Westbrook & Kirk, 2005). Because CBT typically requires fewer than 16 sessions and can be used for a wide variety of conditions, it is a favorite among insurance providers.

Biopsychosocial Approaches

Patient characteristics, the type of problems being addressed, and other variables influence the success of any particular treatment. Consequently, most therapists use the **biopsychosocial approach**, which combines elements of therapy designed to address the biological, psychological, and social underpinnings of an individual case. The therapist focuses on what works for an individual client, without adopting a single theoretical orientation (Lazarus, 2005). For example, a therapist might find that relaxation training seems to help one client while role-playing is more effective with another.

What Are Biological Therapies?

The major types of biological treatments for psychological disorders include medication, electroconvulsive therapy (ECT), psychosurgery, deep brain stimulation, and neurofeedback.

Medication

Medication is the most commonly used of the medical therapies. Particularly in the last 60 years, the discovery of medications that effectively treated psychological disorder has dramatically shaped the outcomes of millions of patients. A comprehensive review of psychoactive medications is clearly beyond the scope of this text, but we will discuss the use of medication for some specific disorders later in this chapter.

Electroconvulsive Therapy (ECT)

Electroconvulsive therapy (ECT) is used in some severe cases of depression that do not respond to other treatments. In ECT, the patient is anesthetized and given a muscle relaxant prior to the induction of general seizures, which are produced by electricity applied through electrodes on the head. Six to 12 treatments, at a rate of three per week, are typically given.

ECT was first used with patients with schizophrenia in the 1930s, with very poor results. However, observations of improved mood in these patients following ECT led to further use with patients diagnosed with major depressive or bipolar disorder. This procedure is used primarily with patients who do not respond to conventional treatments with medication (Medda, Perugi, Zanello, Ciuffa, & Cassano, 2009). Although the exact mode of action of ECT is currently unknown, most patients experience an increase in responsiveness to dopamine and norepinephrine, along with the desired reduction in subjective feelings of depression. Other research has suggested that ECT might stimulate neural growth (Duman & Vaidya, 1998; Ma et al., 2010).

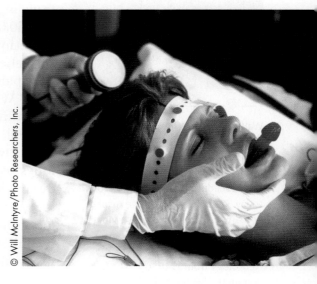

A patient is shown being prepared for electroconvulsive therapy (ECT) for serious depression. The patient is anesthetized before electricity is applied through electrodes to the head, inducing seizures. ECT is believed to increase responsiveness to dopamine and norepinephrine and to stimulate neural growth.

© Will McIntyre/Photo Researchers, Inc.

biopsychosocial approach An integrated approach to therapy that combines treatments addressing the biological, personal, and social underpinnings of psychological disorders.

electroconvulsive therapy (ECT) A biological treatment in which seizures are induced in an anesthetized patient; used primarily in the treatment of mood disorders that have not responded to medication or other treatments.

Trepanation has made a bizarre modern comeback in the form of an alternative medicine or elective procedure. People are actually doing this in their own homes, in a possible variation of the self-injurious behavior we discussed in our learning chapter. They argue that the procedure improves brain circulation and metabolism, but research support for such claims is lacking (Moskalenko et al., 2008).

© AP Photo

Walter Freeman (1895–1972) performed over 3,400 lobotomies at $25 per procedure, despite having no formal training in surgery. Although this procedure is considered barbaric today, Freeman enjoyed the respect of many of his colleagues, serving as cofounder and president of the American Board of Psychiatry and Neurology from 1946 to 1947. He nominated his mentor, Egas Moniz, for the Nobel Prize in Physiology and Medicine, which Moniz won in 1949.

psychosurgery The attempt to improve symptoms of psychological disorders through the use of brain surgery.

deep brain stimulation Electrical stimulation applied through surgically implanted electrodes; used to treat some anxiety and mood disorders.

Although many people have a negative view of ECT, perhaps as a result of reading Ken Kesey's *One Flew Over the Cuckoo's Nest* or viewing the film or play of the same name, ECT is considered as safe as any minor surgery conducted under general anesthesia (American Psychiatric Association [APA], 2001). However, approximately one third of patients experience persistent memory loss following the procedure (Rose, Fleischmann, Wykes, Leese, & Bindman, 2003). This memory loss specifically affects autobiographical memory, discussed in our chapter on memory, which can be impaired for at least six months following treatment (Sackheim et al., 2007).

Psychosurgery As we observed in our first chapter, trepanation, or the drilling of holes in the skull by ancient people, might represent the very first effort to use psychosurgery. Although particular functions might be localized to parts of the brain, it is a giant leap of faith from our current understanding of localization and brain networking to the idea that one can use **psychosurgery** to treat psychological disorders.

Historically, one of the most frequent types of psychosurgery aimed at changing behavior was the frontal lobotomy, which we discussed in our chapter on biological psychology. After observing the calm that resulted following the procedure in chimpanzees, Egas Moniz encouraged his colleagues to try the procedure on psychotic patients in the 1930s (Valenstein, 1986). Walter Freeman popularized the procedure in the United States, traveling in a vehicle he referred to as his "lobotomobile." Between 40,000 and 50,000 patients received the procedure between the 1930s and 1950s, sometimes for very vague problems such as depression in housewives or misbehavior in children (Sabatini, 1997). John Fulton, whose research with chimpanzees had formed the basis for Freeman's operation, was horrified. "What are these terrible things I hear about you doing lobotomies in your office with an ice pick?" he asked Freeman. "Why not use a shotgun?" (Kopell, Machado, & Rezai, 2005, p. 192).

As we have emphasized in several contexts in this textbook, the frontal lobes participate in some of the highest order cognitive functions carried out by the human brain. Consequently, the deliberate damage to the frontal lobes and their connections to other parts of the brain involved with the lobotomy procedure has harmful effects on a person's judgment, personality, initiative, social behavior, and sense of self. Despite the outrage among many in the medical community, frontal lobotomies were performed well into the 1960s, until the use of medications for psychological disorders became an established practice (Sabatini, 1997). Radiation and very precise lesions are still used today to treat small numbers of patients with depression or obsessive-compulsive disorder (Kopell et al., 2005).

Brain Stimulation Brain stimulation has a number of advantages over psychosurgery. Most importantly, most of the effects are reversible. In contrast, once the brain has been damaged by psychosurgery, there is no going back.

Following observations of mood changes in patients undergoing **deep brain stimulation** through surgically implanted electrodes for the relief of

Parkinson's disease, physicians attempted to use stimulation to address obsessive-compulsive disorder and mood disorders. Microelectrodes are surgically inserted into specific parts of the brain, and in many cases, the patient controls the application of any current (Mayberg et al., 2005). Fifty percent of patients with severe depression who had not responded to more conventional treatments achieved improvements in mood following stimulation of the nucleus accumbens (Bewernick et al., 2010). In our chapter on biological psychology, we indicated that the nucleus accumbens was part of a circuit that processes feelings of reward. Stimulating this area improved patients' mood and led to their engagement in more pleasurable activities.

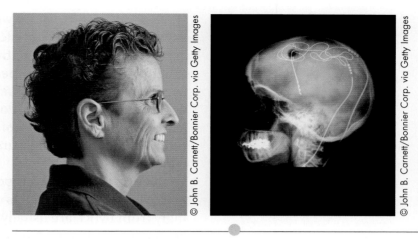

After the successful use of deep brain stimulation for Parkinson's disease, the method was used to treat patients with depression. The image on the right shows where an electrode was implanted in this woman's brain.

Deep brain stimulation requires surgery to implant the microelectrodes. Repeated transcranial magnetic stimulation (rTMS) provides an alternative way to stimulate the brain without surgery. When applied through a handheld device touching the scalp, low-frequency magnetic pulses change activity in underlying cortical regions. Application of rTMS over the auditory cortex reduced instances of auditory hallucinations in patients with schizophrenia for a period of up to 15 weeks (Hoffman et al., 2003). This technique has been recommended for use in depression (see ● Figure 15.8) and some cases of schizophrenia, but it appears to have a negative effect in cases of obsessive-compulsive disorder (OCD; Slotema, Blom, Hoek, & Sommer, 2010).

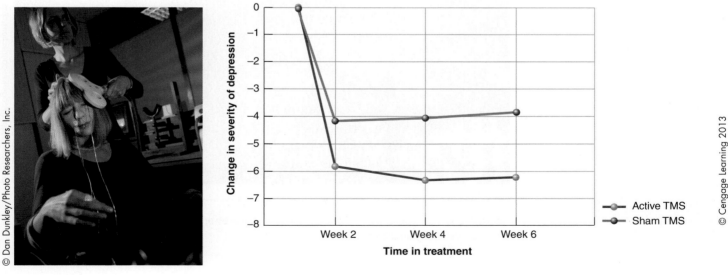

FIGURE 15.8

Effects of rTMS on Depression. Compared to participants with depression undergoing a placebo version of repeated transcranial magnetic stimulation (Sham rTMS), participants receiving active rTMS showed significantly reduced scores on the standard Hamilton Depression Rating Scales. The fact that participants showed rather strong placebo effects in the Sham condition (note the drop in depression at week 2 of "treatment") emphasizes the need for placebo-controlled studies in assessing the effectiveness of all types of treatment. *Source:* Adapted from O'Reardon et al. (2007).

Neurofeedback As we mentioned in our chapter on biological psychology, biofeedback training allows participants to gain some conscious control over some otherwise unattended physical functions. For example, people can be taught to overcome "white coat hypertension," or the classically conditioned spike in blood pressure that occurs when a nurse or doctor (in a lab coat) takes a measurement. By learning to relax instead of becoming tense in this situation, people can reduce their blood pressure, which is not a process we typically try to control.

Neurofeedback is a type of biofeedback that concentrates on the activity of the brain. Recordings of brain activity, usually from EEG but increasingly from fMRI, are usually displayed for the participant, who is trained to keep readings in a desired range. In most cases, people are not consciously aware of what they are doing to comply.

Neurofeedback appears to be promising in the treatment of attention deficit hyperactivity disorder in children (Gevensleben et al., 2009) and appears to reduce the frequency of seizures in patients with epilepsy (Walker, 2010). In a preliminary study using fMRI, patients with depression were able to increase activity in parts of the brain that were most active when they viewed positive images (Linden & Lancaster, 2011).

© Dr. Lise DeLong/cognitive-connections.com

Neurofeedback, a type of biofeedback training that focuses on brain activity, can be used to treat attention deficit hyperactivity disorder in children.

neurofeedback A type of biofeedback used to treat ADHD and seizures by teaching the client to keep measures of brain activity within a certain range.

Summary 15.2

Approaches to Treating Psychological Disorders

Type of therapy	Theoretical perspective	Defining features
Psychoanalysis © Bjanka Kadic/ Alamy	Psychodynamic theory	• Directive therapy • Free association • Dream analysis • Analysis of resistance • Analysis of transference
Humanistic therapy © Catchlight Visual Services/ Alamy	Humanistic theory	• Nondirective therapy • Unconditional positive regard • Reflection • Empathy
Behavior therapy Photo by Stephen Dagadakis, copyright Hunter Hoffman www .vrpain.com, World built by Firsthand Inc.	Behaviorism	• Application of classical and operant learning principles in behavior modification • Based on observed behavior only
Cognitive therapy © Beck Institute for Cognitive Behavior Therapy, 2011	Cognition	• Cognitive restructuring • Cognitive-behavioral therapy (CBT) combines restructuring with behavior modification
Biological treatments © John B. Carnett/Bonnier Corp. via Getty Images	Biology	• Medication • Electroconvulsive therapy (ECT) • Psychosurgery • Brain stimulation • Neurofeedback

How Are Specific Disorders Treated?

As we have mentioned previously, different approaches to treatment have differing success rates when applied to specific types of disorders. In this section, we will outline the typical approaches to the psychological disorders we discussed in our previous chapter.

Treating Anxiety Disorders

Anxiety disorders are typically treated by using medication, cognitive-behavioral treatment, or a combination of the two.

As we discussed in our chapter on psychological disorders, anxiety is associated with a heightened level of brain activity due to anticipated danger. Consequently, most efforts to medicate anxiety attempt to reduce brain activity, or produce a "tranquilizing" effect.

Because GABA is the major inhibitory neurotransmitter in the brain, a common method for slowing brain activity is to enhance the effects of

Psychology *as a* Hub Science

Using Virtual Reality to Treat Anxiety

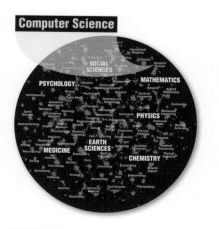

Computer Science

You might expect virtual reality (VR), the presentation of realistic stimuli through a device worn on the head, to be more exciting to video gamers than to therapists. However, this new technology is showing remarkable promise for the treatment of phobias and post-traumatic stress disorder.

As we discussed in this chapter and in our chapter on learning, one of the best ways to address these stress- and fear-related problems is to combine relaxation with a controlled exposure to the fear-producing stimuli. This application of classical conditioning was popularized by Joseph Wolpe in the 1950s (Wolpe, 1958). For example, if a person is afraid of heights, he or she could imagine progressively more stressful situations (climbing a ladder, visiting the Empire State Building) while remaining relaxed.

Eventually, the fear of heights should be reduced.

Imagination is a wonderful capability of the mind, but it does have its limitations. This is where virtual reality comes in. Instead of asking a client to imagine a situation, the scenario can be presented in a very realistic way through the use of VR technology. As our height-phobic client works his or her way through elevators, construction sites, and other high places, wind, vibration, and sound can be added to make the visual experience even more realistic. In addition to treating phobias, virtual reality is being used to help combat veterans recover from PTSD

GABA. As we described in our consciousness chapter, many substances interact with the GABA receptor to produce stronger inhibition in the brain, including alcohol, barbiturates, and benzodiazepines. Each of these types of substance produces a tranquilizing effect on the brain. As these drugs have additive effects with one another and work at the same receptor site, taking combinations of these drugs is frequently fatal due to a life-threatening level of brain inhibition.

Barbiturates, developed in 1903, continue to be quite useful in the treatment of seizures, but their use as a treatment for anxiety is no longer considered desirable. Barbiturates were one of the first of several medications used for psychological treatments to become vastly overprescribed. By the mid-1960s, enough barbiturates were being made to provide every American man, woman, or child with 40 to 50 doses per year (Regan, 2000). The addictive properties of barbiturates, as well as their frequent use in suicides, were definite drawbacks.

The discovery of benzodiazepines after World War II changed the treatment of anxiety dramatically, but like the barbiturates, the benzodiazepines became overused. By the 1970s, chlordiazepoxide (Librium) and diazepam (Valium) were the most frequently prescribed drugs of their day. Alprazolam (Xanax) remains a widely used benzodiazepine, typically prescribed for panic disorder, general anxiety disorder, and premenstrual syndrome. In some cases, alprazolam seems to be helpful in treating major depressive disorder, but its mechanism for doing so is not understood.

Knowing that one of the motivations for alcohol use might be to reduce the anxiety resulting from social events and other stressors can be helpful in avoiding problem drinking. If a person feels like she or he "can't face" a situation without being drunk, it would be more positive to seek professional help rather than continue drinking.

Defense Dept. photo by John J. Kruzel

The U.S. Army is testing "Virtual Iraq," a 360-degree interactive computer-generated environment, as a treatment for soldiers with PTSD. Soldiers are able to relate their traumatic experiences to the therapist, who can then program the environment to reproduce weather conditions, terrain, helicopter flyovers, types of attacks, and sound. Soldiers being treated with virtual reality are being compared with soldiers treated with other traditional psychotherapy approaches and a control group of soldiers on the waiting list for treatment.

(Spira et al., 2006). In these cases, odors from diesel fuel and gunpowder can be added to enhance the reality of the virtual experience.

Research comparing the effectiveness of virtual reality therapies, alone or in conjunction with traditional cognitive-behavioral approaches, suggests that VR therapy alone is about as effective as cognitive-behavioral approaches alone in treating phobias, but might have an advantage in certain situations, such as fear of flying (Krijn et al., 2007). Virtual reality also performed well in comparisons with cognitive-behavioral treatment in cases of post-traumatic stress disorder (Baños et al., 2011). In particular, VR therapy appealed to people with post-traumatic stress disorder who were unwilling to undergo more traditional treatments. Perhaps people who grew up playing video games might find the VR approach more effective and comfortable. ◉

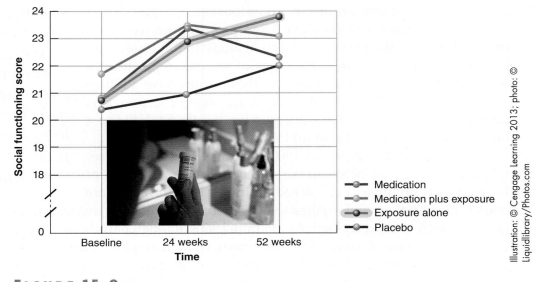

FIGURE 15.9

Comparisons of Treatments in Social Phobia. Medication, exposure therapy (in which the individual is gradually introduced to anxiety-producing situations), and combined medication and exposure therapy appear to produce approximately equal improvements in the functioning of people with social phobia. Scores of social functioning of people randomly assigned to these treatment conditions were significantly better than scores of the placebo group after 24 weeks of treatment. However, when treatment was discontinued after 24 weeks, the medication and medication combined with exposure therapy groups deteriorated at the 1-year follow-up assessment, whereas the exposure alone group continued to improve. These results suggest that patients choosing to use medication should continue treatment to maintain gains in functioning. *Source:* Adapted from Haug et al. (2003).

> Psychoanalysis. Almost went three times—almost. Then I decided what was peculiar about me was probably what made me successful. I've seen some very talented actors go into analysis and really lose it.
>
> —Bette Davis

You might think that tranquilizers would be a logical choice of medication for treating anxiety disorders. Although these drugs are used occasionally, the antidepressants we discuss in a subsequent section are typically much more effective. This result might reflect a common underlying cause for both depression and anxiety.

Behavioral and cognitive-behavioral techniques are commonly used to treat anxiety disorders and, of course, have the advantage over medication of having no side effects. Phobias, for instance, can be treated by gradually exposing the person to the fear stimulus or to other people interacting harmlessly with the fear stimulus while the person relaxes (see ● Figure 15.9). Obsessive-compulsive disorder (OCD) can be treated by training the person to anticipate compulsive behavior, and then to engage in a competing behavior. For example, a compulsive hand-washer could go outside away from faucets and soap to do some gardening. Not only are these treatments helpful for those who do not respond well to medication, but they appear to produce longer-lasting benefits in many cases. People with OCD who received behavioral treatment had fewer symptoms 17 months later than patients who had received, then discontinued, medication alone (Hembree, Riggs, Kozak, Franklin, & Foa, 2003).

Treating Mood Disorders

Although major depressive disorder and bipolar disorder share a common experience of depression, these disorders appear to have different underlying biological roots and respond to different types of treatments.

Treating Major Depressive Disorder Given the wide range of suspected causal factors in depression, it should not come as a surprise to you that treatment approaches are equally diverse. Treatments range from medical to cognitive to behavioral to simple aerobic exercise, and combinations of these approaches are common.

The most popular method for treating major depressive disorder today is the use of medication. Nearly 170 million prescriptions for **antidepressant medications** were written in the United States in 2005 (Stagnitti, 2008). In the United Kingdom, where health statistics are easier to obtain due to nationalized medicine, annual prescriptions for antidepressants went from less than 10 million in 1991 to nearly 40 million in 2009 (Middleton & Moncrieff, 2011). Far from reducing reported problems, this 400% increase in prescriptions was accompanied by an equal increase in the number of disability claims for related disorders. Keep in mind that antidepressant medications are often prescribed for conditions other than major depressive disorder, such as the anxiety disorders discussed earlier. This is still a remarkable number of prescriptions and raises the distinct possibility that like barbiturates and benzodiazepines before them, antidepressants are likely being overprescribed (see ● Figure 15.10). In addition, studies have shown that

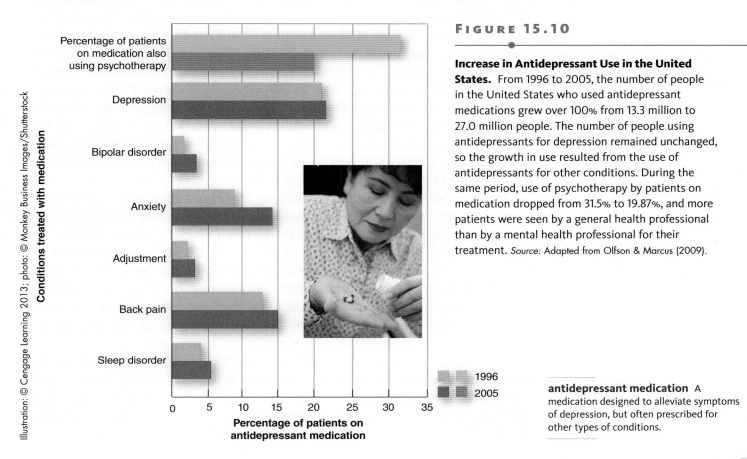

Illustration: © Cengage Learning 2013; photo: © Monkey Business Images/Shutterstock

FIGURE 15.10

Increase in Antidepressant Use in the United States. From 1996 to 2005, the number of people in the United States who used antidepressant medications grew over 100% from 13.3 million to 27.0 million people. The number of people using antidepressants for depression remained unchanged, so the growth in use resulted from the use of antidepressants for other conditions. During the same period, use of psychotherapy by patients on medication dropped from 31.5% to 19.87%, and more patients were seen by a general health professional than by a mental health professional for their treatment. *Source: Adapted from Olfson & Marcus (2009).*

antidepressant medication A medication designed to alleviate symptoms of depression, but often prescribed for other types of conditions.

FIGURE 15.11

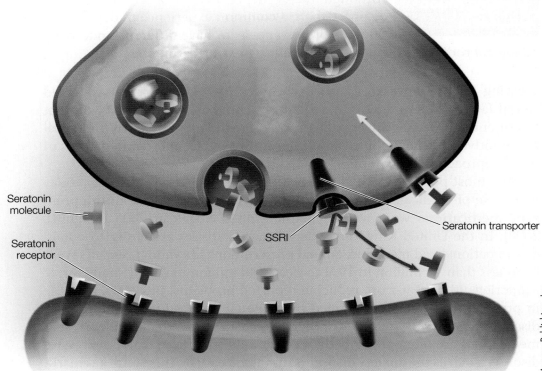

Selective Serotonin Reuptake Inhibitors. The selective serotonin reuptake inhibitors (SSRIs) increase the amount of serotonin in the synaptic gap that is available to interact with serotonin receptors. These drugs achieve this effect by interacting with the serotonin transporters located in the membrane of the neuron releasing the serotonin. This interaction slows the rate of reuptake, or the process by which the neuron retrieves and repackages the molecules of serotonin it has just released.

these medications are effective in severe cases of depression, but do not show any benefits in mild to moderate cases of depression (Fournier et al., 2010).

The most widely prescribed antidepressant medications are the selective serotonin reuptake inhibitors (SSRIs), which include popular brands like Prozac and Zoloft. As their name implies, these medications increase serotonin activity at the synapse by interfering with reuptake of the neurotransmitter, a process we discussed in our biological psychology chapter. As a result, more serotonin is available in the synapse (see ● Figure 15.11). The use of SSRIs is based on a belief that depression results from unusually low serotonin activity and that boosting serotonin activity should therefore improve mood.

In addition to inhibiting the reuptake of neurotransmitters at the synapse, antidepressants provide further benefit by increasing the number of neurons in the hippocampus, at least in rats (Malberg, Eisch, Nestler, & Duman, 2000; Nasrallah, Hopkins, & Pixley, 2010). Stress and depression both appear to reduce the number of neurons found in the hippocampus, and the administration of antidepressants may not only halt this loss but also promote the birth of new neurons in this area. Results from experiments with rats showed a 20 to 40% increase in neurons in the hippocampus in response to administration of antidepressant drugs.

These medications, like any others, have their share of risks and side effects. Increases in thinking about suicide following use of SSRIs, especially among children and youth, have prompted stronger warnings for close supervision by attending physicians (Hall, 2006; Wessely & Kerwin, 2004). Other side effects of SSRIs include nausea, reduction of REM sleep,

headache, weight gain, and sexual dysfunction. Between 30 and 60% of patients treated with SSRIs report problems with sexual activity (Gregorian et al., 2002). SSRIs reduce the activity of nitric oxide (NO), the gaseous neurotransmitter that helps maintain erections in men and genital engorgement in women (Yu et al., 2003). In contrast, erectile dysfunction medications, such as Viagra and Cialis, act by boosting NO activity. When patients fail to respond to medication, other biological treatments might be used to treat depression, such as electroconvulsive therapy (ECT) and repeated transcranial magnetic stimulation (rTMS; Demitrack, 2007; O'Reardon et al., 2007).

In addition to biological treatment options, a number of psychotherapy alternatives are quite successful in alleviating depression. One of the most popular alternatives is the use of cognitive-behavioral therapies (CBT). As we described previously, this approach combines the restructuring of negative cognitions ("nobody loves me" becomes "not everybody loves me, but some people do") and behavioral techniques aimed at increasing the person's activity levels and social skills (Beck, Rush, Shaw, & Emery, 1979). Between 40 and 60% of people with depression treated with CBT not only experience relief from their symptoms but also appear to be less susceptible to repeated bouts of depression than people who use medication alone (Hollon, Thase, & Markowitz, 2002).

People who are depressed also benefit from adding aerobic exercise to their routine (see ● Figure 15.12). A brisk 30-minute walk or jog only three times per week produces the same relief from depression as typical treatment with medication, with none of the side effects (Blumenthal et al., 1999). Not only is exercise an effective treatment for depression, but it might act to prevent depression as well (Ströhle, 2009).

Treating Bipolar Disorder The primary method of treating bipolar disorder is the use of medication. The most commonly prescribed medication is a simple salt, lithium carbonate. Lithium's actions are very specific to bipolar disorder. People who do not have bipolar symptoms show no changes in behavior when given lithium. If we can discover exactly what lithium is doing for patients with bipolar disorder, we should have a much improved understanding of the disorder; however, lithium's actions are not well understood. Lithium appears to both promote the birth of new neurons and prevent further loss of neurons (Quiroz, Machado-Vieira, Zarate, & Manji, 2010). Administration of lithium in patients with bipolar disorder appears to result in increased gray matter relative to patients who are not treated with lithium (see ● Figure 15.13 and ● Figure 15.14).

Unfortunately, lithium carbonate has a number of unpleasant and potentially dangerous side effects. Toxic levels of lithium produce nausea, vomiting, muscular tremor, coma, and seizures. Because of these risks, patients must have regular blood tests to monitor their lithium levels. The unpleasantness of these side effects also contributes to the poor compliance with their treatment plan that characterizes patients with bipolar disorder. These patients are less likely to follow treatment instructions

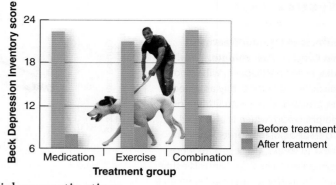

FIGURE 15.12

Exercise and Major Depressive Disorder. Participants with major depressive disorder (MDD) who had not been previously treated were randomly assigned to medication alone, exercise alone, and medication plus exercise groups for a 12-week study period. Because the participants were randomly assigned to groups, there were no statistically significant differences in the severity of their depression prior to treatment. All three treatment groups experienced improvement in their symptoms, as shown by their reduced scores on the Beck Depression Inventory. Although it appears that the medication group might have improved more than the exercise and combination groups, the differences between these three groups were not statistically significant. Therefore, we can conclude that exercise alone was equally effective in reducing symptoms of depression as medication alone or medication in combination with exercise. *Source: Adapted from Blumenthal et al. (1999).*

FIGURE 15.13

Effects of Lithium Treatment on Gray Matter Volume. Newly diagnosed participants with bipolar disorder were randomly assigned to groups treated with lithium or valproic acid, which is also used to treat bipolar disorder. Over the next 16 weeks, these groups were compared to healthy controls using no medications. Gray matter volume increased in the group treated with lithium, but did not change in the healthy controls or in the group treated with valproic acid. These results support the ability of lithium to increase neural growth, which might also explain its effectiveness in treating bipolar disorder. *Source: Adapted from Lyoo et al. (2010).*

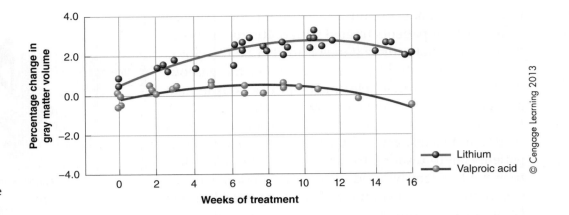

than any other kind of patient on any other type of medication (Sajatovic, Valenstein, Blow, Ganoczy, & Ignacio, 2007). Fortunately, research into alternatives to lithium carbonate is very active, and patients might soon enjoy improved treatment.

Research demonstrating that bipolar disorder is more common in nations in which consumption of seafood is low, discussed in our chapter on psychological disorders, has led to suggestions that dietary omega-3 fatty acids might provide some protection from bipolar disorder (Noaghiul & Hibbeln, 2003). Lower levels of omega-3 fatty acids have been observed in patients with bipolar disorder (Balanzá-Martínez et al., 2011). The use of omega-3 supplements improves symptoms of depression in these patients, but does not seem to have much effect on the symptoms of mania (Balanzá-Martínez et al., 2011). While not a substitute for treatment with lithium, the benefits of omega-3 fatty acids are obtained without any side effects.

You have probably noticed that our discussion of treating bipolar disorder has not emphasized psychotherapy. The vast majority of individuals with bipolar disorder appear to require medication for the alleviation of

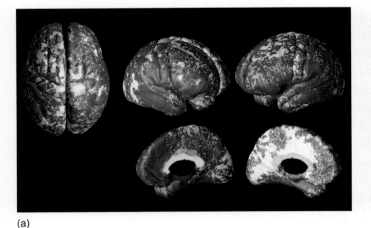

(a)

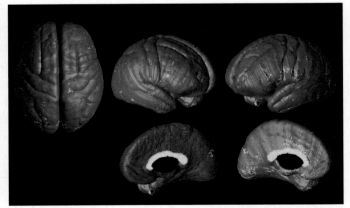

(b)

FIGURE 15.14

Gain in Gray Matter Density With Lithium Use. These images compared gray matter density between patients with bipolar disorder using lithium treatment and control participants (a) and patients with bipolar disorder who were not using lithium treatment and control participants (b). As indicated by the colors (blue = little to no difference and red/white = statistically significant difference), the patients taking lithium experienced considerable growth in gray matter density in many areas of the cerebral cortex. *Source: From Bearden, C. E., et al. (2007). Greater cortical gray matter density in lithium-treated patients with bipolar disorder. Biol Psychiatry, 62: 7–16. Copyright © 2007 Society of Biological Psychiatry/Elsevier, Inc.*

their symptoms, and psychotherapy alone is not considered an option in most cases. However, psychotherapy aimed at assisting the individual and his or her family with coping with bipolar disorder and adhering to treatment is often very beneficial. Even in conditions like bipolar disorder that have strong bases in biology, integrating several perspectives when selecting treatment approaches can produce superior outcomes.

Treating Dissociative and Somatoform/ Somatic Symptom Disorders

As we discussed in our chapter on psychological disorders, the dissociative and somatoform/somatic symptom disorders are characterized by disturbances in identity, memory, or consciousness. Treating these disorders effectively is complicated by our relative lack of information about their causes.

Several dissociative disorders, including dissociative amnesia, fugue, and depersonalization, appear to improve spontaneously over time. In most of these cases, treatment is focused on reducing any depression, stress, or anxiety that might also be present. Although there are no approved medications for the dissociative disorders in general, medication for the depression and anxiety that accompany many cases is common.

Treating Dissociative Identity Disorder (DID) The treatment of dissociative identity disorder can be quite controversial, as is the diagnosis of this condition, discussed in our chapter on psychological disorders.

Some psychotherapists work on the assumption that dissociative identity disorder is a valid diagnostic category that often results from serious trauma, childhood sexual abuse in particular. Treatment is aimed toward integrating the various personalities by first identifying and "working through" the traumatic memories related to the disorder (International

British painter Kim Noble has been diagnosed with dissociative identity disorder (DID). This disorder is characterized by the experience of two or more "personality states." Noble paints quite differently when she feels she is in one of her personality states compared to the others and believes she has improved her well-being by expressing her perceived personalities through her art.

Society for the Study of Dissociation, 2005). Hypnosis is commonly used by these therapists to assist in the recovery and resolution of traumatic memories, but this practice is not well advised. Under hypnosis, a suggestible person might be vulnerable to the manufacture of false memories, and individuals identified as having dissociative identity disorder appear to be far more suggestible than the general public (Frischholz, Lipman, Braun, & Sachs, 1992). In one notable case study, a woman sought therapy to cope with a traumatic event involving her daughter. Her psychiatrist employed hypnosis and convinced her that she had experienced horrific abuse as a child and now had more than 120 separate personalities, including one that was a duck, thereby illustrating the influence therapists can have on the "memories" they help recover (Loftus, 1997).

A particularly damaging finding regarding the state of treatment for dissociative identity disorder is the suggestion that individuals labeled with the disorder subsequently show even worse symptoms (Piper & Merskey, 2004). Critics of the dissociative disorder classification suggest that psychotherapists should restrict their actions to resolving the stress, anxiety, and depression of the individual without referring to dissociation at all.

Cognitive-behavioral therapies (CBT) can be particularly effective in restructuring the distorted perceptions of physical flaws that trouble patients with body dysmorphic disorder. This counselor is using the mirror to help her client think more realistically about her appearance.

Treating Somatoform/Somatic Symptom Disorders Both biological and psychological treatments are commonly used to treat somatoform/somatic symptom disorders, which involve physical symptoms such as pain that have no apparent physical basis.

Among the biological treatments for somatoform/somatic symptom disorders are medication with antidepressants and increases in physical activity. Psychological treatments usually take the form of cognitive-behavioral therapies (CBT). CBT is particularly helpful in cases of body dysmorphic disorder and produces modest improvements in other types of somatoform/somatic symptom disorders (Allen & Woolfolk, 2010). Complicating the treatment of these disorders is the fact that most of these patients are seen by their primary physicians, and relatively few are willing to pursue psychotherapy. Between 50 and 80% of patients referred for psychological treatment by their physicians do not comply, possibly because of their continued belief that they have a real medical condition that has not yet been appropriately diagnosed (Allen & Woolfolk, 2010).

Treating Schizophrenia Prior to the 1950s, effective treatment for schizophrenia was virtually nonexistent. Patients were often subjected to very odd "treatments" that had no basis in any scientific understanding of their condition and that were frankly dangerous in some cases. They were forcibly restrained in lukewarm baths with canvas covers that prevented their escape. "Insulin shock therapy," in which injections of insulin were used to place patients in daily comas, enjoyed a brief fad status, as did the frontal lobotomy discussed earlier in this chapter.

The discovery of effective medications for schizophrenia was accidental (see ● Figure 15.15). A French surgeon, Henri Laborit, was impressed by

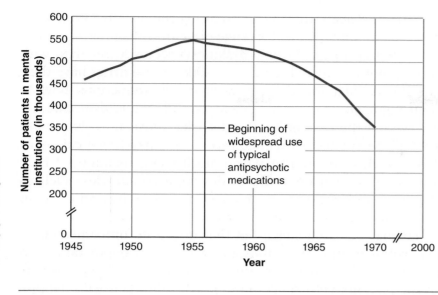

FIGURE 15.15

Effective Medications Changed Outcomes for People With Schizophrenia. The introduction of effective medications for schizophrenia in the 1950s coincided with a substantial reduction in the number of people living in mental institutions in the United States. Keep in mind that the overall population in the United States was growing rapidly at this same time. *Source: Adapted from Freberg (2010), Figure 16.10, p. 464.*

the calming effects of the phenothiazines. He experimented with one of the drugs, chlorpromazine (Thorazine), to reduce stress and shock in his surgical patients. Based on his promising results, Laborit encouraged his psychiatric colleagues to try the drug on their psychotic patients, which they did with dramatic success. A new era of treatment began. Largely as a result of this new type of treatment, institutionalized populations dropped by about 50% in the United States between 1955 and 2000. People responding well to medication could now return to their communities instead of living in institutions.

Initially, nobody understood how the phenothiazines reduced psychosis. One clue came from the fact that high doses of the drug produced symptoms that were very similar to those of Parkinson's disease, such as muscular tremor. Parkinson's was known to result from the degeneration of motor neurons that used dopamine as their primary neurotransmitter. Further research indicated that the phenothiazines acted as dopamine antagonists, blocking dopamine at the receptor site.

The phenothiazines are not without their share of problems. Nearly one quarter of patients with schizophrenia do not respond to these drugs at all (Kane & Freeman, 1994). The drugs successfully reduce psychotic symptoms, such as hallucinations and delusions, but are often less effective in reducing negative symptoms such as social withdrawal and emotional disturbance (Carpenter, Conley, Buchanan, Breier, & Tamminga, 1995). In still other cases, the phenothiazines can produce significant side effects due to their ability to block dopamine activity at the synapse. **Tardive dyskinesia,** (*tardive* means "slow" and *dyskinesia* means "difficulty moving") is a syndrome that results from the use of phenothiazines by some patients. The syndrome produces tremors and involuntary movements, especially of the face and tongue. These problems often continue even when medication stops.

To address these deficits of the phenothiazines, now referred to as "typical" antipsychotic medications, new "atypical" antipsychotic medications, such as clozapine (Clozaril), were introduced. Approximately half of all patients with schizophrenia are now using the atypical antipsychotics (Meltzer, Bobo, Lee, Cola, & Jayathilake, 2010). These newer drugs are often

tardive dyskinesia A movement syndrome that results from the use of medications used to treat symptoms of schizophrenia.

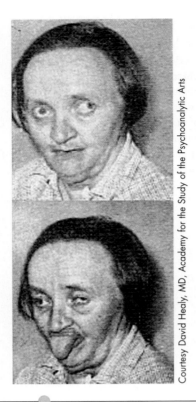

Medications used for schizophrenia often produce a movement disorder known as tardive dyskinesia in patients. This patient is experiencing the intrusive, involuntary movements and tremors that characterize this condition, which is usually permanent. Newer medications for schizophrenia are somewhat less likely to produce tardive dyskinesia, but have their own set of side effects, including diabetes, weight gain, reductions in immune system functioning, aggravation of existing cancers, and seizure disorders.

more effective than the phenothiazines in treating the negative symptoms of schizophrenia, as they affect a wider range of neurotransmitters, including serotonin. Although risk of tardive dyskinesia seems lower than with the typical antipsychotics (Correll & Schenk, 2008), these drugs have their own set of side effects, including diabetes, weight gain, reductions in white blood cell count, aggravation of existing cancers, and seizure disorders.

As we observed in the case of bipolar disorder, most individuals with schizophrenia will be treated with medication, but psychological treatments still have much to offer. The World Health Organization (WHO) noted that people with schizophrenia in developing countries, such as Nigeria, India, and Colombia, were recovering more frequently than patients in the United States and Europe (Hopper, Harrison, Janca, & Sartorius, 2007). Further research suggested that improved outcomes occur when patients remained in their homes and were given opportunities to do meaningful work. These observations led to the use of psychosocial rehabilitation for patients with schizophrenia (Bustillo, Lauriello, Horan, & Keith, 2001). This approach emphasizes providing opportunities to do meaningful work, social skills training, education about schizophrenia and the importance of medication, affordable housing linked to services, and information about symptom management.

Treating Personality Disorders

In our chapter on psychological disorders, we highlighted two examples of personality disorder, antisocial personality disorder and borderline personality disorder.

Treating Antisocial Personality Disorder Finding effective treatments for antisocial personality disorder has a high priority, given the extent of harm individuals in this category inflict on the rest of society. Unfortunately, effective treatments appear elusive.

There are no known medications that specifically reduce antisocial behavior, although many incarcerated individuals are treated with tranquilizing drugs, including antipsychotic and anticonvulsant medications (such as barbiturates), to make their aggressive, violent behavior more manageable. Even if effective medications are eventually discovered, individuals with antisocial personality disorder tend to view themselves as "okay" and not in need of treatment. Compliance with effective treatments is likely to remain a problem.

Psychological treatments for antisocial personality disorder include learning models that emphasize anger control, social skills, and moral reasoning (Goldstein, Glick, & Gibbs, 1998). These models appear to be

Psychosocial rehabilitation for schizophrenia includes opportunities to do useful work. For more than 20 years, Growing Grounds Farm in San Luis Obispo, California, has provided horticultural therapy and vocational training within the setting of a wholesale "green" nursery business. Socializing with peers, engaging in healthy outdoor physical activity, and earning a paycheck contribute to the clients' personal growth.

modestly effective in reducing antisocial behavior in children and youth, but they do not appear to have much benefit for individuals who show evidence of true psychopathy, or lack of guilt and empathy (Hornsveld, Nijman, Hollin, & Kraaimaat, 2008). Individuals with antisocial personality disorder might benefit from training in "character formation" (Salmon, 2004). Addressing the selfishness inherent in people with antisocial personality disorder, therapists can attempt to convince the person that doing the right thing will produce more favorable outcomes (e.g., staying out of prison), even if the person fails to grasp the underlying value of respecting the rights of others. In spite of these efforts, many nations consider this condition untreatable and rely on incarceration of criminals with antisocial personality disorder to protect the public.

Treating Borderline Personality Disorder Once again, we note that no medications are currently approved specifically for the treatment of borderline personality disorder, but medications are frequently prescribed. Among the commonly prescribed medications are antidepressants, antipsychotic medications, mood stabilizers (e.g., lithium), anti-anxiety medications (e.g., benzodiazepines), and anticonvulsants. Because of the potential for self-destructive behavior and serious depression in borderline personality disorder, individuals are occasionally hospitalized for a few days for their own safety.

Psychotherapy for borderline personality disorder often takes the form of cognitive-behavioral therapies. In this case, the individual will learn to manage stress, emotions, and relationships. In particular, psychotherapists emphasize skills aimed at reducing the individual's potential for suicidal thinking and behavior. A therapy specifically designed for individuals with borderline personality disorder, dialectical behavior therapy (DBT), attempts to address symptoms in the order of their importance: reducing suicidal thoughts, reducing behaviors that interfere with therapy, and finally reducing behaviors that interfere with the quality of life (Linehan, Armstrong, Suarez, Allmon, & Heard, 1991). Outcomes using dialectical behavior therapy for borderline personality disorder appear superior to those produced by more conventional treatments with cognitive-behavioral therapies (Linehan et al., 1991).

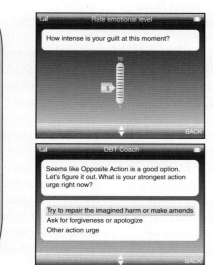

The use of DBT for borderline personality disorder has been simplified by the development of a new smartphone app, which takes the place of keeping diary cards of emotions, events, and problem behaviors. *Source:* Adapted from Rizvi, S. L., et al. (2011). A pilot study of the DBT coach: An interactive mobile phone application for individuals with borderline personality disorder and substance use disorder. *Behavior Therapy 42*, 589–600. Copyright © 2011 Elsevier.

Treating Disorders Emerging in Childhood and Adolescence

All the therapy approaches discussed previously in this chapter have been applied to the treatment of children and adolescents. However, special care must be given to the use of biological therapies in childhood and adolescence, because of the possible adverse effects of these treatments on the development of the nervous system.

Treating Autism Although autism is accompanied by abnormalities in the neurotransmitters serotonin, GABA, and glutamate, no medications have proved effective in alleviating symptoms of autism (Pardo & Eberhart, 2007). This lack of a beneficial result does not mean that medications are not prescribed. One type of antipsychotic medication, described earlier in our section on treatments for schizophrenia, has been approved by the Food and Drug Administration for use in autism and appears helpful in severe cases involving self-injury (Posey, Stigler, Erickson, & McDougle, 2008). Unfortunately, children treated with antipsychotic drugs experience the same side effects as adults. Antidepressants and several other types of drugs are commonly prescribed for children with autism off-label, which

Thinking Scientifically

Hyperbaric Oxygen Therapy and Autism

D esperate parents of children with autism are especially vulnerable to "cures" that enjoy little if any scientific support. Not only might these treatments be ineffective or even harmful, but the parents might neglect established, effective treatments in their search for quick, easy solutions. One such questionable practice is the use of hyperbaric oxygen therapy (HBOT).

HBOT is conducted by placing the individual in a pressurized, oxygen-filled chamber and is typically used to treat scuba divers with the

"bends." This condition results from surfacing too quickly, which produces dangerous oxygen bubbles in the blood. The chamber forces large amounts of oxygen into the body in a short period of time. In addition to treating the bends, HBOT has been used to speed wound healing and to improve cardiac function.

Why would anyone make the jump from scuba divers to children with autism? Two separate observations led to experimentation with HBOT. In some imaging studies, researchers reported that unusual decreases in blood flow to some parts

of the brain had been observed in people with autism (Ryu et al., 1999). Other researchers reported that the brains of individuals with autism appeared to experience inflammation (Pardo, Vargas, & Zimmerman, 2005). Putting these observations together with some promising research on the use of HBOT on stroke patients, who definitely experience reduced oxygen and inflammation in the brain, Daniel Rossignol (2007) performed a number of exploratory studies using HBOT on children with autism. The small number of participants,

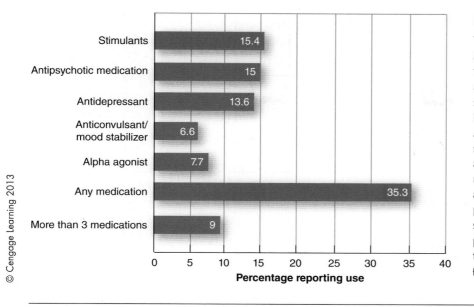

Stimulants — 15.4
Antipsychotic medication — 15
Antidepressant — 13.6
Anticonvulsant/mood stabilizer — 6.6
Alpha agonist — 7.7
Any medication — 35.3
More than 3 medications — 9

Percentage reporting use

© Cengage Learning 2013

FIGURE 15.16

Medications and Autism. Despite the fact that only one medication (risperidone, an antipsychotic medication used to treat schizophrenia and bipolar disorder) has been approved by the U.S. Food and Drug Administration (FDA) for use in autism, large-scale studies show that many other medications are routinely prescribed by psychiatrists and neurologists for children with autism. Alpha agonists are usually prescribed for high blood pressure and have a sedative effect. In this sample, 35.3% of the children had at least one prescription, and 9% had three or more drugs they were taking simultaneously. *Source:* Adapted from Rosenberg et al. (2010).

means that the drugs have not been officially approved for this purpose on the basis of research demonstrating effectiveness (see ● Figure 15.16).

The most commonly used psychological treatment for autism is applied behavior analysis, which builds on the principles of operant conditioning outlined in our chapter on learning (Smith & Lovaas, 1998). Applied behavior analysis focuses on observable, socially important behavior such as language and should produce lasting improvements that generalize to settings outside the therapy setting (Baer, Wolf, & Risley, 1968). Applied behavior analysis often involves therapy that takes up the majority of a child's waking hours, which is a large investment for families in terms of

the lack of control groups, and the use of parental reports of the children's behavior made the positive outcomes of these initial studies difficult to interpret, and on balance this approach still lacks scientific evidence for its efficacy. Nonetheless, the HBOT treatments garnered significant media attention, and many families eagerly sought out the treatments.

Unfortunately, autism is one of those conditions for which quick fixes just aren't possible. Carefully controlled outcome studies have failed to demonstrate any benefits of HBOT with children with autism (Jepson et al., 2010). Not only can the treatment produce negative outcomes,

including seizures, but it is very expensive. One hour of treatment costs about $150, and families report using 40 to 120 hours of HBOT for a total cost of up to $18,000. Families have even purchased the chambers for their own use, at a cost of nearly $30,000. Researchers fear that the time, money, and energy spent on this treatment could be better used for the child's benefit (Jepson et al., 2010). ☼

Courtesy of Summit to Sea/www.hyperbaric-dives.com

Many parents of children with autism are spending large amounts of money on hyperbaric oxygen therapy (HBOT), despite a lack of scientific research demonstrating its beneficial effect. HBOT is currently approved for treating oxygen bubbles in the bloodstream of scuba divers who surface too rapidly (the "bends"), gangrene, and certain types of heart disease.

HOW ARE SPECIFIC DISORDERS TREATED? 777

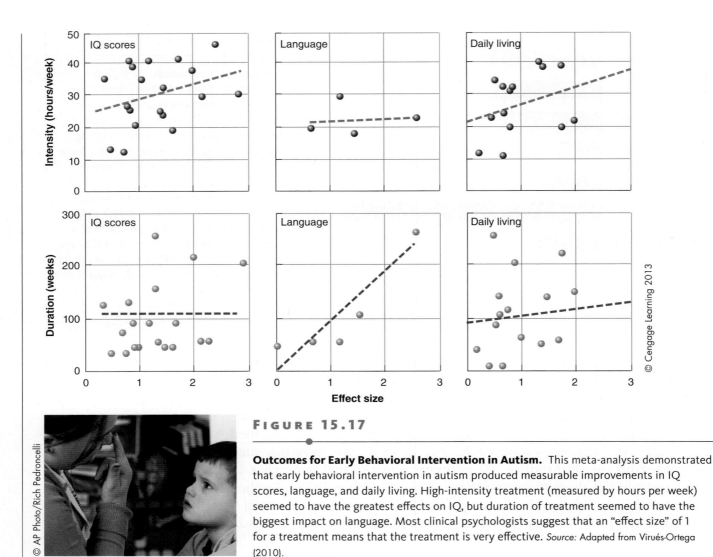

FIGURE 15.17

Outcomes for Early Behavioral Intervention in Autism. This meta-analysis demonstrated that early behavioral intervention in autism produced measurable improvements in IQ scores, language, and daily living. High-intensity treatment (measured by hours per week) seemed to have the greatest effects on IQ, but duration of treatment seemed to have the biggest impact on language. Most clinical psychologists suggest that an "effect size" of 1 for a treatment means that the treatment is very effective. *Source:* Adapted from Virués-Ortega (2010).

time and resources. As shown in ● Figure 15.17, although outcome studies are complicated by the child's initial level of functioning and many other variables, meta-analyses of the outcome of intensive, early-childhood behavioral interventions show a strong positive effect of treatment on language acquisition, but more moderate effects on social skills and daily functioning (Virués-Ortega, 2010).

Because of the severity and lifelong nature of autism, parents of children with autism are especially vulnerable to "cures" that have little research support. Dietary interventions have become popular in recent years, but these appear to have few benefits. People with autism show evidence of excess peptides from gluten (found in wheat) and casein (found in dairy products), but controlled studies do not demonstrate any benefits from restricting these foods (Millward, Ferriter, Calver, & Connell-Jones, 2008). Treatments designed to remove heavy metals from the body are also popular but lack research support (Weber & Newmark, 2007). Even worse, at least one child died from this type of treatment because a physician substituted a toxic chemical for the correct one with a similar name

(Sinha, Silove, & Williams, 2006). Among the other "treatments" that are advertised to parents are hyperbaric oxygen treatment (typically used to treat the "bends" in scuba divers), sensory integration treatment, massage, music, special diets, and animal-assisted therapies.

Treating Attention Deficit Disorder (ADHD) Most children with a diagnosis of attention deficit hyperactivity disorder (ADHD) are treated with medication, either alone or in combination with behavior therapy (Conners et al., 2001). The use of medications for attention problems resulted from yet another accidental discovery. In 1937, Charles Bradley used a stimulant to treat the headaches of a group of children referred to him for learning and behavior problems. The stimulant didn't help too much with the children's headaches, but they began to refer to their medicine as "math pills." It was much easier for them to do their math homework after using the pills.

The most commonly prescribed drugs for ADHD are the closely related stimulants methylphenidate (Ritalin), dextroamphetamine, and a combination of amphetamine salts (Adderall). These drugs increase the activity of dopamine and norepinephrine. Most patients tolerate these medications well, but side effects of weight loss and sleep disturbance can occur. If children take the medications continuously for long periods, growth can also be suppressed. Methylphenidate does produce tolerance, and patients should stop the drug under medical supervision rather than on their own (Ross, Fischhoff, & Davenport, 2002). Although it is chemically quite similar to amphetamine, methylphenidate is not considered an addictive drug given its slower action on the brain (Volkow, Wang, Fowler, & Ding, 2005). Individuals who do not respond well to the stimulant drugs are often treated with nonstimulant drugs that increase norepinephrine activity (Prasad & Steer, 2008).

It might appear odd to treat a disorder that often features hyperactivity, or high levels of impulsive behavior, with a stimulant. Wouldn't it make more sense to try medications that have a calming effect? The rationale for stimulant treatment of ADHD suggests that impulsive hyperactivity occurs if the parts of the brain responsible for planned, thoughtful behavior, such as the basal ganglia and frontal lobes, are not active enough. Raising the activity in these areas theoretically should reduce impulsive behavior. One of the common myths about medications for ADHD, however, is that they are ineffective in people who do not have the disorder. This is not the case at all, and in fact, medications prescribed for ADHD are commonly abused (Arnsten, 2006).

The use of medication for ADHD in the United States is 5 times higher than in any other nation, leading to criticism of the practice (see ● Figure 15.18). In a major long-term study involving thousands of children, researchers found that fewer than half of the children using stimulant medications met even a very casual interpretation of the diagnostic criteria for attention deficit hyperactivity disorder contained in the *Diagnostic and Statistical Manual (DSM)*, which we described in our chapter on psychological disorders (Angold, Erkanli,

Illustration: © Cengage Learning 2013; photo: Courtesy of Bradley Hospital

Dr. Charles Bradley observed the behavior of 30 institutionalized children, who had a variety of problem behaviors, after they were administered benzedrine sulfate, a type of amphetamine used at the time for asthma and other breathing problems. Bradley's observations about the children's "spectacular improvement in school performance" as well as their becoming "emotionally subdued" led to the modern treatment of attention deficit hyperactivity disorder with stimulant medication, including other types of amphetamine.

College students are not the only ones using ADHD medications inappropriately. A survey in the prestigious scientific journal Nature *found that 65% of the scientists who responded knew a colleague who used methylphenidate or similar drugs without a prescription to improve his or her focus and concentration (Maher, 2008).*

FIGURE 15.18

Use of Medication for Treating ADHD. This map of medication use for ADHD from the Centers for Disease Control and Prevention (CDC) shows the same regional variations that we observed in our chapter on psychological disorders for the prevalence of ADHD diagnoses. Together, these data suggest that about half of all children diagnosed with ADHD are prescribed medication. The use of medication produces short-term improvements in about 75 to 80% of children with ADHD. However, children with ADHD who are treated with medication are no better off in adolescence or adulthood than children with ADHD who were not treated with medication. *Source: Adapted from CDC (2003).*

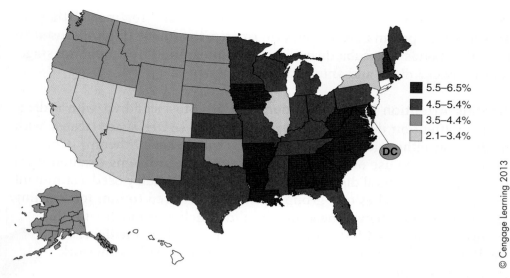

5.5–6.5%
4.5–5.4%
3.5–4.4%
2.1–3.4%

© Cengage Learning 2013

Egger, & Costello, 2000). However, approximately 75 to 80% of children treated with medication alone experience significant improvements on ratings of social compliance and sustained attention (Barkley, 1995). As a result of studies comparing treatment effectiveness, medication continues to be the primary choice in ADHD (Conners et al., 2001). However, these effects are short-term, and research has not demonstrated any long-term benefits of stimulant use on later outcomes in adolescence and adulthood (Loe & Feldman, 2007). In other words, children with ADHD treated with medication do not enjoy superior outcomes later in life compared to children with ADHD that do not receive medication.

Although medications are widely prescribed, behavioral methods for treating ADHD can be helpful. In particular, behavioral parent training, which builds the skills of parents of children with ADHD to use operant conditioning methods effectively, and behavioral classroom management, which extends classical conditioning into the school setting, are especially effective (Pelham & Fabiano, 2008). Another behavioral approach featuring peer-focused treatments in recreational settings has also shown promise (Pelham & Fabiano, 2008). Unfortunately, it is often difficult to maintain the consistency needed for successful behavioral interventions without a great deal of cooperation among teachers, parents, and others working with the child. A combination of individually tailored doses of medication in conjunction with behavioral therapy had the best outcome in a large-sample study of children with ADHD (Hoza, Waschbusch, Pelham, Molina, & Milich, 2000).

Integration of Specific Treatments

Perhaps after reading through the variations in both biological and psychological treatments available for specific types of disorders, you will better appreciate why people who want to be therapists spend such a long time in school perfecting their skills and learning about their options.

Although some disorders seem to defy our currently available treatment methods, we do not want to leave you with the impression that therapy is somehow ineffective. Quite the contrary is true. Compared to the state of available therapies as recently as 60 years ago, psychologists and psychiatrists have made great strides in their ability to alleviate the distress of many millions of people. As we learn more about the causal factors underlying these disorders, as we surely will by pursuing integrative approaches, our abilities to help will expand. At the same time, we are making significant progress in our understanding about the prevention of many of these disorders, which we hope will make these problems a thing of the past.

Summary 15.3

Common Treatments for Psychological Disorders

Disorder	Psychological treatment	Biological treatment
Anxiety *Defense Dept. photo by John J. Kruzel*	• Cognitive-behavioral therapy (CBT)	• Medication with antidepressant or anti-anxiety drugs
Mood disorders *Bearden et al. (2007)*	• CBT	• Medication with antidepressant drugs or lithium carbonate • Electroconvulsive therapy (ECT) • Exercise
Schizophrenia *Courtesy of Transitions-Mental Health Association*	• Psychosocial rehabilitation • Evaluation of expressed emotion	• Medication with antipsychotic drugs
Personality disorders © Cengage Learning 2013; adapted from Rizvi et al. (2011).	• Learning models for antisocial personality disorder • Dialectical behavior therapy for borderline personality disorder	• No effective biological treatments, although medications are sometimes prescribed
Autism *© AP Photo/Rich Pedroncelli*	• Applied behavior analysis	• Antipsychotic medications for self-injury
ADHD *© Cengage Learning 2013*	• Behavior therapy	• Stimulant medications

Interpersonal Relationships
From the Treatment Perspective

We have spent most of our time in this chapter talking about how psychotherapists tackle some of the most challenging psychological disorders, but that is not what they do all the time. The "everyday" problems faced by psychotherapists in their practices can be challenging, too, and the well-being of clients is often at stake.

When a couple is hitting some hard times together, we often hear them advised to seek counseling. Does that work? How often can counselors help people patch up relationships? What do they do to achieve successful outcomes?

One of the biggest problems that drives couples to counseling is infidelity, which we discussed in our chapter on social psychology. The lifetime prevalence of infidelity in married couples in the United States is estimated to be between 20 and 40% (Atkins, Baucom, & Jacobson, 2001). In surveys of psychotherapists who specialize in couples therapy, infidelity is reported to be one of the most damaging situations faced by couples and one of the most difficult for the therapist to treat effectively (Whisman, Dixon, & Johnson, 1997). The therapist's job is further complicated by the impact of the infidelity on the partners' well-being. Many people respond to their partner's infidelity by developing symptoms of depression and anxiety (Gordon, Baucom, & Snyder, 2004).

To assess the outcomes of therapy in cases of infidelity, couples entering therapy with at least one partner indicating concerns about infidelity were compared to couples entering therapy without infidelity concerns (Atkins, Marín, Lo, Klann, & Hahlweg, 2010). The infidelity couples reported greater initial distress and more depression than the other couples. However, by the end of the therapy process, both types of couples had made similar, positive progress. All couples (with or without infidelity), however, still scored rather high on measures of couple distress at the end of their therapy, indicating that in spite of their progress, their relationships were still at risk (see ● Figure 15.19).

One interesting aspect of this study was the wide use of techniques by the couples therapists, which included behavioral therapy, biopsychosocial, and psychodynamic approaches. This study used a large, community sample, so researchers were unable to assign therapists to particular approaches. It is possible that the use of infidelity-specific counseling, emphasizing trust and forgiveness, might have produced even better outcomes for the couples with infidelity. However, even in this less-targeted counseling approach, the results are encouraging. Couples do seem to benefit from seeking counseling for one of the more difficult problems they may face together.

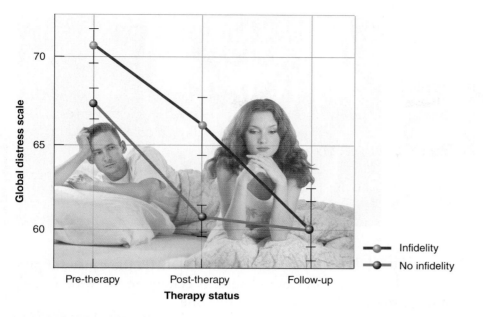

FIGURE 15.19

Response of Couples With and Without Infidelity to Therapy. Couples entering therapy with a history of infidelity showed more initial distress than couples without infidelity, but both types made similar, positive progress after six months of treatment. In a follow-up assessment six months after the end of treatment, or one year since the beginning of the study, both types of couples reported similar, lower levels of distress. *Source:* Adapted from Atkins et al. (2010).

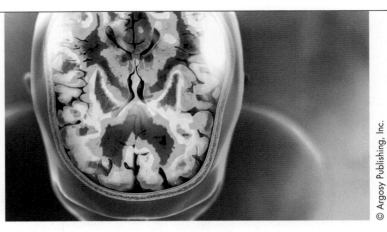
© Argosy Publishing, Inc.

Chapter 15
Reflections

The diversity of theories used to explain the causes of psychological disorders in our previous chapter is echoed in the wide variety of treatment approaches we examined in this one.

Today's theories of causality frequently recognize the need to consider multiple perspectives of psychology, ranging from the biological to the social, to understand why a disorder occurs in one case and not the other. If one identical twin is diagnosed with schizophrenia while the other is not, we need to consider more than genetic explanations to understand schizophrenia.

The necessity of integrating perspectives also characterizes the treatments of disorders. If one person responds to medication for OCD or ADHD and another does not, we cannot rely on medication as our only line of defense. If patients with schizophrenia improve through the use of medication, they may improve even further if they are able to live independently and make at least small contributions to their communities (Shrivastava, Johnston, Shah, & Bureau, 2010). The day of being a "psychoanalytic" or "humanistic" therapist, or adhering strictly to only one set of techniques to the exclusion of others, is past. Today's evidence-based therapist will search the literature for the best, scientifically supported treatments that hold the greatest promise for an individual patient or client. ❮

KEY TERMS The Language of Psychological Science

Be sure you can define these terms and use them correctly.

antidepressant medication, p. 767
behavior therapy, p. 754
biopsychosocial approach, p. 759
brief therapy, p. 746
cognitive behavioral therapy
    (CBT), p. 758
cognitive restructuring, p. 758
counseling, p. 739
couples therapy, p. 747

deep brain stimulation, p. 760
electroconvulsive therapy
    (ECT), p. 759
family therapy, p. 747
free association, p. 750
group therapy, p. 746
humanistic therapy, p. 739
insight therapy, p. 750
neurofeedback, p. 762

person-centered therapy, p. 752
psychiatrist, p. 741
psychoanalysis, p. 749
psychosurgery, p. 760
psychotherapist, p. 741
psychotherapy, p. 737
resistance, p. 751
tardive dyskinesia, p. 773
transference, p. 751

MEDIA RESOURCES

Log in to CengageBrain to access the resources your instructor requires. For this book, you can access:

Psychology **CourseMate** brings course concepts to life with interactive learning, study, and exam preparation tools that support the printed textbook. A textbook-specific website, Psychology **CourseMate** includes an integrated interactive eBook and other interactive learning tools including quizzes, flashcards, videos, and more.

WebTUTOR More than just an interactive study guide, **WebTutor** is an anytime, anywhere customized learning solution with an eBook, keeping you connected to your textbook, instructor, and classmates.

aplia If your professor has assigned **Aplia** homework:
1. Sign in to your account.
2. Complete the corresponding homework exercises as required by your professor.
3. When finished, click "Grade It Now" to see which areas you have mastered, which areas need more work, and detailed explanations of every answer.

The adrenal glands are the source of several important hormones that are released into the bloodstream at times of stress.

The Healthy Mind

16

Stress and Coping, Health Psychology, and Positive Psychology

Learning Objectives

1 Define "stress," identifying key neural and hormonal aspects of Selye's General Adaptation Syndrome.

2 Distinguish between adaptive elements of the short-term stress response with health problems linked to chronic stress.

3 Compare and contrast strategies for coping with stress, including problem-, emotion-, and relationship-focused strategies.

4 Summarize the psychosocial factors associated with smoking, nutrition, alcohol use, and lack of exercise, and develop a behavioral intervention for these problems.

5 Differentiate the aims and principles of positive psychology from other major movements in psychology, as described in our introductory chapter.

6 Distinguish among different meanings of "happiness" (pleasant, good, and/or meaningful lives), and analyze the research evidence on what makes people happy.

© Argosy Publishing, Inc.

We have all had days like the woman in this photo. Whether it comes in relatively minor forms (losing your keys, getting a traffic ticket, doing poorly on an exam) or in very large forms (death of a loved one, serious illness), stress is a fact of life.

We don't know what kind of stress is producing this woman's reactions, but we know a great deal about what is happening to her physically and psychologically in response to her stress. Zooming in, we look at one of her adrenal glands, shown in the larger image. Your adrenal glands are located on top of your kidneys in your lower back, and they are the source of hormones that are dumped into your bloodstream at times of stress. How does feeling stressed get translated into activity by a gland?

Here is how the system works. First, the woman must identify something as a threat to her. Making that cognitive appraisal, or judgment, of her situation, begins a cascade of processes designed to mobilize her to either run (flight) or fight. Messages from her amygdala to her hypothalamus result in the activation of hormones that tell the adrenal glands to release a hormone called cortisol. In our chapter on consciousness, we noted that cortisol levels are naturally high in the morning. In other words, circulating cortisol wakes you up. In response to the cortisol released by the adrenal glands, the body is mobilized for action.

We also have had enough stress in our lives to understand that too much is not a good thing. Once again, if we zoom in, we can understand that our bodies are usually protected from too much circulating cortisol by a feedback loop that reduces cortisol release after circulating levels reach a certain point. It is likely that this feedback loop malfunctions in stress-related disorders, such as depression.

While still at the microscopic level, we might also see that one person's genetic makeup might predispose him or her to have a more or less dramatic response to perceived stressors. By now, you can probably anticipate that we have to zoom back out again to fully understand this situation. These genetic differences between individuals interact with developmental and social factors, such as the possibility that this woman was maltreated as a child or now enjoys a strong social network of family and friends.

We can't make your stress go away, and it is probably not in your best interests for us to do so. Some stress, such as the stress associated with exercise or even surviving a traumatic experience, can have quite beneficial effects on your overall health. Instead we can acquaint you with research findings on coping and resilience that might help you deal with life's inevitable challenges. ⚙

What Is Stress?

College students rarely need much introduction to the concept of stress. They are no strangers to the stress that accompanies worrying about assignments and grades, money matters, world affairs, and relationships. **Stress** is an unpleasant emotional state that results from the perception of danger. The source of stress is referred to as a **stressor**.

The key to our definition is the word *perception*. No one set of stressors reliably produces stress in everybody. People's stressors are highly individual and idiosyncratic. The object of one person's phobia may be another person's beloved, although scaly and slithery, pet. Regardless of the stressor responsible for feelings of stress, once a person perceives that he or she is in some kind of danger, a common and predictable set of responses to the stressor is set in motion.

Psychologists have identified positive outcomes of our responses to stress (Selye, 1975). Stress, by its very nature, is a powerful adaptive response that mobilizes the body's resources to enhance survival in dangerous situations (Meaney, 2010). Although sometimes unpleasant, stress can

© Patrick Tuohy/Shutterstock

Professional athletes like Grace Park have learned to cope with stress in order to perform their best.

stress An unpleasant emotional state that results from the perception of danger.

stressor A stimulus that serves as a source of stress.

motivate us to perform well and makes us healthier in the long run. The exercise we do at the gym is undeniably stressful, but it produces significant benefits down the road. Many of us do some of our best work under time pressure and are not too much the worse for the wear as a result.

However, in other cases, stress can be counterproductive and interfere with our performance and well-being. In extreme cases, as we observed in our chapter on psychological disorders, a diathesis-stress model predicts that stress can contribute to the development of depression, schizophrenia, post-traumatic stress disorder, and other serious conditions. These negative outcomes are more likely when we are unable to cope with or adapt to a stressor. We will be focusing the majority of our discussion on these negative situations.

The Stress Response

Walter Cannon, whom we met in our chapter on motivation and emotion, demonstrated the ability of a number of stressors to activate the sympathetic division of the autonomic nervous system, described in our chapters on biological psychology and on motivation and emotion (Cannon, 1929). Cannon reported that extreme cold, lack of oxygen, and emotional experiences all had the capacity to initiate a "fight or flight" response. During such a response, heart rate, blood pressure, and respiration all increase, while nonessential functions, like digesting food, are inhibited. Stored energy is released, and blood is shunted from the surface of the body to the muscles needed for exertion. These physical responses reflect a process that has been finely tuned through evolution to maximize our survival in emergencies.

Hans Selye identified a General Adaptation Syndrome (GAS), which is our characteristic set of responses to stressors.

Hans Selye, in a research career lasting over 40 years, extended Cannon's findings by studying the effects of stronger, longer lasting stressors. Selye worked primarily with rats, exposing them to a variety of stressors and measuring the amount of time they could subsequently swim before giving up. (They were then rescued, of course.) Cold water, restraint, electric shock, surgery, and having their whiskers cut off were some of Selye's stressors that greatly reduced the amount of time the rats would swim before giving up. Regardless of the nature of the stressor, Selye found that the rats responded with a consistent pattern of behavior, which he labeled the **General Adaptation Syndrome (GAS**; Selye, 1946).

The GAS occurs in three stages (see ● Figure 16.1). An **alarm reaction** is initiated when a stressor is first perceived and identified. Selye's alarm reaction is essentially the same process as Cannon's fight-or-flight response. All possible resources are deployed to survive the danger, and all nonessential systems are inhibited. It is likely that you have had at least one close call while driving a car, and you can probably remember how that felt. Your heart pounds, you breathe rapidly, your hands may be sweaty, and you feel unusually mentally alert and focused. This is precisely the way your autonomic nervous system is supposed to react in an emergency.

Some sources of danger do not go away as quickly as your close call on the freeway. Many students think, "Oh, if only I survive this

General Adaptation Syndrome (GAS) Hans Selye's three-stage model for an organism's response to stressors.

alarm reaction The first stage of the General Adaptation Syndrome, characterized by sympathetic arousal and mental clarity.

FIGURE 16.1

The General Adaptation Syndrome (GAS) Has Three Stages. Hans Selye's General Adaptation Syndrome has three stages: alarm, resistance, and exhaustion. During the alarm stage, all resources are mobilized for "fight or flight." If stress is prolonged, we enter the resistance stage, where we adapt and cope as well as possible. Finally, resources are depleted when we reach the exhaustion stage.

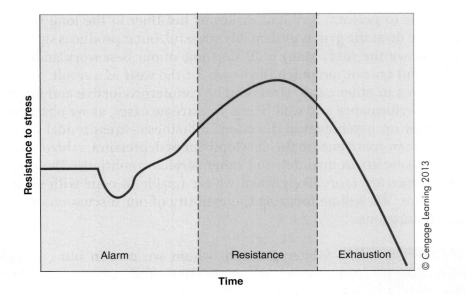

© Cengage Learning 2013

term—everything else will be easy," only to find themselves facing the same problems next term, along with some new ones. One of the challenges of modern living that our ancestors did not face is the need to worry about many future events. For the hunter-gatherer, the challenge was usually surviving that day. In contrast, today's college student may be concerned not only with fairly immediate problems, such as paying the rent and passing a midterm, but also more distant problems of future job markets, world events, climate change, and the future of Social Security. If these uncertainties are perceived as threatening or dangerous, they will act as stressors with the ability to initiate the GAS.

When stressors are prolonged, Selye suggests we enter a stage of **resistance**. During this stage, we continue to experience ongoing stress, which requires us to adapt and cope as well as possible. Although resistance is not as dramatic as the briefer and more intense alarm reaction, it still takes its toll. Under normal circumstances, we alternate between periods of calm and periods of relative arousal. You might calmly enjoy your lunch on the lawn between classes, but feel aroused while taking a quiz in a later class. During the calm periods, we have an opportunity to store nutrients and rest and repair the body. During periods of arousal, such as during the quiz, we expend energy instead of storing it. In the resistance phase of the GAS, we attempt to take care of both arousal and resting functions simultaneously. Neither function operates as smoothly under these circumstances as when it is operating alone. You might get an upset stomach when digesting your lunch is combined with the excitement of giving an oral presentation to your classmates. In contrast to the mental clarity that typically accompanies the brief alarm reaction, judgment during the longer periods of resistance may not be as good.

If stressors are severe and last long enough, a person might reach Selye's **exhaustion** stage. Strength and energy drop to very low levels. As we mentioned in our chapter on psychological disorders, stress is a

During extended periods of stress, judgment can suffer. You might have had the experience of looking back at the decisions you made during a stressful time, scratching your head, and asking, "What was I thinking?"

resistance The second stage of the General Adaptation Syndrome, characterized by coping with ongoing stress.

exhaustion The third and last stage of the General Adaptation Syndrome, characterized by depletion of physical and psychological resources.

risk factor for depression, and the exhaustion stage has much in common with the criteria for major depressive disorder. Exhaustion can even lead to death. Forced marches during war produce higher rates of death than the rate that might be expected to occur due to injuries and lack of food. Similar observations of stress, exhaustion, and death have been made among baboons in Kenya (Sapolsky, 2001). Under normal circumstances, lower status baboons avoid higher status baboons whenever pos-

Older zoos featured cages that often contributed to stress and illness among the animals. Modern zoos go to great lengths to provide more natural, less stressful habitats for their animals in recognition of the stress that often accompanies captivity.

sible. Unfortunately, due to fears of losing their crops, the Kenyan villagers caged the local baboons one year. While caged, the lower status baboons had no way to escape the higher status animals, and many died as a result. They did not die, as you might have guessed, from battle wounds resulting from fights with the higher status animals. Instead, the baboons died from stress-related medical conditions such as cardiovascular disease.

Sources of Stress Stressors exist in the eye of the beholder. Stressing over an exam might seem reasonable to many students, but this behavior might look silly to people stressed by war, poverty, and disease, who would probably be thrilled to have the opportunity to attend college.

Cognitive appraisal models help us to predict when a particular stimulus or event is likely to be a stressor for an individual person (Lazarus, 1966). According to this approach, we make appraisals, or very rapid initial assessments, of potential stressors to determine if they are irrelevant or harmless, positive or negative. Because people appraise situations from the vantage point of their own strengths and experiences, we would expect that a single potential stressor might produce different amounts and intensity of stress for different people.

Despite this variability in response to stressors, we can identify several types of events that are likely to produce significant stress in most people (see ● Figure 16.2). Large-scale disasters, such as the terrorist attacks of 9/11, the Haiti earthquake of 2010, the rash of tornadoes that hit the midwestern and southern United States in 2011, and the 2011 Japanese earthquake and tsunami, typically produce stress in large numbers of people. Post-traumatic stress disorder (PTSD) in New York following 9/11 was estimated to affect 130,000 people in that city alone. In the three to five days following the attacks, 90% of Americans reported feeling unusually stressed (Schuster et al., 2002).

This woman is obviously stressed. Is somebody being injured? Is she in danger? No—she is witnessing the finals of a "rock, paper, scissors" tournament. Cognitive appraisal theories of stress suggest that different people are likely to respond to stimuli with varying levels of stress, based on their individual appraisals of a situation.

FIGURE 16.2

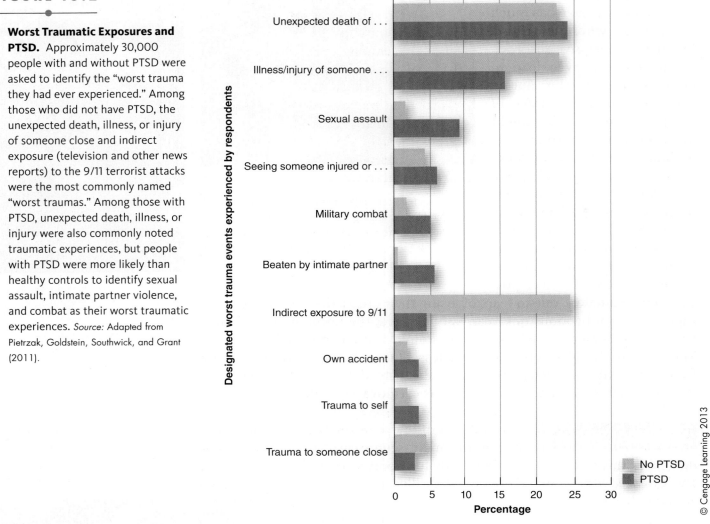

Worst Traumatic Exposures and PTSD. Approximately 30,000 people with and without PTSD were asked to identify the "worst trauma they had ever experienced." Among those who did not have PTSD, the unexpected death, illness, or injury of someone close and indirect exposure (television and other news reports) to the 9/11 terrorist attacks were the most commonly named "worst traumas." Among those with PTSD, unexpected death, illness, or injury were also commonly noted traumatic experiences, but people with PTSD were more likely than healthy controls to identify sexual assault, intimate partner violence, and combat as their worst traumatic experiences. *Source:* Adapted from Pietrzak, Goldstein, Southwick, and Grant (2011).

© Cengage Learning 2013

Stress due to disasters can produce long-range and cross-generational effects. Researchers identified women who witnessed the 9/11 attacks in New York while pregnant and who subsequently developed PTSD (Yehuda et al., 2005). One year later, the women as well as their infants showed indications of long-term, chronic stress. As preschoolers, the children born to the women who were diagnosed with both PTSD and depression following 9/11 showed evidence of higher reactivity to stimuli and more aggressive behavior than did children of terrorism-exposed mothers who did not develop these disorders (Chemtob et al., 2010). The ability of cortisol and other stress hormones to cross the placenta probably accounts for the effects of stress beginning in the prenatal environment (Weinstock, 2005).

As we mentioned in our chapter on psychological disorders, children are especially susceptible to stress and PTSD. Three weeks after the 2004 tsunami, prevalence of PTSD among children in areas of Sri Lanka ranged between 14 and 39% and could be predicted by variables such as family loss and severity of exposure (Neuner, Schauer, Catani, Ruf, & Elbert, 2006). To put these numbers into perspective, we would expect about 10%

of the population to experience PTSD after most large disasters (Kessler, Sonnega, Bromet, Hughes, & Nelson, 1996). Automobile accidents appear to be a major source of PTSD in childhood, with about 25% of children developing the disorder after having been injured in an accident (de Vries et al., 1999).

Although disasters are dramatic, they are obviously not the only sources of stress we face. Changes, including some changes for the better, can also trigger stress. In the 1960s, Holmes and Rahe compiled a list of life events they believed might be correlated with stress and then surveyed participants about the amount of adjustment each event required (Holmes & Rahe, 1967). Subsequently, researchers used the Holmes and Rahe scales to predict vulnerability to physical illness and psychological disorder due to different stressors (Derogatis & Coons, 1993; Scully, Tosi, & Banning, 2000). According to the scales, Christmas is more stressful than minor violations of the law. Getting married is more stressful than being fired from your job. Research results from studies using the Holmes and Rahe scales suggest that we should consider spreading out controllable changes over time. In other words, it may not be the best strategy to graduate from college, get married, move to a new city, and start a new job all at the same time.

Not all psychologists are convinced that "good" life events are as stressful as bad ones, nor are they convinced that change per se is a reliable predictor of stress. Critics of the Holmes and Rahe approach argue that most of the items on their list are quite negative and that these negative items are responsible for more stress (McLean & Link, 1994). It is likely that most of the stress associated with "good" changes occurs when the anticipated event does not live up to the person's expectations. Vacations and holidays may not be inherently stressful, but trying to fulfill unrealistic fantasies about what vacations and holidays *should* be like is probably quite stressful indeed.

Relatively insignificant sources of stress, often referred to as "hassles," can also contribute to a person's overall level of stress. Waiting in long lines, losing your keys, getting a parking ticket, and oversleeping on the day of an important exam are not life-threatening events. However, if enough of these hassles occur within a short period, people begin to react as if something much larger had occurred. The number of hassles people report experiencing predicts psychological symptoms of stress, even when the impact of major life events is factored out (Kanner, Coyne, Schaefer, & Lazarus, 1981). You might hear advice to avoid "sweating the little stuff," because enough little stuff happening at the same time can still impact your well-being (see ● Figure 16.3).

Social relationships and their disruption can be a significant source of stress for many people. When we feel socially isolated, we feel unsafe, and at this point in our discussion, you probably know what happens whenever we feel unsafe—more stress. Because lonely people see the social environment as threatening, they respond with feelings of hostility, stress, pessimism, anxiety, and low self-esteem (Hawkley & Cacioppo, 2010). Their

According to Holmes and Rahe (1967), positive life events, such as weddings and holidays, can be equally or even more stressful than some negative events, such as flunking an important assignment.

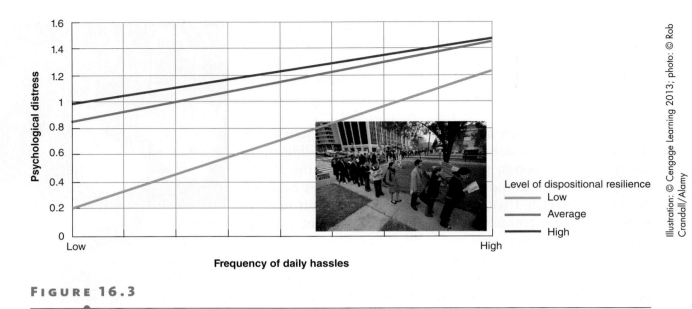

FIGURE 16.3

Hassles Interact With Resilience. The frequency of daily hassles contributes to levels of psychological distress for everybody, but the impact on people who otherwise show little resilience to stress is more dramatic. *Source: Adapted from Martin (2008).*

Feeling socially isolated makes us feel unsafe, which triggers stress responses. Loneliness makes people behave in ways that make them difficult to be around, such as displaying greater pessimism, anxiety, and hostility, beginning a loop of self-fulfilling prophesies and more loneliness.

behavior begins a loop of self-fulfilling prophesies. Thinking that nobody wants to be around them, they begin to act in negative ways that ensure nobody wants to be around them, yet they do not see the reactions of others as related to their own negativity. There are no easy fixes for loneliness, but most people cope more effectively with feelings of loneliness when they consciously attend to the needs of other people rather than focusing on their own situation (Cacioppo & Patrick, 2008).

What Are the Biological Correlates of Stress?

Regardless of the identity of a stressor, once you appraise a stimulus as a danger, you initiate Selye's General Adaptation Syndrome (GAS). The first stage, the alarm stage, is accompanied by a coordinated reaction including physical, cognitive, and behavioral responses to perceived danger. Imagine for a moment that one of your ancient ancestors is out hunting and suddenly finds himself face-to-face with a hungry lion. Physically, the autonomic nervous system will prepare your ancestor for fight or flight. The brainstem, described in our chapter on biological psychology, will initiate the release of the neurotransmitter norepinephrine, which increases vigilance and fear. Cognitively, your ancestor accesses his memory for information about lions, which he hopes will include ideas about how similar situations were handled in the past. Behaviorally, your ancestor carries out his plan for escape. We assume that given your presence today, your ancestor was successful.

Stress and the Amygdala

We can trace the neural pathways that coordinate these responses to potentially dangerous stimuli. Sensory pathways provide information to higher cognitive centers in the cerebral cortex, letting our hunter know that the object in front of him is indeed a lion. Memories of lion behavior, including eating habits, will contribute to accurately identifying the lion as a stressor.

Simultaneously, sensory input travels from the thalamus to the amygdala, which plays an important role in the identification of dangerous stimuli, as discussed in our chapters on biological psychology and on motivation and emotion The amygdala participates in a "fear circuit" that provides a very rapid assessment of a stimulus or situation as potentially dangerous (LeDoux, 2000) . If the amygdala is lesioned, animals no longer respond with conditioned fear to previously learned classically conditioned associations between a stimulus (perhaps a tone or light) and electric shock, an example of classical conditioning we discussed in our chapter on learning (see ● Figure 16.4). Animals with lesions in the amygdala are also unable to learn to respond appropriately to unfamiliar dangerous stimuli (Wilensky, Schafe, Kristensen, & LeDoux, 2006).

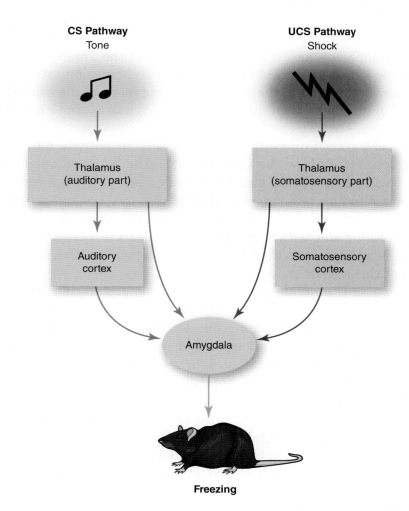

© Cengage Learning 2013

FIGURE 16.4

The Amygdala and Fear. The amygdala participates in a "fear circuit" that provides a very rapid response to a potentially dangerous stimulus. After rats learn a classically conditioned association between a tone that signals the arrival of an electric shock, they will freeze whenever they hear the tone. If the amygdala is lesioned, the rat will no longer freeze when it hears the tone, and it will be unable to learn about new signals for shocks.

Because sensory information can reach the amygdala along routes that are separate from the pathways for information going to the cortex, we might find ourselves frightened by stimuli that we don't immediately understand or consciously view as dangerous (Knight, Nguyen, & Bandettini, 2003). As we mentioned in our chapter on motivation and emotion, a patient who was "blind" because of damage to his visual cortex still showed normal response in his amygdala when shown faces expressing fear (Morris, DeGelder, Weiskrantz, & Dolan, 2001). You might have found yourself feeling anxious while returning to your car after an evening class without really knowing why you are reacting this way, but it is probably a good idea to listen to your amygdala until further information becomes available.

Once the amygdala has identified a stimulus as potentially dangerous, it communicates with the hypothalamus. As we mentioned in our chapter on biological psychology, the hypothalamus most directly commands the autonomic nervous system and the sympathetic division in particular. This part of the autonomic nervous system is responsible for our fight–flight response to danger.

> It's not stress that kills us, it is our reaction to it.
>
> —Hans Selye

Stress, SAM, and the HPA Axis

Perceiving a potential source of danger mobilizes the body's resources using two systems—the **sympathetic adrenal-medullary (SAM) system** and the **hypothalamic-pituitary-adrenal (HPA) axis**. The SAM system initiates the release of adrenaline (also known as epinephrine) and norepinephrine into the bloodstream from the adrenal glands located above the kidneys in your lower back. These chemical messengers circulate to many organs and to the brain, producing many of the immediate, short-lived, fight–flight responses to stress, such as a pounding heart and rapid breathing (see ● Figure 16.5).

Simultaneously, activation of the HPA axis sets an entirely different system in motion. Here's how the circuit works. The hypothalamus (H) communicates with the pituitary gland (P), located just above the roof of your mouth, which in turn tells the adrenal glands (A) to release a hormone known as **cortisol** into the bloodstream. Circulating cortisol boosts the energy available for dealing with a stressor. The HPA axis response to stress can continue much longer than the SAM response, which explains many of the outcomes of chronic stress.

One of the possible outcomes of chronic stress is prolonged high levels of circulating cortisol. Long-term exposure to cortisol can produce a number of harmful effects, including the death of neurons. When rats received daily injections of the rat equivalent of cortisol, neural death began to occur in just a few weeks (Stein-Behrens, Mattson, Chang, Yeh, & Sapolsky, 1994). Identical amounts of neural death occurred if the rats were stressed daily instead of receiving the injections, suggesting that the action of cortisol is responsible for most of the neural damage observed to result from stress. Studies in humans who have a medical condition (Cushing's disease) that results in unusually high cortisol levels suggest that cortisol abnormalities might contribute to reduced hippocampus volume, memory problems, abnormal sleep patterns, and depression (Langenecker et al., 2012). Not only can high levels of cortisol damage neurons, but these same

sympathetic adrenal-medullary (SAM) system A circuit that responds to perceived stressors by initiating the release of epinephrine and norepinephrine into the bloodstream.

hypothalamic-pituitary-adrenal (HPA) axis A circuit that responds to perceived stressors by initiating the release of cortisol into the bloodstream.

cortisol A hormone released into the bloodstream from the adrenal glands.

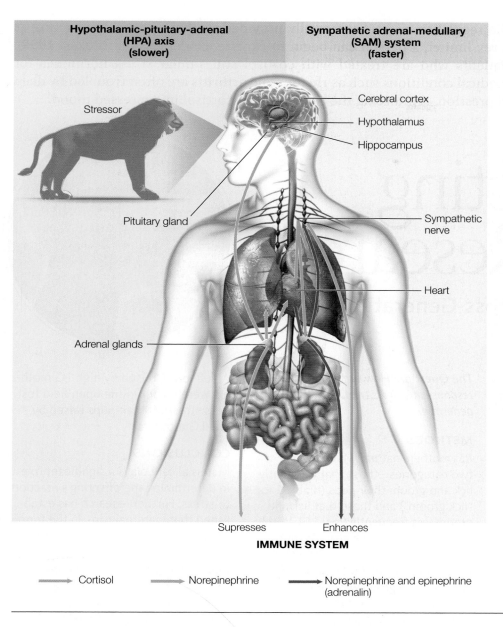

© Argosy Publishing, Inc.

FIGURE 16.5

Two Systems Respond to a Stressor.
In response to the appraisal of a stimulus as a stressor, two systems mobilize the body's resources. The sympathetic adrenal-medullary (SAM) system responds very quickly by initiating the release of epinephrine (adrenaline) and norepinephrine into the bloodstream by the adrenal glands. These chemical messengers initiate many immediate, short-lived responses, such as a pounding heart and rapid breathing. Simultaneously, activation of the hypothalamic-pituitary-adrenal (HPA) axis results in the release of cortisol into the bloodstream by the adrenal glands. Cortisol acts to boost the energy available for dealing with the stress. Cortisol receptors in the hippocampus serve as a feedback loop to keep the system from overreacting. The HPA axis is slower and longer lasting than the SAM response and determines more of the outcomes of chronic stress, such as suppression of the immune system.

levels appear to inhibit the neurogenesis, or birth of new neurons, that might help to offset the damage (Cowen, 2010).

Normally, activity of the HPA axis is regulated by a feedback loop involving the hippocampus (Stokes, 1995). The hippocampus works like a "rev limiter" in an automobile engine that prevents the driver from going over a certain speed. The hippocampus contains large numbers of receptors for cortisol and other stress hormones. When the hippocampus detects high levels of these hormones, it signals the hypothalamus, which in turn tells the adrenal glands to reduce the release of cortisol, and arousal dissipates.

The role of the hippocampus as the rev limiter of the HPA axis might be the bridge between extreme stress and depression. As we observed in our chapter on psychological disorders, many cases of depression are preceded by unusually stressful events. Consistently elevated levels of cortisol due to stress can overwhelm the hippocampus's feedback loop, leading instead to the continuous release of cortisol and constant arousal. Without the regulation of cortisol usually provided by the hippocampus acting as a rev limiter, a person can begin to experience depression (Stokes, 1995). Patients who are treated with cortisol and similar stress hormones for medical conditions such as rheumatoid arthritis are often troubled by deep depression, reinforcing the role of excess cortisol in depressed mood.

Connecting *to* Research

Maternal Care and Cross-Generational Effects on Stress

For many years, psychologists have believed that the care a child receives early in life seems to have long-lasting results, both good and bad, on the child's behavior.

Early research suggested that handling of infant laboratory rats, which in turn stimulated more care by the mother (in the form of licking and grooming the pups), was correlated with later resistance to stress in the pups that lasted well into adulthood (Denenberg, 1964; Levine, 1970). Further research demonstrated that this early experience was correlated with long-term effects on the animals' HPA axis. Specifically, the animals receiving handling or more maternal care showed milder HPA responses to stressors and had more sensitive feedback loops responsive to stress hormones such as cortisol (Liu et al., 1997).

What is there about maternal care that can produce different responses to stress later in life? A clever study that used rat foster mothers was able to answer this question (Francis, Diorio, Liu, & Meaney, 1999).

The Question: How are differences in responses to stress transmitted across generations?

METHODS

Rat mothers naturally fall into one of two categories—those that frequently lick and groom their pups (high-LG for "lick groom") and those that lick and groom less frequently (low-LG). Within 12 hours of birth, one group of pups born to high-LG or low-LG mothers remained with their biological mothers, a second group was adopted by mothers of the same type as their biological mother, and a third group was adopted by mothers whose type was different from their biological mother. The offspring were tested later for stress by observing how much time they would spend in the inner area of a novel open field (rodents in general avoid open space, where they are easily found by predators).

RESULTS

The identity of the mother raising the pup (high-LG or low-LG) had more impact on the pup's later exploration than did the identity of the biological mother (see ● Figure 16.6).

All offspring raised by high-LG mothers were bolder in the open field test (less stressed) than pups raised by low-LG mothers.

CONCLUSIONS

Maternal care plays a significant role in determining the offspring's reaction to stress. Further research has established that maternal care, in the form of LG, is correlated with epigenetic changes to the expression in the pups' hippocampus of a gene affecting receptors for glucocorticoids, a class of hormones that includes cortisol (Meaney et al., 2000; Weaver et al., 2001). Animals with attentive mothers experienced increased expression of glucocorticoid receptor (GR) genes in the hippocampus compared to animals with less attentive mothers (see ● Figure 16.7). Increased expression of GR genes is associated with lower behavioral and hormonal responses to stressors (Meaney, 2010).

Why would we have mechanisms that would allow our genes to behave differently based on how we were raised? Our basic genotype is usually shaped by natural selection over a long period. The types of epigenetic

Not only can the hippocampus fail to regulate cortisol release under conditions of extreme stress, but continued stress can actually damage the hippocampus further. The stressed baboons mentioned earlier in this chapter experienced neural death, particularly in the hippocampus, in addition to their other medical problems (Sapolsky, 2001). People with post-traumatic stress disorder, discussed in our chapter on psychological disorders, also show evidence of having a smaller than average hippocampus (Bossini et al., 2008; Bremner et al., 1995). Having a smaller than average hippocampus might make a person exposed to trauma more vulnerable to the development of PTSD, or elevated levels of cortisol could reduce the size of the hippocampus, or both (Gilbertson et al., 2002; Kasai et al., 2008).

FIGURE 16.6

Exploration by Rat Pups Raised by High- and Low-Licking/Grooming Mothers. The amount of time a rat pup will stay out in the open is highly related to the type of nurture it received. All pups raised by an attentive mother (Hi-LG, or high licking and grooming) explored longer than pups raised by less attentive mothers (Low-LG, or low licking and grooming), regardless of the nurture style used by their biological mother. *Source:* Adapted from Francis, Diorio, Liu, and Meaney (1999).

© Stephen Dalton/Photo Researchers, Inc.

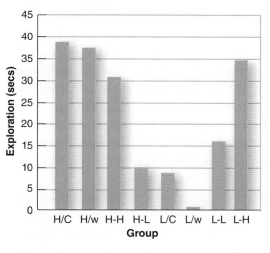

© Cengage Learning 2013

H/C = "High Control"; pups left undisturbed with their own Hi-LG mothers

H/w = "High Cross-fostered"; pups removed and put back with their own Hi-LG mothers

H-H = "High-High"; pups with Hi-LG mother fostered by Hi-LG mother

H-L = "High-Low"; pups with Hi-LG mother fostered by Low-LG mother

L/C = "Low Control"; pups left undisturbed with their own Low-LG mothers

L/w = "Low Cross-fostered"; pups removed and put back with their own Low-LG mothers

L-L = "Low-Low"; pups with Low-LG mother fostered by a Low-LG mother

L-H = "Low-High"; pups with Low-LG mother fostered by a Hi-LG mother

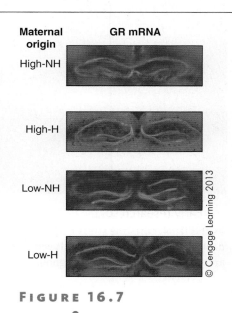

Maternal origin — **GR mRNA**

High-NH

High-H

Low-NH

Low-H

© Cengage Learning 2013

FIGURE 16.7

Nurture Impacts Gene Expression in the Brain. The pups of High-LG mothers show greater expression of glucocorticoid receptors (GR) in the hippocampus, indicated in red. If an experimenter handles infant rat pups, the mother responds with increased licking and grooming when the pups are returned to her. Handling (H) or non-handling (NH) does not change gene expression in pups that are already receiving a lot of attention from their High-LG mothers. However, in Low-LG mothers, pups that are handled (H) experience levels of gene expression that are comparable to the pups of High-LG mothers and that are much higher than non-handled pups of Low-LG mothers (NH). The amount of GR gene expression is associated with resilience to stress later in life. *Source:* Adapted from Francis, Diorio, Liu, and Meaney (1999).

change observed in these rodents can prepare an organism for its more immediate environment. Keep in mind that stress, although unpleasant, is adaptive. If a stressed mother living in a dangerous neighborhood provides minimal care to her children because she herself is stressed, her children enter their environment already predisposed to be reactive to danger. If a mother living in a safer environment is less stressed and provides a great deal of care, her children are likely to survive even though they are less responsive to the stressors they might encounter. ☢

© Sgt. Jessika Malott, 8th MP Bde. Public Affairs/ photo courtesy of U.S. Army

As this family faces the stress of the father's overseas deployment, the mother responds with a tend and befriend approach by comforting her daughter.

tend and befriend An alternative to fight or flight as a response to stressors; possibly more characteristic of females.

Gender Differences in the Stress Response

Although psychologists typically discuss fight or flight as the common response to stressors, an alternate response has been suggested that might be more typical of women's responses to stressors (Taylor, 2006). Noting that from an evolutionary standpoint, a mother with small children is unlikely to find either fight or flight easy to do, these researchers suggest that women are more likely to **tend and befriend** in response to stressors. Soothing frightened children, hiding, and forming social alliances for further protection might be more effective strategies.

Instead of the traditional hormones associated with fight and flight, a tend and befriend response is more closely associated with the release of oxytocin, a hormone related to social bonding that we discussed in our chapters on biological psychology and on motivation and emotion. As we mentioned in our chapter on biological psychology, added oxytocin relieves stress in animals, but only when the animals are in a social group as opposed to being isolated (Taylor & Master, 2010; Yee et al., 2010).

The Epigenetics of Stress

In our chapter on nature and nurture, we discussed the significant role played by the environment in determining if and when a particular gene is expressed. We defined epigenetics as the influence on traits by factors that determine how genes perform; the field of epigenetics explores gene–environment interactions. For example, we observed how both rats and human children who were well nurtured by their mothers showed more resilience to stress later in life. The nurture received from the mother had actually influenced how the genes responsible for producing stress hormones behaved during later stressful experiences (Champagne, Francis, Mar, & Meaney, 2003; Neigh, Gillespie, & Nemeroff, 2009).

Genes and life stress also interact to produce depression. As we observed in our chapter on psychological disorders, depression is often accompanied by dysfunction in systems using the neurotransmitter serotonin. Life stress affects people differently depending on whether they possess a short form or a long form of a gene related to serotonin function. Having the long or short version of the gene interacts with life stress to produce different levels of activity in the amygdala and hippocampus, differences in the pathways connecting the amygdala and hippocampus with other regions of the brain, differences in gray matter, and different levels of rumination, the repetitive rethinking of problems that is particularly characteristic of depressed people (Canli et al., 2006). These gene–stress interactions help explain why some people are more vulnerable to life stress while others seem relatively well protected against stress.

How Does Stress Affect Our Health?

Our stress response was forged by the challenges our hunter-gatherer ancestors were most likely to face. The result is a system that has beneficial effects in the short term, but can lead to negative effects when stress becomes chronic (Cacioppo & Berntson, 2011).

After all, it would not take your ancestors hours, days, months, or years to figure out what to do to escape a hungry lion. For better or for worse, the outcome would be decided quickly. In contrast, many of the stressors we face in modern living are not at all brief, and as a result, we are fairly constantly experiencing Selye's resistance phase, which combines stress and coping. You might be worried about finding a job after you graduate from college, which might be years away. Any long-term, chronic stress has the potential to impact health in negative ways. Not only does responding to stress require large amounts of energy, but while in the resistance stage, you do a less efficient job of storing nutrients and giving your body the rest and repair it needs.

Improved understanding of the relationships between stress and health can guide our quest for physical and psychological well-being.

Stress and the Immune System Very short-term bursts of stress can have a beneficial effect on many biological systems, including the **immune system**, your body's frontline defense against infection and cancer. Participating in a stressful memory task was correlated with an improvement in the response of the immune system, as measured by markers of immune system activity in the saliva of volunteers (Bosch, De Geus, & Kelder, 2001).

However, the immune system does not perform as well in the face of long-term, chronic sources of stress (see ● Figure 16.8). When responding to an emergency, our stress response system prioritizes body functions. Those that are not necessary for handling the immediate emergency are

Many of the dangers faced by these San hunters in South Africa are likely to arise and resolve quickly. Our responses to stress are better suited for short-term stressors than for many of the ongoing, chronic sources of stress we face in industrialized settings.

immune system The body system that defends against infection and cancer.

FIGURE 16.8

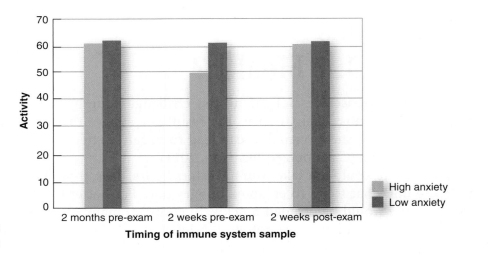

Stress From Exams and Immune Response. Immune system responses were assessed in students at three times: 2 months prior to important exams, 2 weeks prior to the exams, and 2 weeks following the exams. Students were divided on the basis of "trait anxiety," defined by whether a student views exams as stressful (High Trait Anxiety) or as a challenge (Low Trait Anxiety). For the students with high trait anxiety, but not low trait anxiety, the anticipation of upcoming exams produced a temporary drop in function that returned to baseline levels 2 weeks later. *Source:* Adapted from Wadee, Kuschke, Kometz, and Berk (2001).

taken offline. Unfortunately for those suffering from chronic, ongoing stress, one of those expendable systems is the immune system (Thornton, Andersen, Crespin, & Carson, 2007). As a result, stress can lead to greater frequency and severity of illnesses, as you may have noticed immediately following final exam periods (Wadee, Kuschke, Kometz, & Berk, 2001).

Numerous studies indicate that people experiencing chronic stress are more vulnerable to infectious diseases, like colds and the flu (Cohen, Tyrrell, & Smith, 1991). White blood cells, or **lymphocytes**, protect us from invading organisms. Unfortunately, stress hormones directly suppress the activity of lymphocytes (Calcagni & Elenkov, 2006). Flare-ups of both oral and genital herpes are most likely to occur when a person is experiencing unusual stress (Cohen & Herbert, 1996). The progression of HIV infection to AIDS is influenced by a patient's level of stress (Harper et al., 2006). Stressed students show greater vulnerability to the virus responsible for mononucleosis, which normally is kept in check by a robust immune system (Cacioppo & Berntson, 2011). Unfortunately, knowledge of these relationships can place an even greater burden on sick people, who may be led to believe that their illness wouldn't be so bad if they were somehow better at managing stress.

Stress related to our social relationships seems to be especially harmful to our ability to stay healthy. A meta-analysis of almost 300 studies and about 20,000 participants demonstrated that chronic stressors affecting people's social roles (e.g., death of a loved one, divorce) produce the greatest suppression of the immune system (Segerstrom & Miller, 2004). In particular, stressors that are outside a person's sense of control and lead to little hope for improvement have the most damaging effects. Those who are older and already ill are especially susceptible to adverse consequences of stress.

lymphocyte White blood cells; products of the immune system.

Stress and Heart Disease In the 1970s, Meyer Friedman and Ray Rosenman (1974) stimulated a large quantity of research by suggesting that highly competitive workaholics, whom they called **Type A personalities**, were more susceptible to heart disease than the more mellow, laid-back people they called **Type Bs**.

Further study, however, showed that simply being competitive had little to do with increased risk of heart disease. Instead, the Type As who did develop heart problems exhibited a pattern of interpersonal hostility. The Type As most at risk for heart disease were frequently suspicious, angry, and resentful of others. It is possible that their own hostile behavior provoked more hostile situations and reactions from others, confirming their worldview and maintaining their negative behavior. In addition, hostile people are not likely to build up networks of friends and loved ones, who are often our best protectors from the untoward effects of stress (Jackson, Kubzansky, Cohen, Jacobs, & Wright, 2007).

Stress puts the cardiovascular system at risk by affecting the ability of blood vessels to expand when necessary. People whose arteries are already stiff or clogged due to age, poor fitness, or disease often suffer from high blood pressure and might be especially susceptible to heart attacks following stress. In a heart attack, interruptions of blood flow to the heart trigger death of a part of the cardiac muscle. Flexible blood vessels maintain blood flow and blood pressure and lessen the chances of a heart attack. To test the effects of stress on blood flow, healthy participants were given a standardized mental stress task in which colored buttons were to be pushed as quickly as possible in response to flashing lights of the same color (Spieker et al., 2002). For the following 45 minutes, the ability of the participants' blood vessels to expand was reduced by a factor of 50%. A participant's change in blood pressure in response to a stressful situation was predictive of his or her later diagnosis with hypertension, or high blood pressure, which can lead to heart attacks or stroke (Spieker et al., 2002).

Stress, Mood, Sleep, and Obesity As we mentioned in our chapters on biological psychology and on psychological disorders, mood, sleep, and appetite are closely intertwined. A change in one of these behaviors usually results in changes in the others. Long-term, chronic stress can begin a cascade of changes in mood, sleep, and appetite that compromise well-being. Disruptions of sleep due to stress are particularly hazardous to health, as we need sleep as a time to restore our bodies after the challenges of the day. Both sleep quantity and quality are associated with both overall health and cognitive outcomes (Hawkley & Cacioppo, 2010).

Stress frequently serves as a trigger for depressed mood. Self-reports of daily stressors, like having an argument with a friend, were correlated with the participants' mood (Stader & Hokanson, 1998). The ability of stress to alter levels of circulating cortisol, discussed earlier in this chapter, might form the basis for this connection between stress and depressed mood. As we observed in our chapter on psychological disorders, many people diagnosed with depression show signs of abnormal cortisol function (Aihara et al., 2007).

© Jaimie Duplass/Shutterstock

Initial research suggested that having a competitive, workaholic Type A personality was correlated with a higher risk of cardiovascular disease than having a more mellow, relaxed Type B personality. Further research, however, showed that high levels of hostility, not workload and competitiveness, were responsible for the greater risk in some Type As.

Type A personality A competitive, workaholic, and in some cases hostile personality type.

Type B personality A mellow, "laid-back" personality type.

Cortisol is not just released in response to perceived stressors. As we observed in our chapter on consciousness, cortisol also plays a role in maintaining our natural cycles of sleep and waking. Cortisol is released in large quantities early in the morning, contributing to wakefulness. As the day progresses, cortisol levels drop off, reducing wakefulness and setting the stage for sleep. Obviously, if you experience a big jolt of cortisol due to a stressor late in the evening, getting to sleep is going to be difficult, even when you're really very tired. Even when you do manage to get to sleep, high levels of cortisol interfere with good sleep quality (Van Cauter, Leproult, & Plat, 2000). As we observed in our chapter on psychological disorders, both high levels of stress and depression can produce sleep disturbances, especially the experience of waking frequently throughout the night (Koenigsberg et al., 2004).

Mood and sleep can both affect appetite. Among the criteria for major depressive disorder, discussed in our chapter on psychological disorders, are changes in appetite. Some people who are depressed lose weight without dieting, while others gain weight. By now, it shouldn't surprise you to learn that stress, along with depression, can also contribute to obesity. In response to stress-related hormones, fat cells behave differently, growing in both size and number (Kuo et al., 2009). Stressed mice gained much more weight than mice that were not stressed, even when both were fed the same high-fat, high-sugar diet. In addition to this direct effect of stress on appetite, stress can produce indirect effects on obesity by interfering with sleep. Dieters who enjoyed a full-night's sleep lost the same amount of weight as dieters who slept less, but there was a difference in the kind of weight that was lost (Nedeltcheva, Kilkus, Imperial, Schoeller, & Penev, 2010). Dieters who slept well lost a healthy amount of fat. Sleep-deprived dieters lost only half as much fat as the sleeping dieters, and three quarters of their weight loss consisted of precious bone and muscle tissue instead (see ● Figure 16.9).

An Integrated View of Stress and Health We have reviewed a number of studies in this section that demonstrate the adverse effects that chronic, prolonged stress can have on our health. Popular wisdom suggests that people with the highest levels of stress, therefore, should experience the

FIGURE 16.9

Sleep and Diet Interact.
Participants who slept 8.5 hours per night lost about the same amount of weight during a treatment program as participants who slept 5.5 hours per night, but the two groups differed in the amount of body fat and lean body mass that was lost. The 8.5 hours per night sleep group lost more body fat and less lean body mass, which is characteristic of desirable weight loss, than the 5.5 hours per night sleep group. These results remind us that many of our health habits are intimately interconnected, and changing one can have a large effect on others. *Source:* Adapted from Nedeltcheva, Kilkus, Imperial, Schoeller, and Penev (2010).

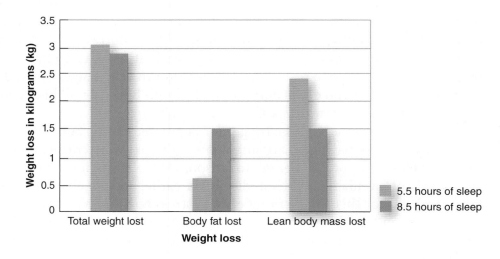

worst health. However, we have already seen one example, the healthy Type As, where this has not been the case. In another study, 5,000 men first reported their stress levels, which were then compared 20 years later to their medical records. Surprisingly, the men who had reported the highest levels of stress had experienced the least amount of heart disease (Macleod et al., 2002). How can we explain these apparently contradictory results?

One approach to reconciling the good health enjoyed by some stressed people with data demonstrating the harmful effects of stress in others is to step back and look at the whole person within his or her environment over the entire life span. Health can be described as not just the absence of disease but instead as the ability to respond to the challenges of being alive (Juster, McEwen, & Lupien, 2010).

Personal factors, including your genes, interact with the parental care you receive, as we discussed previously in this chapter. Other protective factors, such as your social networks and sense of meaning or purpose in life, contribute to your resilience in the face of the negative and cumulative effects of a lifetime of responding to stressors (Cacioppo & Berntson, 2011). These protective factors occur at critical periods, such as the impact of parenting in early childhood, so a complete understanding of protective mechanisms should be examined within the context of life span development. Once we fully understand these protective processes, psychologists should be in the exciting position of being able to design effective interventions for improving health and well-being (see ● Figure 16.10).

Long before vaccinations and antibiotics were available, death rates due to infectious diseases began to drop in the United States. Improved wages and nutrition coupled with more rest time away from work allowed people to recuperate from their daily stresses (Cacioppo & Berntson, 2011).

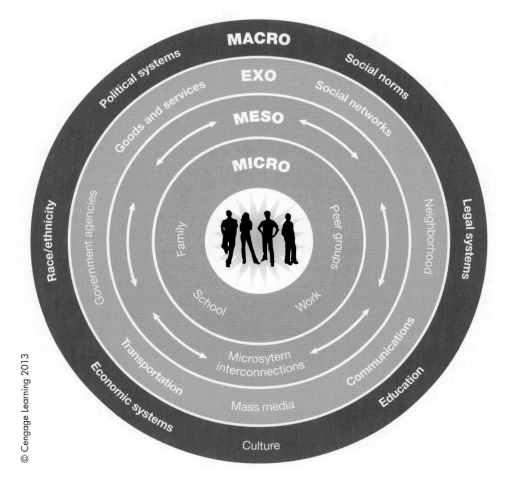

FIGURE 16.10

An Interactive View of Stress and Health. To fully understand how stress impacts health, we place the individual's interactions between genes and experience within a context of family, community, and culture. *Source:* Adapted from Juster, McEwen, and Lupien (2010).

How Can We Cope Effectively With Stress?

Stress is inevitable. That simple statement does not imply that there is nothing you can do about stress. Psychologists have identified a number of strategies people can use to effectively reduce the negative impacts of stress on their happiness and health.

One of the most positive aspects of stress is that we adapt to it over time. Take a minute to jot down the things you found most stressful five years ago and then make a list of the stressors you face today. Would you trade today's list for the one from five years ago? Most people would do so in a heartbeat. Life gets more complicated and often more stressful, but our skills for coping improve at the same time. People tend to report less stress as they get older (Shields, 2004).

Psychology *as a* Hub Science

Belongingness, Stress, Achievement, and Health

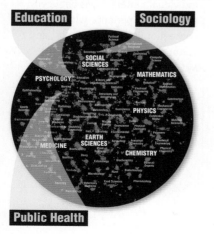

We don't need to tell you that being in college can be stressful. For many students, college can mean new environments, new rules and routines, new social interactions, less sleep, not-so-great eating habits, and more sitting than exercising. Can the application of psychological research make the transition into college easier and less stressful?

We can't make many of these stressors go away, but a simple, one-time intervention at the beginning of the first year of college made a large difference in the academic performance and health of a group of students (Walton & Cohen, 2011). Incoming first-year students at Stanford University were randomly assigned to a control group or a social-belonging group. The social-belonging group read what they thought were the results of a survey of older students, who said that they had worried about fitting in during their first year, but had grown more confident over time. Participants were asked to write an essay comparing their own first-year experiences with the survey results and then deliver a speech based on their essay to a video camera for use with future students. At no time were the participants aware that they were actually experiencing a "treatment" designed to make them see the social stressors of college life as typical of all students and of short duration.

Over the next three years, the participants' grade point averages and health were monitored. The "belongingness" intervention had

Earlier in this chapter, we described the role of cognitive appraisal in identifying a stimulus or event as a stressor. Appraisal plays an important role in coping with identified stressors as well. Once a stressor has been identified, a second set of appraisals occurs that guides our coping responses (Lazarus, 1966). What harm has already occurred? What threats remain? What resources do I need to overcome this challenge?

Managing Stress An obvious starting place for keeping your levels of stress low is to ask whether any stressors can be eliminated. If you feel stressed about having too much to do and too little time to do it, it might be possible to reduce your workload or practice better time management skills. If money is tight, a visit to your campus's financial aid office might provide you with solutions you had not considered. The worst possible approach is to withdraw and avoid stressors, in the vain hope that they will go away. Your latest credit card statement is not going to get better magically if you ignore it. In fact, your emotional response to seeing the statement on your desk every day is likely to get a lot worse over time.

A major variable that predicts our response to stress is the sense of control. Feeling surprised by life or out of control can lead to significant stress. Some of the worst stressors are those that seem to strike randomly, such as being diagnosed with lung cancer when you never smoked (Pietrzak,

The stress of middle school, such as attending school dances, is very real to students at the time, but as we get older and more experienced, our capacity to manage stress improves. With age, people report feeling less stress, even though stressors tend to become more complicated and numerous at the same time.

little impact on the health and grades of European American students, but had significant and positive effects on African American students. Compared to African American students in the control group, the students who had received the one-time reassurance that their concerns about fitting in were normal and not permanent had higher grades, fewer visits to the doctor, and higher subjective happiness (see ● Figure 16.11).

While further research is necessary to know how far these results can be generalized to other students, they do emphasize the importance of how you interpret your situation and whether you feel like you belong to your overall performance, health, and well-being. ❂

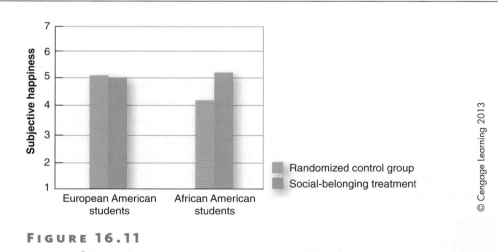

FIGURE 16.11

A Belongingness Intervention Improved the Performance and Health of African American College Students. A one-time treatment aimed at framing the stress of fitting in to the college experience as common to most students and limited in duration significantly improved the grade point averages (GPAs), happiness ratings, and health of African American students at Stanford University 3 years later. European American students did not experience the same treatment-related differences, with both treated and non-treated European American students experiencing the same health and subjective happiness as the treated African American students. This result suggests that "fitting in" was already framed by European American students in positive ways. *Source: Adapted from Walton and Cohen (2011).*

Even when a stressor takes us by surprise, we can regain a sense of control. Viktor Frankl, a Holocaust survivor, developed what he described as "tragic optimism" for coping with unforeseen disasters. Instead of asking why these disasters should happen to us, Frankl recommends that people exert a sense of control by asking, "How can I face this disaster with courage and responsibility?"

Goldstein, Southwick, & Grant, 2011). These seemingly random events undercut our sense of control (if I don't smoke, I am ensuring my lungs will stay healthy).

Many stressors are out of our control. We can't wish our cancer away or magically ensure that enough money appears in our bank accounts to pay this month's bills. However, we can respond to our stressors in ways that reduce our overall stress. This approach is consistent with the elements of positive psychology, which we review later in this chapter. Even if you are struggling with a life-threatening disease, stress can be reduced by educating yourself as much as possible about your condition and participating fully in decisions about your treatment. Residents of nursing homes who have more control over their choice of daily activities live longer than those who are not given such choices (Rodin, 1986). We observed in our chapter on personality that stressors have less effect on people who experience an internal locus of control, which means that they believe most of their outcomes are due to their personal efforts as opposed to luck, chance, or other external forces.

Because of the inevitability of stress, people cope best when they keep themselves as healthy as possible. If you follow good health habits, stress will still deplete your reserves and inhibit your immune system, but a healthy body can take more abuse than an unhealthy one. Students are much more likely to get sick during final exams if they have neglected good eating and sleeping habits all term.

Regular aerobic exercise appears to be especially helpful. In one experiment, patients with heart disease were observed as they engaged in exercise as part of their rehabilitation programs. The exercise reduced the overall stress levels of all participants (Milani & Lavie, 2009). Exercise seemed particularly beneficial for the participants who also scored high on psychosocial stress. None of the high-stress patients who showed the greatest physical benefits from exercise (such as increased oxygen uptake) died in the follow-up period compared to 19% of the high-stress patients who showed relatively low physical benefits from exercise (see ● Figure 16.12). Students would be wise to engage in some level of activity in college to offset the effects of increased stress.

One of the most powerful antidotes to the unhealthy effects of stress is social connectedness and support. Social support from friends and family and belief systems that allow a person to make sense out of the world provide powerful buffers against stress (Montpetit, Bergeman, Deboeck, Tiberio, & Boker, 2010). As we have argued on many occasions in this textbook, people with good social relationships and support are far less vulnerable to adverse health and psychological conditions than people who are lonely and isolated (Cacioppo & Patrick, 2008). In times of distress, people frequently turn to others in an effort to cope. According to a study of responses to the terrorist attacks of 9/11, nearly 100% of the participants reported talking about their thoughts and feelings about the attacks with other people (Schuster et al., 2002). Over 90% reported either praying or engaging in spiritual contemplation appropriate to their faith. Over 60% engaged in relevant public activities. Nearly

Patients who educate themselves about their conditions and participate fully in treatment decisions experience less stress.

© Monkey Business Images/Shutterstock

Illustration: © Cengage Learning 2013; photo: © Alexander Raths/Photos.com

Figure 16.12

Exercise Reduces Mortality in Stressed Cardiac Patients. Patients with cardiovascular disease were assessed for psychosocial stress levels during a rehabilitation program that included exercise. A control group did not have a formal exercise program. Based on their improvement in physical measures following the exercise program, the patients were divided into low and high exercise change groups. In a follow-up 5 years later, high levels of physical improvement due to exercise did not affect the mortality of the low psychosocial stress group, but significantly reduced mortality in the high-stress group. *Source: Adapted from Milani and Lavie (2009).*

40% focused on the needs of others, by donating money or blood to relief efforts.

Understanding the importance of social support for coping helps to explain why people living in poor neighborhoods often experience more stress and have higher rates of depression. Living in a neighborhood where few people know each other or help each other with tasks like child care increases your risk of developing major depressive disorder (Russell & Cutrona, 2010).These socially disconnected neighborhoods become more prevalent as the income of residents decreases, making people living below the poverty line especially vulnerable to stress and depression.

Although it is ideal to receive your social support from other people, having a pet can also provide benefits to your health. Stockbrokers with high blood pressure who lived alone were selected to receive a cat or dog from a local shelter (Allen, 2003). When stressed, the pet owners experienced a much lower increase in blood pressure than their pet-less counterparts. The effect was most obvious among participants who listed few social connections with other people.

Many people find that having religious beliefs helps them cope with stress. People who report having religious beliefs appear to withstand the challenges of unemployment, low income, and widowhood better than people who report no religious beliefs (Diener & Seligman, 2004). Across a number of nations practicing different forms of religion, a higher rate of belief in a god predicts higher ratings of life satisfaction and lower rates of suicide (Helliwell, 2003).

Three Types of Coping Coping with a stressor can take three forms: problem-focused, emotion-focused, and relationship-focused coping (O'Brien & DeLongis, 1996). In each case, positive and negative versions of each style can be observed.

Problem-focused coping is designed to address the problem. If you just flunked an important exam, positive problem-focused coping strategies might include making an appointment with your professor to discuss your options, hiring a tutor, taking a study skills seminar, or joining a study

© Spc. Terence Ewings, 4th AAB PAO, 1st Cav. Div., USD-N/ photo courtesy of U.S. Army

Specialist Lawrence Shipman and Sergeant First Class Jonathan Zeke, a combat stress–relief dog, received an award for their work in reducing the stress of soldiers deployed in Iraq. Shipman notes that Zeke acts as an icebreaker, encouraging soldiers to talk to the behavioral health counselors.

problem-focused coping A response to stress designed to address specific problems by finding solutions.

At times of stress, we often engage in three different types of coping. (a) Problem-focused coping is usually used to solve problems at work. (b) Emotion-focused coping helps us deal with the negative emotions of stress. The use of strategies like overeating, however, can lead to more problems. (c) Relationship-focused coping helps us maintain and strengthen social networks at times of stress.

(a) Problem-focused coping   (b) Emotion-focused coping   (c) Relationship-focused coping

group formed by your classmates. Negative problem-focused coping can include escape and avoidance. Instead of confronting the problem, a student might just stop going to class. Problem-focused coping is more frequently used for work-related stressors (which would include schoolwork) than for interpersonal stressors (like the breakup of an important relationship; Terry, 1994).

Emotion-focused coping helps you deal with the negative emotions associated with a stressor. Flunking an exam might make you feel very sad, discouraged, and depressed. Positive coping with these negative emotions might involve sharing your concerns with your friends or family, taking a break from your studies to enjoy a movie or go for a jog, or, when the negative emotions seem overwhelming, visiting your campus's counseling center for advice. Negative emotion-focused coping, such as eating food you do not need or using alcohol to dull your stress, might simply add to your problems and increase your overall levels of stress.

Relationship-focused coping helps you maintain and protect social relationships in response to stress (O'Brien & DeLongis, 1996). This type of coping also has both positive and negative aspects. For example, people caring for Alzheimer's patients, which can be very stressful, exhibited positive coping (empathy, support, and compromise) as well as negative coping (confronting, ignoring, blaming, and withdrawal; Kramer, 1993).

As we have seen so frequently in our discussions of human behavior, the choice of a coping approach results from interactions between a person and his or her situation (Aldwin, 1994). For example, people who score high on the Big Five trait of neuroticism, which we discussed in our chapter on personality, tend to experience more distress than people with low neuroticism scores (Bolger & Schilling, 1991). When responding to stressors in the work situation, people high in neuroticism are more likely to engage in negative problem-focused coping, such as escaping the situation (O'Brien & DeLongis, 1996). When dealing with interpersonal stress, however, people with high neuroticism use the negative relationship-focused coping strategy of confrontation. People with high neuroticism also cope differently with stress involving close relationships (significant others, family members, close friends) than with stress involving distant

emotion-focused coping A response to stress that targets the negative emotions arising from the situation.

relationship-focused coping A response to stress designed to maintain and protect social relationships.

relationships (coworkers, neighbors). They are much more likely to use a positive relationship-focused coping method, empathy, when dealing with distant relationships than when dealing with close relationships (O'Brien & DeLongis, 1996).

Resilience: Individual Differences in Response to Stress

You might have observed that under the same stressful circumstances, such as an upcoming exam, some students seem very calm and others appear to be in a state of panic. What determines these individual differences in coping?

We have already seen how epigenetic interactions between genes and nurturing can influence later responses to stress. In addition, people differ in **resilience**, or the ability to adapt to life's challenges in positive ways. Resilient people do not ignore feelings of sadness or stress, but like Viktor Frankl, they harness their inner strengths to enable them to remain optimistic and get on with the business of life. In contrast, when people lack resilience, they feel overwhelmed, helpless, and victimized. They become more vulnerable to the use of negative coping strategies, including alcoholism and drug abuse, to escape their problems. Early research in resilience focused on children's ability to thrive even in conditions of poverty, neglect, and abuse (Masten et al., 1999).

Some psychologists refer to individual differences in the ability to cope with stress as resulting from a personality trait of hardiness (Hystad, Eid, Laberg, Johnsen, & Bartone, 2009). As we mentioned in our chapter on personality, a personality trait is likely to be stable and enduring over time. Compared to less hardy people, people with high hardiness experience less threat or disruption in response to the normal stressors of life. Hardiness combines commitment, control, and challenge (Bartone, 2000). People with high commitment see the world as interesting and seek involvement rather than withdrawal. Control refers to an individual's belief in her or his own ability to influence events. Challenge is a state of mind that sees change and new experiences not as negative stressors but as opportunities for learning and personal growth. Among college students, hardiness did not predict grades, but it was negatively correlated with health complaints and stress related to academic work (Hystad et al., 2009) (see ● Figure 16.13).

Other protective factors contributing to individual differences in resilience are cognitive skills, social skills, and flexibility in response to new situations (Garmezy, 1991). Individual differences in resilience might also have their roots in emotion. People who are generally more positive in mood tend to build the resources they need, including strong social networks, to sustain them at difficult times (Cohn, Fredrickson, Brown, Mikels, & Conway, 2009).

Austrian psychiatrist Viktor Frankl (1905–1997) was sent to the dreaded Nazi concentration camp Auschwitz, where he lost his pregnant wife, parents, and brother. Frankl used his experiences in developing his theories of *logotherapy*, after the Greek word for "meaning." The ability to find meaning even in the depths of despair by recalling pleasant memories or helping a suicidal inmate helped Frankl survive the stress and horror surrounding him.

People who write "scripts" for how their life "should" happen, such as thinking that everyone should enjoy a holiday, often experience high stress levels when events take an unexpected turn. Maintaining a flexible approach to meeting your life's goals is far less likely to produce stress.

resilience The ability to adapt to life's challenges in positive ways.

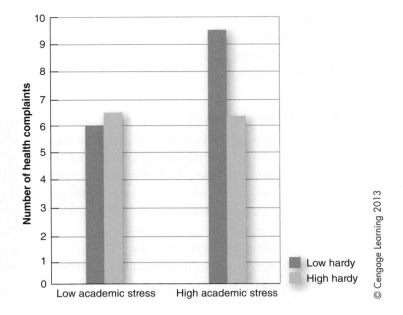

FIGURE 16.13

Hardiness Protects Students From the Health Impacts of Stress. A personality trait of hardiness, which combines commitment, a sense of control, and the appraisal of stressors as challenges, seems to protect college students from the health consequences of high academic stress.

Source: Adapted from Hystad, Eid, Laberg, Johnsen, and Bartone (2009).

© Cengage Learning 2013

Summary 16.1

Stages in Hans Selye's General Adaptation Syndrome

Stage	What's happening?
Alarm	Mobilization of resources for fight or flight
Resistance	Continued coping with chronic stress
Exhaustion	Systems begin to fail

© Ryan Romero

© Sgt. Jessika Malott, 8th MP Bde. Public Affairs/ photo courtesy of U.S. Army

© oliveromg/ Shutterstock

What Is the Relationship Between Psychology and Health?

You might be surprised to see a section about **health psychology** in your psychology textbook. Isn't health the exclusive domain of medical personnel rather than of psychologists? It all depends on how you define *health*. For most of its history, the field of medicine viewed health as a lack of disease (Juster et al., 2010). Treatments were designed to make sick people feel better. In more recent years, health has been more commonly defined as the attainment of a positive state of well-being, rather than simply the absence of disease. Medicine today is more likely to use a **biopsychosocial model** of health, in which health is viewed as the sum of biological (such as genetics, infection, injury), psychological (such as lifestyle, stress, health beliefs), and social factors (such as culture, family, social support). In 1948, the World Health Organization (WHO) proposed a definition that reflects this more contemporary model of health: "a state of complete physical, mental and social well-being and not merely the absence of disease or infirmity" (World Health Organization [WHO], 2003). In addition to making sick people feel better, which of course is an important function of medicine, this new view of health seeks to improve the well-being of people who are not sick (see • Figure 16.14).

One reason for this transition from the biomedical model to the biopsychosocial model is the changing face of health and medicine over the last 100 years or so. Because of improved sanitation and vaccination, the threats to health faced today are quite different from those faced by earlier generations. In 1900, the leading causes of death in the United States were

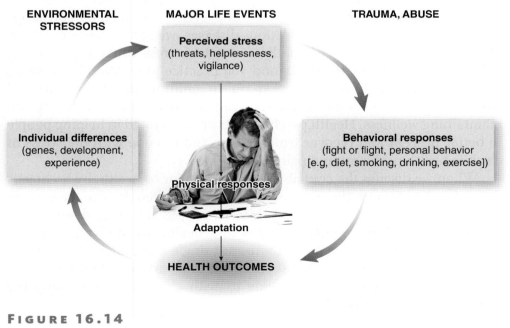

Illustration: © Cengage Learning 2013; photo: © forestpath/Shutterstock

FIGURE 16.14

A Biopsychosocial Model of Health. Health today is viewed as the product of interactions between individual characteristics, life experiences, cognitions, and behavior. *Source:* Adapted from Juster, McEwen, and Lupien (2010).

health psychology A branch of psychology that investigates the relationships between psychological variables and health.

biopsychosocial model A model that sees health as the result of biological, psychological, and social factors.

FIGURE 16.15

Leading Causes of Death in the United States. Over the last 100 years, infectious diseases have been replaced as the major causes of death in the United States by heart disease, cancer, lung disease, and stroke. As medical progress decreases deaths due to these causes, age-related diseases such as Alzheimer's disease have become more common causes of death. *Source:* Adapted from Kochanek, Xu, Murphy, Miniño, and Kung (2011).

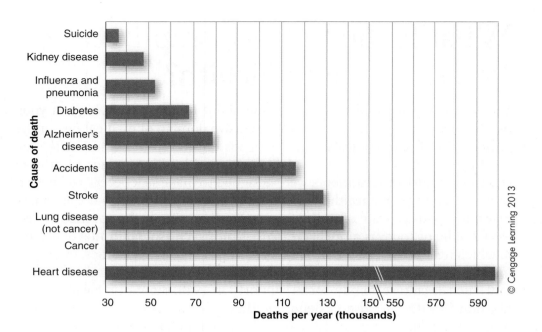

pneumonia, influenza, and tuberculosis, but by 2005, the leading causes of death were heart disease, cancer, lung disease, and stroke (see ● Figure 16.15). In other words, we have gone from facing major threats from infectious, short-duration conditions to noninfectious, long-term conditions. In the last few decades, considerable progress was made in the treatment of heart disease, cancer, and stroke. This improvement in turn has resulted in a larger number of Americans who are living long enough to be diagnosed with age-related conditions such as Alzheimer's disease and Parkinson's disease.

The contemporary leading causes of death just listed (heart disease, cancer, and stroke) form significant interactions with behavior, as their risk factors include obesity, smoking, lack of exercise, and alcohol consumption. Even when we consider infectious diseases, we see evidence of strong behavioral components, such as the amount of stress you're experiencing (Cohen et al., 1991) or the likelihood you practice prevention by washing your hands during flu season and so on. In addition, lifestyle factors and adherence to treatment plans can be extremely important to achieving and maintaining wellness. Health psychologists are interested in helping people to better prevent and recover from disease and to cope with the stress of chronic health problems and pain.

When we discuss the contributions of behavior to health, by no means do we want to "blame the victims" of poor health. People who have never smoked still get lung cancer, and thin, fit people get heart disease. The relationships between lifestyle factors and health are derived from the statistical analyses of large populations, not single individuals. At the same time, understanding that most people engaged in particular behaviors have certain health outcomes can provide us with clues for maintaining the healthiest lifestyles possible.

Behavior and Health

In 2009, *Consumer Reports* conducted a survey of 1,000 Americans to see how many engaged in everyday prevention behaviors (Consumerreports.com, 2009). As shown in Table 16.1, the respondents did rather well in a number

TABLE

16.1 Americans' Safety Practices

Behavior	Yes	No
Use cotton swabs to clean ears	73%	26%
Let your kids play on trampoline	43%	56%
Eat raw dough when making cookies	39%	61%
Use top step of ladder	31%	69%
Fail to use car's seat belt	24%	75%
Drink beer while using power tool or mower	13%	87%
Have a rubber mat in shower	39%	61%
Have a carbon-monoxide detector in home	51%	48%
Eat burgers only well done	67%	32%
Change batteries in smoke alarm annually	79%	21%
Clean lint trap in dryer after each use	81%	18%
Read warnings on prescription medicines	91%	9%
Wear a bike helmet	42%	58%
Wear sunscreen when outside for an extended time	73%	27%

Source: Adapted from Consumerreports.org (2009).

of categories (91% read the warnings that come with a prescription drug, and 87% report not drinking beer while using a power tool or mower), but neglected some obvious preventive steps (58% never wear a bike helmet, 24% report being in a car without using a seat belt, and 27% do not use sunscreen when outdoors for an extended period). We do worry about those 13% who are drinking beer while mowing the lawn. The point is that many of our choices contribute to the prevention of accident and disease.

The behaviors that contribute to our major causes of death include smoking, poor nutrition, alcohol use, and lack of exercise (see ● Figure 16.16).

Tobacco Use Cigarette smoking is considered to be the leading preventable cause of death in the United States, with a direct responsibility in one

FIGURE 16.16

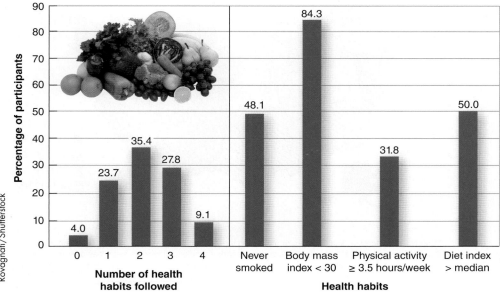

Four Simple Habits Make Major Contributions to Health. Following four simple health habits—never smoking, exercising 30 minutes per day, maintaining a non-obese weight, and eating a healthy diet including fruits and vegetables—reduced overall risk of chronic disease by 78%. Compared to the people who had none of these healthy habits, people doing all four health habits reduced their risk of diabetes by 93%, their risk of heart attack by 81%, their risk of stroke by 50%, and their risk of cancer by 36%. Unfortunately, only 9.1% of a sample of over 20,000 people had all four habits. Most people reported following only one to three of the four health habits. *Source:* Adapted from Ford et al. (2009).

out of five deaths each year (Centers for Disease Control and Prevention [CDC], 2010d). On average, smokers die 13 to 14 years earlier than non-smokers. Tobacco use can lead to additional health problems. Nicotine is a well-established gateway drug, capable of producing epigenetic changes that increase the likelihood of addiction to cocaine (Levine et al., 2011). Tobacco's effects are not restricted to its users. In the United States, exposure to secondhand smoke leads to 3,400 lung cancer deaths, 46,000 heart disease deaths, 430 cases of Sudden Infant Death Syndrome (SIDS), 24,500 low-birth-weight babies, 71,900 pre-term deliveries, and 200,000 episodes of childhood asthma each year (WHO, 2008).

Despite considerable educational efforts aimed at smoking prevention, 19.3% of American adults smoked as of 2010 (Centers for Disease Control and Prevention [CDC], 2011c). Worldwide, rates of smoking are even higher than those found in the United States and other developed countries. According to the World Health Organization (WHO; 2008), two thirds of current smokers live in developing countries, with 30% of smokers residing in China and 10% in India. Gender, race, ethnicity, education, mental health, and income are strong determinants of the likelihood of smoking. Men are more likely to smoke than women (23.5% as opposed to 17.9%). Multirace individuals reported the highest incidence of smoking (29.5%), followed by American Indians/Alaska Natives (23.2%), non-Hispanic Whites (22.1%), non-Hispanic Blacks (21.3%), Hispanics (14.5%), and Asians (12.0%). Smoking drops with increasing education, from 49.1% of individuals with a General Educational Development (GED) certificate to 5.6% of adults with a graduate degree. Poverty plays a strong role in smoking, as 31.1% of adults living below the poverty line compared to 19.4% living above the poverty line report smoking (see ● Figure 16.17).

FIGURE 16.17

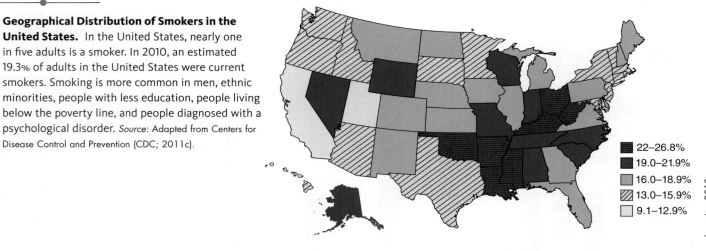

Geographical Distribution of Smokers in the United States. In the United States, nearly one in five adults is a smoker. In 2010, an estimated 19.3% of adults in the United States were current smokers. Smoking is more common in men, ethnic minorities, people with less education, people living below the poverty line, and people diagnosed with a psychological disorder. *Source:* Adapted from Centers for Disease Control and Prevention (CDC; 2011c).

22–26.8%
19.0–21.9%
16.0–18.9%
13.0–15.9%
9.1–12.9%

© Cengage Learning 2013

Percentage of persons age 18 years or more who reported smoking at least 100 cigarettes during their lifetime and who, at the time of the survey, reported smoking cigarettes every day or some days.

Given the carnage produced by tobacco, why do people start smoking and then continue? An understanding of the initiation of tobacco use requires combining many of the different perspectives we have discussed in this textbook—in particular, development, biological psychology, learning, and social psychology.

Most tobacco users begin smoking in childhood or early adolescence, long before decision making abilities are mature. Due to the addictive nature of nicotine, about half of those who experiment with tobacco will continue to use it. In addition to its action on synapses where the neurotransmitter acetylcholine is released, as discussed in our chapter on consciousness, nicotine has the ability to stimulate the dopamine reward circuits of the brain and to produce a particularly unpleasant set of withdrawal symptoms. As we discussed in our chapter on development, adolescence is also a time in which people try out new roles and learn important skills for getting along with peers, making them frequently susceptible to peer pressure. Teens often overestimate how many other people are using tobacco, so they might begin using it to avoid looking "different" (Institute of Medicine [IOM], 1994). Finally, most smokers have friends and parents who also smoke, suggesting a role for social learning (Biglan, Duncan, Ary, & Smolkowski, 1995).

A very troubling aspect of the initiation of smoking is the prevalence of tobacco use among people with diagnosed psychological disorders. Tobacco use among people with schizophrenia and other severe mental illnesses is about 70% in the United States, more than 3 times as high as the 20% of users in the general population as reported by the CDC (Dixon et al., 2007). In addition, the severity of smoking among these individuals, which includes such factors as how many cigarettes are smoked per day, appears to be much higher among people with psychological disorders than in the general population. In a large-scale study of over 50,000 adults who did not live in mental institutions, individuals with serious psychological distress, a global measure of psychological disorder, were much more likely to smoke currently, smoke heavily, and be less likely to quit than individuals without serious psychological distress (Sung, Prochaska, Ong, Shi, & Max, 2011). Although many smokers with psychological disorders report

© Carlos Barria/Reuters

One out of every three cigarettes lit each day is smoked by a person in China, where it is a conventional courtesy for one businessperson to greet another by offering a cigarette. The 2011 ban on smoking in bars, in restaurants, and on transportation does not apply to offices and factories. The ban was required by China's having signed the World Health Organization (WHO) Framework Convention on Tobacco Control 5 years ago. Public health officials fear that the lack of an awareness program and penalties will encourage the population to ignore the ban.

Columbia Pictures/Photofest

Among the many aids used to help people quit smoking are nicotine patches, nicotine gum, and now the electronic cigarette. Johnny Depp's use of an electronic cigarette in the 2011 movie *The Tourist* helped publicize this product. More research is needed to determine if electronic cigarettes will be used as a substitute for real cigarettes or as actual aids for quitting the use of nicotine entirely. Health agencies worldwide are in the process of evaluating the safety of the electronic cigarette.

using cigarettes to feel better, most began smoking long before their symptoms emerged and they were diagnosed with a disorder (Sacco, Termine, & Seyal, 2005). Evidence has begun to emerge supporting a causal role for nicotine in the development of some psychological disorders, especially depression (Husky, Mazure, Paliwal, & McKee, 2008).

People do manage to quit smoking, although some find it difficult. In the United States, ex-smokers now outnumber smokers (47 million to 46 million; Chapman & MacKenzie, 2010). Smokers use a variety of techniques to quit, including simply stopping all use abruptly ("cold turkey"), gradually reducing intake, using nicotine patches and gum or other nicotine replacement tools, counseling and support groups, or some combination of these.

Once again, the social nature of our species plays a role in this process. A person's chances of successfully quitting are reduced by 67% if a spouse smokes, 25% if a sibling smokes, 36% if a friend smokes, and 34% if a coworker smokes (Schroeder, 2008). We are not advocating that a prospective quitter abandon the essential social support needed at a difficult time; rather, we are suggesting that people trying to quit physically separate themselves when friends and family light up. As we noted in our chapter on learning, being exposed to conditioned stimuli, such as the smell of tobacco, can initiate a variety of conditioned behaviors that might make refusing a cigarette very difficult for the person trying to quit.

> Time is the most valuable thing on earth: time to think, time to act, time to extend our fraternal relations, time to become better men, time to become better women, time to become better and more independent citizens.
>
> —Samuel Gompers

Smoking cessation programs can also take advantage of the self-reference effect that we discussed in our chapter on personality and the self. The self-reference effect explains the superior recall for information relevant to the self by suggesting that the self serves as an important schema for organizing information. Participants experiencing interventions for smoking that were tailored to their own lives, needs, interests, and obstacles not only were more successful at quitting smoking but also showed brain activity in parts of the prefrontal cortex believed to participate in thinking about the self (Chua et al., 2011).

The benefits of quitting smoking appear within minutes to hours, as the body begins to repair itself. After 5 years of abstention from smoking, risk of stroke is the same for ex-smokers and nonsmokers. After 10 years of abstention, the risk of lung cancer is cut in half. If the smoker quits before the age of 30 years, life expectancy remains the same as for someone who has never smoked (Doll, Peto, Boreham, & Sutherland, 2004). Eliminating all tobacco smoking in the United States would produce a gain of 1.73 years of life expectancy for an 18-year-old (Stewart, Cutler, & Rosen, 2009).

Nutrition Nutrition plays a significant part in overall physical development, including brain development, and is believed to be responsible for many differences in psychological and health outcomes related to socioeconomic status (Rosales, Reznick, & Zeisel, 2009). People need just the right amount and quality of nutrients to support optimum health and brain functioning, and being either underweight or obese is associated with reduced health. Returning the United States population to normal weight (a BMI between 18.5 and 24.9) would produce about the same

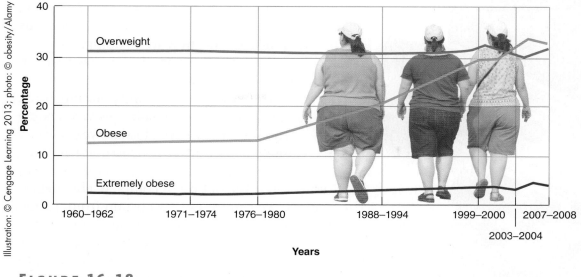

FIGURE 16.18

The Obesity Epidemic. In 1960, fewer than 15% of American adults were obese (BMI ≥ 30), but today about one third are obese. The number of people who are extremely or morbidly obese (BMI ≥ 40) has also climbed during this period. The reasons for the obesity epidemic are not well-understood currently and are likely to be complex. *Source: Adapted from Ogden and Carroll (2010).*

improvement in overall life expectancy as the elimination of smoking (Stewart et al., 2009).

As we mentioned in our chapter on motivation and emotion, not only do we face problems in the form of eating disorders, such as anorexia and bulimia, but the world has also experienced an unprecedented obesity epidemic over the last two decades (see ● Figure 16.18). In the United States, the percentage of obese adults rose from 12% in 1991 to 34% in 2008 (Flegal, Carroll, Ogden, & Curtin, 2010). It is likely that multiple factors have contributed to this change, including our sedentary lifestyle, increases in caloric intake, changes in the types of food we eat, changes in sleep patterns, and social factors.

Obesity increases the rates of many chronic conditions, including heart disease, stroke, diabetes, arthritis, and breast and colon cancers. As we noted previously, maintaining a BMI below 30 (non-obese) was one of the four protective factors associated with much lower risk of disease. The World Health Organization (WHO; 2006) describes low- and middle-income countries as facing a "double burden" of disease, as undernutrition and obesity occur at the same time, often in the same households. A combination of inadequate nutrition prenatally and in childhood followed by exposure to high-calorie but nutrient-poor foods sets the stage for a lifetime of poor health, possibly due to epigenetic factors (Haemer, Huang, & Daniels, 2009).

As was the case in smoking, we can also see evidence of social factors that maintain our eating habits and weight. Our recent history of cheap, fatty, and sugary foods is now colliding with increased rates of poverty due to a downward spiraling economy. Nutritionists have raised the alarm that eating healthy foods is becoming more expensive than ever. Having an obese spouse increases your risk of obesity by 37%, and having obese friends

© Chuck Franklin/Alamy

© Adrian Assalve/iStockphoto

© acilo/iStockphoto

© Arsgera/iStockphoto

One of the challenges we face today is the high cost of eating a healthy diet. If you have $1.50 in your pocket, you can buy about 1,100 calories at McDonald's (pancakes and sausage breakfast) or 250 calories of fresh apples. We can guess which choice financially struggling parents with hungry children are likely to make.

increases your risk by 57% (Christakis & Fowler, 2007). We seem to use the people around us as a measure of "how we're doing."

As we observed in our chapter on motivation and emotion, there are no quick fixes for obesity and poor nutrition. Many of the same challenges face people who want to lose weight that we observed among people attempting to quit smoking. One advantage would-be ex-smokers enjoy, however, is the option of complete abstinence. In contrast, we cannot exactly abstain from eating, but instead must choose to eat differently. Research identifying the contagious aspects of smoking and obesity might actually provide a hopeful note. If people in your social circle begin to eat more healthy diets and maintain healthier weights, perhaps it will become easier for you to do so as well. Although losing weight can seem very difficult, small changes in behavior can be very helpful. People using smaller plates (Wansink, 2006) or larger forks (Mishra, Mishra, & Masters, 2011) unconsciously ate less.

In addition to addressing concerns about obesity, current research in nutrition focuses on the specific nutrients we need for healthy development and psychological well-being. As we mentioned in our chapter on psychological disorders, prevalence of bipolar disorder is much lower in countries consuming large amounts of seafood than in countries where seafood consumption is rare (Noaghiul & Hibbeln, 2003). Although much remains to be explored in this area (increasing intake of seafood or the omega-3 fatty acids it contains has not proved effective in treating bipolar disorder), a further understanding of the consequences of changes in our modern diet should help us achieve a healthier lifestyle.

Alcohol Alcohol is widely used in the United States and in many other countries around the world (see ● Figure 16.19). According to the Centers for Disease Control and Prevention (CDC; 2010a), more than half of the American adult public reported drinking alcohol in the last 30 days. Five percent reported drinking heavily (more than one drink per day for women or two for men), and 15% reported an episode of binge drinking (four drinks on a single occasion for women and five for men).

The devil has put a penalty on all things we enjoy in life. Either we suffer in health or we suffer in soul or we get fat.

—Albert Einstein

The largest threats to health from alcohol use are to the liver, which is responsible for clearing the body of toxins, but alcohol use also contributes to lower life spans because of stroke, high blood pressure, and some cancers (breast, digestive, and liver). Even more dramatic is the loss of potential years of life due to alcohol-related accidents. Alcohol contributes to the loss of 577,729 potential years of life from automobile crashes, 336,763 potential years of life from homicides, and 241,959 potential years of life from suicide (Centers for Disease Control and Prevention [CDC], 2004).

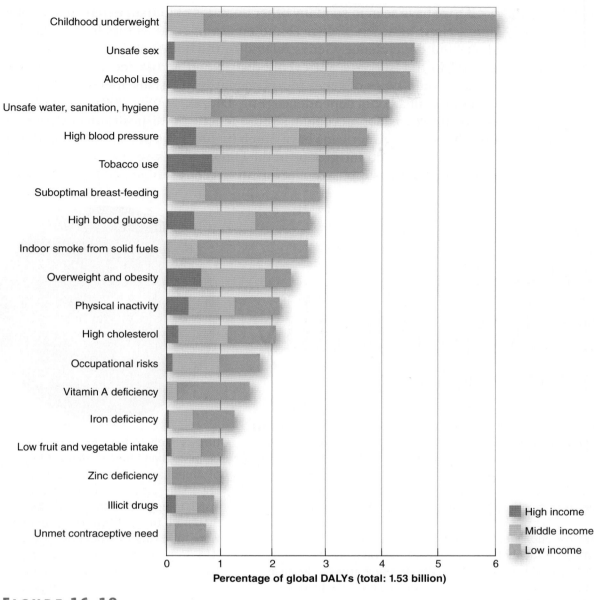

Childhood underweight
Unsafe sex
Alcohol use
Unsafe water, sanitation, hygiene
High blood pressure
Tobacco use
Suboptimal breast-feeding
High blood glucose
Indoor smoke from solid fuels
Overweight and obesity
Physical inactivity
High cholesterol
Occupational risks
Vitamin A deficiency
Iron deficiency
Low fruit and vegetable intake
Zinc deficiency
Illicit drugs
Unmet contraceptive need

High income
Middle income
Low income

Percentage of global DALYs (total: 1.53 billion)

FIGURE 16.19

Alcohol Is the Third-Leading Cause of Worldwide Loss of Disability-Adjusted Life Years (DALYs). The World Health Organization (WHO) reports that worldwide, alcohol is third behind only childhood starvation and unsafe sex (leading to HIV/AIDS) as a cause of loss of years of "healthy life" due to disability and poor health. *Source:* Adapted from World Health Organization (WHO; 2011). Used by permission of WHO.

Alcohol also poses a risk of abuse and dependence for many people. Psychologists define alcohol abuse as repeated use in spite of adverse consequences and alcohol dependence as alcohol abuse accompanied by tolerance, withdrawal, and a compulsive urge to drink more (American Psychiatric Association [APA], 2000). As we observed in our chapter on biological psychology, *tolerance* is defined as the need to administer greater quantities of a drug to maintain the same subjective effect, and *withdrawal* refers to symptoms that occur when a habitually used drug is no longer used.

As we have seen in so many other domains of human behavior, complex interactions between biological and environmental factors lead to alcohol abuse and dependence. Genes related to the body's ability to break down alcohol in the liver are not evenly distributed across the world's populations. Certain types of genes found primarily in Asians are correlated with lower rates of alcohol dependence (Eng, Luczak, & Wall, 2007). To illustrate the need to consider more than simply genetic predisposition, however, we find that Native Americans have much higher rates of alcohol dependence than many other ethnic groups in the United States, in spite of having high prevalence of the supposedly "protective" genes (Ehlers, 2007).

Thinking
Scientifically

Alcohol Consumption and Health

 In the previous section, we outlined some of the challenges of alcohol consumption—dependence, drunk driving, homicide, and suicide. What do we know about any benefits of alcohol consumption?

According to a review published by the National Institute on Alcohol Abuse and Alcoholism (NIAAA), moderate drinkers (defined as an average of one drink per day for women and two for men) consistently outlive abstainers, people who drink less than one drink per week, and heavy drinkers (those who drink more than an average of one to two drinks per day and/or binge drink; Gunzerath, Faden, Zakhari, & Warren, 2004) (see ● Figure 16.20). The major factor responsible for these statistics is reduced risk for heart disease. Alcohol appears to produce this benefit by increasing "good" cholesterol levels, decreasing "bad" cholesterol, reducing blood clotting, reducing blood pressure, and reducing plaque in arteries. Moderate drinkers are

less likely to be hospitalized, are less likely to be disabled, and are less likely to miss work because of stress.

Although many studies using many tens of thousands of participants produce similar results, some caution is in order. These data do not result from true experiments, where we would randomly assign participants to drinking groups, because of the obvious ethical challenges of such a practice. Instead, people self-select into drinking groups, which raises the possibility that factors in addition to alcohol consumption might be involved. Nondrinkers make up about 46% of the adult population of the United States (U.S. Department of Justice, 2002). Another 26% report drinking once per week or less, which does not qualify as "moderate." The remaining 28% combines moderate and heavy drinkers. Most researchers agree that there is a big health difference between drinking one drink per day for 7 days and having seven drinks on Saturday night. Moderate drinking spread out over

time is likely to have more health benefits than binge drinking. Only 6% of American adults reported drinking on more than 21 days out of the last 30, suggesting that of the 28% of moderate to heavy drinkers, very few were following the "healthy" pattern (U.S. Department of Justice, 2002). So statistics showing moderate drinkers living longer are comparing very small groups of people (possibly as few as 6% of the adult population) to a relatively large group of abstainers and light drinkers (about 73% of the adult population) who may show much more variation across multiple health domains.

To make matters more confusing, the cardiovascular benefits of alcohol could be offset by increasing risk for other diseases. For example, alcohol's ability to raise levels of the female hormone estrogen has been suggested as a mechanism for the elevated risk of breast cancer observed in women who drink. Women drinking in the moderate amounts sug-

Many of the same factors that encourage teens to begin smoking also operate to encourage drinking. Most people who go on to abuse alcohol are drinking heavily by late adolescence, and most cases of alcohol dependence are well established by the age of 30 years (Enoch, 2006). This timeline provides insight into when prevention programs are likely to be most effective. Peer pressure, the need to fit in or look cool, overestimates of "everybody's doing it," modeling the behavior of parents and other family members, and the teen's characteristic sense of being immune to harm from risky behaviors can contribute to decisions to begin drinking. Because alcohol reduces anxiety, socially anxious teens are especially at risk for problem drinking. If teens feel more socially competent while drinking, they are likely to continue this practice due to operant conditioning, as described in our chapter on learning. Reduced feelings of anxiety are rewarding, so a person is likely to repeat the behavior (alcohol consumption in this case) that is associated with this reward.

People who are exposed to alcohol at younger ages have the highest risk for alcohol abuse.

gested as beneficial for preventing heart disease (average of one drink per day) experience a 10% increase in breast cancer compared to women who did not drink at all (Gunzerath et al., 2004). With a family history of breast cancer or binge and heavy drinking, the risk of breast cancer goes up even further. Once again, we are not assigning women to drinking groups, and other factors that influence risk of breast cancer might be associated with women's drinking choices.

How can we offer reasonable advice on the basis of these conflicting types of data? Large population data are not particularly helpful when making individual choices. Perhaps at some point in the future, each newborn baby will receive a genetic printout saying "given your family history, here are some health habits you should pursue and here are some behaviors you should not do." In the meantime, we should probably look at our extended families, identify any frequent health weaknesses, and plan our health habits accordingly. ⚙

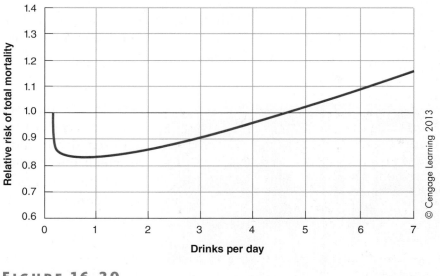

FIGURE 16.20

Drinks per Day and Risk of Mortality. Many studies show a characteristic "J-curve" relationship between the number of drinks consumed and risk of mortality, with people drinking "moderate" amounts of alcohol having a slightly lower risk of mortality than nondrinkers or light drinkers. However, it's important to note that such studies are not true experiments, in which people are randomly assigned to drinking or nondrinking conditions. Many complex variables possibly contribute and interact to produce this result. For example, most studies include previous drinkers in the nondrinker category. These individuals might have quit for medical reasons, which might lead to inflated mortality risk in this group. *Source: Adapted from Di Castelnuovo et al. (2006).*

Among the environmental influences on problem drinking is the age at which a person takes his or her first drink. Individuals exposed to alcohol at earlier ages show a much higher rate of alcohol dependence later in life. Once again, we find that age of first drink interacts with a person's genetic predisposition to alcohol dependence (Agrawal et al., 2009). In yet another example of the epigenetic mechanisms we discussed in our chapter on genetics and evolution, early exposure to alcohol might impact the expression of genes related to problem drinking. Another similar interaction is found between child maltreatment and neglect and genetic vulnerability to alcohol dependence. Not all children who are maltreated go on to become dependent on alcohol, although many do (Shin, Edwards, Heeren, & Amodeo, 2009; Shin, Edwards, & Heeren, 2009). The maltreated children who do not develop drinking problems are likely to be protected by combinations of genetic predisposition and the presence of peer and parental support (Enoch, 2006).

Treatment for very heavy drinkers often requires medical supervision, as withdrawal from alcohol can produce life-threatening seizures. Recall from our biological psychology chapter that alcohol boosts the inhibition produced by GABA, leading to alcohol's classification as a central nervous system depressant. Because withdrawal symptoms are usually the opposite of drug effects, withdrawing from a depressant produces excitation, and too much excitation leads to seizures.

One of the remaining controversies in the treatment of alcohol-dependence is whether or not a person can safely return to moderate drinking. Most psychologists do not believe it is possible for recovered problem drinkers to resume alcohol consumption without relapse. In one 60-year longitudinal study of men with problem drinking, very few returned to moderate drinking without experiencing a relapse (Vaillant, 2003).

Exercise Exercise was not a question for our hunter-gatherer ancestors, for whom physical work meant the difference between death and survival. In today's sedentary lifestyle, in which many workers spend hours commuting in cars to sit for more hours in front of computers, exercise becomes something we have to consciously remember to do. Children in previous generations would dash from school to play out-of-doors, but social changes including lack of supervision at home and safety concerns have led to much less spontaneous, outdoor activity. Parents might prefer that their children stay indoors playing video games rather than ride their bicycles in the neighborhood. For many middle-aged and older adults, loneliness might lead to less physical activity (Hawkley & Cacioppo, 2010; Hawkley, Thisted, & Cacioppo, 2009).

Lack of exercise and sitting are related but different. Today's children and adults in the United States spend an average of 55% of their day sitting while riding in cars, watching television, sitting at work or school, and playing video games or doing other computer work (Matthews et al., 2008). Sitting predicts risk of death independently from a person's level of exercise (see ● Figure 16.21). Although the highest risk of death occurs in obese

© Ariel Skelley/Blend Images/Alamy

In contrast to previous generations, who simply "played," it is not uncommon today to find children as young as 3 to 5 years of age involved with adult-organized formal sports. Further research will be necessary to determine the long-term impacts of this social trend on adult patterns of play and exercising.

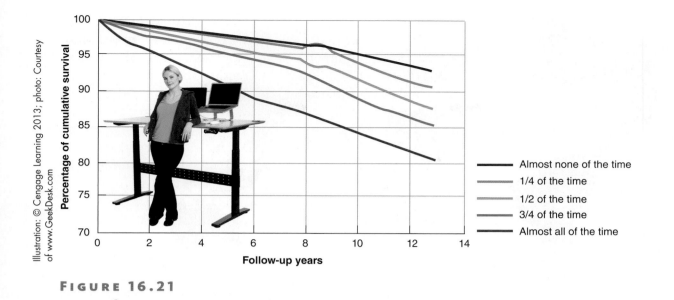

FIGURE 16.21

Time Spent Sitting and Mortality. Data showing decreased survival as a function of the amount of your day spent sitting have led to a market for "standing desks." If you find these desks comfortable, by all means use them, but recall that once again, the sitting data are correlational, and we cannot conclude that sitting *causes* death. We are not randomly assigning people to sitting groups. People who sit all day are very likely to be obese or have other health problems that contribute to their higher risk of mortality. *Source:* Adapted from Katzmarzyk, Church, Craig, and Bouchard (2009).

individuals who spend nearly all their time sitting, the amount of time spent sitting also predicts mortality within a group of very active individuals (Katzmarzyk, Church, Craig, & Bouchard, 2009).

Exercise not only benefits our bodies by keeping muscles and our cardiovascular systems in good shape but also benefits our psychological well-being. A brisk 30-minute walk has emerged as an effective way to treat major depressive disorder, as discussed in our chapter on therapies (Blumenthal et al., 1999). In addition to improving mood, exercise increases cognitive performance, especially in older adults (Kramer, Erickson, & Colcombe, 2006). One mechanism for this improvement could be the increased delivery of oxygen to the brain that results from a fit cardiovascular system. Other research suggests that exercise also has the capacity to boost neurogenesis, the production of new neurons, particularly in the hippocampus of the brain (Fabel & Kempermann, 2008). As you learned from our chapter on biological psychology, the hippocampus plays important roles in learning and memory.

We mentioned in an earlier section that stress can be detrimental to the functioning of the immune system. Exercise can be stressful. Not too surprisingly, we find complex relationships between the amount and type of exercise a person experiences and the response of the immune system. Compared to sedentary people, those who engage in regular moderate exercise enjoy a lower rate of infection (Gleeson, 2007). However, too much of a good thing, in the form of continuous, prolonged, and high-intensity exercise, such as competition in marathons and triathlons, can produce a temporary decrease in immune system function for about one day. Elite athletes, due to their constant and intense training schedules, often

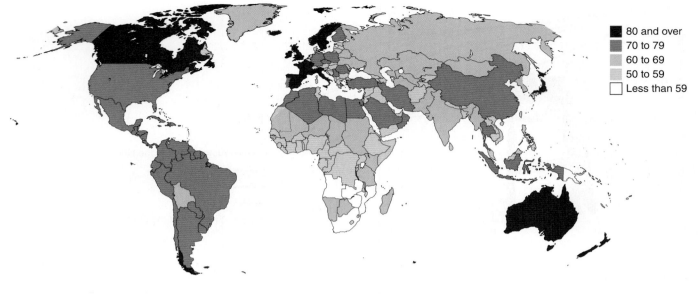

FIGURE 16.22

Culture and Health Interact to Predict Life Expectancy. Many health-related variables, including poverty, education, access to medical care, nutrition, and substance abuse, vary widely from country to country and interact to determine average life expectancy.
Source: Adapted from United Nations (2007).

The map legend reads: 80 and over; 70 to 79; 60 to 69; 50 to 59; Less than 59. © Cengage Learning 2013

experience more minor illnesses, such as sniffles and colds, but the long-term benefits of exercise far outweigh these small vulnerabilities.

Culture and Health

Many health-related variables, including poverty, education, access to medical care, nutrition, and substance abuse, vary widely from country to country and within ethnic groups living in the United States. The United States, despite its high standard of living, ranks 36th among countries of the world in terms of life expectancy, suggesting that wealth alone is not sufficient to guarantee good health (United Nations, 2007) (see ● Figure 16.22).

In the United States, death rates for all ethnic groups have declined over the last decade, but ethnic differences remain. Risk of death is lowest among Asians and Pacific Islanders, and highest among the non-Hispanic Black population (Centers for Disease Control and Prevention [CDC], 2009b). Although life expectancy for White and Black Americans continues to differ, the discrepancy dropped 35% between 1989 and 2007. Whites currently have a life expectancy 4.6 years longer than that of Blacks. Increases in life expectancy across all ethnic groups are due to reductions in the rate of death from leading causes, including heart disease, cancer, chronic respiratory diseases, and stroke.

In addition to ethnic and cultural differences in overall health and health habits, discrepancies occur in mental health. Minorities living in the United States have less access to mental health services, are less likely to receive needed services, receive a poorer quality of care, and are underrepresented in mental health research (Department of Health and Human Services, U.S. Public Health Service, 2007). Not only do these discrepancies burden minorities disproportionately with increased disability, but they contribute to continued poverty and violence affecting the society as a whole.

Among possible variables accounting for increased mental health problems among minorities are poverty, discrimination, and violence. Poverty in particular is an important risk factor for psychological disorders, with people living at the lowest levels of the socioeconomic scale experiencing 2 to 3 times greater rates of psychological disorder (Department of Health and Human Services, U.S. Public Health Service, 2007). The exact prevalence remains unknown, as many people living in poverty do not have access to care. Poverty, discrimination, and violence are obviously stressful and might contribute to higher rates of stress-related health problems and disorders. Distrust of clinicians who might seem to be disrespectful or whose approach is culturally insensitive might also deter people from obtaining the treatment they need.

Culture contributes to risk for suicide. Between 2002 and 2006, the highest rates of suicide in the United States occurred among American Indian and Alaska Natives (16.25 per 100,000). Whites had higher risk of suicide (15.02 per 100,000) than non-Hispanic Blacks, Hispanics, and Asian/Pacific Islander groups (around 6 per 100,000; Centers for Disease Control and Prevention [CDC], 2009a). These data suggest the presence of protective mechanisms within some cultures that offset the negative effects of minority status.

Poverty is a significant risk factor for many types of psychopathology.

An Integrated Understanding of Health Behaviors

If you haven't already noticed this characteristic during our discussions of stress, sleep, nutrition, smoking, alcohol use, and exercise, all these variables interact. Stress can lead to poor sleep, additional consumption of calories, more smoking, more drinking, and less exercise. People who eat poorly are unlikely to sleep well or feel like going to the gym. Smoking reduces weight (the choice of the tobacco industry to market a cigarette to women called "Virginia Slims" was no accident), but of course has negative effects on health that far outweigh that advantage. Problem drinkers, who consume large amounts of alcohol, either cut back on nutritious food or become obese (Breslow & Smothers, 2005). College students often engage in "drunkorexia," or the deliberate restriction of calories prior to planned alcohol consumption for the purpose of avoiding weight gain (Burke, Cremeens, Vail-Smith, & Woolsey, 2010). Most, if not all, of these behaviors are affected by our social context. We eat, drink, and smoke but also exercise more in the company of our fellow human beings.

These interactions in health behaviors remind us of the need to zoom out to look at the whole picture of individuals within their social contexts when we attempt to apply interventions leading to better health (see ● Figure 16.23). We have amassed a significant amount of data on why people engage in a particular problem behavior, whether that is smoking, drinking, or overeating, and we are now in a better position to identify the overlapping patterns of epigenesis, stress, child maltreatment, peer pressure, and motivation that underlie these behaviors.

FIGURE 16.23

The Adverse Childhood Experiences (ACE) Study: An Integrated Model of Health. An example of contemporary research that uses an integrated model of health is the Adverse Childhood Experiences (ACE) Study, currently being undertaken by researchers affiliated with the Centers for Disease Control and Prevention (CDC). The study plans to address identified gaps in our understanding about the relationships between adverse childhood experiences, such as abuse and neglect, and later social, emotional, and cognitive impairments, which in turn could influence the adoption of risky health behaviors.

Source: Adapted from Centers for Disease Control and Prevention (CDC; 2010b).

© Cengage Learning 2013

Summary 16.2

Four Domains of Health Behavior

Domain	Correlates
Smoking	Leading preventable cause of death in the United States
Nutrition	• Obesity increases rates of many chronic diseases, including heart disease, stroke, diabetes, arthritis, and some cancers. • Specific nutrients, not just calories, are necessary for optimum functioning.
Alcohol	Alcohol's main effect on life span is its contribution to accidents, but use is also correlated with liver disease, stroke, high blood pressure, and some cancers.
Exercise	Exercise improves overall health, mood, and cognition.

What Is Positive Psychology?

Although helping people with problems is an important part of psychology, some psychologists have pointed out that there are differences between making people less uncomfortable and helping them live happier, more fulfilling lives. The interventions we explored in our chapter on therapy are designed to alleviate psychological pain, but these treatments are not intended to make people who do not have psychological disorders happier. At the same time, we know a great deal about people with problems, whom we described in our chapter on psychological disorders as representing a small minority of the population. What about the vast majority who lead relatively untroubled, typical lives? As we observed in our chapter on cognition, language, and intelligence, we quite possibly know the least of all about people with unusual strengths, such as talent and genius. The field of **positive psychology** focuses on these relatively neglected areas of behavior and mental processes by using scientific methods to understand positive human experiences and adjustment. A new set of interventions should emerge from this understanding that will guide individuals, families, and communities in their attempts to maximize their potential (Seligman & Csikszentmihalyi, 2000).

William James foreshadowed positive psychology in his 1902 book *The Varieties of Religious Experience.* In this book, James discussed people who achieve "healthy-mindedness" as having an understanding of the "goodness of life" and a soul (a word often used by people in James's era as synonymous with "mind") with "a sky-blue tint" (James, 1905, pp. 79–80). James goes further to speculate about the origins of "healthy-mindedness." For the lucky few, healthy-mindedness occurs naturally and effortlessly. For others, it must be achieved through effort. In this context, James discusses the work of Mary Baker Eddy, founder of the Church of Christ, Scientist, who held some rather modern-sounding beliefs about the relationships between mind and health. For example, Eddy treated one woman, who had not responded to conventional medical treatments, with "unmedicated pellets," or what we now call placebos. The patient made steady progress and eventually recovered (Eddy, 1875).

In spite of James's efforts, psychology continued its fascination with the abnormal and the unhealthy into the 20th century, but did not direct the same energy toward understanding the normal and healthy. Voices of dissent arose from among the humanists, including Abraham Maslow, whom we met in our chapters on motivation and on personality. Maslow argued that psychologists could learn more about human behavior from studying outstanding individuals than by studying people with severe problems. As part of Maslow's thinking about self-actualization, the pinnacle of social motivation in his theory, he took detailed notes on people he admired in a "GHB (Good Human Being) notebook" that he kept between 1945 and 1949 (Lowry, 1973). In addition to making observations of living people he admired, Maslow combed through biographies and autobiographies of famous people looking for common features of "healthy-mindedness."

Running parallel to the humanists' rejection of a negative, sickness model of human behavior were innovations among cognitive and behavioral

In his book *The Varieties of Religious Experience*, William James foreshadowed the development of positive psychology by considering what makes some people "healthy-minded" and others have a "sick soul." James was interested in the work of people such as Mary Baker Eddy, a controversial figure of the day and founder of Christian Science. Eddy believed that thought determined a person's ability to heal.

positive psychology An approach to psychology that emphasizes normal behavior and human strengths.

Martin Seligman (right) and the Dalai Lama (left), spiritual leader of Tibetan Buddhism, discussed the important role of positive emotions at a Mind and Its Potential conference in 2009.

approaches. As we mentioned in our chapter on therapies, Albert Ellis and Aaron Beck were achieving excellent results with cognitive restructuring at about the same time the humanists began reconsidering Freud. Ellis and Beck were able to help their clients with depression see a glass of water as half-full as opposed to half-empty, improving their mood and optimism in the process.

One of the most significant voices leading to contemporary positive psychology approaches is that of Martin Seligman. We discussed his learned helplessness experiments, in which dogs experiencing inescapable shock were subsequently slow to learn other escape behaviors, in our chapter on psychological disorders. Based on these experiments, Seligman proposed that **optimism**, or thinking positively about the future, can be learned as well as helplessness (Seligman, 1990).

While embracing humanistic emphases on human growth and fulfillment, positive psychology differs from the humanistic approach in its emphasis on scientific reasoning and research. Positive psychology has focused on the study of positive emotions, positive traits, and positive institutions.

Positive Emotions

Positive emotions and the experiences that produce them, including happiness, love, gratitude, contentment, and hope, contribute to our well-being. For our social species, it is not an accident that many of the situations, such as promotions at work, marriage, and victories, that produce these positive feelings involve other people who are important to us.

What Is Happiness? We all know happiness when we experience it, and most people certainly prefer the state of happiness to the alternatives of unhappiness and depression. Yet happiness often seems fleeting or transient. The primary reason for this elusiveness is that happiness is typically relative (see ● Figure 16.24). We very quickly adapt to our current circumstances, and it is only change in those circumstances that provokes feelings of happiness or unhappiness.

optimism Thinking positively about the future.

Research with identical twins suggests that we have a happiness "set point" that is largely influenced by genetics (Lykken & Tellegen, 1996). Changes in circumstances might raise or lower happiness from the set point, but the effect would be temporary. However, having a genetic predisposition to be happy or cranky does not mean that a person's behavior has no influence. Instead, people can do a great deal to improve their happiness. Rather than looking for external things to boost happiness, such as a new car or a new nose, looking within is more effective. Happiness can be improved by thinking carefully about what things interfere with our happiness, such as allowing ourselves to stay mad at a partner following an argument, and working to avoid these situations.

One critical factor in people's happiness is the strength of their interpersonal relationships. When participants are asked "What is necessary for your happiness?" or "What is it that makes your life meaningful," nearly everybody talks about their close relationships first—family, friends, and romantic partners (Berscheid & Peplau, 1983). This finding is consistent with one of the ongoing themes of this text—that the social environment plays a central role in human behavior.

Happiness and Marriage Among interpersonal relationships, the institution of marriage is particularly likely to contribute to happiness (see ● Figure 16.25). In a study of over 42,000 Americans beginning in 1972, 40% of married adults, but only 22% of never-married adults, report that they are "very happy" (Davis, Smith, & Marsden, 2006). Eighteen percent of divorced adults report being "very happy," and remarriage increases happiness only in a minority of cases. In a large-scale study that followed 13,000 adults for

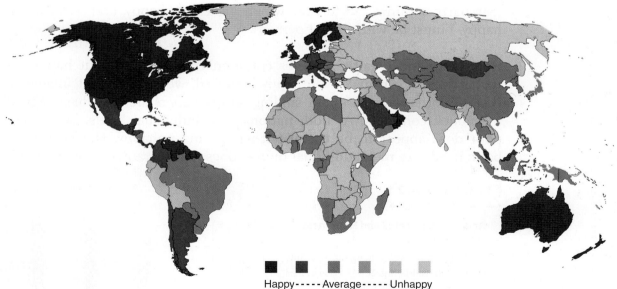

© Cengage Learning 2013

Happy----- Average ----- Unhappy

FIGURE 16.24

Global Happiness. In a study of life satisfaction, health, wealth, and education were the three most important predictors of happiness. The five most happy countries were Denmark, Switzerland, Austria, Iceland, and the Bahamas, with the United States ranked 23, China 82, Japan 90, and Russia 167. *Source:* Adapted from PhysOrg.com (2006).

5 years, people who remained married experienced higher well-being than those who separated or divorced (Waite, Luo, & Lewin, 2009). Among the benefits of marriage are reduced infidelity, longer-lasting relationships, and longer life (Waite & Gallagher, 2001). People who are married and living with their spouse enjoy a significantly lower death rate than those who are unmarried. People who have never married, particularly males, experience an especially high risk for premature death (Kaplan & Kronick, 2006).

Why would marriage make people happy? One possibility is that the relationship between marriage and happiness is a false one, because of the likelihood that happy people produce happy marriages instead of the other way around. Careful research that controls for premarital happiness does not support this hypothesis (Horwitz, White, & Howell-White, 1997). Regardless of how happy you are before marrying, on average being married makes people happier. In case you're thinking of cases you know in which married couples are miserable, time together seems to help. Among the unhappiest couples, only 12% report being unhappy 5 years later. Seventy percent of the formerly unhappy partners report being "very" or "quite" happy (Horwitz et al., 1997).

What is the source of this marital happiness? Traditionally, psychologists have suggested that marital happiness results from the perceptions one partner has of the other. More sophisticated analyses have shown that the factors associated with marital happiness are more complicated (Luo, Zhang, Watson, & Snider, 2010). While it's true that perceptions of your partner influence how satisfied you are in a relationship (I'm with a great person), it is also true that your overall satisfaction with the relationship impacts how you see your partner (I'm happy, so I must be with a great person). Then what is the source of that satisfaction? A major factor in satisfaction with a relationship is how you see yourself perceived by your partner (My partner thinks I'm terrific, which makes me happy, and because I'm happy, I must be with a great person).

Happiness and Wealth Another commonsense notion about happiness is that wealth can make you happy. After all, we see frequent images of ecstatic lottery winners and smiling sports superstars who have signed megabuck contracts. At both national and individual levels, being very poor does appear to be correlated with being unhappy. However, once basic needs are met, additional money does not guarantee happiness (see

© Cengage Learning 2013

FIGURE 16.25

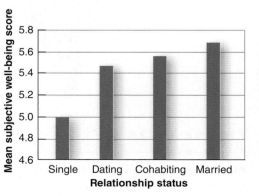

Relationship Status and Happiness.
Many studies have pointed to a strong relationship between being married and subjective well-being. *Source:* Adapted from Soons, Liefbroer, and Kalmijn (2009).

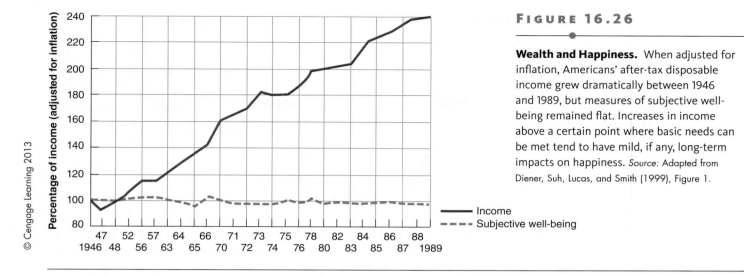

© Cengage Learning 2013

FIGURE 16.26

Wealth and Happiness. When adjusted for inflation, Americans' after-tax disposable income grew dramatically between 1946 and 1989, but measures of subjective well-being remained flat. Increases in income above a certain point where basic needs can be met tend to have mild, if any, long-term impacts on happiness. *Source:* Adapted from Diener, Suh, Lucas, and Smith (1999), Figure 1.

● Figure 16.26). Interviews with the 100 richest people in the United States indicated that they were only slightly happier than average (Diener, Horwitz, & Emmons, 1985).

We return to the idea that happiness occurs because of changing circumstances. Perhaps the 100 richest Americans had simply adapted to their wealthy lifestyles. What about people who suddenly become wealthy? The Camelot Group, which manages the United Kingdom national lottery, reported that winning the lottery did have an impact on happiness (Camelot Group, 2004). Sixty-five percent reported that they were happier following the win, because of financial security and increased freedom. Thirty-five percent said that they were about as happy after winning as before. None reported feeling less happy than before the win. Although the winners traded up in terms of lifestyle (most had bought new cars and new homes), 92% of those who were married when they won were still married to the same spouse.

The correlation between happiness and income has been assumed to reflect the effect of money on happiness. However, longitudinal research suggests that happiness influences income (Cacioppo et al., 2008). As in prior studies, happiness and income in middle-aged and older adults were correlated. However, happiness predicted bigger increases in income, whereas higher income did not predict increases in happiness. Additional analyses by these same researchers further indicated that happy people form better relationships, and these better relationships contribute to larger increases in income, perhaps because of improved job performance, better performance reviews and promotions, and better "networking" opportunities that lead in financially productive directions.

Results from the Gallup World Poll, the first representative sample of all people on the planet, showed that financial wealth and social psychological "wealth" predict different types of well-being across many different cultures (Diener, Ng, Harter, & Arora, 2010). Social psychological wealth was measured by the respect a person received; closeness with family and

Lottery winners do experience an increase in happiness, but they tend to be cautious about changing their lifestyles. Most continue working and attempt to maintain as normal a life as possible.

WHAT IS POSITIVE PSYCHOLOGY?   **833**

friends; the opportunities to learn new things, do what you do best, and choose how to spend your time; and the need to work long hours. A single "happiest nation" measure does not seem supported by the data. Central American and some African nations have greater social psychological wealth than financial wealth, while nations previously in the Soviet bloc experience much higher financial wealth than social psychological wealth. The United States ranks first in financial wealth and 19th in social psychological wealth. Financial wealth predicted global measures of life satisfaction, but social psychological wealth made much stronger predictions of the presence of positive emotions like happiness.

Can We Increase Happiness? Some psychologists have moved past research identifying the causes and correlates of happiness to make recommendations for how to increase individual happiness. Among the steps recommended for improving happiness are practicing time management, exercising regularly, sleeping well, finding interesting work to do, nurturing close relationships, and following a chosen religious faith (Myers, 1993).

Methods for increasing happiness can be tailored to three different types of happiness: the "pleasant life," the "good life," and the "meaningful life" (Seligman, 2002; Seligman & Csikszentmihalyi, 2000). The pleasant life describes the pleasures we enjoy on a moment-to-moment basis. Enjoying a great meal or a beautiful sunset enhances our daily experience. The good life occurs when we are maximizing our strengths in our work, hobbies, and other activities, making time subjectively slow down. The meaningful life describes our ability to focus away from the self to serve others or participate in something more permanent and "larger" than ourselves.

In general, people taking tests designed to assess their involvement with these three types of happiness are happiest overall if either their good life or meaningful life scores are high. If scores on one of these aspects are high, then a high score on the pleasant life can raise overall happiness, like having a cherry on top of an already delicious ice cream sundae. Unfortunately, those who score highest on the pleasant life, without comparable scores on either the good or meaningful lives or both, tend to be less happy (Seligman, 2002). Two reasons help explain why isolated pleasant life scores fail to impact overall happiness very much. First, these scores tend to be highly heritable, which means that you can't do much to improve your sense of pleasure. Some people just seem to respond more intensely than others to pleasurable experiences. Second, these feelings do not last very long and habituate quickly. Think about the last time you had a delicious dessert. The first few bites are fantastic, but the last ones are usually less so. A short time later, you might have completely forgotten how delicious the dessert was.

Even if heritability affects our ability to experience pleasure, positive psychology has some suggestions for enhancing our experiences. How often have you eaten your meals while watching television, reading, or working on your computer? If you try to multitask in this way, it is unlikely that you will derive much pleasure or satisfaction from your food, which

© BlueOrange Studio/Shutterstock

Researchers studying happiness identify three different types. The pleasant life consists of pleasures, like ice cream, that are enjoyed on a moment-to-moment basis. The good life features "flow" and a sense that time is standing still. The meaningful life describes the positive emotions obtained by helping others.

can lead to overeating. Learning to "savor" pleasurable experiences by paying more attention to them can make them more memorable and enjoyable (Bryant & Veroff, 2007).

The good life is somewhat easier to modify than the pleasant life. To enhance your happiness from the good life, all you have to do is identify your strengths and find ways to use them in your important work and hobby activities. During activities that contribute to the good life, people experience **flow**, in which a person is completely absorbed in her or his current activity, usually related to work, problem solving, or creativity (Csikszentmihalyi, 1990, 1996). The word *flow* was chosen to describe this experience on the basis of interviews in which people spontaneously used the metaphor to explain their own experiences. These experiences may qualify as altered states of consciousness and are usually perceived as highly positive. Time appears to stand still for people who are immersed in flow.

People who do not play video games are often astonished by the nearly compulsive attractiveness of the activity for those who do play. However, video games meet many of the criteria for a flow experience (Csikszentmihalyi, 1990). The games have clear goals (reaching the next level, beating a dungeon boss), they provide the opportunity to focus, they encourage a merging of action and awareness (as opposed to self-consciousness), and players generally experience a distortion of subjective time (hours go by very quickly). In addition, games provide instant and precise feedback (you succeed or not), a balance between ability and difficulty (gamers reject games that are either too easy or too challenging), and a sense of personal control (you're the one making the moves). Finally, gaming, like other flow activities, is intrinsically reinforcing. As a matter of fact, many a parent has diabolically used access to gaming as a reinforcer for many other desired behaviors, such as chores or homework. It is likely that video games, at least for some people, tap into a predisposition to find activities that meet these flow criteria to be highly reinforcing.

We are not suggesting that happiness can be found by spending all your time playing video games; instead, we recommend that you seek this type of flow in the work and hobbies you enjoy.

Positive Traits

In an effort to further understand the sources of well-being, positive psychologists have built upon the trait theories we discussed in our chapter on personality. Among the traits that contribute to well-being are hope, resilience, gratitude, and spirituality.

© Masterfile/RF

Hopeful people are capable problem solvers who believe that their goals can be met in the future.

flow A state characterized by complete absorption in a current activity, such as work, problem solving, or creativity.

Hope refers to an expectation that your goals will be met in the future. You are probably hopeful that you will complete your college education and find a good job. The trait of hope is tightly linked to feelings of optimism, or a belief in a positive future. Hope in turn is determined by motivation and planning (Snyder, 1994). Your expectations for a college degree are based on beliefs that you can achieve a degree through hard work and that following your plans will give you the results you desire. Being a hopeful person provides a number of benefits to well-being. Hopeful people withstand more pain and stress, because they believe the future will be better (Snyder et al., 2005). Hopeful people are more capable problem solvers, because they are likely to consider alternate pathways for meeting their goals instead of giving up at the first obstacle. Finally, hopeful people usually enjoy strong social networks, because other people find hope attractive (Snyder, Rand, & Sigmon, 2002). You can test your levels of hope in the following section.

We discussed resilience in an earlier section of this chapter. Resilience not only serves as a buffer for stress but can actually lead to growth following a traumatic experience (Davis & Nolen-Hoeksema, 2009). None of us, of course, likes being traumatized, but when we look back on difficult episodes of our lives, we often feel like a traumatic experience actually led to growth and improved strength. Among the positive changes associated

Experiencing Psychology

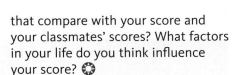

The Trait Hope Scale

Use the following scale to respond to the items listed on the next page. Please select the number that best describes *you* in the space provided.

Scores on this test can range from 8 to 64. To obtain your overall hope score, add your responses to items 1, 2, 4, 6, 8, 9, 10, and 12. (The other items are distractors.) The higher your score, the greater hope you have for the future. The average score among college students in 1991 was 25 (Snyder et al., 1991). How does that compare with your score and your classmates' scores? What factors in your life do you think influence your score? ⚙

with post-traumatic growth are perceptions of the self as a survivor rather than a victim, increased self-confidence and self-efficacy, and greater appreciation for the fragile nature of life. Many people respond to prior trauma with increased compassion for others, closer bonds with family and friends, and enhanced willingness to share emotions. Trauma can also lead people to reduce the value they place on material aspects of life, such as money and possessions, while increasing their sense of what is truly meaningful about life.

As we mentioned in a previous section, the experience of a meaningful life enhances well-being and happiness. Although finding meaning simply refers to recognizing things that are bigger than one's personal existence, some people achieve meaningfulness through religious practice (Myers, 1993). Religious beliefs and practice have also been associated with a long list of health benefits, as most major world religions promote healthier lifestyles (Emmons, Barrett, & Schnitker, 2008). Many people find religious prohibitions to be a helpful tool for resisting the temptation to engage in risky, unhealthy behaviors. Although participation in religious or spiritual activities is a behavior, it is strongly predicted by a person's need for deeper meaning, or trait spirituality (Pargament & Krumrei, 2009).

The idea of individual traits related to well-being has been extended to include shared social values and experiences, resulting in values or virtues. A value can be defined as "an enduring belief that a specific mode of conduct or end state of existence is personally or socially preferable to an opposite or converse mode of conduct or end state of existence" (Rokeach, 1968–1969, p. 5). The voluntary nature of values is stressed by many psychologists, including Gordon Allport, who defines a value as "a belief upon which a man acts by preference" (1961, p. 454). One effort to identify values

© Peter Masa/Staff/Tampa Tribune

Nobody wants to experience trauma, but some survivors report experiencing post-traumatic growth. These four family members attended a Trauma Awareness Day at the hospital that treated them following an explosion of their boat. Mike Atherton, far right, lost both legs and his left arm, but has returned to performing with the Tampa Bay Water Ski Show Team and reports feeling optimistic about his future.

1 Definitely false	2 Mostly false	3 Somewhat false	4 Slightly false	5 Slightly true	6 Somewhat true	7 Mostly true	8 Definitely true

_____ 1. I can think of many ways to get out of a jam.

_____ 2. I energetically pursue my goals.

_____ 3. I feel tired most of the time.

_____ 4. There are lots of ways around any problem.

_____ 5. I am easily downed in an argument.

_____ 6. I can think of many ways to get the things in life that are important to me.

_____ 7. I worry about my health.

_____ 8. Even when others get discouraged, I know I can find a way to solve the problem.

_____ 9. My past experiences have prepared me well for my future.

_____ 10. I've been pretty successful in life.

_____ 11. I usually find myself worrying about something.

_____ 12. I meet the goals I set for myself.

SERVICE Above Self

combined those listed by major world religions and such organizations as the Boy Scouts, Rotary, and Alcoholics Anonymous with data from major personality tests (Franken, 2002). The resulting values are social, cheerful, peaceful, tolerant, kind, generous, trusting, assertive, self-control, self-confidence, communication, leading, and autonomous. Additional lists have added some interesting items, such as "awe" and "forgiving" (Peterson & Seligman, 2004).

One interesting difference between the positive psychologist's discussion of values and the personality psychologist's discussion of traits is the obviously judgmental approach to values. In discussing personality traits, we don't want to think of traits as necessarily good or bad. A variety of personalities, such as the introverted computer programmer and the extroverted salesperson, helps meet the needs of societies. In contrast, the values discussed by positive psychologists are definitely good, and to be without them is definitely not so good. This deviation from being non-judgmental represents a significant departure by the positive psychologists from the humanists, who argue strongly against any type of outward judgments of others.

Do values matter in everyday life? As we have seen in our chapter on social psychology, attitudes and behavior may or may not correlate. However, possessing certain values does seem to correlate with a number of positive outcomes. Participants' self-ratings on the 13 values mentioned earlier are positively correlated with measures of self-esteem (Franken, 2002). In addition, "explosiveness," or a propensity to violence, was negatively correlated with a person's values ratings. As ratings on the values increased, a person's potential for violent behavior decreased. People with high values scores were the least likely to experience alcohol or tobacco addictions or to experience anxiety and depression.

Positive Institutions

Positive psychologists study the roles of institutions such as workplaces, schools, and families in promoting well-being in the community. What characteristics should we strive for in our institutions to raise the likelihood that members of the community will lead satisfying lives? Positive institutions share several features (Peterson, 2006). They share a purpose in the form of institutional goals. Their rules and consequences are fair. They feature a reciprocal caring by the institution for its members and by the members for the institution. A positive institution provides safety for its members and treats them with respect.

One of your goals in completing a college education is probably related to the type of work you'll be able to do as a result. Your future working conditions will have significant influence on your overall well-being. Positive psychologists have identified three different ways people feel about their work (Wrzesniewski, McCauley, Rozin, & Schwartz, 1997). Some people just have "jobs." A job is viewed as a way of supporting your family, and workers with "jobs" emphasize this role without asking more of their work life. A "career" obviously pays the bills, too, but also fulfills workers' needs for status and achievement. Finally, a "calling" satisfies both personal and cooperative goals. The worker pays the bills while gaining both personal

Software giant SAS once again topped the *Fortune* magazine list of best employers. The employer features on-site health care, high-quality child care at a reasonable cost, summer camp for kids, car cleaning, a beauty salon, and a 66,000-square-foot gym. On top of the perks, employees say they love the company because they feel "regarded."

achievement and a sense of contributing to the community. When workers view their employment as a calling, they are less concerned with work conditions, salary, benefits, and status. Positive workplaces facilitate the workers' abilities to meet their personal work-related goals.

Schools from kindergarten through college are particularly important to the health and future of a community. In a manner similar to psychology's emphasis on disorders, most of the research in education has focused on what goes wrong in schools rather than on what schools are doing well. Positive schools promote growth and produce a sense of satisfaction in students. Although this area is sparsely studied, student satisfaction with schools predicts a number of positive outcomes, including higher grades and fewer problem behaviors, even as early as kindergarten (Ladd, Buhs, & Seid, 2000).

Significant challenges face today's families, and identifying what works could provide valuable guidance for many. Family-centered positive psychology (FCPP) focuses on the characteristics of positive families (Sheridan & Burt, 2009). Consistent with the general approach of positive psychology, FCPP identifies the strengths of families rather than emphasizing their failures and weaknesses.

Positive Psychology and the Future

Positive psychology is not without its critics. Among the weaknesses seen in positive psychology are its unintended negative effects on people who face medical and psychological challenges (Held, 2004). Although research does indicate that optimism and health are linked, this finding might give sick people the unfortunate impression that all they have to do to cure their illness is to maintain a positive attitude. A second criticism is related to the integration theme we have featured in this textbook. Positive strengths are valuable, but they are best studied within the entire context of individuals interacting in environments. Positive and negative emotions can certainly coexist, and one cannot fully understand one type of experience without considering the other (Cacioppo, Berntson, Norris, & Gollan, 2011).

It is unlikely that psychology will ever abandon its goal of helping troubled people feel better, but positive psychology's emphasis on "what goes right" is also illuminating. We do not know at this time whether the label of "positive psychology" will drop out of favor like Wundt's structuralism or enjoy the fate of William James's functionalism by becoming so integrated into mainstream psychology that a label is no longer necessary. By applying the same evidence-based criteria we described for evaluating interventions for "negative" behaviors to interventions based on positive psychology, we will figure out the role positive psychology should play in our continued search for understanding the human mind.

Summary 16.3

Types of Happiness

Source of happiness	How to get it	Examples
The pleasant life © BlueOrange Studio/Shutterstock	Savor your experience without trying to multitask.	Turn off the TV when you're trying to enjoy a meal.
The good life © Gaye Gerard/Getty Images	Find ways to incorporate your key strengths into your activities.	Choose an occupation that you truly enjoy, not just one that pays the bills.
The meaningful life SERVICE Above Self "Service Above Self" and the "Service Above Self" Logo are trademarks of Rotary International and used herein with permission.	Focus on something bigger than yourself.	Volunteer for a cause that's important to you.

Interpersonal Relationships
From the Health Psychology Perspective

Relationships don't always turn out in the ways we expect. People do hurt each other. Being hurt can lead to the perception of a very stressful "injustice gap," or a difference between our current situation and how we would like to see a hurt resolved (Exline, Worthington, Hill, & McCullough, 2003). We might choose to respond to a perceived injustice gap with either negative strategies of unforgiveness or positive strategies of forgiveness.

Among the unforgiveness strategies people use are seeking retaliation or revenge, pursuing justice, seeking restitution, or demanding an apology (Worthington & Scherer, 2004). Others attempt to move on with their lives, or they use denial and avoidance to cope. Forgiveness can take two forms—decisional forgiveness and emotional forgiveness (Worthington & Scherer, 2004). Decisional forgiveness leads to a person's treating the transgressor the same way he or she did prior to the betrayal, but can leave anger and other negative emotions still in place. Emotional forgiveness involves the use of empathy, sympathy, compassion, and love to neutralize feelings of unforgiveness.

We mentioned earlier in this chapter that it was not necessarily the workaholic Type As who were susceptible to heart disease, but, rather, hostile people who were more vulnerable. Studies of forgiveness provide some insight into why hostility impacts health in negative ways. Healthy young people prompted to think in unforgiving ways about people who had hurt them personally showed elevated heart rate, skin conductance, muscle tension, and blood pressure compared to participants who were prompted to think about their transgressors with empathy and forgiveness (Witvliet, Ludwig, & Laan, 2001). If just a short period of thinking in unforgiving ways can make these physical changes, it is likely that spending years nursing a grudge is likely to have significant negative impacts on health.

Forgiveness is just one of a number of emotion-focused and relationship-focused coping strategies that we might use to handle relationship stress, and it is not equally effective for every individual. It is likely that the use of forgiveness interacts with personality, relationship quality, social support, and religion to buffer health in response to a betrayal.

© AP Photo/Chuck Robinson

Bud Welch initially turned to alcohol to deal with the grief of losing his 23-year-old daughter, Julie Marie, in the 1995 bombing of the Murrah Federal Building in Oklahoma City. Welch later met with bomber Timothy McVeigh's father and sister, and he spoke publicly against the death penalty. Six months after the bombing, 85% of the victims' families and survivors supported the death penalty for Timothy McVeigh, but that number dropped to nearly half 6 years later. McVeigh was executed in 2001.

Chapter **16**
Reflections

© Argosy Publishing, Inc.

We began this chapter by examining how a person's cognitive appraisal of danger initiated a cascade of physical and psychological outcomes that we call stress. Using a system that has served our species well over the millennia, the identification of a stressor mobilizes the body and mind for fight or flight.

Today, we face stressors that are often quite different from those that were familiar to our ancestors, and we run the risk of initiating this elegant system too often and for too long. As a result, our stress can lead to unwanted outcomes that damage our health and psychological well-being. Our genetic heritage and our developmental history combine to determine our vulnerabilities. Our tendencies to eat well, sleep well, avoid harmful substances, and view the world realistically all interact with our ability to cope with stressful challenges.

But this situation is not helpless or hopeless. The human mind is a master learning machine, and it is capable of assessing an experience and making changes that produce better outcomes in the future. The stressors that terrified us in middle school wouldn't cause us a minute of worry as adults. Our remarkable cognitive capacities can be used to shift our appraisals from "I'm going to die from this" to "This is terrible, but I can do this" while constructing solutions to our problems, perhaps with a little assistance from a good therapist. Our friends and family members provide a safety net of social support, and we return the favor whenever we can. Our strengths of optimism and resilience help us look past our current problems to envision a better future.

These different aspects of mind that we have explored in this chapter and throughout this textbook work together as an integrated machine not just to keep us alive but to provide opportunities for living fully and meaningfully. ‹

KEY TERMS The Language of Psychological Science

Be sure you can define these terms and use them correctly.

alarm reaction, p. 789
biopsychosocial model, p. 813
cortisol, p. 796
emotion-focused coping, p. 810
exhaustion, p. 790
flow, p. 835
General Adaptation Syndrome (GAS), p. 789
health psychology, p. 813

hypothalamic-pituitary-adrenal (HPA) axis, p. 796
immune system, p. 801
lymphocyte, p. 802
optimism, p. 830
positive psychology, p. 829
problem-focused coping, p. 809
relationship-focused coping, p. 810
resilience, p. 811

resistance, p. 790
stress, p. 788
stressor, p. 788
sympathetic adrenal-medullary (SAM) system, p. 796
tend and befriend, p. 800
Type A personality, p. 803
Type B personality, p. 803

MEDIA RESOURCES

Log in to CengageBrain to access the resources your instructor requires. For this book, you can access:

Psychology **CourseMate** brings course concepts to life with interactive learning, study, and exam preparation tools that support the printed textbook. A textbook-specific website, Psychology CourseMate includes an integrated interactive eBook and other interactive learning tools including quizzes, flashcards, videos, and more.

WebTUTOR More than just an interactive study guide, **WebTutor** is an anytime, anywhere customized learning solution with an eBook, keeping you connected to your textbook, instructor, and classmates.

aplia If your professor has assigned **Aplia** homework:
1. Sign in to your account.
2. Complete the corresponding homework exercises as required by your professor.
3. When finished, click "Grade It Now" to see which areas you have mastered, which areas need more work, and detailed explanations of every answer.

References

ABC News: Primetime. (2004). The American sex survey. Retrieved December 12, 2009, from http://abcnews.go.com/images/Politics/959a1AmericanSexSurvey.pdf

Aberson, C. L., Healy, M., & Robero, V. (2000). Ingroup bias and self-esteem: A meta-analysis. *Personality and Social Psychology Review, 4,* 157–173.

Abraham, A., von Cramon, D. Y., & Schubotz, R. I. (2008). Meeting George Bush versus meeting Cinderella: The neural response when telling apart what is real from what is fictional in the context of our reality. *Journal of Cognitive Neuroscience, 20*(6), 965–976.

Abramson, L. Y., Seligman, M. E. P., & Teasdale, J. D. (1978). Learned helplessness in humans: Critique and reformulation. *Journal of Abnormal Psychology, 87,* 49–74.

Achard, S., Salvador, R., Whitcher, B., Suckling, J., & Bullmore, E. (2006). A resilient, low-frequency, small-world human brain functional network with highly connected association cortical hubs. *Journal of Neuroscience, 26*(1), 63–72. doi:10.1523/JNEUROSCI.3874-05.2006

Ackerman, D. (1990). *A natural history of the senses.* New York, NY: Vintage Books.

Adamic, L. A., & Glance, N. (2005, August). *The political blogosphere and the 2004 U.S. election: Divided they blog.* Paper presented at the Eleventh ACM SIGKDD International Conference on Knowledge Discovery and Data Mining, Chicago, Illinois. Retrieved from http://dl.acm.org/citation.cfm?id=1134271&picked=prox

Adams, D. B. (1982). A statistical analysis of the social behavior of the male stumptail macaque (*Macaca arctoides*). *American Journal of Primatology, 2,* 249–273.

Adams, M. J. (2011). Evolutionary genetics of personality in nonhuman primates. In M. Inoue-Murayama, S. Kawamura, & A. Weiss (Eds.), *From genes to animal behavior* (pp. 137–164). Tokyo: Springer Japan.

Adler, A. (1956). The individual psychology of Alfred Adler. In H. L. Ansbacher & R. R. Ansbacher (Eds.). New York, NY: Harper Torchbooks.

Adolphs, R. (2007). Looking at other people: Mechanisms for social perception revealed in subjects with focal amygdala damage. *Novartis Foundation Symposium, 278,* 146–159.

Adolphs, R., Gosselin, F., Buchanan, T. W., Tranel, D., Schyns, P., & Damasio, A. R. (2005). A mechanism for impaired fear recognition after amygdala damage. *Nature, 433,* 68–72.

Adolphs, R., Tranel, D., & Damasio, A. R. (1998). The human amygdala in social judgment. *Nature, 393,* 470–474.

Adolphs, R., Tranel, D., Damasio, H., & Damasio, A. (1994). Impaired recognition of emotion in facial expressions following bilateral damage to the human amygdala. *Nature, 372,* 669–672.

Adolphs, R., Tranel, D., Damasio, H., & Damasio, A. (1995). Fear and the human amygdala. *Journal of Neuroscience, 15,* 5879–5891.

Aftanas, L. I., & Golocheikine, S. A. (2001). Human anterior and frontal midline theta and lower alpha reflect emotionally positive state and internalized attention: High-resolution EEG investigations of meditation. *Neuroscience Letters, 310,* 57–60.

Aftanas, L. I., Varlamov, A. A., Pavlov, S. V., Makhnev, V. P., & Reva, N. V. (2001). Affective picture processing: Event-related synchronisation within individually defined human theta band is modulated by valence dimension. *Neuroscience Letters, 303,* 115–118.

Aggarwal, P., & O'Brien, C. L. (2008). Social loafing on group projects: Structural antecedents and effect on student satisfaction. *Journal of Marketing Education, 30*(3), 255–264. doi:10.1177/0273475308322283

Agrawal, A., Sartor, C. E., Lynskey, M. T., Grant, J. D., Pergadia, M. L., Grucza, R., et al. (2009). Evidence for an interaction between age at first drink and genetic influences on DSM-IV alcohol dependence symptoms. *Alcoholism: Clinical and Experimental Research, 33*(12), 2047–2056. doi:10.1111/j.1530-0277.2009.01044.x

Ahadi, S. A., & Rothbart, M. K. (1994). Temperament, development, and the Big Five. In G. Kohnstamm, C. Halverson, & R. P. Martin (Eds.), *The developing structure of temperament and personality from infancy to adulthood* (pp. 189–207). Hillsdale, NJ: Erlbaum.

Ahadi, S. A., Rothbart, M. K., & Ye, R. (1993). Children's temperament in the U.S. and China: Similarities and differences. *European Journal of Personality, 7*(5), 359–377. doi:10.1002/per.2410070506

Aihara, M., Ida, I., Yuuki, N., Oshima, A., Kumano, H., Takahashi, K., et al. (2007). HPA axis dysfunction in unmedicated major depressive disorder and its normalization by pharmacotherapy correlates with alteration of neural activity in prefrontal cortex and limbic/paralimbic regions. *Psychiatry Research, 155*(3), 245–256.

Ainsworth, M. D. S., Blehar, M. C., Waters, E., & Wall, S. (1978). *Patterns of attachment: A psychological study of the strange situation.* Hillsdale, NJ: Erlbaum.

Ainsworth, M., & Bowlby, J. (1965). *Child care and the growth of love.* London: Penguin Books.

Ajzen, I. (1991). The theory of planned behavior. *Organizational Behavior and Human Decision Processes, 50*(2), 179–211. doi:10.1016/0749-5978(91)90020-t

Åkerstedt, T., & Fröberg, J. E. (1976). Interindividual differences in circadian pattern of catecholamine excretion, body temperature, performance, and subjective arousal. *Biological Psychology, 4,* 277–292.

Alcántara, C., & Gone, J. P. (2008). Suicide in Native American communities: A transactional-ecological formulation of the problem. In M. M. Leach & F. T. L. Leong (Eds.), *Suicide among racial and ethnic minority groups: Theory, research, and practice* (pp. 173–199). New York, NY: Routledge/Taylor & Francis Group.

Alcock, J. (2011). Back from the future: Parapsychology and the Bem affair. Retrieved April 20, 2011, from http://www.csicop.org/specialarticles/show/back_from_the_future

Aldwin, C. (1994). *Stress, coping, and development: An integrative perspective.* New York, NY: Guilford Press.

Alford, J. R., Funk, C. L., & Hibbing, J. R. (2005). Are political orientations genetically transmitted? *American Political Science Review, 99,* 153–167.

Al-Issa, I. (1977). Social and cultural aspects of hallucinations. *Psychological Bulletin, 84*(3), 570–587.

Allen, K. (2003). Are pets a healthy pleasure? The influence of pets on blood pressure. *Current Directions in Psychological Science, 12,* 236–239.

Allen, L. A., & Woolfolk, R. L. (2010). Cognitive behavioral therapy for somatoform disorders. *Psychiatric Clinics of North America, 33*(3), 579–593. doi:10.1016/j.psc.2010.04.014

Allen, L. S., Hines, M., Shryne, J. E., & Gorski, R. A. (1989). Two sexually dimorphic cell groups in the human brain. *Journal of Neuroscience, 9,* 497–506.

Allen, N. B., & Badcock, P. B. T. (2003). The social risk hypothesis of depressed mood: Evolutionary, psychosocial, and neurobiological perspectives. *Psychological Bulletin, 129,* 887–913.

Allison, T., & Cicchetti, D. (1976). Sleep in mammals: Ecological and constitutional correlates. *Science, 194,* 732–734.

Allport, G. W. (1937). *Personality: A psychological interpretation.* New York, NY: Henry Holt.

Allport, G. W. (1961). *Pattern and growth in personality.* Oxford, England: Holt, Reinhart & Winston.

Allport, G. W., & Odbert, H. S. (1936). Trait names: A psycho-lexical study. *Psychological Monographs, 47,* 171.

Allport, G. W., & Postman, L. J. (1945). The basic psychology of rumor. *Transactions of the New York Academy of Sciences, 8,* 61–81.

Alwin, D. F. (1988). From obedience to autonomy: Changes in traits desired in children, 1924–1978. *Public Opinion Quarterly, 52*(1), 33–52.

Amaral, D. G., Schumann, C. M., & Nordahl, C. W. (2008). Neuroanatomy of autism. *Trends in Neurosciences, 31*(3), 137–145.

Ambady, N., & Rosenthal, R. (1993). Half a minute: Predicting teacher evaluations from thin slices of nonverbal behavior and physical attractiveness. *Journal of Personality and Social Psychology, 64*, 431–441.

American Association for the Advancement of Science. (2009). Benchmarks online. Retrieved November 15, 2009, from http://www.project2061.org/publications/bsl/online/index.php?chapter=1

American Foundation for Suicide Prevention (AFSP). (2007). When you fear someone may take their own life. Retrieved July 8, 2007, from http://www.afsp.org/index.cfm?fuseaction=home.viewPage&page_id=F2F25092-7E90-9BD4-C4658F1D2B5D19A0

American Psychiatric Association (APA). (2000). *Diagnostic and Statistical Manual of Mental Disorders—Text Revised*. Washington, DC: Author.

American Psychiatric Association (APA). (2001). *The practice of ECT: Recommendations for treatment, training, and privileging*. Washington, DC: American Psychiatric Press.

American Psychiatric Association (APA). (2011a). Proposed revision. Retrieved August 18, 2011, from http://www.dsm5.org/ProposedRevision/

American Psychiatric Association (APA). (2011b). Timeline. Retrieved August 16, 2011, from http://www.dsm5.org/about/Pages/Timeline.aspx

American Psychological Association (APA). (1996/2007). Statement on the disclosure of test data. Retrieved July 16, 2007, from http://www.apa.org/science/disclosu.html

American Psychological Association (APA). (2005a). Guidelines for ethical conduct in the care and use of animals. Retrieved August 1, 2006, from http://www.apa.org/science/anguide.html

American Psychological Association (APA). (2005b). What is hypnosis? Retrieved April 10, 2007, from http://www.csj.org/infoserv_articles/apa_what_is_hypnosis.htm

American Psychological Association (APA). (2009). Careers in psychology. Retrieved September 24, 2009, from http://www.apa.org/topics/psychologycareer.html

Ames, E. (1997). *The development of Romanian orphanage children adopted to Canada*. Barnaby, British Columbia, Canada: Simon Fraser University.

Ammon, K., & Gandevia, S. C. (1990). Transcranial magnetic stimulation can influence the selection of motor programmes. *Journal of Neurology, Neurosurgery, and Psychiatry, 53*(8), 705–707.

Anand, B., & Brobeck, J. R. (1951). Hypothalamic control of food intake in rats and cats. *Yale Journal of Biology and Medicine, 24*, 123–140.

Anderson, C. A., & Bushman, B. J. (2001). Effects of violent video games on aggressive behavior, aggressive cognition, aggressive affect, physiological arousal, and prosocial behavior. *Psychological Science, 12*(5), 353–359.

Anderson, C. A., & Bushman, B. J. (2002). The effects of media violence on society. *Science, 295*, 2377–2378.

Anderson, C. A., & Dill, K. E. (2000). Video games and aggressive thoughts, feelings, and behavior in the laboratory and in life. *Journal of Personality and Social Psychology, 78*, 772–790.

Anderson, D. R., Huston, A. C., Schmitt, K. L., Linebarger, D. L., & Wright, J. C. (2001). Early childhood television viewing and adolescent behavior: The recontact study. *Monographs for the Society for Research in Child Development, 66*, 1–147.

Anderson, P. W. (1972). More is different. *Science, 177*(4047), 393–396.

Anderson, S. W., Bechara, A., Damasio, H., Tranel, D., & Damasio, A. R. (1999). Impairment of social and moral behavior related to early damage in human prefrontal cortex. *Nature Neuroscience, 2*(11), 1032–1037.

Anderton, B. H. (1997). Changes in the ageing brain in health and disease. *Philosophical Transactions: Biological Sciences, 352*(1363), 1781–1792.

Andrews, G., Steward, G., Allen, B., & Henderson, A. S. (1990). The genetics of six neurotic disorders: A twin study. *Journal of Affective Disorders, 19*, 23–29.

Angold, A., Erkanli, A., Egger, H. L., & Costello, E. J. (2000). Stimulant treatment for children: A community perspective. *Journal of the American Academy of Child and Adolescent Psychiatry, 39*, 975–984.

Anokhin, A. P., Golosheykin, S., & Heath, A. C. (2010). Heritability of individual differences in cortical processing of facial affect. *Behavior Genetics, 40*(2), 178–185. doi:10.1007/s10519-010-9337-1

Anokhin, A. P., Golosheykin, S., Grant, J., & Heath, A. C. (2009). Heritability of risk-taking in adolescence: A longitudinal twin study. *Twin Research and Human Genetics, 12*(4), 366–371. doi:10.1375/twin.12.4.366

Antonov, I., Antonova, I., Kandel, E. R., & Hawkins, R. D. (2003). Activity-dependent presynaptic facilitation and hebbian LTP are both required and interact during classical conditioning in Aplysia. *Neuron, 37*, 135–147.

APS Observer. (2010). Major developments in undergraduate psychology. Retrieved March 11, 2011, from http://www.psychologicalscience.org/observer/getArticle.cfm?id=2643

Armstrong, L., & Jenkins, S. (2000). *It's not about the bike: My journey back to life*. New York, NY: Penguin Putnam.

Arnsten, A. F. (2006). Stimulants: Therapeutic actions in ADHD. *Neuropsychopharmacology, 31*(11), 2376–2383.

Aron, A., Ketay, S., Hedden, T., Aron, E. N., Markus, H. R., & Gabrieli, J. D. E. (2010). Temperament trait of sensory processing sensitivity moderates cultural differences in neural response. *Social Cognitive and Affective Neuroscience, 5*(2–3), 219–226. doi:10.1093/scan/nsq028

Aron, A., Norman, C. C., Aron, E. N., McKenna, C., & Heyman, R. E. (2000). Couples' shared participation in novel and arousing activities and experienced relationship quality. *Journal of Personality and Social Psychology, 78*(2), 273–284.

Aronson, E. (2011). Jigsaw basics. Retrieved August 7, 2011, from http://www.jigsaw.org/pdf/basics.pdf

Aronson, E., & Mills, J. (1959). The effect of severity of initiation on liking for a group. *Journal of Abnormal and Social Psychology, 58*, 177–181.

Asch, S. E. (1951). Effects of group pressure upon the modification and distortion of judgments. In H. Guetzkow (Ed.), *Groups, leadership and men; research in human relations* (pp. 177–190). Oxford, England: Carnegie Press.

Asellus, P., Nordström, P., & Jokinen, J. (2010). Cholesterol and CSF 5-HIAA in attempted suicide. *Journal of Affective Disorders, 125*(1–3), 388–392. doi:10.1016/j.jad.2010.02.111

Aserinsky, E., & Kleitman, N. (1953). Regularly occurring periods of eye motility and concomitant phenomena during sleep. *Science, 118*, 273–274.

Asmundson, G. J. G., & Norton, G. R. (1993). Anxiety sensitivity and its relationship to spontaneous and cued panic attacks in college students. *Behavior Research and Therapy, 31*, 199–201.

Atkins, D. C., Baucom, D. H., & Jacobson, N. S. (2001). Understanding infidelity: Correlates in a national random sample. *Journal of Family Psychology, 15*, 735–749.

Atkins, D. C., Marín, R. A., Lo, T. T. Y., Klann, N., & Hahlweg, K. (2010). Outcomes of couples with infidelity in a community-based sample of couple therapy. *Journal of Family Psychology, 24*(2), 212–216. doi:10.1037/a0018789

Atkinson, Q. D. (2011). Phonemic diversity supports a serial founder effect model of language expansion from Africa. *Science, 332*(6027), 346–349. doi:10.1126/science.1199295

Atkinson, R. C., & Shiffrin, R. M. (1968). Human memory: A proposed system and its control processes. In K. W. Spence & J. T. Spence (Eds.), *The psychology of learning and motivation: Vol. 2. Advances in research and theory* (pp. 89–195). New York: Academic Press.

Atkinson, R. C., & Shiffrin, R. M. (1971). The control of short-term memory. *Scientific American, 225*, 82–90.

Atri, A., Sherman, S., Norman, K. A., Kirchhoff, B. A., Nicolas, M. M., Grecius, M. D., et al. (2004). Blockade of central cholinergic receptors impairs new learning and increases proactive interference in a word paired-associate memory task. *Behavioral Neuroscience, 118*, 223–236.

Austin Alchon, S. (2003). *A pest in the land: New world epidemics in a global perspective*. Albuquerque, NM: University of New Mexico Press.

Averbach, E., & Sperling, G. (1961). Short term storage of information in vision. In C. Cherry (Ed.), *Information theory* (pp. 196–211). London: Butterworth.

Avesani, R., Gambini, M. G., & Albertini, G. (2006). The vegetative state: A report of two cases with a long-term follow-up. *Brain Injury, 20*, 333–338.

Axelrod, R., & Hamilton, W. D. (1981). The evolution of cooperation. *Science, 211*(4489), 1390–1396.

Baars, B. J. (1988). *A cognitive theory of consciousness*. Cambridge, England: Cambridge University Press.

Babad, E., Bernieri, F., & Rosenthal, R. (1991). Students as judges of teachers' verbal and nonverbal behavior. *American Educational Research Journal, 28*, 211–234.

Babiak, P., & Hare, R. D. (2006). *Snakes in suits.* New York, NY: Regan.

Bach, W. G. (2006). The influence of psychoanalytic thought on Benjamin Spock's *Baby and Child Care. Journal of the History of the Behavioral Sciences, 10*(1), 91–94.

Bachman, J. G., & O'Malley, P. M. (1977). Self-esteem in young men: A longitudinal analysis of the impact of educational and occupational attainment. *Journal of Personality and Social Psychology, 35,* 365–380.

Backmaskonline.com. (2011). News. Retrieved July 3, 2011, from http://www.backmaskonline.com/index.php?page=home

Baddeley, A. D. (1966). The influence of acoustic and semantic similarity on long-term memory for word sequences. *Quarterly Journal of Experimental Psychology, 18,* 302–309.

Baddeley, A. D. (1996). Exploring the central executive. *Quarterly Journal of Experimental Psychology, 49A,* 5–28.

Baddeley, A. D., & Hitch, G. J. (1974). Working memory. In G. Bower (Ed.), *The psychology of learning and motivation* (Vol. 8, pp. 47–89). New York: Academic Press.

Baddeley, A. D., Logie, R. H., Nimmo-Smith, I., & Brereton, J. (1985). Components of fluent reading. *Journal of Memory and Language, 24,* 119–131.

Baddeley, A., Eysenck, M. W., & Anderson, M. C. (2009). *Memory.* London: Psychology Press.

Baer, D. M., Wolf, M. M., & Risley, T. R. (1968). Some current dimensions of applied behavior analysis. *Journal of Applied Behavior Analysis, 1*(1), 91–97. doi:10.1901/jaba.1968.1-91

Bahr, S. J., & Hoffmann, J. P. (2010). Parenting style, religiosity, peers, and adolescent heavy drinking. *Journal of Studies on Alcohol and Drugs, 71,* 539–543.

Bahrick, H. P. (1984). Semantic memory content in permastore: Fifty years of memory for Spanish learned in school. *Journal of Experimental Psychology: General, 113,* 1–29.

Bailey, A. A., & Hurd, P. L. (2005). Finger length ratio (2D:4D) correlates with physical aggression in men but not in women. *Biological Psychology, 68,* 215–222.

Bailey, C. H., & Chen, M. C. (1983). Morphological basis of long-term habituation and sensitization in *Aplysia. Science, 220,* 91–93.

Baillargeon, R., Li, J., Gertner, Y., & Wu, D. (2011). How do infants reason about physical events? In U. Goswami (Ed.), *The Wiley-Blackwell handbook of childhood cognitive development* (2nd ed., pp. 11–48). Walden, MA: Wiley-Blackwell.

Baird, A. A., Gruber, S. A., Fein, D. A., Maas, L. C., Steingard, R. J., Renshaw, P. F., et al. (1999). Functional magnetic resonance imaging of facial affect recognition in children and adolescents. *Journal of the American Academy of Child and Adolescent Psychiatry, 38*(2), 195–199.

Baker, T. B., McFall, R. M., & Shoham, V. (2008). Current status and future prospects of clinical psychology: Toward a scientifically principled approach to mental and behavioral health care. *Psychological Science in the Public Interest, 9*(2), 67–103. doi:10.1111/j.1539-6053.2009.01036.x

Bakker, A., Spinhoven, P., van Balkom, A. J. L. M., & van Dyck, R. (2002). Relevance of assessment of cognitions during panic attacks in the treatment of panic disorder. *Psychotherapy and Psychosomatics, 71*(3), 158–161. doi:10.1159/000056283

Balanzá-Martínez, V., Fries, G. R., Colpo, G. D., Silveira, P. P., Portella, A. K., Tabarés-Seisdedos, R., et al. (2011). Therapeutic use of omega-3 fatty acids in bipolar disorder. *Expert Review of Neurotherapeutics, 11*(7), 1029–1047. doi:10.1586/ern.11.42

Balschuna, D., Zuschrattera, W., & Wetzel, W. (2006). Allosteric enhancement of metabotropic glutamate receptor 5 function promotes spatial memory. *Neuroscience, 142,* 691–702.

Baltimore Longitudinal Study of Aging. (2000, March 12). Welcome to the BLSA. Retrieved May 1, 2001, from http://www.grc.nia.nih.gov/branches/blsa/blsanew.htm

Bandura, A. (1965). Influence of models' reinforcement contingencies on the acquisition of imitative responses. *Journal of Personality and Social Psychology, 1,* 589–595.

Bandura, A. (1973). *Aggression: A social learning analysis.* Oxford, England: Prentice-Hall.

Bandura, A. (1990). Perceived self-efficacy in the exercise of personal agency. *Journal of Applied Sport Psychology, 2,* 128–163.

Bandura, A. (1993). Perceived self-efficacy in cognitive development and functioning. *Educational Psychologist, 28,* 117–148.

Bandura, A. (1995). Exercise of personal and collective efficacy in changing societies. In A. Bandura (Ed.), *Self-efficacy in changing societies* (pp. 1–45). New York, NY: Cambridge University Press.

Bandura, A. (2001). Social cognitive theory: An agentic perspective. *Annual Review of Psychology, 52,* 1–26.

Banks, E., & Canfell, K. (2009). Invited commentary: Hormone therapy risks and benefits—The Women's Health Initiative findings and the postmenopausal estrogen timing hypothesis. *American Journal of Epidemiology, 170*(1), 24–28. doi:10.1093/aje/kwp113

Baños, R. M., Guillen, V., Quero, S., García-Palacios, A., Alcaniz, M., & Botella, C. (2011). A virtual reality system for the treatment of stress-related disorders: A preliminary analysis of efficacy compared to a standard cognitive behavioral program. *International Journal of Human-Computer Studies, 69*(9), 602–613. doi:10.1016/j.ijhcs.2011.06.002

Barbaresi, W. J., Katusic, S. K., Colligan, R. C., Weaver, A. L., & Jacobsen, S. J. (2005). The incidence of autism in Olmsted County, Minnesota, 1976–1997: Results from a population-based study. *Archives of Pediatric and Adolescent Medicine, 159,* 37–44.

Barceló, F., & Knight, R. T. (2002). Both random and perseverative errors underlie WCST deficits in prefrontal patients. *Neuropsychologia, 40,* 349–356.

Barclay, P., & Lalumière, M. L. (2006). Do people differentially remember cheaters? *Human Nature, 17*(1), 98–113. doi:10.1007/s12110-006-1022-y

Bard, P. (1934). Emotion: I. The neurohumoral basis of emotional reactions. In C. Murchison (Ed.), *Handbook of general experimental psychology* (pp. 264–311). Worcester, MA: Clark University Press.

Bargh, J. A., & Chartrand, T. L. (1999). The unbearable automaticity of being. *American Psychologist, 54*(7), 462–479.

Bargh, J. A., Chen, M., & Burrows, L. (1996). Automaticity of social behavior: Direct efforts of trait construct and stereotype activation on action. *Journal of Personality and Social Psychology, 71*(2), 230–244.

Barkley, R. A. (1995). *Taking charge of ADHD: The complete, authoritative guide for parents.* New York, NY: Guilford Press.

Barkley, R. A. (1997). *ADHD and the nature of self-control.* New York, NY: Guilford Press.

Barkley, R. A. (2002). Psychosocial treatments for attention-deficit/hyperactivity disorder in children. *Journal of Clinical Psychiatry, 63*(Suppl. 12), 36–43.

Barkley, R. A. (2004). Driving impairments in teens and adults with ADHD. *Psychiatric Clinics of North America, 27*(2), 233–260.

Barkley, R. A., & Cox, D. (2007). A review of driving risks and impairments associated with attention-deficit/hyperactivity disorder and the effects of stimulant medication on driving performance. *Journal of Safety Research, 38*(1), 113–128.

Barlow, D. (1988). *Anxiety and its disorders: The nature and treatment of anxiety and panic.* New York, NY: Guilford Press.

Barlow, H. B. (1972). Single units and sensation: A neuron doctrine for perceptual psychology? *Perception, 1,* 371–395.

Bar-On, R., Tranel, D., Denburg, N. L., & Bechara, A. (2003). Exploring the neurological substrate of emotional and social intelligence. *Brain, 126,* 1790–1800.

Baron, J., & Brown, R. V. (1991). *Teaching decision making to adolescents.* Hillsdale, NJ: Erlbaum.

Baron, R. S. (2005). So right it's wrong: Groupthink and the ubiquitous nature of polarized group decision making. In M. P. Zanna (Ed.), *Advances in experimental social psychology* (Vol. 37, pp. 219–253). San Diego, CA: Elsevier Academic Press.

Baron-Cohen, S. (1991). The development of a theory of mind in autism: Deviance and delay? *Psychiatric Clinics of North America, 14,* 33–51.

Barresi, J., & Moore, C. (1996). Intentional relations and social understanding. *Behavioral and Brain Sciences, 19,* 107–122.

Barrick, M. R., & Mount, M. K. (1991). The Big Five personality dimensions and job performance: A meta-analysis. *Personnel Psychology, 44,* 1–26.

Bartels, A., & Zeki, S. (2000). The neural basis of romantic love. *NeuroReport: For Rapid Communication of Neuroscience Research, 11*(17), 3829–3834. doi:10.1097/00001756-200011270-00046

Bartlett, F. C. (1932/1967). *Remembering: A study in experimental and social psychology.* Cambridge: Cambridge University Press.

Bartone, P. T. (2000). Hardiness as a resiliency factor for United States forces in the Gulf War. In J. M. Violanti, D. Paton, & C. Dunning (Eds.), *Posttraumatic stress intervention: Challenges, issues, and perspectives* (pp. 115–133). Springfield, IL: Charles C. Thomas.

Bartoshuk, L. M. (2000). Comparing sensory experiences across individuals: Recent psychophysical advances illuminate genetic variation in taste perception. *Chemical Senses, 25,* 447–460.

Baruch, I., Hemsley, D. R., & Gray, J. A. (1988a). Differential performance of acute and chronic schizophrenics in a latent inhibition task. *Journal of Nervous and Mental Disease, 176,* 598–606.

Baruch, I., Hemsley, D. R., & Gray, J. A. (1988b). Latent inhibition and "psychotic proneness" in normal subjects. *Personality and Individual Differences, 9,* 777–783.

Bashore, T. R., Ridderinkhof, K. R., & van der Molen, M. W. (1997). The decline of cognitive processing speed in old age. *Current Directions in Psychological Science, 6,* 163–169.

Bateson, M., Nettle, D., & Roberts, G. (2006). Cues of being watched enhance cooperation in a real-world setting. *Biology Letters, 2*(3), 412–414.

Bauer, P. J., & Lukowski, A. F. (2010). The memory is in the details: Relations between memory for the specific features of events and long-term recall during infancy. *Journal of Experimental Child Psychology, 107*(1), 1–14. doi:10.1016/j.jecp.2010.04.004

Bauer, P. J., Larkina, M., & Deocampo, J. (2011). Early memory development. In U. Goswami (Ed.), *The Wiley-Blackwell handbook of childhood cognitive development* (2nd ed., pp. 153–179). Walden, MA: Wiley-Blackwell.

Bauer, R. M. (1984). Autonomic recognition of names and faces in prosopagnosia: A neuropsychological application of the Guilty Knowledge Test. *Neuropsychologia, 22,* 457–469.

Baumeister, R. F., & Leary, M. R. (1995). The need to belong: Desire for interpersonal attachments as a fundamental human motivation. *Psychological Bulletin, 117*(3), 497–529.

Baumeister, R. F., Campbell, J. D., Krueger, J. I., & Vohs, K. D. (2003). Does high self-esteem cause better performance, interpersonal success, happiness, or healthier lifestyles? *Psychological Science in the Public Interest, 4*(1), 1–44.

Baumeister, R. F., Smart, L., & Boden, J. M. (1996). Relation of threatened egotism to violence and aggression: The dark side of high self-esteem. *Psychological Review, 103*(1), 5–33.

Baumeister, R. F., Vohs, K. D., & Tice, D. M. (2007). The strength model of self-control. *Current Directions in Psychological Science, 16*(6), 351–355.

Baumrind, D. (1975). *Early socialization and the discipline controversy.* Morristown, NJ: General Learning Press.

Bavelas, J. B., Hutchinson, S., Kenwood, C., & Matheson, D. H. (1997). Using face-to-face dialogue as a standard for other communication systems. *Canadian Journal of Communication, 22,* 5–24.

Baxter, L. R., Jr., Schwartz, J. M., Bergman, K. S., Szuba, M. P., Guze, B. H., Mazziotta, J. C., et al. (1992). Caudate glucose metabolic rate changes with both drug and behavior therapy for obsessive-compulsive disorder. *Archives of General Psychiatry, 49*(9), 681–689. doi:10.1001/archpsyc.1992.01820090009002

Beaman, A. L., Klentz, B., Diener, E., & Svanum, S. (1979). Self-awareness and transgression in children: Two field studies. *Journal of Personality and Social Psychology, 37,* 1835–1846.

Beaton, A. A. (1997). The relation of planum temporale asymmetry and morphology of the corpus callosum to handedness, gender, and dyslexia: A review of the evidence. *Brain and Language, 60,* 252–322.

Bechara, A., Damasio, H., & Damasio, A. R. (2000). Emotion, decision-making, and the orbitofrontal cortex. *Cerebral Cortex, 10,* 295–307.

Beck, A. T. (1975). *Cognitive therapy and the emotional disorders.* Madison, CT: International Universities Press.

Beck, A. T. (1985). Cognitive therapy, behavior therapy, psychoanalysis, and pharmacotherapy: A cognitive continuum. In M. Mahoney & A. Freeman (Eds.), *Cognition and psychotherapy* (pp. 197–220). New York, NY: Plenum Press.

Beck, A. T., Emery, G., & Greenberg, R. L. (2005). *Anxiety disorders and phobias: A cognitive perspective.* New York, NY: Basic Books.

Beck, A. T., Rush, A., Shaw, B., & Emery, G. (1979). *Cognitive therapy of depression.* New York, NY: Guilford Press.

Becker, A. E., Burwell, R. A., Herzog, D. B., Hamburg, P., & Gilman, S. E. (2002). Eating behaviours and attitudes following prolonged exposure to television among ethnic Fijian adolescent girls. *British Journal of Psychiatry, 180,* 509–514.

Beckerman, S., Erickson, P. I., Yost, J., Regalado, J., Jaramillo, L., Sparks, C., et al. (2009). Life histories, blood revenge, and reproductive success among the Waorani of Ecuador. *Proceedings of the National Academy of Sciences, 106*(20), 8134–8139. doi:10.1073/pnas.0901431106

Beevers, C. G., Gibb, B. E., McGeary, J. E., & Miller, I. W. (2007). Serotonin transporter genetic variation and biased attention for emotional word stimuli among psychiatric inpatients. *Journal of Abnormal Psychology, 116*(1), 208–212. doi:10.1037/0021-843x.116.1.208

Bekerian, D. A., & Bowers, J. M. (1983). Eyewitness testimony: Were we misled? *Journal of Experimental Psychology: Learning, Memory, and Cognition, 9,* 139–145.

Bellugi, U., Wang, P. P., & Jernigan, T. L. (1994). Williams syndrome: An unusual neuropsychological profile. In S. H. Broman & J. Grafman (Eds.), *Atypical cognitive deficits in developmental disorders: Implications for brain function* (pp. 23–56). Hillsdale, NJ: Erlbaum.

Belsky, J. (1999). Modern evolutionary theory and patterns of attachment. In J. Cassidy & P. R. Shaver (Eds.), *Handbook of attachment: Theory, research and clinical applications* (pp. 141–161). New York, NY: Guilford Press.

Bem, D. J. (1972). Self-perception theory. In L. Berkowitz (Ed.), *Advances in experimental social psychology* (Vol. 6, pp. 1–62). New York, NY: Academic Press.

Bem, D. J. (2001). Exotic becomes erotic: Integrating biological and experiential antecedents of sexual orientation. In A. R. D'Augelli & C. J. Patterson (Eds.), *Lesbian, gay, and bisexual identities and youth: Psychological perspectives* (pp. 52–68). New York, NY: Oxford University Press.

Bem, D. J. (2011). Feeling the future: Experimental evidence for anomalous retroactive influences on cognition and affect. *Journal of Personality and Social Psychology, 100*(3), 407–425. doi:10.1037/a0021524

Bennett, W. (1983). The nicotine fix. *Rhode Island Medical Journal, 66,* 455–458.

Berglas, S., & Jones, E. E. (1978). Drug choice as a self-handicapping strategy in response to noncontingent success. *Journal of Personality and Social Psychology, 36*(4), 405–417.

Berkun, M. M., Bialek, H. M., Kern, R. P., & Yagi, K. (1962). Experimental studies of psychological stress in man. *Psychological Monographs, 76*(15), Whole No. 534.

Berlim, M. T., Mattevi, B. S., Belmonte-de-Abreu, P., & Crow, T. J. (2003). The etiology of schizophrenia and the origin of language: Overview of a theory. *Comprehensive Psychiatry, 44*(1), 7–14.

Berman, K. F., Torrey, E. F., Daniel, D. G., & Weinberger, D. R. (1992). Regional cerebral blood flow in monozygotic twins discordant and concordant for schizophrenia. *Archives of General Psychiatry, 49,* 927–934.

Berman, M. G. (2009). In search of decay in verbal short term memory. *Journal of Experimental Psychology: Learning, Memory, and Cognition, 35*(2), 317–333.

Bernhardt, P. C., Dabbs, J. M., Jr., Fielden, J. A., & Lutter, C. D. (1998). Testosterone changes during vicarious experiences of winning and losing among fans at sporting events. *Physiology and Behavior, 65,* 59–62.

Bernstein, D. A. (2011). *Essentials of psychology* (5th ed.). Belmont, CA: Cengage.

Berntson, G. G., Cacioppo, J. T., & Quigley, K. S. (1991). Autonomic determinism: The modes of autonomic control, the doctrine of autonomic space, and the laws of autonomic constraint. *Psychological Review, 98,* 459–487.

Berntson, G. G., Norman, G. J., Bechara, A., Bruss, J., Tranel, D., & Cacioppo, J. T. (2011). The insula and evaluative process. *Psychological Science, 22*(1), 80–86. doi:10.1177/0956797610391097

Berscheid, E., & Peplau, L. A. (1983). The emerging science of relationships. In H. H. Kelley, E. Berscheid, A. Christensen, J. H. Harvey, T. L. Huston, G. Levinger, E. McClintock, L. A. Peplau & D. R. Peterson (Eds.), *Close relationships* (pp. 1–19). New York, NY: Freeman.

Berscheid, E., Snyder, M., & Omoto, A. M. (2004). Measuring closeness: The Relationship Closeness Inventory (RCI) revisited. In D. J. Mashek & A. P. Aron (Eds.), *Handbook of closeness and intimacy* (pp. 81–101). Mahwah, NJ: Erlbaum.

Bewernick, B. H., Hurlemann, R., Matusch, A., Kayser, S., Grubert, C., Hadrysiewicz, B., et al. (2010). Nucleus accumbens deep brain stimulation decreases ratings of depression and anxiety in treatment-resistant depression. *Biological Psychiatry, 67*(2), 110–116. doi:10.1016/j.biopsych.2009.09.013

Biederman, I. (1987). Recognition-by-components: A theory of human image understanding. *Psychological Review, 94,* 115–147.

Biederman, J., Rosenbaum, J. F., Hirshfeld, D. R., Faraone, S. V., Bolduc, E. A., Gersten, M., et al. (1990). Psychiatric correlates of behavioral inhibition in young children of parents with and without psychiatric disorders. *Archives of General Psychiatry, 47*(1), 21–26. doi:10.1001/archpsyc.1990.01810130023004

Biglan, A., Duncan, T. E., Ary, D. V., & Smolkowski, K. (1995). Peer and parental influences on adolescent tobacco use. *Journal of Behavioral Medicine, 18*(4), 315–330. doi:10.1007/bf01857657

Birchler, G. R. (1992). Marriage. In V. B. V. Hasselt & M. Hersen (Eds.), *Handbook of social development: A lifespan perspective.* New York, NY: Plenum Press.

Birnholz, J. C., & Benacerraf, B. R. (1983). The development of human fetal hearing. *Science, 222*(4623), 516–518.

Blair, R. J. R., Mitchell, D. G. V., Richell, R. A., Kelly, S., Leonard, A., Newman, C., et al. (2002). Turning a deaf ear to fear: Impaired recognition of vocal affect in psychopathic individuals. *Journal of Abnormal Psychology, 111*(4), 682–686.

Blair, R. J., Colledge, E., Murray, L., & Mitchell, D. G. (2001). A selective impairment in the processing of sad and fearful expressions in children with psychopathic tendencies. *Journal of Abnormal Child Psychology, 29,* 491–498.

Blake, R., & Sekuler, R. (2006). *Perception,* 5th ed. New York, NY: McGraw-Hill.

Blanchard, R. (1997). Birth order and sibling sex ratio in homosexual versus heterosexual males and females. *Annual Review of Sex Research, 8,* 27–67.

Blanco, C., Okuda, M., Wright, C., Hasin, D. S., Grant, B. F., Liu, S.-M., et al. (2008). Mental health of college students and their non-college-attending peers: Results from the National Epidemiologic Study on Alcohol and Related Conditions. *Archives of General Psychiatry, 65*(12), 1429–1437. doi:10.1001/archpsyc.65.12.1429

Bliss, T. V. P., & Lømo, T. (1973). Long-lasting potentiation of synaptic transmission in the dentate gyrus of the anesthetized rabbit following stimulation of the perforant path. *Journal of Physiology, 232,* 331–356.

Block, J., & Robins, R. W. (1993). A longitudinal study of consistency and change in self-esteem from early adolescence to early adulthood. *Child Development, 64*(3), 909–923.

Bloom, P. (2004). Can a dog learn a word? *Science, 304,* 1605–1606.

Bluck, S., Alea, N., Haberman, T., & Rubin, D. C. (2005). A tale of three functions: The self-reported uses of autobiographical memory. *Social Cognition, 23*(1), 91–117.

Blumenthal, J. A., Babyak, M. A., Moore, K. A., Craighead, W. E., Herman, S., Khatri, P., et al. (1999). Effects of exercise training on older patients with major depression. *Archives of Internal Medicine, 159*(19), 2349–2356.

Blumstein, D. T., Davitian, R., & Kaye, P. D. (2010). Do film soundtracks contain nonlinear analogues to influence emotion? *Biology Letters, 6,* 751–754.

Board, B. J., & Fritzon, K. (2005). Disordered personalities at work. *Psychology, Crime, and Law, 11*(1), 17–32.

Bobo, W. V., & Meltzer, H. Y. (2010). Duration of untreated psychosis and premorbid functioning: Relationship with treatment response and treatment-resistant schizophrenia. *Etiology and Neurobiology, 26,* 74–86.

Bogen, J. E. (1995). On the neurophysiology of consciousness: Part II. Constraining the semantic problem. *Consciousness and Cognition, 4,* 137–158.

Bogen, J. E., Schultz, D. H., & Vogel, P. J. (1988). Completeness of callosotomy shown by magnetic resonance imaging in the long term. *Archives of Neurology, 45,* 1203–1205.

Bohart, A., O'Hara, M., & Leitner, L. (1998). Empirically violated treatments: Disenfranchisement of humanistic and other psychotherapies. *Psychotherapy Research, 8*(2), 141–157. doi:10.1080/10503309812331332277

Boles, S. M., & Miotto, K. (2003). Substance and violence: A review of the literature. *Aggression and Violent Behavior, 8*(2), 155–174.

Bolger, N., & Schilling, E. A. (1991). Personality and the problems of everyday life: The role of neuroticism in exposure and reactivity to daily stressors. *Journal of Personality, 59,* 355–386.

Bond, C. F., & Titus, L. J. (1983). Social facilitation: A meta-analysis of 241 studies. *Psychological Bulletin, 94,* 265–292.

Boomsma, D. I., Willemsen, G., Dolan, C. B., Hawkley, L. C., & Cacioppo, J. T. (2005). Genetic and environmental contributions to loneliness in adults: The Netherlands Twin Register Study. *Behavior Genetics, 35,* 745–752.

Booth, A., Shelley, G., Mazur, A., Tharp, G., & Kittok, R. (1989). Testosterone, and winning and losing in human competition. *Hormones and Behavior, 23,* 556–571.

Boring, E. G. (1942). *Sensation and perception in the history of experimental psychology.* New York: Appleton-Century.

Bornstein, M. H., Kessen, W., & Weiskopf, S. (1976). Color vision and hue categorization in young human infants. *Journal of Experimental Psychology: Human Perception and Performance, 2,* 115–119.

Borsook, D., Becerra, L., Fishman, S., Edwards, A., Jennings, C. L., Stojanovic, M., et al. (1998). Acute plasticity in the human somatosensory cortex following amputation. *Neuroreport, 9,* 1013–1017.

Bosch, J. A., De Geus, E. J. C., & Kelder, A. (2001). Differential effects of active versus passive coping on secretory immunity. *Psychophysiology, 38,* 836–846.

Bossard, J. H. S. (1932). Residential propinquity in marriage selection. *American Journal of Sociology, 38,* 219–224.

Bossini, L., Tavanti, M., Calossi, S., Lombardelli, A., Polizzotto, N. R., Galli, R., et al. (2008). Magnetic resonance imaging volumes of the hippocampus in drug-naïve patients with post-traumatic stress disorder without comorbidity conditions. *Journal of Psychiatric Research, 42*(9), 752–762. doi:10.1016/j.jpsychires.2007.08.004

Bouchard, T. J., Jr., & Loehlin, J. C. (2001). Genes, evolution, and personality. *Behavior Genetics, 31*(3), 243–273. doi:10.1023/a:1012294324713

Bouchard, T., Jr. (1994). Genes, environment, and personality. *Science, 264,* 1700–1701.

Bouchard, T., Jr., Lykken, D. T., McGue, M., Segal, N. L., & Tellegen, A. (1990). Sources of human psychological differences: The Minnesota Study of Twins Reared Apart. *Science, 250,* 223–228.

Bower, G. H. (1981). Mood and memory. *American Psychologist, 36,* 129–148.

Bower, G. H., & Gilligan, S. G. (1979). Remembering information related to one's self. *Journal of Research in Personality, 13*(4), 420–432. doi:10.1016/0092-6566(79)90005-9

Bowlby, J. (1969/1982). *Attachment and loss. Vol 1: Attachment.* New York, NY: Basic Books.

Bowlby, J. (1973/1999a). *Attachment and loss. Vol 2: Separation; Anxiety and anger.* New York, NY: Basic Books.

Bowlby, J. (1973/1999b). *Attachment and loss. Vol 3: Loss; Sadness and depression.* New York, NY: Basic Books.

Bowles, S. (2009). Did warfare among ancestral hunter-gatherers affect the evolution of human social behaviors? *Science, 324,* 1293–1298.

Boyack, K. W., Klavans, R., & Börner, K. (2005). Mapping the backbone of science. *Scientometrics, 64,* 351–374.

Boydell, J., van Os, J., McKenzie, K., Allardyce, J., Goel, R., McCreadie, R. G., et al. (2001). Incidence of schizophrenia in ethnic minorities in London: Ecological study into interactions with environment. *British Medical Journal, 323*(7325), 1336–1338.

Bozarth, M. A., & Wise, R. A. (1986). Involvement of the ventral tegmental dopamine system in opioid and psychomotor stimulant reinforcement. *NIDA Research Monograph, 67,* 190–196.

Bradshaw, C., Kahn, A. S., & Saville, B. K. (2010). To hook up or date: Which gender benefits? *Sex Roles.* doi:10.1007/s11199-010-9765-7

Bransford, J. D., & Johnson, M. K. (1972). Contextual prerequisites for understanding: Some investigations of comprehension and recall. *Journal of Verbal Learning and Verbal Behavior, 11,* 717–726.

Bray, R. M., & Noble, A. M. (1978). Authoritarianism and decisions of mock juries: Evidence of jury bias and group polarization. *Journal of Personality and Social Psychology, 36,* 1424–1430.

Breasted, J. H. (1930). *Edwin Smith papyrus.* Chicago: University of Chicago Press.

Breiter, H. C., Aharon, I., Kahneman, D., Dale, A., & Shizgal, P. (2001). Functional imaging of neural responses to expectancy and experience of monetary gains and losses. *Neuron, 30,* 619–639.

Breland, K., & Breland, M. (1961). The misbehavior of organisms. *American Psychologist, 16,* 681–684.

Brembs, B. (1996). Chaos, cheating and cooperation: Potential solutions to the Prisoner's Dilemma. *Oikos, 76,* 14–24.

Bremner, J. D., Randall, P., Scott, T. M., Bronen, R. A., Seibyl, J. P., Southwick, S. M., et al. (1995). MRI-based measurement of hippocampal volume in patients with combat-related posttraumatic stress disorder. *American Journal of Psychiatry, 152,* 973–981.

Bremner, J. D., Vythilingam, M., Vermetten, E., Nazeer, A., Adil, J., Khan, S., et al. (2002).

Reduced volume of orbitofrontal cortex in major depression. *Biological Psychiatry, 51*(4), 273–279.

Breslow, R. A., & Smothers, B. A. (2005). Drinking pattern and body mass index in never smokers: National Health Survey, 1997–2001. *American Journal of Epidemiology, 161*(4), 368–376.

Bressler, E. R., & Balshine, S. (2006). Laughter paves the way for romance. *Evolution and Human Behavior, 27*, 29–39.

Brewer, M. B., & Gardner, W. (1996). Who is this "we"? Levels of collective identity and self representations. *Journal of Personality and Social Psychology, 71*(1), 83–93.

Brewer, N., Keast, A., & Rishworth, A. (2002). The confidence-accuracy relationship in eyewitness identification: The effects of reflection and disconfirmation on correlation and calibration. *Journal of Experimental Psychology: Applied, 8*, 46–58.

Brewin, C. R., Andrews, B., & Valentine, J. D. (2000). Meta-analysis of risk factors for post-traumatic stress disorder in trauma-exposed adults. *Journal of Consulting and Clinical Psychology, 68*, 748–766.

Brooks, L. (1990). Concept formation and particularizing learning. In P. Hanson (Ed.), *Information, language and cognition* (pp. 141–167). Vancouver, BC: University of British Columbia Press.

Brooks, L., Norman, G., & Allen, S. (1991). Role of specific similarity in a medical diagnostic task. *Journal of Experimental Psychology: General, 120*, 278–287.

Brosnan, S. F. (2010). Behavioral development: Timing is everything. *Current Biology, 20*(3), R98–R100. doi:10.1016/j.cub.2009.12.009

Brosnan, S. F., & De Waal, F. B. (2003). Monkeys reject unequal pay. *Nature, 425*, 297–299.

Brown, G. W., & Harris, T. O. (1989). Depression. In G. W. Brown & T. O. Harris (Eds.), *Life events and illness* (pp. 49–93). New York, NY: Guilford Press.

Brown, J. D., & Mankowski, T. A. (1993). Self-esteem, mood, and self-evaluation: Changes in mood and the way you see you. *Journal of Personality and Social Psychology, 64*(3), 421–430.

Brown, J. D., & Smart, S. A. (1991). The self and social conduct: Linking self-representations to prosocial behavior. *Journal of Personality and Social Psychology, 60*(3), 368–375.

Brown, P., & Elliot, R. (1965). Control of aggression in a nursery school class. *Journal of Experimental Child Psychology, 2*, 103–109.

Brown, R. W., & McNeill, D. (1966). The "tip of the tongue" phenomenon. *Journal of Verbal Learning and Verbal Behavior, 5*, 325–337.

Brown, T. A., & Cash, T. F. (1990). The phenomenon of nonclinical panic: Parameters of panic, fear, and avoidance. *Journal of Anxiety Disorders, 4*, 15–29.

Bruck, M., & Ceci, S. J. (2009). Reliability of child witnesses' reports. In J. L. Skeem, S. O. Lilienfeld, & K. S. Douglas (Eds.), *Psychological science in the courtroom: Consensus and controversy* (pp. 149–171). New York, NY: Guilford Press.

Bruine de Bruin, W., Parker, A. M., & Fischhoff, B. (2007). Individual differences in adult decision-making competence. *Journal of Personality and Social Psychology, 92*, 938–956.

Brune, M. (2006). The evolutionary psychology of obsessive-compulsive disorder: The role of cognitive metarepresentation. *Perspectives in Biology and Medicine, 49*(3), 317–329. doi:10.1353/pbm.2006.0037

Brunelli, M., Castellucci, V., & Kandel, E. R. (1976). Synaptic facilitation and behavioral sensitization in Aplysia: Possible role of serotonin and cyclic AMP. *Science, 194*(4270), 1178–1181. doi:10.1126/science.186870

Bryan, C. J., & Rudd, M. D. (2006). Advances in the assessment of suicide risk. *Journal of Clinical Psychology, 62*(2), 185–200. doi:10.1002/jclp.20222

Bryant, F. B., & Veroff, J. (2007). *Savoring: A new model of positive experience.* Mahwah, NJ: Erlbaum.

Bryant, G. A., & Haselton, M. G. (2009). Vocal cues of ovulation in human females. *Biology Letters, 5*(1), 12–15.

Bryden, M. P. (1982). *Laterality: Functional asymmetry in the intact brain.* New York, NY: Academic Press.

Bulik, C. M., Thornton, L., Root, T. L., Pisetsky, E. M., Lichtenstein, P., & Pedersen, N. L. (2010). Understanding the relation between anorexia nervosa and bulimia nervosa in a Swedish national twin sample. *Biological Psychiatry, 67*(1), 71–77.

Burch, M. R., & Bailey, J. S. (1999). *How dogs learn.* Hoboken, NJ: Howell Book House.

Burger, J. M. (2009). Replicating Milgram: Would people still obey today? *American Psychologist, 64*(1), 1–11. doi:10.1037/a0010932

Burger, J. M., Messian, N., Patel, S., del Prado, A., & Anderson, C. (2004). What a coincidence! The effects of incidental similarity on compliance. *Personality and Social Psychology Bulletin, 30*, 35–43.

Burke, R., & Skrull, T. (1988). Competitive interference and consumer memory for advertising. *Journal of Consumer Research, 15*, 55–68.

Burke, S. C., Cremeens, J., Vail-Smith, K., & Woolsey, C. (2010). Drunkorexia: Calorie restriction prior to alcohol consumption among college freshmen. *Journal of Alcohol and Drug Education, 54*(2), 17–34.

Burns, H. D., Van Laere, K., Sanabria-Bohórquez, S., Hamill, T. G., Bormans, G., Eng, W.-s., et al. (2007). [18F]MK-9470, a positron emission tomography (PET) tracer for in vivo human PET brain imaging of the cannabinoid-1 receptor. *Proceedings of the National Academy of Sciences, 104*(23), 9800–9805. doi:10.1073/pnas.0703472104

Burton, L. A., Henninger, D., Hafetz, J., & Cofer, J. (2009). Aggression, gender-typical childhood play, and a prenatal hormonal index. *Social Behavior and Personality: An International Journal, 37*(1), 105–115.

Buscemi, N., Vandermeer, B., Friesen, C., Bialy, L., Tubman, M., Ospina, M., et al. (2007). The efficacy and safety of drug treatments for chronic insomnia in adults: A meta-analysis of RCTs. *Journal of General Internal Medicine, 22*(9), 1335–1350.

Bushman, B. J. (2002). Does venting anger feed or extinguish the flame? Catharsis, rumination, distraction, anger, and aggressive responding. *Personality and Social Psychology Bulletin, 28*, 724–731.

Bushnell, I. W. R. (2001). Mother's face recognition in newborn infants: Learning and memory. *Infant and Child Development, 10*, 67–74.

Buss, A. H., & Perry, M. (1992). The Aggression Questionnaire. *Journal of Personality and Social Psychology, 63*(3), 452–459. doi:10.1037/0022-3514.63.3.452

Buss, D. M. (1985). Human mate selection. *American Scientist, 73*, 47–51.

Buss, D. M. (1989). Sex differences in human mate preferences: Evolutionary hypotheses tested in 37 cultures. *Behavioral and Brain Sciences, 12*, 1–49.

Buss, D. M. (1996). Evolutionary biology and personality psychology: Toward a conception of human nature and individual differences. In G.-H. Jennings (Ed.), *Passages beyond the gate: A Jungian approach to understanding the nature of American psychology at the dawn of the new millennium* (pp. 108–125). Needham Heights, MA: Simon & Schuster Custom Publishing.

Buss, D. M. (1999). Human nature and individual differences: The evolution of human personality. In L. A. Pervin & O. P. John (Eds.), *Handbook of personality: Theory and research* (2nd ed., pp. 31–56). New York, NY: Guilford Press.

Buss, D. M., & Schmitt, D. P. (1993). Sexual Strategies Theory: An evolutionary perspective on human mating. *Psychological Review, 100*, 204–232.

Buss, D. M., Larsen, R. J., & Westen, D. (1992). Sex differences in jealousy: Evolution, physiology, and psychology. *Psychological Science, 3*, 251–255.

Bustillo, J. R., Lauriello, J., Horan, W. P., & Keith, S. J. (2001). The psychosocial treatment of schizophrenia: An update. *American Journal of Psychiatry, 158*(2), 163–175. doi:10.1176/appi.ajp.158.2.163

Byer, C. O., & Shainberg, L. W. (1995). *Living well: Health in your hands* (2nd ed.). New York, NY: Harper Collins.

Byrne, D. (1961). Interpersonal attraction and attitude similarity. *Journal of Abnormal and Social Psychology, 62*, 713–715.

Caballero, B. (2007). The global epidemic of obesity: An overview. *Epidemiologic Reviews, 29*(1), 1–5. doi:10.1093/epirev/mxm012

Cacioppo, J. T., & Berntson, G. G. (1992). Social psychological contributions to the decade of the brain. *American Psychologist, 47*(8), 1019–1028.

Cacioppo, J. T., & Berntson, G. G. (2001). The affect system and racial prejudice. In J. Bargh & D. K. Apsley (Eds.), *Unraveling the complexities of social life: A festschrift in honor of Robert B. Zajonc* (pp. 95–110). Washington, DC: American Psychological Association.

Cacioppo, J. T., & Berntson, G. G. (2011). The brain, homeostasis, and health: Balancing demands of the internal and external milieu. In H. S. Friedman (Ed.), *The Oxford handbook of health psychology* (pp. 73–91). New York, NY: Oxford University Press.

Cacioppo, J. T., & Decety, J. (2011). An introduction to social neuroscience. In J. Decety & J. T. Cacioppo (Eds.), *The Oxford handbook of social neuroscience* (pp. 3–8). New York, NY: Oxford University Press.

Cacioppo, J. T., & Decety, J. (2011). Social neuro-science: Challenges and opportunities in the study of complex behavior. *Annals of the New York Academy of Sciences, 1224*(1), 162–173. doi:10.1111/j.1749-6632.2010.05858.x

Cacioppo, J. T., & Gardner, W. L. (1999). Emotion. *Annual Review of Psychology, 50,* 191–214.

Cacioppo, J. T., & Hawkley, L. C. (2005). People thinking about people: The vicious cycle of being a social outcast in one's own mind. In K. D. Williams, J. P. Forgas, & W. von Hippel (Eds.), *The social outcast: Ostracism, social exclusion, rejection, and bullying* (pp. 91–108). New York, NY: Psychology Press.

Cacioppo, J. T., & Hawkley, L. C. (2009). Perceived social isolation. *Trends in Cognitive Sciences, 13,* 447–454.

Cacioppo, J. T., & Patrick, W. (2008). *Loneliness: Human nature and the need for social connection.* New York, NY: Norton.

Cacioppo, J. T., & Petty, R. E. (1981). Electro-myograms as measures of extent and affectivity of information processing. *American Psychologist, 36,* 441–456.

Cacioppo, J. T., & Petty, R. E. (1984). The elaboration likelihood model of persuasion. *Advances in Consumer Research, 11,* 673–675.

Cacioppo, J. T., Berntson, G. G., & Klein, D. J. (1992). What is an emotion? The role of somatovisceral afference, with special emphasis on somatovisceral "illusions." *Review of Personality and Social Psychology, 14,* 63–98.

Cacioppo, J. T., Berntson, G. G., Adolphs, R., Carter, C. S., Davidson, R. J., McClintock, M. K., et al. (2002). *Foundations in social neuro-science.* Cambridge, MA: MIT Press.

Cacioppo, J. T., Berntson, G. G., Larsen, J. T., Poehlmann, K. M., & Ito, T. A. (2000). The psychophysiology of emotion. In M. Lewis & J. M. Haviland-Jones (Eds.), *Handbook of emotions* (Vol. 2, pp. 173–191). New York, NY: Guilford Press.

Cacioppo, J. T., Berntson, G. G., Norris, C. J., & Gollan, J. K. (2011). The evaluative space model. In P. Van Lange, A. Kruglanski & E. T. Higgins (Eds.), *Handbook of theories of social psychology* (Vol. 1, pp. 50–72). Thousand Oaks, CA: Sage.

Cacioppo, J. T., Berntson, G. G., Sheridan, J. F., & McClintock, M. K. (2000). Multilevel integrative analyses of human behavior: Social neuroscience and the complementing nature of social and biological approaches. *Psychological Bulletin, 126*(6), 829–843. doi:10.1037/0033-2909.126.6.829

Cacioppo, J. T., Hawkley, L. C., & Thisted, R. A. (2010). Perceived social isolation makes me sad: 5-year cross-lagged analyses of loneliness and depressive symptomatology in the Chicago Health, Aging, and Social Relations Study. *Psychology and Aging, 25*(2), 453–463. doi:10.1037/a0017216

Cacioppo, J. T., Hawkley, L. C., Berntson, G. G., Ernst, J. M., Gibbs, A. C., Stickgold, R., et al. (2002). Lonely days invade the nights: Social modulation of sleep efficiency. *Psychological Science, 13,* 384–387.

Cacioppo, J. T., Hawkley, L. C., Ernst, J. M., Burleson, M., Berntson, G. G., Nouriani, B., et al. (2006). Loneliness within a nomological net: An evolutionary perspective. *Journal of Research in Personality, 40,* 1054–1085.

Cacioppo, J. T., Hawkley, L. C., Kalil, A., Hughes, M. E., Waite, L., & Thisted, R. A. (2008). Happiness and the invisible threads of social connection: The Chicago Health, Aging, and Social Relations Study. In M. Eid & R. Larsen (Eds.), *The science of well-being* (pp. 195–219). New York, NY: Guilford Press.

Cacioppo, J. T., Marshall-Goodell, B. S., Tassinary, L. G., & Petty, R. E. (1992). Rudimentary determinants of attitudes: Classical conditioning is more effective when prior knowledge about the attitude stimulus is low than high. *Journal of Experimental Social Psychology, 28,* 207–233.

Cacioppo, J. T., Norris, C. J., Decety, J., Monteleone, G., & Nusbaum, H. (2009). In the eye of the beholder: Individual differences in perceived social isolation predict regional brain activation to social stimuli. *Journal of Cognitive Neuroscience, 21*(1), 83–92.

Cacioppo, J. T., Petty, R. E., Feinstein, J. A., & Jarvis, W. B. G. (1996). Dispositional differences in cognitive motivation: The life and times of individuals varying in need for cognition. *Psychological Bulletin, 119*(2), 197–253. doi:10.1037/0033-2909.119.2.197

Cacioppo, J. T., Petty, R. E., & Kao, C. F. (1984). The efficient assessment of need for cognition. *Journal of Personality Assessment, 48,* 306–307.

Cacioppo, J. T., Semin, G. R., & Berntson, G. G. (2004). Realism, instrumentalism, and scientific symbiosis. *American Psychologist, 59*(4), 214–223.

Cadoret, R. J., & Cain, C. (1981). Environmental and genetic factors in predicting adolescent antisocial behavior in adoptees. *Psychiatric Journal of the University of Ottawa, 6,* 220–225.

Caggiano, V., Rizzolatti, G., Pomper, J. K., Thier, P., Giese, M. A., & Casile, A. (2011). View-based encoding of actions in mirror neurons of area f5 in macaque premotor cortex. *Current Biology, 21*(2), 144–148.

Cahill, L., Babinsky, R., Markowitsch, H. J., & McGaugh, J. L. (1995). The amygdala and emotional memory. *Nature, 377,* 295–296.

Cain, W. S., & Gent, J. F. (1991). Olfactory sensitivity: Reliability, generality, and association with aging. *Journal of Experimental Psychology: Human Perception and Performance, 17,* 382–391.

Calcagni, E., & Elenkov, I. (2006). Stress system activity, innate and T helper cytokines, and susceptibility to immune-related diseases. *Annals of the New York Academy of Sciences, 1069,* 62–76.

Caldwell, D. F., & Caldwell, M. C. (1976). Cetaceans. In T. A. Sebeok (Ed.), *How animals communicate* (pp. 794–808). Bloomington: Indiana University.

Calvin, W. H. (2004). *A brief history of the mind: From apes to intellect and beyond.* Oxford, United Kingdom: Oxford University Press.

Camelot Group. (2004). Living the dream: Jackpot winners reveal their millionaire lifestyles. Retrieved August 22, 2006, from http://www.camelotgroup.co.uk/Winnerfacts.pdf

Camerer, C. F. (2008). Neuroeconomics: Opening the gray box. *Neuron, 60*(3), 416–419. doi:10.1016/j.neuron.2008.10.027

Canary, D. J., Stafford, L., Hause, K. S., & Wallace, L. A. (1993). An inductive analysis of relational maintenance strategies: Comparisons among lovers, relatives, friends, and others. *Communication Research Reports, 10*(1), 5–14.

Canli, T. (2009). Neuroimaging of personality. In P. J. Corr & G. Matthews (Eds.), *The Cambridge handbook of personality psychology* (pp. 305–322). New York, NY: Cambridge University Press.

Canli, T., Qiu, M., Omura, K., Congdon, E., Haas, B. W., Amin, Z., et al. (2006). Neural correlates of epigenesis. *Proceedings of the National Academy of Sciences, 103*(43), 16033–16038. doi:10.1073/pnas.0601674103

Cannon, M., Kendell, R., Susser, E., & Jones, P. (2003). Prenatal and perinatal risk factors for schizophrenia. In R. M. Murray, P. B. Jones, E. Susser, J. van Os, & M. Cannon (Eds.), *The epidemiology of schizophrenia* (pp. 74–99). Cambridge, England: Cambridge University Press.

Cannon, W. (1927). The James-Lange theory of emotions: A critical examination and an alternative theory. *American Journal of Psychology, 39,* 106–124.

Cannon, W. (1932). *The wisdom of the body.* New York, NY: W. W. Norton.

Cannon, W. B. (1929). *Bodily changes in pain, hunger, fear and rage* (2nd ed.). New York, NY: Harper and Row.

Cannon, W., & Washburn, A. L. (1912). An explanation of hunger. *American Journal of Physiology, 29,* 441–454.

Cantalupo, C., & Hopkins, W. D. (2001). Asymmetric Broca's area in great apes. *Nature, 414,* 505.

Cao, X., Wang, H., Mei, B., An, S., Yin, L., Wang, L. P., et al. (2008). Inducible and selective erasure of memories in the mouse brain via chemical-genetic manipulation. *Neuron, 60*(2), 353–366.

Capela, J. P., Fernandes, E., Remião, F., Bastos, M. L., Meisel, A., & Carvalho, F. (2007). Ecstasy induces apoptosis via 5-HT(2A)-receptor stimulation in cortical neurons. *Neurotoxicology, 28*(4), 868–875.

Capshew, J. H. (1993). Engineering behavior: World War II, Project Pigeon, and the conditioning of B. F. Skinner. *Technology and Culture, 34,* 835–857.

Carballo, J. J., Currier, D., Figueroa, A. E., Giner, L., Kelly, S. A., Sublette, M. E., et al. (2009). Neurobiological underpinnings of suicidal behavior: Integrating data from clinical and biological studies. *European Journal of Psychiatry, 23*(4), 243–259.

Carew, T. J., & Kandel, E. R. (1973). Acquisition and retention of long-term habituation in *Aplysia:* Correlation of behavioral and cellular processes. *Science, 182*(4117), 1158–1160. doi:10.1126/science.182.4117.1158

Carlsmith, J. M., & Anderson, C. A. (1979). Ambient temperature and the occurrence of collective violence: A new analysis. *Journal of Personality and Social Psychology, 37*(3), 337–344.

Carpenter, W. T., Jr., Conley, R. R., Buchanan, R. W., Breier, A., & Tamminga, C. A. (1995). Patient response and resource management: Another view of clozapine treatment of schizophrenia. *American Journal of Psychiatry, 152*, 827–832.

Carskadon, M. A., Wolfson, A. R., Acebo, C., Tzischinsky, O., & Seifer, R. (1998). Adolescent sleep patterns, circadian timing, and sleepiness at a transition to early school days. *Sleep, 21*, 871–881.

Carstensen, L. L., Fung, H. H., & Charles, S. T. (2003). Socioemotional selectivity theory and the regulation of emotion in the second half of life. *Motivation and Emotion, 27*(2), 103–123. doi:10.1023/a:1024569803230

Carstensen, L. L., Isaacowitz, D. M., & Charles, S. T. (1999). Taking time seriously: A theory of socioemotional selectivity. *American Psychologist, 54*(3), 165–181. doi:10.1037/0003-066x.54.3.165

Carstensen, L. L., Turan, B., Scheibe, S., Ram, N., Ersner-Hershfield, H., Samanez-Larkin, G. R., et al. (2010). Emotional experience improves with age: Evidence based on over 10 years of experience sampling. *Psychology and Aging.* doi:10.1037/a0021285

Cartwright, R. D. (1978). *A primer on sleep and dreaming.* Reading, MA: Addison-Wesley.

Carver, C. S., & Scheier, M. F. (1990). Origins and functions of positive and negative affect: A control-process view. *Psychological Review, 97*, 19–35.

Carver, C. S., & Scheier, M. F. (2000). Origins and functions of positive and negative affect: A control-process view. In E. T. Higgins & A. W. Kruglanski (Eds.), *Motivational science: Social and personality perspectives* (pp. 256–272). New York, NY: Psychology Press.

Casanova, M. F., Switala, A. E., Trippe, J., & Fitzgerald, M. (2007). Comparative minicolumnar morphometry of three distinguished scientists. *Autism, 11*(6), 557–569.

Casanova, M. F., van Kooten, I. A., Switala, A. E., van Engeland, H., Heinsen, H., Steinbusch, H. W., et al. (2006). Minicolumnar abnormalities in autism. *Acta Neuropathologica, 112*(3), 287–303.

Caspi, A., Sugden, K., Moffitt, T. E., Taylor, A., Craig, I. W., Harrington, H., et al. (2003). Influence of life stress on depression: Moderation by a polymorphism in the 5-HTT gene. *Science, 301*(5631), 386–389.

Caspi, A., Williams, B., Kim-Cohen, J., Craig, I. W., Milne, B. J., Poulton, R., et al. (2007). Moderation of breastfeeding effects on the IQ by genetic variation in fatty acid metabolism. *Proceedings of the National Academy of Sciences, 104*(47), 18860–18865. doi:10:1073/pnas.0704292104

Cassidy, J. (1988). Child-mother attachment and the self in six-year-olds. *Child Development, 59*(1), 121–134.

Caterina, M. J., Leffler, A., Malmberg, A. B., Martin, W. J., Trafton, J., Petersen-Zeitz, K. R., et al. (2000). Impaired nociception and pain sensation in mice lacking the capsaicin receptor. *Science, 220*, 306–313.

Caterina, M. J., Schumacher, M. A., Tominaga, M., Rosen, T. A., Levine, J. D., & Julius, D. (1997). The capsaicin receptor: A heat-activated ion channel in the pain pathway. *Nature, 389*, 816–824.

Cattell, R. B. (1946/1969). *Description and measurement of personality.* Yonkers, NY: World Book Company.

Cattell, R. B. (1971). *Abilities: Their structure, growth, and action.* Boston: Houghton Mifflin.

CBSNews.com. (2003, October 9). Social rejection is a real pain. Retrieved November 12, 2004, from http://www.cbsnews.com/stories/2003/10/09/health/main577348.shtml

Centers for Disease Control and Prevention (CDC). (2003). State-based prevalence data of ADHD medication treatment. Retrieved from http://www.cdc.gov/ncbddd/adhd/medicated.html

Centers for Disease Control and Prevention (CDC). (2004). Years of potential life lost report, average for United States 2001–2005. Retrieved October 10, 2010, from https://apps.nccd.cdc.gov/ardi/Report.aspx?T=YPLL&P=f214cf69-cad7-496f-ace2-2a09b9d6a126&R=804296a0-ac47-41d3-a939-9df26a176186&M=E2769A53-0BFC-453F-9FD7-63C5AA6CE5D7&L=40071693-2c38-4b92-87aa-21fc57dbc1ab

Centers for Disease Control and Prevention (CDC). (2005). Mental health in the United States: Prevalence of diagnosis and medication treatment for attention deficit/hyperactivity disorder—United States, 2003. Retrieved October 1, 2005, from http://www.cdc.gov/mmwr/preview/mmwrhtml/mm5434a2.htm

Centers for Disease Control and Prevention (CDC). (2007). Healthy aging: Preserving function and improving quality of life among older Americans. Retrieved September 10, 2007, from http://www.cdc.gov/nccdphp/publications/aag/aging.htm

Centers for Disease Control and Prevention (CDC). (2008a). Health, United States, 2008: With special feature on the health of young adults. Retrieved on December 27, 2011, from http://www.cdc.gov/nchs/data/hus/hus08.pdf

Centers for Disease Control and Prevention (CDC). (2008b). Update: Measles—United States, January–July 2008. *MMWR Surveillance Summaries, 57*(33), 893–896.

Centers for Disease Control and Prevention (CDC). (2009a). National suicide statistics at a glance: Suicide rates among persons ages 10 years and older, by race/ethnicity, United States, 2002–2006. Retrieved October 10, 2010, from http://www.cdc.gov/violencepre-vention/suicide/statistics/rates01.html

Centers for Disease Control and Prevention (CDC). (2009b). NCHS data brief. Retrieved October 10, 2010, from http://www.cdc.gov/nchs/data/databriefs/db26.htm

Centers for Disease Control and Prevention (CDC). (2009c). What every woman should know about alcohol and pregnancy. Retrieved on November 25, 2011, from http://www.cdc.gov/Features/AlcoholFreePregnancy/

Centers for Disease Control and Prevention (CDC). (2010a). Alcohol and public health. Retrieved October 10, 2010, from http://www.cdc.gov/alcohol/

Centers for Disease Control and Prevention (CDC). (2010b). Pyramid. Adverse Childhood Experiences (ACE) Study. Retrieved from http://www.cdc.gov/ace/pyramid.htm

Centers for Disease Control and Prevention (CDC). (2010c). Suicide: Facts at a glance. Retrieved November 6, 2010, from http://www.cdc.gov/violenceprevention/pdf/Suicide_DataSheet-a.pdf

Centers for Disease Control and Prevention (CDC). (2010d). Vital signs: Current cigarette smoking among adults aged > 18 years—United States, 2009. Retrieved October 9, 2010, from http://www.cdc.gov/tobacco/data_statistics/mmwrs/byyear/2010/mm59e0907a1/intro.htm

Centers for Disease Control and Prevention (CDC). (2010e). What do we know about tobacco use and pregnancy? Retrieved July 13, 2010, from http://www.cdc.gov/reproductivehealth/tobaccoUsePregnancy/index.htm

Centers for Disease Control and Prevention (CDC). (2011a). Life expectancy. Retrieved July 18, 2011, from http://www.cdc.gov/nchs/fastats/lifexpec.htm

Centers for Disease Control and Prevention (CDC). (2011b). Suicide and self-inflicted injury. Retrieved August 19, 2011, from http://www.cdc.gov/nchs/fastats/suicide.htm

Centers for Disease Control and Prevention (CDC) (2011c). Vital signs: Current cigarette smoking among adults aged ≥ 18 years—United States, 2005–2010. *Morbidity and Mortality Weekly Report.* Retrieved on December 13, 2011, from http://www.cdc.gov/mmwr/pdf/wk/mm60e0906.pdf

Cerella, J., & Hale, S. (1994). The rise and fall in information-processing rates over the life span. *Acta Psychologica, 86*, 109–197.

Chagnon, N. A. (1988). Life histories, blood revenge, and warfare in a tribal population. *Science, 239*, 985–992.

Champagne, F., Francis, D. D., Mar, A., & Meaney, M. J. (2003). Naturally-occurring variations in maternal care in the rat as a mediating influence for the effects of environment on the development of individual differences in stress reactivity. *Physiology and Behavior, 79*, 359–371.

Chaplin, J. P., & Krawiec, T. S. (1979). *Systems and theories of psychology.* New York: Holt, Rinehart, and Winston.

Chapman, R. S. (1995). Language development in children and adolescents with Down syndrome. In P. Fletcher & B. MacWhinney (Eds.), *The handbook of child language* (pp. 641–663). Oxford: Blackwell.

Chapman, S., & MacKenzie, R. (2010). The global research neglect of unassisted smoking cessation: Causes and consequences. *PLoS Medicine, 7*(2), e1000216.

Charmaraman, L., & Grossman, J. M. (2010). Importance of race and ethnicity: An exploration of Asian, Black, Latino, and multiracial adolescent identity. *Cultural Diversity and Ethnic Minority Psychology, 16*(2), 144–151. doi:10.1037/a0018668

Chase, W. G., & Simon, H. A. (1973). Perception in chess. *Cognitive Psychology, 4*, 55–81.

Chatrian, G. (1990). Coma and other states of altered responsiveness and brain death. In D. D. Daly & T. A. Pedley (Eds.), *Current Practice of Clinical Electroencephalography* (pp. 442–443). New York, NY: Raven Press.

Chaudhari, N., Landlin, A. M., & Roper, S. D. (2000). A metabotropic glutamate receptor variant functions as a taste receptor. *Nature Neuroscience, 3,* 113–119.

Chaudhri, N., Sahuque, L. L., & Janak, P. H. (2008). Context-induced relapse of conditioned behavioral responding to ethanol cues in rats. *Biological Psychiatry, 64*(3), 203–210.

Chemtob, C. M., Nomura, Y., Rajendran, K., Yehuda, R., Schwartz, D., & Abramovitz, R. (2010). Impact of maternal post-traumatic stress disorder and depression following exposure to the September 11 attacks on preschool children's behavior. *Child Development, 81*(4), 1129–1141. doi:10.1111/j.1467-8624.2010.01458.x

Chen, S., Boucher, H. C., & Tapias, M. P. (2006). The relational self revealed: Integrative conceptualization and implications for interpersonal life. *Psychological Bulletin, 132*(2), 151–179.

Cherkas, L., Hochberg, F., MacGregor, A. J., Snieder, H., & Spector, T. D. (2000). Happy families: A twin study of humour. *Twin Research, 3,* 17–22.

Chertkow, H., Whitehead, V., Phillips, N., Wolfson, C., Atherton, J., & Bergman, H. (2010). Multilingualism (but not always bilingualism) delays the onset of Alzheimer disease: Evidence from a bilingual community. *Alzheimer Disease and Associated Disorders, 24*(2), 118–125. doi:110.1097/WAD.1090b1013e3181ca1221

Chiao, J. Y., & Blizinsky, K. D. (2010). Culture–gene coevolution of individualism–collectivism and the serotonin transporter gene. *Proceedings of the Royal Society B: Biological Sciences, 277*(1681), 529–537. doi:10.1098/rspb.2009.1650

Chicago Social Brain Network. (2011). *Invisible forces and unseen powers: Gravity, gods, and minds.* Saddle River, NJ: Pearson.

Child, I. L. (1973). *Humanistic psychology and the research tradition: Their several virtues.* Oxford, England: Wiley.

Cho, K., Ennaceur, A., Cole, J. C., & Suh, C. K. (2000). Chronic jet lag produces cognitive deficits. *Journal of Neuroscience, 20,* RC66.

Choi, I., Nisbett, R. E., & Norenzayan, A. (1999). Causal attribution across cultures: Variation and universality. *Psychological Bulletin, 125*(1), 47–63.

Chomsky, N. (1957). *Syntactic structures.* The Hague, Netherlands: Mouton.

Chrea, C., Valentin, D., Sulmont-Rosse, C., Mai, H. L., Nguyen, D. H., & Abdi, H. (2004). Culture and odor categorization: Agreement between cultures depends upon the odors. *Food Quality and Preference, 15,* 669–679.

Christakis, N. A., & Fowler, J. H. (2007). The spread of obesity in a large social network over 32 years. *New England Journal of Medicine, 357*(4), 370–379. doi:10.1056/NEJMsa066082

Christoff, K., Gordon, A. M., Smallwood, J., Smith, R., & Schooler, J. W. (2009). Experience sampling during fMRI reveals default network and executive system contributions to mind wandering. *Proceedings of the National Academy of Sciences, 106*(21), 8719–8724. doi:10.1073/pnas.0900234106

Chua, H. F., Boland, J. E., & Nisbett, R. E. (2005). Cultural variation in eye movements during scene perception. *Proceedings of the National Academy of Sciences, 102,* 12629–12633.

Chua, H. F., Ho, S. S., Jasinska, A. J., Polk, T. A., Welsh, R. C., Liberzon, I., et al. (2011). Self-related neural response to tailored smoking-cessation messages predicts quitting. *Nature Neuroscience, 14*(4), 426–427. doi:10.1038/nn.2761

Chung, B. (2001). Muscle dysmorphia: A critical review of the proposed criteria. *Perspectives in Biology and Medicine, 44*(4), 565–574.

Cialdini, R. B. (2001). *Influence: Science and practice* (4th ed.). Boston, MA: Allyn & Bacon.

Cialdini, R. B., & Goldstein, N. J. (2004). Social influence: Compliance and conformity. *Annual Review of Psychology, 55,* 591–621.

Cialdini, R. B., Borden, R. J., Thorne, A., Walker, M. R., Freeman, S., & Sloan, L. R. (1976). Basking in reflected glory: Three (football) field studies. *Journal of Personality and Social Psychology, 34*(3), 366–375.

Cialdini, R. B., Cacioppo, J., Bassett, R., & Miller, J. (1978). Low-ball procedure for producing compliance: Commitment then cost. *Journal of Personality and Social Psychology, 36,* 463–476.

Cialdini, R. B., Kenrick, D. T., & Baumann, D. J. (1981). Effects of mood on prosocial behavior in children and adults. In N. Eisenberg (Ed.), *The development of prosocial behavior* (pp. 339–359). New York, NY: Academic Press.

Cialdini, R. B., Vincent, J., Lewis, S., Catalan, J., Wheeler, D., & Darby, B. L. (1975). Reciprocal concessions procedure for inducing compliance: The door-in-the-face technique. *Journal of Personality and Social Psychology, 31,* 206–215.

Cipolotti, L., Husain, M., Crinion, J., Bird, C. M., Khan, S. S., Losseff, N., et al. (2008). The role of the thalamus in amnesia: A tractography, high-resolution MRI and neuropsychological study. *Neuropsychologia, 46*(11), 2745–2758.

Clarke, A., & Butler, P. E. (2009). The psychological management of facial transplantation. *Expert Review of Neurotherapeutics, 9*(7), 1087–1100.

Clegg, J., & Sheard, C. (2002). Challenging behaviour and insecure attachment. *Journal of Intellectual Disability Research, 46,* 503–506.

CNN. (1997). Poll U.S. hiding knowledge of aliens. Retrieved March 15, 2011, from http://articles.cnn.com/1997-06-15/us/9706_15_ufo.poll_1_ufo-aliens-crash-site?_s=PM:US

Coan, J. A., Schaefer, H. S., & Davidson, R. J. (2006). Lending a hand: Social regulation of the neural response to threat. *Psychological Science, 17*(12), 1032–1039. doi:10.1111/j.1467-9280.2006.01832.x

Coffey, S., Dansky, B. S., Carrigan, M. H., & Brady, K. T. (2000). Acute and protracted cocaine abstinence in an outpatient population: A prospective study of mood, sleep and withdrawal symptoms. *Drug and Alcohol Dependence, 59,* 277–286.

Cohen, E., Chazan, S., Lerner, M., & Maimon, E. (2010). Posttraumatic play in young children exposed to terrorism: An empirical study. *Infant Mental Health Journal, 31*(2), 159–181. doi:10.1002/imhj.20250

Cohen, S., & Herbert, T. B. (1996). Health psychology: Psychological factors and physical disease from the perspective of human psychoneuroimmunology. *Annual Review of Psychology, 47,* 113–142.

Cohen, S., Tyrrell, D. A., & Smith, A. P. (1991). Psychological stress and susceptibility to the common cold. *New England Journal of Medicine, 325*(9), 606–612.

Cohn, D., & Taylor, P. (2010). Baby boomers approach age 65—glumly. Retrieved July 18, 2011, from http://pewresearch.org/pubs/1834/baby-boomers-old-age-downbeat-pessimism

Cohn, M. A., Fredrickson, B. L., Brown, S. L., Mikels, J. A., & Conway, A. M. (2009). Happiness unpacked: Positive emotions increase life satisfaction by building resilience. *Emotion, 9*(3), 361–368. doi:10.1037/a0015952

Coid, J., Yang, M., Ullrich, S., Roberts, A., Moran, P., Bebbington, P., et al. (2009). Psychopathy among prisoners in England and Wales. *International Journal of Law and Psychiatry, 32*(3), 134–141. doi:10.1016/j.ijlp.2009.02.008

Cole, F. S., Alleyne, C., Barks, J. D. E., Boyle, R. J., Carroll, J. L., Dokken, D., et al. (2011). NIH Consensus Development Conference Statement: Inhaled nitric-oxide therapy for premature infants. *Pediatrics, 127*(2), 363–369. doi:10.1542/peds.2010-3507

Cole, J. (1955). Paw preference in cats related to hand preference in animals and man. *Journal of Comparative and Physiological Psychology, 48,* 137–140.

Cole, M. (1999). Culture in development. In M. H. Bornstein & M. E. Lamb (Eds.), *Developmental psychology: An advanced textbook* (4th ed., pp. 73–123). Hillsdale, NJ: Erlbaum.

Cole, S. W., Hawkley, L. C., Arevalo, J. M. G., & Cacioppo, J. T. (2011). Transcript origin analysis identifies antigen presenting cells as primary targets of socially regulated leukocyte gene expression. *Proceedings of the National Academy of Sciences, 108,* 3080–3085.

Coleman, R. M. (1986). *Wide awake at 3:00 a.m. by choice or by chance?* New York, NY: W. H. Freeman.

College Board, The. (2009). 2009 college-bound seniors: Total group profile report. Retrieved on December 11, 2011, from http://professionals.collegeboard.com/profdownload/cbs-2009-national-TOTAL-GROUP.pdf

Collins, A. M., & Loftus, E. (1975). A spreading activation theory of semantic processing. *Psychological Review, 82,* 407–428.

Collins, A. M., & Quillian, M. R. (1969). Retrieval time from semantic memory. *Journal of Verbal Learning and Verbal Behavior, 8,* 240–247.

Colwell, K., Hiscock-Anisman, C., Memon, A., Rachel, A., & Colwell, L. (2007). Vividness and spontaneity of statement detail characteristics as predictors of witness credibility. *American Journal of Forensic Psychology, 25*(1), 1–25.

Comings, D. E., & Blum, K. (2000). Reward deficiency syndrome: Genetic aspects of behavioral disorders. *Progress in Brain Research, 126,* 325–341.

Committee on Public Education. (2001). Children, adolescents, and television. *Pediatrics, 107*(2), 423–426. doi:10.1542/peds.107.2.423

Connelly, K., & Martlew, M. (1999). *Psychologically speaking: A book of quotations.* Oxford, UK: BPS Books.

Conners, C. K., Epstein, J. N., March, J. S., Angold, A., Wells, K. C., Klaric, J., et al. (2001). Multimodal treatment of ADHD in the MTA: An alternative outcome analysis. *Journal of the American Academy of Child and Adolescent Psychiatry, 40,* 159–167.

Connidis, I. A. (1992). Life transitions and the adult sibling tie: A qualitative study. *Journal of Marriage and the Family, 54*(4), 972–982. doi:10.2307/353176

Connolly, T., & Zeelenberg, M. (2002). Regret in decision making. *Current Directions in Psychological Science, 11,* 212–216.

Conrad, R. (1964). Acoustic confusions in immediate memory. *British Journal of Psychology, 55,* 75–84.

Consumerreports.com. (2009). Risky business. Retrieved October 9, 2010, from http://www.consumerreports.org/cro/money/consumer-protection/risk-taking/risky-business/risky-business.htm; http://www.consumerreports.org/health/healthy-living/health-safety/risk-taking/overview/risk-taking-ov.htm

Cook, C. R., Williams, K. R., Guerra, N. G., Kim, T. E., & Sadek, S. (2010). Predictors of bullying and victimization in childhood and adolescence: A meta-analytic investigation. *School Psychology Quarterly, 25*(2), 65–83. doi:10.1037/a0020149

Cooper, J. (2011). Cognitive dissonance theory. In A. W. Kruglanski, E. T. Higgins, & P. A. M. V. Lange (Eds.), *Handbook of theories of social psychology* (Vol. 1, pp. 377–397). Thousand Oaks, CA: Sage.

Cooper, S. J., & Dourish, C. T. (1990). Multiple cholecystokinin (CCK) receptors and CCK-monoamine interactions are instrumental in the control of feeding. *Physiology and Behavior, 48,* 849–857.

Corballis, M. C. (2004). The origins of modernity: Was autonomous speech the critical factor? *Psychological Review, 111,* 543–552.

Corbett, M. (1991). *American public opinion.* White Plains, NY: Longman.

Coren, S. (1993). The Lateral Preference Inventory for measurement of handedness, footedness, eyedness, and earedness: Norms for young adults. *Bulletin of the Psychonomic Society, 31,* 1–3.

Coren, S. (1996a). *Sleep thieves.* New York, NY: Free Press.

Coren, S. (1996b). Daylight savings time and traffic accidents. *New England Journal of Medicine, 334,* 924.

Corkin, S. (2002). What's new with the amnesic patient H.M.? *Nature Reviews Neuroscience, 3,* 153–160.

Corkin, S., Amaral, D. G., Gonzalez, R. G., Johnson, K. A., & Hyman, B. T. (1997). H.M.'s medial temporal lobe lesion: Findings from magnetic resonance imaging. *Journal of Neuroscience, 17,* 3964–3979.

Cornford, F. M. (1957). *From religion to philosophy: A study in the origins of Western speculation.* New York, NY: Harper Torchbooks.

Correll, C. U., & Schenk, E. M. (2008). Tardive dyskinesia and new antipsychotics. *Current Opinion in Psychiatry, 21*(2), 151–156. doi:110.1097/YCO.1090b1013e3282f53132

Cosmides, L., & Tooby, J. (1997). Evolutionary psychology: A primer. Retrieved July 21, 2009, from http://www.psych.ucsb.edu/research/cep/primer.html

Costa, P. T., & McCrae, R. R. (2011). NEO Personality Inventory-Revised (NEO PI-R). Retrieved July 28, 2011, from http://www4.parinc.com/Products/Product.aspx?ProductID=NEO-PI-R

Courchesne, E. (1997). Brainstem, cerebellar and limbic neuroanatomical abnormalities in autism. *Current Opinion in Neurobiology, 7,* 269–278.

Cowan, N. (2000). The magical number 4 in short-term memory: A reconsideration of mental storage capacity. *Behavioral and Brain Sciences, 24,* 87–185.

Cowen, P. J. (2010). Not fade away: The HPA axis and depression. *Psychological Medicine, 40*(01), 1–4. doi:10.1017/S0033291709005558

Cowey, A., & Stoerig, P. (1991). The neurobiology of blindsight. *Trends in Neuroscience, 14,* 140–145.

Cox, M. J., Owen, M. T., Henderson, V. K., & Margand, N. A. (1992). Prediction of infant-father and infant-mother attachment. *Developmental Psychology, 28*(3), 474–483. doi:10.1037/0012-1649.28.3.474

Craig, A., & Tran, Y. (2005). The epidemiology of stuttering: The need for reliable estimates of prevalence and anxiety levels over the lifespan. *Advances in Speech–Language Pathology, 7*(1), 41–46.

Craig, I. W. (2007). The importance of stress and genetic variation in human aggression. *Bioessays, 29*(3), 227–236.

Craik, F. I. M., & Lockhart, R. S. (1972). Levels of processing: A framework for memory research. *Journal of Verbal Learning and Verbal Behavior, 11,* 671–684.

Craik, F. I. M., & Tulving, E. (1975). Depth of processing and the retention of words in episodic memory. *Journal of Experimental Psychology: General, 104*(3), 268–294. doi:10.1037/0096-3445.104.3.268

Craik, F. I.M., Bialystock, E., & Freedman, M. (2011). *Delaying the onset of Alzheimer disease: Bilingualism as a form of cognitive reserve.* Abstract presented at AAAS, 2011.

Crick, F., & Koch, C. (2003). A framework for consciousness. *Nature Neuroscience, 6,* 119–126.

Csikszentmihalyi, M. (1990). *Flow: The psychology of optimal experience.* New York, NY: Harper and Row.

Csikszentmihalyi, M. (1996). *Creativity: Flow and the psychology of discovery and invention.* New York, NY: HarperCollins.

Cuperman, R., & Ickes, W. (2009). Big Five predictors of behavior and perceptions in initial dyadic interactions: Personality similarity helps extraverts and introverts, but hurts "disagreeables." *Journal of Personality and Social Psychology, 97*(4), 667–684. doi:10.1037/a0015741

Custance, D. M., Whiten, A., & Bard, K. A. (1995). Can young chimpanzees (*Pan troglodytes*) imi-

tate arbitrary actions? Hayes & Hayes (1952) revisited. *Behaviour, 132,* 837–859.

Dabbs, J. M., & Janis, I. L. (1965). Why does eating while reading facilitate opinion change? An experimental inquiry. *Journal of Experimental Social Psychology, 1,* 133–144.

Dabbs, J. M., Jr., & Hargrove, M. F. (1997). Age, testosterone, and behavior among female prison inmates. *Psychosomatic Medicine, 59,* 477–480.

Dabbs, J. M., Jr., & Morris, R. (1990). Testosterone, social class, and antisocial behavior in a sample of 4,462 men. *Psychological Science, 1,* 209–211.

Dabbs, J. M., Jr., Frady, R. L., Carr, T. S., & Besch, N. F. (1987). Saliva testosterone and criminal violence in young adult prison inmates. *Psychosomatic Medicine, 49,* 174–182.

Dahl, R. E., Holttum, J., & Trubnick, L. (1994). A clinical picture of child and adolescent narcolepsy. *Journal of the American Academy of Child and Adolescent Psychiatry, 33,* 834–841.

Daly, R. (2006). Psychiatrists proactive in scope-of-practice battles. *Psychiatric News, 41*(5), 17–34.

Damasio, A. R. (1994). *Descartes' error: Emotion, reason, and the human brain.* New York, NY: Putnam.

Damasio, A. R., & Anderson, S. W. (1993). The frontal lobes. In K. M. Heilman & E. Valenstein (Eds.), *Clinical neuropsychology* (pp. 409–460). New York: Oxford University Press.

Damasio, A. R., Grabowski, T. J., Bechara, A., Damasio, H., Ponto, L. L., Parvizi, J., & Hichwa, R. D. (2000). Subcortical and cortical brain activity during the feeling of self-generated emotions. *Nature Neuroscience, 3,* 1049–1056.

Damasio, A. R., Tranel, D., & Damasio, H. (1991). Somatic markers and the guidance of behavior: theory and preliminary testing. In H. S. Levin, H. M. Eisenberg, & A. L. Benton (Eds.), *Frontal lobe function and dysfunction* (pp. 217–229). New York: Oxford University Press.

Damasio, A., Bellugi, U., Damasio, H., Poizner, H., & Gilder, J. V. (1986). Sign language aphasia during left-hemisphere amytal injection. *Nature, 322,* 363–365.

Damasio, H., Grabowski, T., Frank, R., Galaburda, A. M., & Damasio, A. R. (1994). The return of Phineas Gage: Clues about the brain from the skull of a famous patient. *Science, 264,* 1102–1105.

Dani, J. A., & Harris, R. A. (2005). Nicotine addiction and comorbidity with alcohol abuse and mental illness. *Nature Neuroscience, 8*(11), 1465–1470.

Dapretto, M., Davies, M. S., Pfeifer, J. H., Scott, A. A., Sigman, M., Bookheimer, S. Y., et al. (2006). Understanding emotions in others: Mirror neuron dysfunction in children with autism spectrum disorders. *Nature Neuroscience, 9*(1), 28–30.

Dark, J., Forger, N. G., Stern, J. S., & Zucker, I. (1984). Recovery of lipid mass after removal of adipose tissue in ground squirrels. *American Journal of Physiology, 249*(Pt. 2), R73–R78.

Darwin, C. (1859). *On the origin of species by means of natural selection, or the preservation of favoured races in the struggle for life.* London: John Murray.

Darwin, C. (1871). *The descent of man and selection in relation to sex.* London: John Murray.

Darwin, C. (1872). *The expression of emotions in man and animals.* London: Murray.

David, N., Bewernick, B. H., Cohen, M. X., Newen, A., Lux, S., Fink, G. R., et al. (2006). Neural representations of self versus other: Visual-spatial perspective taking and agency in a virtual ball-tossing game. *Journal of Cognitive Neuroscience, 18*(6), 898–910.

Davidson, P. S. R. (2008). The cognitive and neural bases of flashbulb memories. In E. Dere, A. Easton, L. Nadel, & J. P. Huston (Eds.), *Handbook of behavioral neuroscience* (Vol. 18, pp. 81–97). Amsterdam: Elsevier.

Davidson, R. J., & Irwin, W. (1999). The functional neuroanatomy of emotion and affective style. *Trends in Cognitive Sciences, 3*(1), 11–21.

Davidson, R. J., Putnam, K. M., & Larson, C. L. (2000). Dysfunction in the neural circuitry of emotion regulation—A possible prelude to violence. *Science, 289*, 591–594.

Davis, C. G., & Nolen-Hoeksema, S. (2009). Making sense of loss, perceiving benefits, and posttraumatic growth. In S. J. Lopez & C. R. Snyder (Eds.), *Oxford handbook of positive psychology* (2nd ed., pp. 641–649). New York, NY: Oxford University Press.

Davis, J. A., Smith, T. W., & Marsden, P. V. (2006). General Social Survey (GSS). Retrieved August 22, 2006, from http://www.norc.uchicago.edu/projects/gensoc.asp

Davis, J. L. (2004). Researchers identify alcoholism gene: Alcohol addiction, high anxiety linked to same gene. Retrieved August 21, 2006, from http://www.webmd.com/content/article/87/99592.htm

Davis, J. L., & Rusbult, C. E. (2001). Attitude alignment in close relationships. *Journal of Personality and Social Psychology, 81*, 65–84.

Davis, M. (2007). An introduction to sine-wave speech. Retrieved February 20, 2010, from http://www.mrc-cbu.cam.ac.uk/people/matt.davis/sine-wave-speech/

Dawe, S., Davis, P., Lapworth, K., & McKetin, R. (2009). Mechanisms underlying aggressive and hostile behavior in amphetamine users. *Current Opinion in Psychiatry, 22*(3), 269–273.

Dawkins, R. (1976). *The selfish gene.* Oxford, UK: Oxford University Press.

de Gelder, B., Snyder, J., Greve, D., Gerard, G., & Hadjikhani, N. (2004). Fear fosters flight: A mechanism for fear contagion when perceiving emotion expressed by a whole body. *Proceedings of the National Academy of Sciences, 101*, 16701–16706.

de Lecea, L., Kilduff, T. S., Peyron, C., Gao, X. B., Foye, P. E., Danielson, P. E., et al. (1998). The hypocretins: Hypothalamus-specific peptides with neuroexcitatory activity. *Proceedings of the National Academy of Sciences, 95*(1), 322–327. doi:10.1073/pnas.95.1.322

De Martino, B., Camerer, C. F., & Adolphs, R. (2010). Amygdala damage eliminates monetary loss aversion. *Proceedings of the National Academy of Sciences.* doi:10.1073/pnas.0910230107

De Valois, R. L., & De Valois, K. K. (1980). Spatial vision. *Annual Review of Psychology, 31*, 309–341.

de Vries, A. P., Kassam-Adams, N., Cnaan, A., Sherman-Slate, E., Gallagher, P. R., & Winston, F. K. (1999). Looking beyond the physical injury: Posttraumatic stress disorder in children and parents after pediatric traffic injury. *Pediatrics, 104*, 1293–1299.

Dear Abby. (January 14, 2006). Man ready to scrap marriage after wife wrecks his car. Retrieved August 8, 2006, from http://www.uexpress.com/dearabby/?uc_full_date=20060114

Deary, I. J., Penke, L., & Johnson, W. (2010). The neuroscience of human intelligence differences. *Nature Reviews Neuroscience, 11*, 201–211. doi:10.1038/nrn2793

Deary, I. J., Strand, S., Smith, P., & Fernandes, C. (2007). Intelligence and educational achievement. *Intelligence, 35*(1), 13–21. doi:10.1016/j.intell.2006.02.001

DeCasper, A. J., & Fifer, W. P. (1980). Of human bonding: Newborns prefer their mothers' voices. *Science, 208*, 1174–1176.

DeCasper, A. J., & Spence, M. J. (1986). Prenatal maternal speech influences newborns' perception of speech sounds. *Infant Behavior and Development, 9*, 133–150.

DeCharms, R. (1968). *Personal causation.* New York, NY: Academic Press.

Deci, E. L., & Ryan, R. M. (2000). The "what" and "why" of goal pursuits: Human needs and the self-determination of behavior. *Psychological Inquiry, 11*, 227–268.

Deese, J. (1959). Influence of inter-item associative strength upon immediate free recall. *Psychological Reports, 5*, 305–312.

Del Russo, J. (1971). Observational learning in hooded rats. *Psychonomic Science, 24*, 37–38.

Dement, W. (1960). The effect of dream deprivation. *Science, 131*, 1705–1707.

Dement, W. (1974). *Some must watch while some must sleep.* San Francisco: W. H. Freeman.

Dement, W., & Kleitman, N. (1957). The relation of eye movements during sleep to dream activity: An objective method for the study of dreaming. *Journal of Experimental Psychology, 53*, 339–346.

Demitrack, M. A. (2007). Therapeutic neuromodulation: Clinical and research implications of a new therapeutic platform. *Psychiatric Annals, 37*(3), 165–174.

Demo, D. H. (1992). New families, no families? The transformation of the American home. *Journal of Marriage and the Family, 54*, 464–466.

Denenberg, V. H. (1964). Critical periods, stimulus input, and emotional reactivity: A theory of infantile stimulation. *Psychological Reviews, 71*, 335–351.

DeNeve, K. M., & Cooper, H. (1998). The happy personality: A meta-analysis of 137 personality traits and subjective well-being. *Psychological Bulletin, 124*(2), 197–229. doi:10.1037/0033-2909.124.2.197

Dennett, D. C. (1991). *Consciousness explained.* Boston, MA: Little, Brown, & Co.

Dennis, W. (1966). Age and creative productivity. *Journal of Gerontology, 21*, 1–8.

Department of Health and Human Services, U.S. Public Health Service. (2007). Mental health: Culture, race, and ethnicity. Retrieved October 10, 2010, from http://www.surgeongeneral.gov/library/mentalhealth/cre/execsummary-1.html

Derntl, B., Windischberger, C., Robinson, S., Kryspin-Exner, I., Gur, R. C., Moser, E., et al. (2009). Amygdala activity to fear and anger in healthy young males is associated with testosterone. *Psychoneuroendocrinology, 34*(5), 687–693. doi:10.1016/j.psyneuen.2008.11.007

Derogatis, L. R., & Coons, H. L. (1993). Self-report measures of stress. In L. Goldberger & S. Breznitz (Eds.), *Handbook of stress: Theoretical and clinical aspects* (2nd ed., pp. 200–233). New York, NY: Free Press.

Deschamps, J. C., & Doise, W. (1978). Crossed category membership in intergroup relations. In H. Tajfe (Ed.), *Differentiation between social groups* (pp. 141–158). London: Academic Press.

DeYoung, C. G., Hirsh, J. B., Shane, M. S., Papademetris, X., Rajeevan, N., & Gray, J. R. (2010). Testing predictions from personality neuroscience. *Psychological Science, 21*(6), 820–828. doi:10.1177/0956797610370159

Di Castelnuovo, A., Costanzo, S., Bagnardi, V., Donati, M. B., Iacoviello, L., & de Gaetano, G. (2006). Alcohol dosing and total mortality in men and women: An updated meta-analysis of 34 prospective studies. *Archives of Internal Medicine, 166*(22), 2437–2445. doi:10.1001/archinte.166.22.2437

Di Pellegrino, G., Fadiga, L., Fogassi, L., Gallese, V., & Rizzolatti, G. (1992). Understanding motor events: A neurophysiological study. *Experimental Brain Research, 91*, 176–180.

Diamond, A., & Goldman-Rakic, P. S. (1989). Comparison of human infants and rhesus monkeys on Piaget's AB task: Evidence for dependence on dorsolateral prefrontal cortex. *Experimental Brain Research, 74*, 24–40.

Diamond, D. M., Campbell, A. M., Park, C. R., Halonen, J., & Zoladz, P. R. (2007). The temporal dynamics model of emotional memory processing: A synthesis on the neurobiological basis of stress-induced amnesia, flashbulb and traumatic memories, and the Yerkes-Dodson Law. *Neural Plasticity*, 60803.

Diamond, L. M. (2004). Emerging perspectives on distinctions between romantic love and sexual desire. *Current Directions in Psychological Science, 13*(3), 116–119. doi:10.1111/j.0963-7214.2004.00287.x

Dickens, W. T., & Flynn, J. R. (2001). Heritability estimates versus large environmental effects: The IQ paradox resolved. *Psychological Review, 108*, 346–369.

Diener, E., & Seligman, M. E. P. (2004). Beyond money: Toward an economy of well-being. *Psychological Science in the Public Interest, 5*, 1–31.

Diener, E., Horwitz, J., & Emmons, R. A. (1985). Happiness of the very wealthy. *Social Indicators, 16*, 263–274.

Diener, E., Ng, W., Harter, J., & Arora, R. (2010). Wealth and happiness across the world: Material prosperity predicts life evaluation, whereas psychosocial prosperity predicts positive feeling. *Journal of Personality and Social Psychology, 99*(1), 52–61. doi:10.1037/a0018066

Diener, E., Suh, E. M., Lucas, R. E., & Smith, H. L. (1999). Subjective well-being: Three decades of progress. *Psychological Bulletin, 125*(2), 276–302. doi:10.1037/0033-2909.125.2.276

Dierks, T., Linden, D. E., Jandl, M., Formisano, E., Goebel, R., Lanfermann, H., et al. (1999). Activation of Heschl's gyrus during auditory hallucinations. *Neuron, 22,* 615–621.

DiGrande, L., Perrin, M. A., Thorpe, L. E., Thalji, L., Murphy, J., Wu, D., et al. (2008). Posttraumatic stress symptoms, PTSD, and risk factors among lower Manhattan residents 2–3 years after the September 11, 2001 terrorist attacks. *Journal of Traumatic Stress, 21*(3), 264–273.

DiLalla, L. F., Kagan, J., & Reznick, J. S. (1994). Genetic etiology of behavioral inhibition among 2-year-old children. *Infant Behavior and Development, 17,* 405–412.

Dion, K., Berscheid, E., & Walster, E. (1972). What is beautiful is good. *Journal of Personality and Social Psychology, 24*(3), 285–290. doi:10.1037/h0033731

Ditzen, B., Schaer, M., Gabriel, B., Bodenmann, G., Ehlert, U., & Heinrichs, M. (2009). Intranasal oxytocin increases positive communication and reduces cortisol levels during couple conflict. *Biological Psychiatry, 65*(9), 728–731.

Dixon, D. P. (2008). Informed consent or institutionalized eugenics? How the medical profession encourages abortion of fetuses with Down syndrome. *Issues in Law and Medicine, 24*(1), 3–59.

Dixon, L., Medoff, D. R., Wohlheiter, K., DiClemente, C., Goldberg, R., Kreyenbuhl, J., et al. (2007). Correlates of severity of smoking among persons with severe mental illness. *American Journal on Addictions, 16*(2), 101–110. doi:10.1080/10550490601184415

Dixon, M., & Sweeney, K. (2000). *The human effect in medicine.* Abingdon, United Kingdom: Radcliffe.

Dolinoy, D. C., Huang, D., & Jirtle, R. L. (2007). Maternal nutrient supplementation counteracts bisphenol A-induced DNA hypomethylation in early development. *Proceedings of the National Academy of Sciences, 104,* 13056–13061.

Doll, R., Peto, R., Boreham, J., & Sutherland, I. (2004). Mortality in relation to smoking: 50 years' observations on male British doctors. *British Medical Journal, 328*(7455), 1519. doi:10.1136/bmj.38142.554479.AE

Domhoff, G. W. (2003). *The scientific study of dreams: Neural networks, cognitive development, and content analysis.* Washington, DC: American Psychological Association.

Dopfel, R. P., Schulmeister, K., & Schernhammer, E. S. (2007). Nutritional and lifestyle correlates of the cancer-protective hormone melatonin. *Cancer Detection and Prevention, 31*(2), 140–148.

Dorries, K. M. (1992). Sex differences in olfaction in mammals. In M. J. S. K. L. Chobor (Ed.), *Science of olfaction* (pp. 355–376). New York, NY: Springer Verlag.

Dovidio, J. F., & Gaertner, S. L. (2005). Color blind or just plain blind? The pernicious nature of contemporary racism. *NonProfit Quarterly.* Retrieved October 7, 2009, from http://www.nonprofitquarterly.org/index.php?option=com_content&view=frontpage&Itemid=1

Downing, P. E., Chan, A. W., Peelen, M. V., Dodds, C. M., & Kanwisher, N. (2006). Domain specificity in visual cortex. *Cerebral Cortex, 16*(10), 1453–1461.

Drewnowski, A. (2010). The Nutrient Rich Foods Index helps to identify healthy, affordable foods. *American Journal of Clinical Nutrition, 91*(4), 1095S–1101. doi:10.3945/ajcn.2010.28450D

Dronkers, N. F., Pinker, S., & Damasio, A. (2000). Language and the aphasias. In E. R. Kandel, J. H. Schwartz, & T. M. Jessell (Eds.), *Principles of neural science* (Vol. 4, pp. 1169–1185). New York: McGraw-Hill.

Druett, J. (2007). *Island of the lost: Shipwrecked at the edge of the world.* Chapel Hill, NC: Algonquin.

Dubernard, J.-M., Owen, E. R., Lanzetta, M., & Hakim, N. (2001). What is happening with hand transplants? *The Lancet, 357,* 1711–1712.

Dubovsky, S. L., & Dubovsky, A. N. (2002). *Concise guide to mood disorders.* Arlington, VA: American Psychiatric Publishing.

Dudai, Y. (2004). The neurobiology of consolidations, or, How stable is the engram? *Annual Review of Psychology, 55,* 51–86.

Dulaney, S., & Fiske, A. P. (1994). Cultural rituals and obsessive-compulsive disorder: Is there a common psychological mechanism? *Ethos, 22*(3), 243–283. doi:10.1525/eth.1994.22.3.02a00010

Duman, R., & Vaidya, V. (1998). Molecular and cellular actions of chronic electroconvulsive seizures. *Journal of ECT, 14,* 181–193.

Dunbar, R. I. M., & Shultz, S. (2007). Evolution in the social brain. *Science, 317*(5843), 1344–1347.

Dutton, D. G., & Aron, A. P. (1974). Some evidence for heightened sexual attraction under conditions of high anxiety. *Journal of Personality and Social Psychology, 30,* 510–517.

Dyson-Hudson, N., & Dyson-Hudson, R. (1999). The social organization of resource exploitation in South Turkana. In M. A. Little & P. W. Leslie (Eds.), *Turkana herders of the dry savanna: Ecology and biobehavioural response of nomads to an uncertain environment.* Oxford, England: Oxford University Press.

Dyson-Hudson, R., & Dyson-Hudson, N. (1995). *South Turkana homicide: A proximate view.* Paper presented at the Human Behavior and Evolution Conference, Santa Barbara, CA. Retrieved from http://www.hbes.com/HBES/abst95.htm#South_Turkana

Eastwick, P. W., & Finkel, E. J. (2008). Sex differences in mate preferences revisited: Do people know what they initially desire in a romantic partner? *Journal of Personality and Social Psychology, 94*(2), 245–264. doi:10.1037/0022-3514.94.2.245

Eastwick, P. W., Eagly, A. H., Finkel, E. J., & Johnson, S. E. (2011). Implicit and explicit preferences for physical attractiveness in a romantic partner: A double dissociation in predictive validity. *Journal of Personality and Social Psychology, 101*(5), 993–1011. doi:10.1037/a0024061

Eberhardt, J. L., Davies, P. G., Purdie-Vaughns, V. J., & Johnson, S. L. (2006). Looking deathworthy: Perceived stereotypicality of Black defendants predicts capital-sentencing outcomes. *Psychological Science, 17,* 383–386.

Eccles, R. (2002). The powerful placebo in cough studies? *Pulmonary Pharmacology and Therapeutics, 15*(3), 303–308.

Eddy, M. B. (1875). *Science and health with key to the scriptures.* North Ft. Myers, FL: Helen Wright Publishing.

Egeland, J. A., & Hostetter, A. M. (1983). Amish study, I: Affective disorders among the Amish. *American Journal of Psychiatry, 140,* 56–61.

Eglinton, E., & Annett, M. (1994). Handedness and dyslexia: A meta-analysis. *Perceptual Motor Skills, 79,* 1611–1616.

Ehlers, C. L. (2007). Variations in ADH and ALDH in Southwest California Indians. *Alcohol Research and Health, 30*(1), 14–17.

Eich, J., Weingartner, H., Stillman, R., & Gillan, J. (1975). State-dependent accessibility of retrieval cues and retention of a categorized list. *Journal of Verbal Learning and Verbal Behavior, 14,* 408–417.

Eichel, S. K. D. (2002). Credentialing: It may not be the cat's meow. Retrieved August 5, 2006, from http://users.snip.net/~drsteve/Articles/Dr_Zoe.htm

Einstein, A. (1945). A testimonial from Professor Einstein (Appendix II). In J. Hadamard (Ed.), *An essay on the psychology of invention in the mathematical field* (pp. 142–143). Princeton, NJ: Princeton University Press.

Eisenberger, N. I. (2011). Social pain: Experiential, neurocognitive, and genetic correlates. In A. Todorov, S. T. Fiske, & D. A. Prentice (Eds.), *Social neuroscience: Toward understanding the underpinnings of the social mind* (pp. 229–248). New York: Oxford University Press.

Eisenberger, N. I., Lieberman, M. D., & Williams, K. D. (2003). Does rejection hurt? An fMRI study of social exclusion. *Science, 302,* 290–292.

Ekman, P. (1996). Why don't we catch liars? *Social Research, 63,* 801–817.

Ekman, P., Davidson, R. J., & Friesen, W. V. (1990). The Duchenne smile: Emotional expression and brain physiology II. *Journal of Personality and Social Psychology, 58*(2), 342–353. doi:10.1037/0022-3514.58.2.342

Ekman, P., Friesen, W. V., & Ellsworth, P. (1972). *Emotion in the human face: Guidelines for research and an integration of findings.* London: Pergamon Press.

El Nasser, H., Overberg, P., & Thomassie, J. (2010). Recession affecting every aspect of American life. Retrieved April 19, 2011, from http://www.usatoday.com/news/nation/census/2010-09-28-census-american-community-survey_N.htm

Elbert, T., Pantev, C., Weinbruch, C., Rockstroh, B., & Taub, E. (1995). Increased cortical representation of the fingers of the left hand in string players. *Science, 270,* 305–307.

Elkind, D. (1967). Egocentrism in adolescence. *Child Development, 38,* 1025–1034.

Elkind, D., & Bowen, R. (1979). Imaginary audience behavior in children and adolescents. *Developmental Psychology, 15*, 38–44.

Eller, A., Abrams, D., Viki, G. T., & Imara, D. A. (2007). When my friend's friend is a police officer: Extended contact, cross-categorisation, and public-police relations of black and white people. *South African Journal of Psychology, 37*(4), 783–802.

Ellis Weismer, S., Lord, C., & Esler, A. (2010). Early language patterns of toddlers on the autism spectrum compared to toddlers with developmental delay. *Journal of Autism and Developmental Disorders, 40*(10), 1259–1273. doi:10.1007/s10803-010-0983-1

Ellis, A. (1975). *A new guide to rational living.* Upper Saddle River, NJ: Prentice Hall.

Ellis, H. C., & Hunt, R. R. (1983). *Fundamentals of human memory and cognition.* Dubuque, IA: William C. Brown.

Ellsworth, P. C. (1991). Some implications of cognitive appraisal theories of emotion. *International Review of Studies on Emotion, 1*, 143–160.

Ellsworth, P. C. (1994). William James and emotion: Is a century of fame worth a century of misunderstanding? *Psychological Review, 101*(2), 222–229.

Elman, C. (2011). The midlife years: Human capital and job mobility. In J. L. Angel, J. R. A. Settersten, & R. Settersten (Eds.), *Handbook of sociology of aging* (pp. 245–261). New York, NY: Springer.

Emery, N. J., Capitanio, J. P., Mason, W. A., Machado, C. J., Mendoza, S. P., & Amaral, D. G. (2001). The effects of bilateral lesions of the amygdala on dyadic social interactions in rhesus monkeys (*Macaca mulatta*). *Behavioral Neuroscience, 115*, 515–544.

Emlen, S. T., & Oring, L. W. (1977). Ecology, sexual selection, and the evolution of mating systems. *Science, 197*, 215–223.

Emmons, R. A., Barrett, J. L., & Schnitker, S. A. (2008). Personality and the capacity for religious and spiritual experience. In O. P. John, R. W. Robins, & L. A. Pervin (Eds.), *Handbook of personality psychology: Theory and research* (3rd ed., pp. 634–653). New York, NY: Guilford Press.

Enard, W., Gehre, S., Hammerschmidt, K., Hölter, S. M., Blass, T., Somel, M., et al. (2009). A humanized version of *FOXP-2* affects cortico-basal ganglia circuits in mice, *Cell, 137*(5), pp. 961–971.

Eng, M. Y., Luczak, S. E., & Wall, T. L. (2007). ALDH2, ADH1B, and ADH1C genotypes in Asians: A literature review. *Alcohol Research and Health, 30*(1), 22–27.

Engel, S. M., & Daniels, J. L. (2011). On the complex relationship between genes and environment in the etiology of autism. *Epidemiology, 22*(4), 486–488. doi:10.1097/EDE.0b013e31821daf1c

Enoch, M. A. (2006). Genetic and environmental influences on the development of alcoholism. *Annals of the New York Academy of Sciences, 1094*(1), 193–201. doi:10.1196/annals.1376.019

Eppig, C., Fincher, C. L., & Thornhill, R. (2010). Parasite prevalence and the worldwide distribution of cognitive ability. *Proceedings of the Royal Society B: Biological Sciences,* *277*(1701), 3801–3808. doi:10.1098/rspb.2010.0973

Erikson, E. H. (1963). *Childhood and society.* New York, NY: Norton.

Erikson, E. H. (1968). *Identity: Youth and crisis.* Oxford, England: Norton.

Erol, R. Y., & Orth, U. (2011). Self-esteem development from age 14 to 30 years: A longitudinal study. *Journal of Personality and Social Psychology* (0022-3514). doi:10.1037/a0024299

Eshel, N., Nelson, E. E., Blair, R. J., Pine, D. S., & Ernst, M. (2007). Neural substrates of choice selection in adults and adolescents: Development of the ventrolateral prefrontal and anterior cingulate cortices. *Neuropsychologia, 45*(6), 1270–1279.

Eskelinen, M. H., & Kivipelto, M. (2010). Caffeine as a protective factor in dementia and Alzheimer's disease. *Journal of Alzheimer's Disease, 20* (Supplement 1), 167–174.

Eslinger, P. J., & Damasio, A. R. (1985). Severe disturbance of higher cognition after bilateral frontal lobe ablation: Patient EVR. *Neurology, 35*, 1731–1741.

Evans, P. D., Anderson, J. R., Vallender, E. J., Gilbert, S. L., Malcom, C. M., Dorus, S., et al. (2004). Adaptive evolution of ASPM, a major determinant of cerebral cortical size in humans. *Human Molecular Genetics, 13*, 489–494.

Evans, P. D., Gilbert, S. L., Mekel-Bobrov, N., Vallender, E. J., Anderson, J. R., Vaez-Azizi, L. M., et al. (2005). Microcephalin, a gene regulating brain size, continues to evolve adaptively in humans. *Science, 309*, 1717–1720.

Exline, J. J., Worthington, E. L., Hill, P., & McCullough, M. E. (2003). Forgiveness and justice: A research agenda for social and personality psychology. *Personality and Social Psychology Review, 7*(4), 337–348. doi:10.1207/s15327957pspr0704_06

Eysenck, H. J. (1967). *The biological basis of personality.* Springfield, IL: Charles C. Thomas.

Fabel, K., & Kempermann, G. (2008). Physical activity and the regulation of neurogenesis in the adult and aging brain. *NeuroMolecular Medicine, 10*(2), 59–66. doi:10.1007/s12017-008-8031-4

Fan, Y.-T., Decety, J., Yang, C.-Y., Liu, J.-L., & Cheng, Y. (2010). Unbroken mirror neurons in autism spectrum disorders. *Journal of Child Psychology and Psychiatry, 51*(9), 981–988. doi:10.1111/j.1469-7610.2010.02269.x

Farley, R. (2000). Counting on the census? Race, group identity, and the evasion of politics. *Population and Development Review, 26*, 606–609.

Faurie, C., & Raymond, M. (2004). Handedness frequency over more than ten thousand years. *Proceedings: Biological Sciences/The Royal Society, 271*(Suppl. 3), S43–45.

Fazel, S., & Danesh, J. (2002). Serious mental disorder in 23000 prisoners: A systematic review of 62 surveys. *The Lancet, 359*(9306), 545–550. doi:10.1016/S0140-6736(02)07740-1

Federman, J. (Ed.). (1998). *National Television Violence Study: Executive summary.* Santa Barbara, CA: Center for Communication and Social Policy, University of California.

Fehr, E., & Rockenbach, B. (2004). Human altruism: Economic, neural, and evolutionary perspectives. *Current Opinion in Neurobiology, 14*, 784–790.

Feinberg, I. (1978). Efference copy and corollary discharge: Implications for thinking and its disorders. *Schizophrenia Bulletin, 4*, 636–640.

Feinstein, J. S., Adolphs, R., Damasio, A., & Tranel, D. (2011). The human amygdala and the induction and experience of fear. *Current Biology : CB, 21*(1), 34–38.

Fejfar, M. C., & Hoyle, R. H. (2000). Effect of private self-awareness on negative affect and self-referent attribution: A quantitative review. *Personality and Social Psychology Review, 4*(2), 132–142.

Feldman, M. B., & Meyer, I. H. (2007). Eating disorders in diverse lesbian, gay, and bisexual populations. *International Journal of Eating Disorders, 40*(3), 218–226.

Feldman, R., Weller, A., Zagoory-Sharon, O., & Levine, A. (2007). Evidence for a neuroendocrinological foundation of human affiliation: Plasma oxytocin levels across pregnancy and the postpartum period predict mother-infant bonding. *Psychological Science, 18*(11), 965–970.

Fergusson, D. M., Horwood, L. J., & Ridder, E. M. (2005). Tests of causal linkages between cannabis use and psychotic symptoms. *Addiction Research and Theory, 100*, 354–366.

Ferrari, J. R. (1991). Self-handicapping by procrastinators: Protecting self-esteem, social-esteem, or both? *Journal of Research in Personality, 25*, 245–261.

Ferrari, P. F., Paukner, A., Ionica, C., & Suomi, S. J. (2009). Reciprocal face-to-face communication between rhesus macaque mothers and their newborn infants. *Current Biology, 19*(20), 1768–1772. doi:10.1016/j.cub.2009.08.055

Ferri, C. P., Prince, M., Brayne, C., Brodaty, H., Fratiglioni, L., Ganguli, M., et al. (2005). Global prevalence of dementia: A Delphi consensus study. *Lancet, 366*(9503), 2112–2117.

Festinger, L. (1950). Informal social communication. *Psychological Review, 57*, 271–282.

Festinger, L. (1954). A theory of social comparison processes. *Human Relations, 7*, 117–140.

Festinger, L. (1957). *A theory of cognitive dissonance.* Stanford, CA: Stanford University Press.

Feusner, J. D., Neziroglu, F., Wilhelm, S., Mancusi, L., & Bohon, C. (2010). What causes BDD? *Psychiatric Annals, 40*(7), 349–355.

Fidler, D. J., Most, D. E., Booth-LaForce, C., & Kelly, J. F. (2008). Emerging social strengths in young children with Down syndrome. *Infants and Young Children, 21*(3), 207–220. doi:10.1097/01.IYC.0000324550.39446.1f

Fink, G. R., Markowitsch, H. J., Reinkemeier, M., Bruckbauer, T., Kessler, J., & Heiss, W. D. (1996). Cerebral representation of one's own past: Neural networks involved in autobiographical memory. *Journal of Neuroscience, 16*, 4275–4282.

Fiorito, G., & Scotto, P. (1992). Observational learning in *Octopus vulgaris. Science, 256*, 545–547.

Fischhoff, B., de Bruin, W. B., Parker, A. M., Millstein, S. G., & Halpern-Felsher, B. L. (2010). Adolescents' perceived risk of dying. *Journal of Adolescent Health, 46*(3), 265–269. doi:10.1016/j.jadohealth.2009.06.026

Fisher, P. A., Van Ryzin, M. J., & Gunnar, M. R. (2011). Mitigating HPA axis dysregulation associated with placement changes in foster care. *Psychoneuroendocrinology, 36*(4), 531–539. doi:10.1016/j.psyneuen.2010.08.007

Fisher, R. P., & Geiselman, R. E. (2010). The cognitive interview method of conducting police interviews: Eliciting extensive information and promoting therapeutic jurisprudence. *International Journal of Law and Psychiatry, 33*(5–6), 321–328. doi:10.1016/j.ijlp.2010.09.004

Fiske, S. T. (1998). Stereotyping, prejudice, and discrimination. In D. T. Gilbert, S. T. Fiske, & G. Lindzey (Eds.), *The handbook of social psychology* (4th ed., Vol. 2, pp. 357–411). New York, NY: McGraw-Hill.

Fiske, S. T., Cuddy, A. J. C., Glick, P., & Xu, J. (2002). A model of (often mixed) stereotype content: Competence and warmth respectively follow from perceived status and competition. *Journal of Personality and Social Psychology, 82*(6), 878–902. doi:10.1037/0022-3514.82.6.878

Flegal, K. M., Carroll, M. D., Ogden, C. L., & Curtin, L. R. (2010). Prevalence and trends in obesity among U.S. adults, 1999–2008. *JAMA: The Journal of the American Medical Association, 303*(3), 235–241. doi:10.1001/jama.2009.2014

Fleischman, J. (2002). *Phineas Gage: A gruesome but true story about brain science.* Boston: Houghton Mifflin.

Flexser, A. J., & Tulving, E. (1978). Retrieval independence in recall and recognition. *Psychological Review, 85,* 153–171.

Flom, R., & Bahrick, L. E. (2007). The development of infant discrimination of affect in multimodal and unimodal stimulation: The role of intersensory redundancy. *Developmental Psychology, 43*(1), 238–252. doi:10.1037/0012-1649.43.1.238

Flynn, J. R. (1984). The mean IQ of Americans: Massive gains 1932 to 1978. *Psychological Bulletin, 91*(1), 29–51.

Flynn, J. R. (1999). Searching for justice: The discovery of IQ gains over time. *American Psychologist, 54,* 5–20.

Flynn, J. R. (2006). Efeito Flynn: Repensando a inteligência e seus efeitos [The Flynn Effect: Rethinking intelligence and what affects it]. In C. Flores-Mendoza & R. Colom (Eds.), *Introdução à Psicologia das Diferenças Individuais* (pp. 387–411). Porto Alegre, Brazil: ArtMed.

Fodor, E. M. (1995). Subclinical manifestations of psychosis-proneness, ego strength, and creativity. *Personality and Individual Differences, 18*(5), 635–642. doi:10.1016/0191-8869(94)00196-y

Fogassi, L., Ferrari, P. F., Gesierich, B., Rozzi, S., Chersi, F., & Rizzolatti, G. (2005). Parietal lobe: From action organization to intention understanding. *Science, 308*(5722), 662–667. doi:10.1126/science.1106138

Food and Drug Administration (FDA). (2002). What can I expect before, during, and after liposuction? Retrieved April 20, 2007, from http://www.fda.gov/cdrh/liposuction/expect.html

Ford, E. S., Bergmann, M. M., Kroger, J., Schienkiewitz, A., Weikert, C., & Boeing, H. (2009). Healthy living is the best revenge: Findings from the European Prospective Investigation into Cancer and Nutrition–Potsdam study. *Archives of Internal Medicine, 169*(15), 1355–1362. doi:10.1001/archinternmed.2009.237

Forer, B. R. (1949). The fallacy of personal validation: A classroom demonstration of gullibility. *The Journal of Abnormal and Social Psychology, 44*(1), 118–123. doi:10.1037/h0059240

Forsyth, D. R., & Kerr, N. A. (1999). *Are adaptive illusions adaptive?* Boston, MA: American Psychological Association.

Forsyth, D. R., & Schlenker, B. R. (1977). Attributing the causes of group performance: Effects of performance quality, task importance, and future testing. *Journal of Personality, 45*(2), 220–236. doi:10.1111/j.1467-6494.1977.tb00148.x

Foulkes, D. (1999). *Children's dreaming and the development of consciousness.* Cambridge, MA: Harvard University Press.

Fournier, J. C., DeRubeis, R. J., Hollon, S. D., Dimidjian, S., Amsterdam, J. D., Shelton, R. C., et al. (2010). Antidepressant drug effects and depression severity. *JAMA: Journal of the American Medical Association, 303*(1), 47–53. doi:10.1001/jama.2009.1943

Foutz, A. S., Mitler, M. N., Cavalli-Storza, G. L., & Dement, W. C. (1979). Genetic factors in canine narcolepsy. *Sleep, 1,* 413–421.

Fox, P. W., Hershberger, S. L., & Bouchard, T. J., Jr. (1996). Genetic and environmental contributions to the acquisition of a motor skill. *Nature, 384*(6607), 356–358.

Fox, R., Aslin, R. N., Shea, S. L., & Dumais, S. T. (1980). Stereopsis in human infants. *Science, 207,* 323–324.

Frances, A. (2010, March 1). It's not too late to save "normal": Psychiatry's latest DSM goes too far in creating new mental disorders. *Los Angeles Times.* Retrieved October 31, 2010, from http://articles.latimes.com/2010/mar/01/opinion/la-oe-frances1-2010mar01

Francis, D., Diorio, J., Liu, D., & Meaney, M. J. (1999). Nongenomic transmission across generations of maternal behavior and stress responses in the rat. *Science, 286*(5442), 1155–1158. doi:10.1126/science.286.5442.1155

Frank, M. G., & Ekman, P. (1993). Not all smiles are created equal: The differences between enjoyment and nonenjoyment smiles. *Humor: International Journal of Humor Research, 6*(1), 9–26.

Franke, B., Neale, B., & Faraone, S. (2009). Genome-wide association studies in ADHD. *Human Genetics, 126*(1), 13–50. doi:10.1007/s00439-009-0663-4

Franken, D. (2002). *Personal strengths, positive psychology, optimum psycho-social lifeskills.* Holland, MI: Wellness Publications.

Freberg, K. J. (2011). Intention to comply with food safety messages in a crisis as a function of message source and message reliability. (Doctoral dissertation). Retrieved August 23, 2011, from http://trace.tennessee.edu/utk_graddiss/970/

Freberg, L. A. (2010). *Discovering biological psychology* (2nd ed.). Belmont, CA: Wadsworth/Cengage Learning.

Frederick, J. Z., Dimitri, A. C., & Andrew, N. M. (2007). Associations between media viewing and language development in children under age 2 years. *Journal of Pediatrics, 151*(4), 364–368.

Fredrickson, B. L. (2001). The role of positive emotions in positive psychology: The broaden-and-build theory of positive emotions. *American Psychologist, 56*(3), 218–226. doi:10.1037/0003-066x.56.3.218

Fredrikson, M., Annas, P., Fischer, H., & Wik, G. (1996). Gender and age differences in the prevalence of specific fears and phobias. *Behaviour Research and Therapy, 34*(1), 33–39. doi:10.1016/0005-7967(95)00048-3

Freedman, D. G. (1964). Smiling in blind infants and the issue of innate vs. acquired. *Journal of Child Psychology and Psychiatry, 47,* 171–184.

Freedman, D. G. (1974). *Human infancy: An evolutionary perspective.* Hillsdale, NJ: Erlbaum.

Freud, S. (1900/1953). Interpretation of dreams. In J. Strachey (Ed.), *The standard edition of the complete psychological works of Sigmund Freud* (Vols. 4 and 5). London: Hogarth Press.

Freud, S. (1909/1976). Analysis of a phobia of a five year old boy. *The Pelican Freud library: Case Histories I* (Vol. 8, pp. 169–306). Harmondsworth, England: Penguin Books.

Freud, S. (1938). *The basic writings of Sigmund Freud.* New York, NY: Modern Library.

Freud, S. (1953). *The standard edition of the complete psychological works of Sigmund Freud.* London: Hogarth Press.

Friedman, J. M., & Halaas, J. L. (1998). Leptin and the regulation of body weight in mammals. *Nature, 395*(6704), 673–770.

Friedman, M., & Rosenman, R. H. (1974). *Type A behavior and your heart.* New York, NY: Knopf.

Frisch, R. E. (1983). Fatness, menarche, and fertility. In S. Golub (Ed.), *Menarche: The transition from girl to woman* (pp. 5–20). Lexington, MA: Lexington Books.

Frischholz, E. J., Lipman, L. S., Braun, B. G., & Sachs, R. G. (1992). Psychopathology, hypnotizability, and dissociation. *American Journal of Psychiatry, 149*(11), 1521–1525.

Frith, U., & Frith, U. (1996). A biological marker for dyslexia. *Nature, 382,* 19–20.

Frost, P. (2006). European hair and eye color. *Evolution and Human Behavior, 27,* 85–103.

Fulkerson, J. A., Story, M., Mellin, A., Leffert, N., Neumark-Sztainer, D., & French, S. A. (2006). Family dinner meal frequency and adolescent development: Relationships with developmental assets and high-risk behaviors. *Journal of Adolescent Health, 39*(3), 337–345.

Funder, D. C. (2009). Persons, behaviors and situations: An agenda for personality psychology in the postwar era. *Journal of Research in Personality, 43*(2), 120–126. doi:10.1016/j.jrp.2008.12.041

Gage, F. (2000). *Neurogenesis in the adult brain and spinal cord.* Paper presented at the Society for Neuroscience, New Orleans, LA.

Gailliot, M. T., Baumeister, R. F., DeWall, C. N., Maner, J. K., Plant, E. A., Tice, D. M., et al. (2007). Self-control relies on glucose as a limited energy source: Willpower is more than a metaphor. *Journal of Personality and Social Psychology, 92*(2), 325

Gais, S., & Born, J. (2004). Declarative memory consolidation: Mechanisms acting during human sleep. *Learning and Memory, 11*(6), 679–685.

Galea, S., Ahern, J., Resnick, H., Kilpatrick, D., Bucuvalas, M., Gold, J., et al. (2002). Psychological sequelae of the September 11 terrorist attacks in New York City. *New England Journal of Medicine, 346*(13), 982–987. doi:10.1056/NEJMsa013404

Gallassi, R., Morreale, A., Montagna, P., Cortelli, P., Avoni, P., Castellani, R., et al. (1996). Fatal familial insomnia: Behavioral and cognitive features. *Neurology, 46,* 935–939.

Gallup Poll News Service. (2005). Three in four Americans believe in paranormal. Retrieved October 28, 2009, from http://home.sandiego.edu/~baber/logic/gallup.html

Gallup, G. G. (1970). Chimpanzees: Self-recognition. *Science, 167,* 86–87.

Gallup, G. G., & Suarez, S. D. (1986). Self-awareness and the emergence of mind in humans and other primates. In J. Suls & A. Greenwald (Eds.), *Psychological perspectives on the self: Vol. 3* (pp. 3–26). Hillsdale, NJ: Erlbaum.

Galovski, T., & Lyons, J. A. (2004). Psychological sequelae of combat violence: A review of the impact of PTSD on the veteran's family and possible interventions. *Aggression and Violent Behavior, 9*(5), 477–501. doi:10.1016/s1359-1789(03)00045-4

Galton, F. (1869). *Hereditary genius.* London: Macmillan and Company.

Galvan, A., Hare, T., Voss, H., Glover, G., & Casey, B. J. (2007). Risk-taking and the adolescent brain: Who is at risk? *Developmental Science, 10*(2), F8–F14. doi:10.1111/j.1467-7687.2006.00579.x

Galvani, A. P., & Slatkin, M. (2003). Evaluating plague and smallpox as historical selective pressures for the CCR5-_32 HIV-resistance allele. *Proceedings of the National Academy of Sciences, 100*(25), 15276–15279.

Galyer, K. T., Conaglen, H. M., Hare, A., & Conaglen, J. V. (1999). The effect of gynecological surgery on sexual desire. *Journal of Sex and Marital Therapy, 25,* 81–88.

Gantt, W. H. (1928). Ivan P. Pavlov: A biographical sketch. In I. P. Pavlov (Ed.), *Lectures on conditioned reflexes* (W. H. Gantt, Trans.) (pp. 11–34). New York: International Universities Press.

Garb, H. N., Wood, J. M., Lilienfeld, S. O., & Nezworski, M. T. (2005). Roots of the Rorschach controversy. *Clinical Psychology Review, 25,* 97–118.

Garcia, J., & Koelling, K. W. (1966). Relation of cue to consequence in avoidance learning. *Psychonomic Science, 4,* 123–124.

Gardner, H. (1976). *The shattered mind: The person after brain damage.* New York: Knopf.

Gardner, H. (1983). *Frames of mind: The theory of multiple intelligences.* New York: Basic Books.

Gardner, H. (1999). *Intelligence reframed: Multiple intelligences for the 21st century.* New York: Basic Books.

Gardner, R. A., & Gardner, B. I. (1969). Teaching sign language to a chimpanzee. *Science, 165,* 664–672.

Gardner, W., Gabriel, S., & Lee, A. Y. (1999). "I" value freedom, but "we" value relationships: Self-construal priming mirrors cultural differences in judgment. *Psychological Science, 10*(4), 321–326.

Garfinkel, P. E., Lin, E., Goering, P., Spegg, C., Goldbloom, D., Kennedy, S., et al. (1996). Should amenorrhoea be necessary for the diagnosis of anorexia nervosa? Evidence from a Canadian community sample. *British Journal of Psychiatry, 168*(4), 500–506. doi:10.1192/bjp.168.4.500

Garmezy, N. (1991). Resilience and vulnerability to adverse developmental outcomes associated with poverty. *American Behavioral Scientist, 34*(4), 416–430. doi:10.1177/0002764291034004003

Gawronski, B. (2004). Theory-based bias correction in dispositional inference: The fundamental attribution error is dead, long live the correspondence bias. *European Review of Social Psychology, 15,* 183–217. doi:10.1080/10463280440000026

Gayan, J., Willcutt, E. G., Fisher, S. E., Francks, C., Cardon, L. R., Olson, R. K., et al. (2005). Bivariate linkage scan for reading disability and attention-deficit/hyperactivity disorder localizes pleiotropic loci. *Journal of Child Psychology and Psychiatry, 46,* 1045–1057.

Gazzaniga, M. S. (1967). The split brain in man. *Scientific American, 217,* 24–29.

Gazzaniga, M. S. (2011). *Who's in charge? Free will and the science of the brain.* New York, NY: Ecco.

Gazzola, V., Aziz-Zadeh, L., & Keysers, C. (2006). Empathy and the somatotopic auditory mirror system in humans. *Current Biology: CB, 16,* 1824–1829. doi:10.1016/j.cub.2006.07.072

Geda, Y. E., Roberts, R. O., Knopman, D. S., Christianson, T. J. H., Pankratz, V. S., Ivnik, R. J., et al. (2010). Physical exercise, aging, and mild cognitive impairment: A population-based study. *Archives of Neurology, 67*(1), 80–86. doi:10.1001/archneurol.2009.297

Geiser, S., & Studley, R. (2001). UC and the SAT: Predictive validity and differential impact of the SAT I and SAT II at the University of California. Retrieved November 1, 2009, from http://www.ucop.edu/sas/research/researchandplanning/pdf/sat_study.pdf

Geller, B., Sun, K., Zimerman, B., Luby, J., Frazier, J., & Williams, M. (1995). Complex and rapid cycling in bipolar children and adolescents: A preliminary study. *Journal of Affective Disorders, 34,* 259–268.

Geuze, E., van Berckel, B. N., Lammertsma, A. A., Boellaard, R., de Kloet, C. S., Vermetten, E., et al. (2008). Reduced GABA$_A$ benzodiazepine receptor binding in veterans with post-traumatic stress disorder. *Molecular Psychiatry, 13*(1), 74–83, 73.

Gevensleben, H., Holl, B., Albrecht, B., Vogel, C., Schlamp, D., Kratz, O., et al. (2009). Is neurofeedback an efficacious treatment for ADHD? A randomised controlled clinical trial. *Journal of Child Psychology and Psychiatry, 50*(7), 780–789. doi:10.1111/j.1469-7610.2008.02033.x

Gibson, M. A. (2008). Does investment in the sexes differ when fathers are absent? Sex-biased infant survival and child growth in rural Ethiopia. *Human Nature, 19*(3), 263–276. doi:10.1007/s12110-008-9044-2

Giesbrecht, T., Lynn, S. J., Lilienfeld, S. O., & Merckelbach, H. (2010). Cognitive processes, trauma, and dissociation—Misconceptions and misrepresentations: Reply to Bremner

(2010). *Psychological Bulletin, 136*(1), 7–11. doi:10.1037/a0018068

Gigerenzer, G. (2008). Why heuristics work. *Perspectives on Psychological Science, 3*(1), 20–29.

Gilbert, D. T., & Jones, E. E. (1986). Perceiver-induced constraint: Interpretations of self-generated reality. *Journal of Personality and Social Psychology, 50,* 269–280.

Gilbert, D. T., & Malone, P. S. (1995). The correspondence bias. *Psychological Bulletin, 117*(1), 21–38.

Gilbertson, M. W., Shenton, M. E., Ciszewski, A., Kasai, K., Lasko, N. B., Orr, S. P., et al. (2002). Smaller hippocampal volume predicts pathologic vulnerability to psychological trauma. *Nature Neuroscience, 5*(11), 1242–1247. doi:10.1038/nn958

Gilger, J. W., Hanebuth, E., Smith, S. D., & Pennington, B. F. (1996). Differential risk for developmental reading disorders in the offspring of compensated versus noncompensated parents. *Reading and Writing, 8*(5), 407–417.

Gillihan, S. J., & Farah, M. J. (2005). Is self special? A critical review of evidence from experimental psychology and cognitive neuroscience. *Psychological Bulletin, 131*(1), 76–97.

Gilovich, T. (1993). *How we know what isn't so: The fallability of human reason in everyday life.* New York: Free Press.

Gilovich, T., Medvec, V. H., & Savitsky, K. (2000). The spotlight effect in social judgment: An egocentric bias in estimates of the salience of one's own actions and appearance. *Journal of Personality and Social Psychology, 78*(2), 211–222.

Gilovich, T., Vallone, R., & Tversky, A. (1985). The hot hand in basketball: On the misperception of random sequences. *Cognitive Psychology, 17,* 295–314.

Glanzer, M., & Cunitz, A. R. (1966). Two storage mechanisms in free recall. *Journal of Verbal Learning and Verbal Behavior, 5,* 351–360.

Gleeson, M. (2007). Immune function in sport and exercise. *Journal of Applied Physiology, 103*(2), 693–699. doi:10.1152/japplphysiol.00008.2007

Gleick, J. (1992). *Genius: The life and science of Richard Feynman.* New York: Pantheon.

Glynn, S. M. (1990). Token economy approaches for psychiatric patients: Progress and pitfalls over 25 years. *Behavior Modification, 14,* 383–407.

Godden, D. R., & Baddeley, A. D. (1975). Context-dependent memory in two natural environments: On land and under water. *British Journal of Psychology, 66,* 325–331.

Goetz, C. G., Leurgans, S., Pappert, E. J., Raman, R., & Stemer, A. B. (2001). Prospective longitudinal assessment of hallucinations in Parkinson's disease. *Neurology, 57,* 2078–2082.

Goff, D. C., & Evins, A. E. (1998). Negative symptoms in schizophrenia: Neurobiological models and treatment response. *Harvard Review of Psychiatry, 6*(2), 59–77. doi:10.3109/10673229809000313

Goldsmith, T. H., & Zimmerman, W. F. (2001). *Biology, evolution, and human nature.* New York, NY: John Wiley.

Goldstein, A. P., Glick, B., & Gibbs, J. C. (1998). *Aggression replacement training: A comprehensive intervention for aggressive youth.* Champaign, IL: Research Press.

Goldstein, D. G., & Gigerenzer, G. (2002). Models of ecological rationality: The recognition heuristic. *Psychological Review, 109,* 75–90.

Goldstein, E. B. (2010). *Sensation and perception* (8th ed.). Belmont, CA: Cengage.

Goleman, D. (2006). *Social intelligence.* New York: Random House.

Gollan, J. K., McCloskey, M., Hoxha, D., & Coccaro, E. F. (2010). How do depressed and healthy adults interpret nuanced facial expressions? *Journal of Abnormal Psychology, 119*(4), 804–810. doi:10.1037/a0020234

Gonzalez-Maeso, J., Ang, R. L., Yuen, T., Chan, P., Weisstaub, N. V., Lopez-Gimenez, J. F., et al. (2008). Identification of a serotonin/glutamate receptor complex implicated in psychosis. *Nature, 452*(7183), 93–97.

Gonzalez-Maeso, J., Weisstaub, N. V., Zhou, M., Chan, P., Ivic, L., Ang, R., et al. (2007). Hallucinogens recruit specific cortical 5-HT(2A) receptor-mediated signaling pathways to affect behavior. *Neuron, 53*(3), 439–452.

Goodall, J. (1971). *In the shadow of man.* Boston: Houghton Mifflin.

Gopnik, A., Capps, L., & Meltzoff, A. N. (2000). Early theories of mind: What the theory can tell us about autism. In S. Baron-Cohen, H. Tager-Flusberg, & D. J. Cohen (Eds.), *Understanding other minds: Perspectives from developmental cognitive neuroscience* (2nd ed., pp. 50–72). New York, NY: Oxford University Press.

Gordon, I., Zagoory-Sharon, O., Schneiderman, I., Leckman, J. F., Weller, A., & Feldman, R. (2008). Oxytocin and cortisol in romantically unattached young adults: Associations with bonding and psychological distress. *Psychophysiology, 45*(3), 349–352.

Gordon, K. C., Baucom, D. H., & Snyder, D. K. (2004). An integrative intervention for promoting recovery from extramarital affairs. *Journal of Marital and Family Therapy, 30,* 213–231.

Gordon, N. (2002). Stuttering: Incidence and causes. *Developmental Medicine and Child Neurology, 44*(4), 278–281.

Gorelick, D. A., & Balster, R. L. (1995). Phencyclidine. In F. E. Bloom & D. J. Kupfer (Eds.), *Psychopharmacology, the fourth generation of progress* (pp. 1767–1776). New York, NY: Raven Press.

Gosling, S. D., Mollaghan, D. M., & Van Lange, P. A. M. (2006). Animal research in social psychology: A bridge to functional genomics and other unique research opportunities. In P. A. M. Van Lange (Ed.), *Bridging social psychology: Benefits of transdisciplinary approaches* (pp. 123–128). Mahwah, NJ: Erlbaum.

Gosselin, N., Peretz, I., Johnson, E., & Adolphs, R. (2007). Amygdala damage impairs emotion recognition from music. *Neuropsychologia, 45*(2), 236–244.

Gottesman, C. (2002). The neurochemistry of waking and sleeping mental activity: The disinhibition-dopamine hypothesis. *Psychiatry and Clinical Neurosciences, 56,* 345–354.

Gottesman, I. I. (1991). *Schizophrenia genesis.* New York, NY: W. H. Freeman.

Gottman, J. (2011). Gottman's relationship tips 101. Retrieved June 29, 2011, from http://www.gottman.com/49804/Self-Help-and-Tips.html

Gottman, J., Swanson, C., & Swanson, K. (2002). A general systems theory of marriage: Nonlinear difference equation modeling of marital interaction. *Personality and Social Psychology Review, 6*(4), 326–340. doi:10.1207/s15327957pspr0604_07

Gouin, J.-P., Carter, C. S., Pournajafi-Nazarloo, H., Glaser, R., Malarkey, W. B., Loving, T. J., et al. (2010). Marital behavior, oxytocin, vasopressin, and wound healing. *Psychoneuroendocrinology, 35*(7), 1082–1090.

Gould, E., Reeves, A. J., Graziano, M. S., & Gross, C. G. (1999). Neurogenesis in the neocortex of adult primates. *Science, 386,* 548–552.

Gouldner, A. (1960). The norm of reciprocity: A preliminary analysis. *American Sociological Review, 25,* 161–178.

Grandin, T. (2010). *Thinking in pictures.* New York: Vintage Books.

Granrud, C. E., Haake, J. J., & Yonas, A. (1985). Infants' sensitivity to familiar size: The effect of memory on spatial perception. *Perception and Psychophysics, 37,* 459–466.

Grant, A. M. (2003). The impact of life coaching on goal attainment, metacognition and mental health. *Social Behavior and Personality, 31,* 253–264.

Gray, J. R., & Thompson, P. M. (2004). Neurobiology of intelligence: Science and ethics. *Nature Reviews Neuroscience, 5,* 471–482.

Gray, P. B., Singh, A. B., Woodhouse, L. J., Storer, T. W., Casaburi, R., Dzekov, J., et al. (2005). Dose-dependent effects of testosterone on sexual function, mood, and visuospatial cognition in older men. *Journal of Clinical Endocrinology and Metabolism, 90*(7), 3838–3846.

Greenberg, J., Pyszczynski, T., & Solomon, S. (1986). The causes and consequences of a need for self-esteem: A terror management theory. In R. F. Baumeister (Ed.), *Public self and private self* (pp. 189–212). New York, NY: Springer-Verlag.

Greene, R. W. (2010). Collaborative problem solving. In R. C. Murrihy, A. D. Kidman, & T. H. Ollendick (Eds.), *Clinical handbook of assessing and treating conduct problems in youth* (pp. 193–220). New York: Springer Science + Business Media.

Greenspoon, J., & Ranyard, R. (1957). Stimulus conditions and retroactive inhibition. *Journal of Experimental Psychology, 53,* 55–59.

Greenwald, A. G. (1980). The totalitarian ego: Fabrication and revision of personal history. *American Psychologist, 35*(7), 603–618.

Greenwald, A. G., & Farnham, S. D. (2000). Using the Implicit Association Test to measure self-esteem and self-concept. *Journal of Personality and Social Psychology, 79,* 1022–1038.

Greenwald, A. G., Spangenberg, E. R., Pratkanis, A. R., & Eskenazi, J. (1991). Double-blind tests of subliminal self-help audiotapes. *Psychological Science, 2,* 119–122.

Gregorian, R. S., Golden, K. A., Bahce, A., Goodman, C., Kwong, W. J., & Khan, Z. M. (2002). Antidepressant-induced sexual dysfunction. *Annals of Pharmacotherapy, 36,* 1577–1589.

Grether, J. K., Anderson, M. C., Croen, L. A., Smith, D., & Windham, G. C. (2009). Risk of autism and increasing maternal and paternal age in a large North American population.

American Journal of Epidemiology, 170(9), 1118–1126. doi:10.1093/aje/kwp247

Grimm, S., Beck, J., Schuepbach, D., Hell, D., Boesiger, P., Bermpohl, F., et al. (2008). Imbalance between left and right dorsolateral prefrontal cortex in major depression is linked to negative emotional judgment: An fMRI study in severe major depressive disorder. *Biological Psychiatry, 64*(4), 369–376. doi:10.1016/j.biopsych.2007.05.033

Grisham, J. R., Anderson, T. M., & Sachdev, P. S. (2008). Genetic and environmental influences on obsessive-compulsive disorder. *European Archives of Psychiatry and Clinical Neuroscience, 258*(2), 107–116.

Grossman, M. (2007). *Unprotected.* New York, NY: Sentinel.

Groth-Marnat, G. (2009). *Handbook of psychological assessment* (5th ed.). New York, NY: Wiley.

Guignard, J.-H., & Lubart, T. (2006). Is it reasonable to be creative? In J. C. Kaufman & J. Baer (Eds.), *Creativity and reason in cognitive development* (pp. 269–281). New York, NY: Cambridge University Press.

Gunter, B. (1994). The question of media violence. In J. Bryant & D. Zillmann (Eds.), *Media effects: Advances in theory and research* (pp. 163–211). Hillsdale, NJ: Lawrence Erlbaum Associates.

Gunzerath, L., Faden, V., Zakhari, S., & Warren, K. (2004). National Institute on Alcohol Abuse and Alcoholism report on moderate drinking. *Alcoholism: Clinical and Experimental Research, 28*(6), 829–847. doi:10.1097/01.alc.0000128382.79375.b6

Guzman-Marin, R., Suntsova, N., Stewart, D. R., Gong, H., Szymusiak, R., & McGinty, D. (2003). Sleep deprivation reduces proliferation of cells in the dentate gyrus of the hippocampus in rats. *Journal of Physiology, 549,* 563–571.

Haber, R. N., & Haber, R. B. (1964). Eidetic imagery: I; Frequency. *Perceptual and Motor Skills, 19,* 131–138.

Haber, S. N., & Barchas, P. R. (1983). The regulatory effect of social rank on behavior after amphetamine administration. In P. R. Barchas (Ed.), *Social hierarchies: Essays toward a sociophysiological perspective* (pp. 119–132). Westport, CT: Greenwood Press.

Haemer, M. A., Huang, T. T., & Daniels, S. R. (2009). The effect of neurohormonal factors, epigenetic factors, and gut microbiota on risk of obesity. *Preventing Chronic Disease, 6*(3), A96.

Haier, R. J. (2009). What does a smart brain look like? *Scientific American Mind,* Nov./Dec., 26–33.

Haier, R. J., Jung, R. E., Yeo, R. A., Head, K., & Alkire, M. T. (2005). The neuroanatomy of general intelligence: Sex matters. *NeuroImage, 25,* 320–327.

Haier, R. J., Siegel, B. V., Nuechterlein, K. H., Hazlett, E., Wu, J. C., Paek, J., et al. (1988). Cortical glucose metabolic rate correlates of abstract reasoning and attention studied with positron emission tomography. *Intelligence, 12*(2), 199–217. doi:10.1016/0160-2896(88)90016-5

Halaas, J. L., Gajiwala, K. S., Maffei, M., Cohen, S. L., Chait, B. T., Rabinowitz, D., et al. (1995). Weight-reducing effects of the plasma protein encoded by the obese gene. *Science, 269,* 543–546.

Hall, C. (1951). What people dream about. *Scientific American, 184,* 60–63.

Hall, C., & Van de Castle, R. (1966). *The content analysis of dreams.* New York, NY: Appleton-Century-Crofts.

Hall, W. D. (2006). How have the SSRI antidepressants affected suicide risk? *Lancet, 367*(9527), 1959–1962. doi:10.1016/s0140-6736(06)68860-0

Halmi, K. A., Casper, R. C., Eckert, E. D., Goldberg, S. C., & Davis, J. M. (1979). Unique features associated with age of onset of anorexia nervosa. *Psychiatry Research, 1*(2), 209–215.

Halpern, D. F., Benbow, C. P., Geary, D. C., Gur, R. C., Hyde, J. S., & Gernsbacher, M. A. (2007). The science of sex differences in science and mathematics. *Psychological Science in the Public Interest, 8*(1), 1–51.

Halpern, J. H., & Pope, H. G., Jr. (2003). Hallucinogen persisting perception disorder: What do we know after 50 years? *Drug and Alcohol Dependence, 69*(2), 109–119.

Halverson, M. S., & Bolnick, D. A. (2008). An ancient DNA test of a founder effect in Native American ABO blood group frequencies. *American Journal of Physical Anthropology, 137*(3), 342–347. doi:10.1002/ajpa.20887

Hamel, M., Shaffer, T. W., & Erdberg, P. (2000). A study of nonpatient preadolescent Rorschach protocols. *Journal of Personality Assessment, 75*(2), 280–294. doi:10.1207/s15327752jpa7502_8

Hamermesh, D. S., & Parker, A. M. (2003). Beauty in the classroom: Professors' pulchritude and putative pedagogical productivity. NBER Working Paper No. w9853. Retrieved August 27, 2006, from http://ssrn.com/abstract=425589

Hamilton, W. D. (1964). The genetical evolution of social behaviour: I and II. *Journal of Theoretical Biology, 7,* 1–16, 17–52.

Hamm, A. O., Weike, A. I., Schupp, H. T., Treig, T., Dressel, A., & Kessler, C. (2003). Affective blindsight: Intact fear conditioning to a visual cue in a cortically blind patient. *Brain, 126*(Pt. 2), 267–275.

Hampson, E. (1990). Estrogen-related variations in human spatial and articulatory-motor skills. *Psychoneuroendocrinology, 15*(2), 97–111.

Hampson, E., & Kimura, D. (1988). Reciprocal effects of hormonal fluctuations on human motor and perceptual-spatial skills. *Behavioral Neuroscience, 102*(3), 456–459.

Hänecke, K., Tiedemann, S., Nachreiner, F., & Grzech-Sukalo, H. (1998). Accident risk as a function of hour at work and time of day as determined from accident data and exposure models for the German working population. *Scandinavian Journal of Work, Environment & Health, 24,* 43–48.

Haney, C., Banks, C., & Zimbardo, P. (1973). Interpersonal dynamics in a simulated prison. *International Journal of Criminology and Penology, 1,* 69–97.

Hansen, J., Winzeler, S., & Topolinski, S. (2010). When the death makes you smoke: A terror management perspective on the effectiveness of cigarette on-pack warnings. *Journal of Experimental Social Psychology, 46*(1), 226–228. doi:10.1016/j.jesp.2009.09.007

Hansford, B. C., & Hattie, J. A. (1982). The relationship between self and achievement/performance measures. *Review of Educational Research, 52,* 123–142.

Hare, R. D. (2002). *The predators among us.* Paper presented at the Canadian Police Association Annual General Meeting, St. John's, Newfoundland and Labrador.

Hare, R. D. (2006). Psychopathy: A clinical and forensic overview. *Psychiatric Clinics of North America, 29*(3), 709–724.

Harley, H. E., Xitco, M. J., Jr., Roitblat, H. L., & Herman, L. M. (1998, June). *Imitation of human models by bottlenose dolphins.* Paper presented at the Napoli Social Learning Conference, Naples, Italy.

Harlow, H. (1958). The nature of love. *American Psychologist, 13,* 573–685.

Harlow, H. F., & Harlow, M. K. (1973). Social deprivation in monkeys. In W. T. Greenough (Ed.), *The nature and nurture of behavior: Readings from* Scientific American (pp. 108–116). San Francisco, CA: Freeman.

Harper, C., & Matsumoto, I. (2005). Ethanol and brain damage. *Current Opinion in Pharmacology, 5*(1), 73–78.

Harper, F. K., Schmidt, J. E., Beacham, A. O., Salsman, J. M., Averill, A. J., Graves, K. D., et al. (2006). The role of social cognitive processing theory and optimism in positive psychosocial and physical behavior change after cancer diagnosis and treatment. *Psychooncology, 16,* 79–91.

Harper, K., Sperry, S., & Thompson, J. K. (2008). Viewership of pro-eating disorder websites: Association with body image and eating disturbances. *International Journal of Eating Disorders, 41*(1), 92–95.

Harris, J. R. (1998). *The nurture assumption: Why children turn out the way they do.* New York, NY: Touchstone.

Hart, A. J., Whalen, P. J., Shin, L. M., McInerney, S. C., Fischer, H., & Rauch, S. L. (2000). Differential response in the human amygdala to racial outgroup vs ingroup face stimuli. *Neuroreport, 11,* 2351–2355.

Harvey, A., Watkins, E., Mansell, W., & Shafran, R. (2004). *Cognitive behavioural processes across psychological disorders.* New York, NY: Oxford University Press.

Haselton, M. G., Bryant, G. A., Wilke, A., Frederick, D. A., Galperin, A., Frankenhuis, W. E., et al. (2009). Adaptive rationality: An evolutionary perspective on cognitive bias. *Social Cognition, 27*(5), 733–763. doi:10.1521/soco.2009.27.5.733

Haselton, M. G., Mortezaie, M., Pillsworth, E. G., Bleske-Rechek, A., & Frederick, D. A. (2006). Ovulatory shifts in human female ornamentation: Near ovulation, women dress to impress. *Hormones and Behavior, 51,* 40–45.

Hasin, D. S., Goodwin, R. D., Stinson, F. S., & Grant, B. F. (2005). Epidemiology of major depressive disorder: Results from the National Epidemiologic Survey on Alcoholism and Related Conditions. *Archives of General Psychiatry, 62,* 1097–1106.

Hathaway, S. R., & McKinley, J. C. (1940). A multiphasic personality schedule (Minnesota): I. Construction of the schedule. *Journal of Psychology, 10,* 249–254.

Hathaway, S. R., & McKinley, J. C. (1943). *The Minnesota Multiphasic Personality Inventory manual.* New York, NY: Psychological Corporation.

Hawkley, L. C., & Cacioppo, J. T. (2010). Loneliness matters: A theoretical and empirical review of consequences and mechanisms. *Annals of Behavioral Medicine, 40*(2), 218–227. doi:10.1007/s12160-010-9210-8

Hawkley, L. C., Masi, C. M., Berry, J. D., & Cacioppo, J. T. (2006). Loneliness is a unique predictor of age-related differences in systolic blood pressure. *Psychology and Aging, 21,* 152–164.

Hawkley, L. C., Thisted, R. A., & Cacioppo, J. T. (2009). Loneliness predicts reduced physical activity: Cross-sectional and longitudinal analyses. *Health Psychology, 28*(3), 354–363.

Hayak, Y., Walker, J. R., Li, C., Wong, W. H., Davis, L., Buxbaum, J. D., et al. (2001). Genome-wide expression analysis reveals disregulation of myelination-related genes in chronic schizophrenia. *Proceedings of the National Academy of Sciences, 48,* 4746–4751.

Haycock, P. C. (2009). Fetal alcohol spectrum disorders: The epigenetic perspective. *Biology of Reproduction, 81*(4), 607–617. doi:10.1095/biolreprod.108.074690

Head, A. J., & Eisenberg, M. B. (2010). How college students evaluate and use information in the digital age. Retrieved on December 4, 2011, from http://projectinfolit.org/pdfs/PIL_Fall2010_Survey_FullReport1.pdf

Heatherton, T. F., Wyland, C. L., Macrae, C. N., Demos, K. E., Denny, B. T., & Kelley, W. M. (2006). Medial prefrontal activity differentiates self from close others. *Social, Cognitive, and Affective Neuroscience, 1*(1), 18–25. doi:10.1093/scan/nsl001

Hecht, D. (2010). Depression and the hyperactive right-hemisphere. *Neuroscience Research, 68*(2), 77–87. doi:10.1016/j.neures.2010.06.013

Hecht, S., Shlaer, S., & Pirenne, M.H. (1942). Energy, quanta, and vision. *Journal of General Physiology, 25,* 819–840.

Heider, F. (1958). *The psychology of interpersonal relations.* New York, NY: Wiley.

Held, B. S. (2004). The negative side of positive psychology. *Journal of Humanistic Psychology, 44*(1), 9–46. doi:10.1177/0022167803259645

Helliwell, J. F. (2003). How's life? Combining individual and national variables to explain subjective well-being. *Economic Modeling, 20,* 331–360.

Helpern, J. A., Adisetiyo, V., Falangola, M. F., Hu, C., Di Martino, A., Williams, K., et al. (2011). Preliminary evidence of altered gray and white matter microstructural development in the frontal lobe of adolescents with attention-deficit hyperactivity disorder: A diffusional kurtosis imaging study. *Journal of Magnetic Resonance Imaging, 33*(1), 17–23. doi:10.1002/jmri.22397

Hembree, E. A., Riggs, D. S., Kozak, M. J., Franklin, M. E., & Foa, E. B. (2003). Cognitive-behavioral therapy for panic disorder: A review of treatment elements, strategies, and outcomes. *CNS Spectrums, 8,* 363–371.

Henkel, L. A., & Mather, M. (2007). Memory attributions for choices: How beliefs shape our memories. *Journal of Memory and Language, 57*(2), 163–176. doi:10.1016/j.jml.2006.08.012

Hennenlotter, A., Schroeder, U., Erhard, P., Haslinger, B., Stahl, R., Weindl, A., et al. (2004). Neural correlates associated with impaired disgust processing in presymptomatic Huntington's disease. *Brain, 127*(6), 1446–1453. doi:10.1093/brain/awh165

Herdt, G. H. (1987). *The Sambia: Ritual and gender in New Guinea.* New York, NY: Holt, Rinehart, and Winston.

Herlitz, J., Wiklund, I., Caidahl, D., Hartford, M., Haglid, M., Karlsson, B. W., et al. (1998). The feeling of loneliness prior to coronary artery bypass grafting might be a predictor of short- and long-term postoperative mortality. *European Journal of Vascular and Endovascular Surgery, 16,* 120–125.

Herndon, J. G. (2010). The grandmother effect: Implications for studies on aging and cognition. *Gerontology, 56*(1), 73–79. doi:10.1159/000236045

Herpertz, S. C., Werth, U., Lukas, G., Qunaibi, M., Schuerkens, A., Kunert, H. J., et al. (2001). Emotion in criminal offenders with psychopathy and borderline personality disorder. *Archives of General Psychiatry, 58,* 737–745.

Herrnstein, R. J. (1979). Acquisition, generalization, and discrimination reversal of a natural concept. *Journal of Experimental Psychology: Animal Behavior Processes, 5,* 116–129.

Herrnstein, R. J., & Boring, E. G. (1965). *A source book in the history of psychology.* Cambridge, MA: Harvard University Press.

Herrnstein, R. J., & de Villiers, P. A. (1980). Fish as a natural category for people and pigeons. In G. H. Bower (Ed.), *The psychology of learning and motivation* (Vol. 14, pp. 59–95). New York: Academic Press.

Herrnstein, R. J., & Heyman, G. M. (1979). Is matching compatible with reinforcement maximization on concurrent variable-interval, variable ratio? *Journal of the Experimental Analysis of Behavior, 31,* 209–223.

Herxheimer, A., & Waterhouse, J. (2003). The prevention and treatment of jet lag. *British Medical Journal, 326,* 296–297.

Herz, R. (2003). The effect of verbal context on olfactory perception. *Journal of Experimental Psychology: General, 132,* 595–606.

Hicks, T. V., Leitenberg, H., Barlow, D. H., Gorman, J. M., Shear, M. K., & Woods, S. W. (2005). Physical, mental, and social catastrophic cognitions as prognostic factors in cognitive-behavioral and pharmacological treatments for panic disorder. *Journal of Consulting and Clinical Psychology, 73*(3), 506–514. doi:10.1037/0022-006x.73.3.506

Hinton, D. E., & Good, B. (Eds.). (2009). *Culture and panic disorder.* Stanford, CA: Stanford University Press.

Hirshkowitz, M., & Moore, C. A. (1996). Sleep-related erectile activity. *Neurological Clinics, 14,* 721–737.

Ho, B.-C., Wassink, T. H., Ziebell, S., & Andreasen, N. C. (2011). Cannabinoid receptor 1 gene polymorphisms and marijuana misuse interactions on white matter and cognitive deficits in schizophrenia. *Schizophrenia Research, 128*(1–3), 66–75. doi:10.1016/j.schres.2011.02.021

Ho, M. Y., & Fung, H. H. (2011). A dynamic process model of forgiveness: A cross-cultural perspective. *Review of General Psychology, 15*(1), 77–84. doi:10.1037/a0022605

Hobson, J. M., & McCarley, R. W. (1977). The brain as a dream state generator: An activation-synthesis hypothesis of the dream process. *American Journal of Psychiatry, 134,* 1335–1348.

Hodgkin, A. L., & Huxley, A. F. (1952). A quantitative description of membrane current and its application to conduction and excitation in nerve. *Journal of Physiology, 117,* 500–544.

Hoebel, B. G., & Teitelbaum, P. (1966). Effects of forcefeeding and starvation on food intake and body weight in a rat with ventromedial hypothalamic lesions. *Journal of Comparative and Physiological Psychology, 61,* 189–193.

Hoebel, B. G., Patten, C. S., Colantuoni, C., & Rada, P. V. (2000, November). *Sugar withdrawal causes symptoms of anxiety and acetylcholine release in the nucleus accumbens.* Paper presented at the Society for Neuroscience, New Orleans, LA.

Hoffman, R. E., Hawkins, K. A., Gueorguieva, R., Boutros, N. N., Rachid, F., Carroll, K., et al. (2003). Transcranial magnetic stimulation of left temporoparietal cortex and medication-resistant auditory hallucinations. *Archives of General Psychiatry, 60,* 49–56.

Hofling, C. K., Brotzman, E., Dalrymple, S., Graves, N., & Pierce, C. M. (1966). An experimental study in nurse-physician relationships. *Journal of Nervous and Mental Disease, 143,* 171–180.

Hofstede, G. (1980). *Culture's consequences.* Beverly Hills, CA: Sage.

Hofstede, G. (1984). The cultural relativity of the quality of life concept. *Academy of Management Review, 9*(3), 389–398.

Holder, M. K. (1999). Influences and constraints on manual asymmetry in wild African primates: Reassessing implications for the evolution of human handedness and brain lateralization. (Unpublished doctoral dissertation.) Rutgers University.

Hollander, E., Liebowitz, M. R., Gorman, J. M., Cohen, B., Fyer, A., & Klein, D. F. (1989). Cortisol and sodium lactate-induced panic. *Archives of General Psychiatry, 46*(2), 135–140. doi:10.1001/archpsyc.1989.01810020037007

Hollon, S. D., Thase, M. E., & Markowitz, J. C. (2002). Treatment and prevention of depression. *Psychological Science in the Public Interest, 3*(2), 39–77. doi:10.1111/1529-1006.00008

Holmes, T. H., & Rahe, R. H. (1967). The social readjustment rating scale. *Journal of Psychosomatic Research, 11,* 213–218.

Holt, L. H., Lotto, A. J., & Kluender, K. R. (1998). Incorporating principles of general learning in theories of language acquisition. In M. Gruber, C. D. Higgins, K. S. Olson, & T. Wysocki (Eds.), *Chicago Linguistic Society: Vol. 34. The panels* (pp. 253–268). Chicago: Chicago Linguistic Society.

Holzgrabe, U., Kapkova, P., Alptuzun, V., Scheiber, J., & Kugelmann, E. (2007). Targeting acetylcholinesterase to treat neurodegeneration. *Expert Opinion on Therapeutic Targets, 11*(2), 161–179. doi:10.1517/14728222.11.2.161

Hopper, K., Harrison, G., Janca, A., & Sartorius, N. (2007). *Recovery from schizophrenia: An international perspective; A report from the WHO Collaborative Project, the international study of schizophrenia.* New York, NY: Oxford University Press.

Horn, J. L., & Hofer, S. M. (1992). Major abilities and development in the adult period. In R. J. Sternberg & C. A. Berg (Eds.), *Intellectual development* (pp. 44–99). Cambridge, England: Cambridge University Press.

Horne, J. (1988). *Why we sleep: The functions of sleep in humans and other mammals.* New York, NY: Oxford University Press.

Horney, K. (1923–1937/1967). *Feminine psychology.* New York, NY: Norton.

Hornsveld, R. H., Nijman, H. L., Hollin, C. R., & Kraaimaat, F. W. (2008). Aggression control therapy for violent forensic psychiatric patients: Method and clinical practice. *International Journal of Offender Therapy and Comparative Criminology, 52*(2), 222–233.

Horwitz, A. V., White, H. R., & Howell-White, S. (1997). Becoming married and mental health: A longitudinal study of a cohort of young adults. *Journal of Marriage and the Family, 58,* 895–907.

Houghton, D. P. (2008). Invading and occupying Iraq: Some insights from political psychology. *Peace and Conflict: Journal of Peace Psychology, 14*(2), 169–192. doi:10.1080/10781910802017297

House, J. S., Landis, K. R., & Umberson, D. (1988). Social relationships and health. *Science, 241,* 540–545.

Howsepian, A. A. (1998). In defense of whole-brain definitions of death. *Linacre Quarterly, 65,* 39–61.

Hoza, B., Waschbusch, D. A., Pelham, W. E., Molina, B. S. G., & Milich, R. (2000). Attention-deficit/hyperactivity disordered and control boys' responses to social success and failure. *Child Development, 71,* 432–447.

Hrdy, S. B. (2005). Comes the child before the man: How cooperative breeding and prolonged postweaning dependence shaped human potential. In B. S. Hewlett & S. E. Lamb (Eds.), *Hunter-gatherer childhoods: Evolutionary, developmental and cultural perspectives* (pp. 65–91). New Brunswick, NJ: Transaction Publishers.

Hsu, L. K. G., Chesler, B. E., & Santhouse, R. (1990). Bulimia nervosa in eleven sets of twins: A clinical report. *International Journal of Eating Disorders, 9,* 275–282.

Hubel, D. H., & Livingstone, M. S. (1987). Segregation of form, color, and stereopsis in primate area 18. *Journal of Neuroscience, 7,* 3378–3415.

Hubel, D. H., & Wiesel, T. N. (1959). Receptive fields of single neurons in the cat's striate cortex. *Journal of Physiology, 148,* 574–591.

Hudson, J., Hiripi, E., Pope, H., & Kessler, R. (2007). The prevalence and correlates of eating disorders in the national comorbidity survey replication. *Biological Psychiatry, 61*(3), 348–358.

Hudspeth, A. (1983). The hair cells of the inner ear. *Scientific American, 248,* 54–64.

Hulka, B. S., & Moorman, P. G. (2002). Breast cancer: Hormones and other risk factors. *Maturitas, 42*(Suppl. 1), S95–S105.

Hull, C. L. (1933). *Hypnosis and suggestibility: An experimental approach.* New York: Appleton Century Crofts.

Hull, C. L. (1943). *Principles of behaviour.* New York, NY: Appleton-Century-Crofts.

Humanoid Robotics Group (n.d.). Cog. Retrieved June 9, 2011, from http://www.ai.mit.edu/projects/humanoid-robotics-group/cog/overview.html

Hunt, H. T. (1989). *The multiplicity of dreams.* New Haven, CT: Yale University Press.

Hunt, J., & Eisenberg, D. (2010). Mental health problems and help-seeking behavior among college students. *Journal of Adolescent Health, 46*(1), 3–10. doi:10.1016/j.jadohealth.2009.08.008

Hunt, M. (2007). Borderline personality disorder across the lifespan. *Journal of Women Aging, 19,* 173–191.

Hupka, R. B., Lenton, A. P., & Hutchison, K. A. (1999). Universal development of emotion categories in natural language. *Journal of Personality and Social Psychology, 77,* 247–278.

Hurlemann, R., Wagner, M., Hawellek, B., Reich, H., Pieperhoff, P., Amunts, K., et al. (2007). Amygdala control of emotion-induced forgetting and remembering: Evidence from Urbach-Wiethe disease. *Neuropsychologia, 45*(5), 877–884. doi:10.1016/j.neuropsychologia.2006.08.027

Husky, M. M., Mazure, C. M., Paliwal, P., & McKee, S. A. (2008). Gender differences in the comorbidity of smoking behavior and major depression. *Drug and Alcohol Dependence, 93*(1–2), 176–179.

Huston, A. C., Anderson, D. R., Wright, J. C., Linebarger, D. L., & Schmitt, K. L. (2001). *Sesame Street* viewers as adolescents: The recontact study. In S. M. Fisch & R. T. Truglio (Eds.), *"G" is for growing: Thirty years of research on children and* Sesame Street. Mahwah, NJ: Lawrence Erlbaum Associates.

Huxley, A. (1954). *The doors of perception.* New York, NY: Harper.

Hyde, J. S. (1984). Children's understanding of sexist language. *Developmental Psychology, 20,* 697–706.

Hystad, S. W., Eid, J., Laberg, J. C., Johnsen, B. H., & Bartone, P. T. (2009). Academic stress and health: Exploring the moderating role of personality hardiness. *Scandinavian Journal of Educational Research, 53*(5), 421–429. doi:10.1080/00313830903180349

Iacoboni, M., & Dapretto, M. (2006). The mirror neuron system and the consequences of its dysfunction. *Nature Reviews Neuroscience, 7*(12), 942–951.

Iacoboni, M., & Mazziotta, J. C. (2007). Mirror neuron system: Basic findings and clinical applications. *Annals of Neurology, 62*(3), 213–218.

Iervolino, A. C., Pike, A., Manke, B., Reiss, D., Hetherington, E. M., & Plomin, R. (2002). Genetic and environmental influences in adolescent peer socialization: Evidence from two genetically sensitive designs. *Child Development, 73*(1), 162–174.

Inoue, M., Koyanagi, T., Nakahara, H., Hara, K., Hori, E., & Nakano, H. (1986). Functional development of human eye movement in utero assessed quantitatively with real-time ultrasound. *American Journal of Obstetrics and Gynecology, 155,* 170–174.

Insel, T. R. (2007). Post-traumatic stress disorder research at the National Institute of Mental Health. Retrieved July 18, 2007, from http://www.hhs.gov/asl/testify/2007/05/t20070524a.html

Institute of Medicine (IOM). (1994). *Growing up tobacco free: Preventing nicotine addiction in children and youths.* Washington, DC: National Academy Press.

International Coach Federation (ICF). (2006). What is a coach? Retrieved August 22, 2006, from http://www.coachfederation.org/ICF/For+Coaching+Clients/What+is+a+Coach/

International Society for the Study of Dissociation. (2005). Guidelines for treating dissociative identity disorder in adults. *Journal of Trauma and Dissociation, 6,* 69–149.

Inui, A., Asakawa, A., Bowers, C. Y., Mantovani, G., Laviano, A., Meguid, M. M., et al. (2004). Ghrelin, appetite, and gastric motility: The emerging role of the stomach as an endocrine organ. *FASEB Journal, 18*(3), 439–456.

Isen, A. M., Daubman, K. A., & Nowicki, G. P. (1987). Positive affect facilitates creative problem solving. *Journal of Personality and Social Psychology, 52*(6), 1122–1131. doi:10.1037/0022-3514.52.6.1122

Ishunina, T. A., & Swaab, D. F. (1999). Vasopressin and oxytocin neurons of the human supraoptic and paraventricular nucleus: Size changes in relation to age and sex. *Journal of Clinical Endocrinology and Metabolism, 84*(12), 4637–4644. doi:10.1210/jc.84.12.4637

Ito, T. A., & Urland, G. R. (2003). The influence of processing objectives on the perception of faces: An ERP study of race and gender perception. *Cognitive, Affective, and Behavioral Neuroscience, 5,* 21–36.

Ito, T. A., Chiao, K. W., Devine, P. G., Lorig, T. S., & Cacioppo, J. T. (2006). The influence of facial feedback on race bias. *Psychological Science, 17,* 256–261.

Ittleson, W. H. (1952). *The Ames demonstrations in perception.* Princeton, NJ: Princeton University Press.

Iveson, C. (2002). Solution-focused brief therapy. *Advances in Psychiatric Treatment, 8,* 149–156.

Jabbi, M., Swart, M., & Keysers, C. (2007). Empathy for positive and negative emotions in the gustatory cortex. *NeuroImage, 34*(4), 1744–1753. doi:10.1016/j.neuroimage.2006.10.032

Jackson, B., Kubzansky, L. D., Cohen, S., Jacobs, D. R., Jr., & Wright, R. J. (2007). Does harboring hostility hurt? Associations between hostility and pulmonary function in the Coronary Artery Risk Development in (Young) Adults (CARDIA) study. *Health Psychology, 26*(3), 333–340.

Jackson, J. H. (1884). The Croonian lectures of evolution and dissolution of the nervous system. Lecture 1. *British Medical Journal, 1,* 591–593.

Jakupcak, M., Tull, M. T., McDermott, M. J., Kaysen, D., Hunt, S., & Simpson, T. (2010). PTSD symptom clusters in relationship to alcohol misuse among Iraq and Afghanistan war veterans seeking post-deployment VA health care. *Addictive Behaviors, 35*(9), 840–843. doi:10.1016/j.addbeh.2010.03.023

James, D., & Drakich, J. (1993). Understanding gender differences in amount of talk: A critical review of research. In D. Tannen (Ed.), *Gender and conversational interaction* (pp. 281–312). New York, NY: Oxford University Press.

James, W. (1884). What is an emotion? *Mind, 9,* 188–205.

James, W. (1887). What is an instinct? *Scribner's Magazine, 1,* 355–365.

James, W. (1890). *Principles of psychology.* New York, NY: Henry Holt.

James, W. (1905). *The varieties of religious experience: A study in human nature.* New York, NY: Longmans, Green.

James, W. H. (2006). Two hypotheses on the causes of male homosexuality and paedophilia. [Review]. *Journal of Biosocial Science, 38*(6), 745–761.

Jamison, K. R. (1993). *Touched with fire: Manic-depressive illness and the artistic temperament.* New York, NY: Free Press.

Jamison, K. R. (1995). Manic-depressive illness and creativity. *Scientific American, 272,* 62–67.

Jäncke, L., & Kaufmann, N. (1994). Facial EMG responses to odors in solitude and with an audience. *Chemical Senses, 19,* 99–111.

Janik, V. M., Sayigh, L. S., & Wells, R. S. (2006). Signature whistle shape conveys identity information to bottlenose dolphins. *Proceedings of the National Academy of Sciences, 103,* 8293–8297.

Janis, I. (1971). Groupthink. *Psychology Today, 5,* 43–46, 74–76.

Jansen, K. L. R. (1996). Using ketamine to induce the near-death experience: Mechanism of action and therapeutic potential. In C. Ratsch & J. R. Baker (Eds.), *Yearbook for Ethnomedicine and the Study of Consciousness (Jahrbuch für Ethnomedizin und Bewubtseinsforschung)* (pp. 55–81). Berlin, Germany: VWB Verlag.

Jaques, E. (1965). Death and the midlife crisis. *International Journal of Psychoanalysis, 46,* 502–514.

Jensen, R., & Burgess, H. (1997). Mythmaking: How introductory psychology texts present B. F. Skinner's analysis of cognition. *Psychological Record, 47*(2), 221–232.

Jepson, B., Granpeesheh, D., Tarbox, J., Olive, M., Stott, C., Braud, S., et al. (2010). Controlled evaluation of the effects of hyperbaric oxygen therapy on the behavior of 16 children with autism spectrum disorders. *Journal of Autism and Developmental Disorders, 41*(5), 575–588. doi:10.1007/s10803-010-1075-y

Jepson, T., Ernst, M. E., & Kelly, M. W. (1999). Perspectives on the management of seasonal affective disorder. *Journal of the American Pharmaceutical Association, 39*(6), 822–829.

Jodee. (2010). Prothinspo. Retrieved April 28, 2010, from http://www.prothinspo.com/pro-anatipsandtricksindexpage.html

Johns, M. W. (1991). A new method for measuring daytime sleepiness: The Epworth sleepiness scale. *Sleep, 14*(6), 540–545.

Johnson, J. A. (2009). Wrong and right questions about persons and situations. *Journal of Research in Personality, 43*(2), 251–252. doi:10.1016/j.jrp.2008.12.022

Johnson, M. K., Hashtroudi, S., & Lindsay, D. S. (1993). Source monitoring. *Psychological Bulletin, 114,* 3–28.

Johnson, P. L., Truitt, W., Fitz, S. D., Minick, P. E., Dietrich, A., Sanghani, S., et al. (2010). A key role for orexin in panic anxiety. *Nature Medicine, 16*(1), 111–115. doi:10.1038/nm.2075

Johnson, S. P., & Aslin, R. N. (1995). Perception of object unity in 2-month-old infants. *Developmental Psychology, 31,* 739–745.

Johnson, W. G., Tsoh, J. Y., & Vanrado, P. J. (1996). Eating disorders: Efficacy of pharmacological and psychological interventions. *Clinical Psychology Review, 16,* 457–478.

Johnston, L. D., O'Malley, P. M., Bachman, J. G., & Schulenberg, J. E. (2011). *Monitoring the future: National survey results on drug use, 1975–2010; Volume I: Secondary school students.* Ann Arbor, MI: Institute for Social Research, The University of Michigan.

Jones, E. E., & Nisbett, R. E. (1972). The actor and the observer: Divergent perceptions of the causes of the behavior. In E. E. Jones, D. E. Kanouse, H. H. Kelley, R. E. Nisbett, S. Valins, & B. Weiner (Eds.), *Attribution: Perceiving the causes of behavior* (pp. 79–94). Morristown, NJ: General Learning Press.

Jones, E. E., Rhodewalt, F., Berglas, S., & Skelton, J. A. (1981). Effects of strategic self-presentation on subsequent self-esteem. *Journal of Personality and Social Psychology, 41,* 407–421.

Jones, I. H., & Barraclough, B. M. (1978). Automutilation in animals and its relevance to self-injury in man. *Acta Psychiatrica Scandinavica, 58*(1), 40–47. doi:10.1111/j.1600-0447.1978.tb06918.x

Jones, M. C. (1924). The elimination of children's fears. *Journal of Experimental Psychology, 7,* 382–390.

Jost, J. T., Glaser, J., Kruglanski, A. W., & Sulloway, F. J. (2003). Political conservatism as motivated social cognition. *Psychological Bulletin, 129*(3), 339–375. doi:10.1037/0033-2909.129.3.339

Joyner, K., & Kao, G. (2005). Interracial relationships and the transition to adulthood. *American Sociological Review, 70,* 563–581.

Judge, T. A., Livingston, B. A., & Hurst, C. (2012). Do nice guys—and gals—really finish last? The joint effects of sex and agreeableness on income. *Journal of Personality and Social Psychology, 102*(2), 390–407. doi:10.1037/a0026021

Julesz, B. (1971). *Foundations of cyclopean perception.* Chicago: University of Chicago Press.

Jung, C. G. (1928). *Contributions to analytical psychology.* New York, NY: Harcourt Brace Jovanovich.

Juster, R.-P., McEwen, B. S., & Lupien, S. J. (2010). Allostatic load biomarkers of chronic stress and impact on health and cognition. *Neuroscience and Biobehavioral Reviews, 35*(1), 2–16. doi:10.1016/j.neubiorev.2009.10.002

Juvonen, J. (2005). Myths and facts about bullying in schools. *Behavioral Health Management, 25,* 36–40.

Kagan, J. (1997). Temperament and the reactions to unfamiliarity. *Child Development, 68,* 139–143.

Kagan, J., Kearsley, R. B., & Zelazo, P. R. (1978). *Infancy: Its place in human development.* Cambridge, MA: Harvard University Press.

Kail, R. V., & Cavanaugh, J. C. (2010). *Human Development: A Life-Span View,* 5th ed. (p. 93). Belmont, CA: Wadsworth, Cengage Learning.

Kail, R., & Bisanz, J. (1992). The information-processing perspective on cognitive development in childhood and adolescence. In R. J. Sternberg & C. A. Berg (Eds.), *Intellectual development* (pp. 229–260). New York, NY: Cambridge University Press.

Kamin, L. J. (1968). "Attention-like" processes in classical conditioning. In M. R. Jones (Ed.), *Miami symposium on the prediction of behavior: Aversive stimulation* (pp. 9–31). Miami, FL: University of Miami Press.

Kamin, L. J. (1969). Predictability, surprise, attention, and conditioning. In B. A. Campbell & R. M. Church (Eds.), *Punishment and aversive behavior* (pp. 279–296). New York: Appleton-Century-Crofts.

Kandel, D. B. (1978). Similarity in real-life adolescent friendship pairs. *Journal of Personality and Social Psychology, 36,* 306–312.

Kandel, E. R., & Wurtz, R. H. (2000). Constructing the visual image. In E. R. Kandel, J. H. Schwartz & T. M. Jessell (Eds.), *Principles of neural science* (4th ed., pp. 492–506). New York, NY: McGraw-Hill.

Kane, J. M., & Freeman, H. L. (1994). Towards more effective antipsychotic treatment. *British Journal of Psychiatry 165,* Supplement 25, 22–31. doi:10.1192/bjp.165.1.22

Kaneda, M., & Osaka, N. (2008). Role of anterior cingulate cortex during semantic coding in verbal working memory. *Neuroscience Letters, 436*(1), 57–61. doi:10.1016/j.neulet.2008.02.069

Kang, C., Riazuddin, S., Mundorff, J., Krasnewich, D., Friedman, P., Mullikin, J. C., et al. (2010). Mutations in the lysosomal enzyme–targeting pathway and persistent stuttering. *New England Journal of Medicine, 362*(8), 677–685. doi:10.1056/NEJMoa0902630

Kaniasty, K., & Norris, F. H. (2008). Longitudinal linkages between perceived social support and posttraumatic stress symptoms: Sequential roles of social causation and social selection. *Journal of Traumatic Stress, 21,* 274–281.

Kanner, A. D., Coyne, J. C., Schaefer, C., & Lazarus, R. S. (1981). Comparison of two modes of stress measurement: Daily hassles and uplifts versus major life events. *Journal of Behavioral Medicine, 4,* 1–39.

Kant, I. (1798/1978). *Anthropology from a pragmatic point of view* (V. L. Dodwell, Trans.). Carbondale, IL: Southern Illinois University Press.

Kaplan, H., & Dove, H. (1987). Infant development among the Ache of Eastern Paraguay. *Developmental Psychology, 23,* 190–198.

Kaplan, R. M., & Kronick, R. G. (2006). Marital status and longevity in the United States population. *Journal of Epidemiology and Community Health, 60*(9), 760–765.

Kaplan, R. M., & Saccuzzo, D. P. (2001). *Psychological testing: Principles, applications, and issues* (5th ed.). Belmont, CA: Wadsworth/Thomson Learning.

Karau, S. J., & Williams, K. D. (1993). Social loafing: A meta-analytic review and theoretical integration. *Journal of Personality and Social Psychology, 65,* 681–706.

Karraker, A., DeLamater, J., & Schwartz, C. R. (2011). Sexual frequency decline from midlife to later life. *Journals of Gerontology: Series B. Psychological Sciences and Social Sciences, 66B*(4), 502–512. doi:10.1093/geronb/gbr058

Kasai, K., Yamasue, H., Gilbertson, M. W., Shenton, M. E., Rauch, S. L., & Pitman, R. K. (2008). Evidence for acquired pregenual anterior cingulate gray matter loss from a twin study of combat-related posttraumatic stress disorder. *Biological Psychiatry, 63*(6), 550–556. doi:10.1016/j.biopsych.2007.06.022

Kasper, S., & Wehr, T. A. (1992). The role of sleep and wakefulness in the genesis of depression and mania. *L'Encephale, 18,* 45–50.

Katzenberg, D., Young, T., Finn, L., Lin, L., & Mignot, E. (1998). A CLOCK polymorphism associated with human diurnal preference. *Sleep, 21,* 569–576.

Katzmarzyk, P. T., Church, T. S., Craig, C. L., & Bouchard, C. (2009). Sitting time and mortality from all causes, cardiovascular disease, and cancer. *Medicine and Science in Sports and Exercise, 41*(5), 998–1005 doi:10.1249/MSS.0b013e3181930355

Kavé, G., Eyal, N., Shorek, A., & Cohen-Mansfield, J. (2008). Multilingualism and cognitive state in the oldest old. *Psychology and Aging, 23*(1), 70–78. doi:10.1037/0882-7974.23.1.70

Kawashima, R., Okita, K., Yamazaki, R., Tajima, N., Yoshida, H., Taira, M., et al. (2005). Reading aloud and arithmetic calculation improve frontal function of people with dementia. *Journals of Gerontology: Series A. Biological Sciences and Medical Sciences, 60*(3), 380–384.

Kearney, C. A., & Trull, T. J. (2012). *Abnormal psychology and life: A dimensional approach.* Belmont, CA: Wadsworth/Cengage Learning.

Kearney, C. A., Albano, A. M., Eisen, A. R., Allan, W. D., & Barlow, D. H. (1997). The phenomenology of panic disorder in youngsters: An empirical study of a clinical sample. *Journal of Anxiety Disorders, 11,* 49–62.

Kearns, D. N., Weiss, S. J., Schindler, C. W., & Panlilio, L. V. (2005). Conditioned inhibition of cocaine seeking in rats. *Journal of Experimental Psychology: Animal Behavior Processes, 31,* 247–253.

Keenan, J. P., Nelson, A., O'Connor, M., & Pascual-Leone, A. (2001). Self-recognition and the right hemisphere. *Nature, 409*(6818), 305.

Keith, S. J., Regier, D. A., & Rae, D. S. (1991). Schizophrenic disorders. In L. N. Robins & D. A. Regier (Eds.), *Psychiatric disorders in America* (pp. 33–52). New York, NY: Free Press.

Kellogg, W. N., & Kellogg, L. A. (1933). *The ape and the child.* New York: McGraw-Hill.

Kelly, T. L., Neri, D. F., Grill, J. T., Ryman, D., Hunt, P. D., Dijk, D. J., et al. (1999). Nonentrained circadian rhythms of melatonin in submariners scheduled to an 18-hour day. *Journal of Biological Rhythms, 14,* 190–196.

Keltner, D., & Ekman, P. (2000). Facial expression of emotion. In M. Lewis & J. M. Haviland-Jones (Eds.), *Handbook of emotions* (2nd ed., pp. 236–250). New York, NY: Guilford Press.

Kendall-Tackett, K., & Hale, T. W. (2010). The use of antidepressants in pregnant and breastfeeding women: A review of recent studies. *Journal of Human Lactation, 26*(2), 187–195.

Kendler, K. S., Walters, E. E., Neale, M. C., Kessler, R. C., Heath, A. C., & Eaves, L. J. (1995). The structure of the genetic and environmental risk factors for six major psychiatric disorders in women: Phobia, generalized anxiety disorder, panic disorder, bulimia, major depression, and alcoholism. *Archives of General Psychiatry, 52*(5), 374–383. doi:10.1001/archpsyc.1995.03950170048007

Kennedy, G. C. (1953). The role of depot fat in the hypothalamic control of food intake in the rat. *Proceedings of the Royal Society of London B, 140,* 578–592.

Kenrick, D. T., Griskevicius, V., Neuberg, S. L., & Schaller, M. (2010). Renovating the pyramid of needs: Contemporary extensions built upon ancient foundations. *Perspectives on Psychological Science, 5*(3), 292–314. doi:10.1177/1745691610369469

Kessler, R. C., Adler, L. A., Barkley, R., Biederman, J., Conners, C. K., Greenhill, L. L., et al. (2011). The prevalence and correlates of adult ADHD. In J. K. Buitelaar, C. C. Kan, & P. Asherson (Eds.), *ADHD in adults: Characterization, diagnosis, and treatment* (pp. 9–17). Cambridge: Cambridge University Press.

Kessler, R. C., Angermeyer, M., Anthony, J. C., De Graaf, R., Demyttenaere, K., Gasquet, I., et al. (2007). Lifetime prevalence and age-of-onset distributions of mental disorders in the World Health Organization's World Mental Health Survey Initiative. *World Psychiatry, 6*(3), 168–176.

Kessler, R. C., Berglund, P., Demler, O., Jin, R., Koretz, D., Merikangas, K. R., et al. (2003). The epidemiology of major depressive disorder: Results from the National Comorbidity Survey Replication (NCS-R). *JAMA: Journal of the American Medical Association, 289*(23), 3095–3105.

Kessler, R. C., Chiu, W. T., Demler, O., & Walters, E. E. (2005). Prevalence, severity, and comorbidity of twelve-month DSM-IV disorders in the National Comorbidity Survey Replication (NCS-R). *Archives of General Psychiatry, 62,* 617–627.

Kessler, R. C., Sonnega, A., Bromet, E., Hughes, M., & Nelson, C. B. (1996). Posttraumatic stress disorder in the National Comorbidity Survey. *Archives of General Psychiatry, 52,* 1048–1060.

Kety, S. S., Rosenthal, D., Wender, P. H., & Schulsinger, F. (1968). The types and prevalence of mental illness in the biological and adoptive families of adopted schizophrenics. In D.

Rosenthal & S. S. Kety (Eds.), *The transmission of schizophrenia* (pp. 345–362). Oxford, England: Pergamon Press.

Keys, A., Brozek, J., Henschel, A., Mickelsen, O., & Taylor, H. L. (1950). *The biology of human starvation.* Minneapolis, MN: University of Minnesota Press.

Keysers, C., & Gazzola, V. (2010). Social neuroscience: Mirror neurons recorded in humans. *Current Biology: CB, 20*(8), R353–R354.

Khaw, K.-T., Wareham, N., Bingham, S., Welch, A., Luben, R., & Day, N. (2008). Combined impact of health behaviours and mortality in men and women: The EPIC-Norfolk prospective population study. *PLoS Medicine, 5*(1), e12.

Kiang, L., Witkow, M. R., Baldelomar, O. A., & Fuligni, A. J. (2010). Change in ethnic identity across the high school years among adolescents with Latin American, Asian, and European backgrounds. *Journal of Youth and Adolescence, 39*(6), 683–693. doi:10.1007/s10964-009-9429-5

Kiehl, K. A., Smith, A. M., Hare, R. D., Mendrek, A., Forster, B. B., Brink, J., et al. (2001). Limbic abnormalities in affective processing by criminal psychopaths as revealed by functional magnetic resonance imaging. *Biological Psychiatry, 50*(9), 677–684.

Kieseppä, T., Partonen, T., Haukka, J., Kaprio, J., & Lönnqvist, J. (2004). High concordance of bipolar I disorder in a nationwide sample of twins. *American Journal of Psychiatry, 161*(10), 1814–1821.

Kihlstrom, J. F. (1997). Hypnosis, memory, and amnesia. *Philosophical Transactions of the Royal Society: Biological Sciences, 372.* Retrieved from http://socrates.berkeley.edu/~kihlstrm/hypnosis_memory.htm

Kihlstrom, J. F., & Barnhardt, T. M. (1993). The self-regulation of memory, for better and for worse, with and without hypnosis. In D. M. Wegner & J. W. Pennebaker (Eds.), *Handbook of mental control* (pp. 88–125). Englewood Cliffs, NJ: Prentice-Hall.

Kihlstrom, J. F., & Eich, E. (1994). Altering states of consciousness. In D. Druckman & R. A. Bjork (Eds.), *Learning, remembering, and believing: Enhancing performance* (pp. 207–248). Washington, DC: National Academy Press.

Kikkert, M. A., Ribbers, G. M., & Koudstaal, P. J. (2006). Alien hand syndrome in stroke: A report of 2 cases and review of the literature. *Archives of Physical Medicine and Rehabilitation, 87*(5), 728–732.

Kikuchi, M., Yamada, K., Toyota, T., Itokawa, M., Hattori, E., Yoshitsugu, K., et al. (2003). Two-step association analyses of the chromosome 18p11.2 region in schizophrenia detect a locus encompassing C18orf1. *Molecular Psychiatry, 8*(5), 467–469. doi:10.1038/sj.mp.4001280

Kilham, W., & Mann, L. (1974). Level of destructive obedience as a function of transmitter and executant roles in the Milgram obedience paradigm. *Journal of Personality and Social Psychology, 29,* 696–702.

Kim, H., & Markus, H. R. (1999). Deviance or uniqueness, harmony or conformity? A cultural analysis. *Journal of Personality and Social Psychology, 77,* 785–800.

Kim, K. H., Relkin, N. R., Lee, K. M., & Hirsch, J. (1998). Distinct cortical areas associated with native and second languages. *Nature, 388,* 171–174.

King, P. M., & Kitchener, K. S. (2002). The reflective judgment model: Twenty years of research on epistemic cognition. In B. K. Hofer & P. R. Pintrich (Eds.), *Personal epistemology: The psychology of beliefs about knowledge and knowing* (pp. 37–61). Mahwah, NJ: Erlbaum.

King-Casas, B., Sharp, C., Lomax-Bream, L., Lohrenz, T., Fonagy, P., & Montague, P. R. (2008). The rupture and repair of cooperation in borderline personality disorder. *Science, 321*(5890), 806–810.

Kirk, K. M., Bailey, J. M., & Martin, N. G. (2000). Etiology of male sexual orientation in an Australian twin sample. *Psychology, Evolution and Gender, 2*(3), 301–311.

Kirsch, I., & Lynn, S. J. (1995). The altered state of hypnosis: Changes in the theoretical landscape. *American Psychologist, 50,* 846–858.

Klauke, B., Deckert, J., Reif, A., Pauli, P., & Domschke, K. (2010). Life events in panic disorder—An update on "candidate stressors." *Depression and Anxiety, 27*(8), 716–730.

Klein, S. B., Cosmides, L., & Tooby, J. (2002). Decisions and the evolution of memory: Multiple systems, multiple functions. *Psychological Review, 109,* 306–329.

Kleinmuntz, B., & Szucko, J. J. (1984). A field study of the fallibility of polygraph lie detection. *Nature, 308,* 449–450.

Klima, E. S., & Bellugi, U. (1979). *The signs of language.* Cambridge, MA: Harvard University Press.

Kline, P. (1981). *Fact and fantasy in Freudian theory* (2nd ed.). London, England: Methuen.

Kling, K. C., Hyde, J. S., Showers, C. J., & Buswell, B. N. (1999). Gender differences in self-esteem: A meta-analysis. *Psychological Bulletin, 125,* 470–500.

Kloner, R. A., & Rezkalla, S. H. (2007). To drink or not to drink? That is the question. *Circulation, 116*(11), 1306–1317.

Klonsky, E. D. (2007). The functions of deliberate self-injury: A review of the evidence. *Clinical Psychological Review, 27,* 226–239.

Klonsky, E. D., & Muehlenkamp, J. J. (2007). Self-injury: A research review for the practitioner. *Journal of Clinical Psychology, 63*(11), 1045–1056.

Klüver, H., & Bucy, P. (1939). Preliminary analysis of functions of the temporal lobe in monkeys. *Archives of Neurology and Psychiatry, 42,* 979–1000.

Knickmeyer, R., Baron-Cohen, S., Raggatt, P., & Taylor, K. (2005). Foetal testosterone, social relationships, and restricted interests in children. *Journal of Child Psychology and Psychiatry, and Allied Disciplines, 46*(2), 198–210.

Knight, D. C., Nguyen, H. T., & Bandettini, P. A. (2003). Expression of conditional fear with and without awareness. *Proceedings of the National Academy of Sciences, 100*(25), 15280–15283.

Knowlton, B. J., Squire, L. R., Paulsen, J. S., Swerdlow, N. R., Swenson, M., & Butters, N. (1996). Dissociations within nondeclarative memory in Huntington's disease. *Neuropsychology, 10*(4), 538–548.

Kochanek, K. D., Xu, J., Murphy, S. L., Miniño, A. M., & Kung, H.-C. (2011, March 16). Deaths: Preliminary data from 2009. *National Vital Statistics Reports, 59*(4), 5. Retrieved from http://www.cdc.gov/nchs/data/nvsr/nvsr59/nvsr59_04.pdf

Koeda, T., Seki, A., Uchiyama, H., & Sadato, N. (2011). Dyslexia: Advances in clinical and imaging studies. *Brain and Development, 33*(3), 268–275. doi:10.1016/j.braindev.2010.11.006

Koelega, H. S., & Koster, E. P. (1974). Some experiments on sex differences in odor perception. *Annals of the New York Academy of Sciences, 237*, 234–246.

Koenigsberg, H. W., Teicher, M. H., Mitropoulou, V., Navalta, C., New, A. S., Trestman, R., et al. (2004). 24-h monitoring of plasma norepinephrine, MHPG, cortisol, growth hormone and prolactin in depression. *Journal of Psychiatric Research, 38*(5), 503–511.

Koffka, K. (1935). *Principles of Gestalt psychology.* London, England: Lund Humphries.

Kohlberg, L. (1981). *The philosophy of moral development: Essays on moral development* (Vol. 1). San Francisco, CA: Harper and Row.

Kohlberg, L. (1984). *Essays on moral development: The psychology of moral development* (Vol. 2). San Francisco: Harper & Row.

Kohler, C. G., Turner, T. H., Bilker, W. B., Brensinger, C. M., Siegel, S. J., Kanes, S. J., et al. (2003). Facial emotion recognition in schizophrenia: Intensity effects and error pattern. *American Journal of Psychiatry, 160*, 1768–1774.

Kokis, J. V., Macpherson, R., Toplak, M. E., West, R. F., & Stanovich, K. E. (2002). Heuristic and analytic processing: Age trends and associations with cognitive ability and cognitive styles. *Journal of Experimental Child Psychology, 83*(1), 26–52. doi:10.1016/S0022-0965(02)00121-2

Komarraju, M., Karau, S. J., & Schmeck, R. R. (2009). Role of the Big Five personality traits in predicting college students' academic motivation and achievement. *Learning and Individual Differences, 19*(1), 47–52. doi:10.1016/j.lindif.2008.07.001

Konopka, G., Bomar, J. M., Winden, K., Coppola, G., Jonsson, Z. O., Gao, F., et al. (2009). Human-specific transcriptional regulation of CNS development genes by FOXP2. *Nature, 462*, 213–217.

Kopell, B. H., Machado, A.G., & Rezai, A.R. (2005). Not your father's lobotomy: Psychiatric surgery revisited. In Congress of Neurological Surgeons (2011). *Clinical neurosurgery* (Vol. 52; pp. 192–196). Retrieved on December 10, 2011, from http://book2.neurosurgeon.org/?defaultarticle=&defaultnode=2671&layout=22&pagefunction=Load%20Layout

Kopelman, M. D. (2002). Disorders of memory. *Brain: A Journal of Neurology, 125*(10), 2152–2190. doi:10.1093/brain/awf229

Koscik, T. R., & Tranel, D. (2011). The human amygdala is necessary for developing and expressing normal interpersonal trust. *Neuropsychologia, 49*(4), 602–611. doi:10.1016/j.neuropsychologia.2010.09.023

Kosslyn, S. M. (1978). Measuring the visual angle of the mind's eye. *Cognitive Psychology, 10*, 356–389.

Kosslyn, S. M. (1980). *Image and mind.* Cambridge, MA: Harvard University Press.

Kosslyn, S. M. (1994). *Elements of graph design.* New York: Freeman.

Kosslyn, S. M., Thompson, W. L., Costantini-Ferrando, M. F., Alpert, N. M., & Spiegel, D. (2000). Hypnotic visual illusion alters color processing in the brain. *American Journal of Psychiatry, 157*, 1279–1284.

Kotov, R., Gamez, W., Schmidt, F., & Watson, D. (2010). Linking "big" personality traits to anxiety, depressive, and substance use disorders: A meta-analysis. *Psychological Bulletin, 136*(5), 768–821. doi:10.1037/a0020327

Kozorovitskiy, Y., Hughes, M., Lee, K., & Gould, E. (2006). Fatherhood affects dendritic spines and vasopressin V1a receptors in the primate prefrontal cortex. *Nature Neuroscience, 9*(9), 1094–1095.

Krain, A. L., & Castellanos, F. X. (2006). Brain development and ADHD. *Clinical Psychology Review, 26*(4), 433–444.

Kramer, A. F., Erickson, K. I., & Colcombe, S. J. (2006). Exercise, cognition, and the aging brain. *Journal of Applied Physiology, 101*(4), 1237–1242. doi:10.1152/japplphysiol.00500.2006

Kramer, B. J. (1993). Expanding the conceptualization of caregiver coping: The importance of relationship-focused coping strategies. *Family Relations, 42*(4), 383–391.

Kravitz, D. A., & Martin, B. (1986). Ringelmann rediscovered: The original article. *Journal of Personality and Social Psychology, 50*, 936–941.

Krebs, H., Hogan, N., Hening, W., Adamovich, S., & Poizner, H. (2001). Procedural motor learning in Parkinson's disease. *Experimental Brain Research, 141*, 425–437.

Krijn, M., Emmelkamp, P. M. G., Ólafsson, R. P., Bouwman, M., van Gerwen, L. J., Spinhoven, P., et al. (2007). Fear of flying treatment methods: Virtual reality exposure vs. cognitive behavioral therapy. *Aviation, Space, and Environmental Medicine, 78*(2), 121–128.

Kross, E., Berman, M. G., Mischel, W., Smith, E. E., & Wager, T. D. (2011). Social rejection shares somatosensory representations with physical pain. *Proceedings of the National Academy of Sciences, 108*(15), 6270–6275. doi:10.1073/pnas.1102693108

Krueger, R. F., South, S., Johnson, W., & Iacono, W. (2008). The heritability of personality is not always 50%: Gene-environment interactions and correlations between personality and parenting. *Journal of Personality, 76*(6), 1485–1522.

Kruger, J., & Dunning, D. (1999). Unskilled and unaware of it: How difficulties in recognizing one's own incompetence lead to inflated self-assessments. *Journal of Personality and Social Psychology, 77*, 1121–1134.

Krull, D. S., Loy, M. H.-M., & Lin, J. (1999). The fundamental fundamental attribution error: Correspondence bias in individualist and collectivist cultures. *Personality and Social Psychology Bulletin, 25*, 1208–1219.

Kuhl, B. A., Dudukovic, N. M., Kahn, I., & Wagner, A. D. (2007). Decreased demands on cognitive control reveal the neural processing benefits of forgetting. *Nature Neuroscience, 10*, 908–914. doi:10.1038/nn1918

Kuhl, P. K. (2007). Is speech learning "gated" by the social brain? *Developmental Science, 10*(1), 110–120.

Kuhn, D. (2008). Formal operations from a twenty-first century perspective. *Human Development, 51*(1), 48–55. doi:10.1159/000113155

Kulik, J. A., Mahler, H. I. M., & Moore, P. J. (1996). Social comparison and affiliation under threat: Effects of recovery from major surgery. *Journal of Personality and Social Psychology, 71*, 967–979.

Kuo, L. E., Czarnecka, M., Kitlinska, J. B., Tilan, J. U., Kvetňanský, R., & Zukowska, Z. (2009). Chronic stress, combined with a high-fat/high-sugar diet, shifts sympathetic signaling toward neuropeptide Y and leads to obesity and the metabolic syndrome. In R. Kvetňanský, G. Aguilera, D. Goldstein, D. Jezova, O. Krizanova, E. L. Sabban, & K. Pacak (Eds.), *Stress, neurotransmitters, and hormones: Neuroendocrine and genetic mechanisms* (pp. 232–237). New York, NY: Wiley-Blackwell.

Kurihara, T., Kato, M., Sakamoto, S., Reverger, R., & Kitamura, T. (2000). Public attitudes towards the mentally ill: A cross-cultural study between Bali and Tokyo. *Psychiatry and Clinical Neurosciences, 54*, 547–552.

Kurland, J. A. (1977). Kin selection in the Japanese monkey. *Contributions to Primatology, 12*, 1–145.

Kurtz, R. G., Rozin, P., & Teitelbaum, P. (1972). Ventromedial hypothalamic hyperphagia in the hypophysectomized weanling rat. *Journal of Comparative and Physiological Psychology, 80*(1), 19–25.

Kurzban, R., & Houser, D. (2005). Experiments investigating cooperative types in humans: A complement to evolutionary theory and simulations. *Proceedings of the National Academy of Sciences, 102*, 1803–1807.

Kuster, J. M. (2005). Folk myths about stuttering. Retrieved March 15, 2011, from http://www.mnsu.edu/comdis/kuster/Infostuttering/folkmyths.html

La Barre, W. (1975). Anthropological perspectives on hallucination and hallucinogens. In L. J. West & R. K. Siegel (Eds.), *Hallucinations* (pp. 9–52). New York, NY: John Wiley & Sons.

Ladd, G. W., Buhs, E. S., & Seid, M. (2000). Children's initial sentiments about kindergarten: Is school liking an antecedent of early classroom participation and achievement? *Merrill-Palmer Quarterly: Journal of Developmental Psychology, 46*(2), 255–279.

Lagerspetz, K. M. J., & Lagerspetz, K. Y. H. (1983). Genes and aggression. In E. C. Simmel, M. E. Hahn, & J. K. Walters (Eds.), *Aggressive behavior: Genetic and neural approaches* (pp. 89–102). Hillsdale, NJ: Erlbaum.

Lahey, B. B. (1995). *Psychology: An introduction* (5th ed.). Dubuque, IA: WCB Brown & Benchmark.

Lai, C. S., Fisher, S. E., Hurst, J. A., Vargha-Khadem, F., & Monaco, A. P. (2001). A forkhead-domain gene is mutated in a severe speech and language disorder. *Nature, 413*, 519–523.

Lakin, J. L., Chartrand, T. L., & Arkin, R. M. (2008). I am too just like you: Nonconscious mimicry as an automatic behavioral response to social exclusion. *Psychological Science, 19*(8), 816–822. doi:10.1111/j.1467-9280.2008.02162.x

Lammers, J., Stoker, J. I., Jordan, J., Pollmann, M. M. H., & Stapel, D. A. (2011). Power increases infidelity among men and women. *Psychological Science, 22*(9), 1191–1197.

Lane, A., Young, R., Baker, A., & Angley, M. (2010). Sensory processing subtypes in autism: Association with adaptive behavior. *Journal of Autism and Developmental Disorders, 40*(1), 112–122. doi:10.1007/s10803-009-0840-2

Lane, R. E. (2001). Self-reliance and empathy: The enemies of poverty—and of the poor. *Political Psychology, 22*(3), 473–492. doi:10.1111/0162-895X.00250

Lange, C. G. (1885/1912). The mechanisms of the emotions. In B. Rand (Ed.), *The classical psychologists* (pp. 672–284). Boston, MA: Houghton Mifflin.

Langenecker, S. A., Weisenbach, S. L., Giordani, B., Briceño, E. M., Guidotti Breting, L. M., Schallmo, M.-P., et al. (2012). Impact of chronic hypercortisolemia on affective processing. *Neuropharmacology.* Advance online publication. doi:10.1016/j.neuropharm.2011.07.006

Langley, J. (1921). *The autonomic nervous system.* Cambridge, United Kingdom: Heffer & Sons.

Langlois, J. H., Roggman, L. A., & Rieser-Danner, L. A. (1990). Infants' differential social responses to attractive and unattractive faces. *Developmental Psychology, 26*(1), 153–159.

Largo, R. H., Molinari, L., von Siebenthal, K., & Wolfensberger, U. (1996). Does a profound change in toilet-training affect development of bowel and bladder control? *Developmental Medicine and Child Neurology, 38,* 1106–1116.

Larrick, R. P., Nisbett, R. E., & Morgan, J. N. (1993). Who uses the cost-benefit rules of choice? Implications for the normative status of microeconomic theory. *Organization Behavior and Human Decision Processes, 56,* 331–347.

Lassek, W. D., & Gaulin, S. J. C. (2009). Costs and benefits of fat-free muscle mass in men: Relationship to mating success, dietary requirements, and native immunity. *Evolution and Human Behavior, 30*(5), 322–328. doi:10.1016/j.evolhumbehav.2009.04.002

Latané, B., & Darley, J. M. (1968). Group inhibition of bystander intervention in emergencies. *Journal of Personality and Social Psychology, 10,* 215–221.

Latané, B., Williams, K., & Harkins, S. (1979). Many hands make light the work: The causes and consequences of social loafing. *Journal of Personality and Social Psychology, 37,* 822–832.

Lau, J., & Chan, J. (2009). About critical thinking. Retrieved November 5, 2009, from http://philosophy.hku.hk/think/critical/improve.php

Laumann, E. O., Paik, A., Glasser, D. B., Kang, J.-H., Wang, T., Levinson, B., et al. (2006). A cross-national study of subjective sexual well-being among older women and men: Findings from the global study of sexual attitudes and behaviors. *Archives of Sexual Behavior, 35*(2), 145–161.

Laurence, J.-R., & Perry, C. (1983). Hypnotically created memory among highly hypnotizable subjects. *Science, 222,* 523–524.

Lawrence, E., Rothman, A. D., Cobb, R. J., Rothman, M. T., & Bradbury, T. N. (2008). Marital satisfaction across the transition to parenthood. *Journal of Family Psychology, 22*(1), 41–50.

Lazar, S. W., Bush, G., Gollub, R. L., Fricchinoe, G. L., Khalsa, G., & Benson, H. (2000). Functional brain mapping of the relaxation response and meditation. *NeuroReport, 11,* 1581–1585.

Lazar, S. W., Kerr, C., Wasserman, R. H., Gray, J. R., Greve, D., Treadway, M. T., et al. (2005). Meditation experience is associated with increased cortical thickness. *NeuroReport, 16,* 1893–1897.

Lazarus, A. A. (2005). Multimodal therapy. In J. C. Norcross & M. R. Goldfried (Eds.), *Handbook of psychotherapy integration* (pp. 105–120). New York, NY: Oxford University Press.

Lazarus, R. S. (1966). *Psychological stress and the coping process.* New York, NY: McGraw-Hill.

Le Courteur, A., Bailey, A., Goode, S., Pickles, A., Robertson, S., Gottesman, I., et al. (1996). A broader phenotype of autism: The clinical spectrum in twins. *Journal of Child Psychology and Psychiatry, 37,* 785–801.

Le Lionnais, F. (1960). *The Orion book of time.* New York: Orion.

Lea, M., & Spears, R. (1991). Computer-mediated communication, de-individuation and group decision-making. *International Journal of Man-Machine Studies, 34,* 283–301.

Leaper, C., & Ayres, M. M. (2007). A meta-analytic review of gender variations in adults' language use: Talkativeness, affiliative speech, and assertive speech. *Personality and Social Psychology Review, 11*(4), 328–363. doi:10.1177/1088868307302221

Leary, M. R. (2004). *The curse of the self: Self-awareness, egotism, and the quality of human life.* New York, NY: Oxford University Press.

Leary, M. R., & Downs, D. L. (1995). Interpersonal functions of the self-esteem motive: The self-esteem system as a sociometer. In M. H. Kernis (Ed.), *Efficacy, agency, and self-esteem* (pp. 123–144). NewYork, NY: Plenum.

Leary, M. R., Tambor, E. S., Terdal, S. K., & Downs, D. L. (1995). Self-esteem as an interpersonal monitor: The sociometer hypothesis. *Journal of Personality and Social Psychology, 68,* 518–530.

LeBlanc, S. A. (2003). *Constant battles: The myth of the peaceful, noble savage.* New York, NY: St. Martin's Press.

LeDoux, J. E. (1996). *The emotional brain.* New York, NY: Simon and Schuster.

LeDoux, J. E. (2000). Emotion circuits in the brain. *Annual Review of Neuroscience, 23,* 155–184.

LeDoux, J. E., Cicchetti, P., Xagoraris, A., & Romanski, L. M. (1990). The lateral amygdaloid nucleus: Sensory interface of the amygdala in fear conditioning. *Journal of Neuroscience, 10,* 1062–1069.

Lee, G. P., Meador, K. J., Loring, D. W., Allison, J. D., Brown, W. S., Paul, L. K., et al. (2004). Neural substrates of emotion as revealed by functional magnetic resonance imaging. *Cognitive and Behavioral Neurology, 17*(1), 9–17.

Lee, H. S. (2010). Change in the singular racial concept of American society. *International Area Review, 13*(3), 51–72.

Lee, H., Park, S.-A., Lee, Y.-A., & Cameron, G. T. (2010). Assessment of motion media on believability and credibility: An exploratory study. *Public Relations Review, 36,* 310–312.

Lee, M. R., Okazaki, S., & Yoo, H. C. (2006). Frequency and intensity of social anxiety in Asian Americans and European Americans. *Cultural Diversity and Ethnic Minority Psychology, 12*(2), 291–305. doi:10.1037/1099-9809.12.2.291

Lehrer, E. L. (2006). Age at marriage and marital instability: Revisiting the Becker-Landes-Michael hypothesis. *Journal of Population Economics, 21*(2), 463–484. doi:10.1007/s0048-006-0092-9

Leichsenring, F. (2005). Are psychodynamic and psychoanalytic therapies effective? A review of empirical data. *International Journal of Psychoanalysis, 86,* 841–868.

Leichsenring, F., & Rabung, S. (2008). Effectiveness of long-term psychodynamic psychotherapy: A meta-analysis. *JAMA: The Journal of the American Medical Association, 300*(13), 1551–1565. doi:10.1001/jama.300.13.1551

Leichtman, M. (1995). Behavioral observations. In J. N. Butcher (Ed.), *Clinical personality assessment: Practical approaches* (pp. 251–266). New York, NY: Oxford University Press.

Leiner, H. C., Leiner, A. L., & Dow, R. S. (1991). The human cerebro-cerebellar system: Its computing, cognitive and language skills. *Behavioral Brain Research, 44,* 113–128.

LePine, J. A., & Van Dyne, L. (1998). Predicting voice behavior in work groups. *Journal of Applied Psychology, 83,* 853–868.

Lerner, M. J., & Miller, D. T. (1978). Just world research and the attribution process: Looking back and ahead. *Psychological Bulletin, 85,* 1030–1051.

Leroi, A. M. (2006). The future of neo-eugenics. *EMBO Reports, 7*(12), 1184–1187. doi:10.1038/sj.embor.7400860

Lesku, J. A., Roth, T. C., Rattenborg, N. C., Amlaner, C. J., & Lima, S. L. (2008). Phylogenetics and the correlates of mammalian sleep: A reappraisal. *Sleep medicine reviews, 12(3),* 229–244.

Leung, A. K.-y., Kim, Y.-H., Zhang, Z.-X., Tam, K.-P., & Chiu, C.-y. (2011). Cultural construction of success and epistemic motives moderate American-Chinese differences in reward allocation biases. *Journal of Cross-Cultural Psychology, 43*(1), 46–52. doi:10.1177/0022022111405660

LeVay, S. (1991). A difference in hypothalamic structure between heterosexual and homosexual men. *Science, 253,* 1034–1037.

Levenson, R. W., Ekman, P., & Friesen, W. V. (1990). Voluntary facial action generates emotion-specific autonomic nervous system activity. *Psychophysiology, 27,* 363–384.

Leventhal, H., & Watts, J. C. (1966). Sources of resistance to fear-arousing communications on smoking and lung cancer. *Journal of Personality, 34,* 155–175.

Levine, A., Huang, Y. Y., Drisaldi, B., Griffin, E. A., Jr., Pollak, D. D., Xu, S., et al. (2011). Molecular mechanism for a gateway drug: Epigenetic changes initiated by nicotine prime gene expression by cocaine. *Science Translational Medicine, 3*(107), 1–10.

Levine, M., Taylor, P. J., & Best, R. (2011). Third parties, violence, and conflict resolution. *Psychological Science, 22*(3), 406–412. doi:10.1177/0956797611398495

Levine, S. (1970). The pituitary–adrenal system and the developing brain. *Progress in Brain Research, 32,* 79–85.

Levinson, D., Darrow, C. M., Klein, E. B., Levinson, M. H., & McKee, B. (1976). Periods in the adult development of men: Ages 18–14. *Counselling Psychologist, 6* (1), 21–25.

Lewinsohn, P. M., Klein, D. N., & Seeley, J. R. (1995). Bipolar disorders in a community sample of older adolescents: Prevalence, phenomenology, comorbidity, and course. *Journal of the American Academy of Child and Adolescent Psychiatry, 34,* 454–463.

Lewis, M., & Brooks-Gunn, J. (1979). *Social cognition and the acquisition of self.* New York, NY: Plenum Press.

Lewontin, R. C. (1970). Race and intelligence. *Bulletin of the Atomic Scientists, 26*(3), 2–8.

Li, S.-C., Lindenberger, U., Hommel, B., Aschersleben, G., Prinz, W., & Baltes, P. B. (2004). Transformations in the couplings among intellectual abilities and constituent cognitive processes across the lifespan. *Psychological Science, 15*(3), 155–163.

Lichtenberg, J. D., Lachmann, F. M., & Fosshage, J. L. (2010). *Psychoanalysis and motivational systems: A new look.* New York, NY: Taylor & Francis.

Lichtenstein, E., Harris, D. E., Birchler, G. R., Wahl, J. M., & Schmahl, D. P. (1973). Comparison of rapid smoking, warm, smoky air, and attention placebo in the modification of smoking behavior. *Journal of Consulting and Clinical Psychology, 40,* 92–98.

Lieber, A. L. (1978). Human aggression and the lunar synodic cycle. *Journal of Clinical Psychiatry, 39,* 385–392.

Light, K. C., Grewen, K. M., & Amico, J. A. (2005). More frequent partner hugs and higher oxytocin levels are linked to lower blood pressure and heart rate in premenopausal women. *Biological Psychology, 69*(1), 5–21.

Liguori, A., Hughes, J. R., & Grass, J. A. (1997). Absorption and subjective effects of caffeine from coffee, cola and capsules. *Pharmacology Biochemistry and Behavior, 58*(3), 721–726. doi:10.1016/s0091-3057(97)00003-8

Likert, R. (1932). A technique for the measurement of attitudes. *Archives of Psychology, 140,* 44–53.

Lilly, I. C. (1967). *The mind of the dolphin.* New York: Doubleday.

Lin, A., Adolphs, R., & Rangel, A. (2011). Social and monetary reward learning engage overlapping neural substrates. *Social Cognitive and Affective Neuroscience.* doi:10.1093/scan/nsr006

Linden, D., & Lancaster, T. (2011). P02-341 - Functional magnetic resonance imaging

(fMRI)-based neurofeedback as a new treatment tool for depression. *European Psychiatry, 26*(Suppl. 1), 937. doi:10.1016/s0924-9338(11)72642-6

Linehan, M. M., Armstrong, H. E., Suarez, A., Allmon, D., & Heard, H. L. (1991). Cognitive-behavioral treatment of chronically parasuicidal borderline patients. *Archives of General Psychiatry, 48*(12), 1060–1064. doi:10.1001/archpsyc.1991.01810360024003

Lisman, S. A. (1974). Alcoholic "blackout": State dependent learning? *Archives of General Psychiatry, 30,* 46–53.

Little, A. C., Jones, B. C., DeBruine, L. M., & Feinberg, D. R. (2008). Symmetry and sexual dimorphism in human faces: Interrelated preferences suggest both signal quality. *Behavioral Ecology, 19*(4), 902–908. doi:10.1093/beheco/arn049

Liu, D., Diorio, J., Tannenbaum, B., Caldji, C., Francis, D., Freedman, A., et al. (1997). Maternal care, hippocampal glucocorticoid receptors, and hypothalamic-pituitary-adrenal responses to stress. *Science, 277*(5332), 1659–1662. doi:10.1126/science.277.5332.1659

Livingstone, M. S., & Hubel, D. H. (1984). Anatomy and physiology of a color system in the primate visual cortex. *Journal of Neuroscience, 4,* 309–356.

Livshits, G., Kato, B. S., Wilson, S. G., & Spector, T. D. (2007). Linkage of genes to total lean body mass in normal women. *Journal of Clinical Endocrinology and Metabolism, 92*(8), 3171–3176.

Lloyd-Richardson, E., Perrine, N., Dierker, L., & Kelley, M. L. (2007). Characteristics and functions of non-suicidal self-injury in a community sample of adolescents. *Psychological Medicine, 37,* 1183–1192.

Locke, J. (1690). An essay concerning human understanding. Retrieved September 23, 2009, from http://oregonstate.edu/instruct/phl302/texts/locke/locke1/Book2a.html#Chapter I

Loe, I. M., & Feldman, H. M. (2007). Academic and educational outcomes of children with ADHD: Literature review and proposal for future research. *Ambulatory Pediatrics, 7*(Suppl. 1), 82–90.

Loftus, E. F. (1979). *Eyewitness testimony.* Cambridge, MA: Harvard University Press.

Loftus, E. F. (1997). Creating false memories. *Scientific American, 277*(3), 70–75.

Loftus, E. F. (2003). Our changeable memories: Legal and practical implications. *Nature Reviews Neuroscience, 4,* 231–234.

Loftus, E. F., & Palmer, J. C. (1974). Reconstruction of automobile destruction: An example of the interaction between language and memory. *Journal of Verbal Learning and Verbal Behavior, 13,* 585–589.

Lotto, R. B., & Purves, D. (2000). An empirical explanation of color contrast. *Proceedings of the National Academy of Sciences, USA, 97,* 12834–12839.

Lotto, R. B., & Purves, D. (2002). The empirical basis of color perception. *Consciousness and Cognition, 11,* 609–629.

Lovaas, O. I. (1996). The UCLA young autism model of service delivery. In C. Maurice, G. Green, & S. C. Luce (Eds.), *Behavioral intervention for young children with autism:*

A manual for parents and professionals (pp. 241–248). Austin, TX: PRO-ED, Inc.

Lovaas, O. I., Freitag, G., Kinder, M. I., Rubenstein, B. D., Schaeffer, B., & Simmons, J. Q. (1966). Establishment of social reinforcers in two schizophrenic children on the basis of food. *Journal of Experimental Child Psychology, 4*(2), 109–125.

Lovaas, O. I., Schreibman, L., & Koegel, R. L. (1974). A behavior modification approach to the treatment of autistic children. *Journal of Autism and Developmental Disorders, 4*(2), 111–129. doi:10.1007/bf02105365

Lovett, M. C. (2002). Problem solving. In H. Pashler & D. Medin (Eds.), *Stevens' handbook of experimental psychology: Vol. 2. Memory and cognitive processes* (3rd ed., pp. 317–362). Hoboken, NJ: Wiley.

Lowry, R. (Ed.). (1973). *A. H. Maslow: An intellectual portrait.* Monterey, CA: Brooks/Cole.

Loyola University Health System Office of Media Relations. (2005). The world's smallest baby celebrates health[y] first year at Loyola. Retrieved from http://www.luhs.org/feature/smallest/birthday.htm

Lubow, R. E., & Moore, A. U. (1959). Latent inhibition: The effect of nonreinforced exposure to the conditioned stimulus. *Journal of Comparative and Physiological Psychology, 52,* 415–419.

Lubow, R. E., Ingberg-Sachs, Y., Salstein-Orda, N., & Gewirtz, J. C. (1992). Latent inhibition in low and high "psychotic-prone" normal subjects. *Personality and Individual Differences, 15,* 563–572.

Luo, S., & Zhang, G. (2009). What leads to romantic attraction: Similarity, reciprocity, security, or beauty? Evidence from a speed-dating study. *Journal of Personality, 77*(4), 933–964. doi:10.1111/j.1467-6494. 2009.00570.x

Luo, S., Zhang, G., Watson, D., & Snider, A. G. (2010). Using cross-sectional couple data to disentangle the causality between positive partner perceptions and marital satisfaction. *Journal of Research in Personality, 44*(5), 665–668. doi:10.1016/j.jrp.2010.08.006

Luoma, J. B., & Pearson, J. L. (2002). Suicide and marital status in the United States, 1991–1996: Is widowhood a risk factor? *American Journal of Public Health, 92*(9), 1518–1522. doi:10.2105/ajph.92.9.1518

Luyckx, K., Tildesley, E. A., Soenens, B., Andrews, J. A., Hampson, S. E., Peterson, M., et al. (2011). Parenting and trajectories of children's maladaptive behaviors: A 12-year prospective community study. *Journal of Clinical Child and Adolescent Psychology, 40*(3), 468–478.

Lykken, D. T. (1982). Fearlessness: Its carefree charm and deadly risks. *Psychology Today, 16,* 20–28.

Lykken, D., & Tellegen, A. (1996). Happiness is a stochastic phenomenon. *Psychological Science, 7,* 186–189.

Lynn, M., & Simons, T. (2000). Predictors of male and female servers' average tip earnings. *Journal of Applied Social Psychology, 30,* 241–252.

Lyoo, I. K., Dager, S. R., Kim, J. E., Yoon, S. J., Friedman, S. D., Dunner, D. L., et al. (2010). Lithium-induced gray matter volume increase as a neural correlate of treatment response in bipolar disorder: A longitudinal brain imaging study. *Neuropsychopharmacology, 35*(8), 1743–1750.

Ma, D. K., Marchetto, M. C., Guo, J. U., Ming, G.-l., Gage, F. H., & Song, H. (2010). Epigenetic choreographers of neurogenesis in the adult mammalian brain. *Nature Neuroscience, 13*(11), 1338–1344. doi:10.1038/nn.2672

Maccoby, E. E., & Martin, J. A. (1983). Socialization in the context of the family: Parent-child interaction. In P. Mussen & E. M. Hetherington (Eds.), *Handbook of child psychology: Vol. 4. Socialization, personality, and social development* (pp. 1–101). New York, NY: Wiley.

Maccoby, M. (2003). *The productive narcissist: The promise and perils of visionary leadership.* New York, NY: Broadway Books.

MacDonald, A., & Burrell, S. (2009). Infrequently performed studies in nuclear medicine: Part 2. *Journal of Nuclear Medicine Technology, 37*(1), 1–13.

Macleod, J., Davey Smith, G., Heslop, P., Metcalfe, C., Carroll, D., & Hart, C. (2002). Psychological stress and cardiovascular disease: Empirical demonstration of bias in a prospective observational study of Scottish men. *British Medical Journal, 324,* 1247.

Maggard, M. A., Shugarman, L. R., Suttorp, M., Maglione, M., Sugerman, H. J., Livingston, E. H., et al. (2005). Meta-analysis: Surgical treatment of obesity. *Annals of Internal Medicine, 142*(7), 547–559.

Maguire, E. A., Gadian, D. G., Johnsrude, I. S., Good, C. D., Ashburner, J., Frackowiak, R. S. J., et al. (2000). Navigation-related structural change in the hippocampi of taxi drivers. *Proceedings of the National Academy of Sciences, 97*(8), 4398–4403.

Mahay, J., & Lewin, A. C. (2007). Age and the desire to marry. *Journal of Family Issues, 28*(5), 706–723. doi:10.1177/0192513x06297272

Maher, B. (2008). Poll results: Look who's doping. *Nature, 452,* 674–675.

Maher, B. A. (2001). Music, the brain, and Williams syndrome. *Scientist, 15,* 20.

Mahon, B. Z., & Caramazza, A. (2009). Concepts and categories: A cognitive neuropsychological perspective. *Annual Review of Psychology, 60*(1), 27–51. doi:10.1146/annurev.psych.60.110707.163532

Mahon, B. Z., & Caramazza, A. (2011). What drives the organization of object knowledge in the brain? *Trends in Cognitive Sciences, 15*(3), 97–103. doi:10.1016/j.tics.2011.01.004

Maier, N. (1931). Reasoning in humans. *Psychological Review, 38,* 332–346.

Main, M., & Solomon, J. (1986). Discovery of an insecure-disorganized/disoriented attachment pattern. In T. B. Brazelton & M. W. Yogman (Eds.), *Affective development in infancy* (pp. 95–124). Westport, CT: Ablex.

Malberg, J. E., Eisch, A. J., Nestler, E. J., & Duman, R. S. (2000). Chronic antidepressant treatment increases neurogenesis in adult rat hippocampus. *Journal of Neuroscience, 20,* 9104–9110.

Malle, B. F. (2006). The actor-observer asymmetry in attribution: A (surprising) meta-analysis. *Psychological Bulletin, 132*(6), 895–919. doi:10.1037/0033-2909.132.6.895

Malle, B. F. (2008). Fritz Heider's legacy: Celebrated insights, many of them misunderstood. *Social Psychology, 39*(3), 163–173. doi:10.1027/1864-9335.39.3.163

Malone, E. (2006). Endangered languages. Retrieved August 15, 2006, from http://www.nsf.gov/news/special_reports/linguistics/endangered.jsp

Malt, B. C., & Smith, E. E. (1984). Correlated properties in natural categories. *Journal of Verbal Learning and Verbal Behavior, 23,* 250–269.

Månsson, H. (2000). Childhood stuttering: Incidence and development. *Journal of Fluency Disorders, 25*(1), 47–57. doi:10.1016/s0094-730x(99)00023-6

Mantell, D. M. (1971). The potential for violence in Germany. *Journal of Social Issues, 27,* 101–112.

Mäntylä, T., & Nilsson, L.-G. (1988). Cue distinctiveness and forgetting: Effectiveness of self-generated retrieval cues in delayed recall. *Journal of Experimental Psychology: Learning, Memory, and Cognition, 14*(3), 502–509. doi:10.1037/0278-7393.14.3.502

Marchione, M. (2010). $93,000 cancer drug: How much is a life worth? Retrieved October 9, 2010, from http://finance.yahoo.com/news/93000-cancer-drug-How-much-is-apf-2083419757.html?x=0

Marian, V., & Neisser, U. (2000). Language-dependent recall of autobiographical memories. *Journal of Experimental Psychology: General, 129*(3), 361–368.

Marks, G. A., Shaffery, J. P., Oksenberg, A., Speciale, S. G., & Roffwarg, H. P. (1995). A functional role for REM sleep in brain maturation. *Behavioural Brain Research, 69,* 1–11.

Markus, H. (1977). Self-schemata and processing information about the self. *Journal of Personality and Social Psychology, 35*(2), 63–78. doi:10.1037/0022-3514.35.2.63

Markus, H. R., & Kitayama, S. (1991). Culture and the self: Implications for cognition, emotion, and motivation. *Psychological Review, 98,* 223–253.

Marner, L., Nyengaard, J. R., Tang, Y., & Pakkenberg, B. (2003). Marked loss of myelinated nerve fibers in the human brain with age. *Journal of Comparative Neurology, 462*(2), 144–152.

Marsh, A. A., & Blair, R. J. R. (2008). Deficits in facial affect recognition among antisocial populations: A meta-analysis. *Neuroscience and Biobehavioral Reviews, 32*(3), 454–465.

Marshall, G. D., & Zimbardo, P. G. (1979). Affective consequences of inadequately explained physiological arousal. *Journal of Personality and Social Psychology, 37*(6), 970–988. doi:10.1037/0022-3514.37.6.970

MarsVenus.com. (2007). Retrieved July 19, 2007, from http://www.marsvenus.com/

Martin, A., Wiggs, C. L., Ungerleider, L. G., & Haxby, J. V. (1996). Neural correlates of category-specific knowledge. *Nature, 379,* 649–652.

Martin, J. A., Hamilton, B. E., Sutton, P. D., Ventura, S. J., Menacker, F., Kirmeyer, S., et al. (2008). *Births: Final data for 2006.* Hyattsville, MD: National Center for Health Statistics.

Martin, P. (2008). Moderating effects of dispositional resilience on associations between hassles and psychological distress. *Journal of Applied Developmental Psychology, 30*(1), 53–60. doi:10.1016/j.appdev.2008.10.005

Maslow, A. H. (1943). A theory of human motivation. *Psychological Review, 50,* 370–396.

Maslow, A. H. (1950). *Self-actualizing people: A study of psychological health.* New York, NY: Grune and Stratton.

Mason, M. F., Norton, M. I., Van Horn, J. D., Wegner, D. M., Graftin, S. T., & Macrae, C. N. (2007). Wandering minds: The default network and stimulus-independent thought. *Science, 315*(5810), 393–395. doi:10.1126/science.1131295

Mason, W. A., Capitanio, J. P., Machado, C. J., Mendoza, S. P., & Amaral, D. G. (2006). Amygdalectomy and responsiveness to novelty in rhesus monkeys (*Macaca mulatta*): Generality and individual consistency of effects. *Emotion, 6*(1), 73–81.

Masten, A. S., Hubbard, J. J., Gest, S. D., Tellegen, A., Garmezy, N., & Ramirez, M. (1999). Competence in the context of adversity: Pathways to resilience and maladaptation from childhood to late adolescence. *Development and Psychopathology, 11*(1), 143–169. doi:10.1017/s0954579499001996

Masuda, T., & Nisbett, R. E. (2001). Attending holistically versus analytically: Comparing the context sensitivity of Japanese and Americans. *Journal of Personality and Social Psychology, 81*(5), 922–934. doi:10.1037/0022-3514.81.5.922

Mather, M., & Lavery, D. (2010). In U.S., proportion of married at lowest recorded levels. Retrieved on December 11, 2011, from http://www.prb.org/Articles/2010/usmarriagedecline.aspx

Mathews, T. J., & Hamilton, B. E. (2009). Delayed childbearing: More women are having their first child later in life. Retrieved July 20, 2010, from http://www.cdc.gov/nchs/data/databriefs/db21.htm

Matsumoto, D., & Hwang, H. S. (2011). Cooperation and competition in intercultural interactions. *International Journal of Intercultural Relations, 35*(5), 677–685. doi:10.1016/j.ijintrel.2011.02.017

Matsumoto, D., Consolacion, T., Yamada, H., Suzuki, R., Franklin, B. Paul, S., Ray, R., & Uchida, H. (2002). American-Japanese cultural differences in judgments of emotional expressions of different intensities. *Cognition and Emotion, 16,* 721–747.

Matsumoto, D., Yoo, S. H., Nakagawa, S., et al. (2008). Culture, emotion regulation, and adjustment. *Journal of Personality and Social Psychology, 94*(6), 925–937.

Matthews, C. E., Chen, K. Y., Freedson, P. S., Buchowski, M. S., Beech, B. M., Pate, R. R., et al. (2008). Amount of time spent in sedentary behaviors in the United States, 2003–2004. *American Journal of Epidemiology, 167*(7), 875–881.

Maurer, D., & Maurer, C. (1988). *The world of the newborn.* New York, NY: Basic Books.

Mauro, J. (1992). Bright lights, big mystery. Retrieved August 5, 2006, from http://www.psychologytoday.com/articles/pto-19920701-000030.html

Maxfield, M. C. (1990). *Effects of rhythmic drumming on EEG and subjective experiences*

(Unpublished doctoral dissertation). Institute of Transpersonal Psychology, Menlo Park, CA.

Mayberg, H. S., Lozano, A. M., Voon, V., McNeely, H. E., Seminowicz, D., Hamani, C., et al. (2005). Deep brain stimulation for treatment-resistant depression. *Neuron, 45,* 651–660.

Mayer, J. (1955). Regulation of energy intake and the body weight: The glucostatic theory and the lipostatic hypothesis. *Annals of the New York Academy of Sciences, 63,* 15–43.

Mayer, J. D., & Salovey, P. (1993). The intelligence of emotional intelligence. *Intelligence, 17,* 433–442.

Mayer, J. D., & Salovey, P. (1997). What is emotional intelligence? In P. Salovey & D. Sluyter (Eds.), *Emotional development and emotional intelligence: Educational implications* (pp. 3–31). New York, NY: Basic Books.

Mazur, A., & Booth, A. (1998). Testosterone and dominance in men. *Behavioral and Brain Sciences, 21,* 353–363.

Mazur, A., & Michalek, J. (1998). Marriage, divorce and male testosterone. *Social Forces, 77,* 315–331.

Mazur, A., & Mueller, E. (1996). Facial dominance. In A. Somit & S. Peterson (Eds.), *Research in biopolitics* (Vol. 4, pp. 99–111). London: JAI Press.

Mazure, C. M. (1998). Life stressors as risk factors in depression. *Clinical Psychology: Science and Practice, 5,* 291–313.

McArthur, L. Z., & Berry, D. S. (1987). Cross-cultural agreement in perceptions of baby-faced adults. *Journal of Cross-Cultural Psychology, 18*(2), 165–192. doi:10.1177/0022002187018002003

McCall, M. (1997). The effects of physical attractiveness on gaining access to alcohol: When social policy meets social decision making. *Addiction, 92,* 597–600.

McCall, R. B. (1979). *Infants.* Cambridge, MA: Harvard University Press.

McCann, D., Barrett, A., Cooper, A., Crumpler, D., Dalen, L., Grimshaw, K., et al. (2007). Food additives and hyperactive behaviour in 3-year-old and 8/9-year-old children in the community: A randomised, double-blinded, placebo-controlled trial. *Lancet, 370*(9598), 1560–1567. doi:10.1016/s0140-6736(07)61306-3

McCarley, R. W. (2007). Neurobiology of REM and NREM sleep. *Sleep Medicine, 8*(4), 302

McClelland, D. C. (1953). *The achievement society.* New York, NY: Appleton.

McClelland, D. C. (1985). *Human motivation.* Glenview, IL: Scott, Foresman.

McClelland, D. C., & Boyatzis, R. E. (1982). Leadership motive pattern and long-term success in management. *Journal of Applied Psychology, 67,* 737–743.

McClure, S. M., Li, J., Tomlin, D., Cypert, K. S., Montague, L. M., & Montague, P. R. (2004). Neural correlates of behavioral preference for culturally familiar drinks. *Neuron 44*(2), 379–387.

McComb, K., Baker, L., & Moss, C. (2006). African elephants show high levels of interest in the skulls and ivory of their own species. *Biology Letters, 2*(1), 26–28.

McCrae, R. R., & Costa, P. T. (1985). Updating Norman's "adequacy taxonomy":

Intelligence and personality dimensions in natural language and in questionnaires. *Journal of Personality and Social Psychology, 49,* 710–721.

McCrae, R. R., & Costa, P. T. (1987). Validation of the five-factor model of personality across instruments and observers. *Journal of Personality and Social Psychology, 52,* 81–90.

McCrae, R. R., & Costa, P. T., Jr. (1997). Personality trait structure as a human universal. *American Psychologist, 52*(5), 509–516. doi:10.1037/0003-066x.52.5.509

McCrae, R. R., Kurtz, J. E., Yamagata, S., & Terracciano, A. (2011). Internal consistency, retest reliability, and their implications for personality scale validity. *Personality and Social Psychology Review, 15*(1), 28–50. doi:10.1177/1088868310366253

McDaniel, M. A. (2000). Big-brained people are smarter: A meta-analysis of the relationship between in vivo brain volume and intelligence. *Intelligence, 33,* 337–346.

McEwen, B. S. (2001). Invited Review: Estrogens effects on the brain: Multiple sites and molecular mechanisms. Series: Genome and hormones: Gender differences in physiology. *Journal of Applied Physiology, 91*(6), 2785–2801.

McGaw, S., Shaw, T., & Beckley, K. (2007). Prevalence of psychopathology across a service population of parents with intellectual disabilities and their children. *Journal of Policy and Practice in Intellectual Disabilities, 4,* 11–22.

McGraw, A. P., Mellers, B. A., & Tetlock, P. E. (2005). Expectations and emotions of Olympic athletes. *Journal of Experimental Social Psychology, 41*(4), 438–446. doi:10.1016/j.jesp.2004.09.001

McGuffin, P., Reveley, A., & Holland, A. (1982). Identical triplets: Non-identical psychosis? *British Journal of Psychiatry, 140,* 1–6.

McGuffin, P., Riley, B., & Plomin, R. (2001). Toward behavioral genomics. *Science, 291*(5507), 1232–1249. doi:10.1126/science.1057264

McKay, D. (2011). Methods and mechanisms in the efficacy of psychodynamic psychotherapy. *American Psychologist, 66*(2), 147–148. doi:10.1037/a0021195

McKay, K. E., Halperin, J. M., Schwartz, S. T., & Sharma, V. (1994). Developmental analysis of three aspects of information processing: Sustained attention, selective attention, and response organization. *Developmental Neuropsychology, 10*(2), 121–132. doi:10.1080/87565649409540572

McKelley, R. A., & Rochlen, A. B. (2007). The practice of coaching: Exploring alternatives to therapy for counseling-resistant men. *Psychology of Men and Masculinity, 8*(1), 53–65. doi:10.1037/1524-9220.8.1.53

McKetin, R., McLaren, J., Lubman, D. I., & Hides, L. (2006). The prevalence of psychotic symptoms among methamphetamine users. *Addiction, 101*(10), 1473–1478.

McLean, D. E., & Link, B. G. (1994). Unraveling complexity: Strategies to refine concepts, measures, and research designs in the study of life events and mental health. In W. R. Avison & I. H. Gotlib (Eds.), *Stress and mental health: Contemporary issues and*

prospects for the future (pp. 15–42). New York, NY: Plenum Press.

McNulty, J. K., Neff, L. A., & Karney, B. R. (2008). Beyond initial attraction: Physical attractiveness in newlywed marriage. *Journal of Family Psychology, 22*(1), 135–143. doi:10.1037/0893-3200.22.1.135

McQueeny, T., Schweinsburg, B. C., Schweinsburg, A. D., Jacobus, J., Bava, S., Frank, L. R., et al. (2009). Altered white matter integrity in adolescent binge drinkers. *Alcoholism: Clinical and Experimental Research, 33*(7), 1278–1285.

Meaney, M. J. (2010). Epigenetics and the biological definition of gene x environment interactions. *Child Development, 81*(1), 41–79.

Meaney, M. J., Diorio, J., Francis, D., Weaver, S., Yau, J., Chapman, K., et al. (2000). Postnatal handling increases the expression of cAMP-inducible transcription factors in the rat hippocampus: The effects of thyroid hormones and serotonin. *Journal of Neuroscience, 20*(10), 3926–3935.

Mecca, A. M., Smelser, N. J., & Vasconcellos, J. (Eds.). (1989). *The social importance of self-esteem.* Berkeley, CA: University of California Press.

Medda, P., Perugi, G., Zanello, S., Ciuffa, M., & Cassano, G. B. (2009). Response to ECT in bipolar I, bipolar II and unipolar depression. *Journal of Affective Disorders, 118*(1–3), 55–59. doi:10.1016/j.jad.2009.01.014

Meddis, R., Pearson, A., & Langford, G. (1973). An extreme case of healthy insomnia. *Electroencephalography and Clinical Neurophysiology, 35,* 213–214.

Mednick, S. A., & Kandel, E. (1988). Genetic and perinatal factors in violence. In T. E. Moffitt & S. A. Mednick (Eds.), *Biological contributions to crime causation* (pp. 40–54). Boston, MA: Martinus Nijhoff.

Medvec, V. H., Madey, S. F., & Gilovich, T. (1995). When less is more: Counterfactual thinking and satisfaction among Olympic medalists. *Journal of Personality and Social Psychology, 69*(4), 603–610. doi:10.1037/0022-3514.69.4.603

Meeus, W. H. J., & Raaijmakers, Q. A. W. (1995). Obedience in modern society: The Utrecht studies. *Journal of Social Issues, 51,* 155–175.

Mehl, M. R., Vazire, S., Ramírez-Esparza, N., Slatcher, R. B., & Pennebaker, J. W. (2007). Are women really more talkative than men? *Science, 317*(5834), 82. doi:10.1126/science.1139940

Meltzer, H. Y., Bobo, W. V., Lee, M. A., Cola, P., & Jayathilake, K. (2010). A randomized trial comparing clozapine and typical neuroleptic drugs in non-treatment-resistant schizophrenia. *Psychiatry Research, 177*(3), 286–293. doi:10.1016/j.psychres.2010.02.018

Meltzoff, A. N., Kuhl, P. K., Movellan, J., & Sejnowski, T. J. (2009). Foundations for a new science of learning. *Science, 325*(5938), 284–288. doi:10.1126/science.1175626

Melzack, R., & Wall, P. D. (1965). Pain mechanisms: A new history. *Science, 150,* 971–979.

Melzack, R., & Wall, P. D. (1983). *The challenge of pain.* New York, NY: Basic Books.

Melzack, R., Taenzer, P., Feldman, P., & Kinch, R. A. (1981). Labour is still painful after prepared childbirth training. *Canadian Medical Association Journal, 125*(4), 357–363.

Mendel, G. (1866). Experiments in plant hybrid-ization (W. Bateson & R. Blumberg, Trans.). Retrieved November 27, 2009, from http://www.esp.org/foundations/genetics/classical/gm-65-f.pdf

Mennella, J. A., & Beauchamp, G. K. (1996). The human infant's response to vanilla flavors in mother's milk and formula. *Infant Behavior and Development, 19*, 13–19.

Mennella, J. A., Jagnow, C. P., & Beauchamp, G. K. (2001). Prenatal and postnatal flavor learning by human infants. *Pediatrics, 107*, E88.

Menzel, E. W. (1978). Cognitive mapping in chimpanzees. In S. H. Hulse, H. Fowler, & W. K. Honig (Eds.), *Cognitive processes in animal behavior* (pp. 375–422). Hillsdale, NJ: Erlbaum.

Menzies, L., Chamberlain, S. R., Laird, A. R., Thelen, S. M., Sahakian, B. J., & Bullmore, E. T. (2008). Integrating evidence from neuro-imaging and neuropsychological studies of obsessive-compulsive disorder: The orbito-fronto-striatal model revisited. *Neuroscience and Biobehavioral Reviews, 32*(3), 525–549.

Merritt, L. L., Martin, B. R., Walters, C., Licht-man, A. H., & Damaj, M. I. (2008). The endogenous cannabinoid system modulates nicotine reward and dependence. *Journal of Pharmacology and Experimental Therapeu-tics, 326*(2), 483–492.

Mery, F., & Kawecki, T. J. (2005). A cost of long-term memory in Drosophila. *Science, 308*, 1148.

Merzenich, M. M., & Jenkins, W. M. (1993). Reorganization of cortical representations of the hand following alterations of skin inputs induced by nerve injury, skin island transfers, and experience. *Journal of Hand Therapy, 6*, 89–104.

Merzenich, M. M., Jenkins, W. M., Johnston, P., Schreiner, C., Miller, S. L., & Tallal, P. (1996). Temporal processing deficits of language-learning impaired children ameliorated by training. *Science, 271*, 77–81.

Meyer, D. E., & Schvanevelt, R.W. (1971). Facilitation in recognizing pairs of words: Evidence of a dependence between retrieval operations. *Journal of Experimental Psychol-ogy, 90*, 227–234.

Meyer-Bahlburg, H. F., Dolezal, C., Baker, S. W., & New, M. I. (2008). Sexual orientation in women with classical or non-classical con-genital adrenal hyperplasia as a function of degree of prenatal androgen excess. *Archives of Sexual Behavior, 37*(1), 85–99.

Michalski, D., Kohout, J., Wicherski, M., & Hart, B. (2011). 2009 doctorate employ-ment survey. Retrieved on December 11, 2011 from http://www.apa.org/workforce/publications/09-doc-empl/index.aspx

Middleton, H., & Moncrieff, J. (2011). They won't do any harm and might do some good: Time to think again on the use of antidepres-sants? *British Journal of General Practice, 61*(582), 47–49. doi:10.3399/bjgp11X548983

Mieda, M., Williams, S. C, Richardson, J. A., Tanaka, K., & Yanagisawa, M. (2006). The dorsomedial hypothalamic nucleus as a puta-tive food-entrainable circadian pacemaker. *Proceedings of the National Academy of Sci-ences, 103*(32), 12150–12155.

Milani, R. V., & Lavie, C. J. (2009). Reducing psychosocial stress: A novel mechanism of improving survival from exercise training. *American Journal of Medicine, 122*(10), 931–938. doi:10.1016/j.amjmed.2009.03.028

Milevsky, A., Schlechter, M., Netter, S., & Keehn, D. (2007). Maternal and paternal parenting styles in adolescents: Associations with self-esteem, depression and life-satisfaction. *Jour-nal of Child and Family Studies, 16*(1), 39–47.

Milgram, S. (1963). Behavioral study of obedi-ence. *Journal of Abnormal and Social Psy-chology, 67*, 371–378.

Milgram, S. (1974). *Obedience to authority.* New York, NY: Harper & Row.

Milich, R., & Pelham, W. E. (1986). Effects of sugar ingestion on the classroom and playground behavior of attention deficit disordered boys. *Journal of Consulting and Clinical Psychology, 54*, 714–718.

Milinski, M., Semmann, D., & Jrambeck, H.-J. (2002). Reputation helps solve the "tragedy of the commons." *Nature, 415*, 424–426.

Miller, B. L., Seeley, W. W., Mychack, P., Rosen, H. J., Mena, I., & Boone, K. (2001). Neuro-anatomy of the self: Evidence from patients with frontotemporal dementia. *Neurology, 57*(5), 817–821.

Miller, D. T., & Ross, M. (1975). Self-serving biases in the attribution of causality: Fact or fiction? *Psychological Bulletin, 82*, 213–225.

Miller, G. A. (1956). The magical number seven, plus or minus two: Some limits on our capacity for processing information. *Psycho-logical Review, 63*, 81–97.

Miller, G. A., & Gildea, P. M. (1987). How chil-dren learn words. *Scientific American, 257*, 94–99.

Miller, J. G., & Bersoff, D. M. (1992). Culture and moral judgment: How are conflicts between justice and interpersonal responsibilities resolved? *Journal of Personality and Social Psychology, 62*(4), 541–554.

Millward, C., Ferriter, M., Calver, S., & Con-nell-Jones, G. (2008). Gluten- and casein-free diets for autistic spectrum disorder. *Cochrane Database of Systematic Reviews, 2*, CD003498.

Milner, B. (1966). Amnesia following operation on the temporal lobe. In C. W. M. Whitty & O. L. Zangwill (Eds.), *Amnesia* (pp. 109–133). London: Butterworth.

Milner, B. (1974). Hemispheric specialization: Scope and limitations. In F. O. Schmitt & F. G. Worden (Eds.), *The neurosciences: Third study program.* Cambridge, MA: MIT Press.

Milner, B. (2005). The medial temporal-lobe amnesic syndrome. *The Psychiatric Clinics of North America, 28*, 599–611.

Milner, B., Corkin, S., & Teuber, H. L. (1968). Further analysis of the hippocampal amnesic syndrome: 14-year follow-up study of H.M. *Neuropsychologia, 6*, 215–234.

Mindess, A. (2006). *Reading between the signs* (2nd ed.). Boston, MA: Intercultural Press.

MindSign Neuromarketing. (2010). MindSign services: Neuropolitics. Retrieved June 28, 2010, from http://mindsignonline.com/services_pennsylvania.html

MindSign Neuromarketing. (2011). What is neurocinema? Retrieved July 5, 2011, from http://mindsignonline.com/neurocinema.html

Mineka, S., & Cook, M. (1988). Social learning and the acquisition of snake fear in monkeys. In T. R. Zentall & B. G. Galef (Eds.), *Social learning: Psychological and biological per-spectives* (pp. 51–73). Hillsdale, NJ: Erlbaum.

Mineka, S., Sutton, J., Craske, M. G., Hermans, D., & Vansteenwegen, D. (2006). Contem-porary learning theory perspectives on the etiology of fears and phobias. In M. G. Craske, D. Hermans, & D. Vansteenwegen (Eds.), *Fear and learning: From basic pro-cesses to clinical implications* (pp. 75–97). Washington, DC: American Psychological Association.

Mirnics, K., Middleton, F. A., Marquez, A., Lewis, D. A., & Levitt, P. (2000). Molecular characterization of schizophrenia viewed by microarray analysis of gene expression in prefrontal cortex. *Neuron, 28*, 53.

Mischel, W. (1968). *Personality and assessment.* New York, NY: Wiley.

Mischel, W. (2004). Toward an integrative sci-ence of the person. *Annual Review of Psy-chology, 55*, 1–22.

Mischel, W., & Shoda, Y. (1995). A cognitive-affective system theory of personality: Reconceptualizing situations, dispositions, dynamics, and invariance in personality structure. *Psychological Review, 102*(2), 246–268.

Mischel, W., Ebbesen, E. B., & Raskoff Zeiss, A. (1972). Cognitive and attentional mecha-nisms in delay of gratification. *Journal of Personality and Social Psychology, 21*(2), 204–218. doi:10.1037/h0032198

Mishra, A., Mishra, H., & Masters, T. M. (2012). The influence of bite size on quantity of food consumed: A field study. *Journal of Con-sumer Research.* Advance online publication.

Mitchell, B. A., & Lovegreen, L. D. (2009). The empty nest syndrome in midlife families. *Journal of Family Issues, 30*(12), 1651–1670. doi:10.1177/0192513x09339020

Mobbs, D., Lau, H. C., Jones, O. D., & Frith, C. D. (2007). Law, responsibility, and the brain. *PLoS Biology, 5*(4), 693–700.

Mobbs, D., Petrovic, P., Marchant, J. L., Has-sabis, D., Weiskopf, N., Seymour, B., et al. (2007). When fear is near: Threat imminence elicits prefrontal-periaqueductal gray shifts in humans. *Science, 317*, 1079–1083.

Moberg, T., Nordström, P., Kristiansson, M., & Jokinen, J. (2011). FC04-03 – Serotonin, trauma and violence in attempted suicide. *European Psychiatry, 26*(Suppl. 1), 1830–1830. doi:10.1016/s0924-9338(11)73534-9

Mofenson, L. M. (2010). Protecting the next generation—eliminating perinatal HIV-1 infection. *New England Journal of Medicine, 362*(24), 2316–2318.

Moffitt, T. E., Caspi, A., Taylor, A., Kokaua, J., Milne, B. J., Polanczyk, G., & Poulton, R. (2010). How common are common mental disorders? Evidence that lifetime prevalence rates are doubled by prospective *versus* retrospective ascertainment. *Psycho-logical Medicine, 40*, 899–909. doi:10.1017/S0033291709991036

Moldofsky, H., & Scarisbrick, P. (1976). Induc-tion of neurasthenic musculoskeletal pain syndrome by selective sleep stage deprivation. *Psychosomatic Medicine, 38,* 35–44.

Molina, E., Cervilla, J., Rivera, M., Torres, F., Bellón, J. Á., Moreno, B., et al. (2011). Polymorphic variation at the serotonin 1-A receptor gene is associated with comorbid depression and generalized anxiety. *Psychiatric Genetics, 21*(4), 195–201. doi:10.1097/YPG.1090b1013e3283457a3283448

Monk, C. S., Telzer, E. H., Mogg, K., Bradley, B. P., Mai, X., Louro, H. M. C., et al. (2008). Amygdala and ventrolateral prefrontal cortex activation to masked angry faces in children and adolescents with generalized anxiety disorder. *Archives of General Psychiatry, 65*(5), 568–576. doi:10.1001/archpsyc.65.5.568

Monson, C. M., Taft, C. T., & Fredman, S. J. (2009). Military-related PTSD and intimate relationships: From description to theory-driven research and intervention development. *Clinical Psychology Review, 29*(8), 707–714. doi:10.1016/j.cpr.2009.09.002

Monti, M. M., Vanhaudenhuyse, A., Coleman, M. R., Boly, M., Pickard, J. D., Tshibanda, L., et al. (2010). Willful modulation of brain activity in disorders of consciousness. *New England Journal of Medicine, 362*(7), 579–589. doi:10.1056/NEJMoa0905370

Montpetit, M. A., Bergeman, C. S., Deboeck, P. R., Tiberio, S. S., & Boker, S. M. (2010). Resilience-as-process: Negative affect, stress, and coupled dynamical systems. *Psychology and Aging, 25*(3), 631–640. doi:10.1037/a0019268

Moon, C., Cooper, R. P., & Fifer, W. P. (1993). Two-day-olds prefer their native language. *Infant Behavior and Development, 16,* 495–500.

Moore, B. R. (1992). Avian movement imitation and a new form of mimicry: Tracing the evolution of a complex form of learning. *Behaviour, 122,* 231–263.

Moore, T. E. (1996). Scientific consensus and expert testimony: Lessons from the Judas Priest trial. Retrieved May 26, 2007, from http://www.csicop.org/si/9611/judas_priest.html

Moreno, C., Laje, G., Blanco, C., Jiang, H., Schmidt, A. B., & Olfson, M. (2007). National trends in the outpatient diagnosis and treatment of bipolar disorder in youth. *Archives of General Psychiatry, 64*(9), 1032–1039. doi:10.1001/archpsyc.64.9.1032

Morin, C. M., Culbert, J. P., & Schwartz, S. M. (1994). Nonpharmacological interventions for insomnia: A meta-analysis of treatment efficacy. *American Journal of Psychiatry, 151*(8), 1172–1180.

Morris, J. S., DeGelder, B., Weiskrantz, L., & Dolan, R. J. (2001). Differential extragenicu-lostriate and amygdala responses to presentation of emotional faces in a cortically blind field. *Brain Research, 124*(6), 1241–1252. doi:10.1093/brain/124.6.1241

Morris, M. W., & Peng, K. (1994). Culture and cause: American and Chinese attributions for social and physical events. *Journal of Personality and Social Psychology, 67,* 949–971.

Morse, S., & Gergen, K. J. (1970). Social comparison, self-consistency, and the concept of self. *Journal of Personality and Social Psychology, 16,* 148–156.

Moscovici, S. (1976). *Social influence and social change.* London: Academic Press.

Moscovici, S., & Zavalloni, M. (1969). The group as a polarizer of attitudes. *Journal of Personality and Social Psychology, 12,* 125–135.

Moscovici, S., Lage, S., & Naffrechoux, M. (1969). Influence of a consistent minority on the responses of a majority in a color perception task. *Sociometry, 32,* 365–380.

Moskalenko, Y. E., Weinstein, G. B., Kravchenko, T. I., Mozhaev, S. V., Semernya, V. N., Feilding, A., et al. (2008). The effect of craniotomy on the intracranial hemodynamics and cerebrospinal fluid dynamics in humans. *Human Physiology, 34*(3), 299–305.

Mössner, R., Schuhmacher, A., Schulze-Rauschenbach, S., Kühn, K.-U., Rujescu, D., Rietschel, M., et al. (2008). Further evidence for a functional role of the glutamate receptor gene GRM3 in schizophrenia. *European Neuropsychopharmacology, 18*(10), 768–772. doi:10.1016/j.euroneuro.2008.05.007

Mundorf, N., Weaver, J., & Zillmann, D. (1989). Effects of gender roles and self perceptions on affective reactions to horror films. *Sex Roles, 20*(11), 655–673. doi:10.1007/bf00288078

Mundy, P., Block, J., Delgado, C., Pomares, Y., Van Hecke, A. V., & Parlade, M. V. (2007). Individual differences and the development of joint attention in infancy. *Child Development, 78*(3), 938–954.

Munker, H. (1970). *Farbige Gitter, Abbildung auf der Netzhaut und übertragungstheoretische Beschreibung der Farbwahrnehmung* [Chromatic grids, projection to the retina, and translation theory-based description of the color perception]. München: Habilitationsschrift.

Muraven, M., & Baumeister, R. F. (2000). Self-regulation and depletion of limited resources: Does self-control resemble a muscle? *Psychological Bulletin, 126,* 247–259.

Murdoch, B. B., Jr. (1962). The serial position effect in free recall. *Journal of Experimental Psychology, 64,* 482–488.

Murphy, J. M., Gilligan, C., & Puka, B. (1994). *Moral development in late adolescence and adulthood: A critique and reconstruction of Kohlberg's theory.* New York, NY: Garland.

Murphy, K. D., Rose, M. W., Chinkes, D. L., Meyer, W. J., III, Herndon, D. N., Hawkins, H. K., et al. (2007). The effects of gammahydroxybutyrate on hypermetabolism and wound healing in a rat model of large thermal injury. *Journal of Trauma, 63*(5), 1099–1107.

Murray, H. A. (1938). *Explorations in personality.* New York, NY: Oxford University Press.

Murray, S. L., Holmes, J. G., Gellavia, G., Griffin, D. W., & Dolderman, D. (2002). Kindred spirits? The benefits of egocentrism in close relationships. *Journal of Personality and Social Psychology, 82,* 563–581.

Myers, D. G. (1993). *The pursuit of happiness.* New York, NY: Avon.

Nair, K. S. (1995). Muscle protein turnover: Methodological issues and the effect of aging. *Journals of Gerontology: Series A. Biological Sciences and Medical Sciences, 50,* 107–112.

Narumi, J., Miyazawa, S., Miyata, H., Suzuki, A., Kohsaka, S., & Kosugi, H. (1999). Analysis

of human error in nursing care. *Accident: Analysis and Prevention, 31,* 625–629.

Nasrallah, H. A., Hopkins, T., & Pixley, S. K. (2010). Differential effects of antipsychotic and antidepressant drugs on neurogenic regions in rats. *Brain Research, 1354,* 23–29. doi:10.1016/j.brainres.2010.07.075

National Institute of Child Health and Human Development (NICHHD). (2003). SIDS: Back to sleep public education campaign. Retrieved February 27, 2010, from http://www.nichd.nih.gov/sids/

National Institute of Mental Health (NIH) (2009). What causes ADHD? Retrieved on December 6, 2011, from http://www.nimh.nih.gov/health/publications/attention-deficit-hyperactivity-disorder/what-causes-adhd.shtml

National Sleep Foundation (2008). 2008 Sleep in America poll. Retrieved on December 2, 2011 from http://www.sleepfoundation.org/sites/default/files/2008%20POLL%20SOF.PDF

National Sleep Foundation. (2009). Restless legs syndrome (RLS) and sleep. Retrieved February 27, 2010, from http://www.sleepfoundation.org/article/sleep-related-problems/restless-legs-syndrome-rls-and-sleep

Navara, K. J., & Nelson, R. J. (2007). The dark side of light at night: Physiological, epidemiological, and ecological consequences. *Journal of Pineal Research, 43,* 215–224.

Neal, D. T., & Chartrand, T. L. (2011). Embodied emotion perception: Amplifying and dampening facial feedback modulates emotion perception accuracy. *Social Psychological and Personality Science, 2*(6), 673–678. doi:10.1177/1948550611406138

Nedeltcheva, A. V., Kilkus, J. M., Imperial, J., Schoeller, D. A., & Penev, P. D. (2010). Insufficient sleep undermines dietary efforts to reduce adiposity. *Annals of Internal Medicine, 153,* 435–441.

Negovsky, V. A., & Gurvitch, A. M. (2004). Post-resuscitation disease—a new nosological entity: Its reality and significance. *Resuscitation, 30,* 23–27.

Neigh, G. N., Gillespie, C. F., & Nemeroff, C. B. (2009). The neurobiological toll of child abuse and neglect. *Trauma, Violence, and Abuse, 10*(4), 389–410. doi:10.1177/1524838009339758

Neisser, U. (1967). *Cognitive psychology.* Upper Saddle River, NJ: Prentice-Hall.

Neisser, U. (1981). John Dean's memory: A case study. *Cognition, 9,* 1–22.

Neisser, U., Boodoo, G., Bouchard, T. J., Boykin, A. W., Brody, N., Ceci, S. J., et al. (1996). Intelligence: Knowns and unknowns. *American Psychologist, 51*(2), 77–101.

Nelson, C. A. (2000). The neurological bases of early intervention. In J. P. Shonkoff & S. J. Meisels (Eds.), *Handbook of Early Childhood Intervention,* 2nd ed. (pp. 204–227). Cambridge, MA: Cambridge University Press.

Neuner, F., Schauer, E., Catani, C., Ruf, M., & Elbert, T. (2006). Post-tsunami stress: A study of posttraumatic stress disorder in children living in three severely affected regions in Sri Lanka. *Journal of Traumatic Stress, 19,* 339–347.

Neville, H. J., Bavelier, D., Corina, D., Rauschecker, J., Karni, A., Lalwani, A., et al.

(1998). Cerebral organization for language in deaf and hearing subjects: Biological constraints and effects of experience. *Proceedings of the National Academy of Sciences, 95,* 922–929.

Newcombe, T. M. (1929). *Consistency of certain extrovert-introvert behavior patterns in 51 problem boys.* New York, NY: Columbia University Teachers College Press.

Newell, A., & Simon, H. (1972). *Human problem solving.* Englewood Cliffs, NJ: Prentice Hall.

Newitz, A. (2000). The personality paradox: Industry trend or event. *The Industry Standard.* Retrieved July 16, 2007, from FindArticles.com. http://findarticles.com/p/articles/mi_m0HWW/is_39_3/ai_6667

Newman, T. K., Syagailo, Y. V., Barr, C. S., Wendland, J. R., Champoux, M., Graessle, M., et al. (2005). Monoamine oxidase a gene promoter variation and rearing experience influences aggressive behavior in rhesus monkeys. *Biological Psychiatry, 57*(2): 167–172.

Nielsen, M., & Tomaselli, K. (2010). Overimitation in Kalahari Bushman children and the origins of human cultural cognition. *Psychological Science, 21,* 729–736. doi:10.1177/0956797610368808

Nielsen, T. A., Zadra, A., Simard, V., Saucier, S., Kuiken, D., & Smith, C. (2003). Typical dreams of Canadian university students. *Dreaming, 13,* 211–235.

Noaghiul, S., & Hibbeln, J. R. (2003). Crossnational comparisons of seafood consumption and rates of bipolar disorders. *American Journal of Psychiatry, 160*(12), 2222–2227. doi:10.1176/appi.ajp.160.12.2222

Noelle-Neumann, E. (1984). *The spiral of silence: Public opinion—our social skin.* Chicago, IL: University of Chicago Press.

Nolen-Hoeksema, S. (1991). Responses to depression and their effects on the duration of depressive episodes. *Journal of Abnormal Psychology, 100,* 569–582.

Nolen-Hoeksema, S. (2003). *Women who think too much: How to break free of overthinking and reclaim your life.* New York, NY: Henry Holt.

Nolen-Hoeksema, S., & Girgus, J. S. (1994). The emergence of gender differences in depression during adolescence. *Psychological Bulletin, 115,* 424–443.

Norcross, J. C., & Castle, P. H. (2002). Appreciating the Psy.D.: The facts. *Eye on Psi Chi, 7,* 22–26.

Norman, W. T. (1963). Toward an adequate taxonomy of personality attributes: Replicated factor structure in peer nomination personality ratings. *Journal of Abnormal and Social Psychology, 66,* 574–583.

Nosek, B. A. (2007). Understanding the individual implicitly and explicitly. *International Journal of Psychology, 42*(3), 184–188.

Nowak, M. A. (2006). Five rules for the evolution of cooperation. *Science, 314,* 1560–1563.

O'Brien, T. B., & DeLongis, A. (1996). The interactional context of problem-, emotion-, and relationship-focused coping: The role of the Big Five personality factors. *Journal of Personality, 64*(4), 775–813. doi:10.1111/j.1467-6494.1996.tb00944.x

O'Keefe, J., & Nadel, L. (1978). *The hippocampus as a cognitive map.* Oxford, United Kingdom: Oxford University Press.

O'Reardon, J. P., Solvason, H. B., Janicak, P. G., Sampson, S., Isenberg, K. E., Nahas, Z., et al. (2007). Efficacy and safety of transcranial magnetic stimulation in the acute treatment of major depression: A multisite randomized controlled trial. *Biological Psychiatry, 62*(11), 1208–1216. doi:10.1016/j.biopsych.2007.01.018

O'Rourke, N., & Cappeliez, P. (2005). Marital satisfaction and self-deception: Reconstruction of relationship histories among older adults. *Social Behavior and Personality, 33*(3), 273–282. doi:10.2224/sbp.2005.33.3.273

Ochsner, K. N., Beer, J. S., Robertson, E., Cooper, J., Gabrieli, J. D. E., Kihlstrom, J. F., et al. (2005). The neural correlates of direct and reflected self-knowledge. *Neuroimage, 28,* 797–814.

Ochsner, K. N., Knierim, K., Ludlow, D., Hanelin, J., Ramachandran, T., & Mackey, S. (2004). Reflecting upon feelings: An fMRI study of neural systems supporting the attribution of emotion to self and other. *Journal of Cognitive Neuroscience, 16,* 1746–1772.

Odegard, T. N., Cooper, C. M., Lampinen, J. M., Reyna, V. F., & Brainerd, C. J. (2009). Children's eyewitness memory for multiple real-life events. *Child Development, 80*(6), 1877–1890. doi:10.1111/j.1467-8624.2009.01373.x

Ogden, C. L., & Carroll, M. D. (2010, June). Prevalence of overweight, obesity, and extreme obesity among adults: United States, trends 1960–1962 through 2007–2008. *NCHS Health E-Stats.* Atlanta, GA: Centers for Disease Control and Prevention. Retrieved from http://www.cdc.gov/NCHS/data/hestat/obesity_adult_07_08/obesity_adult_07_08.pdf

Olfson, M., & Marcus, S. C. (2009). National patterns in antidepressant medication treatment. *Archives of General Psychiatry, 66*(8), 848–856. doi:10.1001/archgenpsychiatry.2009.81

Olsho, L. W., Koch, E. G., Halpin, C. F., & Carter, E. A. (1987). An observer-based psychoacoustic procedure for use with young infants. *Developmental Psychology, 23,* 627–640.

Olson, C. K. (2010). Children's motivations for video game play in the context of normal development. *Review of General Psychology, 14*(2), 180–187. doi:10.1037/a0018984

onthemedia.org. (2009). The witnesses that didn't: Transcript. Retrieved August 17, 2011, from http://www.onthemedia.org/2009/mar/27/the-witnesses-that-didnt/transcript/

Orne, M. T., & Evans, F. J. (1965). Social control in the psychological experiment: Antisocial behavior and hypnosis. *Journal of Personality and Social Psychology, 1,* 189–200.

Osaka, M., Osaka, N., Kondo, H., Morishita, M., Fukuyama, H., Aso, T., et al. (2003). The neural basis of individual differences in working memory capacity: An fMRI study. *NeuroImage, 18*(3), 789–797. doi:10.1016/s1053-8119(02)00032-0

Osinsky, R., Reuter, M., Küpper, Y., Schmitz, A., Kozyra, E., Alexander, N., et al. (2008). Variation in the serotonin transporter gene modulates selective attention to threat. *Emotion, 8*(4), 584–588. doi:10.1037/a0012826

Ostfeld, B. M., Esposito, L., Perl, H., & Hegyi, T. (2010). Concurrent risks in sudden infant death syndrome. *Pediatrics,125*(3), 447-453. doi: 10.1542/peds.2009-0038

Owen, M. J., Craddock, N., & Jablensky, A. (2007). The genetic deconstruction of psychosis. *Schizophrenia Bulletin, 33*(4), 905–911.

Padoa-Schioppa, C., & Assad, J. A. (2006). Neurons in the orbitofrontal cortex encode economic value. *Nature, 441,* 223–236.

Paluck, E. L., & Green, D. P. (2009). Prejudice reduction: What works? A review and assessment of research and practice. *Annual Review of Psychology, 60,* 339–367.

Papp, L. A., Klein, D. F., Martinez, J., Schneier, F., Cole, R., Liebowitz, M. R., et al. (1993). Diagnostic and substance specificity of carbon-dioxide-induced panic. *American Journal of Psychiatry, 150,* 250–257.

Pardo, C. A., & Eberhart, C. G. (2007). The neurobiology of autism. *Brain Pathology, 17*(4), 434–447.

Pardo, C. A., Vargas, D. L., & Zimmerman, A. W. (2005). Immunity, neuroglia and neuroinflammation in autism. *International Review of Psychiatry, 17,* 485–495.

Pargament, K. I., & Krumrei, E. J. (2009). Clinical assessment of clients' spirituality. In J. D. Aten & M. M. Leach (Eds.), *Spirituality and the therapeutic process: A comprehensive resource from intake to termination* (pp. 93–120). Washington, DC: American Psychological Association.

Parker, A. M., & Fischhoff, B. (2005). Decision-making competence: External validation through an individual-differences approach. *Journal of Behavioral Decision Making, 18,* 1–27.

Parrilla, L. (2006). O'Malley killer begins his sentence. *The Tribune,* San Luis Obispo, CA, p. B2.

Parrott, A. C. (2007). The psychotherapeutic potential of MDMA (3,4-methylenedioxymethamphetamine): An evidence-based review. *Psychopharmacology, 191*(2), 181–198.

Pascalis, O., & Kelly, D. J. (2009). The origins of face processing in humans: Phylogeny and ontogeny. *Perspectives on Psychological Science, 4*(2), 200–209. doi:10.1111/j.1745-6924.2009.01119.x

Pascual-Leone, A., & Torres, F. (1993). Plasticity of sensorimotor cortex representation of the reading finger in Braille readers. *Brain, 116,* 39–52.

Paterson, D. S., Trachtenberg, F. L., Thompson, E. G., Belliveau, R. A., Beggs, A. H., Darnall, R., et al. (2006). Multiple serotonergic brainstem abnormalities in sudden infant death syndrome. *JAMA: Journal of the American Medical Association, 296*(17), 2124–2132. doi:10.1001/jama.296.17.2124

Patterson, C. J. (2009). Children of lesbian and gay parents: Psychology, law, and policy. *American Psychologist, 64,* 727–736.

Patterson, F. (1978, October). Conversations with a gorilla. *National Geographic,* 438–465.

Patterson, F. (1984). Self-recognition by gorilla (*Gorilla gorilla*). *Gorilla, 7,* 2–3.

Patterson, F. G. P., & Cohn, R. H. (1994). Self-recognition and self-awareness in lowland gorillas. In S. T. Parker, R. W. Mitchell, & M. L. Boccia (Eds.), *Self-awareness in animals and humans: Developmental perspectives* (pp. 273–290). New York, NY: Cambridge University Press.

Patterson, G. R., Chamberlain, P., & Reid, J. B. (1982). A comparative evaluation of parent training procedures. *Behavior Therapy, 13*, 638–650.

Patterson, K. D., & Pyle, G. F. (1991). The geography and mortality of the 1918 influenza pandemic. *Bulletin of the History of Medicine, 65*(1), 4–21.

Paulhus, D. I. (1998). Interpersonal and intrapsychic adaptiveness of trait self-enhancement: A mixed blessing? *Journal of Personality and Social Psychology, 74*, 1197–1208.

Pavlov, I. P. (1906). The scientific investigation of the psychical faculties or processes in the higher animals. *Science, 24*, 613–619.

Pavlov, I. P. (1927). *Conditioned reflexes.* Oxford, United Kingdom: Oxford University Press.

Payne, J. D., Jackson, E. D., Hoscheidt, S., Ryan, L., Jacobs, W. J., & Nadel, L. (2007). Stress administered prior to encoding impairs neutral but enhances emotional long-term episodic memories. *Learning and Memory, 14*(12), 861–868.

Pearce, J. M. S. (2005). A note on aphasia in bilingual patients: Pitres' and Ribot's laws. *European Neurology, 54*, 127–131.

Pearce, M. T., Ruiz, M. H., Kapasi, S., Wiggins, G., & Bhattacharya, J. (2010). Unsupervised statistical learning underpins computational, behavioural, and neural manifestations of musical expectation. *NeuroImage.* doi:10.1016/j.neuroimage.2009.12.019

Pearson Assessments. (2005). MMPI-2. Retrieved August 27, 2006, from http://www.pearsonassessments.com/tests/mmpi_2.htm

Pearson, B. Z., Fernandez, S. C., & Oller, D. K. (1993). Lexical development in bilingual infants and toddlers: Comparison to monolingual norms. *Language Learning, 43*, 93–120.

Pegna, A. J., Landis, T., & Khateb, A. (2008). Electrophysiological evidence for early non-conscious processing of fearful facial expressions. *International Journal of Psychophysiology, 70*(2), 127–136.

Pelham, W. E., & Fabiano, G. A. (2008). Evidence-based psychosocial treatments for attention-deficit/hyperactivity disorder. *Journal of Clinical Child and Adolescent Psychology, 37*(1), 184–214. doi:10.1080/15374410701818681

Pelios, L. V., MacDuff, G. S., & Axelrod, S. (2003). The effects of a treatment package in establishing independent academic work skills in children with autism. *Education and Treatment of Children, 26*, 1–21.

Peltokorpi, V. (2008). Transactive memory systems. *Review of General Psychology, 12*(4), 378–394. doi:10.1037/1089-2680.12.4.378

Penke, L., & Asendorpf, J. B. (2008). Beyond global sociosexual orientations: A more differentiated look at sociosexuality and its effects on courtship and romantic relationships. *Journal of Personality and Social Psychology, 95*, 1113–1135.

Pepperberg, I. M. (1990). An investigation into the cognitive capacities of an African grey parrot (*Psittacus erithacus*). In P. J. B. Slater, J. R. Rosenblatt, & C. Beer (Eds.), *Advances in the study of behavior* (pp. 357–409). New York: Academic Press.

Perani, D., Paulesu, E., Galles, N. S., Dupoux, E., Dehaene, S., Bettinardi, V., et al. (1998). The bilingual brain: Proficiency and age of acquisition of the second language. *Brain, 121*, 1841–1852.

Perfect, T. J., & Askew, C. (1994). Print adverts: Not remembered but memorable. *Applied Cognitive Psychology, 8*(7), 693–703. doi:10.1002/acp.2350080707

Perkins, T., Stokes, M., McGillivray, J., & Bittar, R. (2010). Mirror neuron dysfunction in autism spectrum disorders. *Journal of Clinical Neuroscience, 17*(10), 1239–1243. doi:10.1016/j.jocn.2010.01.026

Pernanen, K. (1991). *Alcohol in human violence.* New York, NY: Guilford Press.

Perry, W. I. (1970). *Forms of intellectual and ethical development in the college years.* New York, NY: Holt, Rinehart and Winston.

Peters, A. (2010). The morphology of minicolumns. In G. J. Blatt (Ed.), *The neurochemical basis of autism* (pp. 45–68). New York, NY: Springer.

Peterson, C. (2006). *A primer in positive psychology.* New York, NY: Oxford University Press.

Peterson, C. C. (1996). The ticking of the social clock: Adults' beliefs about the timing of transition events. *International Journal of Aging and Human Development, 42*(3), 189–203. doi:10.2190/mmdd-f9yp-npn8-720m

Peterson, C., & Seligman, M. E. P. (2004). *Character strengths and virtues: A handbook and classification.* Washington, DC: APA Press and Oxford University Press.

Peterson, C., & Whalen, N. (2001). Five years later: Children's memory for medical emergencies. *Applied Cognitive Psychology, 15*(7), S7–S24. doi:10.1002/acp.832

Peterson, C., Semmel, A., von Baeyer, C., Abramson, L. Y., Metalsky, G. I., & Seligman, M. E. P. (1982). The attributional style questionnaire. *Cognitive Therapy and Research, 6*(3), 287–300.

Peterson, L. R., & Peterson, M. J. (1959). Short-term retention of individual verbal items. *Journal of Experimental Psychology, 58*, 193–198.

Petrides, M., Cadoret, G., & Mackey, S. (2005). Orofacial somatomotor responses in the macaque monkey homologue of Broca's area. *Nature, 435*(7046), 1235–1238. doi:10.1038/nature03628

Petrou, M. (2009). Preimplantation genetic diagnosis. *Hemoglobin, 33*(s1), S7–S13. doi:10.3109/03630260903344838

Petty, R. E., & Cacioppo, J. T. (1981). *Attitudes and persuasion: Classic and contemporary approaches.* Dubuque, IA: Wm. C. Brown.

Petty, R. E., & Cacioppo, J. T. (1986a). *Communication and persuasion: Central and peripheral routes to attitude change.* New York, NY: Springer-Verlag.

Petty, R. E., & Cacioppo, J. T. (1986b). The elaboration likelihood model of persuasion.

Advances in Experimental Social Psychology, 19, 123–205.

Petty, R. E., Cacioppo, J. T., & Kasmer, J. (1988). The role of affect in the elaboration likelihood model of persuasion. In L. Donohew, H. Sypher, & E. T. Higgins (Eds.), *Communication, social cognition, and affect* (pp. 117–146). Hillsdale, NJ: Erlbaum.

Peverly, S. T., Brobst, K. E., & Morris, K. S. (2002). The contribution of reading comprehension ability and meta-cognitive control to the development of studying in adolescence. *Journal of Research in Reading, 25*(2), 203.

Pew Research Center. (2010). The decline of marriage and rise of new families. Retrieved July 18, 2011, from http://pewresearch.org/pubs/1802/decline-marriage-rise-new-families

Phan, K. L., Wager, T., Taylor, S. F., & Liberzon, I. (2002). Functional neuroanatomy of emotion: A meta-analysis of emotion activation studies in PET and fMRI. *NeuroImage, 16*, 331–348.

Phelps, E. A., O'Connor, K. J., Cunningham, W. A., Funayama, E. S., Gatenby, J. C., Gore, J. C., et al. (2000). Performance on indirect measures of race evaluation predicts amygdala activation. *Journal of Cognitive Neuroscience, 12*, 729–738.

PhysOrg.com. (2006, July 28). First ever world map of happiness produced. Retrieved from http://www.physorg.com/news73321785.html

Piacentini, J., & Graae, F. (1997). Childhood OCD. In E. Hollander & D. Stei (Eds.), *Obsessive-compulsive disorders: Diagnosis, etiology, treatment* (pp. 23–46). New York, NY: Dekker.

Pietrzak, R. H., Goldstein, R. B., Southwick, S. M., & Grant, B. F. (2011). Prevalence and Axis I comorbidity of full and partial post-traumatic stress disorder in the United States: Results from Wave 2 of the National Epidemiologic Survey on Alcohol and Related Conditions. *Journal of Anxiety Disorders, 25*(3), 456–465. doi:10.1016/j.janxdis.2010.11.010

Pinker, S. (1994). *The language instinct: The new science of language and mind.* London: Penguin.

Piper, A., & Merskey, H. (2004). The persistence of folly: A critical examination of dissociative identity disorder. Part I. The excesses of an improbable concept. *Canadian Journal of Psychiatry, 49*(9), 592–600.

Pisani, J. (2009). More upper-income workers living paycheck to paycheck. Retrieved on December 11, 2011, from http://www.cnbc.com/id/32862851/

Pitman, R. K., Sanders, K. M., Zusman, R. M., Healy, A. R., Cheema, F., Lasko, N. B., et al. (2002). Pilot study of secondary prevention of posttraumatic stress disorder with propranolol. *Biological Psychiatry, 51*(2), 189–192.

Pitts, F. N., & McClure, J. N. (1967). Lactate metabolism in anxiety neurosis. *New England Journal of Medicine, 277*, 1329–1336.

Plomin, R. (1999). Two views about the nurture assumption. *PsycCRITIQUES, 44*(4), 269–271.

Plomin, R., & Spinath, F. M. (2004). Intelligence: Genetics, genes, and genomics. *Journal of Personality and Social Psychology, 86,* 112–129.

Plotnik, J. M., de Waal, F. B. M., & Reiss, D. (2006). Self-recognition in an Asian elephant. *Proceedings of the National Academy of Sciences, 103*(45), 17053–17057. doi:10.1073/pnas.0608062103

Plous, S. (1993). *The psychology of judgment and decision making.* New York: McGraw-Hill.

Pol, H. E. H., Schnack, H. G., Posthuma, D., Mandl, R. C. W., Baaré, W. F., van Oel, C., et al. (2006). Genetic contributions to human brain morphology and intelligence. *Journal of Neuroscience, 26*(40), 10235–10242. doi:10.1523/jneurosci.1312-06.2006

Polya, G. (1957). *How to solve it.* Garden City, NY: Doubleday.

Pope, H. G., Jr., Kouri, E. M., & Hudson, J. I. (2000). Effects of supraphysiologic doses of testosterone on mood and aggression in normal men: A randomized controlled trial. *Archives of General Psychiatry, 57*(2), 133–140.

Pope, H. G., Katz, D. L., & Hudson, J. I. (1993). Anorexia nervosa and "reverse anorexia" among 108 male bodybuilders. *Comprehensive Psychiatry, 34,* 406–409.

Porter, R. H., Makin, J. W., Davis, L. B., & Christensen, K. M. (1991). An assessment of the salient olfactory environment of formula-fed infants. *Physiology and Behavior, 50,* 907–911.

Posey, D. J., Stigler, K. A., Erickson, C. A., & McDougle, C. J. (2008). Antipsychotics in the treatment of autism. *Journal of Clinical Investigation, 118*(1), 6–14.

Posner, M. I., & Keele, S. W. (1970). Retention of abstract ideas. *Journal of Experimental Psychology, 83,* 304–308.

Poundstone, W. (1983). *Big secrets.* New York, NY: William Morrow.

Poundstone, W. (1992). *Prisoner's dilemma.* New York, NY: Doubleday.

Povinelli, D. J. (1993). Reconstructing the evolution of mind. *American Psychologist, 48,* 493–509.

Prasad, S., & Steer, C. (2008). Switching from neurostimulant therapy to atomoxetine in children and adolescents with attention-deficit hyperactivity disorder: Clinical approaches and review of current available evidence. *Paediatric Drugs, 10*(1), 39–47.

Pratkanis, A. R. (1992). Myths of subliminal persuasion: The cargo-cult science of subliminal persuasion. *Skeptical Inquirer, 16,* 260–272.

Pratt, L. A., & Brody, D. J. (2008, September). Depression in the United States household population, 2005–2006. NCHS Data Brief No. 7. Washington, DC: U.S. Department of Health and Human Services. Retrieved from http://www.cdc.gov/nchs/data/databriefs/db07.pdf

Premack, D. (1965). Reinforcement theory. In D. Levine (Ed.), *Nebraska Symposium on Motivation* (Vol. 13, pp. 3–41). Lincoln: University of Nebraska Press.

Premack, D. G., & Woodruff, G. (1978). Does the chimpanzee have a theory of mind? *Behavioral and Brain Sciences, 1,* 515–526.

Price, E. E., Lambeth, S. P., Schapiro, S. J., & Whiten, A. (2009). A potent effect of observational learning on chimpanzee tool construction. *Proceedings of the Royal Society B.*

Priebe, S. (2006). The provision of psychotherapy: An international comparison. Retrieved August 22, 2006, from http://cep.lse.ac.uk/textonly/research/mentalhealth/Stefan-Priebe_provision-of-incapacity-benefit.pdf

Prinzie, P., Stams, G. J. J. M., Deković, M., Reijntjes, A. H. A., & Belsky, J. (2009). The relations between parents' Big Five personality factors and parenting: A meta-analytic review. *Journal of Personality and Social Psychology, 97*(2), 351–362. doi:10.1037/a0015823

Pronin, E., & Kugler, M. B. (2007). Valuing thoughts, ignoring behavior: The introspection illusion as a source of the bias blind spot. *Journal of Experimental Social Psychology, 43*(4), 565–578. doi:10.1016/j.jesp.2006.05.011

Pronin, E., & Ross, L. (2006). Temporal differences in trait self-ascription: When the self is seen as an other. *Journal of Personality and Social Psychology, 90*(2), 197–209. doi:10.1037/0022-3514.90.2.197

Provine, R. R. (1986). Yawning as a stereotyped action pattern and releasing stimulus. *Ethology, 72,* 109–122.

Psychological Clinical Science Accreditation System (PCSAS). (2011). PCSAS mission. Retrieved August 27, 2011, from http://pcsas.org/mission-function.php

Public Broadcasting Service (PBS). (2005). The story of . . . smallpox—and other deadly Eurasian germs. Retrieved from http://www.pbs.org/gunsgermssteel/variables/smallpox.html

Public Broadcasting Service (PBS). (1998). DNA "fingerprinting." Retrieved December 6, 2009 from http://www.pbs.org/wgbh/aso/resources/guide/outcomesindex.html#DNA

Purves, D., & Lotto, R. B. (2002). *Why we see what we do: An empirical theory of vision.* Sunderland, MA: Sinauer Associates.

Pyszczynski, T., Greenberg, J., & Solomon, S. (1991). A terror management analysis of self-awareness and anxiety: The hierarchy of terror. In R. Schwarzer & R. A. Wicklund (Eds.), *Anxiety and self-focused attention* (pp. 67–85). Amsterdam, Netherlands: Harwood Academic Publishers.

Qin, S., Hermans, E. J., van Marle, H. J. F., Luo, J., & Fernández, G. (2009). Acute psychological stress reduces working memory-related activity in the dorsolateral prefrontal cortex. *Biological Psychiatry, 66*(1), 25–32. doi:10.1016/j.biopsych.2009.03.006

Qiu, D.-l., & Knopfel, T. (2007). An NMDA receptor/nitric oxide cascade in presynaptic parallel fiber-Purkinje neuron long-term potentiation. *Journal of Neuroscience, 27*(13), 3408–3415. doi:10.1523/jneurosci.4831-06.2007

Quillian, M. R. (1966). *Semantic memory* (Doctoral dissertation). Carnegie Institute of Technology, Pittsburgh, PA.

Quiroga, R. Q., Reddy, L., Kreiman, G., Koch, C., & Fried, I. (2005). Invariant visual representation by single neurons in the human brain. *Nature, 435,* 1102–1107.

Quiroz, J. A., Machado-Vieira, R., Zarate, J. C. A., & Manji, H. K. (2010). Novel insights into lithium's mechanism of action: Neurotrophic and neuroprotective effects. *Neuropsychobiology, 62*(1), 50–60.

Raine, A., Lencz, T., Bihrle, S., LaCasse, L., & Colletti, P. (2000). Reduced prefrontal gray matter volume and reduced autonomic activity in antisocial personality disorder. *Archives of General Psychiatry, 57,* 119–127.

Raine, A., Stoddard, J., Bihrle, S., & Buchsbaum, M. (1998). Prefrontal glucose deficits in murderers lacking psychosocial deprivation. *Neuropsychiatry, Neuropsychology, and Behavioral Neurology, 11*(1), 1–7.

Rainville, P., Hofbauer, R. K., Bushnell, M. C., Duncan, G. H., & Price, D. D. (2002). Hypnosis modulates activity in brain structures involved in the regulation of consciousness. *Journal of Cognitive Neuroscience, 14*(6), 887–901).

Rakic, P. (2000). Molecular and cellular mechanisms of neuronal migration: Relevance to cortical epilepsies. *Advances in Neurology, 84,* 1–14.

Ramachandran, V. S. (1998). Consciousness and body image: Lessons from phantom limbs, Capgras syndrome and pain asymbolia. *Philosophical Transactions of the Royal Society of London. Series B, Biological Sciences, 353,* 1851–1859.

Ramachandran, V. S., & Rogers-Ramachandran, D. (2000). Phantom limbs and neural plasticity. *Archives of Neurology, 57,* 317–320.

Ramachandran, V. S. (2006). Mirror neurons and imitation learning as the driving force behind "the great leap forward" in human evolution. Retrieved June 13, 2011, from http://www.edge.org/3rd_culture/ramachandran/ramachandran_p1.html

Ramaekers, J. G., Moeller, M. R., van Ruitenbeek, P., Theunissen, E. L., Schneider, E., & Kauert, G. (2006). Cognition and motor control as a function of [Delta]9-THC concentration in serum and oral fluid: Limits of impairment. *Drug and Alcohol Dependence, 85*(2), 114–122.

Rammstedt, B., & John, O. P. (2007). Measuring personality in one minute or less: A 10-item short version of the Big Five Inventory in English and German. *Journal of Research in Personality, 41*(1), 203–212. doi:10.1016/j.jrp.2006.02.001

Rapkin, A. J., Mikacich, J. A., Moatakef-Imani, B., & Rasgon, N. (2002). The clinical nature and formal diagnosis of premenstrual, postpartum, and perimenopausal affective disorders. *Current Psychiatry Reports, 4,* 419–428.

Rapoport, J. (1989). *The boy who couldn't stop washing: The experience and treatment of obsessive-compulsive disorder.* New York, NY: Dutton.

Rapoport, J. L., Giedd, J. N., Blumenthal, J., Hamburger, S., Jeffries, N., Fernandez, T., et al. (1999). Progressive cortical change during adolescence in childhood-onset schizophrenia: A longitudinal magnetic resonance imaging study. *Archives of General Psychiatry, 56,* 649–654.

Rasmussen, T., & Milner, B. (1977). The role of early left-brain injury in determining lateralization of cerebral speech functions. *Annals of the New York Academy of Sciences, 299,* 355–369.

Ratiu, P., & Talos, I.-F. (2004). The tale of Phineas Gage, digitally remastered. *New England Journal of Medicine, 351*(23), e21.

Rawlins, W. K. (2004). Friendships in later life. In J. F. Nussbaum & J. Coupland (Eds.), *Handbook of communication and aging research* (2nd ed., pp. 273–299). Mahwah, NJ: Erlbaum.

Raz, A., Kirsch, I., Pollard, J., & Nitkin-Kaner, Y. (2006). Suggestion reduces the Stroop Effect. *Psychological Science, 17*, 91–95.

Rebhan, B., Kohlhuber, M., Schwegler, U., Fromme, H., Abou-Dakn, M., & Koletzko, B. V. (2009). Breastfeeding duration and exclusivity associated with infants' health and growth: Data from a prospective cohort study in Bavaria, Germany. *Acta Paediatrica, 98*(6), 974–980. doi:10.1111/j.1651-2227 .2009.01281.x

Reese, H. E., McNally, R. J., & Wilhelm, S. (2010). Facial asymmetry detection in patients with body dysmorphic disorder. *Behaviour Research and Therapy, 48*(9), 936–940. doi:10.1016/j.brat.2010.05.021

Regan, C. (2000). *Intoxicating minds.* London, England: Weidenfeld and Nicolson.

Reichenberg, A., Gross, R., Kolevzon, A., & Susser, E. S. (2011). Parental and perinatal risk factors for autism. In E. Hollander, A. Kolevzon, & J. T. Coyle (Eds.), *Textbook of autism spectrum disorders* (pp. 239–246). Arlington, VA: American Psychiatric Publishing.

Reinisch, J. M., Ziemba-Davis, M., & Sanders, S. A. (1991). Hormonal contributions to sexually dimorphic behavioral development in humans. *Psychoneuroendocrinology, 16*, 213–278.

Reips, U.-D., & Orth, D. (2006). An Internet-based test of the Stock Choice Recognition Heuristic as an investment tool: More successful than experts, market and trust. Retrieved August 15, 2006, from http://www .psychologie.unizh.ch/sowi/reips/poster/ ReipsOrthJDM2005poster.pdf

Reisenzein, R. (1983). The Schachter theory of emotion: Two decades later. *Psychological Bulletin, 94*, 239–264.

Remez, R. E., Rubin, P. E., Pisoni, D. B., & Carell, T. D. (1981). Speech perception without traditional speech cues. *Science, 212*, 947–950.

Rendell, L., Boyd, R., Cownden, D., Enquist, M., Eriksson, K., Feldman, M. W., et al. (2010). Why copy others? Insights from the social learning strategies tournament. *Science, 328*, 208–213. doi:10.1126/science.1184719

Renzulli, J. S., & Delcourt, M. A. (1986). The legacy and logic of research on the identification of gifted persons. *Gifted Child Quarterly, 30*, 20–23.

Rescorla, R. A. (1968). Probability of shock in the presence and absence of CS in fear conditioning. *Journal of Comparative and Physiological Psychology, 66*, 1–5.

Rescorla, R. A., & Wagner, A. R. (1972). A theory of Pavlovian conditioning: Variations in the effectiveness of reinforcement and nonreinforcement. In A. H. Black & W. F. Prokasy (Eds.), *Classical conditioning, Vol. II: Current theory and research* (pp. 64-99). New York: Appleton-Century-Crofts.

Restak, R. (1988). *Mind.* New York: Bantam Dell Publishing Group.

Reyna, V. F. (2008). A theory of medical decision making and health: Fuzzy trace theory.

Medical Decision Making, 28(6), 850–865. doi:10.1177/0272989x08327066

Reyna, V. F., & Farley, F. (2006). Risk and rationality in adolescent decision making: Implications for theory, practice, and public policy. *Psychological Science in the Public Interest, 7*(1), 1–44. doi:10.1111/j.1529-1006 .2006.00026.x

Reyna, V. F., Estrada, S. M., DeMarinis, J. A., Myers, R. M., Stanisz, J. M., & Mills, B. A. (2011). Neurobiological and memory models of risky decision making in adolescents versus young adults. *Journal of Experimental Psychology: Learning, Memory, and Cognition, 37*(5), 1125–1142. doi:10.1037/a0023943

Reznick, J. S. (1999). Can prenatal caffeine exposure affect behavioral inhibition? *Review of General Psychology, 3*(2), 118–132.

Rhodes, N., & Wood, W. (1992). Self-esteem and intelligence affect influenceability: The mediating role of message reception. *Psychological Bulletin, 111*, 156–171.

Rhodewalt, F., Sandonmatsu, D. M., Tschanz, B., Feick, D. L., & Waller, A. (1995). Self-handicapping and interpersonal trade-offs: The effects of claimed self-handicaps on observers' performance evaluations and feedback. *Personality and Social Psychology Bulletin, 21*, 1042–1050.

Riby, D., & Hancock, P. J. B. (2009). Looking at movies and cartoons: Eye-tracking evidence from Williams syndrome and autism. *Journal of Intellectual Disability Research, 53*(2), 169–181. doi:10.1111/j.1365-2788.2008.01142.x

Rice, C. (2009). Prevalence of autism spectrum disorders—Autism and Development Disabilities Monitoring Network, United States, 2006. *MMWR Surveillance Summaries, 58*(SS10), 1–20.

Ridley, M. (2003). *Nature via nurture.* New York: HarperCollins.

Rijnbeek, B., de Visser, S. J., Franson, K. L., Cohen, A. F., & van Gerven, J. M. A. (2003). REM sleep effects as a biomarker for the effects of antidepressants in healthy volunteers. *Journal of Psychopharmacology, 17*(2), 196–203. doi:10.1177/0269881103017002008

Rips, L. (1975). Inductive judgments about natural categories. *Journal of Verbal Learning and Verbal Behavior, 14*, 665–681.

Rips, L., & Collins, A. (1993). Categories and resemblance. *Journal of Experimental Psychology: General, 122*, 468–489.

Riskind, J. H., Moore, R., & Bowley, L. (1995). The looming of spiders: The fearful perceptual distortion of movement and menace. *Behaviour Research and Therapy, 33*(2), 171–178. doi:10.1016/0005-7967(94)e0023-c

Rivers, W. H. R. (1905). Observations on the senses of the Todas. *British Journal of Psychology, 1*, 321–396.

Rivkin, M. J., Davis, P. E., Lemaster, J. L., Cabral, H. J., Warfield, S. K., Mulkern, R. V., et al. (2008). Volumetric MRI study of brain in children with intrauterine exposure to cocaine, alcohol, tobacco, and marijuana. *Pediatrics, 121*(4), 741–750.

Rivkin, M. J., Flax, J., Mozell, R., Osathanondh, R., Volpe, J. J., & Villa-Komaroff, L. (1995). Oligodendroglial development in human fetal cerebrum. *Annals of Neurology, 38*(1), 92–101.

Rizzolatti, G., Fadiga, L., Gallese, V., & Fogassi, L. (1996). Premotor cortex and the recognition of motor actions. *Cognitive Brain Research, 3*(2), 131–141.

Robberson, M. R., & Rogers, R. W. (1988). Beyond fear appeals: Negative and positive persuasive appeals to health and self-esteem. *Journal of Applied Social Psychology, 18*, 277–287.

Roberts, M., & Scanlan, L. (1999). *The man who listens to horses.* New York, NY: Ballantine Books.

Robins, L. N., & Regier, D. A. (Eds.). (1991). *Psychiatric disorders in America: The Epidemiologic Catchment Area Study.* New York, NY: Free Press.

Robins, L. N., Helzer, J. E., & Davis, D. H. (1975). Narcotic use in Southeast Asia and afterward. *Archives of General Psychiatry, 41*, 955–961.

Robinson, B. L., & Shergill, S. S. (2011). Imaging in posttraumatic stress disorder. *Current Opinion in Psychiatry, 24*(1), 29–33 10.1097/ YCO.1090b1013e3283413519.

Robinson, J. A., & Swanson, K. L. (1990). Autobiographical memory: The next phase. *Applied Cognitive Psychology, 4*, 321–335.

Robinson, J. A., & Swanson, K. L. (1993). Field and observer modes of remembering. *Memory, 1*(3), 169–184. doi:10.1080/0965821930 8258230

Rodin, J. (1986). Aging and health: Effects of the sense of control. *Science, 233*, 1271–1276.

Roediger, H. L., III, & Butler, A. C. (2011). The critical role of retrieval practice in long-term retention. *Trends in Cognitive Sciences, 15*(1), 20–27. doi:10.1016/j.tics.2010.09.003

Roenneberg, T., Kuehnle, T., Pramstaller, P. P., Ricken, J., Havel, M., Guth, A., et al. (2005). A marker for the end of adolescence. *Current Biology, 14*, R1038–R1039.

Roesch, S. C., & Amirkhan, J. H. (1997). Boundary conditions for self-serving attributions: Another look at the sports pages. *Journal of Applied Social Psychology, 27*, 245–261.

Roese, N. J., & Summerville, A. (2005). What we regret most . . . and why. *Personality and Social Psychology Bulletin, 31*(9), 1273–1285. doi:10.1177/0146167205274693

Roffwarg, H. P., Muzic, J. N., & Dement, W. C. (1966). Ontogenetic development of the human sleep-dream cycle. *Science, 152*, 604–619.

Rogers, C. R. (1942). *Counseling and psychotherapy: New concepts in practice.* Boston, MA: Houghton Mifflin.

Rogers, C. R. (1951). *Client-centered therapy: Its current practice, implications and theory.* London, England: Constable.

Rogers, C. R. (1980). *A way of being.* Boston, MA: Houghton Mifflin.

Rogers, L. J. (2000). Evolution of hemispheric specialization: Advantages and disadvantages. *Brain and Language, 73*, 236–253.

Rogers, T. B., Kuiper, N. A., & Kirker, W. S. (1977). Self-reference and the encoding of personal information. *Journal of Personality and Social Psychology, 35*(9), 677–688. doi:10.1037/0022-3514.35.9.677

Rohman, L. (2009). The relationship between anabolic steroids and muscle dysmorphia: A review. *Eating Disorders, 17*(3), 187–199.

Rojas, Y., & Stenberg, S.-Å. (2010). Early life circumstances and male suicide—A

30-year follow-up of a Stockholm cohort born in 1953. *Social Science and Medicine, 70*(3), 420–427. doi:10.1016/j.socscimed.2009.10.026

Rokeach, M. (1968–1969). The role of values in public opinion research. *Public Opinion Quarterly, 32,* 547–559.

Rolls, E. T. (2000). The orbitofrontal cortex and reward. *Cerebral Cortex, 10,* 284–294.

Roney, J. R., Hanson, K. N., Durante, K. M., & Maestripieri, D. (2006). Reading men's faces: Women's mate attractiveness judgments track men's testosterone and interest in infants. *Proceedings of the Royal Society of London, Series B: Biological Sciences, 273,* 2169–2175.

Rorschach, H. (1921). Psychodiagnostik: Methodik und Ergebnisse eines wahrnehmungsdiagnostischen Experiments; (Deutenlassen von Zufallsformen). *Arbeiten zur angewandten Psychiatrie* (Vol. 2). Bern: Bircher.

Rosales, F., Reznick, J. S., & Zeisel, S. (2009). Understanding the role of nutrition in the brain and behavioral development of toddlers and preschool children: Identifying and addressing methodological barriers. *Nutritional Neuroscience, 12*(5), 190–202. doi:10.1179/147683009x423454

Rosch, E. (1973). Natural categories. *Cognitive Psychology, 4,* 328–350.

Rosch, E. (1983). Prototype classification and logical classification: The two systems. In E. Scholnick (Ed.), *New trends in cognitive representation: Challenges to Piaget's theory* (pp. 73–86). Hillsdale, NJ: Erlbaum.

Rose, D., Fleischmann, P., Wykes, T., Leese, M., & Bindman, J. (2003). Patients' perspectives on electroconvulsive therapy: Systematic review. *British Medical Journal, 326*(7403), 1363. doi:10.1136/bmj.326.7403.1363

Rose, J. E., Behm, F. M., Murugesan, T., & McClernon, F. J. (2010). Silver acetate interactions with nicotine and non-nicotine smoke components. *Experimental and Clinical Psychopharmacology, 18*(6), 462–469. doi:10.1037/a0021966

Roselli, C. E., Larkin, K., Resko, J. A., Stellflug, J. N., & Stormshak, F. (2004). The volume of a sexually dimorphic nucleus in the ovine medial preoptic area/anterior hypothalamus varies with sexual partner preference. *Endocrinology, 145,* 478–483.

Rosenberg, J., & Tunney, R. J. (2008). Human vocabulary use as display. *Evolutionary Psychology, 6,* 538–549.

Rosenberg, M., Schooler, C., & Schoenbach, C. (1989). Self-esteem and adolescent problems: Modeling reciprocal effects. *American Sociological Review, 54,* 1004–1018.

Rosenberg, R., Mandell, D., Farmer, J., Law, J., Marvin, A., & Law, P. (2010). Psychotropic medication use among children with autism spectrum disorders enrolled in a national registry, 2007–2008. *Journal of Autism and Developmental Disorders, 40*(3), 342–351. doi:10.1007/s10803-009-0878-1

Rosenberg, S. D., Rosenberg, H. J., & Farrell, M. P. (1999). The midlife crisis revisited. In S. L. Willis & J. D. Reid (Eds.), *Life in the middle* (pp. 47–73). San Diego, CA: Academic Press.

Rosenstein, D., & Oster, H. (1988). Differential facial responses to four basic tastes in newborns. *Child Development, 59,* 1555–1568.

Ross, D. C., Fischhoff, J., & Davenport, B. (2002). Treatment of ADHD when tolerance to methylphenidate develops. *Psychiatric Services, 53*(1), 102–102.

Ross, G. W., & Petrovitch, H. (2001). Current evidence for neuroprotective effects of nicotine and caffeine against Parkinson's disease. *Drugs and Aging, 18*(11), 797–806.

Ross, L. (1977). The intuitive psychologist and his shortcomings: Distortions in the attribution process. In L. Berkowitz (Ed.), *Advances in experimental social psychology* (Vol. 10, pp. 174–221). New York, NY: Academic Press.

Rossignol, D. A. (2007). Hyperbaric oxygen therapy might improve certain pathophysiological findings in autism. *Medical Hypotheses, 68*(6), 1208–1227.

Rotge, J.-Y., Langbour, N., Jaafari, N., Guehl, D., Bioulac, B., Aouizerate, B., et al. (2010). Anatomical alterations and symptom-related functional activity in obsessive-compulsive disorder are correlated in the lateral orbitofrontal cortex. *Biological Psychiatry, 67*(7), e37–e38. doi:10.1016/j.biopsych.2009.10.007

Roth, A., & Fonagy, P. (1996). *What works for whom? A critical review of psychotherapy research.* London, England: Guilford Press.

Roth, G., & Dicke, U. (2005). Evolution of the brain and intelligence. *Trends in Cognitive Sciences, 9*(5), 250–257.

Rothbart, M. K. (2007). Temperament, development, and personality. *Current Directions in Psychological Science, 16*(4), 207–212. doi:10.1111/j.1467-8721.2007.00505.x

Rothbart, M. K. (2011). *Becoming who we are: Temperament and personality in development.* New York, NY: Guilford Press.

Rothbart, M. K., & Derryberry, D. (1981). Development of individual differences in temperament. In M. E. Lamb & A. L. Brown (Eds.), *Advances in developmental psychology* (Vol. 1, pp. 37–86). Hillsdale, NJ: Erlbaum.

Rothbart, M. K., Ahadi, S. A., & Evans, D. E. (2000). Temperament and personality: Origins and outcomes. *Journal of Personality and Social Psychology, 78*(1), 122–135.

Rothbart, M. K., Sheese, B. E., Rueda, M. R., & Posner, M. I. (2011). Developing mechanisms of self-regulation in early life. *Emotion Review, 3*(2), 207–213. doi:10.1177/1754073910387943

Rothbaum, B. O., Rizzo, A. S., & Difede, J. (2010). Virtual reality exposure therapy for combat-related posttraumatic stress disorder. *Annals of the New York Academy of Sciences, 1208*(1), 126–132. doi:10.1111/j.1749-6632.2010.05691.x

Rotter, J. B. (1966). Generalized expectancies for internal versus external control of reinforcement. *Psychological Monographs, 80,* 1–27.

Rovee-Collier, C. (1997). Dissociations in infant memory: Rethinking the development of implicit and explicit memory. *Psychological Review, 104,* 467–498.

Rowland, L. W. (1939). Will hypnotized persons try to harm themselves or others? *Journal of Abnormal and Social Psychology, 34,* 114–117.

Ruby, P., & Decety, J. (2001). Effect of subjective perspective taking during simulation of action: A PET investigation of agency. *Nature Neuroscience, 4,* 546–550.

Rucker, D., Padwal, R., Li, S. K., Curioni, C., & Lau, D. C. (2007). Long-term pharmacotherapy for obesity and overweight: Updated meta-analysis. *British Medical Journal, 335*(7631), 1194–1199.

Rule, N. O., Ambady, N., Adams, R. B., Jr., Ozono, H., Nakashima, S., Yoshikawa, S., et al. (2010). Polling the face: Prediction and consensus across cultures. *Journal of Personality and Social Psychology, 98*(1), 1–15. doi:10.1037/a0017673

Rule, N. O., Rosen, K. S., Slepian, M. L., & Ambady, N. (2011). Mating interest improves women's accuracy in judging male sexual orientation. *Psychological Science.* doi:10.1177/0956797611412394

Rusbult, C. E., Martz, J. M., & Agnew, C. R. (1998). The Investment Model Scale: Measuring commitment level, satisfaction level, quality of alternatives, and investment size. *Personal Relationships, 5*(4), 357–391. doi:10.1111/j.1475-6811.1998.tb00177.x

Rushton, D. H., Dover, R., Sainsbury, A. W., Norris, M. J., Gilkes, J. J., & Ramsey, I. D. (2001). Why should women have lower reference limits for haemoglobin and ferritin concentrations than men? *British Medical Journal, 322,* 1355–1357.

Rushton, J. P., Fulker, D. W., Neale, M. C., Nias, D. K. B., & Eysenck, H. J. (1986). Altruism and aggression: The heritability of individual differences. *Journal of Personality and Social Psychology, 50,* 1192–1198.

Russell, D., & Cutrona, C. (2010). *Stressful effects of where you live: Studying the influence of neighborhood context over time.* Paper presented at the World Conference on Stress and Anxiety Research, Galway, Ireland.

Russell, D., Peplau, L. A., & Cutrona, C. E. (1980). The revised UCLA Loneliness Scale: Concurrent and discriminant validity evidence. *Journal of Personality and Social Psychology, 39*(3), 472–480. doi:10.1037/0022-3514.39.3.472

Russo, R., & Mammarella, N. (2002). Spacing effects in recognition memory: When meaning matters. *European Journal of Cognitive Psychology, 14,* 49–59.

Rust, J. (1999). Discriminant validity of the "Big Five" personality traits in employment settings. *Social Behavior and Personality: An International Journal, 27*(1), 99–108.

Ruwaard, J., Lange, A., Schrieken, B., & Emmelkamp, P. M. G. (2011). Efficacy and effectiveness of online cognitive behavioral treatment: A decade of Interapy research. *Studies in Health Technology and Informatics, 167,* 9–14.

Ryu, Y. H., Lee, J. D., Yoon, P. H., Kim, D. I., Lee, H. B., & Shin, Y. J. (1999). Perfusion impairments in infantile autism on technetium-99 methyl cysteinate dimer brain single-photon emission tomography: Comparison with findings on magnetic resonance imaging. *European Journal of Nuclear Medicine, 26*(3), 253–259.

Sabatini, R. M. E. (1997). The history of lobotomy. Retrieved July 29, 2007, from http://www.cerebromente.org.br/n02/historia/lobotomy.htm

Sacco, K. A., Termine, A., & Seyal, A. (2005). Effects of cigarette smoking on spatial working memory and attentional deficits in schizophrenia: Involvement of nicotinic receptor mechanisms *Archives of General Psychiatry, 62*(6), 649–659.

Sackett, G. P. (1966). Monkeys reared in isolation with pictures as visual input: Evidence for an innate releasing mechanism. *Science, 154*, 1468–1473.

Sackeim, H. A., Prudic, J., Fuller, R., Keilp, J., Lavori, P. W., & Olfson, M. (2007). The cognitive effects of electroconvulsive therapy in community settings. *Neuropsychopharmacology, 32*, 244–254.

Sacks, O. (1985). *The man who mistook his wife for a hat, and other clinical tales.* New York, NY: Summit Books.

Sajatovic, M., Valenstein, M., Blow, F., Ganoczy, D., & Ignacio, R. (2007). Treatment adherence with lithium and anticonvulsant medications among patients with bipolar disorder. *Psychiatric Services, 58*(6), 855–863. doi:10.1176/appi.ps.58.6.855

Sakai, Y., Shaw, C. A., Dawson, B. C., Dugas, D. V., Al-Mohtaseb, Z., Hill, D. E., et al. (2011). Protein interactome reveals converging molecular pathways among autism disorders. *Science Translational Medicine, 3*(86), 86ra49. doi:10.1126/scitranslmed.3002166

Sakurai, T., Amemiya, A., Ishii, M., Matsuzaki, I., Chemelli, R. M., Tanaka, H., et al. (1998). Orexins and orexin receptors: A family of hypothalamic neuropeptides and G protein-coupled receptors that regulate feeding behavior. *Cell, 92*(5), 573–585, 1 page following 696.

Salazar, M., & Frincke, J. (2005). Yesterday, today, and tomorrow careers in psychology: 2005 what students need to know. Retrieved on December 10, 2011, from http://www.apa.org/workforce/presentations/2005-wpa.pdf

Salmon, S. (2004). The PEACE curriculum: Expanded aggression replacement training. In A. P. Goldstein, R. Nensén, B. Daleflod, & M. Kalt (Eds.), *New perspectives on aggression replacement training* (pp. 171–188). Chichester, England: Wiley.

SAMHSA (2006). Alcohol dependence or abuse in substate areas. Retrieved from http://www.oas.samhsa.gov/2k6/subStateAlc/subStateAlc.htm

Sanfey, A. G., Rilling, J. K., Aronson, J. A., Nystrom, L. E., & Cohen, J. D. (2003). The neural basis of economic decision-making in the Ultimatum Game. *Science, 300*, 1755–1758.

Santosa, C. M., Strong, C. M., Nowakowska, C., Wang, P. W., Rennicke, C. M., & Ketter, T. A. (2007). Enhanced creativity in bipolar disorder patients: A controlled study. *Journal of Affective Disorders, 100*(1–3), 31–39.

Sapolsky, R. (2001). *A primate's memoir.* New York, NY: Scribner.

Sapolsky, R. M., Krey, L. C., & McEwen, B. S. (1985). Prolonged glucocorticoid exposure reduces hippocampal neuron number: Implications for aging. *Journal of Neuroscience, 5*, 1222–1227.

Sarnoff, I., & Zimbardo, P. (1961). Anxiety, fear, and social affiliation. *Journal of Abnormal and Social Psychology, 62*, 356–363.

Saskatchewan Learning. (2006). Juvenile crime—Time of day. Retrieved July 27, 2007, from http://www.sasked.gov.sk.ca/docs/social/psych30/support_materials/time_of_day.htm

Savage-Rumbaugh, S., Shanker, S. G., & Taylor, T. J. (1998). *Apes, language, and the human mind.* New York: Oxford University Press.

Savine, R., & Sönksen, P. (2000). Growth hormone—Hormone replacement for the somatopause? *Hormone Research, 53*(Suppl. 3), 37–41. doi:10.1159/000023531

Savin-Williams, R. C. (2006). Who's gay? Does it matter? *Current Directions in Psychological Science, 15*(1), 40–44.

Saxena, S. (2003). Neuroimaging and the pathophysiology of obsessive compulsive disorder (OCD). In C. H. Y. Fu, C. Senior, T. Russell, D. Weinberger, & R. Murray (Eds.), *Neuroimaging in psychiatry* (pp. 191–224). London, England: Martin Dunitz.

Saxena, S., Brody, A. L., Maidment, K. M., Smith, E. C., Zohrabi, N., Katz, E., et al. (2004). Cerebral glucose metabolism in obsessive-compulsive hoarding. *American Journal of Psychiatry, 161*, 1038–1048.

Schachter, S. (1951). Deviation, rejection, and communication. *Journal of Abnormal Psychology, 46*, 190–207.

Schachter, S. (1959). *The psychology of affiliation: Experimental studies of the sources of gregariousness.* Stanford, CA: Stanford University Press.

Schachter, S., & Singer, J. (1962). Cognitive, social and physiological determinants of emotional state. *Psychological Review, 69*, 379–399.

Schaffer, C. E., Davidson, R. J., & Saron, C. (1983). Frontal and parietal electroencephalogram asymmetry in depressed and nondepressed subjects. *Biological Psychiatry, 18*, 753–762.

Schaie, K. W. (1996). *Intellectual development in adulthood: The Seattle Longitudinal Study.* Cambridge, England: Cambridge University Press.

Schechter, R., & Grether, J. K. (2008). Continuing increases in autism reported to California's developmental services system: Mercury in retrograde. *Archives of General Psychiatry, 65*(1), 19–24.

Schenck, C. H., Bundlie, S. R., Ettinger, M. G., & Mahowald, M. W. (1986). Chronic behavioral disorders of human REM sleep: A new category of parasomnia. *Sleep, 9*, 293–308.

Schernhammer, E. S., & Schulmeister, K. (2004). Melatonin and cancer risk: Does light at night compromise physiologic cancer protection by lowering serum melatonin levels? *British Journal of Cancer, 90*(5), 941–943.

Schernhammer, E. S., Kroenke, C. H., Dowsett, M., Folkerd, E., & Hankinson, S. E. (2006). Urinary 6.sulfatoxymelatonin levels and their correlations with lifestyle factors and steroid hormone levels. *Journal of Pineal Research, 40*(2), 116–124.

Schimmelmann, B. G., Friedel, S., Nguyen, T. T., Sauer, S., Vogel, C. I. G., Konrad, K., et al. (2009). Exploring the genetic link between RLS and ADHD. *Journal of Psychiatric Research, 43*(10), 941–945. doi:10.1016/j.jpsychires.2009.01.003

Schjedlderup-Ebbe, T. (1922). Beiträge zur Sozialpsychologie des Haushuhns [Contributions to the social psychology of the house chicken]. *Zeitschrift für Psychologie, 88*, 225–252.

Schlaug, G., Forgeard, M., Zhu, L., Norton, A., Norton, A., & Winner, E. (2009). Training-induced neuroplasticity in young children. *Annals of the New York Academy of Sciences, 1169*, 205–208.

Schlaug, G., Jäncke, L., Huang, Y., & Steinmetz, H. (1995). In vivo evidence of structural brain asymmetry in musicians. *Science, 267*, 699–701.

Schmidt, R. J., Hansen, R. L., Hartiala, J., Allayee, H., Schmidt, L. C., Tancredi, D. J., et al. (2011). Prenatal vitamins, one-carbon metabolism gene variants, and risk for autism. *Epidemiology, 22*(4), 476–485. doi:410.1097/EDE.1090b1013e31821d31820e31830.

Schnakers, C., Vanhaudenhuyse, A., Giacino, J., Ventura, M., Boly, M., Majerus, S., et al. (2009). Diagnostic accuracy of the vegetative and minimally conscious state: Clinical consensus versus standardized neurobehavioral assessment. *BMC Neurology, 9*(1), 35.

Schneider, F., Gur, R. C., Koch, K., Backes, V., Amunts, K., Shah, N. J., et al. (2006). Impairment in the specificity of emotion processing in schizophrenia. *American Journal of Psychiatry, 163*, 442–447.

Schober, M. F., & Carstensen, L. L. (2010). Does being together for years help comprehension? In E. Morsella (Ed.), *Expressing oneself/expressing one's self: Communication, cognition, language, and identity* (pp. 107–124). Hove, England: Psychology Press/Taylor & Francis.

Schön, D., Gordon, R., Campagne, A., Magne, C., Astésano, C., Anton, J.-L., et al. (2010). Similar cerebral networks in language, music and song perception. *NeuroImage.* doi:10.1016/j.neuroimage.2010.02.023

Schouwenburg, H. C. (1995). Academic procrastination: Theoretical notions, measurement, and research. In J. R. Ferrari, J. L. Johnson, & W. G. McCown (Eds.), *Procrastination and task avoidance: Theory, research, and treatment* (pp. 71–96). New York, NY: Plenum Press.

Schraw, G., Wadkins, T., & Olafson, L. (2007). Doing the things we do: A grounded theory of academic procrastination. *Journal of Educational Psychology, 99*, 12–25.

Schroeder, S. (2008). Stranded in the periphery — The increasing marginalization of smokers. *New England Journal of Medicine, 358*(21), 2284–2286. doi:10.1056/NEJMe0802708

Schroeder, V., & Kelley, M. (2009). Associations between family environment, parenting practices, and executive functioning of children with and without ADHD. *Journal of Child and Family Studies, 18*(2), 227–235. doi:10.1007/s10826-008-9223-0

Schumann, C. M., Bauman, M. D., Machado, C. J., & Amaral, D. G. (2006). The social brain, amygdala, and autism. In S. O. Moldin & J. L. R. Rubenstein (Eds.), *Understanding autism: From basic neuroscience to treatment* (pp. 227–253). Boca Raton, FL: Taylor and Francis Group.

Schurz, G. (1985). Experimentelle Überprüfung des Zusammenhangs zwischen Persönlichkeitsmerkmalen und der Bereitschaft zum destruktiven Gehorsam gegenüber Autoritäten [Experimental examination of the relationship between personality characteristics and the readiness to destructive obedience to authorities]. *Zeitschrift für experimentelle und angewandte Psychologie, 32*, 160–177.

Schuster, M. A., Stein, L. H., Jaycox, R. L., Marshall, G. N., Elliott, M. N., Zhou, J., et al. (2002). After 9/11: Stress and coping across America. Retrieved August 22, 2006, from http://www.rand.org/pubs/testimonies/2005/CT198.pdf

Schwartz, B. (1984). *Psychology of learning and behavior* (2nd ed.). New York: Norton.

Schwartz, B., Ward, A., Monterosso, J., Lyubomirsky, S., White, K., & Lehman, D. R. (2002). Maximizing versus satisficing: Happiness is a matter of choice. *Journal of Personality and Social Psychology, 83*(5), 1178–1197. doi:10.1037/0022-3514.83.5.1178

Schwartz, C. E., Snidman, N., & Kagan, J. (1999). Adolescent social anxiety as an outcome of inhibited temperament in childhood. *Journal of the American Academy of Child and Adolescent Psychiatry, 38*(8), 1008–1015.

Schwarz, M., & Susswein, A. J. (1992). Presence of conspecifics facilitates learning that food is inedible in *Aplysia fasciata. Behavioral Neuroscience, 106*(2), 250–261.

Schwarz, M., Blumberg, S., & Susswein, A. J. (1998). Social isolation blocks the expression of memory after training that a food is inedible in *Aplysia fasciata. Behavioral Neuroscience, 112*(4), 942–951.

Scott, V., & Gijsbers, K. (1981). Pain perception in competitive swimmers. *British Medical Journal, 283,* 91–93.

Scully, J. A., Tosi, H., & Banning, K. (2000). Life event checklists: Revisiting the Social Readjustment Rating Scale after 30 years. *Educational and Psychological Measurement, 60,* 864–876.

Segall, H. H., Campbell, D. T., & Herskovits, M. J. (1966). *The influence of culture on visual perception.* Indianapolis, IN: Bobbs-Merrill.

Segerstrom, S. C., & Miller, G. E. (2004). Psychological stress and the human immune system: A meta-analytic study of 30 years of inquiry. *Psychological Bulletin, 130,* 601–630.

Sekiguchi, A., & Kawashima, R. (2007). Cognitive rehabilitation—The learning therapy for the senile dementia. *Brain Nerve, 59*(4), 357–365.

Seksel, K., & Lindeman, M. J. (2001). Use of clomipramine in treatment of obsessive-compulsive disorder, separation anxiety and noise phobia in dogs: A preliminary, clinical study. *Australian Veterinary Journal, 79,* 252–256.

Seligman, M. E. P. (1971). Phobias and preparedness. *Behavior Therapy, 2*(3), 307–320. doi:10.1016/s0005-7894(71)80064-3

Seligman, M. E. P. (1987, February). *Predicting depression, poor health, and presidential elections.* Paper presented at the Science and Public Policy Seminar sponsored by the Federation of Behavioral, Psychological and Cognitive Sciences, Washington, DC.

Seligman, M. E. P. (1990). *Learned optimism.* New York, NY: Simon and Schuster.

Seligman, M. E. P. (2002). *Authentic happiness: Using the new positive psychology to realize your potential for lasting fulfillment.* New York, NY: Simon and Schuster.

Seligman, M. E. P., & Csikszentmihalyi, M. (2000). Positive psychology: An introduction. *American Psychologist, 55*(1), 5–14. doi:10.1037/0003-066x.55.1.5

Seligman, M. E., Abramson, L.Y., & Semmel, A. (1979). Depressive attributional style. *Journal of Abnormal Psychology, 88,* 242–247.

Selye, H. (1946). The general adaptation syndrome and the diseases of adaptation. *Journal of Clinical Endocrinology, 6,* 177–231.

Selye, H. (1975). Confusion and controversy in the stress field. *Journal of Human Stress, 1*(2), 37–44.

Senju, A., Maeda, M., Kikuchi, Y., Hasegawa, T., Tojo, Y., & Osanai, H. (2007). Absence of contagious yawning in children with autism spectrum disorder. *Biology Letters, 3*(6), 706–708. doi:10.1098/rsbl.2007.0337

Senju, A., Southgate, V., White, S., & Frith, U. (2009). Mindblind eyes: An absence of spontaneous theory of mind in Asperger syndrome. *Science, 325*(5942), 883–885. doi:10.1126/science.1176170

Sereno, M. I., & Tootell, R. B. H. (2005). From monkeys to humans: What do we now know about brain homologies? *Current Opinion in Neurobiology, 15,* 135–144.

Setchell, J. M., & Wickings, E. J. (2005). Dominance, status signals and coloration in male mandrills (*Mandrillus sphinx*). *Ethology, 111,* 25–50.

Settle, J. E., Dawes, C. T., Christakis, N. A., & Fowler, J. H. (2010). Friendships moderate an association between a dopamine gene variant and political ideology. *Journal of Politics, 72*(4), 1189–1198. doi:10.1017/s0022381610000617

Shallice, T., & Warrington, E. K. (1970). Independent functioning of verbal memory stores: A neuropsychological study. *Quarterly Journal of Experimental Psychology, 22,* 261–273.

Shapira, M., Thompson, C. K., Soreq, H., & Robinson, G. E. (2001). Changes in neuronal acetylcholinesterase gene expression and division of labor in honey bee colonies. *Journal of Molecular Neuroscience, 17,* 1–12.

Shaw, P. J., Cirelli, C., Greenspan, R. J., & Giulio Tononi, G. (2000). Correlates of sleep and waking in *Drosophila melanogaster. Science, 287,* 1834–1837.

Shaw, P., Eckstrand, K., Sharp, W., Blumenthal, J., Lerch, J. P., Greenstein, D., et al. (2007). Attention-deficit/hyperactivity disorder is characterized by a delay in cortical maturation. *Proceedings of the National Academy of Sciences, 104*(49), 19649–19654.

Shaw, P., Greenstein, D., Lerch, J., Clasen, L., Lenroot, R., Gogtay, N., et al. (2006). Intellectual ability and cortical development in children and adolescents. *Nature, 440*(7084), 676–679. doi:10.1038/nature04513

Shaywitz, S. (1996). Dyslexia. *Scientific American, 275,* 98–105.

Shaywitz, S. E., Morris, R., & Shaywitz, B. A. (2008). The education of dyslexic children from childhood to young adulthood. *Annual Review of Psychology, 59,* 451–475.

Shaywitz, S., Shaywitz, B. A., Pugh, K. R., Fulbright, R. K., Constable, R. T., Mencl, W. E., et al. (1998). Functional disruption in the organization of the brain for reading in dyslexia. *Proceedings of the National Academy of Sciences, 95,* 2636–2641.

Shedler, J. (2010). The efficacy of psychodynamic psychotherapy. *American Psychologist, 65*(2), 98–109. doi:10.1037/a0018378

Shepard, R. N. (1990). *Mind sights: Original visual illusions, ambiguities, and other anomalies with a commentary on the play of mind in perception and art.* New York, NY: W. H. Freeman.

Sher, L. (2006). Alcohol consumption and suicide. *QJM: Monthly Journal of the Association of Physicians, 99*(1), 57–61. doi:10.1093/qjmed/hci146

Sheridan, S. M., & Burt, J. D. (2009). Family-centered positive psychology. In S. J. Lopez & C. R. Snyder (Eds.), *Oxford handbook of positive psychology* (2nd ed., pp. 551–559). New York, NY: Oxford University Press.

Sherif, M., Harvey, L. J., White, B. J., Hood, W. R., & Sherif, C. (1961). *The Robbers Cave experiment: Intergroup conflict and cooperation.* Norman, OK: University of Oklahoma Institute of Intergroup Relations.

Sherman, D. K., & Kim, H. S. (2005). Is there an "I" in "team"? The role of the self in group-serving judgments. *Journal of Personality and Social Psychology, 88*(1), 108–120.

Shields, M. (2004). Stress, health, and the benefit of social support. *Health Reports (Statistics Canada, Catalogue 82-003), 15,* 9–38.

Shifren, J. L., Braunstein, G. D., Simon, J. A., Casson, P. R., Buster, J. E., Redmond, G. P., et al. (2000). Transdermal testosterone treatment in women with impaired sexual function after oophorectomy. *New England Journal of Medicine, 343,* 682–688.

Shih, M., & Sanchez, D. T. (2005). When race becomes even more complex: Toward understanding the landscape of multiracial identity and experiences. *Journal of Social Issues, 65*(1), 1–11. doi:10.1111/j.1540-4560.2008.01584.x

Shin, S. H., Edwards, E. M., & Heeren, T. (2009). Child abuse and neglect: Relations to adolescent binge drinking in the National Longitudinal Study of Adolescent Health (AddHealth) Study. *Addiction and Behavior, 34*(3), 277–280. doi:10.1016/j.addbeh.2008.10.023

Shin, S. H., Edwards, E., Heeren, T., & Amodeo, M. (2009). Relationship between multiple forms of maltreatment by a parent or guardian and adolescent alcohol use. *American Journal on Addictions, 18*(3), 226–234.

Shiota, M. N., & Levenson, R. W. (2007). Birds of a feather don't always fly farthest: Similarity in Big Five personality predicts more negative marital satisfaction trajectories in long-term marriages. *Psychology and Aging, 22*(4), 666–675. doi:10.1037/0882-7974.22.4.666

Ship, J. A., & Weiffenbach, J. M. (1993). Age, gender, medical treatment, and medication effects on smell identification. *Journal of Gerontology: Medical Sciences, 48,* M26–M32.

Shrivastava, A., Johnston, M., Shah, N., & Bureau, Y. (2010). Redefining outcome measures in schizophrenia: Integrating social and clinical parameters. *Current Opinion in Psychiatry, 23*(2), 120–126. doi:110.1097/YCO.1090b1013e328336662e

Shu, L. L., Gino, F., & Bazerman, M. H. (2011). Dishonest deed, clear conscience: When cheating leads to moral disengagement and motivated forgetting. *Personality and Social Psychology Bulletin, 37*(3), 330–349. doi:10.1177/0146167211398138

Shute, N. (2000, June 5). A maddening disconnect: Unraveling the mysteries of autism. Retrieved December 16, 2000, from http://www.usnews.com:80/usnews/issue/000605/autism.htm

Sia, C.-L., Tan, B. C. Y., & Wei, K.-K. (2002). Group polarization and computer-mediated communication: Effects of communication cues, social presence, and anonymity. *Information Systems Research, 13*(1), 70–90. doi:10.1287/isre.13.1.70.92

Siegel, J. M. (2001). The REM sleep-memory consolidation hypothesis. *Science, 294,* 1058–1063.

Siegfried, J. (2010). Airlines may charge fat people higher fairs. Retrieved on December 4, 2011, from http://www.examiner.com/airlines-airport-in-national/airlines-may-charge-fat-people-higher-fares

Siegle, G., Sagratti, S., & Crawford, C. (1999). *Effects of rumination and initial severity on response to cognitive therapy for depression.* Paper presented at the Meeting of the Association for the Advancement of Behavior Therapy, Toronto, ON.

Siever, L. J. (2008). Neurobiology of aggression and violence. *American Journal of Psychiatry, 165*(4), 429–442.

Silvia, P. J. (2005). Deflecting reactance: The role of similarity in increasing compliance and reducing resistance. *Basic and Applied Social Psychology, 27,* 277–284.

Simon, H. A. (1957). *Models of man, social and rational: Mathematical essays on rational human behavior.* New York: Wiley.

Simons, D. J., & Chabris, C. F. (1999). Gorillas in our midst: Sustained inattentional blindness for dynamic events. *Perception and Psychophysics, 28,* 1059–1074.

Simons, L. G., & Conger, R. D. (2007). Linking mother-father differences in parenting to a typology of family parenting styles and adolescent outcomes. *Journal of Family Issues, 28*(2), 212–241.

Simpson, D. (2005). Phrenology and the neurosciences: Contributions of F. J. Gall and J. G. Spurzheim. *ANZ Journal of Surgery, 75*(6), 475.

Singer, M. I., Miller, D. B., Guo, S., Slovak, K., & Frierson, T. (1998). *The mental health consequences of children's exposure to violence.* Cleveland, OH: Cuyahoga County Community Mental Health Research Institute, Mandel School of Applied Social Sciences, Case Western Reserve University.

Singer, T., Kiebel, S. J., Winston, J. S., Dolan, R. J., & Frith, C. D. (2004). Brain responses to the acquired moral status of faces. *Neuron, 41,* 653–662.

Singh, D. (1993). Adaptive significance of female physical attractiveness: Role of waist-to-hip ratio. *Journal of Personality and Social Psychology, 65,* 293–307.

Singh, D., Dixson, B. J., Jessop, T. S., Morgan, B., & Dixson, A. F. (2010). Cross-cultural consensus for waist-hip ratio and women's attractiveness. *Evolution and Human Behavior, 31*(3), 176–181. doi:10.1016/j.evolhumbehav.2009.09.001

Sinha, Y., Silove, N., & Williams, K. (2006). Chelation therapy and autism. *British Medical Journal, 333*(7571), 756.

Skene, D. J., Lockley, S. W., & Arendt, J. (1999). Use of melatonin in the treatment of phase shift and sleep disorders. *Advances in Experimental Medicine and Biology, 467,* 79–84.

Skinner, B. F. (1953). Some contributions of an experimental analysis of behavior to psychology as a whole. *American Psychologist, 8,* 69–78.

Skinner, B. F. (1960). Pigeons in a pelican. *American Psychologist, 15,* 28–37.

Skinner, B. F. (1970). *Verbal behavior.* New York: Appleton-Century-Crofts.

Skinner, B. F. (1971). *Beyond freedom and dignity.* New York: Knopf.

Skodol, A. E., & Bender, D. S. (2003). Why are women diagnosed borderline more than men? *Psychiatric Quarterly, 74*(4), 349–360.

Slob, A. K., Bax, C. M., Hop, W. C., Rowland, D. L., & van der Werff ten Bosch, J. J. (1996). Sexual arousability and the menstrual cycle. *Psychoneuroendocrinology, 21,* 545–558.

Slobodchikoff, C. N., Perla, B. S., & Verdoli, J. L. (2009). *Communication and community in an animal society.* Cambridge, MA: Harvard University Press.

Slotema, C. W., Blom, J. D., Hoek, H. W., & Sommer, I. E. (2010). Should we expand the toolbox of psychiatric treatment methods to include Repetitive Transcranial Magnetic Stimulation (rTMS)? A meta-analysis of the efficacy of rTMS in psychiatric disorders. *Journal of Clinical Psychiatry, 71*(7), 873–884. doi:10.4088/JCP.08m04872gre

Slovic, P., Finucane, M., Peters, E., & MacGregor, D.G. (2002). The affect heuristic. In T. Gilovich, D. Griffin, & D. Kahneman (Eds.), *Heuristics and biases* (pp. 397–420). New York: Cambridge University Press.

Smith, C. T., & Fazekas, A. (1997). Amounts of REM sleep and stage 2 required for efficient learning. *Sleep, 26,* 690.

Smith, E. E., & Grossman, M. (2008). Multiple systems of category learning. *Neuroscience and Biobehavioral Reviews, 32*(2), 249–264. doi:10.1016/j.neubiorev.2007.07.009

Smith, E. E., Shoben, E. J., & Rips, L. J. (1974). Structure and process in semantic memory: A feature model for semantic decisions. *Psychological Review, 81,* 214–241.

Smith, T., & Lovaas, I. (1998). Intensive early behavioral intervention with autism: The UCLA Young Autism Project. *Infants and Young Children, 10,* 67–78.

Sneed, D. (2006). Teen murder suspect's judgment could be impaired, says doctor. *The Tribune,* San Luis Obispo, CA, p. B1.

Sneed, J. R., Whitbourne, S. K., & Culang, M. E. (2006). Trust, identity, and ego integrity: Modeling Erikson's core stages over 34 years. *Journal of Adult Development, 13*(3–4), 148–157. doi:10.1007/s10804-007-9026-3

Snyder, C. R. (1994). *The psychology of hope: You can get there from here.* New York, NY: Free Press.

Snyder, C. R., Berg, C., Woodward, J. T., Gum, A., Rand, K. L., Wrobleski, K. K., et al. (2005). Hope against the cold: Individual differences in trait hope and acute pain tolerance on the cold pressor task. *Journal of Personality, 73*(2), 287–312. doi:10.1111/j.1467-6494.2005.00318.x

Snyder, C. R., Harris, C., Anderson, J. R., Holeran, S. A., Irving, L. M., Sigmon, S. T., et al. (1991). The will and the ways: Development and validation of an individual-differences measure of hope. *Journal of Personality and Social Psychology, 60,* 570–585.

Snyder, C. R., Rand, K. L., & Sigmon, D. R. (2002). Hope theory: A member of the positive psychology family. In C. R. Snyder & S. J. Lopez (Eds.), *Handbook of positive psychology* (pp. 257–276). New York, NY: Oxford University Press.

Society for Neuroscience. (2011). About membership. Retrieved from http://www.sfn.org/index.aspx?pagename=membership_About-Membership

Soldan, A., Mangels, J. A., & Cooper, L. A. (2008). Effects of dividing attention during encoding on perceptual priming of unfamiliar visual objects. *Memory, 16*(8), 873–895. doi:10.1080/09658210802360595

Soon, C. S., Brass, M., Heinze, H.-J., & Haynes, J.-D. (2008). Unconscious determinants of free decisions in the human brain. *Nature Neuroscience, 11*(5), 543–545.

Soons, J. P. M., Liefbroer, A. C., & Kalmijn, M. (2009). The long-term consequences of relationship formation for subjective well-being. *Journal of Marriage and Family, 71*(5), 1254–1270. doi:10.1111/j.1741-3737.2009.00667.x

Soria, V., Martinez-Amoros, E., Escaramis, G., Valero, J., Perez-Egea, R., Garcia, C., et al. (2010). Differential association of circadian genes with mood disorders: CRY1 and NPAS2 are associated with unipolar major depression and CLOCK and VIP with bipolar disorder. *Neuropsychopharmacology, 35*(6), 1279–1289. doi:http://www.nature.com/npp/journal/v35/n6/suppinfo/npp2009230s1.html

Sorkhabi, N. (2005). Applicability of Baumrind's parent typology to collective cultures: Analysis of cultural explanations of parent socialization effects. *International Journal of Behavioral Development, 29*(6), 552–563. doi:10.1177/01650250500172640

Soto-Faraco, S., Kingstone, A., & Spence, C. (2006). Integrating motion information across sensory modalities: The role of top-down factors. In S. Martinez-Conde, S. L. Macknik, L. M. Martinez, J. M. Alonso, & P. U. Tse (Eds.), *Progress in brain research* (Vol. 155, Part 2, pp. 273–286). New York, NY: Elsevier.

Sotres-Bayon, F., Cain, C. K., & LeDoux, J. E. (2006). Brain mechanisms of fear extinction: Historical perspectives on the contribution of prefrontal cortex. *Biological Psychiatry, 60*(4), 329–336. doi:10.1016/j.biopsych.2005.10.012

Sowell, E. R., Mattson, S. N., Kan, E., Thompson, P. M., Riley, E. P., & Toga, A. W. (2008). Abnormal cortical thickness and brain-behavior correlation patterns in individuals with heavy prenatal alcohol exposure. *Cerebral Cortex, 18*(1), 136–144. doi:10.1093/cercor/bhm039

Spearman, C. E. (1904). "General intelligence" objectively determined and measured. *American Journal of Psychology, 5,* 201–293.

Spence, S. A., Brooks, D. J., Hirsch, S. R., Liddle, P. F. Meehan, J., & Grasby, P. M. (1997). A PET study of voluntary movement in schizophrenic patients experiencing passivity phenomena (delusions of alien control). *Brain, 120,* 1997–2011.

Sperling, G. (1960). The information available in brief visual presentations. *Psychological Monographs, 74* (whole no. 11).

Sperry, R. W. (1982). Some effects of disconnecting the cerebral hemispheres. *Science, 217,* 1223–1226.

Spiegel, K., Tasali, E., Penev, P., & Van Cauter, E. (2004). Brief communication: Sleep curtailment in healthy young men is associated with decreased leptin levels, elevated ghrelin levels, and increased hunger and appetite. *Annals of Internal Medicine, 141*(11), 846–850.

Spieker, L. E., Hürlimann, D., Ruschitzka, F., Corti, R., Enseleit, F., Shaw, S., et al. (2002). Mental stress induces prolonged endothelial dysfunction via endothelin-A receptors. *Circulation, 105*(24), 2817–2820. doi:10.1161/01.cir.0000021598.15895.34

Spira, J. L., Pyne, J. M., Wiederhold, B., Wiederhold, M., Graap, K., & Rizzo, A. (2006). Virtual reality and other experiential therapies for combat-related posttraumatic stress disorder. *Primary Psychiatry, 13*(3), 58–64.

Sprengnether, M. (1990). *The spectral mother: Freud, feminism and psychoanalysis.* Ithaca, NY: Cornell University Press.

Springer, S. P., & Deutsch, G. (1998). *Left brain, right brain* (5th ed.). New York: Freeman.

Squire, L. R. (1987). *Memory and the brain.* New York, NY: Oxford University Press.

Sroufe, L. A., Carlson, E. A., & Levy, A. K. (2003). Implications of attachment theory for developmental psychopathology. In M. E. Hertzig & E. A. Farber (Eds.), *Annual progress in child psychiatry and child development: 2000–2001* (pp. 43–61). New York, NY: Brunner-Routledge.

Stacher, G. (1986). Effects of cholecystokinin and caerulein on human eating behavior and pain sensation: A review. *Psychoneuroendocrinology, 11*, 39–48.

Stader, S. R., & Hokanson, J. E. (1998). Psychosocial antecedents of depressive symptoms: An evaluation using daily experiences methodology. *Journal of Abnormal Psychology, 107*(1), 17–26. doi:10.1037/0021-843x.107.1.17

Stagnitti, M. N. (2008). Antidepressants prescribed by medical doctors in office based and outpatient settings by specialty for the U.S. civilian noninstitutionalized population, 2002 and 2005. Retrieved November 24, 2010, from http://www.meps.ahrq.gov/mepsweb/data_files/publications/st206/stat206.pdf

Stahl, L. A., Begg, D. P., Weisinger, R. S., & Sinclair, A. J. (2008). The role of omega-3 fatty acids in mood disorders. *Current Opinion in Investigational Drugs, 9*(1), 57–64.

Stanley, S. A., Connan, F., Small, C. J., Murphy, K. G., Todd, J. F., Ghatei, M., et al. (2003). Elevated circulating levels of cocaine- and amphetamine-regulated transcript (CART) in anorexia nervosa. *Endocrine Abstracts, 5,* OC30.

Steblay, N. M., Dysart, J., Fulero, S., & Lindsay, R. C. L. (2001). Eyewitness accuracy rates in sequential and simultaneous lineup presentations: A meta-analytic comparison. *Law and Human Behavior, 25*, 459–474.

Steele, C. M. (1997). A threat in the air: How stereotypes shape intellectual identity and performance. *American Psychologist, 52,* 613–629.

Steele, C. M., & Aronson, J. (1995). Stereotype threat and the intellectual test performance of African Americans. *Journal of Personality and Social Psychology, 69,* 797–811.

Steele, C. M., & Josephs, R. A. (1990). Alcohol myopia: Its prized and dangerous effects. *American Psychologist, 45,* 921–934.

Stefanucci, J. K., & Proffitt, D. R. (2009). The roles of altitude and fear in the perception of height. *Journal of Experimental Psychology: Human Perception and Performance, 35*(2), 424–438. doi:10.1037/a0013894

Steiger, B. (2000). *American Indian medicine dream book.* Atglen, PA: Whitford Press.

Stein-Behrens, B., Mattson, M. P., Chang, I., Yeh, M., & Sapolsky, R. (1994). Stress exacerbates neuron loss and cytoskeletal pathology in the hippocampus. *Journal of Neuroscience, 14,* 5373–5380.

Steinberg, L., & Levine, A. (1997). *You and your adolescent: A parent's guide for ages 10 to 20.* New York, NY: Harper Perennial.

Steinhausen, H.-C., Willms, J., & Spohr, H.-L. (1993). Long-term psychopathological and cognitive outcome of children with fetal alcohol syndrome. *Journal of the American Academy of Child and Adolescent Psychiatry, 32,* 990–994.

Stern, M. B. (1971). *Heads & headlines: The phrenological Fowlers.* Norman: University of Oklahoma Press.

Sternberg, R. J. (1985). *Beyond IQ: A triarchic theory of human intelligence.* New York: Cambridge University Press.

Sternberg, R. J. (1986). *Intelligence applied: Understanding and increasing your intellectual skills.* New York: Harcourt Brace Jovanovich.

Sternberg, R. J. (2004). A triangular theory of love. In H. T. Reis & C. D. Rusbult (Eds.), *Close relationships: Key readings* (pp. 213–227). Philadelphia, PA: Taylor & Francis.

Sternberg, R. J., & Salter, W. (1982). Conceptions of intelligence. In R. J. Sternberg (Ed.), *Handbook of human intelligence* (pp. 3–28). New York: Cambridge University Press.

Sternberg, S. (1966). High speed scanning in human memory. *Science, 153,* 652–654.

Sternberg, S. (1967). Retrieval of contextual information from memory. *Psychonomic Science, 8,* 55–56.

Sternberg, S. (1969). Memory scanning: Mental processes revealed by reaction-time experiments. *American Scientist, 57,* 421–457.

Stevens, D., Charman, T., & Blair, R. J. (2001). Recognition of emotion in facial expressions and vocal tones in children with psychopathic tendencies. *Journal of Genetic Psychology, 162,* 201–211.

Stevens, S. S. (1960). Psychophysics of sensory function. *American Scientist, 48,* 226–252.

Stewart, S. T., Cutler, D. M., & Rosen, A. B. (2009). Forecasting the effects of obesity and smoking on U.S. life expectancy. *New England Journal of Medicine, 361*(23), 2252–2260. doi:10.1056/NEJMsa0900459

Stewart, W. K., & Fleming, L. W. (1973). Features of a successful therapeutic fast of 382 days' duration. *Postgraduate Medical Journal, 49,* 203–209.

Steyn, P., Wallstrom, A., & Pitt, L. (2010). Consumer-generated content and source effects in financial services advertising: An experimental study. *Journal of Financial Services Marketing, 15*(1), 49–61.

Stickgold, R., & Walker, M. P. (2007). Sleep-dependent memory consolidation and reconsolidation. *Sleep Medicine, 8*(4), 331–343.

Stickgold, R., James, L., & Hobson, J. A. (2000). Visual discrimination learning requires sleep after training. *Nature Neuroscience, 3,* 1237–1238.

Stokes, P. E. (1995). The potential role of excessive cortisol induced by HPA hyperfunction in the pathogenesis of depression. *European Neuropsychopharmacology, 5*(Suppl. 1), 77–82. doi:10.1016/0924-977x(95)00039-r

Stoller, R. J., & Herdt, G. H. (1985). Theories of origins of male homosexuality: A cross-cultural look. *Archives of General Psychiatry, 42,* 399–404.

Stone, J., Perry, Z. W., & Darley, J. M. (1997). "White men can't jump": Evidence for the perceptual confirmation of racial stereotypes following a basketball game. *Basic and Applied Social Psychology, 19*(3), 291–306. doi:10.1207/15324839751036977

Strait, D. L., Kraus, N., Parbery-Clark, A., & Ashley, R. (2010). Musical experience shapes top-down auditory mechanisms: Evidence from masking and auditory attention performance. *Hearing Research.* doi:10.1016/j.heares.2009.12.021

Strasburger, V. C. (2007). First do no harm: Why have parents and pediatricians missed the boat on children and media? *Journal of Pediatrics, 151*(4), 334–336.

Straus, S., Richardson, W. S., Glasziou, P., & Haynes, R. B. (2011). *Evidence-based medicine: How to practice and teach E.B.M.* (4th ed.). Edinburgh, Scotland: Churchill Livingstone.

Strauss, G. P., Harrow, M., Grossman, L. S., & Rosen, C. (2010). Periods of recovery in deficit syndrome schizophrenia: A 20-year multi–follow-up longitudinal study. *Schizophrenia Bulletin, 36*(4), 788–799. doi:10.1093/schbul/sbn167

Streissguth, A. P., Aase, J. M., Clarren, S. K., Randels, S. P., LaDue, R. A., & Smith, D. F. (1991). Fetal alcohol syndrome in adolescents and adults. *Journal of the American Medical Association, 264,* 1961–1967.

Strickland, B. R. (1992). Women and depression. *Current Directions in Psychological Science, 1,* 132–135.

Stroebe, W. (2010). The graying of academia: Will it reduce scientific productivity? *American Psychologist, 65*(7), 660–673. doi:10.1037/a0021086

Ströhle, A. (2009). Physical activity, exercise, depression and anxiety disorders. *Journal of Neural Transmission, 116*(6), 777–784. doi:10.1007/s00702-008-0092-x

Stroop, J. R. (1935). Studies of interference in serial verbal reactions. *Journal of Experimental Psychology, 18,* 643–662.

Sugden, K., Arseneault, L., Harrington, H., Moffitt, T. E., Williams, B., & Caspi, A. (2010). Serotonin transporter gene moderates the development of emotional problems among children following bullying victimization. *Journal of the American Academy of Child and Adolescent Psychiatry, 49*(8), 830–840. doi:10.1016/j.jaac.2010.01.024

Sung, H.-Y., Prochaska, J. J., Ong, M. K., Shi, Y., & Max, W. (2011). Cigarette smoking and serious psychological distress: A population-based study of California adults. *Nicotine and Tobacco Research.* doi:10.1093/ntr/ntr148

Suomi, S. J. (2006). Risk, resilience, and gene × environment interactions in rhesus monkeys. *Annals of the New York Academy of Sciences, 1094*(1), 52–62. doi:10.1196/annals.1376.006

Super, C. M. (1976). Environmental effects on motor development: The case of "African infant precocity." *Developmental Medicine and Child Neurology, 18*, 561–567.

Susswein, A. J., Schwarz, M., & Feldman, E. (1986). Learned changes of feeding behavior in *Aplysia* in response to edible and inedible foods. *Journal of Neuroscience, 6*, 1513–1527.

Sutton, R. M., & Douglas, K. M. (2005). Justice for all, or just me? More evidence of the importance of the self-other distinction in just world beliefs. *Personality and Individual Differences, 39*, 637–645.

Svoboda, E., McKinnon, M. C., & Levine, B. (2006). The functional neuroanatomy of autobiographical memory: A meta-analysis. *Neuropsychologia, 44*(12), 2189–2208.

Swaminathan, R., Burrows, G., & McMurray, J. (1982). Energy cost of sodium pump activity in man: An in vivo study of metabolic rate in human subjects given digoxin. *IRCS Medical Science, 10*, 949.

Swap, W. C. (1977). Interpersonal attraction and repeated exposure to rewarders and punishers. *Personality and Social Psychology Bulletin, 3*, 248–251.

Swedo, S. E., Leonard, H. L., Mittleman, B. B., Allen, A. J., Rapoport, J. L., Dow, S. P., et al. (1997). Identification of children with pediatric autoimmune neuropsychiatric disorders associated with streptococcal infections by a marker associated with rheumatic fever. *American Journal of Psychiatry, 154*, 110–112.

Syvalahti, E. K. G. (1994). I. The theory of schizophrenia: Biological factors in schizophrenia. *British Journal of Psychiatry, 164*, 9–14.

Szeszko, P. R., MacMillan, S., McMeniman, M., Chen, S., Baribault, K., Lim, K. O., et al. (2004). Brain structural abnormalities in psychotropic drug-naive pediatric patients with obsessive-compulsive disorder. *American Journal of Psychiatry, 161*(6), 1049–1056.

Szymanski, L., & King, B. H. (1999). Practice parameters for the assessment and treatment of children, adolescents, and adults with mental retardation and comorbid mental disorders. *Journal of the American Academy of Child and Adolescent Psychiatry, 38*(12, Suppl.), 5S–31S.

Tallal, P., Ross, R., & Curtiss, S. (1989). Familial aggregation in specific language impairment. *Journal of Speech and Hearing Disorders, 54*, 167–171.

Tarumi, S., Ichimiya, A., Yamada, S., Umesue, M., & Kuroki, T. (2004). Taijin Kyofusho in university students: Patterns of fear and predispositions to the offensive variant. *Transcultural Psychiatry, 41*(4), 533–546. doi:10.1177/1363461504047933

Taylor, D. A., & Altman, I. (1987). Communication in interpersonal relationships: Social penetration processes. In M. E. Roloff & G. R. Miller (Eds.), *Interpersonal processes: New directions in communication research* (pp. 257–277). Thousand Oaks, CA: Sage.

Taylor, L., Faraone, S. V., & Tsuang, M. T. (2002). Family, twin, and adoption studies of bipolar disease. *Current Psychiatry Reports, 4*, 130–133.

Taylor, P. (2008). Republicans: Still happy campers. Retrieved August 9, 2010, from http://

pewsocialtrends.org/assets/pdf/Republicans-Happiness.pdf

Taylor, S. E. (2002). *The tending instinct: How nurturing is essential to who we are and how we live.* New York, NY: Henry Holt.

Taylor, S. E. (2006). Tend and befriend: Biobehavioral bases of affiliation under stress. *Current Directions in Psychological Science, 15*(6), 273–277. doi:10.1111/j.1467-8721 .2006.00451.x

Taylor, S. E., & Brown, J. D. (1988). Illusion and well-being: A social psychological perspective on mental health. *Psychological Bulletin, 103*, 193–210.

Taylor, S. E., & Master, S. L. (2010). Social response to stress: The tend-and-befriend model. In R. J. Contrada & A. Baum (Eds.), *The handbook of stress science: Biology, psychology, and health* (pp. 101–109). New York, NY: Springer.

Terman, L. (1916). *The measurement of intelligence.* Boston: Houghton Mifflin.

Terman, L. (1925). *Genetic studies of genius: Vol. 1. Mental and physical traits of a thousand gifted children.* Stanford, CA: Stanford University Press.

Terman, L. M., & Oden, M. H. (1959). *Genetic studies of genius: Vol. 5. The gifted group at mid-life.* Stanford, CA: Stanford University Press.

Terrace, H. S. (1979, November). How Nim Chimpsky changed my mind. *Psychology Today*, 65–76.

Terry, D. J. (1994). Determinants of coping: The role of stable and situational factors. *Journal of Personality and Social Psychology, 66*(5), 895–910. doi:10.1037/0022-3514.66.5.895

Testa, M., Quigley, B. M., & Eiden, R. D. (2003). The effects of prenatal alcohol exposure on infant mental development: A meta-analytical review. *Alcohol and Alcoholism, 38*(4), 295–304. doi:10.1093/alcalc/agg087

Tetlock, P. E., Self, W. T., & Singh, R. (2010). The punitiveness paradox: When is external pressure exculpatory—and when a signal just to spread blame? *Journal of Experimental Social Psychology, 46*(2), 388–395. doi:10.1016/j .jesp.2009.11.013

Thacher, P. V. (2008). University students and "the all nighter": Correlates and patterns of students' engagement in a single night of total sleep deprivation. *Behavioral Sleep Medicine, 6*(1), 16031.

Thannickal, T. C., Moore, R. Y., Nienhuis, R., Ramanathan, L., Gulyani, S., Aldrich, M., et al. (2000). Reduced number of hypocretin neurons in human narcolepsy. *Neuron, 27*, 469–474.

Thera*Scribe* [Computer software]. New York, NY: Wiley. Retrieved July 28, 2007, from http://www.wiley.com/legacy/therascribe/default.htm

Thierry, B. (1994). Emergence of social organizations in non-human primates. *Revue Internationale de Systémique, 8*, 65–77.

Thomas, A., & Chess, S. (1977). *Temperament and development.* New York, NY: Brunner/Mazel.

Thomas, A., & Chess, S. (1989). Temperament and personality. In G. A. Kohnstamm, J. E. Bates, & M. K. Rothbart (Eds.), *Temperament in childhood* (pp. 249–261). New York, NY: Wiley.

Thomas, J. L., Wilk, J. E., Riviere, L. A., McGurk, D., Castro, C. A., & Hoge, C. W. (2010).

Prevalence of mental health problems and functional impairment among active component and National Guard soldiers 3 and 12 months following combat in Iraq. *Archives of General Psychiatry, 67*(6), 614–623. doi:10.1001/archgenpsychiatry.2010.54

Thomas, L. A., De Bellis, M. D., Graham, R., & LaBar, K. S. (2007). Development of emotional facial recognition in late childhood and adolescence. *Developmental Science, 10*(5), 547–558.

Thompson, M. A., Callaghan, P. D., Hunt, G. E., Cornish, J. L., & McGregor, I. S. (2007). A role for oxytocin and 5-HT(1A) receptors in the prosocial effects of 3,4 methylenedioxymethamphetamine ("Ecstasy"). *Neuroscience, 146*(2), 509–514.

Thompson, P. M., Giedd, J. N., Woods, R. P., MacDonald, D., Evans, A. C., & Toga, A. W. (2000). Growth patterns in the developing brain detected by using continuum mechanical tensor maps. *Nature, 404*, 190–193.

Thompson, P. M., Vidal, C., Giedd, J. N., Gochman, P., Blumenthal, J., Nicolson, R., et al. (2001). Mapping adolescent brain change reveals dynamic wave of accelerated gray matter loss in very early-onset schizophrenia. *Proceedings of the National Academy of Sciences, 98*, 11650–11655.

Thornhill, R., & Gangestad, S. W. (1994). Fluctuating asymmetry correlates with lifetime sex partner numbers and age at first sex in *Homo sapiens. Psychological Science, 5*, 297–303.

Thornton, L. M., Andersen, B. L., Crespin, T. R., & Carson, W. E. (2007). Individual trajectories in stress covary with immunity during recovery from cancer diagnosis and treatments. *Brain, Behavior, and Immunity, 21*(2), 185–194.

Thorpe, W. H. (1963). *Learning and instinct in animals* (2nd ed.). Cambridge, MA: Harvard University Press.

Thyer, B. A. (2004). What is evidence-based practice? *Brief Treatment and Crisis Intervention, 4*(2), 167–176. doi:10.1093/brief-treatment/mhh013

Tien, A. Y. (1991). Distribution of hallucinations in the population. *Social Psychiatry and Psychiatric Epidemiology, 26*(6), 287–292. doi:10.1007/bf00789221

Tinbergen, N. (1951). *The study of instinct.* New York: Oxford University Press.

Titone, D., Levy, D. L., & Holzman, P. S. (2000). Contextual insensitivity in schizophrenic language processing: Evidence from lexical ambiguity. *Journal of Abnormal Psychology, 109*, 761–767.

Tolman, E. C. (1948). Cognitive maps in rats and men. *Psychological Review, 55*, 189–208.

Tolman, E. C. (1959). Principles of purposive behavior. In S. Koch (Ed.), *Psychology: A study of a science* (Vol. 2, pp. 92–157). New York: McGraw-Hill.

Tolman, E. C., Richie, B. F., & Kalish, D. (1946). Studies in spatial learning: II. Place learning vs. response learning. *Journal of Experimental Psychology, 36*, 221–229.

Tovée, M. J., Reinhardt, S., Emery, J. L., & Cornelissen, P. L. (1998). Optimum body-mass index and maximum sexual attractiveness. *Lancet, 352*, 548.

Travis, F. T. (1993). Respiratory, autonomic, and EEG correlates of transcendental consciousness experiences during transcendental meditation practice. *Society for Neuroscience Abstracts, 18*(1), 574, 515.

Treffert, D. A., & Wallace, G. L. (2002). Islands of genius. *Scientific American, 286,* 76–85.

Triplett, N. (1898). The dynamogenic factors in pacemaking and competition. *American Journal of Psychology, 9,* 507–533.

Trivers, R. L. (1971). The evolution of reciprocal altruism. *Quarterly Review of Biology, 46*(1), 35–57.

Trivers, R., & Burt, A. (1999). Kinship and genomic imprinting. *Results and Problems in Cell Differentiation, 25,* 1–21.

Trockel, M. T., Barnes, M. D., & Egget, D. L. (2000). Health-related variables and academic performance among first-year college students: Implications for sleep and other behaviors. *Journal of American College Health, 49*(3), 125–131. doi:10.1080/07448 480009596294

Troll, L., Neugarten, B. L., & Kraines, R. J. (1969). Similarities in values and other personality characteristics in college students and their parents. *Merrill-Palmer Quarterly, 15,* 323–336.

Trope, Y., & Liberman, N. (2010). Construal-level theory of psychological distance. *Psychological Review, 117*(2), 440–463. doi:10.1037/a0018963

Trout, D. L. (1980). The role of social isolation in suicide. *Suicide and Life-Threatening Behavior, 10,* 10–23.

Trzesniewski, K. H., Donnellan, M. B., & Robins, R. W. (2003). Stability of self-esteem across the life span. *Journal of Personality and Social Psychology, 84,* 205–220.

Tulving, E. (1972). Episodic and semantic memory. In E. Tulving & W. Donaldson (Eds.), *Organization and memory* (pp. 381–403). New York, NY: Academic Press.

Tulving, E. (1983). *Elements of episodic memory.* Oxford, England: Clarendon Press/Oxford University Press.

Tulving, E. (1985). How many memory systems are there? *American Psychologist, 40,* 385–398.

Tulving, E. (1989). Memory: Performance, knowledge, and experience. *European Journal of Cognitive Psychology, 1,* 3–26.

Tulving, E. (1995). Organization of memory. In M. S. Gazzaniga (Ed.), *The cognitive neurosciences* (pp. 839–853). Cambridge, MA: MIT Press.

Tulving, E., & Psotka, J. (1971). Retroactive inhibition in free recall: Inaccessibility of information available in the memory store. *Journal of Experimental Psychology, 87,* 1–8.

Tulving, E., & Thomson, D. M. (1973). Encoding specificity and retrieval processes in episodic memory. *Psychological Review, 80,* 352–373.

Turati, C., Simion, F., Milani, I., & Umiltà, C. (2002). Newborns' preference for faces: What is crucial? *Developmental Psychology, 38*(6), 875–882. doi:10.1037/0012-1649.38.6.875

Turkheimer, E., Haley, A., Waldron, M., D'Onofrio, B., & Gottesman, I. I. (2003). Socioeconomic status modified heritability of IQ in young children. *Psychological Science, 14*(6), 623–628.

Tversky, A., & Kahneman, D. (1973). Availability: A heuristic for judging frequency and probability. *Cognitive Psychology, 5,* 207–232.

Tversky, A., & Kahneman, D. (1974). Judgment under uncertainty: Heuristics and biases. *Science, 185,* 1124–1131.

Tversky, A., & Kahneman, D. (1987). Rational choice and the framing of decisions. In R. M. Hogarth & M. W. Reder (Eds.), *Rational choice: The contrast between economics and psychology* (pp. 67–94). Chicago: University of Chicago Press.

Twenge, J. M., & Crocker, J. (2002). Race and self-esteem: Meta-analyses comparing Whites, Blacks, Hispanics, Asians, and American Indians. *Psychological Bulletin, 128,* 371–408.

Twenge, J. M., Baumeister, R. F., Tice, D. M., & Stucke, T. S. (2001). If you can't join them, beat them: Effects of social exclusion on aggressive behavior. *Journal of Personality and Social Psychology, 81,* 1058–1069.

Tygart, C. E. (2000). Genetic causation attribution and public support of gay rights. *International Journal of Public Opinion Research, 12*(3), 259–275. doi:10.1093/ijpor/12.3.259

U.S. Census Bureau. (2011). About the American Community Survey. Retrieved April 19, 2011, from http://www.census.gov/acs/www/about_the_survey/american_community_survey/

U.S. Department of Education Office of Educational Research and Improvement. (1993). *National excellence: A case for developing America's talent.* Washington, DC: U.S. Government Printing Office.

U.S. Department of Justice. (2002). Drinking in America: Myths, realities, and prevention policy. Retrieved October 28, 2009, from http://www.udetc.org/documents/drinking_in_america.pdf

U.S. Department of Justice. (2006). Crime in the United States. Retrieved October 7, 2007, from http://www.fbi.gov/ucr/cius2006/index.html

U.S. Food and Drug Administration (FDA). (2010). FDA approves new formulation for OxyContin. Retrieved June 11, 2011, from http://www.fda.gov/NewsEvents/Newsroom/PressAnnouncements/ucm207480.htm

Umbel, V. M., Pearson, B. Z., Fernandez, S. C., & Oller, D. K. (1992). Measuring bilingual children's receptive vocabularies. *Child Development, 63,* 1012–1020.

UNdata. (2008). Total fertility rate. Retrieved April 9, 2010, from http://data.un.org/Data.aspx?d=PopDiv&f=variableID%3A54

Underwood, B. J. (1957). Interference and forgetting. *Psychological Review, 64,* 49–60.

United Nations Office on Drugs and Crime. (2001). The seventh United Nations survey on crime trends and the operations of criminal justice systems (1998–2000). Retrieved October 7, 2007, from http://www.unodc.org/unodc/crime_cicp_survey_seventh.html

United Nations. (2007). World population prospects: The 2006 revision. Retrieved September 10, 2011, from http://www.un.org/esa/population/publications/wpp2006/WPP2006_Highlights_rev.pdf

United Nations. (2009, June). World population prospects: The 2008 revision. Retrieved April 16, 2011, from http://data.un.org/Data.aspx?d=PopDiv&f=variableID%3A54

University of Michigan Transportation Research Institute. (2004). Roadway deaths up after 9/11. Retrieved July 7, 2011, from http://www.umtri.umich.edu/content/rr35_4.pdf

Üstün, T. B., Ayuso-Mateos, J. L., Chatterji, S., Mathers, C., & Murray, C. J. L. (2004). Global burden of depressive disorders in the year 2000. *British Journal of Psychiatry, 184*(5), 386–392. doi:10.1192/bjp.184.5.386

Vaillant, G. E. (2003). A 60-year follow-up of alcoholic men. *Addiction, 98*(8), 1043–1051. doi:10.1046/j.1360-0443.2003.00422.x

Vaillant, G. E., & Koury, S. H. (1993). Late midlife development. In G. H. Pollock & S. I. Greenspan (Eds.), *The course of life: Vol. 6. Late adulthood* (Rev. and exp. ed., pp. 1–22). Madison, CT: International Universities Press.

Vaitl, D., Gruzelier, J., Jamieson, G. A., Lehmann, D., Ott, U., Sammer, G., et al. (2005). Psychobiology of altered states of consciousness. *Psychological Bulletin, 131,* 98–127.

Valenstein, E. S. (1986). *Great and desperate cures.* New York, NY: Basic Books.

van Anders, S. M., & Watson, N. V. (2006). Relationship status and testosterone in North American heterosexual and non-heterosexual men and women: Cross-sectional and longitudinal data. *Psychoneuroendocrinology, 31*(6), 715–723.

van Anders, S. M., Hamilton, L. D., & Watson, N. V. (2007). Multiple partners are associated with higher testosterone in North American men and women. *Hormones and Behavior, 51*(3), 454–459.

Van Cauter, E., Leproult, R., & Plat, L. (2000). Age-related changes in slow wave sleep and REM sleep and relationship with growth hormone and cortisol levels in healthy men. *JAMA: Journal of the American Medical Association, 284*(7), 861–868. doi:10.1001/jama.284.7.861

van Hell, J. G., & Tokowicz, N. (2010). Event-related brain potentials and second language learning: Syntactic processing in late L2 learners at different L2 proficiency levels. *Second Language Research, 26*(1), 43–74. doi:10.1177/0267658309337637

Van Knippenberg, D., & Wilke, H. (1992). Prototypicality of arguments and conformity to ingroup norms. *European Journal of Social Psychology, 22,* 141–155.

van Londen, L., Goekoop, J. G., van Kempen, G. M. J., Frankhuijzen-Sierevogel, A. C., Wiegant, V. M., van der Velde, E. A., et al. (1997). Plasma levels of arginine vasopressin elevated in patients with major depression. *Neuropsychopharmacology, 17,* 284–292.

van Veen, V., Krug, M. K., Schooler, J. W., & Carter, C. S. (2009). Neural activity predicts attitude change in cognitive dissonance. *Nature Neuroscience, 12*(11), 1469–1474. doi:10.1038/nn.2413

Vaughn, B. E., & Bost, K. K. (1999). Attachment and temperament: Redundant, independent, or interacting influences on interpersonal adaptation and personality development? In J. Cassidy & P. R. Shaver (Eds.), *Handbook of attachment: Theory, research, and clinical applications* (pp. 198–225). New York, NY: Guilford Press.

Vermetten, E., Schmahl, C., Southwick, S. M., & Bremner, J. D. (2007). Positron tomographic emission study of olfactory induced emotional recall in veterans with and without combat-related posttraumatic stress disorder. *Psychopharmacology Bulletin, 40*(1), 8–30.

Vescio, T. K., Judd, C. M., & Kwan, V. S. Y. (2004). The crossed-categorization hypothesis: Evidence of reductions in the strength of categorization, but not intergroup bias. *Journal of Experimental Social Psychology, 40*(4), 478–496. doi:10.1016/j.jesp.2003.09.005

Vestergaard-Poulsen, P., van Beek, M., Skewes, J., Bjarkam, C. R., Stubberup, M., Bertelsen, J., et al. (2009). Long-term meditation is associated with increased gray matter density in the brain stem. *NeuroReport, 20*(2), 170–174.

Vinokur, R. (2004). Acoustic noise as a non-lethal weapon. *Sound and Vibration, 38*, 19–23.

Virués-Ortega, J. (2010). Applied behavior analytic intervention for autism in early childhood: Meta-analysis, meta-regression and dose-response meta-analysis of multiple outcomes. *Clinical Psychology Review, 30*, 387–399.

Visser, B. A., Ashton, M. C., & Vernon, P. A. (2006). Beyond *g*: Putting multiple intelligences theory to the test. *Intelligence, 34*(5), 487–502. doi:10.1016/j.intell.2006.02.004

Vohs, K. D., & Heatherton, T. F. (2000). Self-regulatory failure: A resource-depletion approach. *Psychological Science, 11*(3), 249–254.

Voineagu, I., Wang, X., Johnston, P., Lowe, J. K., Tian, Y., Horvath, S., et al. (2011). Transcriptomic analysis of autistic brain reveals convergent molecular pathology. *Nature, 474*(7351), 380–384. doi:10.1038/nature10110.

Vokey, J. R. (2002). Subliminal messages. In J. R. Vokey & S. W. Allen (Eds.), *Psychological sketches* (6th ed., pp. 223–246). Lethbridge, Alberta: Psyence Ink.

Volkow, N. D., Wang, G.-J., Kollins, S. H., Wigal, T. L., Newcorn, J. H., Telang, F., et al. (2009). Evaluating dopamine reward pathway in ADHD: Clinical implications. *JAMA: Journal of the American Medical Association, 302*(10), 1084–1091. doi:10.1001/jama.2009.1308

Volkow, N. D., Wang, G.-J., Fowler, J. S., & Ding, Y.-S. (2005). Imaging the effects of methylphenidate on brain dopamine: New model on its therapeutic actions for attention-deficit/hyperactivity disorder. *Biological Psychiatry, 57*(11), 1410–1415.

Vollenweider, F. X., Vollenweider-Sherpenhuyzen, M. F., Bäbler, A., Vogel, H., & Hell, D. (1998). Psilocybin induces schizophrenia-like psychosis in humans via a serotonin-2 agonist action. *NeuroReport, 9*, 3897–3902.

von Brücke, E. W. (1881). *Vorlesungen über Physiologie.* (3rd ed.). Vienna: W. Braumüller.

Vuilleumier, P., Armony, J. L., Driver, J., & Dolan, R. J. (2001). Effects of attention and emotion on face processing in the human brain: An event-related fMRI study. *Neuron, 30*(3), 829–841.

Vygotsky, L. S. (1934/1962). *Thought and language.* Cambridge, MA: MIT Press.

Wadee, A. A., Kuschke, R. H., Kometz, S., & Berk, M. (2001). Personality factors, stress and immunity. *Stress and Health: Journal of the International Society for the Investigation of Stress, 17*(1), 25–40.

Wagner, D. R. (1996). Disorders of the circadian sleep-wake cycle. *Neurological Clinics, 14*, 651–670.

Wagner, U., Fischer, S., & Born, J. (2002). Changes in emotional responses to aversive pictures across periods rich in slow-wave sleep versus rapid eye movement sleep. *Psychosomatic Medicine, 64*(4), 627–634.

Wagner, U., Gais, S., & Born, J. (2001). Emotional memory formation is enhanced across sleep intervals with high amounts of rapid eye movement sleep. *Learning and Memory, 8*(2), 112–119.

Wahlstrom, K. L. (2003). Changing times: Findings from the first longitudinal study of later high school start times. *Bulletin of the National Association of Secondary School Principals (NASSP), 86*, 3–21.

Wainer, H., & Steinberg, L. S. (1992). Sex differences in performance on the mathematics section of the Scholastic Aptitude Test: A bidirectional validity study. *Harvard Educational Review, 62*(3), 323–336.

Wainright, J. L., & Patterson, C. J. (2008). Peer relations among adolescents with female same-sex parents. *Developmental Psychology, 44*(1), 117–126. doi:10.1037/0012-1649 .44.1.117

Waite, L. J., & Gallagher, M. (2001). *The case for marriage: Why married people are happier, healthier, and better off financially.* New York, NY: Random House.

Waite, L. J., Luo, Y., & Lewin, A. C. (2009). Marital happiness and marital stability: Consequences for psychological well-being. *Social Science Research, 38*(1), 201–212. doi:10.1016/j.ssresearch.2008.07.001

Waldinger, R. J., & Schulz, M. S. (2010). What's love got to do with it? Social functioning, perceived health, and daily happiness in married octogenarians. *Psychology and Aging, 25*(2), 422–431. doi:10.1037/a0019087

Walker, A., & Shipman, P. (1996). *The wisdom of the bones: In search of human origins.* New York, NY: Knopf.

Walker, J. (2010). Using QEEG-guided neurofeedback for epilepsy versus standardized protocols: Enhanced effectiveness? *Applied Psychophysiology and Biofeedback, 35*(1), 29–30. doi:10.1007/s10484-009-9123-0

Wallston, K. (2005). Reviews: Control and the psychology of health: Theory, measurement and applications. *Journal of Health Psychology, 10*(2), 301–302.

Walster, E., Aronson, V., & Abrahams, D. (1966). Importance of physical attractiveness in dating behavior. *Journal of Personality and Social Psychology, 4*, 508–516.

Walters, S. (1994). Algorithms and archetypes: Evolutionary psychology and Carl Jung's theory of the collective unconscious. *Journal of Social and Evolutionary Systems, 17*(3), 287–306. doi:10.1016/1061-7361(94)90013-2

Walton, G. M., & Cohen, G. L. (2011). A brief social-belonging intervention improves academic and health outcomes of minority students. *Science, 331*(6023), 1447–1451. doi:10.1126/science.1198364

Wan, C.-S., & Chiou, W.-B. (2010). Inducing attitude change toward online gaming among adolescent players based on dissonance theory: The role of threats and justification of effort. *Computers and Education, 54*(1), 162–168. doi:10.1016/j.compedu.2009.07.016

Wang, J., Horlick, M., Thornton, J. C., Levine, L. S., Heymsfield, S. B., & Pearson, R. S., Jr. (1999). Correlations between skeletal muscle mass and bone mass in children 6–18 years: Influences of sex, ethnicity, and pubertal status. *Growth, Development, and Aging, 63*, 99–109.

Wang, Q. (2008). Emotion knowledge and autobiographical memory across the preschool years: A cross-cultural longitudinal investigation. *Cognition, 108*(1), 117–135. doi:10.1016/j.cognition.2008.02.002

Wang, X. T., Kruger, D. J., & Wilke, A. (2009). Life history variables and risk-taking propensity. *Evolution and Human Behavior, 30*, 77–84.

Wansink, B. (2006). *Mindless eating: Why we eat more than we think.* New York, NY: Bantam.

Wansink, B., & Sobal, J. (2007). Mindless eating. The 200 daily food decisions we overlook. *Environment and Behaviour, 39*, 106–123.

Ward, D. (2006). *Stuttering and cluttering: Frameworks for understanding treatment.* New York, NY: Psychology Press.

Wasserman, R. C., Kelleher, K. J., Bocian, A., Baker, A., Childs, G. E., Indacochea, F., et al. (1999). Identification of attentional and hyperactivity problems in primary care: A report from pediatric research in office settings and the ambulatory sentinel practice network. *Pediatrics, 103*, E 38.

Wasson, R. (1968). *Soma, divine mushroom of immortality.* New York, NY: Harcourt Brace Jovanovich.

Watkins, C. E., Campbell, V. L., & Nieberding, R. (1995). Contemporary practice of psychological assessment by clinical psychologists. *Professional Psychology: Research and Practice, 26*, 54–60.

Watkins, E., & Brown, R. G. (2002). Rumination and executive function in depression: An experimental study. *Journal of Neurology, Neurosurgery, and Psychiatry, 72*, 400–402.

Watson, J. B. (1925). *Behaviorism.* Chicago: University of Chicago Press.

Weaver, I. C. G., La Plante, P., Weaver, S., Parent, A., Sharma, S., Diorio, J., et al. (2001). Early environmental regulation of hippocampal glucocorticoid receptor gene expression: Characterization of intracellular mediators and potential genomic target sites. *Molecular and Cellular Endocrinology, 185*(1–2), 205–218. doi:10.1016/s0303-7207(01)00635-9

Weber, W., & Newmark, S. (2007). Complementary and alternative medical therapies for attention deficit/hyperactivity disorder and autism. *Pediatric Clinics of North America, 54*(6), 983–1006.

Wedekind, C., & Füri, S. (1997). Body odour preferences in men and women: Do they aim for specific MHC combinations or simply heterozygosity? *Proceedings of the Royal Society of London, Series B: Biological Sciences, 264*(1387), 1471–1479. doi:10.1098/rspb.1997.0204

Wegner, D. M. (1986). Transactive memory: A contemporary analysis of the group mind. In B. Mullen & G. R. Goethals (Eds.), *Theories of group behavior* (pp. 185–208). New York, NY: Springer-Verlag.

Wegner, D. M. (1994). Ironic processes of mental control. *Psychological Review, 101*, 34–52.

Wegner, D. M., Erber, R., & Raymond, P. (1991). Transactive memory in close relationships. *Journal of Personality and Social Psychology, 61*(6), 923–929.

Wegner, D. M., Giuliano, T., & Hertel, P. (1985). Cognitive interdependence in close relationships. In W. J. Ickes (Ed.), *Compatible and* incompatible relationships (pp. 253–276). New York, NY: Springer-Verlag.

Weinberger, N. M. (2006). Food for thought: Honeybee foraging, memory, and acetylcholine. *Science Signaling: The Signal Transduction Knowledge Environment, 336,* pe23-. doi:10.1126/stke.3362006pe23

Weingartner, H., Miller, H., & Murphy, D. L. (1977). Mood-state-dependent retrieval of verbal associations. *Journal of Abnormal Psychology, 86,* 276–284.

Weinstock, M. (2005). The potential influence of maternal stress hormones on development and mental health of the offspring. *Brain, Behavior, and Immunity, 19*(4), 296–308.

Weisberg, P., & Waldrop, P. B. (1972). Fixed-interval work habits of Congress. *Journal of Applied Behavior Analysis, 5,* 93–97.

Weiskrantz, L., Barbur, J. L., & Sahraie, A. (1995). Parameters affecting conscious versus unconscious visual discrimination with damage to the visual cortex (V1). *Proceedings of the National Academy of Sciences, 92,* 6122–6126.

Weissman, M. M., Warner, V., Wickramaratne, P., Moreau, D., & Olfson, M. (1997). Offspring of depressed parents: 10 years later. *Journal of Affective Disorders, 15,* 269–277.

Wells, A. (2006). Metacognitive therapy for worry and generalised anxiety disorder. In G. C. L. Davey & A. Wells (Eds.), *Worry and its psychological disorders: Theory, assessment and treatment* (pp. 259–272). Hoboken, NJ: Wiley.

Wells, G. L., & Bradfield, A. L. (1998). "Good, you identified the suspect": Feedback to eyewitnesses distorts their reports of the witnessing experience. *Journal of Applied Psychology, 83,* 360–376.

Wells, G. L., Memon, A., & Penrod, S. D. (2006). Eyewitness evidence: Improving its probative value. *Psychological Science in the Public Interest, 7*(2), 45–75.

Wernicke, C. (1874). *Der aphasische symptomenkomplex.* Breslau, Poland: Cohn & Weigart.

Wertheimer, M. (1912). Experimentelle Studien über das Sehen von Bewegung. *Zeitschrift für Psychologie, 61,* 161–265.

Wessely, S., & Kerwin, R. (2004). Suicide risk and the SSRIs. *JAMA: Journal of the American Medical Association, 292,* 379–381.

Westbrook, D., & Kirk, J. (2005). The clinical effectiveness of cognitive behaviour therapy: Outcome for a large sample of adults treated in routine practice. *Behaviour Research and Therapy, 43,* 1243–1261.

Whisman, M. A., Dixon, A. E., & Johnson, B. (1997). Therapists' perspectives of couples' problems and treatment issues in the practice of couples therapy. *Journal of Family Psychology, 11,* 361–366.

White, G. L. (1980). Physical attractiveness and courtship progress. *Journal of Personality and Social Psychology, 39,* 660–668.

Whitehouse, W. G., Dinges, D. F., Orne, E. C., & Orne, M. T. (1988). Hypnotic hypermnesia: Enhanced memory accessibility or report bias? *Journal of Abnormal Psychology, 97,* 289–295.

Whorf, B. L. (1956). Science and linguistics. In J. B. Carroll (Ed.), *Language, thought, and reality: Selected writings of Benjamin Lee Whorf* (pp. 207–219). Cambridge, MA: MIT Press.

Widmeyer, W. N., & Loy, J. W. (1988). When you're hot, you're hot: Warm-cold effects in first impressions of persons

and teaching effectiveness. *Journal of Educational Psychology, 80*(1), 118–121. doi:10.1037/0022-0663.80.1.118

Widom, C. (1978). A methodology for studying non-institutionalized psychopaths. In R. D. Hare & D. Schalling (Eds.), *Psychopathic behaviour: Approaches to research* (pp. 71–84). Chichester, England: Wiley.

Wiersma, D., Nienhuis, F. J., Slooff, C. J., & Giel, R. (1998). Natural course of schizophrenic disorders: A 15-year follow-up of a Dutch incidence cohort. *Schizophrenia Bulletin, 24,* 75–85.

Wilcox, H. C., Arria, A. M., Caldeira, K. M., Vincent, K. B., Pinchevsky, G. M., & O'Grady, K. E. (2010). Prevalence and predictors of persistent suicide ideation, plans, and attempts during college. *Journal of Affective Disorders, 127*(1–3), 287–294. doi:10.1016/j.jad.2010.04.017

Wilensky, A. E., Schafe, G. E., Kristensen, M. P., & LeDoux, J. E. (2006). Rethinking the fear circuit: The central nucleus of the amygdala is required for the acquisition, consolidation, and expression of Pavlovian fear conditioning. *Journal of Neuroscience, 26*(48), 12387–12396.

Wilke, A., Hutchinson, J. M. C., Todd, P. M., & Kruger, D. J. (2006). Is risk taking used as a cue in mate choice? *Evolutionary Psychology, 4,* 367–393.

Wilkinson, G. S. (1984). Reciprocal food sharing in the vampire bat. *Nature, 308,* 181–184.

Wilkinson, G. S. (1990). Food sharing in vampire bats. *Scientific American, 62,* 76–82.

Williams, H., Conway, M. A., & Cohen, G. (2008). Autobiographical memory. In G. Cohen & M. A. Conway (Eds.), *Memory in the real world* (pp. 21–90). New York, NY: Psychology Press.

Williams, J. H. G. (2008). Self-other relations in social development and autism: Multiple roles for mirror neurons and other brain bases. *Autism Research, 1*(2), 73–90.

Williams, K. D. (2007). Ostracism. *Annual Review of Psychology, 58,* 425–452.

Williams, L. M., Liddell, B. J., Kemp, A. H., Bryant, R. A., Meares, R. A., Peduto, A. S., et al. (2006). Amygdala-prefrontal dissociation of subliminal and supraliminal fear. *Human Brain Mapping, 27*(8), 652–661.

Williamson, A. M., & Feyer, A.-M., (2000). Moderate sleep deprivation produces impairments in cognitive and motor performance equivalent to legally prescribed levels of alcohol intoxication. *Occupational and Environmental Medicine, 57,* 649–655.

Williamson, R. A., Jaswal, V. K., & Meltzoff, A. N. (2010). Learning the rules: Observation and imitation of a sorting strategy by 36-month-old children. *Developmental Psychology, 46*(1), 57–65. doi:10.1037/a0017473

Wilson, A. E., & Ross, M. (2000). The frequency of temporal and social comparisons in people's personal appraisals. *Journal of Personality and Social Psychology, 78,* 928–942.

Wilson, E. O. (1975). *Sociobiology: The new synthesis.* Cambridge, MA: Belknap Prsss.

Wilson, G. D., Cousins, J. M., & Fink, B. (2006). The CQ as a predictor of speed-date outcomes. *Sexual and Relationship Therapy, 21,* 163–169.

Wilson, J. L., Peebles, R., Hardy, K. K., & Litt, I. F. (2006). Surfing for thinness: A pilot study of pro-eating disorder web site usage in adolescents with eating disorders. *Pediatrics, 118*(6), e1635–e1643. doi:10.1542/peds.2006-1133

Wilton, P. (2002). A rule of thumb. *Canadian Medical Association Journal, 167,* 1367.

Wimmer, H., & Perner, J. (1983). Beliefs about beliefs: Representation and constraining function of wrong beliefs in young children's understanding of deception. *Cognition, 13,* 103–128.

Winson, J. (1985). *Brain and psyche.* Garden City, NY: Anchor Press/Doubleday.

Winter, D. G. (2010). Why achievement motivation predicts success in business but failure in politics: The importance of personal control. *Journal of Personality, 78*(6), 1637–1667. doi:10.1111/j.1467-6494.2010.00665.x

Witt, D. M., Carter, C. S., Lederhendler, I. I., & Kirkpatrick, B. (1997). Regulatory mechanisms of oxytocin-mediated sociosexual behavior. *The integrative neurobiology of affiliation* (pp. 287–301). New York, NY: New York Academy of Sciences.

Wittchen, H.-U., & Hoyer, J. (2001). Generalized anxiety disorder: Nature and course. *Journal of Clinical Psychiatry, 62*(Suppl. 11), 15–19.

Wittgenstein, L. (1953). *Philosophical investigations* (G. E. M. Anscombe, Trans.). Oxford, England: Blackwell.

Witvliet, C. v. O., Ludwig, T. E., & Laan, K. L. V. (2001). Granting forgiveness or harboring grudges: Implications for emotion, physiology, and health. *Psychological Science, 12*(2), 117–123. doi:10.1111/1467-9280.00320

Wobber, V., Wrangham, R., & Hare, B. (2010). Bonobos exhibit delayed development of social behavior and cognition relative to chimpanzees. *Current Biology, 20*(3), 226–230.

Woike, B. A., Lavezzary, E., & Barsky, J. (2001). The influence of implicit motives on memory processes. *Journal of Personality and Social Psychology, 81,* 935–945.

Wolfers, J. (2010). How marriage survives. Retrieved April 19, 2011, from http://www.brookings.edu/opinions/2010/1013_recession_marriage_wolfers.aspx

Wolpe, J. (1958). *Psychotherapy by reciprocal inhibition.* Stanford, CA: Stanford University Press.

Wolraich, M. L., Wilson, D. B., & White, J. W. (1996). The effect of sugar on behavior or cognition in children: A meta-analysis. *JAMA: Journal of the American Medical Association, 274,* 1617–1621.

Wood, J. M., Bootzin, R. R., Rosenhan, D., Nolen-Hoeksema, S., & Jourden, F. (1992). Effects of the 1989 San Francisco earthquake on frequency and content of nightmares. *Journal of Abnormal Psychology, 101*(2), 219–224.

Wood, J. M., Nezworski, M. T., & Lilienfeld, S. O. (2003). *What's wrong with the Rorschach? Science confronts the controversial inkblot test.* San Francisco, CA: Jossey-Bass.

Woodworth, M., & Porter, S. (2002). In cold blood: Characteristics of criminal homicides as a function of psychopathy. *Journal of Abnormal Psychology, 111*(3), 436–445.

Woolley, A. W., Chabris, C. F., Pentland, A., Hashmi, N., & Malone, T. W. (2010).

Evidence for a collective intelligence factor in the performance of human groups. *Science, 330,* 686–688.

World Health Organization (WHO). (2003). WHO definition of health. Retrieved October 16, 2010, from http://www.who.int/about/definition/en/print.html

World Health Organization (WHO). (2006). Obesity and overweight. Retrieved October 10, 2010, from http://www.who.int/mediacentre/factsheets/fs311/en/index.html

World Health Organization (WHO). (2008). *WHO report on the global tobacco epidemic, 2008: The MPOWER package.* Geneva, Switzerland: World Health Organization.

World Health Organization (WHO). (2011). The International Classification of Diseases 11th Revision is due by 2015. Retrieved August 16, 2011, from http://www.who.int/classifications/icd/revision/en/index.html

World Health Organization (WHO). (2011, February). Alcohol (Fact Sheet). Retrieved from http://www.who.int/mediacentre/factsheets/fs349/en/index.html

Worthington, E. L., Jr., & Scherer, M. (2004). Forgiveness is an emotion-focused coping strategy that can reduce health risks and promote health resilience: Theory, review, and hypotheses. *Psychology and Health, 19*(3), 385–405.

Wrzesniewski, A., McCauley, C., Rozin, P., & Schwartz, B. (1997). Jobs, careers, and callings: People's relations to their work. *Journal of Research in Personality, 31*(1), 21–33. doi:10.1006/jrpe.1997.2162

Wu, P.-L., & Chiou, W.-B. (2008). Postformal thinking and creativity among late adolescents: A post-Piagetian approach. *Adolescence, 43*(170), 237–251.

Wurtman, R. J. (2005). Genes, stress, and depression. *Metabolism, 54*(5, Suppl. 1), 16–19.

Yalom, I. D. (1995). *The theory and practice of group psychotherapy* (4th ed.). New York, NY: Basic Books.

Yang, M. S., & Gill, M. (2007). A review of gene linkage, association and expression studies in autism and an assessment of convergent evidence. *International Journal of Developmental Neuroscience, 25*(2), 69–85.

Yee, J. R., Frijling, J., Saber, M., Sterlinski, A., Tovar, S., Barlas, L., et al. (2010). *Oxytocin alters the behavioral, cardiovascular, and hormonal responses to a mild daily stressor.* Paper presented at the Society for Neuroscience.

Yee, N. (2006). The demographics, motivations and derived experiences of users of massively-multiuser online graphical environments. *PRESENCE: Teleoperators and Virtual Environments, 15,* 309–329.

Yehuda, R., Engel, S. M., Brand, S. R., Seckl, J., Marcus, S. M., & Berkowitz, G. S. (2005). Transgenerational effects of posttraumatic stress disorder in babies of mothers exposed to the World Trade Center attacks during pregnancy. *Journal of Clinical Endocrinology and Metabolism, 90,* 4115–4118.

Yerkes, R. M., & Dodson, J. D. (1908). The relation of strength of stimulus to rapidity of habit-formation. *Journal of Comparative and Physiological Psychology, 18,* 459–482.

Yotsutsuji, T., Saitoh, O., Suzuki, M., Hagino, H., Mori, K., Takahashi, T., et al. (2003). Quantification of lateral ventricular subdivisions in schizophrenia by high-resolution three-dimensional magnetic resonance imaging. *Psychiatry Research, 122,* 1–12.

Young, F. (2011). The Pearson correlation coefficient. Retrieved on December 12, 2011, from http://forrest.psych.unc.edu/research/vista-frames/help/lecturenotes/lecture11/pearson.html

Young, P. C. (1952). Antisocial uses of hypnosis. In L. M. LeCron (Ed.), *Experimental hypnosis* (pp. 376–409). New York, NY: Macmillan.

Young, S. G., & Claypool, H. M. (2010). Mere exposure has differential effects on attention allocation to threatening and neutral stimuli. *Journal of Experimental Social Psychology, 46*(2), 424–427. doi:10.1016/j.jesp.2009.10.015

Yu, Y. W., Chen, T. J., Wang, Y. C., Liou, Y. J., Hong, C. J., & Tsai, S. J. (2003). Association analysis for neuronal nitric oxide synthase gene polymorphism with major depression and fluoxetine response. *Neuropsychobiology, 47,* 137–140.

Yurgelun-Todd, D. (2007). Emotional and cognitive changes during adolescence. *Current Opinion in Neurobiology, 17*(2), 251–257.

Zadra, A. L., & Pihl, R. O. (1997). Lucid dreaming as a treatment for recurrent nightmares. *Psychotherapy and Psychosomatics, 66,* 50–55.

Zager, A., Andersen, M. L., Ruiz, F. S., Antunes, I. B., & Tufik, S. (2007). Effects of acute and chronic sleep loss on immune modulation of rats. *American Journal of Physiology. Regulatory, Integrative and Comparative Physiology, 293*(1), R504–R509.

Zajonc, R. B. (1965). Social facilitation. *Science, 149*(3681), 269–274.

Zajonc, R. B. (1968). Attitudinal effects of mere exposure. *Journal of Personality and Social Psychology Monograph Supplement, 9,* 1–27.

Zajonc, R. B., & Sales, S. M. (1966). Social facilitation of dominant and subordinate responses. *Journal of Experimental Social Psychology, 2*(2), 160–168.

Zajonc, R. B., Heingartner, A., & Herman, E. (1969). Social enhancement and impairment of performance in the cockroach. *Journal of Personality and Social Psychology, 13,* 83–92.

Zelazo, P. R. (1998). McGraw and the development of unaided walking. *Developmental Review, 18*(4), 449–471. doi:10.1006/drev.1997.0460.

Zerjal, T., Xue, Y., Bertorelle, G., Wells, S., Bao, W., Suling, Z., et al. (2003). The genetic legacy of the Mongols. *American Journal of Human Genetics, 72,* 717–721.

Zhang, T. Y., Chrétien, P., Meaney, M. J., & Gratton, A. (2005). Influence of naturally occurring variations in maternal care on prepulse inhibition of acoustic startle and the medial prefrontal cortical dopamine response to stress in adult rats. *Journal of Neuroscience, 25,* 1493–1502.

Zhang, Y., Proenca, R., Maffei, M., Barone, M., Leopold, L., & Friedman, J. M. (1994). Positional cloning of the mouse obese gene and its human homologue. *Nature, 372,* 425–432.

Zigler, E. (1967). Familial mental retardation: A continuing dilemma. *Science, 155,* 292–298.

Zigler, E., & Hodapp, R. (1986). *Understanding mental retardation.* New York: Cambridge University Press.

Zimbardo, P. G. (1969). The human choice: Individuation, reason, and order vs. deindividuation, impulse and chaos. In W. J. Arnold & D. Levine (Eds.), *Nebraska symposium on motivation* (pp. 237–307). Lincoln, NE: University of Nebraska Press.

Zimmer, C. (2009). On the origin of tomorrow. *Science, 326,* 1334–1336.

Zimmerman, F. J., Gilkerson, J., Richards, J. A., Christakis, D. A., Xu, D., Gray, S., et al. (2009). Teaching by listening: The importance of adult-child conversations to language development. *Pediatrics, 124*(1), 342–349. doi:10.1542/peds.2008-2267

Zito, K. A., Vickers, G., & Robert, D. C. (1985). Disruption of cocaine and heroin self-administration following kainic acid lesions of the nucleus accumbens. *Pharmacology, Biochemistry, and Behavior, 23,* 1029–1036.

Zubin, J., & Spring, B. (1977). Vulnerability: A new view of schizophrenia. *Journal of Abnormal Psychology, 86,* 103–126.

Zuscho, H. (1983). Posttraumatic anosmia. *Archives of Otolaryngology—Head and Neck Surgery, 4,* 252–256.

Zyzak, D. R., Otto, T., Eichenbaum, H., & Gallagher, M. (1995). Cognitive decline associated with normal aging in rats: A neuropsychological approach. *Learning and Memory, 2,* 1–16.

Name Index

Deocampo, J., 532
Department of Health and Human Services, 826–827
Depp, J., 817
Derntl, B., 670
Derogatis, L. R., 793
Derryberry, D., 588
DeRubeis, R. J., 768
Desai, S., 499
Descartes, R., 7–8, 9, 13
Deschamps, J. C., 636
Deutsch, G., 165
De Valois, K. K., 197
De Valois, R. L., 197
De Villiers, P. A., 456
De Visser, S. J., 702–703
De Vries, A. P., 695, 793
De Waal, F. B. M., 239, 666
DeWall, C. N., 385
DeYoung, C. G., 591
Diamond, A., 408, 529
Diamond, D. M., 436
Diamond, L. M., 173, 308
DiCaprio, L., 116
Di Castelnuovo, A., 823
Dicke, U., 110
Dickens, W. T., 496
DiClemente, C., 817
Diener, E., 599, 809, 833
Dierker, L., 370
Dierks, T., 712
Dietrich, A., 690
Difede, J., 696
DiGrande, L., 695
Dijk, D. J., 244
DiLalla, L. F., 687
Dill, K. E., 62–63, 65, 66
Di Martino, A., 729
Dimidjian, S., 768
Dimitri, A. C., 499
Ding, Y.-S., 779
Dinges, D. F., 279
Dinnegan, M., 161
Dion, K., 642
Diorio, J., 798, 799
Di Pellegrino, G., 148
Ditzen, B., 175
Dixon, A. E., 782
Dixon, D. P., 516
Dixon, L., 817
Dixon, M., 366
Dixson, A. F., 659
Dixson, B. J., 659
Dr. Seuss, 136
Dodds, C. M., 131
Dodson, J. D., 320, 652
Doise, W., 636
Dokken, D., 514, 515
Dolan, C. B., 316
Dolan, R. J., 154, 192, 666, 796
Dolderman, D., 657
Dolezal, C., 312
Dolinoy, D. C., 88, 298
Doll, R., 818
Domhoff, G. W., 256
Domschke, K., 690
Donati, M. B., 823
Donnellan, M. B., 601
D'Onofrio, B., 496–497
Dopfel, R. P., 172
Dorries, K. M., 228
Dorus, S., 110
Douglas, K. M., 628
Dourish, C. T., 296
Dove, H., 526
Dover, R., 305
Dovidio, J. F., 350
Dow, R. S., 151
Dow, S. P., 693
Downing, P. E., 131
Downs, D. L., 605, 606
Dowsett, M., 247
Doyle, A. C. See Holmes, S.
Drakich, J., 48
Dressel, A., 240
Drewnowski, A., 820

Drisaldi, B., 816
Driver, J., 154
Dronkers, N. F., 482
Druett, J., 662
Dubernard, J.-M., 134
Dubovsky, A. N., 706
Dubovsky, S. L., 706
Dudai, Y., 438
Dudukovic, N. M., 437
Dugas, D. V., 726
Dulaney, S., 694–695
Dumais, S. T., 204
Duman, R., 759, 768
Dunbar, R. I. M., 110, 145
Duncan, G. H., 277
Duncan, T. E., 817
Dunlap, A., 723
Dunner, D. L., 770
Dunning, D., 603
Dupoux, E., 488
Durante, K. M., 116
Dutton, D. G., 336
Dysart, J., 440
Dyson-Hudson, N., 673
Dyson-Hudson, R., 673
Dzekov, J., 306

Eagly, A. H., 658
Eastwick, P. W., 658, 659
Eaves, L. J., 688, 702
Ebbers, B., 722
Ebbesen, E. B., 493
Eberhardt, J. L., 633
Eberhart, C. G., 776
Eccles, R., 366
Eckert, E. D., 73
Eckstrand, K., 729
Eddy, M. B., 829
Edison, T., 485
Edwards, A., 220
Edwards, E. M., 824
Edward VII, 98
Egeland, J. A., 699
Egger, H. L., 728, 779–780
Egget, D. L., 59
Eglinton, E., 486
Ehlers, C. L., 822
Ehlert, U., 175
Eich, E., 279
Eich, J., 431
Eichel, S. K. D., 279–280, 744
Eichenbaum, H., 443
Eid, J., 811, 812
Eiden, R. D., 61
Einstein, A., 82, 220, 455, 485, 576, 580, 700
Eisch, A. J., 768
Eisen, A. R., 689
Eisenberg, D., 683
Eisenberg, M. B., 643
Eisenberger, N. I., 131, 154, 327, 622, 674
Ekman, P., 329, 330, 332, 334, 335
Elbert, T., 220, 792
Elenkov, I., 802
Eliot, 322
Elizabeth, Queen, 199
Elkind, D., 599
Eller, A., 636
Elliot, R., 375
Elliott, M. N., 791, 808
Ellis, A., 758, 830
Ellis, H. C., 404
Ellis Weismer, S., 725
Ellsworth, P., 330, 341
Elman, C., 558
El Nasser, H., 50
Emery, G., 709, 769
Emery, J. L., 659
Emery, N. J., 154, 323
Emlen, S. T., 115
Emmelkamp, P. M. G., 747, 748, 765
Emmons, R. A., 833, 837
Enard, W., 485
Eng, M. Y., 822
Eng, W.-s., 270

Engel, S. M., 727, 792
Ennaceur, A., 245
Enoch, M. A., 823, 824
Enquist, M., 646
Enseleit, F., 803
Eppig, C., 496
Epstein, J. N., 779, 780
Erber, R., 448
Erdberg, P., 596
Erhard, P., 327
Erickson, C. A., 776
Erickson, K. I., 825
Erickson, M., 746
Erickson, P. I., 116
Erikson, E. H., 549–550, 601
Eriksson, K., 646
Erkanli, A., 728, 779–780
Ernst, J. M., 252, 254, 701
Ernst, M., 162
Ernst, M. E., 246
Erol, R. Y., 551, 602
Ersner-Hershfield, H., 561
Escaramis, G., 702
Eshel, N., 162
Eskelinen, M. H., 271
Eskenazi, J., 419
Esler, A., 725
Eslinger, P. J., 159, 161
Esposito, L., 259
Estrada, S. M., 531
Ettinger, M. G., 250
Eugenie, V., 98
Evans, A. C., 509, 525
Evans, D. E., 588
Evans, F. J., 276
Evans, P. D., 110
Evins, A. E., 715
Exline, J. J., 841
Eyal, N., 487
Eysenck, H. J., 591, 670
Eysenck, M. W., 402, 407

Fabel, K., 825
Fabiano, G. A., 780
Faden, V., 822, 823
Fadiga, L., 148, 389
Falangola, M. F., 729
Fan, Y.-T., 391
Farah, M. J., 608
Faraone, S. V., 687, 706, 728
Farley, F., 547
Farley, R., 634
Farmer, J., 777
Farnham, S. D., 602–603
Farrell, M. P., 555
Fastow, A., 722
Faurie, C., 166
Fazekas, A., 445
Fazel, S., 720
Feder, H. C., 12, 184–185
Federman, J., 672
Fehr, E., 668
Feick, D. L., 603
Feilding, A., 760
Fein, D. A., 135
Feinberg, D. R., 658, 659
Feinberg, I., 608
Feinstein, J. A., 30, 652
Feinstein, J. S., 154
Fejfar, M. C., 598
Feldman, D. E., 780
Feldman, H. M., 780
Feldman, M. B., 301
Feldman, M. W., 646
Feldman, P., 367
Feldman, R., 173
Fergusson, D. M., 717
Fernandes, C., 490
Fernandes, E., 274
Fernández, G., 436
Fernandez, S. C., 487
Fernandez, T., 547
Ferrari, J. R., 292
Ferrari, P. F., 390, 536
Ferri, C. P., 560
Ferriter, M., 778

Festinger, L., 601, 637, 638
Feusner, J. D., 712
Feyer, A.-M., 251
Feynman, R., 500
Fidler, D. J., 493
Fielden, J. A., 127, 307
Fifer, W. P., 216, 514
Figueroa, A. E., 709
Fincher, C. L., 496
Fink, B., 623
Fink, G. R., 422, 423, 609
Finkel, E. J., 658, 659
Finn, L., 247
Finucane, M., 467
Fiorito, G., 389
Fischer, H., 632, 692
Fischer, S., 252, 445
Fischhoff, B., 469, 547
Fischhoff, J., 779
Fisher, C., 707
Fisher, P. A., 99
Fisher, R. P., 334
Fisher, S. E., 103, 484
Fishman, S., 220
Fiske, A. P., 694–695
Fiske, S. T., 631, 632
Fitz, S. D., 690
Fitzgerald, F. S., 712
Fitzgerald, M., 727
Fitzgerald, Z., 712
Flatt, R., 627
Flax, J., 514
Flegal, K. M., 298, 819
Fleischman, J., 159
Fleischmann, P., 760
Fleming, L. W., 295
Flexser, A. J., 430
Flom, R., 521
Flynn, J. R., 67, 110, 496
Foa, E. B., 766
Fodor, E. M., 716
Fogassi, L., 148, 389, 390
Folkerd, E., 247
Fonagy, P., 723, 759
Food and Drug Administration (FDA), 276, 300
Ford, E. S., 815
Forer, B. R., 572
Forgeard, M., 216
Forger, N. G., 300
Formisano, E., 712
Forster, B., 721
Forsyth, D. R., 605, 628
Fosshage, J. L., 749
Foulkes, D., 256
Fournier, J. C., 768
Foutz, A. S., 258
Fowler, J. H., 299–300, 592, 593, 819–820
Fowler, J. S., 779
Fox, P. W., 525
Fox, R., 204, 466
Foye, P. E., 295
Frackowiak, R. S. J., 423
Frady, R. L., 670
Fraga, M., 97
Frances, A., 684
Francis, D., 99, 798, 799, 800
Francks, C., 103
Frank, L. R., 547
Frank, M. G., 332
Frank, R., 159
Franke, B., 728
Franken, D., 837–838
Frankenhuis, W. E., 467
Frankhuijzen-Sierevogel, A. C., 308
Frankl, V., 811
Franklin, B., 333, 739
Franklin, M. E., 766
Franson, K. L., 702–703
Fratiglioni, L., 560
Frazier, J., 705
Freberg, K. J., 643
Freberg, L. A., 773
Frederick, D. A., 306, 467
Frederick, J. Z., 499

Fredman, S. J., 731
Fredrickson, B. L., 571, 811
Fredrikson, M., 692
Freedman, A., 798
Freedman, D. G., 329
Freedman, M., 487
Freedson, P. S., 824
Freeman, H. L., 715, 773
Freeman, S., 603
Freeman, W., 760
Freitag, G., 385
French, S. A., 552
Freud, S., 7, 23–25, 26, 27, 237, 240, 255, 273, 276, 508, 549, 573–578, 739, 748, 749–751, 754
Fricchinoe, G. L., 280
Fried, I., 196
Friedel, S., 259
Friedman, J. M., 295, 297
Friedman, M., 803
Friedman, P., 44
Friedman, S. D., 770
Frierson, T., 672
Fries, G. R., 770
Friesen, C., 257
Friesen, W. V., 330, 332, 335
Frijling, J., 175, 800
Frincke, J., 743, 744
Frisch, R. E., 544–545
Frischholz, E. J., 772
Frith, C. D., 160, 666
Frith, U., 486, 725
Fritzon, K., 722
Froberg, J., 247
Fromme, H., 523
Frost, P., 106
Frost, R., 161
Fryer, R., 291
Fuhrer, D., 4
Fukuyama, H., 408
Fulbright, R. K., 486
Fulero, S., 440
Fuligni, A. J., 551
Fulker, D. W., 670
Fulkerson, J. A., 552
Fuller, R., 760
Fulton, J., 760
Funayama, E. S., 632
Funder, D. C., 624
Fung, H. H., 561, 629
Funk, C. L., 638
Füri, S., 121, 620
Fyer, A., 690

Gabriel, B., 175
Gabriel, S., 610
Gabrieli, J. D. E., 589, 609
Gadian, D. G., 423
Gaertner, S. L., 350
Gage, F., 509, 759
Gage, P., 158–159, 322, 397
Gailliot, M. T., 385
Gais, S., 252, 445
Gajiwala, K. S., 297
Galaburda, A. M., 159
Galea, S., 697
Galilei, G., 47
Gallagher, M., 443, 832
Gallagher, P. R., 695, 793
Gallassi, R., 251
Galles, N. S., 488
Gallese, V., 148, 389
Galli, R., 695, 799
Gallup, G. G., 239
Gallup Poll News Service, 76
Galovski, T., 731
Galperin, A., 467
Galton, F., 90–91
Galvan, A., 547
Galvani, A. P, 126
Galyer, K. T., 306
Gambini, M. G., 262
Gamez, W., 583
Gandevia, S. C., 236
Gandhi, M., 318
Gangestad, S. W., 659

Ganguli, M., 560
Ganoczy, D., 770
Gantt, W. H., 366
Gao, F., 99
Gao, X. B., 295
Garb, H. N., 596
Garcia, C., 702
Garcia, J., 361–362
García-Palacios, A., 765
Gardner, B. I., 482
Gardner, H., 481, 492
Gardner, R. A., 482
Gardner, W., 609, 610, 611
Gardner, W. L., 225
Garfinkel, P. E., 302
Garmezy, N., 811
Gasquet, I., 695, 712
Gassman, M., 500
Gatenby, J. C., 632
Gates, B., 637
Gaulin, S. J. C., 108
Gawronski, B., 626
Gayan, J., 103
Gazzaniga, M. S., 163, 236, 238
Gazzola, V., 389, 390
Geary, D. C., 78
Geda, Y. E., 560
Gehre, S., 485
Geiselman, R. E., 334
Geiser, S., 70
Gellavia, G., 657
Geller, B., 705
Genovese, K., 668
Gent, J. F., 228
George VI, King, 43
Gerard, G., 321
Gergen, K. J., 601
Gernsbacher, M., 78
Gersten, M., 687
Gertner, Y., 533
Gertsch, G., 221
Gesierich, B., 390
Gest, S. D., 811
Geuze, E., 696
Gevensleben, H., 762
Gewirtz, J. C., 367
Ghatei, M., 303
Giacino, J., 264
Gibb, B. E., 571
Gibbs, A. C., 254
Gibbs, J. C., 774
Gibson, M. A., 116
Giedd, J., 131, 509, 525, 547, 714, 715
Giel, R., 737
Giesbrecht, T., 711
Giese, M. A., 149
Gigerenzer, G., 467
Gijsbers, K., 222
Gilbert, D. T., 625, 626
Gilbert, S. L., 110
Gilbertson, M. W., 696, 799
Gildea, P. M., 480
Gilder, J. V., 488
Gilger, J. W., 486
Gilkerson, J., 483
Gilkes, J. J., 305
Gill, M., 726
Gillan, J., 431
Gillespie, C. F., 99, 800
Gilligan, C., 549
Gilligan, S. G., 598
Gillihan, S. J., 608
Gilman, S. E., 302
Gilovich, T., 288, 467, 599
Giner, L., 709
Gino, F., 440
Giordani, B., 796
Girgus, J. S., 700
Giuliano, T., 448
Giulio Tononi, G., 237
Glance, N., 654
Glanzer, M., 411
Glaser, J., 592
Glaser, R., 175
Glasser, D. B., 307
Glasziou, P., 740

Gleeson, M., 825
Gleick, J., 500
Glick, B., 774
Glick, P., 631
Glover, G., 547
Glynn, S. M., 755
Gochman, P., 131, 714, 715
Godden, D. R., 430, 431
Goebel, R., 712
Goekoop, J. G., 308
Goel, R., 716, 717
Goering, P., 302
Goetz, C. G., 715
Goff, D. C., 715
Gogtay, N., 494
Gold, J., 696
Goldberg, R., 817
Goldberg, S. C., 73
Goldbloom, D., 302
Golden, K. A., 769
Goldman-Rakic, P. S., 408, 529
Goldsmith, T. H., 661
Goldstein, A. P., 774
Goldstein, D. G., 467
Goldstein, E. B., 227
Goldstein, N. J., 647
Goldstein, R. B., 792, 807–808
Goleman, D., 492
Gollan, J. K., 52, 323, 704, 705, 840
Gollub, R. L., 280
Golocheikine, S. A., 280
Golosheykin, S., 102, 332
Gompers, J., 818
Gone, J. P., 709
Gong, H., 251
Gonzalez, A, 167
Gonzalez, R. G., 420
Gonzalez-Maeso, J., 270
Good, B., 690
Good, C. D., 423
Goodall, J., 56
Goode, S., 726
Goodman, C., 769
Goodwin, R. D., 698
Gopnik, A., 534
Gordon, A. M., 248
Gordon, I., 173
Gordon, K. C., 782
Gordon, N., 44
Gordon, R., 321
Gore, J. C., 632
Gorelick, D. A., 270
Gorman, J. M., 690
Gorski, R. A., 312
Gosling, S. D., 592
Gosselin, F., 325
Gosselin, N., 324
Gottesman, C., 255
Gottesman, I. I., 496–497, 713, 726
Gottman, J. M., 343, 661
Gouin, J.-P., 175
Gould, E., 173, 509
Gouldner, A., 647
Graae, F., 694
Graap, K., 765
Grabowski, T., 159, 327–328
Graessle, M., 535
Graf, H., 754
Graftin, S. T., 248
Grafton, S., 27
Graham, R., 547
Grandin, T., 455
Granpeesheh, D., 777
Granrud, C. E., 204
Grant, A. M., 745
Grant, B. F., 683, 698, 792, 807–808
Grant, J., 102
Grant, J. D., 824
Grasby, P. M., 608
Grass, J. A., 364
Gratton, A., 582
Graves, K. D., 802
Graves, N., 650
Gray, J., 745
Gray, J. A., 367
Gray, J. R., 280, 281, 493, 496, 591

Gray, P. B., 306
Gray, S., 483
Graziano, M. S., 509
Grecius, M. D., 443
Green, D. P., 635
Greenberg, J., 606
Greenberg, R. L., 709
Greene, R. W., 465
Greenhill, L. L., 728
Greenspan, R. J., 237
Greenspoon, J., 430
Greenstein, D., 494, 729
Greenwald, A. G., 419, 600, 602–603
Gregorian, R. S., 769
Gregory, R. L., 197
Greider, C., 486
Grether, J. K., 726, 727
Greve, D., 280, 281, 321
Grewen, K. M., 308
Griffin, D. W., 657
Griffin, E. A., Jr., 816
Grill, J. T., 244
Grimm, S., 702
Grimshaw, K., 47
Grisham, J. R., 693
Griskevicius, V., 317, 318
Gross, C. G., 509
Gross, R., 59
Grossman, J. M., 551
Grossman, L. S., 737
Grossman, M., 308, 416
Groth-Marnat, G., 741
Gruber, S. A., 135
Grubert, C., 761
Grucza, R., 824
Gruzelier, J., 248, 280, 281
Grzech-Sukalo, H., 244
Guehl, D., 694
Gueorguieva, R., 761
Guerra, N. G., 465
Guerrero, P., 691
Guidotti Breting, L. M., 796
Guignard, J.-H., 553, 554
Guillen, V., 765
Gulyani, S., 258
Gum, A., 836
Gunnar, M. R., 99
Gunter, B., 352
Gunzerath, L., 822, 823
Guo, J. U., 759
Guo, S., 672
Gur, R. C., 78, 333, 670
Gurvitch, A. M., 264
Guth, A., 247
Guze, B. H., 736
Guzman-Marin, R., 251

Haake, J. J., 204
Haas, B. W., 800
Haber, R. B., 456
Haber, R. N., 456
Haber, S. N., 30
Haberman, T., 415
Hadjikhani, N., 321
Hadrysiewicz, B., 761
Haemer, M. A., 819
Hafetz, J., 670
Hagino, H., 714
Haglid, M, 254
Hahlweg, K., 782
Haier, R. J., 493, 494
Hakim, N., 134
Halaas, J. L., 297
Haldane, J. B. S., 96
Hale, S., 532
Hale, T. W., 517
Haley, A., 496–497
Hall, C., 255–256
Hall, G. S., 22, 23
Hall, W. D., 768
Halmi, K. A., 73
Halonen, J., 436
Halperin, J. M., 532
Halpern, D. F., 78
Halpern, J. H., 271
Halpern-Felsher, B. L., 547

Martinez, J., 690
Martinez-Amoros, E., 702
Martlew, M., 96
Martz, J. M., 556
Marvin, A., 777
Marx, G., 592
Masatake, M., 692
Masi, C. M., 313
Maslow, A., 24, 26, 317–318, 580, 829
Mason, M. F., 248, 249
Mason, W. A., 154, 323
Masten, A. S., 811
Master, S. L., 800
Masters, T. M., 820
Masuda, T., 629
Mater, G., 35
Mather, J., 591
Mather, M., 51, 439
Mathers, C., 699
Matheson, D. H., 644
Mathews, T. J., 553
Matsumoto, D., 330, 331, 333, 665
Matsumoto, I., 274
Matsuzaki, I., 295
Mattevi, B. S., 166
Matthews, C. E., 824
Mattson, M. P., 796
Mattson, S. N., 60
Matusch, A., 761
Maurer, C., 522
Maurer, D., 522
Mauro, J., 263
Max, W., 817
Maxfield, M. C., 282
Mayberg, H. S., 761
Mayer, J., 294
Mayer, J. D., 332, 492
Mazur, A., 306, 307, 663
Mazure, C. M., 703, 818
Mazziotta, J. C., 389, 736
McArthur, L. Z., 663
McCall, M., 647
McCall, R. B., 524
McCann, D., 47
McCarley, R. W., 253, 256
McCarthy, J., 727
McCauley, C., 838
McClelland, D. C., 313–314, 316
McClernon, F. J., 364
McClintock, M. K., 110, 621
McCloskey, M., 704, 705
McClure, J. N., 690
McClure, S. M., 476
McComb, K., 240
McCrae, R. R., 581, 582, 583, 594
McCreadie, R. G., 716, 717
McCullough, M. E., 841
McDaniel, M. A., 493
McDermott, M. J., 696
McDougle, C. J., 776
McEwen, B. S., 526, 696, 805, 813
McFall, R. M., 740, 742, 748
McGaugh, J. L., 436
McGaw, S., 500
McGeary, J. E., 571
McGillivray, J., 390
McGinty, D., 251
McGraw, A. P., 288
McGraw, P., 745
McGregor, I. S., 274
McGue, M., 589, 638
McGuffin, P., 101, 713
McGurk, D., 695, 731
McGwire, M., 174
McInerney, S. C., 632
McKay, D., 751
McKay, K. E., 532
McKee, B., 555
McKee, S. A., 818
McKelley, R. A., 745
McKenna, C., 661
McKenzie, K., 716, 717
McKetin, R., 30, 273
McKinley, J. C., 594
McKinnon, M. C., 423
McLaren, J., 273

McLean, D. E., 793
McMeniman, M., 694
McMurray, J., 138
McNally, R. J., 712
McNeely, H. E., 761
McNeill, D., 432
McNulty, J. K., 659
McQueeny, T., 547
McVeigh, T., 841
Meador, K. J., 165
Meaney, M. J., 99, 582, 788, 798, 799, 800
Meares, R. A., 323
Mecca, A. M., 604
Medda, P., 759
Meddis, R., 257
Mednick, S. A., 720
Medoff, D. R., 817
Medvec, V. H., 288, 599
Meehan, J., 608
Meeus, W. H. J., 649
Meguid, M. M., 295
Mehl, M. R., 48
Mei, B., 436
Meisel, A., 274
Mekel-Bobrov, N., 110
Mellers, B. A., 288
Mellin, A., 552
Meltzer, H. Y., 737, 773
Meltzoff, A. N., 382, 483, 534
Melzack, R., 221, 222, 367
Memon, A., 334, 440, 441
Mena, I., 608
Menacker, F., 514
Mencl, W. E., 486
Mendel, G., 105–106
Mendoza, S. P., 154, 323
Mendrek, A., 721
Mennella, J. A., 229, 514, 522
Menzel, E. W., 381
Menzies, L., 693
Merckelbach, H., 711
Merikangas, K. R., 562
Merritt, L. L., 270
Merskey, H., 772
Mery, F., 401
Merzenich, M. M., 220–221, 486
Mesmer, F. A., 276, 739
Messian, N., 647
Metalsky, G. I., 626
Metcalfe, C., 805
Meyer, D. E., 418
Meyer, I. H., 301
Meyer, W. J., III, 251
Meyer-Bahlburg, H. F., 312
Michalek, J., 307
Michalski, D., 35, 36
Michelangelo, 707
Mickelsen, O., 317
Middleton, F. A., 103
Middleton, H., 767
Middleton, K., 316
Mieda, M., 244
Mignot, E., 247
Mikacich, J. A., 699
Mikels, J. A., 811
Milani, I., 522
Milani, R. V., 808, 809
Milevsky, A., 541, 542
Milgram, S., 586, 648–650
Milich, R., 730, 780
Milinski, M., 665
Miller, B. L., 608
Miller, D. B., 672
Miller, D. T., 628
Miller, G., 23
Miller, G. A., 405, 406, 480
Miller, G. E., 802
Miller, H., 431
Miller, I. W., 571
Miller, J., 648
Miller, J. G., 549
Miller, S. L., 486
Mills, B. A., 531
Mills, J., 638
Millstein, S. G., 547

Millward, C., 778
Milne, B. J., 496, 683
Milner, B., 164, 166, 398, 399, 405, 420
Mindess, A., 216
MindSign Neuromarketing, 453, 476
Mineka, S., 389, 692
Ming, G.-l., 759
Minick, P. E., 690
Miniño, A. M., 814
Miotto, K., 670
Mirnics, K., 103
Mischel, W., 493, 588, 622
Mishra, A., 820
Mishra, H., 820
Mitchell, B. A., 558
Mitchell, D. G. V., 154, 720, 721
Mitler, M. N., 258
Mitropoulou, V., 804
Mittleman, B. B., 693
Miyata, H., 245
Miyazawa, S., 245
Mobbs, D., 160, 689
Moberg, T., 709
Moffitt, T. E., 90–91, 93, 95, 569, 683, 703, 720
Mogg, K., 688
Molaison, H., 55, 397–399, 411, 419–420
Moldofsky, H., 251
Molina, B. S. G., 780
Molina, E., 688
Molinari, L., 525
Mollaghan, D. M., 592
Monaco, A. P., 484
Moncrieff, J., 767
Moniz, E., 760
Monk, C. S., 688
Monson, C. M., 731
Montagna, P., 251
Montague, L. M., 476
Montague, P. R., 476, 723
Monteleone, G., 155
Monterosso, J., 502
Monti, M. M., 263, 264
Montpetit, M. A., 808
Moon, C., 215
Moore, A. U., 359
Moore, B. R., 389
Moore, C., 534
Moore, C. A., 250
Moore, K. A., 769, 825
Moore, P. J., 317
Moore, R., 693
Moore, R. Y., 258
Moore, T. E., 419
Moorman, P. G., 275
Moran, P., 720
Moreau, D., 687
Moreno, B., 688
Moreno, C., 705, 706
Morgan, B., 659
Morgan, J. N., 469
Morgan, W. P., 486
Mori, K., 714
Morin, C. M., 758
Morishita, M., 408
Morreale, A., 251
Morris, J. S., 192, 796
Morris, K. S., 548
Morris, M. W., 629
Morris, M., 486, 670
Morse, S., 601
Mortezaie, M., 306
Moscovici, S., 650, 651, 653
Moser, E., 670
Moskalenko, Y. E., 760
Moss, C., 240
Mössner, R., 715
Most, D. E., 493
Mount, M. K., 583
Mountbatten, A., 98

Movellan, J., 382, 483
Mozell, R., 514
Mozhaev, S. V., 760
Muehlenkamp, J. J., 370
Mueller, E., 663
Mulkern, R. V., 518
Mullikin, J. C., 44
Mundorf, N., 454
Mundorff, J., 44
Mundy, P., 522
Munker, H., 180
Muraven, M., 607
Murdoch, B. B., Jr., 410
Murphy, D. L., 431
Murphy, J., 695
Murphy, J. M., 549
Murphy, K. D., 251
Murphy, K. G., 303
Murphy, S. L., 814
Murray, B., 689
Murray, C. J. L., 699
Murray, H. A., 313, 316
Murray, L., 720, 721
Murray, S. L., 657
Murugesan, T., 364
Mustafa, I., 19
Muzic, J. N., 253
Mychack, P., 608
Myers, D. G., 834, 837
Myers, R. M., 531

Nachreiner, F., 244
Nadel, L., 381, 436
Naffrechoux, M., 651
Nahas, Z., 761, 769
Nair, K. S., 553
Nakagawa, S., 331
Nakahara, H., 514
Nakano, H., 514
Nakashima, S., 624
Narumi, J., 245
Nasrallah, H. A., 768
National Institute of Child Health and Human Development (NICHHD), 259
National Institute of Mental Health (NIH), 728
National Sleep Foundation, 244, 259
Navalta, C., 804
Navara, K. J., 246–247
Nazeer, A., 696
Neal, D. T., 338, 339
Neale, B., 728
Neale, M. C., 670, 688, 702
Nedeltcheva, A. V., 804
Neff, L. A., 659
Negovsky, V. A., 264
Neigh, G. N., 99, 800
Neisser, U., 20–21, 26, 431, 489, 496, 600
Nelson, A., 608, 609
Nelson, C. A., 524
Nelson, C. B., 695, 793
Nelson, E. E., 162
Nelson, R. J., 246–247
Nemeroff, C. B., 99, 800
Neri, D. F., 244
Nestler, E. J., 768
Netter, S., 541, 542
Nettle, D., 599
Neuberg, S. L., 317, 318
Neugarten, B. L., 552
Neumark-Sztainer, D., 552
Neuner, F., 792
Neville, H. J., 488
New, A. S., 804
New, M. I., 312
Newcombe, T. M., 588
Newcorn, J. H., 729
Newell, A., 21, 462
Newen, A., 609
Newitz, A., 595
Newman, C., 154
Newman, T. K., 535
Newmark, S., 778
Newton, I., 52

Subject Index/Glossary

"Light at the end of the tunnel"
experience, 264
Light spectrum, 188, 210
Limbic system, 152. *See also* Subcortical
structures
Linear perspective, 200, 201, 202*f*
Lithium, 770, 770*f*
Lobes, 156–157, 157*f*
frontal, 156, 158–160, 161, 162
occipital, 156, 162
parietal, 156, 162–163
temporal, 156–157, 162
Locus of control, 587. A cognitive
expectancy featured in social-
cognitive learning theories of
personality about the source
of individual outcomes; an
external locus of control
sees outcomes as resulting
from luck or chance, while
an internal locus of control
sees outcomes as the result of
individual effort.
Loneliness, sleep and, 254, 255
Longitudinal study, 68. An
experimental design for
assessing age-related changes
in which data are obtained
from the same individuals at
intervals over a long period.
Long-term memory (LTM), 408. The
final stage of the Atkinson-
Shiffrin model that is the
location of permanent
memories, 408–427
levels of processing in, 409–410, 410*f*
moving information into,
409–410
organization in, 425–427
connectionist theories and,
425–426
inferences using schemas and,
426–427
spreading activation model and,
425, 426*f*
retrieval from, 429–435
types of, 413–418 (*See also*
Declarative memory;
Nondeclarative memory)
vs. working memory, 410–412, 411*f*
Long-term potentiation (LTP),
442. The enhancement of
communication between
two neurons resulting from
their synchronous activation,
442–443, 442*f*
Loudness, perception of, 213–214, 213*t*,
214*f*
Love, brain imaging of, 82, 83*f*
LSD (lysergic acid diethylamide),
270–271
Lucid dreaming, 256. A conscious
awareness of dreaming
accompanied by the ability
to control the content of the
dream.
Lymphocyte, 802. White blood cells;
products of the immune
system.
Lysergic acid diethylamide (LSD),
270–271

Magic-eye pictures, 203–204
Magnetoencephalography (MEG), 130*t*
**Major depressive disorder (unipolar
disorder),** 698. A disorder
characterized by lengthy
periods of depressed mood,
loss of pleasure in normal
activities, disturbances in
sleep and appetite, difficulty
concentrating, feelings of
hopelessness, and possible
thoughts of suicide, 698–703.
See also Depression
causes of, 700
integration of perspectives on, 703
prevalence of, 698–699
treating, 767–769, 767*f*, 769*f*
Major histocompatibility complex
(MHC), 121

Mania, 698. A period of unrealistically
elevated mood.
*Man Who Mistook His Wife for a Hat,
The* (Sacks), 260–261
Marijuana (cannabis), 270
Marriage, happiness and, 831–832, 832*f*
Massively multiplayer online role-
playing games (MMORPGs),
379
Master of Divinity (MDiv) degree, 744
Maternal bonding behaviors, 173
Maternal care, stress and, 798–799, 799*f*
MDMA (Ecstasy), 274
Mean, 72. The numerical average of a
set of scores, 67*f*, 72, 73. *See
also* Data
Measure, 59. A method for describing a
variable's quantity.
Median, 72. The halfway mark in a set
of data, with half of the scores
above and half below, 72, 72*f*.
See also Data
Medications. *See also* Antidepressant
medication; Psychoactive drug
antipsychotic, 755, 773–774, 776,
777*f*
for autism, 776–779, 777, 777*f*
biological therapies and, 759
over-the-counter, 217, 271, 516, 517*f*
for schizophrenia, 773*f*
Meditation, 280. A voluntary alteration
of consciousness characterized
by positive emotion and
absence of thought.
cortical thickening and, 280, 281*f*
Medulla, 150. The brainstem structure
that lies just above the spinal
cord, 150–151
vestibular system and, 218–219
Melatonin, 172
Memory, 399. The ability to retain
knowledge, 397–450
adaptive advantage of, 401
biochemistry and, 443
biology of, 442–443
forgetting and, 436–442
improving, 444–447
distribute practice over time,
444–445
mnemonics, 446–447
recite, 445–446
sleep, 445
take tests, 445
information processing and, 399–401
interpersonal relationships from the
perspective of, 448–449
long-term, 408–424
processing, 402–403
retrieval, 400–401, 428–436
sensory, 402–408
subliminal messages and, 418, 419
Meninges, 147
Meningitis, 147
Menopause, 556. The complete
cessation of a woman's
menstrual cycles.
Mental processes, study of, 5
Mere exposure effect, 656. Repeated
exposure increases liking.
Mescaline, 269
Mesoderm, 512
Meta-analysis, 66. A statistical analysis
of many previous experiments
on a single topic, 66–67
insights from, 67*f*
Methamphetamine, 273
Meth mouth, 273
Methylphenidate (Ritalin), 273–274,
729, 779
Microscope, 11, 12*f*
Microwaves, 182, 182*f*, 188
Midbrain, 152. The part of the
brainstem that lies between
the pons and the cerebral
hemispheres.
Midlife, 554–559
cognitive development in, 556, 557
physical development in, 556, 557
social changes in, 558–559, 558*f*
Migration, 106. Movement to a new
location.

Mind, 5. The brain and its activities,
including thought, emotion,
and behavior.
Minnesota Multiphasic Personality
Inventory (MMPI), 595*f*
Mirror neuron, discovery of, 148, 149
Misbehavior of Organisms, The (Breland
and Breland), 382
Mixed longitudinal design, 68. A
method for assessing age-
related changes that combines
the cross-sectional and
longitudinal approaches by
observing a cross-section of
participants over a shorter
period than is used typically in
longitudinal studies.
Mnemonics, 446. Memory aids that
link new information to well-
known information, 446–447
Mode, 72. The most frequently
occurring score in a set of data,
72–73, 73*f*. *See also* Data
Monism, 7–8
Monocular cue, 200. A depth cue that
requires the use of only one
eye, 200–202
Ames room and, 200, 200*f*
depth and, recognizing, 200–202
linear perspective and, 200, 201, 202*f*
moon illusion and, 201–202, 202*f*
Müller-Lyer illusion and, 201, 201*f*
occlusion and, 201
Ponzo illusion and, 201, 202*f*
Mood
health and, 803–804
REM and, 254, 255
Mood disorders, 698–709
bipolar disorder, 703–707, 706–707*f*
major depressive disorder, 698–703,
699*f*
suicide and, 707–709, 708*f*
treating, 767–771, 767*f*, 769*f*, 770*f*
Moon illusion, 201–202, 202*f*
Moral reasoning, Kohlberg's stages of,
548–549, 549*t*
conventional morality, 548–549
postconventional morality, 549
preconventional, 548
Moro reflex, 520*t*
Morpheme, 480. The smallest
component of speech that
carries meaning.
Morphine, 275
Motivated forgetting, 439. Failure to
retrieve negative memories.
Motivation, 289. A process that arouses,
maintains, and guides behavior
toward a goal, 288–319
achievement motivation, 313–314
affiliation and, 315, 315*f*, 316–317
cognitive and social, 313–317
drive and, 290
drive reduction and, 290
vs. emotion, 288–289
forgetting and, 439–440, 441, 442
hierarchy of needs and, Maslow's,
317–318, 317*f*
homeostasis and, 290
hunger and eating and, 292–303
incentives and, 290–291, 291*f*
meaning of, 289–292
in observational learning
priorities and, 317–318
procrastination and, 292, 293
rewards and, 290–291, 291*f*
self-actualization and, 318
set points and, 290
sexual, 303–313
Motor development, 525–527, 526*f*
Motor neuron, 150
Müller-Lyer illusion, 201, 201*f*
Multilingualism, 487–488, 487*f*
Munker illusion, 180
Mushrooms, 269
Mutation, 106. Errors that occur when
DNA is replicated.
Myelin, 133. The insulating material
covering some axons, 133–135
adolescent development and, 547

childhood development and, 525,
525*f*
glia and, 133–135, 133*f*, 134*f*
prenatal development and, 512, 514
propagation and, 137–138, 138*f*

Naïve theories, 533, 533*f*
Narcolepsy, 257. A sleep disorder
characterized by the intrusion
of REM phenomena into
wakefulness, 257–258
orexins and, 258
sleep paralysis and, 257
Naturalistic observation, 56.
An in-depth study of a
phenomenon in its natural
setting, 56–57
Natural selection, 105. The process
by which survival and
reproduction pressures act to
change the frequency of alleles
in subsequent generations,
105–109
adaptation and, 107–109
allele and, 106–107, 107*f*
Darwin and, 105, 115
selections in, 107
Natural utterance, 217*f*
Nature, 89. The contributions of
heredity to our physical
structure and behaviors,
89–92
in developmental themes,
510–511
vs. nurture, 89–90, 91, 92
Near-death experience, 263. An
altered state of consciousness
reported by people who were
close to death due to cardiac
or other medical problems
that features out-of-body
experiences, light at the end
of a tunnel perceptions, and a
state of calmness, 263–265
glutamate and, 264, 265
ketamine and, 264, 265
similarities among documented cases
of, 264
Negative punishment, 373. A method
for reducing behavior by
removing something desirable
whenever the target behavior
occurs.
Negative reinforcement, 372. A
method for increasing
behaviors that allow an
organism to escape or avoid
an unpleasant consequence,
372–373
Neo-Freudian, 578. A theorist who
attempted to update and
modify Freud's original theory
of personality, 578–579
Adler, 578
Horney, 579
Jung, 579
Nerve signaling, speed of, 11–12
Nervous system. *See also* Central
nervous system (CNS);
Peripheral nervous system
(PNS)
childhood development and,
523–525, 524*f*
depressants and, 274–275
prenatal development and, 512, 514
stimulants and, 271–274
Neural communication, 131–143. *See
also* Action potentials
axon and, 132
cell body, 131–132
chemical signaling, 139–141, 140*f*
dendrite, 132
depolarization and, 136, 136*f*,
140–141
electrical signaling, 135–138, 136*f*,
137*f*, 138*f*, 139*f*
excitatory messages and, 140–141
glia, 133–135
hyperpolarization and, 136, 136*f*, 141
inhibitory messages and, 140–141
synapses and, 141

Neurofeedback, 762. A type of biofeedback used to treat ADHD and seizures by teaching the client to keep measures of brain activity within a certain range.

Neuron, 131. A cell of the nervous system that is specialized for sending and receiving neural messages, 131–135. *See also* Action potentials; Neural communication
  interneuron, 150
  mirror, discovery of, 148, 149
  motor neuron, 150
  myelinated, 133–135, 133*f*, 134*f*
  parts of, 132*f*
  sensory neuron, 150
  summation, 141
Neuropolitics, 476, 477*f*
Neuroticism, 582. A Big Five personality trait characterized by anxiety, angry hostility, depression, self-consciousness, impulsivity, and vulnerability.
Neurotransmitter, 139. A chemical messenger that communicates across a synapse, 139–143
  acetylcholine (ACh), 141–142
  antidepressant medications and, 768
  depolarization and, 136, 136*f*, 140–141
  dopamine, 142–143
  endorphins, 143
  excitatory messages and, 140–141
  hyperpolarization and, 136, 136*f*, 141
  norepinephrine (Noradrenalin), 142
  orexins, narcolepsy and, 258
  receptors and, 139–141
  release, 140*f*
  reuptake and, 139, 140
  serotonin, 143
  types of, 139*t*, 141–143
Newborn development, 520–522
  activity, 521
  reflexes, 520, 520*t*
  senses, 521–522, 521*f*, 522*t*
Nicotine, 272, 272*f*
Night terror, 257. A sleep disorder occurring in N-REM sleep in which the sleeper wakes suddenly in great distress, but without experiencing the imagery of a nightmare.
NMDA receptor, 444
Nodes of Ranvier, 137–138, 137*f*
Nonassociative learning, 352. Learning that involves changes in the magnitude of responses to a stimulus
  habituation and, 352–353
  sensitization and, 352–353
Nondeclarative memory, 413. Unconsciously and effortlessly retrieved memories that are difficult to verbalize, including memories for classical conditioning, procedural learning, and priming; also known as implicit memories, 415–418
  classical conditioning and, 416
  declarative memory and, separating from, 420*f*
  priming and, 417–418, 417*f*
  procedural memory and, 416–417
Non-rapid eye movement (N-REM) sleep, 249. The components of sleep characterized by theta and delta wave activity as recorded by EEG and deep physical relaxation.
  benefits of, 251–252
  delta waves and, 250
  human growth hormone and, 251, 252*f*
  mood and, 255
  night terrors and, 257
  pattern of, 251, 251*f*
  sleep-talking and, 250–251
  sleepwalking and, 250
  theta waves and, 249

Norepinephrine (Noradrenalin), 139*t*, 142, 255, 273
Normal distribution, 74. A symmetrical probability function, 74–75
Nucleus accumbens, 155. A subcortical structure that participates in reward and addiction.
Nurture, 89. The contributions of environmental factors and experience to our physical structure and behaviors, 89–92
  in developmental themes, 510–511
  nature *vs.*, 89–90, 91, 92
Nurture Assumption, The (Harris), 540
Nutrition
  health psychology and, 815*f*, 818–820, 819*f*
  pregnancy and, 518–519, 520*f*

Obedience, 648. Compliance with a request from an authority figure, 648–650, 649*f*
Obesity, 297–301
  BMI and, 297–298, 297*f*
  cultural influences on, 298–299
  epidemic, 297*f*
  genetic influences on, 298
  health and, 803–804, 804*f*
  individual influences on, 299
  satiety and, 296, 296*f*
  social influences on, 299, 300*f*
  weight loss and, 300–301
Objectivity, 45. The practice of basing conclusions on facts without influence of personal emotion and bias, 45–46, 47–48
  evidence and, repeatable *vs.* ignored, 48
  observation and, systematic *vs.* hit-or-miss, 47, 48, 48*f*
  vs. subjectivity, 45–46
Object permanence, 529. The ability to form mental representations of objects that are no longer present.
Objects, recognizing, 195–200
  contrast and frequency, 197, 198, 198*f*, 204
  differences in, developmental and individual, 204
  Gestalt psychology and, 198–200, 199*f*
  hierarchical model of, feature detectors and, 195, 196, 197, 197*f*
  mathematical model of, gratings and, 196, 197, 198, 198*f*
Observational learning, 352. Learning that occurs when an organism watches the actions of another. Also known as social learning or modeling, 353, 386–392
  aggression and, Bandura's work on, 388–389
  behaviors influenced by, 387
  cognitive processes in modeling of behavior, 388–387
  cultural transmission of, 391–392
  examples of, 387–388
  imitation and, 353, 389
  mirror neurons and, 389–390, 391
Obsession, 693. An intrusive, distressing thought.
Obsessive-compulsive disorder (OCD), 693. A disorder associated with intrusive obsessions and compulsions, 693–695
  biological explanations of, 693–694, 694*f*
  decision making and, 473
  degeneration of basal ganglia and, 153
  learning explanations of, 694
  social explanations of, 694–695
Occipital lobe, 157. The lobe of the cerebral cortex located at the back of the brain; location of primary visual cortex, 156, 157

  blindsight and, 240, 241
  vision loss and, 240
Occlusion, 201
OCD. *See* Obsessive-compulsive disorder (OCD)
Olfaction, 223. The sense of smell, 223–225. *See also* Chemical senses
  biology of, 223–225
  chemical stimuli in, 223
  olfactory pathways and, 225, 227
  olfactory receptors and, 223–225, 224*f*
  post-traumatic stress disorder and, 228–229
Olfactory bulb, 225. One of two structures below the frontal lobes of the brain that receive input from the olfactory receptors in the nose.
Olfactory nerve, 225. A nerve carrying olfactory information from the olfactory receptors to the olfactory bulbs.
Online research, credibility and, 642, 643*f*
Openness, 583. A Big Five personality trait characterized by an appreciation for fantasy, feelings, actions, ideas, values, and aesthetics.
Operant conditioning, 352. A type of learning in which associations are formed between behaviors and their outcomes, 352, 369–386. *See also* Schedules of reinforcement
  applying, 383–385
    behavior therapies, 385
    token economies, 384, 385
  biological influences on, 382
  cognitive influences on, 381–382
  consequences, 369–370, 369*t*
  negative reinforcement and, 372–373
  positive reinforcement and, 370, 371, 372
  punishment and, 373–375
  schedules of reinforcement, 375–379
  shaping, or method of successive approximations and, 379–380
  social influences on, 382–383
Operationalization, 66. Defining variables in practical terms.
Opiates, 143, 143*f*, 152, 221, 275–276
Opponent process theory, 193. A theory of color vision that suggests we have a red-green color channel and a blue-yellow color channel in which activation of one color in each pair inhibits the other, 193–195
  color vision and, 193–194 , 194*f*, 195
  vs. trichromacy theory, 195
Optic chiasm, 191
Optic disk, 189
Optic nerve, 191. The nerve exiting the retina of the eye.
Optic tracts, 191. Nerve pathways traveling from the optic chiasm to the thalamus, hypothalamus, and midbrain.
Optimism, 830. Thinking positively about the future.
Orbitofrontal cortex, 159. A part of the prefrontal cortex located right behind the eyes that participates in impulse control, 159–160
  abnormalities in, psychological disorders and, 160–162
  damage to, 159–160, 159*f*, 161
  decision making and, 472, 473*f*
  OCD and, 693, 694*f*
  prefrontal cortex and, 159
Orexins, 258, 690
Organ of Corti, 211. A structure located on the basilar membrane that contains auditory receptors.
Origin of Species, The (Darwin), 15, 105

Outgroup
  cooperation, reduction of bias through, 634, 635*f*
  perceptions of, 631–632, 631*f*
Ovaries, 172, 173*f*, 174
Over-the-counter medications, 217, 271, 516, 517*f*
Oxycontin, 276
Oxytocin, 173, 175
  MDMA and, 274
  romantic love and, 307–308, 309*f*

Pain, 221–222. *See also* Somatosensation
  cognitive influences on, 221–222
  gate theory of, 221, 222*f*
  pain messages and, 221
  pain receptors and, 221
  perception of, 221
  placebo effects on, 222
  stress and, 221–222
Palmer reflex, 520*t*
Panic attack, 689. The experience of intense fear and autonomic arousal in the absence of real threat.
Panic disorder, 689. A disorder characterized by repeated panic attacks and fear of future attacks, 689–691
  biological explanations of, 690
  cognitive explanations of, 690
  integrating perspectives on, 691
  social explanations of, 690
Papillae, 226. Small bumps on the tongue that contain taste buds.
Paradoxical sleep, 250
Parapsychology, 76, 77
Parasympathetic nervous system, 170. The part of the autonomic nervous system associated with rest, repair, and energy storage, 170–171
  antagonistic effects on organs served by, 171–172, 171*f*
  function of, 170
  low fat stores and leptin levels and, 294–295
Parenting styles, 540–543, 541*t*, 543*f*
  categories of, 541–542, 541*t*, 543*f*
    authoritarian, 541, 542
    authoritative, 540–542
    indulgent, 540, 542
    uninvolved, 542
  child outcomes and, 543*f*
  cultural influences on, 539
Parietal lobe, 157. The lobe of the cerebral cortex that lies at the top of the head between the frontal and occipital lobes; location of primary somatosensory cortex, 156, 157
  vestibular system and, 219
Parkinson's disease, 142, 153
Partial reinforcement, 375. The reinforcement of a desired behavior on some occasions but not others.
Partial reinforcement effect in extinction, 378. The more rapid extinction observed following continuous reinforcement than following partial reinforcement, 378–379
Partner infidelity, 661, 661*f*
Patriarchal systems, 118
Peer review, 53. The process of having other experts examine research prior to its publication.
Perception, 181. The process of interpreting sensory information, 180–187
  auditory, 209–217
  bottom-up processing and, 183
  gustatory, 223–225, 227–229
  interpersonal relationships and, 231
  measuring
    absolute threshold and, 184*f*, 185

Satiety, 296. A sense of feeling full; not requiring further food, 295–296, 296*f*

Scatter plot, 75, 75*f*

Schachter-Singer two-factor theory, 339. A theory of emotion in which general arousal leads to assessment, which in turn leads to subjective feelings, 338–340, 340*f*

Schedules of reinforcement, 375–379
  comparing schedules, 379
  fixed interval schedules, 377
  fixed ratio schedules, 375–376
  partial reinforcement, 375
  partial reinforcement effect in extinction, 378–379
  variable interval schedules, 377–378
  variable ratio schedules, 376–377

Schema, 427. Set of expectations about objects and situations.
  concepts and, 460
  false memories and, 428, 429
  inferences and, 426–427

Schizophrenia, 712. A disorder characterized by hallucinations, delusions, disorganized thought and speech, disorders of movement, restricted affect, and avolition/asociality, 712–717
  amphetamine use and, 273
  biological factors in, 713–715, 714*f*
  causes of, 713–717
  cocaine use and, 273
  creativity and, 367
  dopamine and, 142
  genetics and, 714*f*
  hallucination and, 712
  hallucinogen use and, 269
  medications for, 773*f*
  psychological factors and, 715–717, 717*f*
  recovery in, 737, 737*f*
  stress and, 717*f*
  symptoms of, 712–713
  therapy for, 772–774, 773*f*

Science, 45. A method for learning about reality through systematic observation and experimentation, 44–54
  critical thinking in, 48–49
  hypothesis in, 52–53
  objectivity in, 45–46, 47–48
  theories in, 49–50, 52

Scotoma, 240, 241

Sea slug, 348, 360

Seasonal affective disorder (SAD), 246. A mood disorder in which depression occurs regularly at the same time each year, usually during the winter months.

Secondary sex characteristics, 545. Physical changes occurring at puberty associated with sexual maturity.

Secure attachment, 538. A pattern of infant-caregiver bonding in which children explore confidently and return to the parent or caregiver for reassurance, 538–540

Seizure, 265. An abnormal level of brain activation with a sudden onset.
  GABA and, 265
  generalized, 265, 266, 266*f*
  partial, 265, 266, 266*f*

Selective serotonin reuptake inhibitors (SSRIs), 768–769, 768*f*

Self, 597. Patterns of thought, feelings, and actions we perceive in our own minds.
  brain and, 608–609, 609*f*
  culture and, modifying effects of, 610, 611*f*
  definition of, 597
  personality and, 597–613
  self-awareness, 598–600, 599*f*

  self-concept, 597–598, 598*f*
  self-esteem, 600–607
  self-regulation, 607–608, 607*f*
  social, 609–613

Self-actualization, 318. A state of having fulfilled your potential, 24–25

Self-awareness, 237, 598. The special understanding of the self as distinct from other stimuli, 598–600, 599*f*
  self-knowledge and, sources of, 599–600

Self-concept, 597. A person's description of his or her own characteristics, 597–598, 598*f*

Self-consciousness, 599*f*

Self-control, 607, 607*f*

Self-efficacy, 587

Self-enhancement to protect self-esteem, use of, 603

Self-esteem, 600. A judgment of the value of the self, 600–607
  academic performance and, 604–605
  advantages of, 604–607
  gender, race, culture and, 602, 603*f*
  juvenile delinquency and, 604–605
  self-enhancement to protect, use of, 603
  social rejection and, signal for, 605, 606*f*
  sources of, 601–602

Self-hypnosis, 742–743

Self-knowledge, sources of, 599–600

Self-regulation, 607–608, 607*f*

Self-schema, 597. A cognitive organization that helps us think about the self and process self-relevant information.

Semantic memory, 413. A general knowledge memory.

Sensation, 181. The process of detecting environmental stimuli or stimuli arising from the body. *See also* Perception
  interpersonal relationships and, 231
  microwaves and ultraviolet waves and, 182, 182*f*
  transduction and, 182

Senses of newborn, 521–522, 521*f*, 522*t*

Sensitization, 352. An increased reaction to many stimuli following exposure to one very strong stimulus, 352–353

Sensorimotor stage, 528. Piaget's stage of development beginning at birth and ending at the age of 2 years and characterized by active exploration of the environment, 528–529

Sensory adaptation. 183. The tendency to pay less attention to a nonchanging source of stimulation.

Sensory homunculus, 219–220

Sensory memory, 402. The first stage of the Atkinson-Shiffrin model that holds large amounts of incoming data for very brief amounts of time, 402–408
  short-term memory and, 403–406
  Sperling's demonstration of duration of, 403*f*
  working memory, 406–408, 406*f*

Sensory neuron, 150

Sensory sensitivity in autism spectrum disorder, 725, 725*f*

Separation anxiety, 538

Serial position effect, 411*f*

Serotonin, 139*t*, 143
  hallucinogens and, 269, 270
  MDMA and, 274
  REM and, 255
  sudden infant death syndrome and, 259

Serotonin transporter gene, 90, 91, 91*f*, 571*f*

Set point, 290. A value that is defended to maintain homeostasis.

Sex and adolescence, 545–546

Sex hormones, 174

Sexual motivation, 303–313
  cross-cultural studies on, 307, 307*f*
  evolutionary psychology perspective of, 303–304, 305
  gender differences in mate preferences, 304, 305, 305*f*
  hormones and, 305, 306–308
    menopause and, 306
    ovulation and menstrual cycle and, 305, 306, 306*f*
    oxytocin, 307–308, 309*f*
    stability of relationships and, 307–308, 308*f*
    testosterone and, 306–307
    vasopressin and, 307–308, 309*f*
  sexual orientation and, 308, 309–313

Sexual orientation, 308. A stable pattern of attraction to members of a particular sex, 308–313
  birth order and, 312
  brain structures and, 312–313, 312*f*
  cross cultural surveys on mate preferences, 304, 305*f*
  determinants of, 309–313
  genetics and, 311
  hormones and, 311, 312
  sexual motivation and, 308, 309–313
  SOI-R and, 310, 311

Sexual selection, 115. The development of traits that help an individual compete for mates, 115–119
  of humor, 118, 119
  parental investment and, 115–116
  traits influenced by, 116

Shaping/method of successive approximations, 379. A method for increasing the frequency of behaviors that never or rarely occur, 379–380

Shift maladaptation syndrome, 244–245, 244*f*

Short-term memory (STM), 403. The second stage of the Atkinson-Shiffrin model that holds a small amount of information for a limited time, 403–406
  chunking and, 405
  rehearsal and, 404–405
  retrieval and, 428, 429

Signal detection, 186. The analysis of sensory and decision making processes in the detection of faint, uncertain stimuli, 186–187
  outcomes in, 186–187, 187*t*
  perception and, 186–187
  two-step process of, 186

Similarity, Gestalt principle of, 199, 199*f*

Simplicity, Gestalt principle of, 200

Sine wave speech, 216, 217*f*

Single cell recording, 130*t*

Sitting, death and, 825*f*

Situational attribution, 624. A judgment assigning the cause of a person's behavior to his or her environment, 629, 629*f*, 651–654
  deindividuation, 653
  group polarization, 653–654, 654*f*
  groupthink, 654
  social facilitation, 651–652
  social loafing, 652

Skin conductance response (SCR), 130*t*

Skinner boxes, 20

Sleep, 243. A normal state of consciousness characterized by reduced awareness of external stimuli, 249–254
  benefits of, 251–255
  circadian rhythms and, 243–247
  health and, 803–804, 804*f*
  loneliness and, 254, 255
  memory and, 445
  regulation, serotonin and, 143
  stages of (*See* Non-rapid eye movement (N-REM) sleep; Rapid eye movement (REM) sleep)

Sleep apnea, 259. A sleep disorder in which the person stops breathing while asleep.

Sleep disorders, 256
  cataplexy, 257–258, 258*f*
  insomnia, 257
  narcolepsy, 257–258
  nightmares, 256–257
  night terrors, 257
  restless legs syndrome and, 259
  sleep apnea, 259
  sudden infant death syndrome and, 259

Sleep spindles, 250

Smell. *See* Olfaction

Social behavior
  altruism and, 113–115
  cooperation and, 113
  culture and, 116–118, 119
  origins of, 112–115
  reciprocal altruism and, 114
  sexual selection and, 115–116
  social interactions and, outcomes of, 113*t*

Social-cognitive learning theory, 587. A theory of personality that features cognition and learning, especially from the social environment, as important sources of individual differences in personality, 586–588
  if-then relationships and, 588
  locus of control and, 587
  reciprocal determinism and, 587
  self-efficacy and, 587

Social facilitation, 651. The presence of other people changes performance, 651–652

Socialization, 620–622, 621*f*, 622*f*. *See also* Social relationships

Social loafing, 652. Reduced motivation and effort shown by individuals working in a group.

Social media, influences of, 642, 643*f*

Social norms, 645. Usually unwritten or unspoken rules for behavior in social settings, 645–651
  compliance, 646–648, 647*f*
  conformity, 645–646, 645*f*
  obedience, 648–650, 649*f*
  power of one, 650–651

Social phobia/social anxiety, 691. A disorder characterized by an unrealistic fear of being scrutinized and criticized by others.
  specific phobia, **692**
  treating, 766*f*, 782, 783*f*

Social psychology, 29. The psychological perspective that examines the effects of the social environment on the behavior of individuals.
  aggression and, 669–673
  attitudes and, 637–640
  attributions of behaviors and, 624–630
  cooperation and competition and, 662–669
  first impressions and, 622–624, 624*f*
  interpersonal relationships from perspective of, 674–675, 674*f*
  persuasion and, 640–644
  prejudice and, 630–636
  situational influences on behavior and, 651–654
  socialization and, 620–622, 621*f*, 622*f*
  social norms and, 645–651
  social relationships and, 655–661

Social rejection, 605, 606*f*

Social relationships, 655–661
  attraction and liking, 656–659, 657*f*
  building, 660, 660*f*
  ending, 661, 661*f*
  maintaining, 660–661

Social self, 609–613
  cultural influences on, 612–613
  interpersonal self, 610–611

Sociocultural influences
  on audition, 216, 217*f*